The Wiley Handbook of What Works in Violence Risk Management

The Wiley Handbook of What Works in Violence Risk Management

Theory, Research and Practice

Edited by

J. Stephen Wormith,

Leam A. Craig,

and

Todd E. Hogue

WILEY Blackwell

This edition first published 2020
© 2020 John Wiley & Sons Ltd

The right of J. Stephen Wormith, Leam A. Craig, and Todd E. Hogue to be identified as the authors of the editorial material in this work has been asserted in accordance with law.

Registered Offices
John Wiley & Sons, Inc., 111 River Street, Hoboken, NJ 07030, USA
John Wiley & Sons Ltd, The Atrium, Southern Gate, Chichester, West Sussex, PO19 8SQ, UK

Editorial Office
111 River Street, Hoboken, NJ 07030, USA

For details of our global editorial offices, customer services, and more information about Wiley products visit us at www.wiley.com.

Wiley also publishes its books in a variety of electronic formats and by print-on-demand. Some content that appears in standard print versions of this book may not be available in other formats.

Library of Congress Cataloging-in-Publication Data

Names: Wormith, J. S., editor. | Craig, Leam, editor. | Hogue, Todd E.,
    editor.
Title: The Wiley Handbook of what works in violence risk management : theory,
    research and practice / J. Stephen Wormith, Leam A. Craig, and Todd E.
    Hogue.
Description: First edition. | Hoboken, NJ : John Wiley & Sons, 2020. |
    Series: What works with offender rehabilitation series | Includes
    bibliographical references and index.
Identifiers: LCCN 2019045102 (print) | LCCN 2019045103 (ebook) | ISBN
    9781119315711 (hardback) | ISBN 9781119315759 (paperback) | ISBN
    9781119315889 (adobe pdf) | ISBN 9781119315971 (epub)
Subjects: LCSH: Violence. | Violent crimes. | Violent offenders.
Classification: LCC HM1116 .H364 2020 (print) | LCC HM1116 (ebook) | DDC
    303.6–dc23
LC record available at https://lccn.loc.gov/2019045102
LC ebook record available at https://lccn.loc.gov/2019045103

Cover Design: Wiley
Cover Image: hidden forest by 1,006 (634 KB) Schwarzes-flimmern (talk | contribs) is licensed under CC
Attribution-Share Alike 3.0 Unported

Set in 10/12.5pt Galliard by SPi Global, Pondicherry, India
Printed and bound in Singapore by Markono Print Media Pte Ltd

10 9 8 7 6 5 4 3 2 1

IN MEMORY OF J. STEPHEN WORMITH

Contents

About the Editors

The late J. Stephen Wormith, Ph.D, was a Professor in the Psychology Department at the University of Saskatchewan (U of S) where he taught in the Department's Clinical Psychology program and its Applied Social Psychology program. He was also the Director of the Centre of Forensic Behavioural Science and Justice Studies, which was also at U of S. Previously he worked as a psychologist in the Correctional Service of Canada (CSC) and was Psychologist-in-Chief for the Ontario Ministry of Community Safety and Correctional Services. He was a Fellow of the Canadian Psychological Association (CPA) and represented CPA at the National Associations Active in Criminal Justice (NACJ). He co-authored the *Level of Service/Case Management Inventory* (2004) with D. A. Andrews and J. Bonta, and participated internationally in research and training on risk assessment. He was on the editorial board of *Criminal Justice and Behavior*, *Psychological Services* and the *Canadian Journal of Criminology and Criminal Justice*. He was also on the Board of Directors of the International Association for Correctional and Forensic Psychology (IACFP). In 2015, he received the Edwin I. Megargee Distinguished Contribution Award from the IACFP. In the following year, he received a Teaching Leadership Award from the American Psychological Association's Division 18, Criminal Justice Section.

Dr. Wormith's research activities have concentrated on the assessment and treatment of offenders and community-based crime prevention initiatives. He consulted with provincial and federal government correctional ministries and for the Royal Canadian Mounted Police (RCMP). He served as an expert witness on matters of offender assessment and treatment. He also coached Pee-wee hockey.

Leam A. Craig, Ph.D, MAE, FBPsS, FAcSS, C.Sci, C.Psychol, EuroPsy., is a Consultant Forensic and Clinical Psychologist and Partner at Forensic Psychology Practice Ltd. He is a Chartered dual Registered Forensic and Clinical Psychologist. He is Hon. Professor of Forensic Psychology at the Centre for Applied Psychology, University of Birmingham, and Visiting Professor of Forensic Clinical Psychology at Birmingham City University. He is a Fellow of the British Psychological Society and the Academy of Social Sciences and Full Member of the Academy of Experts. In 2013 he was the recipient of the Senior Academic Award by the Division of Forensic Psychology for distinguished contributions to academic knowledge in forensic psychology. He has experience working in various forensic settings including prisons, probation and secure forensic psychiatric services throughout England and Wales and Northern Ireland. He is currently a Consultant to the National Probation Service working on the

Offenders with Personality Disorder Pathway. He acts as an expert witness to civil and criminal courts in the assessment of sexual and violent offenders and in matters of child protection. He has previously been instructed by the Catholic and Church of England Dioceses, South African Police Service and the United States Air Force in matters of risk assessment of sexual offenders. In 2015 he co- authored a Ministry of Justice research report into the use of expert witnesses in family law. In 2016 he was appointed as Chair of the British Psychological Society Expert Witness Advisory Group. He sits on the editorial boards of several international journals and has over 100 publications including 12 books published/in press. He is a Series Editor for the *Wiley Handbook on What Works in Offender Rehabilitation* book series for Wiley-Blackwell. His research interests include sexual and violent offenders, personality disorder, forensic risk assessment and the use of psychologists as expert witnesses.

Todd E. Hogue, Ph.D, is a Registered Forensic and Clinical Psychologist and Professor of Forensic Psychology at the University of Lincoln. He started his career in the British Prison Service working primarily with sexual offenders including organising the national training for staff implementing the original Sex Offender Treatment Programme in the UK. He practiced in community mental health and secure residential settings for adolescents before moving to Rampton high secure hospital where he was psychology lead for the development of a specialist Personality Disorder Service and subsequent development of the Peaks Unit as part of the Dangerous and Severe Personality (DSPD) initiative. All his practice has focused on the development of forensic clinical services for individuals who are hard to engage and have high risk sexual and violent offending histories. His research interests include understanding the impact of attitudes towards sexual offenders and the extent to which attitudes impact on risk perception, clinical practice and social policy. The development of new methods of measuring sexual interest / deviant interest using implicit methodologies such as eye-tracking and touch technologies and evaluating the effect of applied practice initiatives on offender care, reintegration and reoffending. Since 2006 he has been Professor of Forensic Psychology at the University of Lincoln where he developed undergraduate and postgraduate in forensic psychology programmes and has published over 50 peer reviewed articles. He now acts as Director of Research for the College of Social Science.

Editors Note: The editors would like to acknowledge and express their appreciation for the administrative assistance provided to this project by Brandon Sparks, a graduate student at the University of Saskatchewan.

About the Contributors

Gina Ambroziak, B.S., has worked for Sand Ridge Secure Treatment Center (SRSTC), Wisconsin's sex offender civil commitment program, for approximately nine years. She is currently the Quality Improvement and Research Supervisor and held previous positions with the program as a Research Analyst and Treatment Specialist. She has been involved in research related to the Structured Risk Assessment – Forensic Version, sex offenders with major mental illness, and outcomes of released sexually violent persons. She obtained her Bachelor of Science in psychology and legal studies from the University of Wisconsin-Madison.

Elizabeth A. Bates, Ph.D., is a Senior Lecturer in Applied Psychology at the University of Cumbria. Her PhD involved exploring the impact of personality and psychopathology on men's and women's intimate partner violence. Her key research interests lie in exploring effective interventions for perpetrators, women's violence and male victims of intimate partner violence.

Elliot Bell, BCA, MA, PGDipClinPsyc, Ph.D., FNZCCP, is a senior lecturer at the University of Otago Wellington, New Zealand. Dr Bell has a clinical background working in New Zealand forensic mental health services in inpatient, community, and prison settings, with mentally disordered and intellectually disabled offenders. He has extensive experience writing court reports and has provided expert witness testimony. Dr Bell maintains a private practice currently. He completed his Masters thesis on psychopathology in people with intellectual disabilities, and his PhD on Theory of Mind in people with schizophrenia. His current research focuses cognitive behaviour therapies, mental health rehabilitation, intellectual disability, forensic rehabilitation, resilience, and psychological factors in the rehabilitation of physical health conditions. He is a Fellow and past Vice President of the New Zealand College of Clinical Psychologists.

Douglas P. Boer, Ph.D., is currently Professor of Clinical Psychology in Psychology at the University of Canberra (Australia). Prior to his current position, he worked as an academic at the University of Waikato, Hamilton, New Zealand for approximately seven years and before that he worked for the Correctional Service of Canada for 14 years in a variety of contexts including sex offender therapist and treatment programme supervisor. He is a consultant to a number of agencies regarding sex offender treatment and the treatment of intellectually disabled individuals who have offended in a violent manner. He has published more than 70 articles and book chapters and edited books, as well as several structured risk assessment manuals for use with sexual offenders. In 2017, Professor Boer was the senior editor on a three volume handbook published by Wiley regarding the theories, assessment and treatment of sexual offending. He is also on a number of editorial boards including the Journal of Intellectual and Developmental Disability, Sexual Offender Treatment, and the British Journal of Forensic Practice. Finally, he is an active clinician, assessor, researcher, and clinical supervisor.

Guy Bourgon, Ph.D., received his PhD from the University of Ottawa and is a clinical psychologist specializing in correctional and criminal justice psychology. With over 30 years clinical experience in the assessment and treatment of adults and youths involved in the criminal justice system, Dr. Bourgon has been dedicated to the development and implementation of empirically validated correctional services. He has published numerous articles on effective correctional treatment services, community corrections and risk assessment. He has extensive international experience in the training and supervision of front-line professionals helping transfer "What Works" to everyday practice. As co-lead for the Strategic Training Initiative in Community Supervision (STICS), an empirically supported and internationally recognized best practice model of community supervision, he is recognized for translating research evidence into useful and practical concepts, skills, and techniques that promote client engagement and facilitate prosocial change.

Gunnar C. Butler, B.A., is currently enrolled as a master's student at Southern Illinois University Carbondale (SIUC). He received his bachelor's degree from SIUC, and has primarily focused on research that aims at reducing recidivism rates throughout interventions. He has worked on projects pertaining to prison programming, as well as a grant that studied the effects of intensive probation.

Nick Chadwick, M.A., is a senior research analyst at Public Safety Canada in Ottawa, Canada. He has contributed to research on the use and implementation of evidence-based practices in community supervision, the utility of assessing dynamic risk and protective factors in the prediction of recidivism, and effective correctional programming.

Leam A. Craig, Ph.D, FBPsS, FAcSS, is a Consultant Forensic and Clinical Psychologist and Partner at Forensic Psychology Practice Ltd. He is Hon. Professor of Forensic Psychology at the Centre for Applied Psychology, University of Birmingham, and Visiting Professor of Forensic Clinical Psychology at Birmingham City University. He is a Fellow of the British Psychological Society and of the Academy of Social Sciences and Full Member of the Academy of Experts. He has experience working in various forensic settings including prisons, probation and secure forensic psychiatric services throughout England and Wales and Northern Ireland. He is currently a Consultant to the National Probation Service working on the Offenders with Personality Disorder Pathway. He has over 100 publications including 12 books published/in press. He is the Series Editor for the *Wiley Handbook on What Works in Offender Rehabilitation* book series for Wiley-Blackwell. His research interests include sexual and violent offenders, personality disorder, forensic risk assessment and the use of expert witnesses in civil and criminal courts (see About the Editors section for more detail).

Andrew Day, Ph.D., is Professor in the Australian Aboriginal and Torres Strait Islander Centre at James Cook University, Australia. Before joining academia he was employed as a clinical psychologist in South Australia and the UK, having gained his Doctorate in Clinical Psychology from the University of Birmingham and his Masters in Applied Criminological Psychology from the University of London. He is widely published in many areas of forensic psychology, with a focus on the development of effective and evidence based approaches to offender rehabilitation.

Michael R. Davis, B.Behav.Sci.(Hons), D.Psych. (Clinical and Forensic), is a forensic and clinical psychologist in full time consulting practice. He is an Adjunct Research Fellow at the Centre for Forensic Behavioural Science at Swinburne University of Technology, an Adjunct Senior Lecturer in the Department of Psychiatry at Monash University, and an Honorary Fellow in the Department of Psychiatry at the University of Melbourne. Dr Davis' practice is divided between forensic assessment (particularly the assessment of risk, sexual deviance, and personality disorder) and providing behavioural investigative advice to law enforcement in cases of sexual and violent crime. He has provided behavioural advice to several police agencies across three continents and is the only mental health professional in Australia to be elected to membership of the International Criminal Investigative Analysis Fellowship. He regularly provides training workshops on risk assessment for clinicians and has conducted hundreds of risk assessments for the courts and in consultation for mental health services, government departments, and private lawyers. Dr Davis serves on the editorial board of the Journal of Investigative Psychology and Offender Profiling.

Louise Dixon, Ph.D., C.Psychol., is a UK-registered Forensic Psychologist and Reader in Forensic Psychology at Victoria University of Wellington where she is the Director of the postgraduate programme in Forensic Psychology. She specialises in the prevention of interpersonal aggression and violence. Primarily, her research has centred on the study of intimate partner violence and abuse, and the overlap with child maltreatment in the family. Louise's research has been funded by the Economic and Social Research Council, Higher Education Funding Council for England, Police Knowledge fund and more recently Ministry of Social Development, NZ. She is a series editor to the *What Works in Offender Rehabilitation* book series for Wiley-Blackwell.

Liam Ennis, Ph.D., is the founder of the Forensic Behavioural Science Group, and an Assistant Clinical Professor in the Department of Psychiatry at the University of Alberta. A registered psychologist with 20 years of experience in the field of violence risk assessment and management, he previously served as the resident psychologist for Alberta Law Enforcement Response Teams, assigned to the Integrated Threat and Risk Assessment Centre (ITRAC) where he provided risk management training and consultation to federal and provincial law enforcement and child protective services regarding intimate partner violence, stalking, and other forms of targeted violence. He is an active researcher and collaborator on the grant-funded Optimizing Risk Assessment for Domestic Violence (ORA-DV) research project.

Ephrem Fernandez, Ph.D., is Professor of Psychology at the University of Texas, San Antonio. His research on anger is directed primarily at the phenomenology and typology of anger, the psychometrics of anger assessment, and integrative therapy for maladaptive anger. He recently edited a book on Treatments for Anger in Specific Populations and co-edited (with Andrew Day) a book on violence. With Sheri Johnson and Charles Carver, he is co-recipient of a Guggenheim Foundation grant to evaluate treatments for aggressive anger. He provides workshops and consulting services on anger, aggression, and violence.

Catherine Garrington, B.Sc. (Hons.), is a registered psychologist and psychology supervisor who has facilitated group and individual treatment for violent and sexual offenders in prison and community corrections settings for over nine years. She is currently a PhD candidate at the University of Canberra, Australia, supervised by Professor Doug Boer, researching the risk assessment of online Child Sexual Exploitation Material (CSEM) offenders.

Nicola Graham-Kevan, Ph.D., is a Professor of Criminal Justice Psychology; the University of Central Lancashire's lead for Violence and Aggression, and a visiting professor at Mittuniversitetet, Sweden. Nicola's research focuses on exploring psychological processes associated with criminal behaviour and victimisation experiences. These processes include those that increase risk (e.g., exposure to adverse childhood and adulthood experiences, dys-regulated emotions) and those that are protective (e.g., post-traumatic growth, compensatory consequences of domestic abuse, interventions). Nicola's interests have led to her collaborating with others across the world including Europe, Asia, America and Oceania. Nationally, Nicola works with stakeholders including UK Offices of the Police and Crime Commissioner; Constabularies, Her Majesty's Prison Service, Community Rehabilitation Companies and third sector charities. She presents her research and delivers training on domestic abuse both nationally and internationally. Nicola has an interest in theoretical models of risk and recovery and how these can be applied to interventions for offenders and victims. Her research has informed programmes currently being delivered across a range of services across many stake-holder organisations. Evaluations of these interventions suggest that they make an important contribution to the quality of life of some of society's most vulnerable people.

L. Maaike Helmus, Ph.D., is an Assistant Professor in Criminology at Simon Fraser University in Vancouver, British Columbia, Canada. Her research has focused on offender risk assessment, particularly regarding risk scale development and validation, and risk assessment for subgroups such as sex offenders, domestic violence offenders, and Indigenous offenders. She is part of the development team for Static-99R, Static-2002R, BARR-2002R, STABLE-2007, ACUTE-2007, VRAG-R, CPORT, and the Risk of Administrative Segregation Tool (RAST). Dr. Helmus also has a particular interest in meta-analysis and statistical approaches to prediction. She is currently co-editor of the journal *Sexual Offender Treatment* and on the editorial board of *Sexual Abuse*. A former Banting postdoc scholar and winner of the Governor General's Gold Medal for her work in risk assessment, Dr. Helmus has been the recipient of numerous grants and awards from organizations including the Association for the Treatment of Sexual Abusers (ATSA) and the Social Sciences and Humanities Research Council of Canada.

Sarah Hilder, M.S.W., is a senior lecturer and researcher in Criminology at Nottingham Trent University. Her research and teaching expertise has centered on working with victims, domestic abuse, gang violence and the sexual exploitation of women and girls, knife crime, sex offender rehabilitation, the supervision and surveillance of high risk sexual and violent offenders. Prior to an academic career she worked for the National Probation Service, as both a main grade and then Senior Probation Officer. Sarah has published academic work on risk assessment and safety planning in situations of domestic abuse, multi-agency working, desistance work, sexual exploitation and female gang members, sexual offending and cross border information exchanges on serious violent or sexual offenders travelling across the EU community. She is well versed in comparative victim and criminal justice work across the European Union (EU) having worked as a senior researcher on two major EU funded projects from 2010-2015.

N. Zoe Hilton, Ph.D., is Senior Research Scientist at the Waypoint Research Institute, Associate Professor of Psychiatry at the University of Toronto, and a registered psychologist. She earned degrees from the University of Southampton, University of Cambridge and University of Toronto. She was the lead on the research team that developed the Ontario Domestic Assault Risk Assessment (ODARA), led the development and evaluation of in-class and online professional training ("ODARA 101"), and continues to study risk assessment with collaborators and students. Her other current research involves understanding how workplace factors impact trauma experiences among forensic and general psychiatric staff, and research with a new cohort of men admitted to a forensic assessment including their pathways to violence, risk and criminogenic needs, and physical health.

Sheilagh Hodgins, Ph.D., F.R.S.C., is currently professor at the Département de Psychiatrie, Université de Montréal and the Institut Universitaire de Santé Mentale de Montréal, and a visiting professor with the Department of Clinical Neuroscience at the Karolinska Institutet. Professor Hodgins has been publishing studies of antisocial behaviour and criminality among persons with schizophrenia since 1992. Initially, large birth cohorts followed into adulthood were examined in order to compare crimes committed by persons with and without schizophrenia. Once it was robustly established that schizophrenia conferred an elevated risk, especially for violent crimes, clinical studies were undertaken to examine physically aggressive behaviour towards others that was also shown to be more common among those with, than without, schizophrenia. Subsequent studies aimed at identifying effective treatments, the neural correlates of early-onset persistent antisocial behaviour among persons with schizophrenia, while others adopted a developmental perspective in order to begin to identify the causal chain of bio-psycho-social factors leading to aggressive behaviour among persons with schizophrenia.

Todd E. Hogue. Ph.D is a Registered Forensic and Clinical Psychologist and Professor of Forensic Psychology at the University of Lincoln. He has worked as a Forensic Psychologist in prison, community and secure mental health settings developing forensic clinical services for individuals who are hard to engage and have high risk, sexual and violent offending histories. His research interests focus mainly on the impact of attitudes on professional judgements and social policy, the use of new technologies such as eye-tracking to assess inappropriate sexual interest and the evaluation of brief interventions to impact on prisoner engagement and wellbeing.

David V. James, Ph.D., is a Consultant Forensic Psychiatrist currently working with Theseus LLP in the field of threat assessment and management. He was formerly a Senior Lecturer in Forensic Psychiatry at University College London. He spent twenty years working with mentally disordered offenders in the U.K.'s National Health Service. He was co-founder of the Fixated Threat Assessment Centre and the National Stalking Clinic. He is co-author of the *Stalking Risk Profile* and of the *Communications Threat Assessment Protocol*. He is an author of some 65 papers in peer-reviewed journals, as well as a dozen book chapters.

Lawrence Jones started his career working in the community with former lifers, serious offenders and high secure hospital patients, after they had been released. He went on to work at HMP Wormwood Scrubs where he trained as a Forensic Psychologist working with Lifers and going on to work in and eventually manage a wing based therapeutic community. He developed and piloted a CBT model for running Therapeutic Communities. He moved from HMP Wormwood Scrubs to Rampton High Secure Hospital where he trained as a Clinical psychologist and worked with people with a personality disorder diagnosis. He then moved to work in the Peaks Unit, also in Rampton Hospital, eventually working as Lead psychologist there, managing the treatment programmes and developing and maintaining specialist services for individuals who have personality disorder diagnoses who have typically not responded to or been able to access services in other high secure settings. More recently he has taken on the role of Head of Psychology at Rampton Hospital. He is a former chair of the Division of Forensic Psychology and teaches on the Sheffield and Leicester Clinical Psychology doctorate courses and the Nottingham University Forensic Psychology Doctorate. He is an honorary (clinical) associate professor at Nottingham University. He has published in a range of areas including therapeutic communities, working with people who have personality disorder diagnoses who have offended sexually, case formulation with people with personality disorder diagnoses, iatrogenic responses to intervention, motivation, offence paralleling behaviour (OPB) and trauma informed care.

Melissa R. Jonnson, BA (Hon.), is a graduate student in the Clinical-Forensic Psychology program at Simon Fraser University. Her research involves the use of risk assessment tools in criminal sentencing, the experiences of sexual and gender minority youths in the justice system, and the role of objectification in intimate partner violence. She takes an interdisciplinary approach to her research, integrating perspectives from Psychology, Criminology, Sociology, and Gender Studies.

Hazel Kemshall is currently Professor of Community and Criminal Justice at De Montfort University. She has research interests in risk assessment and management of offenders, effective work in multi-agency public protection, and implementing effective practice with high risk offenders. She has completed research for the Economic and Social Research Council, the Home Office, Ministry of Justice, the Scottish Government, the Risk Management Authority, and the European Union. She has over 100 publications on risk, including Understanding Risk in Criminal Justice (2003, Open University Press), and Understanding the Community Management of High Risk Offenders (2008, Open University). Her most recent book Working with Risk was published by Polity in 2013. She was appointed to the Parole Board Review Committee in 2011 and is a Board Member of the Risk Management Authority Scotland and has chaired the Risk Management Plan Approval Committee for Orders for Lifelong Restriction. She recently completed research into European information exchange systems on serious violent and sexual offenders who travel across EU borders.

Daryl G. Kroner, Ph.D., is a Professor at the Department of Criminology and Criminal Justice at Southern Illinois University (SIU). He has more than 20 years of experience in the field as a correctional psychologist. During this time, he worked at maximum, medium, and minimum facilities delivering intervention services to incarcerated men. In collaboration with Dr. Jeremy Mills, he has developed several instruments, including the Measures of Criminal Attitudes and Associates (MCAA), Depression, Hopelessness and Suicide Scale (DHS),

Criminal Attribution Inventory (CRAI), Transition Inventory (TI), and the Measures of Criminal and Antisocial Desistance (MCAD). In collaboration with Drs. Morgan and Mills, a book entitled "Changing Lives and Changing Outcomes: A Treatment Program for Justice Involved Persons with Mental Illness has been published by Rutledge. In 2008, Dr. Kroner joined the Department of Criminology and Criminal Justice at SIU. Current research interests include risk assessment, measurement of intervention outcomes, interventions among offenders with mentally illness, and criminal desistance.

Caleb D. Lloyd, Ph.D., completed his doctorate at Carleton University in Ottawa, Canada, and is a Senior Lecturer at the Centre for Forensic Behavioural Science at Swinburne University of Technology, Melbourne, Australia. He directs a program of research on offender change in corrections and the community, with an aim to conduct theoretically informed research with clear practical applications for the correctional system. He has successfully attained funding for his work from federal agencies in Canada and the United States, and is currently serving as Principal Investigator on projects funded by the U.S. Department of Justice (National Institute of Justice) and Victoria Department of Justice and Regulation (Corrections Victoria, Australia). He seeks to be involved in building an international understanding of the psychology of offender change, and collaborates on projects within multiple countries (New Zealand, US, Australia, and Canada).

Caroline Logan, D.Phil., is Lead Consultant Forensic Clinical Psychologist in the Specialist Services Network in Greater Manchester Mental Health NHS Foundation Trust and an Honorary Research Fellow in the School of Medicine at the University of Manchester, England. Presently, she leads the Trust's Personality and Autism Spectrum Disorders Assessment and Liaison Team, and has developed and runs a number of services for people with personality disorder in prison and probation services. She has worked as a researcher and a clinician in forensic mental health and criminal justice services for 22 years, working directly in both roles with clients who are at risk to themselves and others. She also undertakes various consultancy roles with the national health and criminal justice organisations that look after and manage this client group, examining risk assessment and management practice, and proposing and evaluating change. Dr Logan has served on the editorial board or been associate editor of several journals (*International Journal of Forensic Mental Health, Legal and Criminological Psychology, Journal of Forensic Psychiatry and Psychology*). She is the co-author of several sets of national practice guidelines (e.g., *Understanding Personality Disorder* for the British Psychological Society 2006; *Best Practice in Managing Risk* for the Department of Health 2007 and 2009; *Working with Personality Disordered Offenders* for the National Offender Management Service/Department of Health 2015). She is Past President of the International Association of Forensic Mental Health Services (2006-2008), and a past board member of the Scottish Risk Management Authority (2004-2008) and remains attached to the latter organisation in a consultancy role. Dr Logan has also served on a number of Home Office/Ministry of Justice committees on criminal justice issues. She is Chair of the Scientific Advisory Board of the Bergen International Conference on Forensic Psychiatry series (www.bergenconference.no). Dr Logan has on-going research interests in the areas of personality disorder, including psychopathy, and risk and she has a special interest in gender issues in offending behaviour. She has published two books and multiple articles on all these subjects and is currently working on a book on forensic clinical interviewing.

Christopher T. Lowenkamp, Ph.D., received his PhD in Criminal Justice from the University of Cincinnati and is currently a social science analyst for the Administrative Office (AO) of the US Courts, Probation and Pretrial Services Office. Prior to his appointment at the AO, Dr. Lowenkamp was a research professor and the director of the Center for Criminal Justice Research at the University of Cincinnati. Dr. Lowenkamp's research interests include pretrial and post-conviction risk assessment, effective supervision practices, treatment and intervention quality, and program evaluation. Dr. Lowenkamp has been involved in the development of six risk assessments and has published over 25 articles on the topic of risk assessment. He has written numerous practice related curriculum and materials such as Effective Practices In Correctional Settings-II (EPICS-II), Staff Training Aimed at Reduction Re-arrest (STARR), the Post-Conviction Risk Assessment (PCRA), the Pretrial Risk Assessment (PTRA) and the Public Safety Assessment (PSA). Dr. Lowenkamp is internationally recognized as an expert in the field of corrections and has been awarded the Simon Dinitz Award by the Ohio Justice Alliance for Community Corrections, the MacNamara Award by the Academy of Criminal Justice Science, and the Dan Richard Beto Award by the National Association of Probation Executives. Dr. Lowenkamp has been named as one of the top 100 most influential criminologists based on publication records and a top ten scholar based on research grant acquisition.

Wagdy Loza, Ph.D., received his PhD in psychology from Carleton University. He is an Adjunct Assistant Professor (Psychiatry, Queen's University) and ex. Adjunct Professor (Psychology, Carleton University). He is a licensed psychologist (Ontario) and is the founder of the Extremism/terrorism section of the Canadian Psychological Association (CPA). In 2009, he retired from Correctional Service of Canada with almost 30 years of experience in the Correctional/Forensic field. He was the Chief Psychologist of Kingston Penitentiary. He is currently a member of the Ontario Review Board (a government department responsible for releasing Forensic offenders). Dr. Loza's research interests are in the areas of predicting violent and non-violent recidivism with Correctional and Forensic populations, and understanding extremism and terrorism, primarily emanating from the Middle-East. He has more than 45 publications in these areas and offered workshops and presentations in several countries around the world. Dr. Loza has developed two measure to help with predicting violent and non-violent recidivism and Middle-Eastern extremism and terrorism.

Dawn McDaniel, Ph.D., is Research and Evaluation Consultant with the PEAR Institute: Partnerships in Education and Resilience, a joint initiative of Harvard University and McLean Hospital. Dawn received her PhD in Child Clinical Psychology from the University of Southern California, and completed a fellowship in Applied Epidemiology at the Centers for Disease Control and Prevention (CDC). She has worked with large youth-serving organization, such as the Boys & Girls Clubs of America and Outward Bound USA, to refine their social and emotional development strategies, including integrating new measurement tools to maintain continuous quality improvement through national dissemination of evidence-based practices and programs. In her clinical practice and research, she has focused on youth impacted by gangs and trauma exposure and is interested in how social and emotional programming relates to youth resilience.

James McGuire, MA, MSc, Ph.D., is Emeritus Professor of Forensic Clinical Psychology at the University of Liverpool. After some years in self-employment he worked in intellectual disability services and then in a high security hospital. He has provided psycho-legal assessments and reports for criminal courts, parole hearings, and Mental Health Tribunals. He conducted research in probation services, prisons, youth justice, and in addictions services on aspects of psychosocial rehabilitation with offenders, and has designed and evaluated a number of intervention and staff training programmes. He was co-organiser of the What Works series of conferences in the UK in the 1990s. He has authored or edited 15 books and over 150 other publications, has been an invited speaker in 21 countries and has acted as a consultant to criminal justice agencies in several parts of the world.

Martyn Matthews, RNLD, DipCCM(ID), Ph.D., is director of Kestrel Consulting, and was previously National Clinical Practice Leader for IDEA Services, New Zealand. He also has a long association with Otago University, Department of Psychological Medicine, where he completed his PhD investigating psychiatric comorbidity with autism spectrum disorder. Martyn has worked with people with intellectual disabilities or autism spectrum disorders for 30 years, split between his two passions: early intervention for children and families, and developing services for people who have complex behaviours or have come to disability services via the criminal justice system. He has extensive experience in specialist forensic services for people with ID, in secure hospital and in community settings, both in the UK and NZ. Martyn was a member of the NZ Government's Autism Spectrum Disorder Guideline Implementation Group and is a current member of the NZ ASD Living Guideline Group. He is also a member of IASSIDD special interest research groups: Autism, and Challenging Behaviour and Mental Health.

Raymond W. Novaco, Ph.D., is Professor of Psychology and Social Behavior, at the University of California, Irvine. He has extensive expertise on the assessment and treatment of anger with a variety of clinical populations, including those with a history of violence. He received the Best Contribution Award in 1978 from the International Society for Research on Aggression for his book, *Anger Control: The Development and Evaluation of an Experimental Treatment,* the Distinguished Contributions to Psychology Award in 2000 from the California Psychological Association, and, in 2009, the Academic Award from the Division of Forensic Psychology of the British Psychological Society. His co-edited book, "Using Social Science to Reduce Violent Offending" (Oxford University Press) received the 2013 "Best Book" Award from the American Psychology-Law Society. He received a UC Irvine Excellence in Undergraduate Education Award in 2015.

David Nussbaum, Ph. D., C. Psych., received his PhD in Biological Psychology at the University of Waterloo in 1983 and a Post-Doctoral Internship in Clinical and Neuropsychology at the Clarke Institute of Psychiatry. After working as a staff psychologist and Senior Psychologist at the Metro Toronto Forensic Service (METFORS) for 17 years. He taught in the Psychology Department at York University for 20 years, where he now remains as an adjunct professor. He also taught in the Psychology Department at the University of Toronto (Scarborough) for seven years, where he remains a sessional lecturer. Since 2010, he has held a Guest Professorship at the China University of Political Science and Law in Beijing, PRC. He has published approximately 38 peer reviewed journal articles and delivered over 110 peer-reviewed papers at professional and scientific meetings. He served multiple terms as Chair of three sections of the Canadian Psychological Association (CPA) (Criminal Justice, Psychopharmacology, and the Study of Extremism and Terrorism. He was elected a Fellow of both the CPA and APA (Division 55; Society for Pharmacotherapy). He has sat as a Psychology

Member of the Ontario Review Board since 1996. His ongoing research interests include epistemology, behavioural neurobiology, risk assessment and extremism/terrorism. His areas of practice include neuropsychology, forensic psychology and clinical psychology. He recently established the Allan K. Hess Institute for Integrative and Forensic Psychology.

James R. P. Ogloff, B.A., M.A., J.D., Ph.D., is trained as a lawyer and psychologist. He is Foundation Professor and Director of the Centre for Forensic Behavioural Science at Swinburne University of Technology. He is also Executive Director of Psychological Services and Research Forensicare, Victoria's statewide forensic mental health service. He was appointed a Member of the Order of Australia for significant service to education and law as a forensic psychologist, academic, researcher and practitioner. He assesses and assists with the management of some of the most difficult offenders in Australia. He served as British Columbia's first Director of Mental Health Services for Corrections and has been president or chair of professional organisations (i.e., Australian and New Zealand Association of Psychiatry, Psychology and Law; College of Forensic Psychologists of the Australian Psychological Society; Canadian Psychological Association; American Psychology-Law Society). He has published 17 books and more than 275 scholarly articles and book chapters. He has served as editor and associate editor of leading scholarly journals in his field. He is the recipient of the distinguished contributions awards in law and psychology/forensic psychology from the Australian Psychological Society, the Canadian Psychological Association, and the American Psychology-Law Society.

Mark E. Olver, Ph.D., is a Professor and Registered Doctoral Psychologist at the University of Saskatchewan, in Saskatoon, Saskatchewan, Canada, where he is involved in program administration, graduate and undergraduate teaching, research, and clinical training. Prior to his academic appointment, Mark worked as a clinical psychologist in various capacities, including providing assessment, treatment, and consultation services to young offenders in the Saskatoon Health Region and with adult federal offenders in the Correctional Service of Canada. He has published over 110 journal articles and book chapters and his research interests include offender risk assessment and treatment, young offenders, psychopathy, and the evaluation of therapeutic change. He is co-developer of the Violence Risk Scale-Sexual Offense version (VRS-SO) and Violence Risk Scale-Youth Sexual Offense Version (VRS-YSO), and he provides training and consultation services internationally in the assessment and treatment of sexual, violent, and psychopathic offenders.

Devon L.L. Polaschek, Ph.D., DipClinPsyc., is a clinical psychologist and professor of psychology in the School of Psychology and the Joint Director of the Institute of Security and Crime Science, University of Waikato, New Zealand. Her research interests include theory, intervention, and intervention evaluation with serious violent and sexual offenders, family violence, psychopathy, desistance, reintegration and parole. She is the author of more than 110 journal articles, book chapters and government reports, and a fellow of the Association for Psychological Science. Her research has been supported by a decade of funding from the Department of Corrections, in order to develop a better understanding of high-risk violent male prisoners: their characteristics, and what works to reduce their risk of future offending. She has evaluated the effectiveness of correctional programmes for rehabilitating offenders since 1987, and more recently has worked on family violence research projects with various non-governmental organisations and on several different government contracts.

Vernon L. Quinsey Ph.D., received his PhD in Biopsychology from the University of Massachusetts at Amherst in 1970. He was the founding Director of Research at the maximum security Oak Ridge Division of the Mental Health Centre in Penetanguishene, Ontario. In 1988, he moved to Queen's University in Kingston, Ontario, where he is currently Professor Emeritus of Psychology, Biology, and Psychiatry. He has published upwards of 200 articles, including nine books on risk appraisal, sex offenders, violent offenders, clinical judgment, behavioural interventions in forensic institutions, program evaluation, and evolutionary psychology. More information can be found at: http://www.queensu.ca/psychology/people/emeritus-and-retired-faculty/vern-quinsey.

Martin Rettenberger, M.A., Priv.-Doz. Dipl.-Psych. Dr. biol. hum. Habil., is a psychologist and criminologist and serves currently as the director of the Centre for Criminology (Kriminologische Zentralstelle – KrimZ) in Wiesbaden, Germany, and is affiliated as an associate professor at the Department of Psychology at the Johannes Gutenberg-University Mainz, Germany. He previously worked at the Federal Evaluation Centre for Violent and Sexual Offenders (FECVSO) in the Austrian Prison System in Vienna, Austria, and at the Institute of Sex Research and Forensic Psychiatry at the University Medical Center Hamburg-Eppendorf, Germany. Since 2016, he is the secretary general of the International Association for the Treatment of Sexual Offenders (IATSO) and as editor of the IATSO e-journal *Sexual Offender Treatment*.

Tanya Rugge, Ph.D., is a senior research adviser in the Corrections Research Unit at Public Safety Canada in Ottawa, Canada. Over the years she has interviewed numerous offenders and victims, conducted risk assessments, worked with female offenders in clinical settings, and conducted research on recidivism, high-risk offenders, young offenders and Indigenous offenders, and evaluated several restorative justice programs. She has been involved in researching, advancing, and implementing evidence-based practices in community supervision and corrections for over two decades.

Caitlin Sayegh, Ph. D., is an Assistant Professor of Clinical Pediatrics at University of Southern California Keck School of Medicine and a Licensed Clinical Psychologist at Children's Hospital Los Angeles Divisions of Adolescent and Young Adult Medicine and General Pediatrics. Dr. Sayegh specializes in motivation, treatment engagement, medical adherence, and therapy process research. She has worked extensively with gang-involved and juvenile justice-involved clients in research and clinical contexts.

Ralph C. Serin, Ph.D., is a registered psychologist who received his PhD from Queen's University in 1988. He worked in federal corrections from 1975-2003 in various capacities and is now a Professor at Carleton University where he is Director of the Criminal Justice Decision Making Laboratory. He has received research funding from Canadian and US federal agencies; he has consulted with various government agencies in North America, the United Kingdom, Australia and New Zealand; and he is a member of the Correctional Services Advisory and Accreditation Panel in the United Kingdom. Current research interests relate to understanding offender change and decision making at key points within the Criminal Justice System.

Stephane M. Shepherd, Ph.D., is a Visiting Professor at the Department of Mental Health, Bloomberg School of Public Health, Johns Hopkins University and Senior Lecturer at the Centre for Forensic Behavioural Science, Swinburne University of Technology. He conducts research on risk and protective factors for violence and offending and cross-cultural issues in forensic assessment. Dr. Shepherd's research explores cross-cultural issues at the intersection of psychology and the criminal justice system. He has developed an international body of research and writing on risk and protective factors for violence and cultural differences in offending behaviours and mental ill health and the implications for assessment. Dr. Shepherd has pursued these interests through a variety of novel approaches and international working experiences with people in custody and multicultural communities. His contributions have raised awareness for cross-cultural issues in the forensic psychology and general psychology disciplines and have compelled researchers and practitioners alike to ensure that their methods are culturally fair, relevant and non-discriminatory.

Lorraine P. Sheridan, Ph.D., is a Chartered Forensic Psychologist. She completed Europe's first PhD on stalking and has so far published four books and more than 70 papers on the subject. Her research has taken an applied, interventionist angle and she frequently trains professionals involved in investigating stalking crimes. In the UK, Lorraine was a police accredited offender profiler and she compiles psychological reports related to offenders, highlighting the risks posed by known or unknown suspects. She regularly gives case management advice to the police, security personnel, public figures and others on stalking, harassment, violence, risk assessment, threat assessment, malicious communications and similar topics. After a long stint as a senior academic in universities in the UK, Lorraine is now a Senior Lecturer at Curtin University in Perth, Australia. She is a founder member of the Association of European Threat Assessment Professionals. Her risk checklist for stalking has been adopted by most English and Welsh police forces and partner agencies.

John L. Taylor, Ph.D., is Professor of Clinical Psychology at Northumbria University, Newcastle upon Tyne and Consultant Clinical Psychologist and Associate Director for Psychological Services with Northumberland, Tyne & Wear NHS Foundation Trust. Dr Taylor is a chartered clinical and forensic psychologist. He is Chair of the British Psychological Society (BPS) Mental Health Act Advisory Group, a Past President of the British Association for Behavioural and Cognitive Psychotherapies (BABCP), and a former Chair of the BPS Faculty for Forensic Clinical Psychology. Dr Taylor was one of the first two psychologists to be approved as an Approved Clinician in England following the MHA 2007. He has published more than 140 research papers, articles, books and book chapters mainly concerning the mental health and forensic needs of people with intellectual and developmental disabilities. Dr Taylor received an award for *Outstanding Contribution to Applied Practice* from the BPS Faculty for Forensic Clinical Psychology in 2017.

David Thornton, Ph.D., is a forensic psychologist in private practice, based in Madison (Wisconsin). In this capacity, he also works regularly in Illinois, Minnesota, Iowa, New York and England. He holds a part time position as a professor in the department of clinical psychology at the University of Bergen in Norway where he teaches and carries out research. He has previously worked as both the research director and the treatment director of Wisconsin's SVP program and before that led the unit responsible for treatment services designed to reduce recidivism in the national headquarters of Her Majesty's Prison Service for England and Wales. As a practitioner, he specializes in the assessment and treatment of sexual and violent offenders. As a researcher he has been involved in the development of statistical and psychological frameworks for assessing factors that contribute to different kinds of recidivism.

This has led to the creation of statistical instruments like Static-99 and Risk Matrix 2000 as well as psychological models of risk like SRA Need Assessment.

Jodi L. Viljoen, Ph.D., is an Associate Professor of Clinical and Forensic Psychology at Simon Fraser University and the Associate Director of the Institute for the Reduction of Youth Violence. Her research focuses on risk assessment, particularly strategies by which to bridge risk assessment and treatment. Dr. Viljoen is the first author of the Short-Term Assessment of Risk and Treatability: Adolescent Version and an intervention-planning tool called the Adolescent Risk Reduction and Resilient Outcomes Work-Plan. Her consultation work focuses on helping agencies to implement best practices for assessing and managing risk.

Stephen C.P. Wong, Ph.D., is a forensic psychologist and Fellow of the Canadian Psychological Association. He is Adjunct Professor at the University of Saskatchewan, Canada and Swinburne University of Technology, Melbourne and Honorary Professor at the University of Nottingham, UK. His research and clinical interests include assessment and treatment of violent offending, psychopathy, and treatment evaluation. He is the author of more than 100 journal articles, book, book chapters and reports. Steve started his career as a psychologist at the Regional Psychiatric Centre, a maximum-security psychiatric hospital in the Correctional Service Canada. He was later appointed Chief of Psychology and Research, and then Director of Research. In 2008, he left Canada to spend a year as Visiting Professor at the Department of Forensic and Neurodevelopmental Science at Kings College, London. His research interests are best escribed as a blending of applied research and clinical practice with a focus on the assessment and treatment of violent, sexual and psychopathic offenders. He is the lead author of the Violence Risk Scale (VRS) and the VRS sexual offence version (VRS-SO). These clinical tools can be used to assess violence and/or sexual risk for the respective offender groups. Steve and his colleagues also developed the Violence Reduction Programme (VRP) for the treatment of offenders and forensic service users.

The late J. Stephen Wormith, Ph.D., was a Professor in the Psychology Department at the University of Saskatchewan (U of S) and Director of the Centre of Forensic Behavioural Science and Justice Studies, which is also at UofS Previously, he was Psychologist-in-Chief for the Ontario Ministry of Community Safety and Correctional Services. He was a Fellow of the Canadian Psychological Association (CPA). He co-authored the *Level of Service/Case Management Inventory* (2004) with D. A. Andrews and J. Bonta and participated internationally in research and training on risk assessment. He was on the editorial board of *Criminal Justice and Behavior*, *Psychological Services* and the *Canadian Journal of Criminology and Criminal Justice*. He was also on the Board of Directors of the International Association for Correctional and Forensic Psychology (IACFP). Dr. Wormith's research activities have concentrated on the assessment and treatment of offenders. He consulted with provincial and federal government departments and served as an expert witness on matters of offender assessment and treatment. (See About the Editors section for more detail).

Foreword

The very word "violence" evokes strong emotional reactions and alarm in many people. Violent behaviour threatens the physical and psychological integrity of the person and our society goes to great lengths to minimize the threat of violence and protect victims and the community at-large. Acts of criminal violence are met with sanctions that far outweigh non-violent crimes. Violent offenders are incarcerated for longer periods of time than those who commit nonviolent crimes. Offenders who commit homicide may be executed or remain in prison for the rest of their life. Individuals who commit a violent crime and are on probation or parole will be subject to more conditions and longer periods of community supervision. This is particularly so for sex offenders. Many jurisdictions have controls that permit the incarceration of individuals, not for what they have done, but for what they *may* do in the future (e.g., preventative detention, dangerous offender designation).

It is not a surprise that much has been written about violence from both popular and scholarly perspectives. Scholarly books tend to be compartmentalized into silos of theory, assessment, and intervention. Granted a specialized book, for example on assessment will include theory and/or intervention but, these topics are usually addressed in a cursory fashion. Perhaps, this compartmentalization is necessary considering the voluminous literature on each of these three areas. This, however, need not be the case; theory, assessment, and intervention are all closely inter-connected. This edited book by Stephen Wormith, Leam Craig, and Todd Hogue offers a notable exception to the silo approach of addressing the topic of violence. In the text, an impressive array of international experts have been brought together to provide the most recent advances in our theoretical understanding, assessment, and management of violent behaviour.

Part I of the book gives an introduction to the topic and lays out the basic challenges in the field of violent behaviour. The reader is furnished with a comprehensive review of who are the violent, their prevalence in society, and the most recent explanations for their behaviour. We are also introduced to the importance of social context (e.g., gangs) and subgroups of violent offenders (e.g., intimate partner violence) with more in-depth coverage left for later in the text. Of course, specifying who commits violence and under what circumstances, even with a sound theoretical understanding is limited without some guidance on how we can minimize the harm from violent behaviour. Thus, Part I ends with an overview of the effectiveness of treatment for aggressive offenders, both youths and adults.

Various assessment approaches and specialized risk assessment instruments are thoroughly described in Parts II and III. For both the reader who is new to the area of violence and the reader who has spent a significant proportion of his/her career studying violent behaviour, the chapters in these sections of the text are an excellent resource on the assessment of violent offenders. We are exposed to the various general approaches to violence risk assessment and the more commonly used instruments for adults and young offenders with a special emphasis on intimate partner violence and sex offenders (Part II). Part III is a unique and valuable feature of this book. It includes what the editors call "Specialty Clinical Assessments". The chapters here address assessment issues that one would typically find in textbooks devoted to the specific area. Thus, if one wanted to know current thinking on the assessment, for example, of terrorism then the reader would typically consult a text devoted to the whole topic of terrorism and its complexity. In Part III we have a number of "go-to" chapters brought together in one text and should appeal to a broad audience.

The chapters in Parts II and III are critical for what follows in the book, the treatment of violent and aggressive behaviour. Effective interventions are impossible without the reliable assessment of the risk and criminogenic needs of the offender. Too many treatment programs fail because of the inappropriate matching of treatment services to the offender. Parts IV and V deliver in providing the latest evidence on effective treatment and risk management. A number of well-established treatment interventions for violent offenders are presented here. In Part IV, the reader will be pleased with highly readable chapters that address common issues associated with violent behaviour (e.g., alcohol misuse) and the less common (i.e., offenders with intellectual disabilities). Clearly, violence is not limited to a small defined subset of offenders and social contexts. Finally, if society wants to do more than simply isolate the violent from our communities through incarceration then treatment interventions must have the support of criminal justice agencies. A number of examples of how much can be accomplished when criminal justice policies and practice organizations are aligned with the "what works" agenda are presented in Part V.

The editors of this text and the chapter authors must be commended for their scholarly treatment of a difficult topic. They have achieved an empirically based and current account of the theory, assessment, and treatment of violent offenders. This volume will be of considerable use, not only to scholars, but also the practitioners and policy-makers who deal with the issue of violence. When our actions are based on a solid empirical foundation progress is made in minimizing the pain and suffering arising from criminal violence. This is a goal that is shared by the many professionals who have a responsibility to address violent behaviour and who have an obligation to maximize public safety.

James Bonta

Acknowledgements

We are grateful to the contributors of this volume for sharing their experience and expertise and who have worked tirelessly on this project alongside their hectic schedules.

We would like to thank all those at Wiley-Blackwell for their patience and guidance in bringing this project together.

The Wiley Handbook of What Works in Violence Risk Management

Part I
Introduction

1

An Overview of Violent Behaviour from Aggression to Homicide
Theory, Research, and Practice

J. Stephen Wormith[1], Leam A. Craig[2,3,4], and Todd E. Hogue[5]

[1] University of Saskatchewan, Canada
[2] Forensic Psychology Practic Ltd., Sutton Coldfield, UK
[3] Centre for Applied Psychology, University of Birmingham, UK
[4] School of Social Sciences, Birmingham City University, UK
[5] School of Psychology, University of Lincoln, UK

Introduction and Overview

The magnitude and scope of human violence is vast and its manifestations take many forms. As such, it remains one of the terrible ills with which our species must contend. Arguably, it remains as complex and resistant to amelioration as fatal medical conditions such as cancer and 'super bugs', chronic economic issues such as poverty, hunger, and homelessness, and political blights such as warfare, displaced refugees, and ethnic cleansing. Violence, by definition, always has an impact on individuals and often extends to the broader community and society as a whole. Consequently, society has a tremendous responsibility to address violence and to challenge both its causes and its perpetrators. However, the diversity of forms by which violence is enacted dictate that our range of responses must be equally diverse. Social sciences and their allied professions offer a number of important strategies to address violence by furthering theories of violence, generating empirical data about violence, and translating the resulting knowledge into policy and practice. But when it comes to violence, the devil is, quite literally, in the details.

This chapter offers an overview of violence in society and the complex issues that it raises for researchers, clinicians, policy makers, lawmakers, and society at large. It begins with a review of definitions of violence, then describes its behavioural variability, and relates violence to other forms of antisocial behaviour, such as aggression. While being mindful not to burden the reader with endless statistics, it offers sobering data about the magnitude of violence in society and its impact on victims, with a focus on its most severe expression, homicide. Attention is given to some of the more popular and validated theories of violence as they may guide efforts

The Wiley Handbook of What Works in Violence Risk Management: Theory, Research and Practice,
First Edition. Edited by J. Stephen Wormith, Leam A. Craig, and Todd E. Hogue.

to reduce the prevalence of violence in society and to direct further research. In order to be successful, such efforts must use empirically validated assessments, the dramatic proliferation of which is described briefly. This leads to a review of explicit efforts to reduce violence presented in three tiers whereby the criminological concepts of primary, secondary, and tertiary prevention are used to classify violence prevention initiatives (Pease 2002). The chapter ends with a call to arms on many fronts and points to the remaining chapters as a series of promising jumping off points.

Definitions of Violence and Aggression

Because of its diverse forms, a comprehensive, all-inclusive definition of violence is more difficult to craft than one might anticipate. Moreover, disciplines and professions are likely to conceptualize violence in a fashion that reflects their own perspective of human behaviour. It is also important to understand the difference between violence and aggression and to appreciate how the former is situated within the latter, which itself, also requires some thought to define.

There are two key aspects to the concept of aggression. The first is that it entails a conscious effort to harm someone or some people. The second is that the nature of the intended harm can take various forms including physical, emotional, and psychological. Although implied in Glover's (1960) psychoanalytic perspective on crime, Feshbach (1964) was the first to identify two types of aggression that are based on the motivation of the perpetrator and are expressed in two distinct manners. Although various terms have been used over the last half century, the first form of aggression (described as hostile, irritable, reactive, expressive, and conflict-oriented aggression) entails a reaction to some kind of external event, often a slight, insult, or perceived transgression or act of unfairness that generates an emotional, often impulsive and disorganized, reaction to the triggering event. On the other hand, the second form of aggression (described as instrumental, predatory, proactive, purposive, premeditated, and crime-oriented aggression), is motivated by a desire to achieve some specific goal, often the acquisition of material gain, but can also be motivated simply by a desire to inflict some suffering on another individual. It is planned, premeditated, organized, and can take quite some time to orchestrate. In addition, the magnitude of each motivational dimension can vary tremendously, from a verbal insult to a murderous rage and from hurt feelings to the fraudulent acquisition of one's life savings.

In spite of the variation of severity within these two kinds of aggression, empirical examples of their differences abound. Khachatryan et al. (2018) revealed that crime-oriented juvenile homicide was much more likely to involve accomplices (86%) than conflict-oriented crime (37.5%), while conflict-oriented homicide was much more likely to involve firearms (75% vs. 39.5%). Also amongst juvenile offenders, Tecce (2014) found that those who committed instrumental aggression had significantly higher psychopathy scores than those who committed reactive aggression. In the laboratory, alcohol is more likely to increase reactive aggression in persons with higher hostile rumination scores, but not with persons with lower hostile rumination scores (Borders and Giancola 2011). Amongst intimate partner violence (IPV) offenders, instrumental aggressors were significantly more likely to have previously assaulted a family member (33% vs. 15%) and to hold attitudes that condone spousal assault (20% vs. 7%), while reactive aggressors were significantly more likely to have witnessed or been a victim of family violence during their childhood (29% vs. 11%; Ennis et al. 2017). Treatment, such as anger management, has been found to affect violent offenders' potential for reactive aggression, but not proactive aggression (Walters 2009). In a sample of violent offenders in Ontario, Canada, there was a highly negative correlation ($r = -0.57$) between their degree of instrumental and reactive aggression, lending support to the distinction between these two forms of violence (Tapscott et al. 2012). These and many other studies tend to validate this classification system in spite of its simplicity and as Day and Fernandez (2020) note in Chapter 12, the understanding of anger is paramount in the assessment and understanding of violence.

A variation of Feshbach's classification comes from the developmental perspective of Loeber and Stouthamer-Loeber (1998). They noted that overt aggression, which is characterized by anger and confrontation, is often seen in children and adolescents, while covert aggression, which involves greater cognitive sophistication and less emotional reactivity, is more commonly used by adults. Clearly, overt and covert aggression bear resemblance to reactive and proactive aggression. The fact that they emerge at different stages of development lends support for this binary model of aggression and the different motivations and mechanisms that accompany them.

Although this was a helpful distinction in early theoretical work and research on aggression, such a dichotomy is now perceived as simplistic. Aggressive behaviour often has elements of both kinds of motivation (Bushman and Anderson 2001). Moreover, as Buss (1971) pointed out, aggression may be expressed physically or verbally, by taking actions or lack of action (passive aggression), and by acting directly or indirectly (in the absence of the intended victim), resulting in a $2 \times 2 \times 2$ classification system of aggression. The hostile-instrumental characterization also excludes the concept of defensive aggression, which is a response that occurs when a person perceives an imminent threat, typically physical, and often imaginary, as is the case with some serious mental disorders.

Although all interpersonal violence may be described as acts of aggression, not all aggression is physically aggressive (for example, relational aggression, verbal aggression, and passive aggression). In other words, aggression may be perpetrated or attempted with the explicit intent of harming a person or persons psychologically, emotionally, or even by reputation, as we see in Internet-based aggression. Yet 'aggression is the basic ingredient of violent crime … as well as violent behavior that may not necessarily be defined as crime (e.g. legitimate used of force)' (Bartol and Bartol 2016, p. 47). Simply put, violence refers to the more 'serious and extreme' expressions of aggression (Tolan and Guerra 1994, p. 1). Invariably, it is an expression of physical aggression with intent to harm the victim physically. Most forms of violence are antisocial transgressions in that they violate accepted morals, principles, and norms, and are violations of the law in the jurisdiction in which the action occurred. Although there are some differences in unaccepted and criminally defined behaviour across cultures and countries, which is of interest in and of itself, there is notable world-wide agreement as to what constitutes violent behaviour. The destruction of property is commonly included in definitions of both aggression and violence. However, it represents only a small portion, if any, of the kinds of aggression and violence that are examined in this edition.

The Magnitude and Scope of Violence in Modern Society as Illustrated by Homicide

As suggested, violent behaviour can take many different forms and can be expressed in widely different degrees. Examples include various kinds of domestic abuse (child, sibling, spousal, intimate partner, and elder abuse), sexual violence, reactive or impulsive violence, gratuitous violence, violence in the commission of another offence (e.g. armed robbery), ethnic and racial violence, retributive violence, and violence in warfare. It is also important to acknowledge that the prevalence of violence can vary over time and this variation may differ by type of violence, which Kroner and Butler (2020) discuss in Chapter 2. However, the accuracy of these rates and their changes are often treated with suspicion, in part because detected variations may be due to changes in the patterns of victim reporting. Regardless, researchers, government, and criminal justice agencies have an obligation to report such changes as they are detected.

Murder and other forms of homicide are of particular interest in the study of violence for at least three reasons. First, although homicide is not a common expression of violence, it does make a consistent contribution to violent crime figures. In 2013 and 2016, homicide made up 1.2% and 1.4% of all violent crimes in the USA, respectively, claiming the lives of over 15 000 people in the latter year (Federal Bureau of Investigation 2014, 2017). Therefore, its reduction is, or at least should be, a global objective. Other Federal Bureau of Investigation (FBI) categories of violent offences in the USA include aggravated assault (62.2 and 64.2%), robbery (29.6 and 26.6%), and rape (6.8 and 7.7%) during 2013 and 2016, respectively. These offence categories, along with homicide, combined to generate a rate of 367.9 and 386.3 violent crimes per 100 000 persons in the USA during 2013 and 2016, respectively (FBI 2014, 2017). Comparing the violent crime rates to other countries is difficult, if not misleading, due to differences in the definitions for violent crime. For instance, while the FBI's classification encompasses the above four offences, the British Office for National Statistics includes minor physical altercations such as pushing and shoving, harassment, and abuse, even if it does not result in physical harm (Office for National Statistics 2018).

Second, homicide is most easily defined and well documented in crime statistics, partly because of its severity and partly because of its relative ease of detection. Consequently, the 'dark figure' pertaining to homicide (its rate of going undetected or unreported) is relatively low because the more serious crime is the more likely it is to be reported (Skogan 1977). Therefore, this relatively accurate picture of homicide statistics is more apt to reflect real changes in perpetration over time at least within a common jurisdiction in comparison to other forms of violence, such as sexual assault and domestic or IPV, which may be influenced by changes in victims' inclination to report the crime as social mores and police practices change (Fisher et al. 2003; Koss et al. 1987).

Third, the causes and motivations for homicide are as diverse as the causes and motivations for all kinds of violent behaviour (Blackman et al. 2001). Frequently, homicide is not much different than other violent crimes except for the outcome, which, sadly, is often a simple matter of chance. The following studies illustrate this claim. Loeber et al. (2005) found that 95% of young men who had committed homicide had a history of previous violent offending. DiCataldo and Everett (2008) found that ease of access to firearms was sufficient to distinguish juvenile homicide offenders from other juvenile violent offenders, a sentiment later echoed by Farrington et al. (2012). In fact, it is difficult to extrapolate risk factors that can differentiate violent juvenile offenders from homicide-specific offenders (Corrado and Cohen 2014). Risk factors for juvenile homicide include familiar risk factors for juvenile violence, such as prior arrest, child abuse victimization, violent families, parental alcohol use, running away from home, low school achievement, truancy, and frequent school suspensions (Heide 2003). These findings support our contention that the difference between homicide and other violent offending is in large part related to circumstances beyond the characteristics of the perpetrator, such as the availability of firearms and access to advanced medical care, particularly when it comes to the hostile or reactive modes of violence. As such, homicide represents a relatively easily researched proxy, albeit an extreme one, for violent behaviour.

In addition to the legal categorizations of homicide, many of which have similar, but not identical, labels across jurisdictions (e.g. first and second degree murder, voluntary (nonnegligent) and involuntary (negligent) manslaughter/homicide, 'justifiable' homicide, infanticide, mass murder, unintentional homicide, assassination (murder with premeditation), vehicular homicide/manslaughter, injury resulting in death, feticide (death of fetus), regicide, gross negligence manslaughter, and culpable homicide), there are a number of behavioural, situational, and motivation-based classification systems of homicide that illustrate its diversity. One such example is provided by the FBI in the USA (Douglas et al. 2006). Although it suggests four main categories of homicide, these are broken down into numerous subgroups. For example, 'personal cause homicide' which typically occurs as the result of an argument or general altercation and therefore is usually reactive in nature, has 11 subtypes including domestic violence, argument murder, revenge killing, and hostage murder. Criminal enterprise homicide is perpetrated for some kind of material gain and therefore is usually instrumental in nature, or at least begins as such. It includes eight subtypes, such as contract killing, gang-motivated murder, kidnap murder, product tampering, insurance-motivated murder, and felony murder, which occurs during the perpetration of another crime such as robbery, kidnapping, and breaking and entering.

Sexual homicide has four subgroups that are based on an analysis of the crime scene. They included organized, disorganized, and mixed crime scene murders, as well as sadistic sexual murder. Homicide is classified as group-cause homicide when there are multiple perpetrators who share a particular ideology and includes three subtypes, cult murder, extremist murder, and group excitement murder (Bartol and Bartol 2014). As such, homicide represents the tip of a very heterogeneous iceberg of violence. This all makes for some important research data, some of which is described later. However, we are mindful that mind-numbing tables of homicide statistics run the risk of losing one's audience and the real meaning of these numbers, specifically, the fact that each and every data point in these tables constitutes a tragedy that is beyond belief.

Homicide rates vary substantially across countries and to a lesser extent over time. Although one must be mindful of differences in definition, completeness, and accuracy across jurisdictions, the United Nations has reported known homicide rates (homicides per 100 000 people) worldwide for a number of decades (United Nations 2016). In 2015, G8 countries reported the following rates in ascending order: Japan (0.31, in 2014), Italy (0.78), Germany (0.85), the United Kingdom (0.92, in 2014), France (1.58), and Canada (1.68), with the USA (4.88) and Russia (11.31) appearing as moderate and extreme outliers, respectively, and reminiscent of lesser developed countries, such as Cuba (4.72, in 2011), Kazakhstan (4.84), Kyrgyzstan (5.12), and Uruguay (8.42). As dismal as these statistics appear, they are all, with the exception of Uruguay, less than they were in 2003. The average (unweighted) change in the homicide rate was a reduction of 27.63% over this 12-year period. This equates to an average reduction of 1.45 homicides per 100 000 people in each of these 12 countries. Yet the raw numbers, even in these countries, remain disconcerting. Meanwhile some Central and South American countries, such as El Salvador, Honduras, and Venezuela, with their drug-related and political chaos, have gone in the opposite direction, almost doubling (93.44%) their already high rates (108.64, 63.75, and 57.15 per 100 000, respectively for 2015). In sum, from a world view, small gains have been overwhelmed by dramatic losses.

Demographic characteristics of homicide perpetrators, such as the age and gender, have been monitored for many years in most countries and offer a glimpse as to who commits this most serious crime. Although there is no single document that provides age and gender statistics on homicide perpetrators in a standardized manner across countries, a review of international reports offers a reasonably consistent pattern. However, one must also be cognizant of the different base rates of homicide by country when examining the breakdown of perpetrators and victims of homicide by demographics such as age and gender

Homicide offenders are most likely to be young adult males. The FBI reported that males constituted 88.8% of the known homicide perpetrators in the USA during 2016 (Federal Bureau of Investigation 2017). In Canada, males represented 86.04–89.29% of all known homicide offenders between 2012 and 2016 (Statistics Canada 2017). Similar gender trends are found in other developed nations, such as Italy, France, Germany, Russia, and the United Kingdom, where males made up 96, 90, 90, 87, and 76% of homicide perpetrators, respectively (Eurostat 2017; Flatley 2018; Italian National Institute of Statistics 2018; Lysova et al. 2012). Globally, the United Nations' (2014a) Office on Drugs and Crime estimated that 95% of homicide perpetrators are male.

The ages of homicide offenders are relatively similar amongst most industrialized nations, although the specific age range categories differ depending on the reporting agency. There are also some notable differences by country and gender. For instance, in 2016, the most prominent age category amongst male homicide perpetrators was in the 18 to 24 range in Canada and 20 to 24 range for the USA (Federal Bureau of Investigation 2017; Statistics Canada 2017). Across other jurisdictions, prominent age ranges for male perpetrators were similar in France (20–30), Germany (18–20), the UK (16– 24), while slightly older in Italy (25–34; Birkel and Dern 2012; Flatley 2018; Italian National Institute of Statistics 2018; Ministère de la Justice 2017). However, in both Russia and Japan, the average ages were roughly 35 years old (Hiraiwa-Hasegawa 2005; Lysova et al. 2012). Amongst female homicide perpetrators, the most frequent ages in Canada (25–34), Italy (45–54), and the UK (25–34) were moderately to considerably higher than their male counterparts (Flatley 2018; Italian National Institute of Statistics 2018; Statistics Canada 2017).

Clearly, data over time and across most jurisdictions point to young adult males being responsible for a disproportionate amount of homicide in these countries. Both the convergent and divergent statistics are relevant for academics (theoreticians and researchers), criminal justice personnel (law enforcement and correctional practitioners), clinicians (psychiatrists, psychologists, and social workers), and policy makers (politicians and government administrators) to appreciate and to accommodate them in their efforts to quell violence in society. Although these data do not explain the demographic consistency over time and place, nor the differences (for example, age-by-gender), they suggest possible explanatory candidates, that are likely to depend on one's theoretical, ideological, disciplinary, and cultural vantage point. A couple of perspectives deserve mention.

A clear and strong candidate pertains to biological factors, in particular the hormonal differences such as testosterone, that exist simultaneously across age and gender in a pattern that is consistent with the above noted homicide statistics. Although not always popular, a complete understanding of homicide, and violence more generally, must accommodate this pattern (Quinsey 2002). Resistance to accepting this relationship appears to be based on a sense that it leads to a dead end, that intervention cannot overcome our biological condition and, to take the argument to an extreme, may absolve the perpetrator of responsibility or *mens rea*. We do not accept this fatalistic argument. Rather, we believe that the age–gender pattern should direct the above noted groups (academics, criminal justice personnel, clinicians, and policy makers) to consider, in particular, this high-risk, demographically defined group in their theorizing, research, interventions, and policies, as presented later in more detail in a discussion of violence in general.

As the method of homicide may elucidate the motivation for killing and lead to strategies to lessen the occurrence of homicides, the use of weapons in homicide has been of interest to police, criminologists, forensic psychologists, and lawmakers for decades. Although the use and choice of weapon vary quite dramatically by jurisdiction, they have been very consistent within jurisdictions. For example, the use of firearms in the annual commission of homicide between 2005 and 2011 varied in the USA from 58 to 61%, in Canada from 32 to 36%, and in the UK from 6 to 10%. The rate in Germany over two years (2005 and 2006) was 24%, while no data were offered from other G8 countries (United Nations 2016). However, the use of sharp weapons (e.g. knives and swords) during the same time period occurred in the reverse order by country. The UK (37–40%) was followed by Canada (31–37%) and then the USA (11–12%). Italy reported a rate of 27% in 2009. This dramatic variance between countries and their differential use of weapons compared to the minimal difference within countries over time points to cultural variations in these three jurisdictions that are not revealed by these statistics alone.

The situational and interpersonal context of homicide over time and across G8 nations also offers some consistent patterns. Gang-related homicide accounts for substantially different amounts of homicide across international boundaries. It has also become a high-profile type of homicide capturing front-page news and political attention when it occurs. This is particularly the case in Canada, where gangs were implicated in 34.3–48.6% of annual homicides between 2005 and 2011. Gangs were involved in 22.6–24.7% in Japan (2005–2008, only), 9.6–17.9% in Italy, 7.0–15.0% in France (2005–2008, only), and 4.4–5.8% in the USA (other G8 countries were not reported; United Nations 2016). Although some of these differences are likely to be caused by different operational or legal definitions of gangs and one must remain mindful of the different base rates of homicide internationally, the differing rates of gang-related homicide in relation to total homicide is both consistent and substantial, again suggesting cultural variations. Regardless of the rate, gang-related homicides and other violent offences create a serious public safety concern for many communities; as such, many gang violence prevention efforts have been developed, which are discussed further in Chapter 13 (McDaniel and Sayegh 2020).

On the other hand, homicides that occur during the commission of a robbery, and therefore are a criminal enterprise type of crime, are much more consistent across international boundaries. Over a seven-year period (2005–2011), they include Germany (6.2–10.0%), Canada (3.6–7.9%), Japan (4.0–8.4%), Italy (3.7–6.6%) and the USA (5.0–6.1%). Moreover, there was no consistent trend over time, either overall or by individual countries (United Nations 2016). Sadly then, at least for the foreseeable future, we can anticipate that about 5% of homicides will occur as collateral damage during the commission of another crime, particularly robbery.

Victimologists attempt to glean an understanding of crime, including homicide, by investigating the demographics of victims. Amongst G8 countries, while males make up approximately three-quarters of homicide victims in the USA (77.8%), Canada (69.8%), Italy (69.9%), Russia (75.5%), and the UK (70.3%), the male–female divide is more evenly distributed in France (62.1%) Germany (52.7%) and Japan (47.1%). In countries undergoing political, social, or financial unrest, there are particularly large gender discrepancies with males representing the vast majority of homicide victims, as seen in El Salvador (89.0%), Venezuela (91.9%), Nicaragua (92.6%), Honduras (93.2%), Greece (93.4%), and Panama (94.6%; United Nations 2016). This is not to suggest that females are safer in these countries. Rather, males are targeted particularly in less-stable countries, which speaks to the diversity of motives for homicide, and more generally for violence, across cultures.

Table 1.1 Percent of homicides amongst male and female victims that are caused by intimate partner violence (IPV) presented by country and year.

Country	2005	2006	2007	2008	2009	2010	2011	*Average over years*
Male victims								
Canada	12.1	17.4	14.9	16.9	16.2	16.6	14.4	15.5
Germany	19.7	22.2	25.5	23	24.5	24.6	23.0	23.2
Italy	16.0	15.0	15.7	17.0	16.5	18.9	21.1	17.2
United Kingdom	N.D.	14.1	15.8	15.6	15.2	16.3	13.7	15.1
United States	8.2	8.4	8.2	8.9	9.3	9.4	9.7	8.9
Average	14.0	15.5	16.0	16.3	16.3	17.1	16.1	16.0
Female victims								
Canada	66.3	65.0	57.0	61.4	63.6	62.9	60.0	67.3
Germany	39.5	39.8	41.3	43.8	47.8	45.0	50.1	43.9
Italy	64.1	70.8	69.1	74.1	75.1	73.2	73.3	71.4
United Kingdom	N.D.	57.7	62.4	64.9	67.6	65.7	67.5	64.3
United States of America	47.6	44.3	46.6	49.2	48.5	51.5	51.8	48.5
Average over Countries	54.4	55.5	55.3	58.7	60.5	60.7	60.5	59.1

N.D. = No data. Table adapted from United Nations (2016). https://data.unodc.org/#state:0

The demographics of homicide also merit examination by type of homicide in order to understand it more fully. This includes intimate partner homicide, which itself occurs at dramatically different rates by gender (United Nations 2016). To illustrate, a number of important patterns are apparent from Table 1.1. Most dramatically and not surprisingly, when females are victims of homicide, it is much more likely to be in the context of intimate personal violence than it is for males and this difference is consistent both across time and country. For example, an average of 48.5% is found in the USA over seven years and an average of 67.3% in Canada over the same time frame, with an overall average of 59.1% over these five countries (rates were not available for France, Japan, and Russia). The corresponding rates on male homicide victims ranged from 8.9% in the USA to 23.2% in Germany with an average of 16.0% over these five countries. These mean rates for male and female victims also reflect a substantial difference between the percent of homicides that were related to IPV across these five countries. In other words, male victims of homicide in Germany were 2.6 times more likely related to IPV in Germany than they were in the USA. Differences for female victims were less extreme. For instance, female victims in Italy were only 1.6 times more likely to be victims of IPV-related homicide compared to victims in Germany. However, these figures are partly due to the much larger base rate of IPV-related homicide amongst female victims. A cursory inspection of these rates over time is also instructive. Although there is no apparent pattern amongst male victims of IPV-related homicide, a disturbing trend is found amongst female victims whereby the percentage of female victim homicides due to IPV shows a general increase (on average, 6% over these seven years), particularly in Germany, the UK, and the USA.

In sum, there are both consistencies and differences over time, country, and kind of homicide when we examine factors such as motivation, type, method, perpetrator gender, and victim gender. In many ways, by examining the most extreme form of violence, these statistics give us a glimpse of violent crime more generally.

Theories of Aggression and Violence

Although numerous types of theories (e.g. Anderson and Bushman 2002; Heto 2015), let alone specific theories, pertaining to violence, and more generally to aggression, have been proposed over the last century (discussed at length in Chapter 2 by Kroner and Butler), we suggest that they may be categorized into five general types: biological, intrapersonal, social, situational, and integrative. Amongst the biological theories, we include those that are constructed from genetic, biochemical, hormonal, neurological research. Nussbaum (2020) devotes an entire chapter to these later in this work (Chapter 16). Markers for violence that come from these include intellectual disability, poor executive functioning, and Foetal Alcohol Spectrum Disorder (FASD) (Brown et al. 2012; Glenn et al. 2007; Scarpa and Raine 2007; see Gontkovsky 2007 for a review). It is also important to appreciate that these contributors include not only the genetic, ethological, and evolutionary perspectives of human behaviour, commonly summarized as hereditary, but may also have environmental origins. Candidates include environmentally acquired medical conditions such as poor nutrition, exposure to toxic substances, alcohol and drug consumption, head injuries, and physical pain (Murphy et al. 1998; Nkomo et al. 2017; Gontkovsky 2007; Rosenbaum et al. 1994).

Consequently, we now understand that the age-old nature–nurture debate created a false dichotomy, one that simplified a complex reality and divided potentially complementary perspectives, thus inhibiting potentially meaningful advances. For example, thanks to the development of epigenetic research, it is now understood that the activation of a behaviourally related gene may be may be facilitated or inhibited by external factors, some of which, such as maternal care of species as diverse as rats and children, come from the environment (Meaney 2010; Meaney and Szyf 2005). There is no reason to believe that this kind of interaction does not apply to the perpetration of violent behaviour, particularly with the emergence and our developing understanding of the so-called violence or warrior genes (Tiihonen et al. 2015). In this regard, evolutionary theories of violence amongst humans also fall in this category (Duntley and Buss 2004; Lorenz 1966), particularly in that they address the disproportionate amount of male violence in most societies (Daly and Wilson 1994). Yet we are cautious about the over interpretation and over representation of these and other biologically based findings in the popular media, which will only be divisive and establish camps, both popular and academic, that will inhibit our potential for meaningful and accurate understanding of these phenomena. By dismissing this line of inquiry, we would be tying one of our multiple hands behind our backs, hindering us in our search to understand and reduce violent behaviour.

By intrapersonal theories, we refer to two things. The first is the litany of hypothetical constructs that have been proposed over the last 150 years, which have been proposed to capture human cognition and personality. They include psychodynamic structures, cognitive disabilities, and personality characteristics that have been invoked in our efforts to explain violent behaviour. A few notables include the id, ego, and superego, moral disengagement, empathy, self-esteem, self-efficacy, self-control, expectancy, deindividuation, dehumanization, negative affect or discomfort, rumination, and the so-called dark triad consisting of psychopathy, narcissism, and Machiavellianism (Bandura 2002; Baumeister et al. 1996; Baumeister and Boden 1998; Denson 2012; Freud 1920; Gottfredson and Hirschi 1990; Haslam 2006; Larson et al. 2015; Pailing et al. 2014; Zimbardo 1969).

The second is the list of internal, psychological, and cognitive processes that invoke or inhibit the expression of violent behaviour. Examples include the psychodynamic balance between id and super ego, the frustration-aggression sequence and its sociological counterpart, strain, as well as emotionality, displacement, excitation transfer, rationalization and neutralization, hostile attribution, and cognitive processes such as memory scripts (Agnew 1992; Berkowitz 1989, 2003; Baumeister et al. 1996; Dollard et al. 1939; Freud 1920; Huesmann 1998; Lindsay and Anderson 2000; Martinelli et al. 2018; Sykes and Matza 1957; Tsang 2002; Zillmann 1988). Although these personal characteristics and internal processes are often perceived as innate limitations of the individual (as per the preceding paragraph) or learned (as per the following paragraph), they may also be a product of one's social condition, such as poverty (Eron et al. 1997) or familial development, as described in attachment theory (Bowlby 1988; Meloy 2002).

Social theories of violence include social learning, modelling, and various forms of social reinforcement (Bandura 1977; Cohn and Rotton 2006; Mischel and Shoda 1995). Although they are more obviously related to instrumental violence, they also apply to violence that has been triggered by hostility, as when violence has become a socially learned response or anticipated 'solution' to distressing emotions. Theories of social-group influence as illustrated by bullying, gang violence, mob destruction, riots, copycat and contagion violence, including homicide, ideological violence, and terrorism (see Chapter 14, Loza 2020) for an overview of the social and ideological contributors to terrorist activities), all fall into this category. They include feminist theories in their analysis of IPV and sexual violence (Brownmiller 1975; Henderson 2007) and theories about the intergenerational transmission of violence that examine features of violence aside from genetic factors (Eriksson and Mazerolle 2015; Kwong et al. 2003). Finally, reminiscent of the integrative theories described later, general systems theory, first introduced to human services through social work more than forty years ago (Goldstein 1973), goes beyond the interaction of individuals to examine the larger context of families, communities, and society leading to system-level solutions, particularly with reference to family violence (Straus 1973; Murray 2006). Social theories of violence may also invoke some of the internal psychological constructs and processes, such as deindividuation, cited earlier.

Situational theories turn our attention to the external world for elicitors of violent behaviour and may be better described as models for understanding violent behaviour. This can range from a specific image or stimulus in the environment to an event or a situation that has acted as a trigger for violence. A key feature of situational violence is that the behaviour is less likely to have occurred in the absence of a particular trigger. As such, situational theories do not typically address the original motivation for the behaviour but focus on exacerbating features in the environment. Triggers may be inanimate or living, transitory or fixed. Examples include the presence of a weapon, opportunity, temperature, lighting, even a symbolic representation of aggression such as a picture of a weapon (weapons effect; Berkowitz and LePage 1967; Brennan and Moore 2009; Carlson et al. 1990; Cohn 1990; Farrington and Welsh 2002; Steadman 1982). Situational triggers are often dependent on many of the above noted personality features to effect violent behaviour (e.g. Tsang 2002). Notably, a particular situation may have a terrible impact on some people's behaviour and no influence on the behaviour of others, suggesting an intrapersonal-by-situational interaction. Crime prevention by environmental design, typically in public places, is one means of attempting to ameliorate such violence. One is reminded that situational theories are not meant to excuse the behaviour because the trigger is external to the perpetrator. Rather they are meant to obtain a better overall understanding of the causes and contributors to violent behaviour. Moreover, they may facilitate the delivery of interventions that use a relapse prevention model (Pithers 1990).

In spite of the internal variations of the preceding types of theories of violence and their overlap and interaction with each other, Anderson and Bushman (2002) described them as domain-specific theories. By integrated or meta-theories, we refer to efforts made by theoreticians and researchers to combine multiple perspectives about the aetiology of aggression and violence and to do so in a meaningful and integrated fashion. An early example comes from Raine's (1993) sociobiological evolutionary model of psychopathology, which encompassed crime and violence and focused on a genetic-by-environment interaction. A more recent example is the General Aggression Model (GAM; Anderson and Bushman 2002; DeWall and Anderson 2011). The GAM accommodates many of the theories and processes described earlier and integrates them through a cognitive processing and decision model. It posits that individuals process a full range of factors, including past experiences, an assessment of the current scenario, and possible outcomes before deciding to engage in violent behaviour. With time, and more experiences from which one may draw, the process becomes more immediate and part of a lifestyle pattern, particularly when there have been role models to emulate. GAM also considers the process of escalation which often precedes overt violence when individuals misinterpret the meaning of one another's behaviour such that the confrontation culminates in a violent altercation.

I^3 offers another integrative perspective of aggression and violence (Slotter and Finkel 2011). It examines individual factors that promote aggression and how they interact to increase or decrease aggression. The three 'I's include instigating triggers, impelling forces, and inhibiting forces. Instigating triggers draw on the situational theories as they refer to discrete incidents that are likely to invoke violent behaviour. Impelling forces exacerbate the situation, often drawing on the biological and intrapersonal characteristics of the adversaries. Inhibiting forces are those factors that increase the likelihood of a nonviolent resolution to the risky situation. This latter point is a welcome addition to theories of violence as it includes characteristics such as self-regulation in its model. As such, I^3 invokes a hypothetical mathematical equation (i.e. risk = $I_1 + I_2 - I_3$). It offers a potentially valuable perspective to understand various kinds of hostile violence, such as most IPV (Maldonado et al. 2015).

What is important to note about these different types of theories of violence is that each has its own set of approaches to prevention, its foci for assessment, and its remedies for reducing the likelihood of further perpetration. This includes the biological (Raine 2013), the intrapersonal (Leichsenring and Leibing 2003), the psycho-social (McGuire 2008, Chapter 3: McGuire 2020), the situational (Clarke 1995), and the integrative (Gilbert et al. 2017).

Assessment and Prediction of Violent Behaviour

Assessment and prediction is the first crucial prong in the campaign against violence at the individual level and goes hand-in-hand with intervention. Without knowing who to target and what kinds of issues to tackle (i.e. violence-related criminogenic needs), scarce human service resources are likely to be squandered on individuals who are not in need of service and on issues that are unrelated to violent behaviour. This kind of rationale invokes the risk-and-need principle as developed by Andrews and Bonta for the treatment of antisociality more generally (Andrews et al. 1990; Bonta and Andrews 2017). The now well established take-home message to criminal justice administrators and clinicians is to direct treatment services to high-risk offenders (risk principle), to offer services that address the criminogenic needs of clients (need principle), and to do so using behavioural and cognitive behavioural techniques that respect the demographic and psychological attributes of the client (responsivity principle; Andrews et al. 1990; Hanson et al. 2009; Prendergast et al. 2013; Smith et al. 2009). Of course, this lies in the belief that treatment works, in stark contrast to some previous beliefs. See McGuire (2020, Chapter 3) for a lengthy rebuttal to the 'nothing works' movement.

If one is to adhere to these principles, accurate assessments of existing and likely (at risk) offenders is required. Fortunately, this is an area where a great deal of reliable guidance can be taken from a research base that has blossomed over the last forty years and arguably represents one of social sciences' greatest contribution to violence prevention (Andrews et al. 2006). Chapter 4 (Ogloff and Davis 2020) takes us through the journey from unstructured clinical judgements to empirically supported risk assessments and risk management in detail. Garrington and Boer (2020) pick up from there in Chapter 7 and explore the accuracy of several current structured professional judgement tools. Overall, there are at least four main themes that may be derived from the voluminous risk-assessment research.

First, we can predict offending behaviour, including violent acts. Simply said, the best risk-assessment instruments are about 'half-way there', that is to say mid-way between performing no better than chance and being completely accurate (Ogloff and Davis 2020, Chapter 4). Helmus and Quinsey (2020) provide an example of one of the leading violence risk-assessment instruments and discuss the future directions for actuarial risk scales in Chapter 6. The prediction of violent behaviour is not restricted to adults; Viljoen et al. (2020) respond to earlier concerns that it is difficult to assess risk of violence with young offenders in Chapter 11. Given the overrepresentation of intellectual disabilities in correctional populations, it is important to note that risk assessments are also accurate with this population, as Matthews and Bell (2020) demonstrate in Chapter 17. Admittedly, the science and practice of offender violence risk assessment is still quite away from complete accuracy but has far surpassed the realization in the 1970s that violent behaviour simply cannot be predicted with traditional psychiatric assessment procedures (Steadman and Cocozza 1978).

Second, we can identify risk factors that are changeable and when they change, risk changes in the same direction. In particular, so-called third and fourth generation risk-assessment instruments have what has been referred to as *dynamic predictive validity* (Andrews et al. 2006). In an early meta-analysis of offender risk factors, Gendreau et al. (1996) demonstrated that dynamic risk items predicted general recidivism at least as well as static risk items in spite of their greater difficulty to score reliably. Their finding was then replicated with institutional violence and violent recidivism (Campbell et al. 2009). Since then, clear examples of their predictive and incremental (beyond static risk factors) validity have been demonstrated with sexual offenders (Van den Berg et al. 2018), psychopathic offenders (Lewis et al. 2012), forensic patients (Wilson et al. 2013), and young offenders (McGrath and Thompson 2012). Despite the advances noted earlier, more research is required on their dynamic predictive validity in which changes on risk either naturally or by virtue of intervention, are required.

Third, the prediction of specific kinds of antisocial behaviour, including different kinds of violent behaviour, can best be predicted with specialty instruments that have been designed to predict specific kinds of violence. For example, Hilton and Ennis (2020) discuss the role of three risk assessment instruments in the prediction of IPV perpetration in Chapter 8. James and Sheridan (2020) provide an interesting examination of the use of risk assessments in the specific domain of stalking in Chapter 27. Lastly, Rettenberger and Craig (2020) review the use and accuracy of several actuarial risk assessment and structured professional judgement instruments for use with sexual offenders in Chapter 9. A number of these instruments are described in this edition, including the ARMIDILO-S, ERASOR, HCR-20^{V3} ODARA, VRAG-R, VRS-SO, amongst many others (see Table 7.1 in Chapter 7 [Garrington and Boer 2020] for a fuller list).

Fourth, research on offender risk assessment, including violence assessment is continuing unabated and, if anything, is moving at an accelerated rate. This includes research that is devoted to new tools and the improvement of existing tools. The proliferation of new tools, particularly niche tools, are designed to assess a particular subgroup of offenders such as youth (Chapter 11 by Viljoen et al. 2020), sexual offenders (Chapter 9 by Rettenberger and Craig 2020), domestic violence offenders (Chapter 8, by Hilton and Ennis 2020) and offenders with intellectual disabilities (Chapter 17, by Matthews and Bell 2020), or a particular kind of outcome such as stalking behaviour (Chapter 27, by James and Sheridan 2020). Others call for the use of supplementary assessments, such as personality-based measures, to aid in the prediction and prevention of further offending behaviour, as Olver (2020) summarizes in Chapter 10. Other instruments are built around new and innovative ways to determine risk, such as tapping into existing data bases and using more complex algorithms than the longstanding tradition of using simple mathematical calculations, the so-called Burgess (1928) method (e.g. Brennan et al. 2009; Duwe and Rocque 2017). In spite of legal, ethical, and practical concerns about some of these recent directions (Angwin et al. 2016; Wormith 2017), the simple linear progression of risk-assessment generation may be in question as we look to the future (Bonta 1996; Andrews et al. 2006).

Other research is devoted to fine-tuning existing tools, with the release of subsequent editions, new norms (often for demographically defined subgroups of offenders), new and improved scoring directions to increase the reliability of an instrument, and tweaking item weighting to improve predictive validity (e.g. Chapter 6, by Helmus and Quinsey 2020; Chapter 7, by Garrington and Boer 2020; Chapter 8, Hilton and Ennis 2020). Moreover, the use of specific personality assessments is relevant to the process of case conceptualization as one constructs an intervention plan (Chapter 5, by Jones 2020; Chapter 10, by Olver 2020; Chapter 12, by Day and Fernandez 2020).

In sum, there is no excuse for not using empirically validated offender risk assessment for offender violence recidivism when making decisions about the criminal justice processing of violent offenders or referring violent offenders and potential offenders to violence-targeted interventions. Simply, assessment leads to the second prong of crime prevention, effective intervention.

A Collective Response: Three Tiers of Violence Crime Prevention

Following the lead from public health, it is instructive to classify crime prevention, and more specifically violent crime prevention, into three broad approaches (Gordon 1983) even though one particular strategy or programme sometimes falls into multiple categories of violence prevention. Although by 'prevention', we typically think of children and youth, the classification applies to all modes of violence prevention. Primary prevention is also called 'universal' prevention because it consists of strategies that are designed for application at a community or even societal level. These strategies are truly preventive because they are applied 'upstream' before any signs or risk factors for violence emerge. Their merit come from the fact that once risk factors settle into an individual's personality, attitudes, and lifestyle, they become more difficult to overcome. Consequently, primary prevention begins with pre- and post-natal care that includes abstinence of alcohol and drugs, proper nutrition, and family management of preschoolers to avoid some of the early biologically based contributors to violent behaviour (Committee on Preventive Psychiatry 1999).

The development of resilience and protective factors such as self-efficacy, self-regulation, and other 'inhibiting forces', as per the I^3 model, by means of generic programmes for parents and teachers are examples of primary prevention of violent behaviour. Public education campaigns that address violence against women, such as the United Nations' UNiTE to End Violence Against Women (United Nations 2014b) and its Leave No One Behind – End Violence against Women and Girls (United Nations n.d.) campaigns, offer adult-directed examples of primary prevention. Media initiatives at the level of primary prevention can mobilize communities to respond to the potential for violent behaviour, including violent child abuse (Andrews et al. 1995). Another example is the prevention of gang-related violence from a public health perspective (Chapter 13, McDaniel and Sayegh 2020)

Secondary prevention is also known as selective prevention because it targets specific individuals who are at risk for perpetrating violent behaviour or who have shown signs of potentially doing so. They may be at risk because of biological factors such as FASD or ADHD, familial factors such as exposure to, or victimization of, domestic violence, and cognitive factors, such as poor executive functioning. Signs they have displayed may include low frustration tolerance, anger, hostility, poor self-regulation, and nonviolent aggression. The value of secondary prevention is that it is more effective and economical than universal prevention programmes (Hill et al. 2004). Rather than providing services to the general population, it explicitly channels programmatic and clinical resources to groups of individuals who have been empirically shown most likely to become perpetrators of violence. Although primary prevention may be designed for individuals of all ages, secondary prevention programmes are typically directed at children and adolescents (Office of the Surgeon General 2001).

A classic example of secondary prevention is the Perry Preschool Project, which was a cognitive and social development programme directed at preschool children who were at risk for delinquent behaviour. By the age of 40, participants had better rates of various kinds of social, educational, employment, and crime measures including fewer violent crime misdemeanours than randomly assigned control participants (19 vs. 37%; Schweinhart et al. 2005). Other ground-breaking, secondary prevention programmes have focused on cognitive processes that are related to antisocial behaviour including moral reasoning, problem-solving, social skills, and thinking skills of 'behavior disordered' high school students and aggressive boys (Arbuthnot and Gordon 1986; Kazdin et al. 1989). Concerning thinking skills, Lochman's Anger-Coping Intervention successfully reduced aggressive behaviour in high risk, pre-adolescent aggressive boys (Lochman 1992).

Secondary prevention designed to reduce the likelihood of adult-perpetrated violence has not been thoroughly examined. Research on elder abuse provides a minor exception. A meta-analysis on the matter of secondary prevention of elder abuse revealed a positive impact only when the target was use of physical restraints in elder home care, leaving many other dimensions of this form of violence inadequately researched (Ayalon et al. 2016). Mikton and Butchart (2009) found that neither primary nor secondary prevention efforts had consistently demonstrable reductions in parental abuse of children.

Primary and secondary prevention can also be driven by patterns of victimization and the identification and protection of groups who are at high risk of suffering from offending behaviour including violence. Again, the focus tends to be on children who are at risk of child abuse and child sexual abuse. Established and suggested risk factors for child sexual abuse victimization include female gender (Stoltenborgh 2011), cognitive disability (Horner-Johnson and Drum 2006), poverty (MacMillan et al. 2013), and intergenerational history of trauma (Cripps and McGlade 2008). Other factors include young maternal age at first child's birth, growing up in an urban area, and 'parental adversity' including mental health hospitalization or arrest (MacMillan et al. 2013), being in the early teenage years (Cotter and Beaupré 2014), being the victim of other forms of abuse (Fleming et al. 1997; Karayianni et al. 2017), being socially isolated and having a mother with a mental illness (Fleming et al. 1997). To this end, more social scientific research is required to assist in the creation of social policy and programmes to promote both primary and secondary prevention on matters such as child protection (Salter 2018).

Tertiary prevention comprises interventions that are aimed at those who have already exhibited violent behaviour and usually have been processed by criminal justice authorities. It is designed to 'prevent' the problematic behaviour from being repeated. Therefore, offender rehabilitation and treatment fall under the category of tertiary prevention. This can take a myriad of forms, including individual and group modalities, and may be offered in a wide range of community and institutional settings. Of the three types of prevention, tertiary prevention has been most thoroughly researched. Although findings have varied across the spectrum, it has been moderately successful as revealed later in the chapter and in a systematic review of meta-analyses (Chapter 3, McGuire 2020).

Treatment programmes for children and adolescents tend to have broad-based targets of antisocial behaviour that include aggression and violence. Two classic examples for adolescents are Multi-Systemic Therapy (MST) and Functional Family Therapy (FFT). Based on empirically demonstrated areas of risk, MST addresses issues pertaining to the individual, family, peers, school, and community and does so by focusing largely on the family in quite an intense manner (e.g. 60 hours over a four-month period; Henggeler 2011). Repeatedly, it has demonstrated a positive impact on a variety of antisocial behaviours including violent and aggressive behaviour such as sexual offending and externalizing (disrupting) behaviour such as defiance, hostility, and temper tantrums (Borduin et al. 2009; Baglivio et al. 2014). FFT is another widespread, intensive treatment programme in the USA that focuses even more strongly on the family and, unlike MST, less on external factors (Sexton and Turner 2010). Instead, it concentrates on family dynamics, problematic interactions, protective factors with a goal of promoting the inner strength and self-efficacy of all family members. It is equally effective in the treatment of serious and violent adolescents (Baglivio et al. 2014).

Meta-analyses on the effects of treatment with juvenile offenders tend to examine a range of antisocial behaviours, including violence, but also other kinds of aggression and behavioural problems. For example, Lux (2016) demonstrated that MST reduced 'problem behavior' or externalizing (e.g. acting out, aggression, oppositional defiant or conduct disorder) by 15%. Dopp et al. (2017) conducted a meta-analysis on a range of interventions, including MST and FFT, with juveniles having a history of 'serious antisocial behavior' and found that family-based interventions produced long-lasting reductions (2.5 years) in antisocial behaviour relative to usual services ($d = 0.25$, 95% C.I. $= 0.11$–0.39). A small meta-analysis (Hoogsteder et al. 2015) was conducted to investigate the impact of individually-oriented CBT, primarily Mode Deactivation Therapy (Apsche and Ward Bailey 2004) on juveniles who displayed severe aggressive behaviour to the extent that group treatment was not feasible. They found a significant reduction in aggressive behaviour including externalizing, physical aggression, and verbal aggression ($d = 1.139$).

Turning to meta-analyses of treatment for juvenile sexual offenders, Reitzel and Carbonell (2006) found that CBT and adolescent specific treatments such as MST, significantly reduced the rate of sexual offence recidivism (7.37 vs. 18.93%), with no specific advantage to CBT versus other treatment modalities. A more recent meta-analysis (ter Beek et al. 2018) found a moderate treatment effect, a 20.5% reduction in recidivism, with no particular kind of treatment being superior. Another meta-analysis by Soldino and Carbonell-Vayá (2017) considered both the treatment of juvenile and adult sexual offenders together. They found that treatment significantly reduced sexual and general recidivism, but not violent, including violent sexual, recidivism and that MST (for juveniles) was the most successful kind of intervention.

There are many kinds of adult treatment programmes for violent behaviour. Some target precipitators of violence, including frustration, anger, aggression, are discussed at length in Chapter 19 (Novaco 2020). Others focus on a generic outcome, such as generalized violence (Chapter 3, McGuire 2020), while other still target specific forms of violence, often defined by victim characteristics, such as sexual violence and domestic violence including IPV, child abuse, and elder abuse. Dowden and Andrews (2000) conducted the first meta-analysis that looked specifically at violent recidivism following male participation in any kind of violent offender programme and found an overall reduction of 13%. Rather than investigate the impact of treatment by type of offender or type of outcome, they focused on the characteristics of the intervention. Overall, they found a modest treatment effect that was related to the delivery of human service, a focus on criminogenic need, and the use of cognitive-behavioural intervention strategies, but not to the degree of risk of the offender (risk principle). More recently, Henwood et al. (2015) conducted a meta-analysis of CBT and anger-management-based interventions for adult violent offenders. They found a reduction of violent and general offending by 28 and 23%, respectively. They also found a treatment completion effect, whereby those who completed treatment had even greater reductions in violent and general recidivism, 56 and 42%, respectively. However, it has been demonstrated meta-analytically that higher-risk offenders are more likely to drop out of tertiary crime prevention in the first place, thus exaggerating the treatment effect (Olver et al. 2011). Examples of violence reduction programmes in Canada and New Zealand, which also adhere to the principles of risk, need, and responsivity (RNR) and utilize CBT, are described in Chapter 18 (Polaschek and Wong 2020).

Some of these victim-defined types of treatment have been researched sufficiently to allow researchers to conduct meta-analyses of treatment outcome. The systematic reviews and meta-analyses on the treatment of sexual offenders provide an interesting history (Chapter 24, Ambroziak and Thornton 2020). While early studies about the prospects of sexual offender treatment (e.g. Furby et al. 1989; Quinsey et al. 1993) were reminiscent of the pessimism about offender treatment more generally in the 1970s (Martinson 1974), the tide had begun to change by the early 2000s. For example, a systematic review of six earlier reviews and meta-analyses by Craig et al. (2003) found 18 of 19 treatment studies found significant effects and 6 of them were of sufficiently sound methodological quality to have confidence in these results. Then Lösel and Schmucker (2005) conducted one of the early studies that demonstrated quite decisively that the treatment of sexual offenders had a positive impact on their subsequent recidivism with reductions in recidivism being on average 37% lower than that of control participants. Moreover, medical treatment and cognitive-behavioural interventions were most successful. Hanson et al. (2009) took their investigation of offender treatment in another direction.

Following an established pattern in treatment of delinquency generally, they demonstrated that sexual offender treatment reduced sexual recidivism from 19.2 to 10.9%. Moreover, treatment was most effective when it followed the principles of RNR; Andrews et al. 1990), specifically that treatment be directed at moderate- to high-risk offenders, focused on the criminogenic needs of the individual sexual offender, and offered using a cognitive-behavioural format. However, in their meta-analysis, Schmucker and Lösel (2015) found that treatment reduced sexual reoffending by 26.3%, but only CBT significantly reduced recidivism. A meta-analysis on the treatment of sexual offenders against children (Grønnerød et al. 2015) was less encouraging with no overall treatment effect. As a final update, Kim et al. (2016) reviewed these and other meta-analyses on the treatment of adult and juvenile sexual offenders. They revealed an overall positive treatment effect, particularly for interventions with juvenile offenders (3.8 times greater than for adult treatment), for more recent programmes (1.7 times greater) than those in the Craig et al. (2003) review, and when services were delivered in the community (an average 17% reduction on recidivism versus a 10% reduction in custody).

The empirical evidence pertaining to domestic violence and IPV is less clear, which Graham-Kevan and Bates (2020) discuss at length in Chapter 22. Meta-analyses (e.g. Babcock et al. 2004) consistently suggest a small treatment effect, with no difference between type of treatment, which typically is comprised of CBT or a feminist psychoeducational approach, the so-called 'Duluth model' (Pence and Paymar 1993). Similar findings have been found in other meta-analyses and systematic reviews with little change over the last decade, with minimal to no treatment effects demonstrated (Arias et al. 2013; Feder and Wilson 2005; Hester et al. 2014; Waller 2016). Yet there is some evidence that anger management and couples' therapy may be worthwhile avenues to pursue (Gilchrist et al. 2015; Karakurt et al. 2016). Chapter 15 (Dixon and Graham-Kevan 2020) also discusses the importance of functional assessments in curtailing the risk of recidivism for IPV perpetrators, which can help identify why behaviours take place and what may be inhibiting alternative prosocial behaviours. Research on the effectiveness of interventions in other violence-specific areas as defined by the type of violence (e.g. instrumental), type of victim (e.g. elder abuse), type of setting (e.g. institutional violence), or type of context (e.g. road rage) are not sufficiently developed to conduct the convincing meta-analyses that are required to declare evidence-based practice. Other subgroups of offenders who merit specific attention include violent offenders who suffer from personality disorders (see Chapter 20; Logan 2020), those who have a diagnosis of schizophrenia (as discussed in Chapter 21; Hodgins 2020), and those with intellectual and developmental disabilities (see Chapter 23; Taylor 2020). Violent offenders who are high in psychopathy, which Polaschek and Wong (2020) explore in Chapter 18, are also worthy of further attention.

Finally, the case management of violent offenders represents another approach to tertiary prevention of violent crime. This includes violence risk management of violent offenders that is offered through multi-agency partnerships. In Chapter 25, Kemshall and Hilder (2020) provide some European examples of this, which prepares violent offenders for supervision and re-assessment in the community (see Chapter 28 for an overview and a discussion on the merits of including more acute dynamic risk factors; Serin et al. 2020), and which focuses on case managers' interaction with violent offenders at a micro level as exemplified by the Strategic Training Initiative in Case Management (STICS), which is explained in further detail in Chapter 26 (Bourgon et al. 2020). Given the high level of publicity that can coincide with the release of sexual offenders, in Chapter 24 Ambroziak and Thornton (2020) examine the different models used in the management of this group. Not to be forgotten in case management is the growing interest in strengths-based safety planning, which Jones (2020) discusses in Chapter 5.

Future Directions: Global and Local

Violence, particularly in its extreme forms as exemplified in individual ways by sexual assault, child abuse, IPV, and homicide, and in collective ways by war crimes, ethnic cleansing, terrorism, and cultural genocide, is a terrible blight on humanity. The history, magnitude, extent, and variation of violent human behaviour can be overwhelming leaving one with a sense of futility and inertia. Its causes are multiple, its perpetrators are diverse, and its victims can be anybody. When faced with a social ill of this scope, our collective response must be equally varied, such that it addresses violence on as many fronts as it exists with strategies that are undertaken at the individual level, the group level, and the systemic level.

Resources devoted to addressing violence at the individual level have been and will remain an ongoing issue for the long term. Therefore, lobbying for more resources must continue over the foreseeable future. Rationale for such appeal comes from the practical (reductions in recidivism) for juveniles (ter Beek et al. 2018) and adults (Hanson et al. 2009; Henwood et al. 2015) and pragmatic (cost–benefit) for juveniles (Dopp et al. 2014) and adults (Elliott and Beech 2012; French et al. 2010; Sampson et al. 2013; Welsh 2004) to the principled, such as the right to feel and be safe in one's community. A commitment to further research to advance the fight against expressions of violence in all of its various forms is required. Such a commitment must be both preventive and rehabilitative.

As the causes of violence vary, so too must the solutions. This suggests specific strategies that vary with specific kinds of violence, many of which are addressed in this edition. These kinds of violence are reflected in the FBI's classification of homicide into an array of subtypes. To this end, validated assessment tools and evidence-based intervention programmes have emerged and are making inroads in the reduction of violence, one client at a time.

This divide and conquer approach is important, but is incomplete as it tends not to consider the landscape at a societal level. A broad perspective that monitors, examines, and attempts to eradicate violence at, say, a national level or beyond, is also required to progress beyond our current efforts. Such efforts are likely to require political, governmental, nongovernmental organization NGO), and international endorsement and commitment.

There are numerous examples where specific kinds of violence have been tackled in a large systemic fashion. These include commissions that have addressed media violence (Media Violence Commission, International Society for Research on Aggression 2012), domestic and sexual violence (American Bar Association n.d.), youth violence in the UK (The Youth Violence Commission n.d.), child abuse and other forms of family violence (Neave et al. 2016; State of Victoria 2016), and violence against women in the European Union (European Commission n.d.). Other commissions have been mandated to consider the monumental task of addressing all kinds of violence at the national level (National Commission on the Causes and Prevention of Violence 1969), while municipal commissions are tasked to address local issues such as gang violence in the community (e.g. Citizen's Crime Commission of New York City). Numerous truth and reconciliation commissions have been established around the world to address systemic racism and its impact on violence. They are found, not only in South Africa (Republic of South Africa 1995), but in other African countries such as Sierra Leone (Truth and Reconciliation Commission Act 2000) and Morocco (Advisory Council on Human Rights 2009), in G8 countries, such as the USA (Inwood et al. 2016) and Canada (The Truth and Reconciliation Commission of Canada 2015), and in third-world countries, such as Columbia (Marín 2015) and Central American countries (Shifter 2012) where homicide and other forms of violence have been horrific.

However, these commissions, as committed and insightful as they may be, have, by design, a shelf life, a time to conduct their investigation, make their recommendations, and close their doors. With some exceptions such as in Victoria, Australia, where follow-up is legislated (State of Victoria 2017), it would seem, almost by design, they are not afforded an opportunity to make a sustained change in a local community, let alone an entire country. This can produce cynicism about subsequent efforts. Follow-up oversight tends to be left to independent NGOs, journalists, and the victims for whom the commissions were designed to assist in countries as diverse as Canada (Bear and Andersen 2017) and South Africa (Magistad 2017). Sarcastically, journalists have opined that if all of the commissions had worked 'children and families would be safe by now' (Curtis 2016). Political will and pressure is required to change the traditional commission model (United Nations 2006).

Who better to initiate such a movement but the evidence-guided researchers, clinicians, and practitioners who work with violent individuals and their victims on a day-to-day basis (e.g. Koop 1985). Working with other stakeholders, such as victims' advocacy groups, governments should be convinced to take on the task of channelling crime prevention efforts through public policy and into primary, secondary, and tertiary efforts. On another front, researchers and practitioners must work collaboratively, each feeding back findings and observations about violence in all of its forms and its amelioration to one another in a collaborative spirit. The chapters presented in this edition comprise one small effort to this end, but represent the culmination on many and diverse efforts.

References

Advisory Council on Human Rights (2009). *Follow-Up Report on the Implementation of Equity and Reconciliation Commission Recommendations: Main Report.* Rabat, MA: Conseil Consultatif des Droits de l'Homme.

Agnew, R. (1992). Foundation for a general strain theory of crime and delinquency. *Criminology* 30: 47–87.

Ambroziak, G. and Thornton, D. (2020). Sexual violence risk management. In: *What Works in Violence Risk Management: Theory, Research and Practice*, 467–484 (eds. J.S. Wormith, L.A. Craig and T. Hogue). Chichester, UK: Wiley Blackwell.

Anderson, C.A. and Bushman, B.J. (2002). Human aggression. *Annual Review of Psychology* 53: 17–51.

Andrews, A.B., McLeese, D.G., and Curran, S. (1995). The impact of a media campaign on public action to help maltreated children in addictive families. *Child Abuse and Neglect* 19: 921–932.

Andrews, D.A., Bonta, J., and Hoge, R.D. (1990). Classification for effective rehabilitation: rediscovering psychology. *Criminal Justice and Behavior* 17: 19–52.

Andrews, D.A., Bonta, J., and Wormith, J.S. (2006). The recent past and near future of risk and/or need assessment. *Crime and Delinquency* 52: 7–27.

Andrews, D.A., Zinger, I., Hoge, R.D. et al. (1990). Does correctional treatment work? A psychologically informed meta-analysis. *Criminology* 28: 369–404.

Angwin, J., Larson, J., Mattu, S. et al. (2016). Machine bias: there's software used across the county to predict future criminals. And it's biased against blacks. *Propublica.* May 23. https://www.propublica.org/article/machine-bias-risk-assessments-in-criminal-sentencing.

Apsche, J.A. and Ward Bailey, S.R. (2004). Mode deactivation therapy: cognitive-behavioural therapy for young people with reactive conduct disorders or personality disorders who sexually abuse. In: *Children and Young People Who Sexually Abuse: New Theory, Research and Practice Developments* (ed. M.C. Calder), 263–287. Lyme Regis, UK: Russell House Publishing.

Arbuthnot, J. and Gordon, D. (1986). Behavioral and cognitive effects of a moral reasoning develop-ment intervention for high-risk behavior-disordered adolescents. *Journal of Consulting and Clinical Psychology* 54: 208–216.

Arias, E., Arce, R., and Vilariño, M. (2013). Batterer intervention programmes: a meta-analytic review of effectiveness. *Psychosocial Intervention* 22: 153–160.

Ayalon, L., Lev, S., Green, O. et al. (2016). A systematic review and meta-analysis of interventions designed to prevent or stop elder maltreatment. *Age and Aging* 45: 216–227.

Babcock, J.C., Green, C.E., and Robie, C. (2004). Does batterers' treatment work? A meta-analytic review of domestic violence treatment. *Clinical Psychology Review* 23: 1023–1053.

Baglivio, M.T., Jackowski, K., Greenwald, M.A. et al. (2014). Comparison of multisystemic therapy and functional family therapy effectiveness. *Criminal Justice and Behavior* 412: 1033–1056.

Bandura, A. (1977). *Social Learning Theory.* Englewood Cliffs, NJ: Prentice-Hall.

Bandura, A. (2002). Selective moral disengagement in the exercise of moral agency. *Journal of Moral Education* 31: 101–119.

Bartol, C. and Bartol, A. (2014). *Criminal Behavior: A Psychological Approach*, 10e. Upper Saddle River, NJ: Pearson.

Bartol, C.R. and Bartol, A.M. (2016). *Criminal Behavior: A Psychological Approach*, 11e. Boston, MA: Pearson.

Baumeister, R.F. and Boden, J.M. (1998). Aggression and the self: high self-esteem, low self-control, and ego threat. In: *Human Aggression: Theories, Research and Implications for Policy* (eds. R.G. Geen and E. Donnerstein), 111–137. New York: Academic Press.

Baumeister, R.F., Smart, L., and Boden, J.M. (1996). Relation of threatened egotism to violence and aggression: the dark side of high self-esteem. *Psychological Review* 103: 5–33.

Bear, T. and Andersen, C. (2017). Three years later, is Canada keeping its Truth and Reconciliation promises? *Globe and Mail.* April 17. https://www.theglobeandmail.com/opinion/three-years-later-is-canada-keeping-its-truth-and-reconciliation-commission-promises/article34790925.

Berkowitz, L. (1989). Frustration-aggression hypothesis: examination and reformulation. *Psychological Bulletin* 106: 59–73.

Berkowitz, L. (2003). Affect, aggression, and antisocial behavior. In: *Handbook of Affective Sciences* (eds. R.J. Davidson, K. Scherer and H.H. Goldsmith), 804–823. New York: Oxford.

Berkowitz, L. and LePage, A. (1967). Weapons as aggression-eliciting stimuli. *Journal of Personality and Social Psychology* 7: 202–207.

Birkel, C. and Dern, H. (2012). Homicide in Germany. In: *Handbook of European Homicide Research: Patterns, Explanations, and Country Studies* (eds. M.C.A. Liem and W.A. Pridemore), 313–328. New York: Springer.

Blackman, P.H., Leggett, V.L., and Jarvis, J.P. (2001). *The Diversity of Homicide: Proceedings of the 2000 Annual Meeting of the Homicide Research Working Group.* Washington, DC: Federal Bureau of Investigation.

Bonta, J. (1996). Risk-needs assessment and treatment. In: *Choosing Correctional Options that Work: Defining the Demand and Evaluating the Supply* (ed. A.T. Harland), 18–32. Thousand Oaks, CA: Sage.

Bonta, J. and Andrews, D.A. (2017). *The Psychology of Criminal Behavior*, 6e. New York: Routledge.

Borders, A. and Giancola, P.R. (2011). Trait and state hostile rumination facilitate alcohol-related aggression. *Journal of Studies on Alcohol and Drugs* 72: 545–554.

Borduin, C.M., Schaeffer, C.M., and Heiblum, N. (2009). A randomized clinical trial of multisystemic therapy with juvenile sexual offenders: effects on youth social ecology and criminal activity. *Journal of Consulting and Clinical Psychology* 77: 26–37.

Bourgon, N., Chadwick, N., and Rugge, T. (2020). Beyond core correctional practice: facilitating proso-cial change through the strategic training initiative in community supervision. In: *What Works in Violence Risk Management: Theory, Research and Practice*, 505–525 (eds. J.S. Wormith, L.A. Craig and T. Hogue). Chichester, UK: Wiley Blackwell.

Bowlby, J. (1988). *A Secure Base: Clinical Applications of Attachment Theory*. London, UK: Routledge.

Brennan, I.R. and Moore, S.C. (2009). Weapons and violence: a review of theory and research. *Aggression and Violent Behavior* 14: 215–225.

Brennan, T., Dieterich, W., and Ehret, B. (2009). Evaluating the predictive validity of the COMPAS risk and need assessment system. *Criminal Justice and Behavior* 36: 21–40.

Brown, N.N., Connor, P.D., and Adler, R.S. (2012). Conduct-disordered adolescents with fetal alcohol spectrum disorder: intervention in secure treatment settings. *Criminal Justice and Behavior* 39 (6): 770–793.

Brownmiller, S. (1975). *Against our Will: Men, Women, and Rape*. New York: Bantam Books.

Burgess, E.W. (1928). Factors determining success or failure on parole. In: *The Workings of the Indeterminate Sentence Law and the Parole System in Illinois* (eds. A.A. Bruce, E.W. Burgess, J. Landesco, et al.), 221–234. Springfield, IL: Illinois State Board of Parole.

Bushman, B.J. and Anderson, C.A. (2001). Is it time to pull the plug on the hostile versus instrumental aggression dichotomy? *Psychological Review* 108 (1): 273–279.

Buss, A.H. (1971). Aggression pays. In: *The Control of Aggression and Violence* (ed. J.L. Singer), 7–17. New York: Academic Press.

Campbell, M.A., French, S., and Gendreau, P. (2009). The prediction of violence in adult offenders: a meta-analytic comparison of instruments and methods of assessment. *Criminal Justice and Behavior* 36: 567–590.

Carlson, M., Marcus-Newhall, A., and Miller, N. (1990). Effects of situational aggression cues: a quantitative review. *Journal of Personality and Social Psychology* 58: 622–633.

Clarke, R.V. (1995). Situational crime prevention. In: *Building a Safer Society: Strategic Approaches to Crime Prevention. Crime and Justice: A Review of the Research*, vol. 19 (eds. M. Tonry and D. Farrington), 91–150. Chicago, IL: University of Chicago Press.

Cohn, E.G. (1990). Weather and crime. *British Journal of Criminology* 30: 51–64.

Cohn, E.G. and Rotton, J. (2006). Social escape and avoidance (SEA) theory of aggression and violent crime: an integration of psychological and life styles theories of crime an aggression. In: *Perspectives on the Psychology of Aggression* (ed. J.P. Morgan), 1–33. Hauppauge, NY: Nova Science Publishers.

Committee on Preventive Psychiatry (1999). Violent behavior in children and youth: preventive intervention from a psychiatric perspective. *Journal of the American Academy of Child and Adolescent Psychiatry* 38: 235–241.

Corrado, R. and Cohen, I.M. (2014). *A Review of the Research Literature on the Individual-Level Theories of Homicide*. Abbotsford, BC: Centre for Public Safety & Criminal Justice Research, University of the Fraser Valley.

Cotter, A. and Beaupré, P. (2014). Police-reported sexual offences against children and youth in Canada, 2012. *Juristat* (Statistics Canada catalogue #: 85-002-X).

Craig, L.A., Browne, K.D., and Stringer, I. (2003). Treatment and sexual offence recidivism. *Trauma, Violence, & Abuse* 4: 70–89.

Cripps, K. and McGlade, H. (2008). Indigenous family violence and sexual abuse: considering pathways forward. *Journal of Family Studies* 14 (2–3): 240–253.

Curtis, C. (2016). If royal commissions worked children and families would be safe by now. *The Guardian*. April 7. https://www.theguardian.com/commentisfree/2016/apr/07/if-royal-commissions-worked-children-and-families-would-be-safe-by-now (accessed 20 June 2019).

Daly, M. and Wilson, M. (1994). Evolutionary psychology of male violence. In: *Male Violence* (ed. J. Archer), 253–288. London, UK: Routledge.

Day, A. and Fernandez, E. (2020). The importance of understanding anger in the clinical assessment of violence. In: *What Works in Violence Risk Management: Theory, Research and Practice*, 253–264 (eds. J.S. Wormith, L.A. Craig and T. Hogue). Chichester, UK: Wiley Blackwell.

Denson, T.F. (2012). The multiple systems model of anger rumination. *Journal of Personality and Social Psychology* 17: 103–123.

DeWall, C.N. and Anderson, C.A. (2011). The general aggression model. In: *Human Aggression and Violence: Causes, Manifestation, and Consequences* (eds. P.R. Shaver and M. Mikulincer), 15–33. Washington, DC: American Psychological Association.

Dicataldo, F. and Everett, M. (2008). Distinguishing juvenile homicide from violent offending. *International Journal of Offender Therapy and Comparative Criminology* 52: 158–174.

Dixon, L. and Graham-Kevan, N. (2020). Assessing the risk and treatment needs of people who perpetrate intimate partner violence. In: *What Works in Violence Risk Management: Theory, Research and Practice*, 297–314 (eds. J.S. Wormith, L.A. Craig and T. Hogue). Chichester, UK: Wiley Blackwell.

Dollard, J., Doob, L., Miller, N. et al. (1939). *Frustration and Aggression*. New Haven, CT: Yale University Press.

Dopp, A.R., Borduin, C.M., Wagner, D.V. et al. (2014). The economic impact of multisystemic therapy through midlife: a cost-benefit analysis with serious juvenile offenders and their siblings. *Journal of Consulting and Clinical Psychology* 82: 694–705.

Dopp, A.R., Borduin, C.M., White, M.H. II et al. (2017). Family-based treatments for serious juvenile offenders: a multilevel meta-analysis. *Journal of Consulting and Clinical Psychology* 85 (4): 335–354.

Douglas, J.E., Burgess, A.W., Burgess, A.G. et al. (2006). *Crime Classification Manual*, 2e. San Francisco, CA: Jossey-Bass.

Dowden, C. and Andrews, D.A. (2000). Effective correctional treatment and violent reoffending: a meta-analysis. *Canadian Journal of Criminology* 42 (4): 449–467.

Duntley, J.D. and Buss, D.M. (2004). The evolution of evil. In: *The Social Psychology of Good and Evil* (ed. A. Miller), 102–123. New York: Guilford Press.

Duwe, G. and Rocque, M. (2017). Effects of automating recidivism risk assessment on reliability, predictive validity, and return on investment (ROI). *Criminology & Public Policy* 16: 235–269.

Elliott, I.A. and Beech, A.R. (2012). A U.K. cost-benefit analysis of circles of support and accountability interventions. *Sexual Abuse* 25: 211–229.

Ennis, L., Toop, C., Jung, S. et al. (2017). Instrumental and reactive intimate partner violence: offender characteristics, reoffense rates, and risk management. *Journal of Threat Assessment and Management* 4 (2): 61–76.

Eriksson, L. and Mazerolle, P. (2015). A cycle of violence? Examining family-of-origin violence, attitudes, and intimate partner violence perpetration. *Journal of Interpersonal Violence* 30: 945–964.

Eron, L.D., Guerra, N., and Huesmann, L.R. (1997). Poverty and violence. In: *Aggression: Biological, Developmental, and Social Perspectives* (eds. S. Feshbach and J. Zagrodzka), 139–154. Boston, MA: Springer.

European Commission (n.d.). *Say no! Stop violence against women.* http://ec.europa.eu/justice/saynostopvaw/about.html (accessed 20 June 2019).

Eurostat (2017). *Intentional Homicide and Sexual Offences by Legal Status and Sex of the Person Involved – Number and Rate for the Relevant Sex Group.* Luxembourg: European Commission.

Farrington, D.P., Loeber, R., and Berg, M. (2012). Young men who kill: a prospective longitudinal examination from childhood. *Homicide Studies* 16: 99–128.

Farrington, D.P. and Welsh, B.C. (2002). Improved street lighting and crime prevention. *Justice Quarterly* 19: 313–342.

Feder, L. and Wilson, D.B. (2005). A meta-analytic review of court-mandated batterer intervention programs: can courts affect abusers' behavior? *Journal of Experimental Criminology* 1: 239–262.

Federal Bureau of Investigation (2014). *Crime in the United States 2013: Uniform Crime Report.* Washington, DC: US Department of Justice.

Federal Bureau of Investigation (2017). *Crime in the United States 2016: Uniform Crime Report.* Washington, DC: US Department of Justice.

Feshbach, S. (1964). The function of aggression and the regulation of aggressive drive. *Psychological Review* 71 (4): 257–272.

Fisher, B.S., Daigle, L.E., Cullen, F.T. et al. (2003). Reporting sexual victimization to the police and others: results from a national-level study of college women. *Criminal Justice and Behavior* 20: 6–38.

Flatley, J. (2018). *Homicide in England and Wales: Year Ending March 2017*. London, UK: Office for National Statistics.

Fleming, J., Mullen, P., and Bammer, G. (1997). A study of potential risk factors for sexual abuse in childhood. *Child Abuse & Neglect* 21 (1): 49–58.

French, M.T., Fang, H., and Fretz, R. (2010). Economic evaluation of a prerelease substance abuse treatment program for repeat criminal offenders. *Journal of Substance Abuse Treatment* 38: 31–41.

Freud, S. (1920). Beyond the pleasure principle. In: *The Standard edition of the complete psychological works of Sigmund Freud*, vol. 18 (ed. J. Strachey), 7–64. Oxford: Macmillan.

Furby, L., Weinrott, M., and Blackshaw, L. (1989). Sex offender recidivism: a review. *Psychological Bulletin* 105: 3–30.

Garrington, C. and Boer, D. (2020). Structured professional judgement in violence risk assessment. In: *What Works in Violence Risk Management: Theory, Research and Practice*, 145–162 (eds. J.S. Wormith, L.A. Craig and T. Hogue). Chichester, UK: Wiley Blackwell.

Gendreau, P., Little, T., and Goggin, C. (1996). A meta-analysis of the predictors of adult recidivism: what works! *Criminology* 34: 401–433.

Gilbert, F., Daffern, M., and Anderson, C.A. (2017). The general aggression model and its application to violent offender assessment and treatment. In: *The Wiley Handbook of Violence and Aggression* (ed. P. Sturmey), 386–413. New York: Wiley.

Gilchrist, G., Munoz, J.T., and Easton, C.J. (2015). Should we reconsider anger management when addressing physical intimate partner violence perpetration by alcohol abusing males? A systematic review. *Aggression and Violent Behavior* 25: 124–132.

Glenn, A.L., Raine, A., Venables, P.H. et al. (2007). Early temperamental and psychophysiological precursors of adult psychopathic personality. *Journal of Abnormal Psychology* 116 (3): 508–518.

Glover, E. (1960). *The Roots of Crime*. London: Imago Publishing.

Goldstein, H. (1973). *Social Work Practice: A Unitary Approach*. Columbia: University of South Carolina Press.

Gontkovsky, S.T. (2007). Neurobiological bases and neuropsychological correlates of aggression and violence. In: *Psychology of Aggression*, 3e (ed. J.P. Morgan), 101–116. Hauppauge, NY: Nova Science Publishers.

Gordon, R.S. Jr. (1983). An operational classification of disease prevention. *Public Health Reports* 98: 107–109.

Gottfredson, M.R. and Hirschi, T. (1990). *A General Theory of Crime*. Stanford, CA: Stanford University Press.

Graham-Kevan, N. and Bates, E.A. (2020). Intimate partner violence perpetrator programmes. In: *What Works in Violence Risk Management: Theory, Research and Practice*, 437–449 (eds. J.S. Wormith, L.A. Craig and T. Hogue). Chichester, UK: Wiley Blackwell.

Grønnerød, C., Grønnerød, J.S., and Grøndahl, P. (2015). Psychological treatment of sexual offenders against children: a meta-analytic review of treatment outcome studies. *Trauma, Violence, & Abuse* 16 (3): 280–290.

Hanson, R.K., Bourgon, G., Helmus, L. et al. (2009). The principles of effective correctional treatment also apply to sexual offenders: a meta-analysis. *Criminal Justice and Behavior* 36: 865–891.

Haslam, N. (2006). Dehumanization: an integrative review. *Personality and Social Psychology Review* 10: 252–264.

Heide, K.M. (2003). Youth homicide: a review of the literature and a blueprint for action. *International Journal of Offender Therapy and Comparative Criminology* 47: 6–36.

Helmus, L.M. and Quinsey, V.L. (2020). Predicting violent reoffending with the VRAG-R: overview, controversies, and future directions for actuarial risk scales. In: *What Works in Violence Risk Management: Theory, Research and Practice*, 119–144 (eds. J.S. Wormith, L.A. Craig and T. Hogue). Chichester, UK: Wiley Blackwell.

Henderson, H. (2007). Feminism, Foucault, and rape: a theory and politics of rape prevention. *Berkeley Journal of Gender, Law, & Justice* 22: 225–253.

Henggeler, S.W. (2011). Efficacy studies to large-scale transport: the development and validation of multisystemic therapy programs. *Annual Review of Clinical Psychology* 7: 351–381.

Henwood, K.S., Chou, S., and Browne, K.D. (2015). A systematic review and meta-analysis on the effectiveness of CBT informed anger management. *Aggression and Violent Behavior* 25: 280–292.

Hester, M., Lilley, S.-J., O'Prey, L. et al. (2014). *Overview and analysis of research studies evaluating European perpetrator programmes: Working paper 2 from the Daphne III IMPACT Project.* Berlin, Germany: Dissens.

Heto, M.S. (2015). Psychological perspectives of violence. In: *Violent Offenders: Understanding and Assessment* (eds. C.A. Pietz and C.A. Mattson), 3–18. New York: Oxford University Press.

Hill, L.G., Lochman, J.E., Coie, J.D. et al. (2004). Effectiveness of early screening for externalizing problems: issues of screening accuracy and utility. *Journal of Consulting and Clinical Psychology* 72: 809–820.

Hilton, Z. and Ennis, L. (2020). Intimate partner violence risk assessment and management: an RNR approach to threat assessment. In: *What Works in Violence Risk Management: Theory, Research and Practice*, 163–182 (eds. J.S. Wormith, L.A. Craig and T. Hogue). Chichester, UK: Wiley Blackwell.

Hiraiwa-Hasegawa, M. (2005). Homicide by men in Japan, and its relationship to age, resources and risk taking. *Evolution and Human Behavior* 26: 332–343.

Hodgins, S. (2020). Antisocial and aggressive behavior among persons with schizophrenia: evidence and propositions for prevention. In: *What Works in Violence Risk Management: Theory, Research and Practice*, 419–436 (eds. J.S. Wormith, L.A. Craig and T. Hogue). Chichester, UK: Wiley Blackwell.

Hoogsteder, L.M., Stams, G.J.J.M., Figge, M.A. et al. (2015). A meta-analysis of the effectiveness of individually oriented cognitive behavioral treatment (CBT) for severe aggressive behavior in adolescents. *The Journal of Forensic Psychiatry & Psychology* 26 (1): 22–37.

Horner-Johnson, W. and Drum, C.E. (2006). Prevalence of maltreatment of people with intellectual disabilities: a review of recently published research. *Developmental Disabilities Research Reviews* 12 (1): 57–69.

Huesmann, L.R. (1998). The role of social information processing and cognitive schema in the acquisition and maintenance of habitual aggressive behavior. In: *Human Aggression: Theories, Research and Implications for Policy* (eds. R.G. Geen and E. Donnerstein), 73–109. New York: Academic Press.

Inwood, J., Alderman, D., and Barron, M. (2016). Addressing structural violence through US reconciliation commissions: the case study of Greensboro, NC and Detroit, MI. *Political Geography* 52: 57–64.

Italian National Institute of Statistics (2018). *Persons Convicted by Final Judgement - Demographic Characteristics.* Rome: Italian National Institute of Statistics.

James, D. and Sheridan, L. (2020). What works in risk assessment in stalking cases. In: *What Works in Violence Risk Management: Theory, Research and Practice* 527–542 (eds. J.S. Wormith, L.A. Craig and T. Hogue). Chichester, UK: Wiley Blackwell.

Jones, L. (2020). Violence risk formulation: the move towards co-produced 'strengths-based' safety planning. In: *What Works in Violence Risk Management: Theory, Research and Practice*, 99–118 (eds. J.S. Wormith, L.A. Craig and T. Hogue). Chichester, UK: Wiley Blackwell.

Karakurt, G., Whiting, K., van Esch, C. et al. (2016). Couples therapy for intimate partner violence: a systematic review and meta-analysis. *Journal of Marital and Family Therapy* 42 (4): 567–583.

Karayianni, E., Fanti, K.A., Diakidoy, I.A. et al. (2017). Prevalence, contexts, and correlates of child sexual abuse in Cyprus. *Child Abuse & Neglect* 66: 41–52.

Kazdin, A.E., Bass, D., Siegel, T. et al. (1989). Cognitive-behavioral therapy and relationship therapy in the treatment of children referred for antisocial behavior. *Journal of Consulting and Clinical Psychology* 57: 522–535.

Kemshall, H. and Hilder, S. (2020). Effective systems and processes for managing violent offenders in the United Kingdom and the European Union. In: *What Works in Violence Risk Management: Theory, Research and Practice*, 485–504 (eds. J.S. Wormith, L.A. Craig and T. Hogue). Chichester, UK: Wiley Blackwell.

Khachatryan, N., Heide, K.M., and Hummel, E.V. (2018). Recidivism patterns among two types of homicide offenders: a 30-year follow-up study. *International Journal of Offender Therapy and Comparative Criminology* 62 (2): 404–426.

Kim, B., Benekos, P.J., and Merlo, A.V. (2016). Sex offender recidivism revisited: review of recent meta-analyses on the effects of sex offender treatment. *Trauma, Violence, & Abuse* 17 (1): 105–117.

Koop, C.E. (1985). *Surgeon General's workshop on violence and public health.* 27–29 October 1985. DHHS Publication No. HRS-D-MC 86-1. Leesburg, VA: US Department of Health and Human Services (DHHS).

Koss, M.P., Gidycz, C.A., and Wisniewski, N. (1987). The scope of rape: incidence and prevalence of sexual aggression and victimization in a national sample of higher education students. *Journal of Counseling and Clinical Psychology* 55: 162–170.

Kroner, D. and Butler, G.C. (2020). What do we know about violent offending behaviour? In: *What Works in Violence Risk Management: Theory, Research and Practice*, 33–52 (eds. J.S. Wormith, L.A. Craig and T. Hogue). Chichester, UK: Wiley Blackwell.

Kwong, M.J., Bartholomew, K., Henderson, A.J. et al. (2003). The intergenerational transmission of relationship violence. *Journal of Family Psychology* 17: 288–301.

Larson, M., Vaughn, M.G., Salas-Wright, C.P. et al. (2015). Narcissism, low self-control, and violence among a nationally representative sample. *Criminal Justice and Behavior* 42: 644–661.

Leichsenring, F. and Leibing, E. (2003). The effectiveness of psychodynamic therapy and cognitive behavior therapy in the treatment of personality disorders: a meta-analysis. *American Journal of Psychiatry* 160: 1223–1232.

Lewis, K., Olver, M.E., and Wong, S.C.P. (2012). The violence risk scale: predictive validity and linking changes in risk with violent recidivism in a sample of high-risk offenders with psychopathic traits. *Assessment* 20: 150–164.

Lindsay, J.J. and Anderson, C.A. (2000). From antecedent conditions to violent actions: a general affective aggression model. *Personality and Social Psychology Bulletin* 26: 533–547.

Lochman, J.E. (1992). Cognitive-behavioral intervention with aggressive boys: three-year follow-up and preventive effects. *Journal of Consulting and Clinical Psychology* 60: 426–432.

Loeber, R., Pardini, D., Homish, D.L. et al. (2005). The prediction of violence and homicide in young men. *Journal of Consulting and Clinical Psychology* 73 (6): 1074–1088.

Loeber, R. and Stouthamer-Loeber, M. (1998). Development of juvenile aggression and violence: some common misconceptions and controversies. *American Psychologist* 53: 242–259.

Logan, C. (2020). Managing violent offenders with a personality disorder. In: *What Works in Violence Risk Management: Theory, Research and Practice*, 399–418 (eds. J.S. Wormith, L.A. Craig and T. Hogue). Chichester, UK: Wiley Blackwell.

Lorenz, K. (1966). *On Aggression.* New York: Harcourt Brace Jovanovich.

Lösel, F. and Schucker, M. (2005). The effectiveness of treatment for sexual offenders: a comprehensive meta-analysis. *Journal of Experimental Criminology* 1: 117–146.

Loza, W. (2020). Terrorism and ideological violence. In: *What Works in Violence Risk Management: Theory, Research and Practice*, 279–296 (eds. J.S. Wormith, L.A. Craig and T. Hogue). Chichester, UK: Wiley Blackwell.

Lux, J.L. (2016). *Assessing the effectiveness of multisystemic therapy: A meta-analysis.* Doctoral dissertation. Cincinnati, OH: University of Cincinnati.

Lysova, A.V., Shchitov, N.G., and Pridemore, W.A. (2012). Homicide in Russia, Ukraine, and Belarus. In: *Handbook of European Homicide Research* (eds. M. Liem and W. Pridemore), 451–469. New York: Springer.

MacMillan, H.L., Tanaka, M., Duku, E. et al. (2013). Child physical and sexual abuse in a community sample of young adults: results from the Ontario Child Health Study. *Child Abuse & Neglect* 37 (1): 14–21.

Magistad, M.K. (2017). South Africa's imperfect progress, 30 years after the Truth & Reconciliation Commission. *Public Radio International*. 6 April. https://www.pri.org/stories/2017-04-06/south-africas-imperfect-progress-20-years-after-truth-reconciliation-commission

Maldonado, R.C., DiLillo, D., and Hoffman, L. (2015). Can college students use emotion regulation strategies to alter intimate partner aggression-risk behaviors? An examination using I³ theory. *Psychology of Violence* 5: 46–55.

Marín, J.J. (2015). The commissions for the study of violence in Colombia: an analysis of the official devices and narratives of the past and present of violence. In: *The Struggle for Memory in Latin America: Memory, Politics and Transitional Justice* (eds. E. Allier-Montaño and E. Crenzel), 147–163. New York: Palgrave Macmillan.

Martinelli, A., Ackermann, K., Bernhard, A. et al. (2018). Hostile attribution bias and aggression in children and adolescents: a systematic literature review on the influence of aggression subtype and gender. *Aggression and Violent Behavior* 39: 25–32.

Martinson, R. (1974). What works? Questions and answers about prison reform. *The Public Interest* 35: 22–54.

Matthews, M. and Bell, E. (2020). Assessing violent offenders with an intellectual disability. In: *What Works in Violence Risk Management: Theory, Research and Practice*, 349–366 (eds. J.S. Wormith, L.A. Craig and T. Hogue). Chichester, UK: Wiley Blackwell.

McDaniel, D. and Sayegh, C. (2020). Gang violence prevention efforts: a public health approach. In: *What Works in Violence Risk Management: Theory, Research and Practice*, 265–278 (eds. J.S. Wormith, L.A. Craig and T. Hogue). Chichester, UK: Wiley Blackwell.

McGrath, A. and Thompson, A.P. (2012). The relative predictive validity of the static and dynamic domain scores in risk-need assessment of juvenile offenders. *Criminal Justice and Behavior* 39: 250–263.

McGuire, J. (2008). A review of effective interventions for reducing aggression and violence. *Philosophical Transactions of the Royal Society B* 363: 2577–2597.

McGuire, J. (2020). What works with violent offenders: a response to nothing works. In: *What Works in Violence Risk Management: Theory, Research and Practice*, 53–78 (eds. J.S. Wormith, L.A. Craig and T. Hogue). Chichester, UK: Wiley Blackwell.

Meaney, M.J. (2010). Epigenetics and the biological definition of gene x environment interaction. *Child Development* 81: 41–79.

Meaney, M.J. and Szyf, M. (2005). Maternal effects as a model for environmentally-dependent chromatin plasticity. *Trends in Neuroscience* 28: 456–463.

Media Violence Commission, International Society for Research on Aggression (2012). Report of the Media Violence Commission. *Aggressive Behavior* 38: 335–341.

Meloy, R. (2002). Pathologies of attachment, violence and criminality. In: *Handbook of Psychology*, vol. 11 (ed. A. Goldstein), 509–526. New York: Wiley.

Mikton, C. and Butchart, A. (2009). Child maltreatment prevention: a systematic review of reviews. *Bulletin of the World Health Organization* 87: 353–361.

Ministère de la Justice (2017). *Tableau 22. Nombre de condamnations selon l'âge des condamnés et selon la nature de l'infraction. Fichier statistique du casier judiciaire*. Paris: Ministère de la Justice.

Mischel, W. and Shoda, Y. (1995). A cognitive-affective system theory of personality: reconceptualizing situations, dispositions, dynamics, and invariance in personality structure. *Psychological Review* 102: 246–268.

Murphy, J.M., Wehler, C.A., Pagano, M.E. et al. (1998). Relationships between hunger and psychosocial functioning in low-income American children. *Journal of the American Academy of Child & Adolescent Psychiatry* 37: 163–171.

Murray, C.E. (2006). Controversy, constraints, and context: understanding family violence through family systems theory. *The Family Journal: Counseling and Therapy for Couples and Families* 14: 234–239.

National Commission on the Causes and Prevention of Violence (1969). *To Establish Justice, to Insure Domestic Tranquility: Final Report of the National Commission on the Causes and Prevention of Violence.* Washington DC: US Government Printing Office.

Neave, M., Faulkner, P., and Nicholson, T. (2016). *Royal Commission into Family Violence.* Victoria, AU: Victorian Government Printer.

Nkomo, P., Naicker, N., Mathee, A. et al. (2017). The association between environmental lead exposure with aggressive behavior, and dimensionality of direct and indirect aggression during mid-adolescence: birth to twenty plus cohort. *Science of the Total Environment* 612: 472–479.

Novaco, R.W. (2020). Anger treatment with violent offenders. In: *What Works in Violence Risk Management: Theory, Research and Practice*, 385–398 (eds. J.S. Wormith, L.A. Craig and T. Hogue). Chichester, UK: Wiley Blackwell.

Nussbaum, D. (2020). Aggression from a psychobiological perspective: implications for enhanced violent risk assessment and interventions. In: *What Works in Violence Risk Management: Theory, Research and Practice*, 315–348 (eds. J.S. Wormith, L.A. Craig and T. Hogue). Chichester, UK: Wiley Blackwell.

Office for National Statistics (2018). *The Nature of Violent Crime in England and Wales: Year Ending March 2017.* London, UK: Office for National Statistics.

Office of the Surgeon General (2001). *Youth Violence: A Report of the Surgeon General.* Rockville, MD: Office of the Surgeon General.

Ogloff, J. and Davis, M. (2020). From predicting dangerousness to assessing and managing risk for violence: a journey across four generations. In: *What Works in Violence Risk Management: Theory, Research and Practice*, 81–98 (eds. J.S. Wormith, L.A. Craig and T. Hogue). Chichester, UK: Wiley Blackwell.

Olver, M. (2020). Personality-based violent risk assessment. In: *What Works in Violence Risk Management: Theory, Research and Practice*, 203–222 (eds. J.S. Wormith, L.A. Craig and T. Hogue). Chichester, UK: Wiley Blackwell.

Olver, M.E., Stockdale, K.C., and Wormith, J.S. (2011). A meta-analysis of predictors of offender treatment attrition and its relationship to recidivism. *Journal of Consulting and Clinical Psychology* 79: 6–12.

Pailing, A., Boon, J., and Egan, V. (2014). Personality, the dark triad and violence. *Personality and Individual Differences* 67: 81–86.

Pease, K. (2002). Crime reduction. In: *The Oxford Handbook of Criminology* (eds. M. Maguire, R. Morgan and R. Reiner), 947–979. Oxford: Oxford University Press.

Pence, E. and Paymar, M. (1993). *Education Groups for Men Who Batter: The Duluth Model.* New York: Springer-Verlag.

Pithers, W.D. (1990). Relapse prevention with sexual aggressors. In: *Handbook of Sexual Assault* (eds. W.L. Marshall, D.R. Laws and H.E. Barbaree), 343–361. New York: Plenum Press.

Polaschek, D.L.L. and Wong, S.C.P. (2020). Risk-reducing treatment in high-risk psychopathic and violent offenders. In: *What Works in Violence Risk Management: Theory, Research and Practice*, 369–384 (eds. J.S. Wormith, L.A. Craig and T. Hogue). Chichester, UK: Wiley Blackwell.

Prendergast, M.L., Pearson, F.S., Podus, D. et al. (2013). The Andrews' principles of risk, need, and responsivity as applied in drug abuse treatment programs: meta-analysis of crime and drug use outcomes. *Journal of Experimental Criminology* 9: 275–300.

Quinsey, V.L. (2002). Evolutionary theory and criminal behavior. *Legal and Criminological Psychology* 7: 1–13.

Quinsey, V.L., Harris, G.T., Rice, M.E. et al. (1993). Assessing treatment efficacy in outcome studies of sex offenders. *Journal of Interpersonal Violence* 8: 512–532.

Raine, A. (1993). *The Psychopathology of Crime: Criminal Behavior as a Clinical Disorder.* San Diego, CA: Academic Press.

Raine, A. (2013). *The Anatomy of Violence: The Biological Roots of Crime.* New York: Pantheon/Random House.

Reitzel, L.R. and Carbonell, J.L. (2006). The effectiveness of sexual offender treatment for juveniles as measured by recidivism: a meta-analysis. *Journal of Sexual Abuse* 18: 401–421.

Republic of South Africa (1995). *Promotion of National Unity and Reconciliation Act 34 of 1995*. Pretoria, South Africa: Government Printing Works.

Rettenberger, M. and Craig, L.A. (2020). Sexual violence risk assessment. In: *What Works in Violence Risk Management: Theory, Research and Practice*, 183–202 (eds. J.S. Wormith, L.A. Craig and T. Hogue). Chichester, UK: Wiley Blackwell.

Rosenbaum, A., Hoge, S., Adelman, S. et al. (1994). Head injury in partner-abusive men. *Journal of Consulting and Clinical Psycholocy* 62: 1187–1193.

Salter, M. (2018). Child sexual abuse. In: *Routledge International Handbook of Violence Studies* (eds. C.M. Rennison, W.S. Dekeseredy and A. Hall-Sanchez), 276–285. London: Routledge.

Sampson, C.J., James, M., Huband, N. et al. (2013). Cost implications of treatment non-completion in a forensic personality disorder service. *Criminal Behaviour and Mental Health* 23: 321–335.

Scarpa, A. and Raine, A. (2007). Biosocial bases of violence. In: *The Cambridge Handbook of Violent Behavior and Aggression* (eds. D.J. Flannery, A.T. Vazsonyi and I.D. Waldman), 151–169. New York: Cambridge University Press.

Schmucker, M. and Lösel, F. (2015). The effects of sexual offender treatment on recidivism: an international meta-analysis of sound quality evaluations. *Journal of Experimental Criminology* 11: 597–630.

Schweinhart, L.J., Montie, J., Xiang, X. et al. (2005). *Lifetime Effects: The High/Scope Perry Preschool Study through Age 40*. Ypsilanti, MI: High/Scope Press.

Serin, R.C., Lowenkamp, C.T., and Lloyd, C.D. (2020). Managing violent offenders in the community: reentry and beyond. In: *What Works in Violence Risk Management: Theory, Research and Practice*, 543–558 (eds. J.S. Wormith, L.A. Craig and T. Hogue). Chichester, UK: Wiley Blackwell.

Sexton, T.L. and Turner, C.W. (2010). The effectiveness of functional family therapy for youth with behavioral problems in a community practice setting. *Journal of Family Psychology* (3): 339–348.

Shifter, M. (2012). *Countering Criminal Violence in Central America: Council Special Report*. New York: Council on Foreign Relations Press.

Skogan, W.G. (1977). Dimensions of the dark figure of unreported crime. *Crime and Delinquency* 23: 41–50.

Slotter, E.B. and Finkel, E.J. (2011). I³ theory: instigating, impelling, and inhibiting factors in aggression. In: *Human Aggression and Violence: Causes, Manifestations, and Consequences* (eds. P.R. Shafer and M. Mikulincer), 35–52. Washington, DC: American Psychological Association.

Smith, P., Gendreau, P., and Swartz, K. (2009). Validating the principles of effective intervention: a systematic review of the contributions of meta-analysis in the field of corrections. *Victims & Offenders* 4: 148–169.

Soldino, V. and Carbonell-Vayá, E.J. (2017). Effect of treatment on sex offenders' recidivism: a meta-analysis. *Anales de Psicologia* 33 (3): 578–588.

State of Victoria (2016). *Ending Family Violence: Victoria's Plan for Change*. Melbourne, AU: State of Victoria.

State of Victoria (2017). *Violence Rolling Action Plan 2017–2020*. Melbourne, AU: State of Victoria.

Statistics Canada (2017). *Homicide Survey, Victims and Persons Accused of Homicide, by Age Group and Sex, Canada. Table 253–0003*. Ottawa, ON: Canadian Centre for Justice Statistics.

Steadman, H. (1982). A situational approach to violence. *International Journal of Law and Psychiatry* 5: 171–186.

Steadman, H.J. and Cocozza, J. (1978). Psychiatry, dangerousness and the repetitively violent offender. *Journal of Criminal Law and Criminology* 69: 226–231.

Stoltenborgh, M. (2011). A global perspective on child sexual abuse: meta-analysis of prevalence around the world. *Child Maltreatment* 16 (2): 79–101.

Straus, M. (1973). A general systems theory approach to as theory of violence between family members. *Family Sociology/Sociolgie de la Famille* 12: 105–125.

Sykes, G. and Matza, D. (1957). Techniques of neutralization: a theory of delinquency. *American Sociological Review* 22: 664–670.

Tapscott, J.L., Hancock, M., and Hoaken, P.N.S. (2012). Severity and frequency of reactive and instrumental violent offending: divergent validity of subtypes of violence in an adult forensic sample. *Criminal Justice and Behavior* 39 (2): 202–219.

Taylor, J. (2020). Interventions for violent offenders with intellectual and developmental disabilities. In: *What Works in Violence Risk Management: Theory, Research and Practice*, 451–464 (eds. J.S. Wormith, L.A. Craig and T. Hogue). Chichester, UK: Wiley Blackwell.

Tecce, M.P. (2014). *Juvenile psychopathy: Instrumental versus reactive aggression in male and female juvenile offenders*. Doctoral dissertation, Antioch University New England, Keene, NH.

ter Beek, E., Spruit, A., Kuiper, C.H.Z. et al. (2018). Treatment effect on recidivism for juveniles who have sexually offended: a multilevel meta-analysis. *Journal of Abnormal Child Psychology* 46: 543–556.

The American Bar Association (n.d.). *Commission on domestic and sexual violence*. https://www.americanbar.org/groups/domestic_violence.html (accessed 20 June 2019).

The Truth and Reconciliation Commission Act (2000). *Sierra Leone Gazette*. Supplement to vol. CXXXI (9).

The Truth and Reconciliation Commission of Canada (2015). *Honouring the Truth, Reconciling for the Future: Summary of the Final Report on the Truth and Reconciliation Commission of Canada*. Winnipeg, MB: The Truth and Reconciliation Commission of Canada.

The Youth Violence Commission, (n.d.). *Developing policy to address youth violence*. http://yvcommission.com (accessed 20 June 2019).

Tiihonen, J., Rautiainen, M.R., Ollila, H.M. et al. (2015). Genetic background of extreme violent behavior. *Molecular Psychiatry* 20: 786–792.

Tolan, P.H. and Guerra, N. (1994). *What works in reducing adolescent aggression: An empirical review of the field*. Report number F-888. Boulder, CO: The Center for the Study and Prevention of Violence, Institute for Behavioral Sciences, University of Colorado, Boulder.

Tsang, J.-A. (2002). Moral rationalization and the integration of situational factors and psychological processes in immoral behavior. *Review of General Psychology* 6: 25–50.

United Nations (2006). *Rule-of-law tools for post-conflict states: Truth commissions*. Office of the United Nations High Commission for Human Rights. New York: Unit-ed Nations.

United Nations (2014a). *Global Studies on Homicide 2013: Trends/Context/Data*. Vienna: United Nations Office on Drugs and Crime.

United Nations (2014b). *Looking Back: The Year we Oranged the World*. New York: Author.

United Nations (2016). *UNODC Statistics. Table, Homicide: Male and Female Intentional; Homicide Victims Killed by Intimate Partners or Family Members as a Percentage of Total Homicide Victims, by Country/Territory*. New York, NY: United Nations Office on Drugs and Crime.

United Nations (n.d.). *Leave no One behind – End Violence against Women and Girls*. New York: United Nations.

Van den Berg, J.W., Smid, W., Schepers, K. et al. (2018). The predictive properties of dynamic sex offender risk assessment instruments: a meta-analysis. *Psychological Assessment* 30: 179–191.

Viljoen, J.L., Jonnson, M.R., and Shephard, S.M. (2020). Assessing risk for violent, general, and sexual offending in adolescents: recent advances and future directions. In: *What Works in Violence Risk Management: Theory, Research and Practice*, 223–250 (eds. J.S. Wormith, L.A. Craig and T. Hogue). Chichester, UK: Wiley Blackwell.

Waller, B. (2016). Broken fixes: a systematic analysis of the effectiveness of modern and postmodern interventions utilized to decrease IPV perpetration among black males remanded to treatment. *Aggression and Violent Behavior* 27: 42–49.

Walters, G.D. (2009). Anger management training in incarcerated male offenders: differential impact on proactive and reactive criminal thinking. *International Journal of Forensic Mental Health* 8: 214–217.

Welsh, B.C. (2004). Monetary costs and benefits of correctional treatment programs: implications for offender reentry. *Federal Probation* 68 (2): 9–13.

Wilson, C.M., Desmarais, S.L., Nicholls, T.L. et al. (2013). Predictive validity of dynamic factors: assessing risk in forensic psychiatric inpatients. *Law & Human Behavior* 37: 377–388.

Wormith, J.S. (2017). Automated risk assessment: the next generation or a black hole? *Criminology and Public Policy* 16: 281–303.

Zillmann, D. (1988). Cognition-excitation interdependencies in aggressive behavior. *Aggressive Behavior* 14: 51–64.

Zimbardo, P.G. (1969). The human choice: individuation, reason, and order versus deindividuation, impulse, and chaos. In: *Nebraska Symposium on Motivation* (eds. W.D. Arnold and D. Levine), 237–307. Lincoln: University of Nebraska.

2

What Do We Know About Violent Offending Behaviour?

Daryl G. Kroner and Gunnar C. Butler

Southern Illinois University, Carbondale, USA

Overview

Our knowledge of violent behaviour can fall into five interrelated areas; rates of occurrence, explanations/theory, violent behaviour according to type or groups, person-based characteristics, and contextual/environmental factors. The knowledge in each of these areas is interrelated, which makes the categories somewhat artificial. Acknowledging this, the current chapter is structured around these five areas, highlighting a few topics within each area. Rates of occurrence provide a basic understanding of how often violent behaviour occurs within certain groups or contexts. Although not of a causal nature, this information can provide guidance at the policy and service-provider levels. The explanations and theory of violent behaviour can explain much data and give structure to our ideas for a clearer understanding of some of the causal mechanisms that contribute to violent behaviour. Violent behaviour can have unique characteristics according to types (i.e. intimate interpersonal) or groups (i.e. gangs). Personal characteristics are typically robust predictors of violence and contextual/environmental factors have the unique characteristic of being changed through public policy.

Rates of Occurrence

Rates of occurrence of violence differ according to groups (i.e. countries, types of violence, young adult) and according to settings (i.e. prison, psychiatric units). Knowledge of these rates will be beneficial to policy makers and services providers. From a policy perspective, the rates of violence will contribute to determining the amount of resources to adequately manage or ameliorate violent behaviour. Understanding the magnitude over time can assist with long-term planning, contributing to cost–benefit analyses. From a service-provider perspective, knowledge of rate gains inform risk/clinical assessments and the nature and appropriate levels of response. Specially related to violent behaviour assessment, violent rates of occurrence can have some utility. They can act as a comparative reference point in risk assessments (Cunningham and Reidy 1999), but they can also be used inappropriately in trying to alter a validated risk assessment instrument (Harris and Rice 2013). Since violent offending occurs in the context of perpetrators, victims, and specific circumstances, the focus of this section is the prevalence rates of violence according to specialized groups (high risk, mental illness, intimate interpersonal) and settings (prison, psychiatric unit, community parole).

Specialized groups

High risk   High-risk groups, by definition, contribute to the majority of violent behaviour. Understanding the rates of violent behaviour for such a group has direct management and intervention resource implications. A meta-analytic study of risk assessment studies between 1995 and 2011 predicting violence, grouped participants into a high-risk group (Singh et al. 2014). Using nine commonly used risk instruments, the high-risk group was defined by the instrument's manual definition of high risk. From this sample of 13045 participants in 57 international samples, the median annual rate of violent behaviour was 12.9% (Mean = 23.1%). It should be noted that half of the samples reported rates that were either below 6.5% or above 19.0%.

Mental illness   Over the last number of years, researchers have become increasingly interested in the relationship between mental illness and violent behaviour. Evidence suggests that 6% of adults have been diagnosed with a mental illness at some point in their lives (Kessler et al. 2005). Raising concern over understanding this rate is that long hospitalizations pertaining to mental illness no longer occur. This means that more and more people diagnosed with mental illnesses are residing in regular communities. The median hospital stay for a mental illness was forty-one days in 1971, but that number drastically reduced to just over five days (5.4) in 1997 (Choe et al. 2008; Milazzo-Sayre et al. 2000).

One method of examining this relationship is to measure the rates of violent behaviour amongst those who have a mental illness and those who do not have a mental illness. In an Australian study covering 25-years, a sample of convicted offenders with schizophrenia was compared to a community sample matched for age, gender, and place of residence (Wallace et al. 2004). The rate of violent behaviour for the schizophrenic group was 8.2% and for the community matched group, 1.8%. There was a proportionately increase in the rate of violent behaviour over time for the schizophrenic group, but a similar increase occurred for the community sample. These results would indicate that not just one factor, such as deinstitutionalization, would account for rates of violent behaviour amongst those with mental illness. In a representative US sample of schizophrenics, the rate of serious violence was 3.6% and 15.5% for minor violent behaviour (Swanson et al. 2006).

A meta-analytic study of studies including participants with mental illness and violent outcomes between 1983 and 2011 provided the data to determine what percentage of participants were violent (Witt et al. 2013). Amongst this group of 45533 patients, the rate of violence was 18.5%. The nature of the study criteria suggests some biases towards the reporting of violent behaviour, but given the large number of participants over a significant time frame, results are still informative.

Brennan et al. (2000) conducted an epidemiological investigation of a birth cohort in Demark between 1944 and 1947. The study gathered data pertaining to violent arrests and mental illness hospitalizations. Overall, data were available for 335 990 individuals born during that period. The result showed that 4.8% of the sample size was hospitalized for mental illness at some point in their lives. These individuals who were hospitalized committed approximately 26% of all violent crimes situated within Denmark. This is a disproportionate number when considering the small population of those with a mental illness. Breaking this down according to gender, the overall prevalence of mental illness translated to be 2.2% of males and 2.6% of females. The males accounted for 10% of violent crime, whereas the females accounted for 16% of violent crime (Brennan et al. 2000). Men with organic brain syndrome, and women with schizophrenia were at the highest risk of committing violent acts. The findings regarding organic brain syndrome are consistent with previous research (Owen et al. 1998).

Intimate interpersonal and community violence   Focusing on partner violent behaviour for both sexes, a systematic review (1970–2009) of national studies was used to determine the rate of domestic violent behaviour (Esquivel-Santoveña and Dixon 2012). Eleven surveys/studies were retained for the final review. The women victim rates (per 12-month period) ranged from 5.0 (China) to 34.9% (Uganda). The US women victim rate ranged from 7.0 to 11.5%. In a community sample of adults, a 10.1% violent rate of occurrence was reported over the past 12 months (Graham et al. 2002).

Mental health and offenders   In a study of 612 478 incarcerated offenders over a six-year period, the rate of mental illness was calculated within a group that had violent histories (Baillargeon et al. 2010). Within this group, 8.6% had co-occurring psychiatric and substance misuse disorders. For psychiatric disorders alone, the rate was 3.6%. With a sample of 2487 incarcerated offenders, the rate of violent behaviour for a single incident was 17.1% for those with a mental illness and 12.9% for those without one (Walters 2011). The rates for two or more violent incidents were 5.6% (mental illness group) and 3.1% (group without mental illness). The rates for three or more violent incidents were 1.7% (mentally ill group) and 1.2% (non-mentally ill group).

A one-year intake cohort prison sample (n = 79 211) was categorized into those who have a mental illness (n = 7878) and those who did not have a mental illness (n = 71 333) (Baillargeon et al. 2009). The rate of violent behaviour for the index offense was 20.6% for those with a mental illness and 19.8% for those without one. If only measuring assault violence, the rates were 13.0% for the no mental illness group and 21.7% for the schizophrenic group. A sample of 7221 (representing 40% of the state male population) was used to examine institutional victim violence within the past six months (Blitz et al. 2008). The occurrence rate of any inmate-on-inmate incident was 20.5% and for incidents with a weapon, the rate was 14.1%. When the mental illness group was compared to the group without mental illness, the mental illness group had a higher occurrence rate of any inmate-on-inmate incidents (29.2% vs. 18.0%) and incidents with a weapon (19.0% vs. 14.1%).

As with the difference between offenders with mental illness and without, in prison rates of violence, a difference is also found amongst parolees. When the rate of violent offences is compared between parolees with mental illness and parolees without mental illness, the rate is higher for those with mental illness (14.3% vs. 8.0%; Eno Louden and Skeem 2011).

Settings

Psychiatric units Psychiatric units typically have higher rates of violent behaviour compared to other types of institutions. A meta-analytic study that included studies reporting the rate of violent occurrences between 1995 and 2014 provided an overall international rate of violent occurrences (Iozzino et al. 2015). The sample of 23 972 patients over 35 studies suggested a 17% prevalence of violent behaviour for those admitted to an acute psychiatric unit. Units with a greater number of males, greater number of involuntary patients, and patients with alcohol use disorders had higher rates of violent behaviour. With regard to longer stays for patients in a medium secure unit, the rates of violent behaviour were recorded over a 17-year period (1980–1996) (Rutter et al. 2004). Of the 280 patients admitted to the unit, 165 (59%) had one or more violent incidents. The majority of violent incidents (67%) were committed by 18 (6%) of the patients. Within this group, the number of previous prison sentences was the strongest predictor of violent behaviour.

From a sampling frame of 2010–2011, 5005 patients in a forensic mental health unit were followed for three months (O'Shea et al. 2014). The rate of occurrence for violent behaviour during this timeframe was 35.8% (n = 181). These patients accounted for 710 incidents. In summary, the prevalence rates across multiple samples will be approximately 17%, whereas in specific settings the rate can reach 60%.

Prisons A typical finding with rates of violent behaviour in prisons is that the rates vary according to security level, with lower security institutions having lower rates of violent behaviour. During the calendar year of 2002, the Florida state correctional system recorded that 10.9% of all incoming offenders were involved in acts of violent behaviour (Cunningham and Sorensen 2006). With regard to assaults, the overall rate of violent behaviour was 0.9% for minimum, 2.1% for medium, and 7.2% for maximum security levels. A similar overall violent behaviour rate has been found for US federal institutions. With a male sample of 177 767 offenders admitted from 1991 to 1998, the overall violent behaviour rate was 9.6% (Harer and Langan 2001). More serious assaults had a rate of 0.6% and less serious assaults had a rate of 2.7%. At minimum security, the lowest classification score group had a violent behaviour rate of 0.7% and the highest score had a rate of 3.0%. At medium security, the lowest classification score group had a violent behaviour rate of 6.5% and the highest score had a rate of 9.8%. At high security, the lowest classification score group had a violent behaviour rate of 13.1% and the highest score had a rate of 30.2%.

Not only do violent behaviour rates vary according to security level, they can vary according to prison size. Farrington and Nuttall (1980) found that prisons with long-term offenders will have a lower rate of violent behaviour if they are large (2.3% rate with population greater than 500), rather than if they are small (4.7% rate with population less than 300). For short-term prisons, prison size had little effect on the rate of violent behaviour (n less than 500, 4.1% vs. n greater than 500, 4.2%).

Different than solely observing a one-time rate, research has indicated that between 20 and 45% of incarcerated individuals have committed some form of violent behaviour while incarcerated (Cunningham et al. 2005; Sorensen and Cunningham 2010). Consistent with previous research, offenders who are younger than 21, are almost three times more likely to engage in violent behaviour while incarcerated, when compared with other inmates in their thirties. As offenders age, their propensity to commit violent acts decreases (Flanagan 1983). Other factors related to violent behaviour in the prison setting include level of education, prior prison convictions, offence type, and years served. Individuals who have not obtained a high school education, have been sentenced to prison time previously, are serving time for a property offence, or have to serve six to ten years are also at a heightened risk of turning to violent behaviour (Cunningham et al. 2005)

Contrary to popular belief, murderers are not at a heightened risk of committing violent acts while incarcerated, when compared to the rest of the prison population. First-degree murders are actually a population that are least likely to engage in violent behaviour. Only 35% percent of these individuals appear to engage in violent behaviour. Second-degree murders have a prevalence rate near 40%, while individuals convicted of a lesser homicide have a prevalence rate near 34%. All other incarcerated offenders engage in violent behaviour at a prevalence rate of 44.8% (Sorensen and Cunningham 2010).

In summary, rates of occurrence of violent behaviour vary according to groups and settings. These rates have the benefit of providing basic knowledge of violent behaviour for public policy and service providers. The shortcomings of this type of violent behaviour information can occur due to measurement issues, but also because of a lack of understanding of how these rates naturally decrease over time (see Hanson et al. 2014).

Explanations and Theory Related to Violent Behaviour

The violence literature has distinguished proactive (instrumental, cold-blooded) and reactive (hot-blooded, affective defence, impulsive) driven actions. Proactive violent behaviour involves the premeditation of an act, which is generally committed without any emotional outbursts, and reactive violent behaviour is emotionally charged and impulsive in nature. This basic distinction has physiological and behavioural differences, which have been well noted in animal studies. A proactive, predatory attack involves a purposeful and planned behaviour, where the manner of attack, the target, and magnitude of the response is chosen. A reactive defence involves a lowering of the ears, drawing in of the head, and pupillary dilatation (Weinshenker and Siegel 2002).

Proactive and reactive actions can be defined according to internal processes and the type of resultant goals. Proactive actions have a preparation or planning component and are motivated by some type of gain or goals. With proactive actions, external goals are prominent. The amount of control a perpetrator can exert over their behaviour during a violent act is substantially greater than a reactive approach (Stanford et al. 2008). They commit acts of violent behaviour that are methodically thought out, and usually committed without any elements of arousal. Reactive actions are intended to cause injury, typically fuelled by affective states, such as anger, revenge, or frustration. With reactive actions, internal goals are prominent. Reactive perpetrators can be described as short-tempered, and they typically use aggression when they feel as if they are being provoked or threatened. These individuals usually do not have an end goal associated with their violent behaviour, because they act in the heat of the moment (Kockler and Meloy 2007).

The distinction between proactive and reactive driven actions occurs amongst children (Dodge et al. 1997; Poulin and Boivin, 2000), adolescents (Walters and DeLisi 2015), and adults (Walters 2009). Amongst adult offenders, proactive aggression is associated with higher psychopathy scores (Cornell et al. 1996). This study used both prison offenders and forensic patients, and rated offences according to six criteria to place participants into proactive or reactive categories. These researchers concluded that reactive actions are 'the most basic form of

aggression amongst criminal behavior' (p. 788). In fact, other research supports the prominent role of reactive measures in predicting future offending (Peterson et al. 2010; Walters
2011). Yet, others have found high proactive scores to have more of a role in distinguishing
between property and violent delinquency than reactive scores (Miller and Lynam 2006).
Thus, the robustness of the basic conceptual distinction between proactive and reactive
domains is a robust one.

A standardized measure of proactive and reactive behaviours, the Reactive-Proactive
Aggression Questionnaire (Raine et al. 2006), has shown construct validity and reliability
across multiple samples (Baker et al. 2008; White et al. 2015). In a 10-year longitudinal
study (ages 16 and 26), proactive aggression was associated with future antisocial behaviour,
including violence; reactive aggression was associated with future negative affect, most notably
anxiety (Fite et al. 2010). When the Reactive-Proactive Aggression Questionnaire has been
used as an outcome measure, antisocial personality and conduct disorder symptoms are more
strongly related to proactive aggression (Steadham and Rogers 2013). Other indicators of
proactive and reactive actions have demonstrated stronger intervention effects on reactive
actions (Barker et al. 2010). It appears that the proactive and reactive dimensions have different developmental patterns.

A drawback to using past behaviours to predict future behaviours is the potential circularity
of the relationship. To address this, proactive and reactive processes have been psychologically
represented by proactive and reactive antisocial cognitions. These two cognitions have demonstrated relationships with criminal justice outcomes. Using a psychiatric high-risk violent
behaviour sample, two groups defined in relation to proactive and reactive processes were able
to distinguish between past proactive offences (Skeem et al. 2004). Proactive antisocial cognition has been shown to mediate the otherwise poor Psychopathy Checklist Factor 1 (core
personality features) and violent behaviour relationship (Walters and Delisi 2015).

In terms of measurement, a refinement to the psychological conceptualization of proactive and
reactive antisocial cognitions is the development of proactive and reactive criminal thinking
patterns. Walters, using the Psychological Inventory of Criminal Thinking Styles (PICTS; Walters
1995) used three subscales ($2 \times$ Entitlement + [$1.5 \times$ Self-Assertion/Deception] + Historical) to measure the proactive domain and three subscales ($2 \times$ Cutoff + [$1.5 \times$ Problem Avoidance] + Current)
to measure the reactive domain (Walters 2006). With multiple controls and incremental validity
tests, the PICTS proactive and reactive measures have been able to predict past and future offending patterns and also distinguish between respective proactive and reactive-based outcome results
(Carr et al. 2009; Walters 2005, 2007, 2011; Walters et al. 2007). The PICTS proactive measure
has been less amenable to treatment changes (Walters 2006; likely due to the use of static items
of the Historical subscale).

Types of Violence

Gangs

Previous research has found that many gang members exhibit low levels of pro social behaviour and anxiety, but high levels of hyperactivity (Dupéré et al. 2007). Individuals who join
gangs and partake in gang violent behaviour possess a unique set of cognitive traits that set
them apart from the rest of society. Research suggests that if a person possesses psychopathic
personality traits, then there is an increased likelihood of participating in gang activity. More

specifically, the psychopathic trait of impulsive-irresponsible distinguishes gang and non-gang involvement (Chu et al. 2014). In this sample, once attitudes toward associates were entered, the psychopathic trait of impulsive-irresponsible did not remain statistically significant, thereby reducing the importance of this trait.

Other research, though has demonstrated the importance of personality disorders in gang membership. In a higher risk group of identified gang members, antisocial personality disorder rate has been found to be between 50 and 63% (Di Placido et al. 2006). These personality traits, in general, are not readily affected by common forms of informal social control, such as parental supervision. In addition, the use of commitment language does not translate into actions to assist in crime reduction (Smith et al. 2015).

In general, individuals who join gangs have negative perceptions of authority figures, which is one of the most common features of gangs as a whole. This can potentially be problematic, because youth are the most susceptible to succumbing to gang activity and peer pressure. Other cognitive deficiencies that contribute to gang violent behaviour include lower IQ, learning disabilities, mental illness, and low self-esteem (Alleyne and Wood 2012).

Within a prison setting, gang affiliation has been shown to be predictive of assaultive behaviours (Walters and Crawford 2013). In this analysis, gang affiliation was restricted to gang affiliations occurring before the current incarceration. Gang affiliation remained predictive after controlling for age, risk level, criminal thinking, and drug history.

Intimate partner

Drawing upon the reactive and proactive distinction, a 2009 study utilized self-report and partner-report questionnaires to examine male-perpetrated domestic violence (Ennis et al. 2017). This study specifically looked at the severity of intimate violent behaviour in relation to proactive and reactive violence amongst males diagnosed with antisocial personality disorder, borderline personality disorder, or both. Women's personal accounts of the violent acts were also utilized in the results, thereby allowing the researchers to account for certain behaviours and events that led up to the act of domestic violence (Ross and Babcock 2009)

Overall, 124 couples over the age of eighteen were selected for the study. The average age of the respondents was 32 for males and 30 for females. Eighty-three of the one hundred and twenty-four men did not meet criteria for either antisocial personality disorder or borderline personality disorder. Just over 14% (14.5%) of males showed signs of antisocial personality disorder, and just over 18% (18.5%) showed signs of borderline personality disorder. Overall, the study found that women's violent behaviour was the most significant predictor of domestic violence perpetrated by men with antisocial personality disorder. Women's violent behaviour was not an accurate predictor for men diagnosed with borderline personality disorder, or a combination of the two disorders. The researchers found that batterers diagnosed with borderline personality disorder were more likely to act in a reactive fashion, whereas batterers diagnosed with antisocial personality disorder were likely to act proactively (Ross and Babcock 2009).

As noted, there is support for the reactive/proactive distinction amongst intimate partner violence. Building upon this distinction, Babcock and colleagues developed a measure to assess the situational components of interpersonal partner violence (Babcock et al. 2004). They found three components; violence to control, the increased likelihood of violence following the partner's attempt for autonomy or control; violence out of jealously, a jealous response to perceived infidelity; and violence following verbal abuse, the use of verbal abuse, including threats. Other research has confirmed the importance of the second component, jealously, in the prediction of future intimate partner violence (Robinson and Howarth 2012).

Previous research has indicated that many perpetrators immediately react to their partners' behaviours in an effort to reduce arousal internally (Kingsbury et al. 1997). Men with borderline personality disorder reacted immediately to their partner's distress by committing acts of severe violent behaviour, while men diagnosed with antisocial personality disorder or both disorders refrained from immediate violent behaviour when their partners displayed distress. The research found that men with antisocial personality disorder typically premeditate their violent behaviour in an effort to control and dominate their partner. This tends to happen when they sense a threat to their authority, which can happen when a spouse makes a demand or becomes defiant (Babcock et al. 2000), and when they have a distorted definition of an intimate relationship involving domination and control (Ross and Babcock 2009; Tweed and Dutton 1998).

Associated Contributors – Person-Based

Mental illness

Much research and commentary has examined the relationship between mental illness and violent behaviour. In addition to differential occurrence rates of violent behaviour between different mental illness groups (mentally ill vs. non-mentally ill) giving evidence for a relationship between mental illness and violent behaviour, a correlational-type of analysis is also another approach to examine this relationship. The support for and against this relationship has varied considerably.

Many studies find a relationship. Using a sample of 79 211 offenders, the mentally ill group had 16.4% rate of assaultive offenses compared to the non-mentally ill group with a lower 13.0% assault rate (Baillargeon et al. 2009). Silver et al. (2008) used the Survey of Inmates in State and Federal Correctional Facilities (n = 17 248) to examine the mental illness and violent behaviour relationship. They classified the sample into five groups based on crime types; assaultive violent behaviour, property, drug, other, and sexual crime. Both serious and minor mental illness problems distinguished between assaultive violent behaviour and the four other types of crime. This relationship occurred while accounting for a wide variety of control variables.

A meta-analysis of the psychosis and violent behaviour literature overcame specific sample concerns. Douglas et al. (2009) drew upon studies examining the relationship between psychosis and violent behaviour up to 2006. Their results were based on 885 effect sizes with samples that had demonstrated evidence of psychosis. Studies that did not explicitly state the presence of psychosis (i.e. samples described as only having 'mental illness') or solely used self-report to indicate the presence of psychosis were not included in the analysis. Violent behaviour was defined as 'any actual, attempted, or threatened harm to another person or persons' (p. 684). Thus, studies that referred to self-harm or violent behaviour towards an object were not included. Their overall results found psychosis to correspond with a 49–68% increase in violent behaviour, which translated into a small, standardized mean difference score ($d = 0.24$ to 0.32). The conclusion was a small, but reliable, effect for psychosis differentiating between nonviolent behaviour and violent behaviour. Of interest was what moderated this relationship. Studies that occurred in civil psychiatric, correctional, and community settings maintained the psychosis and violent behaviour relationship, whereas forensic psychiatric settings did not give evidence of the psychosis and violent behaviour relationship.

Many other studies do not find a direct relationship (Feder 1991; Langan 2010; Solomon et al. 2002). A number of methodological shortcomings in the research literature may account for these discrepant findings. Covariates of medication compliance (Junginger and McGuire 2004), command hallucinations (McNiel et al. 2000), homelessness (Markowitz 2006), symptom severity (Steadman et al. 2009), and attitudes (Podubinski et al. 2017) factor into this relationship. We will highlight a statistical constraining issue and a methodological shortcoming of the research.

A statistical base rate comment affecting the nature of the mental illness and violent behaviour will help frame subsequent discussions. The base rate of mental illness and violent behaviour is relatively low. Commenting on this feature, Lurigio and Swartz (2000) concluded that the two are 'unlikely to occur together' (p. 54). Even in samples that have a relatively high base rate, such as the MacArthur study (e.g. 25.7% committed at least one violent act over 41 weeks), the rate of violent behaviour that occurred while either delusional or hallucinatory at the time was very low (7.4% delusional and 5.2% hearing voices) (Monahan et al. 2001). Thus, base rate, by itself, will reduce the finding of a strong, robust relationship between mental illness and violent behaviour.

The inclusion or exclusion of criminal justice variables in examining the relationship between mental illness and violent behaviour is a methodological shortcoming that has hampered our understanding of this relationship. Two reasons for not including substantive criminal justice variables are the research paradigms and intervention strategies. A prominent research orientation of mental health researchers is that of a unidirectional view of the relationship between mental illness and criminal justice outcomes. Mental illness is viewed as a direct link, or a causal factor to criminal justice outcomes (Goin 2014; Kooyman et al. 2007; Krelstein 2002; McInerny and Minne 2004; Torrey et al. 1998). If this view is not explicitly stated, it is assumed (Cummins 2006; Roskes et al. 1999). One strong pressure for this orientation is the legal decisions that have involved offenders. Metzner (2002) presented an overview of litigation brought forward by offenders, in which the focus of these court actions was to correct the inadequate levels of mental health care.

This focus on mental illness then guides the formulation of research questions and recommended intervention/management strategies for offenders with mental illness. One research consequence of this assumption is the strong focus on psychiatric symptomatology. For example, in studies using violent behaviour or criminal recidivism as the outcome, predictive/control measures include basic demographics, Diagnostic and Statistical Manual (DSM) diagnoses, and other psychiatric rating scales (i.e. Brief Psychiatric Rating Scale [BPRS]). Many studies do not include basic criminal justice predictors/control measures (e.g. Messina et al. 2004; Odgers et al. 2009; Wallace et al. 2004). If criminal justice predictors are used, they are nonstandardized criminal justice measures (Prince et al. 2007). Although the focus traditionally has been on the establishment of industry performance standards, a basic assumption was that intervention in the psychotic disorders was directly related to criminal justice outcomes.

This lack of integrating interventions for mental illness and criminal justice need areas amongst offenders with mental illness has been acknowledged by some researchers. Cohen and Dvoskin (1992) argue for a separation between addressing mental illness concerns and criminal justice rehabilitation. Similarly, Toch and Adams (1987) state, 'It is that some inmates are *primarily* disturbed and *secondarily* offenders but have been dispensed of as if they were primarily offenders and secondarily (if at all) disturbed' (p. 541, emphasis in original). The advantage of these positions is that there is an acknowledgement that criminal justice need areas (i.e. anger, impulsivity) can have a significant role in determining the behaviour amongst offenders with mental illness (Cohen and Dvoskin 1992; Skeem et al. 2011).

In moving forward, integration of mental health illness and criminal justice variables has been examined with two approaches. One is using a pathways to violent behaviour approach and the other is an additive/multiplicative approach. The pathways research has found an antisocial path can be a distinct pathway. Using a sample of schizophrenic patients, early conduct problems and positive psychotic symptom pathways were found to lead to future violent behaviour (Swanson et al. 2008). This study compared the early conduct group to a non-conduct problem group. The early conduct group committed twice the amount of violent behaviour within the past six months than the non-conduct group. In addition, the likelihood of adult violent behaviour increased with a greater number of childhood conduct problems reported. Positive psychiatric symptoms were not related to adult violent behaviour in the early conduct group. The picture was different for the non-conduct group, in which positive psychiatric symptoms were related to adult violent behaviour. These results of the importance of early problems are further confirmed by a recent meta-analysis. Drawing upon studies conducted between 1983 and 2011, risk domains of negative symptoms, neuropsychological, positive symptoms, treatment, demographic, substance misuse, and criminal history were measured (Witt et al. 2013). Criminal history was the strongest predictor for overall violent behaviour, extreme violent behaviour, and violent behaviour occurring within inpatient settings.

A mediation design was used by Walters (2011) to assess the role of criminal thinking in the mental illness and violent behaviour relationship. This study took place within a prison and criminal thinking was found to partially mediate the relationship between mental illness and subsequent violent behaviour. In a further examination of the role of criminal justice variables, violent history and a major mental illness were used to predict institutional violent behaviour (Walters and Crawford 2014). This study also entered the interaction term of mental illness and violent history into the regression model. In the final model, only the interaction term of mental illness and violent history was statistically significant in predicting institutional violent behaviour. For violent recidivism, only violent history was statistically significant. The predictor of violent history, both as a single predictor and in an interaction, highlights the importance of criminal justice variables in predicting violent behaviour amongst those with mental illness. These results correspond with other research. Amongst a schizophrenic group, younger age, early conduct problems, and prior arrest history were amongst the variables that were more strongly associated with the outcome of serious violent behaviour (Swanson et al. 2006).

Antisocial attitudes

Apart from the violent behaviour literature, attitudes have a robust relationship with behaviour. This relationship between an attitude and future behaviour is supported with meta-analytic studies ($r = 0.56$; k = 128, n = 4598; Glasman and Albarracín 2006). It is not surprising, then, to find that a relationship between antisocial attitudes (in the broad sense, including antisocial beliefs, criminal cognitions) and violent behaviour. The General Criminal Thinking (GCT) score from the PICTS (Walters 2012) has been found to be predictive of institutional assault and fighting (Walters and Crawford 2013). With the assault outcome, age, gang affiliation, and GCT entered into the prediction model, whereas with the fighting outcome, only the age and GCT variables entered into the prediction model. The GCT results are similar to the Control scale from the Measure of Offender Thinking Styles (Mandracchia et al. 2007). The Control scale (i.e. desire for power and control over the self, others, and the environment) was able to distinguish violent offending from nonviolent offending after controlling for demographic, custody, and mental health variables (Mandracchia and Morgan 2012). The Criminal Sentiments Scale – Modified (Simourd 1997) had a weak correlation ($r = 0.17$) with violent re-offending amongst violent offenders (Simourd and van de Ven 1999).

The Self-Appraisal Questionnaire (SAQ; Loza 2005) includes a Criminal Tendencies scale, which measures antisocial attitudes, beliefs, behaviours, and feelings. With an offender sample, the Criminal Tendencies scale had a correlation of 0.35 with violent recidivism (Loza and Loza-Fanous 2000). The total SAQ score's correlation with the same outcome was 0.32. With institutional severe infractions as an outcome, the Criminal Tendencies had a correlation of 0.27 and the total SAQ scale had a correlation also of 0.27 (Loza and Loza-Fanous 2002).

The Criminal Attitudes to Violence Scale (Polaschek et al. 2004) was designed to assess attitudes often found in incarcerated offenders, assuming a history of violent behaviour or adhering to norms of a violent sub-culture. This scale was adequately able to distinguish offender groups who had a history of violent behaviour from those without a history of such behaviour.

In addition to general antisocial attitude scales, attitudes toward violent behaviour scales are indicative of future violent behaviours. The Measures of Criminal Attitudes and Associates (MCAA) scale has a Violent Attitude Scale that assesses attitudes supportive of violent behaviour, attitudes that indicate a tolerance toward violent behaviour, and perceptions that are guided by a willingness to use violent behaviour to obtain a desired goal. With an offender sample, the Violent Attitude Scale was predictive of future violent offending ($r = 0.19$; Mills et al. 2004). In a subsequent study with violent offenders, the Violent Attitude Scale had an $r = 0.19$ relationship with violent recidivism (Mills and Kroner 2006). In this study, the total MCAA scale had an $r = 0.31$ relationship with violent recidivism. In addition, the Violent Attitude Scale made an additional contribution to the prediction of violent behaviour once a standardized risk assessment instrument was included in the prediction model. With a student sample, the Violent Attitude Scale was statistically predictive of violent behaviour, after controlling for positive evaluation of violent behaviour, positive evaluation of violent people, and identification of self as violent (Nunes et al. 2015). These authors postulated that violent cognitions may be distinct from violent attitudes.

Associated Contributors – Contextual Factors

Behaviour is determined by both person-based factors and contexts. In comparing the associations with violence between personal characteristics and contextual factors, personal characteristics have a stronger relationship. The reasons for this difference are not immediately apparent. First, there may be difficulties in assessing contexts and related features (Gadon et al. 2006). For example, it may be more difficult to assess the dynamic nature of contextual change. Second, contexts may be viewed as only having current or temporal relevance and with the passage of time these features become a part of memories, which is a personal characteristic. If this approach is taken, then contexts become very limiting and only provide micro-level type of information (Monahan and Klassen 1982). Third, there can be considerable difference between the perceived and objective components of a context.

Others have covered broad contextual factors, such as stress and social support, social stability, victim availability, family environment, employment setting, availability of substances, victim characteristics, and concentrated poverty (Krnjacki et al. 2016; Kroner et al. 2013; Monahan and Klassen 1982; Otto 2000; Silver et al. 1999). In this review, we will focus on the role of companions, places, and weapons.

Companions

The degree of violent behaviour is also influenced by companions, and this relationship occurs also within forensic and correctional mental health samples. In a Finish study examining violent offence severity amongst homicide offenders with schizophrenia, predictors included positive psychotic symptoms, previous homicidal (attempted) history, and the presence of peers during the offence (Laajasalo and Häkkänen 2006). In the regression model, the presence of companions during the offence was the strongest predictor of offence severity. The companion results in this study confirm what is found in non-mentally ill samples examining violent offence severity (Girard and Wormith 2004). Using the Level of Service Inventory/Risk-Need-Responsivity (LSI/RNR) Companion scale, the results amongst offenders with mental illness demonstrate a weak overall relationship with violent recidivism (Canales et al. 2014). Amongst mental illness sub-groups, only the mood/anxiety group had a relationship between companions and violent recidivism that was above chance.

Amongst offenders without mental illness, the relationship between companions and violent offending appears to be robust. A meta-analytic study of the Level of Service scale studies (1981–2012) reported the relationship between the Companions scale and violent recidivism (Olver et al. 2014). From the sample of 55 440 offenders in 19 studies, the effect size (random) was 0.17, which was the fifth best predictor out of 11 scales. The effect size was the same for both male and female offenders. Using a different method of measuring companions (number and amount of associated time) found similar results. Part A of the MCAA (Mills and Kroner 2004) had a correlation of 0.18 with violent recidivism (Mills et al. 2004).

Places

Using data from a community sample, four places of violent behaviour were assessed; in or near licensed settings, in a public place other than a bar or social event, private social event or gathering, and at the residence of the main participants (Graham et al. 2002). Licensed settings had the greatest occurrence of violent behaviour (30%), followed by a public place (21%). What is of interest is that the violent behaviour expressed in these different places was associated with different personal characteristics. Incidents in a licensed setting most often occurred amongst strangers, involved predominantly males, and more than two people. In these incidents, only 60% were the primary participants and the average emotional impact, measured by positive feelings or no impact after the incident, was low. Public place incidents were distinguished by the occurrence across all ages. Violent behaviour in private social events occurred equally amongst men and women. Residence of the main participants typically involved intimate partners, with 70% of respondents being women. Emotional impact was reported as high, with more than 60% having extreme negative feelings after the incident.

Amongst those who have schizophrenia, household structures (i.e. with family, with non-family, frequent contact) were related to serious violent behaviour in the bivariate analyses (Swanson et al. 2006). When submitted to a regression model with demographic, social, and clinical variables, the household structure was not predictive of serious violent behaviour. Homelessness, though, did remain predictive of future violent behaviour.

The nature of a place also will impact the occurrence of violent behaviour. In assessing 100 census tracts in Seattle, the amount of disorder was measured (Wilcox et al. 2004). The three contributors to this measure were litter or garbage on the street, abandoned houses or buildings, and poor street lighting. This measure of disorder was strongly predictive of violent behaviour. With each unit increase in disorder, violent behaviour increased 132%.

Within a prison environment, a structured review of the literature found that violent behaviour can occur in any part of a prison (Gadon et al. 2006). One exception is the workshop area of a prison. It may be that these areas have higher security or there may be an offender selection process that results in reduced violent behaviour.

Weapons

A quarter of violent incidents in the USA and the UK involve the use of some sort of weapon (Brennan and Moore 2009; Rand and Catalano 2007). A weapon can be defined as an object that is intended to cause physical harm to somebody (Brennan and Moore 2009). Within the USA, individuals between the ages of 13 and 16 have the highest prevalence rates of carrying a weapon (DuRant et al. 1999). Often males who choose to carry guns before the age of 16 do so because of involvement in gangs or a drug-dealing network (Lizotte et al. 2000). The spike in youth violent crime in the 1980s and 1990s, more specifically gun-related violent behaviour, was partially caused by an increased availability of firearms (Huebner et al. 2007). Weapons can be used to both cause harm, and to deter it, Pickett et al. (2005) conducted a study that explored the phenomena. They found that males were more likely to carry weapons associated with proactive aggression (guns, clubs, etc.), while females were found to carry weapons as a form of self-defence. These weapons include mace and pepper spray.

A study conducted in 2000 looked at the prevalence of gun availability in relation to violent behaviour. The study utilized data from the National Incident-Based Reporting System in South Carolina from 1991 to 1994. The scholars found that legitimate gun availability does not increase the rate of violent crimes committed. This essentially means that violent crime does not increase as more and more individuals legally obtain firearms. Illegal gun availability was the only variable in the study that was associated with an increase in violent behaviour. Specifically, the study found that as the number of stolen guns increased, so too did the rate of youth arrested for gun crimes. This is particularly alarming because youth can only obtain guns in illegal ways (Stolzenberg and D'Alessio 2000).

The availability of weapons has a role in multiple types of violent behaviour and contexts. With regard to the presence of weapons in domestic violence, weapons are predictive of future domestic violence, after controlling for a wide number of demographic and situational variables (Robinson and Howarth 2012). In completed adult sexual assaults, when the victim was known, injury was associated with a weapon, whereas when the victim was a stranger injury was associated without a weapon (Quinsey and Upfold 1985). In a study of serial adult sexual offenders, use of a weapon occurred in 39% of the sample (Beauregard and Leclerc 2007). When a weapon was used, the purpose was to prevent the victim from resisting. A lesser purpose of the weapon was to break and enter the residence or to facilitate strangulation.

In a sample of convicted murderers, 1.45% of this group were involved in an incident that used a weapon against another inmate (Sorensen and Cunningham 2007). When the serious injury occurred against a staff, the rate was 0.12%.

Summary

Our understanding of violent behaviour is multidimensional, spanning across the five areas of rates of occurrence, explanations/theory, violent behaviour according to type or groups, person-based characteristics, and contextual/environmental factors. With regard to rates of occurrence, the focus in this review was on specific groups and places, and how the rates change according to these different parameters. It is an oversimplified perspective to suggest general rates when specific groups and specific places can be identified. The explanation of much violent behaviour can be made within a proactive and reactive framework, which has been applied fruitfully to intimate partner violence. By definition, person-based factors and contextual factors each have unique roles in violent behaviour. We highlighted the two potential contributions of mental illness and antisocial attitudes. Contextual contributors were the influence of companions, characteristics of places, and the availability of weapons. Compared to person-based factors, contextual factors are understudied and have not been developed and integrated into our understanding of violent behaviour.

References

Alleyne, E. and Wood, J.L. (2012). Gang membership: the psychological evidence. In: *Youth Gangs in International Perspective* (eds. F.-A. Esbensen and C.L. Maxson), 151–168. New York: Springer.

Babcock, J.C., Costa, D.M., Green, C.E. et al. (2004). What situations induce intimate partner violence? A reliability and validity study of the Proximal Antecedents to Violent Episodes (PAVE) scale. *Journal of Family Psychology* 18 (3): 433–442.

Babcock, J.C., Jacobson, N.S., Gottman, J.M. et al. (2000). Attachment, emotional regulation, and the function of marital violence: differences between secure, preoccupied, and dismissing violent and nonviolent husbands. *Journal of Family Violence* 15 (4): 391–409.

Baillargeon, J., Binswanger, I., Penn, J. et al. (2009). Psychiatric disorders and repeat incarcerations: the revolving prison door. *American Journal of Psychiatry* 166 (1): 103–109.

Baillargeon, J., Penn, J.V., Knight, K. et al. (2010). Risk of reincarceration among prisoners with co-occurring severe mental illness and substance use disorders. *Administration and Policy in Mental Health and Mental Health Services Research* 37 (4): 367–374.

Baker, L.A., Raine, A., Liu, J. et al. (2008). Differential genetic and environmental influences on reactive and proactive aggression in children. *Journal of Abnormal Child Psychology* 36 (8): 1265–1278.

Barker, E.D., Vitaro, F., Lacourse, E. et al. (2010). Testing the developmental distinctiveness of male proactive and reactive aggression with a nested longitudinal experimental intervention. *Aggressive Behavior* 36 (2): 127–140.

Beauregard, E. and Leclerc, B. (2007). An application of the rational choice approach to the offending process of sex offenders: a closer look at the decision-making. *Sexual Abuse: A Journal of Research and Treatment* 19 (2): 115–133.

Blitz, C.L., Wolff, N., and Shi, J. (2008). Physical victimization in prison: the role of mental illness. *International Journal of Law and Psychiatry* 31 (5): 385–393.

Brennan, I.R. and Moore, S.C. (2009). Weapons and violence: a review of theory and research. *Aggression and Violent Behavior* 14 (3): 215–225.

Brennan, P.A., Mednick, S.A., and Hodgins, S. (2000). Major mental disorders and criminal violence in a Danish birth cohort. *Archives of General Psychiatry* 57 (5): 494–500.

Canales, D.D., Campbell, M.A., Wei, R. et al. (2014). Prediction of general and violent recidivism among mentally disordered adult offenders test of the Level of Service/Risk-Need-Responsivity (LS/RNR) instrument. *Criminal Justice and Behavior* 41 (8): 971–991.

Carr, W.A., Rosenfeld, B., Magyar, M. et al. (2009). An exploration of criminal thinking styles among civil psychiatric patients. *Criminal Behaviour and Mental Health* 19 (5): 334–346.

Choe, J.Y., Teplin, L.A., and Abram, K.M. (2008). Perpetration of violence, violent victimization, and severe mental illness: balancing public health concerns. *Psychiatric Services* 59 (2): 153–164.

Chu, C.M., Daffern, M., Thomas, S.D.M. et al. (2014). Criminal attitudes and psychopathic personality attributes of youth gang offenders in Singapore. *Psychology, Crime & Law* 20 (3): 284–301.

Cohen, F. and Dvoskin, J. (1992). Inmates with mental disorders: a guide to law and practice. *Mental & Physical Disability Law Reporter* 16 (4): 462–470.

Cornell, D.G., Warren, J., Hawk, G. et al. (1996). Psychopathy in instrumental and reactive violent offenders. *Journal of Consulting and Clinical Psychology* 64 (4): 783–790.

Cummins, I. (2006). A path not taken? Mentally disordered offenders and the criminal justice system. *Journal of Social Welfare & Family Law* 28: 267–281.

Cunningham, M.D. and Reidy, T.J. (1999). Don't confuse me with the facts: common errors in violence risk assessment at capital sentencing. *Criminal Justice and Behavior* 26 (1): 20–43.

Cunningham, M.D. and Sorensen, J.R. (2006). Actuarial models for assessing prison violence risk revisions and extensions of the Risk Assessment Scale for Prison (RASP). *Assessment* 13 (3): 253–265.

Cunningham, M.D., Sorensen, J.R., and Reidy, T.J. (2005). An actuarial model for assessment of prison violence risk among maximum security inmates. *Assessment* 12 (1): 40–49.

Di Placido, C., Simon, T., Witte, T. et al. (2006). Treatment of gang members can reduce recidivism and institutional misconduct. *Law and Human Behavior* 30 (1): 93–114.

Dodge, K.A., Lochman, J.E., Harnish, J.D. et al. (1997). Reactive and proactive aggression in school children and psychiatrically impaired chronically assaultive youth. *Journal of Abnormal Psychology* 106 (1): 37–51.

Douglas, K.S., Guy, L.S., and Hart, S.D. (2009). Psychosis as a risk factor for violence to others: a meta-analysis. *Psychological Bulletin* 135 (5): 679–706.

Dupéré, V., Lacourse, É., Willms, J.D. et al. (2007). Affiliation to youth gangs during adolescence: the interaction between childhood psychopathic tendencies and neighborhood disadvantage. *Journal of Abnormal Child Psychology* 35 (6): 1035–1045.

DuRant, R.H., Krowchuk, D.P., Kreiter, S. et al. (1999). Weapon carrying on school property among middle school students. *Archives of Pediatrics & Adolescent Medicine* 153 (1): 21–26.

Ennis, L., Toop, C., Jung, S. et al. (2017). Instrumental and reactive intimate partner violence: offender characteristics, reoffense rates, and risk management. *Journal of Threat Assessment and Management* 4 (2): 61.

Eno Louden, J. and Skeem, J. (2011). Parolees with mental disorder: toward evidence-based practice. *Bulletin of the Center for Evidence-Based Corrections* 7 (1): 1–9.

Esquivel-Santoveña, E.E. and Dixon, L. (2012). Investigating the true rate of physical intimate partner violence: a review of nationally representative surveys. *Aggression and Violent Behavior* 17 (3): 208–219.

Farrington, D.P. and Nuttall, C.P. (1980). Prison size, overcrowding, prison violence, and recidivism. *Journal of Criminal Justice* 8 (4): 221–231.

Feder, L. (1991). A comparison of the community adjustment of mentally ill offenders with those from the general prison population: an 18-month followup. *Law and Human Behavior* 15 (5): 477–493.

Fite, P.J., Raine, A., Stouthamer-Loeber, M. et al. (2010). Reactive and proactive aggression in adolescent males examining differential outcomes 10 years later in early adulthood. *Criminal Justice and Behavior* 37 (2): 141–157.

Flanagan, T.J. (1983). Correlates of institutional misconduct among state prisoners. *Criminology* 21 (1): 29–40.

Gadon, L., Johnstone, L., and Cooke, D. (2006). Situational variables and institutional violence: a systematic review of the literature. *Clinical Psychology Review* 26 (5): 515–534.

Girard, L. and Wormith, J.S. (2004). The predictive validity of the Level of Service Inventory-Ontario Revision on general and violent recidivism among various offender groups. *Criminal Justice and Behavior* 31 (2): 150–181.

Glasman, L.R. and Albarracín, D. (2006). Forming attitudes that predict future behavior: a meta-analysis of the attitude-behavior relation. *Psychological Bulletin* 132 (5): 778–822.

Goin, M. (2014). Fiscal fallout: patients in the criminal justice system. *Psychiatric News* 38 (13): 3–4.

Graham, K., Wells, S., and Jelley, J. (2002). The social context of physical aggression among adults. *Journal of Interpersonal Violence* 17 (1): 64–83.

Hanson, R.K., Harris, A.J.R., Helmus, L. et al. (2014). High-risk sex offenders may not be high risk forever. *Journal of Interpersonal Violence* 29 (15): 2792–2813.

Harer, M.D. and Langan, N.P. (2001). Gender differences in predictors of prison violence: assessing the predictive validity of a risk classification system. *Crime & Delinquency* 47 (4): 513–536.

Harris, G.T. and Rice, M.E. (2013). Bayes and base rates: what is an informative prior for actuarial violence risk assessment? *Behavioral Sciences & the Law* 31 (1): 103–124.

Huebner, B.M., Varano, S.P., and Bynum, T.S. (2007). Gangs, guns, and drugs: recidivism among serious, young offenders. *Criminology & Public Policy* 6 (2): 187–221.

Iozzino, L., Ferrari, C., Large, M. et al. (2015). Prevalence and risk factors of violence by psychiatric acute inpatients: a systematic review and meta-analysis. *PLoS One* 10 (6): e0128536.

Junginger, J. and McGuire, L. (2004). Psychotic motivation and the paradox of current research on serious mental illness and rates of violence. *Schizophrenia Bulletin* 30 (1): 21–30.

Kessler, R.C., Chiu, W.T., Demler, O. et al. (2005). Prevalence, severity, and comorbidity of 12-month DSM-IV disorders in the National Comorbidity Survey Replication. *Archives of General Psychiatry* 62 (6): 617–627.

Kingsbury, S.J., Lambert, M.T., and Hendrickse, W. (1997). A two-factor model of aggression. *Psychiatry* 60 (3): 224–232.

Kockler, T. and Meloy, J.R. (2007). The application of affective and predatory aggression to psycholegal opinions. In: *Forensic Psychiatry: Research Trends* (ed. R.C. Browne), 63–83. Hauppauge, NY: Nova Science Publishers, Inc.

Kooyman, I., Dean, K., Harvey, S. et al. (2007). Outcomes of public concern in schizophrenia. *The British Journal of Psychiatry* 191 (50): s29–s36.

Krelstein, M.S. (2002). The role of mental health in the inmate disciplinary process: a national survey. *Journal of the American Academy of Psychiatry and the Law Online* 30 (4): 488–496.

Krnjacki, L., Emerson, E., Llewellyn, G. et al. (2016). Prevalence and risk of violence against people with and without disabilities: findings from an Australian population-based study. *Australian & New Zealand Journal of Public Health* 40 (1): 16–21.

Kroner, D.G., Gray, A.L., and Goodrich, B. (2013). Integrating risk context into risk assessments: the Risk Context Scale. *Assessment* 20 (2): 135–149.

Laajasalo, T. and Häkkänen, H. (2006). Excessive violence and psychotic symptomatology among homicide offenders with schizophrenia. *Criminal Behaviour and Mental Health* 16 (4): 242–253.

Langan, J. (2010). Challenging assumptions about risk factors and the role of screening for violence risk in the field of mental health. *Health, Risk & Society* 12 (2): 85–100.

Lizotte, A.J., Krohn, M.D., Howell, J.C. et al. (2000). Factors influencing gun carrying among young urban males over the adolescent-young adult life course. *Criminology* 38 (3): 811–834.

Loza, W. (2005). *The Self-Appraisal Questionnaire (SAQ): A Tool for Assessing Violent and Non-violent Recidivism*. Toronto, Canada: Mental Health Systems.

Loza, W. and Loza-Fanous, A. (2000). Predictive validity of the Self-Appraisal Questionnaire (SAQ): a tool for assessing violent and nonviolent release failures. *Journal of Interpersonal Violence* 15 (11): 1183–1191.

Loza, W. and Loza-Fanous, A. (2002). The effectiveness of the Self-Appraisal Questionnaire as an offenders' classification measure. *Journal of Interpersonal Violence* 17 (1): 3–13.

Lurigio, A.J. and Swartz, J.A. (2000). Changing the contours of the criminal justice system to meet the needs of persons with serious mental illness. In: *Criminal Justice 2000: Policies, Processes, and Decisions of the Criminal Justice System*, vol. 3 (ed. J. Horney), 45–108. Washington, DC: US Department of Justice, National Institute of Justice.

Mandracchia, J.T. and Morgan, R.D. (2012). Predicting offenders' criminogenic cognitions with status variables. *Criminal Justice and Behavior* 39 (1): 5–25.

Mandracchia, J.T., Morgan, R.D., Garos, S. et al. (2007). Inmate thinking patterns: an empirical investigation. *Criminal Justice and Behavior* 34 (8): 1029–1043.

Markowitz, F.E. (2006). Psychiatric hospital capacity, homelessness, and crime and arrest rates. *Criminology* 44 (1): 45–72.

McInerny, T. and Minne, C. (2004). Principles of treatment for mentally disordered offenders. *Criminal Behaviour and Mental Health* 14 (S1): S43–S47.

McNiel, D.E., Eisner, J.P., and Binder, R.L. (2000). The relationship between command hallucinations and violence. *Psychiatric Services* 51 (10): 1288–1292.

Messina, N., Burdon, W., Hagopian, G. et al. (2004). One year return to custody rates among co-disordered offenders. *Behavioral Sciences & the Law* 22 (4): 503–518.

Metzner, J.L. (2002). Commentary: the role of mental health in the inmate disciplinary process. *Journal of the American Academy of Psychiatry and the Law* 30 (4): 497–499.

Milazzo-Sayre, L.J., Henderson, M.J., Manderscheid, R.W. et al. (2000). Persons treated in specialty mental health care programs, United States, 1997. *Mental Health, United States*: 172–217.

Miller, J.D. and Lynam, D.R. (2006). Reactive and proactive aggression: similarities and differences. *Personality and Individual Differences* 41 (8): 1469–1480.

Mills, J.F. and Kroner, D.G. (2004). *Measures of Criminal Attitudes and Associates (MCAA)*. Ontario: Selby.

Mills, J.F. and Kroner, D.G. (2006). Impression management and self-report among violent offenders. *Journal of Interpersonal Violence* 21 (2): 178–192.

Mills, J.F., Kroner, D.G., and Hemmati, T. (2004). The Measures of Criminal Attitudes and Associates (MCAA): the prediction of general and violent recidivism. *Criminal Justice and Behavior* 31 (6): 717–733.

Monahan, J. and Klassen, D. (1982). Situational approaches to understanding and predicting individual violent behavior. In: *Criminal Violence* (eds. M.E. Wolfgang and N.A. Weiner), 292–319. Thousand Oaks, CA: Sage Publications, Inc.

Monahan, J., Steadman, H., Silver, E. et al. (2001). *Rethinking Risk Assessment: The MacArthur Study of Mental Disorder and Violence*. New York: Oxford University Press.

Nunes, K.L., Hermann, C.A., Maimone, S. et al. (2015). Thinking clearly about violent cognitions: attitudes may be distinct from other cognitions. *Journal of Interpersonal Violence* 30 (8): 1322–1347.

Odgers, C.L., Mulvey, E.P., Skeem, J.L. et al. (2009). Capturing the ebb and flow of psychiatric symptoms with dynamical systems models. *American Journal of Psychiatry* 166 (5): 575–582.

Olver, M.E., Stockdale, K.C., and Wormith, J.S. (2014). Thirty years of research on the Level of Service Scales: a meta-analytic examination of predictive accuracy and sources of variability. *Psychological Assessment* 26 (1): 156–176.

O'Shea, L.E., Picchioni, M.M., Mason, F.L. et al. (2014). Differential predictive validity of the Historical, Clinical and Risk Management Scales (HCR-20) for inpatient aggression. *Psychiatry Research* 220 (1–2): 669–678.

Otto, R.K. (2000). Assessing and managing violence risk in outpatient settings. *Journal of Clinical Psychology* 56 (10): 1239–1262.

Owen, C., Tarantello, C., Jones, M. et al. (1998). Repetitively violent patients in psychiatric units. *Psychiatric Services* 49 (11): 1458–1461.

Peterson, M.A., Skeem, P.D., Hart, B.A. et al. (2010). Analyzing offense patterns as a function of mental illness to test the criminalization hypothesis. *Psychiatric Services* 61 (12): 1217–1222.

Pickett, W., Craig, W., Harel, Y. et al. (2005). Cross-national study of fighting and weapon carrying as determinants of adolescent injury. *Pediatrics* 116 (6): e855–e863.

Podubinski, T., Lee, S., Hollander, Y. et al. (2017). Patient characteristics associated with aggression in mental health units. *Psychiatry Research* 250 (Supplement C): 141–145.

Polaschek, D.L.L., Collie, R.M., and Walkey, F.H. (2004). Criminal attitudes to violence: development and preliminary validation of a scale for male prisoners. *Aggressive Behavior* 30 (6): 484–503.

Poulin, F. and Boivin, M. (2000). Reactive and proactive aggression: evidence of a two-factor model. *Psychological Assessment* 12 (2): 115–122.

Prince, J.D., Akincigil, A., and Bromet, E. (2007). Incarceration rates of persons with first-admission psychosis. *Psychiatric Services* 58 (9): 1173–1180.

Quinsey, V.L. and Upfold, D. (1985). Rape completion and victim injury as a function of female resistance strategy. *Canadian Journal of Behavioural Science* 17 (1): 40–50.

Raine, A., Dodge, K., Loeber, R. et al. (2006). The Reactive-Proactive Aggression Questionnaire: differential correlates of reactive and proactive aggression in adolescent boys. *Aggressive Behavior* 32 (2): 159–171.

Rand, M. and Catalano, S. (2007). *Bureau of Justice Statistics Bulletin: Criminal Victimization, 2006.* Washington, DC: US Department of Justice.

Robinson, A.L. and Howarth, E. (2012). Judging risk: key determinants in British domestic violence cases. *Journal of Interpersonal Violence* 27 (8): 1489–1518.

Roskes, E., Feldman, R., Arrington, S. et al. (1999). A model program for the treatment of mentally ill offenders in the community. *Community Mental Health Journal* 35 (5): 461–472.

Ross, J.M. and Babcock, J.C. (2009). Proactive and reactive violence among intimate partner violent men diagnosed with antisocial and borderline personality disorder. *Journal of Family Violence* 24 (8): 607–617.

Rutter, S., Gudjonsson, G., and Rabe-Hesketh, S. (2004). Violent incidents in a medium secure unit: the characteristics of persistent perpetrators of violence. *Journal of Forensic Psychiatry & Psychology* 15 (2): 293–302.

Silver, E., Felson, R.B., and Vaneseltine, M. (2008). The relationship between mental health problems and violence among criminal offenders. *Criminal Justice and Behavior* 35 (4): 405–426.

Silver, E., Mulvey, E.P., and Monahan, J. (1999). Assessing violence risk among discharged psychiatric patients: toward an ecological approach. *Law and Human Behavior* 23 (2): 237–255.

Simourd, D.J. (1997). The Criminal Sentiments Scale-Modified and Pride in Delinquency Scale: psychometric properties and construct validity of two measures of criminal attitudes. *Criminal Justice and Behavior* 24 (1): 52–70.

Simourd, D.J. and van de Ven, J. (1999). Assessment of criminal attitudes: criterion-related validity of the Criminal Sentiments Scale-Modified and Pride in Delinquency Scale. *Criminal Justice and Behavior* 26 (1): 90–106.

Singh, J.P., Fazel, S., Gueorguieva, R. et al. (2014). Rates of violence in patients classified as high risk by structured risk assessment instruments. *The British Journal of Psychiatry* 204 (3): 180–187.

Skeem, J.L., Manchak, S., and Peterson, J.K. (2011). Correctional policy for offenders with mental illness: creating a new paradigm for recidivism reduction. *Law and Human Behavior* 35 (2): 110–126.

Skeem, J.L., Mulvey, E.P., Appelbaum, P. et al. (2004). Identifying subtypes of civil psychiatric patients at high risk for violence. *Criminal Justice and Behavior* 31 (4): 392–437.

Smith, C., Huey, S.J., and McDaniel, D.D. (2015). Commitment language and homework completion in a behavioral employment program for gang-affiliated youth. *International Journal of Offender Therapy and Comparative Criminology* 59 (5): 502–518.

Solomon, P., Draine, J., and Marcus, S.C. (2002). Predicting incarceration of clients of a psychiatric probation and parole service. *Psychiatric Services* 53 (1): 50–56.

Sorensen, J. and Cunningham, M.D. (2010). Conviction offense and prison violence: a comparative study of murderers and other offenders. *Crime & Delinquency* 56 (1): 103–125.

Sorensen, J.R. and Cunningham, M.D. (2007). Operationalizing risk: the influence of measurement choice on the prevalence and correlates of prison violence among incarcerated murderers. *Journal of Criminal Justice* 35 (5): 546–555.

Stanford, M.S., Houston, R.J., and Baldridge, R.M. (2008). Comparison of impulsive and premeditated perpetrators of intimate partner violence. *Behavioral Sciences & the Law* 26 (6): 709–722.

Steadham, J.A. and Rogers, R. (2013). Predictors of reactive and instrumental aggression in jail detainees: an initial examination. *Journal of Forensic Psychology Practice* 13 (5): 411–428.

Steadman, H.J., Osher, F.C., Robbins, P.C. et al. (2009). Prevalence of serious mental illness among jail inmates. *Psychiatric Services* 60 (6): 761–765.

Stolzenberg, L. and D'alessio, S.J. (2000). Gun availability and violent crime: new evidence from the national incident-based reporting system. *Social Forces* 78 (4): 1461–1482.

Swanson, J.W., Swartz, M.S., Van Dorn, R.A. et al. (2006). A national study of violent behavior in persons with schizophrenia. *Archives of General Psychiatry* 63 (5): 490–499.

Swanson, J.W., Van Dorn, R.A., Swartz, M.S. et al. (2008). Alternative pathways to violence in persons with schizophrenia: the role of childhood antisocial behavior problems. *Law and Human Behavior* 32 (3): 228–240.

Toch, H. and Adams, K. (1987). The prison as dumping ground: mainlining disturbed offenders. *Journal of Psychiatry & Law* 15 (4): 539–553.

Torrey, E.F., Stieber, J., Ezediel, J. et al. (1998). Why do mentally ill individuals end up in jail? In: *Criminalizing the Seriously Mentally Ill: The Abuse of Jails as Mental Health Hospitals* (eds. E.F. Torrey, National Alliance for the Mentally Ill and Public Citizens Health Research Group), 43–57. Washington, DC: National Alliance for the Mentally Ill and Public Citizen's Health Research Group.

Tweed, R.G. and Dutton, D.G. (1998). A comparison of impulsive and instrumental subgroups of batterers. *Violence and Victims* 13 (3): 217–230.

Wallace, C., Mullen, P.E., and Burgess, P. (2004). Criminal offending in schizophrenia over a 25-year period marked by deinstitutionalization and increasing prevalence of comorbid substance use disorders. *American Journal of Psychiatry* 161 (4): 716–727.

Walters, G.D. (1995). The Psychological Inventory of Criminal Thinking Styles part I: reliability and preliminary validity. *Criminal Justice and Behavior* 22 (3): 307–325.

Walters, G.D. (2005). Predicting institutional adjustment with the Lifestyle Criminality Screening Form and Psychological Inventory of Criminal Thinking Styles. *International Journal of Forensic Mental Health* 4 (1): 63–70.

Walters, G.D. (2006). Proactive and reactive composite scales for the Psychological Inventory of Criminal Thinking Styles (PICTS). *Journal of Offender Rehabilitation* 42 (4): 23–36.

Walters, G.D. (2007). Predicting institutional adjustment with the Psychological Inventory of Criminal Thinking Styles composite scales: Replication and extension. *Legal & Criminological Psychology* 12 (1): 69–81.

Walters, G.D. (2009). Effect of a longer versus shorter test-release interval on recidivism prediction with the Psychological Inventory of Criminal Thinking Styles (PICTS). *International Journal of Offender Therapy and Comparative Criminology* 53 (6): 665–678.

Walters, G.D. (2011). Criminal thinking as a mediator of the mental illness-prison violence relationship: a path analytic study and causal mediation analysis. *Psychological Services* 8 (3): 189–199.

Walters, G.D. (2012). Criminal thinking and recidivism: meta-analytic evidence on the predictive and incremental validity of the Psychological Inventory of Criminal Thinking Styles (PICTS). *Aggression and Violent Behavior* 17 (3): 272–278.

Walters, G.D. and Crawford, G. (2013). In and out of prison: do importation factors predict all forms of misconduct or just the more serious ones? *Journal of Criminal Justice* 41 (6): 407–413.

Walters, G.D. and Crawford, G. (2014). Major mental illness and violence history as predictors of institutional misconduct and recidivism: main and interaction effects. *Law and Human Behavior* 38 (3): 238–247.

Walters, G.D. and DeLisi, M. (2015). Psychopathy and violence: does antisocial cognition mediate the relationship between the PCL: YV factor scores and violent offending? *Law and Human Behavior* 39 (4): 350–359.

Walters, G.D., Frederick, A.A., and Schlauch, C. (2007). Postdicting arrests for proactive and reactive aggression with the PICTS proactive and reactive composite scales. *Journal of Interpersonal Violence* 22 (11): 1415–1430.

Weinshenker, N.J. and Siegel, A. (2002). Bimodal classification of aggression: affective defense and predatory attack. *Aggression and Violent Behavior* 7 (3): 237–250.

White, B.A., Gordon, H., and Guerra, R.C. (2015). Callous-unemotional traits and empathy in proactive and reactive relational aggression in young women. *Personality and Individual Differences* 75: 185–189.

Wilcox, P., Quisenberry, N., Cabrera, D.T. et al. (2004). Busy places and broken windows? Toward defining the role of physical structure and process in community crime models. *Sociological Quarterly* 45 (2): 185–207.

Witt, K., van Dorn, R., and Fazel, S. (2013). Risk factors for violence in psychosis: systematic review and meta-regression analysis of 110 studies. *PLoS One* 8 (2): e55942.

3

What Works with Violent Offenders
A Response to 'Nothing Works'

James McGuire

University of Liverpool, Liverpool, UK

Introduction

Reviews of research evidence have had a considerable influence in the field of criminal justice, with particular impact on approaches to offender rehabilitation. In the period before 1990, there was a commonly held view that efforts to change offending behaviour and to reduce criminal recidivism were naïve and fundamentally futile. Today in contrast, most practitioners, researchers, and even many policy makers take a more optimistic view and accept the assembled evidence showing that the so-called 'nothing works' position (Martinson 1974) is untenable. Through methodical work with offenders, informed by research findings ('evidence-based practice'), there is mounting confidence that by enabling individuals to acquire new skills or adopt fresh perspectives on their own behaviour, they can escape a life of crime. While many succeed in doing this at some stage without professional help, it is now possible to facilitate their efforts to do so earlier, and so accelerate the process of desistance.

The grounds for these modified expectations are in the steadily expanding volume of results from a large body of research, brought together in a series of reviews employing meta-analysis. By 2012, a total of 100 such reviews had been published on the effects of 'tertiary' or criminal-justice-based interventions (McGuire 2013). Taking account of further reviews produced since then, alongside other types of initiatives and evaluations of them – such as innovations in schools, policing, situational crime prevention, and drug treatment – the cumulative body of knowledge in this area is now very large (Weisburd et al. 2016, 2017).

The majority of these studies and the reviews of them were concerned with criminal recidivism in general, meaning any kind of reoffending, and only a portion examined rates of committing new offences of specific types. Several of the latter, to be discussed in this chapter, have analysed

The Wiley Handbook of What Works in Violence Risk Management: Theory, Research and Practice,
First Edition. Edited by J. Stephen Wormith, Leam A. Craig, and Todd E. Hogue.
© 2020 John Wiley & Sons Ltd. Published 2020 by John Wiley & Sons Ltd.

the impact of interventions on rates of aggression or violent offending. Contrary to what we might expect, where such data have been reported, evaluations have revealed a trend towards larger effects for offences of personal violence and sexual offences than for acquisitive or property crimes such as theft, fraud, burglary, or criminal damage (Redondo et al. 2002; Travers et al. 2014).

Reducing Aggression and Violence

This chapter focuses therefore on the segment from that large volume of work that is concerned with interventions that address aggression and violent crime, drawing upon but extending previous overviews (McGuire 2008, 2017). In surveying this area however, the present chapter adopts a wide-ranging 'lifespan' approach in considering research from successive phases of development.

There is evidence of both continuity and discontinuity in levels of aggression across developmental phases (Piquero et al. 2012a). That is, although many children may display aggressiveness or may be involved in fighting at some point, only a minority of them will go on to be aggressive in adolescence, and only a fraction of those will commit violent offences in adulthood (Piquero et al. 2012b). Within clinical samples at each of these stages, declining proportions will meet the criteria for psychiatric diagnoses on what has been called the 'externalizing spectrum' (Krueger and Tackett 2016), which includes attention deficit hyperactivity disorder (ADHD) or oppositional/defiant disorder in childhood, conduct disorder in adolescence, and antisocial personality disorder in adulthood (Hofvander et al. 2009).

These overall trends may arise because there are different patterns or trajectories within 'externalizing' problems and also within delinquent or antisocial conduct, as proposed and substantiated by Moffitt (1993, 2003, 2018) and others. It thus appears likely that there is a small proportion of those who act aggressively who continue to do so over extended periods. That finding is commensurate with data suggesting that a small proportion of those who offend is responsible for a relatively large proportion of crimes (Loeber et al. 2008). This then holds out the prospect, if we can identify those at higher risk, of having a proportionately larger effect on the total number of crimes committed.

In what follows I deal in sequence with evaluations of the effects of interventions to reduce non-sexual aggression and violence in six different populations, respectively:

- parent training and related interventions for young children;
- anti-bullying programmes (ABPs) and other methods to reduce aggression in schools;
- interventions with young offenders, usually carried out in juvenile correctional facilities;
- interventions with adult offenders, provided as part of prison or community sentences;
- interventions to reduce or prevent intimate partner violence (IPV);
- treatment of offenders diagnosed with mental disorders and with histories of violence.

The format of the chapter is thus one of a 'review of reviews', focusing on those that are concerned with outcomes that include direct measurement of aggression or violent reoffending, or with variables firmly associated with them as mediators. Results in each area are summarized in tabular form. Within each, reviews are listed in chronological order and in author name order within each year. Some reviews incorporated studies in more than one of the above categories, so could not be neatly allocated under a single heading. Where that occurred they were placed under the heading that reflected the largest share of the studies they reviewed (e.g. the review by Cox et al. 2016).

Where available, effect sizes are reported in one of three forms: as the *standardized mean difference* (Cohen's *d*) between experimental and control samples; as a *correlation coefficient* (Pearson *r*); or as an *odds ratio* or *risk ratio*, which are measures of the relative proportions of those reconvicted and not reconvicted, or of the proportions who have shown improvement or who have not, in the experimental versus comparison conditions (Ellis 2010). With respect to the first of these, the *standardized mean difference*, Cohen (1988) proposed a rough convention which has become widely accepted, of describing effect sizes in the region of 0.20 as small, of 0.50 as moderate, and of 0.80 as large.

This overview can refer only briefly to other areas where there is also valuable evidence on 'what works' in reducing violence. For example Farrington et al. (2017) assembled findings from a total of 50 systematic reviews of the field of *developmental prevention*. This denotes 'community-based programs designed to prevent antisocial behaviour, targeted on children and adolescents, and aiming to change individual, family, or school risk factors' (p. 91). Interventions in this area include a variety of services such as child skills training, home visiting, foster care arrangements, and school-based initiatives. The median effect size obtained, expressed as an odds ratio, was 1.46. This corresponds to a reduction in aggression by one-quarter in those who received interventions as compared to those who did not. As Farrington and his colleagues concluded, 'with regard to practice, these effects are quite large' (p. 102).

Parent training and related interventions

According to research by Tremblay et al. (2004), many children show some form of aggression from an early age, and while most learn to regulate this, a proportion whose behaviour is more problematic show an escalating pattern. Other research suggests that children can learn patterns of aggressiveness as a result of cycles of coercive interactions with their parents (Patterson et al. 1984). Aggression at an early age is of immediate concern in itself: but also because it can be a precursor of problems, including antisocial behaviour and delinquency, later on. Several reviews have brought together evaluations of interventions to reduce aggression in early and middle childhood, and in adolescence.

Table 3.1 lists five reviews or meta-analyses of interventions carried out with parents with the objective of responding to children in ways that will reduce aggression. Some involve methods such as *behavioural parent training* (BPT), in which parents are helped to acquire skills for managing child behaviour problems. As can be seen from Table 3.1, all the published reviews found predominantly positive outcomes. A review of BPT studies was reported by Serketich and Dumas (1996), while McCart et al. (2006) compared the effectiveness of BPT with that of *cognitive-behavioural therapy* (CBT) in reducing aggression and other antisocial behaviour amongst children and young people across a wide range of ages. The mean effect size for child aggression reported by Serketich and Dumas was large (+0.86) but was based only on changes shortly after the training. Post-treatment effect sizes reported by McCart et al. were more modest (+0.47 for BPT and +0.35 for CBT), but included a reported mean effect for cognitive-behavioural interventions of +0.31 at an average eight-month follow-up. Effect sizes reported by Kaminski et al. (2008) were lower, but their review addressed a range of behaviour problems and did not report a separate outcome effect for aggression alone. Focusing on the reduction of conduct problems,

Table 3.1 Reviews of parent training and child behaviour problems including aggression.

Review	Focus	Number of studies	Findings
Serketich and Dumas (1996)	Effectiveness of behavioural parent training (BPT)	26	Focused on aggression and related problem behaviour in children (mean age 6). 18 studies employed random assignment. The mean effect size for child aggression and related behaviour was +0.86 after 9.5 sessions of training, though based only on post-intervention changes.
McCart et al. (2006)	Compared the relative effects of BPT and Cognitive-Behavioural Therapy (CBT) in reducing aggression	41 of BPT, 30 of CBT	Outcome variables recorded were of physical or verbal aggression or delinquency. Mean post-treatment effect sizes for BPT and CBT were respectively +0.47 and +0.35. For CBT, there was a mean effect size of 0.31 at follow-up (average 8 months) across 13 studies.
Kaminski et al. (2008)	Effectiveness of interventions for child behaviour problems	77	Studies addressing a range of child problems: 48 were concerned with aggression, non-compliance, and hyperactivity. The mean effect size was 0.25. The effect for aggression was not reported separately.
Dretzke et al. (2009)	Review of parenting programmes to reduce conduct problems	57	All studies were controlled trials. Some studies compared parent training with no treatment, others with a different type of treatment. Obtained an overall mean effect size of –0.67 in favour of the interventions.
Altafim and Linhares (2016)	Parent training to reduce child maltreatment and behaviour problems	23	Studies evaluated 16 different forms of parent training designed to improve the skills of parents or other caregivers in managing behaviour problems amongst children aged up to 17. No mean effect calculated, but across all studies, on a series of 36 outcomes evaluated, all but four showed measurable improvements.

Dretzke et al. (2009) reported a mean effect size of –0.67 in favour of interventions. Finally Altafim and Linhares (2016) analysed the effectiveness of a series of 16 different types of parent training programmes. These authors did not compute a mean effect size, but they report that in 90% of the studies where relevant changes were evaluated, programmes 'effectively improved' children's behaviour.

ABPs and other school-based interventions

Like parent training, school-based interventions are planned with the purposes of both directly addressing current aggressive behaviour and also of reducing the likelihood of further difficulties at later stages. In relation to school bullying, for example, as well as being a problem in itself, longitudinal research indicates that bullying perpetration is a significant predictor of violence up to 11 years later; that also applies, though to a lesser extent, to being victimized (Ttofi et al. 2012). On the basis of this, it has been suggested that ABPs can be considered as an early form of crime prevention (Ttofi et al. 2011). ABPs are often divided into three types according to the breadth of focus of interventions provided. Some are provided solely to those who have engaged in bullying; others are multi-level, involving different kinds of initiatives; while others employ whole-school or 'universal' interventions.

Table 3.2 lists a series of reviews of interventions designed to reduce bullying or other forms of aggression in schools. Some school-based interventions have a broad range of targets and examine several types of aggression or violence such as fighting or the formation of gangs. The studies located by Wilson and Lipsey (2007; Wilson et al. 2003) are of this type, and were carried out with participant samples ranging from pre-school to the age of 18. In conventional terms the observed mean effect sizes shown in Table 3.2 are relatively small. But as Wilson and Lipsey (2007) note, 'effect sizes of 0.21 and 0.29 represent reductions from a base rate prevalence of 20% to about 15% and 13%, respectively, that is, 25%–33% reductions' (p. S141). As these are mean effect sizes, there are programmes that produce larger decreases, so by identifying their features, interventions can be made more effective.

There has been a largely – although not uniformly – positive pattern of findings from reviews of ABPs. For the most part, the best outcomes have come from universal, whole-school interventions rather than from those with focused or multiple but separate components. Jiménez-Barbero et al. (2012) analysed the findings of five other reviews and 27 primary studies on ABPs with a mixture of research designs, separating the latter into four groups according to the methodological quality of the evaluation. There were similar patterns of findings across all evidence levels in relation to changes in attitudes, beliefs, and behaviours and in the frequency of violent conduct. In a later review of high-quality randomized controlled trials (RCTs), Jiménez-Barbero et al. (2016) found that effect sizes declined as age increased, and also that programmes that lasted less than a year had larger effects. The review by Yeager et al. (2015) also revealed that effect sizes are lower for older adolescents, hence broadly speaking there are smaller effects as age advances. Positive though only small mean effects were also reported by Lee et al. (2015). The largest review in this area, by Ttofi and Farrington (2011) found somewhat larger effects and provides extensive detail on features of the more effective interventions. Running counter to those trends however, the review by Cantone et al. (2015) found that positive effects were short-term with no evidence of lasting gains.

Two other broad-ranging, macro-level overviews or syntheses of other reviews in this area, not included in Table 3.2, sought to obtain a 'big picture' of overall trends. Matjasko et al. (2012) synthesized findings from 15 systematic reviews and 37 meta-analyses on youth violence prevention programmes, including family-based, school-based, community-based, and treatment-specific interventions. Given the variety of studies they included, no mean effect sizes were computed. Instead, outcomes are summarized in terms of proportions of effects in the ranges denoted small, moderate, or large by Cohen (1988). Amongst the family-centred reviews, two found strong effects, nine moderate effects, and three weak effects. Most (11/15) reviews of school-based programmes reported moderate to strong effects on youth violence-related

Table 3.2 Reviews of anti-bullying programmes (ABPs) and other interventions to reduce school aggression.

Review	Focus	Number of studies	Findings
Wilson and Lipsey (2007); Wilson et al. (2003)	Review of interventions designed to reduce aggression or disruptive behaviour in schools	249	Interventions included behavioural strategies, counselling, social skills training programmes, anger management and cognitively based methods; 40% of studies used randomized designs. The mean effect size for universal, school-wide interventions was +0.21 in favour of experimental groups, and for specifically targeted interventions +0.29. The corresponding figure for nonrandomized designs was +0.16.
Ttofi and Farrington (2011)	School-based programmes to reduce bullying (across all tiers of schooling)	44	Meta-analysis of studies with a range of designs. Found an overall effect size (odds ratio) of 1.36 for bullying and 1.29 for victimization. This corresponds to an overall reduction of 17–23% in bullying events in experimental as compared to control samples.
Alford and Derzon (2012)	Review of methods of reducing aggressive and antisocial behaviour	24	All studies showed some positive effect on reduction of violence or antisocial behaviour, but no study obtained positive effects on all the outcomes evaluated. The mean effect sizes obtained were: for physical aggression +0.26, antisocial behaviour +0.15, aggressive/disruptive behaviour +0.12. The authors acknowledged using an 'overly conservative' standard for judging effects (p. 601).
Jiménez-Barbero et al. (2012)	Review of anti-bullying by evidence levels	32: Reviews: 5 randomized controlled trials (RCTs): 12 Quasi-expt. designs: 11 Pre-post designs: 4	Divided studies into four groups by methodological quality of evaluation designs. In all four categories there was a similar pattern of beneficial effects. Studies covered the full school age range. There were similar patterns of findings across all evidence levels in relation to changes in attitudes, beliefs and behaviours and in the frequency of violent behaviour.

Table 3.2 (*Cont'd*)

Review	Focus	Number of studies	Findings
Barnes et al. (2014)	Meta-analysis of cognitive-behavioural interventions to reduce aggression	25	Obtained a mean effect size across all studies of –0.14. The weighted mean effect size, correcting for interdependence within studies was –0.23. In 74% of studies, aggression was lower after treatment. The 'file drawer number', the number of unpublished studies with nil effects needed to overturn the observed effect was 224.
Cantone et al. (2015)	Interventions to reduce bullying and cyber-bullying	17	All included studies were RCTs. Most focused on primary schools; one on adolescents only and 4/17 mainly on them. Positive effects were short-term with no evidence of long-term gains. Better effects were found for universal, whole-school interventions than for those with focused or multi-level components.
Lee et al. (2015)	Effects of school based anti-bullying programmes (ABPs)	13	Aggregate sample size of 19 619, mean effect size of 0.15 favouring interventions. No interventions had negative effects. Those focused on emotional control, peer counselling, and establishing school-wide policies on bullying obtained larger effect sizes than other approaches.
Nocentini et al. (2015)	Use of information and communication technologies (ICTs) in ABPs	13	Only 4 of the 13 programmes were found to be effective. Two using ICTs only were effective and two containing both face-to-face and ICT elements were also effective, thus the added value of ICT could not be established.
Yeager et al. (2015)	Investigation of whether ABP effects vary for different age groups	19	Patterns of bullying changed as age increased. Overall, there was evidence of a decline in the effectiveness of ABPs with increasing age, and some had negative effects for older teenage groups: from age 15 there were iatrogenic outcomes.

(*Continued*)

Table 3.2   (*Cont'd*)

Review	Focus	Number of studies	Findings
Jiménez-Barbero et al. (2016)	Efficacy of ABPs	14 RCTs 8 with children aged >10	Examined the effect of ABPs on frequency of bullying and victimization, and on attitudes to bullying, in a total sample of 30 934 participants. Samples included children in the age range 7–16. Most interventions showed positive effects, with a mean effect size favouring intervention of –0.12, but while the mean effect for those under age 10 was –0.17, effects were smaller for those aged over 10: mean effect for bullying –0.08, for victimization, –0.07.

outcomes, whereas evaluations of treatment-specific interventions had on average moderate effects. In a similar exercise Lester et al. (2017) conducted a synthesis of 31 reviews of interventions for reducing peer aggression in schools. Again due to heterogeneity no mean effect size was reported, but a majority of studies, 58% of 'whole school' programmes and 89% of discrete or 'indicated' interventions, reported positive effects. Thus while for bullying, universal or system-wide approaches appear to produce better effects, for peer aggression (which involves different patterns of behaviour) there are better results from more focused approaches.

Young offenders

The reviews considered so far were mainly concerned with interventions provided in families, schools, or other community settings, often with children below the age of criminal responsibility, or in some cases with adolescents thought to be at risk of involvement in delinquency. Another set of reviews focuses on studies conducted with adjudicated youth: those who have appeared in court and have been given community or custodial sentences. While the volume of research concerned with reducing delinquency in general is large, the proportion of it that has addressed the problem of violent offending and interventions focused specifically on addressing it is more limited. Reviews containing information on this are shown in Table 3.3.

A notable feature of some of these reviews is that the studies they located were carried out with young people likely to be at high risk of further offending, and accordingly regarded as 'chronic' or 'prolific' offenders. As such groups are often responsible for a large proportion of reported crimes, including more serious offences, the benefit of working with them effectively is of considerable practical import. Thus although in all these studies there is a proportion of samples who show little or no response, greater leverage is obtained if there is behaviour change amongst those assessed as being at higher levels of risk. As summarized in Table 3.3, the reviews by Lipsey and Wilson (1998) and Garrido and Morales (2007) both reported small-to-moderate mean effect sizes. Although effect sizes were not calculated by either Limbos et al. (2007) or Cox et al. (2016), some valuable findings emerged. In the Limbos et al. review,

Table 3.3 Reviews of interventions with violent adolescents and young offenders.

Review	Focus	Number of studies	Findings
Lipsey and Wilson (1998)	Meta-analysis of interventions to reduce violence amongst offenders aged 12–20	200 studies: 83 in institutions; 117 in the community.	Found an overall effect of reducing recidivism by 40% in community settings and 30% in custodial settings. The largest and most consistent effects were for structured counselling (mean effect size +0.46), interpersonal skills training (+0.44), behavioural programmes (+0.42), and teaching family homes (+0.39), in which children are fostered by specially trained parent figures. There were different patterns regarding which interventions worked better in community as compared to institutional settings. The review also found some interventions that had no useful effects, notably deterrence-based strategies.
Garrido and Morales (2007)	Review of interventions for serious and chronic violent youth	30	Overall sample size of 6658 followed up over a median of 18 months. Mean effect size for 15 studies that measured serious recidivism (leading to reincarceration) was an odds ratio of 1.354, significantly larger than the mean effect size for general offending of 1.136.
Limbos et al. (2007)	Systematic review of the effectiveness of interventions to prevent youth violence	41	A wide-ranging review including primary, secondary, and tertiary prevention studies. The third group included 11 studies, of which 8 reported positive outcomes. Only 2 of these studies involved random allocation, but both showed positive results of interventions.
Sawyer et al. (2015)	Meta-analysis of studies of long-term prevention or therapeutic programmes	66	Across all studies and combining different sets of outcome variables there was a mean effect size of +0.31 supporting interventions. The mean effect size for official records of violence was higher at +0.42, while that for parental reports of aggression was lower at +0.16. There were no differences in outcomes between randomized and non-randomized designs. Some multicomponent programmes achieved particularly large effects.

(*Continued*)

Table 3.3   (*Cont'd*)

Review	Focus	Number of studies	Findings
Weaver and Campbell (2015)	Meta-analysis of aftercare programmes for juvenile offenders	30	Investigated the effectiveness of aftercare services and supervision for sentenced young offenders re-entering their communities. The mean effect size for general delinquency was a risk ratio of 0.931, meaning no real difference between experimental and control groups. For those aged over 16.5 years whose main offence was violent, the risk ratio was 0.666, a 33% reduction and statistically highly significant.
Cox et al. (2016)	Review of violence prevention and intervention with adolescents in Australia	19	Reviewed studies of bullying (4), alcohol/drug-related violence (5), and other antisocial/violent behaviour (10). Amongst retained studies, 13 were rated as having strong designs; 8 were RCTs. The interventions were of several types and variables recorded were also mixed, with insufficient use of methods specific to violent behaviour. Outcomes were varied, with best results obtained from interventions that focused on skills development.

while overall just under half (49%) of the studies reported effectiveness, amongst those at the tertiary level 82% did so. In the Cox et al. review, findings were more mixed, but there was a pattern within them such that the interventions that emerged with the highest degree of support were predominantly based on imparting and developing interactional and other social-cognitive skills. A more clear-cut finding was reported by Weaver and Campbell (2015), evaluating after-care services. This review found a sizeable impact in reducing reoffending by 33% amongst young offenders in the second half of their teens whose main offence was one of violence.

Amongst young people who become involved in offending from an early age, there is a small number who have been so badly affected by their developmental experiences that even in early adolescence they may already be very resistant to intervention. However, there is evidence of the possibility of carrying out effective work with even the most troubled of them, including those who have been assessed as manifesting features of 'psychopathic disorder' at an early age. These findings come from research carried out at the Mendota Youth Treatment Center in Wisconsin, a specialist unit reserved for young people with histories of repeated violence, who already had several convictions by the age of 14 and were regarded as unmanageable in other institutions. The Mendota Center harnessed what was called a 'decompression' model, to reverse a recurring 'cycle of defiance' that had developed in these young people through successive attempts to control them. This was accompanied by delivery of a structured training programme, *Aggression Replacement Training* (Glick and Gibbs 2010).

At the end of a four-year follow-up period, there was a highly significant reduction in violent reoffending amongst a cohort of 101 Mendota youths as compared to 147 untreated youths, with respective violent recidivism rates of 23 and 44%, and of violent felonies 18 and 37% (Caldwell et al. 2007). The Center's regime was also shown to be economically efficient, yielding a benefit–cost ratio of 7:1 (Caldwell et al. 2006).

Several studies included in the review by Sawyer et al. (2015) involved interventions that contain multiple components. The format of these varies but may incorporate work with both individuals and their families, where interventions are provided in home, school, community, or correctional settings. Some of these have recorded particularly striking outcomes. Borduin et al. (2013) have described three such interventions that produced significant reductions in indicators of aggression and violence, including violent reconviction and reincarceration: *multisystemic therapy*, *multidimensional foster care treatment*, and *functional family therapy*. The review by Sawyer et al. (2015) only included studies with a minimum follow-up period of 1 year; prevention studies had a mean follow-up length of 5.54 years, and intervention studies of 2.72 years. There was no moderating effect of follow-up length on effect size: that is, 'intervention benefits did not decrease over time' (p. 139).

Adult offenders

Over the period 2000–2015 in England and Wales, between 20 and 28% of adults who were given prison sentences had committed offences of violence against the person (Allen and Watson 2017). A further 11–13% had committed offences of robbery, which though primarily an acquisitive offence involves the use of threat or force. Since incarceration in itself does not produce significant reductions in reoffending rates (Cid 2009; Klement 2015; Nagin et al. 2009; Tahamont and Chalfin 2018; Trevena and Weatherburn 2015; Villetaz et al. 2006; Wermink et al. 2010), it is important to test whether any added value can be gained by providing intervention programmes for serving prisoners. Table 3.4 summarizes reviews on the effectiveness of treatment for reducing violent recidivism and also levels of misconduct including violent indiscipline while imprisoned.

Dowden and Andrews (2000) reported one of the earliest reviews of the effect of interventions on violent reoffending by adults. As can be seen from Table 3.4 they found a very wide range of outcomes. While the overall mean effect size was low, that for interventions based on the *risk-needs-responsivity* (RNR) model (Bonta and Andrews 2017) was +0.12, equivalent to recidivism rates of 44% for experimental and 56% for control groups. An important finding was that observed effect sizes were higher when larger numbers of risk-related or criminogenic needs were targeted in interventions; the correlation between the two was +0.69. Thus, while some interventions evidently fail and some can even increase reoffending (Welsh and Rocque 2014) others are associated with significant reductions in violent recidivism.

Jolliffe and Farrington (2009) reviewed data from a series of 11 studies of interventions with adult male violent offenders, amongst which nine also recorded the impact on violent reconviction. Although the mean effect size of 6–7% reduction was rather low, 'the results of this meta-analysis suggest that the nine interventions taken together significantly reduced violent reoffending' (p. 26). In a review of the impact of anger control training on violent reoffending, Henwood et al. (2015) reported a larger effect (28% reduction) than that found by Jolliffe and Farrington. Four of the six studies analysing violent reconviction employed case–control designs, while two used before-and-after designs. Follow-up periods ranged from three months to six years.

Table 3.4 Reviews of interventions with violent adult offenders.

Review	Focus	Number of studies	Findings
Dowden and Andrews (2000)	Interventions to reduce violent reoffending	34	Target offences included general violence, sexual, and domestic assaults. Approximately 70% of the studies focused primarily on work with adults. The mean effect size was low, but there was a sizeable spread amongst the results: effect sizes ranged from −0.22 to +0.63.
French and Gendreau (2006)	Meta-analysis of interventions for reducing prison misconduct	68	Analysed the effects of prison-based treatment programmes on misconduct and on recidivism post-release. All studies employed either a randomized or non-equivalent control group design. Aggregate sample 21 467 offenders, generating a total of 104 effect-size tests. The mean effect size (r) across all studies was 0.14, but was 0.26 amongst 40 studies of behaviourally based programmes, and 0.39 when weighted by sample sizes. Effective programmes were also associated with lower post-release recidivism.
Jolliffe and Farrington (2009)	Review of interventions with violent adult offenders	11	Intervention methods included anger control training, intensive self-management training, a multimodal skills programme, electronic monitoring, and other approaches. Nine studies with a total sample of 1893 offenders were meta-analysed. The mean effect size was low: a reduction in recidivism of 6–7% ($d = 0.14$), equivalent to a drop from a 50% reconviction rate in comparison groups to 43% in treatment groups. The largest outcome effects were for a combined use of anger control, cognitive skills training, role-play, and relapse prevention.
Braga and Weisburd (2012, 2015)	Meta-analysis of studies on reduction of serious gang-related violence	10	Review of the effects of 'pulling levers', a multifaceted intervention entailing direct negotiation with gangs by police, the use of strategies of focused deterrence (applying firmer penalties to gang members' illegal activities), and provision of community resources for those who complied. The reported mean effect size for gun homicides and assaults across experimental sites in different US cities was 0.604.

Table 3.4 (*Cont'd*)

Review	Focus	Number of studies	Findings
Henwood et al. (2015)	Cognitive-behavioural methods of anger management and impact on violent reoffending	14	Studies were divided equally between case–control and before-and-after designs, amongst which 6 measured violent recidivism. The mean effect size, reported as an odds ratio, was 0.72, corresponding to a 28% reduction in risk of reconviction for a violent offence.
Auty et al. (2017)	Reducing prison violence using psychoeducational programmes	21	All studies employed either experimental or quasi-experimental designs; reports covered 17 programmes, most using cognitive-behavioural and social learning methods. Results from both types of designs were mixed, with some positive and statistically significant findings, and moderate effect sizes; others with positive but non-significant trends. The most effective programmes employed a 'staged' approach with prisoners having to complete one phase before proceeding to the next.

Anger control training has been a widely used strategy for attempting to reduce aggression and there are also several reviews dealing with its use in working with people with intellectual disabilities (Ali et al. 2015; Hamelin et al. 2013; Nicoll et al. 2013). These reviews are not included in Table 3.4 as they all reviewed the same small set of primary studies. Vereenooghe and Langdon (2013) reported that anger management produced the largest effect size of any of the treatments tested with this group, with a standardized mean difference of +0.82.

Another population on whom the amount of available research is quite limited is young adults in the age range 18–25, which as a result of changing patterns of employment and education in Western societies has been characterized as a new phase of 'emerging adulthood' (Farrington et al. 2012). McGuire (2015) reviewed a series of 10 evaluations of work with this age range, several of which reported positive outcomes on general recidivism. One study focused on young adult males considered to be at high risk of violent reoffending. Braga et al. (2009) evaluated the *Boston Re-entry Initiative*, which involved the formulation of specially designed release plans for those about to be discharged from prison. To facilitate the transition they were assigned caseworkers, attended a range of programmes, were met on release, and mentored on return to the community. Relative to an untreated comparison group, there was a statistically significant 32.1% reduction in overall arrests and a 37.1% reduction in arrests for violence.

The most successful intervention used to date in addressing serious violent crime amongst young adults is a multicomponent strategy called *Pulling levers*. This emerged from an initial police-led project known as *Operation Ceasefire*, designed to address gang-related gun homicides committed by youths aged under 24 years in Boston (Braga et al. 2001). Police communicated directly with known gang members and made clear to them plans for swift and overwhelming responses to shootings that would disrupt illegal activities on which gangs depended. This was to be strengthened by additional law-enforcement consequences including stiffer plea bargains and sentences; but also by providing more opportunities of other kinds, for example making more community services available to targeted offenders. The approach was subsequently disseminated across several other American cities. A meta-analysis found a moderate-to-large mean effect size of 0.604 across studies in 10 locations, representing a significant drop in key target outcomes, including homicide rates (Braga and Weisburd 2012, 2015).

The remainder of the reviews listed in Table 3.4 brought together evaluations of the impact of interventions designed to reduce rates of prison indiscipline and violence. As part of the review by French and Gendreau (2006) it was possible to calculate 23 effect sizes for the relationship between reductions in prison violations and subsequent recidivism. Interventions that resulted in high reductions in the former were also associated with significant reductions in the latter. The review by Auty et al. (2017) found some positive and encouraging results, but with insufficient consistency to form the basis for any strong conclusions.

Intimate partner violence

A separate and larger set of reviews and meta-analyses has been published concerned with interventions designed to reduce violence against close partners. Attempts to address this problem have taken a variety of forms, from studies of the effectiveness of arrest, to counselling for victims, and treatment of perpetrators by means of *batterer intervention programmes* (BIPs). The last of these has taken several forms, the most widely disseminated of which, the *Duluth programme*, applies principles drawn from feminist criminological theory but combines them with some skills-training elements (Bowen 2011).

Reviews of interventions to address IPV are listed in Table 3.5. The included reviews focus predominantly on evaluations of interventions for perpetrators, but some also encompassed studies of victim-centred methods (e.g. Eckhardt et al. 2013). There is a large body of research on policing interventions (such as the use of arrest, or of 'second responders' who attend after the initial response to a call for assistance) that is not considered here.

As can be seen in Table 3.5, there are some positive outcomes from evaluations in this area. These were reported in reviews such as that of Feder et al. (2008) who integrated results of studies of BIPs which participants were authorized by courts to attend. They located four RCTs and six quasi-experimental evaluations of psychoeducational or cognitive-behavioural programmes. The mean effect size from the RCTs was +0.26; but participants in these studies were assessed as being at low risk of reoffending. Other reviews also reported positive results (Babcock et al. 2004; Karakurt et al. 2016). Still others described positive outcomes but in some studies they were limited to changes in attitudes or awareness and did not include measures of violent behaviour (Ogunsiji and Clisdell 2017). A few reviews do not provide statistical integration of results.

Several other reviews found a mixture of outcomes, with some significant benefits but alongside other non-significant results (e.g. Arias et al. 2013; Eckhardt et al. 2013). In the context of the findings they obtained, other reviewers have drawn pessimistic conclusions. Cluss and Bodea (2011) expressed scepticism over the effectiveness of group programmes and Stover et al. (2009) depicted evidence of positive effects as 'meagre'. In a Cochrane systematic

Table 3.5 Reviews of interventions to reduce or prevent intimate partner violence (IPV).

Review	Focus	Number of studies	Findings
MacMillan et al. (2001); Wathen et al. (2003)	Principally a review of screening for intimate partner violence (IPV) in primary care settings	10	Included a review of batterer intervention studies published in the period 1986–2000: found conflicting evidence regarding the effectiveness of interventions in reducing rates of further IPV.
Stith et al. (2003); McCollum and Stith (2008)	Effectiveness of couples therapy for reducing violence	15	Reviewed 6 experimental, one quasi-experimental and 8 pre-post evaluations of joint treatment. Found some encouraging results but the review contains no quantitative synthesis.
Babcock et al. (2004)	Batterer intervention programmes (BIPs)	22	Located 17 quasi-experimental designs and 5 randomized experiments. Used both police and partner reports as outcomes. Found an average effect size of $d = 0.34$, though due to other factors the effect was estimated to be lower than this.
Feder and Wilson (2005); Feder et al. (2008)	Court-mandated BIPs	10	Reviewed 6 quasi-experimental (QE) evaluations and 4 randomized controlled trials (RCTs) of psychoeducational or Cognitive-Behavioural Therapy (CBT) programmes which low-risk offenders were mandated to attend. Effect size from RCTs was 0.26 and statistically significant; QE results more mixed.
Aos et al. (2006)	General review of adult corrections programmes	11	Included 9 evaluations of educational or cognitive-behavioural interventions for IPV offenders and 2 evaluations of domestic violence courts. Mean effect sizes in both cases were zero.
Stover et al. (2009)	Review of the effect of interventions on perpetrators, victims, couples, and witnesses	21	Compared effects of different interventions by primary treatment focus: batterers (7), victims (6), couples (5) and child witnesses (4). Some studies had multiple measures across the four domains. Interventions for batterers showed high dropout and described as having 'meagre' effects.

(Continued)

Table 3.5   (*Cont'd*)

Review	Focus	Number of studies	Findings
Cluss and Bodea (2011)	Effectiveness of BIPs	22	Does not report statistical integration of findings. Concludes that there is 'very little or no empirically demonstrated effectiveness of the widely available group interventions' (p. 15).
Smedslund et al. (2011)	Cognitive behavioural therapy for physically abusive men	6	Cochrane Collaboration systematic review, RCTs only, 4 included in meta-analysis. The results were inconclusive, with only a small effect size and mainly equivocal results.
Arias et al. (2013)	BIPs	19	Reviewed 13 quasi-experimental and 6 experimental designs, total sample size 18 941. There was a small and non-significant reduction in IPV for Duluth and CBT programmes, but a significant effect for other types of programme.
Eckhardt et al. (2013)	Intervention programmes for perpetrators and victims	20 of CBT or Duluth; 10 of other approaches	Total sample size 20 829. Results were equivocal, but there were some significant results, especially from studies that took account of motivation and readiness to change.
Miller et al. (2013)	Meta-analysis of intervention studies	9 studies with 11 effect sizes	Evaluations of Duluth programmes had an effect size close to zero. Evaluations of four other types of programme showed better results, with a mean 33% reduction in IPV recidivism.
Karakurt et al. (2016)	Systematic review and meta-analysis of couples therapy for reducing IPV	6	Aggregate sample size 470 participants. Found a statistically significant mean effect size of −0.84 favouring intervention, with low heterogeneity in the results, indicating therapy was effective.
Ogunsiji and Clisdell (2017)	Review of interventions to reduce IPV amongst migrant populations	10	All interventions were reported as having positive outcomes for participants, but the recorded variables were in terms of attitudes, knowledge, community engagement, and cultural awareness; no data were available on offences.

review, Smedslund et al. (2011) located six studies of cognitive behavioural therapy for physically abusive men, but the observed mean effect size was small and results were uneven.

One of the possible reasons for the mixed and sometimes null results in this area may arise from the fact that the most widely implemented intervention, the Duluth programme, which is included in many reviews, has not yielded evidence of beneficial effects. Miller et al. (2013) conducted a meta-analysis of nine intervention studies producing 11 effect sizes. The six evaluations of Duluth-model programmes had a near-to-zero average effect. In addition to a lack of supporting evidence, the Duluth programme has also been criticized on ethical grounds (Pender 2012) and in terms of its inadequacy for addressing the complexities of partner violence (Bohall et al. 2016). In contrast, in the review by Miller et al. (2013) evaluations of four other types of programme produced a mean effect of reducing IPV recidivism by 33%.

The overall pattern may be compounded by the finding that IPV programmes often have very high levels of attrition, which can be traced to differences in the circumstances, attitudes, and motivations of participants (Jewell and Wormith 2010). That in turn may be a function of the multiple factors associated with causation of IPV, such that for intervention to be effective, there may be a corresponding need for multiple components, as found with successful interventions for young offenders (as outlined earlier).

A few reviews have been reported of initiatives to address dating and partner violence in adolescent relationships. De La Rue et al. (2014) located 23 studies reporting evaluations of programmes designed for this purpose, finding evidence of significant gains in changed attitudes and reduced acceptance of beliefs that are supportive of male sexual aggression. Four studies reported follow-up information and all found a significant reduction in dating violence. Whitaker et al. (2013) located 19 experimental studies (15 of them RCTs) showing a mixed pattern of results: for example, in some studies there were significant positive outcomes for boys but not girls, while in others the reverse was found. In seven of the nine most 'highly rigorous' studies there was evidence of positive impact. The strongest results were from five community-based programmes (outside schools). Amongst six controlled trials located by De Koker et al. (2014), three reported significant effects in reducing physical or sexual aggression by partners, with effects holding for up to four years afterwards. Effective programmes were delivered at multiple sites (school and community) and focused on relationship skills.

Offenders with mental disorders

Table 3.6 summarizes key findings from reviews of research on interventions to reduce aggression or violence amongst offenders diagnosed with mental disorders. Research in this area presents considerable challenges methodologically, given the diversity of problems experienced by those in this population, together with the practical issues of conducting research in secure hospitals or in community forensic mental health settings.

Given their location in healthcare services, studies in this area are often more focused on clinical or therapeutic change and on symptom reduction rather than with violence. Hence there is often measurement and recording of mediating variables such as anxiety, anger, hostility, or emotional control, and the findings of reviews reflect this emphasis (e.g. Hockenhull et al. 2012). However some reviews also examined effects on aggressive behaviour and on violence. Each of the reviews reports some positive findings on criminal justice outcomes, notably that of Martin et al. (2012), and in two reviews where in-hospital aggression was examined (Frazier and Vela 2014; Ross et al. 2013), as can be seen from Table 3.6 a majority of the studies reported significant effects of interventions. In general

Table 3.6 Reviews of interventions for offenders with mental disorders.

Review	Focus	Number of studies	Findings
Hockenhull et al. (2012)	Systematic review of interventions for offenders with mental disorders and histories of violence	7	All located studies were randomized controlled trials (RCTs) but were confined to evaluating short-term changes such as improvements in anger control, measured by means of psychometric or observational rating scales. Found a mean odds ratio of −0.61 in favour of intervention.
Martin et al. (2012)	Review of interventions for offenders with major mental illnesses including psychoses	25	Combined sample size of 15 678 participants. Found a mean effect size on criminal justice outcomes of +0.19, with significant effects on rates of arrest, time spent in prison, time lapsed before failure, and violent crime; but the impact on reconviction fell below statistical significance.
Morgan et al. (2012)	Review of treatment of major mental disorders (schizophrenia, bipolar disorder, major depression)	26 (mental illness symptoms) 4 (criminal justice outcomes)	Only 4 of the located studies reported outcome data on criminal recidivism, yielding a mean effect size of +0.11. But there were large variations in effects. Three studies reported positive outcomes while the fourth showed a large negative result.
Reidy et al. (2013)	Review of interventions to reduce psychopathic violence	17	Included studies on secure hospital (2), general psychiatric (3), sex offender (7), and adolescent (5) populations assessed as showing features of psychopathy. Found a very mixed pattern of results that was difficult to interpret due to methodological problems, with only a small number of studies reporting positive outcomes.
Ross et al. (2013)	Review of interventions to reduce aggressive behaviour in secure forensic settings	10	Located 2 RCTs, 6 before-and-after studies, and 2 small case series. Given design and measurement variations, no clear trend could be detected in results. Eight studies reported reductions in physical aggression; 6 reported significant reductions on aggression-related variables. However only one found a drop in violent recidivism at follow-up.

Table 3.6 *(Cont'd)*

Review	Focus	Number of studies	Findings
Frazier and Vela (2014)	Review of Dialectical Behaviour Therapy (DBT) for reducing anger and aggression	12	Seven studies were RCTs. No mean effect size was calculated, but 10 of the studies reported significant reductions on measures of anger and/or aggressive behaviour; 2 also found reductions in violent disciplinary infractions in prisons.

then, while conclusions in this area remain tentative, there is evidence of the possibility of reducing aggression and violence.

Research in this area often encounters the question of whether there are some individuals who are unresponsive to intervention, who are 'treatment-resistant'. This may be a residue of long-standing beliefs suggesting that individuals with 'psychopathic' features are 'untreatable' or can even be made worse by treatment (D'Silva et al. 2004). While there is not as yet any extensive evidence that can wholly counter such beliefs, some research results have provided evidence of observable change amongst individuals classified as psychopathic.

For example, in a study of 72 individuals classified as psychopathic, and a further 195 classed as 'potentially' psychopathic, all of whom were under supervision in a probation setting, Skeem et al. (2002) reported that those who attended seven or more sessions were 3.5 times less likely to commit violent offences than those who attended fewer sessions. In a systematic review of 10 studies of the relationship between psychopathic personality and sexual offending, Doren and Yates (2008) found that there was a proportion within many participant samples who had responded constructively to intervention and showed evidence of treatment progress. Their rate of recidivism then became comparable to that of non-psychopathic individuals. In an evaluation of a group-based intervention in a secure psychiatric centre, Wong et al. (2012; Olver and Wong 2013) reported that amongst participants who were classed as psychopathic, three-quarters completed treatment, and following release had a reoffending rate one-third lower than those who did not (60.6% as compared to 91.7%). Each of these findings is at odds with the view that this group is not susceptible to treatment or is unable to change.

Conclusion

There continue to be sizeable challenges facing the area of research summarized here. Across the whole spectrum of the 53 reviews (and three 'mega-reviews') cited in this chapter, and the many studies summarized and analysed within them, there is an assortment of effects. Reviewers often comment on the limited number of studies available, and discrepancies between them that make the drawing of clear conclusions difficult. Although numerous studies have been published, they show considerable heterogeneity, such that when reviewers apply selection criteria, the number meeting successive requirements swiftly declines, leaving few with enough features in common to allow meaningful analysis (Hockenhull et al. 2015).

There are also wide variations in methodological quality, and while there is a sizeable proportion of well-designed experiments involving children and adolescents, that proportion is far lower for research conducted in criminal justice settings. With the use of statistical controls in quasi-experimental evaluations however, and by taking account of moderators in meta-analysis, a sufficient body of findings emerges as the basis for drawing conclusions, and when these precautions are applied the majority of reviews report positive effects of interventions.

Thus across six areas or populations surveyed in the chapter, what can be concluded about whether interventions 'work' to reduce different forms of violence?

- Reviews of the field of parent training and allied interventions designed to reduce aggression in children produce almost uniformly positive results, with effect sizes ranging from 0.25 to 0.86.
- For bullying and other forms of aggressiveness in schools, findings are more varied but again largely positive, with mean effects ranging from 0.12 to 0.29. ABPs succeeded in reducing bullying by almost a quarter on average, with some programmes having larger effects. However a few interventions had no effect, or changes were short-lived, and effect sizes fell in later adolescence.
- For those whose behaviour resulted in entry to the criminal justice system, there are some medium-range effects, with violent reoffending reduced by up to one-third, and good results are achievable with those whose offending is persistent or serious.
- Amongst adult offenders, there is a wide spread of effect sizes, and the mean effect in some reviews is relatively low. However there are also very impressive outcomes with anger-related offending and for members of violent gangs.
- In relation to IPV, the proportion of zero effects is considerably larger, and some reviews found little if anything positive to report. Others however found more encouraging outcomes, but there is as yet no consensus on the most suitable approaches to implement with IPV given the complexity of its causes. Research however shows that it is possible to prevent the onset of a pattern of partner violence amongst young people.
- Finally for those who have acted violently and have also been diagnosed with mental disorders, average effects sizes are also comparatively low. Nevertheless there are again some promising results that point towards future routes for developing more appropriate interventions.

Putting the above in a broader perspective, it is also salutary to keep in mind that even effect sizes that are low in Cohen's (1988) terms can be of considerable practical import: any reduction in violence is a lowering in levels of harm and fear, and can represent significant cost savings both for criminal justice services and for society more widely.

Within the research reviews collected here it is possible to identify features of more consistently effective interventions. The best results usually come from employing combinations of methods that include skill acquisition, development of self-control, and of perspective taking, applied within the framework of the RNR model, adapted according to context. This continues to be the best-supported approach to offender rehabilitation, and proposals to replace it with alternatives drawing on the 'desistance paradigm' or on the concept of 'good lives' are in this author's view based on misplaced criticisms of it, and have not delivered anything of added value either theoretically or empirically.

Amongst the findings reviewed, there is a relationship between the size of effects and the age of participants: better and more consistent outcomes are obtained from evaluations of interventions with children and young people than with adults. In most respects that should not be surprising, as the longer any pattern of behaviour has been established, the more firmly it becomes entrenched and the more difficult it is to change. Prevention, or early intervention, is regarded as the best option in many fields. Nonetheless, there have been some large effect sizes reported from studies with what are often regarded as the most resistant groups, such as seen in the work by Caldwell et al. (2007) with adolescents showing features classed as 'psychopathic', or Braga and Weisburd (2012, 2015) with violent gangs. Moreover, positive effects where obtained usually reflect an impact on those individuals who commit the largest proportion of offences or the most serious kinds of violence.

In addition, information is steadily accumulating on the factors associated with poor outcomes. Future intervention methods, their modes of delivery, levels of organizational support and other elements can therefore be progressively better tailored to the needs of participant groups. Overall, as Thornton (1987) observed when reviewing some of the earliest research on 'correctional treatment', there can be disagreements over how to interpret varied patterns of results. But today as then, the one conclusion that is not supported by the available evidence is the idea that 'nothing works'.

References

Alford, A.A. and Derzon, J. (2012). Meta-analysis and systematic review of the effectiveness of school-based programs to reduce multiple violent and antisocial behavioral outcomes. In: *Handbook of School Violence and School Safety: International Research and Practice*, 2e (eds. S.R. Jimerson, A. Nickerson, M.J. Mayer, et al.), 593–606. New York: Routledge.

Ali, A., Hall, I. Blickwedel, J. et al. (2015). Behavioural and cognitive-behavioural interventions for outwardly-directed aggressive behaviour in people with intellectual disabilities. *Cochrane Database of Systematic Reviews*, 4, Art. No.: CD003406.

Allen, G. and Watson, C. (2017). *UK Prison Population Statistics*. Briefing Paper Number SN/SG/04334. London: House of Commons Library.

Altafim, E.R.P. and Linhares, M.B.M. (2016). Universal violence and child maltreatment prevention programs for parents: a systematic review. *Psychosocial Intervention* 25: 27–38.

Aos, S., Miller, M., and Drake, E. (2006). *Evidence-Based Adult Corrections: What Works and What Does Not*. Olympia, WA: Washington State Institute for Public Policy.

Arias, E., Arce, R., and Vilariño, M. (2013). Batterer intervention programmes: a meta-analytic review of effectiveness. *Psychosocial Intervention* 22: 153–160.

Auty, K.M., Cope, A., and Liebling, A. (2017). Psychoeducational programs for reducing prison violence: a systematic review. *Aggression and Violent Behavior* 33: 126–143.

Babcock, J.C., Green, C.E., and Robie, C. (2004). Does batterers' treatment work? A meta-analytic review of domestic violence treatment. *Clinical Psychology Review* 23: 1023–1053.

Barnes, T.N., Smith, S.W., and Miller, M.D. (2014). School-based cognitive-behavioral interventions in the treatment of aggression in the United States: a meta-analysis. *Aggression and Violent Behavior* 19: 311–321.

Bohall, G., Bautista, M.-J., and Musson, S. (2016). Intimate partner violence and the Duluth model: an examination of the model and recommendations for future research and practice. *Journal of Family Violence* 31: 1029–1033.

Bonta, J. and Andrews, D.A. (2017). *The Psychology of Criminal Conduct*, 6e. London and New York: Routledge.

Borduin, C.M., Dopp, A.R., and Taylor, E.K. (2013). Evidence-based interventions for serious and violent juvenile offenders. In: *What Works in Offender Rehabilitation: An Evidence Based Approach to*

Assessment and Treatment (eds. L. Craig, J. Dixon and T.A. Gannon), 192–210. Chichester: Wiley Blackwell.

Bowen, E. (2011). *The Rehabilitation of Partner Violent Men*. Chichester: Wiley Backwell.

Braga, A.A., Kennedy, D.M., Waring, E.J. et al. (2001). Problem-oriented policing, deterrence, and youth violence: an evaluation of Boston's Operation Ceasefire. *Journal of Research in Crime and Delinquency* 38: 195–225.

Braga, A.A., Piehl, A.M., and Hureau, D. (2009). Controlling violent offenders released to the community: evaluation of the Boston Reentry Initiative. *Journal of Research in Crime and Delinquency* 46: 411–436.

Braga, A.A. and Weisburd, D.L. (2012). The effects of 'Pulling levers' focused deterrence strategies on crime. *Campbell Systematic Reviews* 6.

Braga, A.A. and Weisburd, D.L. (2015). Focused deterrence and the prevention of violent gun injuries: practice, theoretical principles, and scientific evidence. *Annual Review of Public Health* 36: 55–68.

Caldwell, M.F., McCormick, D.J., Umstead, D. et al. (2007). Evidence of treatment progress and therapeutic outcomes among adolescents with psychopathic features. *Criminal Justice and Behavior* 34: 573–587.

Caldwell, M.F., Vitacco, M., and Van Rybroek, G.J. (2006). Are violent delinquents worth treating? A cost–benefit analysis. *Journal of Research in Crime and Delinquency* 43: 148–168.

Cantone, E., Piras, A.P., Vellante, M. et al. (2015). Interventions on bullying and cyberbullying in schools: a systematic review. *Clinical Practice and Epidemiology in Mental Health* 11 (Suppl 1: M4): 58–76.

Cid, J. (2009). Is imprisonment criminogenic? A comparative study of recidivism rates between prison and suspended prison sanctions. *European Journal of Criminology* 6: 459–480.

Cluss, P. and Bodea, A. (2011). *The Effectiveness of Batterer Intervention Programs: A Literature Review & Recommendations for Next Steps*. (Abridged Version). Pittsburgh, PA: University of Pittsburgh and FISA Foundation.

Cohen, J. (1988). *Statistical Power Analysis for the Behavioral Sciences*. Hillsdale, NJ: Erlbaum.

Cox, E., Leung, R., Baksheev, G. et al. (2016). Violence prevention and intervention programmes for adolescents in Australia: a systematic review. *Australian Psychologist* 51: 206–222.

De Koker, P., Mathews, C., Zuch, M. et al. (2014). A systematic review of interventions for preventing adolescent intimate partner violence. *Journal of Adolescent Health* 54: 3–13.

De La Rue, L., Polanin, J.R., Espelage, D.L. et al. (2014). School-based interventions to reduce dating and sexual violence: a systematic review. *Campbell Systematic Reviews* 7.

Doren, D.M. and Yates, P.M. (2008). Effectiveness of sex offender treatment for psychopathic sexual offenders. *International Journal of Offender Therapy and Comparative Criminology* 52: 234–245.

Dowden, C. and Andrews, D.A. (2000). Effective correctional treatment and violent reoffending: a meta-analysis. *Canadian Journal of Criminology and Criminal Justice* 42: 449–467.

Dretzke, J., Davenport, C., Frew, E. et al. (2009). The clinical effectiveness of different parenting programmes for children with conduct problems: a systematic review of randomised controlled trials. *Child and Adolescent Psychiatry and Mental Health* 3: 7.

D'Silva, K., Duggan, C., and McCarthy, L. (2004). Does treatment really make psychopaths worse? A review of the evidence. *Journal of Personality Disorders* 18: 163–177.

Eckhardt, C.I., Murphy, C.M., Whitaker, D.J. et al. (2013). The effectiveness of intervention programs for perpetrators and victims of intimate partner violence. *Partner Abuse* 4: 196–231.

Ellis, P.D. (2010). *The Essential Guide to Effect Sizes: Statistical Power, Meta-Analysis, and the Interpretation of Research Results*. Cambridge: Cambridge University Press.

Farrington, D.P., Gaffney, H., Lösel, F. et al. (2017). Systematic reviews of the effectiveness of developmental prevention programs in reducing delinquency, aggression, and bullying. *Aggression and Violent Behavior* 33: 91–106.

Farrington, D.P., Loeber, R., and Howell, J.C. (2012). Young adult offenders: the need for more effective legislative options and justice processing. *Criminology & Public Policy* 11: 729–750.

Feder, L. and Wilson, D.B. (2005). A meta-analytic review of court-mandated batterer intervention programs: Can courts affect abusers' behaviour? *Journal of Experimental Criminology* 1: 239–262.

Feder, L., Wilson, D.B., and Austin, S. (2008). Court-mandated interventions for individuals convicted of domestic violence. *Campbell Systematic Reviews* 12.

Frazier, S.N. and Vela, J. (2014). Dialectical behaviour therapy for the treatment of anger and aggressive behaviour: a review. *Aggression and Violent Behavior* 19: 156–163.

French, S.A. and Gendreau, P. (2006). Reducing prison misconducts: what works! *Criminal Justice and Behavior* 33: 185–218.

Garrido, V. and Morales, L.A. (2007). Serious (violent and chronic) juvenile offenders: a systematic review of treatment effectiveness in secure corrections. *Campbell Systematic Reviews* 7.

Glick, B. and Gibbs, J.C. (2010). *Aggression Replacement Training: A Comprehensive Intervention for Aggressive Youth*, 3e. Champaign, IL: Research Press.

Hamelin, J., Travis, R., and Sturmey, P. (2013). Anger management and intellectual disabilities: a systematic review. *Journal of Mental Health Research in Intellectual Disabilities* 6: 60–70.

Henwood, K.S., Chou, S., and Browne, K.D. (2015). A systematic review and meta-analysis on the effectiveness of CBT informed anger management. *Aggression and Violent Behavior* 25: 280–292.

Hockenhull, J.C., Cherry, M.G., Whittington, R. et al. (2015). Heterogeneity in the interpersonal violence outcome research: an investigation and discussion of clinical and research implications. *Aggression and Violent Behavior* 22: 18–25.

Hockenhull, J.C., Whittington, R., Leitner, M. et al. (2012). A systematic review of prevention and intervention strategies for populations at high risk of engaging in violent behaviour: update 2002-8. *Health Technology Assessment* 16 (3): 1–145.

Hofvander, B., Ossowski, D., Lundström, S. et al. (2009). Continuity of aggressive antisocial behaviour from childhood to adulthood: the question of phenotype definition. *International Journal of Law and Psychiatry* 32: 224–234.

Jewell, L.M. and Wormith, J.S. (2010). Variables associated with attrition from domestic violence treatment programs targeting male batterers: a meta-analysis. *Criminal Justice and Behavior* 37: 1086–1113.

Jiménez-Barbero, J.A., Hernández, J.A., Esteban, B.L. et al. (2012). Effectiveness of antibullying school programmes: a systematic review by evidence levels. *Children and Youth Services Review* 34: 1646–1658.

Jiménez-Barbero, J.A., Ruiz-Hernández, J.A., Llor-Zaragoza, L. et al. (2016). Effectiveness of anti-bullying programs: a meta-analysis. *Children and Youth Services Review* 61: 165–175.

Jolliffe, D. and Farrington, D.P. (2009). *Effectiveness of Interventions for Adult Male Violent Offenders*. Stockholm: Swedish National Council for Crime Prevention.

Kaminski, J.W., Valle, L.A., Filene, J.H. et al. (2008). A meta-analytic review of components associated with parent training program effectiveness. *Journal of Abnormal Child Psychology* 36: 567–589.

Karakurt, G., Whiting, K., Van Esch, C. et al. (2016). Couple therapy for intimate partner violence: a systematic review and meta-analysis. *Journal of Marital and Family Therapy* 42: 567–583.

Klement, C. (2015). Comparing the effects of community service and imprisonment on reconviction: results from a quasi-experimental Danish study. *Journal of Experimental Criminology* 11: 237–261.

Krueger, R.F. and Tackett, J.L. (2016). The externalizing spectrum of personality and psychopathology: an empirical and quantitative alternative to discrete disorder approaches. In: *The Oxford Handbook of Externalizing Spectrum Disorders* (eds. T.P. Beachaine and S.P. Hinshaw), 79–89. New York: Oxford University Press.

Lee, L., Kim, C.J., and Kim, D.H. (2015). A meta-analysis of the effect of school-based anti-bullying programs. *Journal of Child Health Care* 19: 136–153.

Lester, S., Lawrence, C., and Ward, C.L. (2017). What do we know about preventing school violence? A systematic review of systematic reviews. *Psychology, Health & Medicine* 22: 187–223.

Limbos, M.A., Chan, L.S., Warf, C. et al. (2007). Effectiveness of interventions to prevent youth violence: a systematic review. *American Journal of Preventive Medicine* 33: 65–74.

Lipsey, M.W. and Wilson, D.B. (1998). Effective intervention for serious juvenile offenders: a synthesis of research. In: *Serious and Violent Juvenile Offenders: Risk Factors and Successful Interventions* (eds. R. Loeber and D.P. Farrington), 313–345. Thousand Oaks, CA: Sage.

Loeber, R., Farrington, D.P., Stouthamer-Loeber, M. et al. (2008). *Violence and Serious Theft: Development and Prediction from Childhood to Adulthood*. New York: Routledge.

MacMillan, H.L., Wathen, C.N., and with The Canadian Task Force on Preventive Health Care (2001). *Prevention and treatment of violence against women: Systematic review & recommendations*. CTF-PHC Technical Report #01–4. London, ON: Canadian Task Force.

Martin, M.S., Dorken, S.K., Wamboldt, A.D. et al. (2012). Stopping the revolving door: a meta-analysis on the effectiveness of interventions for criminally involved individuals with major mental disorders. *Law and Human Behavior* 36: 1–12.

Martinson, R. (1974). What works? – questions and answers about prison reform. *The Public Interest* 10: 22–54.

Matjasko, J.L., Vivolo-Kantor, A.M., Massetti, G.M. et al. (2012). A systematic meta-review of evaluations of youth violence prevention programs: common and divergent findings from 25 years of meta-analyses and systematic reviews. *Aggression and Violent Behavior* 17: 540–552.

McCart, M.R., Priester, P.E., Davies, W.H. et al. (2006). Differential effectiveness of behavioural parent-training and cognitive-behavioral therapy for antisocial youth: a meta-analysis. *Journal of Abnormal Child Psychology* 34: 527–543.

McCollum, E.E. and Stith, S.M. (2008). Couples treatment for interpersonal violence: a review of outcome research literature and current clinical practices. *Violence and Victims* 23: 187–201.

McGuire, J. (2008). A review of effective interventions for reducing aggression and violence. *Philosophical Transactions of the Royal Society, B: Biological Sciences* 363: 2577–2597.

McGuire, J. (2013). 'What works' to reduce reoffending: 18 years on. In: *What Works in Offender Rehabilitation: An Evidence Based Approach to Assessment and Treatment* (eds. L.A. Craig, L. Dixon and T.A. Gannon), 20–49. Chichester: Wiley Blackwell.

McGuire, J. (2015). What works in reducing reoffending in young adults? A rapid evidence assessment. Analytical Summary. London: National Offender Management Service.

McGuire, J. (2017). Evidence-based practice and adults: what works? What works best? In: *The Wiley Handbook of Violence and Aggression*, vol. II (ed. P. Sturmey), 803–814. New York: Wiley.

Miller, M., Drake, E., and Nafziger, M. (2013). *What works to reduce recidivism by domestic violence offenders?* Document No. 13-01-1201. Olympia, WA: Washington State Institute for Public Policy.

Moffitt, T.E. (1993). Adolescence-limited and life-course-persistent antisocial behavior: a developmental taxonomy. *Psychological Review* 100: 674–701.

Moffitt, T.E. (2003). Life-course-persistent and adolescence-limited antisocial behaviour: a 10-year research review and a research agenda. In: *Causes of Conduct Disorder and Delinquency* (eds. B.B. Lahey, T.E. Moffitt and A. Caspi), 49–75. New York: Guilford Press.

Moffitt, T.E. (2018). Male antisocial behaviour in adolescence and beyond. *Nature Human Behaviour* 2: 177–186.

Morgan, R.D., Flora, D.B., Kroner, D.G. et al. (2012). Treating offenders with mental illness: a research synthesis. *Law and Human Behavior* 36: 37–50.

Nagin, D.S., Cullen, F.T., and Jonson, C.L. (2009). Imprisonment and reoffending. *Crime and Justice* 38: 115–200.

Nicoll, M., Beail, N., and Saxon, D. (2013). Cognitive behavioural treatment of anger in adults with learning disabilities: a systematic review and meta-analysis. *Journal of Applied Research in Intellectual Disabilities* 26: 47–62.

Nocentini, A., Zambuto, V., and Menesini, E. (2015). Anti-bullying programs and information and communication technologies (ICTs): a systematic review. *Aggression and Violent Behavior* 23: 52–60.

Ogunsiji, O. and Clisdell, E. (2017). Intimate partner violence prevention and reduction: a review of literature. *Health Care for Women International* 38: 439–462.

Olver, M.E. and Wong, S.C.P. (2013). A description and research review of the Clearwater Sex Offender Treatment Programme. *Psychology, Crime & Law* 19: 477–492.

Patterson, G.R., Dishion, T.J., and Bank, L. (1984). Family interaction: a process model of deviancy training. *Aggressive Behavior* 10: 253–267.

Pender, R.L. (2012). ASGW best practice guidelines: an evaluation of the Duluth model. *Journal for Specialists in Group Work* 37: 218–231.

Piquero, A.R., Carriaga, M.L., Diamond, B. et al. (2012a). Stability in aggression revisited. *Aggression and Violent Behavior* 17: 365–372.

Piquero, A.R., Jennings, W.G., and Barnes, J.C. (2012b). Violence in criminal careers: a review of the literature from a developmental life-course perspective. *Aggression and Violent Behavior* 17: 171–179.

Redondo, S., Sánchez-Meca, J., and Garrido, V. (2002). Crime treatment in Europe: a review of outcome studies. In: *Offender Rehabilitation and Treatment: Effective Programmes and Policies to Reduce Re-Offending* (ed. J. McGuire), 113–141. Chichester: Wiley.

Reidy, D.E., Kearns, M.C., and DeGue, S. (2013). Reducing psychopathic violence: a review of the treatment literature. *Aggression and Violent Behavior* 18: 527–538.

Ross, J., Quayle, E., Newman, E. et al. (2013). The impact of psychological therapies on violent behaviour in clinical and forensic settings: a systematic review. *Aggression and Violent Behavior* 18: 761–773.

Sawyer, A.M., Borduin, C.M., and Dopp, A.R. (2015). Long-term effects of prevention and treatment on youth antisocial behavior: a meta-analysis. *Clinical Psychology Review* 42: 130–144.

Serketich, W.J. and Dumas, J.E. (1996). The effectiveness of behavioural parent training to modify antisocial behaviour in children: a meta-analysis. *Behavior Therapy* 27: 171–186.

Skeem, J.L., Monahan, J., and Mulvey, E.P. (2002). Psychopathy, treatment involvement, and subsequent violence among civil psychiatric patients. *Law and Human Behavior* 26: 577–603.

Smedslund, G., Dalsbø, T.K., Steiro, A. et al. (2011). Cognitive behavioural therapy for men who physical abuse their female partner. *Cochrane Database of Systematic Reviews*, 2.

Stith, S.M., Rosen, K.H., and McCollum, E.E. (2003). Effectiveness of couples treatment for spouse abuse. *Journal of Marital and Family Therapy* 29: 407–426.

Stover, C.S., Meadows, A.M., and Kaufman, J. (2009). Interventions for intimate partner violence: review and implications for evidence-based practice. *Professional Psychology: Research and Practice* 40: 223–233.

Tahamont, S. and Chalfin, A. (2018). The effect of prisons on crime. In: *The Oxford Handbook of Prisons and Imprisonment* (eds. J. Wooldredge and P. Smith), 627–650. New York: Oxford University Press.

Thornton, D.M. (1987). Treatment effects on recidivism: a reappraisal of the 'nothing works' doctrine. In: *Applying Psychology to Imprisonment: Theory and Practice* (eds. B.J. McGurk, D.M. Thornton and M. Williams), 181–189. London: Her Majesty's Stationery Office.

Travers, R., Mann, R.E., and Hollin, C.R. (2014). Who benefits from cognitive skills programs? Differential impact by risk and offense type. *Criminal Justice and Behavior* 41: 1103–1129.

Tremblay, R.E., Nagin, D.S., Séguin, J.R. et al. (2004). Physical aggression during early childhood: trajectories and predictors. *Pediatrics* 114: e43–e50.

Trevena, J. and Weatherburn, D. (2015). Does the first prison sentence reduce the risk of further offending? *BOCSAR NSW Crime and Justice Bulletins* 187 16 pp.

Ttofi, M.M. and Farrington, D.P. (2011). Effectiveness of school-based programs to reduce bullying: a systematic and meta-analytic review. *Journal of Experimental Criminology* 7: 27–56.

Ttofi, M.M., Farrington, D.P., and Lösel, F. (2012). School bullying as a predictor of violence later in life: a systematic review and meta-analysis of prospective longitudinal studies. *Aggression and Violent Behavior* 17: 405–418.

Ttofi, M.M., Farrington, D.P., Lösel, F. et al. (2011). The predictive efficiency of school bullying versus later offending: a systematic/meta-analytic review of longitudinal studies. *Criminal Behaviour and Mental Health* 21: 80–89.

Vereenooghe, L. and Langdon, P.E. (2013). Psychological therapies for people with intellectual disabilities: a systematic review and meta-analysis. *Research in Developmental Disabilities* 34: 4085–4102.

Villetaz, P., Killias, M., and Zoder, I. (2006). The effects of custodial vs. non-custodial sentences on re-offending: a systematic review of the state of knowledge. *Campbell Systematic Reviews* 13.

Wathen, C.N., MacMillan, H.L., and with The Canadian Task Force on Preventive Health Care (2003). Prevention of violence against women: recommendation statement from the Canadian Task Force on Preventive Health Care. *Canadian Medical Association Journal* 169: 582–584.

Weaver, R.D. and Campbell, D. (2015). Fresh start: a meta-analysis of aftercare programs for juvenile offenders. *Research on Social Work Practice* 25: 201–212.

Weisburd, D., Farrington, D.P., and Gill, C. (2016). *What Works in Crime Prevention and Rehabilitation: Lessons from Systematic Reviews*. New York: Springer.

Weisburd, D., Farrington, D.P., and Gill, C. (2017). What works in crime prevention and rehabilitation: an assessment of systematic reviews. *Criminology & Public Policy* 16: 415–449.

Welsh, B.C. and Rocque, M. (2014). When crime prevention harms: a review of systematic reviews. *Journal of Experimental Criminology* 10: 245–266.

Wermink, H., Blokland, A., Nieuwbeerta, P. et al. (2010). Comparing the effects of community service and short-term imprisonment on recidivism: a matched samples approach. *Journal of Experimental Criminology* 6: 325–349.

Whitaker, D.J., Murphy, C.M., Eckhardt, C.I. et al. (2013). Effectiveness of primary prevention efforts for intimate partner violence. *Partner Abuse* 4: 175–195.

Wilson, S.J. and Lipsey, M.W. (2007). School-based interventions for aggressive and disruptive behaviour: update of a meta-analysis. *American Journal of Preventive Medicine* 33: S130–S143.

Wilson, S.J., Lipsey, M.W., and Derzon, J.H. (2003). The effects of school-based intervention programs on aggressive behaviour: a meta-analysis. *Journal of Consulting and Clinical Psychology* 71: 136–149.

Wong, S.C., Gordon, A., Gu, D. et al. (2012). The effectiveness of violence reduction treatment for psychopathic offenders: empirical evidence and a treatment model. *International Journal of Forensic Mental Health* 11: 336–349.

Yeager, D.S., Fong, C.J., Lee, H.Y. et al. (2015). Declines in efficacy of anti-bullying programs among older adolescents: theory and a three-level meta-analysis. *Journal of Applied Developmental Psychology* 37: 36–51.

Part II
What Works in Violence Risk Assessment

4

From Predicting Dangerousness to Assessing and Managing Risk for Violence
A Journey Across Four Generations

James R.P. Ogloff and Michael R. Davis
Centre for Forensic Behavioural Science, Swinburne University of Technology and Forensicare, Melbourne, Australia

Introduction

We are not now and probably never will be in a position to be able to determine with certainty who will or will not engage in a violent act. Relying on a range of empirically supported risk factors, though, we can make a reasoned determination of the extent to which those we are assessing share the factors that have been found in others to relate to an increased level of risk. (Mullen and Ogloff 2009)

Assessments of risk for violence, or 'prediction of dangerousness' as it was formerly known,[1] have significant consequences in the criminal justice system and society more widely. On one hand, identifying someone as 'low risk', who is then released from prison only to go on to commit a violent crime, damages the victims and shatters confidence in the justice system. On the other hand, though, identifying someone as 'high risk', who is detained preventatively, but if released would not commit a violent crime, deprives the person of liberty unnecessarily. These consequences speak to the importance of ensuring that violence risk assessments are as accurate as possible.

[1] It is important to note that until the early 1990s, the focus was on the prediction of 'dangerousness' and clinical practice and research focused on determining whether people could be accurately identified as dangerous or not dangerous (Otto 2000). Over time, the narrative has evolved to violence risk assessment, recognizing that risk is not static or dichotomous. Rather, individuals have fewer or greater numbers of risk factors that increase or decrease their likelihood of acting violently. Thus, violence risk assessment includes the identification of such factors, and attempts to prevent violence from occurring through the process of risk management.

The Wiley Handbook of What Works in Violence Risk Management: Theory, Research and Practice,
First Edition. Edited by J. Stephen Wormith, Leam A. Craig, and Todd E. Hogue.
© 2020 John Wiley & Sons Ltd. Published 2020 by John Wiley & Sons Ltd.

Courts have wrestled with the accuracy of risk assessments. For example, in 1978, Thomas Barefoot was convicted of murdering a police officer in Bell County, Texas. A jury found him guilty and, in accordance with the law, a second jury imposed the death penalty on him. One of the questions submitted to the jury, as required by Texas law, was whether there was a probability that Mr. Barefoot would commit further criminal acts of violence and would constitute a continuing threat to society if he was not executed. Based on evidence provided by two psychiatrists, the jury decided in the affirmative and the death penalty was imposed. In what was to become a leading case on future dangerousness, Mr. Barefoot ultimately appealed his case to the US Supreme Court. As part of the grounds for his appeal, Mr. Barefoot argued 'that psychiatrists, individually and as a group, are incompetent to predict with an acceptable degree of reliability that a particular criminal will commit other crimes in the future and so represent a danger to the community'. This position was supported by an Amicus Curiae ('friend of the court') brief submitted by the American Psychological Association arguing, as was the state of the research then, that no one can predict with any degree of reliability that an individual will commit crimes in the future was before the court (Krauss and Sales 2001).

The Supreme Court in *Barefoot v. Estelle* (1983) upheld expert testimony although the majority stated that there was no supporting scientific evidence. Writing for the majority, Justice White, wrote that:

'The suggestion that no psychiatrist's testimony may be presented with respect to a defendant's future dangerousness is somewhat like asking us to disinvent the wheel. In the first place, it is contrary to our cases. If the likelihood of a defendant committing further crimes is a constitutionally acceptable criterion for imposing the death penalty, which it is, *Jurek v. Texas*, 428 U.S. 262, 96 S.Ct. 2950, 49 L.Ed.2d 929 (1976), and if it is not impossible for even a lay person sensibly to arrive at that conclusion, it makes little sense, if any, to submit that psychiatrists, out of the entire universe of persons who might have an opinion on the issue, would know so little about the subject that they should not be permitted to testify.'

The Court reasoned that the testimony complied with the state's rules of evidence and there was no proof that psychiatrists were wrong all of the time regarding future dangerousness, but only wrong more often than not.[2]

This chapter begins with a brief overview of the foundation issues related to violence risk assessment, including terminology, evaluation of accuracy of risk assessment measures, identification of early errors and the importance of base rates in estimating violence risk. We then turn to a discussion of the evolving approaches to violence risk assessment, which has been described as the four generations of risk assessment. Following the review of the progress in violence risk assessment approaches, we describe the two approaches to risk assessment: actuarial assessment and structured professional judgment (SPJ). We then discuss the leading actuarial and SPJ tools that have been developed and evaluated for violence risk assessment: the Violence Risk Appraisal Guide (VRAG), Revised and the Historical Clinical Risk – 20 (HCR – 20), Version 3.

---

[2] Having lost his appeal, Thomas Barefoot was executed on October 30, 1984.

Foundation Issues

The limited research available on 'dangerousness prediction' conducted in the 1970s, and reviewed by Professor John Monahan (1981) around the time of the Barefoot case, showed that 'psychiatrists and psychologists are accurate in no more than one out of three predictions of violent behavior over a several year period' (pp. 47, 49; see also, Cocozza and Steadman 1976). It was found, perhaps not surprisingly, that psychiatrists, psychologists, and release decision-makers tended to make conservative decisions that suggested that people were at risk for dangerousness or violence when, in fact, they were not. For example, Belfrage (1998) found that clinicians found 90% of a group of 640 offenders sentenced to psychiatric treatment in Sweden to be at 'risk of severe criminality;' when, in fact, only 50% went on to commit a crime.

Despite the importance of the question of risk for violence, it is perhaps surprising that it has only been in the past 30–35 years that attempts have been successful to assess an individual's level of risk for violence with some modicum of accuracy. To understand the evolution of risk assessment, it is important to begin with how risk for violence (or dangerousness as it was known) has been defined (Brooks 1974). Traditionally, people were considered to be dangerous or not. For legal decision-making purposes where release discretion was available,[3] those who were deemed dangerous were detained further whilst those who were not seen to be dangerous were released. As noted at the outset of this chapter, this can lead to two possible types of errors, as set out in Table 4.1 below.

Beyond merely identifying the accuracy of risk prediction, consideration has been given to the elements of risk for violence. Brooks (1974) suggested that 'dangerousness' could be analyzed into four components: (i) the magnitude of harm (the hazard); (ii) the probability that the harm will occur (likelihood); (iii) the frequency with which the harm will occur, and (iv) the imminence of the harm (see also, Janus and Meehl 1997).

A more contemporary consideration of risk for violence includes the following elements:

1. Risk for violence is the likelihood of an adverse violent event or outcome.
2. Risk factors are the particular characteristics of the individual being considered that alone, or in combination, lead to an increased risk of violence.

Table 4.1   Violence risk 2×2 contingency table.

	Outcome	
Decision	*Violent*	*Non-Violent*
Detention	True Positive (Correct detention)	False Positive (Erroneous detention)
Release	False Negative (Erroneous release)	True Negative (Correct release)

---

[3] There are many junctures in the law where release discretion is available to legal decision makers. For example, in decisions in criminal matters that are based on a consideration, at least in part, of one's risk for violence include intervention orders, bail, sentences, prison security classification and parole. In the civil context, such decisions include preventative detention, involuntary civil commitment, and civil intervention orders.

3. Risk assessment is an estimation of the likelihood of violent events occurring under particular circumstances within a specified period of time.
4. Risk formulation is a process of summarizing and organizing risk data, and identification of the risk factors. It provides the information base for risk management.
5. Risk management aims to minimize the likelihood of a violent event occurring within the context of the overall management of an individual, to achieve the best possible outcome, and deliver safe, appropriate, effective care.

As the above commentary shows, we have moved quite far from merely trying to determine if one was dangerous or not. Violence risk assessment now extends to understanding and managing the factors that contribute to one's risk for violence to reduce the likelihood of violence occurring.

At least three problems led to the false positive errors made in predicting risk for violence. Firstly, research had not identified empirically-supported risk factors associated with violence. As such, many myths existed about the factors that indicated that one was at risk for being violent. The so-called 'triad' is a good example. For many years, it was incorrectly believed that if one had been prone to encopresis, fire setting, and harming animals as a child, one would be at risk for violence.

Secondly, in addition to failing to identify the correct factors that increased one's level of risk for violence, even when some valid factors were identified, it was difficult for clinicians to systematically assess them or to understand how they went together. For example, if we know that mental illness and substance abuse are two risk factors, what would we consider one's level of risk to be if one had a mental illness but not a substance abuse problem (or vice versa), or if one had both a mental illness and substance abuse problem contemporaneously?

Finally, and perhaps most insidious, is the fact that the base rate of violence in many populations is generally so low that to accurately predict whether an individual will be violent is very difficult. For an example of the effect of base rates on prediction, imagine being in a room of Australian adults. If you were asked to identify the adults who drink coffee, the task would be easy because most Australian adults drink coffee (i.e. the base rate of coffee drinkers is high). Conversely, if you were asked to identify those who do not drink coffee, the task would be prone to failure since so few adults do not drink coffee (i.e. the base rate of non-coffee drinkers is low). Thus, for every non-coffee drinker you correctly identified, you would have probably identified many coffee drinkers in error. The same principle holds true for the prediction of violence. The lower the base rate of violent behaviour in the population, the harder it is to accurately predict who will be violent. Just as with the coffee-drinking example, when the base rate of violence is low those being asked to predict who will be violent are likely to incorrectly identify many more people as being violent than those who are actually violent. This sort of error in prediction is known as a false-positive. Despite the difficulties with predictions of low base rate phenomena, a noted American scholar, Dr. Saleem Shah (1978), noted that 'To say that something is difficult to do (namely, to achieve high levels of accuracy in predicting events with very low base rates) is NOT the same as asserting that the task is impossible and simply cannot be done'. The goal of risk prediction is to maximize the true positive and true negative predictions, whilst simultaneously minimizing the false positive and false negative predictions.

It is important to note that Monahan (1981) qualified his provocative statement, quoted above, in numerous ways in the original monograph. Nonetheless, as the following quotation shows, Monahan (1984) expressed concern only three years after the original quotation by writing that:

'Rarely has research been so uncritically accepted and so facilely generalized by both mental health professionals and lawyers as was this first-generation research on the prediction of violence. The careful qualifications the researchers placed on their findings and the circumscribed nature of the situations to which they might apply were forgotten in the rush to frame a bumper-sticker conclusion – "Psychiatrists and psychologists can't predict violence" – and paste it on every policy vehicle in sight (p. 10).'

This is a less well-known quote than the 'one-third correct' one and, as this chapter will show, the situation has changed rather dramatically – for the better – in the intervening decades.

Approaches to Assessing Risk for Violence

After Monahan's seminal 1981 book in which he discussed violence prediction and made suggestions for improvement in this area, commentators (Andrews et al. 2006; Heilbrun et al. 1999; Otto 1992) identified three major 'generations' of research. More recently, a fourth generation has been introduced (Bonta and Andrews 2016).

The first and second generation of violence risk prediction

Monahan (1984) coined the phrase 'first-generation' risk research in his description of the state of the research in the early 1980s, and his calls for new research strategies (the 'second-generation'). The so-called 'first-generation' of violence research, which occurred in the 1970s and early 1980s, was most heavily criticized for the reasons reviewed above. In particular, first-generation risk assessments were made by clinicians with little structure or guidance. In particular, this unstructured form of clinical judgement 'relies on an informal, "in the head," impressionistic, subjective conclusion, reached (somehow) by a human clinical judge' (Grove and Meehl 1996, pp. 293–294). As the large and growing body of literature clearly shows, though, assessments of risk for violence that are made by clinicians based solely on their unstructured clinical opinion have not been found to be accurate, even if the clinician being asked to make the decision is experienced (Meehl 1954). The essential failure of the so-called 'first generation' of violence risk assessments led many to assert that clinicians were unable to make accurate decisions regarding violence predictions and, as such, any attempt to make such decisions was unethical and beyond the range of knowledge of psychiatrists and psychologists.

After 1981, the 'second generation' of violence prediction research was characterized by a focus on statistical risk prediction, that included a greater focus on shorter-term predictions, situational variables, and specified populations (e.g. Felson and Steadman 1983; Hare and McPherson 1984; Karson and Bigelow 1987; Klassen and O'Connor 1988a, b, c, 1989; Lowenstein et al. 1990; McNiel and Binder 1986, 1989; Monahan 1996; Tardiff and Koenigsberg 1985; see Otto 1992, for a review). During this period, researchers essentially abandoned clinical decision making and some scholars went so far as to say that 'psychologists and psychiatrists act unethically when they render predictions of dangerousness that provide a legal basis for restricting another person's interest in life and liberty' (Ewing 1991). By contrast, in a careful review of the issue, Grisso and Appelbaum (1992) wrote that 'not all predictive statements about future violence are unethical…' (p. 628). In particular, the types of predictive statements that they considered to be ethical are those 'based on actuarial indicators offering probability estimates of future violence for persons manifesting various measurable characteristics' (Grisso and Appelbaum 1993, p. 483).

The debate about whether to predict future danger or violence has almost been laid to rest (Ogloff 2002); however, with the increased research that supports the predictive utility of actuarial and structured professional-risk judgments, one is on firm ethical ground when making predictions – so long as care is taken to ensure that the dimensions discussed later in this chapter are considered.

The second generation of risk assessment culminated in the development of so-called 'actuarial' risk-assessment tools. In contrast to unstructured clinical decision making, so-called actuarial decision making 'involves a formal, algorithmic, objective procedure (e.g. equation) to reach the decision' (Grove and Meehl 1996, pp. 293–294). Unlike unstructured clinical decisions, which are based on decisions made by clinicians drawing upon idiosyncratic information, actuarial tools were developed based upon the statistical relationship between a range of predictive factors and the likelihood of violence. To accomplish this task, researchers reviewed files of prisoners and/or psychiatric patients who had been through the prison system or a psychiatric hospital and coded all of the available data (e.g. demographic factors, criminal and violence history, psychiatric history, substance abuse history). They obtained the criminal records of prisoners or patients following release and identified those who had gone on to re-offend violently. Using statistical analyses, they then identified those factors that, when combined, most reliably related to which people had gone on to re-offend violently. Generally, speaking, research has shown that assessments of risk for violence that are based on actuarial instruments are significantly more accurate than those based on unstructured clinical judgements (Quinsey et al. 1998). Examples of actuarial risk-assessment tools that have been found to be effective will be briefly reviewed later in this chapter.

The third generation of violence risk prediction[4]

A 'third generation' of violence prediction research has been identified (Heilbrun et al. 1999). The third generation has moved beyond the careful identification and measurement of relevant risk factors, which characterized the second-generation work. In the third generation, the assessment or prediction of dangerousness is no longer the task. Rather, clinicians assess an individual's level of risk for violence. The term dangerousness connoted a dichotomous state – either one is or is not 'dangerous'. Using the term risk assessment, essentially resulted in the term 'dangerousness' being divided into the following component parts: (i) risk factors – the variables used to predict aggression, (ii) harm – the amount and type of aggression being predicted, and (iii) risk level – the probability that harm will occur. Thus, risk assessment characterizes the task the way it is currently construed. The clinician carefully considers the variables and factors that contribute to an individual's likelihood of being at risk for violence.

The third generation considers an expanded range of predictor variables relevant to violence. Most important amongst these are dynamic risk variables that are subject to change (i.e. they can change over time and they can be influenced by treatment or other intervention) (Douglas and Skeem 2005). Generally speaking, risk assessment variables can be classed as 'static' (i.e. those that cannot be changed) and 'dynamic' (i.e. those that can change over time). Actuarial

---

[4] It should be noted that there are variations in the characterization of the development of risk assessment over time. Regarding the Risk Need Responsivity model, the third generation focuses primarily on dynamic criminogenic needs (as discussed in the following paragraph) (see Bonta 1996).

risk schemes, such as those developed as part of the second generation of work in the field, were based upon variables that were measured from the past. These historic variables generally could not change over time. For example, if one began being violent as a young person, that fact will not change over time. Dynamic variables, in contrast, are subject to change over time, sometimes rapidly. These variables include such things as state of mind, situational factors, attitudes, plans, support, etc. Taken together, the third-generation approach to violence risk assessment takes into account both static and dynamic variables, thus considering an individual's past, present, and future risk factors that might affect the likelihood of him or her becoming violent.

Finally, the third-generation approach to violence risk assessment moves beyond the mere prediction of risk to the management of risk. Indeed, as Mullen (2000) has noted, the role of the mental health professional in making violence risk predictions is really to identify those risk factors that can be managed, to assist the person with violence control, and to ultimately protect society. As such, the aim of identifying high-risk individuals is to apply risk management strategies so that the predicted violence does not ultimately occur.

The fourth generation of violence risk prediction[5]

As the review of the evolution of violence risk assessment shows, there has been considerable progress since Monahan (1981) first reported that psychologists and psychiatrists were essentially unable to predict risk to any acceptable extent. Current research shows that second- and third-generation risk assessment approaches provide a level of accuracy that now far exceeds chance. Whilst there is still room for improvement, it is not uncommon for research findings to show that when an individual is identified to be a high risk for violent offending, the probability is 80% that the person will be violent in the future (i.e. that 80% of those assessed as high risk will re-offend violently). Recent meta-analyses have confirmed that contemporary approaches to violence risk assessment have moderate to strong predictive validity, particularly for identifying those who are at low risk for violence (Campbell et al. 2009; Fazel et al. 2012; Singh et al. 2011).

Most of the literature on violence risk has focused on the prediction of violent behaviour. However, it has been argued that there are at least two models that may be used in risk assessment: (i) *prediction*, with an emphasis on overall accuracy and employing risk factors that are both static (not changeable through planned intervention) and dynamic (potentially changeable through such intervention), and (ii) *management*, with an emphasis on risk reduction and employing dynamic risk factors. It would seem that the prediction model is the better fit for the evaluation of offenders, subject to post-sentence detention legislation (Doyle and Ogloff 2009) or dangerous offender legislation (see Part XXIV *Criminal Code of Canada*). There is also the question, however, of whether a sexual or violent offender might respond favourably to specialized treatment and lower the long-term risk for re-offending, which is better addressed by the management model.

The conceptual advances in risk assessment are most apparent in four distinguishing considerations: (i) *outcome specification* - what is being assessed, and are threats as well as physical acts of aggression included? The jurisdiction's applicable legal standard and relevant case law are

---

[5] As noted with respect to the third generation above, the characterization for the third and fourth generation varies in the literature. Generally speaking, it is agreed that the fourth generation pertains to the link between risk assessment and case planning/risk management (see Bonta and Andrews 2016).

important. In assessing potential habitual offender status, it seems that re-arrest would be the most likely outcome of interest to the court; (ii) *base rates* – what are the base rates and risk factors for the behaviour being assessed? To some extent, this follows from the first step; a broader definition of aggression, including threats, yields a higher base rate; (iii) *form of communication* – more information is conveyed to the decision-maker if predictive conclusions are communicated in terms such as 'X probability that Y behaviours will occur within Z period of time', and management conclusions in terms such as 'relevant risk factors are A, B, and C; to reduce risk, make interventions A_1, B_1, and C_1,', rather than dichotomous communication such as 'dangerous' or 'not dangerous'; and (iv) *divorce from value judgments* – by specifying what outcome is being assessed, by what factors, and at what risk level or with what intervention implications, the mental health professional may disentangle these issues sufficiently so that there is no need to address non-scientific, value-laden questions such as 'how much risk is enough?' or 'what kind of harm is sufficient?'

The fourth generation of violence risk assessment can be viewed as a further elaboration of the SPJ model that characterized the third generation. Whilst the third generation saw a focus on static and dynamic factors and a move away from a purely predictive approach, recent updates to the range of SPJ tools have seen a greater focus on individualizing the assessment by way of coding not only the presence of risk factors but their relevance to the individual case. Furthermore, risk assessors are now guided through a range of further considerations before making their informed judgments of risk. These include developing risk formulations, identifying the most likely forms of future violence through scenario planning, and considering not only the level of risk for violence, but the risk of serious life-threatening violence and imminent violence. These fourth-generation instruments can be seen as comprehensive assessment protocols that provide not only a predictive component, but a focus on understanding the individual's violence risk and making plans to manage it.

Violence Risk Schemes

A number of risk assessment tools have been developed in the past 20–25 years to facilitate risk assessment (see Borum 1996 for a discussion of the early advances in this regard). There are essentially three types of risk-assessment tools: actuarial measures, SPJ measures, and risk-need tools. In addition, construct rating schemes such as the Hare Psychopathy Checklist-Revised (PCL-R) (Hare 2003) have been found to relate to offending and violence. Finally, as the development of the assessment of risk has progressed, there are now some measures that have been created to predict specific types of behaviour or offending, such as sexual offending, spousal assault, and stalking. However, in this section, we shall highlight the major measures that have been developed for the assessment of risk for general violence, including the VRAG instruments (Harris et al. 1993, 2015; Quinsey 1998), the HCR-20 (Version 3 – Douglas et al. 2013; Version 2 – Webster et al. 1997), and the Level of Service family of instruments (Andrews and Bonta 1995; Andrews et al. 2008).

Actuarial measures

As discussed at the outset of this chapter, so-called 'actuarial risk assessment' measures were developed in the second generation of work on violence risk assessment. The measures were developed to correct the significant errors that were identified with the unstructured clinical judgement approach of the first-generation work. The development of actuarial measures was a desirable advance as a large body of literature in psychology demonstrated the clear superiority of actuarial approaches over clinical judgement in prediction tasks (Dawes et al. 1989; Grove and Meehl 1996; Meehl 1954; Quinsey et al. 1998). These instruments are developed by using statistical analyses to identify and combine risk factors to maximize the ability to accurately predict which people will go on to re-offend or commit violent acts. Such tools typically incorporate clearly-established risk factors for violent and criminal behaviour, including psychopathy, criminal and violence history, and substance abuse, as well as other risk factors that may be related to more specific outcomes.

Dr. Marnie Rice, Dr. Grant Harris, Professor Vernon Quinsey, and others conducted a series of studies on criminal recidivism for mentally-disordered offenders over a long period of time (see Quinsey et al. 1998, and Harris et al. 2015, for reviews). Their work culminated in the development of the VRAG (see Helmus and Quinsey, see Chapter 6). This is a purely *actuarial* instrument that is designed to provide a baseline of risk for violence that is based on past variables and remains static (i.e. unchanging over time). The VRAG was developed on a sample of 618 men admitted to Penetanguishene Mental Health Centre for assessment prior to trial for a violent offence (Quinsey et al. 1998; Rice and Harris 1995; Rice 1997). Approximately half were returned to Pentatanguishene following trial (most having been found Not Guilty by Reason of Insanity); the other half were sentenced to prison following conviction and matched to the first group on age, offence, and offence history. Fifty potential predictor variables that were available in subjects' files were considered. These variables were drawn from the areas of demographic information, criminal history, psychiatric history, and childhood history. A subset of 12 of these items ultimately formed the VRAG.

The researchers used violent recidivism (another offence resulting in re-arrest or rehospitalization) over an average period of seven years to assess outcome. The overall violent recidivism rate was 31%. The correlation between the VRAG score and violent recidivism was 0.44; amongst the strongest relationship that has been found. The VRAG items included: high scores on the PCL-R, having been separated from parents when they were younger than 16 years of age, never having been married, elementary school maladjustment, failure on prior conditional release, property offence history, alcohol abuse history, having a personality disorder, not seriously injuring the victim in the current offence, not having schizophrenia, having a female victim in the index offence, and being young when the current offence was committed.

The researchers also found that the VRAG worked as well for a prison sample as it had for a forensic psychiatric hospital sample. Rice and Harris (1997) extended the original VRAG derivation sample by adding 150 men (increased the sample from 618 to 868) and shortened the outcome period (anyone 'failing' after 3.5 years was considered a success). They found VRAG accuracy levels very comparable for this shorter outcome period. It has since been found to have predictive validity for institutional violence (Hastings et al. 2011), general criminal recidivism (Glover et al. 2002), intimate partner violent recidivism (Hilton et al. 2008), and violent recidivism committed by sexual offenders (Harris et al. 2003).

Recently, the authors of the VRAG have developed a revised version of the VRAG (the VRAG-R; Harris et al. 2015). This was developed on a sample of 1261 offenders, less than half of whom were part of the original VRAG development sample. The authors noted that the despite its demonstrated predictive validity, the original VRAG and its sister instrument the Sex Offender Risk Appraisal Guide (SORAG), were somewhat demanding in terms of both time and training. They also required the use of diagnostic criteria for schizophrenia and personality disorders that were explicitly tied to those in the 1980 edition of the Diagnostic and Statistical Manual (DSM-III; APA 1980). They also required completion of the Hare Psychopathy Checklist (Hare 2003). Accordingly, the authors investigated whether a new tool could be developed that could be used for assessment of violence risk amongst sexual and non-sexual violent offenders. The resulting VRAG-R still comprises 12 items, however, several changes were made. Six of the original items remained: Age at index offence; lived with both parents until age 16, elementary school maladjustment, marital status, non-violent criminal history, and failure on conditional release. The alcohol-abuse item was replaced with a substance-abuse item. The new instrument no longer requires the use of the PCL-R, rather the antisocial facet (facet four) of the PCL-R is utilized. In addition, four new items were added to form the revised version: Violent criminal history, prior admission to corrections, Conduct disorder score, and an item pertaining to sexual offending. The VRAG-R places offenders into one of nine score categories with increasingly higher group recidivism rates. The instrument provides probability estimates at five and 12 years for each of the nine categories.

The VRAG-R has been found to have comparable predictive validity to the original VRAG instrument and is arguably easier to code. Indeed, the original publication by Rice et al. (2013) indicated a very slight non-significant trend towards the VRAG-R (VRAG: r_{pb} = 0.434, AUC = 0.753; VRAG-R: r_{pb} = 0.442, AUC = 0.76). Subsequent analyses by Harris et al. (2015) indicated that the VRAG-R has admirable predictive validity in fixed follow-up periods as high as 20 years (AUC = 0.78). Even at follow-up periods of 36 years, whereby the VRAG-R was at its least accurate, predictive validity was still impressive (AUC = 0.75).

The VRAG, which incorporates the PCL-R, has demonstrated good potential as an actuarial tool for the assessment of future violence risk level amongst those with mental disorder, and prisoners with and without a mental illness. Unfortunately, all of the 12 items on the VRAG, and those on the VRAG-R, are historical in nature (i.e. static items); therefore, the score will not change over time. As an example, the first author assessed an offender in a high-profile case. The person had been in prison for almost 25 years. Over time, whilst in prison, he settled considerably; however, his score on the VRAG only shifted minimally during the 25-year period. Thus, the VRAG is not a useful tool for measuring change over time.

Because of the relative success of the VRAG as a predictor, its authors have argued adamantly that clinicians should abandon clinical judgement in violence risk assessment, in favour of using instruments such as the VRAG exclusively. Their sentiments are captured in the following quotation from the book that describes the VRAG:

> 'In issuing this book, we are calling on clinicians to do risk appraisal in a new way – a way that is different from that in which most of us were trained. What we are advising is not the addition of actuarial methods to existing practice, but rather the complete replacement of existing practice with actuarial methods … Actuarial methods are too good and clinical judgment too poor to risk contaminating the former with the latter.' (Quinsey et al. 1998, p. 171)

Perhaps one can understand the strength of sentiment in the quotation if one considers the general inadequacy of unstructured clinical judgments that were made in the past. However, as we note below, there are limitations with the VRAG and more contemporary approaches, employing so-called SPJs, static and dynamic risk factors, have been found to predict violence as well as the VRAG – and better under some circumstances.

Despite its success as a predictive instrument, the VRAG has a number of limitations that must be considered. As already noted, it cannot be used as a measure of change and the instrument may not be useful for assessing those who have been incarcerated for long periods. Also, the measure consists of a very limited range of predictive items. For example, alcohol abuse was a predictor in the original VRAG whilst substance abuse was not. This was not due to any theoretical reason, but rather because of the nature of the sample. Recall that the validation sample was based on people who were incarcerated between 1965 and 1980. Think of the changes in alcohol use and drug use over that time. In fact, the authors of the VRAG took this into consideration when they developed the VRAG-R, expanding the item to reflect substance abuse rather than simply alcohol problems. Another very serious limitation with actuarial models, such as the VRAG and the VRAG-R, is that they exclude any and all variables outside of those that comprise the instrument. As Melton et al. (2017) wrote, 'once the specific predictors in an actuarial technique are set, all other information is irrelevant' (p. 284). Thus, the actuarial devices do not permit the user to consider factors outside of those in the instrument. Additional risk factors can be crucial in particular cases. For example, the second author once assessed a man who was actuarially deemed to pose a moderate risk for violence. However, during the assessment, he described detailed plans to kill his previous victim upon release from hospital. Such plans do not constitute a risk factor on the VRAG, or indeed any other actuarial risk-assessment instrument, as they do not happen often enough to be considered in tools that are based on lengthy follow-up periods. But, in this case, the plans were clearly important when assessing the risk that this offender posed, particularly to his previous victim. Finally, because the instrument provides very specific scores that relate to the probability of offending violently, the instrument must be validated in any population and sample in which it is used. To date, it has not been validated for use in Australia with any population. Whilst this instrument may have some utility for providing a long-term prediction of violence risk, it is not useful for the clinician involved in treatment or management as it does not identify the risk factors that can be addressed in order to assist the patient in reducing their overall level of risk for violence. Also, it has very limited use for post-sentence detention legislation or, for that matter, release decision-making because of the inability of the measure to assess change in risk over time.

SPJ measures

SPJ is a model of decision-making that, by the traditional definition, is one form of clinical prediction (Douglas et al. 2003). However, the nature and quality of the clinical judgments in contemporary SPJ risk assessment measures differ from traditional clinical judgments in that they are defined as *structured*. Recall that the first generation of risk assessment, and traditional clinical decision making, have been criticized for the impressionistic, unstructured, and idiosyncratic nature of the decisions. By contrast, the SPJ model requires evidence-based decision making by providing guidelines and structure that is intended to capture some of the features related to actuarial decision making that promote consistency, whilst at the same time permitting professional flexibility to consider unique characteristics of individual cases. Like all clinical judgement, there are no fixed, explicit, or algorithmic rules for combining items to come to a clinical decision. However, there is structure imposed on the clinical decision-making process in several important ways. Firstly, the measures specify a list of risk factors that have been found in the research to relate to violence. Secondly, the SPJ measures carefully define and operationalize the risk factors and provide scoring guidelines for the factors. Finally, the measures provide some, albeit admittedly minimal, guidance for the making of final clinical decisions of low, moderate, and high risk (see Garrington and Boer, see Chapter 7).

Contemporary SPJ risk-assessment guidelines also differ in their conception of <u>prediction</u> compared to actuarial instruments. Whilst actuarial instruments, such as the VRAG-R, provide probability measures of the likelihood that one will be violent in the future, the SPJ model reflects recent conceptual developments within the field of violence risk assessment that stress the importance of attending to other features of risk, such as imminence, duration, severity, targets, nature, and management (Hart 1998; Heilbrun et al. 1999; Mulvey and Lidz 1995). When likelihood of violence is the important consideration, the two models differ in terms of the portrayed acuity of the statement. Under the SPJ model, statements about the future are made (i) in relative terms based on comparison to others in similar circumstances, (ii) without affixing numerical probability levels, (iii) in general descriptive, action-facilitating categories (low, moderate, high risk) that are (iv) tied to and defined in part by the degree of anticipated interventions deemed necessary in order to prevent violence, and which are (v) based on the presence of violence risk factors in a present case (whether few or many). In most cases, it is presumed a greater number of risk factors will correspond to a higher likelihood of violence. In some cases, however, only a few risk factors, or even a single one, could require intervention to prevent violence. SPJ measures also tend not to be derived from, and hence tied to, single samples; rather, the risk factors are chosen rationally from thorough consideration of the literature broadly relating to the factors that have been found to relate to violence.

To bridge the gap between research on violence risk assessment and clinical practice, Webster et al. (1997) developed the historical, clinical risk management-20 (HCR-20). The 'HCR-20' was named for the measures 10 historical, 5 clinical, and 5 risk variables. The HCR-20 represents a blend of historical/static variables (i.e. those that are not subject to change over time) and dynamic variables (i.e. those that do change over time). The H-scale focuses on past, mainly static risk factors, the C-scale on current aspects of mental status and attitudes, and the R-scale on future situational features that relate to the likelihood that an individual's level of risk can be managed. A revision of the HCR-20, known as the HCR-20^{V3} was published in 2013 (Douglas et al. 2013). Whilst the risk factors themselves saw only minor changes, the degree of structure and guidance offered to clinicians using the instrument increased considerably. Indeed, the HCR-20^{V3} is the apotheosis of the SPJ approach to risk assessment and includes all of the advances that constitute the fourth generation of this field that were described above. Assessing clinicians are guided through a range of steps including coding the presence of risk factors, coding the individual relevance of the risk factors, developing risk formulations, and scenario planning for future violence. The greatest differences between actuarial instruments and previous iterations of SPJ tools was essentially the fact that the latter included dynamic factors and no algorithm for placing those being assessed into risk categories. With the HCR-20^{V3} and some of the other modern SPJ tools, the differences are far more pronounced. As noted above, the HCR-20^{V3} is a comprehensive set of structured professional guidelines that can assist in not only risk assessment, but also understanding the offender's violence and developing management plans to contain the assessed level of risk.

There is accumulating empirical evidence that the HCR-20, be it the second or third version, is a valid measure of violence risk for use with both males and females and in both inpatient and outpatient settings. The HCR-20 has been validated with samples of civil psychiatric, forensic psychiatric, general-population inmates, mentally-disordered inmates, and young offenders, conducted in Canada, Sweden, the Netherlands, Scotland, Germany, England and the US. These studies have invariably found that HCR-20 scores, and structured clinical risk ratings made by clinicians after completing the HCR-20 guidelines, have a statistically significant relationship with subsequent violence that is comparable to, if not slightly higher at times, to actuarial instruments (see Borum 1996; Dolan and Doyle 2000; Douglas et al. 1999, 2002; Strub et al. 2014). Importantly, and in stark contrast to the views of the proponents of actuarial risk assessment, the predictive validity of structured clinical ratings of risk made after completing the HCR-20 guidelines very often adds incremental predictive validity to any score that can be obtained by summing the risk factors in a pseudo-actuarial fashion (e.g. Douglas et al. 2003; Strub et al. 2014).

Criminogenic risk and need tools

Andrews (1983) initially developed the Level of Supervision Inventory (LSI) in order to assess risk for general criminal offending, identify criminogenic needs (i.e. dynamic risk factors), and inform treatment, supervision, and case management. This was followed by the Level of Service Inventory-Revised (LSI-R; Andrews and Bonta 1995), and the latest versions, the Level of Service/Case Management Inventory (LS/CMI; Andrews et al. 2004) and the Level of Service/Risk, Need, Responsivity (LS/RNR; Andrews et al. 2008). This family of tools uses both static and dynamic factors as the basis for offender assessment (Ogloff and Davis 2004). There is also a version of the LSI for young offenders (Youth Level of Service/Case Management Inventory [YLSI/CMI]; Hoge et al. 2002) that is based on the same theoretical psychology of criminal conduct (PCC) and the risk-needs-responsivity approach to offender rehabilitation.

Section one of the LS/CMI and the LS/RNR consists of 43 items grouped into eight domains that mirror the 'big eight' categories of risk factors identified in the literature (with the number of items in parentheses): Criminal History (8); Education/Employment (9); Family/Marital (4); Leisure/Recreation (2); Companions (4); Alcohol/Drug Problems (8); Pro-criminal Attitude/Orientation (4); and Antisocial Pattern (4) (Andrews et al. 2004, 2008). Unlike the measures that have been discussed thus far, the Level of Service family of instruments were designed to be administered not just by mental health professionals, but by a range of clinical and justice personnel, including probation officers and youth justice workers.

Many of the items across the sub-component areas assess criminogenic needs (i.e. dynamic risk factors). As well as assisting in the identification of risk, the *dynamic* risk indicators are particularly important for targeting the areas where offenders require intervention. By focussing resources on changing the criminogenic needs ('treatment targets'), the chances of an offender succeeding in the community can be increased, and the probability of offending decreased.

The Level of Service instruments have been widely used and researched in many jurisdictions (e.g. Canada, the US, Australia, England, Singapore, and parts of Europe). They have been found to be a strong predictor of recidivism for several offender populations (e.g. male and female offenders, mentally-ill offenders, and Canadian Aboriginal offenders) across institutional and community corrections settings. In a recent meta-analytical review of 30 years of research on the Level of Service instruments, they were found to have significant relationships with general re-offending, and to a slightly lesser extent, violent re-offending (Olver et al. 2014). Interestingly, and perhaps not unexpectedly, the most recent versions of the Level of Service tools (the LS/CMI and LS/RNR) both provide considerably more structure and guidance for users to apply the results directly to treatment and case management efforts.

Whilst this is performed in a somewhat different manner to the SPJ approach exemplified in the HCR-20^{V3}, there are notable parallels in the way that both instruments promote the application of risk assessment to case management.

Summary and Conclusion

As this chapter shows, early research showed that psychiatrists and psychologists were essentially unable to predict risk for violence beyond chance; however, developments, and advances dating from the early 1980s have shown that the accuracy of violence risk assessments has grown dramatically. Incidentally, there are no data available suggesting that psychiatrists have an ability to make more accurate violence risk predictions than psychologists. Regardless of whether the person called upon to make an appraisal of an individual's level of risk for violence is a psychologist or psychiatrist, the professional must have knowledge of the area of violence risk assessment (including sexual offending risk, where relevant), expertise in individual assessment that includes training and experience in the administration and interpretation of standardized tests, and expertise in the assessment and diagnosis of mental disorder (major mental illness and personality disorder).

There have been many conceptual and scientific developments in the field of violence risk assessment in the past two decades. Once thought of as 'predicting dangerousness', and requiring clinicians to make dichotomous predictions of 'dangerous behaviour' at some future point, contemporary risk assessment is more likely to recognize that prevention and management of risk for violence are primary. Rather than being seen as a stable characteristic, the move from predicting 'dangerousness' to assessing risk for violence has seen the emergence of risk approaches and instruments that incorporate both static and dynamic variables.

The presence of psychopathy, substance abuse or dependence, and major mental illness have been reliably found to be amongst the most robust individual factors that have been associated with a risk for violence across many different populations of people. The fact that psychopathy has been found to be a robust predictor of risk for violence is not surprising given the fact that people who score high on the PCL-R must have deficits in a number of areas, including some combination of interpersonal, affective (i.e. expressed emotion), lifestyle, and criminal variables.

Whilst each of the risk factors alone (i.e. psychopathy, substance abuse, or major mental illness) can increase an individual's level of risk for violence, when they are found together, the individual's risk for violence rises again. Drawing on advances in violence risk assessment, statements about future risk are more profitably made as probability statements based upon the presence of risk factors and the likelihood that the risk factors will be managed in the future. Further, in recent years, a number of risk assessment instruments have been developed (see this edition).

In response to the perceived low reliability and validity of clinical predictions, some of these – such as the VRAG and the VRAG-R – have relied on actuarial methods. In response to possible problems associated with actuarial procedures (e.g. the exclusion of relevant but infrequently occurring risk factors, difficulties with generalization, inability to assess change over time, and inability optimally to inform management and prevention), the SPJ model of risk assessment has been proposed and developed. The SPJ model structures the risk factors that are considered by an assessor in a given risk assessment, as well as how they are considered. However, it provides relatively little guidance for actually making decisions about risk level, requiring the clinician to incorporate all of the relevant risk variables following a careful consideration of all of the available information about the individual being assessed (e.g. comprehensive clinical interviews, careful file reviews, and consideration of collateral source information).

The HCR-20[V3] is the primary example of the SPJ model of violence risk assessment. Numerous studies support the reliability and validity of the HCR-20 items and scales. As with the SPJ models, the risk-need tools, such as the Level of Service instruments, have also been found to be useful for assessing risk of re-offending. Generally speaking, though, the Level of Service tools are not as robust in their relationship with violent re-offending per se.

Providing that properly trained and qualified clinicians – usually psychologists and psychiatrists – rely upon up-to-date violence risk tools and research, there can be some degree of confidence in their conclusions. However, if the clinician is reliant exclusively upon an unstructured clinical approach, there is no guarantee that the violence risk assessment will have any modicum of accuracy. Similarly, relying upon rigid actuarial measures that have not been validated in the population from which the offender being assessed is drawn, raises very serious concerns regarding the extent to which the measure is valid for use.

In our view, given the liberty and public safety matters that are at stake in situations where psychiatrists and/or psychologists are called upon to make violence risk predictions, the clinician must be particularly well trained and he or she must rely upon a validated risk assessment protocol.

In all instances where clinicians agree to undertake assessments of risk for the courts or other decision makers, they are obliged to ensure that their evaluations are conducted in accordance with prevailing standards in the profession (Ogloff 2002). Care must be taken to refrain from conducting risk assessments on populations that have not been properly evaluated, particularly where cultural differences might dictate differences for risk factors and on risk assessment instruments.

Taken together, perhaps we can summarize, by saying that when conducted in accordance with the growing body of literature and risk assessment guidelines, clinicians, and legal decision-makers can have some degree of confidence that the decisions that are made are based on a firm and growing scientific base. Whilst still far from perfect, we have moved very far forward in the past 35 years. Nonetheless, as we have emphasized, the possible errors associated with violence risk prediction should give all clinicians, policy makers, and release decision makers alike pause for serious concern and thought (Doyle and Ogloff 2009).

References

American Psychiatric Association (1980). *Diagnostic and Statistical Manual of Mental Disorders*, 3e. Washington, DC: American Psychiatric Association.

Andrews, D.A. (1983). The assessment of outcome in correctional samples. In: *The Measurement of Psychotherapy Outcome in Research and Evaluation* (eds. M. Lambert, E. Christensen and S. DeJulio), 160–201. NY: Wiley.

Andrews, D.A. and Bonta, J. (1995). *LSI–R: The Level of Service Inventory – Revised*. Toronto: Multi-Health Systems.

Andrews, D.A., Bonta, J., and Wormith, J.S. (2004). *The Level of Service/Case Management Inventory*. Toronto: Multi-Health Systems.

Andrews, D.A., Bonta, J., and Wormith, J.S. (2006). The recent past and near future of risk and/or need assessment. *Crime & Delinquency* 52: 7–27.

Andrews, D.A., Bonta, J., and Wormith, J.S. (2008). *The Level of Service/Risk-Need-Responsivity (LS/RNR)*. Toronto, Canada: Multi-Health Systems.

Barefoot v. Estelle, 463 US 880, (1983)

Belfrage, H. (1998). Implementing the HCR-20 scheme for risk assessment in a forensic psychiatric hospital: integrating research and clinical practice. *Journal of Forensic Psychiatry* 9: 328–338.

Bonta, J. (1996). Risk-needs assessment and treatment. In: *Choosing Correctional Options that Work: Defining the Demand and Evaluating the Supply* (ed. A.T. Harland), 18–32. Thousand Oaks, CA: Sage.

Bonta, J. and Andrews, D.A. (2016). *The Psychology of Criminal Conduct*, 5e. New York: Routledge.

Borum, R. (1996). Improving the clinical practice of violence risk assessment: technology, guidelines, and training. *American Psychologist* 51: 945–957.

Brooks, A.D. (1974). *Law, Psychiatry and the Mental Health System*. Boston, MA: Little Brown.

Campbell, M.A., French, S., and Gendreau, P. (2009). The prediction of violence in adult offenders: a meta-analytic comparison of instruments and methods of assessment. *Criminal Justice and Behavior* 36: 567–590.

Cocozza, J. and Steadman, H. (1976). The failure of psychiatric predictions of dangerousness: clear and convincing evidence. *Rutgers Law Review* 29: 1084–1101.

Dawes, R., Faust, D., and Meehl, P. (1989). Clinical versus actuarial judgment. *Science* 243: 1668–1674.

Dolan, M. and Doyle, M. (2000). Violence risk prediction: clinical and actuarial measures and the role of the psychopathy checklist. *British Journal of Psychiatry* 177: 303–311.

Douglas, K.S., Cox, D.N., and Webster, C.D. (1999). Violence risk assessment: science and practice. *Legal and Criminological Psychology* 4: 149–184.

Douglas, K.S., Hart, S.D., Webster, C.D., and Belfrage, H. (2013). *HCR-20v3: Assessing Risk for Violence: User Guide*. Burnaby, British Columbia, Canada: Mental Health, Law and Policy Institute, Simon Fraser University.

Douglas, K.S., Ogloff, J.R.P., and Hart, S.D. (2003). Evaluation of a model of violence risk assessment among forensic psychiatric patients. *Psychiatric Services* 54: 1372–1379.

Douglas, K.S. and Skeem, J.L. (2005). Violence risk assessment: getting specific about being dynamic. *Psychology, Public Policy, and Law* 11: 347–383.

Douglas, K.S., Webster, C.D., Hart, S.D. et al. (eds.) (2002). *HCR-20 Violence Risk Management Companion Guide*. Burnaby, BC: Mental Health Law and Policy Institute, Simon Fraser University.

Doyle, D.J. and Ogloff, J.R.P. (2009). Calling the tune without music: a psycho-legal analysis of Australia's post-sentence legislation. *Australian and New Zealand Journal of Criminology* 42: 179–203.

Ewing, C.P. (1991). Preventive detention and execution: the constitutionality of punishing future crimes. *Law and Human Behavior* 15: 139–163.

Fazel, S., Singh, J.P., Doll, H., and Grann, M. (2012). Use of risk assessment instruments to predict violence and antisocial behaviour in 73 samples involving 24,827 people: systematic review and meta-analysis. *British Medical Journal* 345: e4692.

Felson, R.B. and Steadman, H. (1983). Situational factors in disputes leading to criminal violence. *Criminology* 21: 59–74.

Glover, A.J., Nicholson, D.E., Hemmati, T. et al. (2002). A comparison of predictors of general and violent recidivism among high-risk federal offenders. *Criminal Justice and Behavior* 29: 235–249.

Grisso, T. and Appelbaum, P.S. (1992). Is it unethical to offer predictions of future violence? *Law and Human Behavior* 16: 621–633.

Grisso, T. and Appelbaum, P.S. (1993). Structuring the debate about ethical predictions of future violence. *Law and Human Behavior* 17: 482–485.

Grove, W.M. and Meehl, P.E. (1996). Comparative efficiency of informal (subjective, impressionistic) and formal (mechanical, algorithmic) prediction procedures: the clinical-statistical controversy. *Psychology, Public Policy, and Law* 2: 293–323; pp. 293–294.

Hare, R.D. (2003). *Manual for the Hare Psychopathy Checklist*, 2e, Revised. Toronto, Ontario, Canada: Multi-Health Systems.

Hare, R.D. and McPherson, L.M. (1984). Violent and aggressive behavior by criminal psychopaths. *International Journal of Law and Psychiatry* 7: 35–50.

Harris, G.T., Rice, M.E., and Quinsey, V.L. (1993). Violent recidivism of mentally disordered offenders: the development of a statistical prediction instrument. *Criminal Justice and Behavior* 20: 315–335.

Harris, G.T., Rice, M.E., Quinsey, V.L., and Cormier, C.A. (2015). *Violent Offenders: Appraising and Managing Risk*. Washington, DC, US: American Psychological Association.

Harris, G.T., Rice, M.E., Quinsey, V.L. et al. (2003). A multisite comparison of actuarial risk instruments for sex offenders. *Psychological Assessment* 15: 413–426.

Hart, S.D. (1998). The role of psychopathy in assessing risk for violence: conceptual and methodological issues. *Legal and Criminological Psychology* 3: 121–137.

Hastings, M.E., Krishnan, S., Tangney, J.P., and Stuewig, J. (2011). Predictive and incremental validity of the violence risk appraisal guide scores with male and female jail inmates. *Psychological Assessment* 23: 174–186.

Heilbrun, K., Ogloff, J.R.P., and Picarello, K. (1999). Dangerous offender statutes in the United States and Canada: implications for risk assessment. *International Journal of Psychiatry and Law* 22: 393–415.

Hilton, N.Z., Harris, G.T., Rice, M.E. et al. (2008). An indepth actuarial assessment for wife assault recidivism: the domestic violence risk appraisal guide. *Law and Human Behavior* 32: 150–163.

Hoge, R., Andrews, D.A., and Leshied, A. (2002). *The Youth Level of Service/Case Management Inventory*. Toronto, ON: Multi-Health Systems.

Janus, E.S. and Meehl, P.E. (1997). Assessing the legal standard for predictions of dangerousness in sex offender commitment proceedings. *Psychology, Public Policy, and Law* 3: 33–64.

Karson, C. and Bigelow, L.B. (1987). Violent behavior in schizophrenic patients. *Journal of Nervous and Mental Disease* 175: 161–164.

Klassen, D. and O'Connor, W.A. (1988a). Predicting violence in schizophrenic and non-schizophrenic patients: a prospective study. *Journal of Community Psychology* 16: 217–227.

Klassen, D. and O'Connor, W.A. (1988b). A prospective study of predictors of violence in adult male mental health admissions. *Law and Human Behavior* 12: 143–158.

Klassen, D. and O'Connor, W.A. (1988c). Crime, inpatient admissions, and violence among male mental patients. *International Journal of Law and Psychiatry* 11: 305–312.

Klassen, D. and O'Connor, W.A. (1989). Assessing the risk of violence in released mental patients: a cross-validation study. *Psychological Assessment: A Journal of Consulting and Clinical Psychology* 1: 75–81.

Krauss, D.A. and Sales, B.D. (2001). The effects of clinical and scientific expert testimony on juror decision making in capital sentencing. *Psychology, Public Policy, and Law* 7: 267–310.

Lowenstein, M., Binder, R.L., and McNiel, D.E. (1990). The relationship between admission symptoms and hospital assaults. *Hospital and Community Psychiatry* 41: 311–313.

McNiel, D.E. and Binder, R.L. (1986). Violence, civil commitment, and hospitalization. *Journal of Nervous and Mental Disease* 174: 107–111.

Meehl, P. (1954). *Clinical Versus Statistical Prediction: A Theoretical Analysis and a Review of the Evidence*. Minneapolis: University of Minnesota Press.

Melton, G.B., Petrila, J., Poythress, N., and Slobogin, C. (2017). *Psychological Evaluations for the Courts: A Handbook for Mental Health Professionals and Lawyers*, 4e. New York: Guilford.

Monahan, J. (1981). *Predicting Violent Behavior: An Assessment of Clinical Techniques*. Beverly Hills, CA: Sage Publications.

Monahan, J. (1984). The prediction of violent behavior: toward a second generation of theory and policy. *American Journal of Psychiatry* 141: 10–15.

Monahan, J. (1996). Violence prediction: the last 20 and the next 20 years. *Criminal Justice and Behavior* 23: 107–120.

Mullen, P.E. (2000). Dangerousness, risk, and the prediction of probability. In: *New Oxford Textbook of Psychiatry*, vol. 2 (eds. M.G. Gelder, J.J. Lopez-Ibor and N. Andreasen), 2066–2078. Oxford: Oxford University Press.

Mullen, P.E. and Ogloff, J.R.P. (2009). Assessing and managing the risk of violence towards others. In: *New Oxford Textbook of Psychiatry*, 2e (eds. M. Gelder, J. Lopez-Ibor, N. Andreasen and J. Geddes). Oxford University Press.

Mulvey, E.P. and Lidz, C.W. (1995). Conditional prediction: a model for research on dangerousness to others in a new era. *International Journal of Law and Psychiatry* 18: 129–143.

Ogloff, J.R.P. (2002). Professional, legal, and ethical issues in violence risk management. In: *HCR-20 Violence Risk Management Companion Guide* (eds. K.S. Douglas, C.D. Webster, S.D. Hart, et al.), 59–71. Vancouver, BC: Mental Health Law and Policy Institute, Simon Fraser University.

Ogloff, J.R.P. and Davis, M.R. (2004). Advances in offender assessment and rehabilitation: contributions of the risk-needs-responsivity approach. *Psychology, Crime and Law* 10: 229–242.

Olver, M.E., Stockdale, K.C., and Wormith, J.S. (2014). Thirty years of research on the level of service scales: a meta-analytic examination of predictive accuracy and sources of variability. *Psychological Assessment* 26: 156–168.

Otto, R. (1992). The prediction of dangerous behavior: a review and analysis of "second generation" research. *Forensic Reports* 5: 103–134.

Otto, R.K. (2000). Assessing and managing violence risk in outpatient settings. *Journal of Clinical Psychology* 56: 1239–1262.

Quinsey, V.L., Rice, M.E., Harris, G.T., and Cormier, C.A. (1998). *Violent Offenders: Appraising and Managing Risk*. Washington, DC: American Psychological Association.

Rice, M. (1997). Violent offender research and implications for the criminal justice system. *American Psychologist* 52: 414–423.

Rice, M. and Harris, G. (1995). Violent recidivism: assessing predictive validity. *Journal of Consulting and Clinical Psychology* 63: 737–748.

Rice, M.E. and Harris, G.T. (1997). Cross-validation and extension of the violence risk appraisal guide for child molesters and rapists. *Law and Human Behavior* 21: 231–241.

Rice, M.E., Harris, G.T., and Lang, C. (2013). Validation of and revision to the VRAG and SORAG: the violence risk appraisal guide – revised (VRAG-R). *Psychological Assessment* 25: 951–966.

Shah, S.A. (1978). Dangerousness and mental illness: some conceptual, prediction, and policy dilemmas. In: *Dangerous Behavior: A Problem in Law and Mental Health* (ed. C. Frederick), 153–191. Washington, DC: Government Printing Office.

Singh, J.P., Grann, M., and Fazel, S. (2011). A comparative study of violence risk assessment tools: a systematic review and metaregression analysis of 68 studies involving 25,980 participants. *Clinical Psychology Review* 31: 499–513.

Strub, D.S., Douglas, K.S., and Nicholls, T.L. (2014). The validity of version 3 of the HCR-20 violence risk assessment scheme amongst offenders and civil psychiatric patients. *International Journal of Forensic Mental Health* 13: 148–159.

Tardiff, K. and Koenigsberg, H.W. (1985). Assaultive behavior among psychiatric outpatients. *American Journal of Psychiatry* 142: 960–963.

Webster, C.D., Douglas, K.S., Eaves, D., and Hart, S.D. (1997). *HCR-20: Assessing Risk for Violence (Version 2)*. Burnaby, BC: Mental Health, Law, and Policy Institute, Simon Fraser University.

5

Violence Risk Formation
The Move Towards Collaboratively Produced, Strengths-Based Safety Planning

Lawrence Jones
Nottinghamshire Healthcare NHS Trust, Nottingham, UK

Introduction

The recent interest and increased attention to the area of formulation has highlighted a number of issues that need to be addressed for practitioners working with risk. Cooke and Michie (2013) describe four 'eras' of risk assessment: unstructured clinical judgement, actuarial clinical judgement, risk management and, more recently, the era of risk formulation. Recognizing that both unstructured clinical judgement and the misuse of the insurance-based notion, of actuarial risk assessment were flawed practitioners turned to the use of case formulation as a clinically justifiable processes for assessing risk. Case formulations are parsimonious accounts explaining why an individual is functioning in the way they are. They can focus on a range of behaviours or individual problems or on a specific behaviour/problem (e.g. violence). The accounts involve linking theory to the individual case in a manner that suggests ways of intervening to bring about change. As such, a formulation is an individualized causal model. Ideally, they are developed collaboratively with the individual that they refer to.

Validation criteria for risk formulations are identified by Cooke and Michie as the 'next challenge'. There is no clear framework yet for establishing the validity or reliability of case formulations. Indeed, there are a range of different approaches to formulation that each have a range of explicit or implicit criteria for establishing validity. There are also a range of theoretical explanations and models for violent offending in the literature. Each of these have their own approach to formulation and to testing or establishing the validity of the formulation (e.g. Sturmey and McMurran 2011).

As well as informing risk assessment, formulations are used in designing treatment interventions. Historically, as part of a move towards standardized and manualized interventions,

The Wiley Handbook of What Works in Violence Risk Management: Theory, Research and Practice,
First Edition. Edited by J. Stephen Wormith, Leam A. Craig, and Todd E. Hogue.
© 2020 John Wiley & Sons Ltd. Published 2020 by John Wiley & Sons Ltd.

formulation was neglected in some areas of forensic practice in favour of 'one size fits all' group-based interventions.

Recent failure to replicate outcomes in interventions accredited because of their evidence base, have highlighted the importance of case formulation as a way of tailoring the intervention to the individual case. Indeed, some accredited interventions have evaluations which suggest possible iatrogenic outcomes. It has thus become imperative that individualized interventions are devised and that these are tested for their reliability and validity on a case-by-case basis.

In this chapter, one approach to formulation will be outlined; this approach will adhere to the following set of practitioner values deriving from the need for clinical accountability:

(A)   That practice should follow a scientist practitioner framework (Hayes et al. 1999; Shapiro 2002). This involves applying scientific methodology and application of the current evidence base for 'what works' to the individual case.

(B)   That formulations should be logically coherent causal models of the domain being formulated.

(C)   That formulations should be testable and that the practice of formulation should involve seeking evidence to establish the validity and reliability or otherwise of the formulation.

(D)   That formulations should be accessible, co-produced (done with not done to or for the individual) and ethically and culturally attuned to those who they are being used with.

(E)   That formulations should be focused on strengths as well as deficits.

This chapter explores issues, skills and competencies that practitioners need to take into account when they undertake a formulation of violence risk.

The Relationship Between Formulations and Actuarial Measures of Risk

Actuarial measures of risk are based on – usually predictive – correlational analysis. As such, they do not offer a clear causal model to explain why an individual offended in the way they did. Ward (e.g. Ward and Fortune 2016) has argued that dynamic risk needs to be conceptualized clearly as being about causal processes deriving from theory. In case formulation, these causal processes need to be placed in a developmental narrative, itself an account of multiple interacting causal processes.

Because a particular factor correlates with reconviction does not mean that it is a causal factor. In order to establish the reasons for the correlation the following questions need to be asked:

- Is the observed factor a marker for some other factor or process that is more directly causally linked with the outcome?
- Does the factor mediate the link between some other factor and offending?
- Does the factor moderate the link between some other factor and offending?

For the purposes of formulation, what is needed is a clear **risk mechanism** linking a factor causally with the behaviour being explained. Risk factors on their own are of little use without translating them into contextualized causal processes or risk mechanisms. To illustrate this, the Andrews and Bonta (2003) 'central eight' risk/need factors associated with offending are listed below (see Table 5.1) and each one is linked with examples of risk mechanisms linked with key developmental experiences.

Table 5.1 Examples of developmentally informed risk mechanisms linked with the risk needs responsivity model.

Criminogenic Needs Identified in the RNR model (Andrews and Bonta 2003)	Example of developmental antecedents and Risk Mechanisms associated with each need	Possible Interventions
Procriminal attitudes (thoughts, values, and sentiments supportive of criminal behaviour)	Early violent or sexual abuse linked with longstanding preoccupation with revenge and hypervigilance looking for possible violence in current context. Beliefs in the validity of violence and abusive behaviour as a means of meeting revenge needs. Beliefs about violence being a way of preventing further victimization. Belief about the legitimacy and efficacy of violence deriving from social learning in abusive family contexts. These beliefs impacting on choices about how to manage ambiguous situations and meeting needs.	Working on trauma and trauma reactions using staged approach (e.g. Courtois and Ford 2009). Eye Movement Desensitization and Reprocessing (EMDR) for intrusive thoughts and memories. Developing strategies for feeling safe that do not involve violence. Ensuring that perpetrators are notified to social services and police so that if possible prosecutions can be proceeded with (to prevent further victims and to offer a sense of justice). Exploration of links between victim experiences and those of the victims they have made. Strategy of choices (e.g. Bush 1995)
Antisocial personality (low self-control, hostility, adventurous pleasure seeking, disregard for others, callousness)	Trauma impacting on: Futurelessness (Kerig and Becker 2010) linked with short term perspective, Emotional numbing (Kerig and Becker 2010) linked with lack of sensitivity to i) emotions linked with consequential thinking and behaviour (e.g. anticipatory anxiety or compassion for self in the future) ii) linked with compassion for others iii) a preoccupation with generating sensations because of experience of ongoing numbness	Trauma work using EMDR (Shapiro) Schema Therapy (e.g. Young et al. 2006) or CAT therapy (e.g. Pollock and Stowell-Smith 2006). Compassion focused therapy (e.g. Gilbert and Procter 2006)
Procriminal associates	Not trusting adults or people who have not got a similar background to the self – i.e. due to history of violent abuse, institutional trauma, betrayal trauma (Chakhssi et al. 2014).	Working on building relationships with a non-offender peer group. Building sense of belonging through work and education.

(Continued)

Table 5.1   (*Cont'd*)

Criminogenic Needs Identified in the RNR model (Andrews and Bonta 2003)	Example of developmental antecedents and Risk Mechanisms associated with each need	Possible Interventions
Social achievement (education, employment)	Capacity to think and think about others' minds requires attachment experience to develop (e.g. Fonagy and Target 1997). Truancy, emotional dysregulation. Child abuse alters the normal development of the brain and neural pathways (e.g. Teicher et al. 2002, 2003), this then increases the risk of cognitive impairments later in life (Lupien et al. 2009).	Provision of opportunities to achieve in a 'scaffolded' supportive context. Using relational interventions to foster capacity to mentalize. Using thinking skills training and practise.
Family/marital (marital instability, poor parenting skills, criminality)	Developmental attachment traumas, e.g. loss, rejection, family breakdown leading to problematic attachment styles. These then lead to a cascade of poor relationships in later life. Offending taking place in the context of serial attachment ruptures and disturbances which act as a significant trigger for 'futurelessness' and 'giving up' on values linked with engaging woth the 'social contract'.	Intervention addressing attachment style using, e.g. limited reparenting (Young et al. 2006) or long term attachment based interventions. Psycho-education about attachment. Relationship rupture repair interventions (e.g. Safran et al. 2011)
Substance abuse	Child maltreatment has been strongly related to substance misuse disorders in a range of populations (e.g. Dube et al. 2006; Ducci et al. 2009; Enoch 2011). Substance misuse as a strategy for managing trauma related emotional dysregulation. Substance misuse as a response to neglect and consequent exposure to substance misuse valorizing peer group	Intervening to address trauma difficulties so that 'self-medication' is not required (e.g. EMDR). Work on finding healthy peer groups and healthy social activity. Work on emotional reaction to experiences of social exclusion.

Table 5.1 (*Cont'd*)

Criminogenic Needs Identified in the RNR model (Andrews and Bonta 2003)	Example of developmental antecedents and Risk Mechanisms associated with each need	Possible Interventions
Leisure/recreation (lack of prosocial pursuits)	Neglect in developmental context resulting in significantly limited repertoire of pleasure, relaxation and enjoyment skills.	Provision of structured opportunities to engage in range of leisure and recreational pursuits in a 'scaffolded' and supportive manner. Happiness skills such as learning about how to enjoy things and mindful savouring of recreation

Top Down and Bottom Up Approaches to Looking at the Data

In the process of generating a formulation, the practitioner can use two kinds of model building: top down or bottom up, both of which are essentially qualitative methods.

The top-down method entails examining the available information about the individual with a set of preconceived constructs thought to be relevant to the issue at hand. So, for instance, one might look at an individual's interview and file information and examine the extent to which there is evidence for each of the Risk domains in the Risk-Need-Responsibility (RNR) model, or each of the 'goods' in the good lives model. In this case, the literature guides the potential selection of causal factors in the individual case. In this way, there are a number of sources for practitioners to identify possible areas to explore in generating hypotheses about risk mechanisms. Daffern and Howells (2009) developed a typology of functions of aggressive acts. This kind of typology can be useful in prompting the clinician to explore different functional possibilities. Theoretical models of violence such as the General Aggression Model (e.g. Gilbert and Daffern 2011) can suggest domains for the practitioner to explore with respect to the individual case. Such a theoretical model can only work as a guide to what kinds of factors to explore. Without knowledge of different kinds of variables relevant to violence, derived from the literature, it is possible that the practitioner might miss a significant domain. To use the literature unthinkingly – using 'one size fits all' for example – can result in missing out on the unique developmental history and constellation of contributory factors of the specific case.

Essentially, in applying these models to the individual, the practitioner is engaged in a form of content analysis. The data are scanned with a view to seeing if it 'fits' with a set of preconceived constructs.

Another method is to attempt to 'bracket' – or try to hold back on – any preconceptions and to see what kinds of causal mechanisms emerge from the data. This is more akin to bottom-up qualitative methods like Grounded theory (e.g. Bryant and Charmaz 2007; Henwood and Pidgeon 2006) or Thematic analysis (Braun and Clarke 2006). Once a set of causal themes have been identified, these themes can then be used when looking at the literature to see if there is anything relevant to this kind of process that could be applied to this particular case.

An example of this might be looking at all of the offences of a repeat offender (using serial 'deviant' case analysis (Kelly and Taylor 1981; Needs 1988) and building a model that attempts to explain all the offences. The offences of a particular individual might, for example, all have been committed in the context of:

(a) substance misuse disinhibiting and making them more impulsive
(b) being exposed to opportunities for acquisitive offending involving attacking somebody perceived as weaker than them
(c) periods of unemployment.

Making Logical Inferences Based on the Nomothetic Literature About the Individual Case

Kuyken (2009) advocates that one test of a formulation is that there is evidence to support the psychological mechanism(s) being employed. If there is evidence supporting it, then this evidential support, underpinning the causal mechanism is passed on to the individual case. Interestingly, this offers an alternative source of warranty to that offered by accreditation of 'one size fits all' 'programs'. A scientist practitioner approach (e.g. Barlow et al. 1984) to formulation ensures that a defensible 'treatment justification' is provided. In contexts where all practice can be subjected to critical scrutiny in legal or quasi-legal contexts, it is imperative that a clearly argued logical case is provided for requiring an individual to engage in an intervention and for evidencing that change has taken place.

It is important to establish that the individual case is a good representative of the population that was described in the literature and which is being used to make inferences about it'. Yin (1984) proposes a process for doing this called 'pattern matching'. This is a process whereby a hypothesized pattern or constellation of factors from the literature are applied to the individual case, to see if the individual case matches those used in the study. For example, say a study was done with a group of individuals in Setting A who had an average age of B and had developmental experiences C, D and E and had committed an offence of F. If researchers also found that, for this population, work focusing on beliefs about violence could impact on the chances of being violent again then one might want to use this same intervention with an individual case assessed as having this same demographic profile/pattern. The question becomes, does the constellation of demographic features found in the individual case match those used in the original research? If there is a match between the two patterns, then confidence can be invested in the hypothesis that the individual case will behave in a similar way as was identified in that study.

The Turn Towards Strengths-Based Practice

In recent years, there has been an increasing emphasis on strengths-based practice. Rather than focusing on a 'deficit model' which, it is argued, can have the demoralizing effect of stigmatizing and emphasizing the negative aspects of an individual's presentation, it is important to highlight the strengths, resources and social capital that an individual possesses. The early work by researchers such as Seligman (e.g. Seligman and Csikszentmihalyi 2000) on positive psychology, has been applied to the forensic field and elaborated by Ward's 'Good lives' model (GLM) (e.g. Ward 2002) and, more recently in the health sector, the recovery movement (e.g.

Moore and Drennan 2013). Ward proposes that formulations should look at the underlying needs that were met by offending and the offending lifestyle. Drawing on the literature which suggests that approach goals (i.e. goals that we move towards) are more effective in achieving self-regulation than avoidance goals (i.e. goals that we try to avoid). In the recovery paradigm, strengths are seen as a way of avoiding the stigmatizing impact of diagnosis and being labelled as a particular kind of offender. Stepping away from these processes of 'othering' is at the heart of the recovery model. In forensic settings, this has resulted in a move away from a focus on risk and a move towards a focus on 'safety planning'; looking at how to achieve safety in a person's life as well as in the contexts in which they live.

The implication of positive psychology and GLM for formulation is that instead of formulating when things have gone wrong, the times when an individual has managed crises effectively should be focused on. Times when an individual has managed not to offend when they had an urge to, can also be focused on. Instead of 'problem behaviour' being formulated 'coping pro-social behaviour' or indeed thriving behaviours are explored to develop a psychological model of what caused this and then to follow the solution-focused approach of 'if it works then do more of it' (Jones 2010a). This amounts to an individualized 'what works' approach.

Formulation as Causal Modelling Linking Evidence to Practice

From a scientist practitioner perspective, formulation is an activity that is aimed at identifying, for the individual case, what plausible psychological mechanisms were in play related to the development of risk for the individual case. There is a danger of implicitly using a 'one-size-fits-all' approach if thinking about what the causal mechanism is, in the individual case, is not explored. Identifying that somebody's ruminations about revenge are 'linked with' their violent behaviour is not as useful as knowing that the link was mediated by a set of psychological processes. For example, increased physiological arousal associated with rumination, triggered by trauma memories, that were in turn triggered by trauma reminders or cues in the environment.

Some argue that formulations do not necessarily only need to attempt to be 'true' insofar as they serve an additional function of helping people feel contained and, as such, feel less distressed and alone (Division of Clinical Psychology 2011). From this perspective, a formulation is conceived, at least in part, as a 'convenient fiction' that allows the individual to overcome a sense of being 'other' and not understood. A scientist practitioner approach is not necessarily at odds with this approach. What is critical, however, is that the final formulation be translated into a format that is accessible to the individual to whom it applies. Even more critical perhaps, is the idea that the formulation has been co-produced with the person that it is about. Co-production means collaborating and co-creating the formulation with the person it is being used with (Moore and Drennan 2013).

If the practitioner has a different view from the client, then there needs to be an effort to understand (i) what this difference is about and (ii) what the implications of this difference are.

Sequential Analysis

The question of 'what to formulate' needs to take into account the fact that much offending is the result of a sequence of events as opposed to single episodes. This construal of the problem is captured well by Layne et al.'s (2014a) account of causal factors linked with the analysis of the impact of trauma that is very relevant to causal analysis of violent behaviour. Layne et al. (2014a) talk about 'risk-factor caravans':

> *'Risk factor caravans* [emphasis in original] consist of constellations of causal risk factors that: a) occur, co-occur, and statistically covary; b) 'travel' with their host over time; c) each serve as a risk marker for the occurrence (whether temporally prior, concurrent, or subsequent) and adverse effects of one another; d) intersect with, and exacerbate, the adverse effects of one another in potentially complex ways; e) tend to increase their host's risk for subsequent exposure to, and vulnerability to the adverse effects of, additional risk factors; and f) accumulate in number, accrue, and 'cascade forward' in their cumulative adverse effects across development. In contrast, elements making up risk factor caravans do not necessarily: g) emanate from the same causal origin, h) occur, co-occur, or recur at the same point in time or during the same developmental periods, i) relate in similar ways to other variables, j) carry the same risks, k) exert similar causal effects, l) operate through the same pathways of influence, m) eventuate in the same causal consequences or sequelae, or n) respond in similar ways to the same intervention components .... (p. 53)

This constellatory approach to causal factors can be contrasted with more simple, single-factor models that are derived from data-dredging exercises that fail to differentiate, at a theoretical level, between risk markers, mediating variables and risk factors. Formulation requires a skill set that includes the ability to understand and use causal reasoning. Layne et al. (2014b) provide a useful framework for the interested reader to develop competencies in this area.

A useful approach to a series of offences where there is a process of learning across the offences is the Multiple Sequential Functional Analysis model (Gresswell and Dawson 2010; Gresswell and Hollin 1992; Hart et al. 2011). This approach starts with an initial formulation of an early offence and then uses this as the antecedent to the formulation of a subsequent offence and then, again, using this as the antecedent for the next offence. This analysis allows an understanding of serial offending as a developmental process. This is an elaborated version of the model described above (Kelly and Taylor 1981; Needs 1988) which attempts to identify consistencies across offenses.

Domains and Types of Causal Factor in Formulations

A number of different models of formulation have been used with people who have been violent. Perhaps the most common approach is functional analysis. One example is the SORC model (Setting conditions, Organism variables, Response variables and Consequences; Ireland 2008; Lee-Evans 1994) which has the strength of including critical developmental experiences (see Ireland 2008). However, Jones (In press), notes the importance of looking at offence-related altered states of consciousness in analysing offending, something that historically behavioural analysis has avoided.

Formulations seek to identify different kinds of causal factors. Morton (2004) working in a developmental psychology context identifies a typology of causal factors which, he argues, are fundamentally different in kind. They include biological factors, cognitive/emotional factors (intra-psychic factors including states of consciousness), environmental factors (which include developmental experiences), and behavioural factors. Each of these types of factor (see Table 5.2 below) can be used to conceptualize the different types of causal process commonly known as the '5Ps' model (Weerasekera 1996).

Kinderman and colleagues (e.g. Kinderman 2005; Kinderman and Tai 2007) have highlighted the way in which, generally, biological processes impact on behaviour through the

Table 5.2 Domains for formulation.

	Pre-disposing (distal antecedents)	Precipitating (proximal antecedents)	Presenting	Protective	Perpetuating (including reinforcement)
Biological					
Intrapersonal factors Cognitive/ emotional States of consciousness					
Environmental					
Behavioural					

mediation of psychological processes. So, for instance, the impact of alcohol on an individual's behaviour is mediated by changes in cognition, emotion and states of consciousness linked with the use of alcohol; thinking might be more impulsive and emotional reactions exaggerated for instance.

Fictional Case Study

The following brief example of a formulation aims to illustrate the ways in which this framework can be used:

Peter was brought up by a single mother and in the course of his childhood was violently abused by one of his mother's partners and often witnessed violence against his mother. When he was eight, he was involved in a car crash and was in a coma. Assessment of cognitive functioning after the accident revealed that he had difficulties suggestive of a frontal lobe injury with poor performance on tasks involving problem solving and set shifting. When he was 10, he was sexually abused by a neighbour and began to get into trouble for violent behaviour at school soon after this. He started drinking heavily in his early teens and went on to develop a significant drink problem. He indicated that he had found a group of friends who valued violence as a way of dealing with problems.

He reported that he had always had a good relationship with his grandmother and grandfather. He had spent periods of time living with them as a child and had good memories of this.

In prison, he had started out not coping well. Soon after his arrival into custody, he assaulted another inmate who he found out had committed a sexual offence. When he had discussed this, he indicated that the assault was linked with feelings triggered in relation to his own experience of sexual abuse. Another assault was triggered by the belief that he was not safe, and he reported that the assault was driven by a belief that the only way to feel safe would be to assault the other person first. A formulation of the case using the '5Ps' model is illustrated in Table 5.3.

Testing the validity of case formulations

As indicated above, hypotheses used in a formulation need to be tested if we want to invest them with any degree of confidence (see also Hart & Logan; 2011). Part of this testing

Table 5.3 A formulation of the case using the '5Ps' model.

	Pre-disposing	Precipitating	Presenting	Protective	Perpetuating
Biological	Head injury impacting on frontal lobes	Use of alcohol		Healthy diet	Frontal lobe deficits ongoing. Drink problem.
Cognitive/emotional	Problem solving difficulties. Schema identifying people as un-trustable. Difficulties feeling safe.	Schemas linked with people being un-trustable triggered. State switching from frightened to hostile. Ruminative thoughts about revenge against perpetrator of sexual abuse. Shame and self-loathing linked with blaming self for abuse. Trauma related dissociative state triggered by hostile behaviour of victim. Alcohol linked with increased impulsivity.	Ongoing difficulties with relationships with peers and staff linked with emotional dysregulation and feelings of mistrust. Occasionally violent in custodial setting. Ongoing shame and revenge rumination linked with sexual abuse. Hypervigilance for possibility of violence in prison.	Positive attitudes to psychological interventions. Periods of relative stability in custody linked with being employed in jobs that he found rewarding. Beginning to engage effectively with education for the first time.	Impulsive thinking style. Abused related thinking and emotions. Difficulty maintaining and generalizing change after previous attempts to change.
Environmental	Sexual and violent abuse	Absence of restraining relationships	Capable of triggering punitive reactions from staff.	Some good attachment experiences, e.g. with grandparents.	Exposure to peer group who value violence
Behavioural	History of violent behaviour	Escalation of violent behaviour	Index offence Violent assault	Has evidenced self-regulation attempts and successfully stopping self from offending in past	

process is to look at their validity and reliability. In order to subject hypotheses developed in devising a formulation to the test Haynes et al. (2011) describe a number of procedures for establishing the validity of causal relations.

1. *Logical analysis of casual factors*

   Following John Stuart Mill they propose that we establish:

   (a) The **temporal precedence** of the causal variable. The cause must come before the effect.

   (b) The cause and effect must be **related** (otherwise described as covariation)

   (c) All other explanations of the cause–effect relation must be eliminated.

   They propose exploring, in interview or through observation, a 2×2 matrix that is displayed in Table 5.4.

Table 5.4 Haynes et al. (2011) matrix.

Status of target behaviour	Hypothesized causal variable present	Hypothesized causal variable absent
Target behaviour present	Evidence supporting causation (Necessary Condition) Example: 'How frequently do you feel like hitting people when you feel shame and ruminate'	Evidence against causation Example: 'How frequently do you feel like hitting someone when you do not feel shame and ruminate?'
Target behaviour absent	Evidence against causation Example: 'How frequently do you **not** feel like hitting someone when you feel shame and ruminate?'	Evidence supporting causation (Sufficient condition) Example: 'How frequently do you not feel like hitting someone when you don't feel shame and don't ruminate?'

2. *Predictive validity*

   The 'offence paralleling behaviour' (e.g. Jones 2004, 2010c) paradigm is one way of looking at the predictive validity of a formulation. This is essentially a framework for testing the predictive validity of a formulation and thereby identifying current behaviours that warrant intervention in order to address longstanding behavioural problems.

   If a causal model for a particular kind of problem has been developed, then in order to have confidence in it as a model it needs to be tested. If the target behaviour is violent offending, then specific **causal mechanisms** linking offending to causal factors need to be tested. In the example above, we are asking 'how' or 'in what way does shame and rumination link with offending?'. This could be underpinned by a number of different hypothetical casual mechanisms. It could, for example, be that the individual experiences emotional pain associated with shame and has learned that this pain can be offset by being violent or it could be that they have a belief that they should punish people for making them feel bad. The offence paralleling behaviour framework then suggests that these hypothesized causal mechanisms or **risk mechanisms** be tested, by looking at predictions of sequences or chains of events in the current setting.

   An offence paralleling behaviour prediction for this hypothesis might be: Peter feels unbearable pain when experiencing shame and then tries frantically to avoid it.

   The avoidance doesn't have to be the same as it was at the time of the offence. So, they might use self-harm or substance misuse as strategies for managing unbearable shame; not just violence. Evidence of this pattern playing out in the current context offers support for the veracity of the case formulation. Absence of evidence leads to a return to the formulation to see if it needs to be revised.

3. *Face validity*

Perhaps more than any other kind of validity, face validity with the client, is critical. In order for a formulation of violence risk to be effective as a tool for intervention or indeed as an aid to safety planning, it needs to have face validity. One of the best ways to ensure this is to co-produce the formulation (Moore and Drennan 2013) with the aim of facilitating a process of ownership of the formulation.

Managing the **differences** in formulation between different stakeholders in the process is critical and is perhaps a key role for forensic practitioners. It is important, for example, to explore the kinds of risk factors that the practitioner thinks are important but which the service user does not. Ideally, the level of agreement about the key causal mechanisms and processes between the practitioner and the client is maximized and differences minimized. Similarly, it is important to anticipate differences of opinion between other stakeholders – within the clinical team or even those making judgements about moving on – in order to ensure that work undertaken is going to ensure progress through the system (See Figure 5.1).

It could be argued, however, that the tabulation of factors outlined above (see Table 5.2) does not actually help to integrate information, it is simply a useful typology of variables to encourage the practitioner to explore different **kinds** of relevant causal process. Making formulations accessible and giving them face validity requires integration and an appreciation of the complexity involved.

Integration can come out of thinking about how the different casual factors interact with each other and getting some sense of the 'big picture'.

Two approaches are used to try and achieve this. One is to use diagrams (e.g. Cognitive Analytic Therapy (CAT) Diagrams Pollock and Stowell-Smith 2006) and the other is to try to present the formulation in a narrative format. Both CAT and Schema therapists use letter writing as a way of sharing the formulation in an integrated way with the person that it has been produced with. This can be done with varying degrees of co-production involved. If an account is written and re-written collaboratively with the person about whom the formulation has been made, it can serve as a powerful 'roadmap' for the intervention.

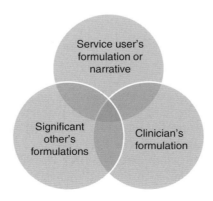

Figure 5.1   Different partially overlapping perspectives.

A narrative account for Peter:

We worked to try to understand why you did the things you did. You described having some horrible experiences when you were young where you were violently and sexually abused. We saw how these experiences left you with a feeling of disgust with yourself and also with people who remind you of the people who offended against you. Whenever you are reminded of these feelings, all those memories from the past come back, and you find it hard to cope with them. You want to get rid of them and the hurt that goes with them. You have learned to use violence as a way of getting rid of these bad feelings.

Diagrams can also be used to illustrate a formulation, see Figure 5.2 below.

Reliability of formulation

Kuyken (2006) and Beiling and Kuyken (2003) summarize the literature on the reliability of cognitive behavioural therapy (CBT) formulations and concludes that it is often poor. When different clinicians attempt to develop formulations for the same material they often come up with different factors or emphasize different factors. The more the process is standardized the greater the degree of congruence between formulations.

In practice, strategies for testing reliability include seeing if the formulation changes over time and seeking peer review.

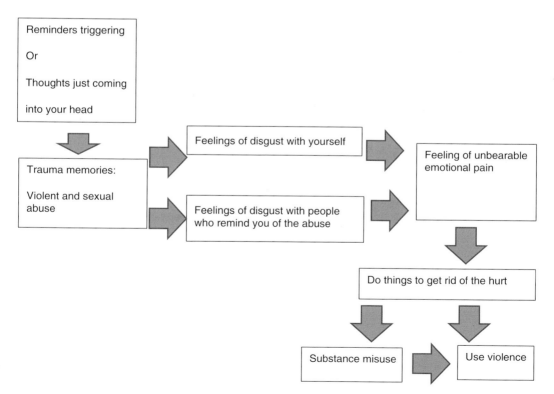

Figure 5.2 Diagram illustrating formulation.

'Strengths-based' approach

Just focussing on the offence runs the risk of increasing the burden of stigma carried by the individual. Moving away from 'offender' identities and towards a more pro-social identity involves identifying strengths (Ward 2002; Woldgabreal et al. 2014).

This can be achieved by exploring a number of strengths-oriented assumptions:

1. Most people who have committed serious offences are not offending most of the time and, therefore, have a significant array of offence evasion skills and skills for meeting needs in a pro-social manner.
2. Offending is aimed at securing a range of 'goods' (Ward) that are a normal part of being a human being and it is possible to secure these same 'goods' through non-offending behaviour.
3. Approach goals have a motivational advantage over avoidance goals.

Instead of doing a formulation of the offence or other offending behaviour, building a formulation of times when the individual had successfully managed *not to offend* or had met the same needs in a non-offending way can be useful (see also Jones 2010a).

Trauma-informed violence formulation

In an attempt to identify the key areas that clinicians need to explore in developing formulations, Johnstone et al. (2018) have taken a critical step in moving towards a trauma-informed systemic model. The Power Threat Meaning framework highlights the following domains as being important for the practitioner to consider in developing a formulation and is explained below.

Power   Powerlessness in different forms is seen as playing a critical role in the development of psychological difficulties, attitudes and beliefs. It is conceptualized as being in the following domains:

> Embodied power, Coercive power, Legal power, Economic and material power, Social and cultural capital, Interpersonal power, Ideological power.

Threat   The experience of threats of different kinds in an individual's life is seen as another critical domain in an individual's life. Threat is conceptualized as happening in the following areas of an individual's life:

> Relational, Emotional, Social/community, Economic/material, Environmental, Bodily, Knowledge and meaning, Value base and beliefs.

Meaning   Meaning is also construed as being critical in shaping an individual's responses. This is seen as deriving from the following domains:

> Ideological meanings, Social discourses, Personal meanings.

Critically, this framework moves away from defining people in terms of what is 'wrong' with them and moves towards identifying 'what happened to them'. This parallels the move in intervention from focussing on the offence – which is seen as perpetuating a stigmatizing and condemnatory personal narrative linked with returning to offending (e.g. Maruna 2001) – to focussing on the individual and building their lifestyles so that they are meeting unmet needs in a way that renders offending obsolete (e.g. Ward).

Deriving treatment targets from the formulation

One of the main purposes of drafting a formulation is to identify treatment targets. This needs to be kept in mind during the process of formulation. The causal factors that are identified need to be ones that are amenable to intervention. It is, moreover, important to be using the process of developing the formulation as an opportunity to think about the critical question of: what kinds of intervention, with what kinds of factor(s), in what contexts, are going to have the biggest impact on the desired outcome. Identifying common factors, that perhaps drive several other key factors, can point towards interventions that have a significant impact through their knock-on effects. As per Figure 5.3, it might be argued that intervening with low mood could impact on violent offending through its impact on three other factors.

The aim here is to identify the most parsimonious target(s) for intervention. However, care needs to be taken to explore the possibility that the assumption that Low mood is the most parsimonious target is not a consequence of implicit assumptions that have shaped the way in which variables have been selected. It might, for example, be more parsimonious to intervene with relationship difficulties as this could have a greater impact on mood and, by implication, the other two factors, Impulsivity and Substance misuse. Testing these hypothesized links between components of the formulation would help the practitioner to clarify the causal processes involved.

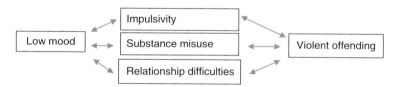

Figure 5.3 Illustration of underlying factor.

Contexts of formulation

Formulation takes place in a number of different contexts within forensic settings.

Formulation in the context of therapy Each therapeutic model has a different epistemology and set of causal factors, or way of describing causal factors, that are given primacy. The practice of formulation can sometimes become biased by a need, in the interests of adherence, to shoehorn each individual into the set of constructs available to the therapeutic model. Whilst it is important within a therapeutic intervention to use constructs from that model, it is debatable whether this is an effective strategy for identifying what the key points of intervention are for an individual. There is possibly a tendency for practitioners to use constructs from their preferred model and thereby running the risk of not entertaining alternative causal factors. Jones (2012) found that few neuropsychological factors were being used in a thematic review of case formulations with people who had offended who had a personality disorder diagnosis; this was not felt to be due to the fact that the practitioners drafting the formulations were mainly working within a schema therapy or cognitive analytic therapy framework. Attempts to use a theory neutral formulation strategy, e.g. Morton diagrams (Jones 2010b) is one way of getting away from this. Whatever formulation model one uses, including theory-neutral ones, they are likely to have implicit assumptions that shape the way the practitioner seeks out causal variables.

Formulations in consultancy work with teams Formulation in the context of consulting to a team might require a different kind of focus than formulations developed in the context of individual clinical work. In this context, formulation is more focused on in-treatment behaviour management problems rather than working on the offence. The aim is also slightly different. The focus is on management rather than on therapeutic change per se (the two agendas can, however, overlap). This has implications for the collaborative nature of the work and the experience of the formulation as 'being known about so you can be controlled' as opposed to 'being known about so that change for the better can be brought about'.

Formulating change processes

It is important to have a clear understanding of what processes are going to be underway in a change process. A formulation can sometimes help the practitioner think about ways in which the intervention can be de-railed and also to identify potentially iatrogenic outcomes (Jones 2007). Identifying how the individual might be expected to respond to the change process, or to risk-management plans, can help with clinical scenario planning. For example, often change processes involve some form of getting worse before getting better (Jones 2007), changes in belief involve going through an emotional process. If the individual cannot tolerate or respond to this process without disengaging, then this needs to be understood and integrated into the intervention and management plan.

Detection evasion skills

A significant proportion of offending goes undetected. Formulation can be used to understand what skills and competencies an individual has in evading detection. Rather than simply focusing on the offending itself, it is useful to understand the post-offending detection and conviction evasion skills (Jones 2004). This is a key part of the offending process.

Some models of formulation make a point of looking at a series of episodes, for example, offences in forensic settings, with a view to identifying what is learned in the course of the offending series (Gresswell and Hollin 1992).

Contextual formulation

Formulation is not just about things relating to the individual. It must also conceptualize the context. This requires exploration of social dynamics of the relationships that the individual is involved with. Often repeating patterns of rejection, real or imagined, are a significant precursor for violent behaviour. Analysis of the ways in which cultural and identity issues influence the context and the individual within it is also critical. Family and friendship dynamics can play a significant factor in the development of offending.

Practitioner Factors Impacting on Utility and Veracity of Formulation

The temptation to 'shoehorn' people into a model, whilst possibly having some heuristic value, runs the risk of missing the identification of significant factors for the individual case. It is difficult not to inadvertently do this. Practitioners have relationships with their theoretical models, not unlike an attachment, and find it hard to take note of non-confirmatory information when this happens. The temptation can then be, consciously or unconsciously, to neglect this kind of information.

Awareness of attachments and being wedded to one's theory are important themes for reflective practise and supervision (Davies 2015). Skills that may be used to offset the potentially biasing impact of avoiding the more challenging emotions of being uncertain and not knowing include the following:

1. allowing oneself to be influenced by what the data, in this case data coming out of attempts to test the validity and reliability of the formulation, is telling us;
2. maintaining an open-minded sense of curiosity;
3. recognizing the kernel of truth in apparently 'irrational' self-formulations of the client and;
4. managing the strong cognitive emotions such as 'feeling of knowing' (e.g. Liu et al. 2007).

Such acknowledging uncertainty and being comfortable with not knowing is very important as a formulation competency.

Overcomplicating formulations can also be a danger and a defensive reaction to uncertainty.

Conclusions

Case formulation has been increasingly recognized as critical to the tasks of intervention and risk assessment with people who have been violent. As a practice, however, formulation has little evidence as yet to support it (cf. Kuyken 2006); this is in no small measure due to the heterogeneity in approaches to creating formulations. This chapter has highlighted some of the problems with case formulation and suggested ways of addressing these concerns by testing reliability and validity. There are a number of different approaches to formulation with people who have been violent currently being used. Hopefully, there will be a common interest in the need to test formulations to see how robust they are in practice. The danger of premature closure in terms of the practitioners understanding of the causal factors involved in offending, is hopefully offset by the emphasis in the formulation process on revisiting the causal model and revising it if it does not stand up to testing.

Key competencies and skill sets need to be developed by practitioners engaged in formulation; this chapter has explored these. These include causal reasoning skills, co-production skills, cultural competencies, self-monitoring and self-reflection skills, skills in acknowledging uncertainty and not knowing, as well as being able to make conjectures and hypotheses and an up-to-date knowledge of the literature on violent offending.

Hopefully, the reader has been stimulated to explore formulation further. Attempts to systematize the approach to formulation can be found in Sturmey and McMurran (2011). Ethical issues are usefully explored in Davies et al. (2013).

The practice of formulation involves both a scientist practitioner skill set and the clinical skills of forming relationships with people who have offended and working towards a clinically meaningful and useful account of why things have happened in the way they have. If nothing else, hopefully this chapter has helped the reader to think about how challenging this task is and how much more research needs to be done to look at better ways of engaging in this complex activity.

References

Andrews, D.A. and Bonta, J. (2003). *The Psychology of Criminal Conduct*, 3e. Cincinnati, OH: Anderson.

Barlow, D.H., Hayes, S.C., and Nelson, R.O. (1984). *The Scientist-Practitioner: Research and Accountability in Clinical and Educational Settings*. New York, NY: Pergamon.

Bieling, P.J. and Kuyken, W. (2003). Is cognitive case formulation science or science fiction? *Clinical Psychology-Science and Practice* 10: 52–69.

Braun, V. and Clarke, V. (2006). Using thematic analysis in psychology. *Qualitative Research in Psychology* 3: 77–101.

Bryant, A. and Charmaz, K. (2007). *The SAGE Handbook of Grounded Theory*. London, UK: Sage.

Bush, J. (1995). Teaching self-risk management to violent offenders. In: *What Works: Reducing Reoffending: Guidelines from Research and Practice* (ed. J. McGuire), 139–154. Chichester, UK: Wiley.

Chakhssi, F., Kersten, T., de Ruiter, C., and Bernstein, D.P. (2014). Treating the untreatable: a single case study of a psychopathic inpatient treated with schema therapy. *Psychotherapy* 51: 447–461.

Cooke, D.J. and Michie, C. (2013). Violence risk assessment: form predicting to understanding- or from what? To why? In: *Managing Clinical Risk a Guide to Effective Practice* (eds. C. Logan and L. Johnstone), 3–26. New York: Routledge.

Courtois, C.A. and Ford, J.D. (2009). *Treating Complex Traumatic Stress Disorders: An Evidence-Based Guide*. New York, NY: The Guilford Press.

Daffern, M. and Howells, K. (2009). The function of aggression in personality disordered patients. *Journal of Interpersonal Violence* 24: 586–600.

Davies, J. (2015). *Supervision for Forensic Practitioners*. London, UK: Routledge.

Davies, J., Black, S., Bentley, N., and Nagi, C. (2013). Forensic case formulation: theoretical, ethical and practical issues. *Criminal Behaviour and Mental Health* 23: 304–314.

Division of Clinical Psychology (2011). *Good Practice Guidelines on the Use of Psychological Formulation*. Leicester, UK: BPS.

Dube, S.R., Miller, J.W., Brown, D.W. et al. (2006). Adverse childhood experiences and the association with ever using alcohol and initiating alcohol use during adolescence. *The Journal of Adolescent Health: Official Publication of the Society for Adolescent Medicine* 38: 444e1–444e10.

Ducci, F., Roy, A., Shen, P.H. et al. (2009). Association of substance use disorders with childhood trauma but not African genetic heritage in an African American cohort. *The American Journal of Psychiatry* 166: 1031–1040.

Enoch, M.A. (2011). The role of early life stress as a predictor for alcohol and drug dependence. *Psychopharmacology* 214: 17–31.

Fonagy, P. and Target, M. (1997). Attachment and reflective function: their role in self-organization. *Development and Psychopathology* 9: 679–700.

Gilbert, F. and Daffern, M. (2011). Illuminating the relationship between personality disorder and violence: Contributions of the General Aggression Model. *Psychology of Violence* 1 (3): 230–244.

Gilbert, P. and Procter, S. (2006). Compassionate mind training for people with high shame and self-criticism. A pilot study of a group therapy approach. *Clinical Psychology and Psychotherapy* 13: 353–379.

Gresswell, D.M. and Dawson, D.L. (2010). Offence paralleling behaviour and multiple sequential functional analysis. In: *Offence Paralleling Behaviour: A Case Formulation Approach to Offender Assessment and Intervention* (eds. L. Jones, J. Shine and M. Daffern), 89–104. London, UK: Wiley Blackwell.

Gresswell, D.M. and Hollin, C.R. (1992). Towards a new methodology for making sense of case material: an illustrative case involving attempted multiple murder. *Criminal Behaviour and Mental Health* 2: 329–341.

Hart, A.J.P., Gresswell, D.M., and Braham, L.G. (2011). Formulation of serious violent offending using multiple sequential functional analysis. In: *Forensic Case Formulation* (eds. P. Sturmey and M. McMurran), 129–152. Oxford, UK: John Wiley & Sons.

Hart, S.D. and Logan, C. (2011). Formulation of violence risk using evidence-based assessments: the structured professional judgment approach. In: *Forensic Case Formulation* (eds. P. Sturmey and M. McMurran), 83–106. Chichester, UK: Wiley Blackwell.

Hayes, S.C., Barlow, D.H., and Nelson-Gray, R.O. (1999). *The Scientist Practitioner Research and Accountability in the Age of Managed Care*, 2e. Boston, MA: Allyn & Bacon.

Haynes, S.N., O'Brien, W.H., and Keawe'aimoku Kaholokula, J. (2011). *Behavioral Assessment and Case Formulation*. Hoboken, NJ: Wiley.

Henwood, K.L. and Pidgeon, N.F. (2006). Grounded theory. In: *Research Methods in Psychology*, 3e (eds. G. Breakwell, S. Hammond, C. Fife-Shaw and J. Smith), 342–365. London, UK: Sage.

Ireland, J. (2008). Conducting individualized theory driven assessments of violent offenders. In: *Violent and Sexual Offenders, Assessment, Treatment and Management* (eds. J. Ireland, C. Ireland and P. Birch), 66–94. London, UK: Willan.

Johnstone, L., Boyle, M., Cromby, J. et al. (2018). *The power threat meaning framework: Towards the identification of patterns in emotional distress, unusual experiences and troubled or troubling behaviour, as an alternative to functional psychiatric diagnosis*. Leicester: British Psychological Society.

Jones, L. (2004). Offence parelleling behaviour (OPB) as a framework for assessment and interventions with offenders. In: *Applying Psychology to Forensic Practice* (eds. A. Needs and G. Towl), 34–63. Blackwell, UK: BPS.

Jones, L. (2007). Iatrogenic interventions with personality disordered offenders. *Behaviour, Crime and Law* 13: 69–79.

Jones, L. (2010a). Working with people who have committed sexual offences with personality disorder diagnoses. In: *Using Time, Not Doing Time: Practitioner Perspectives on Personality Disorder and Risk* (eds. A. Tennant and K. Howells), 125–140. Chichester, UK: Wiley Blackwell.

Jones, L. (2010b). Case formulation with personality disordered offenders. In: *Using Time, Not Doing Time: Practitioner Perspectives on Personality Disorder and Risk* (eds. A. Tennant and K. Howells), 45–61. Chichester, UK: Wiley.

Jones, L. (2010c). Approaches to developing OPB formulations. In: *Offence Paralleling Behaviour: A Case Formulation Approach to Offender Assessment and Intervention* (eds. M. Daffern, L.F. Jones and J. Shine), 71–87. Chichester: Wiley.

Jones, L. (2012). Case formulations for offenders with personality disorder: themes and implications for treatment pathways. International Association of Forensic Mental Health Services Annual conference, Miami.

Jones, L. (2019). New developments in interventions for working with offending behaviour. In: *The Handbook of Correctional Psychology* (eds. D.P.P. Polaschek, A. Day and C.R. Hollin). Chichester, UK: Wiley.

Kelly, D. and Taylor, H. (1981). Take and escape: a personal construct study of car 'theft'. In: *Personal Construct Psychology: Recent Advances in Theory and Practice* (eds. H. Bonarius, R. Holland and S. Rosenberg), 231–239. London, UK: Macmillan.

Kerig, P.K. and Becker, S.P. (2010). From internalizing to externalizing: theoretical models of the processes linking PTSD to juvenile delinquency. In: *Posttraumatic Stress Disorder (PTSD): Causes, Symptoms and Treatment* (ed. S.J. Egan), 33–78. Hauppauge, NY: Nova Science Publishers.

Kinderman, P. (2005). A psychological model of mental disorder. *Harvard Review of Psychiatry* 13: 206–217.

Kinderman, P. and Tai, S. (2007). Empirically grounded clinical interventions: clinical implications of a psychological model of mental disorder. *Behavioural and Cognitive Psychotherapy* 35: 1–14.

Kuyken, W. (2006). Evidence-based case formulation: is the emperor clothed? In: *Case Formulation in Cognitive Behaviour Therapy* (ed. N. Tarrier), 12–35. Hove, UK: Brunner-Routlege.

Kuyken, W., Padesky, C.A., and Dudley, R. (2009). *Collaborative case conceptualization: Working effectively with patients in cognitive-behavioral therapy.* New York: Guilford.

Layne, C.M., Briggs, E.C., and Courtois, C.A. (2014a). Introduction to the special section: using the trauma history profile to unpack risk factor caravans and their consequences. *Psychological Trauma: Theory, Research, Practice, and Policy* 6: S1–S7.

Layne, C.M., Steinberg, J.R., and Steinberg, A.M. (2014b). Causal reasoning skills training for mental health practitioners: promoting sound clinical judgment in evidence-based practice. *Training and Education in Professional Psychology* 8: 292–302.

Lee-Evans, J.M. (1994). Background to behaviour analysis. In: *The Assessment of Criminal Behaviours of Clients in a Secure Setting* (eds. M. McMurran and J. Hodge), 6–34. London, UK: Jessica Kingsley.

Liu, Y., Su, Y., Xu, G., and Chan, R.C. (2007). Two dissociable aspects of feelings of knowing: knowing that you know and knowing that you do not know. *The Quarterly Journal of Experimental Psychology* 60: 672–680.

Lupien, S.J., McEwen, B.S., Gunnar, M.R., and Heim, C. (2009). Effects of stress throughout the lifespan on the brain, behaviour and cognition. *Nat. Rev. Neurosci.* 10: 434–445.

Maruna, S. (2001). *Making Good: How Ex-convicts Reform and Rebuild Their Lives.* Washington, DC: American Psychological Association Books.

Moore, E. and Drennan, G. (2013). Complex forensic case formulation in recovery-oriented services: some implications for routine practice. *Criminal Behaviour and Mental Health* 23: 230–240.

Morton, J. (2004). *Understanding Developmental Disorders: A Causal Modelling Approach.* Oxford: Blackwell.

Needs, A. (1988). Psychological investigation of offending behaviour. In: *Experimenting with Personal Construct Psychology* (eds. F. Fransella and L. Thomas), 493–506. New York, NY: Routledge & Kegan Paul.

Pollock, P.H. and Stowell-Smith, M. (2006). Cognitive analytic therapy applied to offending: theory, tools and practice. In: *Cognitive Analytic Therapy for Offenders: A New Approach to Forensic Psychotherapy* (eds. P.H. Pollock, M. Stowell-Smith and M. Gopfert), 1–42. New York, NY: Routledge/ Taylor & Francis Group.

Safran, J.D., Muran, J.C., and Eubanks-Carter, C. (2011). Repairing alliance ruptures. *Psychotherapy* 48: 80–87.

Seligman, M.E.P. and Csikszentmihalyi, M. (2000). Positive psychology: an introduction. *American Psychologist* 55: 5–14.

Shapiro, D.S. (2002). Renewing the scientist-practitioner model. *Psychologist.* 15: 232–234.

Sturmey, P. and McMurran, M. (2011). *Forensic Case Formulation.* Chichester, UK: Wiley Blackwell.

Teicher, M.H., Andersen, S.L., Polcari, A. et al. (2002). Developmental neurobiology of childhood stress and trauma. *The Psychiatric Clinics of North America* 25: 397–426.

Teicher, M.H., Andersen, S.L., Polcari, A. et al. (2003). The neurobiological consequences of early stress and childhood maltreatment. *Neuroscience and Biobehavioral Reviews* 27: 33–44.

Ward, T. (2002). Good lives and the rehabilitation of offenders: promises and problems. *Aggression and Violent Behavior* 27: 33–44.

Ward, T. and Fortune, C.A. (2016). From dynamic risk factors to causal processes: a methodological framework. *Psychology, Crime & Law* 22: 190–202.

Weerasekera, P. (1996). *Multiperspective Case Formulation: A Step Toward Treatment Integration.* Malabar, FL: Krieger.

Woldgabreal, Y., Day, A., and Ward, T. (2014). The community-based supervision of offenders from a positive psychology perspective. *Aggression and Violent Behavior* 19: 32–41.

Yin, R.K. (1984). *Case Study Research, Design and Methods.* Thousand Oaks, CA: Sage.

Young, J.E., Klosko, J.S., and Weishaar, M.E. (2006). *Schema Therapy A Practitioners Guide.* New York: Guilford.

6

Predicting Violent Reoffending with the VRAG-R
Overview, Controversies, and Future Directions for Actuarial Risk Scales

L. Maaike Helmus[1] and Vernon L. Quinsey[2]

[1] Simon Fraser University Burnaby, Canada
[2] Queen's University Kingston, Canada

Introduction

Assessing an offender's risk to re-offend is one of the most ubiquitous tasks in the criminal justice and forensic psychiatric systems. A formal or informal appraisal of risk informs virtually every decision that is made about offenders, including decisions about granting bail, sentencing, custody placement, treatment options, release from custody, and conditions/frequency of community supervision. Given the potential consequences of a known offender committing a new violent offence, combined with the profound implications for an offender's liberty, risk assessment is an important task that demands the highest attention to evidence-based practice.

The purpose of this chapter is threefold: firstly, to define actuarial risk assessment; secondly, to provide a summary of one of the most frequently used actuarial risk scales for predicting violent recidivism (the VRAG [Violence Risk Appraisal Guide] and its successor, the VRAG-R [Violence Risk Appraisal Guide-Revised]); and thirdly, to give an overview of some emerging issues and controversies in the application of actuarial risk scales (including anticipated future directions). Many of the sections of this chapter are intended to complement and update Harris et al.'s (2015b; Chapter 7) discussion of the criticisms of actuarial risk scales.

Defining Risk Assessment and Actuarial Risk Scales

Risk assessment is an evaluation of an offender's likelihood of re-offending. Unfortunately, the underlying task and purpose of risk assessment is often misunderstood. Importantly, risk assessment is a prognostic, as opposed to a diagnostic, task (Helmus and Babchishin 2017).

The Wiley Handbook of What Works in Violence Risk Management: Theory, Research and Practice,
First Edition. Edited by J. Stephen Wormith, Leam A. Craig, and Todd E. Hogue.
© 2020 John Wiley & Sons Ltd. Published 2020 by John Wiley & Sons Ltd.

This means that risk assessment is not about 'diagnosing' or 'classifying' offenders as recidivists or non-recidivists, given that recidivism by definition cannot exist at the time of assessment – it is about assessing the likelihood of future recidivism. Consequently, risk is a continuous dimension. Offenders are not simply 'dangerous' or 'not dangerous'. They vary in levels of dangerousness and can be ranked according to their risk. This means that risk should be communicated as a continuum and not as a dichotomy (Association for the Treatment of Sexual Abusers 2014), although it is possible that dichotomous decisions will be made, and that risk scales (measuring a continuum of risk) can inform those dichotomous decisions (although different cut-offs may be used for different decisions/purposes). Additionally, diagnosis is a different kind of task than prognosis. For example, determining whether you currently have cancer may be easier than determining whether you will develop cancer in the next five years. Consequently, standards for evaluating the accuracy of risk-assessment scales should be applicable to prognostic tasks and not borrowed from the diagnostic literature (Helmus and Babchishin 2017).

Another important distinction is that risk scales are different than most psychological assessment scales in that they are criterion-referenced, as opposed to norm-referenced (Helmus and Babchishin 2017). Whereas norm-referenced scales are designed to measure how individuals vary on a particular construct (e.g. anxiety, extraversion, psychopathy, intelligence), criterion-referenced scales are designed to maximize accuracy in predicting a particular outcome (e.g. school performance, recidivism; Aiken 1985). This distinction is important because methods of developing and validating scales differ depending on whether the scale is norm- or criterion-referenced. For norm-referenced scales, reliability of the scale increases to the extent that scale items are measuring the same underlying construct (e.g. demonstrated through internal reliability and factor analyses). In contrast, criterion-referenced scales are not intended to measure the same construct. Accuracy is maximized to the extent that the scale measures as many different risk-relevant constructs as possible, directly reducing internal reliability and complicating factor analyses (as efficiency and accuracy are maximized by having as few items as possible from each factor). Given that internal reliability and coherent factor structure are not goals of criterion-referenced scales, these scales should be primarily judged on their accuracy in predicting the outcome of interest, and the extent to which new information adds incremental predictive validity (the degree to which new information captures something predictive not already included in the scale).

Understanding that risk assessment is a prognostic task describing a continuous dimension and that risk scales are criterion-referenced, it is possible to make further distinctions amongst types of structured risk scales. Structured scales use different methods of combining individual factors into an overall assessment of risk (for discussion, see Bonta 1996; Hanson and Morton-Bourgon 2009). This chapter will focus on actuarial risk scales. Following the definition of Meehl (1954), an actuarial risk scale specifies what offender characteristics should be considered (based on their empirical relationship to recidivism) and how to score and mechanically combine them into a total score (either through simple summation or some kind of weighting system). The results are empirically-derived estimates of the probability of some outcome that can be associated with each total score or risk category.

An alternative method of scale development is Structured Professional Judgement (SPJ), where evaluators score items that were selected, based on a combination of research, theory, and clinical practice. However, the evaluators use their clinical judgement to consider additional factors and to form an overall professional assessment of risk. Lastly, another method is mechanical, following the definition of Hanson and Morton-Bourgon (2009); these are like actuarial scales but do not provide empirically-derived recidivism probability estimates.

Additionally, the items of mechanical scales may be selected based on research, theory, or practice (Hanson and Morton-Bourgon 2009). There are two types of mechanical scales. In one, the total score of items in an SPJ scale is used, as opposed to a clinical judgement (this is common in research studies). This is a more mechanized, objective way to use SPJ scales, but it doesn't quite meet the definition of actuarial, and it is not technically SPJ either. The second type comprise scales that do not yet have the research base to be actuarial, but they may become actuarial scales over time, if research supports the items in the scale and produces recidivism estimates. An example is the STABLE-2000, which is a mechanical scale that was later revised into an actuarial scale, called STABLE-2007 (Hanson et al. 2007).

Which approach works best?

A primary advantage of actuarial and mechanical scales is their greater objectivity. It has long been known that mental health professionals, including experienced forensic psychologists and psychiatrists, show poor agreement amongst themselves in predicting violent recidivism and are overly conservative (e.g. Quinsey and Ambtman 1979). The greater the structure in a scale, the more consistent it should be across diverse raters and settings. This has been found in meta-analyses, where there is greater variability in the predictive accuracy of SPJ scales compared to the results of the same scales, but used in a mechanical way (Hanson and Morton-Bourgon 2009; Helmus and Bourgon 2011).

In terms of predictive accuracy, meta-analyses favour actuarial approaches to prediction over professional judgement (Ægisdóttir et al. 2006; Bonta et al. 1998; Dawes et al. 1989; Grove et al. 2000; Hanson and Morton-Bourgon 2009; Mossman 1994), but it depends on the type of task, and the professional judgement in these meta-analyses is typically unstructured. In summarizing the decision making and cognitive science literature, Shanteau (1992) concluded at the time (i.e. before the advent of modern artificial intelligence) that evidence favoured professional judgement in domains such as livestock judges, astronomers, test pilots, soil judges, physicists, mathematicians, accountants, photo interpreters, and insurance analysts. The evidence favoured actuarial approaches for clinical psychologists, psychiatrists, student admissions evaluators, court judges, behavioural researchers, counsellors, personnel selectors, parole officers, polygraph judges, intelligence analysts, and stock brokers. This summary is notably limited to research up until the 1990s. With greater advances in artificial intelligence and predictive models, the list of contexts favouring professional judgement may shrink.

In synthesizing these findings, Shanteau (1992) concluded that actuarial approaches are better at predicting human behaviour (as opposed to physical phenomena), for unique tasks, when feedback is unavailable, and when the environment is intolerant of error. Kahneman (2011) provided a more updated summary of the performance of experts across a variety of tasks, with similar conclusions. According to Kahneman and Klein (2009), expert opinion can be expected to outperform actuarial decisions when the environment is regular (i.e. highly predictable, such as for physical phenomena), the expert has considerable practice, and there are opportunities for timely feedback. These conditions are generally not present in offender risk assessment. The sheer number of diverse predictors of recidivism (e.g. see Bonta and Andrews 2017; Hanson and Morton-Bourgon 2005) suggests that criminal behaviour is not easily predictable with near-perfect accuracy in any given moment (i.e. the number of contingencies are infinite and human behaviour is complex; Hanson 2009), evaluators do not receive timely feedback on their decisions, and the forensic environment is notoriously intolerant of error. Consequently, offender risk assessment fits into the types of tasks that favour actuarial methods.

What kind of information can actuarial risk scales provide?

Actuarial risk scales provide a total score that can be used to provide different types of information. Total scores are often combined into ordinal risk categories or bins, often with a label such as low, moderate, or high risk. Although this interpretive heuristic is frequently reported (e.g. Blais and Forth 2014; Chevalier et al. 2015) and particularly influential to jurors (Varela et al. 2014), there is little consensus across professionals in terms of what the labels actually mean (e.g. Edwards et al. 2002; Hilton et al. 2008; Monahan and Silver 2003; Shaw and Dear 1990; Slovic et al. 2000). In the end, the only way to say what a risk category means is to specify a probability. Given the ambiguity in the use of these qualitative labels describing risk, there are increased efforts in the risk assessment field to move towards more universal definitions of risk categories that are independent of the risk scale being used (e.g. Hanson et al. 2016a, 2017a).

In contrast to the relatively vague terminology of risk labels, there are three quantitative metrics that can be used to summarize the information on an actuarial risk scale: percentiles, risk ratios, and absolute recidivism estimates. Percentiles are commonly used in psychology (particularly for norm-referenced scales) to describe how common or unusual a person's score is in comparison to a reference population (Crawford and Garthwaite 2009). Percentiles have the advantage of being fairly easily defined and communicated and are particularly helpful in decisions for resource allocation. A primary disadvantage of percentiles is that the relationship between percentiles and recidivism is not necessarily linear. In other words, the difference between two risk scores in percentile units may not adequately reflect the difference between two risk scores in terms of the likelihood of recidivism (for further discussion of percentiles, see Hanson et al. 2012).

Risk ratios describe how an offender's risk of recidivism compares to some reference group (e.g. low-risk offenders, or offenders with the median risk score). Risk ratios provide more information than percentiles and are stable across studies despite changes in recidivism rates or follow-up periods (Babchishin et al. 2012b; Hanson et al. 2013). Risk ratios are common in medical risk communication but are rarely used in offender risk scales. Possible barriers to their use include the more complex calculations compared to other metrics for communicating risk (for an example of different computational options, see Hanson et al. 2013), difficulty in communicating them to laypeople (e.g. Varela et al. 2014), and potential for misinterpretation (e.g. overestimation of risk in the absence of base rates; Elmore and Gigerenzer 2005).

Whereas percentiles and risk ratios provide information about the offender's risk *relative* to other offenders, absolute recidivism estimates provide an estimate of the *absolute* probability of recidivism for an offender, based on their score. Neither clinical judgement nor SPJ scales yield an actual probability of re-offending – this metric is uniquely provided by actuarial scales. The recidivism estimates can be generated in a variety of ways (for discussion, see Hanson et al. 2010). Absolute risk information is easy to understand but hard to obtain with high levels of confidence. Likely due to the myriad factors that influence recidivism (e.g. follow-up length, recidivism definition), absolute recidivism estimates tend to be unstable across diverse samples (Helmus et al. 2012b; Helmus and Thornton 2016; Lehmann et al. 2016; Mills et al. 2005; Olver et al. 2014a; Snowden et al. 2007). Given the challenges in producing generalizable recidivism estimates, one potential solution is for jurisdictions to develop their own local norms where possible (for further information and recommendations, see Hanson et al. 2016b).

Ordinal risk categories and absolute recidivism estimates remain the most commonly used despite the subjectivity of the former and the occasional variation over samples of the latter. They are reported in over 80% of Canadian and American hearings for preventative detention, whereas percentiles and risk ratios are reported in less than 40% of evaluations (Blais and Forth 2014; Chevalier et al. 2015). More recently, risk scale developers have begun to call for a decreased emphasis on absolute recidivism estimates, arguing that most decisions can be made on the basis of relative risk information, such as percentiles and risk ratios (Hanson et al. 2016b; Harris et al. 2015a). For example, forensic or correctional administrators with fixed budgets for treatment or supervision would benefit most by differentially providing these resources to higher risk cases. More specifically, if a correctional service has sufficient resources to offer treatment to 15% of their offenders, then using an actuarial risk scale to identify the 15% of offenders representing the highest risk may be sufficient (following the risk principle of effective correctional practice, these are the offenders who should be targeted for treatment[1]; Bonta and Andrews 2017). More generally, the way in which risk is reported must be related to the use to which the estimate is to be put and decision makers should be given information that facilitates their understanding of the estimate. For example, where long-term consequences for community safety and offender liberty are at stake, providing the percentile rank of the offender, his relative risk ratio, and the absolute likelihood of his recidivism are required.

Summary of VRAG and VRAG-R Development and Research

This section describes VRAG-R (Harris et al. 2015b; Rice et al. 2013). As a prelude, we also discuss the VRAG (Quinsey et al. 2006a), its predecessor, because it is the most widely used actuarial instrument for predicting violent recidivism (Archer et al. 2006; Blais and Forth 2014; Neal and Grisso 2014; Singh et al. 2014) and has existed long enough to have received attention from a great many researchers.

The violence risk appraisal guide

The VRAG is an actuarial instrument designed to estimate the likelihood with which a male criminal offender or forensic psychiatric patient will be charged for at least one new violent offence within a 7- or 10-year period of opportunity to re-offend (for more information on the scale, see Harris et al. 1993, 2015b). Opportunity to re-offend refers to ongoing community access (release to the community, a minimum-security psychiatric hospital, or half-way house) and violent offending is defined to include hands-on sex offences. Total scores on the VRAG can be used to provide risk category information (clumped into nine risk bins), percentiles, and recidivism estimates; risk ratios were not developed for the scale. VRAG recidivism estimates were developed based on the observed frequency of post-release charges for violent recidivism over a follow-up period averaging seven years of opportunity. The scale was constructed using a sample of 618 offenders who had been assessed or treated at a maximum-security psychiatric

---

[1] Presuming the hypothetical example is not solely a low-risk population to begin with. This is a simplified example; presumably research, policy, and practical considerations would all predate the determination that 15% of offenders would receive treatment.

facility in Ontario, Canada; most of the assessed-only (untreated) offenders were subsequently sentenced to correctional facilities before their release.

Items were selected for the scale based on the pre-release characteristics of the offenders that were most strongly related to whether they committed a new violent or sexual offence. The scoring system for the items was developed using a method popularized by Nuffield (1982), where a point is added or subtracted to the item levels for each 5% difference from the base rate. For example, if the base rate for violent recidivism is 40%, and offenders with a prior offence on their criminal history re-offend at a rate of 50%, then this item would be given two points (50% is two 5% increases higher than the base rate of 40%). The items are listed in Table 6.1.

The items are defined in Quinsey et al. (2006a) in sufficient detail to conduct applied assessments. More information about the nature of the VRAG items is provided in the discussion of the VRAG-R below but for now a few comments on some of the items will suffice.

Because the items were selected from a larger pool based on their relationship to violent recidivism rather than on theoretical or commonsensical ideas, they are sometimes counterintuitive. The negative relationship between schizophrenia and violence risk is the best exemplar of such an apparently anomalous result. The reason for this relationship becomes apparent on reflection: In studies of the general population, schizophrenia, and other major mental disorders are modest risk indicators (for review, see Walsh et al. 2002) but are much poorer risk indicators than diagnoses of personality disorder, sexual deviance, and substance abuse. Thus, when a sample of offenders is studied, schizophrenia appears to be a protective factor because schizophrenics are being compared to a group composed largely of personality disordered, paraphilic, and/or substance-abusing offenders. Similar considerations apply to some of the other items. Contrary to intuition, offence severity and recidivism are often inversely related, with the lowest rates of recidivism found for murderers (Langan and Levin 2002). Offenders with female victims are generally not homosexual paedophiles, who have high rates of sexual recidivism (Harris and Hanson 2004). Part of the issue with both murderers and offenders with female victims is that a substantial proportion of both groups committed their admission offence against their spouse and such individuals tend to have low rates of violent recidivism (Roberts et al. 2007).

The reader is likely to conjure up visions of spectacular exceptions to the assertions in the preceding paragraph. Domestic murderers who turned out to be serial killers, serial rapists (of women), and so forth. Although anecdotes often feel more powerful and persuasive than data (Kahneman 2011), two considerations temper the force of these objections. The first (and weaker) is that the instrument deals in probabilities not certainties. Secondly, and much more importantly, the items work together, rather than in isolation. It is the combination of items (for example, a pattern of early antisocial behaviour coupled with an adult offence) that yields a high-risk score. The VRAG is, in part, a measure of the persistence of antisocial and criminal behaviour across the lifespan. In the end, however, it is not our theoretical ideas, commonsense notions, or anecdotes derived from our personal experience or reading that count – only the empirical relationship between the actuarial measure and outcome is important.

Accuracy of prediction   The measurement of predictive accuracy is complex and has sometimes been controversial. Firstly, there are two types of predictive accuracy that can be measured: relative and absolute. Relative predictive accuracy (also referred to as discrimination) examines differences in the risk scores of recidivists and non-recidivists (i.e. how well the scale distinguishes the two groups, or is able to rank order offenders in their likelihood of recidivism).

Table 6.1 List and comparison of Violence Risk Appraisal Guide (VRAG) and Violence Risk Appraisal Guide-Revised (VRAG-R) items.

VRAG Items	VRAG-R Items
1) Revised Psychopathy Checklist score (Hare 2003)	1) Antisociality (Facet 4 of PCL-R): Poor behavioural controls, early behavioural problems, juvenile delinquency, revocation of conditional release, criminal versatility.
2) Elementary school maladjustment score	2) Same
3) Meets DSM-III psychiatric criteria for any personality disorder	—
4) Age at time of the index or admission offence (negatively related to recidivism)	3) Same
5) Separation from either parent (except death) under age 16	4) Same
6) Failure on prior conditional release from corrections	5) Same
7) Charges for non-violent offences prior to index offence	6) Same
8) Never married (or equivalent) at time of index offence	7) Same
9) Meets psychiatric criteria for schizophrenia (negatively related to recidivism)	—
10) Most serious victim injury in index offence (negatively related to recidivism)	—
11) Alcohol abuse score	8) History of alcohol or drug problems
12) Female victim in index offence (negatively related to recidivism)	—
—	9) Charges for violent offences before index offence
—	10) Number of prior admissions to correctional institutions
—	11) Conduct disorder before age 15
—	12) Sex offending

Note. The sex offending item assigns scores based on which of the following categories the offender falls in: no known hands-on sex offences, sex offences exclusively against girls under the age of 14, known to have committed at least one hands-on sex offence but not known to fit another category, at least one sex offence against a female victim 14 or older.

In contrast, absolute predictive accuracy (also referred to as calibration) evaluates the correspondence between predicted recidivism rates per risk bin and observed rates in a new sample. Unfortunately, absolute predictive accuracy has been largely neglected in validation studies of most risk scales and we are only beginning to develop consistency in the statistics used to assess it (Helmus and Babchishin 2017).

Despite occasional fads for alternative statistics, the most consistently used and recommended statistic for measuring relative predictive accuracy in the offender risk assessment field has been the Area Under the Curve (AUC) from Receiver Operating Characteristic (ROC) curve analyses (Helmus and Babchishin 2017; Rice and Harris 2005; Swets et al. 2000). The AUC calculates the likelihood that a randomly sampled individual from one outcome group (in this case, violent recidivists) will have a higher score on a predictive instrument than a randomly sampled individual from the other group (those not committing such offences). This probability in the case of the VRAG is approximately 0.75, which is a large effect size (Rice and Harris 2005) and indicates sufficient accuracy to be useful in practical decision making about release and supervision for individual offenders (Harris et al. 2015b). The relative predictive accuracy of the VRAG compares favourably with other methods of predicting violent re-offending (for an extensive review, see Harris et al. 2015b).

Replications Since the VRAG was introduced in the 1990s, there has been about 60 relative predictive accuracy replications around the world, most of which were conducted by individuals unconnected with the VRAG authors. The VRAG, like most actuarial instruments, is very robust upon replication: for example, accuracy (measured with AUCs) in predicting violent recidivism in the community in six studies conducted by the VRAG authors averaged 0.73 and averaged 0.72 in 20 replications conducted by others (Harris et al. 2015b).

There are far fewer replication studies of the recidivism estimates from the VRAG. Two studies using Canadian samples roughly similar to those used in the development of the VRAG have replicated the accuracy of the recidivism estimates (Harris et al. 2002, 2003). In contrast, however, exploratory analyses using measures of outcome somewhat different than that employed in the VRAG construction studies have found that the VRAG probabilities may overestimate violent recidivism in populations that differ from the one used in construction (Mills et al. 2005; Snowden et al. 2007). Given that multi-study analyses for other risk scales have found significant variability in the recidivism rates per score (e.g. Helmus and Thornton 2016; Helmus et al. 2012b; Lehmann et al. 2016; Olver et al. 2014a), it is possible that the VRAG (and VRAG-R) recidivism estimates may not be stable across diverse samples for a variety of reasons (for example, differences in the definition of recidivism, variations in follow-up time, preselection of the sample on risk-related variables, jurisdictional differences, quality of data, and so forth). More replication studies examining this issue are needed.

The violence risk appraisal guide-revised (VRAG-R)

The VRAG-R (first published in Rice et al. 2013; described further in Harris et al. 2015b) was developed primarily to simplify the VRAG scoring system. The biggest change was the substitution of Facet 4 of the Psychopathy Checklist-Revised (PCL-R) (measuring antisociality) for the total PCL-R score. It takes considerable time to score the PCL-R properly, particularly because scoring quite a few of its 20 items involve some judgement. Facet 4 items are amongst the more objective and easily scored. The decision to substitute antisociality for total PCL-R score in the VRAG-R proved prescient because in a field trial of inter-forensic clinician agreement (Edens et al. 2016), scoring of the PCL-R item on the VRAG was strongly associated with rater disagreement in the scoring of the VRAG total score. Moreover, research suggests that Factor 2 of the PCL-R (which contains Facet 4), and even Facet 4 on its own, may be a better predictor of violent recidivism than the total PCL-R score (Leistico et al. 2008; Wormith et al. 2007).

Another simplification is that the VRAG-R includes an item measuring sexual offending, which removes the need for a separate risk scale for sexual offenders (i.e. the Sex Offender Risk Appraisal Guide [SORAG], described in Harris et al. 2015b). The VRAG-R can be used with both violent and sexual offenders with roughly equivalent accuracy (Harris et al. 2015b). Specifically, two items in the VRAG that were found to be not applicable to sex offenders were removed (female victim and victim injury), and the new item measuring sexual offending taps into core offence features that would assess sexual deviance (Mann et al. 2010; e.g. no hands-on sexual offending; paedophilia as indicated by exclusive pattern of offending against young girls). Consequently, the VRAG-R assesses both antisociality and sexual deviance, the two broad domains that predict recidivism for sex offenders (Hanson and Morton-Bourgon 2005).

The VRAG-R correlates very highly with the VRAG ($r = 0.88$) and has nearly identical accuracy of prediction (Rice et al. 2013). Because the VRAG-R is much easier to score without sacrificing predictive accuracy, the developers of the VRAG and VRAG-R recommend use of the latter (Rice et al. 2013). Similar to the original scale, total scores on the VRAG-R can be placed into nine risk bins, and reported in terms of percentiles or recidivism estimates. For the VRAG-R, recidivism estimates are provided based on observed rates after fixed 5- and 12-year periods of follow-up.

The sample of 1261 offenders used for its construction included the offenders used to develop the VRAG. It has 12-items, each scored or weighted according to the direction and magnitude of its relationship to violent (including sexual) re-offending, and then summed to obtain a total score (as with the original VRAG, item weights were identified using the Nuffield method). Table 6.1 lists the VRAG-R items and compares them to VRAG items, noting which are the same, similar, or new. The items are historical (static) in nature and do not change with time, unless of course there is a new offence and the offender is reassessed.

The items are designed to be scored from information contained in the offender's file: a detailed psychosocial history or parole/probation assessment, psychological and psychiatric assessments, court records, criminal history, and psychiatric history. Given adequate information, it is not necessary for the assessor to interview the offender to complete the assessment. To the degree possible, information from multiple sources is used. It is particularly important to attempt to corroborate information obtained from offender self-report. When there is missing information for a particular item, it can be prorated (estimated) according to a formula (see Harris et al. 2015b). Up to four items can be prorated to obtain a valid score. Trained raters show extremely close agreement when independently scoring the same file; the intraclass correlation coefficient for two raters was 0.987 and the standard error of measurement was 2.19 (Harris et al. 2015b).

Theoretical interpretation The principal implication of the results of the research leading to the development of the VRAG-R is the concrete demonstration of the large variation in risk of violent re-offending posed by different offenders. The VRAG-R items are individual-level correlates of crime, most of which have been extensively documented in many societies throughout the world. They are part of a larger class of variables referred to as the universal correlates of crime (Ellis and Walsh 2000). Individual correlates are distinguished from aggregate correlations. Aggregate data are collected at the country, region, or census track level – for example, one can compare the overall crime rates amongst different countries or correlate the association between income disparity and crime in a particular jurisdiction. Correlations based on aggregate data are often different than correlations based on individual data. There is, for example, a very strong association between poverty and crime at the aggregate level (Sampson et al. 1997) but a very weak association between poverty and crime at the level of individuals (Bonta and Andrews 2017). This particular difference may exist simply because most poor people do not commit crimes, although other factors also contribute. Knowing an offender's socioeconomic status, therefore, does not help one in forecasting the likelihood of a particular offender's recidivism.

The items of the VRAG-R were selected empirically, based on their success in predicting violent recidivism, not for theoretical reasons, and therefore do not in themselves constitute a theory of violent offending. The success of the instrument, a result of the predictability of violent offending, does have theoretical relevance, however, in that it constitutes data to be explained by a successful theory.

Overview of Controversies and Future Directions for Actuarial Risk Assessment

This section will discuss some current controversies and future directions for research and application of actuarial risk assessment scales. Although we have focused on the VRAG and VRAG-R in this chapter and will continue to reference it below, the following discussion is broadly applicable to all actuarial offender risk scales. The sections are framed around common questions we are asked, followed by a discussion of our answers. This follows a similar format to Chapter 7 of Harris et al. (2015b), surrounding arguments against actuarial risk assessment methods. This discussion is meant to supplement that chapter and will cover some of the more recent debates in the field.

Risk and protective factors

Risk factors (in this context, offender characteristics) are the items, or the building blocks, of actuarial risk scales. Recently, however, there has been strong empirical and theoretical interest in the discussion of *protective* factors (e.g. Farrington and Ttofi 2011; Lösel and Farrington 2012), often asserted to be a new type of factor heretofore not considered in existing risk assessment scales (e.g. Farrington and Ttofi 2011).

Considering whether protective factors are indeed new constructs for assessment has been complicated by a dizzying array of vague and sometimes conflicting definitions, accompanied by subjectively interpreted examples. It is common for a dissertation, chapter, or article to assert that protective factors are more than just the reverse end of risk factors, but then provide a list of examples that can all be considered a reverse framing of one of the 'Central Eight' (Bonta and Andrews 2017) risk factors for recidivism. Some definitions of protective factors unhelpfully consider them to be any factor associated with lower rates of recidivism (e.g. de Vries Robbé et al. 2015), with the necessary implication that they are merely the inverse of risk factors. If this convention were to be adopted, then some items of the VRAG-R could be reversed and defined as protective (e.g. marital status).

Other definitions have been more nuanced. Lösel and Farrington (2012) subdivide protective factors into 'direct protective', which are factors associated with lower levels of violence (similar to above), and 'buffering protective' which interact with a risk factor to decrease its association with violence. Statistical interactions have not been analysed much in research (for VRAG-R or other scales), and it is always possible that a risk factor could interact with another to reduce its association with violence, suggesting that even commonly perceived risk factors could technically meet this definition of protective. Farrington and Ttofi (2011) have also advanced the idea of promotive factors, which is largely an extension of the idea of direct protective factors, but factors are defined as either solely promotive or solely risk factors based on non-linear relationships with recidivism (e.g. in this conceptualization, a purely linear relationship between a factor and recidivism makes it *both* a promotive and a risk factor). One challenge is the lack of standardized definitions and measurement of risk-relevant constructs which impedes the ability to study replicable non-linear relationships in a way that could support this definition.

Based on current empirical and theoretical work, we remain unconvinced that protective factors are in fact measuring something new (for further discussion of this issue, see Harris and Rice 2015; Helmus 2015, 2018). Importantly, however, the confusion over whether protective factors are unique constructs or opposite ends of existing constructs raises the issue of whether it is necessary to make the distinction at all, although it is the case that a focus on protective factors may contribute to a positive therapeutic milieu and greater offender compliance with intervention efforts.

An alternative conceptualization focusses on the idea of psychologically meaningful risk factors (Mann et al. 2010), or risk-relevant propensities. In psychological assessment, it is assumed that scale items are imperfect indicators of some underlying, not-directly-observable latent trait or construct. In this model, risk factors in a scale are indicators of underlying constructs/propensities related to violence (and ideally, the different items/factors in the scale will assess distinct constructs).[2] For example, an antisocial personality may be a latent psychological construct related to violent recidivism. There are many different items we can use to try and measure this construct, including static, dynamic, and protective items. For example, items that could measure antisociality include history of criminal behaviour (a static item), current cooperation with correctional staff (a dynamic item), and whether the offender has meaningful employment that gives him/her purpose and goals (a protective factor).

Static vs. Dynamic risk factors

Risk factors are often assigned to static (unchanging) and dynamic (changing or changeable) categories. Clinicians are often most interested in dynamic risk factors because they provide a focus for interventions and are commonly perceived as being more relevant than static factors to case management. Although the distinction between static and dynamic predictors is helpful and conceptually necessary, it can often become a false dichotomy, and careful attention must be paid to how these risk indicators are measured and used to avoid confusion. For

---

[2] To clarify the meaning of this in context of the earlier distinction between criterion- and norm-referenced scales, note that risk scales are criterion-referenced and are intended to assess as many different outcome-relevant constructs as possible. Each measured construct in the scale, however, could theoretically be assessed using norm-referenced scales or scale development techniques. So, for example, if there are eight separate constructs relevant to recidivism risk, there could be eight items in the scale, whereby each item reflects a separate norm-referenced assessment. For this reason, the scale items would not be expected to cohere in a factor analysis.

example, substance abuse can be measured by history of substance abuse (static) or by current substance abuse (dynamic). Even risk factors traditionally classified as static may change over time, depending upon whether they are measured over a lifetime or over a much shorter interval. The PCL-R, for example, is generally considered to be static and is coded based on lifetime history, but some of the items, such as manipulativeness, can and do vary over time in prospective studies (Quinsey et al. 2006b). Consequently, a particular item may be static or dynamic, dependent on how it is measured.

The manner in which a risk factor is used also affects the meaning of the distinction between static and dynamic predictors. If one is to measure predictive factors at one point in time and use them to predict the likelihood of re-offending in a lengthy follow-up period, all of the predictors are static from a data analytic perspective. Even changeable variables, such as the provision of, or response to, treatment is static in this analytic sense; they cannot change once the follow-up period has begun.

Keeping in mind that the distinction between static and dynamic is not always clear, and that dynamic risk scales tend to add incrementally to static scales (e.g. Brankley et al. 2017; Helmus 2015), there is a finite amount of variance in recidivism that can be reliably explained, and static risk factors or scales tend to account for more variance than most changeable factors (e.g. Hanson et al. 2015; Helmus 2015); even amongst the Central Eight risk factors, the only static factor (criminal history) generally out-predicts the other seven changeable factors, with the possible exception of antisociality (Bonta and Andrews 2017; Olver et al. 2014b). Consistent with this research, VRAG-R items are largely static in nature and provide a baseline estimate of risk that appears valid for long follow-ups. Dynamic risk scales may add incremental validity to the VRAG-R, although based on research with other scales, the magnitude of improvement is not likely to be large. Dynamic risk scales may, however, be more useful in conceptualizing targets for treatment.

More relevant to case management, including supervision, is the use of dynamic or fluctuating risk indicators to measure imminence. In this scheme, continuously fluctuating (acute) risk factors, such as mood and compliance, that have been shown to forecast antisocial behaviours in the month following their measurement (Quinsey et al. 1997, 2006b) can be used to adjust the level of supervision parameters determined by an actuarial appraisal of long-term risk. This use of prediction is quite different than that involved in the actuarial appraisal of violence risk. Firstly, the prediction concerns a very brief period of opportunity. Secondly, because adjustments in supervision are transient, there are no apocalyptic consequences for civil liberties – thus permitting higher rates of false positives. Thirdly, the outcomes of concern need not be limited to serious violent behaviours – all antisocial behaviours (trashing the place, elopement, and so forth) that are of concern to supervisory staff would be relevant; this expansion of the behaviours to be predicted directly increases the base rate. Similarly, restricting the use of dynamic prediction to those individuals meeting a threshold of actuarially determined long-term risk also increases the base rate. Lastly, because the predictors have all been demonstrated to change and to relate prospectively to the likelihood of antisocial behaviour, they are natural targets for intervention. Although considerable effort will be required to put this scheme on a firm quantitative footing, the evidence shows that it is in principle workable. Research advances in this domain should measure dynamic risk factors at more than two time points, and will likely be aided by more sophisticated statistical techniques designed to assess changes over time (for discussion of methodological issues, see Babchishin 2013; Yang et al. 2017).

Can we override actuarial results?

It is well known (and moreover, obvious) that actuarial risk scales do not include all relevant risk factors. Does that mean that predictive accuracy could be improved by adjusting actuarial results based on external, empirical risk factors not included in the scale? This seems an intuitively defensible approach, but research has consistently found that overriding actuarial results degrades their predictive accuracy. In their meta-analysis, Hanson and Morton-Bourgon (2009) found three studies examining different risk scales, all showing degradations in predictive accuracy when clinicians were allowed to override the results. In a more recent and impressively large study, Wormith et al. (2012) examined the accuracy of the Level of Service/Case Management Inventory (LS/CMI, one of the most frequently used actuarial risk scales for general offenders; see Bonta and Andrews 2017) in predicting general, violent, and sexual recidivism for non-sex offenders ($N > 24\,000$) and sexual offenders ($N > 1900$). The results were the same for both offender types and all three recidivism outcomes: the overrides degraded the accuracy of the scale. Interestingly, the degradations were consistently more pronounced for sex offenders compared to non-sex offenders.

If we know that actuarial risk scales do not incorporate all relevant information, then why don't overrides work? There are many potential reasons for this. Although some evaluators may be capable of identifying empirically-supported risk factors external to the scale, they may not be good at integrating this information. Perhaps the additional risk factors already correlate with existing information in the scale such that the new information does not add incremental accuracy. Or perhaps they overweigh the new information – given how much is already included in the risk scales, additional relevant factors (to the extent that they exist and have been identified by the evaluator) may make only a tiny additional contribution to what is already measured, in most cases not changing the offenders' risk category. The ability to override results may exacerbate a punitive or risk-averse tendency in evaluators, which is seen in findings that evaluators are far more likely to use overrides to increase than to decrease an offender's risk score (Hanson et al. 2015; Wormith et al. 2012). Additionally, where subjectivity is increased, so is the potential for bias. Consequently, it is probable that overrides are influenced by factors irrelevant to recidivism risk. This may also explain why degradation in accuracy is strongest for sex offenders, where there is a strong negative emotional reaction to their offences. This reaction could explain why evaluators were more likely to upgrade risk excessively for sex offenders compared to non-sex offenders (Wormith et al. 2012).

Regardless of the reason for the degradation in accuracy, the research findings are clear that actuarial results should not be adjusted, and this applies to the VRAG-R as well. So, where does this leave the conscientious evaluator who knows that all relevant information is not included in the risk scale, but trying to adjust the scale will only make things worse? It is important to remember that a risk-assessment scale is one piece of information that is used in offender case management decisions. It is an important piece of information and arguably should be given the highest weight, but it is not the sole piece of information. As noted by Hanson (2009), 'scoring an actuarial risk tool is not a risk assessment' (p. 174). If there is information perceived to be crucial to intervention and supervision practices, this must be considered separately from the risk-scale results (Harris et al. 2015).

How can we incorporate treatment completion into the assessment of risk?

The developers of the VRAG-R and most other actuarial methods designed to predict recidivism of various kinds hoped that their instruments would become obsolete with the development of more effective interventions. With a perfectly effective intervention, the only information pertaining to risk a decision maker would need is knowledge of whether the offender received it. More realistically, if a particular intervention had been shown to reduce the likelihood of violent re-offending by a certain amount, that amount could be incorporated into the actuarial estimate of risk via an empirically-derived formula. Alternatively, a measure of response to intervention could be developed that could be used in a similar fashion. We are, at present, very far from this desired objective.

Although there are some treatments/interventions for offenders that have been shown to reduce criminal recidivism (e.g. Andrews et al. 1990; Hanson et al. 2009), this effect depends on the quality of the treatment, how the particular offender responded to the treatment, and likely also on the dose (Bourgon and Armstrong 2005). Additionally, there are very few high-quality research studies on this topic. Establishing the nature and size of treatment effects is sufficiently nuanced and variable, and a prerequisite for establishing their incremental effect in predicting recidivism above and beyond actuarial risk assessments. A great deal of programme development work and rigorous evaluation will be required before the receipt of, or response to, intervention can be reliably used to modify actuarial estimates of risk.

How does static risk change as a function of time spent in the community without re-offending?

One objective, static way of measuring changes in risk may simply be in recording the mere passage of time. Specifically, static actuarial risk scales such as the VRAG-R are designed to predict the occurrence of at least one relevant recidivism event (e.g. violent recidivism) over a lengthy period of opportunity. Intervals of opportunity ranging from 6 months to 49 years have been examined and the VRAG-R has good relative predictive accuracy in all of them (Harris et al. 2015b). The risk scales are scored based on the information that was available before the offender had an opportunity to re-offend (i.e. before they were released to the community after their index offence).

However, one risk-relevant piece of information is whether the offender is presented with opportunities to re-offend, but does not do so. Specifically, offenders are slightly less likely to re-offend with each year of opportunity they complete without re-offending. There is an empirically-derived formula to compute this reduction in risk for the VRAG-R (Harris et al. 2015b, p. 313). Specifically, for each year the offender remained offence-free, the original recidivism probability successively decreases 10% from the previous year. This pattern of results is broadly consistent with research on both sexual and general offenders (Bushway et al. 2011; Hanson et al. 2014a). For example, research on Static-99R (a commonly used actuarial risk scale for sex offenders; Helmus et al. 2012c) has found that for every five years sex-offence free, the initial predicted recidivism rate roughly halves, and there are now structured guidelines to adjust risk levels over time (Hanson et al. 2017b). Note that these adjustments are specific to offenders with opportunity to re-offend (i.e. released to the community). Time spent in forensic or correctional institutions after the initial assessment are not included in these adjustments. In the case of the VRAG-R research, time elapsed in custody was not related to reductions in risk (Harris et al. 2015b).

Do actuarial scales apply cross-culturally?

This question is part of a broader discussion of the extent to which we should expect risk factors to apply across diverse cultures (for a more detailed discussion of international generalizability issues in risk assessment, see Helmus et al. 2011). One of the first challenges pertains to definitions. For example, should they be based on race, ethnicity, or culture? In the US, the research emphasis has been on racial/ethnic groups, often comparing Black, White, and Latino offenders. Research based on racial definitions places greater emphasis on genetic explanations or assumptions, whereas research focusing on ethnic distinctions may be better suited to assess cultural differences, although the two cannot be fully disentangled. Recent research in the US, however, has distinguished between minority offenders born inside vs. outside the US (Boccaccini et al. 2017; Leguizamo et al. 2015), presuming that cultural differences would be stronger for offenders born outside the US. Unfortunately, these analyses are likely confounded by the quality of data available to score the risk scale (e.g. availability of complete and accurate criminal history records).

In Canada, there has been more interest in studying the applicability of risk scales with Indigenous offenders, a group that could be described emphasizing either race or culture (and different offenders could be classified as Indigenous depending on which definition is chosen). Discussions have often focused on cultural differences between Indigenous and non-Indigenous offenders (e.g. *Ewert v. Canada* 2015), suggesting that culture may be of more importance than race. Most research studies, however, have largely avoided this issue by relying on offender self-identification, not making distinctions amongst Indigenous groups (which are incredibly diverse), and not addressing variations in cultural background amongst Indigenous offenders (e.g. those raised in Indigenous communities vs. those raised in predominantly Caucasian urban areas).

Minority groups (however they are defined) may be over-represented or under-represented in correctional systems, and they may, on average, score higher or lower than non-minority populations (Brankley and Lee 2016). However, none of this necessarily means that the same risk factors and scales may not function similarly for these groups. The core issue here is not whether certain racial, ethnic, or cultural groups are over-represented or score as higher risk, but whether the scales have significantly or meaningfully *different* predictive accuracy (relative and absolute) with these groups.

Although crime rates vary substantially cross-culturally (Helmus et al. 2011), there is no *a priori* reason to expect that different risk factors will apply across different racial/cultural/ethnic groups, but this is an important empirical question. Risk scales are defensible to use insofar as they are empirically validated, and the assumption made by an evaluator is that the individual they are assessing is not meaningfully different from the offenders included in the development and validation research on the scale. Given over-representation of minority groups in many correctional systems, the applicability of risk scales with these subgroups is an important and worthwhile research question (Gutierrez et al. 2016; Hart 2016).

In Canada, we are most familiar with research on Indigenous offenders, because this is a contentious issue in Canadian correctional contexts. A recent court decision (*Ewert v. Canada* 2015) and its subsequent appeal has raised questions about the research available and the research that is needed to support the use of actuarial risk scales with Indigenous offenders, and a 2016 Special Issue of the *Journal of Threat Assessment and Management* (volume 3) was devoted to discussion of the available research and the court cases. There seems to be a fairly consistent pattern of research findings whereby actuarial risk scales significantly predict recidivism for Indigenous offenders, but the relative predictive accuracy tends to be lower than for non-Indigenous offenders, though this difference does not always reach statistical significance (Babchishin et al. 2012a; Gutierrez et al. 2013; Helmus et al. 2012a; Olver et al. 2016, 2018; Wilson and Gutierrez 2014).

Additionally, evidence suggests that SPJ risk scales may be problematic to use with Indigenous offenders. One large study has found that evaluators making clinical assessments of risk using an SPJ scale, rated Indigenous offenders as significantly higher risk than non-Indigenous offenders after controlling for all the risk factors considered in the scale (Helmus and Forrester 2014). This suggests that the greater objectivity inherent in actuarial scales may be particularly appropriate for Indigenous offenders, who could face greater discrimination in assessment schemes that allow more discretion.

Regarding other minority groups, the results have been more encouraging. There are several studies finding equivalent predictive accuracy for actuarial risk scales for Black, White, and Latino offenders (Baglivio and Jackowski 2013; Boccaccini et al. 2017; Hanson et al. 2014b; McCafferty 2016; Schwalbe et al. 2006; note that the McCafferty and Schwalbe studies did not examine Latino offenders), with all but the Hanson et al. (2014a) study having sample sizes in the thousands for the minority subgroups. There are, however, some examples of studies with much smaller sample sizes which have found meaningful differences in predictive accuracy across some racial groups (for a review, see McCafferty 2016).

Overall, research suggests that actuarial scales predict significantly better than chance for diverse racial/cultural/ethnic groups. Consequently, they are appropriate and defensible to use for these groups. However, it is also important to note that the relative predictive accuracy of risk scales is sometimes lower for Indigenous offenders, which necessitates additional caution in applying risk scales with this group. The reasons for the lower accuracy are not fully understood (for review and discussion, see Gutierrez et al. 2016), and it is possible that future research in this area will improve the performance of actuarial risk scales with Indigenous offenders. Minimally, the volume of research on this topic in insufficient at the present time (as emphasized in the *Ewert* court decisions) for strong conclusions to be drawn. For the VRAG-R in particular, validation studies are needed with Indigenous offender populations.

Do actuarial scales apply across gender?

The applicability of actuarial risk scales across gender is also an important issue. Like many (but not all) actuarial scales, VRAG and VRAG-R were designed for use with males, and are currently not recommended for female offenders, because there are potentially important differences between male and female offenders. That being said, this is also an area that is in need of further empirical validation.

In contrast to Aboriginal offenders, females are under-represented in the criminal justice system (Snyder 2003), especially in the Canadian federal prison system (which administers custodial sentences of two years or more), where women comprise approximately 5% of the offender population (Public Safety Canada 2013). Women also have lower recidivism rates than men (e.g. Andrews et al. 2012); however, this does not mean that risk factors or scales would necessarily perform differently for this subgroup.

Numerous theories emphasize important differences between male and female offenders, suggesting risk scales developed with males are not necessarily applicable to females, but many of these theories have received little empirical attention (for a review, see Blanchette and Brown 2006). In the general psychology literature, meta-analyses find more support for gender similarities than gender differences, although one of the few robust differences is lower levels of physical aggression amongst women (Hyde 2005).

Andrews et al. (2012) provided helpful terminology for examining the applicability of risk factors with female offenders. The term 'gender neutral' refers to risk factors or scales that predict similarly for male and female offenders. Risk factors are 'specific' when they predict for one gender but not the other (i.e. they could be male-specific or female-specific). And factors are 'salient' if they predict for both genders, but significantly better for one compared to the other (i.e. they could be male-salient or female-salient). In a meta-analysis of 16 studies directly comparing male and female offenders, Smith, Cullen, and Latessa (2009) found that the LSI-R risk scale (which is focused on assessing the Central Eight risk factors) was gender neutral.

In a more recent paper, Andrews et al. (2012) examined the specific domains of the LS/CMI across five samples ($N = 354$ females and 2069 males). The Central Eight risk factors were either gender-neutral or female-salient (substance abuse and criminal history had significantly higher relative predictive accuracy for females compared to males). Whilst this study provides encouraging results for risk assessment with female offenders, more research on violence risk assessment (particularly with the VRAG-R) is needed.

Should we apply group-based recidivism estimates to individuals, and should we report individual confidence intervals?

What makes actuarial risk scales unique is that they provide probability estimates for recidivism linked to specific scores or risk categories. It is possible to make statements such as '45% of people in Bin 7 of the VRAG-R are expected to be charged with a new violent offence after 5 years of follow-up'. These estimates are consistent with other fields (e.g. insurance calculations, weather predictions) and are rooted in the empirical tradition of psychology, which seeks to make generalizations or predictions about human behaviour based on prior information about other individuals. In this scientific endeavour, the larger and more representative the research data are, the greater the confidence in generalizing to new individuals. Applying information from previous groups to individuals with similar characteristics (e.g. the same risk score) is not only defensible practise, but it is the strongest empirical evidence we currently have.

As summarized by Hanson, Thornton, Helmus, and Babchishin (2016b), once we have identified the probability of recidivism associated with a particular score, there are at least three different ways these probabilities can be interpreted in applied risk assessment (Gillies 2000; Greenland 1998). The frequentist approach defines empirical probabilities based on the number of events in a given number of trials, and the observed proportion (e.g. 45 out of 100) cannot directly be applied to an individual/trial (Greenland 1998). Adherents of this approach would say that the recidivism probabilities can be described only in terms of group data (e.g. 'In previous research, 45% of people in Bin 7 of the VRAG-R violently re-offended'), without ascribing a probability of recidivism to any particular individual.

Subjectivist interpretations of probability (e.g. derived from Bayesian analyses) can be directly applied to individuals, making them more intuitively appealing. They describe certainty of beliefs (e.g. 'I am 45% confident that this offender will re-offend'; Greenland 1998). In the example of Bayesian probabilities, they rely on a concept of subjective prior information, which means it is possible that different evaluators arriving at the same actuarial risk score would provide different probability estimates of recidivism, which can be a challenge for decision makers.

Another option is the propensity interpretation (Gillies 2000; Popper 1959), which retains the objectivity of the frequentist approach, but with the conceptual benefits of the Bayesian approach, whereby the empirically-derived estimate can be ascribed to the individual. The propensity approach recognizes that risk is an underlying, continuous property of the individual assessed. Using this interpretation, it is possible to apply the recidivism estimate to the individual (e.g. 'Based on his VRAG-R bin of 7, his probability of violent recidivism is 45% over five years'). Of these three approaches, we believe that the propensity interpretation is most closely aligned with the underlying nature of risk assessment (i.e. measuring offenders on a continuous dimension of risk).

Another confusion that has appeared in the field regarding application of group data to individuals surrounds the issue of individual confidence intervals. In linear regression, where the outcome being predicted is continuous (i.e. a range of possible values), there is a distinction between group and individual confidence intervals around the predicted value. The group confidence interval describes the plausible range of expected mean outcome scores for a group of individuals with the same sample size as that used to generate the confidence intervals. In contrast, the individual confidence interval describes the plausible range of outcome scores for an individual based on their score on the predictor variable.

In recent years, Cooke and colleagues (Cooke and Michie 2009, 2010; Hart and Cooke 2013; Hart et al. 2007) have tried to apply the conceptual and computational distinctions between group and individual confidence intervals to violence risk assessment (which uses logistic regression, not linear regression), and have concluded that individual confidence intervals for recidivism estimates from actuarial risk scales are too wide to provide meaningful information about the recidivism probability of the individual. Unfortunately, the logic and calculations behind individual confidence intervals apply when the outcome is a range of scores, but not for an outcome with only two possible values (recidivist or non-recidivist). When the outcome is dichotomous, there is no distinction between the confidence intervals for the individual or for the group because the variance of the predicted value is fully determined by the mean (specifically, $\sigma^2 = [\bar{X}(1 - \bar{X})]$, using Ward's method). Subsequent articles have consistently concluded that Hart, Cooke, and Michie have incorrectly applied the formulas and logic of linear regression to actuarial risk assessment, and that their recommendations and conclusions are simply not credible (Hanson and Howard 2010; Harris et al. 2007; Imrey and Dawid 2015; Mossman and Sellke 2007). Mossman and Sellke (2007) go so far as to say that the methods employed by Hart, Michie, and Cooke (Hart et al. 2007) 'pile nonsense of top of meaninglessness' (p. 561). Instead of concluding that actuarial recidivism estimates do not provide meaningful information, the most suitable conclusion is that individual confidence intervals (whatever they might be) do not provide meaningful information for dichotomous outcomes.

Will actuarial risk scales work equally well across diverse settings? Some notes on the quality of implementation

Actuarial risk assessment scales are designed to be scored objectively and consistently across diverse raters. This should enhance consistent accuracy across diverse samples and settings. However, merely implementing an actuarial risk assessment scale is not sufficient to ensure predictive accuracy consistent with research studies. Implementing actuarial scales requires care in applying the scale to populations within the appropriate range of applications for the scale (typically specified in the coding manual or development study), as well as ensuring that raters have been appropriately trained on how to score the scale, have access to the necessary information to score the scale, and are motivated to produce accurate and high-quality assessments. Ideally, raters should have access to ongoing support and supervision as coding questions arise. The further raters deviate from the methods and definitions employed in developing the scale, the further the assessment is distanced from the empirical support for the scale.

An interesting example of how implementing the same actuarial risk scale may yield different results comes from the Static-99, the most commonly used sex offender risk assessment scale in North America and Europe (e.g. Archer et al. 2007; Blais and Forth 2014; Neal and Grisso 2014). Both Texas and California have mandated the use of Static-99 by corrections staff, with field studies published to examine its predictive accuracy. Predictive accuracy in Texas was meaningfully lower than previous research and field studies of the scale (AUC = 0.60; Boccaccini et al. 2009). In contrast, California found remarkably high levels of predictive accuracy (AUC = 0.82) – their results were amongst the best of all studies conducted on the scale, or any other actuarial risk scale (Hanson et al. 2014a).

How could two American jurisdictions implementing the same risk scale achieve such remarkably different results? There are some methodological or policy differences that could affect these findings, but at least part of the difference likely has to do with the quality of implementation. The study from Texas provides no information on how the correctional system maintains the quality of their risk assessments. In contrast, California has a remarkably rigorous implementation and quality control system. All staff who use the scale must be trained by someone certified by the Static-99 development team. All staff receive training from a detailed, standardized curriculum and by law, they must be retrained in the scale every two years. Additionally, they must pass scoring tests after training, and ideally, their first 10 to 20 cases are reviewed by a trainer. Novice users are also encouraged to work with a mentor to maintain the quality of their assessments. With such diligent attention paid to the quality of their risk scale implementation, it is not surprising that California has found some of the highest predictive accuracy ever obtained in a field setting for a risk assessment scale.

Research demonstrates that actuarial risk assessment scales are capable of producing high accuracy in predicting recidivism. However, to achieve these results in applied assessments, it is important to administer the scale accurately and conscientiously, paying close attention to the rules and recommendations of the scale developers, and grounding practice in research evidence.

Summary and Next Steps

Risk assessment has important implications for public safety and the civil liberties of offenders. The decisions that these assessments inform are more just, transparent, and accurate when based on structured empirical risk scales. Recent decades have seen considerable advances in violence risk assessment, although some areas require further empirical attention.

Risk assessment scales are best considered to be prognostic and criterion-referenced measurements of a continuous dimension of risk. This conceptualization has important implications for how to best understand and evaluate them. Recent evaluative work has explored the strengths and weaknesses of different ways (such as percentiles, risk ratios, and more empirically defensible labels/definitions for risk levels) to communicate violence risk beyond only a probability. As it stands, application of group-based recidivism estimates (and their associated group confidence intervals) reflects the best available research to guide decisions about recidivism probability. We also believe that propensity-based definitions of probability support extrapolations from group data to an individual's probability of recidivism (e.g. that it is appropriate to say 'this person's estimated risk is X%').

The VRAG and the VRAG-R have become amongst the most widely researched actuarial risk scales for assessing risk of future violence, generally demonstrating large effect sizes. The VRAG-R, in particular, has benefited from years of feedback from frontline users to develop a revised scale that can be scored faster and simpler, with no discernible loss in predictive accuracy.

Although the content and methods behind the VRAG-R are well-supported empirically, it is important to keep abreast of further developments in the field, and to periodically revise actuarial scales (or the recommendations on how to use them) as new research accumulates. In discussing some of the most common questions heard by actuarial risk-scale developers, we believe that static, dynamic, and protective factors are not necessarily distinct constructs, and a more helpful understanding focuses on all of those methods as different indicators of underlying risk-relevant propensities. Static risk factors tend to be amongst the most robust predictors and easiest to measure, and are an important foundation in any risk assessment.

The results of actuarial risk scales should not be overridden by clinical judgement, no matter how unique a particular case is believed to be. Professional judgement has its place, but that place is outside the results of the risk assessment scale. To the extent that actuarial risk scales such as the VRAG-R do not include all relevant information, the wisest course of action is to develop empirically-based structured methods of incorporating this information, such as adjustments to consider the effect of time offence-free post-release from the index offence. Incorporating other factors (e.g. completion of a credible treatment programme) may be possible, but would require considerable additional research. There is also a reasonable expectation of a point of diminishing returns, where additional information (no matter its bivariate relationship with recidivism) becomes successively less likely to add incrementally to predicting recidivism.

Applicability of risk-assessment scales and items across race/ethnicity/culture and gender remains an important area of research and debate. As this evidence base increases, recommendations on the suitable populations for these risk scales may be refined.

Lastly, the quality of a risk assessment is limited by the availability of evidence to support the methods. That being said though, in order to benefit from the empirical support available for risk assessment techniques, it is critical that risk-scale users pay close attention to their practises to ensure they are implementing the scales in a manner consistent with the research base. Careful attention to training, coding manuals/guidance, ongoing support/supervision, and monitoring research advances are all essential in implementing risk scales in applied practice.

Acknowledgement

We would like to thank R. Karl Hanson for his helpful comments on sections of this chapter.

References

Ægisdóttir, S., White, M.J., Spengler, P.M. et al. (2006). The meta-analysis of clinical judgment project: fifty-six years of accumulated research on clinical versus statistical prediction. *The Counseling Psychologist* 34: 341–382.

Aiken, L.R. (1985). *Psychological Testing and Assessment (5)*. Newton, MA: Allyn and Bacon.

Andrews, D.A., Guzzo, L., Raynor, P. et al. (2012). Are the major risk/need factors predictive of both female and male reoffending? A test with the eight domains of the Level of Service/Case

Management Inventory. *International Journal of Offender Therapy and Comparative Criminology* 56: 113–133.

Andrews, D.A., Zinger, I., Hoge, R.D. et al. (1990). Does correctional treatment work? A clinically relevant and psychologically informed meta-analysis. *Criminology* 28: 369–404.

Archer, R.P., Buffington-Vollum, J.K., Stredny, R.V., and Handel, R.W. (2006). A survey of psychological test use patterns among forensic psychologists. *Journal of Personality Assessment* 87: 84–94.

Association for the Treatment of Sexual Abusers (2014). *ATSA Practice Guidelines for Assessment, Treatment Interventions, and Management Strategies for Male Adult Sexual Abusers.* Beaverton, OR: Professional Issues Committee, ATSA.

Babchishin, K.M. (2013). *Sex offenders do change on risk-relevant propensities: Evidence from a longitudinal study of the ACUTE-2007.* Unpublished doctoral dissertation. Carleton University.

Babchishin, K.M., Blais, J., and Helmus, L. (2012a). Do static risk factors predict differently for Aboriginal sex offenders? A multi-site comparison using the original and revised Static-99 and Static-2002 scales. *Canadian Journal of Criminology and Criminal Justice* 54: 1–43.

Babchishin, K.M., Hanson, R.K., and Helmus, L. (2012b). Communicating risk for sex offenders: risk ratios for Static-2002R. *Sexual Offender Treatment* 7 (2): 1–12.

Baglivio, M.T. and Jackowski, K. (2013). Examining the validity of a juvenile offender risk assessment instrument across gender and race/ethnicity. *Youth Violence and Juvenile Justice* 11: 26–43.

Blais, J. and Forth, A.E. (2014). Prosecution-retained versus court-appointed experts: comparing and contrasting risk assessment reports in preventative detention hearings. *Law and Human Behavior* 38: 531–543.

Blanchette, K. and Brown, S.L. (2006). *The Assessment and Treatment of Women Offenders: An Integrated Perspective. Wiley Series in Forensic Clinical Psychology.* Chichester, UK: Wiley.

Boccaccini, M.T., Murrie, D.C., Caperton, J.D., and Hawes, S.W. (2009). Field validity of the Static-99 and MnSOST-R among sex offenders evaluated for civil commitment as sexually violent predators. *Psychology, Public Policy, and Law* 15: 278–314.

Boccaccini, M.T., Rice, A.K., Helmus, L.M. et al. (2017). Field validity of Static-99/R scores in a statewide sample of 34,687 convicted sexual offenders. *Psychological Assessment* 29: 611–623. https://doi.org/10.1037/pas0000377.

Bonta, J. (1996). Risk-needs assessment and treatment. In: *Choosing Correctional Options that Work: Defining the Demand and Evaluating the Supply* (ed. A.T. Harland), 18–32. Thousand Oaks, CA: Sage.

Bonta, J. and Andrews, D.A. (2017). *The Psychology of Criminal Conduct (6).* New York: Routledge.

Bonta, J., Law, M., and Hanson, K. (1998). The prediction of criminal and violent recidivism among mentally disordered offenders: a meta-analysis. *Psychological Bulletin* 123: 123–142.

Bourgon, G. and Armstrong, B. (2005). Transferring the principles of effective treatment into a "real world" prison setting. *Criminal Justice and Behavior* 32: 3–25.

Brankley, A.E., Babchishin, K.M., and Hanson, R.K. (2017). STABLE-2007 demonstrates predictive and incremental validity in assessing risk-relevant propensities for sexual offending: a meta-analysis. Unpublished manuscript.

Brankley, A.E., and Lee, S.C. (2016). *The utility of Static-99R and STABLE-2007 across different ethnic groups: A prospective field study.* Paper presented at the 35th Annual Research and Treatment Conference for the Association for the Treatment of Sexual Abusers in Orlando, FL, USA (2–5 November 2016).

Bushway, S.D., Nieubeerta, P., and Blokland, A. (2011). The predictive value of criminal background checks: do age and criminal history affect time to redemption? *Criminology* 49: 27–60.

Chevalier, C., Boccaccini, M.T., Murrie, D.C., and Varela, J.G. (2015). Static-99R reporting practices in sexually violent predator cases: does norm selection reflect adversarial allegiance? *Law and Human Behavior* 39: 209–218.

Cooke, D.J. and Michie, C. (2009). Erratum. *Law and Human Behavior*, vol. 33, 541.

Cooke, D.J. and Michie, C. (2010). Limitations of diagnostic precision and predictive utility in the individual case: a challenge for forensic practice. *Law and Human Behavior* 34: 269–274.

Crawford, J.R. and Garthwaite, P.H. (2009). Percentiles please: the case for expressing neuropsychological test scores and accompanying confidence limits as percentile ranks. *The Clinical Neuropsychologist* 23: 193–204.

Dawes, R.M., Faust, D., and Meehl, P.E. (1989). Clinical versus actuarial judgment. *Science* 243: 1668–1674.

de Vries Robbé, M., Mann, R.E., Maruna, S., and Thornton, D. (2015). An exploration of protective factors supporting desistance from sexual offending. *Sexual Abuse: A Journal of Research and Treatment* 27: 16–33.

Edens, J.F., Penson, B.N., Ruchensky, J.R. et al. (2016). Interrater reliability of violence risk appraisal guide scores provided in Canadian criminal proceedings. *Psychological Assessment* 28: 1543–1549.

Edwards, A., Elwyn, G., and Mulley, A. (2002). Explaining risk: turning numerical data into meaningful pictures. *British Medical Journal* 324: 827–830.

Ellis, L. and Walsh, A. (2000). *Criminology: A Global Perspective*. Needham Heights, MA: Allyn & Bacon.

Elmore, J.G. and Gigerenzer, G. (2005). Benign breast disease: the risk of communicating risk. *New England Journal of Medicine* 353: 297–299.

Ewert v. Canada, FC 1093 (CanLII), (2015)

Farrington, D.P. and Ttofi, M.M. (2011). Protective and promotive factors in the development of offending. *Antisocial Behavior and Crime: Contributions of Developmental and Evaluation Research to Prevention and Intervention* (eds. T. Bliesener, A. Beelmann and M. Stemmler), 71–88. Cambridge, MA: Hogrefe Publishing.

Gillies, D. (2000). Varieties of propensity. *The British Journal for the Philosophy of Science* 51: 807–835.

Greenland, S. (1998). Probability logic and probabilistic induction. *Epidemiology* 9: 322–332.

Grove, W.M., Zald, D.H., Lebow, B.S. et al. (2000). Clinical versus mechanical prediction: a meta-analysis. *Psychological Assessment* 12: 19–30.

Gutierrez, L., Helmus, L.M., and Hanson, R.K. (2016). What we know and don't know about risk assessment with offenders of Indigenous heritage. *Journal of Threat Assessment and Management* 3: 97–106.

Gutierrez, L., Wilson, H., Rugge, T., and Bonta, J. (2013). The prediction of recidivism with aboriginal offenders: a theoretically informed meta-analysis. *Canadian Journal of Criminology and Criminal Justice* 55: 55–99.

Hanson, R.K. (2009). The psychological assessment of risk for crime and violence. *Canadian Psychology* 50: 172–182.

Hanson, R.K., Babchishin, K.M., Helmus, L.M., and Thornton, D. (2013). Quantifying the relative risk of sex offenders: risk ratios for static-99R. *Sexual Abuse: A Journal of Research and Treatment* 25: 482–515.

Hanson, R.K., Babchishin, K.M., Helmus, L.M. et al. (2017a). Communicating the results of criterion-referenced prediction measures: risk categories for the Static-99R and Static-2002R sexual offender risk assessment tools. *Psychological Assessment* 29: 582–597.

Hanson, R.K., Bourgon, G., Helmus, L., and Hodgson, S. (2009). The principles of effective correctional treatment also apply to sexual offenders: a meta-analysis. *Criminal Justice and Behavior* 36: 865–891.

Hanson, R.K., Bourgon, G., McGrath, R.J. et al. (2016a). *A Five-Level Risk and Needs System: Maximizing Assessment Results in Corrections Through the Development of a Common Language*. Washington, DC: Justice Center Council of State Governments.

Hanson, R.K., Harris, A.J.R., Helmus, L., and Thornton, D. (2014a). High risk sex offenders may not be high risk forever. *Journal of Interpersonal Violence* 29: 2792–2813.

Hanson, R.K., Harris, A.J.R., Letourneau, E. et al. (2017b). Reductions in risk based on time offense free in the community: once a sex offender, not always a sex offender. *Psychology, Public Policy, and Law* 24: 48–63.

Hanson, R.K., Harris, A.J.R., Scott, T.-L., and Helmus, L. (2007). *Assessing the risk of sexual offenders on community supervision: The Dynamic Supervision Project* (User Report No. 2007–05). Ottawa, ON: Public Safety Canada.

Hanson, R.K., Helmus, L., and Thornton, D. (2010). Predicting recidivism among sexual offenders: a multi-site study of Static-2002. *Law and Human Behavior* 34: 198–211.

Hanson, R.K., Helmus, L.M., and Harris, A.J.R. (2015). Assessing the risk and needs of supervised sexual offenders: a prospective study using STABLE-2007, Static-99R, and Static-2002R. *Criminal Justice and Behavior* 42: 1205–1224.

Hanson, R.K. and Howard, P.D. (2010). Individual confidence intervals do not inform decision-makers about the accuracy of risk assessment evaluations. *Law and Human Behavior* 2010: 275–281.

Hanson, R.K., Lloyd, C.D., Helmus, L., and Thornton, D. (2012). Developing non-arbitrary metrics for risk communication: percentile ranks for the Static-99/R and Static-2002/R sexual offender risk tools. *International Journal of Forensic Mental Health* 9: 11–23.

Hanson, R.K., Lunetta, A., Phenix, A. et al. (2014b). The field validity of Static-99/R sex offender risk assessment tool in California. *Journal of Threat Assessment and Management* 1: 102–117.

Hanson, R.K. and Morton-Bourgon, K.E. (2005). The characteristics of persistent sexual offenders: a meta-analysis of recidivism studies. *Journal of Consulting and Clinical Psychology* 73: 1154–1163.

Hanson, R.K. and Morton-Bourgon, K.E. (2009). The accuracy of recidivism risk assessments for sexual offenders: a meta-analysis of 118 prediction studies. *Psychological Assessment* 21: 1–21.

Hanson, R.K., Thornton, D., Helmus, L.M., and Babchishin, K.M. (2016b). What sexual recidivism rates are associated with Static-99R and Static-2002R scores? *Sexual Abuse: A Journal of Research and Treatment* 28: 218–252.

Hare, R.D. (2003). *The Revised Psychopathy Checklist*. Toronto, ON: Multi-Health Systems.

Harris, A.J.R. and Hanson, R.K. (2004). *Sex offender recidivism: A simple question (User Report 2004–03)*. Ottawa, ON: Public Safety and Emergency Preparedness Canada.

Harris, G.T., Lowenkamp, C.T., and Hilton, N.Z. (2015a). Evidence for risk estimate precision: implications for individual risk communication. *Behavioural Sciences and the Law* 33: 111–127.

Harris, G.T. and Rice, M.E. (2015). Progress in violence risk appraisal and communication: a commentary on hypotheses and evidence. *Behavioral Sciences & the Law* 33: 128–145.

Harris, G.T., Rice, M.E., and Cormier, C.A. (2002). Prospective replication of the Violence Risk Appraisal Guide in predicting violent recidivism among forensic patients. *Law and Human Behavior* 26: 377–394.

Harris, G.T., Rice, M.E., and Quinsey, V.L. (1993). Violent recidivism of mentally disordered offenders: the development of a statistical prediction instrument. *Criminal Justice and Behavior* 20: 315–335.

Harris, G.T., Rice, M.E., and Quinsey, V.L. (2007). Abandoning evidence-based risk appraisal in forensic practice: comments on Hart et al. *British Journal of Psychiatry* 190: S60–s65.

Harris, G.T., Rice, M.E., Quinsey, V.L., and Cormier, C.A. (2015b). *Violent Offenders: Appraising and Managing Risk (3)*. Washington, DC: American Psychological Association.

Harris, G.T., Rice, M.E., Quinsey, V.L. et al. (2003). A multi-site comparison of actuarial risk instruments for sex offenders. *Psychological Assessment* 15: 413–425.

Hart, S.D. (2016). Culture and violence risk assessment: the case of *Ewert v. Canada. Journal of Threat Assessment and Management* 3: 76–96.

Hart, S.D. and Cooke, D.J. (2013). Another look at the (im-)precision of individual risk estimates made using actuarial risk assessment instruments. *Behavioral Sciences & the Law* 31: 81–102.

Hart, S.D., Michie, C., and Cooke, D.J. (2007). Precision of actuarial risk assessment instruments: evaluating the 'margins of error' of group v. individual predictions of violence. *British Journal of Psychiatry* 190: s60–s65.

Helmus, L.M. (2015). Developing and validating a risk assessment scale to predict inmate placements in administrative segregation in the Correctional Service of Canada. Doctoral dissertation. Carleton University.

Helmus, L.M. (2018). Sex offender risk assessment: Where are we and where are we going? *Current Psychiatry Reports* 20 (6): 46.

Helmus, L.M. and Babchishin, K. (2017). Primer on risk assessment and the statistics used to evaluate its accuracy. *Criminal Justice and Behavior* 44: 8–25.

Helmus, L.M., Babchishin, K.M., and Blais, J. (2012a). Predictive accuracy of dynamic risk factors for Aboriginal and non-Aboriginal sex offenders: an exploration comparison using STABLE-2007. *International Journal of Offender Therapy and Comparative Criminology* 56: 856–876.

Helmus, L.M. and Bourgon, G. (2011). Taking stock of 15 years of research on the Spousal Assault Risk Assessment guide (SARA): a critical review. *International Journal of Forensic Mental Health* 10: 64–75.

Helmus, L.M. and Forrester, T. (2014). *Static Factors Assessment (SFA): Relationship to release and recidivism outcomes* (Research Report No. R-339). Ottawa, ON: Correctional Service of Canada.

Helmus, L.M., Hanson, R.K., and Morton-Bourgon, K.E. (2011). International comparisons of the validity of actuarial risk tools for sexual offenders, with a focus on Static-99. In: *International Perspectives on the Assessment and Treatment of Sexual Offenders: Theory, Practice, and Research* (eds. D.P. Boer, L.A. Craig, R. Eher, et al.), 57–83. Chichester, West Sussex, U.K.: Wiley.

Helmus, L.M., Hanson, R.K., Thornton, D. et al. (2012b). Absolute recidivism rates predicted by Static-99R and Static-2002R sex offender risk assessment tools vary across samples: a meta-analysis. *Criminal Justice and Behavior* 39: 1148–1171.

Helmus, L.M. and Thornton, D. (2016). The MATS-1 risk assessment scale: summary of methodological concerns and an empirical validation. *Sexual Abuse: A Journal of Research and Treatment* 28: 160–186.

Helmus, L.M., Thornton, D., Hanson, R.K., and Babchishin, K.M. (2012c). Improving the predictive accuracy of Static-99 and Static-2002 with older sex offenders: revised age weights. *Sexual Abuse: A Journal of Research and Treatment* 24: 64–101.

Hilton, N.Z., Carter, A., Harris, G.T., and Sharpe, A.J.B. (2008). Does using nonnumerical terms to describe risk aid violence risk communication? *Journal of Interpersonal Violence* 23: 171–188.

Hyde, J.S. (2005). The gender similarities hypothesis. *American Psychologist* 60: 581–592.

Imrey, P.B. and Dawid, A.P. (2015). A commentary on statistical assessment of violence recidivism risk. *Statistics and Public Policy* 2: 1–28.

Kahneman, D. (2011). *Thinking Fast and Slow*. New York, NY: MacMillan.

Kahneman, D. and Klein, G. (2009). Conditions for intuitive expertise: a failure to disagree. *American Psychologist* 64: 515–526.

Langan, P.A. and Levin, D.J. (2002). *Recidivism of prisoners released in 1994 (Bureau of Justice Statistics Special Report NCJ 193427)*. Washington, DC: US Department of Justice.

Leguizamo, A., Lee, S.C., Jeglic, E.L., and Calkins, C. (2015). Utility of the Static-99 and Static-99R with Latino sex offenders. *Sexual Abuse: A Journal of Research and Treatment* 29: 765–785.

Lehmann, R.J.B., Thornton, D., Helmus, L.M., and Hanson, R.K. (2016). Developing non-arbitrary metrics for risk communication: norms for the risk matrix 2000. *Criminal Justice and Behavior* 43: 1661–1687.

Leistico, A.-M.R., Salekin, R.T., DeCoster, J., and Rogers, R. (2008). A large-scale meta-analysis relating the Hare measures of psychopathy to antisocial conduct. *Law and Human Behavior* 32: 28–45.

Lösel, F. and Farrington, D.P. (2012). Direct protective and buffering protective factors in the development of youth violence. *American Journal of Preventive Medicine* 43: S8–S23.

Mann, R.E., Hanson, R.K., and Thornton, D. (2010). Assessing risk for sexual recidivism: some proposals on the nature of psychologically meaningful risk factors. *Sexual Abuse: A Journal of Research and Treatment* 22: 191–217.

McCafferty, J.T. (2016). Unjust disparities? The impact of race on juvenile risk assessment outcomes. *Criminal Justice Policy Review* 29: 423–442.

Meehl, P.E. (1954). *Clinical Versus Statistical Prediction: A Theoretical Analysis and a Review of the Evidence*. Minneapolis, MN: University of Minnesota Press.

Mills, J.F., Jones, M.N., and Kroner, D.G. (2005). An examination of the generalizability of the LSI-R and VRAG probability bins. *Criminal Justice and Behavior* 32: 565–585.

Monahan, J. and Silver, E. (2003). Judicial decision thresholds for violence risk management. *International Journal of Forensic Mental Health* 2: 1–6.

Mossman, D. (1994). Assessing predictions of violence: being accurate about accuracy. *Journal of Consulting and Clinical Psychology* 62 (4): 783–792.

Mossman, D. and Sellke, T.M. (2007). Avoiding errors about the 'margins of error'. *British Journal of Psychiatry* 191: 561.

Neal, T.M.S. and Grisso, T. (2014). Assessment practices and expert judgment methods in forensic psychology and psychiatry: an international snapshot. *Criminal Justice and Behavior* 41: 1406–1421.

Nuffield, J. (1982). *Parole Decision-Making in Canada: Research Toward Decision Guidelines.* Ottawa, ON: Solicitor General of Canada.

Olver, M.E., Beggs Christofferson, S.M., Grace, R.C., and Wong, S.C.P. (2014a). Incorporating change information into sexual offender risk assessments using the Violence Risk Scale – sexual offender version. *Sexual Abuse: A Journal of Research and Treatment* 26: 472–499.

Olver, M.E., Neumann, C.S., Sewall, L.A. et al. (2018). A comprehensive examination of the psychometric properties of the Hare Psychopathy Checklist-Revised in a Canadian multisite sample of indigenous and non-indigenous offenders. *Psychological Assessment* 30: 779–792.

Olver, M.E., Sowden, J.N., Kingston, D.A. et al. (2016). Predictive accuracy of Violence Risk Scale – sexual offender version risk and change scores in treated Canadian Aboriginal and non-Aboriginal sexual offenders. *Sexual Abuse: A Journal of Research and Treatment* 30: 254–275.

Olver, M.E., Stockdale, K.C., and Wormith, J.S. (2014b). Thirty years of research on the Level of Service scales: a meta-analytic examination of predictive accuracy and sources of variability. *Psychological Assessment* 26: 156–176.

Popper, K.R. (1959). The propensity interpretation of probability. *British Journal for the Philosophy of Science* 10 (37): 25–42.

Public Safety Canada (2013). Corrections and conditional release statistical overview: annual report 2013. (Cat. No.: PS1–3/2013E).

Quinsey, V.L. and Ambtman, R. (1979). Variables affecting psychiatrists' and teachers' assessments of the dangerousness of mentally ill offenders. *Journal of Consulting and Clinical Psychology* 47: 353–362.

Quinsey, V.L., Coleman, G., Jones, B., and Altrows, I. (1997). Proximal antecedents of eloping and reoffending among mentally disordered offenders. *Journal of Interpersonal Violence* 12: 794–813.

Quinsey, V.L., Harris, G.T., Rice, M.E., and Cormier, C.A. (2006a). *Violent Offenders: Appraising and Managing Risk (2).* Washington, DC: American Psychological Association.

Quinsey, V.L., Jones, G.B., Book, A.S., and Barr, K.N. (2006b). The dynamic prediction of antisocial behavior among forensic psychiatric patients: a prospective field study. *Journal of Interpersonal Violence* 21: 1539–1565.

Rice, M.E. and Harris, G.T. (2005). Comparing effect sizes in follow-up studies: ROC area, Cohen's d, and r. *Law and Human Behavior* 29: 615–620.

Rice, M.E., Harris, G.T., and Lang, C. (2013). Validation of and revision to the VRAG and SORAG: the Violence Risk Appraisal Guide-Revised (VRAG-R). *Psychological Assessment* 25: 951–965.

Roberts, A.R., Zgoba, K.M., and Shahidullah, S.M. (2007). Recidivism among four types of homicide offenders: an exploratory analysis of 336 homicide offenders in New Jersey. *Aggression and Violent Behavior* 12: 493–507.

Sampson, R.J., Raudenbush, S.W., and Earls, F. (1997). Neighbourhoods and violent crime: a multilevel study of collective efficacy. *Science* 277: 918–924.

Schwalbe, C.S., Fraser, M.W., Day, S.H., and Cooley, V. (2006). Classifying juvenile offenders according to risk of recidivism: predictive validity, race/ethnicity, and gender. *Criminal Justice and Behavior* 33: 305–324.

Shanteau, J. (1992). Competence in experts: the role of task characteristics. *Organizational Behavior and Human Decision Processes* 53: 252–262.

Shaw, N.J. and Dear, P.R. (1990). How do parents of babies interpret qualitative expressions of probability? *Archives of Disease in Childhood* 65: 520–523.

Singh, J.P., Desmarais, S.L., Hurducas, C. et al. (2014). International perspectives on the practical application of violence risk assessment: a global survey of 44 countries. *International Journal of Forensic Mental Health* 13: 193–206.

Slovic, P., Monahan, J., and MacGregor, D.G. (2000). Violence risk assessment and risk communication: the effects of using actual cases, providing instruction, and employing probability versus frequency formats. *Law and Human Behavior* 24: 271–296.

Smith, P., Cullen, F.T., and Latessa, E.J. (2009). Can 14,737 women be wrong? A meta-analysis of the LSI-R and recidivism for female offenders. *Criminology & Public Policy* 8: 183–208.

Snowden, R.J., Gray, N.S., Taylor, J., and MacCulloch, M.J. (2007). Actuarial prediction of violent recidivism in mentally disordered offenders. *Psychological Medicine* 37: 1539–1549.

Snyder, H.N. (2003). *Juvenile Arrests 2001*. Washington, DC: U.S. Department of Justice, Office of Juvenile Justice and Delinquency Prevention.

Swets, J.A., Dawes, R.M., and Monahan, J. (2000). Psychological science can improve diagnostic decisions. *Psychological Science in the Public Interest* 1: 1–26.

Varela, J.G., Boccaccini, M.T., Cuervo, V.A. et al. (2014). Same score, different message: perceptions of offender risk depend on Static-99R risk communication format. *Law and Human Behavior* 38: 418–427.

Walsh, E., Buchanan, A., and Fahy, T. (2002). Violence and schizophrenia: examining the evidence. *The British Journal of Psychiatry* 180: 490–495.

Wilson, H.A. and Gutierrez, L. (2014). Does one size fit all? A meta-analysis examining the predictive ability of the level of service inventory (LSI) with Aboriginal offenders. *Criminal Justice and Behavior* 41: 196–219.

Wormith, J.S., Hogg, S., and Guzzo, L. (2012). The predictive validity of a general risk/needs assessment inventory on sexual offender recidivism and an exploration of the professional override. *Criminal Justice and Behavior* 39: 1511–1538.

Wormith, J.S., Olver, M.E., Stevenson, H.E., and Girard, L. (2007). The long-term prediction of offender recidivism using diagnostic, personality, and risk/need approaches to offender assessment. *Psychological Services* 4: 287–305.

Yang, M., Guo, B., Olver, M.E. et al. (2017). Assessing associations between changes in risk and subsequent reoffending: an introduction to relevant statistical models. *Criminal Justice and Behavior* 44: 59–84.

7

Structured Professional Judgement in Violence Risk Assessment

Catherine Garrington[1] and Douglas P. Boer[2]

[1] Faculty of Health, University of Canberra, Canberra, Australia
[2] Centre for Applied Psychology, University of Canberra, Canberra, Australia

Introduction

Mental health professionals have long assessed an individual's future risk of violence for the safety of the community and the treatment of the individual. With risk assessments used in mental health, community and criminal justice settings, the importance of accuracy remains paramount. The results of violence risk assessments are often incorporated into decisions regarding mental health and criminal detention, and in criminal sentencing procedures.

There are numerous parties with a vested interest in assessing an individual's potential for future use of violence. These parties include the individual who commits violence, the victim/s of violence and family and/or friends of both. Additional parties include police forces, judicial members, mental health services, correctional services and the general community. However, it is the professionals (psychiatrists, psychologists and other practitioners) who bear the responsibility of completing risk assessments and the ethical accountability of their findings.

Historically, clinical assessments have competed with specific assessment tools to provide predictions of future risk of violence (See Cooper et al. 2008, for a review and case study examples). Clinical decision making relies on the expertise of the assessor, with subjective conclusions reached based on the assessors' knowledge, clinical hypotheses, and experience. In comparison, pure actuarial risk assessments rely solely on data and statistical probability in the absence of human expertise (See Chapter 9, Rettenberger and Craig).

The development of risk assessment methodologies for populations who use violence has remained commensurate with methodological changes in general risk assessment. Progressing through four generations of risk assessment development to the current tools, Structured Professional Judgement (SPJ) tools combine actuarial data with informed clinical assessments and provide recommendations for areas of treatment and management. SPJ tools assist professionals to not only assess an individual's future risk of violence, but also to document changes

The Wiley Handbook of What Works in Violence Risk Management: Theory, Research and Practice,
First Edition. Edited by J. Stephen Wormith, Leam A. Craig, and Todd E. Hogue.
© 2020 John Wiley & Sons Ltd. Published 2020 by John Wiley & Sons Ltd.

in risk and guide interventions, thereby reducing their risk of re-offending. As queried by Klepfisz et al. (2017), without reducing risk of re-offending, what, indeed, is the point of risk assessment?

This chapter will provide a brief overview of the development of violence risk assessment, and review SPJ tools in current usage for populations at risk of future use of violence. A summary of specific cohorts that use violence risk assessment tools will then be surveyed. Finally, we consider current research in this arena, along with ongoing ethical considerations.

First generation risk assessment – unstructured clinical judgement

Initial predictions of risk of violence by mental health professionals were clinical opinions of a violent individual's circumstances based on the professional's hypotheses about the causes of violent behaviour and their own experiences. Although this method was based on perceived expertise, it provided no better than chance prediction of future violence (Ægisdóttir et al. 2006). Ennis and Litwack's (1974) paper highlighted the extraordinary power psychiatric experts have in the courtroom to affect the defendant's liberty and queried both the reliability and validity of unstructured clinical judgements.

As noted by Cooper et al. (2008), mental health professionals in this generation often made subjective clinical opinions and judgements based on their personal experiences. These judgements often did not predict future risk of violence with any degree of accuracy (Cooper et al. 2008). As also discussed in Quinsey (1995), the prediction of criminal violence based on professional induction is a poor predictor of future violence. Further disadvantages include the varying levels of training and experience in expert testimony, assessor susceptibility to bias, lack of ease of replication, context of assessment and ambiguity (Ennis and Litwack 1974).

Second generation risk assessment – actuarial risk assessment instruments

Actuarial risk assessment instruments for violence require the assessor to respond to the presence or absence of pre-set factors to ascertain the possibility of a future violent event occurring. The accumulation of multiple risk factors thus increases an individual's future risk of use of violence. As data is gathered through ongoing research, reference data can be established, and individual scores compared to population scores and group norms. The measurable data is directly linked to outcome variables and provides a statistically valid risk category predicting use of future violence by an individual. Although the accuracy of statistical probability cannot be denied, actuarial risk assessment instruments are prone to group and individual errors. The overall margin of error can impact individual findings (Hart et al. 2007).

Actuarial assessments of violence provide a probability based on static risk factors and does not provide room for the inclusion of dynamic or protective factors. By nature, static factors tend to be historical (for example, criminal history or past use of illicit substances) and thus unchangeable. Critics of actuarial assessment note the absence of the application of clinical knowledge, the inability to weight factors to individual or situational circumstances, the inability to include additional risk factors, and the inability to know exactly where an offender sits in comparison to the group norms (see Hart et al. 2007 and Hart and Cooke 2013).

The static nature of actuarial tools may provide a high degree of accuracy in data comparison of past events but does not account for the human ability to change their behaviours in positive ways. To their detriment, actuarial tools are unable to measure individual change over time and thus do not represent decreases in risk although some tools have attempted to include risk reductions based on time free from detected offending.

Third generation risk assessment – risk/need/responsivity based instruments

Developed in the 1980s, the Risk/Need/Responsivity Model (RNR) highlighted the importance of the inclusion of individual circumstances in the assessment of risk (Andrews et al. 1990). The *Risk Principle* suggests that criminal behaviour can be treated, and that interventions should be provided appropriate to the assessed risk level of the offender. For example, high-risk offenders should receive high levels of intervention, and low-risk offenders, by extension, should receive low levels of intervention. The *Need Principle* stipulates that identified criminogenic needs (i.e. dynamic risk issues) for each offender should be the focus of intervention. The *Responsivity Principle* suggests that intervention is more likely to be effective if it is provided in a way that is commensurate with the offender's learning style (see Andrews and Bonta 2010). Predominantly used in the correctional field, RNR principles can also be applied in general mental health, psychological, and sentencing proceedings (Andrews and Bonta 2010).

Recognizing the need for assessment of dynamic factors, perhaps the most notable example of an RNR-based assessment tool is the Level of Service Inventory – Revised (LSI-R; Andrews and Bonta 1995). The LSI-R is commonly used in correctional services to assess an offender's change in risk of re-offending during a period of supervision. Actuarial in nature, the LSI-R identifies an individual's criminogenic needs based on the completion of a 52-item instrument, including dynamic and changeable risk factors such as changes in employment status. With rescoring recommended every 12 months or upon a major change in circumstances, the LSI-R is able to capture changes in need to either decrease or increase an offender's assessed risk of general re-offending.

With the addition of dynamic risk factors to static risk factors, assessors gained the ability to measure and monitor change over time for each individual when compared to their own previous scores. This approach also provides guidance for risk reduction by providing treatment targets through the identification of relevant dynamic risk factors. For example, assisting a homeless offender to source appropriate accommodation may reduce risk. Whilst providing an individual focus, the RNR model requires repeated administration to capture changes in circumstances, although most likely on a non-onerous (e.g. annual) basis. Andrews and Bonta (2010) emphasized the importance of RNR principles being applied not only in assessment but in treatment programmes, especially in programme integrity and staff training. However, the RNR model retains a risk-oriented focus.

Fourth generation risk assessment – SPJ instruments

Both clinical and actuarial approaches can provide a prediction of violent reoffending in numerical or categorical terms, assigning a level of assessed risk based on static or dynamic factors. SPJ may be viewed as a combination of actuarial and clinical decision making, essentially providing an empirical basis for clinical observations. Similar to actuarial tools, risk factors are scored as absent (0), somewhat present (1), or present (2) and higher overall scores are related to increased future risk of an individual's propensity to be violent. In comparison to either pure clinical or actuarial tools, SPJ tools then guide the assessor to consider a range of factors, form a judgement of risk and assist with case planning and treatment interventions. This provides the basis for the interpretation of the combination of factors relevant to the individual. Although somewhat subjective, the SPJ approach results in the identification of treatment targets and guides risk management based on a structured set of guidelines and summary risk ratings (Falzer 2013). Balancing subjectivity in risk assessment with documentable outcomes, SPJ tools represent an advance in risk assessment by providing specific factors for treatment and the management of an individual's overall risk.

A variety of SPJ tools for specific cohorts have been developed, with predictive validities ranging from low to high. The individuality of predictive validity arises from the identification of factors specific to each cohort. Of especial note is the necessity for validity of static actuarial factors to form the basis to which SPJ dynamic factors are added. The premise a dynamic factor must have descriptive factors to which individual information is matched against during assessment is crucial to SPJ assessments.

The inclusion of dynamic risk factors such as attitudinal, behavioural and social issues provide SPJ risk assessment with broad scope to recognize the human ability to change. This can assist in not only the risk assessment of an individual's capacity for future violence, but can also provide guidance in entering treatment programmes, forming treatment targets and the selection of appropriate interventions. Thus, relying on structured clinical judgement of known correlates of risk for violence provides a fuller picture of an individual's circumstances, risk factors and targeted area/s of need to reduce future re-offending.

Importantly, SPJ tools are designed to be used in conjunction with other risk assessment instruments. In addition, a numerical presentation of the risk level is not recommended, with best practice to present the risk category in conjunction with an explanation (Guy et al. 2012).

Case formulation and SPJ tools

Whilst each risk assessment tool has specific guidelines and scoring criteria, there are generalities in the application of SPJ tools. These include the identification of risk factors, the presence (or absence) of protective factors, a risk formulation, and the development of a treatment or management plan. This may also include scenario planning to consider the future application of identified management strategies, such as in the Historical, Clinical, Risk Management, Version 3 (HCR-20[V3])(Douglas et al. 2013).

Guy et al.'s (2012)' case study highlighted the ways in which SPJ assessments and case formulations can be used to guide treatment. For Mr. S, a psychiatric inpatient, SPJ informed his risk management, privilege level and discharge decisions. With the ability to be rescored if/when Mr. S's circumstances change (for example, inpatient vs. community, absence vs. presence of psychiatric symptoms and/or compliance vs. non-compliance), Guy et al. (2012) successfully apply the SPJ case formulation to a complex case.

Positive practice and protective factors

The rise of the positive psychology movement has impacted risk assessment by shifting the focus from a 'risk' to a 'strengths' perspective. For a brief introduction to positive psychology, prevention and the importance of strengths, please see Seligman and Csikszentmihalyi (2000). In their words (p. 7):

'Treatment is not just fixing what is broken; it is nurturing what is best.'

Assessment instruments that focus solely on risk factors and their management may neglect the contribution positive life actions can make to the reduction of overall risk of future violence. Newer SPJ tools such as the Structured Assessment of PROtective Factors (SAPROF; de Vogel et al. 2011) and Short-Term Assessment of Risk and Treatability (START; Webster et al. 2006) focus on protective factors against violence, either exclusively (SAPROF) or in a balanced risk-strengths model (START). Klepfisz et al. (2017) noted ongoing challenges in defining the term 'protective', and argue the use of terminology such as 'strengths' and 'capabilities' may more clearly indicate not only the presence of a factor but also the willingness of an individual to use it. For example, the presence of a supportive, pro-social relationship is not a protective factor unless the individual is willing and able to engage with the support offered. Although casting some doubt of the application of these factors to violence risk assessment, Klepfisz et al. (2017) encouraged further research.

Polaschek (2017) provided a considered evaluation of whether protective factors are indeed different to risk factors, including the possible relationships between them. Suggesting the action of the protection may be the treatment or change of dynamic risk factors, Polaschek (2017) suggested 'desistance' may be more appropriate terminology and concluded more research is required on this topic.

An exclusive focus on risk factors can be seen by offenders in treatment as focussing only on the negative aspects of their persona. Although terminology more often used in sexual offender treatment, the Self-Regulation Model includes 'avoidance goals', those requiring an offender to avoid certain situations that may increase their risk of re-offending, such as drug use or anti-social peers. The inclusion of positive, or 'approach goals' can provide a more balanced treatment structure that allows the development of self-esteem and reinforcement of pro-social activities (Ward 2000). For further discussion of protective factors and models of offending, please see Ward (2017).

SPJ Assessment Tools

There are a variety of SPJ assessment tools applicable to particular types of violence, or to specific cohorts who use violence. Please see Table 7.1 for an overview of SPJ assessment tools considered in this book for specific violence types and/or cohorts.

Domestic violence

Previously encompassing any violence committed within the family context, domestic violence is now considered to exclude Intimate Partner Violence (IPV). Please see below and Chapter 15 for a consideration of IPV. Thus, the definition of domestic violence generally now includes offences committed by adult children against parents, siblings and other family members. That said, one of the earliest and most researched tools, is the Spousal Assault Risk Assessment Guide (SARA; Kropp et al. 1995). Please see Chapter 8 for further information on domestic violence risk assessment.

Sexual violence

Sexual violence may be committed in a range of contexts. This can include adult and/or child victims. There are SPJ tools specific to the assessment of youth (aged 12–18 years) who have committed sexual violence, including the Estimate of Risk Adolescent Sexual Offence Recidivism (ERASOR; Worling and Curwen 2001) and for the assessment of adults, such as the Sexual Violence Risk – 20 (SVR-20) (Boer et al. 1997).

Table 7.1 Structured professional judgement (SPJ) assessment tools for specific violence type/cohorts.

Violence Type/Cohort	SPJ Assessment Tools	Chapter
Violence (general)	Historical, Clinical, Risk Management, Version 3 (HCR-20^V3)	7
	Structured Assessment of PROtective Factors (SAPROF)	
	Short Term Assessment of Risk and Treatability (START)	
Domestic Violence	Ontario Domestic Assault Risk Assessment (ODARA)	8
Sexual Violence	Estimate of Risk Adolescent Sexual Offence Recidivism (ERASOR)	9
	Risk of Sexual Violence Protocol (RSVP)	
	Sexual Violence Risk – 20 (SVR-20)	
Personality-based Violence	Psychopathy Checklist Revised (PCL-R)	10
	Psychopathy Checklist: Screening Version (PCL: SV)	
Youth Violence	Structured Assessment of Violence Risk in Youth (SAVRY)	11
Anger/Emotional Regulation	Short Anger Measure	12
Gang Violence	Gang Risk of Entry Factors (GREF)	13
Terrorism and Ideological Violence	Extremism Risk Guidelines 22+ (ERG 22+)	14
	Violent Extremism Risk Assessment protocol (VERA-2)	
Intimate Partner Violence (IPV)	Brief Spousal Assault Form for the Evaluation of Risk (B-SAFER)	15
	Spousal Assault Risk Assessment Guide (SARA)	
Violent Offenders with an Intellectual Disability (ID)	Assessment of Risk and Manageability for Individuals with Developmental and Intellectual Limitations who Offend Sexually (ARMIDILO-S)	17
Stalking	Stalking Assessment and Management (SAM)	27
	Stalking Risk Profile (SRP)	

Specifically designed for the youth population, the ERASOR total score has good predictive validity Area Under the Curve ((AUC) = 0.72) (Worling et al. 2012).

The SVR-20 has been subjected to a large variety of research. Of note, it has been found to have good predictive validity for sexual recidivism (AUC = 0.72) (Rettenberger et al. 2011). Systematic reviews including that by Singh et al. (2011) confirm good predictive validity (AUC = 0.70) over multiple studies.

These and other tests were developed within the SPJ framework and are reviewed in Chapter 9 of the present volume.

Personality based violence

Personality disorders have long been proposed as having a causal relationship with violence (see Howard 2015 for a summary). However, whether personality disorders are 'causal', or whether personality traits such as impulsivity and delusions may better explain the over representation of those in the criminal justice system remains an ongoing area of research. Please see Chapter 10 for further discourse on personality-based violence.

Youth violence

Whilst there is no dispute as to the developmental trajectory of teenagers, the position of youth violence as a distinction from adult violence provides opportunities to divert youth from a lifetime of criminal activity. With the possibility of identifying major turning points for behaviour change, the application of youth specific SPJ tools is of vital importance. Youth violence is considered a matter of priority, especially in relation to high-profile violent offences such as school shootings (see Bushman et al. 2016 for a full commentary).

The 24-item Structured Assessment of Violence Risk in Youth (SAVRY; Borum et al. 2000) for those aged between 12 and 18 years, is based on the risk factors of the HCR-20. With three domains (Historical, Social/Contextual, and Individual/Clinical), the SAVRY also includes protective factors. In a study of 121 juvenile offenders, the SAVRY was found to have strong predictive validity of ROC 0.75 and 0.66 for general and violent recidivism respectively at the one-year follow up period (Myers and Schmidt 2008). Of note, this study found no significant differences between male and female juvenile offenders.

A recent study comparing a variety of youth-specific risk assessment tools including the SAVRY, found the addition of protective factors did not improve the tools' predictive validity (Dickens and O'Shea 2018). The authors noted their disappointment with this finding, and strongly encourage further research on protective factors and their applicability to SPJ youth assessment. Please see Chapter 11 for more information on the risk assessment of youth who have committed violent offences.

Anger/emotional regulation

Whilst anger is a feeling commonly experienced within the general population, the expression of this in ways that violently harm others is fortunately less common. The ability to regulate the expression of anger is a learned skill, as is the ability to recognize the emotions underlying this expression. Research has indicated brain function deficits may contribute to the expression of anger (violence), however targeted interventions can improve emotional regulation and executive functioning to reduce violence (Holley et al. 2015). Please see Chapter 12 for further exploration of anger and emotional regulation in relation to violence.

Gang violence

Gangs have long provided like-minded individuals the opportunity to associate and, in criminal contexts, support each other to commit a range of offences. The fairly strong association between gang membership and offending behaviours was captured in a 2016 meta-analysis (Pyrooz et al. 2015). The study noted the strength of this relationship was stronger in United States of America (USA) based gangs than in European gangs and suggested further research into gang organization and structure. It is noted this meta-analysis incorporated 'violence' as one of the search terms for 'offending' and did not provide a breakdown of offending in a violent manner.

At this time, there are no SPJ instruments specific to the assessment of violence by gang members. However, the application of general violence assessment tools can provide utility in assessing an individual's capacity for future violence. It is further noted there are suggested overlaps between youth violence and gang violence (see Ross and Arsenault 2017) and similarities between gang violence and ideological violence (see Pyrooz et al. 2017). Please see Chapter 13 for further discussion on gang violence.

Terrorism and ideological violence

An emerging field of research, SPJ tools have been developed to assess an individual's risk of committing terrorism and ideological violence, and to formulate treatment and management pathways. Sarma (2017) discussed the challenges in assessing this population, noting how the consequences of identification of future risk can have long-term impacts on an individual's freedom. Richards (2018) discussed the importance of SPJ assessments within this cohort, particularly in relation to de-radicalization and release of offenders from custodial settings. Please also see Scarcella et al. (2016) for a review of current risk assessment tools in this field and their notes of caution in methodological construction.

The Violent Extremism Risk Assessment protocol, Version 2 (VERA-2; Pressman and Flockton 2012) is one of the first SPJ tools in this field. The authors of the VERA-2 noted that risk indicators used in assessment tools for general violent offenders are different to individuals with violent extremist views and ideological motivations. Comprising 31 risk indicators, scored on presence or absence, the VERA-2 is designed for repeated scoring to monitor an individual's behaviour change over time, through the provision of targeted intervention and treatment (Pressman 2016). It is noted the VERA-2R was released in 2016 with revised guidelines for application to female populations, youth, and individuals with mental health vulnerabilities.

The Extremism Risk Guidelines 22+ (ERG 22+; Lloyd and Dean 2015) was developed in the United Kingdom (UK) to assess individuals who were convicted of terrorism-related offences. Again emphasizing the importance of individual assessment and the role SPJ plays in this, the ERG 22+ maintains a strong SPJ focus. In contrast to the VERA-2, case formulation with the ERG 22+ includes both the presence or absence of identified factors and the role of the factor in the offence. This case formulation of dynamic needs and treatment targets notably excludes the assessment of past violence, as the authors established this is often absent in the cohort (Lloyd and Dean 2015). Please see Chapter 14 for further discussion of this emerging topic.

Intimate partner violence

Research has both proposed, confirmed and refuted the concept that IPV offenders have different offence pathways and risk factors than generalist violent offenders. For example, a study of 153 imprisoned Spanish males compared characteristics of those convicted for IPV to those convicted for violent offence/s outside the family (Juarros-Basterretxea et al. 2018). The study found no statistical differences and proposed these populations may share a common aetiology. In contrast, Weldon and Gilchrist (2012), through a phenomenological study of implicit theories of IPV offenders, have proposed general differences between IPV offenders and violent offenders. Notably, they propose a differentiation between general attitudes towards violence and how IPV offenders consider cues in a relationship (Weldon and Gilchrist 2012). Please also see Dixon and Graham-Kevan (2011) for further review and discussion of the aetiology of IPV.

SPJ tools specific to assessing the future risk of an individual committing IPV include the SARA (Kropp et al. 1995) and the Brief Spousal Assault Form for the Evaluation of Risk

(B-SAFER; Kropp et al. 2005). It is noted the SARA is also applicable to family violence offenders who commit offence/s against family members other than an intimate partner.

Currently in a third edition, the SARA has been found to accurately predict IPV recidivism (AUC = 0.74), violent recidivism (AUC = 0.74) and general recidivism (AUC = 0.78) (Olver and Jung 2017). Adapted from the SARA, the B-SAFER considers the seriousness of the IPV behaviours and victim characteristics and assists the assessor to form risk scenarios. The B-SAFER has been found to focus the work of police forces when used by assessing officers and improve follow up for high-risk cases (Belfrage and Strand 2012). The authors do provide a note of caution in the application of these findings, as police resources were focussed only on the cases assessed as highest risk on the B-SAFER.

In a Spanish pilot study of men who were imprisoned for violence against their partners, Loinaz (2014) found the B-SAFER to have moderate predictive accuracy of 70% (AUC = 0.76). Further, the same study found the best predictor items on the B-SAFER to be age at first imprisonment, justification of violence and treatment. Males who participated in cognitive-behavioural treatment were found to recidivate at 9.4%, compared to 50% of untreated males (Loinaz 2014).

The B-SAFER has been found by Storay and Strand (2013) to have some relevance to the formulation of risk judgements for female IPV offenders when compared to the data from Belfrage and Strand (2012). Please see Chapter 15 for a full consideration of IPV.

Violent offenders with an Intellectual Disability (ID)

Individuals with decreases in functioning across intellectual, communication and/or functional skills areas have been suggested to be over represented in the criminal justice arena as both offenders and victims (see Hayes 1997). Fogden et al. (2016) summarized data finding individuals with an ID, or Intellectual Development Disorder (IDD), re-offend at significantly higher rates than a community sample, up to three times more likely for males and four times more likely for females. Confirming this in their Australian review, the same authors found the IDD cohort re-offended violently at three times higher rates than the comparable community cohort (Fogden et al. 2016). They note the co-morbidity of mental illness with IDD as contributing to increases in both offending and victimization and encourage further research.

At this time, there are no SPJ tools for general violence risk assessment developed specifically for individuals with an ID that have peer-reviewed research support. However, Boer and colleagues have developed an SPJ framework for the assessment of sexual offenders with an IDD. The Assessment of Risk and Manageability for Individuals with Developmental and Intellectual Limitations who Offend Sexually (ARMIDILO-S; Boer et al. 2013) is an SPJ with some research support (see, for example, Lofthouse et al. 2013) study which found the full instrument had an AUC of 0.92 for intellectually disabled sexual offenders over a six-year follow-up). Boer and colleagues have also produced a General version of the ARMIDILO-S, however the supporting studies have not been peer-reviewed to date (as already noted above). Nonetheless, there is good evidence that tools such as the HCR-20 and START have good to excellent predictive validity for violent behaviour in this cohort (Hounsome et al. 2018). It is noted the HCR-20 scoring guidelines include an Intellectual Disability Supplement (Webster et al. 1997, found to have slightly increased predictive validity when compared to the HCR-20 (AUC = 0.97 and AUC = 0.94 respectively; Verbrugge et al. 2011).

There are numerous methodological challenges in assessing this cohort, notably the variety of definitions in IDD and mental illness, the inability to assess every offender for such conditions, and whether such offenders have been diverted to community-based alternatives rather than correctional services. Further, it is highly likely the risk-taking lifestyles of many violent offenders may contribute to changes in brain structure and intellectual functioning over time. This is suggested as a consequence of violent assaults, illicit substance use, and abuse of legal substances such as alcohol. Please see Chapter 17 for further discussion of this topic.

Other – stalking

Stalking is a unique type of violence, in that there may be no direct act of violence. Rather, the threat or fear of violence is the predominant element of this targeted and intrusive behaviour. The victim may or may not be known to the offender, although has been selected as the recipient of unwanted, repeated contacts. SPJ assessment tools specific to stalking note differences in the typologies of stalking offenders. For examples, see the Stalking Assessment and Management (SAM; Kropp et al. 2008) and the Stalking Risk Profile (SRP; MacKenzie et al. 2009).

The SAM (Kropp et al. 2008) is an SPJ tool for the assessment of stalking behaviours and has been found to have good reliability and concurrent validity when compared to other violence assessment tools (Kropp et al. 2011). However, various research has provided findings supporting the use of the SAM, particularly in relation to risk markers recently present (Shea et al. 2018), and mixed support for ongoing use with findings it did not predict future stalking behaviours (Foellmi et al. 2015). It appears further research in this area is required.

The SRP, developed in Australia by MacKenzie et al. (2009) comprises four domains for assessment (Persistence, Violence, Recurrence, and Psychosocial Damage to the Stalker), and requires separate professional judgements in scoring and treatment target identification. The SRP has been found to have good predictive validity (AUC = 0.66 to 0.68) at the full follow-up period (median 170.43 weeks), with high-risk stalkers re-offending at shorter time periods and more often than low-risk stalkers. With a shorter follow-up time period of six months, differences between risk groups were only statistically significant for targeting of new victims (AUC = 0.75) (McEwan et al. 2016). The authors recommended continued use in correctional and forensic settings and encouraged ongoing research. Please see Chapter 29 for further discussion of stalking risk assessment.

SPJ General Violence Assessment Tools

Three main SPJ tools specifically designed for general violence risk assessment were identified as being in regular use with ongoing research:

- HCR-20[V3]
- SAPROF
- START

Each of these will be considered as stand-alone risk assessment tools (where applicable), and in conjunction with other tools. Tools will also be considered for their application (where tested) to the female populations.

Historical, Clinical, Risk Management, Version 3 (HCR-20^{V3})

First published in 1995 (Webster et al. 1995), revised two years later (Webster et al. 1997) and again in 2013, the HCR-20 comprises 10 historical, 5 clinical and 5 risk management items, and provides an overall estimate of an individual's future risk of violence. The final categorical assessment of future risk relies on the assessors' determination of the presence and relevance of the 20 items. Relevant is considered in terms of an item's contribution to past violence, likely influence on future violence-related decisions, capacity to make alternative, nonviolent choices, and the need to manage the variable through treatment (Douglas et al. 2014).

There is widespread use of the HCR-20 (all versions) in 20 languages and evaluations in 35 countries, and there are numerous studies confirming the HCR-20's validity in all versions (Douglas et al. 2014). Please see meta studies such as Douglas et al. (2010) and the annotated bibliographies by Douglas et al. (2005) and Douglas et al. (2010) for further details. Noting the changes in contemporary SPJ risk assessment since 1997 with especial note to dynamic risk, case formulation and scenario planning, the authors considered it was timely to update the tool.

Retaining the same 20 items as Versions 1 and 2, changes and updates to the HCR-20^{V3} are as follows (Douglas et al. 2014):

- clarification of naming conventions of selected items;
- changes to the content of selected items;
- addition of several subscales;
- increased guidance on individual decision making and risk-management plans that target future risk of violence through the addition of indicators; and
- provision of three rating sheet sets for summary, sub-item and multi-page recording.

For a comprehensive discussion of the updates, please see Douglas et al. (2014).

Of especial note is the inclusion of guidelines for risk scenarios to develop hypothetical situations based on the knowledge of an individual's identified risk factors. Whilst acknowledging the speculative nature of this task, Douglas et al. (2014) emphasize the importance of tailoring various scenarios to known risk factors. Finally, they suggest the development of management strategies that can explain what actions an individual may take in the future. Returning to the RNR principles, the management areas include monitoring, supervision, treatment and victim safety planning (Douglas et al. 2014).

Research: A sample of 106 psychiatric patients transitioning out of residential treatment found high correlations between Version 3 and Version 2 of the HCR-20 (Strub et al. 2014). Further, this study found summary risk ratings added to the associations between the presence and relevance of risk factors for violence at four to six weeks and six to eight months (Strub et al. 2014). This indicates positive findings for the HCR-20^{V3} applicability to the prediction of short- and mid-term violence. Of especial note, the summary risk rating finding provides support to the SPJ argument of reliable clinical assessment though structured guidelines.

Female Populations: The HCR-20 has been found to be a valid predictor of female aggression in inpatients, demonstrating higher predictors than in males (O'Shea et al. 2013). Further, Strub et al. (2014) found the HCR-20^{V3} to be equally predictive of future violence in both male and female populations. However, they encourage further research in this area as differences in gender violence have been proposed.

Whilst the HCR-20^{V3} does not consider protective factors, the SAPROF has been developed for scoring in conjunction with the HCR-20^{V3}.

Structured assessment of protective factors (SAPROF)

Developed in The Netherlands in 2008 and translated for English use in 2009, the SAPROF is a 17-item tool assessing the protective factors of adult violent behaviours. Designed to be used in conjunction with the HCR-20^{V3}, the SAPROF requires assessors to consider the contribution of positive protective factors. The only tool to focus solely on positive protective factors, the SAPROF aims to contribute to the reduction of future violence by identifying the current level of available protection. The identification of 'key' items, strong predictors of future violence risk, and 'goal' items, the treatment targets, provides a categorical assessment of protection based on a lineal scale (see de Vogel et al. 2011).

The Total Integrated Risk Score (TIRS) score is obtained by subtracting the SAPROF protection score from the HCR-20^{V3} risk score. Klepfisz et al. (2017) Note: caution should be used in subtracting total scores from different tools, as they do not necessarily consider the same construct.

Research: The SAPROF has been found to demonstrate change in scores after treatment, with reductions in violent recidivism present for at least one and up to 11 years post treatment (de Vries Robbé et al. 2015). This study comprised 108 male patients at a psychiatric clinic in the Netherlands, sentenced to mandatory treatment as a criminal diversion due to mental health diagnoses. The average length of treatment was 5.65 years (de Vries Robbé et al. 2015). Although these results are encouraging, the significant length of treatment may be a barrier for other populations.

Further, as per its design, the use of the SAPROF in conjunction with the HCR-20^{V3} demonstrates increased predictive validity for a sample of 126 forensic psychiatric patients in the Netherlands (de Vogel et al. 2011). This study found the predictive validity of the SAPROF was significantly increased when used with the HCR-20^{V3}, outperforming that of the HCR-20^{V3} when scored in isolation (AUC 0.80 and 0.72 at one- and two-year follow ups for non-recidivism). deVries Robbé et al. (2011) also note the sensitivity of the change captured by the SAPROF as important for treatment monitoring.

In a sample of 95 (male n = 83, female n = 12) forensic psychiatric inpatients in Japan with a mental health diagnosis, Kashiwagi et al. (2018) found SAPROF scores were predictive of future violence at both 6- and 12-month follow up periods (AUC = 0.87 and 0.85 respectively). Similarly to de Vries Robbé et al. (2011) above, Kashiwagi et al. (2018) found when used in combination with the HCR-20^{V3}, the final score outperformed that of the HCR-20^{V3} alone (AUC 0.87 and 0.78 at 6-month and 12-month follow ups compared to the HCR-20^{V3} only at AUC 0.79 and 0.67). Although this sample included both male and female cohorts, the authors note the sample size was insufficient for independent analysis.

Female Populations: Whilst there are no exclusionary criteria for using the SAPROF for a female population, the authors encourage caution (see www.saprof.com). Tested on a population of mental health clients being released to the community, Viljoen et al. (2016) found SAPROF scores were a better total predictor of violence for the male population (n = 62, AUC = 0.67 to 0.74)) than female (n = 40, AUC = 0.31 to 0.51). Further, they found the SAPROF did not predict any significant use of violence by the female population at any timeframe (Viljoen et al. 2016).

Short-term assessment of risk and treatability (START)

Developed in 2004, the START is a 20-item risk assessment tool designed to assess an individual's short-term future risk of violence across seven domains including risk to others, suicide, self-harm, self-neglect, substance abuse, unauthorized leave, and victimization. These domains form two scales, namely Strengths and Vulnerabilities (Webster et al. (2006).

The above domains then guide assessors to create an intervention (or treatment) plan, directly based on an individual's areas of need. The START scales have both been found to independently predict violent behaviour. In a study of 47 involuntary psychiatric hospital inpatients in Norway, researchers found inpatients with the same or higher strengths scale score than their vulnerability scale score had less likelihood of engaging in violent behaviours during the follow-up period of three months (Nonstad et al. 2010). Although this sample also included female inpatients (n = 8), the female cohort was not analysed as a separate cohort. Similarly, a Canadian study of 30 male psychiatric inpatients found the START to demonstrate predictive validity for short-term prediction of violence during the follow up period of nine months (Wilson et al. 2010).

Research: In a meta-analysis of nine studies and a total of 543 participants, O'Shea and Dickens (2014) found the START to have high internal consistence and interrater reliability. When compared to other tools, the START demonstrated convergent validity between the Vulnerability scale and the HCR-20 total and all subscale scores. Additionally, there were significant positive correlations between the Strengths scale and the SAPROF total score, and significant negative correlations between the Vulnerability scale and the SAPROF total score. However, O'Shea and Dickens (2014) also note the variety in results with varying correlations demonstrated between the START and HCR-20 subscale scores in other studies. Wilson et al. (2010) found the Strengths subscale did not contribute to violence risk as an independent construct.

In relation to the domain relationships, O'Shea and Dickens (2014) found studies to demonstrate overall strong predictive validity for START's risk to others (aggression) domain. Additionally, the self-harm domain also demonstrated good predictive validity, but the self-neglect and victimization scales were not predictive. The authors note the relatively limited studies available at the time of the meta-analysis, and the variability in the construction of each study.

Female Populations: The START has been found to be a stronger predictor of risk to others (aggression) and self-harm in female populations than in male populations (O'Shea and Dickens 2015).

Historische, Klinische, Toekomstige-R (history current behaviour and future) (HKT-R)

Developed and widely used in the Netherlands in 2002, the HKT-30 is an SPJ risk assessment tool presently used in the second version, the HKT-R (Spreen et al. 2014). The HKT-30 had an emphasis on dynamic risk factors, and, similar to the HCR-20, the HKT-30 included the subscales historical, clinical and risk management. Different to the HCR-20, the HKT-30 included a higher number of items in each subscale (11, 13, and 6, respectively), and increased subscale scoring to capture changes in risk. Designed to assess risk for the impending three-month period, the HKT-30 has lately been revised to the HKT-R to expand the applicability to a range of cohorts.

Research: Findings from a study of 347 forensic psychiatric patients released from inpatient treatment in the Netherlands indicated the HKT-R predicated violent re-offending with modest ability (AUC = 0.78) at two years, and lower ability (AUC = 0.63) at five years after discharge. The domains with moderate predictive validity were Historical (AUC =0.75) and Future (AUC =0.71), and total score (AUC =0.78), all at two years after discharge (Bogaerts et al. 2017).

Female Populations: Remaining with Bogaerts et al. (2017), the female cohort of 27 were found not to have committed further offences, either violent or non-violent, during the follow-up periods.

Future Implications

Polaschek (2015) proposed desistance factors and dynamic risk factors belong together. By understanding the factors enabling an offender to persist in offending and factors that maintain desistance from further offending, Polaschek (2015) suggested targeted management will continue to improve. This is consistent with the SPJ approach of both quantifying risk factors, providing guidance on case-plan formulation and treatment and management guidelines.

Roychowdhury and Adshead (2014) remind us that SPJ remains limited to the risk factors contained in each assessment tool. To some extent, this can be mitigated by the recommendation to use SPJ tools in conjunction with other tools. A skilled assessor is able to tailor the clinical formulation of their assessment strategy to the needs of the client.

It is always important to consider the potential for overlap between general and specific types of violence. The SPJ structure not only allows but encourages individual circumstances to be considered in risk assessment, management and treatment. For example, consider an IPV-offender who also commits stalking offences; a youth offender participating in gang violence or a terrorism offender with no history of violence. The use of multiple risk assessment tools will assist professionals to form a more complete analysis of individual circumstances.

A holistic approach to individuals who use both general and specific types of violence will continue to ensure individuals are offered relevant, targeted, and specific management and interventions. Although many intervention strategies such as assessment and treatment programmes are, by necessity, 'one size fits all', the SPJ approach provides guidance for individualized foci within systematic processes.

Ethical Considerations

As with all risk assessment, the consequences must be carefully, and ethically, considered. The assessment of an individual's future risk of violence can impact criminal sentencing, location of sentence served (mental health facility vs. custodial setting), security classifications in custody, access to rehabilitation programmes, determination of release from custody, and level of monitoring in the community.

Roychowdhury and Adshead (2014) provided a unique consideration of the ethical considerations of violence risk assessment when compared to a medical model. Whilst praising the emphasis of SPJ on prevention rather than prediction, they remind assessors of the need to use tools correctly and to complete management plans and risk scenarios. Indeed, Roychowdhury and Adshead (2014) say to do less is harmful and unethical practice. Recommendations include the inclusion of the client in the assessment, firstly by seeking consent and secondly to consider their voice and narrative particularly in scenario generation.

Time remains an essential consideration in all risk assessment, including in the use of SPJ tools. Whilst tools such as the START indicate predictive validity over a short term, the HCR-20[V3] over a medium term, it remains difficult to place a limitation on when tools should be rescored. For example, an SPJ tool scored when an individual is mentally unwell and enters the criminal justice system may yield substantially different results after treatment to address the risk factors.

Finally, transparency and the ability to replicate assessment (inter-relater reliability) remain key to the use of SPJ tools. Again, considering the repercussions upon an individual's freedom or detainment in the criminal justice system, it is imperative equality, fairness and ethical practice remain inherent to all risk assessment practices.

Conclusions

Violence has existed since time immemorial. The risk assessment of violence has progressed through stages of development and continues to do so as research indicates areas for improvement. A convergent approach using actuarial assessment tools in conjunction with SPJ remains the gold standard for risk assessment and case management, and has provided further guidance for professionals to make decisions affecting an individual's life circumstances.

Whilst there is no certainty in risk prediction, the combination of actuarial and clinical approaches to inform SPJ findings ensures progression towards best practice in assessment. Risk assessment cannot operate in isolation from effective case planning, provision of appropriate interventions, flexibility, communication and follow-up assessments. It is anticipated continued research will promote ongoing developments in the SPJ field.

References

Ægisdóttir, S., White, M.J., Spengler, P.M. et al. (2006). The meta-analysis of clinical judgment project: fifty-six years of accumulated research on clinical versus statistical prediction. *The Counseling Psychologist* 34 (3): 341–382.

Andrews, D.A. and Bonta, J. (1995). *The Level of Service Inventory–Revised*. Toronto, Canada: Multi-Health Systems.

Andrews, D.A. and Bonta, J. (2010). Rehabilitating criminal justice policy and practice. *Psychology, Public Policy, and Law* 16 (1): 39–55. https://doi.org/10.1037/a0018362.

Andrews, D.A., Bonta, J., and Hoge, R.D. (1990). Classification for effective rehabilitation: rediscovering psychology. *Criminal Justice and Behavior* 17: 19–52.

Belfrage, H. and Strand, S. (2012). Measuring the outcome of structured spousal violence risk assessments using the B-SAFER: risk in relation to recidivism and intervention. *Behavioral Sciences & the Law* 30: 420–430.

Boer, D.P., Haaven, J., Lambrick, F. et al. (2013). ARMIDILO–S Manual. http://www.armidilo.net (Accessed 14 August 2019).

Boer, D.P., Hart, S.D., Kropp, P.R., and Webster, C.D. (1997). *Manual for the Sexual Violence Risk-20: Professional Guidelines for Assessing Risk of Sexual Violence*. Vancouver, Canada: Mental Health, Law and Policy Institute.

Bogaerts, S., Spreen, M., ter Horst, P., and Gerlsma, C. (2017). Predictive validity of the HKT-R risk assessment tool: two and 5-year violent recidivism in a nationwide sample of Dutch forensic patients. *International Journal of Offender Therapy and Comparative Criminology* 62 (8): 2259–2270.

Bushman, B.J., Newman, K., Calvert, S.L. et al. (2016). Youth violence: what we know and what we need to know. *American Psychologist* 71 (1): 17–39.

Cooper, B.S., Griesel, D., and Yuille, J.C. (2008). Clinical-forensic risk assessment: the past and current state of affairs. *Journal of Forensic Psychology Practice* 7 (4): 1–63.

de Vogel, V., de Vries Robbé, M., de Ruiter, C., and Bouman, Y. (2011). Assessing protective factors in forensic psychiatric practice: introducing the SAPROF. *International Journal of Forensic Mental Health* 10 (3): 171–177.

de Vries Robbé, M., de Vogel, V., Douglas, K., and Nijman, H. (2015). Changes in dynamic risk and protective factors for violence during inpatient forensic psychiatric treatment: predicting reductions in postdischarge community recidivism. *Law and Human Behavior* 39 (1): 53–61.

Dickens, G.L. and O'Shea, L.E. (2018). Protective factors in risk assessment schemes for adolescents in mental health and criminal justice populations: a systematic review and meta-analysis of their predictive efficacy. *Adolescent Research Review* 3: 95–112.

Dixon, L. and Graham-Kevan, N. (2011). Understanding the nature and etiology of intimate partner violence and implications for practice and policy. *Clinical Psychology Review* 31 (7): 1145–1155.

Douglas, K., Hart, S., Webster, C. et al. (2014). Historical-clinical-risk management-20, version 3 (HCR-20V3): development and overview. *International Journal of Forensic Mental Health* 13 (2): 93–108.

Douglas, K.S., Blanchard, A.J.E., Guy, L.S. et al. (2010). HCR-20 violence risk assessment scheme: Overview and annotated bibliography. http://kdouglas.wordpress.com (Accessed 14 August 2019).

Douglas, K.S., Guy, L.S. and Reeves, K.A. (2005). HCR-20 violence risk assessment scheme: Overview and annotated bibliography. Systems and Psychosocial Advances Research Center Publications and Presentations, 335.

Douglas, K.S., Hart, S.D., Webster, C.D., and Belfrage, H. (2013). *HCR-20V3: Assessing Risk for Violence – User Guide*. Burnaby, BC, Canada: Mental Health, Law, and Policy Institute, Simon Fraser University.

Ennis, B. and Litwack, T. (1974). Psychiatry and the presumption of expertise: flipping coins in the courtroom. *California Law Review* 62 (3): 693–752.

Falzer, P. (2013). Valuing structured professional judgment: predictive validity, decision-making, and the clinical-actuarial conflict. *Behavioral Sciences & the Law* 31 (1): 40–54.

Foellmi, M., Rosenfeld, B., and Galietta, M. (2015). Assessing risk for recidivism in individuals convicted of stalking offenses. *Criminal Justice and Behavior* 43 (5): 600–616.

Fogden, B., Thomas, S., Daffern, M., and Ogloff, J. (2016). Crime and victimisation in people with intellectual disability: a case linkage study. *BMC Psychiatry* 16 (1): 170.

Guy, L., Packer, I., and Warnken, W. (2012). Assessing risk of violence using structured professional judgment guidelines. *Journal of Forensic Psychology Practice* 12 (3): 270–283.

Hart, S. and Cooke, D. (2013). Another look at the (im-)precision of individual risk estimates made using actuarial risk assessment instruments. *Behavioral Sciences & the Law* 31 (1): 81–102.

Hart, S., Michie, C., and Cooke, D. (2007). Precision of actuarial risk assessment instruments. *British Journal of Psychiatry* 190 (S49): s60–s65.

Hayes, S. C. (1997). Prevalence of intellectual disability in local courts.

Holley, S.R., Ewing, S.T., Stiver, J.T., and Bloch, L. (2015). The relationship between emotion regulation, executive functioning, and aggressive behaviours. *Journal of Interpersonal Violence* 11 (32): 1692–1707.

Hounsome, J., Whittington, R., Brown, A. et al. (2018). The structured assessment of violence risk in adults with intellectual disability: a systematic review. *Journal of Applied Research in Intellectual Disabilities* 31 (1): e1–e17.

Howard, R. (2015). Personality disorders and violence: what is the link? *Borderline Personality Disorder and Emotion Dysregulation* 2 (12): 2–11.

Juarros-Basterretxea, J., Herrero, J., Fernández-Suárez, A. et al. (2018). Are generalist batterers different from generally extra-family violent men? A study among imprisoned male violent offenders. *The European Journal of Psychology Applied to Legal Context* 10: 8–14.

Kashiwagi, H., Kikuchi, A., Koyama, M. et al. (2018). Strength-based assessment for future violence risk: a retrospective validation study of the Structured Assessment of PROtective Factors for violence risk (SAPROF) Japanese version in forensic psychiatric inpatients. *Annals of General Psychiatry* 17 (1): 5.

Klepfisz, G., Daffern, M., and Day, A. (2017). Understanding protective factors for violent reoffending in adults. *Aggression and Violent Behavior* 32: 80–87.

Kropp, P., Hart, S., Lyon, D., and Storey, J. (2011). The development and validation of the guidelines for stalking assessment and management. *Behavioral Sciences & the Law* 29 (2): 302–316.

Kropp, P.R., Hart, S.D., and Belfrage, H. (2005). *The Brief Spousal Assault Form for the Evaluation of Risk: User Manual*. Vancouver, British Columbia, Canada: ProActiveReSolutions.

Kropp, P.R., Hart, S.D., and Lyon, D.R. (2008). *Stalking Assessment and Management (SAM)*. Vancouver, British Columbia, Canada: Proactive-Resolutions.

Kropp, P.R., Hart, S.D., Webster, C.W., and Eaves, D. (1995). *Manual for the Spousal Assault Risk Assessment Guide*, 2e. Vancouver, BC: British Columbia Institute on Family Violence.

Lloyd, M. and Dean, C. (2015). The development of structured guidelines for assessing risk in extremist offenders. *Journal of Threat Assessment and Management* 2 (1): 40–52.

Lofthouse, R.E., Lindsay, W.R., Totsika, V. et al. (2013). Prospective dynamic assessment of risk of sexual reoffending in individuals with an intellectual disability and a history of sexual offending behaviour. *Journal of Applied Research in Intellectual Disabilities* 26: 394–403.

Loinaz, I. (2014). Typologies, risk and recidivism in partner-violent men with the B-SAFER: a pilot study. *Psychology, Crime & Law* 20 (2): 183–198.

MacKenzie, R.D., McEwan, T.E., Pathe, M.T. et al. (2009). *Stalking Risk Profile: Guidelines for the Assessment and Management of Stalkers*, 1e. Melbourne, Victoria, Australia: StalkInc. and Centre for Forensic Behavioural Science, Monash University.

McEwan, T., Shea, D., Daffern, M. et al. (2016). The reliability and predictive validity of the stalking risk profile. *Assessment* 25 (2): 259–276.

Myers, J.R. and Schmidt, F. (2008). Predictive validity of the Structured Assessment for Violence Risk in Youth (SAVRY) with juvenile offenders. *Criminal Justice and Behavior* 35 (3): 344–355.

Nonstad, K., Nesset, M., Kroppan, E. et al. (2010). Predictive validity and other psychometric properties of the Short-Term Assessment of Risk and Treatability (START) in a Norwegian high secure hospital. *International Journal of Forensic Mental Health* 9 (4): 294–299.

Olver, M. and Jung, S. (2017). Incremental prediction of intimate partner violence: an examination of three risk measures. *Law and Human Behavior* 41 (5): 440–453.

O'Shea, L. and Dickens, G. (2014). Short-Term Assessment of Risk and Treatability (START): systematic review and meta-analysis. *Psychological Assessment* 26 (3): 990–1002.

O'Shea, L. and Dickens, G. (2015). Predictive validity of the Short-Term Assessment of Risk and Treatability (START) for aggression and self-harm in a secure mental health service: gender differences. *International Journal of Forensic Mental Health* 14 (2): 132–146.

O'Shea, L., Mitchell, A., Picchioni, M., and Dickens, G. (2013). Moderators of the predictive efficacy of the historical, clinical and risk Management-20 for aggression in psychiatric facilities: systematic review and meta-analysis. *Aggression and Violent Behavior* 18 (2): 255–270.

Polaschek, D. (2015). Desistance and dynamic risk factors belong together. *Psychology, Crime & Law* 22 (1–2): 171–189.

Polaschek, D. (2017). Protective factors, correctional treatment and desistance. *Aggression and Violent Behavior* 32: 64–70.

Pressman, D.E. (2016). The complex dynamic causality of violent extremism: applications of the VERA-2 risk assessment method to CVE initiatives. In: *Disaster Forensics: Advanced Sciences and Technologies for Security Applications* (ed. A.J. Masys), 249–270. Switzerland: Springer International Publishing.

Pressman, E.D. and Flockton, J. (2012). Calibrating risk for violent political extremists and terrorists: the VERA 2 structured assessment. *The British Journal of Forensic Practice* 14 (4): 237–251.

Pyrooz, D., LaFree, G., Decker, S., and James, P. (2017). Cut from the same cloth? A comparative study of domestic extremists and gang members in the United States. *Justice Quarterly* 35 (1): 1–32.

Pyrooz, D., Turanovic, J., Decker, S., and Wu, J. (2015). Taking stock of the relationship between gang membership and offending. *Criminal Justice and Behavior* 43 (3): 365–397.

Quinsey, V. (1995). The prediction and explanation of criminal violence. *International Journal of Law and Psychiatry* 18 (2): 117–127.

Rettenberger, M., Boer, D.P., and Eher, R. (2011). The predictive accuracy of risk factors in the Sexual Violence Risk-20 (SVR-20). *Criminal Justice and Behavior* 38 (10): 1009–1027.

Richards, J. (2018). High risk or low risk: screening for violent extremists in DDR programmes. *International Peacekeeping* 25 (3): 373–393.

Ross, L. and Arsenault, S. (2017). Problem analysis in community violence assessment: revealing early childhood trauma as a driver of youth and gang violence. *International Journal of Offender Therapy and Comparative Criminology* 62 (9): 2726–2741.

Roychowdhury, A. and Adshead, G. (2014). Violence risk assessment as a medical intervention: ethical tensions. *Psychiatric Bulletin* 38: 75–82.

Sarma, K. (2017). Risk assessment and the prevention of radicalization from nonviolence into terrorism. *American Psychologist* 72 (3): 278–288.

Scarcella, A., Page, R., and Furtado, V. (2016). Terrorism, radicalisation, extremism, authoritarianism and fundamentalism: a systematic review of the quality and psychometric properties of assessments. *PLoS ONE* 11 (12): e0166947.

Seligman, M. and Csikszentmihalyi, M. (2000). Positive psychology: an introduction. *American Psychologist* 55 (1): 5–14.

Shea, D., McEwan, T., Strand, S., and Ogloff, J. (2018). The reliability and predictive validity of the guidelines for Stalking Assessment and Management (SAM). *Psychological Assessment* 30 (11): 1409–1420.

Singh, J.P., Grann, M., and Fazel, S. (2011). A comparative study of violence risk assessment tools: a systematic review and metaregression analysis of 68 studies involving 25,980 participants. *Clinical Psychology Review* 3 (31): 499–513.

Spreen, M., Brand E., ter Horst P. and Bogaerts S. (2014). Handleiding en methodologischeverantwoording HKT-R, historisch, klinische en toekomstige – revisie. Groningen, Netherlands: Dr. van Mesdagkliniek Kliniek.

Storay, J.E. and Strand, S. (2013). Assessing violence risk among female IPV perpetrators: an examination of the B-SAFER. *Journal of Aggression, Maltreatment & Trauma* 22 (9): 964–980.

Strub, D.S., Douglas, K.S., and Nicholls, T.L. (2014). The validity of version 3 of the HCR-20 violence risk assessment scheme amongst offenders and civil psychiatric patients. *International Journal of Forensic Mental Health* 13 (2): 148–159.

Verbrugge, H.M., Goodman-Delahunty, J., and Frize, M.C.J. (2011). Risk assessment in intellectually disabled offenders: validation of the suggested ID supplement to the HCR-20. *International Journal of Forensic Mental Health* 10 (2): 83–91.

Viljoen, S., Nicholls, T., Roesch, R. et al. (2016). Exploring gender differences in the utility of strength-based risk assessment measures. *International Journal of Forensic Mental Health* 15 (2): 149–163.

Ward, T. (2000). Sexual offenders' cognitive distortions as implicit theories. *Aggression and Violent Behavior* 5 (5): 491–507.

Ward, T. (2017). Prediction and agency: the role of protective factors in correctional rehabilitation and desistance. *Aggression and Violent Behavior* 32: 19–28.

Webster, C., Nicholls, T., Martin, M. et al. (2006). Short-Term Assessment of Risk and Treatability (START): the case for a new structured professional judgment scheme. *Behavioral Sciences & the Law* 24 (6): 747–766.

Webster, C.D., Douglas, K.S., Eaves, D., and Hart, S.D. (1997). *HCR-20: Assessing Risk for Violence (Version 2)*. Burnaby, BC, Canada: Simon Fraser University, Mental Health, Law, and Policy Institute.

Webster, C.D., Eaves, D., Douglas, K.S., and Wintrup, A. (1995). *The HCR-20 Scheme: The Assessment of Dangerousness and Risk*. Burnaby, BC, Canada: Forensic Psychiatric Services Commission of British Columbia.

Weldon, S. and Gilchrist, E. (2012). Implicit theories in intimate partner violence offenders. *Journal of Family Violence* 27 (8): 761–772.

Wilson, C., Desmarais, S., Nicholls, T., and Brink, J. (2010). The role of client strengths in assessments of violence risk using the Short-Term Assessment of Risk and Treatability (START). *International Journal of Forensic Mental Health* 9 (4): 282–293.

Worling, J.R., Bookalam, D., and Litteljohn, A. (2012). Prospective validity of the Estimate of Risk of Adolescent Sexual Offence Recidivism (ERASOR). *Sexual Abuse: A Journal of Research and Treatment* 24 (3): 203–223.

8

Intimate Partner Violence Risk Assessment and Management
An RNR Approach to Threat Assessment

N. Zoe Hilton[1] and Liam Ennis[2]

[1] University of Toronto and Waypoint Research Institute, Toronto, Canada
[2] Forensic Behavioural Science Group and University of Alberta, Edmonton, Alberta, Canada

Introduction

There has been steady growth in the practice of assessing an offender's risk of committing a violent offence against a current or former marital, cohabiting, or dating partner (i.e. intimate partner violence; IPV) since structured tools to aid this process appeared in the 1990s and early 2000s. Risk assessment is closely tied to the process of managing offender risk; that is, identifying and intervening with key risk factors in an effort to reduce the likelihood of future IPV. IPV risk assessment and management can be viewed within the framework of the Risk, Needs, and Responsivity (RNR) principles of effective correctional services (Bonta and Andrews 2016). RNR comprises an iterative process of offender assessment and intervention, with a view to enacting the most effective strategies to manage the riskiest offenders in ways that promote the greatest response to intervention. In this chapter, we will describe the RNR model and then examine research on IPV offender risk assessment and treatment needs, showing how the IPV literature can be understood within RNR. Rather than providing a comprehensive review, we will use exemplars to illustrate areas in which existing work appears consistent with RNR, highlight the gaps where the RNR framework may be able to help the field advance, and comment on its applicability to threat assessment. First, we will look briefly at the criminal justice response to IPV and, in particular, the emerging role of threat assessment.

The Wiley Handbook of What Works in Violence Risk Management: Theory, Research and Practice,
First Edition. Edited by J. Stephen Wormith, Leam A. Craig, and Todd E. Hogue.
© 2020 John Wiley & Sons Ltd. Published 2020 by John Wiley & Sons Ltd.

The Criminal Justice Response to IPV

The earliest Western record of the criminal justice response to IPV concerns the Massachusetts Bay Colony which established that wives have the right to be free from bodily correction by their husbands (Pleck 1989) although there is little evidence of how this worked in practice or whether violations were dealt with through formal justice procedures. It is interesting to note that women had freedom from their husband's violence 'unlesse it be in his owne defence upon her assault', (cited by Pleck 1989, p. 22), an early reference to IPV by women. The phrase 'rule of thumb' appears to be a measure in common parlance that came to be used to describe men going unpunished if they beat their wives with a stick no wider than their thumb, but this does not appear to relate to an actual law or common practice (Kelly 1994). By the end of the nineteenth century, domestic violence was a criminal offence in most US states, although perpetrators were not likely convicted except in severe cases (e.g. Hilton and Harris 2009a).

Burris and Jaffe (1983) published the first article describing efforts to increase arrest for IPV, based on experiences in the Canadian city of London, Ontario. A series of studies in US cities attempted to test experimentally the effects of arrest compared with giving a warning or mediating between the couple, with overall results consistent with a desirable effect of arrest (e.g. Maxwell et al. 2002). Prosecution, conviction, and sentencing also became more common, although the evaluation of criminal sanctions to date provides only weak evidence regarding their effectiveness (e.g. Maxwell and Garner 2012). By the early 2000s, some specialized domestic violence courts were established (e.g. Tutty and Koshan 2013) that appear to reduce processing time (e.g. Cissner et al. 2013).

IPV currently places a heavy burden on the criminal justice system. Domestic violence-related occurrences have been described as the single largest category of calls received by police (Klein 2009). During 2013 in Canada, there were more than 90 300 victims of police-reported violence by an intimate partner accounting for over one quarter of all police-reported victims of violent offences (Canadian Centre for Justice Statistics 2015). In an effort to better manage that burden and better protect victims of IPV, law enforcement agencies have increasingly adopted principles and processes of threat assessment.

The development of threat assessment services

Threat assessment refers to 'a set of investigative and operational techniques that can be used by law-enforcement professionals to identify, assess, and manage the risks of targeted violence and its potential perpetrators' (Fein et al. 1995, p. 5). The threat-assessment approach emerged in the 1990s, in the context of a growing awareness within criminal justice that violent events could be anticipated and potentially averted through appropriate intervention, along with changes in US and Canadian stalking laws, protective orders, and growing concerns about violent attacks in public forums (Borum et al. 1999). Threat-assessment practices focus on prevention of violence through early identification and management of potential threats.

Threat assessment is a 'fact-based method of evaluation' (Borum et al. 1999, p. 327) developed by the US Secret Service in its efforts to protect heads of state from targeted violence. Developed based on data about 83 individuals who attacked or attempted to attack public officials in the US during the latter twentieth century (Fein and Vossekuil 1999), its central tenets have since been applied in a wide range of contexts concerning threats of targeted violence, including stalking (Meloy et al. 2012), campus violence (Fein et al. 2002) and work-place violence (Rugala and Isaacs 2003). Threat assessment is predicated on the notion that targeted violence is the result of an understandable and often identifiable process of thinking and behaviour (Borum et al. 1999; Meloy et al. 2014). Whilst both risk assessment and man-agement are fundamental to threat assessment, the structured and empirically-informed approach typical of risk assessment is only part of the threat assessment procedure. Due to its origins in efforts to predict and manage infrequent behaviours (i.e. assassination attempts), threat assessment tends to employ an idiographic approach to identifying case-specific behav-ioural and dynamic indicators presumed to reflect underlying changes in the potential perpe-trator's commitment to violent action.

Increasingly, the principles of threat assessment are being applied by front-line law enforce-ment to inform decision making and resource allocation related to IPV (Ennis et al. 2015; Kropp and Cook 2014; Storey et al. 2013). Threat assessment is appropriate to IPV because: there is an identifiable target, IPV perpetrators often pose an active threat to the victim that will often only be briefly interrupted by arrest as most accused will be returned to the com-munity within 24 hours, and IPV is a precursor to many cases of intimate partner homicide (e.g. Boyce and Cotter 2013; Campbell et al. 2007) a catastrophic and often planned outcome (e.g. Juodis et al. 2014). The RNR principles of effective correctional assessment and crime prevention services now have a burgeoning literature supporting 'what works' in offender intervention and rehabilitation (e.g. Bonta and Andrews 2016). Accordingly, it is beneficial to draw upon this robust literature to inform both the theory and practice of threat assessment.

Risk, Need, and Responsivity

The risk principle states that the intensity of services should be matched with risk, and that more intervention efforts should be put into offenders whose measured risk of recidivism is relatively high. Interaction between offenders with very different levels of risk should be avoided; indeed, offenders deemed to be at low risk of re-offending may fare better without intervention. This principle is key to the process of offender risk assessment, including IPV risk assessment, because effective risk management decisions depend on the offender's appraised risk. Thus, risk assessment is conducted as a first step towards prevention of future offending.

The need principle states that intervention should predominantly target criminogenic needs, which are risk factors that can be changed and whose change is associated with changes in the likelihood of re-offending. Interventions should primarily target criminogenic needs and aim to move them towards individual strengths, such as replacing antisocial behaviour with pro-social skills and activities. Other offender needs that are not related to recidivism might be addressed to help motivate individual change, respond to humanitarian grounds, or otherwise promote positive outcomes for the individual, but they should not be the treatment target. There is substantial evidence indicating the presence of criminogenic needs amongst IPV offenders, which we shall discuss below.

The responsivity principle is founded on the principle that the most effective interventions should be used. In general, interventions that modify behaviours or skills have been found most effective (general responsivity). At the specific level, the manner of implementation should fit the delivery setting and offenders' gender, culture, maturity, cognitive performance, motivation, and humanitarian or related needs (specific responsivity).

Subsidiary principles in the RNR model elucidate the value of supplementing criminal justice interventions with human services for optimizing long-term benefits; attending to multiple risk factors with a variety of interventions; assessing offender strengths, but not to the exclusion of risks; using structured, validated assessment tools to inform each step of assessment and management; and circumscribed use of professional discretion.

The RNR model has been developed largely through research with offenders and tested extensively in community and custodial settings, where greater adherence to its principles is associated with larger effect sizes of the interventions studied (e.g. Bonta and Andrews 2016, p. 230). Its specific application to IPV, however, is underdeveloped. The dominant model in IPV intervention has been the coordinated community response (e.g. Shepard et al. 2002). Although researchers such as Shepard and colleagues report positive effects for offenders who complete batterer treatment programmes within the coordinated model (see also Herman et al. 2014) implementation of the coordinated response itself does not appear to reduce IPV compared with other communities that did not implement the coordinated response model (e.g. Post et al. 2010; Visher et al. 2008). Few studies of IPV treatment have applied robust evaluation methods (e.g. Akoensi et al. 2013) and reviews indicate only small effects (e.g. Babcock et al. 2004; Stover et al. 2009). These discouraging findings have led to calls for integrating RNR into IPV risk assessment and management (e.g. Radatz and Wright 2016; Stewart et al. 2013).

The Risk Principle and IPV Risk Assessment

Radatz and Wright (2016) report that risk assessment is used in batterer intervention programmes, but not consistently or with a view to implementing the risk principle. The intervention literature, though, has generated batterer typology research, which identifies a subtype of IPV offenders who are generally antisocial and pose relatively high risk for serious and persistent IPV (e.g. Holtzworth-Munroe et al. 2003; Huss and Ralston 2008). Various typology systems have identified one, two, or three other types of IPV offender (e.g. those with family-only violence, emotional dysphoria or psychopathology, or low-level antisocial behaviour). Regardless of the number of batterer types, the generally antisocial batterer consistently represents a minority of men posing greater risk of recidivism (e.g. Johnson and Goodlin-Fahncke 2015; Serie et al. 2015; Thijssen and de Ruiter 2011). Building on this existing knowledge, the next step in implementing the risk principle in IPV intervention is to prioritize the highest risk offenders for treatment, especially the most intensive and evidence-based treatment programmes, as well as focused efforts to maintain attendance. The use of empirically-validated risk assessment tools offers a more precise way to identify IPV offenders at greatest risk of recidivism. In this section, we review the tools most commonly validated for IPV offender risk assessment, including an actuarial instrument (Ontario Domestic Assault Risk Assessment: ODARA; Hilton et al. 2010b), a structured professional judgement guide (Spousal Assault Risk Assessment Guide: SARA; Kropp et al. 1999) and the Domestic Violence Screening Instrument (DVSI-R; Williams and Houghton 2004) that includes both a mechanical process and summary risk judgement.

Prediction and prevention

The prediction paradigm is the standard approach for measuring the validity of an offender risk assessment tool, but it does not indicate that a tool is used only to 'predict' an individual outcome without a view to risk management. Testing an assessment tool's accuracy in a statistical prediction model is a necessary step regardless of whether the tool is based on a numerical score from an actuarial instrument, a mechanical sum of risk factors identified through an assessment guide, or a professional judgement of risk categorized as high, moderate, or low. Predictive accuracy is typically assessed using the receiver operating characteristic (ROC) Area Under the Curve (AUC), a statistic that indicates a tool's overall predictive effect size, accounting for sensitivity (true positives) and specificity (avoidance of false positives) for all possible cut-off scores (for details see Chapter 6). The statistic ranges from 0 to 1, such that an AUC of 0.50 indicates no predictive effect and AUCs over 0.5 and up to 1 indicate increasingly large effects in the positive direction (i.e. higher risk assessment scores are associated with greater likelihood of recidivism). Scores on the tools reviewed below all yield moderate AUCs on average; that is, in the range of approximately 0.64–0.70, equivalent to Cohen's *d* of 0.50–0.80 (Rice and Harris 2005).

Spousal assault risk assessment guide (SARA)

The SARA was developed in British Columbia, Canada as a guide to help assessors evaluate some well-established risk factors for IPV and also to individualize the risk assessment task by identifying potentially critical factors or additional risk factors that the assessor considers important to a particular offender's risk (Kropp et al. 1999). The SARA defines IPV (or spousal violence) as 'any actual, attempted, or threatened physical harm perpetrated by a man or woman against someone with whom he or she has, or has had, an intimate, sexual relationship' (Kropp and Gibas 2010). Risk factors were selected based on a review of clinical and empirical literature and a short list of 20 items was identified, covering criminal history, spousal assault history and most recent offence, and psychosocial adjustment (e.g. relationship, employment, substance abuse, mental health, and behavioural problems). Each item is scored between 0 and 2 for a total possible score of 40. Items were selected in part to focus on offender traits and characteristics, rather than on specific behaviours (Kropp and Gibas 2010). The assessor uses multiple sources of information to rate each SARA item, such as interviews with the offender and any victims, standardized measures of intimate partner abuse and substance abuse, review of official records, etc. (Kropp and Gibas 2010). The assessment concludes with a summary risk judgement of low, moderate, or high for the risk of violence against a partner or against another person. In SARA Version 3, these ratings concern case prioritization instead, risk for serious IPV, and imminence of IPV, and the item scoring is removed in favour of the assessor considering how each item has related to IPV in the past and scenarios in which it might contribute to future violence (Kropp and Hart 2015). Inter-rater reliability on the SARA Version 2 total score has been reported to be good (correlations over 0.80) but more variable for the summary risk rating and poorer for the selection of critical items (e.g. Grann and Wedin 2002; Kropp and Hart 2000). Professional training increased the number of risk factors and critical factors that assessors identify, resulting in improved SARA assessments (Storey et al. 2011).

The SARA's predictive accuracy has been replicated in multiple studies, with an average AUC in the moderate effect size range (Helmus and Bourgon 2011; Messing and Thaller 2013). Validation research has been conducted in Canada (e.g. Hilton et al. 2008; Kropp and Hart 2000), the US (Heckert and Gondolf 2004; Williams and Houghton 2004; Wong and Hisashima 2008), Sweden (e.g. Belfrage et al. 2012; Grann and Wedin 2002) and Spain (Andrés-Pueyo et al. 2008) and using samples involved with police (e.g. Andrés-Pueyo et al. 2008; Hilton et al. 2008; Williams and Houghton 2004; Wong and Hisashima 2008), corrections (e.g. Williams and Houghton 2004) and treatment or other evaluations (e.g. Belfrage et al. 2012; Grann and

Wedin 2002; Heckert and Gondolf 2004; Kropp and Hart 2000). To date, the SARA has only been validated for male offenders.

A briefer version of the SARA was designed for police officers to use (Kropp and Hart 2004). A review of the literature, analysis of the performance of SARA items, and pilot test feedback resulted in the Brief Spousal Assault Form for the Evaluation of Risk (B-SAFER), a 10-item tool covering IPV history, attitudes, other serious offending, substance abuse, and relationship, employment, or mental health problems. The assessor evaluates the presence of each item based on interviews with the offender and victim, review of official records, or other sources of information, and rates case prioritization and the risk of life-threatening or imminent violence as high, moderate, or low (Kropp and Hart 2004). Inter-rater reliability for four of the B-SAFER items yielded an average intra-class correlation (ICC) of 0.57, better for criminal history items and poorer for mental health problems (Thijssen and de Ruiter 2011). Test–retest reliability was good following a repeated police contact (ICC = 0.76; Storey et al. 2013). Amongst 40 men released from prison, B-SAFER total score predicted recidivism (return to prison) with an AUC of 0.76 (Loinaz 2014). Both the total score (AUC = 0.70) and the risk summary rating (AUC = 0.69) predicted subsequent IPV reports amongst 249 IPV offenders with police contact in Sweden (Storey et al. 2013).

Ontario domestic assault risk assessment (ODARA)

The ODARA was developed in Ontario, Canada as a tool for police and other front-line responders to IPV. Items were selected based on a follow-up study of men identified in police reports as committing physical violence (or a credible threat of death with a weapon in hand in the victim's presence) against a woman with whom they were or had been married or cohabiting (Hilton et al. 2004). A series of multivariate regression analyses identified the strongest unique predictors of subsequent police reports for a new act of IPV. The final list comprised 13 risk factors, including items related to criminal history, IPV history, the most recent ('index') assault, substance abuse, children, victim concern, and barriers to victim support. Each item is scored 1 if present or 0 if absent, with a prorating procedure for up to five missing items (Hilton et al. 2010b). ODARA scores are associated with an actuarial table indicating the percentage of men scoring higher or lower and the rate of recidivism in the construction and initial validations studies of over 1400 male offenders (Hilton et al. 2010b).

Inter-rater reliability on the ODARA is reported to be excellent, with correlations over 0.90 for researchers and police officers (Hilton et al. 2004). A scoring manual and professional training have resulted in reliable scoring whether in person or online (Hilton and Ham 2015; Hilton et al. 2007). In the construction research, the ODARA had a large predictive effect (AUC = 0.77). The ODARA's predictive value has been replicated in several validation studies with a moderate effect size on average (Helmus and Bourgon 2011; Messing and Thaller 2013) amongst male IPV offenders involved with police (e.g. Gerth et al. 2015; Hilton and Harris 2009b; Hilton et al. 2004, 2008; Jung and Buro 2017; Olver and Jung 2017) or correctional services (Hilton et al. 2010a; Rettenberger and Eher 2012). Most published research has taken place in Canada, with additional studies in Austria (Rettenberger and Eher 2012) and Switzerland (Gerth et al. 2015). Initial meta-analyses reported a significantly higher average AUC for the ODARA than other tools for offender or victim risk assessment (Hanson et al. 2007; Messing and Thaller 2013).

Preliminary research validated the ODARA for female IPV offenders in custody, where it predicted women's post-release IPV recidivism with an AUC of 0.72 (Hilton et al. 2014).

However, women recidivated at a lower rate than indicated by the data used to interpret male offenders' ODARA scores. Consistent with RNR, the authors suggested the ODARA could be used to inform decisions about prioritizing interventions for female offenders, although more research is necessary to permit the development of normative data for women. The Domestic Violence Risk Appraisal Guide (DVRAG) was developed to be used in conjunction with the ODARA when more in-depth case information is available and greater discriminative accuracy amongst higher scoring cases is desired (Hilton et al. 2008, 2010b). It was derived from research identifying assessments that improved on the ODARA's predictive accuracy and that were associated with not only the likelihood of IPV recidivism but also alternative outcomes including the severity and imminence of recidivism. The DVRAG is essentially an algorithm for scoring the 13 ODARA items, some with weighted scores rather than all items being scored dichotomously as in the ODARA, plus the Psychopathy Checklist–Revised (PCL-R; Hare 2003) which contributes from –1 to +6 points to the DVRAG score. Inter-rater reliability for the total DVRAG score was reported to be excellent (ICC = 0.90; Hilton et al. 2008). In cross-validation amongst 346 men with both a police record of IPV and a correctional history, the AUC for IPV was 0.70 (Hilton et al. 2008), and amongst 94 previously incarcerated offenders, the AUC for IPV was 0.713 (Gray 2012). The DVRAG can be scored using PCL-R Facet 4 items in lieu of the PCL-R total score. This modification, known as the DVRAG-4, had an AUC of 0.73 for IPV recidivism in the Hilton et al. (2008) cross-validation sample of 346 men (Hilton and Quinsey 2017).

Domestic violence screening instrument (DVSI and DVSI-R)

The DVSI was developed to respond to the need for empirically-validated IPV risk assessment (Williams and Houghton 2004) and it is used to help assign services and supervision according to risk in Colorado and Connecticut (Williams 2012; Williams and Grant 2006). Its 12 items were selected based on a literature review, statistical analysis of the characteristics that distinguished repeated IPV offenders in a large sample of probationers, and feedback from user focus groups. Items concern domestic and nondomestic criminal history (e.g. conviction, assault, restraining orders, community supervision, weapon use, presence of children during a domestic incident) as well as treatment history for IPV or substance use, unemployment, and variables relating to the victim (separation, restraining order). Using all available sources of information, assessors score each item using response options that vary from 0–1 to 0–3, and sum the items for a total risk score. The revised version (DVSI-R) drops a redundant item concerning restraining orders, and adds summary risk judgments of low, moderate, or high risk for imminent violence to the index victim or to another person (Williams and Grant 2006).

The DVSI tools are scored by probation officers (Williams and Houghton 2004) or by master's level counsellors between offenders' arrest and initial court appearance in order to inform arraignment decisions (Williams 2012). Inter-rater reliability has not been reported but a standard of 80% correct is required in training (Stansfield and Williams 2014). The DVSI tools have been validated with a small-effect size on average (Helmus and Bourgon 2011; Messing and Thaller 2013). The DVSI was first tested in a sample of 1465 men arrested for IPV against a female partner, in which the total score predicted official IPV recidivism with a moderate effect size (AUC = 0.61; Williams and Houghton 2004). In a subsample of 125 cases for whom victim reports were obtained, the DVSI did not predict less serious physical assault (AUC = 0.49) but did predict severe threatening (AUC = 0.68) and very severe physical violence (AUC = 0.65). Other validation studies have been conducted in large US samples of male and female IPV and other family violence offenders (Stansfield and Williams 2014; Williams 2012; Williams and Grant 2006; Wong and Hisashima 2008) as well as a Canadian sample of male IPV offenders involved with police (Hilton et al. 2008). As with the ODARA, research using the DVSI-R indicates that women re-offend less often and less quickly than men overall (Stansfield and Williams 2014). Tests of the DVSI-R summary risk rating have yielded AUCs of 0.62–0.64 (Williams 2012; Williams and Grant 2006; Wong and Hisashima 2008).

The Need Principle and IPV Risk/Need Factors

Many of the best validated offender risk and need factors for general offenders are also associated with IPV offending. There is evidence that criminogenic needs are especially prevalent amongst IPV offenders compared with violent offenders with no IPV history or with nonviolent offenders (Hilton and Radatz 2017). Such research supports a focus on criminogenic treatment needs in IPV-offender interventions, consistent with RNR. Here, we will review the IPV literature using the framework of the 'Central Eight' criminogenic needs.

History of antisocial behaviour

IPV was once considered a problem largely restricted to the family context, but research now indicates that men arrested for IPV or incarcerated with a history of IPV are likely to be 'generally antisocial', representing the most severe and persistent batterer type (e.g. Holtzworth-Munroe et al. 2003). In a Canadian study of over 4000 male correctional inmates with a history of IPV and deemed at moderate or high risk of IPV recidivism using the SARA, over 90% had a previous offence history (Stewart and Power 2014). The prevalence of previous offences was significantly higher than amongst a comparison group of offenders who did not have an identified history of IPV (it is not apparent whether the comparison men were judged at risk of criminal recidivism). The largest group differences were observed for prior violence, including sexual offences. This finding is consistent with other research suggesting that IPV offenders have diverse criminal careers, particularly those at risk of serious and persistent IPV (e.g. Cunha and Gonçalves 2013; Fowler and Westen 2011; Hilton and Eke 2016; Huss and Ralston 2008; Loinaz 2014; Piquero et al. 2006).

A history of antisocial behaviour cannot be changed, but developing noncriminal responses to risky situations and building self-efficacy for using those new behaviours may help reduce repeated antisociality (e.g. Bonta and Andrews 2016, p. 45). For example, relapse-prevention techniques involve the identification of risky situations and planning alternative ways to manage the emotions, thoughts, and behaviours that precipitate an offence (e.g. Dowden et al. 2003). In Correctional Services Canada, family violence programmes train offenders in social and communication skills and relapse-prevention plans, with a high-intensity programme for those at higher appraised risk that also examines developmental influences (Connors et al. 2012, 2013; Stewart et al. 2014). Offenders completing these programmes were almost four times less likely to be charged for any subsequent partner-related offence in a one-year follow up than men who qualified for the programme but did not start or complete it (Stewart et al. 2014). One random controlled trial found a positive effect of assignment to treatment on new incidents involving the partner, attributed to a short-term suppression effect rather than to the programme content itself (Maxwell et al. 2010).

Antisocial personality pattern

Antisocial personality encompasses both behaviour and character. In extreme cases, it is manifested in psychopathy, a condition characterized by glibness, proneness to boredom, callous lack of empathy, irresponsibility, impulsivity, and criminal versatility with early onset of problem behaviour (e.g. Hare 2003). IPV offenders have been found to score lower on measures of psychopathy than other violent offenders, but psychopathy is nevertheless a risk factor for persistent IPV (e.g. Grann and Wedin 2002; Hilton et al. 2001, 2008; Huss and Langhinrichsen-Rohling 2006; Theobald et al. 2016), both independently and in interaction with interpersonal and neighbourhood-level variables (Harris et al. 2011).

Antisocial personality appears resistant to change over time, but breaking the characteristics into static risk factors (e.g. early delinquency), potentially changeable criminogenic needs (e.g. indiscriminative sexual relationships), and responsivity factors (e.g. sensation seeking) may generate new approaches to treatment (Bonta and Andrews 2016, p. 111). A potential avenue is emotion regulation, particularly for treating anger and hostility, both of which appear elevated in both IPV and non-IPV offenders (e.g. Birkley and Eckhardt 2015; Gardner et al. 2014). Cognitive behavioural therapy (CBT) to alter hostile attributions associated with emotionally reactive violence may be of benefit (e.g. Stewart et al. 2014).

Antisocial cognition

Antisocial cognition includes attitudes and beliefs that favour or support criminal behaviour. It also includes rationalizations, such as minimizing the extent or nature of offending behaviour or attempting to justify or provide a rationale for an offence that is favourable to the offender. Amongst IPV offenders, attention has been paid especially to attitudes supportive of interpersonal violence (e.g. Hanson et al. 1997; Robertson and Murachver 2007; Scott and Straus 2007) which are associated with the subsequent onset of IPV (O'Leary et al. 1994) but not consistently with IPV recidivism amongst offenders (e.g. Henning and Holdford 2006; Loinaz 2014). Self-reported anger, also considered a potentially antisocial cognition, has been found to be a proximal predictor of IPV perpetration (Elkins et al. 2013), and in experimental research IPV perpetrators were more likely to endorse abusive behaviours towards a partner under anger-inducing conditions than were a comparison group of men (Nedegaard and Sbrocco 2014).

Antisocial attitudes are typically treated in offender intervention through cognitive behavioural methods. In IPV treatment, attitudes are an important focus, although attention is not on antisocial attitudes so much as attitudes towards women and IPV, and psychoeducational approaches to attitude change are often favoured (Radatz and Wright 2016). Anger management has been a recommended, though controversial, alternative intervention. Eckhardt et al. (2008) recommended intervention for anger because of its association with IPV-treatment dropout, if not exclusive attention to it as a primary treatment target.

Social supports for criminal behaviour

Delinquent peers and gang affiliation are strongly correlated with criminal behaviour (e.g. Bonta and Andrews 2016). Overall, IPV offenders appear less likely than other offenders to have criminal associates, and this need was not associated with higher appraised risk of IPV (Stewart and Power 2014). Having peers who endorse aggression towards women has been identified as a risk factor for committing IPV according to the 'male peer support' model, which sees the abuse of women as a socially learned behaviour (e.g. Godenzi et al. 2001). Much of the evidence for the influence of peer support on IPV comes from research with adolescents and college students, although a self-report study of men from an urban community sample found that negative peer climate (e.g. friends telling jokes about women or hitting their partners) was associated with more frequent IPV perpetration and more injury caused (Schmidt et al. 2016). Criminal associates' influence on IPV recidivism remains to be studied.

Substance use

Problems with alcohol or other drug use are a widely recognized risk/need factor amongst IPV offenders. Most Canadian inmates with a history of IPV exhibit substance abuse problems, and alcohol dependence and drug abuse problems are more severe amongst IPV offenders than other inmates (Stewart and Power 2014). Alcohol use itself has shown a small but consistent association with IPV, including in longitudinal research (e.g. Boden et al. 2013; Loinaz 2014). Severe alcohol use shows stronger associations (Foran and O'Leary 2008; Kraanen et al. 2014) and concurrent substances increase the risk (e.g. Crane et al. 2014; Kraanen et al. 2014; Smith et al. 2012). There is evidence that alcohol acts at a proximate level, being a topic of verbal conflict and increasing the occurrence of IPV incidents (e.g. Katerndahl et al. 2014; Kaufmann et al. 2014; Leonard and Roberts 1998). Applying the need principle to IPV, therefore, requires treating substance abuse. However, community-based IPV treatment often excludes offenders with active substance use problems; at best, some programmes require participants to simultaneously attend substance use treatment (e.g. Radatz and Wright 2016). Elsewhere, integrated treatment for substance abuse and concurrent problems has been shown to be effective (e.g. McKee and Hilton 2017) and a similar approach that treats both substance use and IPV as primary problems may be an appropriate approach to IPV risk management.

Poor marital and family relationships

It is not surprising to find relationship problems amongst IPV offenders. Men with a history of IPV showed higher scores overall than other offenders on an inmate intake assessment designed to capture criminogenic needs compared, and particularly so in the family-marital domain (Stewart and Power 2014). Both male and female IPV perpetrators cite communication problems, control in the relationship, and jealousy as proximal causes of their violence (e.g. Elmquist et al. 2014). Sexual jealousy has been studied as a causal factor in IPV, and reported to be present in over 40% of intimate partner homicides (especially homicide-suicides; Dawson 2005). There is both theoretical and empirical support for jealousy's association with IPV, and more research has been recommended to explicate treatment directions (e.g. Easton and Shackelford 2009). Possibly related to jealousy is insecure attachment; for example, measures of interpersonal dependency were related to use of psychological abuse and level of injury amongst men entering IPV treatment (Mellinger and Carney 2014).

Employment or school problems   Problems with work or school amongst IPV offenders have not been widely studied, although unemployment is a recognized risk factor, appearing on both the SARA and DVSI. Local employment rates are related to men's increased controlling behaviour, but evidence for their association with actual IPV is equivocal (e.g. Harris et al. 2011; Schneider et al. 2016).

Poor use of leisure time Leisure and recreation are considered a criminogenic need to the extent that offenders have little involvement in pro-social recreation and personal interests. In light of empirical support for the finding that sensation seeking is a risk factor for juvenile delinquency (e.g. Raskin White et al. 1985) and chronic antisociality (e.g. Mann et al. 2017), leisure and recreation are thought to be important to the extent that criminally inclined individuals are likely to fill unstructured time with criminogenic behaviour (e.g. substance abuse, associating with antisocial peers), or the actual commission of crimes. However, despite and Bonta and Andrews (2016) finding that the absence of involvement in organized, pro-social leisure activities had a small significant correlation with general recidivism, few studies adequately test the effectiveness of targeting pro-social leisure/recreation for decreasing criminal recidivism. The few existing studies have focused on the effectiveness of after school programmes for reducing juvenile delinquency, and generally reported positive results (e.g. Gottfredson et al. 2004); however, there have not yet been any studies demonstrating poor use of leisure time as a valid criminogenic need for adult IPV perpetrators.

The Responsivity Principle and IPV Treatment

The responsivity principle refers to the notion that the effectiveness of interventions is optimized when those interventions are delivered in a manner that matches the characteristics and general learning style of the offender. General responsivity refers to the use of empirically-supported techniques to restructure attitudes, develop new adaptive skills, and ultimately modify behavioural patterns. For example, research supports CBT as the most effective treatment paradigm for reducing general (e.g. Lipsey et al. 2001) and sexual re-offending (e.g. Hall 1995; Lösel and Schmucker 2005). Consistent with the general responsivity principle, there is evidence that cognitive behavioural methods were most often appropriate for IPV treatment (e.g. Gondolf 2004). Cannon et al. (2016) have observed, however, that in their survey of 238 batterer intervention programmes in the US and Canada only 29% of programmes identified CBT as their primary mode of intervention (Cannon et al. 2016).

Specific responsivity refers to individual characteristics of the offender that may promote or impede his or her ability to benefit from the intervention being provided. Such characteristics might include cognitive deficits, learning disabilities, and poor motivation, as well as the individual offender's personality traits, gender, and so on. Research with sex offenders has found that offenders who complete treatment programmes that did not address the responsivity principle show smaller decreases in recidivism post-treatment than offenders whose treatment programme was tailored to their individual responsivity factors (Hanson et al. 2009).

Little is known about specific responsivity in IPV. IPV treatment providers appear to be aware of the predictors of attrition (Radatz and Wright 2016), many of which are also risk factors for IPV recidivism, such as young age, antisocial personality, substance abuse, prior domestic assaults or criminal history, voluntary referral, unemployment, and lower income and education (e.g. Jewell and Wormith 2010). The similarity of risk factors for recidivism and treatment dropout mean that programme evaluations that fail to control for pre-treatment risk of recidivism can lead to inconclusive results; that is, the apparent relation between noncompletion of IPV treatment and recidivism could be explained by offenders at greatest pre-treatment risk of recidivism being more likely to refuse or quit treatment (Stewart et al. 2013). There is also evidence that some offender characteristics are associated with completion of psychoeducational interventions and others with completion of CBT (Jewell and Wormith 2010), suggesting the need to consider both general and specific responsivity in IPV treatment.

Stewart et al. (2013) suggest tailoring treatment to offender typology and motivation levels to improve retention (although this should not be to the exclusion of general responsivity). For example, the generally antisocial batterer may require more motivation to attend treatment than others, such as the emotionally dysphoric offender, and may require attention to substance use treatment concurrently with other interventions. Relatedly, some researchers see psychopathy as representing diverse treatment responsivity factors rather than an untreatable condition (Polaschek and Daly 2013). Similarly, batterers who present with prominent borderline personality features, such as those characterized as dysphoric/borderline in the IPV typology research (e.g. Holtzworth-Munroe and Stuart 1994), may experience problems with emotional dysregulation that not only serve as a risk factor for future violence but also affect the individual offender's ability to establish a therapeutic relationship with treatment providers and to tolerate the process of treatment.

Finally, culturally-competent care is generally agreed to be important to clinical practice. In IPV treatment, it may be considered necessary in order to allow offenders to speak more freely about the attitudes and practices in their cultural background that contribute to their offending. However, research on IPV programme outcomes as a function of offender ethnicity is equivocal to date (e.g. Stewart et al. 2013).

Responsivity is the least well explored of the RNR principles, and this is particularly true in the realm of IPV. Based on the broader 'what works' literature, we recommend that IPV interventions should be empirically evaluated and supported, and should be tailored to accommodate the characteristics and limitations of each individual perpetrator. That is, IPV interventions should match the general learning styles, motivation and abilities of the offender, as well as his or her personality style, gender, and ethno-cultural considerations (Jung 2017).

Implementing RNR in Threat Assessment

Kropp and Cook (2014) recommended that threat assessors should consider four basic kinds of risk management strategies: monitoring, treatment, supervision, and victim safety planning. We add to this our recommendation that risk management be informed by RNR. Although RNR principles have not been explicitly adapted for threat assessment, they have clear relevance and fit well with the preventative aim and the desire to focus on changeable risk factors that underlie contemporary threat assessment.

Monitoring refers to ongoing assessment and adaptation of risk management (Kropp and Cook 2014). Ideally, monitoring is a collaborative strategy that involves information-sharing amongst all involved in the case (e.g. mental health, law enforcement, probation). Individuals assessed as higher risk warrant correspondingly intensive monitoring in order to identify changes in risk status, which must be focused on observable changes in criminogenic needs. Where monitoring suggests that existing risk management is ineffective, it behoves the threat manager to reconsider the management plan through the lens of RNR. Are the interventions that have been introduced of sufficient intensity relative to assessed degree of risk (i.e. Risk)? Are the criminogenic needs that have been targeted appropriate, and are there additional needs that remain unaddressed (i.e. Need)? Finally, if interventions are ineffective despite appropriate assessment of risk and needs, have identified responsivity factors been effectively addressed, and are there additional characteristics affecting progress (i.e. Responsivity)? For example, a convicted batterer presenting as disruptive and unengaged in group therapy might benefit from adjunctive skills-building sessions to foster emotional regulation and mindfulness skills.

Treatment involves the provision of rehabilitative services intended to facilitate changes in psychosocial functioning and consequent offending. In accordance with the Risk principle, treatment services should be reserved for higher-risk, higher-need offenders. IPV offenders are a heterogeneous group (e.g. Chiffriller et al. 2006; Holtzworth-Munroe et al. 2003) who differ in individual characteristics, nature and severity of psychopathology, and presumably their criminogenic needs (Stewart et al. 2013). Treatment recommendations should, therefore, target the criminogenic needs most relevant for each individual offender and, in accordance with the general responsivity principle, be primarily cognitive-behavioural.

Supervision involves restriction of the offender's rights and freedoms with the intention of making it difficult for the offender to commit a new offence. The most intrusive deprivations should be reserved for the highest-risk cases. Where effective risk management in the community is not plausible, incarceration may be necessary for victim safety. Community supervision restrictions should target the central eight risk factors including prohibitions against alcohol consumption (substance abuse), no contact orders (relationships; social supports for crime such as IPV perpetrators and sympathizers), and keeping the peace (antisocial behaviour).

Victim safety planning

Threat assessment can be partly distinguished from violence risk assessment by the former's focus on victim protection compared to the latter's emphasis on offender management (Meloy et al. 2014). In the context of IPV, the victim's willingness and ability to take self-protective action has a significant impact on third parties' ability to manage risk. Victim safety planning, sometimes referred to as 'target hardening', (Kropp and Cook 2014) refers to efforts to ensure that victims control risk factors within their influence so they are less likely to be attacked or seriously injured. Safety planning consultation, offered by police or social services, is particularly important when a relatively high-risk offender is in the community and there is a likelihood of noncompliance with supervision. IPV victims may be vulnerable due to shared children, mental illness, substance abuse, and financial and emotional dependence that place the victim in need of additional protection and support to engage in self-protective behaviours.

Threat assessment and dynamic risk

Its typically ideographic context means that threat assessment is conducted with a view to capturing assumed fluctuations in recidivism risk by attending to dynamic measures. Change in risk is not well understood in the offender risk assessment literature, and assessors are rightly concerned when offenders appraised as relatively low risk do recidivate, and interpret this as the offenders being temporarily at high risk at the time of recidivism. In part, this apparent contradiction of events reflects assessors' discomfort with the probabilistic nature of risk and a confusion of changeable risk factors with the manner in which a risk factor is measured and used (e.g. Harris and Rice 2015; Helmus and Quinsey this volume).

Ideally, threat assessors could identify and manage risk/need factors whose variation is associated with offence commission, but there is insufficient evidence to guide this practice yet. There is considerable promise in non-IPV research, where desirable individual-level changes in antisocial attitudes, beliefs, associates, and personality as well as social support and substance use have been related to reduced recidivism (Serin et al. 2013). For example, amongst sex offenders, post-treatment change in risk scores was associated with reduced recidivism (e.g. Olver et al. 2015); amongst general offenders, a combination of static measures and change in variables relating to employment, social support, and attitudes improved prediction of re-offending (e.g. Brown et al. 2009); and a lengthy period of living in the community offence-free can indicate a reduction in offenders' risk (e.g. Hanson et al. 2014). Amongst IPV offenders, assessed risk can change after treatment (e.g. Lila et al. 2014); however, any link between dynamic risk and reduced IPV recidivism remains to be investigated.

Conclusion

It is not always clear to assessors how the assessment of risk per se can inform risk management, but the RNR model shows that risk management is a process that is informed by, and responsive to, the assessment of risk. Although evidence for the effectiveness of IPV offender risk management through threat assessment and human services is not currently strong, there is optimism that the application of the RNR principles of effective correctional assessment and crime prevention may have beneficial outcomes (e.g. Radatz and Wright 2016; Stewart et al. 2013). The broader offender rehabilitation field, which was fraught with pessimism in the 1970s, rebounded after the characteristics of relatively more and less effective interventions were teased apart, and the increasing application of RNR following decades of debate over the effectiveness of offender rehabilitation now generates optimism (e.g. Cullen 2013). Likewise, we are optimistic that systematic adoption of RNR in IPV risk assessment and management will yield more effective interventions and greater victim safety.

References

Akoensi, T.D., Koehler, J.A., Lösel, F., and Humphreys, D.K. (2013). Domestic violence perpetrator programs in Europe, part II: a systematic review of the state of evidence. *International Journal of Offender Therapy and Comparative Criminology* 57: 1206–1225.

Andrés-Pueyo, A., López, S., and Álvarez, E. (2008). Assessment of the risk of intimate partner violence and the SARA. *Papeles del Psicólogo* 29: 107–122.

Babcock, J.C., Green, C.E., and Robie, C. (2004). Does batterers' treatment work? A meta-analytic review of domestic violence treatment. *Clinical Psychology Review* 23: 1023–1053.

Belfrage, H., Strand, S., Storey, J.E. et al. (2012). Assessment and management of risk for intimate partner violence by police officers using the Spousal Assault Risk Assessment Guide. *Law and Human Behavior* 36: 60–67.

Birkley, E.L. and Eckhardt, C.I. (2015). Anger, hostility, internalizing negative emotions, and intimate partner violence perpetration: a meta-analytic review. *Clinical Psychology Review* 37: 40–56.

Boden, J.M., Fergusson, D.M., and Horwood, L.J. (2013). Alcohol misuse and criminal offending: findings from a 30-year longitudinal study. *Drug and Alcohol Dependence* 128: 30–36.

Bonta, J. and Andrews, D.A. (2016). *The Psychology of Criminal Conduct*, 6e. New York, NY: Routledge.

Borum, R., Fein, R., Vossekuil, B., and Berglund, J. (1999). Threat assessment: defining an approach for evaluating risk of targeted violence. *Behavioral Sciences & the Law* 17: 323–337.

Boyce, J. and Cotter, A. (2013). *Homicide in Canada, 2012*. Statistics Canada catalogue no. 85-002-X. Ottawa, ON: Statistics Canada.

Brown, S.L., St. Amand, M.D., and Zamble, E. (2009). The dynamic prediction of criminal recidivism: a three-wave prospective study. *Law and Human Behavior* 33: 25–45.

Burris, C.A. and Jaffe, P. (1983). Wife abuse as a crime: the impact of police laying charges. *Canadian Journal of Criminology* 25: 309–318.

Campbell, J.C., Glass, N., Sharps, P.W. et al. (2007). Intimate partner homicide: review and implications of research and policy. *Trauma, Violence & Abuse* 8: 246–269.

Canadian Centre for Justice Statistics. (2015). Family violence in Canada: A statistical profile, 2013. Statistics Canada Catalogue no. 85-002-X. Ottawa, ON: Statistics Canada.

Cannon, C., Hamel, J., Buttell, F., and Ferreira, R.J. (2016). A survey of domestic violence perpetrator programs in the United States and in Canada: findings and implications for policy and intervention. *Partner Abuse* 7: 226–276.

Chiffriller, S.H., Hennessy, J.J., and Zappone, M. (2006). Understanding a new typology of batterers: implications for treatment. *Victims and Offenders* 1: 79–97.

Cissner, A.B., Labriola, M. and Rempel, M. (2013). Testing the effects of New York's domestic violence courts: A statewide impact evaluation. Centre for Court Innovation, Document No.: 242583.

Connors, A.D., Mills, J.F., and Gray, A.L. (2012). An evaluation of intimate partner violence intervention with incarcerated offenders. *Journal of Interpersonal Violence* 27: 1176–1196.

Connors, A.D., Mills, J.F., and Gray, A.L. (2013). Intimate partner violence intervention for high-risk offenders. *Psychological Services* 10: 12–23. 1541–1559.

Crane, C.A., Oberleitner, L.M.S., Devine, S., and Easton, C.J. (2014). Substance use disorders and intimate partner violence perpetration among male and female offenders. *Psychology of Violence* 4: 322–333.

Cullen, F.T. (2013). Rehabilitation: beyond nothing works. *Crime and Justice* 42: 299–376.

Cunha, O. and Gonçalves, R.A. (2013). Intimate partner violence offenders: generating a data-based typology of batterers and implications for treatment. *The European Journal of Psychology Applied to Legal Context* 5: 131–139.

Dawson, M. (2005). Intimate Femicide followed by suicide: Examining the role of premeditation. *Suicide and Life-Threatening Behavior* 35: 76–90. https://doi.org/10.1521/suli.35.1.76.59261.

Dowden, C., Antonowicz, D., and Andrews, D.A. (2003). The effectiveness of relapse prevention with offenders: a meta-analysis. *International Journal of Offender Therapy and Comparative Criminology* 47 (5): 516–528.

Easton, J. and Shackelford, T. (2009). Morbid jealousy and sex differences in partner-directed violence. *Human Nature* 20: 342–350.

Eckhardt, C., Samper, R., and Murphy, C. (2008). Anger disturbances among perpetrators of intimate partner violence: clinical characteristics and outcomes of court-mandated treatment. *Journal of Interpersonal Violence* 23: 1600–1617.

Elkins, S.R., Moore, T.M., McNulty, J.K. et al. (2013). Electronic diary assessment of the temporal association between proximal anger and intimate partner violence perpetration. *Psychology of Violence* 3: 100–113.

Elmquist, J., Hamel, J., Shorey, R.C. et al. (2014). Motivations for intimate partner violence in men and women arrested for domestic violence and court referred to batterer intervention programs. *Partner Abuse* 5: 359–374.

Ennis, L., Hargreaves, T., and Gulayets, M. (2015). The Integrated Threat and Risk Assessment Centre: a program evaluation investigating the implementation of threat management recommendations. *Journal of Threat Assessment and Management* 2: 114–126.

Fein, R.A. and Vossekuil, B. (1999). Assassination in the United States: an operational study of recent assassins, attackers, and near-lethal approaches. *Journal of Forensic Sciences* 50: 321–333.

Fein, R.A., Vossekuil, B. and Holden, G. (1995). Threat assessment: An approach to prevent targeted violence. (Publication NCJ 155000). Washington, DC: US Department of Justice, Office of Justice Programs, National Institute of Justice.

Fein, R.A., Vossekuil, B., Pollack, W.S. et al. (2002). *Threat Assessment in Schools: A Guide to Managing Threatening Situations and to Creating Safe School Climates.* Washington, DC: US Secret Service and US Department of Education.

Foran, H.M. and O'Leary, K.D. (2008). Alcohol and intimate partner violence: a meta-analytic review. *Clinical Psychology Review* 28: 1222–1234.

Fowler, K.A. and Westen, D. (2011). Subtyping male perpetrators of intimate partner violence. *Journal of Interpersonal Violence* 26: 607–639.

Gardner, F.L., Moore, Z.E., and Dettore, M. (2014). The relationship between anger, childhood maltreatment, and emotion regulation difficulties in intimate partner and non-intimate partner violent offenders. *Behavior Modification* 38: 779–800.

Gerth, J., Rossegger, A., Singh, J.P., and Endrass, J. (2015). Assessing the risk of severe intimate partner violence: validating the DyRiAS in Switzerland. *Archives of Forensic Psychology* 2: 1–15.

Godenzi, A., Schwartz, M.D., and DeKeseredy, W.S. (2001). Toward a gendered social bond/male peer support theory of university woman abuse. *Critical Criminology* 10: 1–16.

Gondolf, E.W. (2004). Evaluating batterer counseling programs: a difficult task showing some effects and implications. *Aggression and Violent Behavior* 9: 605–631.

Gottfredson, D.C., Gerstenblith, S.A., Soulé, D.A. et al. (2004). Do After School Programs Reduce Delinquency? *Prevention Science* 5 (4): 253–266. https://doi.org/10.1023/b:prev.0000045359.41696.02.

Grann, M. and Wedin, I. (2002). Risk factors for recidivism among spousal assault and spousal homicide offenders. *Psychology, Crime & Law* 8: 5–23.

Gray, A.L. (2012). Assessing risk for intimate partner violence: A cross-validation of the ODARA and DVRAG within a sample of incarcerated offenders. Master thesis. Carleton University.

Hall, G.C. (1995). Sex offender recidivism revisited: a meta-analysis of recent treatment studies. *Journal of Consulting and Clinical Psychology* 63: 802–809. https://doi.org/10.1037//0022-006x.63.5.802.

Hanson, R.K., Bourgon, G., Helmus, L., and Hodgson, S. (2009). The principles of effective correctional treatment also apply to sexual offenders: a meta-analysis. *Criminal Justice and Behaviour* 36: 865–891. https://doi.org/10.1177/0093854809338545.

Hanson, R.K., Cadsky, O., Harris, A., and Lalonde, C. (1997). Correlates of battering among 997 men: family history, adjustment, and attitudinal differences. *Violence and Victims* 12: 191–208.

Hanson, R.K., Harris, A.J.R., Helmus, L., and Thornton, D. (2014). High-risk sex offenders may not be high risk forever. *Journal of Interpersonal Violence* 29: 2792–2813.

Hanson, R.K., Helmus, L. and Bourgon, G. (2007). The validity of risk assessments for intimate partner violence: A meta-analysis. Public Safety Canada, unpublished report Cat. No.: PS3–1/2007–7.

Hare, R.D. (2003). *The Psychopathy Checklist- Revised*, 2e. Toronto, ON: Multi-Health Systems.

Harris, G.T., Hilton, N.Z., and Rice, M.E. (2011). Explaining the frequency of intimate partner violence by male perpetrators: do attitude, relationship, and neighborhood variables add to antisociality? *Criminal Justice and Behavior* 38: 309–331.

Harris, G.T. and Rice, M.E. (2015). Progress in violence risk assessment and communication: hypothesis versus evidence. *Behavioral Sciences & the Law* 33: 128–145.

Heckert, D.A. and Gondolf, E.W. (2004). Battered women's perceptions of risk versus risk factors and instruments in predicting repeat reassault. *Journal of Interpersonal Violence* 19: 778–800.

Helmus, L. and Bourgon, G. (2011). Taking stock of 15 years of research on the Spousal Assault Risk Assessment Guide (SARA): a critical review. *International Journal of Forensic Mental Health* 10: 64–75.

Helmus, L.M. and Quinsey, V.L. (2019). Predicting violent reoffending with the VRAG-R: overview, controversies, and future directions for actuarial risk scales. In: *What Works in Violence Risk Management: Theory, Research and Practice* (eds. J.S. Wormith, L. Craig and T. Hogue). Wiley.

Henning, K. and Holdford, R. (2006). Minimization, denial, and victim blaming by batterers: how much does the truth matter? *Criminal Justice and Behavior* 33: 110–130.

Herman, K., Rotunda, R., Williamson, G., and Vodanovich, S. (2014). Outcomes from a Duluth model batterer intervention program at completion and long term follow-up. *Journal of Offender Rehabilitation* 53: 1–18.

Hilton, N.Z. and Eke, A.W. (2016). Nonspecialization of criminal careers among intimate partner violence offenders. *Criminal Justice and Behavior* 43: 1347–1363. https://doi.org/10.1177/0093854816637886.

Hilton, N.Z. and Ham, E. (2015). Cost-effectiveness of electronic training in domestic violence risk assessment: ODARA 101. *Journal of Interpersonal Violence* 30: 1065–1073.

Hilton, N.Z. and Harris, G.T. (2009a). Criminal justice responses to partner violence: history, evaluation, and lessons learned. In: *Preventing Partner Violence: Foundations, Intervention, Issues* (eds. J. Lutzker and D. Whitaker), 219–243. Washington, DC: American Psychological Association.

Hilton, N.Z. and Harris, G.T. (2009b). How nonrecidivism affects predictive accuracy: evidence from a cross-validation of the Ontario Domestic Assault Risk Assessment (ODARA). *Journal of Interpersonal Violence* 24: 326–337.

Hilton, N.Z., Harris, G.T., Popham, S., and Lang, C. (2010a). Risk assessment among male incarcerated domestic offenders. *Criminal Justice and Behavior* 37: 815–832.

Hilton, N.Z., Harris, G.T., and Rice, M.E. (2001). Predicting violent recidivism by serious wife assaulters. *Journal of Interpersonal Violence* 16: 408–423. https://doi.org/10.1177/088626001016005002.

Hilton, N.Z., Harris, G.T., and Rice, M.E. (2010b). *Risk Assessment for Domestically Violent Men: Tools for Criminal Justice, Offender Intervention, and Victim Services*. Washington, DC: American Psychological Association.

Hilton, N.Z., Harris, G.T., Rice, M.E. et al. (2004). A brief actuarial assessment for the prediction of wife assault recidivism: the Ontario Domestic Assault Risk Assessment. *Psychological Assessment* 16: 267–275.

Hilton, N.Z., Harris, G.T., Rice, M.E. et al. (2007). Training front-line users in the Ontario Domestic Assault Risk Assessment (ODARA), a tool for police domestic investigations. *Canadian Journal of Police and Security Services* 5: 92–96.

Hilton, N.Z., Harris, G.T., Rice, M.E. et al. (2008). An in-depth actuarial risk assessment for wife assault recidivism: the Domestic Violence Risk Appraisal Guide. *Law and Human Behavior* 32: 150–163.

Hilton, N.Z., Popham, S., Lang, C., and Harris, G.T. (2014). Preliminary validation of the ODARA for female intimate partner violence offenders. *Partner Abuse* 5: 189–203.

Hilton, N.Z. and Quinsey, V.L. (2017). Domestic Violence Risk Appraisal Guide can be scored with PCL-R Facet 4. *Crime Scene* 24: 14–16.

Hilton, N.Z. and Radatz, D. (2017). The criminogenic needs of intimate partner violence offenders. *International Journal of Offender Therapy and Comparative Criminology* 62: 3247–3259.

Holtzworth-Munroe, A., Meehan, J.C., Herron, K. et al. (2003). Do subtypes of maritally violent men continue to differ over time? *Journal of Consulting and Clinical Psychology* 71: 728–740.

Holtzworth-Munroe, A. and Stuart, G.L. (1994). Typologies of male batterers: three subtypes and the difference among them. *Psychological Bulletin* 116: 476–497.

Huss, M.T. and Langhinrichsen-Rohling, J. (2006). Assessing the generalization of psychopathy in a clinical sample of domestic violence perpetrators. *Law and Human Behavior* 30: 571–586.

Huss, M.T. and Ralston, A. (2008). Do batterer subtypes actually matter? Treatment completion, treatment response, and recidivism across a batterer typology. *Criminal Justice and Behavior* 35: 710–724.

Jewell, L.M. and Wormith, J.S. (2010). Variables associated with attrition from domestic violence treatment programs targeting male batterers: a meta-analysis. *Criminal Justice and Behavior* 37: 1086–1113.

Johnson, R.R. and Goodlin-Fahncke, W. (2015). Exploring the effect of arrest across a domestic batterer typology. *Juvenile and Family Court Journal* 66: 15–30.

Jung, S. (2017). *RNR Principles in Practice: In the Management of and Treatment of Sexual Abusers*. Brandon, VT: Safer Society Press.

Jung, S. and Buro, K. (2017). Appraising risk for intimate partner violence in a police context. *Criminal Justice and Behavior* 44: 240–260.

Juodis, M., Starzomski, A., Porter, S., and Woodworth, M. (2014). A comparison of domestic and non-domestic homicides: further evidence for distinct dynamics and heterogeneity of domestic homicide perpetrators. *Journal of Family Violence* 29: 299–313.

Katerndahl, D., Burge, S., Ferrer, R. et al. (2014). Multi-day recurrences of intimate partner violence and alcohol intake across dynamic patterns of violence. *Journal of Evaluation in Clinical Practice* 20: 711–718.

Kaufmann, V.G., O'Farrell, T.J., Murphy, C.M. et al. (2014). Alcohol consumption and partner violence among women entering substance use disorder treatment. *Psychology of Addictive Behaviors* 28: 313–321.

Kelly, H.A. (1994). "Rule of thumb" and the folklaw of the husband's stick. *Journal of Legal Education* 44: 341–365.

Klein, A.R. (2009). *Practical Implications of Current Domestic Violence Research: For Law Enforcement, Prosecutors and Judges*. Washington, DC: US Department of Justice, National Institute of Justice Special Report.

Kraanen, F.L., Vedel, E., Scholing, A., and Emmelkamp, P.M.G. (2014). Prediction of intimate partner violence by type of substance use disorder. *Journal of Substance Abuse Treatment* 46: 532–539.

Kropp, P.R. and Cook, A.N. (2014). Intimate partner violence, stalking, and femicide. In: *International Handbook of Threat Assessment* (eds. J.R. Meloy and J. Hoffmann), 179–194. New York, NY: Oxford.

Kropp, P.R. and Gibas, A. (2010). The Spousal Assault Risk Assessment Guide (SARA). In: *Handbook of Violence Risk Assessment* (eds. R.K. Otto and K.S. Douglas), 227–250. New York, NY: Routledge.

Kropp, P.R. and Hart, S.D. (2000). The Spousal Assault Risk Assessment (SARA) guide: reliability and validity in adult male offenders. *Law and Human Behavior* 24: 101–118.

Kropp, P.R. and Hart, S.D. (2004). *The Development of the Brief Spousal Assault Form for the Evaluation of Risk (B-SAFER): A tool for criminal justice professionals*. Department of Justice Canada Retrieved from https://www.justice.gc.ca/eng/rp-pr/fl-lf/famil/rr05_fv1-rr05_vf1/rr05_fv1.pdf.

Kropp, P.R. and Hart, S.D. (2015). *SARA-V3: User Manual for Version 3 of the Spousal Assault Risk Assessment Guide*. Vancouver, BC: Proactive Resolutions.

Kropp, P.R., Hart, S.D., Webster, C.D., and Eaves, D. (1999). *Spousal Assault Risk Assessment guide (SARA)*, 2e. Toronto, ON: Multi-Health Systems Inc.

Leonard, K.E. and Roberts, L.J. (1998). The effects of alcohol on the marital interactions of aggressive and nonaggressive husbands and their wives. *Journal of Abnormal Psychology* 107: 602–615.

Lila, M., Oliver, A., Catalá-Miñana, A., and Conchell, R. (2014). Recidivism risk reduction assessment in batterer intervention programs: a key indicator for program efficacy evaluation. *Psychosocial Intervention* 23: 217–223.

Lipsey, M.W., Chapman, G.L., and Landenberger, N.A. (2001). Cognitive-behavioral programs for offenders. *The Annals of the Academy of Political and Social Sciences* 578: 144–157.

Loinaz, I. (2014). Typologies, risk and recidivism in partner-violent men with the B-SAFER: a pilot study. *Psychology, Crime & Law* 20: 183–198.

Lösel, F. and Schmucker, M. (2005). The effectiveness of treatment for sexual offenders: A comprehensive meta-analysis. *Journal of Experimental Criminology* 1: 117–146. https://doi.org/10.1007/s11292-004-6466-7.

Mann, F.D., Engelhardt, L., Briley, D.A. et al. (2017). Sensation seeking and impulsive traits as personality endophenotypes for antisocial behavior: evidence from two independent samples. *Personality and Individual Differences* 105: 30–39.

Maxwell, C.D., Davis, R.C., and Taylor, B.G. (2010). The impact of length of domestic violence treatment on the patterns of subsequent intimate partner violence. *Journal of Experimental Criminology* 6: 475–497. https://doi.org/10.1007/s11292-010-9106-4.

Maxwell, C.D. and Garner, J.H. (2012). The crime control effects of criminal sanctions for intimate partner violence. *Partner Abuse* 3: 469–500.

Maxwell, C.D., Garner, J.H., and Fagan, J.A. (2002). The preventive effects of arrest on intimate partner violence: research, policy and theory. *Criminology & Public Policy* 2: 51–80.

McKee, S.A. and Hilton, N.Z. (2017). Co-occurring substance use, PTSD, and IPV victimization: Implications for female offender services. *Trauma, Violence, & Abuse* 20 (3): 303–314.

Mellinger, M.S. and Carney, M.M. (2014). Interpersonal dependency constructs and male perpetrators of intimate partner violence. *Journal of Forensic Social Work* 4: 29–47. https://doi.org/10.1080/1936928x.2013.866608.

Meloy, J.R., Hart, S.D., and Hoffmann, J. (2014). Threat assessment and threat management. In: *International Handbook of Threat Assessment* (eds. J.R. Meloy and J. Hoffmann), 3–17. New York, NY: Oxford.

Meloy, J.R., Hoffmann, J., Guldimann, A., and James, D. (2012). The role of warning behaviors in threat assessment: an exploration and suggested typology. *Behavioral Sciences & the Law* 30: 256–279.

Messing, J.T. and Thaller, J. (2013). The average predictive validity of intimate partner violence risk assessment instruments. *Journal of Interpersonal Violence* 28: 1537–1558.

Nedegaard, R.C. and Sbrocco, T. (2014). The impact of anger on the intimate partner violence decision-making process. *Journal of Family Violence* 29: 613–624.

O'Leary, K.D., Malone, J., and Tyree, A. (1994). Physical aggression in early marriage: Prerelationship and relationship effects. *Journal of Consulting and Clinical Psychology* 62: 594–602.

Olver, M.E., Beggs Christofferson, S.M., and Wong, S.C.P. (2015). Evaluation and applications of the clinically significant change method with the violence risk scale-sexual offender version: implications for risk-change communication. *Behavioral Sciences & the Law* 33: 92–110.

Olver, M.E. and Jung, S. (2017). Incremental prediction of intimate partner violence: an examination of three risk measures. *Law and Human Behavior* 41: 440–453.

Piquero, A.R., Brame, R., Fagan, J., and Moffitt, T.E. (2006). Assessing the offending activity of criminal domestic violence suspects: offense specialization, escalation, and de-escalation evidence from the Spouse Assault Replication Program. *Public Health Reports* 121: 409–418.

Pleck, E. (1989). Criminal approaches to family violence, 1640–1980. *Crime and Justice* 11: 19–57.

Polaschek, D.L.L. and Daly, T.E. (2013). Treatment and psychopathy in forensic settings. *Aggression and Violent Behavior* 18: 592–603.

Post, L., Klevens, J., Maxwell, C. et al. (2010). An examination of whether coordinated community responses affect intimate partner violence. *Journal of Interpersonal Violence* 25: 75–93.

Radatz, D.L. and Wright, E.M. (2016). Integrating the principles of effective intervention into batterer intervention programming: the case for moving toward more evidence-based programming. *Trauma, Violence & Abuse* 17: 72–87.

Raskin White, H., Labouvie, E.W., and Bates, M.E. (1985). The relationship between sensation seeking and delinquency: a longitudinal analysis. *Journal of Research in Crime and Delinquency* 22: 197–211.

Rettenberger, M. and Eher, R. (2012). Actuarial risk assessment in sexually motivated intimate-partner violence. *Law and Human Behavior* 37: 75–86.

Rice, M.E. and Harris, G.T. (2005). Comparing effect sizes in follow-up studies: ROC area, Cohen's d, and r. *Law and Human Behavior* 29: 615–620.

Robertson, K. and Murachver, T. (2007). Correlates of partner violence for incarcerated women and men. *Journal of Interpersonal Violence* 22: 639–655.

Rugala, E.A. and Isaacs, A.R. (2003). Workplace Violence: Issues in Response. Unpublished report: US Department of Justice, National Center for the Analysis of Violent Crime.

Schmidt, M.R., Lisco, C.G., Parrott, D.J., and Tharp, A.T. (2016). Moderating effect of negative peer group climate on the relation between men's locus of control and aggression toward intimate partners. *Journal of Interpersonal Violence* 31: 755–773.

Schneider, D., Harknett, K., and McLanahan, S. (2016). Intimate partner violence in the great recession. *Demography* 53: 471–505.

Scott, K. and Straus, M. (2007). Denial, minimization, partner blaming, and intimate aggression in dating partners. *Journal of Interpersonal Violence* 22: 851–871.

Serie, C.M.B., van Tilburg, C.A., van Dam, A., and de Ruiter, C. (2015). Spousal assaulters in outpatient mental health care: the relevance of structured risk assessment. *Journal of Interpersonal Violence* 32: 1658–1677.

Serin, R.C., Lloyd, C.D., Helmus, L. et al. (2013). Does intra-individual change predict offender recidivism? Searching for the Holy Grail in assessing offender change. *Aggression and Violent Behavior* 18: 32–53.

Shepard, M., Falk, D., and Elliott, B. (2002). Enhancing coordinated community responses to reduce recidivism in cases of domestic violence. *Journal of Interpersonal Violence* 17: 551–569.

Smith, P.H., Homish, G.G., Leonard, K.E., and Cornelius, J.R. (2012). Intimate partner violence and specific substance use disorders: findings from the National Epidemiologic Survey on alcohol and related conditions. *Psychology of Addictive Behaviors* 26: 236–245.

Stansfield, R. and Williams, K.R. (2014). Predicting family violence recidivism using the DVSI-R: integrating survival analysis and perpetrator characteristics. *Criminal Justice and Behavior* 41: 163–180.

Stewart, L.A., Flight, J., and Slavin-Stewart, C. (2013). Applying effective corrections principles (RNR) to partner abuse interventions. *Partner Abuse* 4: 494–534.

Stewart, L.A., Gabora, N., Kropp, P.R., and Lee, Z. (2014). Effectiveness of risk-needs-responsivity-based family violence programs with male offenders. *Journal of Family Violence* 29: 151–164.

Stewart, L.A. and Power, J. (2014). Profile and programming needs of federal offenders with histories of intimate partner violence. *Journal of Interpersonal Violence* 29: 2723–2747.

Storey, J.E., Gibas, A.L., Reeves, K.A., and Hart, S.D. (2011). Evaluation of a violence risk (threat) assessment training program for police and other criminal justice professionals. *Criminal Justice and Behavior* 38: 554–564.

Storey, J.E., Kropp, P.R., Hart, S.D. et al. (2013). Assessment and management of risk for intimate partner violence by police officers using the brief spousal assault form for the evaluation of risk. *Criminal Justice and Behavior* 41: 256–271.

Stover, C.S., Meadows, A.L., and Kaufman, J. (2009). Interventions for intimate partner violence: review and implications for evidence-based practice. *Professional Psychology: Research and Practice* 40: 223–233.

Theobald, D., Farrington, D.P., Coid, J.W., and Piquero, A.R. (2016). Are male perpetrators of intimate partner violence different from convicted violent offenders? Examination of psychopathic traits and life success in males from a community survey. *Journal of Interpersonal Violence* 31: 1687–1718.

Thijssen, J. and de Ruiter, C. (2011). Identifying subtypes of spousal assaulters using the B-SAFER. *Journal of Interpersonal Violence* 26: 1307–1321.

Tutty, L.M. and Koshan, J. (2013). Calgary's specialized domestic violence court: an evaluation of a unique model. *Alberta Law Review* 50: 731–755.

Visher, C.A., Harrell, A., Newmark, L., and Yahner, J. (2008). Reducing intimate partner violence: an evaluation of a comprehensive justice system-community collaboration. *Criminology & Public Policy* 7: 49–523.

Williams, K.R. (2012). Family violence risk assessment: a predictive cross-validation study of the Domestic Violence Screening Instrument-Revised (DVSI-R). *Law and Human Behavior* 36: 120–129.

Williams, K.R. and Grant, S.R. (2006). Empirically examining the risk of intimate partner violence: the Revised Domestic Violence Screening Instrument (DVSI-R). *Public Health Reports* 121: 400–408.

Williams, K.R. and Houghton, A.B. (2004). Assessing the risk of domestic violence reoffending: a validation study. *Law and Human Behavior* 28: 437–455.

Wong, T. and Hisashima, J. (2008). State of Hawaii, 2003–2007: Domestic violence exploratory study on the DVSI and SARA. Report No. 1. Honolulu, HI: Hawaii State Department of Health.

9

Sexual Violence Risk Assessment

Martin Rettenberger[1,2] and Leam A. Craig[3,4,5]

[1]Centre for Criminology (Kriminologische Zentralstelle – KrimZ),
Wiesbaden, Germany
[2]Department of Psychology, Johannes Gutenberg-University (JGU),
Mainz, Germany
[3]Forensic Psychology Practice Ltd, UK
[4]Centre for Applied Psychology, University of Birmingham, Birmingham, UK
[5]School of Social Sciences, Birmingham City University, Birmingham, UK

Introduction

The 'What Works' literature is based on an overarching principle that highlights the need for empirically rigorous evidence-based practice. Over the years, several systems have been developed to aid the evaluation of the quality of evidence on the efficacy of particular therapeutic techniques and assessments with particular groups of people. The focus of this work has been to inform crime reduction. This work has been subsumed under the category 'What Works in the treatment and management of offenders to reduce crime'.

The three main systems of empirical evaluation used to examine the quality of outcome studies that are most often referred to in the literature are: the American Psychological Association (APA) Chambless and colleagues' system (Chambless and Hollon 1998; Chambless and Ollendick 2001; Chambless et al. 1998); Sherman et al.'s (1998) 'levels' system for reviewing the quality of evidence and intervention; and the Cochrane System (Higgins and Green 2006, 2011). Consistent between these systems is the emphasis on the quality of evidence from research studies and the effectiveness of interventions in the field of criminal behaviour. Based on knowledge of what constitutes methodologically robust research, several countries have begun to introduce structured assessment procedures specifically in relation to the assessment of risk of sexual violence amongst sexual offenders. The aim of this chapter is to consider empirically supported techniques and methodologies, as part of a 'What Works' approach, in assessing the risk of sexual violence in sexual offenders.

The Wiley Handbook of What Works in Violence Risk Management: Theory, Research and Practice,
First Edition. Edited by J. Stephen Wormith, Leam A. Craig, and Todd E. Hogue.
© 2020 John Wiley & Sons Ltd. Published 2020 by John Wiley & Sons Ltd.

The Methodology of Sexual Violence Risk Assessment

In modern forensic psychology, there are basically three different methodological approaches to risk assessment (e.g. Boer and Hart 2009; Craig et al. 2008; Hanson 2009): unstructured clinical judgment (UCJ), actuarial risk assessment instruments (ARAIs), and structured professional judgment (SPJ). Intuitively made UCJs – even if done by experienced clinicians – should no longer be taken into account in professional risk assessment settings because they cannot be regarded as a scientific procedure and, therefore, should not be named even 'professional' (Hanson 2009). By far, the most important reason for neglecting UCJ is that – as in other areas of psychological assessment and prediction research – empirical results indicate that structured and standardized risk assessment instruments like ARAIs and SPJ instruments are more accurate in predicting recidivism than unstructured prediction methods (e.g. Bonta et al. 1998; Dawes et al. 1989; Grove and Meehl 1996; Grove et al. 2000). Meta-analytic research has shown that this is also true for sexual offenders (Hanson and Morton-Bourgon 2009).

SPJ instruments like the Sexual Violence Risk-20 (SVR-20; Boer et al. 1997) consists of an empirically derived list of risk and protective factors, whereas scoring is typically based on professional considerations about which items apply best to an individual case. The final risk judgement in SPJ procedures – i.e. if an offender should be classified as low, moderate, or high risk – is primarily based on the professional's judgement using clinical experience, and the professional's theoretical and empirical knowledge about (re-)offending behaviour. ARAIs, on the other hand, represent highly structured risk assessment scales using combinations of empirically determined and thoroughly operationalized predictor variables (e.g. Craig et al. 2008; Hanson and Morton-Bourgon 2009; Quinsey et al. 2006). Based on Meehl's (1954) seminal work about the comparison between actuarial and clinical prediction methods, two core variables of ARAIs are that they use explicit methods of combining the risk factors, and that the total score which usually resulted from adding up the individual item scores to a total sum score is linked to an empirically derived probability figure (Dawes et al. 1989; Hanson and Morton-Bourgon 2009).

The Different Generations of Risk Assessment and the RNR-Model of Offender Rehabilitation

Another kind of categorization of risk assessment methods is based on the influential work of Bonta and Andrews (2007) about their Psychology of Criminal Conduct (PCC) which is not only related to sexual or violent offences but also to all kind of delinquent or criminal behaviour. The focus on the conceptualization of different 'generations' of risk assessment is that risk assessment should not only provide as much as possible predictive accuracy but also information about the opportunities of risk management, i.e. about the potential risk-reducing influence of (therapeutic) interventions and sanctions (Boer and Hart 2009; Hanson and Morton-Bourgon 2007, 2009; Wong et al. 2003). Andrews and Bonta (2010) initially proposed three (in the meantime four) generations of risk assessment: firstly, unstructured-intuitive clinical/professional judgement, secondly, actuarial (i.e. empirically derived) risk assessment methods based on predominantly or exclusively static/historical/biographical risk factors, and thirdly, actuarial risk assessment methods based on dynamic factors or criminogenic needs (Harris and Hanson 2010; Mann et al. 2010). The fourth generation of risk assessment tools attempt to integrate more systematically data about the intervention and monitoring process with a comprehensive permanently up-to-date assessment, a procedure which is usually called 'case management' in non-forensic settings and which is similar to the SPJ procedure (Andrews et al. 2006).

The proliferation of the second-generation risk assessment instruments as well as the development of third- and fourth-generation risk assessment instruments was strongly influenced and supported by the risk-need-responsivity (RNR) model of offender rehabilitation (Andrews and Bonta 2006; Bonta and Andrews 2007; Bonta and Wormith 2013; Harris and Hanson 2010). Andrews and Bonta (2010) suggested that an effective intervention should focus on risk (i.e. the risk potential of the single offender for committing new offences), need (i.e. consideration of empirically proven criminogenic needs in terms of particular treatment goals), and responsivity (i.e. the use of intervention techniques and treatment programmes to which the individual offender's abilities, learning style, motivation, and strengths respond). Today, the RNR-model is regarded as probably the most influential model for the assessment and treatment of offenders (Bonta and Andrews 2007; Ward et al. 2007) and was also successfully proven for sexual offenders (Hanson et al. 2009). In the last-named study, Hanson et al. (2009) reported that treatment programmes which adhered to the RNR principles showed the best results in reducing recidivism in sexual offenders. Because of the consistency of these findings with the general offender rehabilitation literature (Andrews and Bonta 2006; Bonta and Andrews 2007), the authors suggested that the RNR-model should be the most relevant aspect in the design and implementation of interventions for sexual offenders (Hanson et al. 2009).

Second-Generation ARAIs

Validation studies for second-generation ARAIs have consistently demonstrated predictive accuracy across samples and countries including Australia (Allan et al. 2006), Austria (Rettenberger et al. 2010), Belgium (Ducro and Pham 2006), Brazil (Baltieri and de Andrade 2008), Canada (Kingston et al. 2008), Denmark (Bengtson 2008), Germany (Stadtland et al. 2005), New Zealand (Skelton et al. 2006), and the UK (Craig 2008; Craig et al. 2006). In North America and the UK, ARAIs have permeated the entire criminal justice system when assessing potential future risk of sexual recidivism either in civil commitment or parole board assessments (Craig and Beech 2010). Below, we offer a brief summary of the most commonly used and empirically supported ARAIs.

The Static-99 family: The international gold standard of actuarial risk assessment

The Static-99 was developed by R. Karl Hanson and David Thornton (2000) and is today the ARAI most commonly used and best validated for sexual offenders (e.g. Anderson and Hanson 2010; Archer et al. 2006; Hanson and Morton-Bourgon 2009; Helmus et al. 2011). The instrument consists of 10 predominantly static risk factors: age when exposed to risk, any live-in intimate relationship for two or more years, any index offence of nonsexual violence, prior offences of nonsexual violence, prior charges or convictions for sexual offences, prior sentencing dates, any convictions for noncontact sexual offences, any unrelated victims, any stranger victims, and any male victims (for further information see Harris et al. 2003). Although there are 10 risk items, the individual risk factors of a sexual offender add up to a maximum total score of 12 as the risk item 'prior sex offences' is a weighted item, where the score goes from

0 to 3 depending on the number of prior convictions. Depending on the total score, the offender could be assigned to one of four risk categories as well as to relative and absolute risk estimates (Eher et al. 2012a; Helmus et al. 2012; Phenix et al. 2012; for further information see also www.static99.org).

A number of different studies have now investigated the interrater reliability of the Static-99 and usually found excellent results (Anderson and Hanson 2010). In the developmental study, Hanson and Thornton (2000) investigated the predictive accuracy of the Static-99 using four different datasets of $n = 1301$ sexual offenders in Canada and the UK. The Static-99 showed moderate to good predictive accuracy for sexual recidivism (AUC = 0.71) as well as for any violent (including sexual) recidivism (AUC = 0.69). In the following years, a huge amount of further cross-validation studies were published (for overviews see, for example, Anderson and Hanson 2010; Hanson and Morton-Bourgon 2009) including studies with Canadian (Barbaree et al. 2001), Dutch (de Vogel et al. 2004), Belgian (Ducro and Pham 2006), Austrian (Rettenberger et al. 2010), Swedish (Sjöstedt and Långstrom 2001), and UK (Craig et al. 2004, 2006) sexual offender samples. For sexual recidivism, the predictive accuracy values ranged in these studies from moderate (AUC = 0.66; Ducro and Pham 2006) to good validity indices (AUC = 0.76; Sjöstedt and Långstrom 2001).

One of the most important features of the actuarial paradigm of risk assessment is the sole reliance on empirically derived relations between data and the event of interest. Therefore, it is necessary to regulary investigate if revisions of the instrument or specific risk factors are needed. A very intense discussion about the imperative of a revision of the Static-99 and other second-generation ARAIs referred to the question about the risk-related influence of age on the recidivism risk estimates of sexual offenders (Helmus et al. 2012; Prentky et al. 2006; Rettenberger et al. 2013, 2015; Wollert 2006). Although there is usually a broad consensus regarding the inclusion of age items in actuarial risk scales, the question of which age variable should be used (e.g. age at first offence, age at index offence, or age at release from custody), and what weighting method would perform best in the prediction of recidivism has been debated (for a review of the effect of age on sexual recidivism see, for example, Craig 2008; Rice and Harris 2014).

In order to consider the age-related influence on the Static-99-based risk assessment appropriately Helmus, Thornton et al. (2012), argued that the 'age at release' variable in the Static-99 should be weighted more heavily which led to the development of a revised version of the Static-99, the Static-99R. In an independent cross-validation study of this revised version, Rettenberger et al. (2013) examined the influence of several age-related variables on the predictive accuracy of the German version of the Static-99 and compared the predictive accuracy of the original Static-99 and the new Static-99R using a population-based sample of prison-released sexual offenders ($n = 1077$). The results indicated that the original Static-99 (AUC = 0.73) performed better than the age-corrected Static-99R (AUC = 0.71) for sexual recidivism. Whereas Helmus et al. (2012) recommended to switch to the revised age weights when using the Static-99 in applied risk assessment settings, Rettenberger et al. (2013) concluded that their results indicated that – at least for the German version – the original Static-99 yields better predictive accuracy than the age-corrected Static-99R for the prediction of sexual recidivism and, therefore, supported the use of the original version of the instrument.

Further developments of the Static-99R led to the Static-2002 with increased coherence and conceptual clarity (Hanson and Thornton 2003; Helmus et al. 2012). The Static-2002 has 14 items with some items modified from Static-99. For example, the item 'young' on Static-2002 has four age categories rather than two. New items not included in Static-99 are 'any juvenile arrest for sexual offence', 'rate of sexual offending', 'young, unrelated victims', 'any community supervision violation', and 'years free prior to index'. Static-2002 items are grouped into five domains: age, persistence of sex offending, deviant sexual interests, relationship to victims, and general criminality producing five risk categories, low, low-moderate, moderate, moderate-high, and high. Several studies have provided support for the predictive validity of Static-2002 (Haag 2005; Langton et al. 2006, 2007; Martens et al. 2017) with AUC values ranging from 0.71 to 0.76 and the Static-2002 has demonstrated predictive superiority of Static-99 in predicting sexual, violent, and any recidivism, although the difference for sexual recidivism was small (Hanson et al. 2010). The Static-2002 underwent further refinement resulting in the Static-2002R which has identical risk items as the Static-2002 with the exception of upgraded age weights. The revised scale has produced some promising results regarding the predictive accuracy (Babchishin et al. 2012, 2016).

ARAIs provide several types of information that could be of value to decision makers (Hanson et al. 2013). The most prominent and traditional measure of risk are recidivism rate estimates linked to every single total score of an instrument. On the other hand, relative risk measures provide information about an offender's risk relative to other offenders (i.e. to the population to which he/she belongs) and can be quantified by, for example, so-called 'relative risk ratios' or 'percentile ranks' (Hanson et al. 2012). Whereas a meta-analytical review suggested that absolute recidivism rates predicted by the Static-99 varied substantially across samples (Helmus et al. 2012), the relative risk estimate are relatively stable over time and for different settings and jurisdictions (Hanson et al. 2013).

The Risk Matrix 2000 – Sexual and Violence Versions

The Risk Matrix 2000 – Sexual/Violent (Thornton et al. 2003) is today probably the most frequently used second-generation ARAI in the UK (Cortoni et al. 2010; Craig, 2019; Craig et al. 2008) and is based on the Structured Anchored Clinical Judgment Scale (SACJ; Grubin 1998) and on the meta-analytic findings by Hanson and Bussière (1998). The instrument consists of two separate scales, one for measuring the risk of sexual recidivism – the Risk Matrix 2000/Sexual (RM2000/S) –, and the other one for measuring the risk of non-sexual violent recidivism – the Risk Matrix 2000/Violent (RM2000/V). Both subscales were specifically developed for their use with sexual offenders, i.e. the RM2000/V should also be regarded as a second-generation ARAIs for sexual offenders. Additionally, both scale scores can be combined to assess the composite risk for sexual and non-sexual violent re-offence which is called the Risk Matrix 2000/Combined (RM2000/C). The individual risk level which is indicated by four separate risk categories (low, medium, high, and very high) is determined by a two-stage risk assessment process. The first stage of the protocol involves three risk items (age, previous sexual and previous general criminal offences). Points accumulated across these three items are then turned into one of four risk categories, low, medium, high, and very high. The second stage of the protocol considers four risk items (male victim, stranger victim, non-contact sexual offences, and no long-term relationship). If the offender obtains two or three of these risk items, the overall category of risk is raised by one category. If the offender obtained all four risk items, the overall risk category is raised by two categories. In the developmental study Thornton et al. (2003) examined the predictive accuracy of the RM2000/S on a treated ($n = 647$) and an untreated ($n = 429$) sexual offender sample and yielded good AUC-values (AUC = 0.77 assessed after treatment and AUC = 0.75 for the untreated sample, respectively), whereas the RM2000/V obtained even higher validity indices (AUC > 0.78) for the prediction of non-sexual violent recidivism in different long-term samples. Conducting a series of cross-validation studies with different UK samples Craig and colleagues reported varying results for the predictive accuracy of the RM2000 scales (e.g. Craig et al. 2004, 2006): On the one hand, the tools yielded impressive validity indices up to AUC = 0.86 for the prediction of violent including sexual recidivism by the RM2000/V (Craig et al. 2006). On the other hand, in other analyses the predictive accuracy was hardly better than chance (e.g. as indicated by AUC = 0.56 for the prediction of sexual recidivism by the RM2000/S as described in Craig et al. 2004). In a published meta-analysis, Helmus et al. (2013) integrated the findings of 16 unique samples (derived from 14 studies) which have examined the extent to which the RM2000 scales are able to discriminate between recidivists and non-recidivists. Helmus et al. (2013) found that all three RM2000 scales (RM2000/S, RM2000/V and RM2000/C) provided significant predictive power for all recidivism types which were investigated in this meta-analysis (i.e. sexual, non-sexual violent, any violent, non-violent and any recidivism). Due to outcome specificity, the predictive accuracy of the RM2000/S for predicting sexual recidivism performed the best ($d = 0.74$) whilst the RM2000/V had the largest effect size for predicting non-sexual violence ($d = 0.98$). The effect sizes of the RM2000/C were highest for the prediction of non-violent recidivism ($d = 0.92$) and any violent recidivism ($d = 0.81$).

The Sex Offender Risk Appraisal Guide

The Sex Offender Risk Appraisal Guide (SORAG; Quinsey et al. 2006) is another second-generation actuarial risk assessment tool for sexual offenders which was developed by the Canadian research group headed by Vernon L. Quinsey, Marnie E. Rice and Grant T. Harris. Together with the Static-99, the SORAG can be regarded as the most frequently used and best validated instrument internationally (for an overview see, for example, Rice et al. 2010). It is a modification of the Violence Risk Appraisal Guide (VRAG; Quinsey et al. 2006) which was developed to predict violent (including sexual hands-on) recidivism amongst adult male offenders. Therefore, 10 of the 14 items of the SORAG are the same as in the VRAG. The SORAG is conceptualized for sexual offenders to assess violent recidivism risk which includes sexual offences involving physical contact with the victim. The instrument consists of the following 14 weighted items: lived with biological parents up to age 16, elementary school maladjustment, history of alcohol problems, marital status, criminal history for nonviolent offences, criminal history for violent offences, previous convictions for sexual offences, sexual offences against girls under age 14 only, failure on prior conditional releases, age at index offence, Diagnostic and Statistical Manual of Mental Disorders (3rd ed. [DSM-III], American Psychiatric Association [APA] 1980) criteria for any personality disorder, DSM-III criteria for schizophrenia, phallometric test results indicating paedophilia or sexual sadism, and Hare PCL-R score. Based on the total score, the risk assessor can allocate the offender to one of nine risk categories. By means of these risk categories, it is possible to infer to empirically calculated probabilities of violent (including sexual) recidivism after 7 and 10 years at risk, respectively. Furthermore, evaluators can use relative risk ratios in terms of percentile ranks (Quinsey et al. 2006).

Even if the majority of the validation studies were still completed in Anglo-American countries, in the meantime there also exist cross-validation studies from several European countries (e.g. Rettenberger et al. 2017; for further details in other countries see, for example, Harris et al. 2010;

Rice et al. 2010). Harris et al. (2003) concluded that at that time the existing research from several North-American studies (e.g. Barbaree et al. 2001; Nunes et al. 2002; Rice and Harris 1995) have shown the SORAG to have a high accuracy in the prediction of violent (including sexual) recidivism and moderate accuracy in predicting sexual offences. For the prediction of violent (including sexual) recidivism they calculated a median area under the curve (AUC) value of 0.75. Current overviews about the reliability and validity of the SORAG reported more than 50 empirical investigations (Harris et al. 2010; Rice et al. 2010) and in the meta-analysis published by Hanson and Morton-Bourgon (2009) the SORAG was one of the instruments with the strongest predictive power. A few years ago, a revised version of the VRAG (VRAG-R) was developed which should replace both the VRAG and the SORAG (Rice et al. 2013). Compared to its predecessors the VRAG-R is easier to score and, at the same time, obtained similar levels of predictive accuracy as the VRAG and SORAG. A first independent cross-validation using a sexual offender sample from Austria confirmed these conclusions (Gregório Hertz et al. 2019).

The Minnesota Sex Offender Screening Tool (MnSOST) and its Revision (MsSOST-R)

The Minnesota Sex Offender Screening Tool (MnSOST) as well as its revised version, the Minnesota Sex Offender Screening Tool-Revised (MnSOST-R; Epperson et al. 1998, 2000) were developed by the Minnesota Department of Corrections for the recidivism risk assessment of male adult sexual offenders. The MnSOST consists of the following 16 items: number of sexual convictions, length of sexual offending history, sexual offending whilst under supervision, sexual offence committed in a public place, use of threat or force, multiple acts on a single victim, different age groups of victims, offences against a 13–15 year old and being at least 5 years older than the victim, stranger victims, antisocial behaviour during adolescence, substance abuse, employment history, institutional misconduct (one item refers to behavioural misconduct, another one about the use of illicit substances whilst incarcerated), participation in sexual offender treatment programmes during incarceration, and age at the time of release. A later revised version of the MnSOST consists of 17 items and showed good predictive accuracy (AUC = 0.77) for the prediction of sexual recidivism using 6-year follow-up data ($N = 274$; Craig et al. 2008). However, Barbaree et al. (2001) reported a clearly lower predictive validity (AUC = 0.65) using an independent Canadian sample. Further empirical studies about the MnSOST and the revised version, the MnSOST-R, yielded mixed results ranging from poor predictive performance (Bartosh et al. 2003) up to moderate to good predictive accuracy (Epperson et al. 2000; Langton et al. 2002).

Third-Generation ARAIs

Stable and acute dynamic risk factors: The Stable-2007 and Acute-2007

Dynamic risk factors – sometimes also called criminogenic needs or psychologically meaningful risk factors (Mann et al. 2010) – are the core construct of third-generation instruments (Harris and Hanson 2010). The central difference between static risk factors captured in the second-generation ARAIs and these third-generation dynamic risk factors is that they are amenable to changes based on interventions which can lead to risk-related changes in the individual offender. Therefore, dynamic risk factors play a major role in treatment planning and in the monitoring of treatment process and success and have to be regarded today as a cornerstone of effective treatment programme implementation (Hanson et al. 2009).

In 1999, Hanson et al. (2007) initiated the Dynamic Supervision Project (DSP), a prospective-longitudinal field trial about the reliability, validity, and clinical utility of the Acute-2000 and Stable-2000, two predecessor versions of the Stable-2007 and Acute-2007. For the DSP, parole and probation officers from every Canadian province as well as from the US-states of Alaska and Iowa were trained in the application of the Static-99 (which should be used once at the beginning of the supervision process), the Stable-2000 (which should be assessed every six months), and the Acute-2000 (which should be used at every supervisory meeting). A total of 156 parole and probation officers completed these static, stable, and acute risk assessments on $n = 997$ sexual offenders across 16 jurisdictions. After an average follow-up of three years the predictive accuracy of the Static-99 for the prediction of sexual recidivism was expectably high (AUC = 0.74). The same was true for the Acute-2000 (AUC = 0.74), whereas the AUC-value of the Stable-2000 (AUC = 0.64) was considerably lower. Further problems of the Stable-2000 were that, firstly, not all risk factors showed the hypothesized linear relationship with recidivism, and secondly, the instrument showed no incremental predictive accuracy beyond the Static-99. Therefore, the authors made a few minor rating and operationalization changes for some items (deviant sexual interests, lovers/intimate partners, and emotional identification with children) and dropped the three attitude items due to a lack of prognostic relevance. This revised version of the instrument, called the Stable-2007, showed higher predictive accuracy (AUC = 0.67) and incremental predictive power for the prediction of sexual recidivism beyond what was captured by the Static-99 alone (Hanson et al. 2007). A published follow-up study confirmed these promising results (Hanson et al. 2015).

One major result for the Acute-2000 was that only a subset of the included risk factors was significantly related to all outcome measures used in the DSP (sexual, violent, and general criminal recidivism). This result led to a revision of the risk tool, called Acute-2007, and to the separation of two different factors: one factor consisting of acute risk factors relevant for the prediction of violent and sexual recidivism and another general criminality factor which contains all seven specified risk factors. There are only a few independent cross-validation studies of the Stable-2007 and less for the Acute-2007. Eher et al. (2012b) investigated the predictive and incremental validity of the Stable-2000 and the Stable-2007 in a prison-released sample of sexual offenders from Austria ($n = 263$) by using a prospective-longitudinal research design. After an average follow-up period of 6.4 years, the Stable-2007 was significantly related to all outcomes (AUC = 0.67–0.71), whereas the Stable-2000 showed only weak predictive accuracy for the prediction of sexual recidivism (AUC = 0.62). Furthermore, the study provided additional evidence for the incremental validity of the Stable-2007 beyond the second-generation static risk factors (Eher et al. 2012b) which was recently replicated (Etzler et al. 2018). In a further cross-validation study from Austria, Eher et al. (2013) investigated the predictive accuracy of the Static-99 and the Stable-2007 in a sample ($n = 96$) of released male forensic patients hospitalized under mandatory treatment who committed sexually motivated offences. The Static-99 (AUC = 0.86) and the Stable-2007 (AUC = 0.71) were significantly related to sexual re-offending after an average follow-up period of approximately seven years. Again, the Stable-2007 provided evidence for the incremental predictive accuracy beyond the Static-99 (Eher et al. 2013).

The Structured Assessment of Risk and Need Framework

The Structured Assessment of Risk and Need Framework (SARN; Thornton 2002; Webster et al. 2006) is not an actuarial risk instrument in a strict methodological sense (Dawes et al. 1989; Meehl 1954). However, due to its rigorously empirical orientation, it could be regarded conceptually as an actuarial risk tool (Hanson and Morton-Bourgon 2007; Sawyer 1966). In 2002, David Thornton proposed the SRA as a process for evaluating the risk presented by sex offenders (Thornton 2002). The SRA consisted of four subsystems: the first one is called Static Assessment and is based on unchangeable, static risk factors, the second one is called the Initial Deviance Assessment and is based on potentially changeable but relatively stable risk factors, the third one is called *Evaluation of Progress* and is based on the offender's response to treatment, and the fourth one is called *Risk Management* and is based on offence-related, environmental, and other acute risk factors. Furthermore, Thornton (2002) postulated that the main dynamic risk factors fall into four domains: sexual interests, distorted attitudes, socio-affective functioning, and self-management. Within SRA, the term deviance is defined by the extent to which the offender's functioning is dominated by the psychological factors that contribute to his offending. High deviance is defined as an individual showing problems within at least three domains, moderate deviance means that dynamic risk factors are present in one or two domains, and low deviance is defined by the absence of any dynamic risk factor in these domains (Cortoni et al. 2010).

The SARN was developed based on Thornton's SRA-approach and contains 16 items allocated to one of the above-mentioned dynamic risk domains (Craig et al. 2007; Webster et al. 2006): the sexual interests domain contains four subdomains (sexual preoccupation, sexual preference for children, sexualized violence, and other offence-related sexual interests), the distorted attitudes domain has five items (adversarial sexual attitudes, child abuse supportive beliefs, sexual entitlement, rape supportive beliefs, and women are deceitful beliefs), the socio-affective functioning domain exhibited four specified risk factors (grievance thinking, inadequacy, lack of emotional intimacy, and distorted intimacy balance), and the self-management domain consisted of three items (lifestyle impulsiveness, poor problem solving, and poor emotional control). The greater the number of deviancy domains, the greater the treatment need. Craig et al. (2007) calculated a Psychological Deviance Index (PDI) based on the number of deviant domains in a sample of 119 sexual offenders. Of the four dynamic risk domains, the *Sexual Interests* domain obtained a large effect in predicting sexual reconviction over two-years (AUC = 0.86) and five-year follow-up periods (AUC = 0.72). The *Self-Management* factor obtained moderate results (AUC = 0.71) in predicting sexual reconviction at two years. In comparison, the Static-99 obtained moderate accuracy in predicting sexual reconviction, at two-years (AUC = 0.66) and five-years (AUC = 0.60). When the rates of sexual reconviction were compared with the PDI, it was found that the increase in rates of sexual reconviction mirrored the increase in the degree of PDI. When the PDI was grouped into Low (0), Moderate (1–2) and High (3+) categories, the degree of PDI and rates of reconviction were linear at 3, 18, and 40%, respectively. Of the four domains, the Sexual Interests Domain appears to produce the most promising results in predicting sexual reconviction. Psychometric measures of sexual obsession (AUC = 0.71) and paraphilia (AUC = 0.62), as part of the *Sexual Interests* domain, have demonstrated reasonable accuracy in predicting sexual (Craig et al. 2007) as well as clinical assessments of the *Sexual Interests* domain (AUC = 0.65 and 0.68, at two-years and five-years respectively; Tully et al. 2015).

As part of a review of the SARN, to reflect protective factors and make more explicit issues of responsivity as well as desistance (see Laws and Ward 2010), the framework was revised to the Structured Assessment of Risk, Need, and Responsivity (SARNR). The framework continues to be cantered on the four core domains as well as an additional item, Success Factors aimed at being a responsible member of society, actively changing life for the better by working on the things that led to offending in the past, and having a job or being busy. The assessment methodology adopts a triangulation of evidence to identify an individual's risk factors based on: interview data, observation, file review, treatment programme products, and psychometric measures (For a more detailed description of the SARN development, its derivates, and the current status of research, see Craig et al. 2007; Craig & Rettenberger, 2017). The idea of four core dynamic risk domains is consistent with other dynamic frameworks such as the Stable-2007 and Acute-2007 (see Beech and Craig 2012; Craig and Rettenberger 2016).

The Violence Risk Scale – Sexual Offence Version

The Violence Risk Scale–Sexual Offence Version (VRS–SO; Olver et al. 2007; Wong et al. 2003) is a conceptual actuarial third-generation risk assessment instrument (Hanson and Morton-Bourgon 2007; Wong and Olver 2010) and is based predominantly on the Violence Risk Scale (VRS; Wong and Gordon 2006) which was developed for the prediction of general (rather than only sexual) violence. The major theoretical and conceptual underpinnings of the VRS and the VRS–SO were the PCC (Andrews and Bonta 2006) and the RNR-model of effective treatment implementation (Bonta and Andrews 2007; Hanson et al. 2009). The VRS–SO was specifically developed to assess the risk of sexual violence for forensic patients who are considered for release to the community after attending a treatment programme (Wong et al. 2003). The instrument consists of 7 static (age at release, age at first sexual offence, offender type, prior sexual offences, unrelated victims, victim gender, and prior sentencing dates) and 17 dynamic (sexually deviant lifestyle, sexual compulsivity, offence planning, criminal personality, cognitive distortions, interpersonal aggression, emotional control, insight, substance abuse, community support, release to high-risk situation, sexual offending cycle, impulsivity, compliance with community supervision, treatment compliance, deviant sexual preference, and intimacy deficits) items.

The static as well as the dynamic items are both used to determine the recidivism risk of an individual offender (i.e. to fulfil the risk principle), whereas the dynamic variables were developed to identify treatment targets and to measure treatment-induced changes in recidivism risk (i.e. to fulfil the need principle; Wong and Olver 2010). The static and dynamic factors are all rated on a 4-point Likert-scale to reflect the extent of the problems identified by the factors (Wong et al. 2003). The total score represents the individual's current (or pre-treatment) risk and can be differentiated into four risk categories: low (total scores from 0 to 20), moderate-low (21–30), moderate-high (31–40), and high (41–72). Despite this opportunity of using categories, the authors recommend linking the scores of the instrument directly to recidivism risk tables because the meaning of labels such as 'high risk' or 'low risk' could vary substantially between different persons (Hilton et al. 2008; Wong and Gordon 2006; Wong and Olver 2010). The dynamic factors with high ratings are potential treatment targets and should be worked on during therapy.

The first studies about the psychometric properties of the VRS–SO provided evidence for the construct validity (e.g. due to high correlations between the Static-99 and the VRS–SO static items) and indicated a three-factor solution which was labelled *Sexual Deviance*, *Criminality*, and *Treatment Responsivity* (Olver et al. 2007). Furthermore, the internal consistency ($\alpha = 0.81$ for the dynamic items score and $\alpha = 0.84$ for the total VRS–SO score; Olver et al. 2007) as well as the interrater reliability was good to excellent, even for the more complex dynamic items (ICC = 0.74–0.95; Beggs and Grace 2010; Beyko and Wong 2005; Olver et al. 2007). The predictive validity of the VRS–SO was examined by Olver et al. (2007) in a sample of $n = 321$ sexual offenders with an average follow-up period of 10 years. For the prediction of sexual recidivism both the VRS–SO static and the VRS–SO dynamic total sub-scale scores showed significant AUC-values (AUC = 0.74 for the static and AUC = 0.67 for the dynamic items). Furthermore, the dynamic items provided an incremental predictive contribution beyond the static items. The VRS–SO total had with an AUC = 0.72 a predictive accuracy which could be regarded as a large effect size (Rice and Harris 2005). Interestingly, the predictive accuracy for non-sexual violent recidivism was substantially lower than for sexual recidivism, particularly because of a negative predictability of the *Sexual Deviance* subscale of the VRS–SO dynamic part (Olver et al. 2007). Beggs and Grace (2010) investigated the predictive accuracy of the VRS–SO in an independent cross-validation study by using a sample of *n* = 218 child molesters and an average follow-up period of about 4.5 years. In this study, the dynamic items of the VRS–SO obtained a high AUC-value (AUC = 0.80) which was considerably higher than for the static items (AUC = 0.67) and showed again an incremental predictive contribution beyond static items (Beggs and Grace 2010). In a further cross-validation study from Austria, the positive results of the above-mentioned previous studies could be largely replicated (Eher et al. 2015).

Structured Professional Judgement

The Sexual Violence Risk-20

The sexual violence risk-20 (SVR-20) is probably the most commonly used Structured Professional Judgement (SPJ) instrument for the risk assessment of sexual offenders. Boer and Hart (2009) stated that 'the SVR-20 has been evaluated by a variety of researchers in a variety of sites and is the best-validated SPJ for the risk assessment of sexual offenders' (p. 34). The SVR–20 is a structured clinical guideline designed for the assessment of risk for sexual violence in adult sex offenders by a group of forensic scientists who had already done research on SPJ for other offender subgroups. The SVR-20 was developed from a thorough research of the empirical literature and using the clinical expertise of a number of clinicians. To identify relevant risk factors, there were three general principles: The risk factor must be (i) supported by scientific research, (ii) consistent with theory and professional recommendations, and (iii) legally acceptable, that is, consistent with human and civil rights. The SVR-20 consists of 20 items and three domains: psychosocial adjustment (11 items: sexual deviance, victim of child abuse, psychopathy, major mental illness, substance use problems, suicidal, or homicidal ideation, relationship problems, employment problems, past nonsexual violent offences, past nonviolent offences, and past supervision failure), sexual offences (7 items: high-density sex offences, multiple sex offence types, physical harm to victim[s] in sex offences, use of weapons or threats of death in sex offences, escalation in frequency or severity of sex offences, extreme minimization or denial of sex offences, and attitudes that support or condone sex offences), and future plans (2 items: lack of realistic plans and negative attitude towards interventions). The authors developed a manual and worksheets, to support a reliable application of the instrument.

The administration of the SVR-20 can be divided into three general steps of the risk assessment process: Firstly, the 20 items as well as any additional case-specific risk factors have to be coded by an experienced forensic clinician. The items are rated using a 3-point ordinal rating scale as definitely present, possibly or partially present, or absent. In the second step, the evaluator indicates for each present risk factor whether there has been any recent change in the status of that factor within a flexible timeframe. Changes are also coded on a 3-point ordinal rating scale in terms of exacerbation, no change, or amelioration. In the final step, users make a final judgement about the risk of future violence again using a 3-point ordinal rating scale. The final risk judgement should be rated as low, moderate, or high which is also indicating the degree of intervention required in this individual case. For example, a final judgement of high risk would indicate an urgent need to develop and start a comprehensive risk management plan for the individual which would feature more resources than in cases of moderate or low risk.

In comparison to the above-mentioned ARAIs, the state of research about the psychometric properties of the SVR-20 is smaller (de Vogel et al. 2004). The reason is that the SPJ final-risk judgement model is much more complex than the actuarial way of summing up individual item scores. In the meantime, a number of studies provide evidence of the reliability, (predictive) validity, and cross-cultural transferability of the SVR-20 (e.g. Dempster 1998; Dietiker et al. 2007; Hanson and Morton-Bourgon 2007; Macpherson 2003; Rettenberger et al. 2011; Stadtland et al. 2005; de Vogel et al. 2004; for an international review see, for example, Rettenberger et al. 2009).

The SVR-20 items and organization of the protocol has been revised and updated (Boer 2011). Not to invalidate previous research supporting the SVR-20, many of the original 20 items remain although some items have changed or been replaced, allowing for the inclusion of new items (for detail of changes see Craig and Rettenberger 2017). However, to date, there is no published research on the revised SVR–20.

The Risk for Sexual Violence Protocol

The Risk for Sexual Violence Protocol (RSVP) is a set of professional guidelines for the assessment of risk of sexual violence using 22 different risk factors from five different risk domains: history of sexual violence (chronicity of sexual violence, diversity of sexual violence, escalation of sexual violence, physical coercion in sexual violence and psychological coercion in sexual violence), psychological adjustment (extreme minimization or denial of sexual violence, attitudes that support or condone sexual violence, problems with self-awareness, problems with stress or coping and problems resulting from child abuse), mental disorder (sexual deviance, psychopathic personality disorder, major mental illness, problems with substance use and violent or suicidal ideation), social adjustment (problems with intimate relationship, problems with non-intimate relationship, problems with employment and non-sexual criminality), and manageability (problems with planning, problems with treatment and problems with supervision).

According to Craig et al. (2008), the RSVP 'represents the most evolved form of structured professional judgement in the risk assessment and management field' (p. 81). On the one hand, the RSVP and the SVR-20 are very similar in content and have an about 85% overlap of common items (Craig et al. 2008). On the other hand, there is a conceptual difference because the RSVP puts more emphasis on psychological risk factors and development of case management plans. Therefore, it is better suited for evaluations conducted for treatment purposes (Hart and Boer 2010). The SVR-20 was developed for general use by a wide range of professionals, whereas the RSVP was intended primarily for use by sexual offender specialists in management- and treatment-oriented evaluations. Like the SVR-20, the manual of the instrument was also developed from a thorough consideration of the empirical literature and the clinical expertise of a number of clinicians. In order to identify relevant risk factors, there were the same three general principles: The risk factor has to be (i) supported by scientific research, (ii) consistent with theory and professional recommendations, and (iii) legally acceptable, that is, consistent with human and civil rights. The authors developed a comprehensive manual as well as a detailed worksheet, in order to ensure reliable ratings of each risk factor.

The Administration of the RSVP is more detailed and complex than that of the SVR-20 and is divided into six separate steps (Hart et al. 2003). In Step 1, the evaluator gathers information about the individual case guided by recommendations in the user's manual. In Step 2, the evaluator codes the presence of the above-mentioned 22 individual risk factors from five different domains, as well as any case-specific risk factors. The ratings are made for two different timeframes: On the one hand, the evaluator codes whether the risk factor was present more than one year prior to the evaluation and, on the other hand, the evaluator codes whether the risk factor has been present within the year prior to the assessment. The first coding is called 'past' evaluation, the second one 'recent'. Each rating is made using the same 3-point ordinal scale as the SVR-20, which is absent, possibly or partially present, or present. These ratings may be omitted when there is insufficient information.

In Step 3, the user determines the relevance of the individual risk factor. A risk factor would be classified as 'relevant' when the evaluator assesses a risk factor either as functionally or causally related to the offender's recidivism risk or related to a substantial impairment of the effectiveness of risk management strategies such as psychotherapy. The relevance ratings are also made by using a 3-point ordinal scale: Not relevant, possibly or partially relevant, or relevant. In Step 4, users identify and describe the most likely scenarios of future sexual violence by considering the gathered information in Step 1, by considering the risk factors identified as present and relevant in Step 2 and 3, and by considering the probable living circumstances. These scenarios form the basis for the development of risk management strategies. In Step 5, the evaluator has to develop strategies for managing the recidivism risk of the individual case referring to the risk scenarios constructed in Step 4. Hart et al. (2003) suggested four general categories of risk management: monitoring, treatment, supervision, and victim safety planning. In the last step, Step 6, the evaluator makes a final overall risk judgement in this case. The authors encourage the users to deliver judgements about case prioritization, risk of serious physical harm, indications of other possible risk scenarios, need for immediate actions, and critical dates or triggers for case review (Hart et al. 2003). Unfortunately, international data on the psychometric properties of the RSVP is relatively poor. Although there are already translations of the manual in different languages, there are currently only studies from Canada and international research is still scarce.

Conclusions

The ARAIs and SPJ scales discussed here have been rigorously examined and cross-validated with different samples from several countries and arguably meet the 'What Works' overarching principles that highlight the need for empirically rigorous evidence-based practice. The development and promulgation of the standardized risk assessment methodology is certainly one of the most important advances in forensic and criminological psychology in the last few decades. Based on the seminal work of Paul E. Meehl (e.g. Meehl 1954) we are now able to provide reliable and valid prognoses about the recidivism risk of sexual offenders by using comparably easy to score and scientifically sound risk assessment instruments. The more complex and clinically informed instruments provide information about the most relevant and promising (in terms of sustainably risk-reducing) therapeutic aims in sexual offender treatment settings. Taken together, standardized risk assessment instruments should be an integral part of every clinical or correctional institution which has to diagnose, assess, and/or treat sexual offenders.

References

Allan, A., Dawson, D., and Allan, M.M. (2006). Prediction of the risk of male sexual reoffending in Australia. *Australian Psychologist* 41: 60–68.

American Psychiatric Association (1980). *Diagnostic and Statistical Manual of Mental Disorders*, 3e. Washington, DC: American Psychiatric Association.

Anderson, D. and Hanson, R.K. (2010). Static-99: an actuarial tool to assess risk of sexual and violent recidivism among sexual offenders. In: *Handbook of Violence Risk Assessment* (eds. R.K. Otto and K.S. Douglas), 251–267. Oxford, UK: Routledge.

Andrews, D.A. and Bonta, J. (2010). *The Psychology of Criminal Conduct*, 5e. Cincinnati, OH: Anderson.

Andrews, D.A., Bonta, J., and Wormith, S.J. (2006). The recent past and near future of risk and/or need assessment. *Crime and Delinquency* 52: 7–27.

Archer, R.P., Buffington-Vollum, J.K., Stredny, R.V., and Handel, R.W. (2006). A survey of psychological test use patterns among forensic psychologists. *Journal of Personality Assessment* 87: 84–94.

Babchishin, K.M., Hanson, R.K., and Blais, J. (2016). Less is more: using Static-2002R subscales to predict violent and general recidivism among sexual offenders. *Sexual Abuse: A Journal of Research and Treatment* 28: 187–217.

Babchishin, K.M., Hanson, R.K., and Helmus, L. (2012). Even highly correlated measures can add incrementally to predicting recidivism among sex offenders. *Assessment* 19: 442–461.

Baltieri, D.A. and de Andrade, A.G. (2008). Comparing serial and nonserial sexual offenders: alcohol and street drug consumption, impulsiveness and history of sexual abuse. *Revista Brasileira de Psiquiatria* 30: 25–31.

Barbaree, H.E., Seto, M.C., Langton, C.M., and Peacock, E.J. (2001). Evaluating the predictive accuracy of six risk assessment instruments for adult sex offenders. *Criminal Justice and Behavior* 28: 490–521.

Bartosh, D.L., Garby, T., Lewis, D., and Gray, S. (2003). Differences in the predictive validity of actuarial risk assessments in relation to sex offender type. *International Journal of Offender Therapy and Comparative Criminology* 47: 422–438.

Beech, A.R. and Craig, L. (2012). The current status of static and dynamic factors in sexual offender risk assessment. *Journal of Aggression, Conflict and Peace Research* 4 (4): 169–185.

Beggs, S.M. and Grace, R.C. (2010). Assessment of dynamic risk factors: an independent validation study of the violence risk scale: sexual offender version. *Sexual Abuse: A Journal of Research and Treatment* 22: 234–251.

Bengtson, S. (2008). Is new better? A cross-validation of the Static-2002 and the risk matrix 2000 in a Danish sample of sexual offenders. *Psychology, Crime & Law* 14: 85–106.

Beyko, M.J. and Wong, S.C.P. (2005). Predictors of treatment attrition as indicators for program improvement not offender shortcomings: a study of sex offender treatment attrition. *Sexual Abuse: A Journal of Research and Treatment* 17: 375–389.

Boer, D.P. (2011). SVR-20 2nd edition updates. Presented at the Workshop at the New Directions in Sex Offender Practice Conference in Birmingham, England (24th October 2011).

Boer, D.P. and Hart, S.D. (2009). Sex offender risk assessment: research, evaluation, "best-practice" recommendations and future directions. In: *Violent and Sexual Offenders: Assessment, Treatment and Management* (eds. J.L. Ireland, C.A. Ireland and P. Birch), 27–42. Cullompton, UK: Willan Publishing.

Boer, D.P., Hart, S.D., Kropp, P.R., and Webster, C.D. (1997). *Manual for the Sexual Violence Risk-20: Professional Guidelines for Assessing Risk of Sexual Violence*. Vancouver, Canada: The Mental Health, Law and Policy Institute.

Bonta, J. and Andrews, D.A. (2007). *Risk-Need-Responsivity Model for Offender Assessment and Rehabilitation (User Report 2007–04)*. Ottawa, ON: Public Safety Canada.

Bonta, J., Law, M., and Hanson, R.K. (1998). The prediction of criminal and violent recidivism among mentally disordered offenders: a meta-analysis. *Psychological Bulletin* 123: 123–142.

Bonta, J. and Wormith, J.S. (2013). Applying the risk-need-responsivity principles to offender assessment. In: *What Works in Offender Rehabilitation: An Evidence Based Approach to Assessment and Treatment* (eds. L.A. Craig, L. Dixon and T.A. Gannon), 71–93. Malden, MA: Wiley Blackwell.

Chambless, D. and Ollendick, T. (2001). Empirically supported psychological interventions: controversies and evidence. *Annual Review of Psychology* 52: 685–716.

Chambless, D.L., Baker, M.J., Baucom, D.H. et al. (1998). Update on empirically validated therapies, II. *The Clinical Psychologist* 51: 3–16.

Chambless, D.L. and Hollon, S.D. (1998). Defining empirically supported therapies. *Journal of Consulting and Clinical Psychology* 66: 7–18.

Cortoni, F., Craig, L., and Beech, A.R. (2010). Risk assessment of sexual offenders. In: *Transnational Criminology Manual*, vol. 3 (ed. M. Herzog-Evans), 503–527. Nijmegen, Netherlands: Wolf Legal Publishers.

Craig, L.A. (2008). How should we understand the effect of age on sexual reconviction? *Journal of Sexual Aggression* 14: 185–198.

Craig, L.A. (2019). The predictive accuracy of the risk matrix 2000. In: *The SAGE Encyclopaedia of Criminal Psychology* (ed. R.D. Morgan), 1269. Thousand Oaks, CA: Sage Publications.

Craig, L.A. and Beech, A.R. (2010). Towards a guide to best practice in conducting actuarial risk assessments with sex offenders. *Aggression and Violent Behavior* 15: 278–293.

Craig, L.A., Beech, A.R., and Browne, K.D. (2006). Cross-validation of the risk matrix 2000 sexual and violent scales. *Journal of Interpersonal Violence* 21: 612–633.

Craig, L.A., Browne, K.D., and Beech, A.R. (2008). *Assessing Risk in Sex Offenders: A Practitioner's Guide*. Chichester, UK: Wiley.

Craig, L.A., Browne, K.D., and Stringer, I. (2004). Comparing sex offender risk assessment measures on a UK sample. *International Journal of Offender Therapy and Comparative Criminology* 48: 7–27.

Craig, L.A. and Rettenberger, M. (2016). A brief history of sexual offender risk assessment. In: *Treatment of Sexual Offenders: Strengths and Weaknesses in Assessment and Intervention* (eds. D.R. Laws and W. O'Donohue), 19–44. New York, NY: Springer.

Craig, L.A. and Rettenberger, M. (2017). Risk assessment for sexual offenders: where to from here? In: *The Wiley Handbook on the Theories, Assessment and Treatment of Sexual Offending. Volume 2, Assessment* (eds. L. Craig and M. Rettenberger), 1203–1226. Chichester, UK: Wiley Blackwell.

Craig, L.A., Thornton, D., Beech, A.R., and Browne, K.D. (2007). The relationship of statistical and psychological risk markers to sexual reconviction. *Criminal Justice and Behavior* 34: 314–329.

Dawes, R.M., Faust, D., and Meehl, P.E. (1989). Clinical versus actuarial judgement. *Science* 243: 1668–1674.

de Vogel, V., de Ruiter, C., van Beek, D., and Mead, G. (2004). Predictive validity of the SVR-20 and Static-99 in a Dutch sample of treated sex offenders. *Law and Human Behavior* 28: 235–251.

Dempster, R.J. (1998). Prediction of sexually violent recidivism: A comparison of risk assessment instruments. Master thesis. Simon Fraser University.

Dietiker, J., Dittmann, V., and Graf, M. (2007). Gutachterliche Risikoeinschätzung bei Sexualstraftätern. Anwendbarkeit von PCL: SV, HCR-20+3 und SVR-20 [risk assessment of sex offenders in a German-speaking sample: applicability of PCL: SV, HCR-20+3, and SVR-20]. *Nervenarzt* 78: 53–61.

Ducro, C. and Pham, T. (2006). Evaluation of the SORAG and the Static-99 on Belgian sex offenders committed to a forensic facility. *Sexual Abuse: A Journal of Research and Treatment* 18: 15–26.

Eher, R., Matthes, A., Schilling, F. et al. (2012b). Dynamic risk assessment in sexual offenders using STABLE-2000 and the STABLE-2007: an investigation of predictive and incremental validity. *Sexual Abuse: A Journal of Research and Treatment* 24: 5–28.

Eher, R., Olver, M., Heurix, I. et al. (2015). Predicting reoffence in pedophilic child molesters by clinical diagnoses and risk assessment. *Law and Human Behavior* 39: 571–580.

Eher, R., Rettenberger, M., Gaunersdorfer, K. et al. (2013). Über die Treffsicherheit der standardisierten Risikoeinschätzungsverahren Static-99 und Stable-2007 bei aus einer Sicherungsmaßnahme entlassenen Sexualstraftätern [on the accuracy of the standardardized risk assessment procedures Static-99 and Stable-2007 for sexual offenders released from detention]. *Forensische Psychiatrie, Psychologie, Kriminologie* 7: 264–272.

Eher, R., Schilling, F., Haubner-MacLean, T. et al. (2012a). Ermittlung des relativen und absoluten Rückfallrisikos mithilfe des Static-99 in einer deutschsprachigen population entlassener Sexualstraftäter [assessment of the relative and absolute risk of recidivism using Static-99 in a German-speaking population of released sexual offenders]. *Forensische Psychiatrie, Psychologie, Kriminologie* 6: 32–40.

Epperson, D.L., Kaul, J.D. and Hesselton, D. (1998). Final report on the development of the Minnesota Sex Offender Screening Tool—Revised. Paper presented at the 17th Annual Research and Treatment Conference of the Association for the Treatment of Sexual Abusers in Vancouver, Canada (October 1998).

Epperson, D.L., Kaul, J.D., Huot, S.J. et al. (2000). Cross-validation of the Minnesota Sex Offender Screening Tool—Revised. Paper presented at the 19th Annual Research and Treatment Conference of the Association for the Treatment of Sexual Abusers in San Diego, USA (1–4 November 2000).

Etzler, S., Eher, R. & Rettenberger, M. (2018). Dynamic risk assessment of sexual offenders: Validity and dimensional structure of the Stable-2007. Assessment. Advance online publication. https://doi.org/10.1177/1073191118754705

Grove, W.M. and Meehl, P.E. (1996). Comparative efficiency of informal (subjective, impressionistic) and formal (mechanical, algorithmic) prediction procedures: the clinical-statistical controversy. *Psychology, Public Policy, and Law* 2: 293–323.

Grove, W.M., Zald, D.H., Lebow, B.S. et al. (2000). Clinical versus mechanical prediction: a meta-analysis. *Psychological Assessment* 12: 19–30.

Grubin, D. (1998). *Sex Offending against Children: Understanding the Risk*, Police Research Series, Paper 99. London, UK: Home Office.

Haag, A.M. (2005). Do psychological interventions impact on actuarial measures? An analysis of the predictive validity of the Static-99 and Static-2002 on a re-conviction measure of sexual recidivism. Doctoral dissertation. University of Calgary.

Hanson, R.K. (2009). The psychological assessment of risk for crime and violence. *Canadian Psychology* 50: 172–182.

Hanson, R.K., Babchishin, K.M., Helmus, L., and Thornton, D. (2013). Quantifying the relative risk of sex offenders: risk ratios for Static-99R. *Sexual Abuse: A Journal of Research and Treatment* 24: 482–515.

Hanson, R.K., Bourgon, G., Helmus, L., and Hodgson, S. (2009). The principles of effective correctional treatment also apply to sexual offenders: a meta-analysis. *Criminal Justice and Behavior* 36: 865–891.

Hanson, R.K. and Bussière, M.T. (1998). Predicting relapse: a meta-analysis of sexual offender recidivism studies. *Journal of Consulting and Clinical Psychology* 66: 348–362.

Hanson, R.K., Harris, A.J.R., Scott, T.L., and Helmus, L. (2007). *Assessing the Risk of Sexual Offenders on Community Supervision: The Dynamic Supervision Project*, Corrections Research User Report 2007–05. Ottawa, ON: Public Safety Canada.

Hanson, R.K., Helmus, L., and Thornton, D. (2010). Predicting recidivism among sexual offenders: A multi-site study of Static-2002. *Law and Human Behavior* 34: 198–211. https://doi.org/10.1007/s10979-009-9180-1.

Hanson, R.K., Helmus, M.-L., and Harris, A.J.R. (2015). Assessing the risk and needs of supervised sexual offenders: a prospective study using STABLE-2007, Static-99R, and Static-2002R. *Criminal Justice and Behavior* 42: 1205–1224.

Hanson, R.K., Lloyd, C.D., Helmus, L., and Thornton, D. (2012). Developing non-arbitrary metrics for risk communication: percentile ranks for the Static-99/R and Static-2002/R sexual offender risk tools. *International Journal of Forensic Mental Health* 11: 9–23.

Hanson, R.K. and Morton-Bourgon, K. (2007). *The Accuracy of Recidivism Risk Assessment for Sexual Offenders: A Meta-Analysis*, Corrections Research User Report No. 2007–01. Ottawa, ON: Public Safety Canada.

Hanson, R.K. and Morton-Bourgon, K. (2009). The accuracy of recidivism risk assessments for sexual offenders: a meta-analysis of 118 prediction studies. *Psychological Assessment* 21: 1–21.

Hanson, R.K. and Thornton, D. (2000). Improving risk assessment for sex offenders: a comparison of three actuarial scales. *Law and Human Behavior* 24: 119–136.

Hanson, R.K. and Thornton, D. (2003). *Notes on the Development of Static-2002*. Ottawa, ON: Department of the Solicitor General of Canada.

Harris, A.J.R. and Hanson, R.K. (2010). Clinical, actuarial, and dynamic risk assessment of sexual offenders: why do things keep changing? *Journal of Sexual Aggression* 16: 296–310.

Harris, G.T., Rice, M.E., and Quinsey, V.L. (2010). Allegiance or fidelity? A clarifying reply. *Clinical Psychology: Science and Practice* 17: 82–89.

Harris, G.T., Rice, M.E., Quinsey, V.L. et al. (2003). A multisite comparison of actuarial risk instruments for sex offenders. *Psychological Assessment* 15: 413–425.

Hart, S.D. and Boer, D.P. (2010). Structured professional judgement guidelines for sexual violence risk assessment: the Sexual Violence Risk-20 (SVR-20) and risk for sexual violence protocol (RSVP). In: *Handbook of Violence Risk Assessment* (eds. R.K. Otto and K.S. Douglas), 269–294. Oxford: Routledge.

Hart, S.D., Kropp, P.R., Laws, D.R. et al. (2003). *The Risk for Sexual Violence Protocol (RSVP): Structured Professional Guidelines for Assessing Risk of Sexual Violence*. Burnaby, BC: Mental Health, Law, and Policy Institute, Simon Fraser University.

Helmus, L., Babchishin, K.M., and Hanson, R.K. (2013). The predictive accuracy of the risk matrix 2000: a meta-analysis. *Sexual Offender Treatment* 8: 1–20.

Helmus, L., Hanson, R.K., and Morton-Bourgon, K.E. (2011). International comparisons of the validity of actuarial risk tools for sexual offenders, with a focus on Static-99. In: *International Perspectives on the Assessment and Treatment of Sexual Offenders: Theory, Practice, and Research* (eds. D.P. Boer, L.A. Craig, R. Eher, et al.), 57–84. Chichester: Wiley.

Helmus, L., Hanson, R.K., Thornton, D. et al. (2012). Absolute recidivism rates predicted by Static-99R and Static-2002R sex offender risk assessment tools vary across samples: a meta-analysis. *Criminal Justice and Behavior* 33: 1148–1171.

Helmus, L., Thornton, D., Hanson, R.K., and Babchishin, K.M. (2012). Improving the predictive accuracy of Static-99 and Static-2002 with older sex offenders: revised age weights. *Sexual Abuse: A Journal of Research and Treatment* 24: 64–101.

Higgins, J.P.T. and Green, S. (2006). *Cochrane Handbook for Systematic Reviews of Interventions 4.2.6* [updated September 2006]. Chichester, UK: The Cochrane Collaboration.

Higgins, J.P.T. and Green, S. (2011). *Cochrane Handbook for Systematic Reviews of Interventions 5.1.0* [updated March 2011]. Chichester, UK: The Cochrane Collaboration.

Hilton, N.Z., Carter, A.M., Harris, G.T., and Sharpe, A.J.B. (2008). Does using nonnumerical terms to describe risk aid violence risk communication? Clinician agreement and decision making. *Journal of Interpersonal Violence* 23: 171–188.

Kingston, D.A., Yates, P.M., Firestone, P. et al. (2008). Long term predictive validity of the risk matrix 2000: a comparison with the Static-99 and the sex offender risk appraisal guide. *Sexual Abuse: A Journal of Research and Treatment* 20: 466–484.

Langton, C.M., Barbaree, H.E., Harkins, L., and Peacock, E.J. (2006). Sexual offenders response to treatment and its association with recidivism as a function of psychopathy. *Sexual Abuse* 18: 99–120.

Langton, C.M., Barbaree, H.E., Harkins, L. et al. (2002). Evaluating the predictive validity of seven risk assessment instruments for sexual offenders. Paper presented at the 21st Annual Research and Treatment Conference of the Association for the Treatment of Sexual Abusers in Montreal, Canada (October 2002).

Langton, C.M., Barbaree, H.E., Seto, M.C. et al. (2007). Actuarial assessment of risk for reoffense among adult sex offenders: Evaluating the predictive accuracy of the Static-2002 and five other instruments. *Criminal Justice and Behavior* 34: 37–59.

Laws, D.R. and Ward, T. (2010). *Desistance from Sex Offending: Alternatives to Throwing Away the Keys.* New York, NY: Guilford Press.

Macpherson, G.J.D. (2003). Predicting escalation in sexually violent recidivism: use of the SVR-20 and PCL:SV to predict outcome with non-contact recidivists and contact recidivists. *Journal of Forensic Psychiatry & Psychology* 14: 615–627.

Mann, R.E., Hanson, R.K., and Thornton, D. (2010). Assessing risk for sexual recidivism: some proposals on the nature of psychologically meaningful risk factors. *Sexual Abuse: A Journal of Research and Treatment* 22: 191–217.

Martens, R., Rettenberger, M. & Eher, R. (2017). The predictive and incremental validity of the German adaptation of the Static-2002 in a sexual offender sample released from the prison system. Legal and Criminological Psychology, 22, 164–179.

Meehl, P.E. (1954). *Clinical Versus Statistical Prediction: A Theoretical Analysis and a Review of the Evidence.* Minneapolis, MN: University of Minnesota Press.

Nunes, K.L., Firestone, P., Bradford, J.M. et al. (2002). A comparison of modified versions of the Static-99 and the sex offender risk appraisal guide (SORAG). *Sexual Abuse: A Journal of Research and Treatment* 14: 253–269.

Olver, M.E., Wong, S.C.P., Nicholaichuk, T., and Gordon, A. (2007). The validity and reliability of the violence risk scale-sexual offender version: assessing sex offender risk and evaluating therapeutic change. *Psychological Assessment* 19: 318–329.

Phenix, A., Helmus, L. and Hanson, R.K. (2012). Static-99R. Evaluators' workbook. http://www.static99.org/pdfdocs/st-99rworkbookwithsamplesandsummaries.pdf (Accessed 14 August 2019).

Prentky, R.A., Janus, E., Barbaree, H.E. et al. (2006). Sexually violent predators in the courtroom: science on trial. *Psychology, Public Policy, and Law* 12: 357–393.

Quinsey, V.L., Harris, G.T., Rice, M.E., and Cormier, C. (2006). *Violent Offenders: Appraising and Managing Risk*, 2e. Washington, DC: American Psychological Association.

Rettenberger, M., Boer, D.P., and Eher, R. (2011). The predictive accuracy of risk factors in the Sexual Violence Risk-20 (SVR-20). *Criminal Justice and Behavior* 38: 1009–1027.

Rettenberger, M., Briken, P., Turner, D., and Eher, R. (2015). Sexual offender recidivism among a population-based prison sample. *International Journal of Offender Therapy and Comparative Criminology* 59: 424–444.

Rettenberger, M., Haubner-MacLean, T., and Eher, R. (2013). The contribution of age to the Static-99 risk assessment in a population-based prison sample of sexual offenders. *Criminal Justice and Behavior* 40: 1413–1433.

Rettenberger, M., Hucker, S.J., Boer, D.P., and Eher, R. (2009). The reliability and validity of the Sexual Violence Risk-20 (SVR-20): an international review. *Sexual Offender Treatment* 4: 1–14.

Rettenberger, M., Matthes, A., Boer, D.P., and Eher, R. (2010). Actuarial recidivism risk assessment and sexual delinquency: a comparison of five risk assessment tools in different sexual offender subtypes. *International Journal of Offender Therapy and Comparative Criminology* 54: 169–186.

Rettenberger, M., Rice, M.E., Harris, G.T., and Eher, R. (2017). Actuarial risk assessment of sexual offenders: the psychometric properties of the sex offender risk appraisal guide (SORAG). *Psychological Assessment* 29: 624–638.

Rice, M.E. and Harris, G.T. (1995). Violent recidivism: assessing predictive validity. *Journal of Consulting and Clinical Psychology* 63: 737–748.

Rice, M.E. and Harris, G.T. (2005). Comparing effect sizes in follow-up studies: ROC, Cohen's *d* and *r*. *Law and Human Behavior* 29: 615–620.

Rice, M.E. and Harris, G.T. (2014). What does it mean when age is related to recidivism among sex offenders? *Law and Human Behavior* 38: 151–161.

Rice, M.E., Harris, G.T., and Hilton, N.Z. (2010). The violence risk appraisal guide and sex offender risk appraisal guide for violence risk assessment and the Ontario domestic assault risk assessment and domestic violence risk appraisal guide for wife assault risk assessment. In: *Handbook of Violence Risk Assessment Tools* (eds. R.K. Otto and K.S. Douglas), 99–120. Oxford, UK: Routledge/Taylor & Francis.

Rice, M.E., Harris, G.T., and Lang, C. (2013). Validation of and revision to the VRAG and SORAG: the violence risk appraisal guide-revised (VRAG-R). *Psychological Assessment* 25: 951–965.

Sawyer, J. (1966). Measurement and prediction: clinical and statistical. *Psychological Bulletin* 66: 178–200.

Sherman, L.W., Gottfredson, D., MacKenzie, D.L. et al. (1998). *Preventing Crime: What Works, What Doesn't, What's Promising*. Washington, DC: National Institute of Justice.

Sjöstedt, G. and Långstrom, N. (2001). Actuarial assessment of sex offender recidivism risk: a cross-validation of the RRASOR and the Static-99 in Sweden. *Law and Human Behavior* 25: 629–645.

Skelton, A., Riley, D., Wales, D., and Vess, J. (2006). Assessing risk for sexual offenders in New Zealand: development and validation of a computer-scored risk measure. *Journal of Sexual Aggression* 12: 277–286.

Stadtland, C., Hollweg, M., Kleindienst, N. et al. (2005). Risk assessment and prediction of violent and sexual recidivism in sex offenders: long-term predictive validity of four risk assessment instruments. *Journal of Forensic Psychiatry and Psychology* 16: 92–108.

Thornton, D. (2002). Constructing and testing a framework for dynamic risk assessment. *Sexual Abuse: A Journal of Research and Treatment* 14: 139–153.

Thornton, D., Mann, R., Webster, S. et al. (2003). Distinguishing and combining risks for sexual and violent recidivism. *Annals of the New York Academy of Sciences* 989: 225–235.

Tully, R., Browne, K.D., and Craig, L.A. (2015). An examination of the predictive validity of the structured assessment of risk and need treatment needs analysis (SARN-TNA) in England and Wales. *Criminal Justice and Behavior* 42: 509–528.

Ward, T., Mesler, J., and Yates, P. (2007). Reconstructing the risk-need-responsivity model: a theoretical elaboration and evaluation. *Aggression and Violent Behavior* 12: 208–228.

Webster, S.D., Mann, R.E., Carter, A.J. et al. (2006). Inter-rater reliability of dynamic risk assessment with sexual offenders. *Psychology, Crime & Law* 12: 439–452.

Wollert, R. (2006). Low base rates limit expert certainty when current actuarials are used to identify sexually violent predators: an application of Bayes's theorem. *Psychology, Public Policy, and Law* 12: 56–85.

Wong, S.C.P. and Gordon, A.E. (2006). The validity and reliability of the violence risk scale: a treatment-friendly violence risk assessment tool. *Psychology, Public Policy, and Law* 12: 279–309.

Wong, S.C.P. and Olver, M.E. (2010). Two treatment- and change-oriented risk assessment tools: the violence risk scale and the violence risk scale-sexual offender version. In: *Handbook of Violence Risk Assessment Tools* (eds. R.K. Otto and K.S. Douglas), 121–146. Oxford, UK: Routledge/Taylor & Francis.

Wong, S.C.P., Olver, M.E., Nicholaichuk, T.P., and Gordon, A. (2003). *The Violence Risk Scale: Sexual Offender Version (VRS-SO)*. Saskatoon, SK: Regional Psychiatric Centre and University of Saskatchewan.

10

Personality-Based Violence Risk Assessment

Mark E. Olver
University of Saskatchewan, Saskatchewan, Canada

Introduction

Completing an assessment of risk for future violence is a complex and multifaceted task that ideally should involve use of multiple assessment methods, drawing on multiple information sources, and targeting multiple domains of functioning (Boer et al. 1997). Whilst there remains debate about the utility and psychometric appropriateness of certain assessment tools (e.g. actuarial vs. structured professional judgement (SPJ)), the current zeitgeist in risk assessment research and clinical practice has progressed to an expectation that structured forensic measures are used, and that the presence of at least some structure is superior to an absence of structure (Hanson 2009; Mills 2017). But seldom are violence risk assessments limited to rating one or two purpose-built risk assessment tools. Not uncommonly, supplemental measures may be used to augment appraisals of risk, identify special needs, or important responsivity considerations that could have bearing on risk management applications and release decisions.

This chapter focuses on the role and relevance of personality-based measures within the context of violence risk assessment. I begin with an overview of the relevance of personality in violence risk assessment per the risk-need-responsivity (RNR) model (Bonta and Andrews 2017), and then review relevant research and clinical applications of three sets of personality-based metrics that have frequent use in violence risk assessment: (i) multiscale self-report inventories, namely, the Minnesota Multiphasic Personality Inventory-2 (MMPI-2; Butcher et al. 1989) and its variants and the Personality Assessment Inventory (PAI; Morey 1991); (ii) the Hare Psychopathy Checklist Revised (PCL-R; Hare 1991, 2003) and the Psychopathy Checklist: Screening Version (PCL: SV; Hart et al. 1995); and (iii) Diagnostic appraisals of personality pathology, which may be based on the *Diagnostic and Statistical Manual of Mental Disorders*, fifth edition (DSM-5; American Psychiatric Association 2013) or the *International Classification of Diseases*, 11th edition (ICD-11; World Health Organization 2018). Owing to space constraints I will not be covering specific self-report measures of single personality constructs that

The Wiley Handbook of What Works in Violence Risk Management: Theory, Research and Practice,
First Edition. Edited by J. Stephen Wormith, Leam A. Craig, and Todd E. Hogue.
© 2020 John Wiley & Sons Ltd. Published 2020 by John Wiley & Sons Ltd.

can have risk relevance, such as self-report measures of psychopathy, aggression, and hostility, or other indices of personality pathology (e.g. measures of narcissism, Machiavellianism), although there is an abundance of excellent measures.

Personality and its positioning within the RNR model

Personality has special relevance within the context of the RNR model. Briefly, the risk principle states that treatment intensity should be matched to the risk level of the individual, such that higher-risk persons receive a higher dosage of treatment, whilst lower risk persons receive few or minimal services. The need principle posits that criminogenic needs, that is, dynamic risk factors that may have causal relevance for criminal behaviour, should be prioritized for intervention. Finally, the responsivity principle speaks to the 'how of treatment', that is, the manner in which services should be delivered to promote client engagement and gain. General responsivity asserts that cognitive behavioural methods of behaviour change should be used in offender programmes, whilst specific responsivity features the tailoring of service delivery to the unique presenting characteristics of correctional clientele that can impact response to services (e.g. cognitive ability, learning style, culture, motivation, and personality).

The RNR model is embedded within a broader General Personality and Cognitive Social Learning theory (GPCSL) of criminal conduct, identifying the central predisposing factors and covariates of criminal behaviour. The 'Central Eight' feature prominently within the GPCSL as a collection of criminogenic needs to be prioritized for risk reduction services, per the need principle; these include criminal history and seven dynamic areas of education/employment, family/marital, antisocial peers, alcohol/drug problems, leisure/recreation, antisocial attitudes, and antisocial personality pattern. The latter is a personality dimension characterized by early and diverse antisocial behaviour, procriminal attitudes, and a pattern of generalized trouble (e.g. poor work/education history; Andrews et al. 2004), all of which have direct overlap with a diagnosis of antisocial personality disorder (ASPD). From an RNR standpoint, presence of an antisocial personality pattern would generally signify greater violence risk, it constitutes a criminogenic need area, and by its very nature, would warrant sensitive therapeutic engagement strategies per the responsivity principle to maximize client gain. In essence then, personality can have risk relevance and may warrant direct assessment within the context of a broader violence risk appraisal. The following section commences with a review of two prominent multiscale self-report measures of personality and psychopathology through an RNR lens: the MMPI-2 and its variants and the PAI.

Multiscale Self-Report Inventories

MMPI-2 and its variant   The MMPI-2 (Butcher et al. 1989) is a 567-binary item multiscale self-report measure of personality, psychopathology, and emotional functioning. In common with its predecessor, the original 550-item MMPI (Hathaway and McKinley 1943), are 10 basic clinical scales (numbered 0 through 9) and three validity scales measuring response sets and impression management biases. The MMPI-2, however, has numerous additional validity scales (e.g. response inconsistency, overreporting of psychopathology, impression management), supplemental scales, content scales, and other specialty scales (e.g. Psychopathology Five, Restructured Clinical Scales) designed to enhance the assessment of clinically relevant domains. Other variants of the MMPI-2 include the MMPI Adolescent (MMPI-A; Butcher et al. 1992) and the 388-item MMPI-Restructured Form (MMPI-RF; Ben-Porath and Tellegen 2008).

The MMPI-2 is one of the most heavily researched and frequently used tools in psycho-legal proceedings (Otto 2002). Surveys of forensic psychologists demonstrate the MMPI scales to be the most heavily used multiscale inventories, with more than two thirds of those surveyed reporting to use it in their forensic evaluations (Archer et al. 2006; Bow et al. 2010). Particularly common uses include fitness to stand trial and criminal responsibility assessments (Borum and Grisso 1995), personal injury assessment (Boccaccini and Brodsky 1999), child custody evaluations (Bow et al. 2010), and prison classification (Megargee and Bohn 1979). The MMPI scales tend to encounter few legal challenges when presented in expert testimony, unless used for purposes that have not been empirically validated (Otto 2002). There is an extensive literature examining use of the MMPI scales with offender populations in correctional or criminal justice contexts.

Forensically-based MMPI profiles, subtypes, and correlates   A rather large line of research exists examining MMPI profiles amongst different offender groups, most typically variants on sexual and violent offenders (see Davis and Archer 2010 for a review). The volume of research has tended to examine patterns of codetypes or profile elevations differentiating certain groups of offenders, or used cluster analytic procedures to identify subgroups based on their profile of scores. The potential value of a reliable profile or codetype could offer insights into possible aetiology or inform other clinical applications, such as diagnosis or treatment planning. The classic Megargee and Bohn (1979) study was the first of its kind, identifying 10 subtypes of offenders through cluster analysis of their MMPI profiles from a general prison sample of 1345 men, labelled alphabetically from A (Abel) to J (Jupiter). The Megargee and Bohn (1979) typology has not been replicated. Subsequent cluster analyses have been performed on the MMPI profiles in diverse offender samples with the results yielding anywhere from two clusters (usually comprising a disordered and non-disordered group; e.g. Spaans et al. 2009) up to eight clusters (Duthie and McIvor 1990) depending on sample size and composition, setting, and clustering methodology.

The 4-9/9-4 codetype is particularly common in offender samples, including sexually and nonsexually violent offenders, with high scores on both scales generally being associated with high levels of antisociality, aggression, and delinquency. Other patterns such as 4-8/8-4 (Armentrout and Hauer, 1978; Erickson et al. 1987; Hall et al. 1991), 4-5 (Hall et al. 1991), 4-6-8, 4-8-2, or 4-8-9 (Kalichman et al. 1989; Quinsey et al. 1980) have been identified amongst sexual offenders. In a meta-analysis of MMPI profiles of homicide offenders across 14 studies and 30 datasets, the most frequent pattern to emerge was 4-6-8 profile, characteristic of angry, resentful, hostile, suspicious, and impulsive offenders (Craig 2008). Although these scales were frequently elevated in isolation or in tandem with another (e.g., 4-8/8-4), Craig (2008) concluded that no general MMPI profile exists for homicide offenders. That said, there has been much inconsistency, contradictory findings, or failed efforts to generate a reliable codetype or profile (Freeman et al. 2005; Hall 1987; Hall et al. 1986; Lustig 2012; Matsuzawa 2010; Shechory et al. 2013; Tomak et al. 2009; Valliant and Antonowicz 1992).

MMPI associations with RNR criteria   The utility of the MMPI scales in RNR-based applications can be demonstrated through significant associations with forensically relevant measures and criterion variables (e.g. recidivism, treatment completion). First, per the risk principle, a sizeable literature exists examining associations between MMPI scores and important forensic criteria, such as recidivism; that is, the extent to which the MMPI can accurately discriminate recidivists from non-recidivists on the basis of test scores. In their meta-analytic review of sex offender recidivism predictors, Hanson and Morton-Bourgon (2004) found Scale 2 (D) failed to predict any recidivism criteria ($d = -0.01-0.10$), Scale 5 (Mf) predicted sexual recidivism ($d = 0.42$) but no other outcomes ($d = -0.19-0.16$), whilst Scale 4 (Pd) predicted all types of recidivism (sexual $d = 0.43$, violent $d = 0.28$, and general $d = 0.28$), and Scale 9 (Ma) predicted violent and general ($d = 0.44$ and 0.47, respectively) but not sexual ($d = 0.16$) recidivism. Additional MMPI-based recidivism research has found Scale 4 or its restructured counterpart (RC-4) to predict recidivism in domestically violent offenders ($r = 0.16$) (Sellbom et al. 2008), general probationers ($d = 0.81$) (Tarescavage et al. 2014), and treated sexual offenders (Area Under the Curve, AUC = 0.57–0.67) (Olver et al. 2018). Subsequent MMPI prediction studies on sex offender samples have found Scales 6 and 9 to be predictive of recidivism, as well as Scale 5 amongst clergy sex offenders (Ellsworth 2014), and Scale combinations of 4, 6, 8, and 9 in a mixed sample of treated sex offenders (Olver et al. 2018).

Second, per the need principle, some MMPI-2 scales can also have shared risk variance by virtue of their associations with risk assessment measures or other structured forensic measures correlated with recidivism. Specifically, research has demonstrated Scales 4 and 9 to be individually correlated with Factor 2 of the Psychopathy Checklist-Revised (PCL-R; Hare 1991, 2003) (Brandt et al. 1997) as well as sexual violence measures of risk and need, particularly on indices of general antisociality, as have Scales 6, 7, and 8 (Olver et al. 2018). MMPI-2-RF scales have also been identified as specific markers for several Historical Clinical Risk-20 Version 3 (HCR-20V3; Douglas et al. 2011) items, with Scales RC4 and RC9, Aggression (AGG), Substance Abuse (SUB), and Family Problems (FML) featuring particularly prominently (Tarescavage et al. 2016).

Finally, per the responsivity principle, MMPI correlates exist with offender client features that can have a bearing on response to services. For instance, some studies have found low Scale 5, high L, and elevations on any of Scales 4, 6, and 9 to predict offender treatment noncompletion (Clegg et al. 2011; Kalichman et al. 1990; Lawson 1997; Miner and Dwyer 1995) although such associations are not consistent in the literature (Geer et al. 2001; Hunter 2000; Olver et al. 2018). Moreover, further associations have been found between MMPI indicators of faking good, such as higher scores on K or L, and sex offender denial (Baldwin and Roys 1998; Clark 1997; Karle-Brueck 2003). Other lines of research have found elevations across most of the 10 basic clinical scales to be correlated with slower speed of processing, lower education, and poorer nonverbal cognitive processing in a sex offender sample, suggesting that MMPI elevations may have implications not only for risk and need, but also responsivity (Olver et al. 2018).

PAI

The PAI (Morey 1991) is a 344-item self-report measure of personality, psychopathology, and emotional functioning; it is essentially designed for a common purpose as the MMPI-2, and is a key competitor to the tool. Although it has a much shorter psychometric research and clinical tradition than the MMPI scales (by nearly 50 years), the PAI has amassed an impressive body of research and currently stands as one of the most frequently used self-report inventories with offender populations. The PAI consists of 4 validity scales, 11 major clinical scales (assessing psychopathology), 5 treatment scales (assessing areas that may be a focus of clinical attention such as aggression and suicidal ideation), and 2 interpersonal scales (dominance [DOM] and warmth). Amongst the several unique features of the PAI is a four-point ordinal scale for the individual items (scored 0–3), its grade four reading level, shorter overall length, and the presence of two personality disorder (PD) diagnostic scales (Antisocial Features or ANT, and Borderline Features or BOR) amongst the 11 major clinical scales. Nine of the 11 major clinical scales can also be broken down into specific subscales; for instance, ANT is further broken down to three subscales of Antisocial Actions (ANT-A), Egocentrism (ANT-E), and Stimulus Seeking (ANT-S).

PAI associations with RNR criteria   In terms of RNR applications, selected scales from the PAI have been shown to predict various forms of community recidivism as well as institutional misconducts (per the risk principle). The ANT, AGG, BOR, and DOM scales have received particular research attention in this regard, as they tap personality, interpersonal, and behavioural constructs that have particular relevance to offender populations. The earliest examination of the predictive accuracy of the PAI found that ANT full scale and ANT-E subscale scores significantly predicted recidivism ($r = 0.26$ and 0.27, respectively) in a sample of 78 female offenders, although the other two ANT subscales did not (Salekin et al. 1998). Subsequent investigations have found the ANT, AGG, and DOM scales to predict violent and nonviolent community recidivism (AUCs = 0.57–0.63) in a large sample (N = 1412) of sex offenders screened for civil commitment (Boccaccini et al. 2010), and for scores on the ANT and AGG total scales and all of their subscales except AGG-V (Verbal Aggression) to predict violent and general recidivism (AUCs = 0.62–0.75) amongst offenders who attended a prison-based addictions treatment programme (Ruiz et al. 2014). In the latter, DOM, BOR as well as measures of Alcohol (ALC) and Drug (DRG) problems and Treatment Rejection (RXR) were generally weak and nonsignificant predictors of community recidivism. In another large US sample (N = 1545) of prison inmates, Hendry et al. (2013) found the ANT and AGG scales to be generally weak predictors of a range of community recidivism outcomes. Finally, a recent Canadian PAI study featuring a sample of sex offenders found the ANT total and subscales significantly predicted violent and general recidivism (Jung et al. 2017).

Much more research has examined the predictive efficacy of the aforementioned PAI scales for institutional infractions. Hendry et al. (2013) found the ANT and AGG total scales and subscales performed better as predictors of institutional misconducts (significant rs = 0.11–0.24), and support for these scales in the prediction of institutional behaviour problems have been found across several offender samples (Buffington-Vollum et al. 2002; Caperton et al. 2004; Edens et al. 2002; Newberry and Shuker 2012; Reidy et al. 2016), including women offenders (Skopp et al. 2007). The BOR scale has also been found to predict institutional misconducts in offender samples (Percosky et al. 2013; Skopp et al. 2007).

Per the need principle, selected PAI subscales have been shown to correlate with forensic measures of recidivism risk, again illustrating risk relevance of select scales. The ANT scale and its three subscales specifically, have been found to correlate significantly with the PCL-R and PCL: SV, particularly their chronic antisocial lifestyle features (Edens et al. 2000; Salekin et al. 1998), actuarial sexual violence risk tools such as the Static-2002R (Jung et al. 2017), and general actuarial risk assessment tools such as the Offender Group Reconviction Scale (Newberry and Shuker 2012).

Finally, the PAI has several responsivity correlates, indicating that certain scale elevations reflect correctional client characteristics that affect service delivery and engagement. One line of research has demonstrated certain PAI elevations to be associated with behaviours indicative of difficulties in forensic treatment. For instance, PAI Treatment Rejection (RXR) and Positive Impression Management (PIM) have been found to be significantly correlated with measures of sexual offender minimization and denial (Jung and Daniels 2012). Moreover, in a multisite US sample of male offenders attending a residential drug treatment programme, high AGG, ANT, and BOR scores predicted a number of treatment interfering behaviours (e.g. aggression, disruptive behaviours, noncompliance) as well as decreased therapeutic gains (Magyar et al. 2012). High scores on BOR and over reporting of psychopathology (negative impression management or [NIM]), and low scores on PIM, also predicted disruptive institutional treatment behaviour in a small sample of civilly committed sex offenders; however, AGG, ANT, and DOM did not predict these criteria, contrary to aforementioned findings (Boccáccini et al. 2013).

The PAI has also demonstrated diagnostic efficiency for certain mental health diagnoses, which may have particular relevance as per the responsivity principle and non-criminogenic need. For instance, in a small sample of prison inmates at a psychiatric facility, Edens and Ruiz (2008) found PAI scales assessing depression (DEP) and anxiety-related disorders (ARD) had good diagnostic accuracy for mood disorder and post-traumatic stress disorder, respectively; however, PAI schizophrenia (SCZ) score had poor diagnostic accuracy for psychotic spectrum illnesses. Jung and Dowker (2016) also found violent offenders scored higher on ANT total and subscales than sex offenders and have more pronounced alcohol and drug problems as measured by the ALC and DRG respectively, but were not substantively different on most major mental health indices.

Conclusions on the Use of Multiscale Personality Inventories in Violence Risk Assessment

Research has shown that selected scales from the MMPI-2, its variants, and the PAI can predict various forms of recidivism, converge with established risk assessment measures, and have linkages to other forensically relevant criteria, such as treatment completion, cognitive ability, denial, and so forth. Problematic profiles on these tools can be indicative of serious mental health problems, which may have prognostic relevance for future violence. More importantly, they may impact response to services and identify unique treatment needs. Individuals scoring particularly high on ANT and BOR (i.e. two or more SDs above the mean) may well be candidates for cluster B personality diagnoses, such as ASPD or borderline PD (discussed in further detail later in this chapter). These diagnoses may have implications for risk as well as forecast behavioural challenges in treatment. The MMPI-2 and PAI are not designed to appraise risk for violence or other recidivism outcomes, but their rich research traditions, respect in psycho-legal proceedings, and clinical versatility suggest that their application in this context as adjunctive measures is warranted.

Hare PCL-R and PCL: SV

The Hare PCL-R and PCL: SV are symptom construct rating scales designed to assess the clinical syndrome of psychopathy, a serious PD characterized by the remorseless, selfish use of others and a persistent pattern of socially destructive (and often criminal) behaviour that violates social norms. Interpersonally, psychopathic individuals are deceitful, manipulative, grandiose, and superficially charming. Affectively, psychopathic persons lack guilt or remorse and have a limited capacity for empathy and emotional experience. And behaviourally, psychopathy is characterized by a chronically impulsive, irresponsible, and antisocial lifestyle marked by frequent and varied criminal activity.

Instrument description

Hare developed the original Psychopathy Checklist (PCL; Hare 1980) as a 22-item symptom construct rating scale designed to provide a psychometrically sound measurement of the psychopathy construct. In the years to follow, two items were removed to generate the structurally similar PCL-R. The PCL-R comprises 20 items, each rated on a three-point scale of 0 (characteristic absent), 1 (possibly/partially present), and 2 (characteristic present) as with all PCL measures. Possible PCL-R scores range from 0 to 40 and represent the extent to which the individual represents the prototypical psychopath. Conventionally, a cut score of 30 has been used to characterize psychopathy, although higher scores on the tool are informative and relevant. For instance, the mean score amongst North American male offenders is 22 (SD = 7), and thus a score of 30 is more than a full standard deviation above the mean. The PCL: SV is a shorter, 12-item variant of the PCL-R developed to provide a briefer assessment of the syndrome, particularly in the context of limited time and resources. There is also a youth variant of the PCL-R termed the Psychopathy Checklist: Youth Version (PCL: YV; Forth et al. 2003). The PCL measures are typically scored following a review of relevant file and collateral information and a clinical interview.

Factor analytic research (Hare 2003) supports a four-factor model of the PCL-R, in which 18 of the 20 items are organized into four correlated first-order factors (referred to as facets most frequently in the literature): Interpersonal (superficiality, grandiosity, deceitfulness, manipulation), Affective (lack of remorse, callousness, shallow emotions, failure to accept responsibility), Lifestyle (proneness to boredom, parasitic, lacks goals, impulsivity, irresponsibility), and Antisocial (poor behaviour controls, early behaviour problems, juvenile delinquency, release failure, criminal versatility). In turn, the four first-order factors or facets, are subsumed by two broader second-order factors: Factor 1, which encompasses the Interpersonal and Affective facets, and Factor 2, which subsumes the Lifestyle and Antisocial facets of the syndrome. (Factors 1 and 2 comprised the original factor structure of the PCL and PCL-R.) Scores on the PCL-R overall, and on its constituent factors and facets have important RNR implications and utility within risk assessment, as will be discussed next.

Predictive Accuracy for Recidivism: Implications for Risk and Need

The PCL-R was not designed with the intention of appraising risk for violence or other recidivism outcomes, but it is used frequently to assist with this task and has predictive accuracy for some outcomes that is comparable to established risk assessment tools, consistent with the risk principle. At least 11 meta-analyses have examined the predictive accuracy of the PCL-R and its derivatives for community-based recidivism, including violence, whilst four have examined the predictive accuracy of the tool for behaviour problems within prison or hospital settings, and one, the most comprehensive to date (Leistico et al. 2008), examined the predictive accuracy of the tool for antisocial conduct (institutional or community) in general as well as community recidivism. These meta-analyses are summarized in Table 10.1 and then aggregated using

Table 10.1 Summary of meta-analyses of the Hare Psychopathy Checklist Revised (PCL-R) and its derivatives in the prediction of recidivism.

Study	Psychopathy Checklist (PCL) variant	Measure	Recidivism	k	n	ES
Salekin et al. (1996)	PCL/PCL-R	Total score	General	10	4620	d = 0.55
Hemphill et al. (1998)	PCL/PCL-R	Total score	General	7	1275	r/d = 0.27/0.57
			Violent	6	1374	r/d = 0.27/0.57
			Sexual	1	178	r/d = 0.23/0.53
Gendreau et al. (2002)	PCL/PCL-R	Total score	General	30	4385	r/d = 0.23/0.48
			Violent	26	4823	r/d = 0.21/0.44
Walters (2003)	PCL/PCL-R	Factor 1	General	26	NR	r/d = 0.15/0.30
			Violent	27	NR	r/d = 0.18/0.37
			Sexual	5	NR	r/d = 0.05/0.10
			Institutional	50	NR	r/d = 0.18/0.37
		Factor 2	General	26	NR	r/d = 0.32/0.68
			Violent	27	NR	r/d = 0.26/0.54
			Sexual	5	NR	r/d = 0.08/0.16
			Institutional	50	NR	r/d = 0.28/0.58
Hanson and Morton-Bourgon (2005)	PCL/PCL-R	Total score	Sexual	13	2783	d = 0.29
Guy et al. (2005)	PCL-R	Total score	Institutional	38	5381	r/d = 0.29/0.61
		Factor 1	Institutional	25	3219	r/d = 0.21/0.43
		Factor 2	Institutional	25	3219	r/d = 0.27/0.56
Hanson et al. (2007)	PCL-R	Total score	Spousal assault	2	736	d = 0.60
Edens et al. (2007)	Psychopathy Checklist: Youth Version (PCL: YV)	Total score	General	20	2787	r/d = 0.24/0.50
			Violent	14	2067	r/d = 0.25/0.52
			Sexual	4	654	r/d = 0.07/0.21
		Factor 1	General	15	2157	r/d = 0.18/0.37
			Violent	12	1776	r/d = 0.19/0.39
			Sexual	3	437	r/d = 0.03/0.09

Table 10.1 (*Cont'd*)

Study	Psychopathy Checklist (PCL) variant	Measure	Recidivism	k	n	ES
		Factor 2	General	15	2157	r/d = 0.29/0.61
			Violent	12	1776	r/d = 0.26/0.54
			Sexual	3	437	r/d = 0.08/0.24
Leistico et al. (2008)	PCL/PCL-R	Total score	General	62	11140	d = 0.50
			Institutional	45	6137	d = 0.53
		Factor 1	General	29	5439	d = 0.37
			Institutional	30	3898	d = 0.41
		Factor 2	General	29	5439	d = 0.64
			Institutional	29	3848	d = 0.51
Campbell et al. (2009)	PCL/PCL-R	Total score	Violent	24	4757	r/d = 0.27/0.57
			Institutional	5	626	r/d = 0.14/0.28
	Psychopathy Checklist: Screening Version (PCL: SV)	Total score	Institutional	7	504	r/d = 0.22/0.45
Olver et al. (2009)	PCL: YV	Total score	General	20	2335	r/d = 0.28/0.58
			Violent	20	2547	r/d = 0.25/0.57
			Sexual	4	547	r/d = 0.07/0.21
Yang et al. (2010)	PCL: SV	Total score	Violent	8	2506	d = 0.65
	PCL-R	Total score	Violent	16	3854	d = 0.55
		Factor 1	Violent	13	3895	d = 0.22
		Factor 2	Violent	13	3995	d = 0.61
Hawes et al. (2013)	PCL-R	Total score	Violent	13	3467	d = 0.55
			Sexual	20	5239	d = 0.40
		Factor 1	Violent	8	1538	d = 0.08
			Sexual	13	2838	d = 0.17
		Factor 2	Violent	8	1454	d = 0.63
			Sexual	13	2838	d = 0.44

Note: k = number of studies, n = participants, ES = effect size Cohen's d or correlation r. For r/d ES, r was the original unit of aggregation and converted to d using formulae/tables from Rice and Harris (2005). NR = not reported.

Table 10.2 Aggregation of predictive accuracy findings from Psychopathy Checklist Revised (PCL-R) measures and their derivatives.

PCL measure	K meta-analyses	Recidivism criterion	Median d	Mean unweighted d
Total score	7	General	0.55	0.54
	8	Violent	0.56	0.56
	5	Sexual	0.29	0.33
	3	Institutional	0.50	0.49
Factor 1	3	General	0.37	0.35
	4	Violent	0.30	0.27
	3	Sexual	0.10	0.12
	3	Institutional	0.41	0.40
Factor 2	3	General	0.64	0.64
	4	Violent	0.58	0.58
	3	Sexual	0.24	0.28
	3	Institutional	0.56	0.55

median and unweighted mean Cohen's d for PCL total and factor scores in Table 10.2 (i.e. a meta-analysis of meta-analyses). PCL: YV meta-analyses are included for completeness and given that some reviews focusing on the adult versions of the tool also included youth samples in their final effect size tally. Using rubric from Cohen (1992), d values of 0.20, 0.50, and 0.80 correspond to small/low, medium, and large/high predictive accuracy, respectively. Several themes from the tables are noteworthy.

Firstly, the PCL scales broadly demonstrate moderate predictive accuracy for general and violent recidivism and even future intimate partner violence; demonstrably weaker predictive accuracy has been shown for the prediction of sexual recidivism with a small to moderate effect size overall. Of note, however, is that available research has supported an interaction between psychopathy and deviant sexual interests (what Hare [1999, p. 189] termed, the 'deadly combination'), such that the presence of high levels of psychopathy and sexual deviance (e.g. sexual attraction to violence, children, or other paraphilia) amplify risk for sexual violence and other outcomes. The Hawes et al. (2013) meta-analysis found that the combination of psychopathy and sexual deviance in tandem was associated with a threefold increase in risk for sexual violence (odds ratio = 2.80–3.21, k = 6).

A second theme is that Factor 2 tends to outpredict Factor 1 for all recidivism outcomes, and thus has greater criminogenic relevance. The Yang et al. (2010) meta-analysis used multi-level modelling to control for sample, setting, and other study features and found that Factor 1 was not a significant predictor of future violence, although Factor 2 alone and the PCL-R total score had comparable predictive accuracy to other tools. When aggregated across meta-analyses (Table 10.2), for general and violent recidivism, Factor 1 has median and mean d values ranging from 0.27 to 0.35 whilst Factor 2 is more than double with aggregate d values ranging from 0.58 to 0.64. Similar disparities in effect size magnitude are seen for sexual recidivism and institutional recidivism. Although the predictive efficacy of the four facets has yet to be subjected to meta-analytic aggregation, research to date has demonstrated the Antisocial facet to generally be the most consistent predictor of violent recidivism, followed by the Lifestyle facet (e.g. Olver and Wong 2015; Olver et al. 2013; Wormith et al. 2007), and in some cases, the Affective facet, particularly in higher risk samples (Hare 2016; Olver et al. 2013).

A third issue pertaining to risk, and not reflected in the tables, is use of the PCL-R with female offenders and racial minority groups; the use of the tools with these populations has been greeted with some controversy. Although evidence exists for the predictive accuracy of the PCL-R for recidivism amongst women offenders, findings have been inconsistent (Eisenbarth et al. 2012; Hastings et al. 2011; Nicholls et al. 2004; Salekin et al. 1998), and the field could stand to benefit from further psychometric research on the tool with females. Relatively limited psychometric research has been conducted on the predictive properties of the PCL scales with racial minority offender samples. Olver et al. (2013), in a sample of 435 federally incarcerated adult male offenders in Canada, found moderate to high predictive accuracy of PCL-R total, Lifestyle, and Antisocial facet scores for violent, nonviolent, and general recidivism amongst Indigenous and non-Indigenous subgroups (AUCs = 0.63–0.75); the Interpersonal and Affective facets did not predict any recidivism outcomes. In an expansion of this work in a sample of 1163 men, broadly moderate to high predictive accuracy was found for all PCL-R scale components for violent and general recidivism across both ancestral groups (Olver et al. 2017). Of note, high predictive accuracy was found for PCL-R total scores in the prediction of both outcomes for both broad ancestral groups (AUCs = 0.71–0.73). The use of the PCL measures with Indigenous men provides one example of applicability of the tool with persons of diversity; care needs to be taken to be sensitive to cultural considerations in use of these tools and the assessment of this construct with vulnerable populations.

From the perspective of the need principle, perhaps not surprisingly, men scoring high on the PCL scales also tend to be high need. Simourd and Hoge (2000), for instance, in a sample of 321 Canadian federal inmates, found that men scoring 30 or higher on the PCL-R also had significantly greater concerns on each of the Central Eight domains as assessed by the Level of Service Inventory-Revised (LSI-R; Andrews and Bonta 1995). Psychopathic offenders also displayed more entrenched criminal attitudes as assessed via self-report. Elsewhere, psychometric research has demonstrated the PCL-R, and Factor 2 in particular, to be associated with higher scores on conventional risk assessment tools and measures of criminogenic need (Douglas et al. 2005; Olver and Wong 2009; Wong and Gordon 2006; Wormith et al. 2007).

Therapeutic Responses of Psychopathic Offenders: Implications for Responsivity and Violence Risk Management

The profile of PCL-R factor and facet scores can also have important implications for response to service delivery and risk management. Wong (2015) noted that the interpersonal and affective features of Factor 1 represent a set of responsivity considerations; that is, men who display prominent features of such traits are prone to engaging in treatment interfering behaviours such as aggressive or abusive behaviour, staff splitting, antagonizing co-patients, and engaging in manipulative and boundary violating behaviours to name but a few. Meta-analytic research has demonstrated high PCL-R scores, or a psychopathy diagnosis proper, to be amongst the strongest predictors of attrition from correctional treatment programmes (Olver et al. 2011). Finer grained examination has demonstrated the PCL-R Affective facet (i.e. callous and unemotional features) to be uniquely associated with sex offender treatment noncompletion (Olver and Wong 2011), decreased therapeutic progress (Olver et al. 2013), and weaker working alliances, particularly the emotional bond formed between client and therapist (DeSorcy et al. 2017).

In the context of violence risk assessment and management, high PCL-R Factor 1 scores identify an individual for whom special engagement strategies may need to be utilized by treatment teams to retain difficult clients in treatment. Research supports the stability of Factor 1 and demonstrates it to generally be a weaker and less consistent predictor of recidivism. Wong's (2015) two-component model for the treatment of psychopathic offenders thus recommends service providers to manage the treatment interfering behaviours associated with Factor 1 as a responsivity issue, and to prioritize treatment services to targeting the risks and needs associated with Factor 2 to manage violence risk and reduce recidivism. Although the effectiveness of treatment for psychopathic offenders remains a contentious issue, some promising results using evidence informed approaches have been attained in terms of recidivism reduction (see Salekin et al. 2010, Thornton and Blud 2007; and Wong et al. 2012 for a review and updated empirical findings).

A final relevant issue for use of the PCL measures in violence risk assessment concerns the reliability of scores in real-world settings; that is, do independent raters completing clinical PCL-R ratings on the same client yield similar results? Extant research has suggested that field reliability, as this is called, has been lower than seen in research contexts, particularly in US jurisdictions, and that allegiance effects also exist in legal proceedings; specifically, evaluators have been found to yield ratings that confer an advantage to whichever side of the case (i.e. prosecution or defence) they have been retained (Edens et al. 2010; Murrie et al. 2009). This is also tempered by some recent findings from Canadian legal proceedings showing that the field reliability of the PCL-R can be quite high, for instance, in Canadian criminal proceedings (Edens et al. 2016) and that clinical and research-based ratings of the PCL-R can yield high agreement (Harris et al. 2013).

Conclusions on Use of the Hare PCL-R and Its Variants in Violence Risk Assessment

In conclusion, substantial research support exists for the use of the PCL scales in the context of violence risk assessment, although important cautions are noteworthy. Firstly, Hare (2003) cautioned that the PCL-R should not be used as a standalone measure of risk of violence or other recidivism outcomes; it should be used in tandem with other purpose-built measures of risk and need, preferably at least one additional measure that can assess dynamic risk variables to guide treatment planning and the possibility of capturing changes in risk therein. Indeed, research demonstrates that formalized risk assessment measures tend to be incremental to the PCL in the prediction of recidivism (e.g. Olver and Wong 2009; Olver et al. 2013). Secondly, the PCL total score is the most comprehensive and robust quantity of the tool, with the largest accumulation of research support for predictive accuracy, and the greatest stability in effect size magnitude across different populations, samples, and settings. In most instances, the total score is the metric used in tandem with other measures to couch appraisals of violence risk. Clearly individuals scoring high on the tool are likely to pose a concern for recidivism and warrant a greater allocation of risk management resources. Thirdly, the PCL-R factor and facet profile can be very meaningful. High scores on the Interpersonal and Affective dimensions can speak to important responsivity considerations, specifically, that the individual may be at risk for treatment interfering behaviours and programme attrition, thus signalling the need for additional attention, care, communication, and management resources on the part of staff to retain the individual in treatment to maximize the potential for benefit and gain. Finally, the PCL scales can be rated reliably, although troubling field reliability findings, particularly in some US jurisdictions, speak to the potential for rater drift and allegiance effects in adversarial proceedings.

Diagnostic Approaches

Forensic settings, in custody (hospital and prison) and the community (probation and parole), bring with them higher base rates of various mental health concerns, compared to that of non-offender community-based samples. Whilst a formal DSM-5 or ICD-10 diagnosis may not be the centrepiece of a violence risk assessment, it can have relevance within the RNR framework and may well be a matter of personal discretion whether diagnoses, if present, are identified and communicated as part of the overall assessment. Certain diagnoses, however, have relevance – they may be associated with increased risk for violence, decreased risk for violence, or bear no substantive link to violence. This final section offers a commentary on the role of PD (formerly DSM Axis II) diagnosis in the context of violence risk assessment based specifically on DSM-5 and its predecessors.

Relevant PD diagnoses

According to the DSM-5 'The essential features of a personality disorder are impairments in personality (self and interpersonal) functioning and the presence of pathological personality traits' (APA 2013, p. 645). In contrast to other mental health diagnoses which have a phasic waxing and waning of symptoms (i.e. most people are not constantly psychotic, anxious, or depressed), PDs quite literally infiltrate every interpersonal nook and cranny in one's relational world. Fundamentally, PDs are a disorder involving the self and its relationship to others; a constellation of maladaptive personality traits. One does not cease to be PD at a dinner party, in a social conversation, in a bus queue, at the office, or in a prison setting for that matter. The context, however, will certainly moderate the expression of symptoms (e.g. a borderline patient may be less inclined to fly off the handle in an executive meeting at work after a perceived affront, than they may in a private conversation at the office water cooler after hours). The Cluster B PDs (histrionic, narcissistic, borderline, and antisocial) have particular salience in forensic samples; this is the dramatic, emotional, erratic cluster characterized by emotional volatility, behavioural impulsivity, and relationship instability. Research identifies a 50–75% base rate for PD in general within forensic institutional settings, and comparable frequencies for ASPD, which is the most common PD diagnosis in offender samples (Guy et al. 2008; Kingston et al. 2015).

RNR Implications of PD diagnoses for violence risk assessment

Research has shown that PD diagnoses in general, and some of the Cluster B syndromes in particular, have important RNR implications. Firstly, as per the risk principle, existing research has found higher rates of general and violent recidivism for PD in general and ASPD in particular. In a meta-analysis of criminogenic and psychopathological predictors of recidivism, Bonta et al. (2014) found that antisocial personality pattern was a significant predictor of general ($d = 0.41$, $k = 30$) and violent ($d = 0.57$, $k = 26$) recidivism, as were formal clinical diagnoses of ASPD or psychopathy ($d = 0.54$, $k = 16$, and $d = 0.66$, $k = 14$, respectively), and any PD ($d = 0.44$, $k = 9$, and $d = 0.41$, $k = 12$, respectively). Hanson and Bussière's (1998) meta-analysis of sex offender recidivism predictors found ASPD ($r = 0.14$, $k = 6$) and PD ($r = 0.16$, $k = 3$) diagnoses to be significantly predictive of sexual recidivism. Secondly, just as existing research has demonstrated psychopathic offenders to be of higher need in a variety of domains, the aforementioned lines of research have similarly demonstrated offenders with PD diagnoses, and ASPD more specifically, to also have a greater density of criminogenic needs, particularly those overlapping with the Central Eight, per the need principle (Kingston et al. 2015; Wormith et al. 2007).

Finally, per the responsivity principle, PD diagnoses have also been found to be associated with increased risk for attrition from offender treatment programmes. In a meta-analysis of offender treatment attrition featuring 114 studies, Olver et al. (2011) found that diagnoses of ASPD were significantly associated with higher rates of noncompletion from correctional programmes in general, as well as attrition from sex offender and domestic violence treatment programmes. Any PD, and BPD in particular, were also associated with increased rates of attrition from correctional programmes in general, whilst any PD also predicted attrition from sex offender treatment. The results make sense conceptually; PD diagnosis, and specifically ASPD and BPD, forecast interpersonal problems that are likely to come out in therapeutic contexts, inpatient, outpatient, group, or individual.

Conclusions on the role and relevance of personality in violence risk assessment

The assessment of personality can have considerable relevance to violence risk assessment when viewed through the lens of RNR. The common thread amongst personality assessment schemes with this sort of relevance, whether these be multiscale self-report inventories, clinical rating scales such as the PCL measures, or diagnostic approaches, entails the assessment of personality pathology broadly speaking, particularly antisocial personality/psychopathy and domains indicative of general antisociality (e.g. interpersonal aggression). Per the risk principle, formal relevant measures are capable of discriminating recidivists from non-recidivists with acceptable levels of accuracy, and individuals with diagnoses of antisocial personality or psychopathy have significantly higher rates of a broad range of recidivism outcomes. In turn, these measures and diagnostic groups are associated with a higher density of criminogenic needs, which may be prioritized for risk reduction services, per the need principle. Finally, PD in general, and antisocial personality and psychopathy in particular, embody a number of specific responsivity considerations. Broadly speaking, this is an interpersonal style and behavioural pattern than can translate into treatment interfering behaviours potentially prognostic of attrition; in the context of violence risk assessment, service providers can be alerted to these considerations so that challenging clientele can be retained in, and potentially benefit from, treatment.

In conclusion, it is important to bear in mind that personality-based approaches are neither exclusive or exhaustive; however, these approaches can be a useful adjunct to be used in tandem with formalized static and dynamic risk assessment measures to inform violence risk appraisal, intervention planning, and risk management.

References

American Psychiatric Association (2013). *Diagnostic and Statistical Manual for Mental Disorders Fifth Edition (DSM-5)*. Washington, DC: Author.

Andrews, D.A. and Bonta, J. (1995). *Level of Service Inventory-Revised (LSI-R): An Offender Assessment System*. User's guide. Toronto, ON: Multi-Health Systems.

Andrews, D.A., Bonta, J., and Wormith, J.S. (2004). *Level of Service/Case Management Inventory (LS/CMI): An Offender Assessment System*. User's guide. Toronto, ON: Multi-Health Systems.

Archer, R.P., Buffington-Vollum, J.K., Stredny, R.V., and Handel, R.W. (2006). A survey of psychological test use patterns among forensic psychologists. *Journal of Personality Assessment* 87: 84–94.

Armentrout, J.A. and Hauer, A.L. (1978). MMPIs of rapists of adults, rapists of children, and non-rapist sex offenders. *Journal of Clinical Psychology* 34: 330–332.

Baldwin, K. and Roys, D.T. (1998). Factors associated with denial in a sample of alleged adult sexual offenders. *Sexual Abuse: Journal of Research and Treatment* 10: 211–226.

Ben-Porath, Y.S. and Tellegen, A. (2008). *Minnesota Multiphasic Personality Inventory-2-RF (MMPI-2-RF)*. Minneapolis, MN: University of Minnesota Press.

Boccaccini, M.T. and Brodsky, S.L. (1999). Diagnostic test use by forensic psychologists' emotional injury cases. *Professional Psychology: Research and Practice* 30: 253–259.

Boccaccini, M.T., Murrie, D.C., Hawes, S.W. et al. (2010). Predicting recidivism with the personality assessment inventory in a sample of sex offenders screened for civil commitment as sexually violent predators. *Psychological Assessment* 22: 142–148.

Boccaccini, M.T., Rufino, K.A., Jackson, R.L., and Murrie, D.C. (2013). Personality assessment inventory scores as predictors of misconduct among sex offenders civilly committed as sexually violent predators. *Psychological Assessment* 25: 1390–1395.

Boer, D.P., Hart, S.D., Kropp, P.R., and Webster, C.D. (1997). *Manual for the Sexual Violence Risk-20: Professional Guidelines for Assessing Risk of Sexual Violence*. Vancouver, BC: Institute against Family Violence and the Mental Health, Law, and Policy Institute, Simon Fraser University.

Bonta, J. and Andrews, D. (2017). *The Psychology of Criminal Conduct*, 6e. New York, NY: Routledge.

Bonta, J., Blais, J., and Wilson, H.A. (2014). A theoretically informed meta-analysis of the risk for general and violent recidivism for mentally disordered offenders. *Aggression and Violent Behavior* 19: 278–287.

Borum, R. and Grisso, T. (1995). Psychological tests use in criminal forensic evaluations. *Professional Psychology: Research and Practice* 26: 465–473.

Bow, J.N., Flens, J.R., and Gould, J.W. (2010). MMPI-2 and MCMI-III in forensic evaluations: a survey of psychologists. *Journal of Forensic Psychology Practice* 10: 37–52.

Brandt, J.R., Kennedy, W.A., Patrick, C.J., and Curtin, J.J. (1997). Assessment of psychopathy in a population of incarcerated adolescent offenders. *Psychological Assessment* 9: 429–435.

Buffington-Vollum, J., Edens, J.F., Johnson, D.W., and Johnson, J.K. (2002). Psychopathy as a predictor of institutional misbehavior among sex offenders: a prospective replication. *Criminal Justice and Behavior* 29: 497–511.

Butcher, J.N., Dahlstrom, W.G., Graham, J.R. et al. (1989). *The Minnesota Multiphasic Personality Inventory-2 (MMPI-2)*. Minneapolis, MN: University of Minnesota Press.

Butcher, J.N., Williams, C.L., Graham, J.R. et al. (1992). *Minnesota Multiphasic Personality Inventory-Adolescent (MMPI-A)*. Minneapolis, MN: University of Minnesota Press.

Campbell, M.A., French, S., and Gendreau, P. (2009). The prediction of violence in adult offenders: a meta-analytic comparison of instruments and methods of assessment. *Criminal Justice and Behavior* 36: 567–590.

Caperton, J.D., Edens, J.F., and Johnson, J.K. (2004). Predicting sex offender institutional adjustment and treatment compliance using the personality assessment inventory. *Psychological Assessment* 16: 187–191.

Clark, M.W. (1997). *Characteristics of juvenile sex offenders who admit versus those who deny their offenses.* Unpublished dissertation. Malibu, CA: Pepperdine University.

Clegg, C., Fremouw, W., Horacek, T. et al. (2011). Factors associated with treatment acceptance and compliance among incarcerated male sex offenders. *International Journal of Offender Therapy and Comparative Criminology* 55: 880–897.

Cohen, J. (1992). A power primer. *Psychological Bulletin* 112: 155–159.

Craig, R.J. (2008). MMPI-based forensic psychological assessment of lethal violence. In: *Forensic Psychology and Neuropsychology for Criminal and Civil Cases* (ed. H.V. Hall), 393–416. Boca Raton, FL: Taylor & Francis Group.

Davis, K.M. and Archer, R.P. (2010). A critical review of objective personality inventories with sex offenders. *Journal of Clinical Psychology* 66: 1254–1280.

DeSorcy, D.R., Olver, M.E., and Wormith, J.S. (2017). Working alliance and psychopathy: linkages to treatment outcome in a sample of treated sexual offenders. *Journal of Interpersonal Violence.* Ahead of print publication doi: https://doi.org/10.1177/0886260517698822.

Douglas, K.S., Hart, S.D., Webster, C.D., and Belfrage, H. (2011). *Historical Clinical Risk Management (Version 3): Professional Guidelines for Evaluating Risk of Violence [Draft 2.1].* Vancouver, BC: Mental Health, Law, and Policy Institute, Simon Fraser University.

Douglas, K.S., Yeomans, M., and Boer, D.P. (2005). Comparative validity analysis of multiple measures of violence risk in a sample of criminal offenders. *Criminal Justice and Behavior* 32: 479–510.

Duthie, B. and McIvor, D.L. (1990). A new system for cluster-coding child molester MMPI profile types. *Criminal Justice and Behavior* 17: 199–214.

Edens, J.F., Boccaccini, M.T., and Johnson, D.W. (2010). Inter-rater reliability of the PCL-R total and factor scores among psychopathic sex offenders: are personality features more prone to disagreement than behavioral features? *Behavioral Sciences and the Law* 28: 106–119.

Edens, J.F., Buffington-Vollum, J.K., Colwell, K.W. et al. (2002). Psychopathy and institutional misbehavior among incarcerated sex offenders: a comparison of the psychopathy checklist-revised and the personality assessment inventory. *International Journal of Forensic Mental Health* 1: 49–58.

Edens, J.F., Campbell, J.S., and Weir, J.M. (2007). Youth psychopathy and criminal recidivism: a meta-analysis of the psychopathy checklist measures. *Law and Human Behavior* 31: 53–75.

Edens, J.F., Hart, S.D., Johnson, D.W. et al. (2000). Use of the personality assessment inventory to assess psychopathy in offender populations. *Psychological Assessment* 12: 132–139.

Edens, J.F., Penson, B.N., Ruchensky, J.R. et al. (2016). Interrater reliability of violence risk appraisal guide scores provided in Canadian criminal proceedings. *Psychological Assessment* 28: 1543–1549.

Edens, J.F. and Ruiz, M.A. (2008). Identification of mental disorders in an in-patient prison psychiatric unit: examining the criterion-related validity of the personality assessment inventory. *Psychological Services* 5: 108–117.

Eisenbarth, H., Osterheider, M., Nedopil, N., and Stadtland, C. (2012). Recidivism in female offenders: PCL-R lifestyle factor and VRAG show predictive validity in a German sample. *Behavioral Sciences and the Law* 30: 575–584.

Ellsworth, P.J. (2014). A recidivism prediction study of the MMPI/MMPI-2 scores of catholic clergy sex offenders: Identifying personality-based risk markers. Doctoral dissertation. Fielding Graduate University.

Erickson, W.D., Luxenberg, M.G., Walbek, N.H., and Seely, R.K. (1987). Frequency of MMPI two-point code types among sex offenders. *Journal of Consulting and Clinical Psychology* 55: 560–570.

Forth, A.E., Kosson, D.S., and Hare, R.D. (2003). *Psychopathy Checklist: Youth Version (PCL: YV)*. Toronto: Multi-Health Systems.

Freeman, K.A., Dexter-Mazza, E.T., and Hoffman, K.C. (2005). Comparing personality characteristics of juvenile sex offenders and non-sex offending delinquent peers: a preliminary investigation. *Sexual Abuse: A Journal of Research and Treatment* 17: 3–12.

Geer, T.M., Becker, J.V., Gray, S.R., and Krauss, D. (2001). Predictors of treatment completion in a correctional sex offender treatment program. *Journal of Offender and Comparative Criminology* 45: 302–313.

Gendreau, P., Goggin, C., and Smith, P. (2002). Is the PCL-R really the "unparalleled" measure of offender risk? A lesson in knowledge cumulation. *Criminal Justice and Behavior* 29: 397–426.

Guy, L.S., Edens, J.F., Anthony, C., and Douglas, K.S. (2005). Does psychopathy predict institutional misconduct among adults? A meta-analytic investigation. *Journal of Consulting and Clinical Psychology* 73: 1056–1064.

Guy, L.S., Poythress, N.G., Douglas, K.S. et al. (2008). Correspondence between self-report and interview-based assessments of antisocial personality disorder. *Psychological Assessment* 20: 47–54.

Hall, G.C.N. (1987). WAIS-R and MMPI profiles of men who have sexually assaulted children: evidence of limited utility. *Journal of Personality Assessment* 53: 404–412.

Hall, G.C.N., Graham, J.R., and Shepherd, J.R. (1991). Three methods of developing MMPI taxonomies of sexual offenders. *Journal of Personality Assessment* 56: 2–13.

Hall, G.C.N., Mairo, R.D., Vitaliano, P.P., and Proctor, W.C. (1986). The utility of the MMPI with men who have sexually assaulted children. *Journal of Consulting and Clinical Psychology* 54: 493–496.

Hanson, R.K. (2009). The psychological assessment of risk for crime and violence. *Canadian Psychology* 50: 172–182.

Hanson, R.K. and Bussière, M.T. (1998). Predicting relapse: a meta-analysis of sexual offender recidivism studies. *Journal of Consulting and Clinical Psychology* 66: 348–362.

Hanson, R.K., Helmus, L. and Bourgon, G. (2007). *The validity of risk assessments for intimate partner violence: A meta-analysis*. Corrections Research User Report No. 2007–07. Ottawa, ON: Public Safety Canada.

Hanson, R.K. and Morton-Bourgon, K. (2004). *Predictors of sexual recidivism: An updated meta-analysis*. Corrections Research: User Report 2004–02. Ottawa, ON: Public Safety Canada.

Hanson, R.K. and Morton-Bourgon, K. (2005). The characteristics of persistent sexual offenders: a meta-analysis of recidivism studies. *Journal of Consulting and Clinical Psychology* 73: 1154–1163.

Hare, R.D. (1980). A research scale for the assessment of psychopathy in criminal populations. *Personality and Individual Differences* 1: 111–119.

Hare, R.D. (1991). *The Psychopathy Checklist Revised*. Toronto, ON: Multi-Health Systems.

Hare, R.D. (1999). Psychopathy as a risk factor for violence. *The Psychiatric Quarterly* 70: 181–197.

Hare, R.D. (2003). *The Psychopathy Checklist Revised*, 2e. Toronto, ON: Multi-Health Systems.

Hare, R.D. (2016). Psychopathy, the PCL-R, and criminal justice: some new findings and current issues. *Canadian Psychology* 57: 21–34.

Harris, G.T., Rice, M.E., and Cormier, C.A. (2013). Research and clinical scoring of the psychopathy checklist can show good agreement. *Criminal Justice and Behavior* 40: 1349–1362.

Hart, S.D., Cox, D.N., and Hare, R.D. (1995). *The Hare Psychopathy Checklist: Screening Version (PCL: SV)*. Toronto, ON: Multi-Health Systems.

Hastings, M.E., Krishnan, S., Tagney, J.P., and Stuewig, J. (2011). Predictive and incremental validity of the violence risk appraisal guide score with male and female jail inmates. *Psychological Assessment* 23: 174–183.

Hathaway, S.R. and McKinley, J.C. (1943). *Minnesota Multiphasic Personality Inventory*. Minneapolis, MN: University of Minnesota Press.

Hawes, S.W., Boccaccini, M.T., and Murrie, D.C. (2013). Psychopathy and the combination of psychopathy and sexual deviance as predictors of sexual recidivism: meta-analytic findings using the psychopathy checklist-revised. *Psychological Assessment* 25: 233–243.

Hemphill, J.F., Hare, R.D., and Wong, S. (1998). Psychopathy and recidivism: A review. *Legal and Criminological Psychology* 3: 139–170.

Hendry, M.C., Douglas, K.S., Winter, E.A., and Edens, J.F. (2013). Construct measurement quality improves predictive accuracy in violence risk assessment: an illustration using the personality assessment inventory. *Behavioral Sciences and the Law* 31: 477–493.

Hunter, L.M. (2000). Use of selected MMPI-A factors in the prediction of clinical outcomes in a community-based treatment program for juvenile sexual offenders. Doctoral dissertation. Virginia Consortium for Professional Psychology.

Jung, S. and Daniels, M. (2012). Conceptualizing sex offender denial from a multifaceted framework: investigating the psychometric qualities of a new instrument. *Journal of Addictions & Offender Counseling* 33: 2–17.

Jung, S. and Dowker, B.A. (2016). Responsivity factors among offenders. *Journal of Offender Rehabilitation* 55: 148–167.

Jung, S., Toop, C., and Ennis, L. (2017). Identifying criminogenic needs with the personality assessment inventory with males who have sexually offended. *Sexual Abuse* 30 (8): 992–1009.

Kalichman, S.C., Shealy, L., and Craig, M.E. (1990). The use of the MMPI in predicting treatment participation among incarcerated adult rapists. *Journal of Psychology and Human Sexuality* 3: 105–119.

Kalichman, S.C., Szymanowski, D., McKee, G. et al. (1989). Cluster analytically derived MMPI profile subgroups of incarcerated adult rapists. *Journal of Clinical Psychology* 45: 149–155.

Karle-Brueck, H.R. (2003). Denial in convicted sex offenders: A preliminary examination, Doctoral dissertation. The University of Iowa.

Kingston, D.A., Olver, M.E., Harris, M. et al. (2015). The relationship between mental disorder and recidivism in sexual offenders. *International Journal of Forensic Mental Health* 14: 10–22.

Lawson, K.A. (1997). Prediction of premature termination of adult male sexual offenders from outpatient treatment. Doctoral dissertation. Florida State University.

Leistico, A.R., Salekin, R.T., DeCoster, J., and Rogers, R. (2008). A large-scale meta-analysis relating the Hare measures of psychopathy to antisocial conduct. *Law and Human Behavior* 32: 28–45.

Lustig, L. (2012). The MMPI-2-RF and the MCMI-III on internet sex offenders. Doctoral dissertation. Alliant International University.

Magyar, M.S., Edens, J.F., Lilienfeld, S.O. et al. (2012). Using the Personality Assessment Inventory to predict male offenders' conduct during and progression through substance abuse treatment. *Psychological Assessment* 24: 216–225.

Matsuzawa, Y.K. (2010). MMPI-2 characteristics of internet sex offenders. Doctoral dissertation. Pepperdine University.

Megargee, E.I. and Bohn, M.J. (1979). *Classifying Criminal Offenders: A New System Based on the MMPI.* Beverly Hills, CA: SAGE.

Mills, J.F. (2017). Violence risk assessment: a brief review, current issues, and future directions. *Canadian Psychology/Psychologie Canadienne* 58: 40–49.

Miner, M.H. and Dwyer, S.M. (1995). Analysis of dropouts from outpatient sex offender treatment. *Journal of Psychology and Human Sexuality* 7: 77–93.

Morey, L.C. (1991). *The Personality Assessment Inventory: Professional Manual.* Odessa, FL: Psychological Assessment Resources.

Murrie, D.C., Boccaccini, M.T., Turner, D.B. et al. (2009). Rater (dis)agreement on risk assessment measures in sexually violent predator proceedings. *Psychology, Public Policy, and Law* 15: 19–53.

Newberry, M. and Shuker, R. (2012). Personality Assessment Inventory (PAI) profiles for offenders and their relationship to institutional misconduct and risk of reconviction. *Journal of Personality Assessment* 94: 586–592.

Nicholls, T.L., Ogloff, J.R.P., and Douglas, K.S. (2004). Assessing risk for violence among male and female civil psychiatric patients: the HCR-20, PCL:SV, and VSC. *Behavioral Science and the Law* 22: 127–158.

Olver, M.E., Coupland, R.B.A., and Kurtenbach, T.J.E. (2018). Risk-need-responsivity applications of the MMPI-2 in sexual offender assessment. *Psychology Crime and Law* 24: 806–830.

Olver, M.E., Lewis, K., and Wong, S.C.P. (2013). Risk reduction treatment of high risk psychopathic offenders: the relationship of psychopathy and treatment change to violent recidivism. *Personality Disorders, Theory, Research, and Treatment* 4: 160–167.

Olver, M.E., Neumann, C.S., Sewall, L.A. et al. (2017). A comprehensive examination of the predictive properties of the Hare psychopathy checklist-revised in a Canadian multisite sample of Indigenous and non-Indigenous offenders. *Psychological Assessment* 30 (6): 779–792.

Olver, M.E., Neumann, C.S., Wong, S.C.P., and Hare, R.D. (2013). The structural and predictive properties of the PCL-R in Canadian Aboriginal and non-Aboriginal offenders. *Psychological Assessment* 25: 167–179.

Olver, M.E., Stockdale, K.C., and Wormith, J.S. (2009). Risk assessment with young offenders: a meta-analysis of three assessment measures. *Criminal Justice and Behavior* 36: 329–353.

Olver, M.E., Stockdale, K.C., and Wormith, J.S. (2011). A meta-analysis of predictors of offender treatment attrition and its relationship to recidivism. *Journal of Consulting and Clinical Psychology* 79: 6–21.

Olver, M.E. and Wong, S.C. (2009). Therapeutic responses of psychopathic sexual offenders: treatment attrition, therapeutic change, and long-term recidivism. *Journal of Consulting and Clinical Psychology* 77: 328.

Olver, M.E. and Wong, S.C.P. (2011). Predictors of sex offender treatment dropout: psychopathy, sex offender risk, and responsivity implications. *Psychology Crime and Law* 17: 457–471.

Olver, M.E. and Wong, S.C.P. (2015). Short and long-term recidivism prediction of the PCL-R and the effects of age: a 24-year follow-up. *Personality Disorders, Theory, Research, and Treatment* 6: 97–105.

Otto, R. (2002). Use of the MMPI-2 in forensic settings. *Journal of Forensic Psychology Practice* 2: 71–91.

Percosky, A.B., Boccaccini, M.T., Bitting, B.S., and Hamilton, P.M. (2013). Personality assessment inventory scores as predictors of treatment compliance and misconduct among sex offenders participating in community based treatment. *Journal of Forensic Psychology Practice* 13: 192–203.

Quinsey, V.L., Arnold, L.S., and Pruesse, M.G. (1980). MMPI profiles of men referred for a pretrial psychiatric assessment as a function of offence type. *Journal of Clinical Psychology* 36: 410–417.

Reidy, T.J., Sorenson, J.R., and Davidson, M. (2016). Testing the predictive validity of the Personality Assessment Inventory (PAI) in relation to inmate misconduct and violence. *Psychological Assessment* 28: 871–884.

Rice, M.E. and Harris, G.T. (2005). Comparing effect sizes in follow-up studies: ROC area, Cohen's d, and r. *Law and Human Behavior* 29: 615–620.

Ruiz, M.A., Cox, J., Magyar, M.S., and Edens, J.F. (2014). Predictive validity of the Personality Assessment Inventory (PAI) for identifying criminal reoffending following completion of an in-jail addiction treatment program. *Psychological Assessment* 26: 673–678.

Salekin, R., Worley, C., and Grimes, R. (2010). Treatment of psychopathy: a review and brief introduction to the mental model approach for psychopathy. *Behavioral Sciences and the Law* 28: 235–266.

Salekin, R.T., Rogers, R., and Sewell, K.W. (1996). A review and meta-analysis of the psychopathy checklist and psychopathy checklist-revised: predictive validity of dangerousness. *Clinical Psychology: Science and Practice* 3: 203–215.

Salekin, R.T., Rogers, R., Ustad, K.L., and Sewell, K.W. (1998). Psychopathy and recidivism among female inmates. *Law and Human Behavior* 22: 109–127.

Sellbom, M., Ben-Porath, Y.S., Baum, L.J. et al. (2008). Predictive validity of the MMPI-2 Restructured Clinical (RC) scales in a batterers' intervention. *Journal of Personality Assessment* 90: 129–135.

Shechory, M., Weiss, J.M., and Weinstain, R. (2013). Differentiating offenders by index offense and personality inventories: the characteristics of adult probationers in Israel. *International Journal of Offender Therapy and Comparative Criminology* 57: 312–331.

Simourd, D.J. and Hoge, R.D. (2000). Criminal psychopathy: a risk-and-need perspective. *Criminal Justice and Behavior* 27: 256–272.

Skopp, N.A., Edens, J.F., and Ruiz, M.A. (2007). Risk factors for institutional misconduct among incarcerated women: an examination of the criterion-related validity of the personality assessment inventory. *Journal of Personality Assessment* 88: 106–117.

Spaans, M., Barendregt, M., Muller, E. et al. (2009). MMPI profiles of males accused of severe crimes: a cluster analysis. *Psychology Crime and Law* 15: 441–450.

Tarescavage, A.M., Glassmire, D.M., and Burchett, D. (2016). Introduction of a conceptual model for integrating the MMPI-2-RF into HCR-20V3 violence risk assessments and associations between the MMPI-2-RF and institutional violence. *Law and Human Behavior* 40: 626–637.

Tarescavage, A.M., Luna-Jones, L., and Ben-Porath, Y.S. (2014). Minnesota Multiphasic Personality Inventory-2-Restructured Form (MMPI-2-RF) predictors of violating probation after felonious crimes. *Psychological Assessment* 26: 1375–1380.

Thornton, D. and Blud, L. (2007). The influence of psychopathic traits on response to treatment. In: *The Psychopath: Theory, Research and Practice* (eds. H. Hervé and J.C. Yuille), 505–539. Mahwah, NJ: Lawrence Erlbaum Associates.

Tomak, S., Weschler, F.S., Ghahramanlou-Holloway, M. et al. (2009). An empirical study of the personality characteristics of internet sex offenders. *Journal of Sexual Aggression* 15: 139–148.

Valliant, P.M. and Antonowicz, D.H. (1992). Rapists, incest offenders, and child molesters in treatment: cognitive and social skills training. *International Journal of Offender Therapy and Comparative Criminology* 36: 221–230.

Walters, G. (2003). Predicting institutional adjustment and recidivism with the psychopathy checklist factor scores: a meta-analysis. *Law and Human Behavior* 27: 541–558.

Wong, S.C.P. (2015). Treatment of violence prone individuals with psychopathic personality traits. In: *Integrated Treatment of Personality Disorder: A Modular Approach* (eds. J. Livesley, G. Dimaggio and J. Clarkin), 345–376. New York, NY: Guildford.

Wong, S.C.P. and Gordon, A. (2006). The validity and reliability of the violence risk scale: a treatment-friendly violence risk assessment tool. *Psychology, Public Policy, and Law* 12: 279–309.

Wong, S.C.P., Gordon, A., Gu, D. et al. (2012). The effectiveness of violence reduction treatment for psychopathic offenders: empirical evidence and a treatment model. *International Journal of Forensic Mental Health* 11: 336–349.

World Health Organization (2018). *International Classification of Diseases 11th Revision*. Geneva, CH: Author.

Wormith, J.S., Olver, M.E., Stevenson, H.E., and Girard, L. (2007). The long term prediction of offender recidivism using diagnostic, personality, and risk/need approaches to offender assessment. *Psychological Services* 4: 287–305.

Yang, M., Wong, S.C.P., and Coid, J. (2010). The efficacy of violence prediction: a meta-analytic comparison of nine risk assessment tools. *Psychological Bulletin* 136: 740–767.

11

Assessing Risk for Violent, General, and Sexual Offending in Adolescents
Recent Advances and Future Directions

Jodi L. Viljoen[1], Melissa R. Jonnson[1], and Stephane M. Shepherd[2]

[1] Simon Fraser University, Burnaby, Canada
[2] Centre for Forensic Behavioural Science, Swinburne University of Technology, Hawthorn, Australia

Introduction

Justice and mental health clinicians are often asked to assess the likelihood that an adolescent will engage in violence or other forms of offending (Singh et al. 2014a; Viljoen et al. 2010b). Indeed, youth justice agencies in many American states and Canadian provinces mandate that risk assessments be conducted with adolescents who have been convicted of a criminal offence (Hannah-Moffat et al. 2009; Wachter 2015). The purpose of these risk assessments is to guide treatment-planning and legal decision-making, such as decisions about what type of supervision an adolescent may require.

Knowledge on how to best assess risk in adolescents has grown considerably over the past decade. Although adult risk assessment tools still vastly outnumber adolescent risk assessment tools, researchers have nevertheless developed a variety of risk assessment tools for adolescents (e.g. Borum et al. 2006; Hoge and Andrews 2002, 2011). Furthermore, despite early concerns that it may be more difficult to predict reoffending in adolescents than adults, studies have found that leading adolescent risk assessment tools can significantly predict reoffending over follow-up periods of two years or more (Olver et al. 2009; Singh et al. 2011). Yet another sign of progress is that many professionals and criminal justice agencies have adopted risk assessment tools, and integrated them into routine practice. For instance, in a survey of psychologists who were members of forensic profession/al organizations, over 97% of psychologists reported using these tools at least once in a while, and 61% reported using these tools always or almost always (Viljoen et al. 2010a).

The Wiley Handbook of What Works in Violence Risk Management: Theory, Research and Practice,
First Edition. Edited by J. Stephen Wormith, Leam A. Craig, and Todd E. Hogue.
© 2020 John Wiley & Sons Ltd. Published 2020 by John Wiley & Sons Ltd.

However, a number of challenges remain. Despite a growing body of research on the predictive validity of tools, little is known about the clinical utility of risks assessments, or how courts, professionals, and administrators use adolescent risk assessments to guide decision-making. For instance, do risk assessments ensure that adolescent offenders receive services to address their needs? Are existing adolescent risk assessment tools equally relevant for female and male adolescents and for ethnic minority and non-minority groups, or are tailored approaches needed for some populations? Given that adolescence is a period of enormous developmental change, how frequently should professionals reassess adolescents' risk? Finally, although many would agree that protective factors should play an important role in adolescent risk assessments, how should protective factors be conceptualized and measured? What new information can they add? In this chapter, we review developmental considerations and existing best practises for adolescent risk assessment. Then, following this, we address these outstanding questions, proposing some future directions for the field of adolescent risk assessment.

Adolescent Development and Its Relevance to Risk Assessment

Adolescence refers to the period of time between the onset of puberty and the acquisition of independence (Steinberg 2014). Chronologically, this is commonly defined as the ages of 10–18 (APA 2002). However, within many modern Western societies, individuals often do not attain full independence until later than 18 (Arnett 2000). For instance, many people aged 18–25 continue to reside with their parents and attend post-secondary training rather than holding down full-time employment. Thus, more recently, the period of 18–25 years has been recognized as a transitional period, which is either included within the period of adolescence, broadly defined (APA 2002), or is recognized as a separate developmental period referred to as *emerging adulthood* (Arnett 2000). In this chapter, our emphasis is on adolescents (aged 10–18). However, as justice and mental health systems often retain some jurisdiction over youth up until their early 20s, we also include some discussion of emerging adults (aged 18–25).

To appropriately assess adolescents' risk for violence and offending, it is essential to have a solid understanding of adolescent development and the role it plays in offending. Although adolescents (and emerging adults) are more likely than any other age group to be arrested (Hirschi and Gottfredson 1983; Piquero et al. 2015), studies suggest that aggression peaks in early childhood and then declines with age (Broidy et al. 2003; Côté et al. 2006; Nagin and Tremblay 1999). However, whereas aggression and minor offences committed by children are typically handled informally, or are required to do so by law (e.g. Youth Criminal Justice Act 2002), society exhibits less tolerance when these behaviours are committed by adolescents (Tremblay 2006).

Although adolescents are often expected to be responsible and adult-like, adolescents are more developmentally predisposed to offending than adults. In particular, compared to adults, adolescents aged 18 or younger are more impulsive (Shulman et al. 2016), more sensitive to the rewards of risk-taking (Shulman et al. 2016), and less likely to consider long-term consequences of risk behaviours (Steinberg et al. 2009), all of which contribute to an increased likelihood of offending (Sweeten et al. 2013). These developmental differences between adolescents and adults appear to stem, at least in part, to ongoing brain development (Casey et al. 2011; Steinberg 2010). In particular, the subcortical region of the brain, which is associated with sensitivity to rewards, is activated prior to the full development of the prefrontal cortical region, which is associated with planning and control of behaviour. As such, adolescent functioning, in some ways, is similar to a car that accelerates quickly but does not yet have a reliable set of brakes (Casey et al. 2011).

Although maturational processes and brain development play a role in adolescent offending, so do environmental factors. Adolescents spend less time with parents and more unsupervised time with peers than children (Larson et al. 1996). Compared to adults, they are more impressionable and susceptible to peer influence (Albert et al. 2013; Steinberg and Monahan 2007), and make riskier decisions when in the presence of peers (Smith et al. 2014). Adolescents are also influenced by their parents. Even if their parents are rejecting, unavailable, or have significant personal difficulties (e.g. substance use, criminality), adolescents can do little to change their home environment. Thus, not surprisingly, peer relationships and negative parenting, are robust predictors of offending during adolescence (Hoeve et al. 2009; Lipsey and Derzon 1998).

As adolescents mature, many show significant reductions in offending or stop offending altogether (Sweeten et al. 2013). In general, adolescents who first begin to exhibit illegal behaviours during adolescence (i.e. adolescent-onset) are more likely to desist from offending than those who first exhibit behaviour problems during childhood (i.e. childhood-onset; Moffitt et al. 2002; Roisman et al. 2010). Nevertheless, some adolescent-onset offenders continue to engage in antisocial behaviour as young adults, and show a variety of other life problems as young adults (e.g. substance use, financial difficulties; Moffitt et al. 2002).

Together, these findings on adolescent development have several implications for risk assessment. Firstly, given that developmental factors, such as impulsivity and sensation-seeking, contribute to adolescent offending (e.g. Sweeten et al. 2013), practitioners should ensure that they attend to these factors in their risk assessments. Also, as adolescents are more 'contextually bound' than adults (Hoagwood et al. 2001, p. 1181), environmental factors are particularly important to assess (e.g. peers, parenting). As such, practitioners should use assessment approaches that include such factors and are developmentally-informed.

Secondly, practitioners should be mindful that, in general, many adolescents tend to desist from criminal behaviours over time, and thus avoid assuming that adolescents are high risk for ongoing criminal behaviour. That said, waiting for adolescents to 'age out' of crime is inadequate, especially as legal sanctions (e.g. incarceration) are ineffective at reducing re-offending and may even heighten risk by interfering with developmental processes that might be protective (e.g. acquisition of impulse control skills; Dmitrieva et al. 2012; Lambie and Randell 2013). Instead, practitioners should do all that they can to ensure that adolescents are provided with evidence-based interventions (e.g. multisystematic therapy, cognitive-behavioural therapy; Andrews and Bonta 2010; Henggeler 2016; Landenberger and Lipsey 2005).

Finally, given that a number of developmental changes and transitions occur during adolescence (e.g. changes in peers, romantic relationships, schools), practitioners should reassess risk regularly, such as every six months (Viljoen et al. 2012b; Vincent et al. 2012b). However, as described later in this chapter, the 'shelf-life' of adolescent risk assessments remains unclear, and as such, further research is needed.

Evidence-Based Risk Assessment Tools

Decisions based on information from adolescent risk assessment instruments can have serious ramifications for adolescents' liberties and public safety. For instance, inaccurately judging an adolescent to be high risk might mean that an adolescent is placed in unnecessarily restrictive settings (e.g. incarcerated), whereas inaccurately judging an adolescent to be low risk might result in a failure to prevent violence and harm that may have otherwise been avoidable through risk management efforts. As such, it is important that practitioners use the best available approaches, namely validated risk assessment tools. Although risk assessment tools do not have perfect predictive validity, they outperform unstructured clinical judgement, and are more transparent and legally defensible (see Ægisdóttir et al. 2006; Grove and Meehl 1996).

Thus, in this section, we review evidence-based risk assessment tools for adolescents (see Viljoen et al. 2016a for a more detailed review of psychometric properties). We focus on tools that are widely available rather than tools designed for in-house use by a particular agency (i.e. 'homegrown' tools; Vincent et al. 2009). Similar to Vincent et al. (2009), we define evidence-based risk assessment tools as tools which: (i) have a manual, (ii) include empirically-supported and developmentally-relevant risk factors (e.g. delinquent peers, parental supervision), (iii) have adequate interrater reliability (IRR) based on at least one peer-reviewed study, and (iv) have predictive validity in at least two peer-reviewed studies, including at least one study by an independent party who did not develop the tool.[1] Ideally, evidence should also be available regarding predictive validity across diverse populations (e.g. female and male adolescents, adolescents from ethnic minority groups, adolescents of varying ages). We identified four widely used adolescent risk assessment tools that met these criteria, including tools for violence (Structured Assessment of Violence Risk in Youth [SAVRY]), general offending (Youth Level of Service/Case Management Inventory [YLS/CMI]), and sexual offending (Estimate Risk of Adolescent Sexual Offense Recidivism [ERASOR], Juvenile Sex Offender Assessment Protocol-II [J-SOAP-II]). We also identified several new tools that have emerging research support, Structured Assessment of Protective Factors for violence risk-Youth Version(SAPROF:YV), Short-Term Assessment of Risk and Treatability: Adolescent Version [START:AV], Violence Risk Scale-Youth Version [VRS-YV], Youth Assessment and Screening Instrument [YASI]) Table 11.1 provides a brief summary of the risk scales. Below, we review published studies on these tools, with an emphasis on meta-analyses, where available.

Structured assessment of violence risk in youth

The Structured Assessment of Violence Risk in Youth (SAVRY) (Borum et al. 2006) is designed to assess risk for violence in female and male adolescents aged 12–18. It consists of 24 risk factors which are rated as Low, Moderate, or High. These factors are organized into three domains: Historical (e.g. childhood history of maltreatment), Social/Contextual (e.g. peer delinquency), and Individual/Clinical (e.g. substance use). The Social/Contextual and Individual/Clinical sections are conceptualized as dynamic or modifiable. The SAVRY also includes six protective factors (e.g. resilient personality traits) which are rated as Present or Absent based on the youths' functioning during the preceding year. Rather than summing up scores, evaluators use their professional judgement to make a Summary Risk Rating regarding whether the youth's overall risk for future violence is Low, Moderate, or High. This approach is consistent with the structured professional judgement (SPJ) model. Although the SAVRY manual does not include directions on intervention-planning, a separate risk management tool called the Adolescent Risk Reduction and Resilient Outcomes Work-Plan (ARROW; Viljoen

---

[1] Although Vincent et al. (2009) note that risk assessment tools should have evidence of internal structure (e.g. internal consistency, factor structure), we did not include this information in our review, as there is some debate about the extent to which concepts such as internal consistency apply to risk assessment tools (Douglas et al. 2011).

Table 11.1 Risk assessment tools for adolescents.

Risk Tool	Outcome the Tools is Designed to Predict	Risk Factors	Protective Factors	Timeframe for Rating and Reassessment	Forms/Structure for Risk Management
Evidence-Based Risk Assessment Tools					
Structured assessment of violence risk in youth (SAVRY)	Violence	24 risk factors (low, moderate, high) in historical, individual, and social-contextual domains	6 protective factors (present/absent)	Dynamic factors are rated based on past year	Not included in manual, but ARROW was designed to accompany SAVRY
Youth level of service/Case management inventory (YLS/CMI 2.0)	Any offending	42 risk/needs factors (present, absent) in 8 domains (e.g. Peers)	7 strengths (present/absent)	Dynamic factors are rated based on current functioning or past year	Includes forms for supervision and case management plans
Estimate of risk of adolescent sexual offense recidivism (ERASOR)	Sexual offending	25 risk factors (present, partially present, not present) in 5 domains (4 dynamic, 1 static)	Not included, but authors have developed DASH-13	Dynamic factors are rated based on the past 6 months	Not included in manual
Juvenile sex offender assessment protocol-II (J-SOAP-II)	Sexual and general offending	28 risk factors (absent, possibly present, clearly present) in 4 domains (2 dynamic, 2 static)	Not included	Dynamic are rated factors based on past 6 months, reassess within 6 months	Not included in manual

(Continued)

Table 11.1 (Cont'd)

Risk Tool	Outcome the Tools is Designed to Predict	Risk Factors	Protective Factors	Timeframe for Rating and Reassessment	Forms/Structure for Risk Management
Emerging Risk Assessment Tools					
SAPROF-YV	Violence	Not included	16 protective factors (7-point scale) in resilience, motivation, relational, and external domains	Items are rated based on expected functioning in the 'upcoming 6 months'	Not included in manual
Short-term assessment of risk and treatability: adolescent version (START:AV)	Harm to others (e.g. violence, offending) Harm to youth (e.g. victimization, suicide)	25 vulnerabilities (low/moderate/high) in individual, relationships/environment, and intervention domains	25 strengths (low/moderate/high) in individual, relationships/environment, and intervention domains	Items are rated based on past 3 months, reassess every 3 months	Includes form for formulation, scenario-planning, and intervention-planning
Violence risk scale-youth version (VRS-YV)	Violence	4 stable and 19 dynamic risk factors (scored 0, 1, 2, or 3)	Not included	Stage of change (4-category scale) is rated pre- and post-treatment	No separate forms, but includes assessment of treatment-related change
Youth Assessment and Screening Instrument (YASI)	General offending	90 risks and needs factors (dichotomous, count-based, and Likert items) in one static domain (i.e. Legal History) and 9 dynamic domains (e.g. School)	46 strengths (dichotomous, count-based, and Likert items) in 7 strengths domains (e.g. School)	Items are rated based on past 3 months, past 2 years, or lifetime occurrence	Includes case planning software

Note: Our criteria for evidence-based tools is provided on p. 7. Tools are roughly ordered from those with the most to least research evidence.

et al. 2014a) was recently developed to accompany the SAVRY. The ARROW provides a structured process for intervention-planning by compiling best practice intervention strategies for each of the SAVRY risk and protective factors.

The SAVRY has consistently demonstrated good to excellent IRR in research settings (e.g. when rated by research assistants). For example, studies have identified intraclass correlation coefficients (ICCs, most of which appear to be based on two-way random effects models with absolute agreement)[2] in the range of 0.67–0.97 for the SAVRY risk total, and ICCs in the range of 0.72–0.95 for the summary risk ratings (Borum et al. 2010; Hilterman et al. 2014; Lodewijks et al. 2010; Penney et al. 2010). One study also reported that the SAVRY has good to excellent IRR when used in the field (i.e. when rated by juvenile probation officers), with ICCs ranging from 0.71 for summary risk ratings to 0.86 for SAVRY total scores (Vincent et al. 2012a).

With respect to predictive validity, a meta-analytic review of nine SAVRY studies found that the SAVRY risk total is a moderate predictor of general (weighted r [r_w] = 0.33), violent (r_w = 0.31), and nonviolent (r_w = 0.38) recidivism (Olver et al. 2009). Similarly, another meta-analytic review of nine SAVRY studies reported a median area under the receiver operating characteristic curve (AUC)[3] value of 0.71 in predicting serious recidivism, which represents a large effect size (Singh et al. 2011). With respect to the SAVRY protective factors, a number of studies, but not all, have indicated that total scores on protective factors significantly predicts the absence of re-offending (e.g. Lodewijks et al. 2010; Penney et al. 2010). However, research is mixed as to whether SAVRY protective factors provide incremental validity over SAVRY risk factors (e.g. Lodewijks et al. 2010; Schmidt et al. 2011).

Support for predictive validity has been found in a range of samples (e.g. adolescent offenders, forensic/psychiatric patients, adolescents in specialized school programmes; Gammelgård et al. 2008; Hilterman et al. 2014; McGowan et al. 2011; Penney et al. 2010). Although findings vary somewhat, most evidence suggests that the predictive accuracy of the SAVRY is similar across male and female adolescents (e.g. Gammelgård et al. 2008; Penney et al. 2010). Some studies have reported that predictive validity may be higher amongst Caucasian adolescents than some ethnic minority groups (e.g. Hispanic American youth, culturally and linguistically diverse youth in Australia; Shepherd et al. 2014; Vincent et al. 2011). However, research is limited. Also, although one study found that predictive validity may be lower in younger adolescents (aged 12–15) than older adolescents (aged 16–18; Viljoen et al. 2008), other studies have found comparable predictive validity across age (e.g. Vincent et al. 2012d).

Youth level of service/case management inventory

The Youth Level of Service/Case Management Inventory (YLS/CMI) (Hoge and Andrews 2002) and its revision (YLS/CMI 2.0; Hoge and Andrews 2011) are designed to assess general re-offence risk in adolescent offenders aged 12–18. The YLS/CMI was derived from a

---

[2] ICCs have a theoretical range of 0.00–1.00, with larger coefficients representing higher levels of interrater agreement. Cicchetti (1994) provides the following interpretation guidelines for single measure ICCs: below 0.40 reflect poor clinical significance, those between 0.40 and 0.59 reflect fair clinical significance, those between 0.60 and 0.74 reflect good clinical significance, and those between 0.75 and 1.00 reflect excellent clinical significance.

[3] AUCs have a theoretical range of 0.00–1.00, with 0.50 representing a chance level of predictive accuracy. According to criteria provided by Rice and Harris (2005), AUCs between 0.56 and 0.63 reflect small effect sizes, AUCs between 0.64 and 0.70 reflect medium effect sizes, and AUCs that meet or exceed 0.71 reflect large effects sizes.

commonly-used adult measure, the Level of Service Inventory – Revised (Andrews and Bonta 1995). The YLS/CMI 2.0 includes 42 risk/needs items divided into 8 subscales (i.e. Prior and Current Offences, Family Circumstances/Parenting, Education/Employment, Peer Associations, Substance Abuse, Leisure/Recreation, Personality/Behaviour, and Attitudes/ Orientation). These subscales map onto what are referred to as the central eight risk factors, a model which has considerable research support. Each of the risk/needs items is rated as Present or Absent. With the exception of the Prior and Current Offences subscale, items are rated based on current functioning or functioning during the past year (Hoge and Andrews 2011). The items are scored dichotomously and then summed to generate a total score and risk level rating (Low, Moderate, High, Very High). Raters may adjust or override a youth's risk classification. In addition to its 42 risk/needs items, the tool includes seven strengths ratings; strengths ratings are made for each subscale except for Prior and Current Offences. It also includes a checklist of 53 factors, such as learning disabilities and trauma, that may affect a youth's response to interventions. Finally, the measure provides forms for developing supervision and case management plans.

The YLS/CMI 2.0 has been found to have acceptable IRR in a couple of studies (Chu et al. 2015; Zeng et al. 2014). In particular, ICCs for total scores were good and ICCs for subscales ranged from fair to perfect, based on absolute agreement (Chu et al. 2015; Zeng et al. 2014). IRR results for the earlier version of this tool, the YLS/CMI, are also positive (e.g. Catchpole and Gretton 2003).

In addition, the YLS/CMI 2.0 has shown good predictive validity. In a study with young offenders from Singapore, YLS/CMI 2.0 Total Scores significantly predicted general re-offending with moderate effect sizes (i.e. AUCs = 0.64–0.67; Chu et al. 2015). Similarly, meta-analyses have found that the earlier version of this tool, the YLS/CMI, significantly predicted general re-offending as well as violent re-offending, with moderate correlations (i.e. weighted $r\,[r_w]$ = 0.32 and 0.26, respectively; Olver et al. 2009; see also Olver et al. 2014).

Based on a meta-analytic review, the predictive validity of the YLS/CMI for general recidivism appears to be similar for female and male adolescents (i.e. r_{pb} = 0.25 and 0.28, respectively, k = 69 effect sizes; Pusch and Holtfreter 2017), and for Indigenous and non-Indigenous youth (i.e. r_w = 0.35 and 0.32, respectively, k = 5 studies; Olver et al. 2009). Also, research has suggested that the YLS/CMI's predictive validity is fairly similar for younger adolescents (i.e. age 12–15) and older adolescents (i.e. age 16–18; Viljoen et al. 2009; Olver et al. 2012).

Estimate of risk of adolescent sexual offence recidivism

The Estimate of Risk of Adolescent Sexual Offence Recidivism (ERASOR) (Worling and Curwen 2001) is designed to predict the risk of sexual recidivism in adolescents aged 12–18 who have a history of sexual assault. It is a 25-item checklist of risk factors arranged into four putatively dynamic risk sections (Sexual Interests and Behaviours, Psychosocial Functioning, Family/Environment, and Treatment) and one static risk section (History of Sexual Assaults). Each risk factor is rated as Present, Possibly or Partially Present, or Not Present in the past six months, or Unknown. After evaluators complete the tool, they use structured professional judgement to derive an overall estimate of the level of risk (i.e. Low, Moderate, or High) for future sexual violence. Although the ERASOR does not incorporate protective factors, Worling (2013) has developed an experimental, 13-item checklist to investigate potential protective factors for adolescent sexual offenders (Desistence for Adolescents Who Sexually Harm; DASH-13). The DASH-13 includes items relating to sexual health (e.g. interest in age-appropriate partners) and pro-social functioning (e.g. compassion for others). The psychometric properties of this new tool are under investigation (see Zeng et al. 2015).

The ERASOR has evinced good to excellent levels of interrater agreement across both research and clinical contexts. Most research has identified ICCs in the range of 0.88–0.90 for the ERASOR total score, and ICCs in the range of 0.78–0.87 for the summary risk rating (Rajlic and Gretton 2010; Viljoen et al. 2009; Worling 2004; Worling et al. 2012). However, one study reported only fair IRR for the ERASOR total score and summary risk rating (ICCs = 0.49 and 0.43, respectively; Chu et al. 2012).

In terms of predictive validity, a meta-analytic examination of 10 studies found that the ERASOR significantly predicted sexual re-offending with moderate effects sizes (AUC = 0.66) and general re-offending with small effect sizes (AUC = 0.59; Viljoen et al. 2012c). However, AUCs have ranged considerably and some studies have reported null results (i.e. AUCs – 0.50–0.74 for sexual recidivism, and 0.53–0.67 for general recidivism; Hempel et al. 2013).

Due to the low rate of female adolescent sexual offending, research has not yet investigated the predictive validity of the ERASOR for females. In addition, studies comparing predictive validity across racial and ethnic groups are not yet available. One study found that ERASOR total scores were better able to predict general re-offending in adolescents aged 16–18 than in those aged 12–15, but research is limited (Viljoen et al. 2009).

Juvenile sex offender assessment protocol-II

Like the ERASOR, the intended use of the Juvenile Sex Offender Assessment Protocol-II (J-SOAP-II) is to estimate the risk of re-offending in adolescents aged 12–18 who have been adjudicated for sexual offences (Prentky and Righthand 2003). However, unlike the ERASOR, it is designed to predict both sexual and nonsexual recidivism and is only intended for use with males. The J-SOAP-II is composed of 28 risk factors that comprise four subscales, two of which address putatively dynamic risk factors (Intervention and Community Stability/Adjustment) and two of which address static risk factors (Sexual Drive/Preoccupation and Impulsive/Antisocial Behaviour). Each risk factor is rated as Absent (0), Possibly Present (1), or Clearly Present (2) and item scores are summed to obtain a total score. The youth should be reassessed for risk at a minimum of every six months. Community Stability/Adjustment factors, in particular, are rated based on the preceding six months. Currently, the J-SOAP-II does not include cut-off scores to classify youth into categories of risk. However, higher scores represent a greater risk to reoffend.

Overall, the J-SOAP-II has yielded good to excellent IRR (Cicchetti 1994), with most studies reporting total score ICCs of ≥0.70 using the two-way, random effects approach with absolute agreement (e.g. ICC = 0.71, Aebi et al. 2011; ICC = 0.70; Martinez et al. 2007; ICC = 0.94; Rajlic and Gretton 2010) Findings for the four subscales have been more mixed, with IRR coefficients ranging from poor to excellent (i.e. ICCs range from 0.42 to 0.93; Aebi et al. 2011; Caldwell and Dickinson 2009; Martinez et al. 2007; Rajlic and Gretton 2010).

Predictive validity has been demonstrated by some (e.g. Aebi et al. 2011; Martinez et al. 2007; Prentky et al. 2010; Rajlic and Gretton 2010), but not all (e.g. Caldwell and Dickinson 2009; Chu et al. 2012; Viljoen et al. 2008) of the studies examining the psychometric properties of the J-SOAP-II. However, a meta-analysis of 15 studies estimated the overall predictive validity of J-SOAP-II total scores to be in the moderate range for sexual re-offending (AUC = 0.67) and nonsexual re-offending (AUC = 0.66; Viljoen et al. 2012c).

Several studies have involved samples of adolescents from diverse ethnic groups (Fanniff and Letourneau 2012; Martinez et al. 2007). However, none of these has directly tested whether the predictive validity of the J-SOAP-II is moderated by ethnicity. Although the J-SOAP-II is designed for *adolescents*, some evidence indicates that the J-SOAP-II total score may also significantly predict sexual recidivism in *pre-adolescents* (i.e. aged 11 and younger) over a 7-year follow-up period (AUC = 0.80; Prentky et al. 2010). However, other research has found that the J-SOAP-II is significantly less effective in predicting post-discharge recidivism in younger adolescents (i.e. aged 12–15), as compared to older adolescents (i.e. aged 16–19; Viljoen et al. 2008).

Emerging Risk Assessment Tools

In addition to the tools reviewed above, several tools appear promising based on initial research, such as one published, peer-reviewed predictive validity study or unpublished studies.

Structured assessment of protective factors for violence risk-youth version

The SAPROF-YV (de Vries Robbé et al. 2015) is a measure of protective factors for violence, which is intended to be used in conjunction with a risk-focused assessment tool, such as the SAVRY or the YLS/CMI. Adapted from the Structured Assessment of Protective Factors for Violence Risk for adults (de Vogel et al. 2011), it can be used with adolescents aged 12–18. For emerging adults (e.g. 18–19), evaluators are advised to make case-by-case determinations of whether the SAPROF-YV or the adult version of this tool is preferable. The SAPROF-YV includes 16 protective factors that fall into four scales: Resilience, Motivation, Relational, and External. Each factor is rated on a seven-point scale (i.e. 2, 2–, 1+, 1, 1–, 0+, 0). Items are rated for the 'near future', which is defined as the 'future situation in the upcoming 6 months' (p. 30). After rating items, professionals make a Final Protection Judgement using an SPJ approach. Then, this information is integrated with youths' results from a risk-focused tool (e.g. SAVRY) to make a Final Risk Judgement.

In an initial validation study, the SAPROF-YV Total Score was found to have excellent IRR (de Vries Robbé et al. 2017). Furthermore, higher SAPROF-YV scores significantly predicted lower rates of violent re-offending during a six-month follow-up. Predictive validity was demonstrated in both male adolescents (aged 13–17) and male emerging adults (aged 18–23).

Short-term assessment of risk and treatability: adolescent version

The Short-Term Assessment of Risk and Treatability: Adolescent Version (START:AV) (Viljoen et al. 2014b, 2016b) is a developmentally-informed adaptation of the START (Webster et al. 2009) that is designed to assess risk for multiple types of adverse outcomes (Viljoen et al. 2012b). These outcomes fall into two categories: (i) harm to others/rule violations (i.e. violence, non-violent offences, substance abuse, unauthorized absences), and (ii) harm to the adolescent (i.e. suicide, non-suicidal self-injury, victimization, health neglect). The START:AV is intended for use with adolescents aged 12–18. It can also be used with emerging adults who have not yet achieved independence, such as those who are still residing with caregivers, or receiving services within the youth justice or youth mental health systems (Viljoen et al. 2014b). The START:AV has 25 items that fall into three domains: Individual Adolescent (e.g. impulse control), Relationships and Environment (e.g. peers), and Responses to Interventions (e.g.

plans). Also, there is an optional item on Culture, which is intended for use with adolescents from ethnic, racial, and cultural minority groups. For each item, youth are rated as Low, Moderate, or High in Strengths and Low, Moderate, or High in Vulnerabilities based on youths' recent functioning (i.e. the past three months). Youths' recent and lifetime history of adverse events is also rated on eight domains (e.g. history of violence, victimization). Professionals then use this information to make a Summary Risk Rating of whether a youth poses a Low, Moderate, or High risk for each of the future adverse outcomes (e.g. violence) within the next three months (or another short-term period), at which time risk is reassessed. Drawing from recent developments in adult risk assessment (e.g. Douglas et al. 2013), the START:AV includes case formulation (i.e. the process of developing an explanatory model for the youths' behaviour) and scenario-planning (i.e. trouble-shooting and planning for risk situations that may occur in the future). It also includes forms for intervention-planning and monitoring treatment progress.

As a new tool, research is at an early stage. However, thus far, the START:AV's IRR appears acceptable. One study reported that the IRR for the Strengths and Vulnerabilities total scores fell within the excellent range (ICCs = 0.92 and 0.86 respectively; Viljoen et al. 2012a). Two published, peer-reviewed studies have examined the predictive validity of the START:AV. In a study with adolescent offenders on probation, START:AV Vulnerabilities total scores, Strengths total scores, and risk estimates significantly predicted official arrests for any and violent crimes, as well as self-reported any and violent offending (Viljoen et al. 2012a). The START:AV also predicted victimization, street drug use, and suicide ideation. In a study with adolescent forensic patients, the START:AV Vulnerabilities total scores, Strengths total scores, and the risk estimated for violence towards others predicted verbal aggression, property damage, and physical aggression (Sher et al. 2017). However, the START:AV did not predict self-injury in that study. This may be due to low base rates, but requires further investigation. Viljoen, Beneteau, et al. (2012a) found that predictive validity of the START:AV was not moderated by sex differences; it predicted similarly well for female and male youth. However, Sher et al. (2017) reported that, whilst the START:AV total Strengths and Vulnerability scores were significantly related to adverse outcomes for males at a three-month follow-up (e.g. verbal and physical aggression), no significant associations were identified for females. At the present time, no published studies have examined racial/ethnic differences or age differences in predictive validity (see Bhanwer et al. 2016 for a review of unpublished studies).

Violence risk scale-youth version

The Violence Risk Scale-Youth Version (VRS-YV) (Wong et al. 2004–2011) was developed to assess violence risk in youth. It was adapted for adolescents from an adult tool, the Violence Risk Scale (Wong and Gordon 2009). As the age ranges of youth in the justice system can vary across locations, its authors define youth to encompass the age range specified by the local youth justice system (e.g. in Canada, this is age 12–18). The VRS-YV includes 4 stable and 19 dynamic risk factors which are rated on a four-point scale (0, 1, 2, or 3). In addition, a unique feature of the VRS-YV (and the VRS) is that it is informed by the transtheoretical model of change (Prochaska et al. 1992). As such, in addition to rating risk level, professionals rate the youth's stage of change on a four-category scale (i.e. Precontemplation/Contemplation, Preparation, Action, or Maintenance). These stages of change ratings are made both prior to and following treatment so that professionals can examine improvements over the course of treatment, such as whether a youth progressed from the precontemplation stage to the action stage on any of the targeted risk factors.

In a study by Stockdale et al. (2014), the VRS-YV was found to have excellent IRR (i.e. ICCs = 0.90 for Total score), and moderate to large predictive validity for total general and violent recidivism (AUC for Total score = 0.73 and 0.77, respectively). Furthermore, predictive validity was strong for male and female youth, and for Indigenous and non-Indigenous youth, suggesting generalizability across diverse populations of youth.

Youth assessment and screening instrument

The Youth Assessment and Screening Instrument (YASI) (Orbis Partners 2000) was developed based on the Case Management Assessment Protocol (Barnoski 2003) for use with justice-involved girls and boys aged 12–18 in both community supervision and custody settings (Jones et al. 2016). It is designed to assess risk for general recidivism and is available in two versions: Pre-Screen and Full Assessment. The Full Assessment contains 90 items that are arranged into one static risk domain (Legal History) and nine dynamic need domains (e.g. Family, School, Mental Health). For seven of the dynamic need domains, a strength score is also generated (e.g. Family, School). The Pre-Screen is used to triage justice-involved youth for further assessment and intervention, and it consists of 34 out of the 90 items from the Full Assessment. Items on the Pre-Screen and Full Assessment are rated based on either the past three months, the past two years, or the youth's lifetime. Forty-five items on the Full Assessment and eight items on the Pre-Screen are scored on Likert-type scales ranging from three- to seven-points, whereas the remaining items are dichotomous, age-based (e.g. age at first police contact), or count-based (e.g. number of police contacts). The Pre-Screen and Full Assessment each provide a risk/needs score and a strength score for each domain, along with an overall risk/needs score and an overall strength score, which are calculated by summing the relevant item scores. These overall scores are then used to classify youth as low, moderate, or high risk for recidivism, and low, moderate, or high in strengths.

One study that assessed the match between staff members' and experts' YASI ratings reported an ICC of 0.63 for total scores and ICCs ranging from 0.50 to 0.79 for subscale scores (Kennealy et al. 2017). Also, a study of 464 juvenile offenders on community supervision in Alberta, Canada found that the Pre-Screen accurately predicted general and violent re-offending over an 18-month follow-up period (AUC = 0.79; Jones et al. 2016). Predictive accuracy was similar across Indigenous (AUCs = 0.79–0.80) and non-Indigenous youth (AUCs = 0.77–0.80); however, the Pre-Screen was less accurate in predicting general re-offending for female adolescents (AUC = 0.68) than it was for male adolescents (AUC = 0.82).

Psychopathic Features and Adolescent Risk Assessments

Although measures of psychopathy are *not* risk assessment tools per se, they are widely used in adolescent risk assessments (Viljoen et al. 2010a). Assessing psychopathic features carries both potential benefits and potential risks. On the one hand, identifying early features of psychopathy can be important to treatment-planning. Studies indicate that adolescents with psychopathic features are more likely than other youth to engage in violence (Edens et al. 2007), and may require intensive and specialized treatment (Manders et al. 2013). On the other hand, the application of psychopathy to youth has engendered some apprehension. Several psychopathic symptoms (i.e. impulsivity, impression management) may resemble developmentally normative behaviours (Edens and Vincent 2008; Seagrave and Grisso 2002; Shepherd and Strand 2015). Also, researchers have raised concerns about whether labelling adolescents as psychopathic can be stigmatizing and potentially misleading (Edens and Vincent 2008), as psychopathic features change over time, often decreasing as adolescents mature (Cauffman et al. 2016). Thus, in assessing psychopathic features in adolescents, practitioners should use caution. For instance, practitioners should use well-validated measures. In addition, there is professional consensus against labelling adolescents as 'psychopaths' (Forth et al. 2003; Viljoen et al. 2010a).

Hare psychopathy checklist: Youth version

The Hare Psychopathy Checklist: Youth Version (PCL:YV) (Forth et al. 2003) is the most widely-used approach for assessing psychopathic features in adolescents. It is intended for use with adolescents aged 12–17, and was adapted from a widely used adult measure, the Hare Psychopathy Checklist – Revised (PCL-R; Hare 2003). The PCL:YV has 20 items which are individually scored on a three-point scale (0, 1, or 2) based on the youth's lifetime functioning. Similar to the adult version, the PCL:YV has a two-factor structure which encompasses four facets of the disorder. Factor 1 encompasses an interpersonal facet (e.g. manipulative/deceiving behaviours) and an affective facet (e.g. lack of empathy/remorselessness). Factor 2 encompasses a behavioural facet (e.g. social deviancy) and antisocial facet (e.g. criminal/problem behaviours; Forth et al. 2003). Some studies have also found a three-factor structure of the PCL:YV, which does not include an antisocial factor (Jones et al. 2006; Kosson et al. 2013; Neumann et al. 2006). The construct is measured dimensionally and there is no official diagnostic cut-off point on the instrument (Forth et al. 2003). This is intentional given that the available evidence supporting the life-course stability of the disorder into young adulthood remains equivocal (see Cauffman et al. 2016; Hawes et al. 2014; Hemphala et al. 2015).

The PCL:YV total score has produced strong internal consistency and IRR estimates (e.g. two-way, mixed effects ICC for total score = 0.91; Cauffman et al. 2009; absolute agreement ICC for total score = 0.99; Shepherd and Strand 2016). In addition, the PCL:YV has been found to predict general and violent recidivism across international cohorts of adolescent offenders in custodial and community settings (e.g. Asscher et al. 2011; Edens et al. 2007; Olver et al. 2009; Welsh et al. 2008). Studies have also reported significant associations with problem behaviours (e.g. Penney and Moretti 2007) and institutional misconduct (e.g. Edens and Campbell 2007; Shaffer et al. 2015). Moreover, the PCL:YV has demonstrated comparable predictive validity with commonly used violence risk assessment tools (Catchpole and Gretton 2003; Hilterman et al.2014; Schmidt et al. 2011). That said, the PCL:YV's predictive capability appears to stem largely from the behavioural/antisocial domains (facets 3 and 4) rather than the interpersonal/affective features (facets 1 and 2; Edens et al. 2007; Olver et al. 2009; Walters 2014).

Some questions have been raised about the PCL:YV's generalizability across diverse populations. Specifically, studies exploring the predictive validity of the PCL: YV for female young offenders have produced mixed findings (Edens et al. 2007; Odgers et al. 2005; Vincent et al. 2008) signifying potential gender differences in the presentation and manifestation of the disorder (Strand et al. 2016; Tsang et al. 2015; Wynn et al. 2012). In addition, some researchers have observed low predictive validity in some ethnic minority groups (e.g. Indigenous Australian adolescent offenders; Shepherd and Strand 2016), emphasizing the need for further research, particularly research that is driven by clear hypotheses about how race and ethnicity may be relevant to the assessment of psychopathy.

Conclusions about the state of the field

In summary, great strides have been made in assessing risk for violence and re-offending in adolescents. Each of above-described risk assessment tools have been found to significantly predict violence and/or general re-offending in adolescents. Furthermore, risk assessment tools have been shown to outperform unstructured clinical judgement (Hilterman et al. 2014), indicating that using these tools is clearly preferable to the alternative, namely clinical intuition.

Of the tools reviewed, which tool(s) should practitioners use? This depends, in part, on the type of risk being assessed (e.g. sexual re-offence risk, violent re-offence risk, general re-offence risk). For instance, if the goal is to assess sexual re-offending, practitioners should use tools designed specifically for this purpose (e.g. ERASOR), as sex offence-specific tools appear to achieve higher validity for predicting sexual re-offending than do more general tools (e.g. SAVRY; Viljoen et al. 2012c). However, in many cases, predictive validity appears to be quite similar between tools (e.g. SAVRY vs. YLS/CMI; Shepherd et al. 2014). In such cases, other features of a tool may be relevant to consider in deciding which approach to use (e.g. time-frames for reassessments, inclusion of protective factors, guidelines for intervention-planning; see Table 11.1).

Although practitioners now have a range of tools to choose from, even the best available approaches have limitations. Specifically, risk assessments tools' predictive validity is generally moderate rather than large (Olver et al. 2009). Some authors have described this as 'ceiling' or 'sound barrier' of risk prediction (Menzies et al. 1985; Skeem and Monahan 2011), a barrier that is caused by the inherent complexity of predicting future behaviour. However, even if it is not feasible to significantly surpass this barrier, there are a number of other possible directions by which to improve the field of adolescent risk assessment. For instance, as described below, researchers can focus on the utility of risk assessment tools for intervention-planning and service delivery, and examine the applicability of tools to diverse populations.

Future Directions

Diverse populations

Questions have been raised about the universality of risk assessment tools – that is, whether risk assessment tools, which are largely manufactured on the behavioural patterns, attitudes, worldviews, social norms and expectations of white youth (primarily male), should extend to all youth irrespective of their race/ethnicity, sex, or age (Shepherd and Lewis-Fernandez 2016; Shepherd et al. 2014). Although some studies suggest that tools, such as the YLS/CMI, predict re-offending in minority and non-minority youth with similar accuracy (e.g. Olver et al. 2012, 2014), other studies suggest that risk assessment tools may not perform as well in youth who are racially, ethnically, or linguistically diverse (e.g. Shepherd et al. 2014, 2015). Similarly, although some researchers have reported comparable levels of predictive validity across gender (Olver et al. 2009), others have found poorer predictive validity for female than male youth on some tools (e.g. Jones et al. 2016). Studies on the differential predictive validity of tools across age are, again, somewhat mixed (e.g. Viljoen et al. 2008; Vincent et al. 2012d), and there is a near absence of research on the predictive validity of adolescent risk assessment tools for pre-adolescents (aged 10 or 12) and emerging adults (aged 18–25). As such, it is unclear whether tools generalize across age groups or require adaptation.

Given these scarce and inconsistent findings, further research is needed with respect to the predictive validity of tools across diverse subgroups (e.g. race/ethnicity, sex, age). To provide greater clarity and cohesiveness for such investigations, researchers should test specific hypotheses about how factors relevant to a person's race/ethnicity, sex, and age could affect the psychometric properties of tools (see Shepherd et al. 2015). For instance, researchers should test whether tools are properly calibrated for different groups (Shepherd and Lewis-Fernandez 2016). Tools might over-predict risk in some groups (i.e. high false positives) and under-predict risk in other groups (i.e. high false negatives). If these types of systematic biases do occur, they could lead to unfair penalties or consequences (e.g. incarceration) for certain subgroups. In addition, researchers can examine measurement invariance, that is, the extent to which tools measure the same latent or underlying construct across groups (Hart 2016; Shepherd and Lewis-Fernandez 2016). Rather than examining factors such as race/ethnicity and sex separately, researchers should, where possible, examine the intersection between these factors. To adequately study such topics however, there is a need for studies with larger sample sizes, greater statistical power, and more sophisticated statistical approaches (e.g. moderator analyses to test statistical differences in predictive validity across groups).

Even if future research does show that some tools are 'adequate' for diverse populations, it may nevertheless be possible to improve upon these existing approaches so that they are more sensitive or responsive to diversity. For instance, does modifying existing tools through research and consultation (e.g. cultural experts) lead to improved treatment engagement, better predictions, or more effective and respectful risk management efforts? Modifications or adjustment to tools could range in scope from very small to very large, and take various forms.

One possible modification would be to 'weight' risk and protective factors somewhat differently for different subgroups (e.g. culturally-, gender-, or developmentally-*salient factors*). For instance, whilst victimization and mental health factors may predict re-offending in both male and female youth, it may be especially important for females (Kerig and Schindler 2013), as illustrated by research on gendered-pathways to crime (Chesney-Lind et al. 2008; Daly 1992; Salisbury and Van Voorhis 2009). A second possible modification would be to consider additional factors for particular subgroups (i.e. culturally-, gender-, or developmentally-*specific factors*). For instance, factors such as racial discrimination (Walsh et al. 2015), ethnic identity (Rivas-Drake et al. 2014), and acculturation (Smokowski et al.2009), have been shown to contribute to offending and violence amongst adolescents from racial and ethnic groups (Shepherd 2015, 2016a), suggesting these factors should be additional considerations in risk assessments. A third possible modification would be to adjust the rating criteria for certain items. For instance, when instruments are applied to youth from collectivist cultures, items pertaining to family disruption or parental supervision may need to be reinterpreted to better align with collectivist parenting philosophies and an emphasis on extended families (Shepherd and Esqueda 2018). Importantly, prior to making such modifications, further research would be needed to determine the viability and need for such an approach. Furthermore, if any modifications are made to tools, it would need to be done systematically and carefully. For instance, if new factors are added, it would necessitate the development of new norms and interpretative guidelines. If rating criteria are adjusted, clear operational definitions would need to be developed, so as to avoid unstructured and unguided judgments.

In addition to testing possible adaptations to tool, researchers could develop and evaluate approaches to increase professionals' understanding of the relevance of culture, gender, and development in risk assessments (Shepherd 2016b), such as training programmes and other initiatives to enhance cultural competence (i.e. ensuring that professionals have knowledge and skills) and cultural safety (i.e. conducting interview-based risk assessments and providing services in a manner that clients' cultural identity is not diminished or disempowered; Kirmayer 2012; Papps and Ramsden 1996). For instance, in countries such as Canada, Australia, New Zealand, and the US, Indigenous populations are overrepresented in the justice system due to a long history of colonization and harmful policies, and resulting social and economic disadvantages (McCaslin and Boyer 2009). It is critical for professionals to understand this history, as it positions risk within broader social and historical contexts rather than attributing 'fault' to individual adolescents.

Protective factors

Many professionals and researchers consider protective factors to be an important component of adolescent risk assessments (Viljoen et al. 2010a). Indeed, compared to adult risk assessment tools, adolescent tools are more likely to include protective factors. The SAVRY, for instance, was amongst the first risk assessment tools for adolescents or adults to include protective factors. Although such tools have greatly advanced our understanding of protective factors, these early measures of protective factors are brief (e.g. 6 items) and use fairly crude ratings (i.e. dichotomous categories; see Table 11.1). As such, there is need for a new generation of protective factors measures that capture a broader range of factors. New tools such as the SAPROF-YV, START:AV, and YASI aim to help address this gap.

However, more pressing than the need for more sophisticated tools, is the need for greater clarity regarding definitions and conceptualizations of protective factors. For instance, are protective factors simply the *strong* end or *protective* end of risk factors (e.g. high school commitment vs. low school commitment; Loeber and Farrington 2012; Lösel and Farrington 2012; Ttofi et al. 2016)? Or do some constructs have only a protective end, with no corresponding risk end? Do protective factors directly reduce risk regardless of a youths' risk level (consistent with a compensatory model, i.e. direct or main effects; Lösel and Farrington 2012; Zimmerman et al. 2013)? Are they especially important in reducing risk for high-risk vs. low-risk youth (consistent with a buffering model, i.e. interaction effect)? Until these conceptual issues are better resolved, the study of protective factors will may be met with some scepticism.

Researchers should also investigate how protective factors can best contribute to risk assessments (e.g. prediction, treatment-planning). Thus far, research indicates that protective factors may not consistently provide incremental validity over risk factors (e.g. Hilterman et al. 2014). However, incremental validity is a high bar to surpass, especially as the SAVRY includes only six protective factors, with four times as many risk factors. Furthermore, even if protective factors do not provide incremental validity or outperform risk factors in predicting re-offending, there may be other reasons to assess protective factors. For instance, research in child clinical psychology suggests that assessing strengths rather than solely deficiencies may enhance treatment engagement (Cox 2006).

Also, protective factors might be important to treatment-planning. As hypothesized by the Risk-Need-Responsivity (RNR) model (Bonta and Andrews 2017), treatment might be more effective when it is tailored to youths' strengths (see Singh et al. 2014b). It could even be argued that assessing protective factors is important from an ethical perspective. Indeed, professional practice guidelines assert that assessing strengths is necessary to providing a balanced perspective of adolescents (e.g. APA Task Force on Evidence-Based Practice for Children and

Adolescents 2008). This may be especially important in the context of risk assessments, as such assessments may create potentially stigmatizing labels that adolescent might carry with them for long periods of time.

Changes in risk

Adolescence is a period of enormous developmental change. As a result, researchers have emphasized the importance of regularly reassessing risk (Vincent et al.2012b). Indeed, there are several reasons why it may be important to routinely reassess risk in adolescents and adults (Viljoen et al. 2017a). According to the *shelf-life* hypothesis, risk assessments may expire over time. Thus, tools may be better at predicting short-term vs. long-term re-offending. According to the *dynamic change* hypothesis, increases in scores may signal a period of heightened re-offending. For instance, if an adolescents' risk level increases from moderate to high this might serve as a warning that the adolescent is more susceptible to re-offend in the immediate future. Finally, according to the *familiarity* hypothesis, assessors may become more familiar with youth at each reassessment, leading to greater accuracy in their predictions. Currently, research on these possibilities is limited. However, one longitudinal study of adolescents on probation failed to find support for any of these hypotheses (Viljoen et al. 2017a). Other adolescent research has suggested that short-term predictions may be more accurate than long-term predictions, consistent with the shelf-life hypothesis (Olver et al. 2012; Worling et al. 2012; see Viljoen et al. 2017a for a review). This suggests a need for further research.

One possible reason why reassessment may not automatically improve predictions is that tools may have limited sensitivity to change, or at least in some contexts. Sensitivity to change is defined as the extent to which a tool is able to detect changes in risk (see Viljoen et al. 2017c). It includes *internal sensitivity* (i.e. whether the score on a tool changes over time) and *external sensitivity* (i.e. whether changes in the score on the tool correspond with an external indicator of change, such as re-offending; Husted et al. 2000; Viljoen et al. 2017c). Importantly, sensitivity is context-dependent, meaning that a tool may be sensitive to change in some contexts but not others (Beaton et al. 2001). Although research is scarce, initial research suggests that the SAVRY and J-SOAP-II capture changes amongst youth in intensive treatment programmes (Viljoen et al. 2017b), suggesting adequate internal sensitivity in this context. However, tools such as the SAVRY and YLS/CMI may be less able to detect short-term change amongst youth on probation receiving the usual services (Viljoen, Shaffer et al. 2017). Research is also mixed as to whether changes in risk predict subsequent changes in offending (i.e. external sensitivity; Clarke et al. 2017; Viljoen et al. 2017a, b). Moreover, contrary to expectations, the SAVRY and YLS/CMI do not appear to be any more sensitive to change than the PCL:YV, nor do the putatively 'dynamic' sections of the SAVRY or YLS/CMI appear to be any more dynamic that the historical factors sections amongst adolescents on probation (Viljoen, Shaffer, et al. 2017).

Thus, more research on tools' sensitivity to change is clearly needed. Beyond evaluating existing approaches for measuring change, researchers should examine possible means by which to enhance the predictive validity of tools (i.e. specifying narrower and clearer time-frames for rating items such as past six months rather than the past year; see Table 11.1). There is also a need for research on trajectories or patterns of change in adolescents, and mechanisms or underlying explanations for these changes (e.g. developmental maturation, treatment, life events).

Risk management and interventions

Predicting that a youth is likely to re-offend has little if any value if nothing is done to manage or address this risk. Thus, in most cases the ultimate purpose of risk assessment is not simply to predict the likelihood of violence, but also to help manage and prevent violence (Douglas et al. 2014; Hart and Logan 2011). By gathering information about a youths' risk factors, protective factors, and likelihood of re-offending, professionals should be better able to tailor interventions accordingly. Specifically, consistent with the RNR model, offenders should receive interventions which are commensurate with their risk level (risk principle), target their criminogenic needs (needs principle), and be delivered in a manner that enhances treatment response (responsivity principle; Andrews and Bonta 2010).

However, it is unclear if risk assessments do, in fact, lead to better risk management efforts. Studies with young offenders indicate that even after youth are assessed via a tool, less than half of the criminogenic needs that are identified are addressed through interventions (e.g. Bonta et al. 2008; Peterson-Badali, Skilling, and Haqanee 2015; Singh et al. 2014b; Vieira et al.2009). Thus, in many cases, youths' treatment needs continue to remain unmet. Furthermore, a sizable proportion of professionals do not apply the results of risk assessments to guide their risk management efforts (Krysik and LeCroy 2002; Shook and Sarri 2007). Instead, some professionals view risk assessment tools as 'just another form' to complete (see Hannah-Moffat et al. 2009).

Whilst some studies have reported more positive results (e.g. Luong and Wormith 2011), overall, findings indicate that although risk assessment tools may be a starting point to risk management, they are not sufficient in and of themselves (Flores et al. 2003; Vincent et al. 2012c). Researchers should, therefore, investigate strategies to help bridge this gap between the theory of risk assessment and real-world practice (Peterson-Badali et al. 2015). In particular, researchers should examine how the implementation of a tool (e.g. amount of training and direction provided to agencies) affects outcomes. Initial research has emphasized that tools may only result in benefits (e.g. better match between risk level and intensity of services) when implemented carefully (Vincent et al. 2016).

In addition, researchers should examine whether providing professionals with further structure, guidance, or training improves the link between risk assessment and risk management. Most risk assessment tools provide very little if any direct guidance on how to apply the tool to develop risk management plans (see Table 11.1). However, just as structure can improve risk assessments, so too might structure improve risk management efforts (Bosker and Witteman 2016). To explore this possibility, researchers have started to develop structured intervention-planning forms (such as those included in the YLS/CMI and START:AV), risk management tools (such as the ARROW), and training programmes (such as Strategic Training in Community Supervision; Bonta et al. 2011; see Chapter 26 by Bourgon et al.).

Conclusions

The field of adolescent risk assessment has progressed rapidly, achieving numerous milestones during the past decade. Rather than relying on adult measures, researchers have designed and/or adapted several tools specifically for adolescents, thereby bringing greater attention to developmental considerations. Researchers have conducted a variety of studies on these tools, thus providing evidence to support their IRR and predictive validity. Moreover, professionals from various disciplines (e.g. psychology, psychiatry) and youth justice agencies (e.g. probation) have widely adopted such measures, thereby helping the field to achieve a higher standard of practise.

However, even with these achievements, in our view, some of the most important and most difficult questions still lay ahead, namely: How can we best ensure that risk assessments are culturally-informed, developmentally-informed, and gender-appropriate? What role should protective factors play in risk assessments? How can we measure changes in risk? And what steps can we take to ensure that the use of risk assessment tools translate into better professional practices and better outcomes for youth? Even though predictive validity studies are still needed, researchers also need to tackle these other questions. Although this will mean moving beyond traditional, file-based predictive validity studies and developing new innovations for research and practice, such efforts may ultimately help to enhance the potential value of risk assessments for court systems, justice and mental health agencies, service providers, and adolescents themselves.

References

Aebi, M., Plattner, B., Steinhausen, H.-C., and Bessler, C. (2011). Predicting sexual and nonsexual recidivism in a consecutive sample of juveniles convicted of sexual offences. *Sexual Abuse: Journal of Research and Treatment* 23: 456–473.

Ægisdóttir, S., White, M.J., Spengler, P.M. et al. (2006). The meta-analysis of clinical judgment project: Fifty-six years of accumulated research on clinical versus statistical prediction. *Counseling Psychologist* 34: 341–382.

Albert, D., Chein, J., and Steinberg, L. (2013). The teenage brain: peer influences on adolescent decision making. *Current Directions in Psychological Science* 22: 114–120.

American Psychological Association (2002). *Developing Adolescents: A Reference for Professionals*. Washington, DC: American Psychological Society.

American Psychological Association Task Force on Evidence-Based Practice for Children and Adolescents (2008). *Disseminating Evidence-based Practice for Children and Adolescents: A Systems Approach to Enhancing Care*. Washington, DC: American Psychological Association.

Andrews, D.A. and Bonta, J. (1995). *Level of Service Inventory-Revised*. Toronto, ON: Multi-Health Systems.

Andrews, D.A. and Bonta, J. (2010). Rehabilitating criminal justice policy and practice. *Psychology, Public Policy, and Law* 16: 39–55. https://doi.org/10.1037/a0018362.

Arnett, J.J. (2000). Emerging adulthood. A theory of development from the late teens through the twenties. *American Psychologist* 55: 469–480.

Asscher, J.J., van Vugt, E.S., Stams, G.J.J.M. et al. (2011). The relationship between juvenile psychopathic traits, delinquency and (violent) recidivism: A meta-analysis. *Journal of Child Psychology and Psychiatry* 52: 1134–1143.

Barnoski, R. (2003). *Changes in Washington State's Jurisdiction of Juvenile Offenders: Examining the Impact*. Olympia, WA: Washington State Institute of Public Policy.

Beaton, D.E., Bombardier, C., Katz, J.N., and Wright, J.G. (2001). A taxonomy for responsiveness. *Journal of Clinical Epidemiology* 54: 1204–1217.

Bhanwer, A., Shaffer, C., and Viljoen, J.L. (2016). *Short-Term Assessment of Risk and Treatability: Adolescent Version (START:AV) Annotated Bibliography*. Burnaby, BC: Simon Fraser University.

Bonta, J. and Andrews, D.A. (2017). *The Psychology of Criminal Conduct*, 6e. New York, NY: Routledge.

Bonta, J., Bourgon, G., Rugge et al. (2011). An experimental demonstration of training probation officers in evidence-based community supervision. *Criminal Justice and Behavior* 38: 1127–1148.

Bonta, J., Rugge, T., Scott, T. et al. (2008). Exploring the black box of community supervision. *Journal of Offender Rehabilitation* 47: 248–270.

Borum, R., Bartel, P., and Forth, A. (2006). *Manual for the Structured Assessment for Violence Risk in Youth (SAVRY)*. Odessa, FL: Psychological Assessment Resources.

Borum, R., Lodewijks, H., Bartel, P.A., and Forth, A.E. (2010). Structured assessment of violence risk in youth (SAVRY). In: *Handbook of Violence Risk Assessment* (eds. K. Douglas and R. Otto), 63–80. New York, NY: Routledge.

Bosker, J. and Witteman, C. (2016). Finding the right focus: improving the link between risk/needs assessment and case management in probation. *Psychology, Public Policy, and Law* 22: 221–233.

Broidy, L.M., Nagin, D.S., Tremblay, R.E. et al. (2003). Developmental trajectories of childhood disruptive behaviors and adolescent delinquency: a six-site, cross-national study. *Developmental Psychology* 39: 222–245.

Caldwell, M.F. and Dickinson, C. (2009). Sex offender registration and recidivism in juvenile sexual offenders. *Behavioral Sciences & the Law* 27: 941–956.

Casey, B.J., Jones, R.M., and Somerville, L.H. (2011). Braking and accelerating of the adolescent brain. *Journal of Research on Adolescence* 21: 21–33.

Catchpole, R.E.H. and Gretton, H.M. (2003). The predictive validity of risk assessment with violent young offenders: a 1 year examination of criminal outcome. *Criminal Justice & Behavior* 30: 688–708.

Cauffman, E., Kimonis, E.R., Dmitrieva, J., and Monahan, K.C. (2009). A multimethod assessment of juvenile psychopathy: comparing the predictive utility of the PCL:YV, YPI, and NEO PRI. *Psychological Assessment* 21: 528–542.

Cauffman, E., Skeem, J., Dmitrieva, J., and Cavanagh, C. (2016). Comparing the stability of psychopathy scores in adolescents versus adults: how often is "fledgling psychopathy" misdiagnosed? *Psychopathy, Public Policy, and Law* 22: 77–91.

Chesney-Lind, M., Morash, M., and Stevens, T. (2008). Girls troubles, girls' delinquency, and gender responsive programming: a review. *Australian & New Zealand Journal of Criminology* 41: 162–189.

Chu, C.M., Lee, Y., Zeng, G. et al. (2015). Assessing youth offenders in a non-Western context: the predictive validity of the YLS/CMI ratings. *Psychological Assessment* 27: 1013–1021.

Chu, C.M., Ng, K., Fong, J., and Teoh, J. (2012). Assessing youth who sexually offended: the predictive validity of the ERASOR, J-SOAP-II, and YLS/CMI in a non-western context. *Sexual Abuse: A Journal of Research and Treatment* 24: 153–174.

Cicchetti, D.V. (1994). Guidelines, criteria, and rules of thumb for evaluating normed and standardized assessment instruments in psychology. *Psychological Assessment* 6: 284–290.

Clarke, M.C., Peterson-Badali, M., and Skilling, T. (2017). The relationship between changes in dynamic risk factors and the predictive validity of risk assessments among youth offenders. *Criminal Justice and Behavior* 44: 1340–1355.

Côté, S.M., Vaillancourt, T., LeBlanc, J.C. et al. (2006). The development of physical aggression from toddlerhood to pre-adolescence: a nation wide longitudinal study of Canadian children. *Journal of Abnormal Child Psychology* 34: 71–85.

Cox, K.F. (2006). Investigating the impact of strength-based assessment on youth with emotional or behavioral disorders. *Journal of Child and Family Studies* 15: 287–301.

Daly, K. (1992). Women's pathway to felony court: feminist theories of law-breaking and problems of representation. *Review of Law and Women's Studies* 2: 11–52.

de Vogel, V., de Vries Robbé, M., de Ruiter, C., and Bouman, Y.A. (2011). Assessing protective factors in forensic psychiatric practice: introducing the SAPROF. *The International Journal of Forensic Mental Health* 10: 171–177.

de Vries Robbé, M., Geers, M., Stapel, M. et al. (2015). *SAPROF Youth Version: Guidelines for the Assessment of Protective Factors for Violence Risk in Juveniles* (English version). Utrecht, NL: Forum Educatief.

de Vries Robbé, M., Veldhuizen, A., Vullings, K. et al. (2017). *Protective factors for juvenile and young adult boys and girls*. Manuscript submitted for publication.

Dmitrieva, J., Monahan, K.C., Cauffman, E., and Steinberg, L. (2012). Arrested development: the effects of incarceration on the development of psychosocial maturity. *Development and Psychopathology* 24: 1073–1090.

Douglas, K.S., Hart, S.D., Groscup, J.L., and Litwack, T.R. (2014). Assessing violence risk. In: *The Handbook of Forensic Psychology*, 4e (eds. I.B. Weiner and R.K. Otto), 385–441. Hoboken, NJ: Wiley.

Douglas, K.S., Hart, S.D., Webster, C.D., and Belfrage, H. (2013). *Historical, Clinical, Risk Management (Version 3): Professional Guidelines for Evaluating Risk of Violence.* Burnaby, BC: Mental Health, Law, and Policy Institute.

Douglas, K.S., Skeem, J.L., and Nicholson, E. (2011). Research methods in violence risk assessment. In: *Research Methods in Forensic Psychology* (eds. B. Rosenfeld, S.D. Penrod, B. Rosenfeld and S.D. Penrod), 325–346. Hoboken, NJ: Wiley.

Edens, J.F. and Campbell, J.S. (2007). Identifying youths at risk for institutional misconduct: a meta-analytic investigation of the psychopathy checklist measures. *Psychological Services* 4: 13–27.

Edens, J.F., Campbell, J.S., and Weir, J.M. (2007). Youth psychopathy and criminal recidivism: a meta-analysis of the psychopathy checklist measures. *Law and Human Behavior* 31: 53–75.

Edens, J.F. and Vincent, G.M. (2008). Juvenile psychopathy: a clinical construct in need of restraint? *Journal of Forensic Psychology Practice* 8: 186–197.

Fanniff, A.M. and Letourneau, E.J. (2012). Another piece of the puzzle: psychometric properties of the J-SOAP-II. *Sexual Abuse: A Journal of Research and Treatment* 24: 378–408.

Flores, A.W., Travis, L.F., and Latessa, E.J. (2003). *Case Classification for Juvenile Corrections: An Assessment of the Youth Level of Service/Case Management Inventory (YLS/CMI): Final report.* Washington, DC: National Institute of Justice.

Forth, A.E., Kosson, D.S., and Hare, R.D. (2003). *Hare Psychopathy Checklist: Youth Version.* Toronto, ON: Multi-Health Systems.

Gammelgård, M., Koivisto, A., Eronen, M., and Kaltiala-Heino, R. (2008). The predictive validity of the Structured Assessment of Violence Risk in Youth (SAVRY) among institutionalised adolescents. *Journal of Forensic Psychiatry & Psychology* 19: 352–370.

Grove, W.M. and Meehl, P.E. (1996). Comparative efficiency of informal (subjective, impressionistic) and formal (mechanical, algorithmic) prediction procedures: the clinical–statistical controversy. *Psychology, Public Policy, and Law* 2: 293–323.

Hannah-Moffat, K., Maurutto, P., and Turnbull, S. (2009). Negotiated risk: actuarial illusions and discretion in probation. *Canadian Journal of Law and Society* 24: 391–409.

Hare, R. (2003). *Manual for the Hare Psychopathy Checklist – Revised*, 2e. Toronto, ON: Multi-Health Systems.

Hart, S.D. (2016). Culture and violence risk assessment: the case of Ewert v. Canada. *Journal of Threat Assessment and Management* 3: 76–96.

Hart, S.D. and Logan, C. (2011). Formulation of violence risk using evidence-based assessments: the structured professional judgment approach. In: *Forensic Case Formulation* (eds. P. Sturmey and M. McMurran), 83–106. Chichester, UK: Wiley.

Hawes, S.W., Mulvey, E.P., Schubert, C.A., and Pardini, D.A. (2014). Structural coherence and temporal stability of psychopathic personality features during emerging adulthood. *Journal of Abnormal Psychology* 123: 623–633.

Hempel, I., Buck, N., Cima, M., and van Marle, H. (2013). Review of risk assessment instruments for juvenile sex offenders: what is next? *International Journal of Offender Therapy and Comparative Criminology* 57: 208–228.

Hemphala, M., Kosson, D., Westerman, J., and Hodgins, S. (2015). Stability and predictors of psychopathic traits from mid-adolescence through early adulthood. *Personality and Social Psychology* 56: 649–658.

Henggeler, S.W. (2016). Community-based interventions for juvenile offenders. In: *APA Handbook of Psychology and Juvenile Justice* (eds. K. Heilbrun, D. DeMatteo and N.S. Goldstein), 575–595. Washington, DC: American Psychological Association.

Hilterman, E.B., Nicholls, T.L., and van Nieuwenhuizen, C. (2014). Predictive validity of risk assessments in juvenile offenders: comparing the SAVRY, PCL:YV, and YLS/CMI with unstructured clinical assessments. *Assessment* 21: 324–339.

Hirschi, T. and Gottfredson, M. (1983). Age and the explanation of crime. *American Journal of Sociology* 89: 552–584.

Hoagwood, K., Burns, B.J., Kiser, L. et al. (2001). Evidence-based practice in child and adolescent mental health services. *Psychiatric Services* 52: 1179–1189.

Hoeve, M., Dubas, J.S., Eichelsheim, V.I. et al. (2009). The relationship between parenting and delinquency: a meta-analysis. *Journal of Abnormal Child Psychology* 37: 749–775.

Hoge, R.D. and Andrews, D.A. (2002). *The Youth Level of Service/Case Management Inventory Manual and Scoring Key*. Toronto, ON: Multi-Health Systems.

Hoge, R.D. and Andrews, D.A. (2011). *Youth Level of Service/Case Management Inventory 2.0 (YLS/CMI 2.0): User's Manual*. Toronto, ON: Multi-Health Systems.

Husted, J.A., Cook, R.J., Farewell, V.T., and Gladman, D.D. (2000). Methods for assessing responsiveness: a critical review and recommendations. *Journal of Clinical Epidemiology* 53: 459–468.

Jones, N.J., Brown, S.L., Robinson, D., and Frey, D. (2016). Validity of the youth assessment and screening instrument: a juvenile justice tool incorporating risks, needs, and strengths. *Law and Human Behavior* 40: 182–194.

Jones, S., Cauffman, E., Miller, J.D., and Mulvey, E. (2006). Investigating different factor structures of the psychopathy checklist: youth version: confirmatory factor analytic findings. *Psychological Assessment* 18: 33–48.

Kennealy, P.J., Skeem, J.L., and Hernandez, I.R. (2017). Does staff see what experts see? Accuracy of front line staff in scoring juveniles' risk factors. *Psychological Assessment* 29: 26–34.

Kerig, P.K. and Schindler, S.R. (2013). Engendering the evidence base: a critical review of the conceptual and empirical foundations of gender-responsive interventions for girls' delinquency. *Laws* 2: 244–282.

Kirmayer, L.J. (2012). Rethinking cultural competence. *Transcultural Psychiatry* 49 (2): 149–164.

Kosson, D.S., Neumann, C.S., Forth, A.E. et al. (2013). Factor structure of the Hare Psychopathy Checklist: Youth Version (PCL:YV) in adolescent females. *Psychological Assessment* 25: 71–83.

Krysik, J. and LeCroy, C.W. (2002). The empirical validation of an instrument to predict risk of recidivism among juvenile offenders. *Research on Social Work Practice* 12: 71–81.

Lambie, I. and Randell, I. (2013). The impact of incarceration on juvenile offenders. *Clinical Psychology Review* 33: 448–459.

Landenberger, N.A. and Lipsey, M.W. (2005). The positive effects of cognitive-behavioral programs for offenders: a meta-analysis of factors associated with effective treatment. *Journal of Experimental Criminology* 1: 451–476.

Larson, R.W., Richards, M.H., Moneta, G. et al. (1996). Changes in adolescents' daily interactions with their families from ages 10 to 18: disengagement and transformation. *Developmental Psychology* 32: 744–754.

Lipsey, M.W. and Derzon, J.H. (1998). Predictors of violent or serious delinquency in adolescence and early adulthood: a synthesis of longitudinal research. In: *Serious & Violent Juvenile Offenders: Risk Factors and Successful Interventions* (eds. R. Loeber and D.P. Farrington), 86–105. Thousand Oaks, CA: Sage.

Lodewijks, H.P.B., de Ruiter, C., and Doreleijers, T.A.H. (2010). The impact of protective factors in desistance from violent reoffending: a study in three samples of adolescent offenders. *Journal of Interpersonal Violence* 25: 568–587.

Loeber, R. and Farrington, D.P. (2012). Advancing knowledge about direct protective factors that may reduce youth violence. *American Journal of Preventive Medicine* 43 (2, Suppl. 1): S24–S27.

Lösel, F. and Farrington, D.P. (2012). Direct protective and buffering protective factors in the development of youth violence. *American Journal of Preventive Medicine* 43 (2, Suppl. 1): S8.

Luong, D. and Wormith, J.S. (2011). Applying risk/need assessment to probation practice and its impact on the recidivism of young offenders. *Criminal Justice and Behavior* 38: 1177–1199.

Manders, W.A., Deković, M., Asscher, J.J. et al. (2013). Psychopathy as predictor and moderator of multisystemic therapy outcomes among adolescents treated for antisocial behavior. *Journal of Abnormal Child Psychology* 41 (7): 1121–1132.

Martinez, R., Flores, J., and Rosenfeld, B. (2007). Validity of the Juvenile Sex Offender Assessment Protocol-II (J-SOAP-II) in a sample of urban minority youth. *Criminal Justice and Behavior* 34: 1284–1295.

McCaslin, W.D. and Boyer, Y. (2009). First Nations communities at risk and in crisis: justice and security. *Journal of Aboriginal Health* 5 (3): 61–87.

McGowan, M.R., Horn, R.A., and Mellott, R.N. (2011). The predictive validity of the Structured Assessment of Violence Risk in Youth in secondary educational settings. *Psychological Assessment* 23: 478–486.

Menzies, R.J., Webster, C.D., and Sepejak, D.S. (1985). Hitting the forensic sound barrier: predictions of dangerousness in a pre-trial psychiatric clinic. In: *Dangerousness: Probability and Prediction, Psychiatry and Public Policy* (eds. C.D. Webster, M.H. Ben-Aron and S.J. Hucker), 115–143. New York, NY: Cambridge University Press.

Moffitt, T.E., Caspi, A., Harrington, H., and Milne, B.J. (2002). Males on the life-course-persistent and adolescence-limited antisocial pathways: follow-up at age 26 years. *Development and Psychopathology* 14: 179–207.

Nagin, D. and Tremblay, R.E. (1999). Trajectories of boys' physical aggression, opposition, and hyperactivity on the path to physically violent and nonviolent juvenile delinquency. *Child Development* 70: 1181–1196.

Neumann, C.S., Kosson, D.S., Forth, A.E., and Hare, R.D. (2006). Factor structure of the Hare Psychopathy Checklist: Youth Version (PCL:YV) in incarcerated adolescents. *Psychological Assessment* 18: 142–154.

Odgers, C.L., Moretti, M.M., and Reppucci, N.D. (2005). Examining the science and practice of violence risk assessment with female adolescents. *Law and Human Behavior* 29: 7–27.

Olver, M.E., Stockdale, K.C., and Wong, S.P. (2012). Short and long-term prediction of recidivism using the youth level of service/case management inventory in a sample of serious young offenders. *Law and Human Behavior* 36: 331–344.

Olver, M.E., Stockdale, K.C., and Wormith, J.S. (2009). Risk assessment with young offenders: a meta-analysis of three assessment measures. *Criminal Justice and Behavior* 36: 329–353.

Olver, M.E., Stockdale, K.C., and Wormith, J.S. (2014). Thirty years of research on the level of service scales: a meta-analytic examination of predictive accuracy and sources of variability. *Psychological Assessment* 26: 156–176.

Orbis Partners (2000). *Youth Assessment Screening Inventory (YASI)*. Ottawa, ON: Author.

Papps, E. and Ramsden, I. (1996). Cultural safety in nursing: the New Zealand experience. *International Journal for Quality in Health Care* 8: 491–497.

Penney, S.R., Lee, Z., and Moretti, M.M. (2010). Gender differences in risk factors for violence: an examination of the predictive validity of the Structured Assessment of Violence Risk in Youth. *Aggressive Behavior* 36: 390–404.

Penney, S.R. and Moretti, M.M. (2007). The relation of psychopathy to concurrent aggression and antisocial behavior in high-risk adolescent girls and boys. *Behavioral Sciences & the Law* 25: 21–41.

Peterson-Badali, M., Skilling, T., and Haqanee, Z. (2015). Examining implementation of risk assessment in case management for youth in the justice system. *Criminal Justice and Behavior* 42: 304–320.

Piquero, A.R., Gonzalez, J.R., and Jennings, W.G. (2015). Developmental trajectories and antisocial behavior over the life-course. In: *The Development of Criminal and Antisocial Behavior: Theory, Research and Practical Applications* (eds. J. Morizot and L. Kazemian), 75–88. Cham, CH: Springer International Publishing.

Prentky, R.A., Li, N., Righthand, S. et al. (2010). Assessing risk of sexually abusive behavior among youth in a child welfare sample. *Behavioral Sciences & The Law* 28: 24–45.

Prentky, R.A. and Righthand, S. (2003). *Juvenile Sex Offender Assessment Protocol II (J-SOAP-II) Manual*. Washington, DC: U.S. Department of Justice, Office of Justice Programs, Office of Juvenile Justice and Delinquency Prevention.

Prochaska, J.O., DiClemente, C.C., and Norcross, J.C. (1992). In search of how people change: applications to addictive behaviors. *American Psychologist* 47: 1102–1114.

Pusch, N. and Holtfreter, K. (2017). Gender and risk assessment in juvenile offenders: a meta-analysis. *Criminal Justice and Behavior* 45: 56–81.

Rajlic, G. and Gretton, H.M. (2010). An examination of two sexual recidivism risk measures in adolescent offenders: the moderating effect of offender type. *Criminal Justice and Behavior* 37: 1066–1085.

Rice, M.E. and Harris, G.T. (2005). Comparing effect sizes in follow-up studies: ROC Area, Cohen's d, and r. *Law and Human Behavior* 29 (5): 615–620.

Rivas-Drake, D., Syed, M., Umaña-Taylor, A. et al. (2014). Feeling good, happy, and proud: a meta-analysis of positive ethnic–racial affect and adjustment. *Child Development* 85: 77–102.

Roisman, G.I., Monahan, K.C., Campbell, S.B. et al. (2010). Is adolescence-onset antisocial behavior developmentally normative? *Development and Psychopathology* 22: 295–311.

Salisbury, E.J. and Van Voorhis, P. (2009). Gendered pathways: a quantitative investigation of women probationers' paths to incarceration. *Criminal Justice and Behavior* 36: 541–566.

Schmidt, F., Campbell, M.A., and Houlding, C. (2011). Comparative analyses of the YLS/CMI, SAVRY, and PCL:YV in adolescent offenders: a 10-year follow-up into adulthood. *Youth Violence and Juvenile Justice* 9: 23–42.

Seagrave, D. and Grisso, T. (2002). Adolescent development and the measurement of juvenile psychopathy. *Law and Human Behavior* 26: 219–239.

Shaffer, C., McCuish, E., Corrado, R.R. et al. (2015). Psychopathy and violent misconduct in a sample of violent young offenders. *Journal of Criminal Justice* 43: 321–326.

Shepherd, S. and Strand, S. (2016). The PCL:YV and re-offending across ethnic groups. *Journal of Criminal Psychology* 6: 51–62.

Shepherd, S.M. (2015). Finding color in conformity: A commentary on culturally specific risk factors for violence in Australia. *International Journal of Offender Therapy & Comparative Criminology* 59: 1297–1307.

Shepherd, S.M. (2016a). Criminal engagement and Australian culturally and linguistically diverse populations: challenges and implications for forensic risk assessment. *Psychiatry, Psychology and Law* 23: 256–274.

Shepherd, S.M. (2016b). Violence risk instruments may be culturally unsafe for use with indigenous patients. *Australasian Psychiatry* 24: 565–567.

Shepherd, S.M., Adams, Y., McEntyre, E., and Walker, R. (2014). Violence risk assessment in Australian Aboriginal offender populations: a review of the literature. *Psychology, Public Policy, and Law* 20: 281–293.

Shepherd, S.M. and Esqueda, C.W. (2018). Indigenous perspectives on violence risk assessment – a thematic analysis. *Punishment & Society* 20: 599–627.

Shepherd, S.M. and Lewis-Fernandez, R. (2016). Forensic risk assessment and cultural diversity – contemporary challenges and future directions. *Psychology, Public Policy, and Law* 22: 427–438.

Shepherd, S.M., Luebbers, S., Ferguson, M. et al. (2014). The utility of the SAVRY across ethnicity in Australian young offenders. *Psychology, Public Policy, and Law* 20: 31–45.

Shepherd, S.M., Luebbers, S., and Ogloff, J.P. (2014). Are youth violence risk instruments interchangeable? Evaluating instrument convergence in a sample of incarcerated adolescent offenders. *Journal of Forensic Psychology Practice* 14: 317–341.

Shepherd, S.M., Singh, J.P., and Fullam, R. (2015). Does the youth level of service/case management inventory generalize across ethnicity? *International Journal of Forensic Mental Health* 14: 193–204.

Shepherd, S.M. and Strand, S. (2015). The utility of the Psychopathy Checklist: Youth Version (PCL: YV) and the Youth Psychopathic Trait Inventory (YPI) – is it meaningful to measure psychopathy in young offenders? *Psychological Assessment* 28: 405–415.

Sher, M., Warner, L., McLean, A. et al. (2017). A prospective validation study of the START:AV. *Journal of Forensic Practice* 19: 115–129.

Shook, J.J. and Sarri, R.C. (2007). Structured decision making in juvenile justice: judges' and probation officers' perceptions and use. *Children and Youth Services Review* 29: 1335–1351.

Shulman, E.P., Smith, A.R., Silva, K. et al. (2016). The dual systems model: review, reappraisal, and reaffirmation. *Developmental Cognitive Neuroscience* 17: 103–117.

Singh, J.P., Desmarais, S.L., Hurducas, C. et al. (2014a). International perspectives on the practical application of violence risk assessment: a global survey of 44 countries. *International Journal of Forensic Mental Health* 13: 193–206.

Singh, J.P., Desmarais, S.L., Sellers, B.G. et al. (2014b). From risk assessment to risk management: matching interventions to adolescent offenders' strengths and vulnerabilities. *Children and Youth Services Review* 47: 1–9.

Singh, J.P., Grann, M., and Fazel, S. (2011). A comparative study of violence risk assessment tools: a systematic review and metaregression analysis of 68 studies involving 25,980 participants. *Clinical Psychology Review* 31: 499–513.

Skeem, J.L. and Monahan, J. (2011). Current directions in violence risk assessment. *Current Directions in Psychological Science* 20 (1): 38–42.

Smith, A.R., Chein, J., and Steinberg, L. (2014). Peers increase adolescent risk taking even when the probabilities of negative outcomes are known. *Developmental Psychology* 50: 1564–1568.

Smokowski, P.R., David-Ferdon, C., and Stroupe, N. (2009). Acculturation and violence in minority adolescents: a review of the empirical literature. *Journal of Primary Prevention* 30: 215–263.

Steinberg, L. (2010). Commentary: a behavioral scientist looks at the science of adolescent brain development. *Brain and Cognition* 72: 160–164.

Steinberg, L. (2014). *Age of Opportunity: Lessons from the New Science of Adolescence*. Boston, MA: Houghton Mifflin Harcourt.

Steinberg, L., Graham, S., O'Brien, L. et al. (2009). Age differences in future orientation and delay discounting. *Child Development* 80: 28–44.

Steinberg, L. and Monahan, K.C. (2007). Age differences in resistance to peer influence. *Developmental Psychology* 43: 1531–1543.

Stockdale, K.C., Olver, M.E., and Wong, S.P. (2014). The validity and reliability of the Violence Risk Scale–Youth Version in a diverse sample of violent young offenders. *Criminal Justice and Behavior* 41: 114–138.

Strand, S., Luebbers, S., and Shepherd, S.M. (2016). Psychopathic features in young incarcerated females. *Journal of Criminal Psychology* 6: 63–75.

Sweeten, G., Piquero, A.R., and Steinberg, L. (2013). Age and the explanation of crime, revisited. *Journal of Youth and Adolescence* 42: 921–938.

Tremblay, R.E. (2006). Prevention of youth violence: why not start at the beginning? *Journal of Abnormal Child Psychology* 34: 481–487.

Tsang, S., Schmidt, K.M., Vincent, G.M. et al. (2015). Assessing psychopathy among justice involved adolescents with the PCL:YV: an item response theory examination across gender. *Personality Disorders: Theory, Research, and Treatment* 6: 22–31.

Ttofi, M.M., Farrington, D.P., Piquero, A.R., and DeLisi, M. (2016). Protective factors against offending and violence: results from prospective longitudinal studies. *Journal of Criminal Justice* 45: 1–3.

Vieira, T.A., Skilling, T.A., and Peterson-Badali, M. (2009). Matching court-ordered services with treatment needs: predicting treatment success with young offenders. *Criminal Justice and Behavior* 36: 385–401.

Viljoen, J.L., Beneteau, J.L., Gulbransen, E. et al. (2012a). Assessment of multiple risk outcomes, strengths, and change with the START:AV: a short-term prospective study with adolescent offenders. *International Journal of Forensic Mental Health* 11: 165–180.

Viljoen, J.L., Brodersen, E., Shaffer, C. et al. (2014a). *Adolescent Risk Reduction and Resilient Outcomes Work-Plan*. Burnaby, BC: Simon Fraser University.

Viljoen, J.L., Cruise, K.R., Nicholls, T.L. et al. (2012b). Taking stock and taking steps: the case for an adolescent version of the short-term assessment of risk and treatability. *International Journal of Forensic Mental Health* 11 (3): 135–149.

Viljoen, J.L., Elkovitch, N., Scalora, M.J., and Ullman, D. (2009). Assessment of reoffense risk in adolescents who have committed sexual offenses: predictive validity of the ERASOR, PCL:YV, YLS/CMI, and Static-99. *Criminal Justice and Behavior* 36: 981–1000.

Viljoen, J.L., Gray, A.L., and Barone, C. (2016a). Assessing risk for violence and offending in adolescents. In: *Learning Forensic Assessment* (eds. R. Jackson and R. Roesch), 357–388. New York, NY: Routledge.

Viljoen, J.L., Gray, A.L., Shaffer, C. et al. (2017a). Does reassessment of risk improve predictions? A framework and examination of the SAVRY and YLS/CMI. *Psychological Assessment* 29 (9): 1096–1110.

Viljoen, J.L., Gray, A.L., Shaffer, C. et al. (2017b). Changes in J-SOAP-II and SAVRY scores over the course of residential, cognitive-behavioral treatment for adolescent sexual offending. *Sexual Abuse: Journal of Research And Treatment* 29 (4): 342–374.

Viljoen, J.L., MacDougall, E.A.M., Gagnon, N.C., and Douglas, K.S. (2010a). Psychopathy evidence in legal proceedings involving adolescent offenders. *Psychology, Public Policy, and Law* 16: 254–283.

Viljoen, J.L., McLachlan, K., and Vincent, G.M. (2010b). Assessing violence risk and psychopathy in juvenile and adult offenders: a survey of clinical practices. *Assessment* 17: 377–395.

Viljoen, J.L., Mordell, S., and Beneteau, J.L. (2012c). Prediction of adolescent sexual reoffending: a meta-analysis of the J-SOAP-II, ERASOR, J-SORRAT-II, and Static-99. *Law and Human Behavior* 36: 423–438.

Viljoen, J.L., Nicholls, T.L., Cruise, K.R. et al. (2014b). *Short-Term Assessment of Risk and Treatability: Adolescent Version (START:AV) – User Guide*. Burnaby, BC: Mental Health, Law, and Policy Institute.

Viljoen, J.L., Nicholls, T.L., Cruise, K.R. et al. (2016b). *START:AV knowledge guide: a Research Compendium on the START:AV Strength and Vulnerability Items*. Burnaby, BC: Simon Fraser University.

Viljoen, J.L., Scalora, M., Cuadra, L. et al. (2008). Assessing risk for violence in adolescents who have sexually offended: a comparison of the J-SOAP-II, J-SORRAT-II, and SAVRY. *Criminal Justice and Behavior* 35: 5–23.

Viljoen, J.L., Shaffer, C.S., Gray, A.L., and Douglas, K.S. (2017c). Are adolescent risk assessment tools sensitive to change? A framework and examination of the SAVRY and the YLS/CMI. *Law And Human Behavior* 41 (3): 244–257.

Vincent, G.M., Chapman, J., and Cook, N.E. (2011). Risk-needs assessment in juvenile justice: predictive validity of the SAVRY, racial differences, and the contribution of needs factors. *Criminal Justice & Behavior* 38: 42–62.

Vincent, G.M., Guy, L.S., Gershenson, B.G., and McCabe, P. (2012a). Does risk assessment make a difference? Results of implementing the SAVRY in juvenile probation. *Behavioral Sciences & The Law* 30: 384–405.

Vincent, G.M., Guy, L.S. and Grisso, T. (2012b). Risk assessment in juvenile justice: A guidebook for implementation. Models for Change. http://njjn.org/uploads/digital-library/Risk_Assessment_in_Juvenile_Justice_A_Guidebook_for_Implementation.pdf (Accessed 15 August 2019).

Vincent, G.M., Guy, L.S., Perrault, R.T., and Gershenson, B. (2016). Risk assessment matters, but only when implemented well: a multisite study in juvenile probation. *Law and Human Behavior* 40: 683–696.

Vincent, G.M., Odgers, C.L., McCormick, A.V., and Corrado, R.R. (2008). The PCL: YV and recidivism in male and female juveniles: a follow-up into young adulthood. *International Journal of Law and Psychiatry* 31: 287–296.

Vincent, G.M., Paiva-Salisbury, M.L., Cook, N.E. et al. (2012c). Impact of risk/needs assessment on juvenile probation officers' decision making: importance of implementation. *Psychology, Public Policy, and Law* 18: 549–576.

Vincent, G.M., Perrault, R.T., Guy, L.S., and Gershenson, B.G. (2012d). Developmental issues in risk assessment: implications for juvenile justice. *Victims and Offenders* 7 (4): 364–384.

Vincent, G.M., Terry, A.M., and Maney, S.M. (2009). Risk/needs tools for antisocial behavior and violence among youthful populations. In: *Handbook of Violence Risk Assessment and Treatment: New Approaches for Mental Health Professionals* (ed. J.T. Andrade), 337–424. New York, NY: Springer.

Wachter, A. (2015). Statewide risk assessment in juvenile probation. Pittsburgh, PA: National Center for Juvenile Justice. *Juvenile Justice: Geography, Policy, Practice & Statistics* (July), 1–4.

Walsh, S.D., Fogel-Grinvald, H., and Shneider, S. (2015). Discrimination and ethnic identity as predictors of substance use and delinquency among immigrant adolescents from the FSU and Ethiopia in Israel. *Journal of Cross-Cultural Psychology* 46: 942–963.

Walters, G.D. (2014). Predicting self-reported total, aggressive, and income offending with the youth version of the psychopathy checklist: gender-and factor-level interactions. *Psychological Assessment* 26: 288–298.

Webster, C.D., Martin, M., Brink, J. et al. (2009). *Manual for the Short Term Assessment of Risk and Treatability (START) (Version 1.1)*. Coquitlam, BC: British Columbia Mental Health & Addiction Services.

Welsh, J.L., Schmidt, F., McKinnon, L. et al. (2008). A comparative study of adolescent risk assessment instruments. *Assessment* 15: 104–115.

Wong, S. and Gordon, A. (2009). *Manual for the Violence Risk Scale*. Saskatoon, Saskatchewan, Canada: University of Saskatchewan.

Wong, S., Lewis, K., Stockdale, K., and Gordon, A. (2004–2011). *The Violence Risk Scale-Youth Version*. Saskatoon, SK: University of Saskatchewan.

Worling, J.R. (2004). The Estimate of Risk of Adolescent Sexual Offense Recidivism (ERASOR): preliminary psychometric data. *Sexual Abuse: A Journal of Research and Treatment* 16: 235–254.

Worling, J.R. (2013). Desistence for Adolescents who Sexually Harm (DASH-13). http://www.drjamesworling.com/uploads/8/7/7/6/8776493/dash-13_2013.pdf (Accessed 15 August 2019).

Worling, J.R., Bookalam, D., and Litteljohn, A. (2012). Prospective validity of the Estimate of Risk of Adolescent Sexual Offense Recidivism (ERASOR). *Sexual Abuse: A Journal of Research and Treatment* 24: 203–223.

Worling, J.R. and Curwen, T. (2001). *Estimate of Risk of Adolescent Sexual Offense Recidivism, Version 2.0*. Toronto, ON: Ontario Ministry of Community and Social Services.

Wynn, R., Hoiseth, M.H., and Pettersen, G. (2012). Psychopathy in women: theoretical and clinical perspectives. *International Journal of Women's Health* 4: 257–263.

Youth Criminal Justice Act 2002, (S.C. c. 1).

Zeng, G., Chu, C.M., Koh, L.L., and Teoh, J. (2014). Risk and criminogenic needs of youth who sexually offended in Singapore: an examination of two typologies. *Sexual Abuse* 27 (5): 479–495, Advance online publication.

Zeng, G., Chu, C.M., and Lee, Y. (2015). Assessing protective factors of youth who sexually offended in Singapore: preliminary evidence on the utility of the DASH-13 and the SAPROF. *Sexual Abuse: A Journal of Research and Treatment* 27 (1): 91–108.

Zimmerman, M.A., Stoddard, S.A., Eisman, A.B. et al. (2013). Adolescent resilience: promotive factors that inform prevention. *Child Development Perspectives* 7 (4): 215–220.

Part III
What Works in Specialty Clinical Assessments

12

The Importance of Understanding Anger in the Clinical Assessment of Violence

Andrew Day[1] and Ephrem Fernandez[2]

[1] University of Melbourne, Melbourne, Australia
[2] University of Texas at San Antonio, San Antonio, USA

Introduction

Towards the close of the last century two youths in the US, Eric Harris and Dylan Kleibold, were admitted to a juvenile diversion programme. Although the programme identified anger as a problem that required attention (Officer.com 2016), they were both released within a couple of weeks, after which they continued to vent their anger on websites. And then, on April 20, 1999, they committed a mass shooting and bombing at Columbine High School, causing 13 fatalities and almost twice that number of injuries. The pair had committed what was the deadliest school shooting in American history. This tragedy highlights how the experience of anger has the potential to influence aggressive and violent behaviour and, we hope, highlights the importance of comprehensively reviewing anger in any clinical assessment. This comes from an understanding that anger is often a key risk factor for violence; not only because it is a common antecedent to aggression (Novaco et al. 2001) but also because it is treatable and thus there is the potential to reduce the occurrence of the range of negative outcomes that are related to aggression and violence. In fact, there is robust evidence that the cognitive-behavioural treatment of anger does lead to reliable clinical improvement (see Deffenbacher et al. 2002; Fernandez et al. 2018a), with observable effects evident on post-treatment measures of both aggression (DiGiuseppe and Tafrate 2003) and violent re-offending (Serin et al. 2013). It comes as no surprise then, that items relating to anger feature in most contemporary structured violence risk assessment tools, including the Historical-Clinical-Risk Management-20 version 3 (HCR-20v3; Douglas et al. 2013) and the Violence Risk Scale (VRS; Wong and Gordon 1999). And yet, in this chapter we propose that there are good reasons to think very carefully about how to best assess anger and how to

The Wiley Handbook of What Works in Violence Risk Management: Theory, Research and Practice,
First Edition. Edited by J. Stephen Wormith, Leam A. Craig, and Todd E. Hogue.
© 2020 John Wiley & Sons Ltd. Published 2020 by John Wiley & Sons Ltd.

interpret the meaning and relevance of test results. We suggest, as many others have, that anger is neither a necessary nor a sufficient condition for either aggression or violence to occur and that careful and comprehensive assessment will always be required if we are to understand how anger is associated with an increased risk of violence in the particular individual being assessed. Our approach is simple: to review some of the assumptions that are occasionally made about both the association between anger and violence and the stereotypes that are sometimes held about violent offenders. We then consider some of the approaches that are currently used to assess anger. We conclude that a careful and individualized assessment will always be required if good decision-making is to follow.

Assumptions About Anger

Assumption 1: Getting angry is always a bad thing

It is sometimes assumed that feeling angry is always unhelpful or unhealthy, particularly in those who have acted violently in the past. And yet, it is also clear that anger is a normal and, often, functional emotion that serves to mobilize psychological resources, energize behaviour, and protect self-esteem (Taylor and Novaco 2005). Over 30 years ago now, Averill (1983) clearly demonstrated that anger is part and parcel of everyday life. His studies revealed that two thirds of people report becoming angry one to two times during the week (although this figure rises to seven experiences of anger over a week when daily records are kept). Averill also reported that anger is typically quite intense; when respondents were asked to rate the intensity of their anger on a 10-point Likert scale (ranging from 'very mild' to 'very intense – as angry as most people ever become'), the mean rating was 7.1 with the majority (79%) of all responses falling above the scale midpoint. In addition, one in five people reported that their anger lasted for more than one day (although the median duration of anger was one hour), and their responses were equally aggressive (verbal and/or physical responses) and non-aggressive (e.g. talking calmly or engaging in calming activities). The important point to take from Averill's work is not only that anger is an emotion that is frequently experienced in the normal population, but also that is often quite intense and commonly associated with aggressive behaviour – even though the aggression reported in Averill's studies was not of the type that would be considered to be violent in a clinical or criminal justice context.

Whilst feeling angry is a normal human experience, it is also potentially healthy. Understanding the difference between functional and dysfunctional anger is always going to be important. By the *Diagnostic and Statistical Manual for Mental Disorders – Fifth Edition* (DSM-5; APA, 2013) definition of mental disorder, for example, anger should be considered to be a disorder if it is 'a syndrome characterized by clinically significant disturbance in an individual's cognition, emotion regulation, or behaviour that reflects a dysfunction in the psychological, biological, or developmental processes underlying mental functioning' (p. 20). It follows that a diagnosis may not be applicable for a person who gets angry frequently – even when he or she has a history of aggression and violence. In fact, efforts to ensure that those who have acted violently in the past should *never* be allowed to feel angry may well be counter-productive. There is, for example, ample evidence that anger does have communicative value and, when properly expressed, might even be productive in negotiating conflict (Tamir et al. 2008); on the other hand, anger suppression can be detrimental to both interpersonal relations and cardiovascular health (Fernandez and Smith 2016).

Assumption 2: Anger is fixed and always related to dysfunction in the individual

Howells et al. (2008) have observed that whilst an individual may engage in an isolated act of aggression, she or he may not have a general disposition to act in this way. Thus anger, like anxiety, can be either situational or dispositional. Sandwiched between this state–trait distinction is angry mood, or what is often referred to as irritability. As with sad or anxious mood, angry or irritable mood fluctuates slightly in magnitude, is finite in duration, but is definitely more protracted in time than an emotional episode. In short, it is possible to experience many different forms of anger, ranging all the way from discrete emotional episodes through to longer lasting mood states, motivational dynamic traits and, finally, to relatively stable enduring personality traits (Eckhardt et al. 2004).

It is particularly important to remember that although state, trait, and mood forms of anger can all give rise to the behavioural expression of aggression, they need not do so. Rather, anger can be expressed in a variety of ways of which aggression is simply one (e.g. Fernandez 2008). Aggression itself can be further differentiated as verbal or physical, direct or indirect, passive or active, all of which vary in terms of the hurts or harms that result. Accordingly, it becomes important to consider how different angry states, moods, and traits may be tied to different types of aggression and violent behaviour.

Traditionally, the focus in most assessments of anger is on the individual. And yet, by definition, interpersonal aggression occurs in a relational context; sometimes in a dyad, sometimes in groups, and sometimes between individual and community. This is an important caveat to the use of assessment tools that cannot account for the ways in which behaviour is inevitably a function of the situation or context in which it occurs (Kinderman 2005). This means that a range of different factors beyond an individual's ability to regulate angry feelings will always be relevant to any adequate understanding of his or her violence. This requires consideration of the social, familial, community, public policy and cultural context in which anger, aggression and, indeed, violence arise (Day and Fernandez 2015).

Assumption 3: Violent behaviour always results from a loss of temper

Classifications often draw on the idea of either 'anger-mediated' or 'reactive' violence (which follows a triggering event, an internal state of emotional arousal, and an impulse to hurt or harm), or of 'instrumental' or 'proactive' violence (where the intention is to obtain some reward and arousal is not present). Although this distinction is clearly an oversimplification – it has been established, for example, that violent acts commonly serve more than one function, often incorporate both emotional and goal-driven components and are triggered by other affective states (see Anderson and Bushman 2002; Daffern et al. 2007) – it clearly highlights the different ways in which both the under- and over-control of angry emotion can both be associated with violence. Much less is understood about over-controlled anger than under-controlled anger, although Megargee's (1966) account remains relevant. He described how violence can result from the excessive inhibition of anger and the build-up of arousal. In these circumstances, anger is chronically inhibited – to the extent that this style of regulation can be meaningfully conceptualized as a stable personality trait that is also characterized by excessive compliance with the demands of others and apparent stoicism.

The importance of assessing both under- and over-controlled emotional regulation is illustrated in a study by Eckhardt et al. (2008). They used cluster analysis to show how anger was low in one subgroup of perpetrators of intimate partner violence, a second group scored highly on measures of anger expression, and the third was labelled moderately anger–inexpressive. They concluded that although the majority of partner-abusive men do not present with anger-related disturbances, understanding different anger presentations is important for developing appropriate treatment responses.

Assumption 4: Men are angrier and more violent than women

There is a substantial literature to indicate that males are generally more physically aggressive than females (e.g. Bennett et al. 2005), with gender differences attenuated as the seriousness of aggression increases.[1] The occurrence of verbal aggressiveness has, however, been shown to be similar across genders. An important issue here is whether aggression and violence serve different functions in males than in females; whether the antecedent conditions giving rise to aggression are different and whether the purposes or goals of aggressive acts differ for the two sexes (Howells et al. 2008). A review by Graves (2006) concluded that there is empirical support for: a stronger association between aggression and internalizing conditions (such as depression) in females; greater inhibition of physically aggressive behaviour in females; and a stronger association between aggression and physical and sexual victimization in females. There is also evidence that males and females express anger in different ways; the latter being more indirect (see Archer 2004). One of the most interesting findings from Averill's (1982, 1983) studies, however, was the lack of difference between men and women in terms of the intensity or duration of anger that they reported.

The Clinical Assessment of Anger

One of the most obvious difficulties in identifying a consistent approach to anger assessment is the lack of any accepted diagnostic or classification system. In fact, anger (and aggression) problems have received surprisingly little attention in the most widely used classification systems, despite being clearly implicated in a number of different diagnoses including Posttraumatic Stress Disorder and some personality disorders, such as Passive Aggressive Personality Disorder (see below) (Deffenbacher 2003; Fernandez and Johnson 2016). One diagnosis in DSM that is quintessentially concerned with anger as well as aggression is Intermittent Explosive Disorder (IED) which is considered next as it is helpful for clinicians who work in the field of violence to become familiar with the criteria for diagnosing IED.

Diagnosing intermittent explosive disorder

In the latest version of DSM-V (APA, 2013), IED is grouped within the category called 'Disruptive, Impulse-control and Conduct Disorders' that also include conditions such as pyromania and kleptomania. As such, it is conceptualized fundamentally as a problem of self-control of emotions and/or behaviours, and specifically as a problem that violates the rights of others and/or conflicts significantly with societal norms. Put simply, individuals with IED are characterized as having anger outbursts that are disproportionate to the level of provocation

---

[1] Although differences in the prevalence of aggression for males and females may be less clear-cut in violence between intimate partners; see Archer (2004).

experienced. Of course, there is no calibration system to dictate what is proportionate and what is not, and this is where clinical judgement is invoked. Even violence which is generally abhorred may seem explainable, if not exculpable, when various predisposing, precipitating and exacerbating factors are taken into account. Therefore, the clinician must have sufficient understanding of the complexities of the individual's inherent vulnerability, developmental history and cultural context before reaching such a diagnosis.

The DSM-V criteria for IED are summarized[2] as follows:

(A)   Recurrent uncontrolled outbursts of aggressiveness as indicated by either
   (i)   verbal behaviour (e.g. tantrums, tirades) or physical attacks on persons, property, animals (without resulting in damage or injury though), or
   (ii)   three outbursts per year that result in damage/injury
(B)   Degree of aggressiveness during outbursts is grossly out of proportion to provocation or to any precipitating event.
(C)   Aggressive outbursts are impulsively fuelled by anger and not premeditated and not for the sake of tangible objective (e.g. money, power)
(D)   Marked distress or impairment in the individual are often associated with financial or legal consequences.
(E)   Chronological age is at least six years (or equivalent developmental level).
(F)   Not better explained by another mental disorder or to another medical condition or to the physiological effects of a substance.

An additional feature worthy of evaluation is remorse. As pointed out by Berner (2007), as in other impulse control disorders, acting on the urge brings relief only to be accompanied later by remorse whilst mounting tension can result when the impulse is resisted.

Within the US, 3.9% of the population will be diagnosable with IED at some time during a one-year period and 7.3% will be diagnosable at some time in their life (Kessler et al. 2006). The 12-month and lifetime prevalence rates are much lower in Japan (Yoshimasu and Kawakami 2011) and even in countries where widespread and persistent violence is commonplace (e.g. Iraq; see Al-Hamzawi et al. 2012).

Diagnosing passive aggressive personality disorder

As clinicians and attorneys often strive to point out in legal proceedings, many acts of violence are premeditated rather than impulsive (or triggered by so-called 'anger attacks'). Anger may also be concealed and acted upon in a covertly aggressive manner so as to produce violent consequences. The diagnosis most consistent with such a presentation is Passive Aggressive Personality Disorder (PAPD). Mentioned in the very first edition of DSM, DSM-IV consigned this diagnosis to an Appendix (warranting further study) and it was finally omitted from the 'official' list of personality disorders in DSM-V. Clinical researchers nonetheless maintain that PAPD is reliably diagnosable and internally consistent as a diagnostic category, and is more prevalent and no less valid than any other personality disorder (Wetzler and Morey

---

[2] A more detailed review of the epidemiology, aetiology, and prognosis of IED can be found in Fernandez and Johnson (2016).

1999; Wetzler and Jose 2012). In DSM, the term passive aggressive personality is still recognized as a legitimate diagnosis but within a category called 'Unspecified Personality Disorder'.

In clinical parlance, passive aggressive traits are still highly relevant to any adequate understanding of anger, if not in terms of a formal diagnostic label. There is some heterogeneity in the diagnosis but generally PAPD encompasses resistance, uncooperativeness and even covert tactics that can become destructive (e.g. Hopwood and Wright 2012). This is illustrated by Yanes et al. (2010) who described a depressed patient with co-occurring passive aggressiveness in the form of resistance to requests and oblique methods of communication. In another clinical case, a depressed patient was deemed passive aggressive on the grounds that she was also 'chronically irritable, argumentative, scornful, disdainful' (Thomas 1994, p. 212). Even though such antagonism does not constitute violence as such, it can have extremely hurtful consequences – whether this be in marital relationships, occupational settings, or in the military where the phenomenon was first documented (as reported by Lane 2009).

We include a brief description of PAPD in this chapter as a point of contrast with IED. Both entail 'aggression' with possible destructive consequences, but with strikingly different styles of expression. Nonetheless, both are ultimately aimed at the same goal of countering or redressing a wrongdoing. It is also important to note that because passive aggressiveness is known to be transient, it is conceivable that what starts out as a relatively controlled release of covert anger can turn into an uncontrolled 'explosion' of anger, and conversely, the urge to explode with anger, when curtailed, may devolve into an alternate response that is also maladaptive. Clinicians will no doubt be attuned to these subtleties and complexities in the expression of anger which, in turn, call for very different approaches to treatment.

The Psychometric Assessment of Anger

The more precise quantification and qualitative differentiation of anger seems to fall largely within the purview of psychometric assessment through self-report tests. Fernandez et al. (2015) have recently reviewed the psychometric properties of a number of the most commonly used anger assessments (see also Ronan et al. 2011). They note that the first psychological measures of anger or hostility (the Cook-Medley Hostility Scale; Cook and Medley 1954, the Overcontrolled Hostility Scale; Megargee et al. 1967, and the Hostility & Direction of Hostility Questionnaire; Caine et al. 1967) all emerged out of the Minnesota Multiphasic Personality Inventory (MMPI). Accordingly, these tools all conceptualize anger as a monolithic construct and were soon superseded by instruments that deconstruct anger across multiple dimensions. Three of the most commonly used are summarized in Table 12.1, although over 20 different psychometric tests of anger have now been published in the psychological literature. Some of these overlap with each other, whilst others tap into different aspects of anger.

The choice of which specific instrument to use should be largely determined by the population of interest (e.g. community, psychiatric, forensic) and the particular construct of interest (e.g. anger or hostility, arousal vs. expression of anger, and different subtypes of anger), as well as the purpose of the assessment. Evidence-based assessment protocols have been developed to help with this task, applying specific criteria to evaluate some of the tools that are commonly used in practice. For example, Hunsley and Mash (2007, 2008) have argued that psychologists should opt for instruments that are psychometrically strong. In addition to evidence of reliability, validity, and clinical utility, measures should also have appropriate norms for norm-referenced interpretation and/or replicated supporting evidence regarding the accuracy

Table 12.1 Three commonly used self-report measures of anger.

Scale name	Description
Anger Disorders Scale (ADS; DiGiuseppe and Tafrate 2004).	The ADS contains a total of 18 subscales divided into five domains. The Provocations domain comprises: (i) scope of anger provocations; and (ii) hurt/social rejection. The Arousal domain comprises: (i) physiological; (ii) duration; and (iii) episode length. The Cognitions domain comprises: (i) suspicion; (ii) resentment; (iii) rumination; and (iv) impulsivity. The Motives domain comprises: (i) tension reduction; (ii) coercion; and (iii) revenge. The Behaviours domain comprises: (i) anger-in; (ii) physical aggression; (iii) verbal expression; (iv) indirect aggression; (v) passive aggression; and (vi) relational aggression. A Short Form with three subscales (expression, anger-in, and vengeance) is also available.
Novaco Scales (NASPI; Novaco 2003).	The Novaco Anger Scale and Provocation Inventory contains 25 scenarios that are potentially anger provoking. In addition, there are 60 items for assessing cognitive, behavioural, and arousal-related aspects of anger, as well as anger-regulatory efforts. Data from various versions of the Novaco scales have been reported in several anger treatment outcome studies.
State–Trait Anger Expression Inventory-2 (STAXI-2; Spielberger 1999).	The STAXI-2 is probably the most widely used instrument for assessing anger. Anger is considered as both an emotional state, varying across time, situation and intensity, as well as a stable personality trait, reflecting a person's tendency to experience anger frequently or intensely.

Source: adapted from Fernandez (2013).

(i.e. sensitivity, specificity, predictive power, etc.) of cut-off scores used for criterion-referenced interpretation. This extends to individual characteristics, with a need for psychometric tests to be sensitive to an individual's age, gender, race, ethnicity, as well as specific cultural factors. Fernandez et al.'s (2015) review concludes that, in general, most of these newer anger self-report measures live up to psychometric standards of reliability and validity and are convenient to administer and score. They do, however, note that factor structure is not always stable, and that test–retest reliability is often indeterminate, thus limiting the value of some tools for treatment evaluation purposes. Casey et al. (2012) have also made the useful observation that not all psychometric properties apply to all assessment purposes – whilst group validity statistics (e.g. sensitivity, specificity, positive and negative predictive power) are relevant to diagnosis and prognosis, they are much less relevant when an assessment is used for treatment monitoring or evaluation purposes. Thus, what is considered to be a 'good' test will always relate to the specific purpose for which it is being used.

One of the simpler (and therefore most convenient and useful) tests is, in our view, the Short Anger Measure (Gerace and Day 2014). This 12-item test taps into two of the important phenomena that are the focus of this chapter: anger and aggression. Designed for use with forensic populations, the Short Anger Measure was developed for screening purposes, for monitoring the association between anger and aggressive impulses, and for setting treatment goals. When used in a sample of adult male offenders, the instrument as a whole evidenced high internal consistency and temporal stability. The correlation between these two factors measured by this tool (labelled 'angry feelings' and 'aggressive impulses') supports the common association between anger and aggression.

A possible complement to the Short Anger Measure is the Anger Parameters Scale (Fernandez et al. 2014, 2018a, Henderson 2016) which, unlike other tools, assesses five different parameters of anger activity. The first parameter is frequency, which measures how often someone experiences anger (high vs. low). The second parameter, duration, taps into how long anger persists (short vs. long). Intensity refers to the magnitude at which anger is experienced (weak vs. strong). Latency is the dimension that measures how quickly anger arises after the anger-provoking stimulus (slow responses are permitted. Scores for each parameter range from 0 to 24; the higher the scores, the more that parameter tends towards maladaptiveness (thus, elevated scores on all parameters would mean high frequency, long duration, strong magnitude, quick latency, and low threshold). The Anger Parameters Scale has been psychometrically evaluated and found to have factorial validity, temporal stability, and internal consistency (Fernandez 2010, 2014; Henderson 2016), although full normative data have yet to be reported.

Considerations when using self-report tools to assess anger

There are a number of important considerations involved in the use of self-report measures that any assessor should be aware of when assessing anger. For example, and as noted earlier in this chapter, although many measures are norm-referenced they all de-contextualize anger and, as a consequence, provide limited insight into the specific nature of the angry experience. An additional, and ongoing, problem is motivational and response distortion (see Helmes et al. 2015). Responses to items included in any self-report measure are easily distorted and, therefore, treatments and interventions based on scores from such scales need to be considered carefully. This is a particular issue when assessing anger given the likelihood that many of those referred for assessment will feel pressured to attend (and sometimes may be legally coerced; Day and Vess 2013). This can significantly reduce the quality of information that is provided. Novaco (2013) has described this is in the following way:

> 'At the outset, it must be understood that people who are in forensic or other custodial settings should be expected to "mask" their anger, as they are unlikely to perceive gain in disclosing it. Instead, they are inclined to respond on a "need to know" basis – telling you what they think they need for you to know.' (p. 215)

Clearly, a range of other factors may also be responsible for biased responding, ranging all the way from deliberate conscious dissimulation to inadequate self-insight and/or a lack of conscious awareness of one's anger and hostility. It is for this reason that many assessors take care to use assessments that are specifically designed to assess impression management tendencies. Fernandez et al. (2018c) have, however, recently cautioned against the use of the Marlowe-Crowne Social Desirability Scale (Crowne and Marlowe 1960) given that a number of items ask directly about anger. When these items are rated in the direction of low anger, the ratings are automatically scored in the direction of high social desirability.

Of course, in an ideal world, any assessment would also utilize behavioural observations of anger, or at least the behavioural expression of anger through aggression (see Suris et al. 2004 for a review of these tools). Previous attempts to develop behavioural measures of aggression in forensic settings have typically centred around staff incident reports and disciplinary infractions. Official recording systems have, however, been criticized for only measuring the most consequential acts of violence (e.g. Yudofsky et al. 1986) and for underestimating aggressive behaviour by ignoring incidents of verbal abuse, aggression against property, and unsuccessful attempts at violence (Arboleda-Florez et al. 1994). The Modified Overt Aggression Scale (MOAS; Kay et al. 1988) is one measure that attempts to accurately and reliably measure aggression. It is a modification of a scale developed by Yudofsky et al. (1986) designed to assess four categories of aggression in psychiatric patients: verbal aggression; aggression against property; auto-aggression (against the self); and physical aggression. A total of 16-items, four items from each category, are rated on a five-point scale representing increasing levels of severity. These scores are then weighted to give a total score reflecting the overall seriousness of the aggression over a fixed period of time. The scale is reported to have acceptable internal reliability, interrater reliability, and validity (Kay et al. 1988) and has been successfully used in a prison setting with prisoner behaviour rated by correctional officers (Watt and Howells 1999).

Conclusions

Definitions of anger typically describe anger as a subjective feeling that is negative in valence and interwoven with specific cognitions and motivations, whilst also typified by psychophysiological and facial activation patterns. This highlights the many different facets of anger and draws attention to a number of different aspects of anger that might be assessed. The antecedents of anger are likely to vary for each individual, as is the way in which angry emotion is expressed. A key goal of any assessment then is to understand the triggers for angry arousal (provocations) and how these are interpreted and responded to against the backdrop of sociocultural norms. This can be the basis of a tentative diagnosis. Given suggestions that the defining cognitive component of anger is appraised wrongdoing and its motivational component is the desire to counter or redress the wrongdoing (see Fernandez et al. 2015), these are also important assessment targets which can only be understood through a detailed clinical interview in which the assessee recounts different occasions in which she or he has felt angry. An analysis of these accounts can then be supplemented by psychometric assessment which allows the person's scores to be placed in relation to 'normal' anger as experienced by the general community as well as establishing a baseline that can be used to assess if, and when, change occurs.

There are, however, many different ways that anger regulation problems can impact upon violence risk (Day and Vess 2013) and these need to be carefully considered. It is insufficient to conclude that a person who regularly feels angry will be at risk of acting violently without an attempt to articulate the mechanisms through which this occurs. This also requires careful consideration of the type of behaviour that is being predicted. In our view, it is particularly useful to assess the nature of the relationship between anger and each of Zahn et al.'s (2004) six dimensions of violence: (i) the level of action of the behaviour (individual, interpersonal, collective); (ii) the nature and degree of force; (iii) the outcome including extent of injury; (iv) the type of injury (e.g., physical harm, emotional degradation, interpersonal dominance); (v) the nature and significance of the target(s); and (vi) whether or not the actions were intentional. It is only in this way that anger can be linked to the specific behaviour that is of concern and under specific circumstances whilst also always considering issues relevant to imminent risk to others.

In summary, the routine administration of tests, or even the completion of a standardized interview proforma is not, in itself, likely to be sufficient. And so, the assessment of anger is inherently a decision-making task that involves the formulation and testing of hypotheses. It is here that the case formulation approach (see Delle-Vergini and Day 2016) is central to forming an opinion about the most appropriate intervention and management strategies.

References

Al-Hamzawi, A., Al-Diwan, J.K., Al-Hasnawi, S.M. et al. (2012). The prevalence and correlates of inter-mittent explosive disorder in Iraq. *Acta Psychiatrica Scandinavica* 126: 219–228.

American Psychiatric Association (2013). *Diagnostic and Statistical Manual of Mental Disorders, Fifth edition (DSM-5)*. Washington, D.C.: American Psychiatric Publishing.

Anderson, C.A. and Bushman, B.J. (2002). Human aggression. *Annual Review of Psychology* 53: 27–51.

Arboleda-Florez, J., Crisanti, A., Rose, S., and Holley, H. (1994). Measuring aggression on psychiatric inpatient units: development and testing of the Calgary General Hospital Aggression Scale. *International Journal of Offender Therapy and Comparative Criminology* 38: 183–204.

Archer, J. (2004). Sex differences in aggression in real-world settings: a meta-analytic review. *Review of General Psychology* 8: 291–322.

Averill, J.R. (1982). *Anger and Aggression. An essay on Emotion*. New York: Springer.

Averill, J.R. (1983). Studies on anger and aggression: implications for theories of emotion. *American Psychologist* 38: 1145–1160.

Bennett, S., Farrington, D.P., and Huesmann, L.R. (2005). Explaining gender differences in crime and violence: the importance of social cognitive skills. *Aggression and Violent Behavior* 10: 263–288.

Berner, J.E. (2007). Intranasal ketamine for intermittent explosive disorder: a case report. *Journal of Clinical Psychiatry* 68: 1305.

Caine, T.M., Foulds, G.A., and Hope, K. (1967). *Manual of the Hostility and Direction of Hostility Questionnaire (HDHQ)*. London: University of London Press.

Casey, S., Day, A., Ward, T., and Vess, J. (2012). *Foundations of Offender Rehabilitation*. Oxford: Routledge Publishing.

Cook, W.W. and Medley, D.M. (1954). Proposed hostility and pharisaic-virtue scales for the MMPI. *Journal of Applied Psychology* 38: 414–418.

Crowne, D.P. and Marlowe, D. (1960). A new scale of social desirability independent of psychopathology. *Journal of Consulting Psychology* 24: 349–354.

Daffern, M., Howells, K., and Ogloff, J. (2007). What's the point? Toward a methodology for assessing the function of psychiatric inpatient aggression. *Behaviour Research and Therapy* 45: 101–111.

Day, A. and Fernandez, E. (2015). *Preventing Violence in Australia: Policy, Practice and Solutions*. Leichardt, NSW, Australia: Federation Press.

Day, A. and Vess, J. (2013). Targeting anger in forensic populations. In: *Treatments for Anger in Specific Populations: Theory, Application, and Outcome* (ed. E. Fernandez), 158–175. New York, NY: Oxford University Press.

Deffenbacher, J.L. (2003). Anger disorders. In: *Aggression: Psychiatric Assessment and Treatment* (ed. E.F. Coccaro), 89–112. New York, US: Marcel Dekker, Inc.

Deffenbacher, J.L., Oetting, E.R., and DiGiuseppe, R.A. (2002). Principles of empirically supported interventions applied to anger management. *The Counseling Psychologist* 30: 262–280.

Delle-Vergini, V. and Day, A. (2016). The forensic case formulation. *Journal of Forensic Practice* 18: 240–250.

DiGiuseppe, R. and Tafrate, R. (2003). Anger treatment for adults: a meta-analytic review. *Clinical Psychology: Science and Practice* 10: 70–84.

DiGiuseppe, R. and Tafrate, R.C. (2004). *Anger Disorders Scale: Manual*. Toronto, ON: Multi Health Systems.

Douglas, K.S., Hart, S.D., Webster, C.D., and Belfrage, H. (2013). *HCR-20v3: Assessing Risk for Violence: User Guide*. Burnaby, BC: Mental Health, Law, and Policy Institute, Simon Fraser University.

Eckhardt, C., Norlander, B., and Deffenbacher, J. (2004). The assessment of anger and hostility: a critical review. *Aggression and Violent Behavior* 9: 17–43.

Eckhardt, C.I., Samper, R.M., and Murphy, C.M. (2008). Anger disturbances among perpetrators of intimate partner violence: clinical characteristics and outcomes of court-mandated treatment. *Journal of Interpersonal Violence* 23: 1600–1617.

Fernandez, E. (2008). The angry personality: a representation on six dimensions of anger expression. In: *International Handbook of Personality Theory and Testing: Vol. 2: Personality Measurement and Assessment* (eds. G.J. Boyle, D. Matthews and D. Saklofske), 402–419. London, UK: Sage Publications.

Fernandez, E. (2010). Toward an integrative psychotherapy for maladaptive anger. In: *The International Handbook of Anger: Constituent and Concomitant Biological, Psychological, and Social Processes* (eds. M. Potegal, G. Stemmler and C. Spielberger), 499–514. New York: Springer.

Fernandez, E. (2013). *Treatments for Anger in Specific Populations: Theory, Application, and Outcome.* Oxford, UK: Oxford University Press.

Fernandez, E., Arevalo, I., Torralba, A., and Vargas, R. (2014). Norms for five parameters of anger: how do incarcerated adults differ from the community? *International Journal of Forensic Mental Health* 13: 18–24.

Fernandez, E., Day, A., and Boyle, G.J. (2015). Measures of anger and hostility in adults. In: *Measures of Personality and Social Psychological Constructs* (eds. G.J. Boyle, D.H. Saklofske and G. Matthews), 74–100. London, UK: Academic Press.

Fernandez, E. and Johnson, S.L. (2016). Anger in psychological disorders: Prevalence, presentation, etiology, and prognostic implications. *Clinical Psychology Review* 46: 124–135.

Fernandez, E., Kiageri, V., Guharajan, D., and Day, A. (2018a). Anger parameters in parolees undergoing psychoeducation: temporal stability, social desirability bias and comparison with non-offenders. *Criminal Behaviour and Mental Health* 28: 174–186.

Fernandez, E., Malvaso, C., Day, A., and Guharajan, D. (2018b). 21st century Cognitive-Behavioral Therapy for anger: a systematic review of research design, methodology, and outcome. *Cognitive and Behavioural Psychotherapy* 46: 385–404.

Fernandez, E. and Smith, T.W. (2016). Anger, hostility, and cardiovascular disease in the context of interpersonal relationships. In: *Handbook of Psychocardiology* (eds. M. Alvarenga and D.G. Byrne), 665–683. New York: Springer Sciences.

Fernandez, E., Woldgabreal, Y., Guharajan, D. et al. (2018c). Social Desirability Bias Against Admitting Anger: Bias in the Test-Taker or Bias in the Test? *Journal of Personality Assessment* 9: 1–9.

Gerace, A. and Day, A. (2014). The Short Anger Measure (SAM): Development of a measure to assess anger in forensic populations. *The Journal of Forensic Nursing* 10: 44–49.

Graves, K.N. (2006). Not always sugar and spice: expanding theoretical and functional explanations of why females aggress. *Aggression and Violent Behavior* 11: 131–140.

Helmes, E., Holden, R.R., and Ziegler, M. (2015). Response bias, malingering, and impression management. In: *Measures of Personality and Social Psychological Constructs* (eds. G.J. Boyle, D.H. Saklofske and G. Matthews), 16–43. London, UK: Academic Press.

Henderson, M.M. (2016). The anger parameters scale and the anger expressions scale: A psychometric study. Master thesis. The University of Texas at San Antonio.

Hopwood, C.J. and Wright, A.G.C. (2012). A comparison of passive–aggressive and negativistic personality disorders. *Journal of Personality Assessment* 94: 296–303.

Howells, K., Daffern, M., and Day, A. (2008). Aggression and violence. In: *The Handbook of Forensic Mental Health* (eds. K. Soothill, M. Dolan and P. Rogers), 351–374. Cullompton, UK: Willan.

Hunsley, J. and Mash, E.J. (2007). Evidence-based assessment. *Annual Review of Clinical Psychology* 3: 57–79.

Hunsley, J. and Mash, E.J. (2008). Developing criteria for evidence-based assessment: an introduction to assessments that work. In: *A Guide to Assessments That Work* (eds. J. Hunsley and E.J. Mash), 3–14. New York, NY: Oxford University Press.

Kay, S.R., Wolkenfeld, F., and Murrill, L.M. (1988). Profiles of aggression among psychiatric patients: I. Nature and prevalence. *The Journal of Nervous and Mental Disease* 176: 539–546.

Kessler, R.C., Coccaro, E.F., Fava, M. et al. (2006). The prevalence and correlates of DSM-IV intermittent explosive disorder in the national comorbidity survey replication. *Archives of General Psychiatry* 63: 669–678.

Kinderman, P. (2005). A psychological model of mental disorder. *Harvard Review of Psychiatry* 13: 206–217.

Lane, C. (2009). The surprising history of passive-aggressive personality disorder. *Theory & Psychology* 19: 55–70.

Megargee, E.I. (1966). Undercontrolled and overcontrolled personality types in extreme antisocial aggression. *Psychological Monographs* 80: 1–29.

Megargee, E.I., Cook, P.E., and Mendelsohn, G.A. (1967). Development and validation of an MMPI scale of assaultiveness in overcontrolled individuals. *Journal of Abnormal Psychology* 72: 519–528.

Novaco, R.W. (2003). *The Novaco Anger Scale and Provocation Inventory: Manual*. Los Angeles, CA: Western Psychological Services.

Novaco, R.W. (2013). Reducing anger-related offending. In: *What Works in Offender Rehabilitation: An Evidenced Based Approach to Assessment and Treatment* (eds. L.A. Craig, L. Dixon and T.A. Gannon), 211–236. New York, NY: Wiley-Blackwell.

Novaco, R.W., Ramm, M., and Black, L. (2001). Anger treatment with offenders. In: *Handbook of Offender Assessment and Treatment* (ed. C.R. Hollin), 281–296. Chichester, UK: Wiley.

Officer.Com (2016). Columbine: Background, planning & preparation. https://www.officer.com/tactical/ems-hazmat/article/12243909/columbine-background-planning-preparation (Accessed 16 August 2019).

Ronan, G.F., Dreer, L., Maurelli, K. et al. (2011). *Practitioner's Guide to Empirically Supported Measures of Anger, aggreSsion, and Violence [ABCT Clinical Assessment Series]*. New York, NY: Springer.

Serin, R.C., Lloyd, C.D., Helmus, L. et al. (2013). Does intra-individual change predict offender recidivism? Searching for the Holy Grail in assessing offender change. *Aggression and Violent Behavior* 18: 32–53.

Spielberger, C.D. (1999). *Professional Manual for the State-Trait Anger Expression Inventory-2 (STAXI-2)*. Odessa, FL: Psychological Assessment Resources.

Suris, A., Lind, L., Emmett, G. et al. (2004). Measures of aggressive behavior: overview of clinical and research instruments. *Aggression and Violent Behavior* 9: 165–227.

Tamir, M., Mitchell, C., and Gross, J.J. (2008). Hedonic and instrumental motives in anger regulation. *Psychological Science* 19: 324–328.

Taylor, J.L. and Novaco, R.W. (2005). *Anger Treatment for People with Developmental Disabilities*. Chichester, UK: John Wiley & Sons.

Thomas, G.V. (1994). Mixed personality disorder with passive-aggressive and avoidant features. In: *Personality Disorders from the Perspective of the Five-Factor Model* (eds. P.T. Costa Jr. and T.A. Widiger), 211–215. Washington, DC: American Psychological Association.

Watt, B. and Howells, K. (1999). Skills training for aggression control: evaluation of an anger management programme for violent offenders. *Legal and Criminological Psychology* 4: 285–300.

Wetzler, S. and Jose, A. (2012). Passive-aggressive personality disorder: the demise of a syndrome. In: *The Oxford Handbook of Personality Disorders* (ed. T.A. Widiger), 674–693. New York, NY: Oxford University Press.

Wetzler, S. and Morey, L.C. (1999). Passive-aggressive personality disorder: the demise of a syndrome. *Psychiatry: Interpersonal and Biological Processes* 62: 49–59.

Wong, S.C.P. and Gordon, A. (1999). *Manual for the Violence Risk Scale (Version 2)*. Saskatchewan, Canada: University of Saskatchewan.

Yanes, P.K., Tiffany, S.T., and Roberts, J.E. (2010). Cognitive therapy for co-occurring depression and behaviors associated with passive-aggressive personality disorder. *Clinical Case Studies* 9: 369–382.

Yoshimasu, K. and Kawakami, N. (2011). Epidemiological aspects of intermittent explosive disorder in Japan; prevalence and psychosocial comorbidity: findings from the World Mental Health Japan Survey 2002–2006. *Psychiatry Research* 186: 384–389.

Yudofsky, S.C., Silver, J.M., Jackson, W. et al. (1986). The Overt Aggression Scale for the objective rating of verbal and physical aggression. *American Journal of Psychiatry* 143: 35–39.

Zahn, M.A., Brownstein, H.H., and Jackson, S.L. (2004). *Violence: From Theory to Research*. Newark, NJ: LexisNexis Anderson Publishing.

13

Gang Violence Prevention Efforts
A Public Health Approach

Dawn McDaniel[1] and Caitlin Sayegh[2]

[1] Quality for Youth, LLC, Atlanta, USA
[2] University of Southern California Keck School of Medicine,
Los Angeles, USA

Introduction

The US prevalence of gang affiliation was estimated at 2% for youth ages 5–17 years in 2010 (Pyrooz and Sweeten 2015). The risk of homicide and injury is greater for gang-affiliated youth, compared to their same age peers, which is particularly concerning as the number of gang-related homicides increased 20% from 2011 to 2012 (Egley et al. 2014). In terms of violent victimization, it was estimated that 1.7% of children in the US experienced a group or gang-related assault in 2011 (Finkelhor et al. 2013).

Previous intervention efforts to reduce gang involvement have had negligible effects (Klein and Maxson 2006). Preventing youth from joining gangs is critical, as research has shown that gang entry has serious generational health consequences (Augustyn et al. 2014). The public health approach has been used to address a variety of types of violence, including youth violence, child maltreatment and intimate partner violence. In addition, the public health sector has had great success in using this model to target other complex health behaviours, such as tobacco use, motor vehicle crashes and coronary heart disease (Rosenberg et al. 1992).

This chapter reviews the public health approach to gang violence prevention, particularly as it has been applied in the US. This approach involves four steps that are grounded in the best available research (Dahlberg and Krug 2002; Haegerich et al. 2013). The chapter covers each step and discusses its application to gang violence prevention. In the first step, which is to describe and monitor the problem, we review several national databases that report gang violence statistics. In the second step, which is to identify risk, protective, and promotive factors, we review the socio-ecological model and its relationship to these contextual factors. In the third step, the development and evaluation of prevention programmes, we review universal, selected, and indicated gang-prevention programmes. Finally, in the fourth step, we review a framework to help understand factors that contribute to the broad dissemination and implementation of the prevention programmes.

Define and Monitor the Problem

Public health focuses on societal or population-based problems, not just the health of individuals. Often information used to define and monitor health problems is called public health surveillance data. These data are used to explore how health problems are distributed across populations. Knowing more about the impact of a problem on a population provides insight into where to focus and how to tailor prevention strategies to maximize their positive impact.

Public health researchers typically begin surveillance efforts by establishing a 'case definition' of a health problem that they intend to monitor (Lee et al. 2010). Case definitions need to be specific enough to ensure that the data elements are consistent and comparable over time. A group of gang researchers collaborated to create a standardized definition for gangs (Klein and Maxson 2006). They defined gangs as 'any durable, street-oriented youth group whose involvement in illegal activity is part of its group identity' (Klein and Maxson 2006, p. 4). This definition excludes motorcycle gangs, prison gangs, and other more traditionally adult groups, such as organized crime gangs. To encourage use of this definition, a compilation of measurement tools was developed for use in studying gang violence (Weerman et al. 2009). Despite the creation of this case definition and set of tools, the case definitions used in surveillance efforts in the US are vary state-by-state or even by law enforcement jurisdiction. Therefore, surveillance data in the US is limited in its ability to show trends or accurate comparisons.

In public health, incidents of health problems or persons with health conditions that meet the case definition are often called 'cases' or 'case-patients'. Researchers examine basic case counts to track health problems across populations. In addition, researchers often gather details to better understand the case characteristics. Ethnicity, tattoos, gang colours, territory, and gang names are examples of possible case characteristics of youth gangs. It is also important to identify the 'time, person, and place' associated with the public health problem.

The National Youth Gang Survey is the only nationally representative survey on gang violence in the US (Egley et al. 2014). This survey gathers data from more than 2500 law enforcement agencies, including all police departments in cities of 50 000 or more, all suburban departments, and a random selection of rural and small city police and sheriffs' departments (Egley et al. 2014). The instrument asks each agency about gang activity, and estimates the number of gangs and gang members, the number of gang homicides, and other characteristics that describe the city's gang problems (Egley et al. 2014). The survey allows each agency to determine the youth or young adults that they are willing to identify as a gang, based on local and state definitions. Survey data indicated that, in 2012, there were an estimated 850 000 gang members and 2363 gang-related homicides in the US.

The Center for Disease Control and Prevention (CDC)'s National Violent Death Reporting System (NVDRS) is a public health surveillance system that has collected information since 2003 on violent deaths, including gang-related homicides, across a number of states in the US (Centers for Disease Control and Prevention 2012; Parks et al. 2014). This surveillance system regularly tracks new cases of gang homicides over time to identify ongoing trends and patterns. This system also provides case details with regard to place of death, such as the counts by states and cities, or the place of injury, such as street or residence. As far as the persons involved, the system captures demographic characteristics of both the victim and any known suspects. For example, NVDRS data in 2013 indicated that 3.0% of homicides/legal intervention deaths were gang-related (National Center for Injury Prevention and Control 2016). The definition of a gang homicide in this system is influenced by local and state definitions.

Several other surveillance systems capture information important for understanding gang violence at the community level. For instance, some surveillance systems track the impact of gang violence in terms of injuries and violence victimization. An example of this type surveillance is hospital-based injury surveillance systems that monitor gang-related injuries. This type of surveillance is often used to better understand non-fatal injuries related to gang violence in urban areas. Violence victimization is also an important indicator of the impact and severity of gang violence. An example of this type of surveillance system is the National Survey of Children's Exposure to Violence (NatSCEV), which tracks gang presence and group/gang assaults (Crimes Against Children Research Center 2016).

Whilst there is some public health surveillance of gang violence, much more work is needed to better understand the scope of the problem and its societal impact. A standard case definition for gangs is still not used across these surveillance systems. Until there is consistency in how gangs are defined, surveillance of gang violence is going to continue to be very challenging (Esbensen et al. 2001; Klein and Maxson 2006; O'Brien et al. 2013). In particular, it is difficult to interpret and compare data across studies since various definitions are used. A broad definition of a gang may lead to an overestimate of the gang problem, whereas a narrow definition may lead to an underestimate. If data are not comparable, then it is difficult to make decisions on the severity of the problem, where there is an identified need and where resources should be allocated.

Risk and Protective Factors: Socio-Ecological Model

The second step of the public health model is to identify risk factors that increase risk, protective factors that protect against or buffer risk, and promotive factors that promote positive behaviours. The socio-ecological model, based on Bronfenbrenner's work is a systems framework that organizes and simplifies the complex set of factors and relationships that contribute to gang violence. The model outlines the levels of influence between an individual and their social environment, including relationships, community, and society (Bronfenbrenner 1979). Several studies have used this model to better understanding factors associated with gang affiliation (McDaniel 2012; Merrin et al. 2015).

At the individual level, the person's psychological, behavioural, biological, and personal history factors are examined (Merrin et al. 2015). For example, in a review of 20 studies since 1990, Klein and Maxson (2006) found that consistent predictors of joining a gang include the following: problem behaviours, such as reactivity, aggressiveness, and impulsivity; a youth's experience of negative life events; and a youth's attitudes towards delinquent behaviour. Matsuda's (2014) more recent review of the literature found similar individual-level risk factors, such as disruptive behaviours, previous delinquency, risk seeking, impulsivity, negative life events, blocked opportunities, antisocial beliefs, tolerance of deviance, positive view of alcohol and drugs, etc. Matsuda (2014) provided a nuanced discussion of the research on whether male sex and ethnic minority status are individual risk factors for gang entry, highlighting biases that may inflate estimates of gang membership in these demographic groups.

At the relationship level, the individual's close relationships are examined, such as his or her peers, parents, or mentors (Merrin et al. 2015). When youth are involved in gangs, their rates of participation in crimes and violence go above and beyond levels expected by their peers (even their delinquent non-gang peers) (Esbensen et al. 2001). An explanation for this finding is that the gang has an exaggerating influence on an individual's negative behaviours, encouraging participation in violence and crime typically not engaged in without the peer influence. Having delinquent peer relationships is a consistently supported risk factor for gang membership (Klein and Maxson 2006). There is also preliminary evidence that having pro-social peers can be a protective factor, reducing the likelihood of gang entry (Matsuda 2014). Regarding families, most studies also show support for the association of lack of parental supervision with gang membership (Klein and Maxson 2006). However, at the other end of the spectrum, family support might be protective as it strongly influences a gang-affiliated youth's decisions to leave the gang (Decker 2009).

At the community level, social relationships, including those influenced by school and neighbourhood, as well as the gangs themselves are examined (Merrin et al. 2015). Klein and Maxson (2006) found inconclusive support for school and neighbourhood influence on gang affiliation. Yet, relatively few studies (Watkins and Taylor 2016) have examined factors such as the presence of gangs in a youth's school and/or a youth's feelings of safety in school. More research is needed to understand relationships between gang affiliation and risks at this level of the socio-ecological model.

Finally, at the societal level, social and cultural norms and policies that maintain economic and social inequality amongst groups are examined (Merrin et al. 2015). Whilst little research has examined youth gang affiliation and societal level influences, there is work done on the emergence of gangs and societal level influences. In this literature, city size, economic deprivation, social instability, racial/ethnic composition of the community, and poverty were all found to play a role in the emergence of gangs in a community (Klein and Maxson 2006). Given the importance of social and cultural norms on gang formation, societal level risks and protective factors deserve more research attention. Whilst much of gang prevention efforts are aimed towards preventing youth gang entry, interventions at the societal level may be able to prevent gang formation and persistence.

Whilst the socio-ecological model is useful for organizing contextual factors, research has found inconclusive evidence for the impact of all these domains on predicting gang affiliation (Klein and Maxson 2006). Specifically, there is weak and inconclusive evidence for community or societal influences, although there is clear evidence for individual and peer and family factors (Klein and Maxson 2006). Also, whilst gang research has primarily focused on risk, more research is needed to understand the protective and promotive factors that contribute to youth remaining uninvolved in gangs even though they exhibit many of the risks typically associated with gang affiliation. Theory on youth resilience suggests that potential promotive factors for gang affiliation include: racial/ethnic identity, relationships with adults and pro-social involvement (Zimmerman et al. 2013). These factors are critical for prevention programmes as it is easier for a programme to focus on enhancing a youth's protective or promotive factors than reduce an exposure to a risk.

Prevention Programmes

The third step of the public health model is to develop and evaluate prevention programmes. In public health, intervention is often seen as involving a spectrum of programmes, strategies, and policies aimed to address root causes of public health problems at the individual, relationship, community, and societal levels (Runyan and Freire 2008). Some of these efforts are similar to those traditionally used with gang violence, such as law enforcement strategies that involve policing and incarcerating gang-involved youth. However, public health widens the opportunities to intervene by attempting to prevent problems, like gang involvement and violence, before they begin.

In public health, prevention programmes are often structured in three categories, which relate to the group of interest (Mercy et al. 2002). The first category, universal prevention programmes are offered, regardless of risk for gang involvement or violence, to groups such as school-aged youth. The second category, selected prevention programmes are aimed at youth considered at-risk for gang involvement or violence. Finally, the third category, indicated prevention programmes are aimed at youth who are already involved in gangs or gang violence. This public health framework is very similar to Brantingham and Faust's (1976) crime prevention categories, such that universal prevention is similar to the term 'primary prevention', selected prevention is similar to 'secondary prevention', and indicated is similar to 'tertiary prevention'.

In a recent meta-analysis, Huey and colleagues found 38 controlled evaluations of gang prevention and intervention programmes (Huey et al. 2016). Whilst aimed at gang prevention, 14 of the programmes did not measure gang-related outcomes. Of those that did, only five reported significant reductions in gang-involvement. The meta-analysis indicated that gang prevention and intervention programmes had a small, but statistically significant effect on gang involvement ($d = 0.29$). They also found substantial heterogeneity in outcomes that suggest some programmes may be highly effective and others less so. Due to the small sample of available studies, potential moderators could not be examined; however, the meta-analysis did identify several gang intervention evaluations that had a strong design despite mixed intervention effects. These gang prevention and intervention programmes, along with others, are discussed in this section.

The socio-ecological model, which was used to better understand the risk and protective factors related to gang violence, can also be used to organize gang prevention and intervention programmes. This model outlines key levels of intervention, such as individual risks, dysfunctional relationships, and school or community issues that might exacerbate violence, and larger societal issues that contribute to violence, such as social and economic inequalities and social norms on how to handle conflict. Table 13.1 provides examples of programmes organized along two dimensions: (i) public health prevention categories and (ii) socio-ecological levels. This list is not exhaustive, but it highlights programmes that specifically examined gang outcomes.

Universal Prevention Programmes. Universal prevention programmes are generally open to all interested youth, regardless of risk, are often less intense in terms of programme dosage and start at a young age. To prevent gang involvement, these programmes would typically start with 8–10 year olds, prior to the onset of many of the risks associated with gangs. Universal prevention programmes might include community youth development programmes or school-based health programmes. These programmes often occur in communities at high-risk for gang violence; however, youth are not targeted to participate in these programmes based on individual level risk factors. Whilst a critique of these programmes is that they can be costly and an inefficient way to deliver a programme as only a small portion of the population will even be gang involved. Universal prevention programmes may have secondary outcomes, other than the reduction of gang violence, that are important to note, such as reducing substance abuse, high-risk sexual behaviour, school dropout, early pregnancy and parenthood, family problems, and

Table 13.1 Gang prevention programmes organized by public health prevention category and socio-ecological level.

	Individual level	Family level	Community level
Universal Prevention Programmes	Gang Resistance Education and Training (GREAT) Programme: GREAT is an example of a school-based, universal gang violence prevention curriculum aimed at middle-school students (Esbensen et al. 2012). The lessons include the development of self-management skills, social skills, and drug abuse education. Law enforcement officers lead each lesson. Whilst the first evaluation of the GREAT programme reported no effect on gang membership or delinquency, the second evaluation with a revised curriculum found that students who received the programme had 39% lower odds of gang membership compared to a control group (Esbensen et al. 2011).	No programmes were identified.	No programmes were identified.
Selected Prevention Programmes	The Gang Prevention Through Targeted Outreach (GPTTO) approach, developed by the Boys and Girls Club of America, is an example a selected prevention programme (Arbreton and McClanahan 2002). GPTTO aims to attract and recruit youth at risk of joining gangs into Clubs that include interest-based activities and case management. GPTTO targets 'hard-to-reach' youth through direct outreach and referrals from schools, community agencies, and police or probation departments. GPTTO attendance was associated with delayed onset of at least one gang behaviour (i.e. wearing gang colours), as well as less contact with juvenile justice system, fewer delinquent behaviours, improved school outcomes, and more productive use of after-school hours.	The Montreal Prevention Treatment Program (MPTT) is an example of a prevention programme that targets a selected population at the family level (Tremblay et al. 1996). This programme was intended for disruptive boys in early elementary school. The programme included parent training and social-skills training for the children. MPTT led to statistically significant reductions in gang involvement, substance abuse, and self-reported delinquency. In terms of gang involvement, at 12 years of age, 3% of the participants in the Montreal Prevention Treatment Programme were gang-involved compared to 20% in the group that was not treated.	An example of a prevention programme for a selected population at the community-level is the Logan Square Prevention Project (Godley and Velasquez 1998). This programme was focused on creating a coalition of neighbourhood agencies to provide 'a comprehensive array of school and community-based prevention services to reduce substance use and gang involvement among inner-city Latino youth' (p. 89). Results indicated that gang involvement was significantly lower amongst a post-prevention programme cohort compared to a pre-prevention cohort.

| Indicated Prevention Programmes | The Wraparound Project at University of San Francisco/San Francisco General Hospital is one example of an indicated hospital-based prevention programme (Smith et al. 2013). The Wraparound Project identifies youth with violence-related injuries who are at high-risk for recurrent injury and rehospitalization. The programme provides youth with case management services that vary in intensity by youth risk-level. Housing, substance abuse services. This programme decreased the rate of rehospitalization from 16 to 4.5% for youth at high risk of recurrent injury (Smith et al. 2013). | No programmes were identified. | Spergel's Comprehensive Community-wide Gang Programme Model is an example of an indicated prevention programme implemented at the community-level (Spergel et al. 2001). The Comprehensive Programme involved collaborating with local organizations and law enforcement to decrease violence and delinquency through intensive contacts with gang youth. The Comprehensive Model was implemented in six different US cities, and showed mixed results. However, in Bloomington-Normal there were significant reductions in gang membership. |

Note: No societal level prevention strategies have been investigated, and therefore there is no fourth column for this level.

unstable employment (Krohn et al. 2011). The only universal prevention programme we found in our review that explicitly examined gang outcomes was the Gang Resistance Education and Training (GREAT) Programme. This universal prevention programme is facilitated by police officers in middle-school classrooms, and has been tested in several cities across the US including Albuquerque, NM, Portland, OR, Greeley, CO, Nashville, TN, Philadelphia, PA, Chicago, IL, and Dallas/Fort Worth, TX (see Table 13.1 for outcomes).

Selected Prevention Programmes: To identify youth at-risk for gang involvement, it is important to understand which definition of gangs is being used, the risk factors for gang involvement, the common trajectories and tools to assess these factors. Accuracy in the identification and recruitment of at-risk youth is critical. The Gang Risk of Entry Factors tool was developed to assess youth at risk for gang involvement to inform eligibility for selected prevention programmes (Hennigan et al. 2015). In a validation study, this tool was used to identify high-risk youth, and then one to two years later interviews were conducted on these youth and confirmed that 100% of boys reported current gang members, 81% of boys reported former gang members and 74% of boys reported hanging out with the gang. Similarly, almost all the girls who were identified as high risk endorsed some degree of involvement in gangs in their interviews. In addition, this tool provides information on a youth's pattern of risk and protective factors, which is helpful for tailoring the programmatic efforts and ensuring the right population is identified for intervention.

Selected prevention programmes are often more focused, intense and require more resources than universal programmes. For example, because these youth show signs of potential risks, more supervision and training is often beneficial to those facilitating the programme. Instead of teachers or afterschool professionals facilitating the programme, professionals with specialized mental or behavioural health training, such as counsellors, nurses, healthcare providers, social workers or psychologists are sometimes required. In our review of the literature, selected prevention programmes were the most common type of prevention programme (Table 13.1). Three programmes were identified: the Gang Prevention Through Targeted Outreach programme, which targets risk at the individual level at Boys & Girls Clubs (Arbreton and McClanahan 2002), the Montreal Prevention Treatment Programme, which targets risk at the family level (McCord et al. 1994) and the Logan Square Prevention Project, which targets risk at the community level (Godley and Velasquez 1998).

Indicated Prevention Programmes: Indicated prevention programmes intervene with youth involved in gangs or gang violence in order to reduce their rates of gang violence, re-arrest, and possibly gang affiliation. These programmes face a number of barriers, which might make them less effective than the selected and universal approaches. A consistent finding is that if these programmes utilize a group approach, there is the possibility of iatrogenic effects because deviancy training can occur between group members (Dodge et al. 2006). In addition, these programmes need to be fitting for the populations they are serving. Thus, they are often in the communities where there is gang activity and socio-economic disorder. As with selected prevention programmes, indicated programmes, must be able to accurately identify and recruit youth involved in gangs. Reliably reaching the intended population is often one of the greatest challenges for indicated prevention programmes (Lipsey 2009). One strategy for reaching gang-involved youth is to implement programmes through the juvenile justice system. However, a recent study shows that gang involvement significantly reduces the effectiveness of evidence-based interventions in juvenile justice settings (Boxer et al. 2015).

An example of an indicated prevention programme targeting the individual level is identifying and intervening with patients who are recovering in the hospital after an injury like a gunshot wound. These prevention programmes are particularly important when addressing gang violence as the risk for retaliatory violence and rehospitalization is high. The Wraparound Project (Smith et al. 2013) is an example of a programme at the individual level that identifies youth with violence-related injuries who are at high-risk for recurrent injury and rehospitalization (see Table 13.1).

Spergel's Comprehensive Community-wide Gang Programme Model is an example of an indicated prevention programme implemented at the community level (Spergel et al. 2001). This programme involved a coordination between local organizations and law enforcement to decrease violence and delinquency through intensive contacts with gang youth. The model was implemented in six cities nationwide (Riverside, CA, San Antonio, TX, Mesa, AZ, Tucson, AZ, Bloomington-Normal, IL), but was only effective in three cities: Bloomington-Normal, IL, Mesa, AZ, and Riverside, CA. The cities with success implemented the programme with high fidelity to the programme model.

Whilst risks and protective factors occur at multiple levels of the socio-ecological model, the majority of gang-prevention programmes reviewed intervened at the individual level. An effective delinquency intervention which targets individual, family, and community levels, Multisystemic Therapy, has been shown to be equally effective at preventing re-arrest for gang and nongang youth (Boxer et al. 2017). Future research should investigate whether multisystemic therapy (MST) can prevent gang entry or facilitate gang exit. Furthermore, universal programmes that target youth prior to gang entry were rare. More work is needed in the development and evaluation of programmes that intervene early, i.e. ages 8–10, before the formation of delinquent peer groups, that are focused on multiple levels of the youth's socio-ecological context, particularly the family level and that are for universal and selected population. Often delinquency prevention programmes are seen as synonymous with gang prevention programmes. Yet, outcomes specific to gang involvement are often not examined in these programmes and, as a consequence, their effect on gang involved youth is unknown (Huey et al. 2016). Whilst there are shared risks between delinquency and gang outcomes, there are also unique characteristics of gang-affiliated populations that likely require tailored intervention. Therefore, until more work is done evaluating gang-prevention programmes, we are left with few choices we can feel confident in for our gang-prevention efforts.

Dissemination and Implementation of Programmes and Strategies

The fourth step in the public health model of violence preventions is to determine how to most effectively disseminate and implement prevention programmes. In this section, we will review a framework to better understand factors that contribute to the broad dissemination and implementation of the prevention programmes. Addressing public health problems, like gang violence, necessitates an understanding of the best available prevention programmes to meet the needs of the impacted population. Traditional approaches to planning, delivery, and evaluation RE-AIM Model is a framework that was developed to examine the public health impact of interventions (Glasgow et al. 2006). This framework goes beyond efficacy to better understand the real-world environment and the value of investing in the programme.

Many behavioural health interventions from those that target specific behaviours, such as physical activity, condom use and smoking cessation, to those focus on general well-being and chronic disease prevention have used the RE-AIM Model. A meta-analyses found over 80 studies that examined at least one of the RE-AIM factors (Harden et al. 2015). Whilst the

RE-AIM framework has great utility for better understanding gang prevention programmes, it has not yet been applied to these programmes.

Five individual- and organizational-level factors make up RE-AIM: reach, effectiveness, adoption, implementation, and maintenance.

- Reach: The percentage and representativeness of programme participants (i.e. inclusion criteria, exclusion criteria, participation rate, generalizability);
- Effectiveness: The impact of the programme on the targeted behavioural outcomes, quality of life, and other indicators (i.e. results for one follow-up, intent-to-treat analysis, quality-of-life, or potential negative outcomes, moderation analysis, percentage attrition);
- Adoption: The percentage and representatives of settings and intervention staff that agree to deliver a programme (i.e. programme location, programme staff, method of identifying staff to deliver programme, level of staff expertise, inclusion/exclusion criteria for setting or staff)
- Implementation: Programme fidelity and resources (i.e. intervention duration and frequency, protocol delivered as intended, cost of implementation);
- Maintenance: At the individual level, the extent to which programme participants maintain behavioural change long-term and at the setting level the degree to which the programme is sustained over time within the organizations delivering it. (i.e. indicators of programme-level maintenance, alignment with organizational mission, measures of cost of maintenance).

The RE-AIM framework is particularly suited for programmes that target multiple levels of the socio-ecological context. Knowing that public health programmes have the potential to reach a large number of individuals, especially universal programmes, the framework focuses on understanding the nuances that distinguish risk levels of programme participants and non-participants (Glasgow et al. 2006). It also has an attunement to the external validity of programmes, or the ability to which they understand the setting, population, and long-term organizational needs. These factors are particularly important to understanding the fit of a programme to a setting and population.

Discussion

Public health has had great success in addressing complex health behaviours by defining and understanding the problem, understanding the factors that change risks and protective factors, designing programmes to address these factors, and finally implementing and evaluating these programmes to provide a foundation to judge their public impact (Rosenberg et al. 1992). In this chapter, we have illustrated how utilizing a similar approach has great potential to reduce gang affiliation and subsequent violence. However, putting the public health model into action to prevent gang involvement will require collaboration to occur on many levels. Youth, families, and many community organizations will have to work together in new ways to address this problem.

There are several areas that represent gaps in the current gang-prevention landscape. For instance, the public health model highlights the utility of universal prevention programmes that can reduce gang entry and related violence. However, there are few examples of universal prevention programmes that expressly aim to prevent gang entry. Based on our review of risk, protective, and promotive factors, universal prevention programmes that promote self-regulation skills for children and positive parenting practices for adults could reduce gang prevalence long before selected or indicated prevention programmes are necessary. Promising programmes that could fill this gap include Incredible Years or the Triple P Positive Parenting Programme (Hahlweg et al. 2010). However, recruiting parents for universal participation in such programmes can be challenging. It would likely be easier to recruit for selected prevention perhaps because parents would be more motivated to participate if they already recognize behaviour problems in their children (Robinson et al. 2016).

Whether universal, selected, or indicated, gang prevention efforts at the societal level are scarce. However, there is growing international research that has contrasted the policy responses to gangs in the US vs. other nations (Esbensen and Maxson 2012). For instance, both governmental and cultural differences between the US and Scandinavian countries (e.g. quality of social welfare programmes, perceptions of who is responsible for stopping gangs) may impact gang prevention policy (Esbensen and Maxson 2012). It could be another promising gang prevention strategy to evaluate the impact of different societal approaches to gangs and borrow effective methods across national borders. In the US, since policy might vary state-by-state, surveillance systems, like NVDRS, could be used to measure the impact of these policies on gang prevention efforts.

In summary, the field of public health highlights the need to develop more gang prevention strategies in the universal category, and at the community and societal levels (w. National Center for Injury Prevention and Control 2009). Similar to successes with motor vehicle collisions (World Health Organization 2013), prevention efforts that focus on policy change is likely to be the most promising approach. For example, promoting the safe use and safe storage of weapons, and enforcing curfews for youth might all have an impact on gang entry. Applying the public health model to defining and understanding the problems associated with gangs, identifying key risk, protective, and promotive factors, developing prevention programmes, and implementing and evaluating them, could provide useful guidance in efforts to prevent youths' involvement in gangs and gang violence.

References

Arbreton, A.J. and McClanahan, W.S. (2002). *Targeted Outreach: Boys & Girls Clubs of America's Approach to Gang Prevention and Intervention*. Philadelphia, PA: Office of Juvenile Justice and Deliquence Prevention, US Department of Justice.

Augustyn, M.B., Thornberry, T.P., and Krohn, M.D. (2014). Gang membership and pathways to maladaptive parenting. *Journal of Research on Adolescence* 24 (2): 252–267.

Boxer, P., Kubik, J., Ostermann, M., and Veysey, B. (2015). Gang involvement moderates the effectiveness of evidence-based intervention for justice-involved youth. *Children and Youth Services Review* 52: 26–33. https://doi.org/10.1016/j.childyouth.2015.02.012.

Brantingham, P.J. and Faust, F.L. (1976). A Conceptual Model of Crime Prevention. *Crime & Delinquency* 22 (3): 284–296. https://doi.org/10.1177/00111287760220030.

Bronfenbrenner, U. (1979). *The Ecology of Human Development*. Cambridge, MA: Harvard University Press.

Centers for Disease Control and Prevention (2012). Gang homicides – five U.S. cities, 2003–2008. *Morbidity and Mortality Weekly Report* 61 (3): 46–51.

Crimes Against Children Research Center. (2016). National Survey of Children's Exposure to Violence (NatSCEV). http://www.unh.edu/ccrc/projects/natscev.html (Accessed 16 August 2019).

Dahlberg, L. and Krug, E. (2002). Violence: a global public health problem. In: *World Health Report on Violence and Health* (eds. E.G. Krug, L.L. Dahlberg and J.A. Mercy), 1–22. Geneva, CH: World Health Organization.

Decker, S.H. (2009). Leaving the gang: Problems and prospects. Presentation at the Justice Research and Statistics Association National Conference in St. Louis, USA (22–23 October 2009).

Dodge, K.A., Dishion, T.J., and Lansford, J.E. (2006). *Deviant Peer Influences in Intervention and Public Policy for Youth*. Washington, DC: Society for Research in Child Development.

Egley, A., Howell, J., and Harris, M. (2014). *Highlights of the 2012 National Youth Gang Survey*. Washington, DC: US Department of Justice.

Esbensen, F.-A. and Maxson, C.L. (2012). *Youth Gangs in International Perspective: Results from the Eurogang Program of Research*. New York, NY: Springer.

Esbensen, F.-A., Peterson, D., Taylor, T.J., and Osgood, D. (2012). Results from a multi-site evaluation of the G.R.E.a.T. program. *Justice Quarterly* 29 (1): 125–151.

Esbensen, F.A., Peterson, D., Taylor, T.J. et al. (2011). Evaluation and evolution of the gang resistance education and training (GREAT) program. *Journal of School Violence* 10 (1): 53–70.

Esbensen, F.-A., Winfree, L., He, N., and Taylor, T. (2001). Youth gangs and definitional issues: when is a gang a gang, and why does it matter? *Crime & Delinquency* 47 (1): 105.

Finkelhor, D., Turner, H.A., Shattuck, A., and Hamby, S.L. (2013). Violence, Crime, and Abuse Exposure in a National Sample of Children and Youth: An Update. *JAMA Pediatrics* 167 (7): 614. https://doi.org/10.1001/jamapediatrics.2013.4.

Glasgow, R.E., Klesges, L.M., Dzewaltowski, D.A. et al. (2006). Evaluating the impact of health promotion programs: using the RE-AIM framework to form summary measures for decision making involving complex issues. *Health Education Research* 21 (5): 688–694.

Godley, M.D. and Velasquez, R. (1998). Effectiveness of the Logan Square prevention project: interim results. *Drugs & Society* 12 (1–2): 87–103.

Haegerich, T.M., Mercy, J., and Weiss, B. (2013). What is the role of public health in gang membership prevention? In: *Changing Course: Preventing Gang Membership* (eds. T.R. Simon, N.M. Ritter and R.R. Mahendra), 31–50. Atlanta, GA: National Institute of Justice (NIJ) and Centers for Disease Control and Prevention (CDC).

Hahlweg, K., Heinrichs, N., Kuschel, A. et al. (2010). Long-term outcome of a randomized controlled universal prevention trial through a positive parenting program: is it worth the effort? *Child and Adolescent Psychiatry and Mental Health* 4 (1): 1–14.

Harden, S.M., Gaglio, B., Shoup, J.A. et al. (2015). Fidelity to and comparative results across behavioral interventions evaluated through the RE-AIM framework: a systematic review. *Systematic Reviews* 4 (155): 1–13.

Hennigan, K.M.K., Kathy, A., Vindel, F., and Maxson, C.L. (2015). Targeting youth at risk for gang involvement: validation of a gang risk assessment to support individualized secondary prevention. *Children and Youth Services Review* 56: 86–96.

Huey, S., Lewine, G., and Rubenson, M. (2016). Brief review and meta-analysis of gang intervention trials in North America. In: *Gang Transitions and Transformations in an International Context* (eds. C.E. Maxson and F.A. Esbensen), 217–233. Geneva, CH: Springer International Publishing.

Klein, M.W. and Maxson, C.L. (2006). *Street Gang Patterns and Policies*. New York, NY: Oxford University Press.

Krohn, M.D., Ward, J.T., Thornberry, T.P. et al. (2011). The cascading effects of adolescent gang involvement across the life course. *Criminology* 49 (4): 991–1028.

Lee, L.M., Thacker, S.B., and Louis, M.E.S. (2010). *Principles & Practice of Public Health Surveillance*. New York, NY: Oxford University Press.

Lipsey, M.W. (2009). The primary factors that characterize effective interventions with juvenile offenders: A meta-analytic overview. *Victims & Offenders* 4 (2): 124–147. https://doi.org/10.1080/15564880802612573.

Matsuda, K.N. (2014). Risk factors for gang membership. In: *Encyclopedia of Criminology and Criminal Justice* (eds. G. Bruinsma and D. Weisburd), 4476–4485. New York, NY: Springer.

McCord, J., Tremblay, R.E., Vitaro, F., and Desmarais-Gervais, L. (1994). Boys' disruptive behaviour, school adjustment, and delinquency: the Montreal prevention experiment. *International Journal of Behavioral Development* 17 (4): 739–752.

McDaniel, D.D. (2012). Risk and protective factors associated with gang affiliation among high-risk youth: a public health approach. *Injury Prevention* 18 (4): 253–258.

Mercy, J., Butchart, A., Farrington, D., and Cerdá, M. (2002). Youth violence. In: *World Report on Violence and Health* (eds. E.G. Krug, L.L. Dahlberg, J.A. Mercy, et al.), 23–56. Geneva, CH: World Health Organization.

Merrin, G.J., Hong, J.S., and Espelage, D.L. (2015). Are the risk and protective factors similar for gang-involved, pressured-to-join, and non-gang-involved youth? A social-ecological analysis. *American Journal of Orthopsychiatry* 85: 522–535.

National Center for Injury Prevention and Control (2009). *CDC Injury Research Agenda 2009–2018*. Atlanta, GA: Centers for Disease Control and Prevention.

National Center for Injury Prevention and Control (2016). *Injury Prevention & Control: Data & Statistics (WISQUARS): Violent Deaths 2003–2013*. Atlanta, GA: Centers for Disease Control and Prevention.

O'Brien, K., Daffern, M., Chu, C.M., and Thomas, S.D.M. (2013). Youth gang affiliation, violence, and criminal activities: a review of motivational, risk, and protective factors. *Aggression and Violent Behavior* 18 (4): 417–425.

Parks, S.E., Johnson, L.L., McDaniel, D.D., and Gladden, M. (2014). Surveillance for violent deaths: national violent death reporting system, 16 states, 2010. *Morbidity and Mortality Weekly Report: Surveillance Summaries* 63 (1): 1–33.

Pyrooz, D.C. and Sweeten, G. (2015). Gang membership between ages 5 and 17 years in the United States. *Journal of Adolescent Health* 56 (4): 414–419.

Robinson, L., Adair, P., Coffey, M. et al. (2016). Identifying the participant characteristics that predict recruitment and retention of participants to randomised controlled trials involving children: a systematic review. *Trials* (294): 1–17.

Rosenberg, M.L., O'Carroll, P.W., and Powell, K.E. (1992). Let's be clear: violence is a public health problem. *JAMA* 267 (22): 3071–3072.

Runyan, C.W. and Freire, K.E. (2008). Developing interventions when there is little science. In: *Handbook of Injury and Violence Prevention* (eds. L.S. Doll, S.E. Bonzo, D.A. Sleet, et al.), 411–431. Atlanta, GA: Springer.

Smith, R., Dobbins, S., Evans, A. et al. (2013). Hospital-based violence intervention: risk reduction resources that are essential for success. *Journal of Trauma and Acute Care Surgery* 74 (4): 976–982.

Spergel, I.A., Sosa, R.V., and Wa, K.M. (2001). *Evaluation of the Bloomington-Normal Comprehensive Gang Program*. Chicago, IL: US Department of Justice, Office of Juvenile Justice and Delinquency Prevention.

Tremblay, R., Masse, L., Pagani, L., and Vitaro, F. (1996). From childhood physical aggression to adolescent maladjustment: the Montreal prevention experiment. In: *Preventing Childhood Disorders, Substance Abuse, and Delinquency*, vol. 3 (eds. R.D. Peters and R.J. McMahon), 268–298. Thousand Oaks, CA: Sage.

Watkins, A.M. and Taylor, T.J. (2016). The prevalence, predictors, and criminogenic effect of joining a gang among urban, suburban, and rural youth. *Journal of Criminal Justice* 47: 133–142.

Weerman, F.M., Maxson, C.L., Esbensen, F.-A. et al. (2009). Eurogang Program Manual: Background, development, and use of the Eurogang instruments in multi-site, multi-method comparative research. https://www.umsl.edu/ccj/Eurogang/EurogangManual.pdf.

World Health Organization (2013). *Global Status Report on Road Safety 2013:Ssupporting a Decade of Action*. Geneva, CH: World Health Organization.

Zimmerman, M.A., Stoddard, S.A., Eisman, A.B. et al. (2013). Adolescent resilience: promotive factors that inform prevention. *Child Development Perspectives* 7 (4): 215–220.

14

Terrorism and Ideological Violence

Wagdy Loza

Queen's University (Psychiatry), Kingston, Canada

Introduction

This chapter concentrates on Middle Eastern Terrorism (MET), with particular emphasis on ideologically related terrorism. MET was selected because it has been a major international concern since the four coordinated terrorist attacks on September 11, 2001 in New York, Virginia, and Pennsylvania (collectively referred to as 9/11). It is one of the most serious threats currently facing the world, the other forms of terrorism are minor in comparison to the MET as they are not causing as much damage as the MET, and because it has become a focus of the emerging articles on the subject of terrorism.

At the beginning of this chapter important issues that help with understanding ideologically-related terrorism are briefly reviewed. Issues reviewed include the history of ideologically-related terrorism, definition, characteristics of terrorists, the goals of modern-day terrorists, the psychological and social impact of terrorism, a typology of terrorists, the magnitude and extent of ideologically-based terrorism. In the next section, the motivation and justification for terrorism will be presented. This section will include the religious influences and ideologies, religiously-related ideologies and recruitment of new terrorists, and the use of religiously-related ideologies in terrorist training. In the third section, a brief description of the following two measures will be reported: the Assessment and Treatment of Radicalization Scale (ATRS) and the Violent Extremism Risk Assessment (VERA). In the fourth section, issues regarding prevention and intervention will be discussed. The fifth section will deal with research on ideologically-related terrorism and, finally, the chapter will end with the summary and conclusion.

Understanding Ideologically-Related Terrorism

A brief history of ideologically-related terrorism The history of ideologically related Terrorism goes back to 66–73 CE, when the Sicarii (the dagger men) in Jerusalem assassinated Jewish collaborators, Roman occupiers, and terrorized the residents of Jerusalem

The Wiley Handbook of What Works in Violence Risk Management: Theory, Research and Practice, First Edition. Edited by J. Stephen Wormith, Leam A. Craig, and Todd E. Hogue.
© 2020 John Wiley & Sons Ltd. Published 2020 by John Wiley & Sons Ltd.

(Reid 2003). In 782, Charlemagne killed 4500 captive Saxons who rebelled against forced conversion to Roman Catholicism (Svirsky 2016). From 1090 to 1256, the assassins (the hashishun), in Jerusalem, murdered Muslim Sunni leaders, and other governing rulers. They wanted to turn their society into a purely Islamic community (Pedahzur 2005). In the thirteenth century, Hindu thugs strangled their victims and buried them to please Goddess Kali (Rapoport 1984). In 1572, Christian terrorists committed the St. Bartholomew's Day massacre in which it is estimated that up to 100000 French Protestants were killed by Catholic mobs. In 1784, Moroccan pirates hijacked US ships as a form of jihad (holy war) against Christians (Lee 2008). More recently, Jewish groups known as the Irgun, Stern gangs, Kach, and Kahane Chai committed terrorism to establish and expand the state of Israel (Stern 2003). There are also several terrorist groups that used Christianity to justify their terrorism, such as Saints for Christ (Stern 2003) and Warriors for Divine Justice (Drummond 2002). These groups committed terrorist acts because they opposed abortion and homosexuality. Similarly, since early 1900s the Muslim Brotherhood (MB; its roots go back to 1928 and have recently been declared a terrorist organization in Egypt and some Arab countries) have been implicated in the murder of the Egyptian President Anwar Sadat in 1981, and the murder or attempted murder of several prime ministers and highly ranked government officials, diplomats, tourists, academics, writers, and others who oppose their extreme views (Hafez 2003). More recently, after the ousting of president Morsi from governing Egypt in the summer of 2013, the MB have been held responsible and are currently being persecuted for killing thousands of citizens (Blaydes and Rubin 2008), attacking police stations, and burning government buildings and between 60 and 80 churches. They are still committing terrorist's attacks in northern Sinai killing military and police personnel. The MB is also described as the founding father of today's radical Muslim activism (Bakker and Meijer 2012).

Since the terrorist attacks on 9/11 in the United States, and to this day, many terrorist acts around the world have been well publicized. The most extraordinary terrorist attacks, however, were committed by Al-Qaeda and involved a series of airplane crashes (including into the twin towers of the World Trade Centre), in New York in 2001, a series of bombings in Madrid in 2004, and in Bali and London in 2005 (Silke 2008). Since 2105, there has been a new wave of terrorism around the world supported by the Islamic State of Iraq and Syria (ISIS). ISIS (formerly Da'esh, IS, ISIL), was formed in April 2013, it is now one of the main jihadist groups fighting against Syria and Iraq armed forces.

Definition of terrorism   There is no consensus about a single definition of terrorism that has been accepted universally (Ganor 2008). In 2002, the Counterterrorism Committee of the U.N. General Assembly drafted a definition of terrorism. It defines terrorism as 'the act of destroying or injuring civilian lives or the act of destroying or damaging civilian or government property without the expressly chartered permission of a specific government, thus, by individuals or groups independently or governments on their own accord and belief, in the attempt to effect some political change' (Stevens 2005). In the United States, different agencies have accepted the term 'terrorism' to mean 'the premeditated, politically motivated violence perpetrated against non-combatant targets by subnational groups or clandestine agents' (Stevens 2005). In Canada, section 83.01 of the *Criminal Code defines* terrorism as an act committed 'in whole or in part for a political, religious or ideological purpose, objective or cause, with the intention of intimidating the public'(*Criminal Code,* R.S.C. 1985, c. C-46, s. 83.01).

Characteristics of terrorists   The main characteristics of terrorist action are the calculated use of unexpected, shocking, and unlawful violence against non-combatants (Drummond 2002; Laqueur 1987). Terrorists do not operate according to the rules of war (Stevens 2005). Terrorism is meant to produce a huge psychological impact (Mahmood 2001). There are several reasons given for the use of terrorist activity including the following: to create high profile impact on the public with the goal of undermining public confidence in their own government; to make routine social activity difficult; to inflict as much damage as possible; to seek vengeance; and to create physical pain and paralysing psychological emotions such as panic, chaos, unrest, fear, paranoia, anxiety, anger, grief, and a sense of tragedy (Ardila 2002; Furnish 2005; Hudson 1999; Lawal 2002; McCauley 2002; Reid 2002; Thackrah 2004).

The goals of modern-day terrorists   The majority of contemporary terrorist acts are linked to extremist ideologies, beliefs, and attitudes originating in the Middle-East. The ultimate goal of these terrorists is to establish a 'true' Muslim state (Caliphate) and, eventually, to impose pure Islamic societies in the entire world governed by a strict application of Shariah law (Yaseen 2007) after establishing caliphate system (Lindeborg 2002; Wicker and Lieto 2007). The perpetrators feel that Jihad is the means to achieve this ultimate goal. Extreme religious ideologies play a central role in radicalizing potential terrorists and recruiting and indoctrinating them into the foundational extremist ideology. ISIS clearly demonstrates these ideologies, goals, and methods. In the process to establish their goals, they cause disruption to routine life activities, inflict as much damage as possible, seek vengeance, and create physical pain and paralysing psychological emotions, such as panic, chaos, unrest, fear, paranoia, anxiety, anger, grief, and a sense of tragedy (Ardila 2002; Furnish 2005; Grieger 2006; Hudson 1999; Lawal 2002; McCauley 2002; McDermontt and Zimbardo 2007; Reid 2002; Thackrah 2004). They also attempt to intimidate or coerce a government or civilian population to accede to demands supportive of their underlying ideology or cause (Drummond 2002; Laqueur 1987).

The psychological and social impact of terrorism   The psychological effects of a major national trauma can affect, not only those who experience it firsthand, but all those who witness it via television and other media (Silver et al. 2002). The more visible a terrorist attack, the greater the probability that it will trigger psychiatric problems in the general public (Galea et al. 2002). Psychiatric problems of all kinds, most particularly trauma, may increase a victim's use of alcohol, tobacco products, illicit drugs, or result in resumption of same, which in turn can contribute to long term health problems, problems in the family, and increased rates of injury, assault, and crime (Grieger 2006). Other studies have reported that affected people may develop acute stress, Post-Traumatic Stress Disorder (PTSD), or other psychiatric problems. PTSD, depression, burnout, anxiety, sleep disorders, and substance abuse have been linked to terrorist incidents that resulted in many victims (Beutler et al. 2007); and physical issues such as cardiovascular problems (Holman et al. 2008). Grieger (2006) reported that the September 11, 2001 terrorist attack in New York led to widespread anxiety all over the United States and an increase in the prevalence of some emotional and behavioural problems, and other personality disorders. Recently, French pharmacists reported that the consumption of anxiety medication rose by 20% nationwide (Gurfinkiel 2015) since France's Charlie Hebdo, the French satirical magazine that published cartoons of the prophet Muhammed, attacks in January 2015.

A typology of terrorists   Several typologies have been suggested to categorize terrorists. Only the typologies that are related to Middle-eastern terrorists' ideologies are reported here. Reid (2001, 2010) defined seven different subtypes of terrorists. One, the 'unwavering true believer' possesses hardcore, deeply held religious beliefs. Two, the 'affiliating true believer' is anxious and dependent, and in need of a (often older) person to idealize and follow. Three, the 'opportunistic true believer' has joined the group for power, control, dominance, and wealth. His real cause is himself and he has a need to be admired. Four, the 'criminal true believer' often has a criminal background and is involved for the love of violence and control. Five, the 'betrayer true believer' is not personally wedded to the group's belief or mission, rather he has a personal need to avenge perceived past mistreatment. Six, the 'psychotic true believer' joined the group because extremist beliefs fit his psychotic worldview and his delusions and hallucinations. Seven, the 'fledgling true believer' is an immature or inexperienced person on route to becoming one of the above six subtypes. His susceptibility to recruitment comes either from personal suffering or indoctrination. His developing hatred, which is derived either from victimization or by seeing his family suffer, is further fostered and redirected by a charismatic leader against an external enemy.

The Magnitude and Extent of Ideologically-Based Terrorism: a Post 9/11, a Brief Review

In 2006, it was estimated that over 1000 terrorist organizations were active in more than one hundred countries (Zillmer 2006); from 2001 to 2007 terrorists have attempted over 30 attacks against European Union countries (Wicker and Lieto 2007); that from 2002 to 2005 an average of four terrorist attacks occurred annually in different countries, killing an average of 214 people each year (Mylorie 2008); and, that in Canada 54 groups were listed as terrorist entities in 2019 (Public Safety Canada 2019). Further, it is estimated that since 9/11, terrorists having middle-eastern religious ideologies are responsible for killing over 26 000 and wounding 50 000 in attacks in over 50 countries. Examples of terrorist acts committed before 9/11 are those that occurred in Algeria that killed thousands of people, and those in Kenya and Tanzania, Beirut, Israel, and Mumbai (Alstad 2007). Furthermore, in 2005 and 2006 respectively, Australian and Canadian security agencies thwarted plans to assassinate members of government, parliament, and the destruction of important buildings, such as government buildings, parliaments, the stock exchange, broadcasting buildings, the opera house, etc. Terrorists were also planning to behead the Prime Minster of Canada (in 2006).

The results of a few research projects demonstrate the prevalence of Middle Eastern extreme ideologies amongst some Muslims around the world. For example, in an opinion poll of one thousand US Muslims conducted in 2007, 8 % believed that suicide attacks on civilian targets are sometimes or often justified in order to defend their religion. Another survey conducted in 2006 involving Muslims in Britain, France, Germany, and Spain indicated that 7 to 16% of participants felt that suicide attacks are sometimes or often justified (McCauley and Scheckter 2008). In addition, 5% of US Muslims were favourable towards Al-Qaeda, and 8% justified suicide attacks. This translates to 70 000 adult US Muslims with radicalized opinions in relation to the War on Terrorism (McCauley and Scheckter 2008).

In addition, British Muslims who reported their primary identity as being Muslim held more positive views towards jihad and martyrdom than their fellow Muslim citizens who reported their dominant identity as British (Ansari et al. 2006). Likewise, 13% of British Muslims believe the persons who bombed the London subway system in July 2005 were martyrs for Islam, and 49% believe US military actions in Iraq are an attack against Islam (Wicker and Lieto, 2007). Recently, Pipes (2015) reported that there have been over 27 000 attacks globally connected to Middle-Eastern ideology since 9/11, or more than 5 per day. Also, Chiaramonte (2016) reported two studies which found that the deadly toll of terrorism around the globe has jumped nearly 800% in the past five years, an average of nearly 30 000 people per year have been killed by terrorists between 2010 and the end of 2015. Chiaramonte (2016) also reported a study that indicated that 'Whilst the Islamic State is responsible for at least 10 780 deaths since 2013, the rise of other extremist groups like Boko Haram and Al Shabbab in Africa has accounted for tens of thousands of terror deaths in the past five years'.

Similarly, Kassam (2016) reported findings from seven different surveys results. One; an ICM poll from 2006 indicated that 20% of British Muslims sympathized with the 7 July 2005 London bombers who participated in the killing of 52 and injuring hundreds, and 31 % of younger British Muslims endorsed or excused these bombings. According to NOP Research there are roughly three quarters of a million terror-sympathizing people in the UK. Twenty-seven percent of those polled in the United Kingdom say they had sympathy with the attacks on Charlie Hebdo, with 78% supporting punishment for the publication of cartoons featuring Muhammed, and 68% supporting the arrest and prosecution of British people who 'insult Islam'. Two; according to World Public Opinion, 2009 (Kassam 2016) at the University of Maryland, 61% of Egyptians, 32% of Indonesians, 41% of Pakistanis, 38% of Moroccans, 83% of Palestinians, 62% of Jordanians, and 42% of Turks appear to endorse or sympathize with attacks on American. Three; a 2013 study found that 16% of young Muslims in Belgium believed that state terrorism is 'acceptable', whilst 12% of young Muslims in Britain said that suicide attacks against civilians in Britain can be justified. Four; Pew Research from 2007 found that 26% of young Muslims in America believed suicide bombings are justified, with 35% in Britain, 42% in France, 22% in Germany, and 29% in Spain feeling the same. Five; Muslims who are more devout or dedicated to Islam are three times more likely to believe that suicide bombings are justified. Six; whilst just 5 % of UK Muslims said they would not report a terror attack being planned, the number increased to 18% amongst young British Muslims. Seven, the BBC found that 36% of 16- to 24-year old Muslims believe that if a Muslim converts to another religion they should be punished by death. Another research survey on a sample of Canadian Muslims from Ottawa indicated that 19% approve of the MB organization, and 9% agree that all governments would be better if they were ruled under the Caliphate (McCauley et al. 2011). Also, Rusin (2008) reported that Muslims in Canada indicated their support for punishing people who deserted Islam. Muslim children in Amsterdam as young as eight years of age have been found to exhibit anti-western and anti-democratic values (Pressman 2008).

Consistent with these research findings, Canadian research indicates the prevalence of Middle Eastern extremist ideologies amongst samples from western and nonwestern countries (Ahmed et al. 2013; Loza 2010, 2011; Loza et al. 2010, 2013). Consistent with these findings, the Senate of Canada (2014) reported that the problem of radicalization is widely entrenched and embedded amongst Somali, Bangladeshi, and Pakistani Canadians. Unfortunately, the prevalence of these ideologies may have contributed to the home-grown terrorism that we have seen of late on members of the Royal Canadian Mounted Police (RCMP) and parliament.

Motivation and justification for terrorism

MET has been explained as a phenomenon that has multiple motivations, justifications, and explanations. The majority of the provided explanations are based on sociological, economical, psychological, and political factors, rather than on religious explanations (see review by Loza 2006). It has been suggested that the prevalence of extremist ideologies amongst the populations in the western countries is due to the fact that European countries have allowed asylum for hardcore extremists who escaped prosecution or who served prison time for extremism in their native Middle Eastern or Asian countries prior to immigrating to Europe. These extremists, under the democratic systems, were allowed to spread the extreme religious views that they were prohibited from proliferating in their own countries (Vidino 2005).

Religious ideologies influences   Although several theories have attempted to explain the motivating factors underlying the phenomenon of terrorism, the strongest and most influential factor underpinning terrorism is the religious influences and related ideologies. This is because common themes in the Middle Eastern ideologies that underlie the majority of recent terrorist acts committed around the world are religiously based.

Supporting this argument, are reports that indicate that; (i) Extreme religious ideologies play a central role in in radicalizing young Muslims, recruiting, and indoctrinating them into the terrorist ideology (Ibrahim 1980, 1988; Isam 2006; Schwind 2005); (ii) Ideology has been described as the most important driving force for terrorism because it defines all aspects involved in this enterprise: setting up goals of the organization and its structure, help with recruitment, defining the roles of leaders and members, and the strategies to be used. Ideology also determines the target to be attacked and the method to use (Silber and Bhatt 2007; Gunaratna and Bin Ali 2007); (iii) It is accepted that the majority of terrorist acts that the world has witnessed in the last few years have been linked to extremist religious ideologies, (Gunaratna 2009; Loza 2006; Moghaddam 2005), beliefs (Borum 2004), and attitudes that originated from the Middle-East. The underlying dominator of these ideologies are religiously based; (iv) Religious ideology is important for many groups because terrorists believe that they are serving the will of God (Hronick 2006). Post (1990) suggested that the most dangerous terrorist is likely to be a religious terrorist; (v) A great deal of training time is spent on understanding the organization's ideological tenets and spiritual preparation because of the importance of religious ideology (Lia 2008); (vi) Religious terrorists are willing to endure much higher human costs than secular terrorists (Blaydes and Rubin 2008).

Other reports indicated that by 2004 46% of terrorist groups in Egypt were religiously based (Blaydes and Rubin 2008). Results from 35 incarcerated Palestinians indicated that their attitude regarding suicide terrorism is related more to religion than other reasons such as economic or social reasons (Post et al. 2003). Hoffman (1993) suggested that about half of the most dangerous terrorist groups are primarily motivated by religion. These terrorists believe that God commands them to commit terrorism for their (religiously-based) cause.

The common theme in these ideologies is that Islamic states were no longer purely Islamic and that Muslims were 'living' in 'Jahiliaya' (the age of ignorance which prevailed in the Arabian peninsula before the revelation of Islam to the prophet Mohammed) (Ibrahim 1980). Consequently, it was contended that there must be a continuous state of war between the house of peace (Islamic countries) and the house of war (non-Muslim countries). This state should continue until the nonbelievers, 'the infidels', are converted to Islam, killed or enslaved, or subjugated to the Muslim community as inferior and pay extra taxes in order for them to retain their lives and property (Dhimmi status). The current manmade rules must be overturned in favour of the laws made by God as contained in the Qur'an. Western civilization with its democracy and modernity is viewed as morally corrupt, and Islam possesses the values that are needed for a good and just world. The Muslim societies have decayed and become vulnerable to Western intrusion because Muslims have strayed from their religion. A just world will only be guaranteed and achieved by going back to the true Islam. Infidels must be fought until they become weak, their state disappears, and they submit to the law of Islam. The adherence to the purest sources of Islam is necessary for saving Muslim societies from the ills of our time. There must be a revival of religion and a relationship between God and man via da'wa (call to God, which is considered fard'ayn (a duty incumbent on every Muslim to participate in the Islamic reform of society and state), and Jihad, with the eventual goal of establishing the true Muslim state and creating pure Islamic societies all over the world. Thus, it is the duty of every Muslim to wage holy war against the unbelievers or the infidels. (Hafez 2003; Ibrahim 1988; Isam 2006; Lotfi et al. 1993; Sageman 2004; Schwind 2005; Wickham 2002).

Other expectations followed from this ideology. Loyalty is required of all Muslims to the religion of Islam, rather than to their country or to a secular political system (El-Tuhami 1997). Islamic religion is better than other religions (Locicero and Sinclair 2008). 'It is individual obligation, on every Muslim to prepare his equipment, to make up his mind to engage in Jihad, and to get ready for it until the opportunity is ripe and God decrees a matter which is sure to be accomplished' (Wickham 2013 p. 26). 'The shari'a principles prohibits the sale, production, distribution of alcohol; applying the hudoud (qur'anic punishment for serious crimes like murder and adultery); establishing penalties for breaking the fast during the holy month of Ramadan, and reconciling the laws governing marriage and divorce with shari'a mandates. Under the same principles homosexuals are punished, and inheritance issues are regulated according to Islam laws', (Wickham 2013, p. 31). 'Jews are inherently corrupt and duplicitous, cursed by God' (Wickham 2013, p. 33).

Other ideological themes that are promoted to promote terrorism include the following. The martyr is saved from the punishment of the grave. He is saved from the great terror (the Day of Judgement). On his head is placed a crown of dignity, Nations weaken when people love the world too much and despise death, Weakness occurs when the person loves life and hates death. On the Day of Resurrection, the blood of the Martyr smells like musk, there is nothing more beloved to Allah than the drop of blood shed in the Path of Allah, The Martyr wishes to return to the World in order to be killed again. The motto of the Egyptian MB, founded in 1928, is a manifesto for 'Jihadist Martyrdom' and reflects the ideological backgrounds for terrorists. It states 'Allah is our objective. The Prophet is our leader. The Qur'an is our law. Jihad is our way. Dying in the way of Allah is our highest hope'. All these teaching are designed to communicate to young Muslims that the West is the source of all evil, the Muslim religion is the only right one, that when Islam does not prevail then bigotry and hatred have free reign, and that there is no negotiation with nonbelievers (Israeli 1988; Littman 2005; Manji 2003; Sayyed 2005).

Religiously related ideologies and recruitment of new terrorists The use of religiously related ideologies is essential for the recruitment of new terrorists and encouraging them to commit terrorist acts. Because of the importance of ideology, all ISIS cadres undergo training in which they are filled with ideology that allows them to deem all others as apostates who should be killed (Speckhard and Yayla 2015). The main goal of using ideology is to shame young Muslims, especially urging them to feel victimized by Western governments for taking a 'stance against Islamism' (Kassam 2016). They aspire to develop grievances, anger, and desire for revenge. To achieve their goals recruiters usually lecture about the political problems Muslims are facing around the world, and how their lands and wealth was imperialized. To recruit specifically for ISIS, the recruiters talk about how the Syrian soldiers were raping their sisters and that they should be sending birth control pills to their sisters if they chose not to fight them (Speckhard and Yayla 2015). The following examples offer a detailed review of how terrorist ideologies are used to recruit new terrorists.

First, recruiters use verses from the Qur'an (the Holy book of Islam Qur'an; Maududi 1991) such as: 'O Believers, do not take Jews nor the Christians as your friends: they are one another's friends only' (5:51, p. 177); 'Go fighting with them till there is no more a state of tribulation and Allah's way is established instead' (2–193, p. 45); 'I am now going to fill the hearts of the disbelievers with awe: so smite their necks and beat every joint of their bodies' (8:12–14, p. 279); 'Strike terror into the enemies of Allah and your enemies' (8:60, p. 287); 'The punishment of those who wage war against Allah and His Messenger and run about to spread mischief in the land is this: they should be put to death or crucified or their alternate hands and feet should be cut off, or they should be banished from the land' (5:33, p. 171). There are many similar verses (see Schwind 2005).

The second example to explain how terrorist ideologies are used to recruit new terrorists comes from a series lectures and sermons that are posted on the Internet which are easily accessible (http://www.alminbar.com/khutbaheng/1478.htm). "A martyr has six bounties: He will be forgiven with the first drop of his blood that is spilt; He will see his place in Paradise (at the time of death); He will be saved from the 'Great Horror' (on the Day of Judgement): A Crown of Dignity will be placed on his head, which contains many corundum's, each one being more precious than this life and all that it contains; He will have 72 Women of Paradise; and, he will be allowed to intercede for 70 of his family members (who would have otherwise gone to hell)". "There is no doubt that the sacrificing of one's soul for the sake of Allah in order to defeat His enemies and support Islam is the very highest level. This is of course martyrdom". "The Prophet (Peace be upon him) said: 'I swear by the One in Whose Hands my soul is, I wish that I would fight for the sake of Allah (i.e. Jihad) and get martyred, then return and fight again and get martyred, then return and fight again and get martyred'". "We asked the Prophet (Peace be upon him) about this verse and he replied: 'Their (i.e. the martyrs souls) will live inside green birds that dwell in designated lamps which hang on the throne of Allah, they will roam freely in Paradise as they please, then return to these lamps'". "The pain that a martyr feels at the time of death will be reduced so greatly that he will only feel as if he was stung by a mosquito". Moreover, the finest dwellings in Paradise are those of the martyrs. "The angels spread their wings over the body of a martyr as a form of honour, dignity, and respect. Amongst all the dwellers of Paradise, only the martyrs would wish to return to this life". "For he would wish to return and get killed 10 times due to the honour that he received (in Paradise)". "It is vital that the Muslims exert every effort to spread the love for achieving martyrdom just like the pious early generations of Muslims did. We must continue on the same road that they were on". "Any Muslim who forsakes his fellow Muslim at a time when his honour and sanctity are being attacked will have Allah forsaking him at the time when needs His support the most. Any Muslim who supports his fellow Muslim at a time when his honour and sanctity are being attacked will have Allah supporting him at the time when needs His support the most".

The third example to explain how terrorist ideologies are used to recruit new terrorists, comes from a series of videoed sermons and lectures by Anwar Al Awlaki promote jihad and martyrdom. They include four sites that include the following titles: (i). "Those who stay behind from jihad fisabilillah" (for God's sake; https://www.youtube.com/watch?v=HB3uD9zubfA); (ii) The meaning of Jihad (https://www.youtube.com/watch?v=nDD6FNM895M); (iii) Constants on the path of jihad (https://www.youtube.com/watch?v=yQcGnbZ-N9o); and (iv) Allah is preparing us for victory (https://www.youtube.com/watch?v=_vJdv-HX28o). In these sermons and lectures Al Awlaki encourages young Muslims to commit jihad and martyr themselves. His sermons include statements such as "Victory will not come but through the blood of the martyrs. Those who would like to see their lords in the abode of the prophets; they scarified themselves, offered their souls and bloods for the sake of their religion. People of giving and granting are the people of excellence and pride. The sun of steadfastness has risen. We may return the light faith and glorious might by men who have divorced/forsaken this world and its immorality. We have revived the UMMA (Islamic community) of glory and assured victory. The Islamic state has risen by the blood of the righteous".

In one of his lecture or sermons Al Awlaki's blames those who are not involved in Jihad. Some of his statements include: Those who have neglected jihad have put themselves in the position of exclusion from the mercy of Allah. Deprived themselves from the greatest reward. He questions what is it that makes "you stay back and neglect Jihad" and "stay away from the pass of success". "Why you have not joined the ranked of el-mujahedeen?" "Why holding back yourself and wealth" He then proceeded to say it must be for one of the following reasons that keeping you away from ALLAH: The desire to live a long life. The attachment to family, friend, and wealth. The desire to do good deeds before fighting jihad. The love of a beautiful wife. "Your position of power or love of a comfortable lifestyle. Nothing else could be holding you back". He then scolds his listeners by saying: can't you hear the call of Allah directed at you? He cites a verse from the Quran: "O you who have believed! What was amiss with you that, when you were asked to march forth in the way of Allah, you clung to the earth? What! Did you prefer the life of this world to the life of the Hereafter? If it is so, you should know that all these provisions of this worldly life will prove to be but little in the Hereafter. If you will not march forth, Allah will inflict on you a painful chastisement, and will substitute other people for you" (Al-Tauba, 38–39, p. 301). He asked his audience to listen carefully to how he will respond to each of the reasons that is holding them back from jihad. Then they will come to realize that "nothing but yourself and the Shitan (Devile) that is preventing you from jihad". He then discussed the possible reasons for people to be reluctant to participate in jihad and explained the folly of these reasons. He ends up his sermons by encouraging his audience to go ahead and get involved in jihad and martyrdom, appealing to a number of values and rationales: One, Cowardness: He argued that no one can "delay his time (of death)"; On the Day of Judgement there is fear (for the nonbelievers), but the martyr does not feel the pain of death, except the sting of insect. Then he says "my brother why miss out on this opportunity?" "After death you will be spared the punishment of the grave, spared the questioning of the angels in the graves, you will be tranquil in the Day of Judgement when everyone else will be terrified. Your soul inside of birds flying in paradise. Can you see the difference between dying natural death and as a martyr?" Two, attachments to family: to this he reasoned "Wordily life is enjoyment of delusion". "It does not make sense to leave all the good things in heaven because worldly life, particularly that you are dying anyway. Your family if they love you or hate you they will leave you for the Day of Judgement you will be going there alone. On the Day of Judgement everyone will wish to sacrifice parents, wife, and children if it saves them from the hill fires;"

The third motive is the, love of wealth, to which he rationalized that "Why don't you leave voluntarily as you will leave it anyway?" "In the Day of Judgment you will be asked how you made this money, what you did with it…etc. Allah said poor Muslims will lead the rich to paradise by 500 years;" Four, love for your children and caring for them: to this he reasoned that "Allah will care for them more than you. He cared for them whilst in the womb. If you advise them… they will hate you after;" and Five, your friends: to this he argued against attachment to friends more than the desire to fight and martyr themselves.

The fourth example to explain how terrorist ideologies are used to recruit new terrorists, comes from a series Shiek Yakan who is another prominent speaker whose lectures and sermons have promoted jihad. He stated "all powers have allied against us, such as the Crusaders (that is, Christians), the Communists, the Zionists, and the idolaters; we have become the lowest people on earth. They have seized our land and our wealth and our blood, to the point that the blood of the Muslim has become, in their view, the cheapest blood …. How many youth have died on the gallows … how many women … how many nursing children … and all the whilst, the Muslims have been sleeping!… This bitter reality with which Muslims live everywhere imposes on each one an individual duty (fard'ayn) to work for change" (Wickham 2002, p 141).

The common theme of these sermons and lectures is to emphasize the importance of jihad as mandated by religion and to urge the audience to commit jihad by shaming them.

The use of religiously related ideologies in terrorist training   Example of using ideology in the training of terrorists could be drawn from the ISIS training programme which focuses on ideologies that promote jihad. Trainers usually cite verses from the Qur'an and other references sacred to all participants. They also use many lectures and sermons by prominent preachers - like the ones just mentioned- to promote the validity of their argument (i.e. the call for sacrificing oneself for the sake of Allah). This makes it difficult, and impossible for those undergoing such training to question what they are being taught by the trainers. The material presented coupled with the powerful personalities of the trainers who are described as kind, gentle, highly charismatic, well educated, impressive, and knowledgeable and are well trained in Islamic law, and very convincing, persuades them to be martyrs, and makes them highly vulnerable to accepting the violent interpretations of Islam without questioning or challenging teachers and texts. (Speckhard and Yayla 2015).

Assessment measures for ideologically related terrorism

There are now countless risk and risk/need assessment measures commonly used to assess violent offenders in the correctional and forensic mental health population. However, they were not designed for terrorist offenders, nor have they been standardized on them. The reliability and validity of these scales for use with extremists/terrorists have not been demonstrated. There are now at least two measures that have been specifically designed to measure middle-eastern extremism/terrorism.

The assessment and treatment of radicalization scale   The Assessment and Treatment of Radicalization Scale (ATRS, Loza 2007) is a theoretically driven, empirically validated, self-report instrument that was constructed to quantitatively measure Middle Eastern extremist ideologies on risk areas that are reported in the research literature. The ATRS consists of six subscales and a total scale, with each subscale designed to tap into a prominent ideological theme promoted by Middle Eastern extremists: The first subscale reflects negative Attitudes Towards Israel. The Israeli-Palestinian conflict is a core source of grievance for many Middle Eastern extremists (Ameen 1993; Mokaitis 2006). The second subscale is Political Views, which measures the key political views that are advocated by Middle Eastern extremists (e.g. opposing secular laws and governments and advocating for the implementation of the Sharia Islamic law) (Ibrahim 1988; Mokaitis 2006). The third subscale assesses participants' Attitudes Towards Women. Muslim extremists' attitudes about women are mainly repressive, were historically foreign to many Middle Eastern countries, and were not a part of their culture prior to the 1970s (Kanany-Minesot 1995). The fourth subscale measures negative Attitudes Towards Western Culture. Middle Eastern extremists have been vocal in their rejection of western culture (Mazarr 2007; Mokaitis 2006; Tanveer 2005), claiming that western civilization is corrupt (McCauley 2002) and that the west is trying to undermine the Muslim religion (Orbach 2001). Extremists generally emphasize the prevalence of negative attitudes in Muslim countries towards non-Muslim cultures (Littman 2005; Manji 2003; Mokaitis 2006; Sayyed 2005).

The fifth subscale, Religiosity, assesses the respondents 'commitment to their religion. Extremists draw heavily on their religious convictions and beliefs to support and justify their cause and to recruit new pools of extremists (Hafez 2003; Ibrahim 1988; Isam 2006; Lotfi et al. 1993; Mokaitis 2006; Sageman, 2004; Schwind 2005). Some questions in this subscale tap into extreme religious views that are common in the Middle East. The sixth subscale, Condoning Fighting, measures views that not only condone fighting but also promote acts of violence as a means of destroying infidels (i.e. atheists and nonbelievers in Islam) in order to achieve one world under the Islamic religion (Sageman 2004; Schwind 2005). A final, seventh subscale, is a validity scale. Several research studies conducted by Loza and his colleagues on participants from Australia, Canada, Egypt, and South Africa demonstrate the reliability and validity of the ATRS (Ahmed et al. 2013; Loza 2010, 2011; Loza et al. 2010, 2013). The results of the study that included participants from four countries and included the largest number of participants of all studies (Loza et al. 2010) indicates that:

(a) The range of coefficient alphas (CA) for the ATRS subscales was 0.68–0.90. Only one scale has CA of 0.61. All items correlated significantly with their respective subscales. The correlations between ATRS subscale scores and the total score ranged from 0.77 to 0.93, and the differences between the upper and lower limits of the confidence intervals were small ranging from 0.007 for one scale the attitude towards Israel and -0.007 for the rest of the subscales. The subscale/subscale correlations ranged from 0.31 to 0.88.

(b) The Muslim participants always scored significantly higher than the Christians and the other religion/atheist groups on all the ATRS scales, the other religion/atheist group scored consistently lower than the Muslims and Christians.

(c) To investigate the trend of participant responses on the ATRS, participants

were grouped into low (total scores of ≤3), medium (>3 to ≤17), and high (>17) scoring groups, with approximately 33% in each group. Results indicate that 96.09% of the Muslims' scores fell in the high group, 47.78% of the Christians scores fell in the medium group, and 54.68% of the participants in the other religion/atheist category fell in the low group.

The violent extremism risk assessment The Violent Extremism Risk Assessment (VERA; Pressman 2009) is a structured professional judgement (SPJ) style tool to assess risk in a particular subpopulation who may commit violence based on ideologically motivated extremism.

The tool includes 28 items organized under five headings: Attitudinal Items (10 items); Contextual Items (4 items); Historical Items (6 items); Protective Items (5 items); and Demographic Items (3 items). Using the format and structure of traditional SPJ tools, the VERA guides the assessor to consider and score (e.g. low, moderate, and high risk), risk factors identified in the literature as relevant. The Attitudinal section of the VERA is comprised of 10 items assessing an individual's attachment to ideology, perception of injustice, perception of target, identity issues, and empathy. The four contextual items guide the assessor to consider the social environment of the individual, and the six historical items look to factors associated exposure to violence, violence training, and glorification of violent action. The fourth category guides the evaluator to seek out information that could serve to be protective for the individual. As with other SPJ tools, rehabilitation efforts focus on dynamic or changing factors whilst strengthening protective factors. Pressman refers to the VERA as 'a conceptual "research" tool intended to generate debate and discussion' Pressman (2009) aptly points out that because there are very few imprisoned terrorists in Canada, it is extremely difficult to validate such risk assessment tools due to low sample sizes.

Prevention and intervention

Prevention   Unless the terrorist-related ideologies are thoroughly understood by populations around the world, terrorism-related ideologies and terrorist actions will continue. It is with a great deal of naiveté on the part of Western populations and governments about Islamic terrorist ideology that these types of ideologies were allowed to spread to Western countries, particularly amongst Muslim youth (Loza 2006). As this type of terrorism cannot be defeated either by military or by law and order means alone (Bin Hassan 2006), it is crucial that counter recruitment and prevention programmes be developed and utilized proactively. The population, particularly the young, need to be inoculated from the terrorists' ideologies', their media, and their methods and strategies for attracting and radicalizing new recruits.

For example, internet sites can be developed to expose and challenge extreme ideologies, and to help with early identification of possible terrorists and engage/intervene with them. A component of the school curriculum, as well as discussions for parents and interested community members explaining the techniques used by recruiters may reduce the number of students who are vulnerable to these recruiters. For example, it would be helpful for both public safety officials and the public at large to understand the process by which recruiters tried, over time, to convince a young girl from Brussels to join ISIS. Specifically, how was she initially treated kindly, what kind of issues were discussed in the process of recruiting her, and was she how later subjected to threats to herself, her family, and friends, if she did not comply with recruiter's demands to immediately join ISIS (Burke 2015)

Intervention and rehabilitation

As predicted (Loza 2006), extremism, and terrorism have increased in the last decade. There is now an urgent need for the development of rehabilitation programmes for those who have been convicted of ideologically related terrorist acts, many of whom are now in prisons. In recent years, prison authorities in the West have observed many offenders being converted to Islam by some of the Muslim groups in prison espouse extreme ideologies (Loza 2010). It is reported that radicalization is occurring in prisons throughout the world (Cilluffo et al. 2007; Gilmore 2007; Popeo 2005; Siegel 2006; Travis 2006), and violent Islamist extremism is taking root in prisons amongst offenders (Dunleavy 2015; Moghaddam 2008). As demonstrated below, examples attesting to this phenomenon are plenty.

The MB grew stronger in Egypt in the 1950s and 1960s, and radicalized many others. El-Zawahiri, one of the Muslim brothers, promoted his message whilst in prison. El-Zarqaui, who committed brutal terrorist attacks in Iraq, was indoctrinated whilst in prison. Baker, the ISIS chief, and some of his colleagues were incarcerated in an Iraqi prison. Mohamed Bouyeri, the terrorist who murdered the Dutch filmmaker Theo van Gough, was radicalized whilst in prison. The notorious British 'shoe bomber', converted to Islam whilst incarcerated in Great Britain and attempted to explode a passenger aircraft. A foiled plot to attack numerous government and Jewish targets in California was devised inside New Folsom State Prison by members of an extreme Islamic group. The two gunmen involved in the Paris attack in 2015 at the Charlie Hebdo office were radicalized in prison. The man who shot a policewoman and four hostages at a kosher grocery in Paris before being killed by police, is said to have come under the influences of radical jihadists whilst in a French prison. The two of the Madrid train bombers were radicalized whilst in prison. The man who attempted to detonate a dirty bomb in Chicago and who also conspired to kill people overseas was radicalized in prison. The Amedy Coulibaly Montrouge shooter, in which municipal police officer Clarissa Jean-Philippe was shot and killed, and was the hostage-taker and gunman in the Porte de Vincennes siege in which he killed four hostages converted to radical Islam whilst serving time in Fleury-Merogis Prison. Salah Abdeslam the individual responsible for the recent terror attacks in both Paris and Brussels that killed over 150 people in 2015, spent time in prison.

The need for developing and delivering intervention and rehabilitation programmes in prison becomes apparent when the following reported statistics are considered. Early in 2016, it was reported that one in five prisoners in the United Kingdom's top security gaols is now Muslim, a rise of 23% from just five years ago. Pew data from 2011 revealed that Muslims made up 9% of state and federal prisoners though at the time Muslims made up just 0.8% of the U.S. population. In 2008, it was reported that about 60–70% of all inmates in [France's] prison system are Muslim, though Muslims make up only about 12% of the country's population (Kassam 2016).

Experience from other countries indicates that the majority of religious programming has not produce the kind of results that were anticipated (Loza 2015). Thus multifaceted, interdisciplinary rehabilitation programmes need to be developed that focuses on targeting their extremist beliefs, ideologies, attitudes, and attributions that promote Jihad. This could be accomplished by countering extreme ideologies with other ideologies that are not religiously based. Both prevention and intervention should involve teams of professionals including a moderate Muslim cleric (Imam/Sheik) qualified to offer religious counselling and is well versed in the issues related to Middle-Eastern extremism/terrorism as well as a psychologist, and counsellors with expertise and thorough understanding of issues related to terrorism ideologies. Many salient issues related to terrorist's ideologies are alien to Western culture and consequently not easily understood through theoretical means. Thus utilizing 'experts', who have acquired their expertise through media and self-directed readings, should be avoided. Unfortunately, involvement of these 'experts' has been, and will continue, to cause more harm than good.

The need for research on ideologically related terrorism

Ideologically related terrorism is a very complex problem that, unfortunately, is poorly understood and there is no clear definition of the constructs involved in their study (Drummond 2002; Mahmood 2001; Mazarr 2004. It requires the understanding and thorough knowledge of the religious, cultural, psychological, historical, political, linguistic, and social backgrounds of the populations from which many of the terrorists' ideologies originate. It also requires a thorough understanding of the terrorists' belief systems, cognitions, organization, decision making processes, personality dynamics, and motivations (Hudson 1999; Merari 2000). Thus, there is a need for multifaceted research that utilizes experts from several disciplines such as sociology, political science, police science, psychiatry, psychology, and other professions to fully explore the various dimensions of the phenomenon (Dernevik et al. 2009; Loza 2006). Since the MB is described as the founding father of today's radical Muslim activism (Bakker and Meijer 2012), it affords an appropriate target population for any study. In particular, what are its methods of recruitment and socializing, the socio-economic class composition of its base, the sources of its finances, and the activities of its local cells and branch offices (Wickham 2013).

The psychological part of such a plan would include further exploration of important issues of terrorist ideologies, recruitment, and training. They might include religion-based violence, the influence of religious teachings on extremists' and terrorists' values, beliefs, attitudes, attributions, motivations, cognitive and emotional states. They might also consider the effect of the environment and peers, the process of recruiting, the group dynamics that exist in these organizations including leader-follower relations, the organization of terrorist groups, their decision making processes, and the personality variables involved in the functioning of these groups (Loza 2015). In spite of the difficulties and serious problems facing researchers who are willing to venture in this difficult field of study there is still a great need for research that will address the just mentioned important issues

Conclusion

Extremist and terrorist ideology has been a major concern to the extent that Stern (1999) has suggested that terrorism be considered a danger to the security of civilization. The importance of addressing the MET ideology cannot be overstated. MET must be an international effort to fight their ideology. Using military and other security measures alone will not be enough. It is not a long-lasting solution. The international community must come together to fight the MET ideologies. Psychologists who have proper background in MET can play a major role in the efforts to combat MET. Their area of expertise qualifies them to deal with personalities mentioned in the typology section by design intervention programmes for them.

References

Ahmed, A.G., Audu, M.D., Loza, W., and Maximenco, A. (2013). The prevalence of extreme middle-eastern ideologies among some Nigerians. *International Journal of Social Science Studies* 1: 161–167.

Alstad, J. (2007). Islamist get insulted, we get beheaded. http://www.familyfriendsfirearms.com/forum/archive/index.php/t-51964.html&s=4da25ee443a3fc4e80083099b400ae6d (Accessed 16 August 2019).

Ameen, H.A. (1993). El-Shabab Wa Azmit El-Tatarrof [The youth and the problem of extremism]. In: *El-Mowagha: Gzoor El-Erhab, The confrontation: Roots of Terrorism*, 10–18. Cairo, EG: Egyptian Organization for Publishing Books.

Ansari, H., Cinnirella, M., Rogers, M.B. et al. (2006). Perceptions of martyrdom and terrorism amongst British Muslims. In: *Proceedings of the British Psychological Society Seminar Series Aspects of Terrorism and Martyrdom, eCOMMUNITY* (ed. M.B. Rogers, C.A. Lewis, K.M. Loewenthal, et al.), 1–5.

Ardila, R. (2002). The psychology of the terrorist: behavioural perspective. In: *The Psychology of Terrorism: Volume I, a Public Understanding*, Psychological Dimension to War and Peace (ed. C.E. Stout), 9–16. Westport, CT: Praeger.

Bakker, E. and Meijer, R. (2012). *The Muslim Brotherhood in Europe*. New York, NY: Columbia University Press.

Beutler, L.E., Reyes, G., Franco, Z., and Housley, J. (2007). The need for proficient mental health professionals in the study of terrorism. In: *Psychology of Terrorism* (eds. B. Bongar, L. Brown, L. Beutler, et al.), 32–55. Oxford, UK: Oxford University Press.

Bin Hassan, M.H. (2006). Key considerations in counterideological work against terrorist ideology. *Studies in Conflict & Terrorism* 29: 531–558.

Blaydes, L. and Rubin, L. (2008). Ideological reorientation and counterterrorism: confronting militant Islam in Egypt. *Terrorism and Political Violence* 20: 461–479.

Borum, R. (2004). *Psychology of terrorism*. Tampa: University of South Florida.

Burke, J. (2015). The story of a radicalization: "I was not myself." https://www.theguardian.com/profile/jasonburke (Accessed 16 August 2019).

Chiaramonte, P. (2016) Bloody tide: Terror deaths increased 8-fold since 2010, says study. *Fox News* (28 March). https://www.foxnews.com/world/bloody-tide-terror-deaths-increased-8-fold-since-2010-says-study (Accessed 16 August 2019).

Cilluffo, F.J., Cardash, S.L., and Whitehead, A.J. (2007). Radicalization: behind bars and beyond borders. *The Brown Journal of World Affairs* 13 (2): 113–122.

Dernevik, M., Beck, A., Grann, M. et al. (2009). The use of psychiatric and psychological evidence in the assessment of terrorist offenders. *The Journal of Forensic Psychiatry & Psychology* 20: 508–515.

Drummond, J.T. (2002). From northwest imperative to global jihad: social psychological aspect of the construction of the enemy, political violence, and terror. In: *The Psychology of Terrorism: A Public Understanding*, Psychological Dimension to War and Peace (ed. C.E. Stout), 49–96. Westport, CT: Praeger.

Dunleavy, P. (2015). Another ex-con, another terrorist attack – the danger in closing Gitmo. *Investigative Project* (9 January). https://www.investigativeproject.org/4729/guest-column-another-ex-con-another-terrorist (Accessed 16 August 2019).

El-Tuhami, M. (1997). *Hinama Yokatel el-Malik bi-el-Selah el-Abiad*. Cairo, Egypt: Rose-El-Yossef.

Furnish, T. (2005). Beheading in the name of Islam. *Middle East Quarterly* 2: 51–57.

Galea, S., Ahern, J., Resnick, H. et al. (2002). Psychological sequelae of the September 11 terrorist attacks in New York City. *New England Journal of Medicine* 346 (13): 982–987.

Ganor, B. (2008). Terrorist organization typologies and the probability of a boomerang effect. *Studies in Conflict & Terrorism* 31: 269–283.

Gilmore, H. (2007, December 2). Inmates studying al-Qaeda manual. "The Sydney Morning Herald".

Grieger, T. (2006). Psychiatric and societal impacts of terrorism. *Psychiatric Times* 23 (7). Retrieved from https://www.psychiatrictimes.com/articles/psychiatric-and-societal-impacts-terrorism.

Gunaratna, R. (2009). Terrorist rehabilitation: A global imperative. Symposium presented at the International Conference on Terrorist Rehabilitation in Singapore (24–26 February 2009).

Gunaratna, R. and Bin Ali, M. (2007). The countering the ideology of Jemmah Islamiyah: a point-by-point approach. *The ICFAI Journal of International Relations* 1: 65–84.

Gurfinkiel, M. (2015). France's moment of truth. The Middle East Forum. http://www.meforum.org/4980/france-momentof-Truth (Acceddes 16 August 2019).

Hafez, M.M. (2003). *Why Muslims Rebel: Repression and Resistance in the Islamic World*. Boulder, CO: Lynnes Rienner Publishers, Inc.

Hoffman, B. (1993). *"Holy terror:" the Implications of Terrorism Motivated by a Religious Imperative*. Santa Monica, CA: Rand Corporation.

Holman, E.A., Silver, R.C., Poulin, M. et al. (2008). Terrorism, acute stress, and cardiovascular health. *Achieves of General Psychiatry* 65: 73–80.

Hronick, M.S. (2006). Analyzing terror: researchers study the perpetrators and the effects of suicide terrorism. *National Institute of Justice Journal* 254: 8–11.

Hudson, R.A. (1999). *The Sociology and Psychology of Terrorism: Who Becomes a Terrorist and why?* Washington, DC: Library of Congress.

Ibrahim, S.E. (1980). Anatomy of Egypt's militant Islamic groups: methodological note and preliminary findings. *International Journal of Middle East Studies* 12: 423–453.

Ibrahim, S.E. (1988). Egypt's Islamic activism in the 1980s. *Third World Quarterly* 10: 632–657.

Isam, E. (2006). *Karitat Iktrak El-Ikwan Wa-El-Irhabieen Lil El-Taleem El-Masry*. Cairo, Egypt: Rose-El-Yoss.

Israeli, R. (1988). The charter of Allah: the platform of the Islamic resistance movement (Hamas). In: *The 1988–1989 Annual on Terrorism* (eds. Y. Alexander and A.H. Foxman), 99–129. Dordercht, NL: Martinus Nijhoff Publishers.

Kanany-Minesot, G.H. (1995). The Saudi-Islamic invasion to Egypt: A blind apostasy from civilization and a multi-violation of human rights. *The Copts: Christians of Egypt* 22: 23.

Kassam, R (2016). DATA: Young Muslims in the west are a ticking time bomb, increasingly sympathising with radicals, terror. *Breitbart* (22 March). http://www.breitbart.com/london/2016/03/22/polling-muslims-in-the-west-increasingly-sympathise-with-extremism-terror (Accessed 16 August 2019).

Laqueur, W. (1987). *The Age of Terrorism*. Toronto, ON: Little, Brown, and Company.

Lawal, O. (2002). Social-psychological considerations in the emergence and growth of terrorism. In: *The Psychology of Terrorism: Programs and Practices in Response and Prevention*, Psychological Dimension to War and Peace (ed. C.E. Stout), 23–32. Westport, CA: Praeger.

Lee, M.E. (2008). The fallacy of grievance-based terrorism. *Middle East Quarterly* 15: 71–79.

Lia, B. (2008). Doctrines for jihadi terrorist training. *Terrorism and Political Violence* 20: 518–542.

Lindeborg, L. (2002). The intellectual fathers of fundamentalism: Osama's library. *World Press Review* 49 (1): 1–4.

Littman, D.G. (2005). *Infidels "Jihad and Martyrdom" as Taught in Saudi Arabian and Egyptian Schools: "A Culture of Hate Based on 'Jihad and Martyrdom': Saudi Arabian and Egyptian Schoolbooks Today"*. New York, NY: Midstream.

Locicero, A. and Sinclair, S.J. (2008). Terrorism and terrorist leaders: insights from developmental and ecological psychology. *Studies in Conflict & Terrorism* 31: 227–250.

Lotfi, S. H., Ali, M., & Kamel, G. (1993). El-Mowagha: Tadbeek El-Sharia El-Eslamiah Been El-Haqiqa Wa-Shiaraat El-Fitnah. [The confrontation: Applying the Islamic Sharia between truth and rhetoric of splitting among Muslims.] Cairo, Egypt: Egyptian Organization of Publishing Books.

Loza, W. (2006). The psychology of extremism and terrorism: a middle-eastern perspective. *Journal of Aggression & Violent Behavior* 12: 141–155.

Loza, W. (2007). *The assessment and treatment of radicalization scale*. Unpublished manuscript.

Loza, W. (2010). The prevalence of middle-eastern extreme ideologies among some Canadian offenders. *Journal of Interpersonal Violence* 25: 919–928.

Loza, W. (2011). The prevalence of middle-eastern extreme ideologies among some Canadians. *Journal of Interpersonal Violence* 26: 1388–1400.

Loza, W. (2015). *The Need for Effective Intervention Programs to Prevent Extremism and Terrorist Recruitment in Western Countries with Special Emphasis on Canada*. Toronto, ON: The Mackenzie Institute.

Loza, W., Abd-El-Fatah, Y., Prinsloo, J. et al. (2010). The prevalence of extreme middle eastern ideologies around the world. *Journal of Interpersonal Violence* 26: 522–538.

Loza, W., Bhawanie, S., Nussbaum, D., and Maximenco, A. (2013). Assessing the prevalence of extreme middle-eastern ideologies among some new immigrants to Canada. *International Journal of Social Science Studies* 1: 154–160.

Mahmood, C.K. (2001). Terrorism, myth, and the power of ethnographic praxis. *Journal of Contemporary Ethnography* 30: 520–545.

Manji, I. (2003). *The Trouble with Islam: A Wake-Up Call for Honesty and Change*. Toronto, ON: Random House.

Maududi, S.A.A. (1991) The Holy Book of Islam Qur'an. Translation and brief notes with text. Rana Allah Dad Khan, Islamic Publication (Private) Ltd. Pakistan. I.C.N.A Book Service, Scarborough, Ontario.

Mazarr, M. (2004). The psychological sources of Islamic terrorism: alienation and identity in the Arab world. *Policy Review* 125: 39–69.

Mazarr, M. (2007). *Unmodern men in the modern world: Radical Islam, terrorism, and the war on modernity*. Cambridge: Cambridge University Press.

McCauley, C. (2002). Psychological issues in understanding terrorism and the response to terrorism. In: *The Psychology of Terrorism: Theoretical Understandings and Perspectives*, Psychological Dimension to War and Peace (ed. C.E. Stout), 3–29. Westport, CT: Praeger.

McCauley, C., Leuprecht, C., Hataley, T. et al. (2011). Tracking the war of ideas: a poll of Ottawa Muslims. *Terrorism and Political Violence* 23 (5): 804–819.

McCauley, C. and Scheckter, S. (2008). What's special about U.S. Muslims? The war on terrorism as seen by Muslims in the United States, Morocco, Egypt, Pakistan, and Indonesia. *Studies in Conflict & Terrorism* 31: 1024–1103.

McDermontt, P. and Zimbardo, P.G. (2007). The psychological consequences of terrorist alerts. In: *Psychology of Terrorism* (eds. B. Bongar, L. Brown, L. Beutler, et al.). Oxford, UK: Oxford University Press.

Merari, A. (2000). Terrorism as a strategy of struggle: past and future. In: *The future of terrorism* (eds. M. Taylor and J. Horgan). London: Frank Cass.

Moghaddam, F. (2005). The staircase to terrorism: a psychological exploration. *American Psychologist* 60: 160–169.

Moghaddam, F. M. (2008). Violent Islamist extremism in Global Context. Statement to the United States Senate Committee on Homeland Security and Governmental Affairs. Retrieved March 15, 2009, from http://www.homelandsecuritynews.info/2008/07/violent-islamist-extremism-in-global-context/.

Mokaitis, T.R. (2006). *The "New" Terrorism: Myths and Reality*. Westport, CT: Praeger.

Orbach, B. (2001). Usama Bin Laden and Al-Qa'ida: origins and doctrines. *Middle East Review of International Affairs* 5: 54–68.

Pedahzur, A. (2005). *Suicide terrorism*. Cambridge, UK: Polity Press.

Pipes, D. (2015). How terrorism harms radical Islam. Retrieved (2015-01-10) http://www.washingtontimes.com/news/2015/jan/9/daniel-pipes-how-terrorism-harms-radical-islam/print/).

Popeo, J.W. (2005). Combating radical Islam in prisons within legal dictates of the free exercise clause. *Criminal and Civil Confinement* 32: 135–160.

Post, J. (1990). Terrorist psycho-logic: terrorist behaviour as a product of psychological forces. In: *Origins of Terrorism* (ed. W. Reich), 25–40. Cambridge, UK: Cambridge University Press.

Post, J., Sprinzak, E., and Denny, L. (2003). The Terrorists in their own words: Interviews with 35 incarcerated Middle-Eastern Terrorists. *Terrorism and Political Violence* 15: 1.

Pressman, D.E. (2008). Exploring the sources of radicalization and violent radicalization: some transatlantic perspectives. *Journal of Security Issues* 2 (1): 1–23.

Pressman, D.E. (2009). *Risk Assessment Decisions for Violent Political Extremism*. Ottawa, ON: Public Safety Canada.

Public Safety Canada. (2019). Currently listed entities. https://www.publicsafety.gc.ca/cnt/ntnl-scrt/cntr-trrrsm/lstd-ntts/crrnt-lstd-ntts-en.aspx (Accessed 16 August 2019).

Rapoport, D.C. (1984). Fear and trembling: terrorism in three religious traditions. *The American Political Science Review* 78: 658–677.

Reid, W.H. (2001). Psychological aspects of terrorism. *Journal of Psychiatric Practice* 7: 422–425.

Reid, W.H. (2002). Controlling political terrorism: practicality, not psychology. In: *The Psychology of Terrorism: A Public Understanding*, Psychological Dimension to War and Peace (ed. C.E. Stout), 1–8. Westport, CT: Praeger.

Reid, W.H. (2003). Terrorism and forensic psychiatry. *The Journal of the American Academy of Psychiatry and the Law* 31 (3): 285–288.

Reid, W.H. (2010). When lawyers call clinicians. *Journal of Psychiatric Practice* 16 (4): 253–257.

Rusin, D. J. (2008). Fear stalks Muslim apostates in the West. *American Thinker* (3 August). http://www.americanthinker.com/2008/08/fear_stalks_muslim_apostates_i.html (Accessed 16 August 2019).

Sageman, M. (2004). *Understanding terror networks*. Philadelphia: University of Pennsylvania Press.

Sayyed, T. (2005). A Muslim in a Jewish land. *Aish* (2 December). http://www.aish.com/h/iid/48916537.html (Accessed 16 August 2019).

Schwind, R. L. (2005). The London bombings: hatred in Islam, civil society and the Umma. *Islam Review*. http://docshare.tips/the-london-bombings-hatred-in-islam-civil-society-and-the-umma-by-r-l-schwind_57744a2ab6d87fbb328b4823.html

Senate of Canada. (2014). Proceedings of the Standing Senate Committee on National Security and Defence. https://sencanada.ca/en/Content/Sen/Committee/412/SECD/11ev-51766-e

Siegel, P.C. (2006). Radical Islam and the French Muslim prison population. *Terrorism Monitor* 15: 4–6.

Silber, M.D. and Bhatt, A. (2007). *Radicalization in the West: The Homegrown Threat*. New York, NY: New York City Police Department.

Silke, A. (2008). Holy warriors: exploring the psychological process of jihad radicalization. *European Journal of Criminology* 5: 99–123.

Silver, R.C., Holman, A., McIntosh, D. et al. (2002). Nationwide longitudinal study of psychological responses to September 11. *Journal of the American Medical Association* 288: 1235–1244.

Speckhard, A. and Yayla, A. (2015). Eyewitness accounts from recent defectors from Islamic state: why they joined, what they saw, why they quit. *Perspectives on Terrorism* 9 (6): 95–118.

Stern, J. (1999). *The Ultimate Terrorists*. Cambridge, MA: Harvard University press.

Stern, J. (2003). *Terror in the Name of God: Why Religious Militants Kill*. New York, NY: HarperCollins Publishers Inc.

Stevens, M.J. (2005). What is terrorism and can psychology do anything to prevent it? *Behavioural Sciences and the Law* 23: 507–526.

Svirsky, M. (2016). If ISIS came to your town would you convert to Islam? *Clarion Project* (21 April). https://clarionproject.org/if-isis-came-your-town-would-you-convert-islam-2 (Accessed 16 August 2019).

Tanveer, A. (2005). Muslim "marginal man". *Policy* 21: 35–41.

Thackrah, J.R. (2004). *Dictionary of Terrorism*, 2e. London, UK: Routledge.

Travis, A. (2006). Prisons failing to tackle terror recruitment. *The Guardian* (2 October). https://www.theguardian.com/uk/2006/oct/02/prisonsandprobation.terrorism (Accessed 16 August 2019).

Vidino, L. (2005). The Muslim Brotherhood's conquest of Europe. *Middle East Quarterly* 12 (1): 25–34.

Wicker, C. and Lieto, A. (2007). *International Lessons Learned and Recommendations for Combating Domestic Islamic Terrorism*. Carlisle, PA: U.S. Army War College.

Wickham, C.R. (2002). *Mobilizing Islam: Religion, Activism, and Political Change in Egypt*. New York, NY: Columbia University Press.

Wickham, C.R. (2013). *The Muslim Brotherhood: Evolution of an Islamist Movement*. Princeton, NJ: Princeton University Press.

Yaseen, E. (2007). Al tatarof el-ideology wa makater el hokoma el denia. *Al-Ahram Newspaper* (20 September). http://english.ahram.org.eg/

Zillmer, E.A. (2006). The psychology of terrorists: Nazi perpetrators, the Baader-Meinhof gang, war criminals in Bosnia, and suicide bombers. In: *Military Psychology: Clinical and Operational Applications* (eds. C.H. Kennedy and E.A. Zillmer), 331–359. New York, NY: The Guilford Press.

15

Assessing the Risk and Treatment Needs of People Who Perpetrate Intimate Partner Violence

Louise Dixon[1] and Nicola Graham-Kevan[2]

[1] Victoria University of Wellington, Wellington, New Zealand
[2] University of Central Lancashire, Preston, UK

Introduction

Aggression and violence within intimate relationships has been deemed a significant international problem that affects people across all demographic boundaries (Esquivel-Santoveña and Dixon 2012). The average yearly prevalence rate of physical intimate partner violence (IPV) has been estimated at 15% in several nationally representative studies of US adult couples (e.g. Schafer et al. 1998), with other countries reporting lifetime rates of physical IPV against women (no comparable figures for men are available) at 13% in urban Japan to between 40 and 50% in Samoa, and rural locations in Bangladesh, Tanzania, Ethiopia, and Peru (Garcia-Moreno et al. 2006). Annual crime victimization statistics in England and Wales estimated that 1.6 million people (1.1 million women and 500 000 men) experienced some type of partner abuse in the year studied with 30% reporting repeat victimization in this self-report survey (Office of National Statistics [ONS] 2016). More stringent criminal justice data reports that 34% of men convicted of a domestic violence offence in England and Wales, deemed to be of moderate to high risk of re-offending, and who did not receive intervention, were proven to re-offend (any offence that led to a caution, court conviction, reprimand, or warning) within a two-year period from the date of their sentence (Bloomfield and Dixon 2015).

Considering the magnitude of IPV it is, therefore, not surprising that its prevention is of paramount concern to society. One way to achieve violence prevention is to manage risk which requires risk assessment. Risk assessment has been defined by Kropp et al. (2002) as 'the process of speculating in an informed way about the aggressive acts a person might commit and to determine the steps that should be taken to prevent those acts and minimize their negative

The Wiley Handbook of What Works in Violence Risk Management: Theory, Research and Practice,
First Edition. Edited by J. Stephen Wormith, Leam A. Craig, and Todd E. Hogue.
© 2020 John Wiley & Sons Ltd. Published 2020 by John Wiley & Sons Ltd.

consequences' (p. 147). In other words, this technique has the potential to achieve two main objectives: (i) Estimate a person's likelihood of future harm; and (ii) identify the factors associated with a person's offending behaviour, which can inform risk reduction through the treatment, supervision, and management of those needs. As such, it can inform professional decision making in a variety of settings, for example, in determining bail, sentencing, and release from hospital and prison, victim safety planning, prioritization of resources to victims, and in informing the treatment of people who offend. It is, therefore, essential that risk assessments provide accurate estimations of a person's risk; overestimation can result in unnecessary incarceration and intense treatment and supervision of the individual concerned, whilst underestimation can increase the risk of harm to the public via inadequate treatment and supervision (Boer and Hart 2009).

Different approaches to the risk assessment of offending behaviour have been developed and evaluated in the literature (e.g. Bonta and Andrews 2017). The exact method undertaken in a risk assessment will depend on the objective to be achieved and the information available to the assessor. However, despite the notion that different tools can facilitate a different purpose, the debate in the risk literature has focused on which approach is most effective in identifying risk of recidivism. There is also little agreement however, about how to establish professional standards for risk assessment and communicate risk information (Kropp 2009).

This chapter aims to provide an evidence-based guide to the risk assessment of an individual who has perpetrated IPV, where the focus is on determining the person's *treatment needs* to aid risk reduction. In doing so, we consider the need for the assessor to conduct assessments that are informed by the evidence in the IPV, wider aggression, and corrections literature. First, we discuss key findings in the IPV and aggression literature that should shape the assessment, before considering the role of correctional principles (Risk-Need-Responsivity, Bonta and Andrews 2017) and individual case formulation in determining explanations for the aggressive episodes and individual treatment needs.

The need for evidence-informed risk assessment

In considering the evidence-base for risk assessment, it is first important to note that robust research on the nature and aetiology of IPV should inform the potential areas for assessment. The use of empirical findings is essential to guide assessment as, pragmatically, there is a limited amount of time available to an assessor, who will often have to rely on incomplete information (Neal and Grisso 2014). Theories of IPV and general aggression that have been developed and validated through research should determine the assessment content and guide explanations for the person's offending behaviour to increase accuracy. However, psychological science has struggled to provide widely-accepted explanations of IPV due to the position that many professionals who work in the area of family violence take in explaining the phenomenon. Typically understood as a social problem of violence against women, explanations have centred on sociological factors. This has resulted in psychologically-informed models of aggression (that are commonplace in explanations of other types of sexual and violent crime) not being applied readily to the field of IPV (Dixon and Graham Kevan 2011). Therefore, we first provide a brief overview of key knowledge on the nature and aetiology of IPV that should guide risk assessment.

What Is the Nature of IPV and Who Are the Perpetrators?

Research consistently shows that IPV can happen to people across sexualities, gender identities, marital statuses, ethnicities, cultures, and ages (Dixon and Graham Kevan 2011; Dixon and Polaschek 2018; Esquivel-Santoveña and Dixon 2012). Examination of this research shows the need for an inclusive approach to defining and responding to IPV. Furthermore, a wide range of acts have been shown to constitute IPV, with most definitions describing physical, psychological, emotional, and sexual violence, and in more recent times, controlling behaviours (e.g. Home Office 2018). Indeed, it is important that the full range of behaviour is considered in assessments of IPV to inform estimates of risk, and monitor risk over time. For example, sexual violence has been shown to be indicative of more serious physical violence (Hines and Douglas 2016) and longitudinal research shows that controlling behaviours may be a precursor to physical aggression (Graham Kevan 2007). Thus, knowledge about some behaviours can indicate the likelihood of the presence of other behaviours.

In order to capture the complexity of IPV, we have developed an inclusive and broad definition that can act as a useful heuristic in understanding what encompasses this phenomenon (Dixon and Graham Kevan 2011). We expand on that definition here to be inclusive of all of the groups mentioned above and define IPV as any form of aggression and/or controlling behaviour used against a current or past intimate partner of any gender, ethnicity, culture, sexual orientation, or relationship status (married, co-habiting, dating), and across age.

Avoiding bias in assessment via inclusivity

We strongly suggest that it is important for the assessor to understand IPV in an inclusive and broad manner to ensure that they are open to examining all forms of aggression by anyone, thus reducing any cognitive bias of the assessor in the assessment process. If, for example, the assessor expects the man in a heterosexual relationship to be the aggressor then they may fail to consider the possibility of male victimization or reciprocal aggression between partners. Indeed, research shows that reciprocal aggression is the most common form of IPV (e.g. Straus 1990; Straus and Gelles 1985; Straus et al. 1980), and contrary to popular conception, it can result in high levels of injury (e.g. LaRoche 2008; Whitaker et al. 2007) and increase the risk of physical harm to children living with IPV (Slep and O'Leary 2005).

If gender inclusivity and reciprocity is dismissed from the outset, the assessor will fail to consider the role of relationship dynamics in the violence. Capaldi et al. (2007) stress the importance of this dynamic in the assessment of aggressive interchanges between members of a couple, finding that females under 26 years of age were more likely to initiate aggression than men. The role of understanding reciprocity to aid successful treatment outcomes is denoted by research that shows cessation of violence by one member of the couple is highly dependent on the cessation of violence by the other member (Straus et al. 1996). In addition to failing to consider the client's risk of harm from their intimate partner, the risk of harm that intimate partner may pose to others in the family unit will also be overlooked. Indeed, the literature shows a high level of co-occurrence between IPV and child maltreatment (Dixon and Smith Slep 2017). However, applying a gender-inclusive approach to risk assessment can prove difficult as evidence has been mainly centred on men's aggression with little consideration of relationship dynamics, the role of reciprocal aggression, female perpetration, or same sex IPV.

To date, the majority of actuarial and structured professional judgement (SPJ) tools are developed and primarily validated with men who offend in heterosexual relationships.

How Is IPV Best Explained?

A gendered explanation

Theories are developed to explain why phenomena exist and persist (Ward 2014). They are important in shaping explanations about why problem behaviour (like IPV) occurs which inherently suggests the course of action that could be carried out to reduce or eliminate the problem (Loseke et al. 2005). The most commonly adhered to theory of IPV is a gendered theory which views IPV primarily as a problem of men's violence to women that occurs as a result of societal patriarchal rules and beliefs that encourage male dominance over women (e.g. Dobash and Dobash 1979). Women's aggression, if it occurs, is proposed to be motivated by self-defence, retaliation, or pre-emptive self-defence (Respect 2008). This theory views patriarchy as a direct cause of men's violence towards their female partner and that change rests with altering society's and the individual perpetrator's belief structure. Interventions designed solely from this perspective do not address individual factors (Dutton 2006).

However, there is a lack of empirical support for a gendered theory of IPV (e.g. Dutton and Corvo 2006). The evidence shows that IPV is perpetrated by same-sex couples (Walters et al. 2010), men *and* women in heterosexual relationships, and that women's aggression is not primarily carried out in self-defence (e.g. Straus 2011; Hines and Douglas 2016). Furthermore, research has not found a consistent relationship between measures that reflect patriarchy, such as male domination, men's sex role ideology, and partner violence (e.g. Dutton 1995; Hotaling and Sugarman 1986), with some research demonstrating that the man's patriarchal values are associated with lower rates of partner violence in families (e.g. Campbell 1992; Mihalic and Elliott 1997). This is in line with research that shows hostile and benevolent sexism are highly correlated and together comprise ambivalent sexism, the socially acceptable version of which will be expressed in a given society (Glick and Fiske 1996). In accordance with this finding, normative beliefs pertaining to IPV in Western society have been shown to be chivalrous rather than patriarchal (Sorenson and Taylor 2005), which, authors have argued, serve to reduce the prevalence of violence by men towards women (Archer 2000; Felson 2002). Indeed, experimental studies have found that men will choose to act less aggressively to females than male targets under the same levels of provocation (Cross et al. 2011). Therefore, a theory that exclusively focuses on explaining men's violence towards women is clearly limited and an assessor following this perspective runs the risk of failing to consider important empirical evidence in their assessment, rendering their conclusions inaccurate. Furthermore, treatment programmes incorporating this theoretical perspective have typically resulted in small-effect sizes (Babcock et al. 2004). Indeed, the efficacy of interventions for IPV in general have been described as modest at best (Stewart et al. 2013) which suggest that improvements in theory and resulting practice need to be made.

In an attempt to recognize the heterogeneity of couples experiencing IPV, Johnson (1995, 1999, 2006) proposed that there are different types of IPV that can be identified according to the level of physical violence and pattern of power and control used by both members of the couple. His typology is, therefore, based on differences in the outcome variable of interest, physical aggression and controlling behaviour. He identified Coercive

Controlling Violence (CCV) (formerly known as patriarchal or intimate terrorism) to describe physical IPV perpetrated in the context of high levels of control where the recipient was either non-violent or engaged in non-controlling violence (the latter termed Violence Resistance [VR]). Where both members of the couple acted out CCV this was termed Mutual Violent Control (MVC). Situational Couple Violence (SCV) described physical aggression borne out of conflict and perpetrated in the absence of high levels of control in the relationship (formerly known as common couple violence). He hypothesized that SCV would be perpetrated by both men and women at approximately equal rates and be explained by conflict, and that CCV would be primarily perpetrated by men and explained by patriarchal motives. Indeed, his research showed that 96.9% of people classified into CCV were men compared to 55% of SCV where the perpetrator was the man, and that 96.1% of people classified as VR were women (Johnson 1999). He also proposed that the sample used to investigate IPV could over select for each type, with clinical or 'shelter' samples producing higher rates of CCV and VR, and community or 'survey' samples producing higher levels of SCV due to the limited opportunities that people experiencing controlling relationships would have to take part in a community-based survey. Indeed, this was supported with 93.5 and 93.9% of people classified into CCV and VR respectively from shelter samples. SCV was less prescriptive with 64% of people categorized into SCV from community-survey samples.

However, the samples that Johnson (1999) utilized to proxy 'shelter' and 'survey' samples were non-random and included (respectively) 1) women who had experienced a violent relationship and had primarily been in contact with the courts or women's shelters and 2) women residing in the same neighbourhood and matched to each of those women. First, a randomized sample of people was therefore not obtained in the 'survey' sample on which to test his theory. Indeed, Johnson (1999) acknowledges that this matched neighbourhood sample will 'over-represent violent relationships relative to a random sample' (p. 12). Considering that pro-criminal peers are a risk factor for crime in general (Bonta and Andrews 2017), matching groups based on women's neighbourhood status increases the likelihood that the partners of 'shelter' and 'survey' sample groups know each other. This potentially over selects for male criminality and aggressiveness. Second, clinical services, where men who have experienced victimization may present, were not sampled. It cannot be concluded that male victims of CCV are scarce using research methodology that excludes them by default.

Other research refutes Johnson's (1999) findings and shows that although IPV can be categorized by high and low control, the groups are not limited to different samples or genders. For example, research with men and women in a large representative community sample in Canada shows that approximately 40% of victims of CCV are men, who experience the same levels of severity as women victims of CCV (LaRoche 2008). Therefore, whilst Johnson's (1999) explanation of IPV is useful because it draws attention to the different types of aggression and the need to view both members of the couple to fully understand IPV, it is arguably a rather simplistic account of complex behaviour. We argue that it is dangerous to rely on a theory to guide assessment and treatment that is not well supported by robust evidence and, to do so, may compromise the comprehensiveness and accuracy of the assessment. Assuming that a person exhibiting a certain type of offending behaviour will present via different referral sources and will be of a particular gender, could prove misleading and result in inappropriate decisions regarding service provision and treatment. Examining the literature that describes the aetiology of IPV and its nature shows that a more complex explanation of IPV is warranted (e.g. Bell and Naugle 2008).

Gender-inclusive explanations

A gender-inclusive approach to understanding IPV has been proposed as an alternative to the gendered perspective (see Dixon and Graham Kevan 2011). This perspective aims to understand why individuals or couples engage in IPV, with an emphasis on the role of individual differences on people's behaviour, rather than the wider effects of society on men's behaviour. This perspective can account for the aforementioned evidence about the nature of IPV and the multiple risk factors that have been associated with IPV (discussed in the next section). Therefore, it welcomes the use of psychological input in explaining IPV and in the design of assessment and intervention. However, gender-inclusive theory is an umbrella term that can allude to a variety of theories that provide different explanations for the possibility of both men and women being perpetrators and/or victims of IPV, such as social learning theory, power theory and personality theories (see Bell and Naugle 2008; Birkley and Eckhardt 2015). It is important to note that whilst different theoretical approaches can provide gender-inclusive explanations of IPV, further tests and development of theoretical models for IPV need to be made (Bell and Naugle 2008; Bogat et al. 2005).

Attempts have been made to develop a framework that accounts for the various factors that empirical research has associated with the occurrence of IPV and that are found at different levels of an individual's social world. Dutton's (2006) 'Nested Ecological Model' provides a multilevel, multifactorial framework to understand individual differences in intimate partner aggression. The model presents risk factors at four social levels: the Macrosystem (broad cultural values and beliefs); the Exosystem (subculture factors such as peer-group influence, work-related stress); the Microsystem (immediate context in which violence occurs such as couple or family interaction pattern); and the Ontogenic Level (individual factors such as personality, cognitions, and emotions). The model allows for the possibility that risk factors will interact in different ways for different individuals. Thus, people in similar social circumstances with different individual risk profiles may not all behave in the same manner, just as people with similar individual risk profiles but different social circumstances may also not behave in the same manner. The model also allows for the possibility that patriarchal social norms may play a role for some people, but not others. Tests of factors within a multilevel model have been undertaken with some success (Stith et al. 2004). Such an ecological approach arguably draws on evidence to inform an explanation of intimate partner aggression and is proving a useful heuristic in guiding the assessment of treatment need (Hamel 2005).

Although this model provides a framework to explain the various risk factors or symptoms of IPV, it does not provide a theoretical explanation of how the risk markers and outcome behaviours arose. This is necessary as recent research on dynamic risk and protective factors has identified theoretical problems that limit their utility in explaining offending behaviour and in directing interventions (Ward 2016; Ward and Fortune 2016). Bell and Naugle (2008) do provide a theoretical framework of IPV that takes into account the context of perpetration and considers proximal variables related to IPV episodes. This approach is particularly useful for clinical assessment, allowing the assessor to identify contextually relevant variables for treatment. However, such theories provide a topographic overview of variables associated with IPV perpetration (Birkley and Eckhardt 2015). There are few meta-theoretical explanations of IPV perpetration that provide predictive, or process–level models, hypothesizing how multiple factors interact to cause aggression. The field is highlighting the need for meta-theoretical approaches that do not restrict the explanation of IPV perpetration to one set of risk factors (Birkley and Eckhardt 2015). Of course, theory needs to be tested by experience and adapted in light of results of that experience. However, as Bell and Naugle (2008) assert, it is challenging to design a study that tests a complex theoretical framework in its entirety and therefore, for now at least, clinicians will have to look towards discrete studies that test particular parts of such theory to gauge its accuracy in explaining IPV.

Are People Who Commit IPV a Heterogeneous Group?

We have seen from Johnson's (1995, 1999, 2006) work discussed above that the literature has recognized the heterogeneity of IPV. In addition to the focus on differences between couples based on control motives, research has examined differences in the personality and psychopathology of people who have perpetrated IPV and has consistently shown heterogeneity (e.g. Babcock et al. 2003; Dixon and Browne 2003; Holtzworth-Munroe et al. 2000). This suggests that different theoretical explanations are needed to account for the variation in distal and proximal antecedents.

Holtzworth-Munroe and Stuart (1994) proposed a developmental model of male IPV perpetration. Informed by a review of the literature, they proposed that three types of men could be identified using three dimensions of severity and generality of violence, and psychopathology/personality disorder. They hypothesized that the combination of key distal and proximal antecedents would be associated with the development of one of three subtypes. The Family Only (FO) offender was proposed to use less severe violence, infrequently, towards family members and possess low levels of poor communication skills with their partner, mild impulsivity and dependency on their partner. The Generally Violent/Antisocial (GVA) offender was proposed to use moderate to severe levels of violence towards family members and others, and possess the highest levels of impulsivity, antisocial personality, substance abuse and criminality. The Dysphoric/Borderline (DB) offender was proposed to use moderate-high severity violence, primarily towards family members, and possess the highest levels of psychological distress, emotional volatility, borderline personality characteristics, depression, anger, and dependency on, and preoccupation with, intimate partners. Holtzworth-Munroe et al. (2000) validated the typology and demonstrated the presence of a fourth subcategory, namely the Low-level antisocial (LLA) offender that falls midway between the GVA and DB on the three dimensions used to create the taxonomy.

How should heterogeneity impact assessment?

Amongst the reasons proposed for the modest effect sizes of treatment is that heterogeneity of participants, in terms of their criminogenic needs and learning styles and abilities, is not taken into account in evaluations, and thus differences in response to treatment by perpetrators with varying needs will not be taken into account (Stewart et al. 2013). This limitation may, in part, reflect the normative/legal nature of offence categories, which fail to accurately reflect the psychological and social problems associated with violence (Ward and Heffernan 2017). Research has thus attempted to match offender type to the treatment model used. In a randomized test, Saunders (1996) demonstrated that the recidivism rate for men with antisocial personality characteristics was lower when they received structured cognitive-behavioural intervention compared to a process-psychodynamic intervention, and the opposite effect was found for men characterized by dependent traits. To the best of our knowledge, despite the positive effects of this experiment, research has not since tested the interaction between personality/offender type and treatment type. Other research has shown that typologies predict attrition rates and treatment outcomes. Indeed, the Holtzworth-Munroe and Stuart (1994) GVA and DB subgroups are associated with poor intervention outcomes, being the least likely to complete programmes (Langhinrichsen-Rohlin et al. 2000) and most likely to participate in post-intervention recidivism (Dutton et al. 1997; Jones and Gondolf 2001; Langhinrichsen-Rohlin et al. 2000).

However, research has not shown stability in typologies over time (see Holtzworth-Munroe et al. 2003), making it difficult to allocate a specific approach to treatment for different types. Some researchers have also questioned the need for such typological research to inform treatment concluding that 'one size fits all.' White and Gondolf (2000) examined the personality profiles and treatment implications of 100 men enrolled on batterer programmes. The authors concluded that the majority of men exhibited narcissistic or avoidant traits that were suited to a cognitive behavioural treatment (CBT) approach, with only 15% evidencing severe personality pathology that they suggest would warrant adjunct psychiatric services or an individualized treatment approach. Gondolf and White (2001) also demonstrated that of 122 men who repeatedly assaulted their female partners in a 15-month post-treatment follow up, the majority (60%) had no 'serious personality dysfunction or psychopathology'; only 11% had personality profiles suggestive of primary psychopathic disorder. No significant differences in personality dysfunction or psychopathology arose between men who did not reassault, who reassaulted once, or who repeatedly reassaulted their partner. The authors concluded that the 'majority of repeat reassaulters did not evidence personality dysfunction or psychopathology that, alone, would prevent them from benefiting from the gender-based cognitive-behavioral group interventions' (p. 366–377). However, these studies were based on clinical analysis of individual personality profiles coupled with clinical judgments of the best treatment approach. Unlike Saunders' (1996) study, no experimental manipulation of treatment type took place to examine the interaction of treatment type, personality type, and recidivism. A lack of evidence examining this interaction is not proof of a lack of effect.

Therefore, we conclude that more research in this area is needed to warrant robust conclusions about the utility of typologies in informing assessment and treatment. Indeed, the Holtzworth-Munroe and Stuart (1994) typology has informed most research in this area and they have been critiqued on conceptual and methodological grounds (Brasfield 2015). Although risk factors statistically related to repeat assault are well developed in the IPV field, explanations of the aetiology of behaviour are not. Development of comprehensive theories of offending behaviour could also aid the development of psychologically-informed risk factor checklists, which together could better inform treatment design and planning.

In summary, from a clinical perspective addressing the risk and treatment needs that are specifically related to a person's 'type' of IPV is logical. However, at present, typological research is not at the stage to inform treatment content or design with accuracy. As Holtzworth-Munroe and Meehan (2004) have before us, we warn against the misuse of classification systems. Currently, typological research does not equate to explanatory categories and should not be used as such. The construction of typologies is a classificatory not an explanatory task. At best, current frameworks that highlight the heterogeneity in dynamic risk factors provide a useful heuristic to inform individual case formulation of IPV episodes. Indeed, the need for individual case formulation to accompany the identification of treatment need via other methods (e.g. actuarial tools) is commonly proposed (Stewart et al. 2013; Ireland 2009) and would certainly prove useful in planning alternative treatment approaches for the 15% of offenders that White and Gondolf (2000) identified were unlikely to benefit from the mainstream programmes used in their study.

Applying Evidence in the Risk Assessment of IPV Treatment Need

The role of RNR in the assessment of IPV risk and need

Considering the lack of firm direction that research into typologies currently pose for policy and practice, and the limited resources for treatment that different organizations will likely have to contend with, Stewart et al. (2013) suggest that the best course of action to date may be a practical approach to matching treatment and offender type based on offender risk level. Differences in treatment readiness and outcome between the Holtzworth-Munroe and Stuart (1994) types are between the lower risk (FO and LLA) and higher risk (DB and GVA) categories (Eckhardt et al. 2008). Therefore, Stewart et al.'s (2013) proposal to use two treatment programmes that address the specific multifaceted treatment needs and dosage requirements of lower risk and higher risk offenders makes practical sense.

The principles of Risk-Need-Responsivity (RNR) have been shown to be effective contributors to treatment with people who criminally offend and have been proposed as important determinants in the theory of 'what works' in offender rehabilitation (Bonta and Andrews 2017). Indeed, treatment that adheres to none of the principles has resulted in an effect size of (r) – 0.02 compared to treatment that adheres to all principles which has an effect size of (r) 0.26 (Bonta and Andrews 2017). Therefore, the principles have proved popular in correctional psychology research and practice in Canada, the UK, the USA, Australia, and New Zealand (Stewart et al. 2013). We will now consider how the principles lend themselves to addressing the risk and treatment needs of people who perpetrate IPV.

Risk The *risk* principle promotes matching the intensity and dosage of treatment to the risk of recidivism posed by the person. In other words, people deemed at higher risk receive the highest intensity levels of treatment. Little or no treatment is offered to people deemed to be lower risk who have been shown less likely to re-offend without treatment, and show minimal reductions, or in fact higher rates of offending, in response to intensive treatment (Bonta and Andrews 2017). However, currently the IPV literature is limited, showing few replicable findings to demonstrate the efficacy of an RNR approach to IPV treatment. For example, Gondolf (2004) did not find support for more intensive treatment having beneficial effects for men categorized at higher risk of re-offending. In contrast Stewart et al. (2014b) attained tentative evidence of effectiveness for moderate- and high-intensity family violence treatment programmes and Bloomfield and Dixon (2015) found significant yet small effects for offenders deemed at moderate and high risk of reoffending.

Stewart et al. (2013) recommend that where interventions for people who are assessed at low risk are mandatory in an organization's policy that the intervention be shorter, less intense, and include the opportunity for couples' counselling where both members are willing. This approach to IPV intervention allows prioritization of resources. Intuitively, it seems risky not to intervene with people assessed at the lowest risk of IPV assault. This is an especially important point where children reside in the family unit considering the high co-occurrence rate of the different forms of family violence (Dixon and Smith Slep 2017). Risk should be considered within the context of the family unit where relevant (Dixon and Browne 2003). Although some police and victim report data show that the majority of people will not re-offend against a partner across long time periods, regardless of whether they receive interventions or not (e.g. Maxwell et al. 2001; Statistics Canada 2006), the effects of their behaviour on healthy functioning and communication within the family, or the risk of harm posed to the child or other family members, are unknown. Risk of harm posed to a child residing in a home characterized by IPV should be assessed separately to risk of IPV recidivism. Although risk factors for child maltreatment and IPV overlap to some extent, perpetrators who commit both forms of family violence present with distinct profiles compared to those who commit one form of abuse (Dixon and Smith Slep 2017). A person assessed at low risk of IPV recidivism may therefore be at high risk of child maltreatment. Therefore, we caution that the complex dynamics of family violence should be considered carefully before applying correctional principles to the arena of family violence treatment – treatment outcomes should not just focus on reduction of aggression towards the intimate partner if the intergenerational cycle of violence is to be prevented. Further research needs to identify if people assessed at the lowest risk of physical IPV recidivism are also at the lowest risk of other types of IPV (e.g. psychological aggression and controlling behaviours) and family violence (e.g. child maltreatment).

Best methods   The need to accurately and reliably identify a person's risk level has led to a growing knowledge base on the risk factors that predict violence recidivism, and much debate about the best methods and measures by which to achieve this. The literature is peppered with discussion about the four generations of measures available (e.g. Bonta and Andrews 2017; Hilton et al. 2010), with most concluding that unstructured clinical judgement is inferior to second-generation actuarial risk assessment instruments (ARAIs). ARAIs classify risk through actuarial methods and are thus comprised of items statistically related to risk of recidivism (Hilton et al. 2010). In the IPV literature, this includes measures such as the Ontario Domestic Assault Risk Assessment (ODARA; Hilton et al. 2004) and the Domestic Violence Risk Appraisal Guide (DVRAG; Hilton et al. 2008) that rank men on their risk of physical IPV recidivism to female intimate partners and the frequency and severity of that violence. Although developed with men, the instrument is also validated for use with females who perpetrate IPV, however, the development of absolute risk associated with ODARA scores for women is still needed (Waypoint 2016).

Although ARAIs have proven validity, they have been criticized for their lack of testing by authors independent of the measure's development (Boer and Hart 2009). Furthermore, actuarial scales are most useful when validated in the setting they are used in (Boer and Hart 2009) which is not always possible as differences in ages, ethnicity, and legal context are difficult to control. Another factor to consider is their reliance on static or historical risk factors that have an empirical relationship, yet lack a theoretical relationship, with recidivism (Boer and Hart 2009). The need to identify stable and acute dynamic risk factors has been noted in order to understand those changeable factors related to criminal behaviour (criminogenic need). Static and dynamic items are incorporated into SPJ instruments that guide the clinical judgement of professionals. Indeed, this is in line with the *need principle*, which states that treatment should be tailored to target reductions in dynamic risk factors associated with recidivism (e.g. positive attitudes to violence, problems with emotional regulation).

SPJ instruments are derived from reviews of the international literature and consider a broad range of factors. As such, it has been argued that they are less affected by the immediate context in which they are used, thus reducing the chances of error arising from the mismatch between the context the tool was derived in and the context in which the offender is being assessed (Boer and Hart 2009). In addition, such tools allow for the assessment of likelihood of re-offending in addition to the assessment of treatment need, service provision and management of the person in question. One widely used SPJ tool is the Spousal Assault Risk Assessment (Kropp et al. 2015), which provides a checklist and framework within which to assess the risk of future violence in people arrested for spousal assault. In addition, it can guide risk management strategies and assist in monitoring risk for domestic repeat assault. This could also be described as a fourth-generation tool incorporating static and dynamic risk assessment that aims to guide service and supervision strategies, although their utility in the IPV field has not yet been determined (Stewart et al. 2013).

Need   Research highlights several dynamic risk factors, or criminogenic needs, associated with an increased risk of IPV perpetration. For example, attitudes supporting violence against an intimate partner, relationship discord and communication skill deficits in relationships, alcohol, and drug use, interpersonal dependency, jealousy, emotional regulation, and self-control issues have been highlighted as consistently related to IPV perpetration (e.g. Capaldi et al. 2012; Kropp 2009; Stewart et al. 2013). However, there is little consideration as to how IPV can be explained in couples (Capaldi et al. 2012). Furthermore, whilst limited research on factors that dynamically reduce the likelihood of IPV risk (i.e. change in a criminogenic need factor corresponds with change in likelihood of recidivism) exists, evidence suggests some factors have been found to have protective qualities, including: parental monitoring, support, and encouragement of non-violent behaviour for adolescents; high friendship quality; social support and tangible help (Capaldi et al. 2012). However, these factors are not currently incorporated into risk assessment instruments.

Although the majority of risk factors are displayed at similar levels in men and women (e.g., O'Leary et al. 2007), some differences have been noted. Capaldi et al. (2012) found alcohol use and internalizing behaviours, including depression and low self-esteem, to be greater risk factors for women/girls than men/boys. Alternatively, Spencer et al.'s (2016) meta-analysis found differences in the strength of only three risk factors for men and women: family of origin violence exposure, a demand/withdrawal communication pattern, and alcohol abuse were more predictive of perpetration for men. It is important to explore the robustness of any gender differences and the impact that has on considerations for gender-specific risk assessment; at present, the majority of tools are developed with male offenders.

Furthermore, despite research that has tried to market IPV as a special type of aggression (e.g. Dobash and Dobash 1979), studies demonstrate the similarity of risk factors associated with general violence and IPV (e.g. Hanson and Wallace-Capretta 2004), with studies failing to determine that a specific IPV risk assessment tool is superior to other tools that predict general violence recidivism (e.g. Hanson et al. 2007). Therefore, whether or not IPV warrants specific assessment tools outside of those used for other forms of violence remains undecided.

Responsivity   In line with the specific *responsivity* principle, which states that treatment style should meet the learning style and abilities of the person in question, the assessor who is looking to inform treatment planning should also consider factors that may affect responsivity to treatment in their assessment. In IPV, these may include factors such as clinical psychopathy, motivation for treatment, whether the treatment approach is appropriate for the gender of the person being assessed, or, considering our earlier discussion on typologies, the type of risk profile they present with. Therefore, a wide approach to risk assessment can be a wise approach, especially for people who fall into categories that are poorly understood. For example, there is a dearth of information about IPV risk for perpetrators who: are women; identify as a gender and sexual minority group; have intellectual disabilities; are from age, cultural, and ethnic groups that differ from those on whom the tools were developed. Indeed, New Zealand Police incorporated the ODARA tool into their assessment of IPV incidents and preliminary investigation showed the typical scores gained with the NZ population differed widely from those gained in Canada (New Zealand Family Violence Clearing House 2012). Furthermore, tools are typically built around the prediction of physical harm and do not consider the risk of other forms of aggression experienced by people victimized by their intimate partner.

Functional Assessment

It is clear from the above discussion that many questions need to be addressed to inform the efficacy of actuarial tools in the IPV arena. Although much debate in the RNR literature has focused on which risk assessment tools are superior, we apply the thinking of Boer and Hart (2009) to the field of IPV that 'a good risk assessment needs both our clinical wisdom and the input from structured assessment procedures such as ARAIs or SJP guideline tests' (p. 37). This is necessary considering the under-developed nature of the IPV literature, especially with certain groups of people. The exact format of an assessment will vary depending upon its purpose, the characteristics of the person requiring the assessment and the information that is available to the assessor (Harkins and Beech 2009). Indeed, in the case of an IPV risk and treatment need assessment, it makes sense to take a broader approach than using ARAIs in isolation, including an individualized assessment of offender need that takes a detailed developmental and learning history and arrives at conclusions about the motivation of aggressive and non-aggressive behaviour and client strengths.

Frameworks such as functional assessment are useful to help clinicians understand the complexities of human aggression and tailor treatment to meet individual needs (see Ireland 2009). Functional assessment seeks to explain the function of the target behaviour for the individual, specifically: (i) why a behaviour occurred at a particular time and in a particular context, and; (ii) what immediate problem the behaviour sought to solve. Functional assessment is a process to identify the controlling biopsychosocial variables of a specific behaviour. These include the individual's biology, environment, their emotional triggers, and the associated cognitions. Based on developmental, cognitive-behavioural, and neurological approaches to understanding human behaviour, functional assessments aid the understanding of the multitude of influences (both past and present) that, together, help us to understand the reinforcers in the individual's environment.

The assessment process is interactive, where the professional and the client work collaboratively to identify the factors that increase and decrease the risk that a behaviour will occur. In addition, it enhances the participant's insight, problem-solving, and risk management skills (Harvey et al. 2015). Participants learn through this process that their environment (both past and present) influences their behaviour. It allows the identification of what factors have been motivating the behaviour by identifying the positive (gaining something good) and negative (removing something aversive) reinforcers for that individual.

Assessing developmental history is a necessity in all aggression assessments. The importance of a thorough examination of a perpetrator's developmental and learning history is highlighted by research which consistently finds that exposure to adversity in childhood is associated with a range of problematic behaviours in adulthood that are also 'risk factors' for IPV. These include sexual violence (e.g. Levenson and Socia 2016), substance use (e.g. Fuller-Thomson et al. 2016; Sachs-Ericsson et al. 2016), and poor adult mental health (e.g. Afifi et al. 2008). Adverse childhood experiences (ACEs) also directly and indirectly predict subsequent IPV perpetration and victimization (Brown et al. 2015). This has led researchers to call for a trauma-informed approach to understanding and intervening in IPV (e.g. Birkley and Eckhardt 2015; Slabber 2012) as well as a need to understand the potential neurocognitive and psychological impact of ACEs that may be a key treatment need for many IPV perpetrators (e.g. vulnerability to experiencing dysregulated emotions during relationship conflict).

Importantly, functional approaches can not only facilitate understanding of why a behaviour is taking place but also what may be inhibiting the use of alternative behaviours. They are also able to explore issues related to the function of nonaggressive behaviours which is particularly useful as it can help clinicians focus on client strengths rather than adopting a deficit model (Ireland 2009).

There is a wealth of research supporting the efficacy of interventions for problem behaviour which are directed by an understanding of its function (Hanley 2012). Most of these involve nonforensic populations (e.g. Hawkins and Axelrod 2008). Interventions based on function-based principals are more effective than nonfunction-based behavioural interventions (e.g. Miller and Lee 2013;). Ivanoff and Schmidt (2010) identified several Cognitive Behavioural models of treatment that are based upon functional assessment methods including Dialectical Behaviour Therapy (DBT; Linehan 1993a, b), Acceptance and Commitment Therapy (ACT; Hayes et al. 1999), Functional Analytic Psychotherapy (FAP; Kohlenberg and Tsai 1991), and Barlow's Unified Treatment for Emotional Disorders (Barlow et al. 2004). These treatments are based on the assumption that 'it is possible to offer a comprehensive and individualized assessment by identifying a specific behaviour to change, and then evaluating past environments that have produced the behaviour' (p. 83).

Conclusion

In comparison to other forms of violent behaviour, IPV is an area where the evidence base has been slow to develop, arguably hampered by politically motivated explanations of the behaviour, affecting the design of effective assessment and treatment programmes. In this chapter, we have argued the need to draw on the wider aggression and corrections literature, in addition to evidence in the IPV field, to inform the assessment of risk and treatment need. Whilst a psychologically-informed evidence base of IPV is growing, there are still gaps in the literature making it difficult to provide comprehensive evidence-based assessments, especially for certain groups (e.g. men experiencing harm, and women perpetrating harm in heterosexual relationships). Therefore, the importance of using validated measures, where possible, in conjunction with an individualized assessment, such as a functional assessment, is proposed as a useful and necessary way forward. Although empirically-driven tools are useful in guiding likelihood prediction, other approaches should be used in conjunction with such measures when the need to inform clinical decisions about treatment and management is required.

Indeed, the application of knowledge from the field of correctional psychology to the assessment of IPV risk and treatment need is promising. RNR principles have proved useful in interventions with correction populations and therefore, it is plausible to assume that they may have some utility in the IPV arena. However, first, we caution that more knowledge is needed before firm conclusions can be made about its safe applicability to assessment and treatment with this population. Considering the overlap of different forms of family violence and the lack of knowledge about risk of harm posed to other family members, we caution against withholding interventions from the groups at lowest risk of recidivism until robust research can inform this decision. We also note that RNR principles do not negate the need for better explanations of IPV to inform the content and style of intervention. Although the efficacy of treatment that adheres to the RNR principles is better than treatment that does not, effect sizes are small. The development of better explanations of IPV and resulting psychologically-informed risk factors and assessment tools may determine more effective treatment designs. As the current evidence clearly highlights the complexity of the aetiology of IPV, we advocate for the development of evidence-based, meta-theoretical, and process-level theories that account for the contextual and developmental histories of the assessee in addition to their interaction with their partner and the situation in which the aggression takes place. Inclusivity is of paramount importance in such theories considering the wide range of individuals who can perpetrate and experience IPV. Such comprehensive explanations are arguably the cornerstone for the development of psychologically-informed risk and treatment approaches to reduce family harm.

References

Afifi, T.O., Enns, M.W., Cox, B.J. et al. (2008). Population attributable fractions of psychiatric disorders and suicide ideation and attempts associated with adverse childhood experiences. *American Journal of Public Health* 98: 946–952.

Archer, J. (2000). Sex differences in aggression between heterosexual partners: a meta-analytic review. *Psychological Bulletin* 126 (5): 651–680.

Babcock, J.C., Green, C.E., and Robie, C. (2004). Does batterer's treatment work? A meta-analytic review of domestic violence treatment. *Clinical Psychology Review* 2: 1023–1053.

Babcock, J.C., Miller, S.A., and Siard, C. (2003). Toward a typology of abusive women: differences between partner only and generally violent women in the use of violence. *Psychology of Women Quarterly* 27: 153–161.

Barlow, D.H., Allen, L.B., and Choate, M.L. (2004). Toward a unified treatment for emotional disorders. *Behavior Therapy* 3: 205–230.

Bell, K.M. and Naugle, A.E. (2008). Intimate partner violence theoretical considerations: moving towards a contextual framework. *Clinical Psychology Review* 28: 1096–1107.

Birkley, E.L. and Eckhardt, C.I. (2015). Anger, hostility, internalizing negative emotions, and intimate partner violence perpetration: a meta-analytic review. *Clinical Psychology Review* 37: 40–56.

Bloomfield, S. and Dixon, L. (2015). *An Outcome Evaluation of the Integrated Domestic Abuse Programme (IDAP) and Community Domestic Violence Programme (CDVP): Analytic Summary*. London, UK: National Offender Management service.

Boer, D.P. and Hart, S.D. (2009). Sex offender risk assessment: research, evaluation 'best-practice' recommendations and future directions. In: *Violent and Sexual Offenders: Assessment, Treatment and Management* (eds. J.L. Ireland, C.A. Ireland and P. Birch), 27–41. Devon, UK: Willan.

Bogat, G.A., Levendosky, A.A., and von Eye, A. (2005). The future of research on intimate partner violence: person-oriented and variable-oriented perspectives. *American Journal of Community Psychology* 36: 49–70.

Bonta, J. and Andrews, D.A. (2017). *The Psychology of Criminal Conduct*, 6e. New York, NY: Routledge.

Brasfield, R. (2015). Revisiting the derivation of batterer subtypes. *Journal of Interpersonal Violence* 30: 3467–3478.

Brown, M.J., Perera, R.A., Masho, S.W. et al. (2015). Adverse childhood experiences and intimate partner aggression in the US: sex differences and similarities in psychosocial mediation. *Social Science and Medicine* 131: 48–57.

Campbell, J.C. (1992). Prevention of wife battering: insights from cultural analysis. *Response to the Victimization of Women & Children* 14 (3): 18–24.

Capaldi, D.M., Kim, H.K., and Shortt, J.W. (2007). Observed initiation and reciprocity of physical aggression in young, at-risk couples. *Journal of Family Violence* 22: 101–111.

Capaldi, D.M., Knoble, N.B., Shortt, J.W., and Kim, H.K. (2012). A systematic review of risk factors for intimate partner violence. *Partner Abuse* 3: 231–280.

Cross, C.P., Tee, W., and Campbell, A. (2011). Gender symmetry in intimate aggression: an effect of intimacy or target sex? *Aggressive Behavior* 37: 268–277.

Dixon, L. and Browne, K.D. (2003). The heterogeneity of spouse abuse: a review. *Aggression and Violent Behavior* 268: 1–24.

Dixon, L. and Graham Kevan, N. (2011). Understanding the nature and etiology of intimate partner violence and implications for practice and policy. *Clinical Psychology Review* 31: 1145–1155.

Dixon, L. and Polaschek, D. (2018). Using the research evidence to inform the assessment and treatment of intimate partner aggression. In: *The International Handbook on Human Aggression: Current Issues and Perspectives* (eds. J.L. Ireland, P. Birch and C.A. Ireland), 205–215. Florence, KY: CRC Press.

Dixon, L. and Smith Slep, A.M. (2017). Intimate partner violence and child maltreatment. In: *What Works in Child Maltreatment: An Evidence Based Approach to Assessment and Intervention in Child Protection* (eds. L. Dixon, D.P. Perkins, C.E. Hamilton Giachritsis and L.A. Craig), 97–109. Chichester, UK: Wiley-Blackwell.

Dobash, R.P. and Dobash, R.E. (1979). *Violence Against Wives*. New York, NY: The Free Press.

Dutton, D.G. (1995). Male abusiveness in intimate relationships. *Clinical Psychology Review* 15: 567–581.

Dutton, D.G. (2006). *Rethinking Domestic Violence*. Vancouver, BC: UCB Press.

Dutton, D.G., Bodnarchuk, M., Kropp, R. et al. (1997). Client personality disorders affecting wife assault post-treatment recidivism. *Violence and Victims* 12: 37–50.

Dutton, D.G. and Corvo, K. (2006). Transforming a flawed policy: a call to revive psychology and science in domestic violence research and practice. *Aggression and Violent Behavior* 11: 457–483.

Eckhardt, C., Holtzworth-Munroe, A., Norlander, B. et al. (2008). Readiness to change, partner violence subtypes, and treatment outcomes among men in treatment for partner assault. *Violence and Victims* 23: 446–475.

Esquivel-Santoveña, E.E. and Dixon, L. (2012). Investigating the true rate of physical intimate partner violence: a review of nationally representative surveys. *Aggression and Violent Behavior* 17: 208–219.

Felson, R.B. (2002). *Violence and Gender Reexamined*. Washington, DC: APA.

Fuller-Thomson, E., Roane, J.L., and Brennenstuhl, S. (2016). Three types of adverse childhood experiences, and alcohol and drug dependence among adults: an investigation using population-based data. *Substance Use and Misuse* 51: 1451–1461.

Garcia-Moreno, C., Jansen, H.A.F.M., Ellsberg, M. et al. (2006). Prevalence of IPV: findings from the WHO multi-country study on women's health and domestic violence. *The Lancet* 368: 1260–1269.

Glick, P. and Fiske, S. (1996). The ambivalent sexism inventory: differentiating hostile and benevolent sexism. *Journal of Personality and Social Psychology* 70 (3): 491–512.

Gondolf, E.W. (2004). Evaluating batterer counseling programs: a difficult task showing some effects and implications. *Aggression and Violent Behavior* 9: 605–631.

Gondolf, E.W. and White, R.J. (2001). Batterer program participants who repeatedly reassault: psychopathic tendencies and other disorders. *Journal of Interpersonal Violence* 16: 361–380.

Graham Kevan, N. (2007). Power and control in relationship aggression. In: *Family Interventions in Domestic Violence: A Handbook of Gender Inclusive Theory and Treatment* (eds. J. Hamel and T.L. Nicholls), 87–108. New York, NY: Springer.

Hamel, J. (2005). *Gender-Inclusive Treatment of Intimate Partner Abuse: A Comprehensive Approach*. New York, NY: Springer.

Hanley, G.P. (2012). Functional assessment of problem behavior: dispelling myths, overcoming implementation obstacles, and developing new lore. *Behavior Analysis in Practice* 5 (1): 54–72.

Hanson, R.K., Helmus, L., and Bourgon, G. (2007). *The Validity of Risk Assessments for Intimate Partner Violence: A Meta-Analysis*. Ottawa, ON: Public Safety Canada.

Hanson, R.K. and Wallace-Capretta, S. (2004). Predictors of criminal recidivism among male batterers. *Psychology, Crime & Law* 10: 413–427.

Harkins, L. and Beech, A. (2009). Assessing the therapeutic needs of sex offenders. In: *Violent and Sexual Offenders: Assessment, Treatment and Management* (eds. J.L. Ireland, C.A. Ireland and P. Birch), 97–122. Devon, UK: Willan.

Harvey, J., Rogers, A., and Law, H. (2015). *Young People in Forensic Mental Health Settings: Psychological Thinking and Practice*. Hampshire, UK: Palgrave Macmillan.

Hawkins, R. and Axelrod, M.I. (2008). Increasing the on-task homework behavior of youth with behavior disorders using functional behavioral assessment. *Behavior Modification* 32: 840–859.

Hayes, S.C., Strosahl, K., and Wilson, K.G. (1999). *Acceptance and Commitment Therapy: An Experiential Approach to Behavior Change*. New York, NY: Guilford Press.

Hilton, N.Z., Harris, G.T., and Rice, M.E. (2010). *Risk Assessment for Domestically Violent Men: Tools for Criminal Justice, Offender Intervention, and Victim Services*. Washington, DC: APA.

Hilton, N.Z., Harris, G.T., Rice, M.E. et al. (2004). A brief actuarial assessment for the prediction of wife assault recidivism: the Ontario domestic assault risk assessment. *Psychological Assessment* 16: 267–275.

Hilton, N.Z., Harris, G.T., Rice, M.E. et al. (2008). An in-depth actuarial assessment for wife assault recidivism: the domestic violence risk appraisal guide. *Law and Human Behavior* 32: 150–163.

Hines, D.A. and Douglas, E.M. (2016). Sexual aggression experiences among mal victims of physical partner violence: prevalence, severity and health correlates for male victims and their children. *Archives of Sexual Behavior* 45: 1133–1151.

Holtzworth-Munroe, A., Meehan, C., Herron, K. et al. (2000). Testing the Holtzworth-Munroe and Stuart (1994) batterer typology. *Journal of Consulting and Clinical Psychology* 68: 1000–1019.

Holtzworth-Munroe, A., Meehan, C., Herron, K. et al. (2003). Do subtypes of maritally violent men continue to differ over time? *Journal of Consulting and Clinical Psychology* 71: 728–740.

Holtzworth-Munroe, A. and Meehan, J.C. (2004). Typologies of men who are martially violent: scientific and clinical implications. *Journal of Interpersonal Violence* 19: 1369–1389.

Holtzworth-Munroe, A. and Stuart, G.L. (1994). Typologies of male batterers: three subtypes and the differences among them. *Psychological Bulletin* 116: 476–497.

Home Office (2018). Domestic abuse: How to get help. https://www.gov.uk/guidance/domestic-abuse-how-to-get-help (Accessed 16 August 2019).

Hotaling, G.T. and Sugarman, D.B. (1986). An analysis of risk markers in husband to wife violence: the current state of knowledge. *Violence and Victims* 1: 101–124.

Ireland, J.L. (2009). Conducting individualized theory-driven assessments of violent offenders. In: *Violent and Sexual Offenders: Assessment, Treatment and Management* (eds. J.L. Ireland, C.A. Ireland and P. Birch), 68–93. Devon, UK: Willan.

Ivanoff, A. and Schmidt, H. (2010). Functional assessment in forensic settings: a valuable tool for preventing and treating egregious behavior. *Journal of Cognitive Psychotherapy* 24: 81–91.

Johnson, M.P. (1995). Patriarchal terrorism and common couple violence: two forms of violence against women. *Journal of Marriage and the Family* 57: 283–294.

Johnson, M.P. (1999). Two types of violence against women in the American family: Identifying patriarchal terrorism and common couple violence. Paper presented at the annual meeting of the National Council on family relations in Irvine, CA (10–15 November 1999).

Johnson, M.P. (2006). Conflict and control: gender symmetry and asymmetry in domestic violence. *Violence Against Women* 12: 1003–1018.

Jones, A.S. and Gondolf, E.W. (2001). Time-varying risk factors for re-assault among batterer program participants. *Journal of Family Violence* 16: 345–359.

Kohlenberg, R.J. and Tsai, M. (1991). *Functional Analytic Psychotherapy: Creating Intense and Curative Therapeutic Relationships*. New York, NY: Plenum.

Kropp, P.R. (2009). Intimate partner violence risk assessment. In: *Violent and Sexual Offenders: Assessment, Treatment and Management* (eds. J.L. Ireland, C.A. Ireland and P. Birch), 43–58. Devon, UK: Willan.

Kropp, P.R., Hart, S.D., Lyon, D.R., and LePard, D.A. (2002). Managing stalkers: coordinating treatment and supervision. In: *Stalking and Psychosexual Obsession: Psychological Perspectives for Prevention Policing, and Treatment* (eds. J.C.W. Boon and L. Sheridan), 141–163. Chichester, UK: Wiley.

Kropp, P.R., Hart, S.D., Webster, C.D., and Eaves, D. (2015). *Spousal assault risk assessment guide: Users manual*. New York, NY: Multi Health Systems.

Langhinrichsen-Rohlin, J., Huss, M.T., and Ramsey, S. (2000). The clinical utility of batterer typologies. *Journal of Family Violence* 15: 37–53.

LaRoche, D. (2008). *Context and Consequences of Domestic Violence against Men and Women in Canada 2004: Living Conditions, April*. Québec City, PQ: Institut de la Statistique du Québec.

Levenson, J.S. and Socia, K.M. (2016). Adverse childhood experiences and arrest patterns in a sample of sexual offenders. *Journal of Interpersonal Violence* 31: 1883–1911.

Linehan, M.M. (1993a). *Cognitive Behavioral Treatment of Borderline Personality Disorder*. New York, NY: Guilford.

Linehan, M.M. (1993b). *Skills Training Manual for Treating Borderline Personality Disorder*. New York, NY: Guilford.

Loseke, D.R., Gelles, R.J., and Cavanaugh, M.M. (2005). Controversies in conceptualisation. In: *Current Controversies on Family Violence* (eds. D.R. Loseke, R.J. Gelles and M.M. Cavanaugh), 1–4. Thousand Oaks: CA. Sage.

Maxwell, C., Garner, J.H., and Fagan, J.A. (2001). *The Effects of Arrest on Intimate Partner Violence: New Evidence from the Spouse Assault Replication Program*. Washington, DC: U.S. Department of Justice, Office of Justice Programs.

Mihalic, S.W. and Elliott, D. (1997). A social learning theory model of marital violence. *Journal of Family Violence* 12: 21–47.

Miller, F.G. and Lee, D.L. (2013). Do functional behavioral assessments improve intervention effectiveness for students diagnosed with ADHD? A single-subject meta-analysis. *Journal of Behavioral Education* 22 (3): 253–282.

Neal, T.S. and Grisso, T. (2014). The cognitive underpinnings of bias in forensic mental health evaluations. *Psychology, Public Policy, and Law* 20: 200–211.

New Zealand Family Violence Clearing House. (2012). ODARA tool reveals high levels of risk. www.nzfvc.org.nz/news/odara-tool-reveals-high-levels-risk (Accessed

Office for National Statistics (2016). *Intimate Personal Violence and Partner Abuse*. London, UK: ONS.

O'Leary, K.D., Smith Slep, A.M., and O'Leary, S.G. (2007). Multivariate models of men's and women's partner aggression. *Journal of Consulting and Clinical Psychology* 75: 752–764.

Respect (2008). Respect position statement: Gender and domestic violence. Respect. https://nzfvc.org.nz/sites/nzfvc.org.nz/files/Respect%20Statement.pdf (Accessed 16 August 2019).

Sachs-Ericsson, N.J., Rushing, N.C., Stanley, I.H., and Sheffler, J. (2016). In my end is my beginning: developmental trajectories of adverse childhood experiences to late-life suicide. *Aging and Mental Health* 20: 139–165.

Saunders, D.G. (1996). Feminist-cognitive-behavioral and process-psychodynamic treatments for men who batter: interaction of abuser traits and treatment models. *Violence and Victims* 11: 393–414.

Schafer, J., Caetano, R., and Clark, C.L. (1998). Rates of intimate partner violence in the United States. *American Journal of Public Health* 88: 1702–1704.

Slabber, M. (2012). *Community-Based Family Violence Interventions*. Wellington, NZ: Department of Corrections.

Slep, A.M.S. and O'Leary, S.G. (2005). Parent and partner violence in families with young children: rates, patterns and connections. *Journal of Consulting and Clinical Psychology* 73: 435–444.

Sorenson, S. and Taylor, C. (2005). Female aggression toward male intimate partners: an examination of social norms in a community-based sample. *Psychology of Women Quarterly* 29 (1): 78–96.

Spencer, C., Cafferky, B., and Stith, S.M. (2016). Gender differences in risk markers for perpetration of physical partner violence: results from a meta-analytic review. *Journal of Family Violence* 31: 981–984.

Statistics Canada. (2006). Family violence in Canada: A statistical profile 2006 (Catalogue No. 85-224XIE). Ottawa, ON: Author.

Stewart, L.A., Flight, J., and Salvin-Stewart, C. (2013). Applying effective correction principles (RNR) to partner abuse interventions. *Partner Abuse* 4: 494–534.

Stewart, L.A., Gabora, N., Allegri, N., and Stewart, M.C. (2014a). Profile of female perpetrators of intimate partner violence in an offender population: implications for treatment. *Partner Abuse* 5: 168–188.

Stewart, L.A., Gabora, N., Kropp, P.R., and Lee, Z.C. (2014b). Effectiveness of risk-needs-responsivity-based family violence programmes with male offenders. *Journal of Family Violence* 29: 151–164.

Stith, S.M., Smith, D.B., Penn, C.E. et al. (2004). Intimate partner physical abuse perpetration and victimization risk factors: a meta-analytic review. *Aggression and Violent Behavior* 10: 65–98.

Straus, M.A. (1990). The National Family Violence Surveys. In: *Physical Violence in American Families: Risk Factors and Adaptations to Violence in 8145 Families* (eds. M.A. Straus and R.J. Gelles), 3–15. New Brunswick, NJ: Transaction Publishers.

Straus, M.A. (2011). Gender symmetry and mutuality in perpetration of clinical-level partner violence: empirical evidence and implications for prevention and treatment. *Aggression and Violent Behavior* 16: 279–288.

Straus, M.A. and Gelles, R.J. (1985). Is family violence increasing? A comparison of 1975 and 1985 national survey rates. Paper presented at the American Society of Criminology in San Diego, USA (13–17 November 1985).

Straus, M.A., Gelles, R.J., and Steinmetz, S.K. (1980). *Behind Closed Doors: Violence in the American Family*. New York, NY: Anchor Books.

Straus, M.A., Hamby, S.L., Boney-McCoy, S., and Sugarman, D.B. (1996). The revised conflict tactics scales (CTS2). *Journal of Family Issues* 17: 283–316.

Walters, M.L., Chen, J., and Brieding, M.J. (2010). *The National Intimate Partner and Sexual Violence Survey (NISVS): 2010 Findings on Victimization by Sexual Orientation*. Atlanta, GA: National Center for Injury Prevention and Control Centers for Disease Control and Prevention.

Ward, T. (2014). The explanation of sexual offending: from single factor theories to integrative pluralism. *Journal of Sexual Aggression* 20: 130–141.

Ward, T. (2016). Dynamic risk factors: scientific kinds or predictive constructs. *Psychology, Crime & Law* 22 (1–2): 2–16.

Ward, T. and Fortune, C.A. (2016). The role of dynamic risk factors in the explanation of offending. *Aggression and Violent Behavior* 29: 79–88.

Ward, T. and Heffernan, R. (2017). The role of values in forensic and correctional rehabilitation. *Aggression and Violent Behavior* 37: 42–51.

Waypoint. (2016). The Ontario Domestic Assault Risk Assessment (ODARA): Fact sheet. http://www.waypointcentre.ca/UserFiles/Servers/Server_9960/File?ODARA%20Fact%20Sheet%20v0116.pdf (Accessed 16 August 2019).

Whitaker, D.J., Haileyesus, T., Swahn, M., and Saltzman, L.S. (2007). Differences in frequency of violence and reported injury between relationships with reciprocal and nonreciprocal intimate partner violence. *American Journal of Public Health* 97: 941–947.

White, R.J. and Gondolf, E.W. (2000). Implications of personality profiles for batterer treatment. *Journal of Interpersonal Violence* 15: 467–488.

16

Aggression from a Psychobiological Perspective
Implications for Enhanced Violent Risk Assessment and Interventions

David Nussbaum

Allen K. Institute for Integrative and Forensic Behavioural Science,
Vaughn, Ontario, Canada
University of Toronto, Scarborough, Canada

State-of-the-Art of Violence Risk Prediction

Since the early 1980s (e.g. Kroll and Mackenzie 1983; Stokman 1984), researchers and forensic/correctional mental health professionals have advanced clinicians' ability to foretell more accurately, which individuals are more or less likely to engage in violent recidivism. Previously, psychiatrists provided intuitive and primarily subjective and unstructured clinical judgements of 'dangerousness' that not surprisingly were shown, upon empirical examination, to be invalid (see Chapter 3). In the 1970s, more rigorous approaches were initiated to improve upon this 'low bar'. The two predominant approaches consist of the more objective and algorithmic (if rigid and atheoretical) actuarial algorithms (e.g. the Violent Risk Assessment Guide or VRAG; Harris et al. 1993) and the relatively more subjective but still empirically informed structured clinical judgement (SCJ; e.g. the Historical Clinical Risk-20; Webster et al. 1997). A third prominent approach to risk assessment involves a theoretical component predicated on social learning theory as applied to criminal behaviour in general and risk prediction. The psychology of criminal behaviour (Andrews and Bonta 1994, 2010) presents a theoretical account of criminal behaviour amalgamating tenets of social learning theory, psychoanalytical insights and criminological strain theory. The applied focus speaks to three central principles of offender rehabilitation: Risk, Needs and Responsivity (or RNR; e.g. Andrews et al. 2011). Concisely, the Risk Principle dictates the appropriate amount of correctional/rehabilitative services required to reduce recidivism as determined empirically. The (Criminogenic) Needs Principle refers to putative dynamic causes of criminal behaviour that have been supported empirically. These empirically-identified criminogenic needs suggest

The Wiley Handbook of What Works in Violence Risk Management: Theory, Research and Practice,
First Edition. Edited by J. Stephen Wormith, Leam A. Craig, and Todd E. Hogue.

effective targets for intervention. The Responsivity principle states that in light of offender's differences in learning style and interests, intervention programmes must be tailored to 'fit' the service delivery parameters to optimize the likelihood of success. The RNR model has generated a suite of instruments to evaluate risk levels and identify targets for correctional intervention. These consist of the Level of Service (LS) instruments including the Level of Service Inventory-Revised (Andrews and Bonta 1995) and its derivative Level of Service Inventory/Case Management (LSI/CM; Andrews et al. 2004), that adds an explicate translation of the identified R-N-R items into case management specifics. The LSI in its various forms (Andrews et al. 2008) allows for 'professional over-ride' for rare cases where a salient element of the specific case, necessitates that the mental health professional over-ride the routine conclusions suggested by the particular LSI conclusion.

Beyond these predominant methods, other researchers have developed empirically-validated techniques for assessing risk for violent recidivism and suggestions for successful interventions including a novel self-report measure called the Self-Assessment Questionnaire (SAQ; Loza et al. 2004) and the Violent Risk Scale (VRS; Wong and Gordon 2006). A number of researchers have developed more specific risk instruments for narrower offender subtypes. Amongst instruments for predicting sexual recidivism are The Static-99 and Static 2002/R (Hanson et al. 2012) and the Sex Offender Recidivism Appraisal Guide, or SORAG (Quinsey et al. 1995).

For young offenders, there is the Structured Assessment of Violent Recidivism in Youth or SAVRY (Borum et al. 2010) and Psychopathy Checklist Revised-Youth Version, (PCL-R YV; Forth et al. 2003). For violent domestic offenders there are the Spousal Aggression Risk Assessment (SARA; Kropp and Hart 2000) and the Ontario Domestic Risk Appraisal Guide (ODARA; Hilton et al. 2004). Nussbaum (2006) presented a comprehensive treatment of these and other empirically-tested violent risk prediction techniques. Andrews et al. (2006) provided a historical/conceptual classification of violent risk prediction falling into one of four generations. Table 16.1 reflects the essence of that classification system.

In everyday correctional and forensic practice, many institutions and professionals tasked with providing an estimate of a specific release candidate's likelihood for recidivating violently use two or three instruments from any or all generations. This practice is reassuring when decisions from discrepant instruments and methodologies converge and concur. However, the precise way that potentially conflicting conclusions are integrated and rationalized remains less clear.

Purpose of this chapter

The purpose of this chapter is not to theoretically analyse or empirically question the predictive validity of existing conceptualizations and very positive heuristic value of currently used methods in the practice of risk assessment and management. However, it is instructive to consider a few salient, if occasionally underappreciated, limitations to understand why it is advantageous to explore alternative conceptualizations of violent risk assessment and management.

The actuarial approach per se developed from very successful procedures intended to serve the insurance industry to set policy rates to ensure that the companies would charge policy-holders appropriate fees based on pre-existing group risk factors. Actuarial success in the insurance context meant that sufficient funds would be available to i) pay out the insurance

Table 16.1 Generations of risk assessment instruments.

Generation	General Descriptors	Major Examples
First Generation:	Unstructured Professional Opinion: Subjective	Idiosyncratic Clinical Opinion
First Generation Modified:	Structured Professional Judgement: Cognizant of Empirically Identified Risk Factors	HCR-20
Second Generation:	Pure Actuarial: Static, Historical	PCL-R-2 VRAG
Third Generation:	Theoretically Grounded, Empirically Validated, Dynamic as well as Historical Risk Items, Individual Dynamic Risk Factors Identify Intervention Targets	LSI LSI-R SAG
Fourth Generation:	Extension of Third Generation; Guidance from Intake through Case Closure Successful Interventions can Mitigate Risk Estimate	LS/CMI

claims when the predicted insured events arose, ii) cover all of the costs involved in running the business (e.g. advertising, commissions, office rentals, personnel fees), and iii) have enough left over for a healthy profit. In the insurance example, distinct group risk levels determine specific group premiums by insured individuals who share common risk factors and empirically-determined levels of risk. However, these group statistics do not predict whether, within a particular risk group, it is Ms. Jones or Ms. Smith who would be the one to die at age 55, or which 18–24-year-olds would, or would not be, involved in a traffic collision. In the criminal justice system, it is not the group that is being assessed but the individual.

A second issue involves the outcome variable that existing risk instruments seek to predict. Typically, this involves whether or not an individual will commit a future act of criminal violence, or in the case of the VRAG, whether an individual *is charged* with a future violent offence. However, as will be described later, different individuals tend to commit violent acts that differ in terms of what triggers, motivates, sustains, and terminates the aggressive action. Further, most violent recidivists tend to have similar triggering situations and underlying motivational purposes across violent crimes (Levi et al. 2010). This broader scope including instigating contexts, idiosyncratic triggers, maintenance characteristics and termination cues for different types of aggression imply that greater predictive accuracy, selection of treatment targets, therapeutic/correctional methods and outcome criterion measures is possible for individual offenders. To realize this goal, it is necessary to identify i) the aggression type most typical for the individual offender, ii) cues triggering specific pathways initiating these aggression types, iii) process-oriented and measurable risk factors for each type of aggression and iv) optimal interventions to alter the aggressive response patterns triggered by typical eliciting contexts for each violent offenders.

To achieve these goals, this chapter will first present a novel context to understanding behaviour before turning to the chapter's major focus on two domains neglected within the classical violent risk prediction literature; specifically, aggression and biological theory.

Acknowledging the existence of an extensive social psychology literature on aggression, the primary focus of this chapter will be on the biologically-related systemic approach to understanding the contexts, causes, objectives, and reasons for aggression types, psychobiological mechanisms that 'drive' these aggression systems, and the control mechanisms that regulate their initiation, maintenance, and termination. The chapter will then provide existing empirical data to show how existing psychometric measures can successfully identify individuals whose aggression types conformed to the utilized aggression model. Finally, the chapter will provide a glimpse into how it may be possible to harness recent technology, in conjunction with selected decision-making tasks, to enhance the basic understanding of psychobiological mechanisms of aggression and, more precisely, interpret individuals' psychological test results, selection of specific criminogenic intervention targets and determine success or lack thereof of intervention goals.

A Reductionistic Approach to Understanding Behaviour: General Considerations

Within the psychobiological paradigm, it is necessary to define behaviour reductionistically as 'expressed information' rather than in the 'upward' direction as 'the externally observable actions of the organism' (Nussbaum 2001, p. 127) as suggested by Watson. Our brains are capable of storing vast amounts of diverse information in different, but intercommunicating, specialized networks. Were all of this information expressed simultaneously, actions would be chaotic. Consequently, the fundamental organizing principle of behaviour is the inhibition of information irrelevant to the environment in which the individual finds herself. Second, relevant information must be organized and sequenced to respond effectively to environmental signals and demands. Third, environmental cues inducing a response can result from the 'inside environment' (interoceptively) or from the environment external to the body (exteroceptively) including, of course, social environments. Fourth, different bits of information may promote different actions and travel via neuronal processes for integration to decision-making nodes. Activated decision nodes remain inhibited for brief durations to allow other relevant information to contribute to the outcome (Noorani and Carpenter 2016). The amount of time permitted for admission of relevant information is limited and subject to individual differences. Fifth, in many ways, psychological space is not linear but curvilinear. Moderate levels of a trait generally result in appropriate responses to an environmental cue or opportunity (i.e. trigger) but extremely low or high levels of the trait typically result in an inappropriate response, albeit for very different reasons. This will become crucial when discussing core differences between Primary (e.g. Hare 1980, 1991, 2003) and Secondary (Karpman 1947) psychopathy. These and other psychological intricacies and dynamics highlight problems with defining what should be behavioural outcome variables rather than legal constructs such as criminal charges that confound different behaviours under identical legal categories. Legal constructs originate from philosophical, ethical, moral, and historical ideals that are appropriate and necessary to identify behaviours and behavioural outcomes that merit a range of governmental sanctions. Presently, psychological measures and constructs accurately describe, passably predict but at best, only putatively 'explain' behaviours.[1]

---

[1] A full exposition of this position is beyond the purview and scope of the present chapter. A full treatment of the position is nearing completion.

Additionally, it is important to differentiate between atypical behaviours that originate from abnormal environments but possess well-functioning brains from atypical behaviours that result entirely from genetics such as Huntington's disease. Huntington's is determined by a mutation of the Huntingtin (HTT) gene that provides the chemical template for producing the huntingtin protein (Moss et al. 2017). Mutations in the HTT gene cause an excessive number (40–120) of Cytosine Adenine Guanine (CAG) repeats that in turn, produce elongated huntingtin proteins, that split into smaller fragments that bind to each other and disrupt normal neuronal function (NIMH 2018). In contrast, individuals raised in homes where antisocial behaviour is modelled and reinforced can internalize criminal behaviour by normal processes of vicarious learning and operant conditioning.

Non-genetic biological causes of atypical behaviour also exist. Perhaps the most obvious example is damage to the frontal lobes of the brain that often produce marked differences in cognition, motivational states, emotional lability, and motor efficiency. Perhaps most relevant for criminal behaviour, frontal lobe insults dysregulate different aspects of behaviour depending on the precise location within the frontal lobe and extent of the injury. Finally, many illegal actions that attract attentional systems result from a combination of individual neurobiological characteristics that bias information processing to preferentially attend to, subsequently 'learn' inappropriate patterns for achieving their needs and wants, and typically respond to challenging situations in less than optimal ways. When these characteristic responses exceed legal thresholds for negatively affecting other people's rights and safety, the legal system must intervene to maintain public safety and order.

The task before the psychobiologically-oriented correctional and forensic psychologist is to identify and classify criminal behaviours in a way that directly maps to the proximal brain systems and networks that process requisite information. This endeavour extends to regulatory systems that govern how easily and quickly an unsound decision is crafted and implemented. More distally, the constitutional structures and processes and triggering environmental contexts that contribute hierarchically to the specific offences is necessary for a full appreciation of the contributory pathways to criminal conduct. Distilling this mass of information into a feasible set of coherent procedures consistent with the complex underlying system represents the applied challenge.

Science, Levels of Organization and the Resultant Change in Classification of Psychopathology

In general, organization of the natural sciences is hierarchical. Higher levels of scientific phenomena observed at the higher levels of organization are defined and explained by constructs and mechanisms falling lower in the organizational hierarchy. More concretely, organisms are defined by their distinct constituent organ systems that, in turn, are defined by their specific cell structures and functions. Cells are defined by their organelles, and organelles defined by their macromolecules. Macromolecules are defined by their molecules, molecules by their atoms, and atoms by their subatomic particles. Table 16.2 summarizes the hierarchical structure of the family of natural sciences.

This epistemological structure is becoming germane to the forthcoming classification of psychopathology that seeks to avoid the serious and related issues endemic to DSM and ICD symptom count systems (Clark et al. 2017). These involve i) the heterogeneity of symptoms within a set of diagnostic criteria (e.g. mixtures of perceptual, cognitive,

Table 16.2 Hierarchical structure of natural sciences.

Natural Science	Representative Constituents
Biology	Eco-system; Organism, Organ Systems, Organelles, Genes
Molecular Biology/Biochemistry/ Organic Chemistry	DNA, Nucleotides, Proteins, Amino Acids, Carbohydrates
Chemistry	Molecules
Physics	Atoms, Protons, Electrons, Neutrons, Sub-Atomic Particles (e.g. Neutrinos, Pi Mesons, Strings, Quarks, etc.)

Table 16.3 Summary of the Research Oriented Diagnostic Criteria (RoDC) framework: five domains and seven pillars.

External and Internal Physical and Social Environments

Domains	Genes	Molecules	Cells	Circuits	Physiology	Behaviour	Self-Report
Negative Valence Systems							
Positive Valence Systems							
Cognitive Systems							
Systems for Social Processing							
Arousal/Modulatory Systems							

Source: Based on Cuthbert and Insel (2013).

motivational, emotional, and self-regulation symptoms that reflect operations of distinct information processing systems in the brain) and ii) homogeneity of symptoms across diagnoses (e.g. impulsivity occurring in many diagnoses including Bipolar Mood Disorder, ADHD, Psychopathy, Schizophrenia and Borderline Personality Disorder). The currently percolating Research Oriented Diagnostic Criteria (RoDC) will replace the existing DSM and ICD classification systems in due course. This makes it imperative that psychologists and other behavioural experts become equipped to appreciate and move comfortably between the various identified levels of conceptual and mechanistic information processing. Table 16.3 provides a schematic of the new RoDC meta-system for classification of psychopathology.

Neurodevelopment, responsive to external and internal environmental states, begins on the left with genes, proceeding to specific chemical products that constitute cells, organized during early development in the brain into discrete, specialized information-processing units that form interacting circuits to determine function at the physiological level manifested as overt behaviour or internal information reported by the individual. The blanks in this puzzle will be completed when behavioural neuroscientists 'fill in the blanks' to provide definite concrete knowledge of how behaviours emerge from both optimal and impaired circuits, and trace backward from behaviour to gene.

The RoDC framework will undoubtedly stimulate considerable research and discovery from top-to-bottom and side-to-side within the matrix. A few conceptual caveats remain. First, behaviour appears to remain defined as overtly observable actions (even self-reports are overt and observable). Second, from the RoDC framework, one might believe that genes directly and immutably direct molecular construction and thereby ultimately control behavioural deterministically. The presupposition that 'genes are behavioral destiny' has long been debated in psychology circles, with a more recent consensus that genes and the environment interact to shape biological (and for the purposes of this chapter, neurobiological) development, that in turn, influences different behavioural domains, some more than others (e.g. Zaky 2015). Yet the interactive mechanisms whereby environments affected genes remained obscure and therefore unaddressed even by many who accepted the interactive paradigm. This resigned analyses of the interactions to the statistical sphere that while helpful, left a more precise understanding wanting.

More importantly, a number of recently discovered important mechanisms by which gene–environment interactions occur, are now reasonably well understood. The most detailed mechanism that accounts for how expression of genes (i.e. protein synthesis) is modulated by environmental influences without changing DNA codon sequences is called epigenetics (Cowell n.d.; Felsenfeld 2014; Villota-Salazar et al. 2016). In order to appreciate this section of the chapter, an introduction to the very basic building blocks and mechanisms of molecular biology is necessary.

A Brief Primer on Molecular Biology and Molecular Genetics

In overview, the genetic code consists of the sequential information contained in Deoxyribonucleic Acid (DNA), converted to various formats of Ribonucleic Acid (RNA) that, in turn, assembles genetically-determined sequences of lengthy amino acid chains known as proteins. Proteins serve two major purposes. First, they provide definitive structural elements for all cells of the body. Structural features of cells differentiate kidney cells (nephrons) from muscle or brain cells (neurons). Structural features of cells are intimately associated with specific cell function. Amongst various structural proteins of paramount importance for behaviour are the neuronal receptor proteins that are necessary for the nervous system's information processing. Enzymes are the second type of proteins, serving as catalysts to increase rates of chemical reactions in cells by up to a million-fold. Variations in enzymes determine which cellular reactions will be favoured over others and determine function. We now look at the central dogma of molecular biology: DNA -> *transcription* RNA-> *translation* Protein (Smith 2008). Verbally, 'the coded genetic information hardwired into DNA is transcribed into individual transportable cassettes, composed of messenger RNA (mRNA); each mRNA cassette contains the program for synthesis of a particular protein (or small number of proteins)' (NCBI 2007). Because information processing in the brain (e.g. learning/memory formation) is associated with protein synthesis, this brief review is limited to protein synthesis and does not describe cell replication. Figure 16.1 provides schematic diagrams of DNA and RNA with their double- and single-helix backbones and respective nucleotide base pairings differing only in the substitution of Uracil for Thymine in RNA.

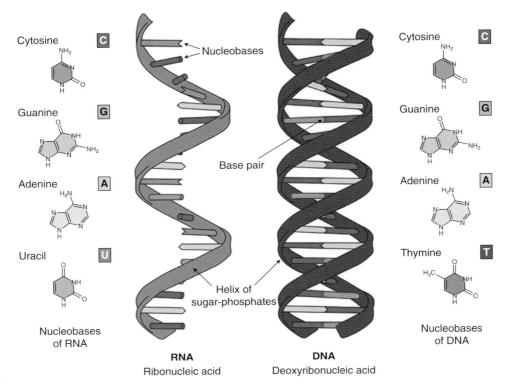

Figure 16.1   Schematic diagrams of DNA and RNA. Source: Helmenstine (2018).

Deoxyribonucleic acid (DNA)

More specifically, the nucleotide, deoxyribonucleic acid (DNA), consists of multiple chains of three subunits consisting of a i) nitrogenous base, ii) a 5-carbon sugar (deoxyribose) and iii) one or more or more phosphate groups. Nitrogenous bases occur in two varieties; Pyrimidines defined by their single six-member ring and the double-ring Purines with their attached five and six rings. Cytosine (C) and Thymine (T) are the pyrimidine bases in DNA whilst Adenine (A) and Guanine (G) are the Purines in DNA (Staroscik 2011). The deoxyribose sugar provides the structural backbone of DNA's double helix. Sequences of nitrogenous base pairings encode genetic information in DNA. In DNA, the purine Adenine (A) always pairs with the pyrimidine thymine (T) (A-T pairing). The pyrimidine cytosine (C) always pairs with the purine guanine (G) (C-G pairing). Relatively weak hydrogen bonds achieve the ionic bonding between these base pairs. Three pairing sequences (e.g. A-T, A-T, C-G) within the double helix, known as code for specific amino acids and consequently named 'triplet codons'. The DNA alphabet results from the exhaustive set of possible A-T and C-G triplet codon sequences. The resulting triplet codons each specified a particular amino acid with the sequence following the precise order of the nucleotide base pairings on the DNA strand. Genes code for particular proteins and contain different numbers of triplet codons depending on the number of constituent amino acids. (See below).

Gene regulation

Each cell contains the complete set of genetic information to produce every protein used in the body, yet within every organ system, individual cells produce only the proteins appropriate and necessary for that organ's structural and functional needs. Obviously, segments of the total DNA/gene package that would produce inappropriate proteins for the type of cells that they reside in are permanently inactivated, whilst segments that produce proteins necessary for their particular cell type are inhibited when not needed but activated when chemical signals inform the gene of the need for production of a given protein. This mechanism, called DNA or gene regulation, permits cells to alter their gene expression patterns to trigger developmental pathways, respond to environmental stimuli, or adapt to new food sources. By regulating the type and rate of protein synthesis and degradation, each cell controls its own structural and functional destiny (Scitable 2010).

In its' 'resting state' (i.e. when DNA is not involved in gene expression), it exists in its classical double-helix form as shown in Figure 16.1. Additionally, these very lengthy double-stranded DNA chains wrap themselves around histone proteins to prevent the double helix from being unravelled and split. That unravelling and separation of the double strands make it possible for the DNA encased genetic code to be 'fingerprinted' and transcribed by the single-stranded RNA (described immediately below). Transcription initiation is the key aspect of gene expression. Two DNA sequence elements 'promote' the process by facilitating the RNA polymerase enzyme to recognize where the relevant protein-coding gene begins. Referred to as promotor sequences, the two DNA promoter signs contain 35 and 10 base pairs respectively. These promotor sequences function much like indentations that help readers recognize where a paragraph begins. The genes are analogous to words constructed from the triplet codon-determined 'letters'. 'Sentences' composed of amino acid words combine to form 'paragraphs' of protein that are operational units performing their own specific role in the overall functioning of the cell. Using three-dimensional stereotaxic fit, RNA polymerase is able to recognize and quickly binds to appropriate promoter sequences. Regulatory proteins known as activators and repressors regulate this interaction of RNA polymerase with promoter sequences by positively or negatively affecting the fit between promoter sequences and RNA polymerase (Cheriyedath 2016). Cheriyedath (2016) provides a brief but comprehensive overview of gene regulation in a two-and-a-half minute YouTube video available on the referenced URL.

Ribonucleic acid (RNA)

Although DNA in every cell contains the necessary genetic blueprint to construct a duplicate individual or synthesize all necessary proteins in the body, DNA remains in the cell nucleus whilst protein synthesis occurs outside the cell nucleus in an organelle called the ribosome. RNA is the macromolecule charged with first transcribing (i.e. copying) the genetic code directly from DNA, and exiting the cell nucleus and then translating the copied DNA instructions into the genetically determined sequence of amino acids. There are distinct types of RNA to accomplish these two sub-tasks (Scoville 2017).

Messenger RNA (or mRNA) has the main role in transcription, or the first step in making a protein from a DNA blueprint. The mRNA is made up of nucleotides found in the nucleus that come together to make a complementary sequence to the DNA found there. The enzyme that puts this strand of mRNA together is called RNA polymerase. Three adjacent nitrogen bases in the mRNA sequence is called a codon and they each code for a specific amino acid that will then be linked with other amino acids in the correct order to make a protein.

Before mRNA can move on to the next step of gene expression, it must first undergo some processing. There many regions of DNA that do not code for any genetic information. These non-coding regions are still transcribed by mRNA. This means the mRNA must first cut out these sequences, called introns, before it can be coded into a functioning protein. The parts of mRNA that do code for amino acids are called exons. The introns are cut out by enzymes and only the exons are left. This now single strand of genetic information is able to move out of the nucleus and into the cytoplasm to begin the second part of gene expression called translation (Scoville 2017). Helmenstine (2018) provides a more detailed account of DNA and RNA mechanisms.

Proteins and amino acids

Proteins, the ultimate product of genetic information, consist of lengthy chains of amino acids (e.g. 100 to many thousands) joined by peptide linkages. Amino acids consist of two distinct but fixed ends common to all amino acids, attached to distinctive radical segments. The two fixed ends include the Amine group consisting of a single Nitrogen and two Hydrogen atoms symbolized and NH_2. The other end consists of the carboxyl group containing single Carbon and Hydrogen atoms and two Oxygen atoms, symbolized as COOH. Figure 16.2 provides a general representation of an amino acid.

This carboxyl group contributes the 'acid' portion of the nomenclature. It falls to the 20 different 'radicals' linked to both the Amine and Carboxyl ends to provide specificity to each essential amino acid.

The 'triplet alphabet code' exists within DNA for the specification of the ultimate amino acid sequence that determines the precise structure for all proteins in the body. The DNA–amino-acid sequence code is provided in Figure 16.3. The coloured circles contain three letter abbreviations for the various 20 amino acids used by humans (e.g. alanine, arginine, asparagine, aspartic acid, cysteine, glutamic acid, glutamine, glycine, histidine, isoleucine, leucine, lysine, methionine, phenylalanine, proline, serine, threonine, tryptophan, tyrosine, and valine). Note that three codons are used to signal the end of a transcription process (UAA, UAG, and UGA).

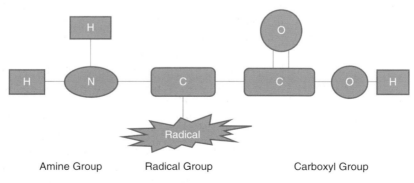

Key: C = Carbon   H = Hydrogen   N = Nitrogen   O = Oxygen

Figure 16.2   General representation of an amino acid.

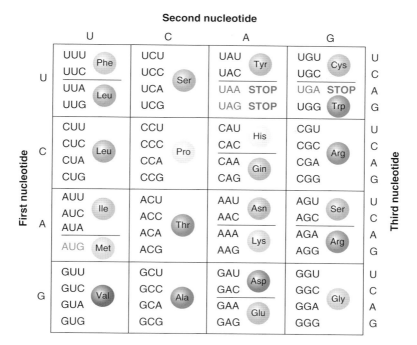

Figure 16.3 DNA->RNA amino acid code. Source: Scitable (2014).

Figure 16.4 presents structural diagrams showing the 20 amino acids. Note the highlighted defining radicals for each amino acid. For a more detailed elaboration of the protein synthesis process, see Clancy and Brown (2008). Additionally, an excellent video of the symphonic integration of the protein synthesis process over time may be found at: https://www.youtube.com/watch?v=8wAwLwJAGHs

Up to this point, the sequence of basic biological information suggests that genes (DNA) transmit information through the various forms of RNA to link specific sequences of amino acids that constitute proteins which serve to provide structural and functional characteristics of all of the body's cells including neurons. Neurons are responsible for information processing ultimately expressed as observed behaviour. Stahl (2013) described the now discredited 'classical' model for biological determination of behaviour, and specifically inherited mental disorders, as 'a single abnormal gene can cause a mental illness. That is, an abnormal gene product would produce an abnormal gene product, which, in turn, would lead to neuronal malfunction that directly causes a mental illness' (Stahl 2013, p. 115).

At least three different lines of reasoning explain why the classical theory is mistaken in explaining any complex behaviour such as mental disorders and aggression. The first two relate to the way behavioural sciences describe complex behaviours. Genotypes refer to the complete complement of an individual organism's genetic information. Phenotype refers to the observed outcome of genetic expression, including what appear to be inherited behaviours. As noted above, complex behaviours result from numerous contributory organizations of relevant information. Attempts to construct meaningful typical or atypical behaviour constructs often conflate statistically associated aspects of higher order behaviour descriptors (i.e. symptoms) processed by distinct neurobiological systems and mechanisms. Obviously, no single gene can relate to a phenotype that results from neutrally distinct informational components. Information

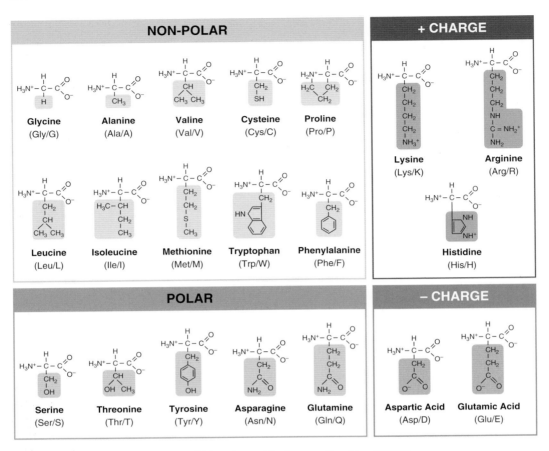

Figure 16.4 Structural diagram of 20 amino acids. Source: Prephixa (2018).

processed within different areas of the CNS construct complex phenotypes dependent on location within the CNS, resident neurotransmitters and receptor subtypes that are products of alternate and independent sections of the genetic code.

In classical genetic terminology, polygenetic inheritance refers to a single trait that is determined by more than one gene. So, for many characteristics, whether physical or psychological, a 'one-gene-one trait' is illusory. This becomes more problematic with diagnostic systems (e.g. DSM or ICD), legal (e.g. criminal) and psychological designations (e.g. 'psychopath') that combine many traits or symptoms, each of which reflects the confluence of multiple gene products. Conversely, pleiotropy refers to situations where a single gene contributes to more than a single trait. This presents another reason why there is no exclusive one-to-one mapping between genes and behavioural traits. Just to complicate matters a bit more, traits controlled by a group of non-allelic genes called 'polygenic traits' (Alleles connote genes that appear in slightly different forms. Although different alleles affect the identical trait, different alleles can produce different forms of the trait when expressed). Due to contributions from many source genes, typically at different locations on different chromosomes, polygenic blueprints produce traits possessing a spectrum of variation such as gradations of height or hair colour. Most behavioural characteristics involve polygenic inheritance rather than 'monogenic inheritance' where traits, including disease, result from a single gene or allele consistent with classical Mendelian inheritance.

In an effort to 'move' the heritable component of behaviour (or physical condition) closer to the gene, researchers have developed the concept of an 'endophenotype'. The construct invented by biologists, seeking to understand why specific types of grasshoppers gravitated to a particular geographic area. Rather than attempt to correlate general features to the genetic contributors to geographic preferences, the biologists sought smaller and more obscure units to relate them more reliably to specific grasshopper genes. Gottesman and Shields (1973) adopted the term for psychiatry noting that diseases were often too large and complex to relate to specific genes and sought more pure aspects of a disease to map to particular genes. However, as shown empirically by their meta-analysis of two measures of working memory and schizophrenia, the use of endophenotypes, although perhaps more reliably measured and stable than diagnoses, are not more helpful in mapping to specific genes. Stahl (2013) summarized the failure of the Symptom-Endophenotype model as:

> 'Another theory, the symptom endophenotype model posits that rather than genes causing mental illness, genes cause individual symptoms, behaviors, personalities, or temperaments. Thus, an abnormal gene encoding for a symptom, behavior, or trait would cause neuronal malfunction leading to that symptom, behavior or trait. However, no genes for personality or behavior have been identified, and there is no longer any expectation that such a discovery might be made ...' (p. 116).

Although people since ancient times realized through uncontrolled observation that a number of interpersonal differences and specific typical and atypical traits tended to run in families, a precise pattern of this heritability has eluded modern thinkers. No clear genetically programmed deterministic models can reliably account for complex behaviours such as mental disorders and aggression. It is now universally accepted based on extensive evidence summarized above that the genetic code determines all potential protein structure in the body including those involved in the structure and function of its 'major psychological information processing module', the CNS. Consequently, the issue at hand becomes whether the yet uncertain relationship between genes (via their gene products) and complex behaviours is the result of incomplete pieces of data within the preceding set of constructs, or perhaps a re-conceptualization of the relationship between genes and their expression is necessary. A relatively recent set of discoveries surfaced with profound implications for understanding the imperfect gene-behaviour relationship. This field is called epigenetics. It offers a detailed set of mechanisms for resolving the longstanding nature-nurture controversy. It asserts that genes are not destiny but it is interactions with the environment, especially early in life that programme which genes will or will not be permitted the ability to express themselves and thereby influence development, general health and mental health.

Epigenetics

As previously mentioned, every somatic cell in the body possesses the complete store of genetic information in its nucleus to produce all types of somatic cells in the body. Yet each type of cell expresses only proteins necessary and sufficient for the specific structure and function of its particular type of cell. The overwhelming amount of information must be prevented from being expressed, or cells would be a chaotic complex of liver-muscle-kidney-brain-retina-intestine-hair-germ, etc. cells, making cell and species function and survival impossible. The question requiring an answer was what mechanism(s) regulates gene expression to ensure appropriate cell specificity as well as sculpting characteristics to fit environments without altering the remarkably stable DNA structure during development and across generations?

Felsenfeld (2014) provides a detailed history of the protean epigenetic construct. Epigenetic literally means 'above the gene' implying that genes themselves (DNA sequences) are not altered but are activated or inactivated. Here, we focus on the current understanding of epigenetic processes in gene regulation. We have described in outline the DNA->mRNA->tRNA->rRNA-> protein synthesis process above. Currently, epigenetics is the study of how this transcription-translation process is controlled. We can consider the linear sequence bases of each DNA strand its primary structure. Permanent covalent bonds join adjacent segments (i.e. bases, sugars, and phosphate groups) within each strand of DNA. Hydrogen bonds join base pairs together, with A-T pairs using two hydrogen bonds and C-G pairs utilizing three hydrogen bonds for this purpose. Through electrostatic forces, the joined strands produce the characteristic double-helix structure that folds. This can be considered DNA's secondary structure feature. To initiate the transcription process, helicases disrupt the hydrogen bonds. This allows mRNA to form its anti-codons from the exposed DNA strands as described above.

Two sets of 'locks' in DNA's inactive state (i.e. when not available for transcription) make it impossible for DNA and RNA polymerases to access separated strands and initiate transcription. To appreciate these mechanisms, Figure 16.6 presents the tertiary and quaternary structures of DNA.

Figure 16.5 depicts two additional spatial arrangements for DNA. The first involves the 'chromatin' structure. Chromatin refers to the cell's compliment of DNA, RNA, and protein.

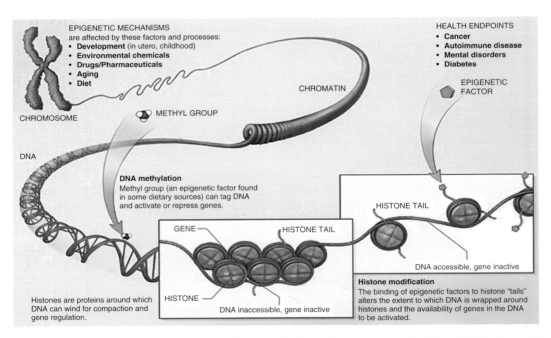

Figure 16.5 Epigenetic mechanisms. Source: National Institutes of Health (2018)- http://commonfund.nih.gov/epigenomics/figure.aspx.

When inactive, DNA segments wrap tightly around proteins called histones. DNA winds 1.65 times around 8 histone proteins to form a 'nucleosome'. Nucleosomes, in turn, fold further to form chromatin fibres of approximately 30 nm (nm) in length. Chromatin fibres continue to fold into loops approximately 300 mn long that are compressed. The 300 nm fibres are compressed and folded to produce 250 nm-wide fibres that subsequently coil tightly into the chromatids of a chromosome. This wrapping greatly compacts the volume of DNA and functionally makes it impossible for transcription to occur since the histone stool firmly locks the DNA (Annunziato 2008). Histones' tails protrude at intervals along the histones that function during the inactive state as 'DNA locks'. Epigenetic factors serve as 'Keys' to unlock and lock.

More specifically, methyl groups (i.e. one carbon and three hydrogen atoms symbolized as CH_3) can bind to chromatin (usually to a cytosine base) and attract subsequent protein binding that blocks access to the DNA transcription activators. Methylation thus compacts the DNA and silences the relevant gene. Methylation can also occur to histones to silence the genes wrapped around them. Methylation turns genes off whether at the Chromatin (DNA) or histone site (Erickson 2016).

A second epigenetic mechanism is acetylation where an acetyl group (composed of constituent methyl and carboxyl groups; e.g. $Ch_3 – COOH$) alters the structure of chromatin and unlike methylation, serves to activate the gene for protein synthesis. Acetylation (or addition of an acetyl group) to histones is accomplished by enzymes called Histone Acetyltransferases (HATs). Conversely, enzymes called histone deacetylases (HDAC) remove acetyl groups from histones and thereby silence the nearby gene, curbing the protein synthesis. These processes alternate to induce protein synthesis when needed and terminate it when the cell has a sufficient supply of that protein (Erikson 2016). Non-coding sections of RNA (ncRNA) are transcribed from DNA but are not translated into proteins. They help regulate gene expression at the transcription level in histone modification, DNA methylation and gene silencing amongst others. Note than none of these mechanisms alter DNA sequences (Erickson 2016).

Making epigenetics interesting for psychology and the nature–nurture issue is that during cell replication, daughter cells retain previously established epigenetic marks. This influences how cells will respond later in life. For example, methylation patterns are preserved even in germ (haploid, egg, or sperm) cells, meaning that the methylation patterns can be passed along to the next generation by either parent. The epigenome refers to the entire set of epigenetic modifications along an individual's complete store of DNA (i.e. the genome). The epigenome responds to the environment and is therefore not static but dynamic, and heritable. See Syzf (2017) for a comprehensive and comprehensible summary for epigenetic processes in generational transmitted behaviors.

Aggression Theory, Biological Systems and the Brain

The four generations of violent risk instruments described above have succeeded empirically despite not utilizing two areas of potentially specifically relevant and rich ongoing theory development[2] and empirical investigation. These two areas include Aggression Theory and the

---

[2] I note that the Psychology of Criminal Conduct approach by Andrews and Bonta (2010) and their co-workers fruitfully utilized general social learning theory in developing their successful approach to criminal conduct, but did not employ aggression theory per se or differentiate between different aggression types in identifying unique risk factors or intervention targets.

Biology of Aggression. The focus of this chapter is not social theories of aggression, so I note only selected developments in this domain. Bandura's (1961) classic observational learning experiment established the specific causal role of social learning in eliciting aggression in children in a rigorous laboratory setting. Subsequently, more nuanced variations of learning theory have focused on social information processing, cognitive associations, and cognitive script theory (Dodge and Coie 1987; Huesmann 1988; Huesmann and Eron 1989; Bushman and Huesman 2014; McQuillan et al. 2017). A common feature across these theoretical variants is a recognition of contextualization of aggression within particular social learning environments. This implies that expression of the aggression in the form of physical violence is more likely in situations that bear some conceptual or experiential similarity to the environment in which the learned response took place. Anderson and Bushman (2002) provided a synthesis of pre-existing cognitive, emotional, and momentary arousal findings in aggression research as mediators of stable individual differences and situational triggers in producing aggressive responses. Known as the General Aggression Model (or GAM), they posited that the persistence of aggression shown in earlier work is attributable to stable knowledge structures (scripts) that constitute personality by guiding interpretations of interpersonal/social environments and subsequently drive behavioural responses to specific social contexts. Anderson and Bushman (2002) also differentiated between hostile aggression (with a primary intent to harm the victim, is impulsive, anger based, and a response to some provocation) and instrumental aggression (conceived as a premeditated attempt to achieve some goal with the harm directed as the victim as a means to achieve the goal). The authors cited a number of research studies supportive of social learning approaches to understanding the causes of aggression and violence. However, the GAM and its differentiation between hostile (aka 'reactive') aggression and Instrumental (or 'predatory') aggression is not explicitly incorporated into any standardized risk assessment instrument. Lastly, the GAM does not incorporate any biological insights into aggression.

The I³ Model (verbalized as 'I cubed') is a contemporary 'general purpose' metatheory of behaviour that has been applied to aggression (see Finkel and Hall 2018, for a current explication and supportive empirical review). Applicable across a very wide range of behavioural contexts, the three I's include:

(a) Instigation, or the contextual information that initiates or triggers the behaviour,
(b) Impellance refers to the strengths of personal and situational factors that generate a proclivity to engage in the behaviour in question, and
(c) Inhibition that refers to the sum of how personal and situational factors afford the individual the ability to overcome the proclivity to engage in the behaviour.

Thus, in a very general way, the I³ formalizes the notion that behaviours require initiators, forces to maintain the behaviour and information to terminate the behaviour. Each 'I' represents a vector with a characteristic strength and path determining the impact that each factor exerts on other nodes in the five-node model. In the case of aggressive behaviour, the nodes consist of Instigation, Impellance, Inhibition, Proclivity to Aggress, and finally, Aggressive Behaviour. For eating behaviour or mating behaviour, the proclivity terms would reflect different Instigators, Impellance Factors and Inhibitors. Lastly, for a particular behaviour to occur and then cease, factors conductive to its Initiation, Impellance and ultimately Inhibition must concur; a situation referred to as a 'Perfect Storm'. Twelve different pathways link these five nodes. Finkel and Hall (2018) present a number of examples of dispositional and contextual constructs that serve to increase or decrease the strength of Instigator and Impellance vectors. A confluence of these factors produces 'The Perfect Storm' that brings about a strong display of the behaviour in question.

The I³ Model provides an interesting general organizing framework for thinking about aggression and many other behaviours. Additionally, Finkel and Hall (2018) cite a number of studies that are consistent with, and consequently supportive of, the I³ Model. Nor does the I³ metatheory intrinsically predict the content of the various I's for any particular behavioural domain. However, the I³ Model does not appear to have influenced risk assessment practice to any great degree, nor is there an intrinsic link to the neurobiology of aggression or specific aggression types.

This brief review leads to an examination of a significant extant literature that does provide guidance with respect to types of violence that implicitly involves instigating contexts, sustaining forces and purposes for termination of aggression. Additionally, because this research was done during the mid- to late-twentieth century, it provides links between distinct aggression types and associated and distinct neurobiological characteristics. After a general description of the Animal Aggression Typology, the chapter will describe the application of the Animal Aggression Typology to violent human criminality, explicate links between neurobiology and specific aggression types, provide initial supportive empirical evidence and suggest opportunities for further advances.

Moyer's animal aggression model: A functional typology with neuroanatomical support

Before reviewing biological approaches to understanding aggression, it is imperative to appreciate the soundly and precisely defined psychological constructs to uncover the underlying biological mechanisms. This holds for correspondences between psychological phenomena and genetic, epigenetic, hormonal, pharmacological, neuroanatomical, neurophysiological, or personality level correspondences. This is because precise biological/neurobiological mechanisms drive specific aspects of information processing. Incorrectly conceptualized, defined, or measured psychological constructs will not be able to map seamlessly to the corresponding biological mechanism. This is analogous to two teams digging extensive tunnels who hope to meet in the middle. If either (or both) teams are a few degrees off target, they will not meet in the middle. The less specific the psychological construct, the less possible it is to find the biological analogues involved in its processing. Taking the notion one step further, Panskepp (2008) has suggested that rather than define emotions in terms of psychological features, they are better defined by observing responses to stimulation of various centres in the limbic system. With this is mind, we now turn to a more nuanced typology of aggression.

Moyer (1968) observed that behaviours of all types are contextualized within experienced environments in service of different goals. In a very general sense, this is manifested by clothing we chose to wear with coats being worn over home clothing in cold winter environments and short sleeves and possibly short pants or bathing suits worn during hot summer days. Providing a seasonal context affords a more precise understanding and prediction of which type of clothing one choses before leaving home in the morning. Similarly, based on earlier studies of animal aggression, Moyer (1968) identified seven types of aggression observed in mammals and described their neural and hormonal initiation, maintenance and termination. The seven include:

1. Predatory/Instrumental
2. Irritable/Anger/Frustration/Insult-Based,
3. Defensive/Fear-Based, ('Flight or, if escape unlikely, Fight')
4. Territorial (invasion by intruder)
5. Maternal (perceived threat to mother's offspring),
6. Inter-male competition (usually over females and mating opportunities), and
7. Sexual.

The above classification system emphases the context-dependent nature of aggression and the diversity of situations that trigger aggression. Valzelli (1981) provided a very detailed account of distinct and overlapping neuroanatomical, hormonal, and pharmacological (i.e. neurotransmitters and neuromodulators) characteristics for each of these aggression types. Examining the seven aggression types, it becomes evident that a number of them are representative of violence that forensic and correctional psychologists encounter in their day-to- day practise. Nussbaum et al. (1997) suggested that the greater specificity intrinsic to this typology might provide heuristic advantage over simply classifying offenders based on whether they are violent or non-violent as 'fuzzier' classifications will obscure meaningful differences between the various types. The question became how to optimally translate the typology into a viable clinical procedure and provide evidence of proof of concept.

A clinical translation of Moyer's typology: Theory and empirical support

The first step was to decide which of the seven types most readily applied to the criminal justice system. Maternal aggression was the most obvious outlier for two complimentary reasons. First, were someone to attack a child and the child's mother were to defend the child by inflicting harm upon the attacker, the law would in all likelihood not charge the mother with assault as people have the right to defend themselves and their children. Secondly, the incidence of over-zealous mothers convicted of assault and subsequently incarcerated would appear to be extremely rare.

The second type that was dismissed from further consideration was the inter-male aggression, not because it might not be a human problem but because competitive fights between males over females tends not to be a prevalent problem within the criminal justice system. There may be societies in which one man will still fight another man to claim a contested woman in marriage, but in contemporary societies, men (and women) appear to have devised more subtle and often devious methods with which to compete for potential partners. In any event, frank inter-male violence in contemporary societies to achieve mating opportunities represent an understudied and undetermined number of violent offenders.

Although sexual offenders certainly comprise a formidable number and clinically challenging group of offenders, that area perhaps has been better studied than the violent offender domain and a series of typologies within the sex-offender universe exists (e.g. Martínez-Catena et al. 2017; Prentky et al. 1985). Additionally, Moyer (1968) considered sexual aggression in the animal kingdom as a unitary phenomenon, involving male on female forced sex. This situation is far more complex in human sexual offenders with heterosexual and homosexual paedophilia and diverse rapist classifications already established. Consequently, we omitted sexual aggression as a target for further consideration. This left the first four types on Moyer's list as primary foci for research.

The majority of criminal acts committed in Canada can be classified as 'impulsive' or 'unplanned'. This is related to what others refer to as 'reactive aggression'. However, delivery of Irritable Aggression and Defensive Aggression occur within distinct emotional envelopes; those of anger and fear. Conflating them under the undifferentiated term 'emotional' induces more 'fuzziness' that in turn obscures potentially important differences. At the neuroanatomical level, Harmon-Jones et al. (2004) demonstrated empirically that 'approach emotional/motivational systems' including anger appear associated with greater activity in the left frontal lobe, which is consistent with Irritable aggressors approaching their intended victims. 'Avoidance emotional/motivational systems' including fear appear processed in the right hemisphere (e.g. Fetterman et al. 2013) but the evidence for this is less strong. At the pharmacological and neuroendocrine levels, testosterone is central in processing anger (Carré et al. 2014). Fear reflects first nor-epinephrine and if sustained more than a few minutes, cortisol. At the personality level, individuals showing excessive fear responses suffer from trait anxiety rather than trait anger. Indeed, when recalling that avoidance mechanisms associate with an increase in right frontal activation, the question arises as to how fear-induced Defensive Aggression ever occurs. One possible resolution is intrinsic to the 'Flight or Fight Syndrome' is the primary 'escape action' that morphs into fight only when the escape flight is blocked. Conceivably, when the organism perceives that their escape is frustrated, fear turns to anger, inducing left hemispheric activation and an approach attack. However, it is not truly a fear delivered attack, but an anger-related attack induced by the initial or triggering fear response. Providing anxiolytics or anxiety disorder focused cognitive therapy for an individual suffering from a primary anger issue would be counter-productive, and unlikely to facilitate a reduction in proneness to violence. Consequently, Moyer's model makes a neurobiologically valid and clinically necessary division of Reactive Aggression into Predatory and Irritable Types.

Nussbaum, Saint Cyr and Bell (1997) initially suggested that Moyer's Animal Aggression Typology was applicable to human criminal behaviour. They proposed that three of Moyer's aggression types mapped to the majority of instances of criminal violence. These included: i) Predatory (or Instrumental) Aggression, ii) Irritable (Anger-initiated) Aggression and iii) Defensive (or Fear-initiated) Aggression. Given clinical realities with mentally disordered offenders (MDOs), they postulated two-sub-types of Defensive Aggression: i) Realistic Defensive Aggression reflecting lawful acts of self-defence, and ii) Unrealistic Defensive Aggression resulting from delusional persecutory beliefs, that if reality-based would justify an act of self-defence. In light of the sharp increase of prevalence and severity of gang-related violent crime, a fourth of Moyer's types, Territorial Aggression appears a worthy addition to the human criminal typology. Figure 16.6 summarizes the types of criminal aggression. Note that Realistic Defensive Aggression is not included because it should not be a concern for the criminal justice system. Additionally, each aggression type has an implicit context for initiating the aggressive act, goals for persistence of the attack and an end state when the function of the aggressive act is complete that terminates the aggressive act. Consequently, the model intrinsically satisfied the three I's of the I^3 Model.

Further, distinct and measurable psychological characteristics relate directly to each of the aggression types. Predatory/Instrumental Aggression in criminals reflects animals during predation, who are motivated by a tangible and identifiable goal, and involves only sufficient violence to achieve the goal (i.e. cats kill with a single bite to the back of the neck). Motivating humans who engage in instrumental aggression is acquisition of some tangible item, whether

Aggression Typology

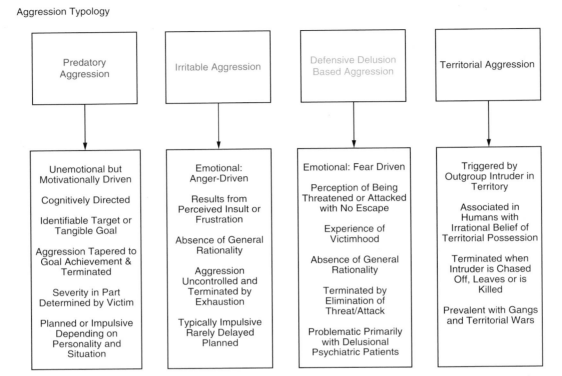

Figure 16.6 Updated adaptation of Moyer's animal aggression typology to criminal aggression types.

concrete (money, televisions, cars, etc.) or less frequently encountered in the criminal justice system, symbolic (e.g. ranking positions in a social hierarchy). Unlike other forms of aggression (described below) Predatory aggression occurs in the absence of strong emotions such as anger towards or fear of the prey. Affiliative emotions, (i.e. empathy) with the prey are also absent. Often, planning assists predatory aggression. Emotional inhibition enhances the cognitive planning process. Empathic tigers would have starved to death being unable to kill cute and innocent deer and antelope. Similarly, predators are not angry at their prey nor are they fearful of their prey. Predatory aggression continues until the individual obtains the goal or attainment becomes impossible. A successful outcome (or escape of the prey) terminates these purposeful aggressive acts.

In other circumstances, unexpected opportunities for immediate gain can generate unplanned acts of predatory aggression in impulsive individuals. Their impulsivity may be a factor in the over-representation of impulsive offenders in custodial setting since their ability to plan and avoid detection is often 'short-circuited' by their more quickly primed motivational system and relatively slower acting and less powerful inhibitory system.

Distinctive psychobiological mechanisms are responsible for initiating, motivating, and regulating the distinct aggression types. Considering each of the contributing neurobiological systems in the complex overall decision-making process is unhelpful because they interact. Figure 16.7 (below) illustrates an existing decision-making model containing eight empirically established neurotransmitters, neuromodulators, and hormones (Nussbaum et al. 2011). Fundamental to understanding this figure, a set of activating and inhibiting transmitters,

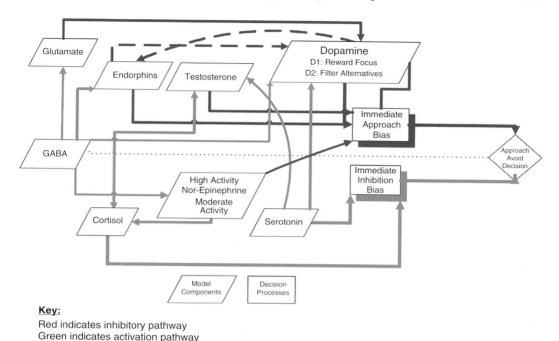

Key:
Red indicates inhibitory pathway
Green indicates activation pathway
Dashed line indicates synergistic effects within Approach or Inhibition components. (See text for details)

Figure 16.7 An eight-element motivational decision-making model.

neuromodulators and hormones exist that favour either pursing or terminating pursuit of the goal. Elements above the central horizontal line (i.e. Dopamine, Testosterone, Endorphins (aka endogenous opioids) and Glutamate synergistically bias the decision-making towards immediate gratification. Alternately, Serotonin, Nor-Epinephrine, and Cortisol bias the decision-making process to avoid the gratification. Glutamate, the most prevalent inhibitory neurotransmitter in the brain, serves to facilitate or inhibit the process, depending on which of the other elements are more effectively inhibited (Nussbaum et al. 2011). Individual differences exist in not only the strength of these systems but also how quickly they activate (i.e. their rise time). The decision-making system utilizes a temporally sensitive weighting of all of these (and quite possibly other) information processing elements to either activate or inhibit the behaviour in question. One major advantage of appreciating the decision-making model lies in its 'parsimony' as it applies to the different aggression types by re-weighting the same decision-making elements components, avoiding conceptually distinct frameworks to explain for different aggression variants.

Predatory/instrumental aggression

To appreciate the mechanism in action, consider an individual who perceives an arising opportunity for tangible gratification. A dopaminergic response is primed and two distinct dopamine receptor types help focus attention on the object of gratification (D1 Receptors) and filter out alternative stimuli and activities (D2 Receptors). Exclusive dopamine activity would portend a consummatory response. Enhancing this tendency to repeat the experience further is increased by greater Testosterone release that energizes the behaviours in question. Additionally, higher

Endorphin activation, co-localized with DA in the VTA, intensifies the pleasurable experience and further increases the likelihood of repeating the behaviour (i.e. reinforcement). Glutamate's role is to link the eliciting stimulus and effective actions in memory. However, often there are greater negative consequences associated with deciding to pursue immediate gratification, perhaps most poignantly illustrated in addictions and criminal behaviour.

Negative consequences fall into two broad categories; cognitive and emotional. To illustrate, a cognitive negative outcome may result from signing a contract to receive a modest payday loan to offset a current debt of $ 1000 but may entail a 30% annual rate of interest that is apparent if someone stops and thinks about information contained in the 'fine print' of the loan agreement. Ignoring it entails a far greater cost than the 20% credit card penalty. Negative emotional decision-making under intense states of fear or anger that 'short-circuit' cognitive processing. Dopamine-Testosterone-Endorphin driven decision-making underlies impulsive Predatory/ Instrumental aggression. In Predatory/Instrumental prone individuals, an effective glutamate/ memory system enhances the 'acquisitonal triad'. Those susceptible to impulsive predatory behaviours (i.e. involving immediate tangible gratification without accessing calculated long-term risks) show ineffective serotonergic inhibition that would afford a realistic cost–benefit analysis that would inhibit pursuit under conditions of negative expectations. Additionally, such individuals lack a sense of fear of being apprehended reflecting muted anxiety/fear signalling involving Nor-Epinephrine and Cortisol. Strongly reactive 'stop and think' (Serotonergic) or anxiety (Nor-Epinephrine/Cortisol) systems could effectively terminate pursuit of risky, immediate goals. GABA in these individuals is more effective in directly inhibiting Nor-epinephrine and indirectly Cortisol and thereby favouring an immediate approach bias.

Clinicians and correctional officers working with individuals with histories of repeated instances of Predatory aggression (or addictions) often report expressions of ostensibly sincere intent to reform their lives and desist from Predatory aggression (or addictions) in future. Even if honestly expressed, such statements occur in offices and other environments devoid of potentially Dopamine, Endorphin, and Testosterone arousing factors such as a potential article to steal or drug to ingest. Under such conditions, the individual is in 'default mode' and weak Serotonin reactivity is sufficient to have the individual 'stop and think' about what is right and socially desirable. However, this is not predictive of negation of future aggression because criminal predation occurs when environmental opportunities 'ramp up' Dopamine, Endorphin, and Testosterone levels to the extent sluggish and muted inhibitory Serotonin, Nor-epinephrine, and Cortisol levels are unequal to the task of over-riding the 'see it, want it, do it' approach decision-making bias. Additionally, GABA circuits that might inhibit Dopamine, Endorphin, and Testosterone are also relatively silent in such individuals, further diminishing inhibitory tendencies and strengths.

Irritable/anger-based aggression

The second important and prevalent aggression type for criminal behaviour is Irritable Aggression. Environmental experience that induce anger or frustration in a susceptible individual are likely to end with an aggressive action towards the perceived cause of the irritation or, in their absence, an available substitute. With respect to the model, changes in feelings of anger are associated with changes in testosterone levels (e.g. Peterson and Harmon-Jones 2012; Wagels et al. 2018). At least in adolescents coupling the male steroid hormones testosterone and its adrenal gland precursor, dehydroepiandrosterone (DHEA) with reductions in cortisol is predictive of externalizing disorders (Han et al.2015). This makes intuitive sense because socially dominant people, utilize anger to achieve prominence, and are unlikely to experience fear, which would serve to inhibit expression and utility of testosterone-induced anger in service of their dominance needs. Consequently, individuals who typically exhibit Irritable Aggression exhibit highly reactive and intense Testosterone responses to frustration, coupled with relatively weak and slow acting Nor-epinephrine and subsequent Cortisol (stress) responses. Additionally, anger-prone individuals generally do not stop and think about alternative ways of proactively dealing with potentially anger-inducing situations. Consequently, sluggish and minimal levels of Serotonin recruitment under anger provoking situations would favour expression of anger and anger-based aggression over reasoned responses to mitigate the anger intensity and initiate a more efficacious result for all parties. Similarly, after a victim is rendered defeated, even to the point of loss of consciousness, the Irritable Aggressor does not seek to acquire the victim's wallet or purse suggesting that Dopamine and Endorphin responsivity is muted during Irritable Aggression. Extreme violence (AKA 'overkill') is understandable given the excessive energy afforded by the principle element of Irritable Aggression, Testosterone. Minimal responsivity of Serotonin is consistent with the senselessness of overkill. Muted Cortisol responses prove inadequate to inhibit the more robust Testosterone responses, consistent with the lack of anxiety or fear evident in Irritable aggressive acts. Similarly, weak Serotonin recruitment in such individuals bias the behavioural decision against stopping, stepping back from the aggravating or frustrating situation and thinking about non-aggressive solutions to deal with the provocation. It is possible that in irritable aggressors, GABA inhibits memory formation (Glutamate) that would help form memories to use for in corrective adjustments when similar social environments recur in future.

This may also explain why, not infrequently, irritable aggressors express what appears to be genuine remorse, and provide cognitively coherent arguments for why they will not engage in such harmful and spiteful behaviour in future. Although such remonstrations may actually be sincere when expressed, an assessor cannot neglect the reality that these and similar sentiments are expressed after commission of a crime and arrest. Whilst in police or clinicians' offices, Testosterone levels are moderate to low, and 'typical' Serotonin levels under such conditions are more than adequate to inhibit the situationally reduced Testosterone levels. However, in 'real world' social interactions, testosterone levels are increased significantly in anticipation of an impending physical confrontation, and weak Serotonin responses prove unequal to the task of effectively reducing heightened Testosterone that mark Irritable aggressors.

Defensive aggression

The experience of intense fear activates the 'flight or fight syndrome', prompting an initial response set to avoid the threat, and if that possibility is unavailable or blocked, a fallback option of attacking the source of the threat. The eliciting stimulus induces an upsurge in Nor-epinephrine that, after a few minutes, induces production and release of the glucocorticoid Cortisol, the stress-related hormone, Cortisol. Cortisol is a product of the HPA (Hypothalamic–Pituitary–Adrenal) axis. In response to low levels of circulating Cortisol, the hypothalamus secretes CRH (corticotrophin-releasing hormone) that travels to the pituitary gland where it in turn releases ACTH (adrenocorticotropic hormone). Blood born ACTH travels throughout the body entering the adrenal gland via specialized surface receptors. ACTH initiates production of Cortisol in the outer layer of the adrenal gland (adrenal cortex) from which Cortisol enters the blood stream, increasing its concentration level, where rising levels extinguish further production of ACTH thereby regulating Cortisol levels via a 'negative feedback loop'. Cortisol plays a role in regulating energy metabolism and the immune system amongst other functions. Acutely elevated levels of Cortisol in response to threatening cues are imme- diately advantageous in providing enhanced levels immediate energy, attentional focus (espe- cially on the threatening stimulus) and visual acuity amongst other benefits.

Individuals differ in their susceptibility to stress responses, including 'rise time' of Cortisol secretion, extent of cortisol release and duration of Cortisol elevations. The negative effects of stress on the brain were known for decades, perhaps most authoritatively encapsulated by Sapolsky (1996).

Persistent elevations of Cortisol, either due to ongoing stress or physiological dis-regulation are harmful physically and mentally. The most notable physical difficulties include increased weight gain, blood pressure, cholesterol, heart disease (components of 'Metabolic Syndrome'), and decreased immune function (rendering individuals susceptible to infections) and reduced bone density. Psychological sequelae include anxiety, depression, memory impairments, disor- ganized thinking and consequently impaired decision-making (Bergland 2013).

McEwen (2000) and his colleagues have provided an updated understanding of the rela- tionship of stress to the brain and behaviour. Essentially, as Selye (1950) posited, the initial 'Adaptation Response' becomes maladaptive over time. The current term, 'Allostasis' refers to the processes by which the body responds to stressors to successfully adapt, maintain homeo- stasis, and survive. When extended, these processes are disruptive to ongoing functioning and actually promote a variety of dysfunctional states including bodily diseases and behavioural disturbances. The negative consequences of drawing on energy and other psychophysiological reserves over time is called Allostatic Load. The brain's interpretation of events is the central hub of the process in its capacities to perceive, interpret and respond to external conditions. Again, individual differences exist with respect to perception and evaluation of potential stress- ors and subsequent responses.

At the neural level, high Cortisol concentrations are associated with reduced hippocampal and frontal lobe volumes. The hippocampus is functionally associated with memory formation and control of the immune system. The frontal lobes are associated with higher cognitive pro- cessing (e.g. abstraction, problem solving organization or collectively, Executive Functions), including decision-making. This is believed to result from the neurotoxic actions of glucocor- ticoids such as Cortisol that initially beginning with erasing dendritic connections between neurons in the hippocampus and pre-frontal cortex thereby undermining memories and inhib- itory/organizational influence. Additionally, activity in the amygdala that processes stimulus intensity related to positive emotions (Bonnet et al.2015) and fear (Kryklywy et al.2013) is increased. Alterations in sensitivity to stress may begin with relatively severe adverse childhood experiences that appear to persist into adulthood, likely via epigenetic mechanisms described earlier. Negatively affected systems include the brain (most notably, smaller prefrontal cortex and hippocampal volumes and exaggerated amygdala activation), the endocrine system (ele- vated HPA activation) and the immune system (increased levels of inflammation; Danese and McEwen 2012). Hill et al. (2013) provide additional details of amygdalar stress responses, and a potential pharmacological approach to limiting them.

Behaviourally, individuals prone to Defensive Aggression show lower than usual thresholds for perceiving threats and heightened levels of anxiety and reactivity to potential threats and stressors. They tend to show disorganization of thinking and difficulties in problem solving when confronted by threats or feeling intimidated. Although this may represent a minority of cases within the general offender population, MDOs (i.e. forensic psychiatric patients) often respond to delusional or unrealistic perceptions of threats with violence, under neural mecha- nisms akin to realistic acute stress responses in non-mentally ill individuals. The 'psychopatho- logical switch' for these individuals is the misperception of a relatively benign or minor threat as a serious and imminent threat. Such delusions or hallucinations are often the kernel of successful and appropriate mental health defences in MDOs with diagnoses such as schizophrenia, paranoid type and delusional disorder, persecutory type.

This background provides clear implications for the pattern of pharmacological elements underlying decision-making in Defensive Aggression. Such individuals have intensely responsive Nor-epinephrine and Cortisol systems that focus initially on the potential threat and subsequently disorganizes effective thinking and problem solving respectively. Possible 'social escape paths' in this hyper-aroused state remain ignored and a fallback physical attack becomes dominant in the behavioural hierarchy. Serotonin responding is slow and weak, precluding a 'stop and think' approach to the eliciting situation. GABA inputs in the amygdala, similar to what happens in anxiety disorders, are inadequate to inhibit the powerful Nor-epinephrine/Cortisol response. Successful acts of Defensive Aggression, as Irritable Aggressive acts, do not result in theft of victims' possessions, underscoring the non-involvement of Dopamine and Opioids in Defensive aggression. Possibly, the initial impulse is escape that would move the attacker away from the threat. When the perception of an escape opportunity vanishes either by reality, or by cognitive or social misrepresentation, the 'program' may shift to frustration and anger, prompting the attack approach with characteristics of Irritable Aggression. This may explain the overkill often displayed in acts of Defensive aggression. However, the initiation of Defensive Aggression, and its distinctiveness, derives from the environment that triggers its occurrence.

Territorial aggression

Gangs and their 'turfs' represent a contemporary and serious instance of Territorial Aggression that is very relevant to the criminal justice system. Urban geographers have presented detailed empirical descriptions and derived models concerning the frequency and intensity of gang conflicts. For example, Radil et al. (2010) employed spatialized network analysis to consider the joint influences of territorial geography and rivalry networks to understand better gang violence, with data generated from gang turf-related violence in Los Angeles. Valasik and Tita (2018) presented an extensive review of different aspects of territorial aggression related to gang-related turf violence. Amongst numerous factors, Valasik and Tita reported that the recent surge in global resettlement has led to fluidity of geographic boundaries. Contributors to attack of intruders onto turfs include protection of drug markets and supplies, and safety from individuals from other groups who may have presented conflicted histories. Reportedly, maintenance of street safety was one purportedly 'legitimate' purpose for establishment of the Mafia in New York around the turn of the twentieth century.

Perhaps doing some injustice to this extensive, well-developed, and nuanced literature, it would appear that Territorial Aggression, (i.e. aggression triggered by an outgroup member passing into another groups territory) could well be considered as a composite of Defensive and Predatory/Instrumental aggression types. The home turf group perceives the intruder as a potential threat to resources (drug supplies and markets, and possibly other commodities) providing a concrete tangible and material purpose to the perceived threat. It is also possible that individuals at different levels of gang hierarchies attach different psychological weights to these conjoint aspects of the perceived trigger. The gang leader may fear theft of their drug source or supplies, or jeopardy of the local market by the intruder(s), with the emphasis on loss of opportunity for economic gain. Members occupying lower rungs of the gang hierarchy may fear direct physical attack. Perhaps these uncertainties could be resolved by examining the nature of attacks as per the spontaneous, impulsive, and angry vs. timed, coordinated and organized nature of attacks on intruders related to the origin of different attacks within gang hierarchies and which gang's turf. These observations could serve as a starting point for future research. Territorial is the aggression type most in need of further study from a biological perspective. Consequently, no further discussion is presented here.

Existing Support for the Model

Three peer-reviewed empirical studies exist that are consistent with the model's ability to reflect essential features of the different types. The first paper (Levi et al. 2010) demonstrated support for the model in a Canadian provincial offender sample convicted of summary (misdemeanour) offences subject to incarceration of less than two years. The second paper empirically supported the model within a group of MDOs in the forensic programme in a Canadian psychiatric hospital. The third supported the typology in a set of MDOs in a Norwegian forensic psychiatric unit.

Levi et al. (2010) studied 89 offenders broken down by history into groups of 25 Predatory, 34 Irritable, and 30 Non-Aggressive (i.e. convicted of fraud, theft, impaired driving, etc.) offenders between the ages of 18 and 55. Inter-rater reliability for this classification from their Canadian Police Information Centre (CPIC) records was very high (Kappa = 0.93). This demonstrates that at least in this diverse offender sample, reliable classification of individuals in terms of aggression type was achievable based on their documented criminal histories.

Individuals were administered a number of psychometric tests. Executive function was measured by letter fluency (CFL), attention (via the Integrated Visual and Auditory CPT; IVA; Sandford and Turner 2000), and motivational regulation (Block 5 of the Iowa Gambling Task (IGT; Bechara 2007; Bechara et al. 1997).[3] Relevant personality trait measures included anger (STAXI-II, Spielberger 1999) and, noting that violent offenders of all types are rarely cooperative, the Cooperativeness scale from the Temperament and Character Inventory (TCI; Cloninger et al. 1993). Together, these 5 variables were able to successfully classify 84.2% of the aggressive participants and 73.3% of the nonaggressive participants, for a combined successful classification rate of 80.5% between aggressive and non-aggressive groups.

For a more nuanced test of the ability of theoretically selected psychometric measures to distinguish between the Predatory and Irritable aggression types, the authors performed a second more focused discriminant function analysis. The six retained variables reflected cognitive control (IVA Full Scale Response Control, Full Scale Attention Control), trait anger (STAXI-II Trait Anger) and personality scales (Personality Assessment Inventory [PAI], Morey 1991) reflecting motivational regulation (PAI Drug Scale) and aggressive tendencies (PAI Physical Aggression and PAI Aggressive Attitudes scales). Combined, this combination successfully

---

[3] The standardized computerized scoring method for the IGT (Bechara 2007) divides the 100 trials into five 20-trial blocks, and provides totals for individual blocks and the total 100 items in terms of advantageous minus disadvantageous deck choices. Advantageous decks produce game dollar accumulations (i.e. winnings) over numerous choices over the course of the task, whilst disadvantageous choices result in cumulative losses. The standard interpretation of IGT scores is that they reflect individuals' abilities to resist selecting from decks resulting in substantial immediate gains and occasional but much larger losses in favour of decks more typically associated with smaller gains but much smaller occasional losses. Interpretation of the IGT has been broken down into components of attraction to large rewards and insensitivity to future costs; e.g. Cantrell et al. (2008). Since most individuals require approximately 60 trial to comprehend the task, scores from Block 4 and 5 are most sensitive to the hypothesized deficiencies. There is an extensive literature on impaired performance on the IGT and difficulties in real-life decision-making (e.g. Cunha et al. 2011; Verdejo-Garcia et al. 2006, 2007).

classified 78.1% of the Irritable offenders and 68.0% of the Predatory offenders, with an overall success rate of 73.7% consistent with their classification based on their CPIC histories.

Five points bear noting. First, this was the initial attempt to select psychological variables to tap accurately behavioural proxies for neurobiological variables and was quite although not near perfectly, successful. Newer psychometric measures may prove more successful. Second, identifying specific aggression types is potentially critical in moving interventions forward as it affords a more precise targeting of an individual's areas in need of intervention. There is no need to provide an individual with an exclusively Defensive Aggression history sessions in Anger Management, nor is an Irritable Aggressor likely to benefit from attempts at moral suasion. Third, electrophysiological measures such as GSR/EDR and EEG could enhance the assessment armamentarium (e.g., Coan and Allen 2003). Changes in physiological responding after appropriate interventions would provide an objective reflection of changes in physiological responding to challenge stimuli. Fourth, insights provided by the model can provide specific physiological interventions for study including neurofeedback and more specific medication use. Fifth, the observations and conclusions reached to date remains preliminary and considerable replication and extension are necessary before widespread implementation occurs in isolation.

Bass and Nussbaum (2010) conducted a study that utilized two distinct methods for scoring the IGT to differentiate between acts of Predatory (n = 7) and Irritable (n = 11) aggression serious enough to require seclusion. Beyond the standard method, Yechiam et al. (2007) developed a mathematical scoring system for the IGT that provides scores for three cognitive decision-making components including i) attention, ii) learning, and iii) response-choice consistency. The authors hypothesized that individuals committing Predatory aggression would show distinct deficits using the original 'motivational' scoring system, whilst those engaging in Irritable aggression, being more cognitively impaired would be differentiated on the basis of lower scores on Yechiam et al.'s (2007) cognitive scoring algorithm and not the original motivational protocol. Results supported the hypotheses. The traditional motivational scoring of the IGT predicted Predatory seclusions but the cognitive scores did not. Conversely, Yechiam's et al.'s cognitive scoring system predicted only Irritable seclusions but not Predatory seclusions. Contrasting the Predatory seclusion group with a combination of the Irritable and (delusional) Defensive seclusion groups produced the following result:

Figure 16.8 shows the increasing separation between the Predatory seclusion group from the Irritable and Defensive seclusion groups with successive blocks. Indeed, the Predatory group's performance continued to deteriorate over time whilst the Irritable and Delusional Defensive did not perform well, but plateaued in the random responding, or impaired range. This may not be atypical of MDO groups as found by others in general offender samples (Beszterczey et al. 2013).

To evaluate the aggression typology model, Urheim et al. (2014) developed a 13-item questionnaire named the Aggressive Incident Motives Evaluation Scale (AIMES). Urheim et al. (2014) had hospital staff routinely administer the AIMES in a high security forensic psychiatric ward in a Norwegian hospital. AIMES responses reflecting 1652 incidents from 28 patients were analysed by both exploratory and confirmatory factor analyses. The authors concluded that:

For the most part, the scale items loaded on the factors as predicted, and the model was able to explain 61% of the data variance. Irritable incidents were the most common, but elevated scores for instrumental characteristics were found as well. High psychopathy scores were associated with incidents scoring high values on both irritable and instrumental dimensions, and low values on the defensive dimensions. (p. 141)

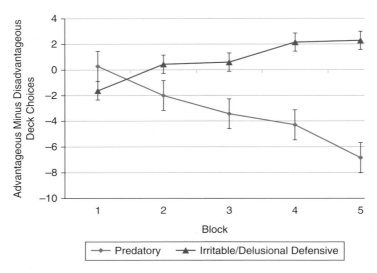

Figure 16.8   The Number of 'advantageous' deck choices minus the number of 'disadvantageous' deck choices per block separated by aggression group. Note: error bars represent standard deviation.

Two major points derive from Urheim et al.'s (2014) study. First, the relationship between psychopathy and Predatory aggression was evident in these Norwegian psychiatric patients. Second, the 13 item AIMES proved an appropriate psychometric instrument to capture the three aggression types in a psychiatric forensic patient sample. This adds confirmatory evidence to the validity of the proposed typology.

Empirical Support Summary

In summary, there is elementary evidence from three studies for the model. The studies used different methodologies (e.g. psychometric instruments, questionnaire) in criminal and mentally disordered samples. These are collectively preliminary and optimal choices of psychometric instruments to capture functional levels of the different aggression types and their neurobiological information processing systems is not at hand. However, the data are encouraging and the different types make intuitive sense and have distinct treatment implications.

Future Perspectives

Psychopaths present special challenges for criminal justice systems because they persistently engage in serious crimes, including violent crimes, and are difficult but not necessarily impossible to treat (Langton et al. 2006; Wong 2018). From the model's perspective, one difficulty with psychopathy is that unlike many criminals, psychopaths can commit all three types of aggression. The most obvious type is Predatory aggression and psychopath's avarice and acquisitive violence is legendary. Not surprisingly, there are reports of highly reactive dopaminergic sensitivity to opportunities for immediate gratification in psychopaths (e.g. Buckholtz et al. 2010) Psychopaths can become extremely angry and are frequently involved in anger-based aggression that involves extreme vindictive violence. Finally, when they feel that their position (usually of social dominance) in an antisocial hierarchy is threatened. Consequently, all aggression types and their underlying pathophysiology must be addressed adding to the complexity of the system needing remediation.

Another issue concerns integration of specific neuropsychological instruments and electrophysiological monitoring that can shed light on the extent of the information-processing pathology during assessment and the extent that interventions are successful. Identification of the underlying neurobiological information processing modules suggest specific psychometric measures to capture their functionality for individuals. Adding electrophysiological measures to reflect objectively the activation and magnitude of physiological systems relevant to decision-making processes will corroborate and enhance psychometric measures. These include GSR/EDR that reflect systems underlying fear and anxiety (e.g. Romano et al. 2017) and eye-blink frequency (EBF) that reflects performance and reinforcement-related dopamine activity (e.g. Jongkees and Colzato 2016; van de Groed et al. 2017, but see Sescousse et al. 2018). Earlier inconsistencies noted in utilizing single electrophysiological measures to predict different aspects of behaviour is not surprising as behavioural decisions reflect inputs from numerous neural systems and subsystems. Understanding the model alerts the scientist and the practitioner to the need to consider how the relevant neurobiological constitution of any particular individual biases their decision-making processing when responding to specific environments. Significant work is necessary to realize this potential.

References

Anderson, C.A. and Bushman, B.J. (2002). Human aggression. *Annual Review of Psychology* 53: 27–51.

Andrews, D.A. and Bonta, J. (1994). *The Psychology of Criminal Conduct*. Cincinnati, OH: Anderson Publishing Co.

Andrews, D.A. and Bonta, J. (1995). *The Level of Service Inventory-Revised*. Toronto, ON: Multi-Health Systems.

Andrews, D.A. and Bonta, J. (2010). *The Psychology of Criminal Conduct*, 5e. Cincinnati, OH: Anderson Publishing Co.

Andrews, D.A., Bonta, J., and Wormith, J.S. (2006). The recent past and near future of risk and/or need assessment. *Crime & Delinquency* 52 (1): 7–27.

Andrews, D.A., Bonta, J., and Wormith, J.S. (2011). The risk-need-responsivity (RNR) model: does adding the good lives model contribute to effective crime prevention? *Criminal Justice and Behavior* 38 (7): 735–755.

Andrews, D.A., Bonta, J., and Wormith, S.J. (2004). *The Level of Service/Case Management Inventory (LS/CMI)*. Toronto, ON: Multi-Health Systems.

Andrews, D.A., Bonta, J., and Wormith, S.J. (2008). *The Level of Service/Risk-Need-Responsivity (LS/RNR)*. Toronto, ON: Multi-Health Systems.

Annunziato, A.T. (2008). DNA packaging: nucleosomes and chromatin. *Nature Education* 1: 26.

Bandura, A., Ross, D., and Ross, S.A. (1961). Transmission of aggression through imitation of aggressive models. *The Journal of Abnormal and Social Psychology* 63 (3): 575–582.

Bechara, A. (2007). *Iowa Gambling Task Professional Manual*. Lutz, FL: Psychological Assessment Resources, Inc.

Bechara, A., Damasio, H., Tranel, D., and Damasio, A.R. (1997). Deciding advantageously before knowing the advantageous strategy. *Science* 275: 1293–1295.

Bergland, C. (2013). Cortisol: Why the "stress hormone" is public enemy no. 1. *Psychology Today* (22 January). https://www.psychologytoday.com/ca/blog/the-athletes-way/201301/cortisol-why-the-stress-hormone-is-public-enemy-no-1 (Accessed 20 August 2019).

Beszterczey, S., Nestor, P.G., Shirai, A., and Harding, S. (2013). Neuropsychology of decision making and psychopathy in high-risk ex-offenders. *Neuropsychology* 27 (4): 491–497.

Bonnet, L., Comte, A., Tatu, L. et al. (2015). The role of the amygdala in the perception of positive emotions: an "intensity detector". *Frontiers in Behavioral Neuroscience* 9 (178): 1–12.

Borum, R., Lodewijks, H., Bartel, P.A., and Forth, A.E. (2010). Structured assessment of violence risk in youth (SAVRY). In: *Handbook of Violence Risk Assessment; Handbook of Violence Risk Assessment* (eds. R.K. Otto and K.S. Douglas), 63–79. New York, NY: Routledge/Taylor & Francis Group.

Buckholtz, J.W., Treadway, M.T., Cowan, R.L. et al. (2010). Mesolimbic dopamine reward system hypersensitivity in individuals with psychopathic traits. *Nature Neuroscience* 13 (4): 419–421.

Bushman, B.J. and Huesmann, L.R. (2014). Twenty-five years of research on violence in digital games and aggression revisited: a reply to Elson and Ferguson (2013). *European Psychologist* 19: 47–55.

Cantrell, H., Finn, P.R., Rickert, M.E., and Lucas, J. (2008). Decision making in alcohol dependence: insensitivity to future consequences and comorbid disinhibitory psychopathology. *Alcoholism: Clinical and Experimental Research* 32 (8): 1398–1407.

Carré, J.M., Iselin, A.R., Welker, K.M. et al. (2014). Testosterone reactivity to provocation mediates the effect of early intervention on aggressive behavior. *Psychological Science* 25 (5): 1140–1146.

Cheriyedath, S. (2016). Regulation of gene expression. *News Medical* (23 August). https://www.news-medical.net/life-sciences/Regulation-of-Gene-Expression.aspx (Accessed 20 August 2019).

Clancy, S. and Brown, W. (2008). Translation: DNA to mRNA to protein. *Nature Education* 1: 101.

Clark, L.A., Cuthbert, B., Lewis-Fernández, R. et al. (2017). Three approaches to understanding and classifying mental disorder: ICD-11, DSM-5, and the national institute of mental Health's research domain criteria (RDoC). *Psychological Science in the Public Interest* 18 (2): 72–145.

Cloninger, C.R., Svrakic, D.M., and Przybeck, T.R. (1993). A psychobiological model of temperament and character. *Archives of General Psychiatry* 50: 975–990.

Coan, J.A. and Allen, J.J.B. (2003). Frontal EEG asymmetry and the behavioral activation and inhibition systems. *Psychophysiology* 40 (1): 106–114.

Cowell, I. (n.d.). Epigenetics - It's not just genes that make us. British Society for Cell Biology. https://bscb.org/learning-resources/softcell-e-learning/epigenetics-its-not-just-genes-that-make-us (Accessed 20 August 2019).

Cunha, P.J., Bechara, A., de Andrade, A.G., and Nicastri, S. (2011). Decision-making deficits linked to real-life social dysfunction in crack cocaine-dependent individuals. *The American Journal on Addictions* 20 (1): 78–86.

Cuthbert, B.N. and Insel, T.R. (2013). Toward the future of psychiatric diagnosis: the seven pillars of RDoC. *BMC Medicine* 11 (126): 1–8.

Danese, A. and McEwen, B.S. (2012). Adverse childhood experiences, allostasis, allostatic load, and age-related disease. *Physiology & Behavior* 106 (1): 29–39.

Dodge, K.A. and Coie, J.D. (1987). Social-information-processing factors in reactive and proactive aggression in children's peer groups. *Journal of Personality and Social Psychology* 53 (6): 1146–1158.

Erickson, B. (2016). Epigenetics lecture. https://www.youtube.com/watch?v=qdpRZoiJBAE (Accessed 20 August 2019).

Felsenfeld, G. (2014). *A Brief History of Epigenetics*. Rockville, MD: National Center for Biotechnology Information.

Fetterman, A.K., Ode, S., and Robinson, M.D. (2013). For which side the bell tolls: the laterality of approach-avoidance associative networks. *Motivation and Emotion* 37: 33–38.

Finkel, E.J. and Hall, A.N. (2018). The I^3 model: a metatheoretical framework for understanding aggression. *Current Opinion in Psychology* 19: 125–130.

Forth, A.E., Kosson, D., and Hare, R. (2003). *The Hare Psychopathy Checklist: Youth Version*. New York, NY: Multi-Health Systems.

Gottesman, I.I. and Shields, J. (1973). Genetic theorizing and schizophrenia. *British Journal of Psychiatry* 122: 15–30.

Han, G., Miller, J.G., Cole, P.M. et al. (2015). Adolescents' internalizing and externalizing problems predict their affect-specific HPA and HPG axes reactivity. *Developmental Psychobiology* 57 (6): 769–785.

Handy, D.E., Castro, R., and Loscalzo, J. (2011). Epigenetic modifications: basic mechanisms and role in cardiovascular disease. *Circulation* 123: 2145–2156.

Hanson, R.K., Lloyd, C.D., Helmus, L., and Thornton, D. (2012). Developing non-arbitrary metrics for risk communication: percentile ranks for the static-99/R and static-2002/R sexual offender risk tools. *The International Journal of Forensic Mental Health* 11 (1): 9–23.

Hare, R. (2003). *The Hare Psychopathy Checklist-Revised (PCL-R)*, 2e. Toronto, ON: Multi-Health Systems.

Hare, R.D. (1980). A research scale for the assessment of psychopathy in criminal populations. *Personality and Individual Differences* 1: 111–119.

Hare, R.D. (1991). *The Hare Psychopathy Checklist—Revised*. Toronto, ON: Multi-Health Systems.

Harmon-Jones, E., Vaughn-Scott, K., Mohr, S. et al. (2004). The effect of manipulated sympathy and anger on left and right frontal cortical activity. *Emotion* 4: 95–101.

Harris, G.T., Rice, M.E., and Quinsey, V.L. (1993). Violent recidivism of mentally disordered offenders: the development of a statistical prediction instrument. *Criminal Justice and Behavior* 20 (4): 315–335.

Helmenstine, A.M. (2018). The differences between DNA and RNA. ThoughtCo. https://www.thoughtco.com/dna-versus-rna-608191 (Accessed 20 August 2019).

Hill, M.N., Kumar, S.A., Filipski, S.B. et al. (2013). Disruption of fatty acid amide hydrolase activity prevents the effects of chronic stress on anxiety and amygdalar microstructure. *Molecular Psychiatry* 18 (10): 1125–1135.

Hilton, N.Z., Harris, G.T., Rice, M.E. et al. (2004). A brief actuarial assessment for the prediction of wife assault recidivism: the Ontario domestic assault risk assessment. *Psychological Assessment* 16: 267–275.

Huesmann, L.R. (1988). An information processing model for the development of aggression. *Aggressive Behavior* 14 (1): 13–24.

Huesmann, L.R. and Eron, L.D. (1989). Individual differences and the trait of aggression. *European Journal of Personality* 3 (2): 95–106.

Jongkees, B.J. and Colzato, L.S. (2016). Spontaneous eye blink rate as predictor of dopamine-related cognitive function - a review. *Neuroscience and Biobehavioral Reviews* 71: 58–82.

Karpman, B. (1947). Passive parasitic psychopathy: toward the personality structure and psychogenesis of idiopathic psychopathy (anethopathy). Part II: mechanisms, processes, psychogenesis. *Psychoanalytic Review* 34: 198–222.

Kroll, J. and Mackenzie, T.B. (1983). When psychiatrists are liable: risk management and violent patients. *Hospital & Community Psychiatry* 34 (1): 29–37.

Kropp, P.R. and Hart, S.D. (2000). The spousal assault risk assessment (SARA) guide: reliability and validity in adult male offenders. *Law and Human Behavior* 24 (1): 101–118.

Kryklywy, J.H., Nantes, S.G., and Mitchell, D.G.V. (2013). The amygdala encodes level of perceived fear but not emotional ambiguity in visual scenes. *Behavioural Brain Research* 252: 396–404.

Langton, C.M., Barbaree, H.E., Harkins, L., and Peacock, E.J. (2006). Sex offenders' response to treatment and its association with recidivism as a function of psychopathy. *Sexual Abuse: Journal of Research and Treatment* 18 (1): 99–120.

Levi, M.D., Nussbaum, D.S., and Rich, J.B. (2010). Neuropsychological and personality characteristics of predatory, irritable, and nonviolent offenders: support for a typology of criminal human aggression. *Criminal Justice and Behavior* 37 (6): 633–655.

Loza, W., Cumbleton, A., Shahinfar, A. et al. (2004). Cross-validation of the self-appraisal questionnaire (SAQ): an offender risk and need assessment measure on Australian, British, Canadian, Singaporean, and American offenders. *Journal of Interpersonal Violence* 19 (10): 1172–1190.

Martínez-Catena, A., Redondo, S., Frerich, N., and Beech, A.R. (2017). A dynamic risk factors-based typology of sexual offenders. *International Journal of Offender Therapy and Comparative Criminology* 61 (14): 1623–1647.

McEwen, B.S. (2000). Allostasis and allostatic load: implications for neuropsychopharmacology. *Neuropsychopharmacology* 22 (2): 108–124.

McQuillan, M.E., Kultur, E.C., Bates, J.E. et al. (2017). Dysregulation in children: origins and implications from age 5 to age 28. *Development and Psychopathology* 30 (2): 695–713.

Morey, L.C. (1991). *Personality Assessment Inventory*. Odessa, FL: Psychological Assessment Resources.

Moss, D.J.H., Pardiñas, A.F., Langbehn, D. et al. (2017). Identification of genetic variants associated with Huntington's disease progression: a genome-wide association study. *The Lancet Neurology* 16 (9): 701–711.

Moyer, K.E. (1968). Kinds of aggression and their physiological basis. *Communications in Behavioral Biology, Part A* 2: 65–87.

National Institutes of Health. (2018). A scientific illustration of how epigenetic mechanisms can affect health. http://commonfund.nih.gov/epigenomics/figure (Accessed 20 August 2019).

NCBI. (2007). Central dogma of biology: Classic view. https://www.ncbi.nlm.nih.gov/Class/MLACourse/Modules/MolBioReview/central_dogma.html (Accessed 20 August 2019).

NIMH. (2018). Huntington disease. https://ghr.nlm.nih.gov/condition/huntington-disease (Accessed 20 August 2019).

Noorani, R. and Carpenter, R.H.S. (2016). The LATER model of reaction time and decision. *Neuroscience and Biobehavioral Reviews* 64: 229–261.

Nussbaum, D. (2001). Psychologists should be free to pursue prescription privileges: a reply to Walters. *Canadian Psychology* 42: 126–130.

Nussbaum, D. (2006). Recommending probation and parole. In: *The Handbook of Forensic Psychology*, 3e (eds. I.B. Weiner and A.K. Hess), 426–483. Hoboken, NJ: Wiley.

Nussbaum, D., Honarmand, K., Govoni, R. et al. (2011). An eight component decision-making model for problem gambling: a systems approach to stimulate integrative research. *Journal of Gambling Studies* 27 (4): 523–563.

Nussbaum, D., Saint Cyr, J., and Bell, E. (1997). A biologically derived, psychometric model for understanding, predicting and treating tendencies toward future violence in humans. *American Journal of Forensic Psychiatry* 18 (4): 35–50.

Panksepp, J. (2008). Carving natural emotions: kindly from bottom-up but not top-down. *Journal of Theoretical and Philosophical Psychology* 28: 395–422.

Peterson, C.K. and Harmon-Jones, E. (2012). Anger and testosterone: evidence that situationally-induced anger relates to situationally-induced testosterone. *Emotion* 12 (5): 899–902.

Prentky, R., Cohen, M., and Seghorn, T. (1985). Development of a rational taxonomy for the classification of rapists: the Massachusetts treatment center system. *Bulletin of the American Academy of Psychiatry & the Law* 13 (1): 39–70.

Prephixa. (2018). Which part of an amino acid's structure makes it unique from other amino acids? [Forum]. *Socratic* (11 March). https://socratic.org/questions/which-part-of-an-amino-acid-s-structure-makes-it-unique-from-other-amino-acids (Accessed 20 August 2019).

Quinsey, V.L., Rice, M.E., and Harris, G.T. (1995). Actuarial prediction of sexual recidivism. *Journal of Interpersonal Violence* 10: 85–105.

Radil, S.M., Flint, C., and Tita, G. (2010). Spatializing social networks: using social network analysis to investigate geographies of gang rivalry, territoriality, and violence in Los Angeles. *Annals of the Association of American Geographers* 100: 307–326.

Romano, M., Roaro, A., Re, F. et al. (2017). Problematic internet users' skin conductance and anxiety increase after exposure to the internet. *Addictive Behaviors* 75: 70–74.

Sandford, J.A. and Turner, A. (2000). *Integrated Visual and Auditory Continuous Performance Test [Manual]*. Richmond, VA: Brain Train.

Sapolsky, R. (1996). Why stress is bad for your brain. *Science* 273: 749–750.

Scitable. (2010). Gene expression. Nature Education. https://www.nature.com/scitable/topicpage/gene-expression-14121669 (Accessed 20 August 2019).

Scitable. (2014). The information in DNA determines cellular function via translation. Nature Education. https://www.nature.com/scitable/topicpage/the-information-in-dna-determines-cellular-function-6523228 (Accessed 20 August 2019).

Scoville, H. (2017). Four types of RNA. ThoughtCo. https://www.thoughtco.com/types-of-rna-1224523 (Accessed 20 August 2019).

Selye, H. (1950). Stress and the general adaptation syndrome. *British Medical Journal* 17: 1384–1392.

Sescousse, G., Ligneul, R., van Holst, R.J. et al. (2018). Spontaneous eye blink rate and dopamine synthesis capacity: preliminary evidence for an absence of positive correlation. *European Journal of Neuroscience* 47 (9): 1081–1086.

Smith, A. (2008). Nucleic acids to amino acids: DNA specifies protein. *Nature Education* 1 (1): 126.

Spielberger, C.D. (1999). *State-Trait Anger Expression Inventory-2*. Lutz, FL: Psychological Assessment Resources.

Stahl, S.M. (2013). *Stahl's Essential Psychopharmacology: Neuroscientific Basis and Practical Applications*. Cambridge, UK: Cambridge University Press.

Staroscik, A. (2011). Nucleotides in DNA. http://scienceprimer.com/nucleotides-dna (Accessed 20 August 2019).

Stokman, C.L. (1984). Dangerousness and violence in hospitalized mentally ill offenders. *Psychiatric Quarterly* 56 (2): 138–143.

Szyf, M. (2017). How early life experience is written into DNA. TED. https://www.ted.com/talks/moshe_szyf_how_early_life_experience_is_written_into_dna#t-466774 (Accessed 20 August 2019).

Urheim, R., Rypdal, K., Melkevic, O. et al. (2014). Motivational dimensions of inpatient aggression. *Criminal Behavior and Mental health* 24: 141–150.

Valasik, M. and Tita, G. (2018). Gangs and space. In: *The Oxford Handbook of Environmental Criminology* (eds. G.J.N. Bruinsma and S.D. Johnson), 839–867. Oxford, UK: Oxford University Press.

Valzelli, L. (1981). *Psychobiology of Aggression and Violence*. New York, NY: Raven.

van de Groep, I.H., de Haas, L.M., Schutte, I., and Bijleveld, E. (2017). Spontaneous eye blink rate (EBR) predicts poor performance in high-stakes situations. *International Journal of Psychophysiology* 119: 50–57.

Verdejo-Garcia, A., Bechara, A., Recknor, E.C., and Perez-Garcia, M. (2006). Decision-making and the Iowa gambling task: ecological validity in individuals with substance dependence. *Psychologica Belgica* 46 (1–2): 55–78.

Verdejo-García, A., Rivas-Pérez, C., Vilar-López, R., and Pérez-García, M. (2007). Strategic self-regulation, decision-making and emotion processing in poly-substance abusers in their first year of abstinence. *Drug and Alcohol Dependence* 86 (2–3): 139–146.

Villota-Salazar, N.A., Mendoza-Mendoza, A., and González-Prieto (2016). Epigenetics: from the past to the present. *Frontiers in Life Science* 9: 347–370.

Wagels, L., Votinov, M., Kellermann, T. et al. (2018). Exogenous testosterone enhances the reactivity to social provocation in males. *Frontiers in Behavioral Neuroscience* 12 (37): 1–11.

Webster, C.D., Douglas, K.S., Eaves, D., and Hart, S.D. (1997). *HCR-20: Assessing Risk for Violence (Version 2)*. Vancouver, BC: Simon Fraser University.

Wong, S.C.P. (2018). A treatment framework for violent offenders with psychopathic traits. In: *Handbook of Personality Disorders: Theory, Research, and Treatment*, 2e (eds. W.J. Livesley and R. Larstone), 629–644. New York, NY: Guilford Press.

Wong, S.C.P. and Gordon, A. (2006). The validity and reliability of the violence risk scale: a treatment-friendly violence risk assessment tool. *Psychology, Public Policy, and Law* 12 (3): 279–309.

Yechiam, E., Veinott, E.S., Busemeyer, J.R., and Stout, J.C. (2007). Cognitive models for evaluating basic decision processes in clinical populations. In: *Advances in Clinical Cognitive Science: Formal Modeling of Processes and Symptoms* (ed. R.W.J. Neufeld), 81–111. Washington, DC: American Psychological Association.

Zaky, E.A. (2015). Nature, nurture, and human behavior; an endless debate. *Journal of Child and Adolescent Behavior* 3 (6): 1–4.

17

Assessment of Risk of Violent Offending for Adults with Intellectual Disability and/or Autism Spectrum Disorder[1]

Martyn Matthews[1] and Elliot Bell[2]

[1] Kestrel Consulting, Wellington, New Zealand
[2] University of Otago, Wellington, New Zealand

Introduction

The effective assessment of the risk of offending in people with intellectual disabilities (IDs) and/or autism spectrum disorder (ASD) is of major interest to practitioners in the field of forensic mental health, and to the wider criminal justice and disabilities sectors. Decisions about treatment, level of security, management strategies and future placement all require effective risk assessments to guide them, so it is essential that any instruments or procedures used are reliable and offer meaningful predictive validity. As Lindsay et al. (2008) noted, this is particularly pertinent for ID offenders, as level of security and length of detention have been found to not necessarily equate to current level of risk, with longer time in detention and higher levels of security than other offender populations.

Research regarding the use of risk assessment tools for ID offenders has taken a number of different approaches to identify and define this population (Lindsay et al. 2017). This is problematic when comparing studies claiming predictive validity for a population where the same tool, but different definitions, has been used to identify the sample. For example, some studies include those with borderline ID (IQ 71–84) in ID samples whilst others only include those with IQ < 70, and in others it is not clearly stated what proportion of the sample has ID

---

[1] This chapter was intended to be written by Bill Lindsay, one of the key figures in the development of approaches to the assessment and treatment of offending behaviour in adults with intellectual disabilities. Bill has had a major in influence on my work, and I suspect on that of many of you who will be reading this chapter. His wisdom is missed by many.

The Wiley Handbook of What Works in Violence Risk Management: Theory, Research and Practice,
First Edition. Edited by J. Stephen Wormith, Leam A. Craig, and Todd E. Hogue.
© 2020 John Wiley & Sons Ltd. Published 2020 by John Wiley & Sons Ltd.

(Murphy 2015). Similarly with ASD, studies may include individuals who have screened positive for ASD features in their ASD sample populations, whilst others include only those who have a formal diagnosis made by a psychiatrist or psychologist (King and Murphy 2014).

The most commonly applied definition of ID remains that from the *Diagnostic and Statistical Manual of Mental Disorders-IV* (DSM-IV; American Psychiatric Association 2000) and is characterized by significantly impaired intellectual functioning (IQ < 70) and deficits in adaptive functioning in two or more domains. By this definition, approximately 2–3% of the population would have an ID. Typically, severity descriptors are used to identify the degree of intellectual impairment experienced by the individual. These are: mild ID (IQ 55–70), moderate ID (IQ 40–55) severe ID (IQ 25–40) and profound ID (IQ < 25). The term 'borderline intellectual functioning' is used to describe those with an IQ between 71 and 84. The most recent edition of the *DSM* (*DSM-5*; American Psychiatric Association 2013) takes a broader approach to defining ID, based on overall level of functioning. Though measure of IQ has been removed from the definition, it is still included in the descriptive text.

ASD is a complex neurodevelopmental disorder, and within the *DSM-5* encompasses the previous diagnoses of autistic disorder, Asperger's disorder and pervasive developmental disorder. The core features of autism are impairments in social communication and restricted, repetitive and inflexible patterns of behaviour and/or thinking. Symptoms may range in severity and impact on the individual's life trajectory in many domains.

Despite the passing of seven decades since Kanner (1943) and Asperger's (1944) original identification of the disorder, and the great progress in assessment, diagnosis, and treatment in children, research into effective interventions for adults is limited. Social, educational, and employment outcomes in adulthood for people with ASD are often poor, with only 20% of individuals having good or very good outcomes and a mere 14% being married or in a long-term relationship (Howlin and Moss 2012). Further, adults with ASD experience higher rates of comorbid psychiatric illness than the general population and have an increased risk of neurological disorders, particularly epilepsy and tic disorders (Canitano and Vivanti 2007), although epilepsy is most common in those who also have severe IDs (Smith 2009). With regard to comorbid psychiatric disorders, anxiety, and depression are most common (Gotham et al. 2015; Hofvander et al. 2009; Lugnegård et al. 2011), but also bipolar disorder (Joshi et al. 2013) and attention deficit hyperactivity disorder (ADHD) (Matthews et al. 2018).

It is important to consider that the way violent or aggressive behaviour is viewed by disability services can be significantly different to the view of the same behaviour within mental health, forensic, or correctional services. Aggressive behaviour by people with IDs is most frequently viewed as 'challenging behaviour' arising from the individuals' difficulties with communicating or understanding and managing their emotions. Challenging behaviour has been defined as 'culturally abnormal behaviour(s) of such an intensity, frequency, or duration that the physical safety of the person or others is likely to be placed in serious jeopardy, or behaviour which is likely to seriously limit use of, or result in, the person being denied access to, ordinary community facilities' (Emerson 2001, p. 4).

In practise, this means that service providers are more likely to adopt an approach such as Positive Behaviour Support where the emphasis is on changing external factors including living environment and communication strategies, to better match the individuals' needs and to focus on improving quality of life (LaVigna and Willis 2012). However, there is a recognized need for some people with IDs to have increased levels of security and supervision, and many jurisdictions have developed specialized services within corrections, forensic mental health or disability services to meet the needs of this population. Such services typically take a more legal perspective where challenging behaviours are viewed more explicitly as 'offending behaviours'.

Due to variations in how ID is identified, and the way criminal behaviour is conceptualized across different populations and services, it is difficult to identify what proportion of adults with ID will be considered more broadly to have violence issues or, more specifically, to be involved with the criminal justice system as suspects or be detained. However, a review by Murphy (2015) indicates that 10–13% of adults using specialist ID support services in the UK would fit a definition of 'mentally-disordered offender'.

Despite significant interest and a rapid increase in research regarding the risk assessment of offenders with IDs, the published literature is scant when compared to that relating to main-stream offender populations. However, there is sufficient literature to indicate that the use of empirically-derived assessment tools is useful for this population, and furthermore that both the application of some mainstream offender assessments and the use of ID-specific assess-ments have their place in assessing the risk of further offending by people with ID. There has also been a steady increase in literature relating to offending by people with ASD, which has focused largely on those who do not have comorbid IDs.

The subsequent sections of this chapter provide an overview of general offender risk assess-ment tools which have been applied to offenders with IDs and/or ASD. In addition, tools designed specifically for the assessment of ID offenders are reviewed.

Offenders with Intellectual Disabilities

The use of general violence risk assessment tools for offenders with intellectual disabilities

There is increasing evidence that a number of risk assessment tools designed for general offender populations are useful in assessing the risk of future offending in those with IDs (Lindsay et al. 2017; Pouls and Jeandarme 2015). Despite this increasing general evidence, we cannot consider all risk assessment instruments valid for ID offenders. As Sturmey et al. (1991) note, it is possible that using an instrument for a different population to that for which it was designed may reduce its validity. Therefore, instruments designed to assess the risk of violence in general for non-ID mentally disordered offenders need to undergo validation research with offenders with ID before they can be recommended for this population (Fitzgerald et al. 2011). The following sections provide an overview of such validated tools, along with the cor-responding evidence of effectiveness. In addition to the literature relating to specific tools, there have been a number of systematic reviews conducted in the area of risk assessment of offenders with ID which provide additional comprehensive statistical analyses (see Hounsome et al. 2018, and Pouls and Jeandarme 2015 for recent examples).

Actuarial Assessments   Actuarial assessment methods and tools are derived from theoretical factor analysis of sample populations of offenders. Historically, proponents of actuarial assess-ment of risk of violence suggest that only these methods can be accurate and that clinical judgement is prone to under- or over-estimating risk (Sreenivasan et al. 2000) and lacks inter-rater reliability and predictive validity. The actuarial assessment instruments described in the following section have shown adequate validity in ID-offender populations and been found to provide similar or better predictive validity as for non-ID samples.

The Violence Risk Appraisal Guide (VRAG) The VRAG (Harris et al. 1993), a 12-item actuarial tool, is one of the most widely used offender risk assessment tools. It was designed to assess the long-term likelihood of violent or sexually-violent re-offending. The 12 items comprise historical static variables (e.g. history of alcohol problems, criminal history, age at index offence and psychopathy score as measured by the Psychopathy Checklist-Revised [PCL-R] and Psychopathy Checklist-Screening Version [PCL-SV]). The VRAG has been widely used and validated with offenders with an ID across a range of settings from community to highly-secure forensic facilities (Gray et al. 2007). For example, Fitzgerald et al. (2013) compared the reliability and validity of VRAG scores across 25 ID and 45 non-ID offenders from four medium-secure units in the UK who were followed over a six-month period. Findings indicated that the VRAG was more effective in predicting future violence in ID offenders than the non-ID participants with an Area Under the Curve (AUC) of 0.78 compared with 0.66.

The Psychopathy Checklist-Revised (PCL-R) and Psychopathy Checklist-Screening Version (PCL-SV) Psychopathy is known to occur in individuals with ID (Morrissey et al. 2007a) and, as is the case in other offender populations, is associated with limited treatment outcomes (Harris and Rice 2006). Psychopathy, as conceptualized by Hare (1991), refers to a constellation of traits clustering across two factors, i) being selfish, callous, lacking remorse and using others; and ii) experiencing a chronically unstable, deviant, and antisocial lifestyle. The PCL-R (Hare 1991) and PCL-SV have been found to have adequate reliability and validity in identifying this severe personality disorder in sample populations of offenders with ID (Boer et al. 2004; Morrissey et al. 2005). Whilst the PCL-R was not designed as a risk assessment instrument, it is a component of both the VRAG and HCR-20 and has demonstrated predictive validity for ID offenders (Gray et al. 2007). Morrissey et al. (2005) evaluated the PCL-R with a sample of 212 male ID offenders from high, medium and low secure and community settings. Internal consistency for the total scale score was considered good, with Cronbach's Alpha being 0.81. Interrater reliability was 0.89 for the full scale and 0.84 for factor 1 and 0.83 for factor 2. The PCL-R comprises 20 items which measure behaviours and personality traits indicative of psychopathic personality disorder. Each item is rated on a three-point scale: 0-does not apply, 1-applies somewhat, and 2-definitely does apply to the person.

The predictive validity of the PCL-R has been further evaluated by Morrissey et al. (2007a, 2007b), comparing it with HCR-20, a well-validated instrument that uses the structured clinical judgement approach to assess general risk of violence. In this study, 73 individuals with ID who had been previously assessed using PCL-R and HCR-20 were followed up after two years. Results indicated that the PCL-R was valid for use in this population and that individuals with higher PCL-R scores had poorer outcomes and were less likely to progress from high- to medium-secure or community environments.

The PCL-SV is a shorter version of the PCL and comprises 12 test items. It has been validated for use with ID offenders by Gray et al. (2007) who concluded that the PCL-SV was effective in predicting both violent and general offending in the ID population. Morrissey (2005, 2006) developed a guideline for the use of the PCL-R and PCL-SV for individuals with ID. The guideline provides both general advice on scoring the PCL-R and specific guidance on the interpretation of individual test items.

Offender Group Reconviction Scale (OGRS) The OGRS (Copas and Marshall 1998) is a criminogenic risk assessment instrument which originally examined six variables containing criminal history and social-demographic items and is designed to provide a two-year probability of re-offending in general offender populations. Four further criminal history variables were added in 1999 (Taylor 1999) in order to increase the scale's ability to predict future sexual and violent offending, and a further revision (Francis et al. 2007) was published in 2009. The OGRS has also been shown to have good predictive validity for general recidivism in mentally-disordered offenders (Gray et al. 2004), with an AUC of 0.762 for violent reconviction (Snowden et al. 2007).

The OGRS has been validated for use with ID offenders (Fitzgerald et al. 2011; Gray et al. 2007) and has been shown to be effective in predicting future violent offending. However, as the tool measures reconviction rates and people with ID are more likely to be diverted into alternate pathways and not convicted, the OGRS may overestimate the risk of reconviction by as much as a factor of two (Fitzgerald et al. 2011).

Dynamic Appraisal of Situational Aggression (DASA)   The DASA (Ogloff and Daffern 2006) was developed for short-term (daily) assessment of risk of violence in high-risk psychiatric populations. A single study has evaluated the use of the DASA for ID offenders. Barry-Walsh et al. (2009) tested the DASA on a population which incorporated individuals detained in a high-secure service for ID offenders within a wider sample of patients in a psychiatric hospital. Twenty-four hours post an initial assessment, psychiatric nurses recorded whether there had been aggression to other patients, staff, or property. DASA had good predictive validity for aggression towards staff (AUC = 0.80) and had moderate predictive validity for all types of aggression (AUC = 0.69).

Structured Professional Judgement (SPJ) Tools   The SPJ approach provides professionals with a framework in which to conduct risk assessment which reflects current theoretical, empirical, and clinical knowledge about violence and ensures that a minimum set of risk factors is always considered (Department of Justice 2005). From a clinical practice viewpoint, the SPJ approach has several advantages over actuarial-only approaches. Most significantly, they add evidence-based dynamic (contextual) factors to static (historical) risk factors. This produces an explanatory model or formulation to inform individualized risk management plans, rather than the risk categorization or likelihood ratios produced by actuarial instruments. This has been shown to be particularly important for ID offenders, where the support environment has a very significant effect on the likelihood of future violent behaviour (Blacker et al. 2011; Boer et al. 2004; Lindsay and Beail 2004).

HCR-20   The HCR-20 (Webster et al. 1997) is the most widely used tool in forensic mental-health risk assessment and comprises historical (static), clinical (dynamic) and risk (future) management items which are designed to assist professionals in making a formulation of an individual's risk of future violent behaviour. Version three of HCR-20 (Douglas et al. 2013) has a number of changes which were made both in response to user feedback and advances in SPJ research. These changes include the addition of sub-items for more complex risk factors, the removal of the requirement to use either the PCL-R or PCL-R(SV), and a set of indicators to help with risk formulation (Douglas et al. 2014). The HCR-20 has been evaluated in over 200 studies, including at least eight studies with samples of ID offenders (Pouls and Jeandarme 2015).

In addition to the scoring criteria contained in the HCR-20 manual, further guidance and adaptation for assessing ID offenders has been produced (Boer et al. 2010) and further validated (Verbrugge et al. 2011), and is shown in Table 17.1. The HCR-20 has been found to

Table 17.1 Intellectual disability (ID) supplement to HCR-20, Boer et al. (2010).

Subscales	Items	Adaptation
Historical		
H1	Previous violence	Examine intent and severity of aggressive behaviour
H2	Young age at first violent incident	Consider mental age
H3	Relationship instability	Scoring adjusted to include nonintimate relationships
H4	Employment problems	Scoring adjusted to broaden definition of employment
H5	Substance use problems	Examine intentionality of drug and alcohol use
H6	Major mental illness	Operationally defines IQ levels but does not change the scoring
H7	Psychopathy	Employ guidelines by Morrissey 2006
H8	Early maladjustment	Consider reason for maladjustment and out- of-home placement
H9	Personalitydisorder	Scoring adjusted to consider longer development of PD: Score of 1 when PD present and aged under 25
H10	Prior supervision Failure	Scoring adjusted to include any sort of imposed supervision in addition to legally imposed ones
Clinical		
C1	Lack of insight	Do not automatically score 1 or 2 based on ID. Consider insight as related to offending
C2	Negative attitudes	Greater time in interview may be necessary to obtain
C3	Active symptoms of major mental illness	Emphasizes this is limited to what is described MMIs in H6 and not ID
C4	Impulsivity	Do not assume impulsivity. Include evaluation of motor and emotional impulsivity and their relationship with violence
C5	Unresponsive to treatment	Scoring adjusted to consider intentionality of noncompliance. Evaluate appropriateness of treatment (match between client and treatment)
Risk Management		
R1	Plans lack feasibility	Additionally considers the ability and willingness
R2	Exposure to destabilizers	Considers the types of typical destabilizers that may be different
R3	Lack of personal support	Scoring adjusted so active support not automatically scored as 0. Evaluate quality and level of support provided
R4	Noncompliance with remediation attempts	Scoring adjusted to consider association between intervention and offending behaviour as opposed to intervention related to other adaptive needs of the client
R5	Stress	Scoring adjusted to broaden definition of serious stressors

be as effective in predicting violence for ID offenders as for other mentally disordered offenders without IDs (Kells 2011; Lindsay et al. 2008; O'Shea et al. 2015). Further, Verbrugge et al. (2011) concluded that the HCR-20 had good predictive validity in offenders with ID and that Boer et al.'s ID-specific supplement provided a small improvement in this regard.

The Short-Term Assessment of Risk and Treatability (START)   The START (Webster et al. 2004, 2009) is an SPJ tool comprising 20 items designed to assess dynamic risk factors. Unlike most other forensic risk assessment tools, which are designed to assess long-term risk, the START has been developed to assess short-term risk for a range of factors which include violence, self-harm, absconding, self-neglect, and victimization. The START also assesses strengths or attributes of the individual which may be protective factors in reducing their risk. It has been evaluated in one small study (Inett et al. 2014) involving a sample of people with ID (*n* = 27). The results of this study indicate that the START tool has moderate-to-good predictive validity for physical aggression (AUC = 0.71) and property damage (AUC = 0.73) over the 30-day period for which it was designed.

Assessment tools designed for adults with ID

Due to historical concerns about the validity of mainstream and forensic mental-health risk assessment instruments, a number of specialist tools have been developed which assess the risk of violence and/or sexual violence in people with IDs. These instruments vary in complexity from the straightforward approach of the Current Risk of Violence scale (CuRV; Lofthouse 2016) which is designed for completion by non-clinical staff, through to the comprehensive and multi-faceted Assessment of Risk and Manageability of Individuals with Developmental and Intellectual Limitations who Offend (ARMIDILO-S; Boer et al. 2004). Some of these tools have had limited but promising results in field testing and are worthy of consideration because of their focus on dynamic factors more likely to occur for offenders with ID than for those in other populations. These factors include living environment and characteristics of, and relationship with, support staff, family, and significant others (Boer et al. 2007; Lofthouse et al. 2014).

Assessment of Risk and Manageability of Individuals with Developmental and Intellectual Limitations Who Offend Sexually (ARMIDILO-S)   The ARMIDILO-S is a hybrid risk assessment and management system, primarily developed for sexual offending, which brings actuarial scales (used as a baseline) together with a process for assessing dynamic factors, into a model for evaluating and managing the risk of sexual and violent offending (Boer et al. 2004). A unique feature of the instrument is that it separates environmental variables, such as living situation and level of support, from offender variables.

Whilst it has not yet been extensively tested in research, results are promising, and two studies show that ARMIDILO-S has moderate to good predictive validity. Blacker et al. (2011) found AUCs of 0.83 for the stable dynamic items and 0.76 for the acute dynamic items in predicting violent recidivism. Interestingly, the predictive validity results for sexual re-offending were a little lower, with AUCs of 0.61 and 0.73 for stable and acute items respectively. Lofthouse et al. (2013) evaluated the ARMIDILO-S in relation to the prediction of sexual recidivism and found good predictive validity for total and subscale scores (AUC of 0.92, 0.81, and 0.90 for the total, environmental and offender subscale scores, respectively). The authors concluded that the ARMIDILO-S performed better than the Static-99 and VRAG, which were used for comparison.

Current Risk of Violence (CuRV)   CuRV (Lofthouse 2016) is a 34-item risk assessment tool which examines dynamic risk factors for violence in adults with ID. The instrument uses a structured clinical judgement approach, with each item having a descriptor and a yes or no rating. The test items comprise individual personality/attitudinal factors, the presence of verbal and physical aggression, health factors and factors related to the living/support environment. A single published study (Lofthouse et al. 2014) indicated moderate to good predictive validity over a five-month period, with the area under the curve (AUC) between 0.72 and 0.77.

The Dynamic Risk Assessment and Management System (DRAMS)   The DRAMS (Lindsay et al. 2004) is an assessment for dynamic/proximal risk factors in people with IDs. The initial field trial of the DRAMS involved staff working in a hospital secure unit completing assessments of 10 individuals, with a total of 45 assessments over a three-month period. The relationship between DRAMS assessments and 'aggressive incidents' (identified via a major incident reporting system) was calculated. Four items were found to have high reliability: mood, psychotic symptoms, self-regulation, and compliance with routine, as did total score. Two further items were found to have moderate reliability: antisocial behaviour and problems with thinking/attitudes. For a further three items: substance abuse, renewal of emotional relationships and victim access, no participant rated on them. The authors concluded that DRAMS may effectively predict aggressive incidents, particularly in residential settings. Subsequent publications have been limited to a study of validity (Steptoe 2008), which found that DRAMS had good concurrent validity with the Ward Anger Rating Scale, and a study of user perception (Murphy 2005).

The Short Dynamic Risk Scale (SDRS)   The SDRS (Quinsey 2004) is an eight-item brief risk of violence assessment tool for people with IDs, where the instrument items are derived from two measures of dynamic risk factors designed for use with mentally-disordered offenders: the Problem Identification Checklist (Rice et al. 1990) and Proximal Risk Factor Scale (Quinsey et al. 1997). The items included are scored on a scale ranging from 0 = no problem through to 4 = severe problem and cover the areas of hostile attitude, coping skills, anxiety, anger, verbal aggression, empathy, and self-care/household management. Lindsay et al. (2008) found the SDRS had good interrater reliability (88.6%) and was effective in predicting future violence in a sample of 145 male ID offenders across community, low-, and medium-secure settings, with an AUC of 0.71. Further, Lindsay et al. (2008) also compared the predictive validity of a range of risk assessment instruments in the same study, including VRAG and HCR-20, and concluded that the predictive validity of SDRS was as accurate as other instruments in predicting future incidents of violence.

Offenders with ASD

Risk of violence assessment with offenders who have asd

ASD is a heterogenous disorder, therefore, clinicians need to consider degree of severity of ASD as this can be wide-ranging. Further, ASD can be comorbid with ID and/or other neurodevelopmental or psychiatric disorders (White et al. 2017). As a result of this heterogeneity, and the frequency of comorbid psychiatric disorders, there is significant complexity in the challenge of undertaking risk of violence assessment in individuals with ASD, with both autism-related and non-ASD factors to consider. This section of the chapter will summarize: (i) research on the known rates of violent offending for individuals with ASD who do not have an ID, (ii) risk factors for offending, and (iii) the use of standardized risk assessment tools for individuals with ASD. The range of studies evaluating risk assessment instruments for offenders with ASD is extremely limited, so literature describing best-practice approaches was also reviewed.

The prevalence of violent offending by adults with ASD   High-profile crimes committed by individuals diagnosed with or suggested to have ASD, such as the shooting at Sandy Hook Elementary School by Adam Lanza, may have contributed to a public perception that there is a causative relationship between autism and violence (Maras et al. 2015). Further, despite increased research into the association between autism and crime, there is limited evidence available which either supports or refutes this perception that autistic people can be violent and dangerous (King and Murphy 2014). However, as noted, adults with ASD form a very heterogeneous group and it is unlikely that a clear causative link between autism and violence or other criminal behaviour could be established.

There is limited and sometimes conflicting information about the prevalence of adults with ASD in the criminal justice system (King and Murphy 2014), though there is evidence of over-representation in forensic mental-health populations, with estimates between 1.5 and 18% (Im 2016; Tromans et al. 2018). These reports have not conclusively shown that individuals with ASD are any more likely to commit violent offences than other offenders, though higher rates of arson were found in one study (Mouridsen et al. 2008). King and Murphy (2014) conducted a systematic review of published studies relating to people with ASD in the criminal justice system. Whilst they noted that 'the poor quality of much of the research and variation of both methodologies and specific focus in each study allows only tentative conclusions' (p. 2727), they did find sufficient evidence to argue that people with ASD committed the same or fewer offences as people without ASD and that those with ASD were likely to be dealt with outside of the criminal justice system. This conclusion is supported by Heeramun et al. (2017) who, in a large study using data from the Stockholm Youth Court, ($n = 295\,734$, of which 5739 had ASD) found a higher adjusted relative risk for the ASD population than for the overall sample (1.39), but a lower relative risk when ASD was adjusted for comorbid ADHD or conduct disorder (0.85). Furthermore, in a comprehensive review of the literature on ASD and violence, Im (2016) concluded that there was no evidence that people with ASD were more violent than the general population.

Risk factors for violent offending in ASD   In addition to criminogenic risk factors in general populations, Howlin (2004) proposed four factors that could be considered to increase the risk of people with ASD behaving aggressively or committing criminal acts:

- Social naivety, increasing vulnerability to being manipulated by others into committing a criminal act;
- The disruption of usual routines or over-rigid adherence to their own rules, leading to distress and subsequent aggression;
- Misinterpreting or misunderstanding social situations or rules triggering aggression;
- Obsessional interests leading to offending in the pursuit of that interest, perhaps exacerbated by a failure to recognize the implications of such behaviour.

From a theoretical viewpoint, ASD-specific predisposing factors for violence are postulated to result from observed deficits in neuro and social cognition. These include well-established impairments in theory of mind, social communication and executive functioning (Ozonoff and McEvoy 1994; Tager-Flusberg 2000; Volkmar and McPartland 2014). Though there is much research which has investigated these factors and their association with ASD, there is very limited research which investigates these factors in relation to ASD and aggressive or violent behaviour. Comorbid psychopathy or anti-social personality disorder has also been suggested as a predisposing factor for violence in individuals with ASD. However, evidence suggests that there is no causative link between ASD and psychopathy, although some individuals have both disorders (Rogers et al. 2006).

One of a very few studies looking at both predisposing and precipitating factors for offending by adults with ASD (Allen et al. 2008) describes factors identified in offending for 16 men with ASD from a range of community, residential, and secure settings. Although that sample was small, its findings were consistent with the ASD-related factors described by Howlin (2004), and also identifies several additional precipitating factors for offending. Some of these factors are similar to those for non-autistic offenders, for example, family conflict, sexual rejection and deterioration in mental health, whilst others appear to be more closely associated with difficulties with flexibility of thinking and behaviour, including change of living situation or change in professional support. Two factors, bullying and social rejection, appear linked to communication and social skills deficits experienced by people with ASD.

With regard to specific ASD-related risk factors for violence, a number of studies provide further broad support for Howlin's (2004) four factors. For example, Lerner et al. (2012) found that a combination of impaired theory of mind, emotion regulation difficulties and impaired moral reasoning increased likelihood of offending. Recent reviews by Im (2016), White et al. (2017) and King and Murphy (2014) also support the position that ASD-specific factors are as important as typical criminogenic and clinical risk factors measured by standardized risk assessment instruments when assessing risk of violence in people with ASD.

Psychiatric comorbidity also appears to have a significant role in offending by adults with ASD. Haw et al. (2013) found that 73.3 of offenders with ASD in a secure setting had comorbid psychiatric disorders, most commonly schizophrenia or other psychotic disorder (35.6%), but also ADHD (11%). Although 77.8% had a lifetime history of violence against others, this was significantly lower than a comparison group of mentally-disordered offenders who did not have ASD. Use of alcohol and other substances was substantially lower in the ASD group than the comparison mentally-disordered offender group.

In a large Swedish retrospective study of risk of violent offending for a sample of adults with ASD (Långström et al. 2009), the authors identified 31 individuals (7%) who had been convicted of violent, non-sexual offences. In the Swedish criminal justice system, mentally-disordered offenders are not diverted prior to sentencing. Rather, the individual's mental disorder is considered in sentencing options. Odds ratios were calculated for a number of risk variables, with the presence of comorbid psychiatric disorder having an OR of 4.21 (95%CI). Similarly, in another Swedish study, Heeramun et al. (2017) found that, after adjusting for comorbid ADHD or conduct disorder, the relative risk for those with ASD was lower than other offenders (0.85). The strongest predictors were male gender, comorbid psychiatric condition, parental criminal or psychiatric history and low socioeconomic status.

In summary, current evidence suggests that there is a complex interplay between typical criminogenic factors, clinical factors and ASD-specific neurobiological factors that may predispose some people with ASD to violence (Allely et al. 2014). The influence of typical criminogenic needs seems to be less than in other populations with regard to violence exhibited by people with ASD. However, substance abuse, unemployment, young age, male, low socioeconomic status (Chaplin and McCarthy 2014) and criminality of parents (Del Pozzo et al. 2018) have been identified as factors for consideration in risk assessment. The influence of psychiatric comorbidity has stronger empirical support, with the studies previously outlined and four systematic reviews (Allely 2018; Im 2016; King and Murphy 2014; White et al. 2017) identifying it as a significant factor in violent offending by people with ASD. Regarding ASD-specific factors, Howlin's proposed factors to explain criminal behaviour by people with ASD make sense when considering the nature of the disorder, though they have not been evaluated in research. However, there is evidence that deficits in social cognition (e.g. impairments in theory-of-mind and empathy) and neurologically-based emotion regulation problems are factors in violent offending by people with ASD (Im 2016).

The use of standardized risk assessment tools for adults with ASD At the present time, there are very few studies evaluating the use of standardized risk assessment tools for autistic adults. Murphy (2013) evaluated the usefulness of the HCR-20 in assessing the risk of violence amongst a small sample of offenders with ASD. Three historical items consistently received high scores: relationship instability (90%), early maladjustment (75%) and suspected or diagnosed personality disorder (80%). These findings are consistent with suggestions that emotion dysregulation is a key mechanism that contributes to violence in people with ASD. One clinical item, lack of insight (85%), and one risk item, vulnerability to future stress (100%), also frequently scored highly. Murphy concluded that whilst some of the standard HCR-20 risk items were present for the sample, there were other ASD-specific factors which contributed significantly to their level of risk and that the influence of the typical risk items was unclear.

Best practice recommendations in risk assessment and management for autistic adults With the limited research into assessments which may be valid predictors of future violence in individuals with ASD, a number of authors have outlined what they consider best practice for this population (Barkham et al. 2013; Chaplin and McCarthy 2014; Murphy 2013; White et al. 2017). This guidance suggests that assessment of risk of violence for offenders with ASD should consider the same risk factors as for other populations and standardized tools should be used. However, risk formulation also needs to include consideration of autism-specific factors including theory of mind deficits and social naivety, emotion regulation and executive functioning difficulties, and needs to consider the impact and management of comorbid psychiatric disorders.

Conclusions

The science of violence risk assessment is an evolving field, but the available evidence suggests that several instruments which predict future violence for offenders in correctional or forensic mental health populations can be applicable and are valid for offenders with IDs, although there is some way to go in establishing a significant evidence base. The picture is less clear when considering risk of violence for those with ASD, particularly considering the very limited research into the validity of risk assessment instruments in this population.

Many of the instruments available have only been tested and validated on small sample populations of offenders with ID, particularly the ID-specific tools. This is not surprising, given the small and specialist nature of the ID forensic field in comparison to the wider forensic mental health and correctional fields. Most of the studies published so far use sample populations who are residing in specialist secure units and only a small number of studies compare rates with offenders with ID living in the community or with a non-ID sample. The variation in definitions of recidivism is a further complication, with some studies using incident data whilst others use reconviction or compulsion under other legal orders such as the Mental Health Act 1983 in the UK.

One area of similarity between ID offender and those with ASD is the influence of comorbid psychiatric disorders on violent offending. There is sufficient evidence to indicate that when assessing risk of future violence in both these populations, a comprehensive mental health assessment should always be completed alongside any risk assessment, and the two assessments be used in formulation and risk management planning (Chaplin and McCarthy 2014; King and Murphy 2014; Murphy 2010).

A further significant consideration for both populations is the context of violent offending. Dynamic contextual variables such as family or staff support, or living environment have been found to have a greater influence for individuals with ID than other groups of violent offenders, and there is emerging evidence that this is also for individuals with ASD (Gunasekaran 2012; Murphy 2013). However, validating an instrument specifically for assessing risk of future violence in individuals with ASD is problematic as outlined previously; ASD is both complex and heterogeneous in presentation. It may be more beneficial if future research on violence and autism focused on the specific factors that lead some individuals with ASD to behave violently, rather than whether those with ASD show higher rates of violence than other populations (Maras et al. 2015).

The need to closely examine dynamic risk variables for adults with ID has led to pragmatic solutions in the development of assessment tools, often drawing on wider sources of information than typical actuarial or SPJ instruments. Specialist services for offenders with ID, particularly those which are community based, have workforces which are largely non-professional. However, these staff have extensive knowledge of the people they provide support to, including current risks. The DRAMS (Lindsay et al. 2004), CuRV (Lofthouse et al. 2014) and ARMIDILO-S (Boer et al. 2004) all take advantage of the knowledge of dynamic risk variables held by direct support workers or other care providers and uses this knowledge in risk formulation and in developing management plans. The limited published research indicates that an approach incorporating the knowledge and experience of non-professional staff can produce valid and reliable instruments, which consider the unique and dynamic risk variables for the individual being assessed.

Whilst there is not currently an evidence base for the use of these instruments for offenders with ASD, the sample population used in scale development often had offenders with ID as their primary diagnosis, but who also had ASD. The flexible and dynamic nature of these instruments would indicate that they could potentially be used when assessing risk of violence in offenders with ASD, but further research is needed to validate this. Chaplin and McCarthy (2014) also comment that the HCR-20 (v.3; Douglas et al. 2013), with its ability to incorporate wider sources of information and contextual/dynamic variables, may be more effective than previous versions in predicting risk of violence and in developing effective risk formulations and management plans for offenders with ASD.

The intent of this chapter was to provide a summary of the tools available, along with the supporting evidence as to reliability, predictive validity and utility. At the present time, drawing absolute conclusions regarding which specific tools to recommend is not possible given the current evidence base, with varying definitions and distributions of ID, methodological differences, and the uses of both modified and unmodified versions of some instruments (Table 17.2 provides a summary of the instruments discussed, their predictive validity and use of any modifications or specialist guidelines). However, current evidence indicates that of the static risk assessments, VRAG may offer the best long-term prediction of future violence for ID offenders. In relation to SPJ tools, the HCR-20 has good predictive validity for ID offenders and, with the modifications made in version three, can take into account the contextual factors particular to this population. The evidence base for ID-specific dynamic risk assessment instruments is small but developing and these instruments show promise in short-term prediction and are very useful for determining both security and treatment needs. For offenders with ASD, there is no evidence for predictive validity of any tool, meaning clinicians are reliant on best practice advice, which at present means using a standardized instrument, but incorporating ASD-specific factors into risk formulation and management plans. A combination of two assessments (static/historical combined with proximal/dynamic) or a hybrid assessment may offer the greatest utility for clinicians and support service providers.

Table 17.2 Assessment tools with demonstrated moderate or good predictive validity for risk of violence in people with intellectual disability (ID) and autism spectrum disorder (ASD).

Assessment	Instrument type	Tool used unadapted for ID/ASD		With Adaptation/ guidance for ID/ASD		Tool designed for ID/ASD	
		ID	ASD	ID	ASD	ID	ASD
Mainstream							
VRAG	Actuarial	✓✓		✓✓			
PCL-R	Actuarial	✓		✓			
PCL-SV	Actuarial	✓		✓✓			
OGRS	Actuarial	✓✓					
HCR-20	SPJ	✓✓	*	✓✓			
START	SPJ	✓					
ID Specific							
ARMIDILO- S	Hybrid SPJ/ Dynamic					✓✓	
DRAMS	SPJ/Dynamic					✓	
SDRS	Dynamic					✓	
CuRV	SPJ/Dynamic					✓✓	

✓ = moderate AUC = 0.70–0.74, ✓✓ = good AUC > 0.75, * = tool used but AUC not published.

References

Allely, C.S. (2018). A systematic PRISMA review of individuals with autism spectrum disorder in secure psychiatric care: prevalence, treatment, risk assessment and other clinical considerations. *Journal of Criminal Psychology* 8 (1): 58–79.

Allely, C.S., Minnis, H., Thompson, L. et al. (2014). Neurodevelopmental and psychosocial risk factors in serial killers and mass murderers. *Aggression and Violent Behavior* 19 (3): 288–301.

Allen, D., Evans, C., Hider, A. et al. (2008). Offending behaviour in adults with Asperger syndrome. *Journal of Autism and Developmental Disorders* 38 (4): 748–758.

American Psychiatric Association (2000). *Diagnostic and Statistical Manual of Mental Disorders: DSM-IV-TR*. Washington, DC: Author.

American Psychiatric Association (2013). *Diagnostic and Statistical Manual of Mental Disorders: DSM-5*. Washington, DC: Author.

Asperger, H. (1944). Die "autistischen psychopathen" im kindesalter. *European Archives of Psychiatry and Clinical Neuroscience* 117 (1): 76–136.

Barkham, E., Gunasekaran, S., and Lovelock, C. (2013). Medium secure care: forensic aspects of autism and Asperger's syndrome. *Journal of Intellectual Disabilities and Offending Behaviour* 4 (1/2): 9–16.

Barry-Walsh, J., Daffern, M., Duncan, S., and Ogloff, J. (2009). The prediction of imminent aggression in patients with mental illness and/or intellectual disability using the dynamic appraisal of situational aggression instrument. *Australasian Psychiatry* 17 (6): 493–496.

Blacker, J., Beech, A.R., Wilcox, D.T., and Boer, D.P. (2011). The assessment of dynamic risk and recidivism in a sample of special needs sexual offenders. *Psychology, Crime & Law* 17 (1): 75–92.

Boer, D.P., Frize, M., Pappas, R. et al. (2010). Suggested adaptations to the HCR-20 for offenders with intellectual disabilities. In: *Assessment and Treatment of Sexual Offenders with Intellectual Disabilities: A Handbook* (eds. L.A. Craig, W.R. Lindsay and K.D. Browne), 177–192. Chichester, UK: Wiley.

Boer, D.P., McVilly, K.R., and Lambrick, F. (2007). Contextualizing risk in the assessment of intellectually disabled individuals. *Sexual Offender Treatment* 2 (2): 1–5.

Boer, D.P., Tough, S., and Haaven, J. (2004). Assessment of risk manageability of intellectually disabled sex offenders. *Journal of Applied Research in Intellectual Disabilities* 17 (4): 275–283.

Canitano, R. and Vivanti, G. (2007). Tics and Tourette syndrome in autism spectrum disorders. *Autism* 11 (1): 19–28.

Chaplin, E. and McCarthy, J. (2014). Autism spectrum disorder and offending – a UK perspective. *Autism Spectrum Quarterly* (Summer): 14–16.

Copas, J. and Marshall, P. (1998). The offender group reconviction scale: a statistical reconviction score for use by probation officers. *Journal of the Royal Statistical Society: Series C (Applied Statistics)* 47 (1): 159–171.

Del Pozzo, J., Roché, M.W., and Silverstein, S.M. (2018). Violent behavior in autism spectrum disorders: who's at risk? *Aggression and Violent Behavior* 39: 53–60.

Department of Justice (2005). *The Development of the Brief Spousal Assault Form for the Evaluation of Risk (B-SAFER): A Tool for Criminal Justice Professionals*. Ottawa, ON: Department of Justice.

Douglas, K.S., Hart, S.D., Webster, C.D., and Belfrage, H. (2013). *HCR-20 (Version 3): Assessing Risk of Violence – User Guide*. Burnaby, BC: Mental Health, Law, and Policy Institute, Simon Fraser University.

Douglas, K.S., Shaffer, C., Blanchard, A.J.E. et al. (2014). *HCR-20 Violence Risk assessment Scheme: Overview and annotated bibliography*. HCR-20 Violence Risk Assessment White Paper Series, #1. Burnaby, BC: Mental Health, Law, & Policy Institute, Simon Fraser University.

Emerson, E. (2001). *Challenging Behaviour: Analysis and Intervention in People with Severe Intellectual Disabilities*. Cambridge, UK: Cambridge University Press.

Fitzgerald, S., Gray, N.S., Alexander, R.T. et al. (2013). Predicting institutional violence in offenders with intellectual disabilities: the predictive efficacy of the VRAG and the HCR-20. *Journal of Applied Research in Intellectual Disabilities* 26 (5): 384–393.

Fitzgerald, S., Gray, N.S., Taylor, J., and Snowden, R.J. (2011). Risk factors for recidivism in offenders with intellectual disabilities. *Psychology, Crime & Law* 17 (1): 43–58.

Francis, B., Soothill, K., and Humphreys, L. (2007). *Development of a Reoffending Measure Using the Police National Computer Database*. Lancaster, UK: Lancaster University.

Gotham, K., Brunwasser, S.M., and Lord, C. (2015). Depressive and anxiety symptom trajectories from school age through young adulthood in samples with autism spectrum disorder and developmental delay. *Journal of the American Academy of Child & Adolescent Psychiatry* 54 (5): 369–376.

Gray, N.S., Fitzgerald, S., Taylor, J. et al. (2007). Predicting future reconviction in offenders with intellectual disabilities: the predictive efficacy of VRAG, PCL-SV, and the HCR-20. *Psychological Assessment* 19 (4): 474–479.

Gray, N.S., Snowden, R.J., MacCulloch, S. et al. (2004). Relative efficacy of criminological, clinical, and personality measures of future risk of offending in mentally disordered offenders: a comparative study of HCR-20, PCL:SV, and OGRS. *Journal of Consulting and Clinical Psychology* 72 (3): 523–530.

Gunasekaran, S. (2012). Assessment and management of risk in autism. *Advances in Mental Health and Intellectual Disabilities* 6 (6): 314–320.

Hare, R.D. (1991). *The Hare Psychopathy Checklist-Revised: Manual*. Toronto, ON: Multi-Health Systems Incorporated.

Harris, G.T. and Rice, M.E. (2006). Treatment of psychopathy. In: *Handbook of Psychopathy* (ed. C. Patrick), 555–572. New York, NY: Guilford.

Harris, G.T., Rice, M.E., and Quinsey, V.L. (1993). Violent recidivism of mentally disordered offenders: the development of a statistical prediction instrument. *Criminal Justice and Behavior* 20: 315–335.

Haw, C., Cooke, L., and Radley, J. (2013). Characteristics of male autistic spectrum patients in low security: are they different from non-autistic low secure patients? *Journal of Intellectual Disabilities and Offending Behaviour* 4 (1/2): 24–32.

Heeramun, R., Magnusson, C., Gumpert, C.H. et al. (2017). Autism and convictions for violent crimes: population-based cohort study in Sweden. *Journal of the American Academy of Child & Adolescent Psychiatry* 56 (6): 491–497.

Hofvander, B., Delorme, R., Chaste, P. et al. (2009). Psychiatric and psychosocial problems in adults with normal-intelligence autism spectrum disorders. *BMC Psychiatry* 9 (35): 1–9.

Hounsome, J., Whittington, R., Brown, A. et al. (2018). The structured assessment of violence risk in adults with intellectual disability: a systematic review. *Journal of Applied Research in Intellectual Disabilities* 31 (1): 1–17.

Howlin, P. (2004). *Autism and Asperger Syndrome: Preparing for Adulthood*. New York, NY: Routledge.

Howlin, P. and Moss, P. (2012). Adults with autism spectrum disorders. *Canadian Journal of Psychiatry* 57 (5): 275–283.

Im, D.S. (2016). Template to perpetrate: an update on violence in autism Spectrum disorder. *Harvard Review of Psychiatry* 24 (1): 14–35.

Inett, A., Wright, G., Roberts, L., and Sheeran, A. (2014). Predictive validity of the START with intellectually disabled offenders. *The Journal of Forensic Practice* 16 (1): 78–88.

Joshi, G., Biederman, J., Petty, C. et al. (2013). Examining the comorbidity of bipolar disorder and autism spectrum disorders: a large controlled analysis of phenotypic and familial correlates in a referred population of youth with bipolar I disorder with and without autism spectrum disorders. *The Journal of Clinical Psychiatry* 74 (6): 578–586.

Kanner, L. (1943). Autistic disturbances of affective contact. *Nervous Child* 2: 217–250.

Kells, M. (2011). The psychometric assessment of offenders with an intellectual disability. Doctoral dissertation. University of Birmingham.

King, C. and Murphy, G.H. (2014). A systematic review of people with autism spectrum disorder and the criminal justice system. *Journal of Autism and Developmental Disorders* 44 (11): 2717–2733.

Långström, N., Grann, M., Ruchkin, V. et al. (2009). Risk factors for violent offending in autism spectrum disorder: a national study of hospitalized individuals. *Journal of Interpersonal Violence* 24 (8): 1358–1370.

LaVigna, G.W. and Willis, T.J. (2012). The efficacy of positive behavioural support with the most challenging behaviour: the evidence and its implications. *Journal of Intellectual & Developmental Disability* 37 (3): 185–195.

Lerner, M.D., Haque, O.S., Northrup, E.C. et al. (2012). Emerging perspectives on adolescents and young adults with high- functioning autism spectrum disorders, violence, and criminal law. *The Journal of the American Academy of Psychiatry and the Law* 40 (2): 177–190.

Lindsay, W.R. and Beail, N. (2004). Risk assessment: actuarial prediction and clinical judgement of offending incidents and behaviour for intellectual disability services. *Journal of Applied Research in Intellectual Disabilities* 17 (4): 229–234.

Lindsay, W.R., Hogue, T.E., Taylor, J.L. et al. (2008). Risk assessment in offenders with intellectual disability: a comparison across three levels of security. *International Journal of Offender Therapy and Comparative Criminology* 52 (1): 90–111.

Lindsay, W.R., Michie, A.M., Finlay, C., and Taylor, J.L. (2017). Offenders with intellectual and developmental disabilities. In: *The Routledge International Handbook of Forensic Psychology in Secure Settings* (eds. J.L. Ireland, C.A. Ireland, M. Fisher and N. Gredecki), 40–54. New York, NY: Routledge.

Lindsay, W.R., Murphy, L., Smith, G. et al. (2004). The dynamic risk assessment and management system: an assessment of immediate risk of violence for individuals with offending and challenging behaviour. *Journal of Applied Research in Intellectual Disabilities* 17 (4): 267–274.

Lofthouse, R. (2016). Assessing and managing risk with adults with intellectual disabilities (ID). Doctoral dissertation. Liverpool University.

Lofthouse, R., Lindsay, W.R., Totsika, V. et al. (2013). Prospective dynamic assessment of risk of sexual reoffending in individuals with an intellectual disability and a history of sexual offending behaviour. *Journal of Applied Research in Intellectual Disabilities* 26 (5): 394–403.

Lofthouse, R., Lindsay, W.R., Totsika, V. et al. (2014). Dynamic risk and violence in individuals with an intellectual disability: tool development and initial validation. *The Journal of Forensic Psychiatry & Psychology* 25 (3): 288–306.

Lugnegård, T., Hallerbäck, M.U., and Gillberg, C. (2011). Psychiatric comorbidity in young adults with a clinical diagnosis of Asperger syndrome. *Research in Developmental Disabilities* 32 (5): 1910–1917.

Maras, K., Mulcahy, S., and Crane, L. (2015). Is autism linked to criminality? *Autism* 19 (5): 515–516.

Matthews, M., Bell, E., and Mirfin-Veitch, B. (2018). Comparing psychopathology rates across autism spectrum disorders and intellectual disabilities. *Advances in Mental Health and Intellectual Disabilities* 12 (5/6): 163–172.

Mental Health Act. (1983). https://www.gov.uk/government/publications/code-of-practice-mental-health-act-1983 (Accessed 20 August 2019).

Morrissey, C. (2005). Guidelines for use of the PCL-R and SV in adults with ID. https://www.researchgate.net/publication/257890698_Guidelines_for_use_of_the_PCL-R_and_SV_in_adults_with_ID (Accessed 20 August 2019).

Morrissey, C. (2006). Assessment of psychopathy in offenders with intellectual disabilities. Doctoral dissertation. University of Leicester.

Morrissey, C., Hogue, T.E., Allen, C. et al. (2007a). Predictive validity of the PCL-R in offenders with intellectual disability in a high secure hospital setting: institutional aggression. *The Journal of Forensic Psychiatry & Psychology* 18 (1): 1–15.

Morrissey, C., Hogue, T.E., Mooney, P. et al. (2005). Applicability, reliability and validity of the psychopathy checklist-revised in offenders with intellectual disabilities: some initial findings. *International Journal of Forensic Mental Health* 4 (2): 207–220.

Morrissey, C., Mooney, P., Hogue, T.E. et al. (2007b). Predictive validity of the PCL-R for offenders with intellectual disability in a high security hospital: treatment progress. *Journal of Intellectual & Developmental Disability* 32 (2): 125–133.

Mouridsen, S.E., Rich, B., Isager, T., and Nedergaard, N.J. (2008). Pervasive developmental disorders and criminal behaviour: a case control study. *International Journal of Offender Therapy and Comparative Criminology* 52 (2): 196–205.

Murphy, D. (2010). Extreme violence in a man with an autistic spectrum disorder: assessment and treatment within high-security psychiatric care. *The Journal of Forensic Psychiatry & Psychology* 21 (3): 462–477.

Murphy, D. (2013). Risk assessment of offenders with an autism spectrum disorder. *Journal of Intellectual Disabilities and Offending Behaviour* 4 (1/2): 33–41.

Murphy, G.H. (2015). *People with Learning Disabilities and Offending Behaviours: Prevalence, Treatment, Risk Assessment and Services*. Canterbury, UK: NHS.

Murphy, L. (2005). Users' views of a dynamic risk assessment system. *Nursing Times* 101 (33): 35–37.

Ogloff, J.R. and Daffern, M. (2006). The dynamic appraisal of situational aggression: an instrument to assess risk for imminent aggression in psychiatric inpatients. *Behavioral Sciences & the Law* 24 (6): 799–813.

O'Shea, L.E., Picchioni, M.M., McCarthy, J. et al. (2015). Predictive validity of the HCR-20 for inpatient aggression: the effect of intellectual disability on accuracy. *Journal of Intellectual Disability Research* 59 (11): 1042–1054.

Ozonoff, S. and McEvoy, R. (1994). A longitudinal study of executive function and theory of mind development in autism. *Development and Psychopathology* 6 (3): 415–431.

Pouls, C. and Jeandarme, I. (2015). Risk assessment and risk management in offenders with intellectual disabilities: are we there yet? *Journal of Mental Health Research in Intellectual Disabilities* 8 (3–4): 213–236.

Quinsey, V. L. (2004). Risk assessment and management in community settings. Offenders with Developmental Disabilities, 131–141.

Quinsey, V.L., Coleman, G., Jones, B., and Altrows, I.F. (1997). Proximal antecedents of eloping and reoffending among supervised mentally disordered offenders. *Journal of Interpersonal Violence* 12 (6): 794–813.

Rice, M.E., Harris, G.T., Quinsey, V.L., and Cyr, M. (1990). Planning treatment programs in secure psychiatric facilities. *Law and Mental Health: International Perspectives* 5: 162–230.

Rogers, J., Viding, E., James Blair, R. et al. (2006). Autism spectrum disorder and psychopathy: shared cognitive underpinnings or double hit? *Psychological Medicine* 36 (12): 1789–1798.

Smith, K. (2009). The assessment of and differences among intellectually disabled adults with comorbid autism spectrum disorders and epilepsy. Doctoral dissertation. Louisiana State University.

Snowden, R.J., Gray, N.S., Taylor, J., and MacCulloch, M.J. (2007). Actuarial prediction of violent recidivism in mentally disordered offenders. *Psychological Medicine* 37 (11).

Sreenivasan, S., Kirkish, P., Garrick, T. et al. (2000). Actuarial risk assessment models: a review of critical issues related to violence and sex-offender recidivism assessments. *Journal-American Academy of Psychiatry and the Law* 28 (4): 438–448.

Steptoe, L. (2008). Construct validity, reliability and predictive validity of the dynamic risk assessment and management system (DRAMS) in offenders with intellectual disability. *Legal and Criminological Psychology* 13 (2): 309–321.

Sturmey, P., Reed, J., and Corbett, J. (1991). Psychometric assessment of psychiatric disorders in people with learning difficulties (mental handicap): a review of measures. *Psychological Medicine* 21 (1): 143–155.

Tager-Flusberg, H. (2000). Understanding the language and communicative impairments in autism. *International Review of Research in Mental Retardation* 23: 185–205.

Taylor, R. (1999). *Predicting Reconvictions for Sexual and Violent Offences Using the Revised Offender Group Reconviction Scale*. London, UK: Home Office.

Tromans, S., Chester, V., Kiani, R. et al. (2018). The prevalence of autism spectrum disorders in adult psychiatric inpatients: a systematic review. *Clinical Practice and Epidemiology in Mental Health* 14: 177–187.

Verbrugge, H.M., Goodman-Delahunty, J., and Frize, M.C.J. (2011). Risk assessment in intellectually disabled offenders: validation of the suggested ID supplement to the HCR-20. *International Journal of Forensic Mental Health* 10 (2): 83–91.

Volkmar, F. and McPartland, J.C. (2014). From Kanner to DSM-5: autism as an evolving diagnostic concept. *Annual Review of Clinical Psychology* 10: 193–212.

Webster, C.D., Douglas, K.S., Eaves, D., and Hart, S.D. (1997). Assessing risk of violence to others. In: *Impulsivity: Theory, Assessment, and Treatment* (eds. C.D. Webster and M.A. Jackson), 251–277. New York, NY, US: Guilford Press.

Webster, C.D., Martin, M., Brink, J. et al. (2004). *Short-Term Assessment of Risk and Treatability (START)*. Port Coquitlam, BC: Forensic Psychiatric Services Commission and St. Joseph's Healthcare.

Webster, C.D., Martin, M.L., Brink, J. et al. (2009). *Manual for the Short-Term Assessment of Risk and Treatability (START) (Version 1.1)*. Port Coquitlam, BC: Forensic Psychiatric Services Commission and St. Joseph's Healthcare.

White, S.G., Meloy, J., Mohandie, K., and Kienlen, K. (2017). Autism spectrum disorder and violence: threat assessment issues. *Journal of Threat Assessment and Management* 4 (3): 144–163.

Part IV
What Works in Violence Intervention

18

Risk-Reducing Treatment in High-Risk Psychopathic and Violent Offenders

Devon L.L. Polaschek[1] and Stephen C.P. Wong[2]

[1] University of Waikato, Hamilton, New Zealand
[2] University of Saskatchewan, Saskatchewan, Canada

Introduction

The tertiary prevention of human violence through psychologically-informed interventions is an important component of any overall societal commitment to reducing the harm to mental and physical health that violence causes. Societal systems charged with the care and management of people with convictions for violence (e.g. Corrections, forensic mental health) are engaged in various ways with this commitment. This chapter examines 'what works' to reduce violence through psychological treatment programmes in custodial settings with high-risk violence-prone offenders. We consider general treatment issues, and focus on two examples of treatment programmes that have shown evidence of effectiveness with male offenders from Canada and New Zealand.

The Target Client Group

In keeping with the empirical research findings that underpin the Risk principle of the Risk-Need-Responsivity (RNR) model (Bonta and Andrews 2016), programmes that reduce recidivism will have the most impact on those at greatest risk of reconviction. In general, those most at risk of reconvictions of any type are also most likely to acquire violent reconvictions; and treatment programmes should aim to reduce criminality in general, including violence propensity. To put it the other way around, targeting those most at risk of violence will result in the selection of a group of people with diverse and extensive conviction histories,

The Wiley Handbook of What Works in Violence Risk Management: Theory, Research and Practice,
First Edition. Edited by J. Stephen Wormith, Leam A. Craig, and Todd E. Hogue.
© 2020 John Wiley & Sons Ltd. Published 2020 by John Wiley & Sons Ltd.

whose next offence is most likely to be a non-violent crime because of the much higher baserate of the latter.[1] This observation is confirmed by longitudinal research (Farrington 2007; Henry et al. 1996).

Further, treatment programmes should target a wide range of changeable risk factors, not just those that show a direct and straightforward relationship to violence because, for example, the precursors of an offence (e.g. alcohol abuse, hostile cognition, anger). Research on the social psychology of aggression is helpful in identifying a number of specific factors that can contribute to violent *acts* (e.g. aggressive cognitive scripts; Gilbert and Daffern 2010). But in these high-risk violent offenders, addressing risk factors that are less obviously linked to specific violent acts will also be helpful in supporting desistance. Usually, these are factors that contribute to a generally antisocial *lifestyle* (e.g. criminal attitudes, criminal peers, lack of prosocial release plans). For example, New Zealand research showing a link between marijuana use and assault leads to speculation that the mechanism was contact with other criminals (Arseneault et al. 2000). Similarly, a person with no release plans may drift back into criminogenic environments where it is much easier to get caught up in new crimes. Also of note is that most studies of precursors of crime and subsequent offending behaviours are correlational investigations that do not imply causation.

Theories from developmental psychology and life-course criminology (Farrington 2003, 2007; Moffitt 1993) are helpful in conceptualizing in a developmental context the characteristics of those referred for treatment, typically men in their early to mid-thirties (Burns et al. 2011; Kilgour and Polaschek 2012; Kirkpatrick et al. 2010; Lewis et al. 2013). They often present at assessment with little motivation to change, are argumentative and hostile, emotionally volatile and impulsive, mistrustful, lacking persistence, and markedly negative about anything that reminds them of being under the control of authority figures, such as being in school. A number of these features that readily disrupt treatment may also be linked to recidivism in their own right. Consequently, treatment programmes for violent offenders must accommodate the inevitable: the treatment process will be challenging, and the design of interventions needs to accommodate these challenges.

Theoretical Influences on Treatment and the Main Phases of Treatment

The theoretical bases of treatment approaches for violent offenders are often not clearly articulated. The origins of violence and crime are understood in biopsychosocial terms, and in treatment, the social context is especially important (Wong et al. 2007). Social learning and social cognitive theories, theories of social influence, cognitive therapy theories, and theories about the creation and function of the therapeutic alliance all shape the key processes of change in treatment (Bonta and Andrews 2016). Therapists work to create a strong bond between themselves and offenders that is based on mutual respect and liking. This bond then becomes a conduit for therapists' influence over offender behaviour. As therapists, we do what we can to persuade and motivate/cajole participants to try new behaviour, to re-evaluate the way they have always understood the world to work, and to stay with the programme long enough to see if it will benefit them. Therapist approval or disapproval can shape behaviour, although of

---

[1] We recognize that there are occasional cases where an offender with little or no previous history of adjudicated crime or any prior antisocial behaviour commits a single very serious offence (e.g. homicide). Empirically, such a person is likely to be a low-risk offender and would therefore not benefit from risk reducing treatment.

course, other offenders and other staff also influence behaviour through their positive (or negative) social support.

The preferred mode of treatment delivery includes a group format (Wong and Gordon 2013). In a group, processes of influence are often established in the first phase of intensive treatment, where offenders are socialized to the treatment process, develop at least a minimal level of respect and trust with other group members, and begin the process of developing self-reflective skills and insight into their own behaviour and its causes. Specific treatment theories that are useful at this stage include those that shed light on group formation and functioning (e.g. Yalom 2005), helping therapists to formulate how to work with the group's process to achieve particular goals. Useful treatment techniques also include motivational interviewing and the transtheoretical model of change; motivating participants to engage in treatment and in behavioural change is a prominent issue in the early stages of treatment. In order to take part effectively in this phase of the programme, offenders may also need to learn specific social skills such as giving and receiving feedback.

Recognizing one's individual treatment needs goes hand in hand with developing engagement in a change process. In this first phase of treatment, participants are typically introduced to the social-learning or cognitive-behavioural model and, in particular, learn to identify the origins of their own patterns of behaviour, both distal origins (e.g. 'where did I learn that?') and proximal origins (i.e. 'my violent behaviour occurs not out of the blue; but following one or more identifiable sequences of events and responses'). Theory and research on the Relapse Prevention Model and violent offence processes (Chambers et al. 2009) are useful for behavioural pattern identification, though it is worth noting that high-risk violent offenders will often have more than one typical 'offence process or cycle'.

Although this first phase may be the most crucial to engaging participants in the change process, high-risk offenders can lose motivation or derail the process at any time. A variety of additional strategies may be necessary to retain and re-engage offenders in treatment including the use of individual therapy sessions, behavioural contracting, and techniques for working with personality difficulties, such as Dialectical Behaviour Therapy and mindfulness training.

The central part of the treatment programme (Phase two) is typical of cognitive-behavioural programmes. For example, violent offenders often hold particular schemata that they may never have questioned, and that serve to maintain criminal and violent behaviour (e.g, Polaschek et al. 2009). These distorted ways of thinking may be a core part of the identity of an offender. Collaborative and Socratic techniques may be used to expose and gradually undermine these ingrained thinking patterns which have often helped the offender to make sense of the world in an earlier developmental stage, but may now be preventing the client from coping with pro-social activities and successful desistance. A substantial part of this phase of treatment is skills teaching and building core competencies that will serve the offender well in many parts of his or her life (e.g. managing volatile affect, communication skills, relationship skills, cognitive, and behavioural self-regulation and problem-solving). The assumption behind these components is that treatment should make it easier for offenders to behave pro-socially, to achieve desired pro-social goals more successfully (e.g. parenting), and to generally take a more reflective, personally, and interpersonally skilful approach to their lives. This approach may sound naïvely optimistic for people who have multiple risk factors and little motivation to work on them, but our research has shown that most offenders in our adult prison programmes want to desist, and indeed already have been trying to do so prior to the sentence leading to their referral (Polaschek and Yesberg 2015). These desires may wax and wane depending on their life circumstances. Therefore, treatment may help them recognize the kind of work they need to do to succeed, to view positive changes as a win-win life choice, and then to set about desisting more consistently. Interestingly, graduates of these RNR-based programmes may show increased agency for desistance following treatment compared to relatively-untreated counterparts (Polaschek 2013), and changes that reduce scores on dynamic risk factors as a consequence benefit other parts of their lives as well, not just their offending-related difficulties (Coupland 2015).

Given learning difficulties, short-attention spans and negative attitudes towards formal learning, skills teaching works best when it is active, with plenty of opportunities for modelling, practise with supportive feedback, and when the newly learned skills can produce tangible positive results. The learned skills and risk reduction usually do not have a simple one-to-one correspondence. Even generic problem solving or cognitive restructuring skills can be useful in reducing several different dynamic risk factors such as problems with alcohol and drugs, relationship and interpersonal problems, not to mention general social functioning such as gaining a better understanding of how others' minds work.

The third phase of treatment variously focuses on consolidating change, and preparing for the future. Based on developments in the sex-offender field, offender-treatment programmes in the 1990s and 2000s often included a relapse-prevention plan, which identified idiosyncratic chains of events that could lead to re-offending, and the coping strategies offenders could use to disrupt the chain. The preparation of such 'safety plans' offers a key opportunity to review what has been learned and to think about its application, and so helps the offender evaluate treatment progress and areas of remaining vulnerability.

In addition, programmes can explicitly address practical preparations for a post-treatment environment. Ideally, those who have made good progress in treatment go on to a supportive environment where they can continue to build on their progress with additional reintegration steps (e.g. work parole). Alternatively, in some cases, with good support, treatment completers may be released more or less directly into the community. As such, this final, third phase of treatment may be about rebuilding community-based pro-social capital, finding accommodation, and addressing other release-specific needs. (Dickson et al. 2013, 2016; Polaschek and Kilgour 2013). The advantage of including this preparation in the treatment programme itself, rather than delegating the planning process to a separate part of the system, such as a parole service, is that it can be more fully integrated with, and informed by, the treatment process (see High Risk Special Treatment Unit [HRSTU] example below).

Assessment of Dynamic Factors for Treatment

Several tools support the clinical assessment of violent offenders, identifying changeable risk and protective factors relating to recidivism (See Table 18.1 for a list of commonly assessed factors). We are most familiar with the *Violence Risk Scale* (*VRS*; Wong and Gordon 2006) which has 20 dynamic and 6 static items. This is the only tool that uses the measurement of treatment change (operationalized as progression on a stage of change continuum adapted from the Transtheoretical Model of Change) to adjust pre-treatment risk scores based on treatment progress. Each VRS item is scored on a 4-point rating scale (0, 1, 2, or 3) where higher scores indicate a stronger relationship with violent behaviour. Dynamic factors that are rated either a 2 or 3 are considered to be appropriate treatment targets. Each dynamic predictor identified as a treatment target is rated pre- and post-treatment to assess progression from

Table 18.1 Common dynamic risk factors for treatment of high-risk violent offenders (and strategies for their remediation).

- Difficulty in regulating emotion (distress tolerance, mindfulness, relaxation training)
- Offence-supportive beliefs (cognitive restructuring, thought diaries, behavioural testing)
- Criminal peers/family (strategies for managing risks posed by continued association, skills for developing and enhancing pro-social supports)
- Low self-control, rapid, ill-thought-out responses, lack of direction ('impulsivity'; identifying valued goals and strategies, cost–benefit analyses, distress tolerance, problem-solving)
- Substance abuse (specific treatment aimed at moderation or abstinence, emotional management strategies, mindfulness, self-control training, relapse prevention)
- Aggressive communication style (positive communication skills, assertiveness training, non-aggressive conflict resolution).
- Volatile or antisocial intimate relationship (relationship and communication skills, problem-solving, non-violent conflict resolution)
- Unstable, under-engaged, unskilled work, education, or training history (identifying preferred work activities, specific vocational skills training, goal setting and self-regulation, impulse control, problem-solving and communication skills).
- Unstructured leisure time (goal setting, employment, identifying valued activities and planning structured day)
- Low pro-social community support (assistance in developing relationships with key community agencies; remediation of dysfunctional family relationships, rebuilding relationships with pro-social family members or friends, and developing structured plans with support people).
- Few or no plans for managing high-risk situations (developing understanding of pathways to offending, identifying and developing resources and plans for acute risk management).
- Poor compliance with sentence requirements (self-control skills, cost–benefit analyses, pro-social relationship building skills, problem-solving, commitment to pro-social lifestyle).

a less advanced to a more advanced stage of change; the progression can be translated into a quantitative reduction in risk.

Other instruments that can be used to determine treatment needs include the Historical Clinical Risk-20 (HCR-20: Douglas et al. 2013), the Structured Assessment of PROtective Factors for violence risk (SAPROF: de Vogel et al. 2012), and the Level of Supervision/Case Management Inventory (LS-CMI: Andrews et al. 2004). All of these measures have a number of uses, including establishing current level of risk, prioritizing areas for immediate attention, identifying key goals for treatment change, monitoring treatment gains, and operationalizing the relative contributions of various factors to understanding what comprises current risk, and identifying what still requires further attention following treatment.

The process of gathering assessment information for these tools and feeding it back to the potential participant affords an opportunity to engage the offender with the programme and begins to build the collaborative relationship that is needed to be successful in treatment. There are multiple positive strategies for addressing dynamic risk factors (as Table 18.1 suggests). Rather than just leaving an offender with a sense of having multiple serious deficits, assessment is the first point at which a preliminary understanding can be reached on how therapist and participant can work together to build capabilities to ameliorate or provide protection against negative influences embedded in those factors; that is, constructing a risk-based case formulation and sharing it with the offender. Sometimes in group treatments, therapists simply gather assessment information and then put it aside. Feeding back assessment results requires the therapist to develop a good grasp of the specific details of how that individual should engage with and may benefit from the programme. Alternatively, such a review may reveal a lack of fit between the client's needs and what the programme has to offer.

Evaluating offenders' Treatment Progress and Change

Whether a programme is highly manualized or more flexible, there are always opportunities to personalize the treatment experience, making it more meaningful for the offender, and providing a stronger basis for engagement. The evaluation of treatment change is one such opportunity. Having completed an initial assessment to identify the key dynamic risk factors and possible interventions, and having engaged the offender in the treatment programme, reviews of progress can consolidate both therapists' and offenders' perceptions of progress or lack of it. In order to conduct such a review, the treatment staff will need to have gathered up their own observations and those of others about the offender's behaviour since the last review (or assessment) for the progress review. Although self-report always has weaknesses, sometimes it is the only realistic source of key types of information, and it can also usefully complement behavioural observation. For example, custodial staff may have observed new behaviour, but motivations for the behaviour can only be elicited from conversation with the offender. Furthermore, the absence of previous antisocial behaviour often can only be detected by talking with the offender, since by definition, there may be nothing to observe.

A tool like the VRS can be used to assist the focus of progress reviews both with the treatment team and the offender. We have also developed a systematic method for observing, understanding, and communicating about such behaviour. Offence Analogue Behaviours (OABs) are defined as the offender's antisocial or otherwise maladaptive behaviours that serve similar functions to his offending (e.g. intimidating staff, running an illicit 'shop' for other prisoners). Offence Replacement Behaviours (ORBs) are the opposite: pro-social or adaptive acts that can achieve the intended results but without the negative consequences (e.g. using conflict resolution skills to address grievances). Documenting and discussing ORBs and OABs are meaningful methods of understanding and capturing evidence indicative of change (see Gordon and Wong 2009, 2010; Mooney and Daffern 2013). Training across all staff in identifying ORBs and OABs increases attention to the functions of participants' behaviour and again provides a common language for gathering evidence of change.

Programmes that Work with Violent Offenders

There is surprisingly sparse evidence that intensive treatment for violent offenders works: that is, it results in a reduction in the expected level of recidivism or shows changes on factors reliably predictive of recidivism (Polaschek 2017). A number of jurisdictions provide custodial interventions for medium- to high-risk violent offenders; for example, in several Australian states (e.g. Victoria: Klepfisz et al. 2014; New South Wales: Ware et al. 2011), and the UK (Bennett 2014; Saradjian et al. 2013). But as yet, few have been subject to rigorous research. Two of the longer ongoing programmes will be described in more detail here. They were developed independently of each other, but have a number of overlapping elements, and both have been the focus of external research. The first is the *Aggressive Behavior Control* (ABC) programme, which began at the forensic maximum-security Regional Psychiatric Centre

(RPC) in Saskatoon, Saskatchewan, Canada around 1993 (Lewis et al. 2013; Wong and Gordon 2013; Wong et al. 2007), and which, over time, developed into the *Violence Reduction Program* (VRP); a more comprehensive and flexible approach that was subsequently adopted elsewhere (Tyrer et al. 2010).[2] The second is a programme that began in 1998 as the Violence Prevention Unit (VPU) at Rimutaka prison (Polaschek et al. 2005) and now runs in dedicated treatment units in four men's prisons in New Zealand; known as the High-Risk Special Treatment Units (HRSTUs).

These two programmes conform to the RNR model, are broadly cognitive-behavioural and social-learning based, and recruit similar male prisoners for treatment. Both primarily use group treatment, which has the advantage of providing an immediate social context in which to make changes. Both programmes work with a majority or a substantial number of indigenous prisoners. Although developed independently, the structure of the two programmes is remarkably similar. However, there are some important differences too. Whereas New Zealand's HRSTU programmes are designed for male prisoners with relatively low current security levels, at high risk of reimprisonment, and largely free of mental disorder, the VRP is intended to address the needs of a wider range of people, including some forensic patients, prisoners in individual or group treatment, and offenders in the community.

The HRSTUs run a closed-group format with a relatively inflexible manualized approach that has a cohort of 10 men moving together through the programme to completion. This approach creates a strong sense of 'we-ness' in the group, but cannot accommodate those who may need a break from the treatment or the group, or who need more time on particular parts of the programme. The ABC programme was better able to accommodate short breaks away from the programme, and although the newer VRP can be run in closed groups, it can also accommodate a rolling group format. Progression through the programme is based on the achievement of specific goals and tasks, and progress is judged using structured observations (See OABs and ORBs above; Wong and Gordon 2013). For example, the incidence of OAB and ORB can be used as indicator of the extent of treatment progress. The gradual replacement of the 'bad' (OABs) by the 'good' behaviours (ORBs) should be a valid and objective indication of violence reduction related treatment improvements. The OABs and ORBs are the 'raw' data that can be used in conjunction with other observations to rate VRS item stages of change discussed earlier.

The RPC environment that housed the ABC programme was also somewhat different from that in the New Zealand prison units. The RPC, which was an accredited psychiatric hospital within the Correctional Services of Canada when the ABC programme was developed, was staffed with a range of mental-health and correctional professionals – psychologists, psychiatrists, and nurses as well as parole and correctional officers – a sort of hybrid hospital-prison environment. The proper functioning of the ABC, which was but one programme within the RPC, required the collaboration of the mental health and the correctional multidisciplinary team. The overall regime, inevitably, had both mental-health and correctional features. Group treatment sessions were conceptualized as occurring in a residential environment that provided natural opportunities both for participants to try out new behaviour and practise new skills, but also for staff to interact with residents in a change-supportive manner: modelling pro-social behaviour, and using contingent reinforcement and (less often) punishment to influence prisoners.

---

[2] The VRP is a modified version of the ABC programme, which, due to a changing client profile, is no longer being offered. Seriously mentally disordered or learning-disabled offenders, rather than violence prone offenders, have now been given priority for treatment at the RPC.

A substantial number of offenders with aboriginal background are in the ABC programme. Consistent with the Responsivity principle, some components in the ABC catered specifically to aboriginal offenders, such as the sweat lodge and the pipe ceremonies carried out during the programme. However, both aboriginal and non-aboriginal offenders participated in the same overall ABC programme described above. Prior to release to the community, contacts with community support, both aboriginal and non-aboriginal services, were re-established to the extent possible.

By contrast, the prison units that house the HRSTU programmes, although dedicated for that use, still are in many other respects like any other prison unit. In the early years, other than the formal group treatment programme at the Rimutaka unit, which occupied prisoners for two-to- three hours per day, there were few of the usual additional recreational and employment activities that are otherwise needed to structure a pro-social day, because the unit was too small to justify the additional infrastructure. Only in the last five years or so have these programmes moved to a hybrid model, where the unit regime itself is treated as a *community of change*: a limited version of a therapeutic community. As with the ABC programme, the treatment environment thus represents an extension of group sessions, with an emphasis on 'walking the walk' (practising newly learned skills), belonging to a community and supporting one another, collective decision-making, and commemoration of important moments in community life, such as a new group starting the programme. However, aside from the pairs of therapists or facilitators who run each group, and one or two additional psychological staff, the HRSTUs are mainly staffed with regular prison officers running a routine custodial regime.

Another strength of the HRSTUs is the approach to working with mainly Māori participants. No claim could be made that the treatment programme is based on an indigenous model but, wherever possible within the broader social learning framework adapted from Western psychology, traditional Māori principles and practices are incorporated into unit life, and examples of stories, proverbs and concepts from Te Ao Māori (the Māori world) are woven through the programme itself. In the reintegration phase of the programme, it is not uncommon for whānau hui (extended family gatherings) to be organized by treatment staff in conjunction with the prisoner, for the purpose of repairing and restoring family relationships damaged by years of crime and imprisonment, and enlisting help with the process of preparing for release.

Do these Programmes Work?

Given that these programmes were developed independently of each other, their similarities are notable. They are also unusual in sharing a body of empirical research about their effects, and about the client group with which they work.

Outcome evaluations: A broad-spectrum approach

Most outcome evaluations are undertaken to answer the general question of whether a programme works in reducing recidivism. These evaluations yield evidence that is essential to correctional administrators and policy-makers, and, to a limited extent, to programme designers. For the latter, such evaluations do not pin-point what needs changing to make a failed programme work, or how to make a working programme work better. Given the low likelihood that a randomized control trial for a programme for high-risk violence-prone offenders will gain approval, it is not surprising that the best evaluations of these two programmes are quasi-experimental in design. Several different methods have been used to create comparison groups that are as equivalent as possible; the design of each evaluation is discussed below, along with the results and any limitations in the methodology.

VRP/ABC outcome research

Because the VRP is newer, outcome research is mainly based on the ABC programme; results would be expected to generalize to the VRP given the overall similarity of the two programmes and target populations. A 2005 evaluation was undertaken with 31 offenders residing in a super-maximum-security prison because they had committed very serious offences (e.g. murders and hostage taking) whilst incarcerated and then were transferred to the super-maximum prison. They participated in the ABC Programme, with the aim of reintegrating them to a lower security prison post-treatment. More than four-fifths of the offenders qualified for a transfer to a low-security facility and remained there over a 20-month follow-up period. They also showed lower institutional offence rates post-reintegration compared to pre-reintegration (Wong et al. 2005). Although by methodological standards, this would be regarded as a low-quality design, given the absence of a comparison group, it does illustrate an important and often overlooked application of treatment to achieve valuable goals *inside* a custodial institution. Reductions in antisocial behaviour such as those reported here represent significant changes for these super maximum-security participants, make the post-treatment institutional environment potentially safer for custodial staff, save considerable money in reduced security costs, and render participants eligible for a wider range of programmes available to general population offenders.

In both Canada and New Zealand, adult criminal gang members comprise a significant proportion of the treatment population, and bring with them substantial additional treatment responsivity challenges. Di Placido et al. (2006) examined the effects of treatment on recidivism for 40 identified gang members from 28 gangs, most of whom completed the ABC programme. They were case-matched with a sample of gang members who also entered the RPC, but did not start or did not complete treatment for various reasons (e.g. noncompliance, voluntary withdrawal, admitted only for assessment for parole board appearance). Community recidivism rates over 24 months for the two samples were compared. Members of each sample were on average about 24 years of age – rather younger than the average in other RPC samples (e.g. Lewis et al. 2013) – with about 20 criminal convictions pre-treatment. Their criminal history and recidivism risk were comparable (based on the General Statistical Information on Recidivism tool; Bonta et al. 1996, as cited in Di Placido et al. 2006) and they were serving six-year sentences on average. After being in treatment for about eight months, the treated gang sample had a significantly lower incidence of court-adjudicated violent and non-violent convictions, significantly fewer major institutional misconducts and, if they had recidivated violently, committed significantly less serious violent offences than the matched gang comparisons (Di Placido et al. 2006).

A second study extended findings regarding the gang members' responses to treatment by assessing its impact on institutional security placements, segregation time, and institutional misconducts. This time, 68 gang-member treatment completers were matched on key demographic and criminological characteristics with 56 gang members who had received significantly less treatment because they were treatment dropouts or were required to leave the programme prior to treatment completion. Members of both groups had extensive criminal, violent, and incarceration histories with no significant difference between groups. Almost 90% of both groups were also diagnosed with substance-use disorder and about 75% with Antisocial Personality Disorder (DSM-IV; American Psychiatric Association 1994). Month-by-month security classification data during the three-year pre-treatment and similarly during the three-year post-treatment were compared between the treated and comparison groups. There was no difference between the two groups during the three pre-treatment years, but the treatment group received a significantly lower security classification in two of the three post-treatment years than the comparison group. A very similar pattern of results was obtained when time in segregation for institutional misconduct was used as the outcome variable (Brulotte et al. 2011).

The results of these studies are noteworthy as few studies have examined gang members' responses to treatment. However, the methods used to construct the comparison group can be problematic, because treatment dropouts are often found to have more behavioural concerns including higher rates of recidivism compared to treatment completers, thus creating the impression of a treatment effect where there is none (Lösel 2001). However, the fact that there was no difference in the outcome variables (security classifications and segregation time) between the two groups in the three pre-treatment years suggested that they were comparable in the outcome measures. The group difference post-treatment, therefore, were more likely attributable to treatment effects.

New Zealand HRSTU outcome research

The HRSTU programmes in New Zealand have a series of outcome evaluations that support their effectiveness with several different recidivism measures. The first had a relatively weak design conducted with treatment completers from the first of these units, which opened in 1998: the VPU at Rimutaka prison. The first 22 completers were compared with a convenience sample of untreated offenders who were statistically equivalent in offence history but differed in ethnicity. Over more than two years of follow-up, programme cases had half the reconviction rate for violence of comparison men (32% cf. 63%), but there were no significant differences for non-violent reconviction or reimprisonment (Polaschek et al. 2005). Pertinently, at this time, the programme was intended to target specifically violent crime.

A later evaluation (Polaschek 2011) used a more robust design in that non-completers were also included. Each programme starter was individually matched on several risk-related variables to an untreated comparison prior to investigating recidivism rates. During the intervening period the programme had developed a wider focus on reducing criminal propensity per se, rather than just violence risk, and had increased the criminal risk level required for entry, from a minimum 40% likelihood of returning to prison in the next five years, to at least a 70% likelihood. Over a mean of 3.5 years of follow-up, a significant difference was found for any new conviction (i.e. all types), for high-risk treatment completers compared to their matched untreated comparisons (83% vs. 95%; $\varphi = 0.19$, $p = 0.04$), with no corresponding increase in negative outcomes for non-completers compared to *their* matches (93% vs. 89%). High-risk completers also had a lower rate of violent reconviction, but it was nonsignificant (62% vs. 72%; $\varphi = 0.11$). There were no significant effects for medium-risk cases.

Since that time, the three newer units have opened, and there has been steady progress in the development of the model, with the introduction of the *community of change*, and more recently, a more rigorous integrity monitoring process. The Department of Corrections routinely monitors the outcomes of these programmes as part of annual reporting to the New Zealand Government,[3] and the results demonstrate a treatment effect, even though increasingly the comparison men also have had some form of intervention. The most recent academically peer-reviewed evaluation of these programmes was conducted as part of the New Zealand Parole Project (see below). It compared 121 treatment completers and 154 men who had not attended the programme (but 70% of whom had undertaken some other form of programme) who were paroled between 2010 and 2013. On four recidivism outcomes over the first 12 months following release – breach of parole, reconviction (excluding parole breaches), reconviction for violence, and reconviction leading to reimprisonment – treated men were less likely to be convicted. Effect sizes (φ) for these differences ranged between 0.15 and 0.21 and all were statistically significant (Polaschek et al. 2016).

How Does Treatment Work?

Few programmes for violent offenders can show that they 'work' in terms of reduced likelihood of recidivism, and prison misconducts and reduced security levels for example. Such results are important for myriad material decisions (e.g. resource allocation, parole release). But for theorists, programme providers, and those who need to identify which participants have responded to programme involvement, asking *how* treatment works is a much more interesting and relevant question.

Research from the *ABC* programme provides one type of answer. A sample of 150 male mostly high-risk violent offenders with significant psychopathic traits (mean VRS score = 60, which is approximately 1 *sd* above the normative sample mean, or more; mean PCL-R = 26, with 64% scoring greater than 25) was treated in the programme for about eight months. Participants were released and followed up for approximately five years in the community. Changes in *VRS* dynamic factor scores – indicating reduced risk for violence at the end of treatment – were linked to reduction in the likelihood of violent recidivism in the community (Lewis et al. 2012; Olver et al. 2013). Such changes were still evident after controlling for psychopathy, initial recidivism risk, ethnicity, or time spent in custody after programme completion and before release.

Analyses using the New Zealand Parole Project dataset have been addressing this question in a slightly different way: by investigating how treatment completers differ from men who did not undertake the programme on indices measured *after* treatment completion. For example, men who have completed the HRSTU programmes are paroled earlier in their sentence, and leave prison with significantly lower VRS scores, and higher engagement in change on VRS dynamic risk factors, better release plans, and a greater commitment to desistance. Two months after release their parole officers have built better relationships with them, rate them as having lower dynamic risk and higher-protective factors in the community, and evaluate their lifestyles as being of higher quality. All of these variables predict the lower recidivism of the HRSTU-treated men (reported above in Polaschek 2015; Polaschek and Yesberg 2015; Polaschek et al. 2016, 2018).

---

[3] See http://www.corrections.govt.nz/__data/assets/pdf_file/0007/811546/Annual_Report_2014-15_full_report.pdf p. 41 for the most recent recidivism outcome statistics.

Treating Violent Offenders with Psychopathy

High PCL-psychopathy scores are the norm in high-risk violent offender programmes; for example, Psychopathy Checklist: Screening Version (Hart et al. 1995) data from the Rimutaka HRSTU yielded mean scores of 19.5 (Polaschek and Ross 2010), which is above the recommended diagnostic cut-off of 18 for a diagnosis of psychopathy.

Consequently, research on the effectiveness of treatment programmes for high-risk violent offenders provides some of the best current evidence that people with psychopathy are treatable (Polaschek and Daly 2013); that is, they *can* show lower levels of recidivism after treatment, and those reductions *can* be mediated by changes in treatment on dynamic risk factors. But, with such a small research literature, and some nonsignificant or even negative results (Rice et al. 1992), replication should be a high priority.

For example, Wong and colleagues reported an evaluation of the treatment efficacy of a sample of high Psychopathy Checklist-Revised (PCL-R) offenders ($n = 32$) who participated in the ABC programme for about nine months in comparison with matched untreated controls ($n = 32$; Wong et al. 2012). The inclusion criteria of psychopathy was assessed using a cut-off score of 25 on the PCL-R (Hare 2003) and the matching was done using a computerized algorithm from a pool of 270 former Correctional Services of Canada research participants; they were matched on race, age, criminal history, VRS as well as PCL-R total, F1, and F2 scores as closely as possible (with no significant difference between groups), and followed up in the community for a mean of 7.4 years for each sample. All were high-risk, violence-prone offenders with significant psychopathic traits (mean PCL-R scores of 28.6 and 28.0 for the treated and comparison groups, respectively). On follow-up, the treated and matched groups were statistically equivalent on the number of violent, and non-violent reconvictions and new sentencing dates and time to first reconviction: although there was a trend towards better performance for the treated compared to the matched group. However, compared to the untreated group, the treated group had significantly shorter aggregated sentences (the summed length of all sentences accrued was 27.7 vs. 56.4 months, respectively, $p < 0.05$). Sentence length in Canada has been shown to be a reasonable proxy for the level of violence or severity of offending (see Di Placido et al. 2006). So treatment appeared to be associated with a harm-reduction effect, based on this index. Whilst it should be noted that this was the only result that was significant of 11 comparisons, it is likely that the treatment length of nine months was inadequate to produce optimal outcomes for participants who were both very high risk and suffering from a serious psychopathic disorder. The small sample size also reduced statistical power, making it more difficult to detect significant group differences.[4]

The authors contend that risk-reduction programmes such as the VRP can reduce violent recidivism, even amongst particularly high-risk and personality disordered/psychopathic individuals. This view is consistent with more recent appraisals of treatment for people with high levels of psychopathy (Polaschek 2014), and with treatment outcome evaluations with high-psychopathy samples that match on criminal risk rather than psychopathy (e.g. Polaschek 2011). In relation to the same programme (the Rimutaka HRSTU), no significant differences in PCL scores were found between those who completed and those who did not complete the programme (Polaschek 2010), and PCL:SV scores did not predict the strength of the therapeutic alliance.

---

[4] Or, in terms of *the New Statistics* (Cumming 2012), a number of small- to medium-effect sizes were found, but with correspondingly wide confidence intervals, indicating imprecise estimations.

Polaschek and Ross (2010) also found that the amount of change made during treatment on the VRS was not related to PCL:SV scores, and PCL:SV scores did not predict recidivism for violence (Polaschek 2008). However, contrary results have been found with ABC programme completers; men with higher PCL-R scores showed less change on the VRS, and were more likely to be reconvicted for violence. The affective facet score of the PCL-R – from the subscale that contains items associated with emotional superficiality, glibness, detachment, and lack of remorse – also predicted less change on the VRS, and both violent and any reconviction after treatment (Olver et al. 2013).

Building on earlier work on how to approach the treatment of psychopathic offenders (Wong and Hare 2005) together with more recent research and conceptual advances on psychopathy, correctional treatment and risk assessment, Wong (2013) and colleagues proposed a two-component model to guide risk-reduction treatment of psychopathy (Wong et al. 2012). Briefly, PCL-R Factor 1 characteristics are conceptualized as driving treatment-disrupting behaviour (the Responsivity aspect of RNR) whilst Factor 2 characteristics are viewed as the relevant targets for treatment to reducing violence risk (the Need aspect of RNR). Although the PCL-R is primarily a static index of risk, there is evidence to suggest that dynamic risk factors for violence that can be operationalized by tools such as the VRS are essentially proxies of Factor 2 features (Wong et al. 2012). Treatment is theorized to be most likely to succeed if Factor 1-related treatment disruptive behaviours are appropriately managed during treatment delivery whilst proxies of Factor 2 features conceptualized as dynamic risk factors are targeted for treatment to realize changes that could result in risk reduction.

To conclude, high psychopathy scores have been used to identify clients with challenging and disruptive behaviours during treatment. But people at high risk of violence also present as challenging participants routinely and, to date, there is little evidence that psychopathy represents any special kind of barrier to the treatment of high-risk violent offenders that is aimed at reducing criminal risk if treatment providers are sufficiently skilled in managing the treatment disruptive behaviours evidenced by these clients.

Conclusions

The psychologically-informed treatment of violent offenders has progressed substantially since the days when brief anger-management interventions were first adapted for use in correctional environments (e.g. Novaco and Welsh 1989). Over the last 20 years or so, the development of actuarial risk assessment, and the accumulation of findings on effective interventions for offenders has led to multi-factorial and multi-modal group programmes for offenders who previously might have been considered untreatable, because of their high levels of needs and difficult, treatment-resistant characteristics. We can be fairly confident that our best treatments for these offenders can reduce reconvictions, but there is still much to learn about how they do so.

References

American Psychiatric Association (1994). *Diagnostic and Statistical Manual of Mental Disorders*, 4e. Washington DC: American Psychiatric Association.

Andrews, D.A., Bonta, J., and Wormith, J.S. (2004). *The Level of Service/Case Management Inventory (LS/CMI)*. Toronto, ON: Multi-Health Systems.

Arseneault, L., Moffitt, T.D., Caspi, A. et al. (2000). Metnal disorders and violence in a total birth cohort. *Archives of General Psychiatry* 57: 979–986.

Bennett, A.L. (2014). The Westgate service and related referral, assessment, and treatment processes. *International Journal of Offender Therapy and Comparative Criminology* 59: 1580–1604.

Bonta, J. and Andrews, D.A. (2016). *The Psychology of Criminal Conduct*, 6e. London, UK: Routledge.

Brulotte, J., Di Placido, C., Gu D. et al. (2011). Treatment can reduce security requirements for gang members. Unpublished manuscript.

Burns, T., Fazel, S., Fahy, T. et al. (2011). Dangerous severe personality disordered (DSPD) patients: characteristics and comparison with other high risk offenders. *International Journal of Forensic Mental Health* 10: 127–136.

Chambers, J.C., Ward, T., Eccleston, L., and Brown, M. (2009). The pathways model of assault: a qualitative analysis of the assault offender and offense. *Journal of Interpersonal Violence* 24: 1423–1449.

Coupland, R.B.A. (2015). An examination of dynamic risk, protective factors, and treatment-related change in violent offenders. Doctoral dissertation. University of Saskatchewan.

Cumming, G. (2012). *Understanding the New Statistics: Effect Sizes, Confidence Intervals, and Meta-Analysis*. New York, NY: Routledge.

de Vogel, V., de Ruiter, C., Bouman, Y., and de Vries Robbé, M. (2012). *SAPROF: Structured Assessment of Protective Factors for Violence Risk*, 2e. Utrecht, NL: Van der Hoeven Kliniek.

Di Placido, C., Simon, T.L., Witte, T.D. et al. (2006). Treatment of gang members can reduce recidivism and institutional misconduct. *Law and Human Behavior* 30: 93–114.

Dickson, S.R., Polaschek, D.L.L., and Casey, A.R. (2013). Can the quality of high-risk violent prisoners' release plans predict recidivism following intensive rehabilitation? A comparison with risk assessment instruments. *Psychology, Crime and Law* 19: 371–389.

Dickson, S.R., Polaschek, D.L.L. and Wilson, M.J. (2016). How do plans enhance desistance? Translating release plans into parole experiences for high risk parolees. Manuscript under review.

Douglas, K.S., Hart, S.D., Webster, C.D., and Belfrage, H. (2013). *HCR-20 V3: Assessing risk for violence—User guide*. Burnaby, BC: Mental Health, Law, and Policy Institute, Simon Fraser University.

Farrington, D.P. (2003). Key results from the first forty years of the Cambridge study in delinquent development. In: *Taking Stock of Delinquency: An Overview of Findings from Contemporary Longitudinal Studies* (eds. T.P. Thornberry and M.D. Krohn), 137–183. New York, NY: Kluwer/Plenum.

Farrington, D.P. (2007). Origins of violent behavior over the life span. In: *The Cambridge Handbook of Violent Behavior and Aggression* (eds. D.J. Flannery, A.T. Vazsonyi and I.D. Waldman), 19–48. Cambridge, UK: Cambridge University Press.

Gilbert, F. and Daffern, M. (2010). Intergrating contemporary aggression theory with violent offender treatment: how thoroughly do interventions target violent behavior. *Aggression and Violent Behavior* 15: 167–180.

Gordon, A., and Wong, S.C.P. (2009). The offence analogue and offence reduction behaviour rating guide. Unpublished user manual.

Gordon, A. and Wong, S.C.P. (2010). Offence analogue behaviours as indicators of criminogenic need and treatment progress in custodial settings. In: *Offence Paralleling Behaviour: A Case Formulation Approach to Offender Assessment and Intervention* (eds. M. Daffern, L. Jones and J. Shine), 171–183. Chichester, UK: Wiley.

Hare, R.D. (2003). *The Hare Psychopathy Checklist-Revised Technical Manual*, 2e. Toronto, ON: Multi-Health Systems.

Hart, S., Cox, D., and Hare, R. (1995). *Manual for the Psychopathy Checklist: Screening Version (PCL:SV)*. Toronto, ON: Multi-Health Systems.

Henry, B., Caspi, A., Moffitt, T.E., and Silva, P.A. (1996). Temperamental and familial predictors of violent and nonviolent criminal convictions: age 3 to age 18. *Developmental Psychology* 32: 614–623.

Kilgour, T.G. and Polaschek, D.L.L. (2012). *Breaking the Cycle of Crime: Special Treatment Unit Evaluation Report*. Wellington, NZ: Department of Corrections Psychological Services.

Kirkpatrick, J.T., Draycott, S., Freestone, M. et al. (2010). A descriptive evaluation of patients and prisoners assessed for dangerous and severe personality disorder. *The Journal of Forensic Psychiatry and Psychology* 21: 264–282.

Klepfisz, G., O'Brien, K., and Daffern, M. (2014). Violent offenders' within-treatment change in anger, criminal attitudes, and violence risk: associations with violent recidivism. *International Journal of Forensic Mental Health* 13: 348–362.

Lewis, K., Olver, M.E., and Wong, S.C.P. (2013). The violence risk scale: predictive validity and linking treatment changes with recidivism in a sample of high risk and personality disordered offenders. *Assessment* 20: 150–164.

Lösel, F. (2001). Evaluating the effectiveness of correctional programs: bridging the gap between research and practice. In: *Offender Rehabilitation in Practice* (eds. G.A. Bernfeld, D.P. Farrington and A.W. Leschied), 67–92. Chichester, UK: Wiley.

Moffitt, T.E. (1993). Adolescence-limited and life-course-persistent antisocial behavior: a developmental taxonomy. *Psychological Review* 100: 674–701.

Mooney, J.L. and Daffern, M. (2013). The offence analogue and offence reduction behaviour rating guide as a supplement to violence risk assessment in incarcerated offenders. *International Journal of Forensic Mental Health* 12: 255–264.

Novaco, R.W. and Welsh, W.N. (1989). Anger disturbances: cognitive mediation and clinical prescriptions. In: *Clinical Approaches to Violence* (eds. K. Howells and C.R. Hollin), 39–60. Chichester, UK: Wiley.

Olver, M.E., Lewis, K., and Wong, S.C.P. (2013). Risk reduction treatment of high risk psychopathic offenders: the relationship of psychopathy and treatment change to violent recidivism. *Personality Disorders: Theory, Research, and Treatment* 4: 160–167.

Polaschek, D.L.L. (2008). *Rimutaka Violence Prevention Unit Evaluation Report V: Interim/Progress Report on Prospective Evaluation*. Wellington, NZ: New Zealand Department of Corrections.

Polaschek, D.L.L. (2010). Treatment non-completion in high-risk violent offenders: looking beyond criminal risk and criminogenic needs. *Psychology, Crime & Law* 16: 525–540.

Polaschek, D.L.L. (2011). High-intensity rehabilitation for violent offenders in New Zealand: reconviction outcomes for high- and medium-risk prisoners. *Journal of Interpersonal Violence* 26: 664–682.

Polaschek, D.L.L. (2013). Psychological treatment of high-risk violent prisoners: Can parole research help us understand how it works? Invited Keynote Address at the 11th Annual Forensic Psychology Conference at the University of New South Wales in Sydney, Australia (29–30 October 2013).

Polaschek, D.L.L. (2014). Adult criminals with psychopathy: common beliefs about treatability and change have little empirical support. *Current Directions in Psychological Science* 23: 296–301.

Polaschek, D.L.L. (2015). Reintegration, rehabilitation, or both? Unpacking factors that contribute to community outcomes for high risk violent offenders. Paper presented at the Keynote address at the Third North American Corrections and Criminal Justice Psychology Conference in Ottawa, USA (4–6 June 2015).

Polaschek, D.L.L. (2017). Prevention of recidivism in violent and aggressive offenders. In: *The Wiley Handbook of Violence and Aggression* (ed. P. Sturmey), 183–205. Chichester, UK: Wiley.

Polaschek, D.L.L., Calvert, S.W., and Gannon, T.A. (2009). Linking violent thinking: implicit theory-based research with violent offenders. *Journal of Interpersonal Violence* 24: 75–96.

Polaschek, D.L.L. and Daly, T. (2013). Treatment and psychopathy in forensic settings. *Aggression & Violent Behavior* 18: 592–603.

Polaschek, D.L.L. and Kilgour, T.G. (2013). New Zealand's special treatment units: the development and implementation of intensive treatment for high-risk male prisoners. *Psychology, Crime & Law* 11: 511–526.

Polaschek, D.L.L. and Ross, E.C. (2010). Do early therapeutic alliance, motivation, and change readiness predict therapy outcomes for high risk violent prisoners? *Criminal Behaviour and Mental Health* 20: 100–111.

Polaschek, D.L.L., Wilson, N.J., Townsend, M., and Daly, L. (2005). Cognitive-behavioral rehabilitation for high-risk violent offenders: an outcome evaluation of the violence prevention unit. *Journal of Interpersonal Violence* 20: 1611–1627.

Polaschek, D.L.L. and Yesberg, J.A. (2015). Desistance in high-risk prisoners: pre-release self-reported desistance commitment and perceptions of change predict 12-month survival. *Practice: The New Zealand Corrections Journal* 3 (1): 24–29.

Polaschek, D.L.L., Yesberg, J.A., Bell, R.K. et al. (2016). Intensive psychological treatment of high-risk violent offenders: outcomes and pre-release mechanisms. *Psychology, Crime & Law* 22: 344–365.

Polaschek, D.L.L., Yesberg, J.A., and Chauhan, P. (2018). A year without a conviction: an integrated examination of potential mechanisms for successful re-entry in high-risk violent prisoners. *Criminal Justice and Behavior* 45: 425–446.

Rice, M.E., Harris, G.T., and Cormier, C.A. (1992). An evaluation of a maximum security therapeutic community for psychopaths and other mentally disordered offenders. *Law and Human Behavior* 16: 399–412.

Saradjian, J., Murphy, N., and McVey, D. (2013). Delivering effective therapeutic interventions for men with severe personality disorder within a high secure prison. *Psychology, Crime & Law* 11: 433–477.

Tyrer, P., Duggan, C., Cooper, S. et al. (2010). The successes and failures of the DSPD experiment: the assessment and management of severe personality disorder. *Medicine, Science and Law* 50: 95–99.

Ware, J., Cieplucha, C., and Matsuo, D. (2011). The Violent Offenders Therapeutic Programme (VOTP)—rationale and effectiveness. *Australasian Journal of Correctional Staff Development* 6: 1–12.

Wong, S. and Gordon, A. (2006). The validity and reliability of the violence risk scale: a treatment-friendly violence risk assessment tool. *Psychology, Public Policy, and Law* 12: 279–309.

Wong, S. and Gordon, A. (2013). The violence reduction program: a treatment program for violence prone forensic clients. *Psychology, Crime & Law* 11: 461–475.

Wong, S., Gordon, A., and Gu, D. (2007). Assessment and treatment of violence-prone forensic clients: an integrated approach. *British Journal of Psychiatry* 190 (suppl. 49): s66–s74.

Wong, S.C.P. (2013). Treatment of psychopathy in correctional settings. In: *Textbook on Correctional Psychiatry* (eds. O. Thienhaus and M. Piasecki), 6-1–6-26. New York, NY: Civic Research Press.

Wong, S.C.P., Gordon, A., Gu, D. et al. (2012). The effectiveness of violence reduction treatment for psychopathic offenders: empirical evidence and a treatment model. *International Journal of Forensic Mental Health* 11: 336–349.

Wong, S.C.P. and Hare, R.D. (2005). *Guidelines for a Psychopathy Treatment Program*. Toronto, ON: Multi-Health Systems.

Wong, S.C.P., Van der Veen, S., Leis, T. et al. (2005). Reintegrating seriously violent and personality disordered offenders from a super- maximum security institution into the general offender population. *International Journal of Offender Therapy and Comparative Criminology* 49: 362–375.

Yalom, I.D. (2005). *The Theory and Practice of Group Psychotherapy*. New York, NY: Basic Books.

19

Anger Treatment with Violent Offenders

Raymond W. Novaco
University of California, Irvine, USA

Introduction

Asserting that therapeutic interventions for anger have efficacy for reducing the violent behaviour of criminal offenders is a proposition that has been met with scepticism. Anger treatment, conducted as a cognitive-behavioural therapy (CBT), has well-demonstrated effectiveness in reducing anger (curiously, it has been a captivating topic having 11 meta-analyses), but there has been some controversy about whether that efficacy extends to violence and to offender populations. Indeed, most anger-intervention studies have simply not included measures of physical aggression, much less violent re-offending. Since physical aggression is a prime criterion for offender populations and since 'anger management' has often been promoted as an intervention strategy for offenders in both institutional and community settings, it behoves us to be grounded in understanding the rationale, utility, and efficacy for anger treatment as a psychotherapeutic remedy for offenders' violent behaviour.

The impetus for anger management as an intervention for violent offenders has many pathways. Violence is an ever-present social reality, conspicuous in trans-national conflicts and terrorism (see Chapter 14), as well as criminal behaviour. It is an international public health problem, reflected in the World Health Organization's extensive attention to violence in intimate partner relationships (e.g. Garcia-Moreno et al. 2015), and other epidemiological research, such as the Wolf et al. (2014) study of ecological variables associated with violence in 169 countries. A United States Center for Disease Control study that examined violence as a public health problem (Corso et al. 2007) reported that the costs associated with non-fatal injuries and deaths due to violence in the year 2000 were more than $70 billion. In the UK, the total economic and social costs of violence in 2008/09 were estimated to be £29.9 billion (Bellis et al. 2012). Soares (2006) estimated the welfare costs of violence across 73 countries and put the yearly cost in Latin America to be 5.7% of GDP.

The Wiley Handbook of What Works in Violence Risk Management: Theory, Research and Practice,
First Edition. Edited by J. Stephen Wormith, Leam A. Craig, and Todd E. Hogue.
© 2020 John Wiley & Sons Ltd. Published 2020 by John Wiley & Sons Ltd.

Harm-doing behaviour draws the attention of societal gatekeepers, and anger's symbolic, intuitive, and empirical association with violence, 'madness', and psychopathology (Novaco 2010) pulls for its relevance. Our humanistic spirit and scientific aspirations implore us to attenuate violence (see Chapter 1), and that ambition easily reaches for anger control. Beyond its violence-engendering role, anger adversely affects prudent thought, core relationships, work performance, and physical health. Hence, community caretakers, social scientists, and clinical professionals seek remedies for anger dysregulation with an eye towards violence reduction.

To be sure, violence is complexly determined, entailing biological, sociocultural, economic, and political causation, and anger is neither a necessary or sufficient condition for it. Contemporary attention to the genetic origins of violence and its neurobiological correlates often seem to ignore the elementary point that the dynamics of violent behaviour inevitably entail multifactorial interplay. For example, the contribution of genetic polymorphisms seems to be unevenly established and relatively weak (Iofrida et al. 2014; Vassos et al. 2014). The genetic risk for violence involves interactive processes with environmental stress or adversity (Ferguson and Beaver 2009). Despite the monoamine oxidase A gene (MAOA) being tagged as a 'warrior gene' having significance for aggression in laboratory studies (e.g. the 'hot sauce' study by McDermott et al. 2009), for life aggressive behaviour, such as intimate partner violence, MAOA, and serotonin transporter gene polymorphisms account for only a small proportion of variance in physical aggression perpetration (Stuart et al. 2014). In contrast, anger is strongly associated with intimate partner violence, as shown in meta-analyses (Birkley and Eckhardt 2015; Norlander and Eckhardt 2005), and anger has been found to mediate the relationship between combat-related post-traumatic stress disorder (PTSD) and partner abuse (Taft et al. 2007), as well as community violence (Novaco and Chemtob 2015). Whether one seeks to ascertain the consequences of violence exposure, such as childhood maltreatment or combat trauma, or understand the activation of violent behaviour, be it 'road rage' eruptions, bar fights, domestic violence assaults, or vengeful retaliation episodes, anger is conspicuously a core factor. Importantly, it is a viable treatment target.

Therapeutic interventions for anger have taken various forms, but whether 'anger management' has programmatic merit for violent offenders is an issue that has had some detractors. Novaco (2013), in addressing the 'What Works' agenda, cast the criticisms as threefold: (i) anger being deemed 'irrelevant' for violent behaviour; (ii) anger management being thought to be too 'weak' for reducing violent offending; and (iii) anger management not 'reaching' the psychological needs of clients. The first of these challenges has been put forth by critics who have not taken on board the 'neither necessary nor sufficient' premise regarding the anger-aggression relationship (long fundamental to anger-control psychotherapy), or who have relied on studies with poor anger assessment methodologies, or who have insufficient knowledge of research that has substantiated anger as a causally-relevant antecedent of violent behaviour.

The second criticism, which concerns anger management interventions being too weak, is indeed an important one, springing from studies done in prison systems in Australia by very proficient anger researchers (e.g. Heseltine et al. 2010; Howells et al. 2005). Both this 'weak' intervention criticism and the 'does not reach the needs' criticism have similar underpinnings. What one reaches is dependent on how far and how long one stretches, and many anger interventions have been insufficiently intensive. A major shortcoming of prison-based anger management programmes is that they are typically delivered at the psycho-educational level. In some studies, the participants have not had sufficiently high anger scores and should not have been included for an anger intervention. However, in the studies by Howells and his colleagues, *high-anger* prisoners in the treatment condition, whilst not found to have lowered anger or aggression, did improve in social functioning, clinical problem level, and self-harm risk. Serious anger problems, however, appear as a multi-layered clinical condition (Howells and Day 2003) and require more treatment time than brief anger-management programmes provide. Anger treatment, in its original and ongoing framing, is intended to be an adjunctive therapy, not a substitute for psychotherapy for complex problems.

To further serve the discussion of 'what works' in the management of violence risk, this chapter will provide an overview of studies regarding anger as a risk factor for violence in offender populations and regarding psychotherapeutic interventions for anger conducted with violent offenders, both adults and adolescents. In addition, attention will be drawn to variation in modes of anger-treatment delivery, including protocol specification and a case-formulated orientation, and to the importance of anger/aggression assessment methodology.

Anger as a Relevant Violence Risk Factor

Anger impels aggressive behaviour, yet it is neither necessary nor sufficient. Anger's aggression activation occurs particularly when its intensity overrides regulatory control mechanisms, which may be otherwise attenuated by factors such as substance use. This overall conception has been generally accepted amongst aggression scholars since Bandura (1973), and Konecni (1975) put forward an anger-aggression bi-directional causality model. As an approach motivation system affect (Carver and Harmon-Jones 2009), anger is inherently a disposition to respond aggressively, but aggression is not an automatic consequence of anger, as it is regulated by inhibitory control mechanisms that are engaged by internal and external cues (Anderson and Bushman 2002; Bandura 1973). Physical constraints, expectations of punishment or retaliation, empathy, consideration of consequences, and pro-social values operate as regulatory controls on aggressive behaviour. The experience of anger creates a readiness to respond with aggression, but that disposition may be otherwise directed, suppressed, or reconstituted. Dysregulated anger – when anger's activation, its expression, and its ongoing experience occur without appropriate controls – is strongly associated with most forms of violence.

Anger and violence amongst forensic psychiatric patients

The problem of violence in psychiatric hospitals was brought to the fore by Fottrell (1980) in a study at three British hospitals, as 10% of the patients had been violent, but that finding was eclipsed by Larkin et al. (1988) at a large British Special Hospital (forensic), where 36.6% of the patients were assaultive in a six-month interval. Anger was slow to get attention as a predictor of violence in the forensic hospital context. Novaco and Renwick (1998) found anger to be predictive of patient assaults over an 18-month period at Scotland's high security forensic hospital. Studies with multiple control variables show anger to be related to violent behaviour by psychiatric patients in forensic hospitals during and after hospitalization (Doyle and Dolan 2006a, b; Linaker and Busch-Iversen 1995; McDermott et al. 2008; Moeller et al. 2016; Novaco and Taylor 2004) and by Wang and Diamond (1999) amongst offenders receiving inpatient psychiatric treatment at an adult male psychiatric prison hospital. That body of research on anger as a violent behaviour predictor is accompanied by studies with non-forensic psychiatric patients on their post-discharge violent behaviour, as predicted by anger (e.g. Sadeh and McNeil 2013; Skeem et al. 2006; Swogger et al. 2012, Ullrich et al. 2014). The violent behaviour of long-term psychiatric patients residing in non-hospital facilities was also found to be predicted by anger in a prospective study by Bulgari et al. (2017). In addition, studies with military populations that have examined violent behaviour or risk of violence in the context of combat-PTSD, and which have controlled for numerous background and psychological distress factors, including depression and PTSD, have found anger to contribute to the largest proportion of variance in the violence criteria (Novaco and Chemtob 2015; Novaco et al. 2012).

Anger and violence by incarcerated offenders

The argument that anger is not relevant to the violent behaviour of offenders is predicated on studies such as that of Loza and Loza-Fanous (1999) and of Mills and Kroner (1999), both of which were conducted in Canadian prisons – neither study found anger to be predictive of 'violence', but the average anger scores in both studies was low, compared to other studies using the same measures – the Spielberger State-Trait Anger Expression Scale (STAXI, Spielberger 1996) and the Novaco Anger Scale (NAS, Novaco 2003). Indeed in the Loza and Loza-Fanous (1999) study, their State Anger Means (10.8–12.4) approached the lowest possible score (10) for that STAXI subscale (thus suggesting a response validity problem), and their violence criterion was a recidivism risk rating. Yet, the viability and validity of doing anger assessment with prison populations has been well demonstrated in many studies (e.g. Baker et al. 2008; Lindqvist et al. 2005; Sutter et al. 2002), including with Canadian prisoners (Ford 1991; Mills et al. 1998).

A meta-analytic review by Chereji et al. (2012) of nine studies concerning violence amongst offender populations that had an anger assessment component found a large-effect size (Cohen's $d = 0.86$) for anger. They concluded that 'anger has a significant predictive role in eliciting violent offences' (p. 71), but that is a stretch as the 'violence' index in some studies was self-report and the 'prediction' was not always prospective/longitudinal. However, the review by Chereji et al. (2012) missed a number of proper studies on anger and violence with adult and adolescent incarcerated offenders. Regarding juveniles' offending in institutions, there are robust studies on anger as a prospective predictor of violence. Butler et al. (2007) found that an anger screen predicted severe rule violations and intensive supervision placement for aggressive behaviours. DeLisi et al. (2010), in a large study with 813 California Youth Authority wards, found that anger on intake was significantly related to assaults on staff, assaults on youth wards, and other aggressive misconduct, controlling for 14 background and mental health variables. Cornell et al. (1999), using two anger instruments, found convergence in their predicting institutional physical aggression. Similarly, Kimonis et al. (2011) found that anger was a robust predictor of lifetime and institutional violence amongst incarcerated juvenile offenders.

Regarding adult offenders, anger has been found to be a strong predictor of violence – e.g. meta-analyses on partner violence (Birkley and Eckhardt 2015; Norlander and Eckhardt 2005) and in the studies covered by Chereji et al. (2012) concerning other offender populations. In addition, a study with adult offenders on parole or probation in Melbourne by Roberton et al. (2015) found anger to be significantly related to life history of aggression, controlling for age and education. Mela et al. (2008), in research with 285 Canadian prison inmates, reported that reductions in anger were associated with reductions in institutional offending.

In summary, the proposition that anger is significantly related to the violent behaviour of criminal offenders and forensic hospital patients is anchored in a substantial amount of research, thus providing a robust rationale for anger treatment as a therapeutic remedy for violence.

Anger Therapeutic Interventions as Violence Remedies

A chronological narrative of illustrative studies with control groups on anger treatment with offenders was presented in Novaco (2013). There was then ample reason for optimism about psychotherapeutic interventions for anger – particularly CBT programmes – being efficacious in reducing anger for offenders, but evidence was thin with respect to aggressive behaviour outcomes. To be sure, some studies on anger management conducted in prisons had not shown anger reduction – e.g. research in Australia by Howells and his colleagues (Heseltine et al. 2010; Howells et al. 2005; Watt and Howells 1999) – but there were numerous studies with offenders that produced anger treatment gains. A central problem, however, was (and remains) that most anger intervention studies, including those with non-offender populations, simply do not incorporate measures of physical aggression, much less violent re-offending. There are now additional anger treatment studies with offenders, as well as some with adolescents not covered in Novaco (2013), to boost the optimistic outlook.

Treatment for anger is predicated on engagement by the client. Facilitating client 'readiness' is challenged by client background adversities, multifaceted comorbidities, and resource limitations in treatment facilities, as Howells and Day (2003) smartly formulated. Nevertheless, evidence for anger treatment efficacy in reducing anger is substantial. Eleven meta-analyses have been published, involving numerous clinical populations (for offenders, Henwood et al. 2015), which overall have found medium to strong effect sizes, thus indicating that approximately 75% of those receiving anger treatment improved compared to controls. It is generally agreed that CBT approaches have greatest efficacy, including for people with intellectual disabilities (IDs) (cf. meta-analysis by Nicoll et al. 2013), which is in accord with the Andrews et al. (1990) general and specific responsivity principles.

The offender-focused meta-analysis by Henwood et al. (2015) on CBT-informed anger management entailed controlled studies pertaining to reductions in recidivism amongst adult male offenders. Of the 11 studies in their review, five were conducted in prison settings, four in secure rehabilitation centres, and two in the community. They found, associated with treatment, an overall risk reduction of 23% for general recidivism and 28% for violent recidivism. When they examined treatment completion as a defining characteristic, the risk reduction for violent recidivism was 56%. However, it is a bit of a stretch for some of the included studies to have been tagged as 'anger management' interventions, when anger-focused treatment was only part of the overall intervention, such as in the New Zealand prison Violence Prevention Unit (VPU) studies – e.g. Polaschek et al. (2005) (see Chapter 19).

More broadly, however, it is reassuring that, when multifaceted offender programmes were reviewed in meta-analyses by Landenberger and Lipsey (2005) and by Dowden and Andrews (2000), reduced recidivism was associated with programmes having an anger control component. Landenberger and Lipsey's (2005) review covered 58 studies of CBT programmes on recidivism of adult and juvenile offenders, 20 of which incorporated anger control as a treatment element. After controlling for method variables, participant characteristics, quality of implementation, and CBT emphasis, their regression model found that having an anger control component in the intervention was significantly related to the effect size for reduced recidivism. Landenberger and Lipsey defined 'anger control' as 'training in techniques for identifying triggers and cues that arouse anger and maintaining self-control' (p. 466). Similarly, the meta-analysis by Dowden and Andrews (2000) of 35 primary studies of correctional treatment programmes had found those that targeted 'negative affect/anger' were positively and significantly associated with effect size in reducing violent recidivism.

To be sure, the incorporation of an anger control component into broader intervention programmes, such as Aggression Replacement Training (Goldstein et al. 1987) or the New Zealand VPU programme (e.g. Polaschek et al. 2005) is different from a focused anger therapeutic intervention that then receives focused evaluation of efficacy; yet the Landenberger and Lipsey and the Dowden and Andrews meta-analytic reviews certainly provide a boost for the value of delivering anger treatment to violent offenders. Similarly, Dialectical Behavior Therapy (DBT), which is a major form of CBT and has an anger control component, has been implemented in many studies for the treatment of anger and aggressive behaviour. A review by Frazier and Vela (2014) identified nine RCTs in that regard and concluded that DBT was a promising approach for reducing anger and aggression. One of those studies (Shelton et al. 2009) was conducted with male and female prisoners, and there were significant treatment gains in anger, in self-reported aggression, and also disciplinary infractions. Further, a meta-analysis of individually-oriented CBTs for severe aggressive behaviour amongst adolescents by Hoogsteder et al. (2015) identified six studies (which qualified if involving anger-management training, skills training, and cognitive restructuring) that, overall, showed a large effect size ($d = 1.14$). Other favourable anger treatment findings pertinent to offenders can be seen in the review by Gilchrist et al. (2015) regarding interventions for physical intimate partner violence by alcohol-abusing males. They identified four RCTs of CBT interventions that had anger management components, two of which found greater reductions in IPV perpetration for the treatment condition than for comparison interventions. Whilst evidence for anger treatment lowering physical aggression and recidivism is relatively sparse, these various meta-analyses on multifaceted offender programmes having an anger control component do provide a supportive empirical base.

Anger interventions with adolescent offenders

The vast major of research on anger treatment with offenders has been with adults, but there have been encouraging results with adolescent offenders. CBT interventions for anger in adolescence in general have demonstrated efficacy, as reflected in medium to strong effect sizes in the meta-analysis by Sukhodolsky et al. (2004) and a review by Cole (2008). A meta-analysis specific to adolescents with special educational needs by Ho et al. (2010) found a medium effect regarding anger dimensions, and a small to medium effect for aggressive behaviour. Regarding offenders, Feindler et al. (1986) did pioneering work with institutionalized adolescents; however, since then few studies have involved juvenile offenders and controlled trials. A 4-session anger management intervention by Snyder et al. (1999) reduced anger and antisocial behaviours in an RCT with adolescents in an inpatient psychiatric facility. Anger control CBT has also shown effectiveness in reducing anger and aggressive behaviour in a controlled study by Robinson et al. (2002) with adolescents having chronic behaviour problems and by Sukhodolsky et al. (2009) with behaviour problem adolescents affected by Tourette's Syndrome. Another form of CBT, Aggression Replacement Training – which has three components: anger control, social skills, and moral reasoning – has shown effectiveness in lowering anger and aggressive behaviour in controlled studies with juveniles by Kaya and Buzlu (2016) in a prison in Istanbul, and by Hornsveld et al. (2015) at an outpatient forensic clinic in Rotterdam.

Treatment modalities: Group-based programmes vs. An individual-based CBT

The platform from which anger treatment is delivered may be a crucial intervention dimension. Howells and Day and their colleagues (e.g. Heseltine et al. 2010; Howells et al. 2005; Watt and Howells 1999) generally found low efficacy for their anger management programmes, which were group-based interventions, largely delivered in prisons. They have highlighted anger problem complexity and insufficient intensity of treatment as potential sources of ineffectiveness and have found that anger declined when 'treatment readiness' was present. A recent anger management group intervention by McGonigal et al. (2018) implemented with prison inmates through a 12-week group programme was successful in reducing anger, but not aggressive behaviour incidents. The McGonigal et al. study was limited in its anger assessment methodology and also by not having a well-defined anger treatment protocol. In contrast to prison-based studies, a group-format 20-session anger management programme conducted at England's Broadmoor high-security hospital with 86 patients who had been referred for treatment over a 10-year period was found by Wilson et al. (2013) to produce significant reductions in anger on a number of subscales on a self-report 'Anger Assessment Profile' instrument and by the STAXI. Wilson and her colleagues also found that treatment completers, compared to non-completers, had significant reductions in physical aggression incidents and self-harm incidents at follow-up time points.

Regarding offenders in the community, Trimble et al. (2015) in a study with probationers in Northern Ireland examined outcomes of a nine-session anger management group programme, finding significant improvements in anger scores on various STAXI subscales, which was also associated with readiness for change. An individual-based anger management programme implement by Henwood et al. (2018) with offenders in the community in Malta, produced significant anger symptom reduction (assessed by one instrument with various subscales) at post-treatment and follow-up. Whilst these results from community-based studies are good, their anger assessment schemes were limited, and they did not measure aggression.

In contrast to most anger intervention programmes with offenders, Taylor and Novaco (2005) put forward an individually-based anger treatment that was conducted with male forensic hospital patients having IDs, but the therapeutic protocol has broad applicability across clinical populations. It is a modified 'stress inoculation' anger treatment (Novaco 1977), delivered twice-weekly for 18 sessions by qualified, chartered psychologists. The protocol (fully provided in Taylor and Novaco 2005) includes a preparatory/motivational phase for fostering treatment engagement and building basic skills, such as emotion awareness, self-monitoring, relaxation strategies and goal setting. It is a case-formulated CBT that targets attentional and cognitive appraisal processes, promotes arousal reduction capabilities, and enhances problem-solving and behavioural skills. The therapeutic approach builds the client's self-regulatory proficiencies. Our research approach has involved multiple modes of anger assessment, and the intervention work has been grounded in extensive anger and aggressive behaviour studies with the hospital population (e.g. Novaco and Taylor 2004, 2008; Taylor and Novaco 2013). In our initial treatment outcome study (Taylor et al. 2005) the anger treatment was compared to an anonymously assigned, matched waiting-list control condition where treatment-as-usual was received. Assessments on multiple anger self-report instruments (STAXI, NAS, and Provocation Inventory) and a staff-rated measure were obtained at screening, pre-treatment, post-treatment, and four-month follow-up. In mixed-model repeated measures analysis, significant differences in favour of the anger treatment were obtained on

NAS and PI measures, and marginal effects were obtained for STAXI measures. Staff-rated anger declined more strongly through follow-up in the treatment condition.

In that Taylor et al. (2005) study and other anger treatment studies that we conducted around that time, hospital assaultive behavioural measures were not incorporated, but more recently we found (Novaco and Taylor 2015), for a cohort of 50 patients, significant reductions in physical assaults, comparing the 12-month interval prior to anger treatment with the 12-months after treatment. The odds of a patient being physically assaultive declined significantly after anger treatment, being 2.57 times higher before treatment. Generalized estimating equations controlled for age, gender, IQ, length of stay, and violent offence history. Importantly, we found that those reductions in physical assaults were associated with reductions in anger and increases in anger regulation that occurred during the course of anger treatment, assessed by STAXI and NAS patient self-reported anger and by hospital staff rated anger. Further, we found (Taylor et al. 2016) that significant reductions in aggressive behaviour also occurred for verbal abuse, verbal threats to staff, and physical assaults to either staff or patients. However, we did not find a significant reduction in incidents involving property damage.

What is being highlighted here is that this anger intervention, implemented in a forensic hospital with patients having serious problems with anger and violent behaviour, is a protocol-driven CBT treatment that has been evaluated by an extensive anger/aggression methodology.

Implications and Conclusions

Acting-out harm-doing behaviour draws the attention of gatekeepers, but anger provides the driving force – the sources of which have complex origins, including a traumatic abuse history, which is well-known, but also IDs – e.g. anger and aggression were the predominant index problems for both male and female offenders in a cohort of 247 consecutive referrals in a 13-year interval to a community forensic service in Scotland (Lindsay et al. 2006) (see Taylor, Chapter 23). Violence in prisons is known to be commonplace, but it is also prevalent in hospitals. A review of violence towards nurses internationally found that 55% of nurses in psychiatric settings experienced physical assault, and 73% experienced verbal assault annually (Spector et al. 2014). Studies with 348 psychiatric staff at a large forensic hospital in California found that 70% experienced physical assault in the previous 12 months, and 45% felt 'unsafe' or 'very unsafe' at work (Kelly et al. 2015, 2016). Being assaulted by patients was associated with staff depression, controlling for background, personality, and conflict exposure variables. That the Taylor and Novaco anger intervention was associated with a 55.9% reduction in physical assaults carries significance for the welfare of both staff and patients, for the hospital's therapeutic milieu, and for hospital administration.

As noted at the outset, anger treatment is an adjunctive therapy. When someone's violent behaviour is a product of other major risk factors, such as alcohol or substance abuse (cf. Wolf et al. 2014), other interventions may need to have priority, and even the anger treatment may require adaptation (e.g. Walitzer et al. 2015; Zarshenas et al. 2017). An important area beckoning for development in the anger treatment domain for offenders is the interface of anger with imagined violence, as bearing on violent behaviour (Moeller et al. 2017) – forensic populations generally have an ample supply of personal memories of violence experiences with which to craft images of violence enactments.

A broad spectrum of CBT approaches to forensic populations appear in Tafrate and Mitchell (2014), whose book's scope includes schema-based therapies, CBT for criminal thought processes, motivational interviewing, and strength-based 'good-lives' approaches. Day and Vess (2013) provide an informative analysis and a rich set of suggestions for treating the anger problems of forensic clients. Beyond anger control, when the larger aim is to reduce violent offending, the chapters in Dvoskin et al. (2012), as well as the present volume, provide an elaborated account of the complexities, achievements, and prospects.

Anger is not only a dynamic risk factor for violence, it constitutes an important forensic mental health treatment need. High-anger patients often have traumatic histories, replete with abandonment and rejection, and with economic and psychological impoverishment. For them, anger becomes an entrenched mode of reactance to aversive experiences, and it can underpin inertia against therapy programmes. The cognitive-behavioural treatment of anger has been shown to have applicability to a wide range of client populations and clinical disorders. Prisoners and forensic hospitalized patients with long-standing aggression histories, mental disorder, and even IDs can be engaged in CBT-anger treatment and have been shown to benefit, with resultant reductions in violent behaviour. Thus, we are fortified in providing therapeutic remedies for anger dyscontrol when aiming to reduce violent behaviour.

References

Anderson, C.R. and Bushman, B.J. (2002). Human aggression. *Annual Review of Psychology* 53: 27–51.

Andrews, D.A., Bonta, J., and Hoge, R.D. (1990). Classification for effective rehabilitation: rediscovering psychology. *Criminal Justice and Behavior* 17: 19–52.

Baker, M.T., Van Hasselt, V.B., and Sellers, A.H. (2008). Validation of the Novaco Anger Scale in an incarcerated offender population. *Criminal Justice and Behavior* 35: 741–754.

Bandura, A. (1973). *Aggression: A Social Learning Analysis*. Englewood Cliffs, NJ: Prentice Hall.

Bellis, M.A., Hughes, K., Perkins, C., and Bennett, A. (2012). *Protecting People Promoting Health: A Public Health Approach to Violence Prevention for England*. Liverpool, UK: Centre for Public Health.

Birkley, E. and Eckhardt, C.I. (2015). Anger, hostility, internalizing negative emotions, and intimate partner violence perpetration: a meta-analytic review. *Clinical Psychology Review* 30: 40–56.

Bulgari, V., Iozzino, L., Ferrari, C. et al. (2017). Clinical and neuropsychological features of violence in schizophrenia: a prospective cohort study. *Schizophrenia Research* 181: 124–130.

Butler, M.A., Loney, B.R., and Kistner, J. (2007). The Massachusetts youth screening instrument as a predictor of institutional maladjustment in severe male juvenile offenders. *Criminal Justice and Behavior* 34 (4): 476–492.

Carver, C.S. and Harmon-Jones, E. (2009). Anger is an approach-related affect: evidence and implications. *Psychological Bulletin* 135: 183–204.

Chereji, S.V., Pintea, S., and David, D. (2012). The relationship of anger and cognitive distortions with violence in violent offenders' population: a meta-analytic review. *European Journal of Psychology Applied to Legal Context* 4: 59–77.

Cole, R.L. (2008). A systematic review of cognitive-behavioural interventions for adolescents with anger-related difficulties. *Educational and Child Psychology* 25: 27–47.

Cornell, D.G., Peterson, C.S., and Richards, H. (1999). Anger as a predictor of aggression among incarcerated adolescents. *Journal of Consulting and Clinical Psychology* 67: 108–115.

Corso, P.S., Mercy, J.A., Simon, T.R. et al. (2007). Medical costs and productivity losses due to interpersonal and self-directed violence in the United States. *American Journal of Preventive Medicine* 32 (6): 474–482.

Day, A. and Vess, J. (2013). Targeting anger in forensic populations. In: *Treatments for Anger in Specific Populations* (ed. E. Fernandez), 158–175. New York, NY: Oxford Press.

DeLisi, M., Caudill, J.W., Trulson, C.R. et al. (2010). Angry inmates are violent inmates: a Poisson regression approach to youthful offenders. *Journal of Forensic Psychology Practice* 10 (5): 419–439.

Dowden, C. and Andrews, D.A. (2000). Effective correction treatment and violent reoffending: a meta-analysis. *Canadian Journal of Criminology* 42: 449–467.

Doyle, M. and Dolan, M. (2006a). Predicting community violence from patients discharged from mental health services. *The British Journal of Psychiatry* 189: 520–526.

Doyle, M. and Dolan, M. (2006b). Evaluating the validity of anger regulation problems, interpersonal style, and disturbed mental state for predicting inpatient violence. *Behavioral Science & the Law* 24: 783–798.

Dvoskin, J., Skeem, J.L., Novaco, R.W., and Douglas, K.S. (2012). *Applying Social Science to Reduce Violent Offending*. New York, NY: Oxford University Press.

Feindler, E.L., Ecton, R.B., Kingsley, D., and Dubey, D.R. (1986). Group anger-control training for institutionalized psychiatric male adolescents. *Behavior Therapy* 17 (2): 109–123.

Ferguson, C.J. and Beaver, K.M. (2009). Natural born killers: the genetic origins of extreme violence. *Aggression and Violent Behavior* 14: 286–294.

Ford, D. (1991). Anger and irrational beliefs in violent inmates. *Personality and Individual Differences* 12: 211–215.

Fottrell, E. (1980). A study of violent behaviour among patients in psychiatric hospitals. *British Journal of Psychiatry* 136: 216–221.

Frazier, S.N. and Vela, J. (2014). Dialectical behavior therapy for the treatment of anger and aggressive behavior: a review. *Aggression and Violent Behavior* 19: 156–163.

Garcia-Moreno, C., Hegarty, K., D'Oliveira, A.F.L. et al. (2015). Violence against women and girls 2: the health-systems response to violence against women. *Lancet* 385: 1567–1579.

Gilchrist, G., Munoz, J.T., and Easton, C.J. (2015). Should we reconsider anger management when addressing physical intimate partner violence perpetration by alcohol abusing males? A systematic review. *Aggression and Violent Behavior* 25: 124–132.

Goldstein, A.P., Glick, B., Reiner, S. et al. (1987). *Aggression Replacement Training: A Comprehensive Intervention for Aggressive Youth*. Champaign, IL: Research Press.

Henwood, K.S., Browne, K.D., and Chou, S. (2018). A randomized controlled trial exploring the effects of brief anger management on community-based offenders in Malta. *International Journal of Offender Therapy and Comparative Criminology* 62: 785–805.

Henwood, K.S., Chou, S., and Browne, K.D. (2015). A systematic review and meta-analysis on the effectiveness of CBT informed anger management. *Aggression and Violent Behavior* 25: 280–292.

Heseltine, K., Howells, K., and Day, A. (2010). Brief anger interventions with offenders may be ineffective: a replication and extension. *Behaviour Research and Therapy* 48: 246–250.

Ho, B.P.V., Carter, M., and Stephenson, J. (2010). Anger management using a cognitive-behavioural approach for children with special education needs: a literature review and meta-analysis. *International Journal of Disability, Development and Education* 57: 245–265.

Hoogsteder, L.M., Stams, G.J.J.M., Figge, M.A. et al. (2015). A meta-analysis of the effectiveness of individually oriented cognitive behavioral treatment (CBT) for severe aggressive behavior in adolescents. *Journal of Forensic Psychiatry & Psychology* 26: 22–37.

Hornsveld, R.H.J., Kraaimaat, F.W., Muris, P. et al. (2015). Aggression replacement training for violent young men in a forensic psychiatric outpatient clinic. *Journal of Interpersonal Violence* 30: 3174–3191.

Howells, K. and Day, A. (2003). Readiness for anger management: clinical and theoretical issues. *Clinical Psychology Review* 23: 319–337.

Howells, K., Day, A., Williamson, P. et al. (2005). Brief anger management programs with offenders: outcomes and predictors of change. *Journal of Forensic Psychology & Psychology* 16: 296–311.

Iofrida, C., Palumbo, S., and Pelegrini, S. (2014). Molecular genetics and antisocial behavior: where do we stand? *Experimental Biology and Medicine* 239: 1514–1523.

Kaya, F. and Buzlu, S. (2016). Effects of aggression replacement training on problem-solving, anger and aggressive behaviour among adolescents with criminal attempts in Turkey: a quasi-experimental study. *Archives of Psychiatric Nursing* 30: 729–735.

Kelly, E., Fenwick, K., Brekke, J.S., and Novaco, R.W. (2016). Well-being and safety among inpatient psychiatric staff: the impact of conflict, assault, and stress reactivity. *Administration and Policy in Mental Health and Mental Health Services Research* 43: 703–716.

Kelly, E.L., Subica, A.M., Fulginiti, A. et al. (2015). A cross-sectional survey of factors related to inpatient assault of staff in a forensic psychiatric hospital. *Journal of Advanced Nursing* 71 (5): 1110–1122.

Kimonis, E.R., Ray, J.V., Branch, J.R., and Cauffman, E. (2011). Anger mediates the relation between violence exposure and violence perpetration in incarcerated boys. *Child & Youth Care Forum* 40: 381–400.

Konecni, V.J. (1975). The mediation of aggressive behavior: arousal level versus anger and cognitive labeling. *Journal of Personality and Social Psychology* 32: 706–712.

Landenberger, N.A. and Lipsey, M.W. (2005). The positive effects of cognitive-behavioral programs for offenders: a meta-analysis of factors associated with effective treatment. *Journal of Experimental Criminology* 1: 451–476.

Larkin, E.S., Murtagh, S., and Jones, S. (1988). A preliminary study of violent incidents in a special hospital (Rampton). *British Journal of Psychiatry* 153: 226–231.

Linaker, O.M. and Busch-Iversen, H. (1995). Predictors of imminent violence in psychiatric inpatients. *Acta Psychiatrica Scandinavia* 92: 250–254.

Lindqvist, J.K., Daderman, A.M., and Hellstrom, A. (2005). Internal reliability and construct validity of the Novaco Anger Scale-1998-S in a sample of violent prison inmates in Sweden. *Psychology, Crime & Law* 11: 223–237.

Lindsay, W.R., Steele, L., Smith, A.H.W. et al. (2006). A community forensic disability service: twelve year follow up of referrals, analysis of referral patterns and assessment of harm reduction. *Legal and Criminological Psychology* 11: 113–130.

Loza, W. and Loza-Fanous, A. (1999). Anger and prediction of violent and non-violent offenders' recidivism. *Journal of Interpersonal Violence* 14: 1014–1029.

McDermott, B.E., Quanbeck, C.D., Busse, D. et al. (2008). The accuracy of risk assessment instruments in the prediction of impulsive versus predatory aggression. *Behavioral Sciences & the Law* 26: 759–777.

McDermott, R., Tingley, D., Cowden, J. et al. (2009). Monoamine oxidase A gene (MAOA) predicts behavioral aggression following provocation. *Proceedings of the National Academy of Sciences of the United States of America* 106: 2118–2123.

McGonigal, P.T., Dixon-Gordon, K.L., Bernecker, S.L., and Constantino, M.J. (2018). An open trial of an anger management treatment in a correctional facility: preliminary effectiveness and predictors of response. *Journal of Forensic Psychiatry and Psychology* 29 (5): 774–781.

Mela, M., Balbuena, L., Duncan, C.R. et al. (2008). The STAXI as a measure of inmate anger and a predictor of institutional offending. *Journal of Forensic Psychiatry and Psychology* 19: 396–406.

Mills, J.M. and Kroner, D.G. (1999). Anger as a predictor of institutional misconduct and recidivism in a sample of violent offenders. *Journal of Interpersonal Violence* 18: 282–294.

Mills, J.M., Kroner, D.G., and Forth, A.E. (1998). Novaco Anger Scale: reliability and validity within an adult criminal sample. *Assessment* 5: 237–248.

Moeller, S.B., Gondan, M., and Novaco, R.W. (2017). Anger, violent images, and physical aggression among male forensic inpatients. *Personality and Individual Differences* 105: 268–274.

Moeller, S.B., Novaco, R.W., Heinola, V., and Hougard, H. (2016). Validation of the Novaco Anger Scale-Provocation Inventory (Danish) with non-clinical, clinical, and offender samples. *Assessment* 23: 624–636.

Nicoll, M., Beail, N., and Saxon, D. (2013). Cognitive behavioural treatment for anger in adults with intellectual disabilities: a systematic review and meta-analysis. *Journal of Applied Research in Intellectual Disabilities* 26: 47–62.

Norlander, B. and Eckhardt, C. (2005). Anger, hostility, and male perpetrators of intimate partner violence: a meta-analytic review. *Clinical Psychology Review* 25: 119–152.

Novaco, R.W. (1977). Stress inoculation: a cognitive therapy for anger and its application to a case of depression. *Journal of Consulting and Clinical Psychology* 45: 600–608.

Novaco, R.W. (2003). *The Novaco Anger Scale and Provocation Inventory (NAS-PI)*. Los Angeles, CA: Western Psychological Services.

Novaco, R.W. (2010). Anger and psychopathology. In: *International Hanbook of Anger* (eds. M. Potegal, G. Stemmler and C. Spielberger), 465–497. New York, NY: Springer.

Novaco, R.W. (2013). Reducing anger-related offending: what works. In: *What Works in Offender Rehabilitation: An Evidence-Based Approach to Assessment and Treatment* (eds. L.A. Craig, L. Dixon and T.A. Ganon), 211–236. Chichester, UK: Wiley.

Novaco, R.W. and Chemtob, C.M. (2015). Violence associated with combat-related posttraumatic stress disorder: the importance of anger. *Psychological Trauma: Theory, Research, Practice, and Policy* 7: 485–492.

Novaco, R.W. and Renwick, S.J. (1998). Anger predictors of assaultiveness of forensic hospital patients. *Behaviour and Cognitive Therapy Today*: 199–208.

Novaco, R.W., Swanson, R.D., Gonzalez, O.I. et al. (2012). Anger and post-combat mental health: validation of a brief anger measure with U.S. soldiers post-deployed from Iraq and Afghanistan. *Psychological Assessment* 24: 661–675.

Novaco, R.W. and Taylor, J.L. (2004). Assessment of anger and aggression in offenders with developmental disabilities. *Psychological Assessment* 16: 42–50.

Novaco, R.W. and Taylor, J.L. (2008). Anger and assaultiveness of male forensic patients with developmental disabilities: links to volatile parents. *Aggressive Behavior* 34: 380–393.

Novaco, R.W. and Taylor, J.L. (2015). Reduction of assaultive behavior following anger treatment of forensic hospital patients with intellectual disabilities. *Behaviour Research and Therapy* 65: 52–59.

Polaschek, D.L.L., Wilson, N.J., Townsend, M.R., and Daly, L.R. (2005). Cognitive-behavioral rehabilitation for high-risk violent offenders. *Journal of Interpersonal Violence* 20: 1611–1627.

Roberton, T., Daffern, M., and Bucks, R.S. (2015). Beyond anger control: difficulty attending to emotions also predicts aggression in offenders. *Psychology of Violence* 5: 74–83.

Robinson, T.R., Smith, S.W., and Miller, M.D. (2002). Effects of a cognitive-behavioral intervention on responses to anger by middle school students with chronic behavior problems. *Behavioral Disorders* 27: 256–271.

Sadeh, N. and McNeil, D.E. (2013). Facets of anger, childhood sexual victimization, and gender as predictors of suicide attempts by psychiatric patients after hospital discharge. *Journal of Abnormal Psychology* 122: 879–890.

Shelton, D., Sampl, S., Kesten, K.L. et al. (2009). Treatment of impulsive aggression in correctional settings. *Behavioral Sciences and the Law* 27: 787–800.

Skeem, J.L., Schubert, C., Odgers, C. et al. (2006). Psychiatric symptoms and community violence among high-risk patients: a test of the relationship at the weekly level. *Journal of Consulting and Clinical Psychology* 74 (5): 967–979.

Snyder, K.V., Kymissis, P., and Kessler, K. (1999). Anger management for adolescents: efficacy of brief group therapy. *Journal of the American Academy of Child & Adolescent Psychiatry* 38 (11): 1409–1416.

Soares, R.R. (2006). The welfare costs of violence across countries. *Journal of Health Economics* 25: 821–846.

Spector, P.E., Zhou, Z.E., and Che, X.X. (2014). Nurse exposure to physical and nonphysical violence, bullying, and sexual harassment: a quantitative review. *International Journal of Nursing Studies* 51 (1): 72–84.

Spielberger, C.D. (1996). *State-Trait Anger Expression Inventory: Professional Manual*. Lutz, FL: Psychological Assessment Resources.

Stuart, G.L., McGeary, J.E., Shorey, R.C. et al. (2014). Genetic associations with intimate partner violence in a sample of hazardous drinking men in batterer intervention programs. *Violence Against Women* 20: 385–400.

Sukhodolsky, D.G., Kassinove, H., and Gorman, B.S. (2004). Cognitive-behavioral therapy for anger in children and adolescents: a meta-analysis. *Aggression and Violent Behavior* 9: 247–269.

Sukhodolsky, D.G., Vitulano, L.A., Carroll, D.H. et al. (2009). Randomized trial of anger control training for adolescents with Tourette's syndrome and disruptive behavior. *Journal of the Academy of Child and Adolescent Psychiatry* 48: 413–421.

Sutter, J.M., Byrne, M.K., Byrne, S. et al. (2002). Anger in prisoners: women and different from men. *Personality and Individual Differences* 32: 1087–1100.

Swogger, M.T., Walsh, Z., Homaifar, B.Y. et al. (2012). Predicting self- and other-directed violence among discharged psychiatric patients: the roles of anger and psychopathic traits. *Psychological Medicine* 42 (2): 371–379.

Tafrate, R.C. and Mitchell, D. (2014). *Forensic CBT: A Handbook for Clinical Practice*. Chicester, UK: Wiley Blackwell.

Taft, C.T., Street, A.E., Marshall, A.D. et al. (2007). Posttraumatic stress disorder, anger, and partner abuse among Vietnam combat veterans. *Journal of Family Psychology* 21: 270–277.

Taylor, J.L. and Novaco, R.W. (2005). *Anger Treatment for People with Developmental Disabilities: A Theory, Evidence, and Manual Based Approach*. London, UK: Wiley.

Taylor, J.L. and Novaco, R.W. (2013). A brief screening instrument for emotionally unstable and dissocial personality disorder in male offenders with intellectual disabilities. *Research in Developmental Disabilities* 34: 546–553.

Taylor, J.L., Novaco, R.W., and Brown, T. (2016). Reductions in aggression and violence following cognitive behavioural anger treatment for detained patients with intellectual disabilities. *Journal of Intellectual Disability Research* 60: 126–133.

Taylor, J.L., Novaco, R.W., Gillmer, B. et al. (2005). A controlled trial of individual cognitive-behavioural anger treatment for people with mild-borderline intellectual disabilities and histories of aggression. *British Journal of Clinical Psychology* 44: 367–382.

Trimble, T.J., Shevlin, M., Egan, V. et al. (2015). An evaluation of a brief anger management programme for offenders managed in the community using cross-lagged panel models. *Journal of Criminal Psychology* 5: 124–136.

Ullrich, S., Keers, R., and Coid, J.W. (2014). Delusions, anger, and serious violence: new findings from the MacArthur violence risk assessment study. *Schizophrenia Bulletin* 40: 1174–1181.

Vassos, E., Collier, D.A., and Fazel, S. (2014). Systematic meta-analyses and field synopsis of genetic association studies of violence and aggression. *Molecular Psychiatry* 19: 471–477.

Walitzer, K.S., Deffenbacher, J.L., and Shyhalla, K. (2015). Alcohol-adapted anger management treatment: a randomized controlled trial of an innovative therapy for alcohol dependence. *Journal of Substance Abuse Treatment* 59: 83–93.

Wang, E.W. and Diamond, P.M. (1999). Empirically identifying factors related to violence risk in corrections. *Behavioral Sciences & the Law* 17 (3): 377–389.

Watt, B.C. and Howells, K. (1999). Skills training for aggression control: evaluation of an anger management programme for violent offenders. *Legal and Criminological Psychology* 4: 285–300.

Wilson, C., Gandolfi, S., Dudley, A. et al. (2013). Evaluation of anger management groups in a high-security hospital. *Criminal Behavioural and Mental Health* 23: 356–371.

Wolf, A., Gray, R., and Fazel, S. (2014). Violence as a public health problem: an ecological study of 169 countries. *Social Science and Medicine* 104: 220–227.

Zarshenas, L., Baneshi, M., Sharif, F., and Sarani, E.M. (2017). Anger management in substance abuse based on cognitive behavioral therapy: an interventional study. *BMC Psychiatry* 17 (375): 1–5.

20

Managing Violent Offenders with a Personality Disorder

Caroline Logan[1,2]

[1] Greater Manchester Mental Health NHS Foundation Trust, Manchester
[2] University of Manchester, Manchester, UK

Introduction

In cross-sectional, community-based surveys conducted throughout Western Europe and America, the prevalence of personality disorder in the general (non-clinical) population is estimated to lie somewhere between 4 and 15% (Tyrer et al. 2015). Prevalence estimates vary as much as they do because of the use of different sampling (e.g. urban vs. rural) and assessment methods (e.g. self-report vs. interview), in addition to a more general problem with poor diagnostic reliability (Paris 2010; Tyrer et al. 2015). Credible studies using validated methods and measures suggest point prevalence estimates of diagnosable personality disorder of between 4 and 6% (e.g. Coid et al. 2006; Huang et al. 2006), with the condition being detected less frequently in studies carried out in European centres compared to those in North and South America. Estimates of the prevalence of personality disorder across the lifetime are, in general, higher than are point prevalence estimates – nearer 10% (e.g. Oltmanns et al. 2014); more people have had or have warranted a diagnosis of a personality disorder at some point in their lives than experience the condition at any one point in time. Obsessive–compulsive and avoidant personality disorders tend to be the most frequently identified conditions in community samples, in addition to personality disorder not otherwise classified (e.g. Oltmanns et al. 2014; Torgersen et al. 2001), and disorders of any kind are more regularly diagnosed amongst men compared to women (e.g. Coid et al. 2006). Psychopathy, a particular form of severe personality disorder of interest to correctional and forensic services (e.g. Patrick 2007, 2018), has an estimated prevalence in the general population of between 0.6 and 1.2% (e.g. Coid et al. 2009; Neumann and Hare 2008), and it is also more frequently diagnosed in men than in women (Nicholls et al. 2005).

The Wiley Handbook of What Works in Violence Risk Management: Theory, Research and Practice,
First Edition. Edited by J. Stephen Wormith, Leam A. Craig, and Todd E. Hogue.
© 2020 John Wiley & Sons Ltd. Published 2020 by John Wiley & Sons Ltd.

In contrast to community samples, amongst men, women, and young people involved in mental health services as either out- or inpatients, the prevalence of personality disorder, usually as a comorbid or co-occurring diagnosis, increases substantially to between 25 and 50% (Beckwith et al. 2014; Moran et al. 2000; Newton-Howes et al. 2010). Borderline personality disorder is commonly identified in such service users, often in combination with other conditions such as a substance use disorder, a mood or anxiety disorder, or post-traumatic stress disorder (e.g. Pagura et al. 2010; Skodol et al. 2011). Symptom presentation amongst mental health service users is often complex and harmful behaviour more frequent, though it is mostly directed towards the self (e.g. self-neglect, self-injury, increased vulnerability to exploitation by others) or played out in the relationships they have or try to have with their intimates, peers, and colleagues (Samuels 2011). In contrast to community-based non-clinical samples, personality disorder is more commonly diagnosed in women engaged with mental health services compared to men, most likely because of the greater willingness of women to seek help compared to men (Tyrer et al. 2015).

Amongst men, women, and young people detained in correctional settings and in forensic psychiatric facilities, personality disorder is thought to be most prevalent. Studies suggest a diagnosis of one or more personality disorders in between 64 and 78% of men, between 42 and 50% of women (Coid et al. 2002; Fazel and Danesh 2002), and in upwards of 84% of young people detained in such facilities (e.g. Lader et al. 2003). Unsurprisingly, antisocial personality disorder is the most commonly diagnosed condition, especially amongst men, followed by paranoid personality disorder, and borderline personality disorder is the most commonly diagnosed condition amongst women (e.g. Fazel and Danesh 2002). In those detained in forensic psychiatric hospitals, the prevalence of personality disorder diagnoses appears to increase with the level of security offered by the detaining authority, with rates upwards of 71% reported in studies of the patients of high-secure hospitals in England (e.g. Blackburn et al. 2003; Coid et al. 1999). Psychopathy is thought to occur at high rates in correctional and forensic psychiatric samples also, with lifetime rates of 10–16% and 7% having been reported amongst incarcerated men and women, respectively (Hare 2003; see also Nicholls et al. 2005). Amongst offenders in prisons and mentally-disordered offenders in hospitals, comorbidity is considered the rule rather than the exception (e.g. Dolan-Sewell et al. 2001). Symptom severity is regarded as highly significant in a great many cases (Blackburn et al. 2003), meaning that harmful behaviour, often severe, towards the self and others, is a common occurrence (e.g. McMurran and Howard 2009). Symptom and, therefore, behaviour management are important objectives of practitioners in prisons and forensic hospitals as well as those taking charge of such clients when they are eventually discharged and returned to the community to live (Dowsett and Craissati 2008).

The subject of this chapter is the management of such offenders, both within the establishments in which they are detained for the duration of their spell in custody and, in the community following release. This chapter will focus on those men, women, and young people who have personality disorder and who have been harmful to others in the past, and who are regarded as being at risk of harmful behaviour again in the future. The first part of this chapter will explore what is currently understood about the link between personality disorder and violence, that is, why the presence of such a condition in an individual may make violence more likely and under what circumstances. The relevance of understanding this link is made clear in the section that follows, on formulation, which is the process of explaining such a link in the individual case for the purpose of effective intervention and, ultimately, managed risk. The second part of the chapter provides a review of options for the formulation-based risk management of personality-disordered offenders with a history of violence, both when in detention and when returned to the community. It will be proposed that it is only when risk management is based on an understanding – or formulation – of the meaning or function of violence to the individual that it stands a chance of being proportionate, transparent and, ultimately, effective. The chapter will end with some concluding comments and a set of good practice recommendations.

The Link Between Personality Disorder and Violence

Overview of the possible links between personality disorder and violence

As noted above, personality disorder appears to exist at a high level of prevalence and severity in offenders detained in prisons and forensic mental health facilities. Personality disorder appears particularly relevant to those who are harmful towards others (e.g. McMurran and Howard 2009). Why is this the case? A number of models may explain the possible link. A first model is where personality disorder or some aspect of this particular condition (variable A) has a direct influence on the individual's decision to use violence against another person (variable B), irrespective of the influence of any other variable. For example, personality disorder (A) has a *direct* or *main* effect on the individual's ability to accurately appraise and appropriately respond to social situations involving complex interpersonal conflict or demand – he or she perceives threat in the behaviour of another person who is engaging with them for whatever purpose – and the person chooses violence (B) as a way of diminishing or controlling or protecting themselves from that threat.

A second model is where the effect of personality disorder (variable A) on the decision to use violence (variable B) is *mediated* through a third variable (variable C), either fully or partially; that is, the third variable functions as a mediator to the extent that it transmits the relationship between (A) and (B). Where a mediator (C) accounts for all of the variance explained previously by the independent variable (A), this is full mediation. This is in contrast to partial mediation in which the effect of the independent variable (A) on the dependent variable (B) is reduced markedly, but not completely, by the presence of the mediator variable (C) in the model. The effect of the independent variable (A) on the dependent variable (B) is therefore *indirect.* For example, it may be the case that substance misuse mediates the relationship between personality disorder (A) and the decision to use violence in interpersonal situations (B). In the full mediation model, personality disorder (A) directly and wholly influences the individual's decision to use substances harmfully (C), such as to manage their labile mood and overwhelming emotions, which in turn directly and completely influences the individual's decision to use violence against another person (B). Alternatively, in the partial mediation model, personality disorder (A) causes the person to use alcohol harmfully (C), and both personality disorder and alcohol make independent contributions to violence (B).

A third model is that the effect of personality disorder (A) on the decision to use violence (B) is buffered or *moderated* by variable C; that is, variable C affects 'the direction and/or strength of the relationship between an independent or predictor variable and a dependent or criterion variable' (Baron and Kenny 1986, p. 1174). Thus, the moderating variable specifies the conditions under which a significant relationship between the independent and dependent variables is observed. For example, it may be predicted that the perceived quality of social support (C) acts as a buffer in the relationship between personality disorder (A) and the decision to use violence (B). Thus, in an individual who perceives that they have good-quality social support, the association between personality disorder and violent behaviour may be weak or non-existent. For individuals who believe that they have inadequate or poor-quality social support, however, the relationship between personality disorder and the decision to use violence in situations involving interpersonal conflict may be strong and direct. A 'pure' moderating effect would be observed if the relationship between personality disorder (A) and violence (B) was reduced to zero for one particular level of social support (C), namely support that is perceived to be of high quality. All three models – main, mediating, and moderating effects – are illustrated in Figure 20.1.

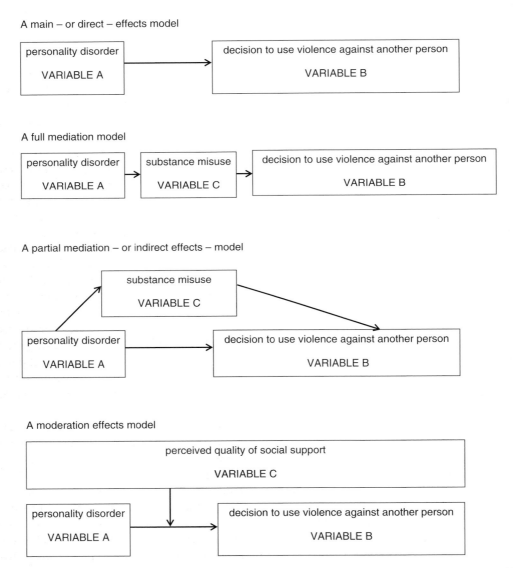

Figure 20.1 Illustration of the main, mediating and moderating effects of the independent variable, personality disorder (A), on the dependent variable, violence (B).

Therefore, there are a number of ways in which the link between personality disorder (A) and violence (B) could be characterized. What guidance does empirical research offer in an effort to determine which or in what circumstances the different links may be identified?

The challenge of establishing empirically the relationships between personality disorder and violence

In reality, because personality disorder is such a heterogeneous concept, and violent behaviour has potentially multiple antecedents in addition to personality disorder, and because personality problems evolve over time through a complex pattern of positive and negative reinforcement (McMurran and Howard 2009), the true nature of any relationship will be a challenge to scrutinize in empirical research in anything other than a piecemeal fashion (Duggan and Howard 2009). In order to try to capture the link between personality disorder and violence – to account for how one may bring about or indeed *cause* the other – certain conditions have to be met in research on the subject (Duggan and Howard 2009; Howard 2015).

First, there must be covariation between the two variables of interest – personality disorder (A) and violence (B) – such that they change together and in more or less direct proportion to one another (Haynes 1992). Thus, as the severity of personality disorder increases, so too does the severity of violence and/or the frequency with which it is observed. Further, were this condition to be met, one may conclude that the severity of personality disorder is associated with an increase in the *risk* of violence, the potential for violence in the future. One thing that affects the ability of empirical research to capture this covariation is knowledge of what the key mediating and moderating variables (C) are in the relationship between personality disorder and violence – knowing what these are and how they impact on this relationship determines the likelihood with which the primary relationship may be observed and understood.

Second, the presumed causal variable should precede the dependent variable in time (Haynes 1992). That is, if personality disorder is a cause of violence – it has a main effect on violence – then personality disorder (the antecedent) should *precede* violent behaviour in time (the consequence). This temporal sequence is problematic to establish in the personality disorder and violence fields because of the relative dearth of longitudinal studies, which is the only research method that has the potential to confirm such a relationship. Also, given the fact that personality and hence personality disorder is a combination of both biological or genetic inheritance (nature) and the individual's interactions with the social, psychological, and physical world in which they are raised (nurture) (Livesley 2003), personality (disorder) and the circumstances that may lead to the decision to use violence in any particular instance are incredibly intertwined.

For example, a dysfunctional young person may put himself into social situations for which he has an inadequate range of resources to bring to bear on its management. He uses aggression and then violence to deal with the conflict that arises between him and the other person. He suffers the consequences of that choice (arrest), which leads to restrictions in his liberty (imprisonment) and exposure to even more risky social situations with equally dysfunctional young people (his peers in prison), compounding his problems and reinforcing his reliance on violence as a way of protecting himself when he feels at risk. When his liberty is restored to him, he is limited in his options for employment and activity because he has a criminal record. So, he continues to associate with people like himself who are similarly limited, thus further reinforcing the attitudes and beliefs that underpin his personality and his reliance on violence as a problem-solving aid. Thus, such a person experiences fewer and fewer opportunities to develop and practice a more extensive repertoire of strategies with which to cope with disagreement, frustration, and conflict with others, and his existing traits and strategies become more entrenched and inflexible because they are functional in the settings to which he feels restricted. And so on. Personality directs behaviour, which in turn influences outcomes for the individual and his or her chances of adapting to new situations; variable A may cause variable B, but the effects of B impact, in turn, on A in a vicious feedback loop that has the potential to cycle endlessly across the formative years of a person's life, making the process of disentangling cause and effect all the more problematic, even within a longitudinal research design.

Third, for personality disorder to be identified as a cause of violence, alternative explanations for the apparent relationship between the two variables should be excluded or at least accounted for (Haynes 1992). Thus, in relation to the previous section, all (partial) mediators and moderators (C) should be identifiable and their effects understood and be regarded as insufficient as to entirely account for the violent outcome (B); it cannot be the case that the only way that personality disorder (A) causes violence (B) is because of the effect of a third variable (C). Thus, personality disorder would not cause violence if the entire influence of personality disorder was on substance misuse (C), which, in turn, was the cause of violence (the full mediation model illustrated in Figure 20.1). Once again, disentangling the direct and indirect influence of variables such as personality disorder on violence is problematic, regardless of the research design used.

The final necessary and sufficient condition to be met in order to capture the causal link between personality disorder and violence is the demonstration of a logical connection between the two variables (Haynes 1992) – in what way, or *how*, does personality disorder cause violence? It is in respect of this condition that a very great deal has been said, although much of it speculative and with little empirical backing, and only some of it directly tied to personality disorder per se. That said, this work warrants some consideration for the suggestions it makes and its impetus to theory development and research.

Why might personality disorder cause violence?

Rather than consider the imperfect personality constructs as laid down in the diagnostic handbooks of the American Psychiatric Association (APA) (the *Diagnostic and Statistical Manuals 5th edition*, or DSM-5, APA 2013) and the World Health Organisation (WHO) (the *International Classification of Diseases 10th edition*, WHO 1992) and their link to violence, it may be more fruitful to consider instead the elemental components of personality pathology and their respective associations (Lynam 2011). Personality pathology, especially the patterns observed in the antisocial and borderline presentations, may influence the decision to use violence through the common elements or mechanisms of hostile or paranoid (non-delusional) attributions, poor affect regulation, poor impulse control, and/or self-interest or narcissism (e.g. Nestor 2002). Therefore, violence is more likely in a person who assumes that the conduct of another person communicates threat or malign intent – the other person's actions are seen as critical if not persecutory, rather than innocent or meaningless – and the individual reacts accordingly with anger or self-defensive action (Howard 2015). Alternatively, labile mood incorporating as it does emotional arousal and reactivity, results in poor situational appraisals and poor appraisals of the emotions of others, which, in combination with poor impulse control, is more likely to lead to ill-judged and unmanaged responses and the escalation of conflict. Poor impulse control – a tendency to act quickly, with urgency, and without planning in response to internal and external stressors, without regard for the consequences for oneself or others (Bjørkly 2013; Few et al. 2015) – as a symptom of personality disorder as opposed to any other condition may impact significantly on conflict management. And in those with an overly valued sense of self-worth, such as may be seen in individuals with antisocial and narcissistic personality disorder presentations and psychopathy, and intermittently in those with paranoid and borderline traits, challenges can threaten egotism (e.g. Baumeister et al. 1996). That is, challenge or perceived criticism can threaten the individual's exaggerated sense of self-worth and entitlement, increasing the risk of intolerable feelings such as shame, guilt, or humiliation, to which he or she may respond with self-righteous aggression or violence in proportion to the nature and scale of the injury experienced (Logan and Johnstone 2010). Such aggression and violence may be impulsive, such as in one's actual or perceived self-defence, but it can also be controlled – or premeditated, or instrumental – as in violence for the purpose of revenge. And whilst violence is often associated with negative emotional states (anger, fear, jealousy), it can also correlate with positive affect as in the case of violence triggered by excitement or greed or as a form of sensation-seeking (Howard 2015), all of which may be linked to traits in disordered personality presentations.

More recent research has examined higher-order personality factors or traits called internalizing (an anxious-inhibited pattern) and externalizing (an acting out pattern). When both internalizing and externalizing traits are judged to be high in an individual, as they might be in a person with both antisocial and borderline traits, their presence is associated with high levels of hostility, lack of positive emotions, poor impulse control, and sensation- or excitement-seeking, in addition to disinhibition (low competence, low self-determination) and antagonism (Uliaszek and Zinbarg 2015). There is evidence that this combination of both high externalizing and high internalizing traits is associated with violence in those with personality disorder (Howard 2015; Nestor 2002).

The application of specific theories such as these to understand the functional links between personality pathology and violence are essential route maps to understanding or formulating the link between personality and past and future violence potential in the individual case (Logan and Johnstone 2010). In the context of more general theories relating to personality and its development, such as attachment theory, and models relating to schema organization or object relations (e.g. Johnstone and Dallos 2013), understanding the possible ways in which dysfunctional personalities can result in violent conduct in the individual becomes more feasible. And it is to formulation in the individual case that we will now turn.

Formulation

Definition and purpose

Formulation is the process of generating one or more linked hypotheses about the underlying mechanism of a complex presenting problem, such as violent conduct, in order to prepare an action plan to facilitate and direct positive change (Kuyken et al. 2009). Assessment findings are directly linked to ameliorative action via or because of the formulation (Logan 2017). *Risk* formulation is a critical component of any violence risk management plan, because it gathers together and makes sense of information generated in the course of an assessment of the individual, on the basis of which a bespoke, proportionate, and harm reducing if not preventing plan is prepared. Thus, the preparation of a formulation discourages the preparation of risk management plans based on salient features of the individual, such as a diagnosis (e.g. anti-social personality disorder) or the nature of their violence (e.g. intimate partner violence). Instead, formulation-based risk management is expected to be based on an understanding of the development of the problem over the course of the individual's life, the meaning or function of the problem behaviour to that person – the reason why they *choose* to engage in this activity as opposed to any other – and the most feasible ways of changing behaviour patterns and personal circumstances in order to reduce dependence upon it (Sturmey and McMurran 2011).

The process of developing a formulation requires the organization of the information available about the person and their problem behaviour. Various schemes exist, such as the 4Ps model (where relevant information is organized in terms of **p**redisposing or vulnerability factors, **p**recipitating or trigger factors, **p**erpetuating or maintenance factors, and **p**rotective factors) (Weerasekera 1996) or the 3Ds model (organizing information in terms of **d**rivers or motivators, **d**estabilisers, and **d**isinhibitors) (Douglas et al. 2013; Hart and Logan 2011). Regardless of which organizational framework is chosen, assessment information relating to the problem behaviour to be managed must be organized in some way so as to expose to the view of the observer the mechanism of the problem's origins and maintenance, as well as the risk of its recurrence. Formulation also involves other people; it should be prepared based on a mutual understanding of the problem, ideally agreed with the individual with the problem. Drawing clients into such a process as this encourages their commitment to its explanation and to the modification of the problem, as well as improvements in the compassion felt by the writer for the client whose behaviour can often seem repellent or unfathomable (e.g. Ramsden et al. 2014).

The key undertaking of the formulation process is the generation of connections amongst different pieces of information about the person with the problem – the past with the present and future, their experiences with their responses, their personality with their violence. This is exactly where the substantial theories of person and personality development – such as attachment theory – and the more specific ones relating to personality problems and violence, such as those described above, come into play as guides to the practitioner writing the formulation. Theories, large or small, direct the practitioner to the information about the client most relevant to the task of formulation and suggest ways in which these pieces of information may be connected and how these connections may play out in the future (Johnstone and Dallos 2013). The theoretical underpinnings of formulation are essential and a piece of narrative text is arguably not a formulation unless there is evidence of this kind of guidance being used to derive it; such a process brings the world of research and evidence-based practice to bear on one's theoretical model of the individual (Tarrier 2006).

However, formulation is also about action – indicators of the direction of travel for the more detailed risk management plan to follow (Persons 1989). Indeed, it may be argued that a narrative statement may not be described as a formulation unless it contains *both* an explanation of the underlying mechanism of the person's presenting problem *and* the general focus of risk management activity. This ensures that formulation is not just an explanation of the past but also a framework for managing the future. Finally, a formulation is a critical communication aid, a vital component of any clinical report, evaluation of risk, and risk management plan. Ideally brief, to ensure they are read, formulations should be between a paragraph in length and several pages, depending on their purpose (e.g. to inform colleagues to promote consistent multidisciplinary working with a client, to encourage more psychologically-informed working practices with the person) (Logan 2016). In addition, they should be free from unnecessary jargon or complexity. These conditions met, a piece of narrative text explaining an individual's use of violence and the role of personality disorder in its occurrence both in the past and the future, may be regarded as an essential element of risk management, a requirement that will now be illustrated.

The Role of Formulation in Violence Risk Management

Definition and purpose

Consider the following scenario: John, who is 35-years of age, has a history of intimate partner violence. He has convictions for violent assault on three intimate partners, as well as on family members and peers, often in the context of alcohol abuse, which itself tends to occur in response to emotional distress and anxiety. John's most recent and abused partner has left him because of his violence towards her, for which he has most recently spent 36 months in prison. They have a child, a son, who is five-years of age. John wishes access to his son, but his ex-partner and the social services involved with the family are concerned about the boy's exposure to his father and the specific risk of violence to the child. In prison, John was diagnosed with antisocial personality disorder with borderline traits. He was also diagnosed with post-traumatic stress disorder, a diagnosis linked to his experiences whilst serving in the British Army, and alcohol dependence. In prison, John engaged in a two-year treatment programme for men with personality disorder and has been released from prison to probation services that are psychologically informed and supported, and where formulation-based risk management is the standard. John has engaged with this entire process – it has been very hard work for him, but, overall, he has been motivated to receive and work with treatment since the start because he desperately wants his relationship with his son to be different from his abusive relationship with his own father. Also, whilst he knows that his relationship with the child's mother is over and that he is to blame for that, he wishes to be able to communicate with her about their son and in a way that is civil, healthy, and enduring.

John's engagement with treatment resulted in the preparation of a case formulation. This formulation, called a level 3 formulation (NOMS/NHSE 2015; see also, Logan 2017), explained in a little under four pages John's problems, their development, and their remediation through intervention. The formulation also proposed a link between his problems and his risk of harm to others, and provided broad directions of travel in respect of future risk management, including further interventions. A shorter version of this formulation was prepared addressing just the issue of risk of future violence – a so-called level 2 formulation, which was just over a page in length and explained John's risks in a way that would be helpful and sufficient for the needs of his probation officer and the staff in the approved premises to which he has been released. John's level 2 formulation is as follows:

> This is a formulation of John. The focus of this formulation is John's risk of aggression and violence. John is at risk of being physically harmful towards others, most particularly, those individuals on whom he feels some form of reliance or dependence, such as his intimate partners or family friends, or some of his peers to whom he is close. He is thought to be at risk of being harmful in the future because he has been harmful towards such individuals in the past, many times, and he has paid heavily for being so. The purpose of this formulation is to try to explain John's risk of aggression and violence in order that everyone – John himself, and those practitioners working with him – is in the best position to understand what is going on for him

and to support him towards more helpful ways of communicating what he feels and obtaining what he needs from others. This formulation is based on what we have come to understand about John during the course of his engagement in a two-year intensive treatment programme for men with personality problems linked to their risk of harm. This formulation has been prepared with John so we feel it reflects both our views and his, which is essential because we see the key to managed risk as being the existence of a collaborative relationship with John. We might not always agree about things, but we must always work together to resolve difficulties and challenges when they arise.

John is 35 years of age now, but he has been through a lot in his life. When he was a young boy, the only child of his parents, he witnessed a great many instances of his father beating his mother. His father drank a lot and he would hurt John's mother when he was drunk. John was terrified of his father, so much so that when he heard his father and mother fighting downstairs and his mother pleading for her safety, John would wet the bed. It was an awful time for him that ended only when his father died in a road traffic accident – he was driving a car while drunk, and in the accident he caused, he also killed a young mother and her baby driving home from a family gathering. John was 9 when his father died. Things improved a little after that, in the sense that John was not so afraid. But his mother became depressed – she felt so guilty about the young mother and her baby – and John's frightened feelings about his father became angry feelings towards his mother as she withdrew into herself and seemed not to notice him or care. As soon as he was able, John joined the army and left home.

John liked the army from the start. He loved the discipline, the hard, physical work, knowing exactly where he stood, and what was expected of him. He did well to begin with. He went to Iraq when he was just 18 years of age. There, things started to get hard for him. He was angry a lot of the time. His mother did not keep in contact with him. He felt lonely and he would form close bonds with other soldiers that would make them feel a bit suffocated by him and their efforts to distance themselves from him felt very rejecting. He got into trouble for fighting. He drank too much when he was not on duty, which caused him more problems with aggression and fighting. Then he witnessed three of his friends being killed and two more seriously injured in an incident when they were out on patrol. John fell apart. He returned to the UK and within a year, was medically discharged from the army. His drinking got worse as he depended on it more and more to help him numb his feelings. He had a number of relationships in which he couldn't handle his feelings of insecurity with his partners. With them, he seemed to turn into the kind of man his father was, and he hated himself for that. He felt like his life was spiralling out of control and he was drinking and fighting with the people he needed the most just to feel like he had any kind of control. He was arrested for his first violent offence when he was 24 – he punched his girlfriend and put her into hospital with multiple fractures to her face. She left him. On his release from prison, another relationship ended the same way.

On his release from prison after his second sentence, a new relationship seemed to offer more safety for John. He made an effort to drink less, he got a job, they made a home together. And then this partner – Dee – became pregnant with his child. John felt very uncomfortable. He was very jealous of the unborn child, and Dee's devotion to her pregnancy. He began to fear the child's birth, that he would be irrelevant to her once the child arrived. And when his son did arrive, this is what he felt happened. Dee only had time for the boy, or so it seemed. And so, the aggression and then violence started there too. John wanted to hurt Dee, to punish her, for preferring the child to him. He wanted to hurt her because he felt she was abandoning him, that she didn't care about him like his father hadn't cared and his mother too. He was so upset that all this was happening in his life and he did not know what to do about it. He drank more to numb the bad feelings he had, which made him awful to be with, so that Dee did eventually leave him. One night, when he was drunk, he went to her mother's house and forced his way in. In front of Dee's mother and their son, John battered Dee unconscious. He only stopped when the police wrestled him to the ground and took him away.

The root of John's violence is his terrible insecurity in his relationships with others. When he assaulted Dee, he was fearful every day, his feelings of guilt and shame and loss and emptiness were out of control, his drinking a clumsy and ineffective coping strategy, his behaviour more disinhibited as a result. He did not feel safe enough with other people to be civil to them, and the distance between them all and him seemed to get bigger and bigger. He felt so lonely and he had no idea how to feel or act differently.

In prison, John was referred to a specialist unit, a treatment service for men who are at high risk of violence because of personality problems. John wanted this referral and pursued it with his probation officer once he found out he was eligible for consideration. He transferred there eight months into his 36-month sentence. It was incredibly hard for him and he almost got deselected twice for fighting within the first three months of starting. But then on his 33rd birthday, Dee sent to him a card scrawled on by their son. There was no message from her, but the connection with his son changed everything for John. Completing the two-year programme was the hardest thing John has ever done, and he knows that it will remain hard for him for a long time to be different from how he has been for so much of his life. However, he understands himself so much better now – what are his strengths and weaknesses – and strong feelings like shame and guilt do not overwhelm him like they did before. But most importantly, he thinks, he has skills that he can use to try to solve problems and resolve difficulties with others before they get too bad. He can talk about what is going on inside him, and he is empowered by the understanding and interest of others.

John is approaching the very end of his sentence. Through his son's social worker, he maintains contact with the boy. He has written to Dee and her mother to express his deep regret for what he did. Dee's mother did not reply, but Dee did and wished him well and expressed the hope that they would be able to get on in the future for the sake of the boy. Encouraged, motivated anew, John is preparing for life in the community once again. He knows it will be a challenge, but he is committed to three things: (1) to not drinking again, ever; (2) to making his life more organized, like with a job and decent accommodation; and (3) being open and honest with people, starting with the staff in the post-release hostel to which he will shortly be transferred. Potential flashpoints will be when he feels messed around or let down, or when he feels overwhelmed by stress. In return, John would appreciate it if the staff could be patient with him while he manages the transition and understanding when he falters.

This formulation of John's harm potential is an explanation of his risks to others, most especially his intimate partners and his son. Its purpose is to inform those to whom it matters in terms of trying to manage that risk on a day-to-day basis; it's purpose is to help them understand what John's risks are and why, and what their role is in helping him to manage them. By creating more understanding, there is a reasonable expectation that their working relationship with John may be better than it might otherwise have been, had that understanding not been in place. Indeed, some commentators have gone so far as to recommend the formulation process as the means by which compassion may be encouraged for a group of people for whom compassion is usually in very short supply (Ramsden et al. 2014; Shaw et al. 2017), despite its frequent justification. This is not excusing the person for the harmful things they have done in their lives or for the distress they have caused to others. It is, instead, an attempt to understand that behaviour and outcome in the context in which it occurs *in order to* encourage alternative ways of meeting one's personal needs other than through the use of aggression and violence. Further, and with reference to the first part of this chapter, the formulation of John's harm potential is an illustration of what is likely to be the partial mediating effect of his consumption of alcohol (mediating variable C) on the relationship between his personality (A) and his violence potential (B).

Key requirements for managing violent offenders with personality disorder

John Livesley, arguably the foremost contributor to working with people with personality disorders in the current time, describes common factors in the treatment and management of people with this condition (see Livesley et al. 2017). These common factors provide guidance for working with individuals – like John – whose personality problems are tied up with other mental health difficulties and harmful behaviour. Common factors are (i) a structured approach, that is, a pre-planned direction of travel rather than one that is merely reactive to problems or crises, (ii) a treatment or working alliance with the client in whose quality both are encouraged to invest, (iii) consistency of approach across time and in everyone working with the same client, (iv) validation, that is, the practitioner's recognition and affirmation of the legitimacy of the client's experience, (v) developing and maintaining motivation to change, and (vi) meta-cognition, that is, promoting self-reflection, encouraging greater self-awareness, self-observation, and self-knowledge (Livesley et al. 2017).

Bateman and Krawitz (2013) identify similar intervention commonalities in their work with men and women with borderline personality disorder, specifically: (i) practitioners should work with people with personality disorders as a matter of choice, and in services that have a commitment to working with this client group; (ii) the therapeutic or working alliance is key, featuring an agreement with the client about goals and objectives whose achievement is discussed collaboratively rather than being imposed on the client; (iii) empathy and validation are central aspects of each encounter; and (iv) collaborative work is structured, planned, monitored, and evaluated, and delivered by practitioners who are supported and clinically supervised in their work, and organized under a strategy for work with this group of clients (Bateman and Krawitz 2013).

With respect to the treatment of men and women with personality disorder who have a history of violence towards others, dedication to common factors derived from Livesley et al. (2017) and Bateman and Krawitz (2013) are recommended (see Table 20.1). This is because they have the potential to create productive working alliances between practitioners of whatever kind, and their clients.

Using John as an illustrative example, his impending discharge to an approved premise staffed by practitioners who want to be there, and who have skills and support to help them work with men like John, is ideal. However, to enable the appropriate management of flashpoints or triggers for aggression and violence, John will also require an approach that is focused on further developing his understanding of himself and his application of different techniques to better understand and respond to others. In addition, he will continue to need encouragement to use appropriate, helpful ways of coping with his emotions. He will need all the staff in the approved premises to support him in these goals in similar ways, and to try to recognize when it is hard for him and to use distraction techniques when he seems preoccupied by negative feelings. In addition, it would be advisable for them to take the initiative on providing this support rather than wait for him to ask for help. He is much more likely to feel understood and looked after, and therefore secure and safe to be himself if that is the case. John also wants frequent reminders of his son and help to remember that the prospect of a decent relationship with him in the future is what he is doing it all for – his motivational hook, as it were. Therefore, a formulation of John such as the one above, provides a rationale for the use of particular approaches with him over others and in full knowledge of the value of them to him.

Table 20.1   A set of recommendations for working therapeutically with personality disordered offenders.

1) Only organizations with a *commitment* to working with people with personality disorders, and practitioners who *want* to work with people with personality disorders and who have been provided with the *knowledge* and *skills* and with the *support* and *clinical supervision* with which to do so, should be encouraged to undertake this work.

2) Work with people with personality disorders should be *planned* and *structured* throughout rather than crisis-driven and unguided by any underlying principle linked to recovery and managed risk.

3) The *therapeutic alliance* – the collaborative working relationship between client and practitioner – is key and should be both nurtured and protected by the individuals involved and the service within which the client is held or managed.

4) Collaborative work with the client, and the approach taken by all practitioners involved, should be as *consistent* as it is possible to be.

5) Practitioners should seek to *validate* the client's valid experiences, that is, recognize and affirm the legitimacy of what they feel.

6) Practitioners should encourage, develop, and maintain the client's *motivation* to change, whilst recognizing that they may require assistance with the skills necessary to achieve and maintain positive change and support when times are hard.

7) Practitioners should also promote *self-reflection* in clients, encourage greater *self-awareness*, and foster *self-observation* and greater *self-knowledge*.

8) Finally, collaborative work with clients should be *monitored* and *evaluated*.

Source: derived from Livesley (2017) and Bateman and Krawitz (2013).

Options for violence risk management in custodial settings: An example in England and Wales

It is recommended that violence risk management for men and women with personality disorder is underpinned by a formulation of the individual's risk and personality problems and how the one is linked to the other (e.g. Douglas et al. 2013; NOMS/NHSE 2015). Further, it is recommended that interventions are organized around common factors consistent with the ones listed in Table 20.1 above. In reality, a minority of offenders with personality problems have a formulation, or a formulation-based approach to their detention in general and risk management in particular. However, a recent development in England and Wales demonstrates that the widespread use of formulation to guide risk management is possible and potentially valuable. In 2011, the Offender Personality Disorder (OPD) Strategy was launched. The successor to the Dangerous and Severe Personality Disorder Programme (Duggan 2011), the OPD Strategy proposed to affect the lives and detention of thousands of offenders with personality problems by improving wellbeing and the knowledge, attitudes, and skills of the practitioners working with them. The OPD Strategy has facilitated the development of a range of treatment services in prisons in England and Wales – services like the Beacon Unit at Her Majesty's Prison (HMP) Garth in the north of England, the likes of which John attended, which is a two-year treatment programme for men with personality problems linked to their violent or sexually-violent offending. A comparable service for women in the north of England is the Rivendell Service in HMP New Hall, which also offers a two-year treatment programme.

There are also treatment services for men and women in high-secure prisons, and a number of pre-and post-treatment facilities intended to prepare offenders for treatment and help them to consolidate gains post-treatment, facilities called psychologically informed planned environments or PIPEs. Democratic therapeutic communities are also part of the OPD Strategy. Further, across England and Wales, mental-health practitioners have been embedded into probation services to improve knowledge and skills and support the development of collaborative formulations to improve the way probation officers understand and work with their clients. These are environments where their daily organization, the behaviour of staff, decision-making, actions, and culture are informed and planned on the basis of psychological principles. Therefore, there exists now a range – or a pathway – of resources in HM Prison and Probation Service in England and Wales for men and women with personality problems, all funded and supported by the principles of the Strategy, key amongst which, is that interventions and risk management should be guided by formulation. Because of the prominence of formulation, and the paucity of research on its efficacy, a set of six standards have been developed on the basis of which the quality of narrative formulations can be judged (NOMS/NHSE 2015; see also Logan 2017). Such a set of standards, and the description of formulations at different levels (as alluded to above) depending on who the formulation is for and how well the client is known to services, has created a platform for research designed to test the assumption that formulation promotes effective risk management.

However, in the absence of such services, such as, if an offender with personality disorder is unable to access OPD Strategy services, perhaps because they have a too brief sentence or they are not referred or are refused, risk management largely consists of physical containment, structured daily living but without a focus on personality problems, and access to programmes dedicated to offending behaviour rather than the personality difficulties that might be driving it. Whilst offending behaviour programmes are in themselves invaluable and indeed essential for changing harmful patterns of behaviour, the underlying personality problems that are thought to be influencing the offending behaviour are not directly addressed; that is, the 'dose' of intervention on offer as well as its target is not sufficient or precise. This leaves the potential for the offending behaviour to resume once treatment ceases because the person has not learned less harmful alternatives to offending as a way of having their needs recognized or addressed – and unaddressed causes have the potential to generate the same harmful outcomes as before. Some offenders may access prison health care because of their capricious mood or unstable behaviour, and medication and some time-limited interventions may be available. However, outside of the OPD Strategy, concerted interventions for men and women in prison with personality disorder are limited in England and Wales and elsewhere. For someone like John, accessing a personality disorder treatment service and being released from prison into the care of a post-release hostel that is run as a PIPE offers a significant opportunity for offenders like him to elect to make choices in how they run the rest of their lives.

Options for violence risk management in community settings

What happens to violent offenders with personality disorder released into the community? Multi-agency public protection arrangements are one helpful way of extending risk management beyond the confines of prison (e.g. Kemshall 2008). Such arrangements have the potential to manage the individual's opportunity to re-offend and support the person's access to resources that may act protectively against risk factors, resources such as accommodation and income security, substance misuse counselling or services, or offending behaviour programmes in the community. And for many people, multi-agency public protection arrangements are sufficient to 'hold' them until they are more established living in the community (Dowsett and Craissati 2008; Logan 2011).

However, there are challenges when a person with a history of violence and personality disorder is no longer subject to oversight by probation services yet requires access to mental health services still for the treatment of their personality disorder or co-occurring diagnoses. Men and women with a history of violence are unattractive prospects for community-based mental health services who tend not to see it as their primary responsibility to work with clients they regard as better suited to forensic mental health services. Further, the model of care best suited to individuals with personality problems is a prolonged engagement built on strengths and managing the threat of crises *before* they arise, when busy community mental health services are often accessed only when the client is acutely unwell and for time limited periods.

Therefore, there is much that limits the delivery of risk management services for men and women with personality disorder and a history of violence and good practice is patchier than is either recommended or desired. However, there are options available and several important guiding principles.

First, as in Table 20.1, the *common factors* in working with people with personality disorder apply to this cohort, as much as if not more, than to any other. Probation and mental health services should strategize their approach to people with personality disorder, to include those with significant histories of offending behaviour. Pathways of care within mental health services, and between mental health services and other agencies, such as prison and probation, should be mapped.

Second, specialized personality disorder treatment services – or community mental health services that will accept people for treatment who have a primary diagnosis of personality disorder – are a challenge to access. They are expensive to set up (costs include those related to training of practitioners and supervision) and their caseloads tend to be small and with a slow turnover. In the main, people with personality problems are managed by more generalist mental health practitioners (psychiatrists, psychologists, nurses) or in services where other conditions are the primary diagnosis (such as substance misuse services). The *structured clinical management* model of care described by Bateman and Krawitz (2013) is ideally suited to just such practitioners as a first line of intervention. Personality disordered former offenders with convictions for violence may benefit greatly from such an approach. However, they may require the support of forensic services to access such a provision, such as through the offer of supervision or risk assessment and management guidance specifically in order that those generalist service providers feel confident enough to take such individuals on. In reality, structured clinical management delivered by community mental health services with the option of support from forensic mental health services – coordinated under a strategy for such work – is a most pragmatic way forward.

Third, working with this group of clients requires the *cooperation* of more than one agency. The needs of personality disordered former offenders at risk of violence will not be met just by multi-agency public protection arrangements or by mental health services; attention is required to more mundane matters relating to social functioning and engagement, such as housing and financial security, employment and access to physical health resources, legal advice and advocacy (Dowsett and Craissati 2008; Risk Management Authority 2016). Such multi-agency cooperation should be enshrined in service level agreements (SLAs) or local inter-agency strategies, guided by national initiatives such as *Personality Disorder: No Longer a Diagnosis of*

Exclusion (Department of Health 2003) in the UK. However, multi-agency cooperation at this level is a challenge to achieve.

Why are services for high-risk personality disordered offenders so problematic to organize? The answer is not clear. People with personality disorder are a challenge to work with when practitioners and service managers do not have the knowledge or skills – or interest or enthusiasm – to work with them. The further away one goes from dedicated and supported personality disorder-specific services, the more likely such resistance will be found. Even within personality disorder services, problems are regularly encountered as the difficulties of the clients are projected onto the staff and the staff play out these difficulties amongst themselves, draining energy and motivation to address the problems at source (Murphy and McVey 2010).

Conclusions

There is a danger that high-risk personality disordered offenders are overlooked because they are not thought to be as deserving of interventions as individuals with other conditions, such as schizophrenia (Hart 2011). Yet, severe presentations of personality disorder clearly affect more people for longer, in an unremitting course, with far more extensive social and financial costs. Further, they have the significant potential to shorten the life expectancy of those with the disorder as well as those they encounter. When the costs incurred by this group of people against individuals and society as a whole are compared to the cost of schizophrenia, regarded by the WHO as the most disabling of conditions, action is clearly required (Hart 2011; Kreis et al. 2016; Moran et al. 2016). And such action is possible and achievable, and potentially life-changing. How? There follow a number of good practice recommendations derived from the work discussed in this chapter, which are proposed as guidance to practitioners intent on improving the lives and prospects of some of the most challenging and concerning clients in their care.

Good Practice Recommendations

- Multi-agency collaboration is essential when working with clients with personality disorder and at risk of violence. Such individuals have complex needs spanning multiple areas of concern and jurisdiction (e.g. criminal justice, mental health, safeguarding) and over prolonged periods of time – from conviction, sentence, and community-based supervision and resettlement. However, one agency needs to take the lead as, without clear leadership and accountability, gaps will open up through which clients will invariably fall.
- The treatment and management of personality-disordered clients who have been and may yet be violent again should be psychologically-informed and formulation-driven, and led by psychologically trained and supervised practitioners who focus on relationships and the social context in which service users live and engage in harmful behaviours.
- Treatment should involve a range of approaches (e.g. treatment for the core personality disorder, treatment for associated conditions, practical support to attain secure housing and financial security). These various approaches should be derived from and integrated around an overarching model of care – a strategy – that incorporates everything required by an individual, which is, in turn, woven into an integrated treatment pathway extending from referral to discharge. The range of interventions identified as necessary should address the problems presented by the client and the variety of reinforcing experiences and beliefs most relevant to their perpetuation in a systematic and coordinated way.

- A primary target within any intervention for high-risk personality-disordered offenders is addressing their engagement and motivation to change. Treatment dropout and compliance have to be addressed because it is almost inevitable that they will be factors in the delivery of what will probably be quite lengthy interventions with often quite ambivalent clients. It is critical that motivation to change is addressed – and with some care, and early on – because of the potential in its absence for treatment to be regarded as not meaningful and disengagement to ensue. Motivation and engagement can be addressed by taking an approach to treatment that is credible and interesting, and that assists clients to decide themselves that change might be helpful, to identify what that change might be and look like in practice, and to choose real change rather than merely compliance. Simply telling offenders that they need to change and dictating the changes required is unlikely to be a successful motivational approach (Harris et al. 2005).
- Therefore, clients should be a key stakeholder in interventions on their behalf.
- Early intervention targets should include the development of practical skills – in relation to helpful stress and emotion management, cognitive flexibility and impulse control, goal-setting, and responsible sensation-seeking. Clients should be encouraged to develop skills in relation to problem-solving generally and interpersonal problem-solving specifically. Such skills will prepare them for more intensive treatment, if available.
- Entirely consistent with the risk-needs-responsivity-principle (Andrews and Bonta 2010), learning style and the extent of need should be directly related to the nature, delivery, and 'dose' of interventions. To try to deliver the same package of care to everyone – to assume that 'one size fits all' – is to ignore the individual and to invite disengagement.
- Finally, evaluation should be a part of all mental health interventions – why administer interventions unless we know they are having the desired effect? Key targets for evaluation with clients with personality disorder will be personal outcomes of relevance to the individual (e.g. family contact), factors related to risk of further harmful behaviour, health, and mental health improvements, and the economic benefits of treatment (e.g. employment).

References

American Psychiatric Association (2013). *Diagnostic and Statistical Manual of Mental Disorders*, 5e. Washington, DC: American Psychiatric Association.

Andrews, D.A. and Bonta, J. (2010). *The Psychology of Criminal Conduct*, 5e. New Providence, NJ: Matthew Bender & Company.

Baron, R.M. and Kenny, D.A. (1986). The moderator-mediator variable distinction in social psychological research: conceptual, strategic, and statistical considerations. *Journal of Personality and Social Psychology* 51: 1173–1182.

Bateman, A.W. and Krawitz, R. (2013). *Borderline Personality Disorder: An Evidence-Based Guide for Generalist Mental Health Professionals*. Oxford, UK: Oxford University Press.

Baumeister, R.F., Smart, L., and Boden, J.M. (1996). Relation of threatened egotism to violence and aggression: the dark side of high self-esteem. *Psychological Review* 103: 5–33.

Beckwith, H., Moran, P.F., and Reilly, J. (2014). Personality disorder prevalence in psychiatric outpatients: a systematic literature review. *Personality and Mental Health* 8: 91–101.

Bjørkly, S. (2013). A systematic review of the relationship between impulsivity and violence in persons with psychosis: evidence or spin cycle? *Aggression and Violent Behaviour* 18: 753–760.

Blackburn, R., Logan, C., Donnelly, J., and Renwick, S. (2003). Personality disorders, psychopathy and other mental disorders: co-morbidity among patients at English and Scottish high-security hospitals. *Journal of Forensic Psychiatry & Psychology* 14: 111–137.

Coid, J., Bebbington, P., Jenkins, R. et al. (2002). The National Survey of Psychiatric Morbidity among prisoners and the future of prison healthcare. *Medicine, Science and the Law* 42: 245–250.

Coid, J., Kahtan, N., Gault, S., and Jarman, B. (1999). Patients with personality disorder admitted to secure forensic psychiatry services. *British Journal of Psychiatry* 175: 528–536.

Coid, J., Yang, M., Tyrer, P. et al. (2006). Prevalence and correlates of personality disorder in Great Britain. *British Journal of Psychiatry* 188: 423–431.

Coid, J., Yang, M., Ullrich, S. et al. (2009). Prevalence and correlates of psychopathic traits in the household population of Great Britain. *International Journal of Law and Psychiatry* 32: 65–73.

Department of Health (2003). *Personality Disorder: No Longer a Diagnosis of Exclusion*. London, UK: HM Stationary Office.

Dolan-Sewell, R.T., Krueger, R.F., and Shea, M.T. (2001). Co-occurrence with syndrome disorders. In: *Handbook of Personality Disorders: Theory, Research, and Treatment* (ed. J. Livesley), 84–104. New York, NY: Guilford Press.

Douglas, K.S., Hart, S.D., Webster, C.D., and Belfrage, H. (2013). *HCR-20: Assessing Risk for Violence*, 3e. Burnaby, BC: Mental Health, Law and Policy Institute, Simon Fraser University.

Dowsett, J. and Craissati, J. (2008). *Managing Personality Disordered Offenders in the Community: A Psychological Approach*. London, UK: Routledge.

Duggan, C. (2011). Dangerous and severe personality disorder. *British Journal of Psychiatry* 198: 431–433.

Duggan, C. and Howard, R. (2009). The 'functional link' between personality disorder and violence: a critical appraisal. In: *Personality, Personality Disorder and Violence* (eds. M. McMurran and R. Howard), 19–37. Chichester, UK: Wiley.

Fazel, S. and Danesh, J. (2002). Serious mental disorder in 23,000 prisoners: a systematic review of 62 surveys. *The Lancet* 359: 545–550.

Few, L.R., Lynam, D.R., and Miller, J.D. (2015). Impulsivity-related traits and their relation to DSM-5 section II and III personality disorders. *Personality Disorders: Theory, Research, and Treatment* 6: 261–266.

Hare, R.D. (2003). *The Psychopathy Checklist-Revised*. Toronto, ON: Multi-Health Systems.

Harris, D., Attrill, G., and Bush, J. (2005). Using choice as an aid to engagement and risk management with violent psychopathic offenders. *Issues in Forensic Psychology* 5: 144–151.

Hart, S.D. (2011). Understanding and treating clients with psychopathy: A way forward. Keynote presentation at the 2nd International Bergen Conference on Forensic Psychiatry in Bergen, Norway (15–17 November 2011).

Hart, S.D. and Logan, C. (2011). Formulation of violence risk using evidence-based assessments: the structured professional judgment approach. In: *Forensic Case Formulation* (eds. P. Sturmey and M. McMurran), 83–106. Chichester, UK: Wiley-Blackwell.

Haynes, S.N. (1992). *Models of Causality in Psychopathology: Toward Dynamic, Synthetic, and Nonlinear Models of Behavior Disorders*. Upper Saddle River, NJ: Prentice Hall.

Howard, R. (2015). Personality disorders and violence: what is the link? *Borderline Personality Disorder and Emotion Dysregulation* 2: 12.

Huang, B., Grant, B.F., Dawson, D.A. et al. (2006). Race-ethnicity and the prevalence and co-occurrence of diagnostic and statistical manual of mental disorders 4th edition, alcohol and drug use disorders and axis I and II disorders: United States, 2001 to 2002. *Comprehensive Psychiatry* 47: 252–257.

Johnstone, L. and Dallos, R. (2013). *Formulation in Psychology and Psychotherapy: Making Sense of people's Problems*, 2e. London, UK: Routledge.

Kemshall, H. (2008). *Understanding the Community Management of High Risk Offenders*. Maidenhead, UK: Open University Press.

Kreis, M.K.F., Hoff, H.A., Belfrage, H., and Hart, S.D. (2016). *Psykopati (Psychopathy: What Is it and What Can we Do About It?)*. Copenhagen, DE: Hans Reitzels Forlag.

Kuyken, W., Padesky, C.A., and Dudley, R. (2009). *Collaborative Case Conceptualization: Working Effectively with Clients in Cognitive-Behavioral Therapy.* New York, NY: Guilford Press.

Lader, D., Singleton, N., and Meltzer, H. (2003). Psychiatric morbidity among young offenders in England and Wales. *International Review of Psychiatry* 15: 144–147.

Livesley, W.J. (2003). *Practical Management of Personality Disorder.* New York, NY: Guilford Press.

Livesley, W.J. (2017). *Integrated modular treatment for borderline personality disorder: A practical guide to combining effective treatment methods.* Cambridge: Cambridge University Press.

Livesley, W.J., Dimaggio, G., and Clarkin, J. (2017). *Integrated Modular Treatment for Borderline Personality Disorder: A Practical Guide to Combining Effective Treatment Methods.* Cambridge, UK: Cambridge University Press.

Logan, C. (2011). Managing high-risk personality disordered offenders: lessons learned to date. In: *'Dangerous' People: Policy, Prediction and Practice* (eds. B. McSherry and P. Keyser), 233–247. Oxford, UK: Routledge.

Logan, C. (2016). Risk formulation: the new frontier in risk assessment and management. In: *Treatment of Sex Offenders: Strengths and Weaknesses in Assessment and Intervention* (eds. D.R. Laws and W.T. O'Donohue). New York, NY: Springer.

Logan, C. (2017). Formulation for forensic practitioners. In: *Handbook of Forensic Mental Health Services* (eds. R. Roesch and A. Cook), 153–178. New York, NY: Routledge.

Logan, C. and Johnstone, L. (2010). Personality disorder and violence: making the link through risk formulation. *Journal of Personality Disorders* 24: 610–633.

Lynam, D.R. (2011). Psychopathy and narcissism). *The handbook of narcissism and narcissistic personality disorder: Theoretical approaches, empirical findings, and treatments* (eds. W.K. Campbell and J.D. Miller), 272–282. Hoboken, New Jersey: John Wiley & Sons Inc.

McMurran, M. and Howard, R. (2009). *Personality, Personality Disorder and Violence: An Evidence Based Approach.* Chichester, UK: Wiley.

Moran, P., Jenkins, R., Tylee, A. et al. (2000). The prevalence of personality disorder among UK primary care attenders. *Acta Psychiatrica Scandinavica* 102: 52–57.

Moran, P., Romaniuk, H., Coffey, C. et al. (2016). The influence of personality disorder on the future mental health and social adjustment of young adults: a population-based, longitudinal cohort study. *The Lancet Psychiatry* 3: 636–645.

Murphy, N. and McVey, D. (2010). *Treating Personality Disorder: Creating Robust Services for People.* London, UK: Routledge.

National Offender Management Service, & NHS England (2015). *Working with Personality Disordered Offenders: A Practitioner's Guide.* London, UK: Authors.

Nestor, P.G. (2002). Mental disorder and violence: personality dimensions and clinical features. *American Journal of Psychiatry* 159: 1973–1978.

Neumann, C.S. and Hare, R.D. (2008). Psychopathic traits in a large community sample: links to violence, alcohol use, and intelligence. *Journal of Consulting and Clinical Psychology* 76: 893–897.

Newton-Howes, G., Tyrer, P., Anagnostakis, K. et al. (2010). The prevalence of personality disorder, its comorbidity with mental state disorders, and its clinical significance in community mental health teams. *Social Psychiatry and Psychiatric Epidemiology* 45: 453–460.

Nicholls, T.L., Ogloff, J.R., Brink, J., and Spidel, A. (2005). Psychopathy in women: a review of its clinical usefulness for assessing risk for aggression and criminality. *Behavioral Sciences and the Law* 23: 779–802.

Oltmanns, T.F., Rodrigues, M.M., Weinstein, Y., and Gleason, M.E. (2014). Prevalence of personality disorders at midlife in a community sample: disorders and symptoms reflected in interview, self, and informant reports. *Journal of Psychopathology and Behavioral Assessment* 36: 177–188.

Pagura, J., Stein, M.B., Bolton, J.M. et al. (2010). Comorbidity of borderline personality disorder and post-traumatic stress disorder in the US population. *Journal of Psychiatric Research* 44: 1190–1198.

Paris, J. (2010). Estimating the prevalence of personality disorders in the community. *Journal of Personality Disorders* 24: 405–411.

Patrick, C.J. (2007). *Handbook of Psychopathy*. New York, NY: Guilford Press.

Patrick, C.J. (2018). *Handbook of Psychopathy*, 2e. New York, NY: Guilford Press.

Persons, J.B. (1989). *Cognitive Therapy in Practice: A Case Formulation Approach*. New York, NY: Norton.

Ramsden, J., Lowton, M., and Joyes, E. (2014). The impact of case formulation focussed consultation on criminal justice staff and their attitudes to work with personality disorder. *Mental Health Review Journal* 19: 124–130.

Risk Management Authority (2016). *Standards and Guidelines for Risk Management*. London, UK: Author.

Samuels, J. (2011). Personality disorders: epidemiology and public health issues. *International Review of Psychiatry* 23: 223–233.

Shaw, J., Higgins, C., and Quartey, C. (2017). The impact of collaborative case formulation with high risk offenders with personality disorder. *Journal of Forensic Psychiatry and Psychology* 28: 777–789.

Skodol, A.E., Grilo, C.M., Keyes, K.M. et al. (2011). Relationship of personality disorders to the course of major depressive disorder in a nationally representative sample. *American Journal of Psychiatry* 168: 257–264.

Sturmey, P. and McMurran, M. (2011). *Forensic Case Formulation*. Chichester, UK: Wiley.

Tarrier, N. (2006). *Case Formulation in Cognitive Behaviour Therapy: The Treatment of Challenging and Complex Clinical Cases*. London, UK: Routledge.

Torgersen, S., Kringlen, E., and Cramer, V. (2001). The prevalence of personality disorders in a community sample. *Archives of General Psychiatry* 58: 590–596.

Tyrer, P., Reed, G.M., and Crawford, M.J. (2015). Classification, assessment, prevalence, and effect of personality disorder. *The Lancet* 385: 717–726.

Uliaszek, A.A. and Zinbarg, R.E. (2015). An examination of the higher-order structure of psychopathology and its relationship to personality. *Journal of Personality Disorders* 29: 183–202.

Weerasekera, P. (1996). *Multiperspective Case Formulation: A Step towards Treatment Integration*. Malabar, FL: Krieger Publishing Company.

World Health Organization (1992). *The ICD-10 Classification of Mental and Behavioural Disorders: Clinical Descriptions and Diagnostic Guidelines*. Geneva, CH: World Health Organization.

21

Antisocial and Aggressive Behaviour Amongst Persons with Schizophrenia
Evidence and Propositions for Prevention

Sheilagh Hodgins

Département de Psychiatrie et Addictologie, Université de Montréal, Centre de recherche de l'Institut universitaire en santé mentale de Montréal, Canada

Introduction

Robust evidence confirms that persons with schizophrenia[1] are at increased risk of engaging in non-violent crime, at higher risk of engaging in violent crime, and at even higher risk of killing as compared to the general population where they live (Alden et al. 2007; Brennan et al. 2000; Erb et al. 2001; Fazel et al. 2009; Hodgins 1992; Large et al. 2009; Tiihonen et al. 1997; Wallace et al. 2004). Whilst the risk associated with violence by persons with schizophrenia is higher in females than males[2], more males than females are convicted or found not guilty due to a mental disorder for a violent crime.

Not all incidents of aggressive behaviour lead to prosecution. Studies show that persons with schizophrenia, or who are developing schizophrenia, are more likely than persons without this disorder to engage in aggressive behaviour towards others (Hodgins et al. 2007; Walsh et al. 2001). Whilst rates of convictions for violent crimes are lower amongst woman than men with schizophrenia, several studies suggest that the prevalence of aggressive behaviour is similar (Dean et al. 2006; Hodgins et al. 2007; Teplin et al. 2005). Importantly, the correlates of violent offending and of physically aggressive behaviour towards others when patients are living in the community are similar (Hodgins et al. 2007).

---

[1] Schizophrenia is a severe mental disorder, one type of psychotic disorder, that typically onsets in late adolescence or early adulthood. It negatively impacts all aspects of functioning throughout adult life. Schizophrenia affects approximately 0.7% of the population.

[2] The difference in the prevalence of violence between women with and without schizophrenia is greater than the difference in the prevalence of violence between men with and without schizophrenia.

The Wiley Handbook of What Works in Violence Risk Management: Theory, Research and Practice,
First Edition. Edited by J. Stephen Wormith, Leam A. Craig, and Todd E. Hogue.
© 2020 John Wiley & Sons Ltd. Published 2020 by John Wiley & Sons Ltd.

People with schizophrenia and a history of violence towards others require treatment both for schizophrenia and for aggressive, and often, antisocial behaviour. Whilst the evidence base on the effectiveness of treatments for schizophrenia is solid, there is some evidence of the effectiveness of cognitive-behavioural interventions in reducing antisocial and aggressive behaviours in this population, and of various court orders requiring compliance with mental health treatments. However, presently, these treatments are provided only after heinous crimes have been committed, even though, in the large majority of cases, both the schizophrenia and the antisocial/aggressive behaviours were present many years earlier. This chapter reviews evidence showing that effective treatments could be provided much earlier in the lives of offenders with schizophrenia and hypothesizes that a re-organization of mental health services to this end would reduce human suffering and costs to the health and criminal justice systems.

Knowledge of evidence-based treatments for offenders with schizophrenia

There is a consensus that individuals with schizophrenia who commit violent crimes, and/or who engage in aggressive behaviour towards others in the community, require both treatment for schizophrenia and interventions aimed at reducing aggressive behaviour. There are several reviews of studies of the effectiveness of treatments for schizophrenia, treatments for aggressive behaviour amongst persons with schizophrenia, and of programmes providing interventions for both schizophrenia and aggressive behaviour. Some studies (Haddock et al. 2009; Jotangia et al. 2015; Rees-Jones et al. 2012; Yip et al. 2013) and systematic reviews (Rampling et al. 2016) focus on components of treatment offered within forensic psychiatric hospitals or prisons. There are a few descriptions of multi-faceted programmes within forensic hospitals (Yates et al. 2005) or prisons (Ashford et al. 2008; Birchwood et al. 2014; Cullen et al. 2012a, b; Morgan et al. 2014). Additionally, there are studies of interventions provided in the community, some specifically for severely mentally-ill offenders discharged from the criminal justice system (Wenzlow et al. 2011), and other studies focusing on various types of court orders such as outpatient commitment orders (Swartz et al. 2016), probation orders (Livingston et al. 2015), and mandated housing (Reif et al. 2014) that require individuals to comply with treatment or return to hospital or prison, and others provide comprehensive reviews of various types of interventions (Hockenhull et al. 2012; Kolla and Hodgins 2013; Morgan et al. 2012; Quinn and Kolla 2017). This literature confirms that simply increasing the intensity of traditional psychiatric treatment for schizophrenia does not reduce aggressive behaviour (Walsh et al. 2001). And importantly, it demonstrates the need for multiple interventions that target both schizophrenia and antisocial/aggressive behaviours that are coordinated, integrated into an individual treatment programme, and continued over the long-term.

The evidence base on the treatment of schizophrenia is more robust than knowledge of treatments of offenders with schizophrenia. Evidence about effective treatments for schizophrenia derives from large multi-site, randomized controlled trials and meta-analyses. This evidence shows that people with schizophrenia show the best outcomes when they receive antipsychotic medication, psychoeducation about the illness, resilience focused individual therapy, supported education and employment (Kane et al. 2015). These interventions also need to be coordinated by a case manager and continue through many decades, so as to limit time in hospital and maximize independent community living.

The evidence base for the effective reduction of antisocial/aggressive behaviours amongst persons with schizophrenia is limited by several factors. One, traditional psychiatric community treatment that involves providing antipsychotic medication and following patients to ensure compliance likely reduces antisocial/aggressive behaviours to some extent (Fazel et al. 2014; Swanson et al. 2008). Two, the population of offenders with schizophrenia is heterogeneous as to treatment needs and engagement and compliance with treatments and these differences have not yet been taken into consideration in trials of treatment effectiveness. Three, there are huge practical difficulties in running randomized controlled trials in settings where offenders with schizophrenia are treated (Müller-Isberner 2017), and especially in running trials with adequate statistical power. Despite the limited evidence base, present findings consistently show that when both problems – schizophrenia and antisocial/aggressive behaviours – are targets of treatment, outcomes are improved.

People with schizophrenia who engage in aggressive behaviour towards others require intensive treatment over many decades of adult life, that involves multiple interventions integrated and coordinated on an individual basis, in order to live independently and safely within the community. These treatment needs are substantial, difficult to co-ordinate over time, and appear at first glance to be very expensive. However, if these interventions reduce readmissions to hospitals, especially to forensic hospitals that are considerably more costly even than general psychiatric wards, and, violence towards others, as well, and antisocial behaviours, it is likely that they would be cost-effective. Presently, these interventions are not provided until after individuals have committed a serious crime, even though their need for such treatments was evident, usually many years before, as was their risk of engaging in antisocial/aggressive behaviours. Further, offenders with schizophrenia include sub-types that differ as to treatment needs and engagement and compliance with treatment. Subsequent sections of the chapter describe the evidence to support the proposition that there exist sub-types of offenders with schizophrenia who present differing treatment needs and that assessment and treatment of aggressive and antisocial behaviour could, and should, be initiated when they emerge.

Recent evidence about the development of schizophrenia

Schizophrenia is a disorder of abnormal neural development that begins at conception. The abnormal neural development is reflected by characteristics of children who will subsequently present schizophrenia (Welham et al. 2009) including lower than average IQ (Dickson et al. 2012), deficits in working memory and in recognizing emotions in faces of others (Dickson et al. 2013), motor abnormalities (Walker et al. 1994), high levels of internalizing and externalizing problems, and psychotic-like-experiences (Welham et al. 2009). Consequently, the onset of schizophrenia is essentially a worsening of symptoms and deficits that have always been present.

Parents of individuals with schizophrenia, and other family members, present high levels of similar mental disorders and of antisocial behaviour (Silverton 1988). Thus, many parents of children who subsequently develop schizophrenia are unable to develop warm positive relationships with their children, and they provide them with non-optimal parenting that often includes physical and sexual abuse (Fisher et al. 2009; Hodgins et al. 2005). As their children grow up, and schizophrenia onsets, these parents and other family members do not provide a resource for their ill relative. Further, children presenting the antecedents of schizophrenia are at increased risk to be bullied by peers (Arseneault et al. 2011). Maltreatment by parents, other family members, and peers in childhood is associated with subsequent antisocial/aggressive behaviours (Vachon et al. 2015). For example, in a sample of 162 men with severe mental illness[3] recruited within general psychiatric services, 32% had experienced maltreatment in childhood and maltreatment was associated with a threefold increase in the likelihood that the victim would commit a violent assault (Bruce and Laporte 2015).

By the time an offender with schizophrenia is identified, he or she has a long history of emotional and behavioural problems, motor problems, lower than average intelligence, and difficulties in understanding social situations. These difficulties are often associated with poor academic functioning and low levels of psychosocial functioning as well as physical victimization. Importantly, these characteristics, and notably psychotic-like-experiences, are associated with an elevated risk of aggressive behaviour (Kinoshita et al. 2011).

Recent evidence about schizophrenia and antisocial and aggressive behaviours

The first study that compared crime by persons with and without a diagnosis of schizophrenia within a large birth cohort showed that behaviour problems in childhood/adolescence preceding the onset of schizophrenia characterized many of the offenders with schizophrenia (Hodgins 1992). Subsequent studies confirmed that as in the general population, amongst persons with schizophrenia, the presence of conduct disorder[4] (CD) in childhood/adolescence greatly increased the risk of violent, and non-violent crime. For example, we examined a sample of 248 men with schizophrenia aged, on average, 39 years old. CD prior to age 15 was associated with a 2.6-fold increase in the risk of a violent offence, and a fourfold increase in risk of a non-violent offence. Both associations remained significant after adjusting for lifetime diagnoses of alcohol or drug abuse/dependence. The associations of numbers of CD symptoms prior to age 15 with violent and non-violent crimes were linear, positive, and statistically significant (Hodgins et al. 2005). We replicated these associations in a sample of patients with severe mental illness (74% with schizophrenia), in their late thirties, who we recruited in general psychiatric services in the UK and showed again that CD in childhood/adolescence was associated with an increased risk of violent and non-violent crime both amongst males and females. Other studies report similar results (Hodgins et al. 2008). Not all persons with schizophrenia who present CD prior to age 15 will meet criteria for Antisocial Personality Disorder (ASPD) in adulthood. One study however, showed that men with prior CD who developed ASPD showed similar numbers of violent and non-violent crimes as did non-mentally ill offenders with CD/ASPD (Hodgins and Côté 1993).

Measuring aggressive behaviour amongst adults living in the community is a challenge. The MacArthur Community Violence Instrument (Steadman et al. 1998) was specifically

---

[3] Severe mental illness includes psychotic disorders and usually bipolar disorder. In most studies that defined samples as suffering from severe mental illness, most participants present schizophrenia.

[4] According to the *Diagnostic and Statistical Manual* (American Psychiatric Association), since version III, Conduct Disorder (CD) is only diagnosed before age 15 and this diagnosis is required for a diagnosis of Antisocial Personality Disorder (ASPD) after age 18. CD indexes a repetitive and persistent pattern of behaviour in which the basic rights of others or major age appropriate social norms or rules are violated (American Psychiatric Association, 2013). The criteria for CD also include destruction of property, deceitfulness, theft, and serious violations of rules, and various types of aggressive behaviours towards other people and animals. Importantly, it is possible to make diagnoses of CD and ASPD in the absence of aggressive behaviour. The requirement of CD for the adult diagnosis of ASPD is based on robust evidence from prospective longitudinal studies of the early onset and persistence of antisocial behaviour. Thus, the DSM requirement that the diagnosis of ASPD is only given if CD was present prior to age 15 is supported by a substantial body of research. By contrast, the diagnosis of Dissocial Personality Disorder as defined in the *ICD-10* (World Health Organization, 1992) is not consistent with the robust evidence of a behavioural syndrome of persistent violation of social norms that onsets in childhood and continues through adult life (Hodgins et al. 2018).

developed to assess aggressive behaviour amongst individuals with mental disorders. Evidence shows that when interviewed with this instrument, patients with severe mental illness report aggressive behaviour similar to that reported by collateral informants with whom they are in close contact. Consequently, self-reports of aggressive behaviour by persons with schizophrenia are considered to be valid. We used this instrument to assess aggressive behaviour in the 248 men with schizophrenia described above. CD and the number of CD symptoms were associated with aggressive behaviour, controlling for life-time diagnoses of substance use disorders, substance misuse measured objectively and subjectively, medication compliance, and obligatory care (Hodgins et al. 2005). Again, we used this instrument to assess aggressive behaviour in the UK sample of men and women with severe mental illness described above. We found that childhood/adolescent CD was also associated with aggressive behaviour towards others after adjusting for substance misuse (Hodgins et al. 2008). A US study designed to measure the effectiveness of various medications for schizophrenia included only patients with a history of compliance with medication. Even in this sample that is biased against the inclusion of participants with antisocial/aggressive behaviour, two or more CD symptoms remained associated with aggressive behaviour in the past six months after controlling for substance misuse (Swanson et al. 2006).

In clinical samples of adults with schizophrenia, the prevalence of CD is approximately 20% amongst both women and men (Hodgins et al. 1998), but for example in the UK sample of inpatients with severe mental illness, CD prior to age 15 characterized 42.0% of the men and 22.4% of the women (Hodgins et al. 2008). Amongst patients with schizophrenia in forensic services the prevalence of CD is even higher, and amongst those in correctional facilities it is further elevated (Hodgins et al. 1998). Amongst juvenile delinquents, a prospective, longitudinal study in Denmark showed that a disproportionate number were developing schizophrenia. The study examined all the offenders aged 15–19 years old in 1992. Of the 780 who were still alive in Denmark in 2001, 3.3% had developed schizophrenia as compared to the expected 0.7%. The odds of developing schizophrenia amongst those with a history of violent criminal offending (as compared to those with only non-violent offending) was 4.59 (1.54–13.74; Gosden et al. 2005). Children with CD are exposed earlier than other children to alcohol and drugs (Robins and McEvoy 1990) and by adolescence almost all of them misuse substances (Nock et al. 2006). Not surprisingly then, we have shown that males who were treated for substance misuse in adolescence were four times more likely than other males to subsequently develop schizophrenia, and that females treated in adolescence for substance misuse were seven times more likely than other females to develop schizophrenia (Hodgins et al. 2016). Prospective studies have shown that cannabis is an additional causal factor for schizophrenia amongst individuals at genetic risk for schizophrenia. Yet, it is those with CD who are most likely to use cannabis and thereby to increase the likelihood of schizophrenia (Malcolm et al. 2011).

Recent studies of men with CD prior to schizophrenia are beginning to show that these men differ not only in behaviour from other men with schizophrenia, but also as to brain structure and functioning. For example, we used magnetic resonance imaging (MRI) to examine grey matter volumes amongst men with schizophrenia and prior CD, comparing them both to men with schizophrenia and no CD and to offenders with CD and no severe mental illness, as well as to healthy non-offenders (Schiffer et al. 2013). The two groups with schizophrenia were similar in terms of age of onset and duration of illness, levels of psychotic symptoms, and medication. The two groups with CD were similar as to number of CD symptoms, lifelong aggressive behaviour, and number of criminal convictions. The men with schizophrenia and prior CD, as compared to those with schizophrenia and no history of anti-social/aggressive behaviour, displayed: (i) increased grey matter volumes in the hypothala-mus, the left putamen, the right cuneus/precuneus, and the right inferior parietal cortex after controlling for age, alcohol, and drug misuse; and (ii) decreased grey matter volumes in the inferior frontal region. Thus, amongst men with schizophrenia those with prior CD showed distinct abnormalities of brain structure. But they also showed an important similarity to the non-mentally ill offenders with prior CD: increased grey matter volumes of the hypothalamus and the inferior and superior parietal lobes, which were not associated with substance misuse. Aggressive behaviour, both prior to age 15 and over the lifespan, was positively correlated with the grey matter volume of the hypothalamus. The amygdala–hypothalamus–periaque-ductal grey system within the midbrain is thought to mediate reactive aggression in response to a real or perceived threat (Blair 2012; White et al. 2016). In another study, offenders with schizophrenia and prior CD showed neural activations similar to those of non-mentally ill offenders with prior CD and different from other men with schizophrenia and no CD when completing Theory of Mind tasks (Brune 2005). Further, those with schizophrenia and CD performed Theory of Mind tasks better than other men with schizophrenia and no CD (Schiffer et al. 2017). These studies suggest that men with schizophrenia and prior CD, pre-sent some neural abnormalities that are similar to those presented by other men with schizo-phrenia and other neural abnormalities that are similar to non-mentally ill men with prior CD. Another indication that men with schizophrenia and prior CD present a distinct pattern of neural abnormalities is their weaker response than other patients with schizophrenia to antipsychotic medication (Swanson et al. 2008).

Antisocial/aggressive behaviour that emerges in childhood characterizes many offenders with schizophrenia. By adolescence, they are misusing substances and engaging in delinquency. In the great majority of cases, neither the antisocial/aggressive behaviours nor the developing schizophrenia are treated, even though several different parenting and community programmes have been shown to be effective in reducing CD (Hawkes 2013). From mid to late adoles-cence, psychotic symptoms become more intense and it is now well established that a long duration of untreated symptoms is associated with poorer outcomes (Bechdolf et al. 2012; McFarlane et al. 2014; Perez et al. 2015; Srihari et al. 2016). Taken together, this evidence strongly suggests that offenders with schizophrenia who have a history of antisocial/aggres-sive behaviour that goes back to childhood might benefit from evidence-based rehabilitation programmes that specifically target antisocial/aggressive behaviours. Consequently, many countries have established specialized outpatient treatment programmes for individuals pre-senting prodromal symptoms of schizophrenia, sometimes referred to as Ultra-High-Risk clin-ics. Treatment programmes for youth presenting both the prodrome of schizophrenia and antisocial/aggressive behaviour and/or juvenile delinquency have recently been proposed (Purcell et al. 2012).

Do psychotic symptoms 'cause' aggressive behaviour?

One of the principal symptoms of schizophrenia are positive psychotic symptoms (hallucina-tions, delusions). It is often assumed that these psychotic symptoms 'cause' aggressive behav-iour amongst people with schizophrenia. During an acute episode of psychosis, when positive psychotic symptoms are very high, many men and women with schizophrenia engage in aggressive behaviour (Hodgins and Riaz 2011; Krakowski and Czobor 2004). Usually, indi-viduals experiencing an acute episode of psychosis are hospitalized, often involuntarily.

Regardless of whether they are in hospital, or living in the community, they present an elevated risk of violence that is directly associated with their positive psychotic symptoms. However, within days of initiating treatment with antipsychotic medication both the psychotic symptoms and the aggressive behaviour begin to decline. Once positive psychotic symptoms are reduced by the use of antipsychotic medication, some people with schizophrenia remain at increased risk of aggressive behaviour and this increased risk is associated with factors such as young age, male sex, CD, substance use, depression, and victimization (Hodgins and Klein 2016). All evidence indicates that antipsychotic medication is necessary both to reduce positive symptoms and also aggressive behaviour. A study of a large population cohort showed that when persons with schizophrenia were taking antipsychotic medications, rates of violence were lower than during periods when they did not have medication (Fazel et al. 2014). Similarly, studies of patients with schizophrenia living in the community show lower rates of aggressive behaviour amongst those receiving medication than those who do not take medication (van Dorn et al. 2013). Importantly, maintaining positive symptoms at a low level is necessary to allow persons with schizophrenia to participate in learning-based treatments, both those targeting deficits related to schizophrenia such as psychoeducation, supported education and housing, and cognitive remediation, and those targeting antisocial/aggressive behaviours and substance misuse. As noted above however, antipsychotic medication may be less powerful in reducing aggressive behaviour amongst patients with schizophrenia and CD/ASPD than amongst others with schizophrenia (Volavka et al. 2012). Thus, antipsychotic medication constitutes one critical component of treatment for all persons with schizophrenia, including offenders and those with a history of antisocial/aggressive behaviour. Whilst necessary, however, antipsychotic medication is insufficient either as a treatment for schizophrenia or for aggressive behaviour.

Offending prior to first treatment for schizophrenia

Most (72%) people with schizophrenia who will commit a criminal offence, do so prior to first contact with mental health services (Wallace et al. 2004). This fact is reflected in the results of a recent meta-analysis showing that 35% of individuals who contacted services for a first episode of psychosis had previously committed at least one assault (Large and Nielssen 2011). Another meta-analysis showed that the risk of homicide is 15.5 times higher in individuals experiencing a first episode of psychosis who were not treated as compared to the general population (Nielssen and Large 2010).

We conducted another study in London of all patients experiencing a first episode of psychosis who sought treatment in one mental health trust (Hodgins et al. 2011). The sample included 168 men and 133 women, on average 30 years old, most of whom presented schizophrenia and the others major affective disorders. Official criminal records were obtained from the Home Office Offenders' Index and the Police National Computer (PNC). We defined convictions to include both convictions and judgments of not guilty by reason of insanity or diminished responsibility. Prior to onset of psychosis, 33% of the men and 10% of the women had been convicted of at least one offence, and 19.9% of the men and 4.6% of the women had been convicted of at least one violent crime. The most common offences amongst males were violence against the person, theft and other offences, and amongst women theft, violence against the person, and fraud. Another recent study of a large sample of patients recruited from clinics in England that specifically treat individuals presenting with a first episode of psychosis shows similar results. The patients were categorized according to self-reports of delinquency prior to contact with mental health services: 48.5% low, 28.7% as stable moderate, 13.2% stable high, and 9.7% early adolescent-onset high-to-moderate (Winsper et al. 2013). In another study of men being treated in clinics for first episodes of psychosis in East London, during the first year, 26% engaged in minor violence (simple assault without injury or weapon use) and 12% in serious violence (assault resulting in injury or involving use of a lethal weapon, threat with a lethal weapon, or sexual assault) (Coid et al. 2013).

A Vicious Circle – Victimization and Aggressive Behaviour

As we noted, a significant proportion of individuals who develop schizophrenia have experienced maltreatment in childhood. Childhood maltreatment is associated with alterations to brain structures that remain throughout adulthood (Herringa et al. 2013; McCrory et al. 2010; Teicher and Samson 2016). Adults with schizophrenia are also at increased risk to experience physical victimization (Walsh et al. 2003). Amongst persons with schizophrenia, both childhood maltreatment and physical vicitimization in adulthood are associated with aggressive behaviour towards others (Hodgins et al. 2007; Sariaslan et al. 2016). Amongst the adults, their own aggressive behaviour is the strongest predictor of victimization (Hiday et al. 1999; Hodgins et al. 2007; Walsh et al. 2003). This replicated finding suggests that individuals with schizophrenia live in environments where aggressive behaviour is used to resolve conflicts. In some of these incidents, they are the aggressor and in others the victim. These findings suggest that persons with schizophrenia may fare better if they do not live in neighbourhoods where crime, and thereby the risk of victimization, is elevated. Further, patients with schizophrenia may require interventions teaching them how to avoid victimization such as not being intoxicated in a public place, not buying and using drugs, not engaging in behaviours that frighten others such as shouting in a public place, and how to resolve interpersonal conflicts without resorting to aggressive behaviour.

Pathways into care

In a cross-country study, 232 men with schizophrenia were recruited in Canada, Finland, Germany, and Sweden. They were assessed during the two weeks preceding discharge from hospital. Figure 21.1 illustrates the onset of offending with admissions to general adult psychiatric wards and to forensic psychiatric hospitals. Of the 158 patients recruited within forensic psychiatric hospitals, 123 (78%) had previously been admitted to a general adult psychiatric ward, and only 35 (22%) were first admitted to a forensic service. The 123 with a history of treatment in general psychiatric services included 49 who had committed a crime prior to their first admission to general psychiatry, 21 who committed a first crime when in the community between admissions to general psychiatry, and 53 who were sent to forensic services after committing a crime. Amongst the 74 men with schizophrenia recruited in general adult services, 18 had a history of criminality, 8 prior to their first admission and 10 after. We compared the patients who had committed a crime before first admission to general psychiatric services ($n = 59$) with those who had not committed crimes ($n = 56$) on factors that were present at first admission. In a multivariable logistic regression model, three factors were independently associated with crime before first admission. CD /ASPD were associated with a sixfold increase in the risk of offending, having been institutionalized before age 18 years was associated with a threefold increase in offending, and alcohol dependence was associated with a fourfold

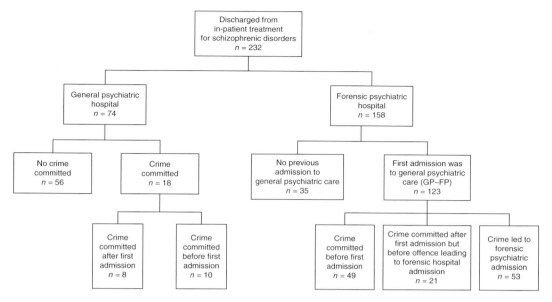

Figure 21.1   Treatment in general and forensic psychiatric services in relation to timing of offending amongst men with schizophrenia. Source: originally published in Hodgins and Müller-Isberner (2004).

increase in offending. Further, the men with schizophrenia who had committed crimes prior to first admission to clinical services obtained significantly higher ratings for deficient affective experience (facet 2) of the Psychopathy Checklist-Revised (PCL-R; Hare 2003) than those with no crime. As can be seen in Figure 21.1, some of the patients committed their first crime after first admission to general psychiatry services but before the crime that led to admission to a forensic hospital ($n = 21$). These patients, as compared to the non-offenders, were 5.8 times (95% CI 1.79–18.99) more likely to have a history of behaviour problems and 4.3 times (95% CI 1.27–14.53) more likely to present alcohol abuse or dependence. The large confidence intervals (CI) indicate, however, that a proportion of the patients who did begin offending after first admission to general psychiatry were not characterized by these or other factors that we measured (Hodgins and Müller-Isberner 2004).

   Three groups of these men with schizophrenia were compared on factors that were present at discharge, the groups being general psychiatric patients, patients who had admissions to general psychiatry before being admitted to forensic services, and patients admitted directly to forensic services. The three groups of patients differed on symptoms measured in the days preceding discharge to the community. Those treated in general psychiatric services were discharged with significantly higher levels of positive psychotic symptoms (hallucinations, delusions), negative symptoms (anhedonia, lack of motivation), and depression than those discharged by forensic psychiatric services. The three groups of patients did not differ on total Historical, Clinical, Risk Management Scale (HCR-20; Webster et al. 1997) scores, but importantly, the general psychiatric patients obtained lower H scores than those initially treated in general psychiatry and subsequently in forensic services, and higher C and R scores than both groups of patients treated in forensic services. Additionally, the patients initially treated in general psychiatric services, and later in forensic services, obtained higher PCL-R scores than either those in general psychiatry or those first admitted to forensic psychiatry (Hodgins et al. 2006).

The evidence described above, and that from other studies, shows that at first admission to psychiatric services most individuals with schizophrenia who will commit a criminal offence have already done so. Consequently, they can be identified. However, when general adult psychiatric services admit a person experiencing their first episode of psychosis, they usually do not assess past antisocial/aggressive behaviours and criminality, and consequently they do not manage it nor attempt to treat it. Most Western countries have now established within psychiatric services what are referred to as 'first-episode clinics'. These clinics usually include both inpatient and outpatient services. Patients contacting such specialized first-episode clinics are usually experiencing an acute episode of psychosis. The first step in treatment is antipsychotic medication, followed by psychoeducation that teaches patients about their illness and the treatments that they need over the long-term. Once positive psychotic symptoms have been reduced, assessment of past antisocial/aggressive behaviour and offending could be undertaken. Those with a childhood history of CD do not differ from others with schizophrenia as to symptom profiles or age of onset schizophrenia (Moran and Hodgins 2004), but they are relatively easy to identify from self-reports, reports from parents and older siblings, and from juvenile justice records. The challenge is to adequately treat both the schizophrenia and the life-long pattern of antisocial/aggressive behaviour that is accompanied by antisocial attitudes and ways of thinking that seriously, and negatively, impact engagement with services (Hodgins et al. 2007, 2009, 2011; Marion-Veyron et al. 2015). A second type of patient, less numerous than those with prior CD, can also be identified, although with somewhat more difficulty. They have recently begun engaging in aggressive behaviour as schizophrenia onset. Often their families deny their aggressive behaviour. Present evidence suggests the need for treatment with antipsychotic medication and other effective treatment for schizophrenia, plus treatments to prevent substance misuse.

Aggressive behaviour and offending amongst patients with schizophrenia in general adult psychiatric services

Given the findings on crime and aggressive behaviour prior to first treatment for schizophrenia, it is not surprising that studies of inpatient samples show very elevated rates of criminality and antisocial/aggressive behaviours. Studies of inpatients with severe mental illness show high rates of convictions for violent crimes and self and collateral reports of aggressive behaviour (Bruce et al. 2014). For example, in the study of 205 inpatients with severe mental illness from a UK inner city mental health trust, most of whom suffered from schizophrenia, official criminal records indicated that 46.7% of the men and 16.5% of the women had at least one conviction for a violent crime, and on average, the violent offenders had each been convicted of more than two crimes. Additionally, 42% of the men and 21% of the women reported having engaged in at least one serious assault over their lifetime, and 49% of the men and 39% of the women reported committing an assault in the previous six months (Hodgins et al. 2007). The 82 men with criminal records had committed 1792 crimes and the 23 female offenders had committed 458 crimes. Two years later, the patients with criminal records had not received any treatments aimed at reducing criminality, or antisocial/aggressive behaviour, including none for substance misuse (Hodgins et al. 2009). Thus, general adult services do not provide treatments aimed at specifically reducing antisocial/aggressive behaviour or preventing recidivism. The extent to which general adult psychiatric services neglect to assess and treat antisocial/aggressive behaviour amongst persons with schizophrenia is further illustrated by a study of 668 individuals who had been convicted for threatening to kill. Individuals with schizophrenia were significantly over-represented and more likely than the others to commit a homicide in the subsequent 10 years (Warren et al. 2008).

However, general adult psychiatric services do provide antipsychotic medication and encourage patients to take it continuously. As noted, these medications do reduce, to some extent, the risk of antisocial/aggressive behaviour amongst people with schizophrenia but may have less effect amongst those with CD/ASPD. Within prisons, the proportions of inmates with schizophrenia who take antipsychotic medication may be lower. In a UK study of prisoners convicted for sexual or violent offences, 94 were found to suffer from schizophrenia, of whom 75 received at least minimal treatment, and 53 continued to receive treatment after discharge. Whether not taking medication was due to inadequate mental health care or refusal by inmates is not known. However, the consequences were consistent with previous evidence of a preventive effect of medications on violence. During the two years after discharge, violence was reported by 50% of the offenders who received no treatment, 27% of those treated in prison, and 25% of those who received treatment both in prison and after release (Hodgins 2014).

The forensic approach to treatment

As the evidence described above indicates, general adult psychiatric services historically, and still typically, limit their assessments and treatment to schizophrenia. By contrast, forensic psychiatric services treat both the schizophrenia and the antisocial/aggressive behaviour. Using data from our international multi-site study (Hodgins and Müller-Isberner 2004), we used prospectively collected data to compare outcomes of men with schizophrenia who were treated in general adult services or in forensic services. The forensic patients had been hospitalized, on average, for four years, but during most of those years they had gradually spent more and more time in the community. The admission of the general psychiatric patients just prior to study entry, lasted, on average, seven months. During two years after discharge, significantly more of the general patients (29%) than the forensic patients (12%) engaged in aggressive behaviour. There were no incidents of rape or use of guns. There were five incidents involving knives, one of which led to death, one to a minor injury, and three in which the victims were not injured. Two other incidents led to major injuries, 16 to minor injuries, and the other incidents caused no physical injuries to the victim. The average number of incidents perpetrated by patients from forensic and general services did not differ. However, the three incidents that caused severe injury to victims were perpetrated by forensic patients. In a multivariate model, neither negative symptoms, medication non-compliance, obligatory care, alcohol, or drug use was associated with aggressive behaviour. Each positive symptom in the six months preceding the aggressive incident was associated with a 1.2 times increase in risk of aggressive behaviour and CD/ASPD was associated with more than a fourfold increase in risk of aggressive behaviour. The numbers of positive and negative symptoms of psychosis were higher at discharge amongst the general patients and remained higher throughout the follow-up period. Thus, the forensic approach succeeded not only in reducing aggressive behaviour more effectively than general psychiatric services but also in treating schizophrenia. Since the forensic hospitals treated greater proportions of patients at the highest risk of aggressive, that is, those with comorbid CD/ASPD, than the general psychiatric hospitals, the results suggested that interventions provided by the forensic hospitals were successful in reducing antisocial/aggressive behaviours (Hodgins et al. 2007). In the first randomized controlled trial evaluating the effectiveness of the Reasoning and Rehabilitation Programme (Ross et al. 1988) for reducing aggressive behaviour amongst male forensic patients with schizophrenia, many patients failed to complete the programme. The likelihood of non-completion was increased 13 times by a Psychopathy Checklist: Screening Version (Hart et al. 1995) score of 16 or higher, six times by a diagnosis of ASPD, and six times by a recent violent incident (Cullen et al. 2011). This finding again reflects the challenge of treating patients with schizophrenia with a life-long history of antisocial/aggressive behaviour regardless of the setting.

Similarly, amongst patients with schizophrenia living in the community, intensifying contact with a case manager had no effect on reducing aggressive behaviour (Walsh et al. 2001), nor did assertive case management, but forensic assertive case management that targeted both schizophrenia and antisocial/aggressive behaviour had a positive effect on both (Kolla and Hodgins 2013). When patients with schizophrenia are living in the community, evidence shows that court orders to comply with treatments do increase compliance and reduce violence (Swartz et al. 2016). However, appropriate and adequate treatments must be available in order to achieve these outcomes.

Despite treating patients with schizophrenia at the highest risk for violence, evidence showed that patients discharged from forensic psychiatric hospitals were less likely than those discharged from general psychiatric services to engage in aggressive behaviour towards others and showed lower levels of symptoms. Similarly, community treatment that focuses on both schizophrenia and antisocial/aggressive behaviour limits violent behaviour amongst persons with schizophrenia.

What will work to prevent violence by persons with schizophrenia?

This chapter has reviewed the extant literature on antisocial/aggressive behaviours and crime amongst persons with schizophrenia. As described, the accumulated evidence shows that most individuals with schizophrenia who will offend have either been prosecuted within the juvenile justice system or have assaulted another person prior to their first contact with psychiatric services. Most of these individuals would meet criteria for CD prior to age 15 and they present a high risk of continuing to offend through adulthood. Taken together, existing knowledge indicates that clinics for individuals developing schizophrenia and clinics for individuals experiencing their first episode of psychosis need to identify those with a past history of antisocial/aggressive behaviour and provide them with treatments targeting not only schizophrenia but also these unwanted behaviours. This proposal has the potential to reduce antisocial/aggressive behaviour by persons with schizophrenia. However, such patients usually present antisocial attitudes and ways of thinking along with antisocial/aggressive behaviour. Thus, it is essential to develop strategies for convincing them not only to take antipsychotic medications and learn about schizophrenia and the triggers of onset of an acute episode, but also, to learn not to engage in antisocial/aggressive behaviours. The effectiveness of court orders to comply with treatments, both for schizophrenia and the antisocial/aggressive behaviours, and of minimum wage whilst they take part in cognitive-behavioural treatments are worthy of investigation. Such a reorganization of mental health services would involve moving forensic expertise to general adult psychiatry.

A further step towards preventing crime by persons with schizophrenia could be taken by targeting at-risk adolescents. Questionnaires could be used to screen juvenile delinquents and adolescents in treatment for substance misuse and refer those reporting psychotic-like-experiences for a more intensive clinical assessment, and if needed, treatment. The possibility of primary prevention – that is preventing the onset of schizophrenia – requires prospective, longitudinal investigations of children presenting the known antecedents of schizophrenia.

In such a study, the subgroup presenting CD could be distinguished and provided with additional interventions that are known to effectively reduce conduct problems.

References

Alden, A., Brennan, P., Hodgins, S., and Mednick, S. (2007). Psychotic disorders and sex offending in a Danish birth cohort. *Archives of General Psychiatry* 64 (11): 1251–1258.

American Psychiatric Association (2013). *Diagnostic and statistical manual of mental disorders*, 5e. Arlington, VA: Author.

Arseneault, L., Cannon, M., Fisher, H.L. et al. (2011). Childhood trauma and children's emerging psychotic symptoms: a genetically sensitive longitudinal cohort study. *The American Journal of Psychiatry* 168 (1): 65–72.

Ashford, J.B., Wong, K.W., and Sternbach, K.O. (2008). Generic correctional programming for mentally ill offenders: a pilot study. *Criminal Justice and Behavior* 35 (4): 457–473.

Bechdolf, A., Wagner, M., Ruhrmann, S. et al. (2012). Preventing progression to first-episode psychosis in early initial prodromal states. *The British Journal of Psychiatry* 200 (1): 22–29.

Birchwood, M., Michail, M., Meaden, A. et al. (2014). Cognitive behaviour therapy to prevent harmful compliance with command hallucinations (COMMAND): a randomised controlled trial. *The Lancet Psychiatry* 1 (1): 23–33.

Blair, R.J.R. (2012). Considering anger from a cognitive neuroscience perspective. *Wiley Interdisciplinary Reviews: Cognitive Science* 3 (1): 65–74.

Brennan, P.A., Mednick, S.A., and Hodgins, S. (2000). Major mental disorders and criminal violence in a Danish birth cohort. *Archives of General Psychiatry* 57 (5): 494–500.

Bruce, M., Cobb, D., Clisby, H. et al. (2014). Violence and crime among male inpatients with severe mental illness: attempting to explain ethnic differences. *Social Psychiatry and Psychiatric Epidemiology* 49 (4): 549–558.

Bruce, M. and Laporte, D. (2015). Childhood trauma, antisocial personality typologies and recent violent acts among inpatient males with severe mental illness: exploring an explanatory pathway. *Schizophrenia Research* 162 (1–3): 285–290.

Brune, M. (2005). "Theory of mind" in schizophrenia: a review of the literature. *Schizophrenia Bulletin* 31: 21–42.

Coid, J.W., Ullrich, S., Kallis, C. et al. (2013). The relationship between delusions and violence: findings from the East London first episode psychosis study. *JAMA Psychiatry* 70 (5): 465–471.

Cullen, A.E., Clarke, A.Y., Kuipers, E. et al. (2012a). A multi-site randomized controlled trial of a cognitive skills programme for male mentally disordered offenders: social-cognitive outcomes. *Psychological Medicine* 42 (3): 557–569.

Cullen, A.E., Clarke, A.Y., Kuipers, E. et al. (2012b). A multisite randomized trial of a cognitive skills program for male mentally disordered offenders: violence and antisocial behavior outcomes. *Journal of Consulting and Clinical Psychology* 80 (6): 1114–1120.

Cullen, A.E., Soria, C., Clarke, A.Y. et al. (2011). Factors predicting dropout from the reasoning and rehabilitation program with mentally disordered offenders. *Criminal Justice and Behavior* 38 (3): 217–230.

Dean, K., Walsh, E., Moran, P. et al. (2006). Violence in women with psychosis in the community: prospective study. *The British Journal of Psychiatry* 188: 264–270.

Dickson, H., Calkins, M.E., Kohler, C.G. et al. (2013). Misperceptions of facial emotions among youth aged 9-14 years who present multiple antecedents of schizophrenia. *Schizophrenia Bulletin* 40 (2): 460–468.

Dickson, H., Laurens, K.R., Cullen, A.E., and Hodgins, S. (2012). Meta-analyses of cognitive and motor function in youth aged 16 years and younger who subsequently develop schizophrenia. *Psychological Medicine* 42 (4): 743–755.

Erb, M., Hodgins, S., Freese, R. et al. (2001). Homicide and schizophrenia: maybe treatment does have a preventive effect. *Criminal Behaviour and Mental Health* 11 (1): 6–26.

Fazel, S., Grann, M., Carlström, E. et al. (2009). Risk factors for violent crime in schizophrenia: a national cohort study of 13,806 patients. *The Journal of Clinical Psychiatry* 70 (3): 362–369.

Fazel, S., Zetterqvist, J., Larsson, H. et al. (2014). Antipsychotics, mood stabilisers, and risk of violent crime. *The Lancet* 384 (9949): 1206–1214.

Fisher, H., Morgan, C., Dazzan, P. et al. (2009). Gender differences in the association between childhood abuse and psychosis. *The British Journal of Psychiatry* 194 (4): 319–325.

Gosden, N.P., Kramp, P., Gabrielsen, G. et al. (2005). Violence of young criminals predicts schizophrenia: a 9-year register-based followup of 15- to 19-year-old criminals. *Schizophrenia Bulletin* 31 (3): 759–768.

Haddock, G., Barrowclough, C., Shaw, J.J. et al. (2009). Cognitive-behavioural therapy v. social activity therapy for people with psychosis and a history of violence: randomised controlled trial. *The British Journal of Psychiatry* 194 (2): 152–157.

Hare, R.D. (2003). *Manual for the Revised Psychopathy Checklist*, 2e. Toronto, ON: Multi-Health Systems.

Hart, S.D., Cox, D.N., and Hare, R.D. (1995). *The Hare Psychopathy Checklist: Screening Version*. Toronto, ON: Multi-Health Systems.

Hawkes, N. (2013). NICE recommends training programmes for parents to tackle children's antisocial behaviour. *BMJ* 346: f1984.

Herringa, R.J., Birn, R.M., Ruttle, P.L. et al. (2013). Childhood maltreatment is associated with altered fear circuitry and increased internalizing symptoms by late adolescence. *Proceedings of the National Academy of Sciences of the United States of America* 110 (47): 19119–19124.

Hiday, V.A., Swartz, M.S., Swanson, J.W. et al. (1999). Criminal victimization of persons with severe mental illness. *Psychiatric Services* 50 (1): 62–68.

Hockenhull, J.C., Whittington, R., Leitner, M. et al. (2012). A systematic review of prevention and intervention strategies for populations at high risk of engaging in violent behaviour: update 2002–2008. *Health Technology Assessment* 16 (3): 1–152.

Hodgins, S. (1992). Mental disorder, intellectual deficiency, and crime. *Archives of General Psychiatry* 49 (6): 476.

Hodgins, S. (2014). Among untreated violent offenders with schizophrenia, persecutory delusions are associated with violent recidivism. *Evidence-Based Mental Health* 17 (3): 75.

Hodgins, S., Alderton, J., Cree, A. et al. (2007). Aggressive behaviour, victimization and crime among severely mentally ill patients requiring hospitalisation. *The British Journal of Psychiatry* 191: 343–350.

Hodgins, S., Calem, M., Shimel, R. et al. (2011). Criminal offending and distinguishing features of offenders among persons experiencing a first episode of psychosis. *Early Intervention in Psychiatry* 5 (1): 15–23.

Hodgins, S., Checknita, D., Lindner, P. et al. (2018). Antisocial personality disorder. In: *Handbook of Forensic Neuroscience* (eds. A. Beech, A.J. Carter, R. Mann and P. Rotshtein), 229–272. Oxford, United Kingdom: Wiley.

Hodgins, S. and Côté, G. (1993). Major mental disorder and antisocial personality disorder: a criminal combination. *The Bulletin of the American Academy of Psychiatry and the Law* 21 (2): 155–160.

Hodgins, S., Côté, G., and Toupin, J. (1998). Major mental disorders and crime: an etiological hypothesis. In: *Psychopathy: Theory, Research and Implications for Society* (eds. D. Cooke, A. Forth and R.D. Hare), 231–256. Dordrecht: Kluwer Academic Publishers.

Hodgins, S., Cree, A., Alderton, J., and Mak, T. (2008). From conduct disorder to severe mental illness: associations with aggressive behaviour, crime and victimization. *Psychological Medicine* 38 (7): 975–987.

Hodgins, S., Cree, A., Khalid, F. et al. (2009). Do community mental health teams caring for severely mentally ill patients adjust treatments and services based on patients' antisocial or criminal behaviours? *European Psychiatry* 24 (6): 373–379.

Hodgins, S. and Klein, S. (2016). New clinically relevant findings about violence by people with schizophrenia. *Canadian Journal of Psychiatry* 62 (2): 86–93.

Hodgins, S., Larm, P., and Westerman, J. (2016). Individuals developing schizophrenia are hidden among adolescent substance misusers. *Psychological Medicine* 46 (14): 3041–3050.

Hodgins, S. and Müller-Isberner, R. (2004). Preventing crime by people with schizophrenic disorders: the role of psychiatric services. *The British Journal of Psychiatry* 185: 245–250.

Hodgins, S., Müller-Isberner, R., and Allaire, J.-F. (2006). Attempting to understand the increase in the numbers of forensic beds in Europe: a multi-site study of patients in forensic and general psychiatric services. *International Journal of Forensic Mental Health* 5 (2): 173–184.

Hodgins, S., Müller-Isberner, R., Freese, R. et al. (2007). A comparison of general adult and forensic patients with schizophrenia living in the community. *International Journal of Forensic Mental Health* 6 (1): 63–75.

Hodgins, S. and Riaz, M. (2011). Violence and phases of illness: differential risk and predictors. *European Psychiatry* 26 (8): 518–524.

Hodgins, S., Tiihonen, J., and Ross, D. (2005). The consequences of conduct disorder for males who develop schizophrenia: associations with criminality, aggressive behavior, substance use, and psychiatric services. *Schizophrenia Research* 78 (2–3): 323–335.

Jotangia, A., Rees-Jones, A., Gudjonsson, G.H., and Young, S. (2015). A multi-site controlled trial of the R&R2MHP cognitive skills program for mentally disordered female offenders. *International Journal of Offender Therapy and Comparative Criminology* 59 (5): 539–559.

Kane, J.M., Robinson, D.G., Schooler, N.R. et al. (2015). Comprehensive versus usual community care for first-episode psychosis: 2-year outcomes from the NIMH RAISE early treatment program. *The American Journal of Psychiatry* 173: 362–372.

Kinoshita, Y., Shimodera, S., Nishida, A. et al. (2011). Psychotic-like experiences are associated with violent behavior in adolescents. *Schizophrenia Research* 126 (1–3): 245–251.

Kolla, N. and Hodgins, S. (2013). Treatment of people with schizophrenia who behave violently towards others: a review of the empirical literature on treatment effectiveness. In: *What Works in Offender Rehabilitation: An Evidence-Based Approach to Assessment and Treatment* (eds. L. Craig, L. Dixon and T.A. Gannon), 319–339. Chichester, UK: Wiley Blackwell.

Krakowski, M. and Czobor, P. (2004). Gender differences in violent behaviors: relationship to clinical symptoms and psychosocial factors. *The American Journal of Psychiatry* 161 (3): 459–465.

Large, M. and Nielssen, O. (2011). Violence in first-episode psychosis: a systematic review and meta-analysis. *Schizophrenia Research* 125 (2–3): 209–220.

Large, M., Smith, G., and Nielssen, O. (2009). The relationship between the rate of homicide by those with schizophrenia and the overall homicide rate: a systematic review and meta-analysis. *Schizophrenia Research* 112 (1–3): 123–129.

Livingston, J.D., Chu, K., Milne, T., and Brink, J. (2015). Probationers mandated to receive forensic mental health services in Canada: risks/needs, service delivery, and intermediate outcomes. *Psychology, Public Policy, and Law* 21 (1): 72–84.

Malcolm, C.P., Picchioni, M.M., DiForti, M. et al. (2011). Pre-morbid conduct disorder symptoms are associated with cannabis use among individuals with a first episode of psychosis. *Schizophrenia Research* 126 (1–3): 81–86.

Marion-Veyron, R., Lambert, M., Cotton, S.M. et al. (2015). History of offending behavior in first episode psychosis patients: a marker of specific clinical needs and a call for early detection strategies among young offenders. *Schizophrenia Research* 161 (2–3): 163–168.

McCrory, E., de Brito, S.A., and Viding, E. (2010). Research review: the neurobiology and genetics of maltreatment and adversity. *Journal of Child Psychology and Psychiatry, and Allied Disciplines* 51 (10): 1079–1095.

McFarlane, W.R., Susser, E., McCleary, R. et al. (2014). Reduction in incidence of hospitalizations for psychotic episodes through early identification and intervention. *Psychiatric Services* 65 (10): 1194–1200.

Moran, P. and Hodgins, S. (2004). The correlates of comorbid antisocial personality disorder in schizophrenia. *Schizophrenia Bulletin* 30 (4): 791–802.

Morgan, R.D., Flora, D.B., Kroner, D.G. et al. (2012). Treating offenders with mental illness: a research synthesis. *Law and Human Behavior* 36 (1): 37–50.

Morgan, R.D., Kroner, D.G., Mills, J.F. et al. (2014). Treating justice involved persons with mental illness: preliminary evaluation of a comprehensive treatment program. *Criminal Justice and Behavior* 41 (7): 902–916.

Müller-Isberner, R. (2017). The use of scientific evidence about schizophrenia and violence in clinical services: a challenge that is not being met. *Canadian Journal of Psychiatry* 62: 84–85.

Nielssen, O. and Large, M. (2010). Rates of homicide during the first episode of psychosis and after treatment: a systematic review and meta-analysis. *Schizophrenia Bulletin* 36 (4): 702–712.

Nock, M.K., Kazdin, A.E., Hiripi, E., and Kessler, R.C. (2006). Prevalence, subtypes, and correlates of DSM-IV conduct disorder in the national comorbidity survey replication. *Psychological Medicine* 36 (5): 699–710.

Perez, J., Jin, H., Russo, D.A. et al. (2015). Clinical effectiveness and cost-effectiveness of tailored intensive liaison between primary and secondary care to identify individuals at risk of a first psychotic illness (the LEGs study): a cluster-randomised controlled trial. *The Lancet Psychiatry* 2 (11): 984–993.

Purcell, R., Fraser, R., Greenwood-Smith, C. et al. (2012). Managing risks of violence in a youth mental health service: a service model description. *Early Intervention in Psychiatry* 6 (4): 469–475.

Quinn, J. and Kolla, N. (2017). From Clozapine to Cognitive Remediation: A Review of Biological and Psychosocial Treatments for Violence in Schizophrenia. The Canadian Journal of Psychiatry, 62(2), 94–101.

Rampling, J., Furtado, V., Winsper, C. et al. (2016). Non-pharmacological interventions for reducing aggression and violence in serious mental illness: a systematic review and narrative synthesis. *European Psychiatry* 34: 17–28.

Rees-Jones, A., Gudjonsson, G., and Young, S. (2012). A multi-site controlled trial of a cognitive skills program for mentally disordered offenders. *BMC Psychiatry* 12: 44.

Reif, S., George, P., Braude, L. et al. (2014). Recovery housing: assessing the evidence. *Psychiatric Services* 65 (3): 295–300.

Robins, L.N. and McEvoy, J.P. (1990). Conduct problems as predictors of substance abuse. In: *Straight and Devious Pathways from Childhood to Adulthood* (eds. L.N. Robins and M. Rutter), 182–204. New York, NY: Cambridge University Press.

Ross, R.R., Fabiano, E.A., and Ewles, C.D. (1988). Reasoning and rehabilitation. *International Journal of Offender Therapy and Comparative Criminology* 32: 29–35.

Sariaslan, A., Lichtenstein, P., Larsson, H., and Fazel, S. (2016). Triggers for violent criminality in patients with psychotic disorders. *JAMA Psychiatry* 73 (8): 796–803.

Schiffer, B., Leygraf, N., Müller, B.W. et al. (2013). Structural brain alterations associated with schizophrenia preceded by conduct disorder: a common and distinct subtype of schizophrenia? *Schizophrenia Bulletin* 39 (5): 1115–1128.

Schiffer, B., Pawliczek, C., Müller, B.W. et al. (2017). Neural mechanisms underlying affective theory of mind in violent antisocial personality disorder and/or schizophrenia. *Schizophrenia Bulletin* 43 (6): 1229–1239.

Silverton, L. (1988). Crime and the schizophrenia spectrum: a study of three Danish cohorts. In: *Biological Contributions to Crime Causation*, NATO ASI Series, Series D: Behavioural and Social Sciences, vol. 40 (eds. T.E. Moffitt and S.A. Mednick), 183–210. Dordrecht, NL: Springer Netherlands.

Srihari, V.H., Jani, A., and Gray, M. (2016). Early intervention for psychotic disorders: building population health systems. *JAMA Psychiatry* 73 (2): 101–102.

Steadman, H.J., Mulvey, E.P., Monahan, J. et al. (1998). Violence by people discharged from acute psychiatric inpatient facilities and by others in the same neighborhoods. *Archives of General Psychiatry* 55: 393–401.

Swanson, J.W., Swartz, M.S., van Dorn, R.A. et al. (2006). A national study of violent behavior in persons with schizophrenia. *Archives of General Psychiatry* 63 (5): 490–499.

Swanson, J.W., Swartz, M.S., van Dorn, R.A. et al. (2008). Comparison of antipsychotic medication effects on reducing violence in people with schizophrenia. *The British Journal of Psychiatry* 193 (1): 37–43.

Swartz, M.S., Bhattacharya, S., Robertson, A.G., and Swanson, J.W. (2016). Involuntary outpatient commitment and the elusive pursuit of violence prevention: a view from the United States. *Canadian Journal of Psychiatry* 62 (2): 102–108.

Teicher, M.H. and Samson, J.A. (2016). Annual research review: enduring neurobiological effects of childhood abuse and neglect. *Journal of Child Psychology and Psychiatry, and Allied Disciplines* 57 (3): 241–266.

Teplin, L.A., McClelland, G.M., Abram, K.M., and Weiner, D.A. (2005). Crime victimization in adults with severe mental illness: comparison with the national crime victimization survey. *Archives of General Psychiatry* 62 (8): 911–921.

Tiihonen, J., Isohanni, M., Räsänen, P. et al. (1997). Specific major mental disorders and criminality: a 26-year prospective study of the 1966 northern Finland birth cohort. *The American Journal of Psychiatry* 154 (6): 840–845.

Vachon, D.D., Krueger, R.F., Rogosch, F.A., and Cicchetti, D. (2015). Assessment of the harmful psychiatric and behavioral effects of different forms of child maltreatment. *JAMA Psychiatry* 72 (11): 1135–1142.

van Dorn, R.A., Desmarais, S.L., Petrila, J. et al. (2013). Effects of outpatient treatment on risk of arrest of adults with serious mental illness and associated costs. *Psychiatric Services* 64 (9): 856–862.

Volavka, J., Swanson, J.W., and Citrome, L.L. (2012). Understanding and managing violence in schizophrenia. In: *Comprehensive Care of Schizophrenia: A Textbook of Clinical Management*, 2e (eds. J.A. Lieberman and R.M. Murray), 262–290. New York, NY: Oxford University Press.

Walker, E.F., Savoie, T., and Davis, D. (1994). Neuromotor precursors of schizophrenia. *Schizophrenia Bulletin* 20 (3): 441–451.

Wallace, C., Mullen, P.E., and Burgess, P. (2004). Criminal offending in schizophrenia over a 25-year period marked by deinstitutionalization and increasing prevalence of comorbid substance use disorders. *The American Journal of Psychiatry* 161 (4): 716–727.

Walsh, E., Gilvarry, C., Samele, C. et al. (2001). Reducing violence in severe mental illness: randomised controlled trial of intensive case management compared with standard care. *BMJ* 323 (7321): 1093.

Walsh, E., Moran, P., Scott, C. et al. (2003). Prevalence of violent victimisation in severe mental illness. *The British Journal of Psychiatry* 183: 233–238.

Warren, L.J., Mullen, P.E., Thomas, S.D.M. et al. (2008). Threats to kill: a follow-up study. *Psychological Medicine* 38 (4): 599–605.

Webster, C.D., Douglas, K., Eaves, D., and Hart, S. (1997). *HCR:20: Assessing Risk for Violence, Version 2*. Burnaby, BC: Mental Health Law and Policy Institute, Simon Fraser University.

Welham, J., Isohanni, M., Jones, P., and McGrath, J. (2009). The antecedents of schizophrenia: a review of birth cohort studies. *Schizophrenia Bulletin* 35 (3): 603–623.

Wenzlow, A.T., Ireys, H.T., Mann, B. et al. (2011). Effects of a discharge planning program on Medicaid coverage of state prisoners with serious mental illness. *Psychiatric Services* 62 (1): 73–78.

White, S.F., VanTieghem, M., Brislin, S.J. et al. (2016). Neural correlates of the propensity for retaliatory behavior in youths with disruptive behavior disorders. *The American Journal of Psychiatry* 173 (3): 282–290.

Winsper, C., Singh, S.P., Marwaha, S. et al. (2013). Pathways to violent behavior during first-episode psychosis: a report from the UK National EDEN Study. *JAMA Psychiatry* 70 (12): 1287–1293.

World Health Organization (1992). *The ICD-10 classification of mental and behavioural disorders: Clinical descriptions and diagnostic guidelines.* Geneva: World Health Organization.

Yates, K., Kunz, M., Czobor, P. et al. (2005). A cognitive, behaviorally based program for patients with persistent mental illness and a history of aggression, crime, or both: structure and correlates of completers of the program. *The Journal of the American Academy of Psychiatry and the Law* 33 (2): 214–222.

Yip, V.C.-Y., Gudjonsson, G.H., Perkins, D. et al. (2013). A non-randomised controlled trial of the R&R2MHP cognitive skills program in high risk male offenders with severe mental illness. *BMC Psychiatry* 13: 267.

22

Intimate Partner Violence Perpetrator Programmes
Ideology or Evidence-Based Practice?

Nicola Graham-Kevan[1] and Elizabeth A. Bates[2]

[1] University of Central Lancashire, Preston, UK
[2] University of Cumbria, Carlisle, UK

Introduction

The 'what works' approach to evidence-based practice has emphasized the need for systematic reviews and meta-analyses to explore the effectiveness of correctional interventions; indeed, the most effective interventions and programmes incorporate the risk, need, responsivity principles (Andrews and Bonta 2010; Prendergast et al. 2013) and this may have no impact or even increase domestic violence (Welsh and Rocque 2014). In this chapter, we will explore current approaches to Intimate Partner Violence (IPV) perpetrator programmes and contrast these with the empirical evidence in terms of treatment need and treatment efficacy. Some alternative approaches will be explored and conclusions drawn as to the way forward.

Current Theoretical Models and Influences

Models derived from feminist and gendered perspectives on IPV (e.g. Dobash and Dobash 1979; Schwartz and DeKeseredy 2003) suggest it is a problem of men's violence towards women that has its roots in patriarchy. The premise being that men are motivated to control and dominate their female partner due to their expectations around male privilege (Pence and Paymar 1993), hence IPV is caused by male gender and patriarchy. From this perspective, a psychoeducational programme to re-educate men about their use of control and violence against women appears an appropriate choice. The Duluth Model was established in the United States in 1981 as an intervention derived from the Duluth Domestic Abuse Intervention Project (Pence and Paymar 1993) in Duluth, Minnesota. This curriculum was developed by activists

The Wiley Handbook of What Works in Violence Risk Management: Theory, Research and Practice,
First Edition. Edited by J. Stephen Wormith, Leam A. Craig, and Todd E. Hogue.
© 2020 John Wiley & Sons Ltd. Published 2020 by John Wiley & Sons Ltd.

within the battered women's movement and five battered women (Pence and Paymar 1993) who believed domestic violence was caused by men's patriarchal ideology. Within such programmes the 'Power and Control Wheel' is positioned centrally as a tool for men to understand their need for power and the behaviours they use to maintain control over women. Women's aggression within this model is either ignored or understood as self-defensive. As a model, it continues to be influential in current programmes and interventions in the UK, US, and Canada (Bates et al. 2017) and in Europe (Graham-Kevan 2007). This is in spite of a lack of supportive data for the theoretical assumptions (e.g. patriarchal beliefs; Smith 1990; Sugarman and Frankel 1996; coercive control as a male prerogative; Bates et al. 2014; Carney and Barner 2012; Graham-Kevan and Archer 2009) or treatment components (e.g. Feder and Forde 2000).

There is a wealth of research detailing empirical problems with this model (e.g. Bohall et al. 2016; Dixon and Graham-Kevan 2011; Dutton and Corvo 2007; Stuart 2005) to the extent that some authors present a coherent argument as to why referring to, or directly delivering Duluth type programmes may contravene professional ethics (Corvo et al. 2008) and be inconsistent with guidelines for working with clients (e.g. Pender 2012; U.S. Department of Health and Human Services 2008).

Programmes based on the Duluth model fail to address the lack of sex-differences in IPV in western nations (Archer 2000, 2006), in young couples (Wincentak et al. 2016), women's propensity for verbal aggression (Stockdale et al. 2013), physical aggression (Archer 2002, 2006; Bair-Merritt et al. 2010) control towards their male partners (Bates and Graham-Kevan 2016; Graham-Kevan and Archer 2009; Straus and Gozjolko 2016), men's victimization (Hines and Douglas 2010; Hines et al. 2007), IPV in same-sex couples (Badenes-Ribera et al. 2016; Finneran and Stephenson 2013), the prevalence of bidirectional violence (Langhinrichsen-Rohling et al. 2012), the overlap of IPV and other types of familial (Choenni et al. 2017) and non-familial violence (e.g. aggression; Bates et al. 2014; Farrington et al. 2017), substance use (Birkley and Eckhardt 2015; Spencer et al. 2016), and the range of risk factors that are known to be predictive of IPV perpetration (Capaldi et al. 2012; Spencer et al. 2016; Thornton et al. 2010, 2012).

Indeed, IPV's association with a broad range of problematic behaviours such as smoking (Crane et al. 2013), problem gambling (Dowling et al. 2016); and substance use (Cafferky et al. 2018) suggest problems with impulsivity (Leone et al. 2016) which may be best understood from a trauma-informed approach. Such approaches recognize the impact of exposure to adverse childhood experiences (Smith-Marek et al. 2015) and the resulting neurocognitive changes such as dysregulated emotions (Gardner et al. 2014; Harding et al. 2013; Iverson et al. 2014) which manifest in poor stress tolerance and high positive (Dir et al. 2016) and negative urgency (Blake et al. 2018). Therefore, psychoeducational approaches such as Duluth or Duluth/Cognitive Behavioural Therapy (CBT) hybrid may be unsuccessful as they fail to target core treatment needs such as emotion dysregulation (Birkley and Eckhardt 2015).

Using a trauma-informed approach allows a more gender-inclusive approach (e.g. Dutton 2010; Hamel 2007) to research and intervention with IPV perpetrators, it leads to a focus on individual circumstances rather than preconceived gender attributions. This includes studying IPV alongside other forms of aggression, rather than seeing it as having a special aetiology (e.g. Felson 2002) and considering it within other aggression models such as the General Aggression Model (Anderson and Bushman 2002) or Finkel's I³ Theory (Finkel 2007). By recognizing the heterogeneous nature of IPV offenders as a group, it is possible to tailor interventions to make them more effective. For example, this may include recognizing the importance of salient factors on the development of conflict resolution strategies in relationships such as adverse childhood experiences (Miller et al. 2013), as well as the current factors acting as barriers to effective management of conflict such as anger and hostility (Norlander and Eckhardt 2005), internalized negative emotions (Birkley and Eckhardt 2015) and attachment anxiety (Dutton 2006).

The Gate-Keepers

Within the US and UK there are barriers to implementing alternative approaches to Duluth informed programmes. Within the UK, there is an organization called 'Respect' which provides accreditation to programmes that meet their standards for working with IPV perpetrators and their victims. Respect (2012) indicates the accreditation standard applies to any organizations working with men who use violence towards their female partners and such accreditation is currently only available for programmes where it is a male using violence towards a female, thus excluding same-sex and female-perpetrator programmes. Programmes that are accredited through this organization must 'hold men accountable for their violence which originates in their sense of entitlement and male privilege'; it is strictly against the accreditation criteria to discuss any motive or circumstance which could count as excusing the violence (e.g. alcohol or substance misuse) and, at no point in their criteria, is there any indication that women can be violent, or that relationships can contain mutual violence.

Within the UK, Respect is very influential in terms of lobbying the Government around IPV policy and practice. Respect's continued belief in a feminist model of IPV may explain their current endorsement of their approach based on the findings of Project Mirabel which was evaluated by Kelly and Westmarland (2015). This study sought to address some of the issues previously seen with Duluth IPV perpetrators evaluations, by evaluating Respect's accredited programmes on a large scale using a control group. They compared their treatment group with a matched control group and found 'there to be no significant differences in reductions in violence and abuse' (p. 8). This should have been the headline finding but unfortunately the authors (Kelly and Westmarland 2015) and Respect chose to ignore their own research findings and instead claimed that men who completed Respect-accredited programmes largely desisted from using physical and sexual violence as well as other forms of abuse (Respect 2012) Their 'evidence' for this (and many other claims within the report) comes from comparing all those surveyed at baseline to only those still engaged and prepared to take part in the research 12 months later. So, for physical aggression, their data compared pre-programme responses from 99 participants to the responses from the 52 remaining participants post-programme. Such a comparison is fundamentally flawed empirically; research has demonstrated that treatment dropouts and completers are significantly different on a number of variables including drug use, criminal history and previous domestic violence offences (Jewell and Wormith 2010). The authors are either extremely naive in terms of research understanding, which is inconsistent with the design of the pilot which was good, or deliberately chose to present findings in such a manner to imply a success they did not find. Additionally, this report is not peer reviewed and does not, therefore, adhere to What Works principles. Unfortunately, some advocacy groups appear more wedded to their ideology than evidence, using 'false facts' (Gelles 2007) or manipulating figures (Graham-Kevan 2007; Straus 2007) to control the narrative.

Similar problems exist in the US and Europe, where lobbyists are allowed to dictate policy, creating a stifling effect at best, but often a chilling effect on innovation due to fear of being seen as not 'pro-women/victim'. This effect may explain why the evidence presented below has failed to significantly shift policy or practice.

Partner Abuse Review of Domestic Violence Perpetrator Programmes

Recently, there have been a number of reviews commissioned to explore current domestic violence perpetrator provision in several areas of the world. Within recent issues of the journal *Partner Abuse* there have been reviews published from the UK (Bates et al. 2017), US, and Canada (Cannon et al. 2016), Sub-Saharan Africa (McCloskey et al. 2016), Latin American and the Caribbean (Santoveñada and da Silva 2016), and South Asian and Middle Eastern countries (Niaz et al. 2017).

Bates et al. (2017) reviewed provision within the UK by surveying providers (e.g. prisons, probation services, private providers). The response rate to their survey was very low (only 10%) and one of their main discussion points in their results was about the lack of willingness to engage by those they had contacted. With such ideological debate and political controversy, providers and those working in the area had viewed such a review with suspicion around motives, funding, and how the results would be used. Within the responses that were received, the majority of provision was still aimed at men who had abused their female partners. There was evidence of continuing dominant influence of the Duluth/feminist model, which is often mixed with some CBT approaches. The authors concluded that the Duluth model is still very influential within practice in the UK and that it is something that is significantly impeding practice moving forward in terms of reducing IPV offending. UK researchers have called for more evidence-based practice within the area and an end to the 'immunity' from the requirement to evidence efficacy that the model seems to enjoy (e.g. Dixon and Graham-Kevan 2011; Dixon et al. 2012). Researchers from Canada (Corvo et al. 2008) have made similar calls. US researchers have literally been calling for this for over 25 years (e.g. Straus 1992; Winstok and Straus 2016).

As with the UK, the US provision is regulated and accredited but again is not grounded in evidence-based practice (Hamel 2016). The majority of services and intervention policies focus of women as victims and target men as perpetrators utilizing psychoeducational programmes (Shernock and Russell 2012). There is little tailoring of interventions to meet the needs of the perpetrators (Maiuro and Eberle 2008). Cannon et al. (2016) reviewed the provision within the US. Almost half the treatment providers reported believing that patriarchy was an important causal factor in IPV perpetration with a much lower proportion considering personality and reciprocal aggression as being important. This discrepancy indicated that those providing treatment may not be aware of current research in the area. Cannon et al. (2016) concluded that such an insufficient knowledge of important risk factors in IPV perpetration is a significant issue and one that needs to be considered by those working in policy and practice.

Although the US and UK reviews shared many similar issues and findings with significant overlap in the current models and practice, the other reviews raised different matters for consideration. In their review of Latin America and the Caribbean, Santoveñada and da Silva (2016) found there was a strong focus on victim services for IPV with only relatively recent discussion about the need for effective interventions to include both victim and perpetrator services. They found effectiveness of the programmes varied with some reporting over 90% rates of re-offending. In Latin America, there is currently no policy or practice in place to assess the efficacy of programmes being used, which is a concern. Participants reported feeling that standards/criteria were inadequate for current provision and discussed the heterogeneity of perpetrators that required tailored interventions. The authors concluded there was also a need to ensure inclusivity and that ethnic minorities are considered within programmes so they may be adapted to indigenous populations. They further concluded there was a need to tailor interventions towards younger people as the relationship dynamics may differ in important ways.

In their review of IPV in Sub-Saharan Africa, McCloskey et al. (2016) describe the high prevalence of IPV within these nations with it being known to affect 36% of the population. The authors found that community-based interventions and engagement were much more strongly emphasized in Africa than in the US and Europe. They concluded that there were some programmes in their regions showing promise, with the evidence was suggesting behavioural.

Across all the reviews, Hamel (2016) commented that despite much of the empirical research detailing high levels of female perpetrated IPV, nearly all programmes within this review were directed towards male perpetrators. He goes on to argue that too often training programmes for working with perpetrators are not grounded in up-to-date, rigorous research, although he also acknowledged that interest in evidence-based practice in this area is growing.

Reviews of the Effectiveness of Programmes

Whilst the *Partner Abuse* reviews aimed to explore the current IPV programmes found across the world, there have been other reviews that have more specifically explored the effectiveness of this current provision. For example, Babcock et al. (2004) performed a meta-analysis ($N = 22$ studies) that evaluated treatment programmes for domestically-violent men, and found minimal effects, concluding that the current interventions are inadequate in reducing recidivism much beyond the effect of arrest and other criminal justice sanctions. Feder et al. (2008) performed a systematic review to assess efforts of court-mandated interventions. When utilizing official reports there was a modest effect seen in terms of effectiveness but this disappeared when using victim reports; the authors attributed this to high attrition of victims within the studies they reviewed. For quasi-experimental designs that used a no-intervention/treatment comparison there was inconsistent findings that suggested there was actually a harmful effect. Psychological treatments that cause harm are often difficult to identify due to methodological difficulties including client drop out, increases in variance, longer-term deterioration and independent replication (Lilienfeld 2007). The authors concluded there are doubts about the effectiveness of these current programmes in reducing re-offending.

Eckhardt et al. (2013) explored and reviewed all studies published since 1990 that used either a randomized control trial or a quasi-experimental design, where they compared an intervention to a relevant comparison group. This resulted in a review of 20 studies of 'traditional' programmes, 10 further studies that looked at alternative programmes and also some programmes for victims. The review concluded that there continued to be an inability to draw firm conclusions about the effectiveness of the programmes due to the ambiguous results and serious methodological problems with the evaluations. Within the studies reviewed, there were mixed results with around half of the results demonstrating the traditional (Duluth informed) programmes were more effective than the controls; however, when the more seriously methodologically flawed studies are removed this positive effect became less substantial. There was little evidence favouring one intervention over any of the others in terms of the traditional treatment models. The review did find some hope in the shape of alternative programmes that utilize work around motivation and readiness to change.

Vigurs et al. (2016) performed a review of reviews in line with the 'What Works' literature for the UK's College of Policing. The review focused on programmes delivered and accredited by the Criminal Justice System in the country of origin. The authors once again concluded that there was insufficient evidence to be able to identify the clear impact of programmes on perpetrators or other outcomes. Furthermore, there was no evidence from the reviews that could lead them to conclude that one type of programme or curriculum was more effective than another. None of the programmes within the reviews were tailored or adapted in any way. There was little evidence of the need to recognize and accommodate the heterogeneity of perpetrators and their relationship dynamics, despite this responsivity being a key part of the Risk-Needs-Responsivity (RNR) principles. Instead, there appeared to be an assumption that the development of an effective programme would be sufficient to address all perpetrators of IPV.

Duluth/CBT hybrids

Due to CBT programmes generally being the treatment of choice for non-IPV programmes, psychologists attempted to improve the efficacy of Duluth-based group outcomes with the addition of CBT. CBT is proven to be effective to some extent in treating anger (Del Vecchio and O'Leary 2004; Saini 2009) and substance abuse (Wexler 2013). Unfortunately, rather than CBT enhancing Duluth programmes, it appears that Duluth programmes appeared to remove any CBT effect and this left Duluth/CBT hybrids with similarly disappointing outcomes to the pure Duluth model men's groups (Babcock et al. 2004; Eckhardt et al. 2013; Feder and Wilson 2005). It highlights the effect of treatment delivery having minimal effect when the ideological basis of the programme is flawed. Therefore, as there is no evidence that any current programmes are effective at reducing IPV (e.g. Eckhardt et al. 2013; Feder and Wilson 2005) there is an urgent need to explore alternative approaches.

Bates et al.'s (2017) review further found that there was only a small proportion of their sample (23.8%) involved external evaluators or agencies, and 57.1% did not collect any data, or have any awareness of whether programme completers went on to re-offend. Whereas, Eckhardt et al. (2013) in their review, found that research design impacted on how favourable the results were from the traditional programmes. Those using randomized control trials found no significant effectiveness whereas those using quasi-experimental methods were more likely to show favourable results compared to no-treatment control groups. Similar to that found in Babcock et al.'s (2004) meta-analysis, as the research design improves and becomes more rigorous, the likelihood of finding significance in effectiveness declines. Eckhardt et al. (2013) further highlighted the serious limitations with current research and evaluation exploring effectiveness in this area. Methodologically speaking, they are mostly US based and have small sample sizes and suffer from similar issues to studies in other Criminal Justice topics.

Research has also demonstrated or discussed issues with high rates of offender attrition (e.g. Jewell and Wormith 2010) which conflates the comparison when pre- and post-comparisons are made, as well as not being clear about penalties for non-compliance (e.g. Vigurs et al. 2016), and findings of current studies often represent group effects rather than individual effects which is an issue when IPV offenders and perpetrators are such a heterogeneous group (Eckhardt et al. 2013). Feder et al. (2008) highlight four concerns with studies in their review: lack of generalizability due to small, restricted samples; reliance on official reports of recidivism; low victim reports and the validity of using a treatment drop-out group as a comparison. It seems that as programmes have become more in demand, the influence of research in practice that is valued in other areas (e.g. in developing therapies for mental health issues) has never been seen as critical or integral to the development of IPV interventions (Birkley and Eckhardt 2015; Eckhardt et al. 2013).

Alternative models of intervention

By applying empirically-grounded theory and evidence-based practice to the design and delivery of new types of intervention, it is possible to preserve the dignity of those receiving the intervention (Ortega and Busch-Armendariz 2014), work within professional guidelines and ethical practice, enhance victim safety, and be pro-science.

There is emerging evidence for interventions that utilize new approaches that are more consistent with current clinical approaches to behaviour change. Zarling et al. (2017) explored the impact of an Acceptance and Commitment Therapy (ACT)-based programme (Achieving Change Through Values-Based Behaviour [ACTV]; Lawrence et al. 2014) on post-programme recidivism. They compared data on a sample of 3474 men who, following their arrest for IPV were court-mandated to an intervention programme (non-randomized either ACTV or Duluth/CBT). Comparing incidence and frequency of new criminal charges 12 months post-intervention for the entire intent-to-treat sample and treatment completers only they found that ACTV participants had significantly fewer charges on average than Duluth/CBT participants. Although, ACTV had higher drop-out than Duluth/CBT groups, the higher success rate of ACTV emerged for both treatment completers and non-completers.

Similarly, an unpublished evaluation of a trauma-informed programme that utilized Dialectical Behaviour Therapy (DBT) approaches and piloted in a male prison in the UK, Inner Strength, found that in their sample of released programme completers (18 men) there was no evidence of any IPV-(or other offences) related charges, cautions, or call-outs approximately 12 months post-release. Although there was no control group, the author of the report (Graham-Kevan 2014) used the Offender Group Reconviction Scale (OGRs) scores which allowed a comparison of actual reconviction rates to the expected reconviction rates. The mean ORGs score for the cohort was 71 which predicts that 35% of the cohort would have another offence within six months. Therefore, the programme appears to have been successful in preventing re-offending (both domestic-violence related and non-domestic violence) within the first 12 months post release. A longer-term evaluation is currently being conducted by Oxford University. Another positive feature of this programme, unlike the ACTV, was that it had very lower attrition (98.5% completion based on a sample of 68 men).

Working with one member of a couple dyad may hinder long-term behaviour change, therefore, the use of couples' programmes are a viable option (Karakurt et al. 2016). Armenti and Babcock (2016) conducted a systematic review of research on couples/conjoint treatment. The use of couples' therapy is worthy of investigation with some caution; agencies must carefully screen for couples where both partners wish to stay together, neither partner is afraid of the other, and the violence within the relationship is the result of escalating conflict rather than a systematic attempt to exert coercive control one over the other. They concluded that conjoint approaches for IPV are empirically promising. They comment that although '… the political barriers are steep, perhaps in no other field will finding an effective intervention have a greater impact on changing public policy and the safety of women and families' (p. 120).

There are increasing calls for programmes to address IPV in same-sex relationships, particularly as research suggests that it is as common as IPV in heterosexual relationships (Langhinrichsen-Rohling et al. 2012). Longobardi and Badenes-Ribera (2017) reviewed the literature and found that research suggests that same-sex IPV appears in many aspects similar to heterosexual IPV in terms of the range of abusive behaviours used (physical, psychological, sexual) and the common pattern of bi-directional violence (Langhinrichsen-Rohling et al. 2012). Additional risks include the role of internalized homophobia, experiences of discriminations and whether the individuals are 'out' in terms of their sexuality. Longobardi and Badenes-Ribera (2017) called for the integration of heterosexual and same-sex treatment need factors into programmes for those experiencing IPV in same-sex relationships.

Conclusion

The Duluth Model, as a basis for understanding treatment need for IPV perpetrators (male, female, or both members of the dyad) is flawed. Reducing any complex human behaviour to simplistic explanatory models is unlikely to lead to understanding and in areas were complexity is a given, such as relationship behaviours, it is utterly futile. The assertion of the Duluth's authors (Pence and Paymar 1993) that IPV is a socialized act taught to men due to patriarchal societal norms, encouraging, or even expecting them to use power and control within their relationships with women, rather than from underlying psychological problems or intergenerational patterns of violence lacks empirical support in western nations. Using such a model is no longer defensible, as Corvo et al. (2008) argue when they stated '[Duluth informed models suffer from a]… failure to consider research evidence, failure to utilize evidence-based practices or best-practice protocols, inadequate assessment diagnosis, failure to connect assessment to treatment, failure to develop individual treatment plans, and failure to provide treatment appropriate to the client's needs' (pp. 323–324). Professionals have a duty of care to their clients as well as the client's family and community. The use of interventions with no proven efficacy is inherently unethical. Theoretical frameworks are critical in guiding practitioners and professionals in their practice (Dixon and Graham-Kevan 2011) so it is imperative that practice is informed by rigorous evidence. There have been calls for 'urgent' additional research with rigorous designs for over a decade (e.g. Wathen and MacMillan 2003), but still with there being relatively little progress in this area.

The politics that exist within the area of IPV research and intervention, may be the issue that is preventing evidence-based practice (Bates 2016) and delaying the progression of effective programmes. Whilst the Duluth model, and its proponents, still hold such power and influence within the area, significant advances in interventions are hindered and so reductions in IPV prevalence rates remain unlikely. The Duluth model seems to have experienced an 'immunity' from needing external empirical evaluation; the political concerns here appear more important than rigorous scientific practice (Corvo et al. 2008, p. 112). Whilst the lack of effectiveness is known in academia (e.g. Eckhardt et al. 2013) and within the Criminal Justice system (e.g. Vigurs et al. 2016), individual clinicians and practitioners are unlikely to be aware of this. Coupled with this, the ability of a practitioner to recognize when an intervention is not working is not strong (Chapman et al. 2012; Hannan et al. 2005). Therefore, the internally consistent and intuitive nature of the Duluth model is likely to be appealing to those conscientious, well-meaning and sincere practitioners and clinicians who deliver it. This will largely be due to a general lack of understanding in regards to the merits of evidence-based practice and lack of practitioner engagement in such research (Green 2008).

Service providers and practitioners could build on those approaches that have shown promise with domestic-abuse perpetrators such as motivational interviewing (Vigurs et al. 2015). As many domestic-abuse perpetrators are comorbid with common issues including serious mental illness, personality disorders and substance abuse (Slabber 2012) professionals should also seek to utilize best practice from interventions outside of the IPV sphere such as DBT (Dixon et al. 2012). Additionally, as offenders in general, including domestic-violence perpetrators, are likely to have experienced adverse childhood experiences then interventions that are trauma-informed should be explored (Birkley and Eckhardt 2015; Slabber 2012).

References

Anderson, C.A. and Bushman, B.J. (2002). Human aggression. *Annual Review of Psychology* 53: 27–51.

Andrews, D.A. and Bonta, J. (2010). *The Psychology of Criminal Conduct*, 5e. London, UK: Routledge.

Archer, J. (2000). Sex differences in aggression between heterosexual partners: a meta-analytic review. *Psychological Bulletin* 126: 651–680.

Archer, J. (2002). Sex differences in physically aggressive acts between heterosexual partners: a meta-analytic review. *Aggression and Violent Behavior* 7 (4): 313–351.

Archer, J. (2006). Cross-cultural differences in physical aggression between partners: a social-role analysis. *Personality and Social Psychology Review* 10 (2): 133–153.

Armenti, N.A. and Babcock, J.C. (2016). Conjoint treatment for intimate partner violence: a systematic review and implications. *Couple and Family Psychology: Research and Practice* 5 (2): 109–123.

Babcock, J.C., Green, C.E., and Robie, C. (2004). Does batterer's treatment work? A meta-analytic review of domestic violence treatment. *Clinical Psychology Review* 23: 1023–1053.

Badenes-Ribera, L., Bonilla-Campos, A., Frias-Navarro, D. et al. (2016). Intimate partner violence in self-identified lesbians: a systematic review of its prevalence and correlates. *Trauma, Violence, & Abuse* 17 (3): 284–297.

Bair-Merritt, M.H., Shea Crowne, S., Thompson, D.A. et al. (2010). Why do women use intimate partner violence? A systematic review of women's motivations. *Trauma, Violence, & Abuse* 11 (4): 178–189.

Bates, E.A. (2016). Current controversies within intimate partner violence: overlooking bidirectional violence. *Journal of Family Violence* 31 (8): 937–940.

Bates, E.A. and Graham-Kevan, N. (2016). Is the presence of control related to help-seeking behavior? A test of Johnson's assumptions regarding sex-differences and the role of control in intimate partner violence. *Partner Abuse* 7 (1): 3–25.

Bates, E.A., Graham-Kevan, N., and Archer, J. (2014). Testing predictions from the male control theory of men's partner violence. *Aggressive Behavior* 40 (1): 42–55.

Bates, E.A., Graham-Kevan, N., Bolam, L.T., and Thornton, A.J. (2017). A review of domestic violence perpetrator programs in the United Kingdom. *Partner Abuse* 8 (1): 3–46.

Birkley, E.L. and Eckhardt, C.I. (2015). Anger, hostility, internalizing negative emotions, and intimate partner violence perpetration: a meta-analytic review. *Clinical Psychology Review* 37: 40–56.

Blake, K.R., Hopkins, R.E., Sprunger, J.G. et al. (2018). Relationship quality and cognitive reappraisal moderate the effects of negative urgency on behavioral inclinations toward aggression and intimate partner violence. *Psychology of Violence* 8 (2): 218.

Bohall, G., Bautista, M.J., and Musson, S. (2016). Intimate partner violence and the Duluth model: an examination of the model and recommendations for future research and practice. *Journal of Family Violence* 31 (8): 1029–1033.

Cafferky, B.M., Mendez, M., Anderson, J.R., and Stith, S.M. (2018). Substance use and intimate partner violence: a meta-analytic review. *Psychology of Violence* 8 (1): 110–131.

Cannon, C., Hamel, J., Buttel, F., and Ferreira, R.J. (2016). A survey of domestic violence perpetrator programs in the United States and Canada: findings and implications for policy and intervention. *Partner Abuse* 7 (3): 226–276.

Capaldi, D.M., Knoble, N.B., Shortt, J.W., and Kim, H.K. (2012). A systematic review of risk factors for intimate partner violence. *Partner Abuse* 3 (2): 231–280.

Carney, M.M. and Barner, J.R. (2012). Prevalence of partner abuse: rates of emotional abuse and control. *Partner Abuse* 3 (3): 286–335.

Chapman, C.L., Burlingame, G.M., Gleave, R. et al. (2012). Clinical prediction in group psychotherapy. *Psychotherapy Research* 22: 673–681.

Choenni, V., Hammink, A., and van de Mheen, D. (2017). Association between substance use and the perpetration of family violence in industrialized countries: a systematic review. *Trauma, Violence, & Abuse* 18 (1): 37–50.

Corvo, K., Dutton, D., and Chen, W.Y. (2008). Toward evidence-based practice with domestic violence perpetrators. *Journal of Aggression, Maltreatment & Trauma* 16 (2): 111–130.

Crane, C.A., Hawes, S.W., and Weinberger, A.H. (2013). Intimate partner violence victimization and cigarette smoking: a meta-analytic review. *Trauma, Violence, & Abuse* 14 (4): 305–315.

Del Vecchio, T. and O'Leary, K.D. (2004). Effectiveness of anger treatments for specific anger problems: a meta-analytic review. *Clinical Psychology Review* 24 (1): 15–34.

Dir, A.L., Banks, D.E., Zapolski, T.C. et al. (2016). Negative urgency and emotion regulation predict positive smoking expectancies in non-smoking youth. *Addictive Behaviors* 58: 47–52.

Dixon, L., Archer, J., and Graham-Kevan, N. (2012). Perpetrator programs for partner violence: are they based on ideology or evidence? *Legal and Criminological Psychology* 17: 196–215.

Dixon, L. and Graham-Kevan, N. (2011). Understanding the nature and etiology of intimate partner violence and implications for practice and policy. *Clinical Psychology Review* 31: 1145–1155.

Dobash, R.E. and Dobash, R.P. (1979). *Violence Against Wives: A Case Against the Patriarchy*. London, UK: Open Books.

Dowling, N., Suomi, A., Jackson, A. et al. (2016). Problem gambling and intimate partner violence: a systematic review and meta-analysis. *Trauma, Violence, & Abuse* 17 (1): 43–61.

Dutton, D.G. (2006). *The Abusive Personality: Violence and Control in Intimate Relationships*, 2e. New York, NY: Guilford Press.

Dutton, D.G. (2010). The gender paradigm and the architecture of anti-science. *Partner Abuse* 1: 5–25.

Dutton, D.G. and Corvo, K. (2007). The Duluth model: a data-impervious paradigm and a failed strategy. *Aggression and Violent Behavior* 12: 658–667.

Eckhardt, C.I., Murphy, C.M., Whitaker, D.J. et al. (2013). The effectiveness of intervention programs for perpetrators and victims of intimate partner violence. *Partner Abuse* 4 (2): 196–231.

Farrington, D.P., Gaffney, H., and Ttofi, M.M. (2017). Systematic reviews of explanatory risk factors for violence, offending, and delinquency. *Aggression and Violent Behavior* 33: 24–36.

Feder, L. and Forde, D.R. (2000). *Test of the Efficacy of Court Mandated Counseling for Domestic Violence Offenders: The Broward Experiment, Executive Summary*. Washington, DC: National Institute of Justice.

Feder, L. and Wilson, D.B. (2005). A meta-analytic review of court-mandated batterer intervention programs: can courts affect abusers' behavior? *Journal of Experimental Criminology* 1 (2): 239–262.

Feder, L., Wilson, D.B., and Austin, S. (2008). Court-mandated interventions for individuals convicted of domestic violence. *Campbell Systematic Reviews* 12: 1–46.

Felson, R.B. (2002). *Violence and Gender Re-Examined*. Washington, DC: American Psychological Association.

Finkel, E.J. (2007). Impelling and inhibiting forces in the perpetration of intimate partner violence. *Review of General Psychology* 11: 193–207.

Finneran, C. and Stephenson, R. (2013). Intimate partner violence among men who have sex with men: a systematic review. *Trauma, Violence, & Abuse* 14 (2): 168–185.

Gardner, F.L., Moore, Z.E., and Dettore, M. (2014). The relationship between anger, childhood maltreatment, and emotion regulation difficulties in intimate partner and non-intimate partner violent offenders. *Behavior Modification* 38 (6): 779–800.

Gelles, R.J. (2007). The politics of research: the use, abuse, and misuse of social science data – the cases of intimate partner violence. *Family Court Review* 45 (1): 42–51.

Graham-Kevan, N. (2007). Domestic violence: research and implications for batterer programmes in Europe. *European Journal on Criminal Policy and Research* 13 (3–4): 213–225.

Graham-Kevan, N., (2014). Forest Bank interim report on Inner Strength pilot. Available from the author.

Graham-Kevan, N. and Archer, J. (2009). Control tactics and partner violence in heterosexual relationships. *Evolution and Human Behavior* 30 (6): 445–452.

Green, L.W. (2008). Making research relevant: if it is an evidenced-based practice, where's the practice-based evidence? *Family Practice* 25: i20–i24.

Hamel, J. (2007). Toward a gender-inclusive conception of intimate partner violence research and theory: part 1 – traditional perspectives. *International Journal of Men's Health* 6 (1): 36–53.

Hamel, J. (2016). Domestic violence perpetrator programs around the world Latin America and the Caribbean (editorial). *Partner Abuse* 7 (3): 223–225.

Hannan, C., Lambert, M.J., Harmon, C. et al. (2005). A lab test and algorithms for identifying clients at risk for treatment failure. *Journal of Clinical Psychology* 61: 155–163.

Harding, H.G., Morelen, D., Thomassin, K. et al. (2013). Exposure to maternal-and paternal-perpetrated intimate partner violence, emotion regulation, and child outcomes. *Journal of Family Violence* 28 (1): 63–72.

Hines, D.A., Brown, J., and Dunning, E. (2007). Characteristics of callers to the domestic abuse helpline for men. *Journal of Family Violence* 22: 63–72.

Hines, D.A. and Douglas, E.M. (2010). Intimate terrorism by women towards men: does it exist? *Journal of Aggression, Conflict and Peace Research* 2 (3): 36–56.

Iverson, K.M., McLaughlin, K.A., Adair, K.C., and Monson, C.M. (2014). Anger-related dysregulation as a factor linking childhood physical abuse and interparental violence to intimate partner violence experiences. *Violence and Victims* 29 (4): 564–578.

Jewell, L.M. and Wormith, J.S. (2010). Variables associated with attrition from domestic violence treatment programs targeting male batterers: a meta-analysis. *Criminal Justice and Behavior* 37 (10): 1086–1113.

Karakurt, G., Whiting, K., Esch, C. et al. (2016). Couples therapy for intimate partner violence: a systematic review and meta-analysis. *Journal of Marital and Family Therapy* 42 (4): 567–583.

Kelly, L. and Westmarland, N. (2015). *Domestic Violence Perpetrator Programmes: Steps Towards Change. Project Mirabal Final Report*. London, UK: London Metropolitan University and Durham University.

Langhinrichsen-Rohling, J., Selwyn, C., and Rohling, M.L. (2012). Rates of bidirectional versus unidirectional intimate partner violence across samples, sexual orientations, and race/ethnicities: a comprehensive review. *Partner Abuse* 3 (2): 199–230.

Lawrence, E., Langer Zarling, A., and Orengo-Aguayo, R. (2014). *Achieving Change Through Value-Based Behavior (ACTV)*. Iowa City, IA: University of Iowa Foundation.

Leone, R.M., Crane, C.A., Parrott, D.J., and Eckhardt, C.I. (2016). Problematic drinking, impulsivity, and physical IPV perpetration: a dyadic analysis. *Psychology of Addictive Behaviors* 30 (3): 356–366.

Lilienfeld, S.O. (2007). Psychological treatments that cause harm. *Perspectives on Psychological Science* 2 (1): 53–70.

Longobardi, C. and Badenes-Ribera, L. (2017). Intimate partner violence in same-sex relationships and the role of sexual minority stressors: a systematic review of the past 10 years. *Journal of Child and Family Studies* 26 (8): 2039–2049.

Maiuro, R. and Eberle, J. (2008). State standards for domestic violence perpetrator treatment: current status, trends, and recommendations. *Violence and Victims* 23 (2): 133–155.

McCloskey, L.A., Boonzier, F., Steinbrenner, S.Y., and Hunter, T. (2016). Determinants of intimate partner violence in Sub-Saharan Africa: a review of prevention and intervention programs. *Partner Abuse* 7 (3): 277–315.

Miller, A.J., Worthington, E.J., Hook, J.N. et al. (2013). Managing hurt and disappointment: improving communication of reproach and apology. *Journal of Mental Health Counseling* 35 (2): 108–123.

Niaz, U., Hassan, S., and Tariq, Q. (2017). Situational analysis of intimate partner violence interventions in South Asian and Middle Eastern countries. *Partner Abuse* 8 (1): 47–88.

Norlander, B. and Eckhardt, C. (2005). Anger, hostility, and male perpetrators of intimate partner violence: a meta-analytic review. *Clinical Psychology Review* 25 (2): 119–152.

Ortega, D. and Busch-Armendariz, N. (2014). Elite knowledge or the reproduction of the knowledge of privilege. *Social Work Doctoral Education* 29 (1): 5–7.

Pence, E. and Paymar, M. (1993). *Education Groups for Men Who Batter: The Duluth Model*. New York, NY: Springer Publishing Company.

Pender, R.L. (2012). ASGW best practice guidelines: an evaluation of the Duluth model. *The Journal for Specialists in Group Work* 37 (3): 218–231.

Prendergast, M.L., Pearson, F.S., Podus, D. et al. (2013). The Andrews' principles of risk, needs, and responsivity as applied in drug treatment programs: meta-analysis of crime and drug use outcomes. *Journal of Experimental Criminology* 9: 275–300.

Respect (2012). *Respect Accreditation Standard*, 2e. London, UK: Author.

Saini, M. (2009). A meta-analysis of the psychological treatment of anger: developing guidelines for evidence-based practice. *Journal of the American Academy of Psychiatry and the Law Online* 37 (4): 473–488.

Santoveñada, E.E. and da Silva, T. (2016). Domestic violence intervention programs for perpetrators in Latin America and the Caribbean. *Partner Abuse* 7 (3): 316–352.

Schwartz, M.D. and DeKeseredy, W.S. (2003). Review of "sexual assault on the college campus.". *Journal of Community and Applied Social Psychology* 13: 80–81.

Shernock, S. and Russell, B. (2012). Gender and racial/ethnic differences in criminal justice decision making in intimate partner violence cases. *Partner Abuse* 3 (4): 501–530.

Slabber, M. (2012). *Community-Based Domestic Violence Interventions: A Literature Review – 2012*. Wellington, NZ: Department of Corrections.

Smith, M.D. (1990). Patriarchal ideology and wife beating: a test of a feminist hypothesis. *Violence and Victims* 5: 257–273.

Smith-Marek, E.N., Cafferky, B., Dharnidharka, P. et al. (2015). Effects of childhood experiences of family violence on adult partner violence: a meta-analytic review. *Journal of Family Theory and Review* 7 (4): 498–519.

Spencer, C., Cafferky, B., and Stith, S.M. (2016). Gender differences in risk markers for perpetration of physical partner violence: results from a meta-analytic review. *Journal of Family Violence* 31 (8): 981–984.

Stockdale, L., Tackett, S., and Coyne, S.M. (2013). Sex differences in verbal aggression use in romantic relationships: a meta-analytic study and review. *Journal of Aggression, Conflict and Peace Research* 5 (3): 167–178.

Straus, M.A. (1992). Sociological research and social policy: the case of family violence. *Social Forum* 7: 211–237.

Straus, M.A. (2007). *Validity of Cross-National Research Based on Convenience Samples: The Case of the International Dating Violence Study Data*. Durham, NH: Family Research Laboratory.

Straus, M.A. and Gozjolko, K.L. (2016). Concordance between partners in "intimate terrorism": a comparison of two typologies. *Aggression and Violent Behavior* 29: 55–60.

Stuart, R.B. (2005). Treatment for partner abuse: Time for a paradigm shift. *Professional Psychology: Research and Practice* 36 (3): 254–263.

Sugarman, D.B. and Frankel, S.L. (1996). Patriarchal ideology and wife-assault: a meta-analytic review. *Journal of family violence* 11 (1): 13–40.

Thornton, A.J.V., Graham-Kevan, N., and Archer, J. (2010). Adaptive and maladaptive traits as predictors of violent and non violent offending behavior in men and women. *Aggressive Behavior* 36: 177–186.

Thornton, A.J.V., Graham-Kevan, N., and Archer, J. (2012). Prevalence of women's violent and nonviolent offending behavior: a comparison of self-reports, victims' reports, and third-party reports. *Journal of Interpersonal Violence* 27: 1399–1427.

U. S. Department of Health and Human Services (2008). *Substance Abuse Treatment: Group Therapy*. Washington, DC: Author.

Vigurs, C., Quy, K., Schucan-Bird, K., and Gough, D. (2015). *A Systematic Review of Motivational Approaches as a Pre-Intervention for Domestic Violence Perpetrator Programs*. London, UK: College of Policing.

Vigurs, C., Schucan-Bird, K., Quy, K., and Gough, D. (2016). *The Impact of Domestic Violence Perpetrator Programs on Victim and Criminal Justice Outcomes: A Systematic Review of Reviews (SRR) of Research Evidence*. London, UK: College of Policing.

Wathen, C.N. and MacMillan, H.L. (2003). Interventions for violence against women: scientific review. *Journal of the American Medical Association* 289 (5): 589–600.

Welsh, C.C. and Rocque, M. (2014). When crime prevention harms: a review of systematic reviews. *Journal of Experimental Criminology* 10: 245–266.

Wexler, D.B. (2013). *The STOP Domestic Violence Program: Group Leader's Manual*. New York, NY: W. W. Norton & Co.

Wincentak, K., Connolly, J., and Card, N. (2016). Teen dating violence: A meta-analytic review of prevalence rates. *Psychology of Violence* 7 https://doi.org/10.1037/a0040194.

Winstok, Z. and Straus, M.A. (2016). Bridging the two sides of a 30-year controversy over gender differences in perpetration of physical partner violence. *Journal of Family Violence* 31 (8): 933–935.

Zarling, A., Bannon, S., & Berta, M. (2017). Evaluation of acceptance and commitment therapy for domestic violence offenders. *Psychology of Violence*. Advance online publication.

23

Interventions for Violent Offenders with Intellectual and Developmental Disabilities

John L. Taylor

Northumbria University, Newcastle-upon-Tyne, UK

Introduction

The life experiences of people with intellectual and developmental disabilities (IDD) are conducive to the activation of anger and aggression, particularly when child abuse punctuates their family backgrounds. In a secure IDD service involving 108 male inpatients, Novaco and Taylor (2004) found that childhood physical abuse was significantly related to staff-rated aggressive behaviour in a one-week interval and to case records of physical assaults since hospital admission; it was also significantly related to multiple measures of patient-rated anger and to staff-rated anger (Novaco and Taylor 2008). Beyond physical abuse history, it was found that exposure to the anger/aggression displays of 'volatile parents' (i.e. the witnessing of parents' anger/aggression) was significantly related to patients' anger and aggressive behaviour in a triangulation of self-report, staff-rated, and archival measures, controlling for background covariates that included childhood physical abuse. The conclusion was that the patients' anger and aggression is at least partially a product of the trauma of abuse exposure.

The environmental settings and social circumstances in which many people with IDD live are intrinsically constraining, potentially threatening, unrewarding and limited in satisfaction. Recurrent thwarting of physical, emotional, and interpersonal needs can potentiate anger activation. Cognitive deficits can impair effective coping with frustrating or aversive events and impoverished support systems limit problem-solving options.

In this chapter, the prevalence of aggression amongst people with IDD is outlined, the impact of aggression on services users and those supporting them, and the links between anger and aggression is discussed before psychopharmacological, behavioural and cognitive-behavioural approaches to treatment are described in some detail.

The Wiley Handbook of What Works in Violence Risk Management: Theory, Research and Practice,
First Edition. Edited by J. Stephen Wormith, Leam A. Craig, and Todd E. Hogue.
© 2020 John Wiley & Sons Ltd. Published 2020 by John Wiley & Sons Ltd.

Prevalence of Aggression and People with IDD

Various surveys of populations of people with IDD have found high rates of what has been termed 'challenging behaviour,' in which aggression features prominently. Harris (1993) conducted a survey of service providers concerning 1362 children and adults with developmental difficulties in England. The overall prevalence of aggression was found to be 17.6%. Harris's study included both hospitals and community daycare facilities. The prevalence rate for aggressive behaviour in the hospitals (38%) was more than three times greater than that found in the community day facilities (11%).

In a similarly conducted survey regarding a population of children and adults with intellectual disability in Queensland, Australia, Sigafoos et al. (1994) found that 11% of the total population of 2412 people were identified by service providers as exhibiting aggressive behaviour, and there was considerable variation as a function of residential setting. The prevalence of aggressive behaviour was 35% for those in institutions, 17% in community-based group homes, and 3% in other community accommodations (giving an average community prevalence rate of 10%).

Emerson et al. (2001), in a total population study carried out in two health authority districts in North West England, used a 'key informant' questionnaire to gather information on the presence of a range of challenging behaviours. From the 2189 children and adults with intellectual disabilities screened, 7% were found to have shown serious aggressive behaviour in the past month. More recently, Crocker et al. (2006) in a survey of care staff supporting 3165 adults with IDD receiving community rehabilitation services in Quebec, Canada found that 24% had been physically aggressive during a 12-month period.

Results consistent with these service-provider surveys were obtained by Smith et al. (1996) in a study involving home interviews with key persons providing care for 2277 adults with developmental disabilities in Leicestershire, England. The prevalence of aggression (40% plus) for residents of National Health Service (NHS) institutional settings was described as being significantly higher than that for those residing in the community. In a similar study by Hill and Bruininks (1984), interviews regarding maladaptive behaviour were conducted with direct care staff working with 236 residents with mental retardation in community- and public-residential facilities across the US. From the data presented in Hill and Bruininks' paper, it is calculated that, for the 2491 residents included in this study, the overall prevalence of behaviour causing injury to others, across all age ranges, was 27%. The rate for this behaviour amongst residents, new admissions, and re-admissions in public facilities averaged 37%. For those people residing in community facilities, the prevalence of the same category of behaviour was 16%.

In a population-based sample of 101 adults with intellectual disabilities randomly selected from the social services department register in South Wales in the UK, using a questionnaire-based interview procedure with carers and, where possible, clients, Deb et al. (2001) found that 23% of participants had histories of severe and/or frequent aggressive behaviour. In a larger community study involving interviews with 3165 adult service users and their carers in England, Tyrer et al. (2006) found that 14% had been physically aggressive. Prevalence was higher amongst male, younger and more disabled participants.

In a study using diagnostic categories of behaviour observed over a 6-month period, Cooper et al. (2009) found that 6% of 1023 adults with IDD in a geographically-defined area of Scotland reached the criteria for physical aggression (i.e. physical aggression must have occurred on at least three occasions in the preceding 6-month period).

The epidemiological research described above that used survey and interview procedures across three continents indicates that aggression, and by implication anger, is a significant issue amongst community populations and inpatient samples of people with IDD.

Impact of Aggression for Patients, Staff and Services

The studies by Harris (1993), Hill and Bruininks (1984), Sigafoos et al. (1994) and Smith et al. (1996) above show that levels of aggression for people with IDD residing in institutional settings are 2–4 times higher than for those in community settings. Rates of physical aggression are higher again for people with IDD detained in secure settings (McMillan et al. 2004; Novaco and Taylor 2004). This is unsurprising as Lakin et al. (1983) found that aggression was the primary reason for people with IDD to be admitted and re-admitted to institutional settings. O'Brien et al. (2010) found that for 477 people (354 men and 123 women) with IDD referred over a 12-month period to services in three regions in the UK due to offending and antisocial behaviour, physical aggression (50%) followed by verbal aggression (30%) were the most common reasons for people being referred to services. It appears that, as a result of the high levels of aggression found in IDD populations, disproportionate numbers of people with IDD (1 in 13 of the total) are being detained in hospitals for compulsory treatment in England under the *Mental Health Act 1983* on the basis of their 'abnormally aggressive' or 'seriously irresponsible' behaviour (Health and Social Care Information Centre 2014).

Many aspects of institutional-living can elicit feelings of frustration, helplessness, injustice and anger (Taylor and Novaco 2005). They include little, if any, personal choice, limited opportunities for the development of intimate or mutually-supportive relationships, and limited opportunities for meaningful occupational or work-related opportunities. Cramped living conditions with little privacy and over-heated, poorly-designed buildings add to conditions that are conducive to anger activation and related aggression (Levey and Howells 1991).

In an NHS Protect (2015) report on physical assaults experienced by NHS staff the highest rate in the country (i.e. 1352 assaults per 1000 staff over a 12-month period) was reported in the country's only remaining specialist IDD Trust located in the North West of England. In their study of violence faced by staff in an IDD service of an NHS Trust in the UK, Kiely and Pankhurst (1998) found that 81% of respondents reported suffering physical assault at the hands of service-users during the previous 12 months. Bromley and Emerson (1995) found that the emotional responses of IDD services staff to episodes of service-user aggression included annoyance (41%), anger (24%), and fear (19%). Staff in the Kiely and Pankhurst (1998) study reported a range of reactions following violent incidents including ignoring the perpetrator, increased wariness and caution in their contact with the assailant, and loss of confidence in their ability to work competently. Jenkins et al. (1997) found that staff working with clients with IDD and challenging behaviour (including aggression) were significantly more anxious than staff working with non-challenging clients. These phenomena are consistent with the process of staff 'burnout' (Edwards and Miltenberger 1991), are associated with high staff turnover (Whittington and Wykes 1991) and thus have clear implications for quality of care provided to patients.

Links Between Anger and Aggression

Anger is a negatively-toned emotion that is subjectively experienced as an aroused state of antagonism towards someone or something perceived to be the source of an aversive event. It is triggered situationally by events perceived to constitute deliberate provocations by an instigator towards oneself or others for whom one is protective (e.g. family and friends). Provocations usually take the form of insults, unfair treatment, or deliberate blocking of goals. Anger is prototypically experienced as a justified response to some perceived wrong, slight or injustice. Whilst anger is situationally triggered by temporally proximal events, it is shaped and facilitated by previous experience (Novaco and Taylor 2008).

Anger is as a normal human emotion that is hard-wired for survival (Novaco 2000). It has considerable adaptive value. Anger can help maintain one's self-esteem and dignity when confronted by provocation, insult or unjust treatment. In the face of danger, anger can help individuals to mobilize psychological resources and prime behaviours to deal with threat. It can communicate negative sentiment to others, potentiate the ability to face up to and redress grievances, and boost perseverance and determination to overcome obstacles to resolve conflict (Novaco 2000).

Recurrent, intense and poorly-controlled anger adversely affects emotional and physical health and is disruptive of social relationships that sustain personal well-being. It is associated with subjective psychological distress and is commonly observed in a range of mental health and emotional problems including: personality, psychosomatic and conduct disorders; schizophrenia, bipolar mood and organic disorders as well as in conditions resulting from trauma (Novaco and Taylor 2006).

Whilst it is neither necessary nor sufficient for aggression to occur, in mental health services anger has been shown to be predictive of physical aggression both prior to and following admission to hospital (Doyle and Dolan 2006a; Novaco 1994) and also following discharge from hospital (Doyle and Dolan 2006b; Swogger et al. 2012). In a secure service for offenders with IDD in the UK, Novaco and Taylor (2004) found the number of physical assaults was significantly related to anger, even when controlling for age, length of stay, IQ, violent offence history, and salient personality variables.

Treatment for Anger and Aggression

Given the high prevalence of aggression amongst populations of people with IDD, its impact on individuals and staff and services supporting them, and the strong association and predictive relationship of anger with aggression, then anger dysregulation is a legitimate target for therapeutic intervention for people with IDD who are aggressive and potentially violent. However, because anger is a frequent precursor of aggression and violence, its treatment can be perplexing for therapists who may be wary of the risks that such clients present to their own safety. Engaging chronically angry people in therapy is difficult as they can be treatment avoidant and attempts to achieve clinical change can be undermined by the adaptive functions of anger and by its embeddedness in the client's sense of self and personal worth (Taylor and Novaco 2005). Angry thinking and behaviour that is strongly attached to a client's character and self-worth is not easily or readily relinquished. Deficits in cognitive functioning can add to the challenges of anger regulation from the standpoint of both clients and those who seek to help them therapeutically.

Psychopharmacological Treatment

Challenging behaviour, primarily aggression, is the main reason for people with IDD to be prescribed psychotropic medication (Aman et al. 1987; Robertson et al. 2000) and antipsychotics are most the commonly used psychotropic drugs over prolonged periods (Paton et al. 2011).

The main types of psychotropic medications that have been used to treat challenging behaviour including aggression in people with IDD are antidepressants, anticonvulsants and antipsychotics. Willner (2015) reviewed the evidence for the use of pharmacological treatments targeted on the serotonin, y-aminobutyric acid (GABA) and dopamine neurochemical systems as these are implicated in the activation and inhibition of aggressive behaviour. No controlled studies for the use of antidepressants (specific serotonin reuptake inhibitors) or anticonvulsants (e.g. sodium valproate) in reducing aggression in people with IDD were identified. The evidence from three older controlled studies to support the use of lithium (a mood stabilizer) in managing aggression in people with IDD (Craft et al. 1987; Tyrer et al. 1984, 1993) was judged to be equivocal, especially when the toxicity of this compound is taken into account.

Previously Matson et al. (2000) reviewed the use of psychopharmacology with people with IDD and various behavioural and psychological difficulties. They reported that despite the very large numbers of people with IDD prescribed medication for aggression, very little research specific to that area had been reported in the 10-year period studied. Although Matson et al. reviewed, in total, 72 studies published between 1990 and 1999, they found only 14 studies that attended specifically to the control of aggression that *partially* met the methodological criteria for inclusion in their review. Whilst most of these studies reported significant reductions in aggression following treatment, all contained serious methodological flaws. The authors suggest that for the 12 studies that utilized antipsychotics, it is likely that their effects were a consequence of indiscriminate suppression of aggressive and other adaptive behaviour, that can in turn result in serious side-effects.

An earlier review by Baumeister et al. (1998) concerning the use of neuroleptic medication for aggression in people with IDD in studies published between 1957 and 1995 could only identify three studies that met their inclusion criteria. They concluded that the evidence for the efficacy of neuroleptic medication in reducing aberrant behaviour, including aggression, is weak. They asserted that the effects of these compounds on individuals with IDD are highly variable and unpredictable and they lack specificity with regard to target behaviours.

Brylewski and Duggan (1999) reviewed 20 randomized controlled trials of antipsychotic medication for challenging behaviour in people with IDD published between 1966 and 1994. They found that only three of these studies met *The Cochrane Library*[1] criteria used for studies in their analyses. These studies were described as short and poorly reported, involving small numbers of participants, drugs that were not used widely in the UK, and dependent measures of aggression and challenging behaviour with limited reliability and validity. Brylewski and Duggan concluded that there was no evidence of whether antipsychotic medication treatment helps or harms adults with IDD and challenging behaviour, and that its continued use without trial-based evidence is ethically questionable.

Later reviews have been more positive about the use of neuroleptics to treat aggression in people with IDD (e.g. Deb & Unwin 2007; Haessler and Reis 2010). This optimism relates

---

[1] The Cochrane Library publishes databases that contain different types of high-quality, independent evidence to inform healthcare decision-making: http://www.cochranelibrary.com.

mainly to studies involving risperidone (a second-generation *atypical* antipsychotic) used with children and adolescents with IDD. Only two controlled trials of risperidone involving adults with IDD have reported positive results in treating aggression (Gagiano et al. 2005; Zarcone et al. 2001) and a more recent single-blind study has supported the efficacy of risperidone and olanzapine over first-generation *typical* antipsychotics (Amore et al. 2011). Contrary to these positive results, Tyrer et al. (2008) reported on a randomized controlled trial in which placebo was found to be superior to both risperidone and haloperidol (a typical antipsychotic) in the treatment of aggressive challenging behaviour in adults with IDD.

In summary, there is some limited evidence for the use of low doses of risperidone for the treatment of aggression of IDD although the effect of this medication on such behaviour, in common with other psychotropic medication, is likely to be due to dampening of behaviour generally, including inhibition of adaptive behaviour. Also, as Willner (2015) pointed out, although risperidone and other atypical antipsychotics are less toxic then typical antipsychotics, they do nonetheless have significant side-effects such as weight gain and sedation. Alternative safer interventions therefore need to be considered. This is particularly so given recent National Institute for Health and Care Excellence (NICE) recommendations that antipsychotic medication should be used to manage challenging behaviour only if psychological or other interventions alone do not work within an agreed time; and they should be used only in combination with psychological or other interventions (National Collaborating Centre for Mental Health 2015).

Behavioural Interventions

The most significant literature concerning the treatment of aggression in people with IDD involves interventions based on applied behavioural analysis principles. In their early review of 162 studies of 'decelerative' interventions for behaviour problems in people with IDD published between 1981 and 1985, Lennox et al. (1988) found that for subjects with aggression problems more intrusive interventions, such as time-out, aversion techniques and medication, were more likely to be used than for other classes of behaviour problems. Less intrusive and more constructive treatment approaches such as environmental change and contingency management were found to be marginally more effective than intrusive and restrictive techniques (Table 2, p. 498 in Lennox et al., 1988).

Scotti et al. (1991) improved on the Lennox et al. (1988) review by carrying out a meta-analysis of interventions for problem behaviour in people with IDD. In this review, which included 403 studies reported in 18 major journals between 1976 and 1987, Scotti et al. found that compared with other classes of behaviour problems, physical aggression/tantrum behaviours were associated with significantly lower treatment effects. Overall, less intrusive interventions, including environmental change and positive practice, were generally more effective than the most intrusive techniques such as aversive stimulation and restraint (see Scotti et al. (1991) Table 6, p. 244).

Carr et al. (2000), in a review of non-contingent reinforcement (NCR: the presentation of reinforcement independent of behaviour) as a treatment for 'aberrant' behaviour in people with IDD, considered 15 studies published between 1977 and 2000 with aggression as the target behaviour. Most of these studies involved people with moderate–severe levels of IDD. NCR involves the delivery of the reinforcer for a specific challenging behaviour to the individual on a response-independent basis in order to reduce or extinguish the target behaviour.

Carr et al. (2000) concluded from their review that whilst NCR is a promising approach for the treatment of problem behaviour, including aggression, it has not yet been evaluated outside of extremely well-controlled experimental settings. Transferability and generalization effects had not been explored and the schedule-thinning in the studies reported would be difficult to replicate in routine clinical or naturalistic settings.

Whitaker (1993) reviewed psychological methods for reducing aggression in people with IDD. He found little evidence for the effectiveness of self-control procedures including self-monitoring, contingency control and self-instruction. This was the case particularly with people with greater levels of disability and associated cognitive and language deficits. The bulk of the literature incorporated into Whitaker's (1993) review is concerned with contingency management using behavioural methods with people with lower levels of disability ('moderate', 'severe' or 'profound' – see Whitaker (1993) Tables 3–12, pp. 21–36). The review findings suggest that for these approaches to be effective in reducing aggression they need to be delivered consistently and they require high-staff ratios. There are significant problems in successfully implementing these approaches with low-frequency aggression and in settings without paid-staff support.

As noted above, much of the evidence concerning the effectiveness of behavioural interventions for challenging behaviour, including aggression, in people with IDD involved participants in the moderate–severe-profound ranges of intellectual functioning. Didden et al. (2006) sought to address this issue by conducting a meta-analysis of single-subject research concerning behavioural treatment of challenging behaviour in people with 'mild mental retardation'. They identified 80 papers published between 1980 and 2005 that involved 119 participants who were treated for *externally maladaptive behaviour* (e.g. verbal aggression, physical aggression, destructive behaviour), *socially disruptive behaviour* (e.g. elopement, disruptive behaviour, stealing, non-compliance), and *internally maladaptive behaviour* (e.g. self-injury, sleep problems, food refusal, depressive behaviour). Although Didden et al. (2006) concluded that behavioural interventions for challenging behaviours are effective with people with mild ID, the treatment effects reported across all studies in the meta-analysis indicate *questionable* effectiveness according to the interpretive schemes provided by Scruggs et al. (1986) and Scotti et al. (1991) respectively. Unfortunately, IQ means, standard deviations and ranges were not reported for participants in this meta-analysis, and the mean age of participants being just 14.5 years. The *external destructive* category (incorporating aggressive and destructive behaviour) showed the lowest and thus most questionable treatment effects amongst the challenging behaviours included in the analysis (see Didden et al. (2006) Tables 2 and 3, pp. 294–295).

In a more recent review of small *n* and single-case research on interventions for reducing challenging behaviour in IDD, Heyvaert et al. (2012) carried out a meta-analysis of 285 studies reporting on 598 participants with a mean age of 18 years published between 2000 and 2011. Just 16% of participants with IDD were in the mild range of disability, and 23%, 31% and 30% were in the moderate, severe and profound ranges respectively. Unfortunately, the level of IDD could not be analysed as a potential moderator of treatment effectiveness because of missing data. The authors reported that, on average, the behavioural interventions (chiefly antecedent control) for challenging behaviour were 'highly effective', especially for people with autism. They noted, however, that the intervention effects varied significantly over the studies included in the analysis and also between study participants. Further, and importantly in the context of this chapter, the interventions were significantly less effective for participants displaying outwardly directed aggression (i.e. aggression and destructive behaviour) when compared to those with other types of challenging behaviour (mainly stereotyped and self-injurious behaviour).

There is a significant body of evidence that behavioural interventions based on applied behavioural analysis principles can be effective in reducing challenging behaviour in people with IDD. The bulk of the evidence supporting these interventions, however, concerns children/adolescents and people with greater levels of disability in the moderate–severe-profound ranges. Relatively little research in this area concerns adults with mild and borderline IDD or mental health and emotional problems such as anxiety, depression and anger. Particularly pertinent to offenders with IDD, it would seem to be the case that these interventions are least effective when targeted on outwardly-directed aggression and violence compared with higher-frequency stereotypic, self-injurious and compulsive behaviours most commonly associated with people with more severe disabilities. As violent offenders with IDD, particularly those who come to the attention of the criminal justice system, tend to be relatively high functioning and demonstrate low frequency but serious aggression and violence (Novaco and Taylor 2015) then alternative approaches to treatment need to be considered.

Cognitive Behavioural Interventions

Behavioural approaches utilizing antecedent control do not encourage self-regulation of behaviour. Once the intervention is withdrawn, or there are changes in the environment, aggressive behaviour is likely to recur. Self-actualization through the promotion of internalized control of behaviour is intrinsic to the skills training components of cognitive-behavioural approaches developed for use with people with IDD (Taylor et al. 2008). For these reasons, there is increasing interest in cognitive behavioural anger treatment for people with IDD.

Taylor (2002), and Taylor and Novaco (2005) reviewed a number of case studies and uncontrolled group-anger treatment studies involving individual and group cognitive behavioural therapy (CBT) approaches incorporating arousal reduction, skills training and self-monitoring. Generally, case studies have produced good outcomes in reducing anger and aggression and improvements have been maintained at short-term follow-up. Many of these case studies (e.g. Black and Novaco 1993; Murphy and Clare 1991; Rose and West 1999) have been conducted in hospital and community settings with individuals who have histories of aggressive behaviour.

There have also been a small number of case studies of cognitive behavioural anger treatment involving offenders with ID that have yielded positive outcomes. Lindsay et al. (2003) reported on six men with mild ID all of whom had been involved with the Criminal Justice System for reasons of aggression and violence. Anger treatment involved group therapy that included: psychoeducation, arousal reduction, role-play, problem solving, and stress inoculation through imagination of anger-provoking situations. Treatment was assessed using self-report measures, reports of aggressive incidents and an anger diary. All measures improved significantly and these improvements were maintained at 15-month follow up. None of the participants had been violent at the four-year follow-up.

In another single case study, Novaco and Taylor (2006) described individual anger management training for a man who was referred for violent behaviour in a medium-secure setting. Self-report for anger and response to provocation was significantly reduced. Care staff observations of reductions in violence were convergent with these findings and improvements were maintained to four-month follow up. Allan et al. (2001) report treatment for five women with mild to borderline IDD, who all had been convicted for violence. Treatment was similar to that described by Lindsay et al. (2003), with significant improvements following intervention and at 15-month follow up. Only one of the women had a further incident of violence and improved scores on the self-reported inventories were maintained. Whilst these case evaluations have generally demonstrated positive outcomes, they have all been uncontrolled demonstrations of clinical effectiveness.

In summary, there have been numerous case studies and case series reports of group-based anger management treatments using cognitive-behavioural approaches for people with mild to severe levels of IDD that have indicated promising outcomes in spite of substantial flaws and weaknesses in study methods and designs. In addition, group studies using cognitive behavioural interventions have resulted in significant pre- and post-treatment reductions in anger in clients with mild–moderate IDD living in the community. Further, there have been a small number of pre-and post-treatment group studies incorporating follow-up phases that have found improvements in anger following CBT that were maintained between 3- and 12-months follow-up.

There have now been 13 studies concerning CBT interventions for anger problems that have incorporated control conditions (see Taylor and Novaco 2018 for a description of these studies including design, setting, participants, treatment format, and outcomes). These studies have utilized mainly psychoeducational CBT approaches delivered by trained therapists that focus on behavioural skills training and have yielded significant improvements on self- and informant-rated anger measures over wait-list control groups that were maintained at up to 9-months follow-up. It can be concluded from this research that group and individual cognitive behavioural anger treatment for people with mild, moderate and borderline IDD living in community and inpatient settings can result in significant improvements in self- and informant-rated anger. Furthermore, gains on these outcome measures are generally maintained at follow-up. However, the largest and most expensive study of psychological treatment involving 179 people with IDD (Willner et al. 2013) reported no significant improvements for the primary study outcome measure (self-reported anger reactivity) or observer-rated aggression following intervention or at follow-up. There are, however, some issues with this study. Potential participants with greatest difficulties with anger and aggression that required immediate intervention were excluded, the intervention was delivered by 'lay therapists' (day-services staff), and the 12-session psychoeducational group intervention did not include the full range of CBT techniques as these were too difficult for 'minimally-trained therapists' (p. 289).

Nicoll et al. (2013) systematically reviewed 12 studies of cognitive behavioural treatment for anger in adults with intellectual disabilities published between 1999 and 2011. Nine studies were included in a quality appraisal and meta-analysis that yielded large uncontrolled effect sizes (average effect size = 0.88; 0.84 for group interventions and 1.01 for individual treatment). The authors concluded that there is an 'emerging evidence base' (p. 60) for CBT anger interventions, albeit based on a small number of studies.

Taylor and colleagues have evaluated individual cognitive-behavioural anger treatment with detained male patients with IDD and significant histories of violence in a linked series of studies (Taylor et al. 2002, 2004, 2005). The 18-session treatment package included a six-session broadly psychoeducational and motivational preparatory phase; followed by a 12-session treatment phase based an individual formulation of each participant's anger problems and needs, following the classical cognitive-behavioural stages of cognitive preparation, skills acquisition, skills rehearsal and then practise *in vivo*. These studies showed significant improvements on self-reported measures of anger disposition, reactivity and imaginal provocation following intervention in the treatment groups compared with scores for the control groups, and these differences were maintained for up to four-months following treatment.

The impact of these anger interventions on aggressive behaviour, including physical vio-lence, has been investigated empirically on only a few occasions (e.g. Allan et al. 2001; Lindsay et al. 2003). In a larger study involving 47 people with IDD and histories of aggression, Lindsay et al. (2004) showed that following a community-group anger intervention, 14% of participants had been aggressive during follow-up, compared with 45% of people in a control condition.

Taylor et al. (2016) described an evaluation of the impact of the cognitive behavioural anger treatment described earlier (e.g. Taylor et al. 2005) on violent behaviour by offenders with IDD living in secure forensic hospital settings. Violence incident data were collected retro-spectively from hospital case notes over a 24-month period. The participants in this study were 44 men and 6 women referred by their clinical teams for anger treatment on the basis of their histories of aggression and/or current presentation. The total number of physical attacks against staff and patients fell from 319 in the 12 months before treatment to 153 in the 12-month period following treatment. This represents a reduction in physical attacks, after treat-ment of 56%. Importantly, the reduction in physical assaults was associated with measured reductions in anger over the course of treatment as indexed by several anger measures vali-dated for use with this population. Novaco and Taylor (2015) demonstrated that these reduc-tions in physical assaults were associated with reductions in self- and informant-rated anger disposition, reactivity and control as a result of CBT anger treatment.

There appears to be an emerging research evidence base to support the use of cognitive behavioural anger interventions in the treatment of adults, including offenders with IDD and histories of aggression and violence. This applies both in terms of improvements on self-report and informant anger dependent measures that are associated with significant reductions in the incidence of post-treatment aggression. Despite the limitations in the research concerning these CBT-anger interventions, the NICE guideline on challenging behaviour and people with IDD recommends that consideration is given to 'individual psychological interventions for adults with an anger management problem. These interventions should be based on cogni-tive-behavioural principles and delivered individually or in groups over 15–20 hours.' (National Collaborating Centre for Mental Health 2015, p. 255).

Conclusions

Aggression is common amongst people with IDD and is associated with experiences of deprivation, abuse and neglect. The consequences of aggression for people with IDD, and those supporting them can be significant and serious, including incarceration for long peri-ods and exposure to harmful treatments and harsh regimes. Anger is a normal human emo-tion that can be functional. Anger is neither necessary nor sufficient for the activation of aggression, but it is strongly associated with, and can be predictive of, aggression in people with IDD. Given its association with aggression, anger is a legitimate target for treatment people with IDD who display aggression and violence. The evidence base for psychological interventions is relatively well developed in this area, with a number of studies demonstrat-ing effectiveness in reducing aggression. Cognitive behavioural treatment, in particular, is supported by NICE guidelines. More research is required to examine the sustainability and generalizability of these effects and further elucidation of the active ingredients of and effective targeting of different treatments to different population subgroups (e.g. children, adults, mild and more severe levels of IDD). Despite it being widely used, the evidence supporting the use of medication for the treatment of aggression in this population is very limited. Such treatments should be used with caution and only after consideration has been given to psychological intervention.

References

Allan, R., Lindsay, W.R., MacLeod, F., and Smith, A.H.W. (2001). Treatment of women with intellectual disabilities who have been involved with the criminal justice system for reasons of aggression. *Journal of Applied Research in Intellectual Disabilities* 14: 340–347.

Aman, M.G., Richmond, G., Stewart, A.W. et al. (1987). The aberrant behavior checklist: factor structure and the effect of subject variables in American and New Zealand facilities. *American Journal on Mental Deficiency* 91: 570–578.

Amore, M., Bertelli, M., Villani, D. et al. (2011). Olanzapine versus risperidone in treating aggressive behaviours in adults with intellectual disabilities: a single blind study. *Journal of Intellectual Disability Research* 55: 201–218.

Baumeister, A.A., Sevin, J.A., and King, B.H. (1998). Neuroleptics. In: *Psychotropic Medications and Developmental Disabilities: The International Consensus Handbook* (eds. S. Reiss and M.G. Aman), 130–150. Columbus, OH: Ohio State University.

Black, L. and Novaco, R.W. (1993). Treatment of anger with a developmentally handicapped man. In: *Casebook of the Brief Psychotherapies* (eds. R.A. Wells and V.J. Giannetti), 143–158. Boston, MA: Springer.

Bromley, J. and Emerson, E. (1995). Beliefs and emotional reactions of care staff working with people with challenging behavior. *Journal of Intellectual Disability Research* 39: 341–352.

Brylewski, J. and Duggan, L. (1999). Antipsychotic medication for challenging behaviour in people with learning disability. *Journal of Intellectual Disability Research* 43: 360–371.

Carr, J.E., Coriaty, S., Wilder, D.A. et al. (2000). A review of "noncontingent" reinforcement as treatment for the aberrant behavior of individuals with developmental disabilities. *Research in Developmental Disabilities* 21: 377–391.

Cooper, S.-A., Smiley, E., Jackson, A. et al. (2009). Adults with intellectual disabilities: prevalence, incidence and remission of aggressive behaviour and related factors. *Journal of Intellectual Disability Research* 53: 217–232.

Craft, M., Ismail, I.A., Kristanamurti, D. et al. (1987). Lithium in the treatment of aggression in mentally handicapped patients: a double blind trial. *The British Journal of Psychiatry* 150: 685–689.

Crocker, A.G., Mercier, C., Lachapelle, Y. et al. (2006). Prevalence and types of aggressive behaviour amongst adults with intellectual disabilities. *Journal of Intellectual Disability Research* 50: 652–661.

Deb, S., Thomas, M., and Bright, C. (2001). Mental disorder in adults with intellectual disability. 2: the rate of behaviour disorders among a community-based population aged between 14 and 64 years. *Journal of Intellectual Disability Research* 45: 506–514.

Deb, S. and Unwin, G.L. (2007). Psychotropic medication for behaviour problems in people with intellectual disability: a review of the current literature. *Current Opinion in Psychiatry* 20: 461–466.

Didden, R., Korzilius, H., van Oorsouw, W., and Sturmey, P. (2006). Behavioral treatment of challenging behaviors in individuals with mild mental retardation: meta-analysis of single subject research. *American Journal on Mental Retardation* 111: 290–298.

Doyle, M. and Dolan, M. (2006a). Evaluating the validity of anger regulation problems, interpersonal style, and disturbed mental state for predicting inpatient violence. *Behavioral Sciences and the Law* 24: 783–798.

Doyle, M. and Dolan, M. (2006b). Predicting community violence from patients discharged from mental health services. *British Journal of Psychiatry* 189: 520–526.

Edwards, P. and Miltenberger, R. (1991). Burnout among staff members at community residential facilities for persons with mental retardation. *Mental Retardation* 29: 125–128.

Emerson, E., Kiernan, C., Alborz, A. et al. (2001). The prevalence of challenging behaviours: a total population study. *Research in Developmental Disabilities* 22: 77–93.

Gagiano, C., Read, S., Thorpe, L. et al. (2005). Short and long-term efficacy and safety of risperidone in adults with disruptive behaviour disorders. *Psychopharmacology* 179: 629–636.

Haessler, F. and Reis, O. (2010). Pharmacotherapy of disruptive behavior in mentally retarded subjects: a review of the current literature. *Developmental Disabilities Research Reviews* 16: 265–272.

Harris, P. (1993). The nature and extent of aggressive behaviour amongst people with learning difficulties (mental handicap) in a single health district. *Journal of Intellectual Disability Research* 37: 221–242.

Health & Social Care Information Centre (2014). Inpatients formally detained in hospitals under the Mental Health Act 1983, and patients subject to supervised community treatment: Annual report, England, 2013/14. London, UK: National Health Service.

Heyvaert, M., Maes, B., Van den Noortgate, W. et al. (2012). A multilevel meta-analysis of single-case and small-n research on interventions for reducing challenging behavior in persons with intellectual disabilities. *Research in Developmental Disabilities* 33: 766–780.

Hill, B.K. and Bruininks, R.H. (1984). Maladaptive behavior of mentally retarded individuals in residential facilities. *American Journal of Mental Deficiency* 88: 380–387.

Jenkins, R., Rose, J., and Lovell, C. (1997). Psychological well-being of staff working with people who have challenging behaviour. *Journal of Intellectual Disability Research* 41: 502–511.

Kiely, J. and Pankhurst, H. (1998). Violence faced by staff in a learning disability service. *Disability and Rehabilitation* 20: 81–89.

Lakin, K.C., Hill, B.K., Hauber, F.A. et al. (1983). New admissions to a national sample of public residential facilities. *American Journal on Mental Retardation* 88: 13–20.

Lennox, D.B., Miltenberger, R.G., Spengler, P., and Erfanian, N. (1988). Decelerative treatment practices with persons who have mental retardation: a review of five years of the literature. *American Journal on Mental Retardation* 92: 492–501.

Levey, S. and Howells, K. (1991). Anger and its management. *Journal of Forensic Psychiatry* 1: 305–327.

Lindsay, W.R., Allan, R., MacLeod, F. et al. (2003). Long-term treatment and management of violent tendencies in men with intellectual disabilities convicted of assault. *Mental Retardation* 41: 47–56.

Lindsay, W.R., Allan, R., Parry, C. et al. (2004). Anger and aggression in people with intellectual disabilities: treatment and follow-up of consecutive referrals and a waiting list comparison. *Clinical Psychology and Psychotherapy* 11: 255–264.

Matson, J.L., Bamburg, J.W., Mayville, E.A. et al. (2000). Psychopharmacology and mental retardation: a 10 year review (1990-1999). *Research in Developmental Disabilities* 21: 263–296.

McMillan, D., Hastings, R.P., and Coldwell, J. (2004). Clinical and actuarial prediction of physical violence in a forensic intellectual disability hospital: a longitudinal study. *Journal of Applied Research in Intellectual Disabilities* 17: 255–265.

Murphy, G. and Clare, I. (1991). MIETS: A service option for people with mild mental handicaps and challenging behaviour or psychiatric problems. *Mental Handicap Research* 4: 180–206.

National Collaborating Centre for Mental Health (2015). *Challenging Behaviour and Learning Disabilities: Prevention and Interventions for People with Learning Disabilities Whose Behaviour Challenges. NICE Guideline 11- Methods, Evidence and Recommendations*. London, UK: The British Psychological Society & The Royal College of Psychiatrists.

NHS Protect (2015). Tables showing the number of physical assaults on NHS staff in 2014/15: National summary by sector type. London, UK: National Health Service.

Nicoll, M., Beail, N., and Saxon, D. (2013). Cognitive behavioural treatment for anger in adults with intellectual disabilities: a systematic review and meta-analysis. *Journal of Applied Research in Intellectual Disabilities* 26: 47–62.

Novaco, R.W. (1994). Anger as a risk factor for violence among the mentally disordered. In: *Violence and mental disorder: Developments in risk assessment* (eds. J. Monahan and H. Steadman), 21–59. Chicago, IL: University of Chicago Press.

Novaco, R.W. (2000). Anger. In: *Encyclopedia of psychology*, vol. 1 (ed. A.E. Kasdin), 170–174. Washington DC: American Psychological Association.

Novaco, R.W. and Taylor, J.L. (2004). Assessment of anger and aggression in offenders with developmental disabilities. *Psychological Assessment* 16: 42–50.

Novaco, R.W. and Taylor, J.L. (2006). Cognitive-behavioural anger treatment. In: *Handbook of Adult Clinical Psychology: An Evidence Based Practice Approach* (eds. M. McNulty and A. Carr), 978–1009. London, UK: Routledge.

Novaco, R.W. and Taylor, J.L. (2008). Anger and assaultiveness of male forensic patients with developmental disabilities: links to volatile parents. *Aggressive Behavior* 34: 380–393.

Novaco, R.W. and Taylor, J.L. (2015). Reduction of assualtive behaviour following anger treatment of forensic hospital patients with intellectual disabilities. *Behaviour Research and Therapy* 65: 52–59.

O'Brien, G., Taylor, J.L., Lindsay, W.R. et al. (2010). A multi-centre study of adults with learning disabilities referred to services for antisocial or offending behaviour: demographic, individual, offending and service characteristics. *Journal of Learning Disabilities and Offending Behaviour* 1: 5–15.

Paton, C., Flynn, A., Shingleton-Smith, A. et al. (2011). Nature and quality of antipsychotic prescribing practice in UK psychiatry of intellectual disability services. *Journal of Intellectual Disability Research* 545: 665–674.

Robertson, J., Emerson, E., Gregory, N. et al. (2000). Receipt of psychotropic medication by people with intellectual disability in residential settings. *Journal of Intellectual Disability Research* 44: 666–676.

Rose, J. and West, C. (1999). Assessment of anger in people with intellectual disabilities. *Journal of Applied Research in Intellectual Disabilities* 12: 211–224.

Scotti, J.R., Evans, I.M., Meyer, L.H., and Walker, P. (1991). A meta-analysis of intervention research with problem behavior: treatment validity and standards of practice. *American Journal on Mental Retardation* 96: 233–256.

Scruggs, T.E., Mastropieri, M.A., Cook, S.B., and Escobar, C. (1986). Early intervention for children with conduct disorders: a qualitative synthesis of single-subject research. *Behavioral Disorders* 11: 260–271.

Sigafoos, J., Elkins, J., Kerr, M., and Attwood, T. (1994). A survey of aggressive behavior among a population of persons with intellectual disability in Queensland. *Journal of Intellectual Disability Research* 38: 369–381.

Smith, S., Branford, D., Collacott, R.A. et al. (1996). Prevalence and cluster typology of maladaptive behaviours in a geographically defined population of adults with learning disabilities. *British Journal of Psychiatry* 169: 219–227.

Swogger, M.T., Walsh, Z., Homaifar, B.Y. et al. (2012). Predicting self- and other-directed violence among discharged psychiatric patients: the roles of anger and psychopathic traits. *Psychological Medicine* 42: 371–379.

Taylor, J.L. (2002). A review of assessment and treatment of anger and aggression in offenders with intellectual disability. *Journal of Intellectual Disability Research* 46: 57–73.

Taylor, J.L., Lindsay, W.R., and Willner, P. (2008). CBT for people with intellectual disabilities: emerging evidence, cognitive ability and IQ effects. *Behavioural & Cognitive Psychotherapy* 36: 723–733.

Taylor, J.L. and Novaco, R.W. (2005). *Anger Treatment for People with Developmental Disabilities: A Theory, Evidence and Manual Based Approach*. Chichester, UK: Wiley.

Taylor, J.L. and Novaco, R.W. (2018). Treatment for anger, aggression and violence. In: *The Wiley Handbook on Offenders with Intellectual and Developmental Disabilities: Research, Training and Practice* (eds. W.R. Lindsay and J.L. Taylor). Chichester, UK: Wiley-Blackwell.

Taylor, J.L., Novaco, R.W., and Brown, T. (2016). Reductions in aggression and violence following cognitive behavioural anger treatment for detained hospital patients with intellectual disabilities. *Journal of Intellectual Disability Research* 60: 126–133.

Taylor, J.L., Novaco, R.W., Gillmer, B., and Thorne, I. (2002). Cognitive-behavioural treatment of anger intensity among offenders with intellectual disabilities. *Journal of Applied Research in Intellectual Disabilities* 15: 151–165.

Taylor, J.L., Novaco, R.W., Gillmer, B.T. et al. (2005). Individual cognitive-behavioural anger treatment for people with mild-borderline intellectual disabilities and histories of aggression: a controlled trial. *British Journal of Clinical Psychology* 44: 367–382.

Taylor, J.L., Novaco, R.W., Guinan, C., and Street, N. (2004). Development of an imaginal provocation test to evaluate treatment for anger problems in people with intellectual disabilities. *Clinical Psychology & Psychotherapy* 11: 233–246.

Tyrer, F., McGrother, C.W., Thorp, C.F. et al. (2006). Physical aggression towards others in adults with learning disabilities: prevalence and associated factors. *Journal of Intellectual Disability Research* 50: 295–304.

Tyrer, P., Oliver-Africano, P.C., Ahmed, Z. et al. (2008). Risperidone, haloperidol, and placebo in the treatment of aggressive challenging behaviour in patients with intellectual disabilities: a randomised controlled trial. *The Lancet* 371: 57–63.

Tyrer, S.P., Aronson, M.E., and Lauder, J. (1993). Effect of lithium on behavioural factors in aggressive mentally handicapped subjects. In: *Lithium in Medicine and Biology* (eds. N.J. Birch, C. Padgham and M.S. Hughes), 119–125. Carnforth, UK: Marius Press.

Tyrer, S.P., Walsh, A., Edwards, D. et al. (1984). Factors associated with a good response to lithium in aggressive mentally handicapped subjects. *Progress in Neuro-psychopharmacology and Biological Psychiatry* 8: 751–755.

Whitaker, S. (1993). The reduction of aggression in people with learning difficulties: a review of psychological methods. *British Journal of Clinical Psychology* 32: 1–37.

Whittington, R. and Wykes, T. (1991). Coping strategies used by staff following assault by a patient: an exploratory study. *Work and Stress* 5: 37–48.

Willner, P. (2015). The neurobiology of aggression: implications for the pharmacotherapy of challenging behaviour by people with intellectual disabilities. *Journal of Intellectual Disability Research* 59: 82–92.

Willner, P., Rose, J., Jahoda, A. et al. (2013). Group-based cognitive-behavioural anger management for people with mild to moderate intellectual disabilities: cluster randomized controlled trial. *British Journal of Psychiatry* 203: 288–296.

Zarcone, J.R., Hellings, J.A., Crandall, K. et al. (2001). Effects of risperidone on aberrant behaviour of persons with developmental disabilities: I. A double-blind crossover study using multiple measures. *American Journal of Mental Retardation* 106: 525–538.

Part V
What Works in Violence Risk Management

24

Sexual Violence Risk Management

Gina Ambroziak[1],[*] and David Thornton[2,3]

[1] Department of Health Services, Wisconsin, USA
[2] Independent Practice, USA
[3] Department of Clinical Psychology, University of Bergen, Bergen, Norway

Introduction

This chapter examines different models and strategies for managing sexual offenders. Risk management of sexual offenders differs from that of non-sexual offenders in important ways, including the level of public alarm, the seriousness of potential failures, the level and duration of risk, and the kinds of factors that contribute to re-offence risk. These differences have led to the development of specialized management strategies for sexual offenders.

Public alarm over sexual offenders is exceptionally high, fed by lurid media accounts (e.g. Zgoba 2004). In contrast to other issues, the moral panic surrounding sexual offences has not faded (Calleja 2016). Sexual offender management laws are shaped by policy makers' responses to constituents' concerns, whose perceptions are often driven by sensationalized media coverage of extreme cases (Sample and Kadleck 2008). The mere prospect of the release of a sexual offender can lead to public protest, acts of vandalism towards intended placements, and letters to newspapers and legislators. Sexual assault can have serious negative effects, including increased risk for future physical and mental-health issues (e.g. Chen et al. 2010). Unfortunately, sexual-assault survivors are often solely defined in terms of their victimization. There tends to be a perception that trauma experienced by all victims is dreadful, defining, and enduring rather than something they can move beyond (McCartan 2016). These factors combine to ensure that agencies responsible for the management of sexual offenders are highly motivated to manage risk in a credible way. Effective risk management of

* The views expressed are those of the author and not necessarily those of the Wisconsin Department of Health Services.

The Wiley Handbook of What Works in Violence Risk Management: Theory, Research and Practice,
First Edition. Edited by J. Stephen Wormith, Leam A. Craig, and Todd E. Hogue.
© 2020 John Wiley & Sons Ltd. Published 2020 by John Wiley & Sons Ltd.

sex offenders is critical for public safety and for promoting public confidence in the system (Kemshall 2009). Isolated failures are highlighted and provoke outrage whilst many successes go unacknowledged.

Surprisingly, given the degree of concern, the rate of known sexual recidivism by sexual offenders is much lower than the rate of non-sexual recidivism by men with a history of non-sexual offending. About two-thirds of violent, property and drug offenders released from American prisons in 2005 were re-arrested for a new crime within three years (Durose et al. 2014). By contrast, over five years of follow up, the sexual recidivism rate for sexual offenders is typically under 10% (Hanson et al. 2016). Put another way, approximately 90% of sexual offenders have no detected sexual offences over a five-year follow up. Almost all non-sexual recidivism by non-sex offenders occurs in the first three years after release. In contrast, about half of sexual offenders' sexual recidivism happens after five years – at least for Low- and Moderate-risk sexual offenders (Hanson et al. 2014). Thus, whilst the risk of recidivism presented by non-sexual offenders is high but concentrated in the first few years after release, the risk of sexual recidivism by sexual offenders is relatively low, but persists over longer periods of time. A consequence of these differences is that systems for managing sexual offenders seek to prevent relatively rare events, but require vigilance over many more years. Notably, however, the rate of sexual offending, along with the rate of violent offending more generally, has been declining (Finkelhor and Jones 2012; U.S. Department of Justice 2014).

Risk factors identified for sexual recidivism only partially overlap with risk factors for non-sexual recidivism. Major risk factors for general recidivism include antisocial behaviour, antisocial associates, poor/absent family/marital circumstances, and problems with alcohol and other drugs (Bonta and Andrews 2017). These factors tend to co-occur in what might be described as a general antisociality. This antisocial syndrome contributes to sexual offending, but sexual deviancy is also a major contributor – both a history of sexual offending and offence-related sexual interests – that is relatively independent of general criminality (Brouillette-Alarie et al. 2017). Thus, whilst risk-management systems for sexual offenders need to attend to the usual risk factors for general offending, they also need to consider someone who is not generally criminal but may still present a significant risk stemming from intense levels of offence-related sexual deviancy.

We begin by reviewing and comparing general models of sexual-offender management and proceed to exploration of specific intervention strategies developed and applied to sexual offenders. Unfortunately, many of the management policies employed have been instituted due to reactional public outrage to rare events, rather than thoughtful implementation based on sound empirical support. Whilst such policies may be intuitively appealing, many run contrary to what is known about sexual offending. Polices aimed at managing sexual-violence risk tend to have the following issues: (i) they often stem from faulty assumptions about sexual offences (e.g. myths about stranger danger or the inevitability of re-offence); (ii) they cast a wide and undiscerning net without regard for the heterogeneity amongst known sexual offenders; (iii) they employ extreme and enduring measures that waste resources; and (iv) they focus inordinately on known sexual offenders despite compelling evidence that the vast majority of sexual offences are committed by persons without a known history of sexual offending. These issues produce policies that may provide a false sense of security, but are minimally effective for reducing sexual offending. Evidence to support the effectiveness of various strategies will be reviewed, limiting the present focus to adult male sexual offenders.

Models of Sexual Offender Management

The containment model

The Containment Model has been popular for managing sexual offenders since the late 1990s. An early description of the model can be found in English et al. (1997). The approach combines assertions about the typical nature of sexual offenders with a five-component model for managing them.

The assumptions may be summarized as follows:

(A) Sexual offenders are planful, secretive and manipulative. These characteristics are central features of their overall lifestyle, the way they commit offences, and how they respond to supervisors and therapists.

(B) Sexual offenders are typically high-functioning individuals who use well-developed social skills to commit offences.

(C) Sexual offenders have well-developed systems for concealing the harm they inflict on others.

(D) Most sexual offenders commit a large number of offences and have a sustained propensity to reoffend.

(E) Once someone becomes a sexual offender, they cannot be cured any more than someone with epilepsy can be cured.

The main components of the Containment Model can be described as follows.

1. The primary focus is on the well-being of the community and the protection and recovery of victims of sexual offences. This leads to agencies freely sharing information about sexual offenders without regard to the usual protections of confidentiality. The lives of offenders are severely restricted whenever these restrictions are believed to enhance public safety or protect persons who have been victimized.

2. Provision of sexual offender specific treatment. Sexual offenders are held accountable for preventing recurrence of the types of thoughts and feelings that preceded past crimes. They are trained to monitor and control dangerous thoughts, fantasies, and feelings.

3. Official supervision and monitoring apply pressure through clear expectations and use of sanctions to ensure compliance with specialized treatment and supervision conditions.

4. Regular polygraph examinations are used to elicit a full history of offending, including undetected offences, and monitor ongoing fantasies and behaviours that influence access to victims.

5. Collaboration within and between disciplines and agencies. Information gathered through the polygraph can inform the therapist about treatment progress and inform supervising agencies about how to restrict the offender's life. For example, if polygraph disclosure indicated that the individual previously used a pet dog to attract children, he might be restricted from having a pet dog, and being found with a newly-purchased dog collar might provide the basis for revocation.

6. Consistent policies to support the above process and hold sexual offenders fully accountable. Thus Alford pleas (in US law is a guilty plea in criminal court where the offender does not admit to the criminal act and asserts innocence), plea bargaining sexual offences into non-sexual offence charges, and referral to diversion programmes are all discouraged.

7. Quality control of the implementation of the containment process. Since the approach has to be sustained for many decades, there is a tendency for it to become compromised over time. Quality controls lead to continuous escalation of the rigour with which the approach is implemented.

In later writings, proponents of the containment approach have emphasized that victims of sexual offences rarely disclose offences to authorities. Consequently, they argue that official statistics, records of offending, or risk-assessment instruments based on them are likely to be misleading (English et al. 2016).

A number of concerns might be raised about this approach. These include the attitudes propagated towards sexual offenders, implications for undermining a therapeutic alliance in treatment, the evidence underlying the assumptions upon which the approach is based, the expense of public resources required for implementation, and the relevance of the approach for prevention of sexual offending.

A professional trained in this approach is naturally suspicious of sexual offenders. Their behaviours are continuously appraised for potential manipulation, deceit, and deviance. The therapeutic relationship is essentially adversarial. Treatment providers do not need to create a therapeutic alliance; this becomes the responsibility of the offender. This approach easily drifts towards a punitive, counter-therapeutic relationship. Overt oppositional reactions are sanctioned; compliant behaviour is easily attributed to manipulative deception. It is difficult for a professional with this attitude to recognize any sexual offender as genuinely presenting a low risk for re-offending, despite the evidence that sexual recidivism rates amongst most sexual offenders are actually quite low. The approach implicitly treats all sexual offenders as presenting a high risk throughout their lifetime. Apparent reductions in risk are viewed with suspicion. Consequently, recognition of real reductions in recidivism risk is very difficult.

The evidence underlying the assumptions upon which this approach is based is weak. Clearly, some sexual offenders do use grooming and manipulation techniques to create offence opportunities and work to conceal their offending from those who would otherwise intervene. In addition, following conviction, they often make excuses for their behaviour or deny guilt. In these respects, however, they are quite similar to other kinds of criminals. Where they differ from other kinds of criminals, however, is that a significant proportion of sexual offenders are not generally antisocial and can often behave in responsible and pro-social ways in other aspects of their lives. For example, on the Psychopathy Checklist – Revised (Hare 2003), child molesters mean score on the antisocial facet is about a standard deviation lower than that of the pooled offender sample. There is no evidence that, as a group, they are particularly more deceptive than general criminals except about their sexual offences.

It is also true that some sexual offenders have committed a large number of offences against many victims. However, tables purporting to demonstrate that the typical sexual offender has many victims are often distorted by the disproportionate contribution of a small number of very prolific offenders on the mean numbers of victims (Abel et al. 1987). The tables are also distorted by the inclusion of marginal incidents, which would not normally be prosecuted, such as cooperative sex between teenagers. Depending on their age and jurisdiction, such behaviour may be illegal, but it is also commonplace in the US; it is not what people commonly have in mind when thinking about sexual offences.

Evidence that sexual offenders have typically committed a large number of sexual offences prior to conviction is frequently used to infer that their offending will continue after release. This, however, is simply speculation, with no direct evidence that the majority of sexual offenders re-offend after being sanctioned. Modern studies of representative samples of released sexual offenders followed over many years typically find rather few of them re-offend. One may suspect that whilst only 10% of sexual offenders are re-arrested, the rest re-offend without getting caught. Again, this is purely speculation. We know that the longer individuals with a history of sexual offending are out in the community without a detected sexual offence, the lower their risk for being arrested for sexual offences becomes (Hanson et al. 2014). Indeed, after five 'offence-free' years in the community, the likelihood of arrest for future sexual offences for many sexual offenders is little different than the rate of 'out of the blue' sex offences for criminals with no known history of sexual offending (Kahn et al. 2017).

Implementing the Containment Model is expensive, assuming that sexual offenders need to be closely supervised, polygraphed, and provided with specialized treatment indefinitely. This involves many resources, which increase over time, as more and more individuals are supervised in this way. Compared to traditional supervision, such as probation, the intensive supervision schemes based on containment make more extensive use of specialized components, such as polygraph, penile plethysmograph (a physiological measure of sexual arousal), and global positioning systems (GPS) monitoring (Buttars et al. 2016). Consequently, these management systems tend to employ more specialized (Burchfield and Mingus 2008) and smaller (Zevitz and Farkas 2000) caseloads. Whilst this may be a more cost-effective approach compared to incarceration (Zevitz and Farkas 2000), the increased frequency and intensity of monitoring and other supervision efforts require substantial investment. It is also common in such intensive regimes for a substantial proportion of offenders to be revoked to confinement for technical rule breaking, rather than committing additional sexual offences (Buttars et al. 2016; Duwe 2015). Vigorous revocation practices are not surprising given the pressure on supervising agents to prevent serious supervision failures. They are exceptionally attuned to the liability of a re-offence. The lens through which they view sexual offenders as a group – seeing them as more risky, manipulative, and deceitful – likely influences the management strategies employed and the interpersonal dynamics between the clients and agents (Bailey and Sample 2017).

Multi-agency public protection arrangements

Multi-Agency Public Protection Arrangements (MAPPAs) were introduced in England and Wales by the *Criminal Justice Act* of 2003 and were elaborated by subsequent guidance. A detailed description can be found in MAPPA Guidance 2012, a document jointly supported by Her Majesty's Prison Service, the Probation Service, and the Association of Chief Police Officers. It is available through the justice.gov.uk website. The following account draws closely on this source. In essence, MAPPA is a set of arrangements whereby relevant agencies share information regarding sexual or violent offenders and coordinate their response in a risk management plan. MAPPAs are established in each of the 42 criminal justice areas in England and Wales.

Under MAPPA, the Responsible Authority has a duty to ensure that the risks posed by certain sexual and violent offenders are assessed and managed appropriately. The Responsible Body is the police, prison, and the probation trusts for the area working together. Other agencies, such as social services, the National Health Service, and Job Centres, have a duty to cooperate with the Responsible Authority in relation to particular aspects of the offender's life. Within each area, a MAPPA Coordinator is commonly appointed. Information is shared between agencies via a secure database.

Persons convicted of most sexual offences are required to register their addresses with the police and are subject to MAPPA. Police forces will routinely visit registered sexual offenders. The frequency is determined by an assessment of level of risk. The great bulk of persons subject to MAPPA are managed at Level I. At this level, information is shared and ordinary agency procedures are followed to manage the individual. For individuals at Level II, a MAPPA meeting is held to facilitate agency coordination. At Level III senior agency involvement is invoked, allowing significant resources to be committed. The Prison Service plays a central role, and planning begins at least six months prior to release for those who will be subject to MAPPA.

Risk assessment is central to MAPPA. All relevant agencies are expected to contribute. For example, the police provide results of a static actuarial risk assessment using Risk Matrix 2000 (Thornton et al. 2003) and share criminal intelligence. The probation service provides information about compliance with supervision, dynamic risk and protective factors, and potential interventions. The Prison Service may report offence-paralleling behaviour observed whilst in custody and the offender's response to interventions. Social services contribute information about relevant children or vulnerable adults. Mental health services may provide information regarding the offender's mental health and relevant clinical interventions. Local Authorities and Registered Social Landlords may provide information about suitable accommodation and the success of current arrangements.

MAPPA risk management plans are guided by an approach developed by Hazel Kemshall commonly referred to as the Four Pillars of Risk Management (National Offender Management Service 2014). These are Supervision, Monitoring & Control, Interventions & Treatment, and Victim Safety Planning. Supervision includes supportive contacts with professionals and agencies designed to strengthen protective factors. Monitoring and Control refer to more coercive procedures to reduce opportunities for offending through restrictions on offenders' activities and living arrangements, surveillance, and/or polygraph examinations. Interventions and Treatment refer to treatment programmes designed to help individuals manage their risk factors. The plan also incorporates contingency plans to allow for rapid and effective response if the risk management plan is not sufficient to manage risk. Guidance is provided on the kinds of factors that may signal deterioration.

Compared to the Containment Model, the MAPPA system manages offenders with a lighter touch and is guided by empirically-supported risk assessment methods. The most intrusive and expensive containment methods are only adopted for the most risky cases. Consequently, it is more cost-effective and adheres more closely to principles of the risk, need, responsivity model (Bonta and Andrews 2017).

Sexual Offender Registration and Community Notification

Sexual Offender Registration and Notification (SORN) policies were initially developed as a law enforcement tool, but have evolved to include publically available internet databases and proactive-community alerts about the release of sexual offenders. The implementation of modern SORN laws began in the 1990s; all US States had enacted some variation of them by the end of 1997 (Terry 2015). The creation and expansion of these laws occurred in the wake of tragic, high-profile cases usually involving the abduction, sexual assault, and/or murder of children. Registration entails the collection and storage of identifying information such as name, photo, and address. This information was intended to facilitate law-enforcement investigations, but has now expanded to allow widespread public access. Whilst registration is one of the most widely implemented sexual-offender policies, the US is one of the only countries to make this information publically available (Vess et al. 2013). Notification alerts members of the public to information about offenders through searchable online databases as mentioned, and in a more targeted manner with flyers, door-to-door alerts, or convened meetings for members of communities in advance of offenders moving in nearby.

Based on the specific details and the nature of the offence, individuals are assigned to a tier that determines how frequently they must register, for how long, and who has access to their information. The idea behind SORN is that public awareness of offenders would allow citizens to take precautionary measures to promote their safety. Additionally, registered individuals are expected to be deterred from committing offences believing that increased surveillance would lower the likelihood of committing an offence without being apprehended.

Research findings using a variety of methodological approaches have generally indicated a lack of effect of SORN on sexual recidivism (Adkins et al. 2000; Letourneau et al. 2010; Sandler et al. 2008; Schram and Milloy 1995; Vasquez et al. 2008; Zevitz 2006). The policies may, however, expedite offence detection and arrest (Freeman 2012; Schram and Milloy 1995). Having registry information accessible to law enforcement appears to have more potential, but the positive impact may actually be diluted by notification components and broad application (Letourneau et al. 2010; Prescott and Rockoff 2011). Unfortunately, requirements for levels of management (tier designations) are linked to offence convictions, rather than empirically-validated measures of risk that more accurately predict recidivism (Harris and Lobanov-Rostovsky 2010; Zgoba et al. 2016).

The success of the open access portion of SORN is conditional on the public accessing (accurate) registry information and using the information to take actions that increase their safety (Boyle et al. 2014). However, surveys indicate that the majority of the public do not access the registry, and amongst those who do, only a fraction respond by taking preventive measures (Anderson and Sample 2008; Boyle et al. 2014; Sample et al. 2011). Further, it is unclear whether taking such steps actually provides any protective effects (Bandy 2011). Yet, the public feels safer having access to the information (Boyle et al. 2014) and tends to support such policies (Levenson et al. 2007; Sample et al. 2011).

Research has also shown that SORN often has unintended consequences. For sexual offenders, these effects frequently entail the loss of relationships, social isolation, and hopelessness that may actually exacerbate their risk for re-offence. In more extreme cases, offenders may be subject to verbal threats or physically assaulted (Levenson and Cotter 2005a). SORN policies may also negatively impact victims. The prospect of community notification may decrease victims' willingness to report abuse. Dissemination of offence charges may inadvertently reveal the identity of the victim (Edwards and Hensley 2001).

These measures substantially increase resource requirements (Zevitz and Farkas 2000). Offender failure to register, however, is not associated with increased risk for sexual recidivism (Duwe and Donnay 2010; Levenson et al. 2009). Furthermore, the resources required for SORN will only increase as the number of offenders required to register inevitably grows due to the lengthy durations of the registration requirements, which range from 15 years to lifetime. Setting aside the dubious merits of these laws more generally, their broad application and enduring nature are largely unnecessary. A non-trivial number of sexual offenders pose no higher risk for sexual offending than non-sexual offenders (Kahn et al. 2017). Additionally, whilst sexual offenders' risk may persist longer than that of non-sexual offenders, risk does remit with age (Helmus et al. 2012) and time offence-free in the community (Hanson et al. 2014).

In summary, there is little evidence to suggest current SORN policies reduce sexual recidivism. Limiting public access to registry information might mitigate unintended consequences that destabilize and disrupt re-integration. The majority of the public does not access registries, but support these policies that do little other than reinforce naïve myths about sexual offenders. Successfully addressing such myths might help shift policies in directions that actually promote community safety. Many myths about sexual offenders are deeply entrenched, but educational efforts can influence certain attitudes (Kleban and Jeglic 2012). Increasing awareness of the nature of sexual offending, rather than alarming the public about low-risk offenders, would be a more effective means to promote safety measures. For example, knowing that the overwhelming majority of sexual offences are committed by persons with no history of sexual offending (Levenson and Zgoba 2016; Sandler et al. 2008), and that most sexual offences are committed by individuals related to or known by the victim (e.g. Prescott and Rockoff 2011) might contribute to more effective preventive strategies. Using classification schemes built on empirical evidence would also increase community safety and permit more efficient use of limited resources (Zgoba et al. 2016). Reconsidering default duration requirements, along with relaxation of reporting mechanisms with demonstrated compliance and desistance over time might also conserve resources without compromising public safety.

Residency Restrictions and GPS Monitoring

Residency restrictions and exclusionary safety zones

Management strategies may also restrict the living arrangements of sexual offenders and/or monitor their movement. Since the 1990s, states have been enacting residency restrictions that prohibit sexual offenders from living within varying distances (500–2500 ft) of areas where children may be present, such as schools and parks. The belief is that prohibiting offenders from living near these areas will protect children and other potential victims. The public views these measures as a common sense strategy to prevent victimizations; many citizens take a strong 'not in my backyard' stance against sexual offenders living in their communities. There is wide support for such policies, often based on misperceptions of sexual offenders as predators targeting child victims unknown to them. Citizens typically favour exclusion zones of 500 ft or more, rarely considering that exclusionary zones for a given offender might want to take into account the type of sexual crime committed (Anderson et al. 2015).

Research has failed to find evidence to support these restrictions (Blood et al. 2008; Zandbergen et al. 2010) and called into question the very basis of the laws. Most sexual offenders make contact with and offend against child victims in private settings, and the vast majority offend against children with whom they have had a sustained relationship through familial ties or close adult acquaintances (Calkins et al. 2015; Colombino et al. 2009). In the rare instances where sexual offenders approach children in public spaces, they typically travel further from their homes than most residential restrictions require to avoid recognition (Duwe et al. 2008). These facts highlight the futility of residency restrictions to prevent sexual offences, since offending is tied to *relational* proximity rather than *geographic* proximity (Colombino et al. 2009). Whilst offenders against adult victims are more likely to initiate victim contact in public places, residency restrictions are specifically geared towards the protection of children (Colombino et al. 2011).

Given the locations used to create exclusion zones in many statutes (e.g. schools, day-cares, parks, churches, even bus stops), residence availability to registered sexual offenders may be virtually non-existent in densely populated areas. Wider buffer zones around these areas can dramatically increase these effects (Barnes et al. 2009; Chajewski and Mercado 2009), but even small buffer distances may leave few viable housing options (Zandbergen and Hart 2006). Such residential restrictions essentially amount to banishment in many non-rural areas. In recent years, these statutes have begun to be struck down as unconstitutional (Levenson 2016).

Severely limiting viable housing options for offenders contributes to greater isolation, forcing them to reside in socially disorganized neighbourhoods and increasing problems for accessing treatment services and living with supportive family members (Levenson 2008; Levenson and Cotter 2005b; Levenson and Hern 2007; Zandbergen and Hart 2006). Destabilizing factors such as homelessness and transience make it more difficult to monitor and track offenders (increasing strain on limited resources), and contribute to higher rates of sexual recidivism – the very behaviours the statutes were designed to reduce (e.g. Lee et al. 2016; Levenson 2016).

As currently implemented, residency restrictions are ineffective. The strategy might be improved if applied to very selective and specific types of offenders. A viable alternative to residency restrictions might be exclusionary child-safety zones. This approach could prohibit sexual offenders from loitering in specific locations where children congregate, rather than restricting where they are permitted to live, and might achieve the intended purpose with greater success (Colombino et al. 2011; Levenson 2008; Zandbergen et al. 2010).

GPS monitoring

Another approach to monitoring and restricting the movements of known sexual offenders is through electronic monitoring using GPS. Whilst not a new technology, its implementation as a strategy for managing sexual offenders has increased over the past decade. Proliferation of this strategy can, again, be tied to well-intentioned policies implemented in response to public reactions following a tragic event (Levenson and D'Amora 2007). As a surveillance tool, electronic monitoring systems can be used passively – storing data that can later be referenced – or actively – generating real-time check-ups of an individual's location and triggering alerts if certain criteria are met. Active monitoring allows for prompt responses to potential violations, such as an individual entering an unapproved location. Inclusion zones can be used to verify that the individual is at home or work when required.

Beyond the limits of the technology itself (i.e. malfunctions that generate false positives or fail to capture true positives), the impact of electronic monitoring surveillance is constrained in that it relies on pre-identifying risky locations, and knowing *where* offenders are at any given time may be minimally informative. Further, evidence regarding the efficacy of the approach is mixed. Some research has found better outcomes, in terms of rule compliance and recidivism (e.g. Gies et al. 2012), whilst other studies have produced less promising results (Tennessee Board of Probation 2007; Turner et al. 2010). The most consistent findings have been increased cost and workload for supervising agents (Omori and Turner 2015; Turner et al. 2010; Zevitz and Farkas 2000). Resources are disproportionately allocated to surveillance at the expense of other important facets of risk management (Payne and DeMichele 2011). Lifetime GPS monitoring for some sexual offenders will increase strain on resources as individuals are continually added to the system. GPS monitoring devices also present barriers for individuals in securing certain kinds of employment and accessing pro-social supports and can interfere with treatment sessions (Bales et al. 2010; Burchfield and Mingus 2008; Tennessee Board of Probation 2007).

Like SORN and residence restrictions, electronic monitoring is viewed by the public as an effective strategy, particularly amongst citizens who embrace 'stranger danger' myths (Budd and Mancini 2015). However, the technology has greater potential for creating a false sense of security whilst draining resources that could be allocated to more effective strategies. GPS monitoring has potential as a management tool for the assessment of rate of adherence, but limitations and potential drawbacks should be recognized. As with the other strategies, selective use under appropriate circumstances and refraining from lifetime requirements would reduce the burden on already scarce resources.

Sexual Offender Civil Commitment

In 1990, Washington State enacted the first modern civil commitment law for sexual offenders. Since that time, 19 other States and the Federal Government have followed suit.[1] These laws allow for the indefinite and involuntary commitment of certain sexual offenders after their criminal sentences. The use of sexual offender civil commitment (SOCC) as a management strategy is contentious (Janus 2007). Objections focus on the constitutionality of the practice, as well as relative benefit in light of the economic and social costs. Whilst programmatic structures and statutory language vary across programmes, civil commitment of a sexual offender generally requires three criteria to be met: (i) a history of a qualifying sexual offence; (ii) a mental disorder or abnormality that predisposes the individual to commit sexual offences; and (iii) a high likelihood of perpetrating acts of sexual violence in the future. Intended to be applied only to individuals at the very highest risk, SOCC programmes commit a very small subset of those screened as they exit the prison system (Thornton and Kelley 2016). Civilly committed offenders are referred to as sexually violent persons/predators (SVPs) or sexually dangerous persons. Preventing these high-risk offenders from returning to the community has probably contributed to a reduction in sexual recidivism rates (Duwe 2014). The same study also emphasized the need to implement intermediate management strategies and recognized that the returns will diminish should the net be cast too widely.

At least half of SOCC programmes include a conditional or supervised release (SR) component, allowing for offender placements in the community rather than in secure inpatient facilities. Some programmes allow for community management of the offenders from the outset of their commitment, based on their level of risk. Others are designed to place the offenders back in the community only after they have progressed through inpatient treatment programmes. The extent to which SR is employed within SOCC programmes varies widely, with some programmes having managed only a handful of clients and others having managed hundreds (Schneider et al. 2016).

Wisconsin's programme, for example, has placed about a quarter of SVPs into the community under SR (Cram and Ambroziak 2016). Just over three-quarters of these clients spent a year or more under SR; the median total time was two years. About two-thirds of clients fell in the high or moderate-high recidivism risk categories according to the Static-99R, the most widely used actuarial risk assessment tool (Helmus et al. 2012). In addition to high actuarial

---

[1] Pennsylvania is an outlier in that it is aimed solely at managed juvenile sexual offenders.

Table 24.1 Most common reasons for supervised release revocation.

Violation	% of Clients
Unapproved contact or activity	25.6
Lying, providing inaccurate information, or failed polygraphs	24.1
Unapproved use of technology – internet, computer, cell phone, cable, gaming system	16.5
Financial Violations – including unapproved lending/borrowing of money, purchasing on credit	15.8
Offence-related interests apparently activated with no imminent risk	15.0
Unapproved intimate relationship or unapproved, but legal sexual contact (including solicitation or attempts to establish)	14.3
Possession of sexually explicit but legal materials	13.5

Less common violations are not included. Revocation may be based on multiple types of violations.

risk, these clients also exhibit many dynamic psychological risk factors that contribute to increased risk of re-offending. Despite the heightened risk for re-offending, only 2% of clients have ever been charged with a new sexual offence whilst under SR, although an additional 5% engaged in relatively minor but illegal sexual behaviour that was not charged (e.g. touching the buttocks of a stranger during a supervised shopping trip).

Other rule violations were quite common amongst Wisconsin SR clients, however, as shown in Table 24.1. Over 85% of revocations were based on multiple types of violations. Of those returned to custody for violations, 95% were due to circumstances other than illegal sexual behaviour. A few clients did engage in behaviours that put them at potentially imminent risk for sexual offending, such as a client with a history of offending against children having unapproved and unsupervised contact with a child. A frequent violation that resulted in custody was evidence of active offence-related interests without direct evidence that the client was at imminent risk for re-offending. These interests may have been identified by the client's self-report of deviant sexual fantasies or discovery of photograph collections of children. Identifying and addressing risky behaviours and situations, and intervening prior to the occurrence of a sexual offence, is precisely the purpose of risk management. The overwhelming majority of SR clients in Wisconsin have been managed safely in the community with supervision and monitoring. In coordination with other supportive services, including community-based sexual offender treatment, the Wisconsin SR programme has been quite successful. Other SOCC programmes report similarly low sexual recidivism rates for clients under SR (Schneider et al. 2016). Exaggerated fears and misperceptions that SVPs released under supervision are exceptionally dangerous are clearly unwarranted. These programmes demonstrate that even high-risk sexual offenders can be safely managed in the community with proper allocation of social resources.

Roughly one-third of Wisconsin SR clients have progressed through legal proceedings to be unconditionally discharged from their civil commitment, raising concerns about their re-entry into the community. An unpublished dataset (Ambroziak et al. 2016) includes outcome data from 48 Wisconsin SVPs who had their commitments discharged following SR. In contrast to the very low rate of sexual recidivism whilst under SR, the recidivism rate for the discharged clients without the structure, support, and supervision was 19%. Survival analysis life tables looking at the timing of sexual offences, when they occurred, show the proportion of clients who remain offence-free after three years was 0.95 under SR. In contrast, for those discharged following SR the proportion remaining offence-free after three years was only 0.78. Figure 24.1 depicts survival curves for the two groups, which are significantly different ($p < 0.05$). Those who did sexually re-offend following discharge did so quite rapidly, some within one month after release. All of the sexual re-offences occurred within two years following release, a rather unique pattern compared to what is typically seen in released sexual offender samples. These results show that the services provided under the Wisconsin SR programme are effective for managing the risk posed by these clients. The findings are persuasive, particularly in light of the fact that the subset of SR clients who had their commitments discharged were presumably at lower risk for re-offending than those remaining under SR, or their petitions for discharge would not have been granted. The rate of sexual recidivism for SVPs discharged following SR is substantially higher. It should be noted, however, that the vast majority of individuals in both samples, once deemed to be at exceptionally high risk for re-offending, did not re-offend following re-integration into the community.

SVPs face enormous challenges to re-integrate into the community, whether under SR or discharged. Typically, they have not been competitively or gainfully employed for many years and few have pro-social, supportive ties in the community. Hostile community responses, housing difficulties and generally unstable release environments combine to further intensify the difficulties. Under such daunting re-integration prospects, it is not surprising that some civilly committed sexual offenders do not petition the courts for release. Many are understandably apprehensive about being released without stable social networks, adequate job prospects, and other supportive services.

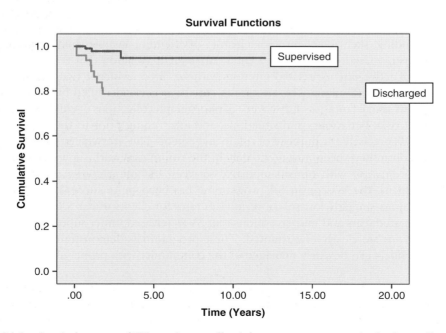

Figure 24.1 Survival curves of Wisconsin sexually violent persons – supervised release clients under community supervision and following unconditional discharge.

Circles of Support and Accountability

One particularly encouraging intervention is Circles of Support and Accountability (COSA; Wilson et al. 2005). Like other measures designed to manage sexual offenders, COSA originated in response to a high-profile case – the release of a repeat child molester who had reached his warrant expiry in Canada. Unlike other approaches, however, this strategy was developed proactively rather than in a reaction to a sensationalized re-offence event. It also promotes community collaboration and re-integration, rather than relying on social isolation and ostracism.

In 1994, a repeat child molester was released to a barrage of negative media attention and public backlash, and members of a local religious organization volunteered to assist with the offender's re-integration (Wilson et al. 2007). The COSA approach provides offenders assistance and support, whilst also holding them accountable. The basic COSA design identifies the offender as the 'Core Member' of the Circle. Community volunteers form an 'Inner Circle' of support, and specialized professionals in the field, such as psychologists, law enforcement, social and workers form an 'Outer Circle' of assistance and oversight.

Research from the early pilot programme to initiatives in other jurisdictions internationally have been positive (Bates et al. 2013; Duwe 2013; Wilson and McWhinnie 2013; Wilson et al. 2005, 2009). Results include positive perspectives of key stakeholders, reduction of sexual and violent recidivism, and positive returns on investment. This strategy has the most potential for high-risk offenders (Duwe 2013), and the *supportive* aspect of the model is critical to its success. The approach may be less effective to the extent that accountability is overemphasized and the focus on risk becomes intensified (Fox 2016).

A major challenge for COSA implementation is the recruitment of suitable volunteers, perhaps due to public perceptions and misperceptions of sexual offenders. Encouragingly, there are a few recent examples of the public holding less extreme views, such as favouring rehabilitation when given the context that treatment can be effective (Mancini and Budd 2016) and supporting the prospect of involving volunteers in rehabilitation efforts (Höing et al. 2016). A shift in the public mindset away from persistently punitive approaches would likely benefit risk management efforts.

COSA creates the opportunity for community members to actively engage in reducing sexual assaults. In contrast to approaches that focus on shaming, isolating, and banishing sexual offenders, the COSA model allows the public to take a more constructive approach to achieve the desired outcome. COSA improves the lives of offenders, by promoting well-being and providing social support for living offence-free (e.g. Fox 2016; Höing et al. 2016). It also benefits the community by lowering sexual recidivism (e.g. Bates et al. 2013). Further, it has financial payoffs, through a marked return on investment (Duwe 2013). Enhancing public safety and promoting supportive community re-integration for offenders need not be competing aims.

Conclusions

Individuals with a history of sexual offences garner neither sympathy nor support from the general public. Opinions reflect a myriad of misperceptions reinforced through the sensationalized media coverage of unusual but horrific sexual crimes. So long as policies and management practices designed to address sexual offending are driven by these misperceptions, our success is likely to be limited. So one critical question to be addressed might be how best to influence 'negative stagnant views on sex-offender management and crime policy that are based on distorted perceptions' (Mancini and Budd 2016, p. 794). Implemented approaches should demonstrate measurable effects on public safety, not simply reassure faulty perceptions (e.g. Erooga 2008). There must be concerted efforts to resist policy development based on public outrage to rare, infamous cases. With finite resources and high stakes for negative outcomes, management strategies must be developed rationally, and the impact of implemented strategies must be empirically evaluated with respect to both financial and preventative effectiveness.

Different models relying on multidisciplinary teams have been developed to manage individuals with a history of sexual offending. The Containment Model is based on questionable assumptions that result in a suspicious, adversarial, and largely inflexible approach. In contrast, MAPPAs offer a more flexible strategy, creating risk management plans around empirically-supported risk assessment and allocating resources more efficiently based on characteristics specific to the offender.

Other strategies have yielded varying degrees of success. Registration and community notification policies have major flaws, but might be improved with modifications. Residency restrictions are ineffective and may actually exacerbate risk rather than manage it. GPS monitoring requires substantial resources with limited evidence supporting its effectiveness to reduce sexual recidivism.

Civil commitment likely has an impact in reducing sexual offences. However, it is contentious, costly, and should be applied on a very limited basis. Amongst those who do warrant civil commitment, many can be and are safely managed in the community. COSA are an especially promising strategy. Importantly, risk management will be most effective when strategies are proportionate to risk level, not poured indiscriminately into low-risk individuals who do not need it.

The vast majority of sexual offences are committed by first-time offenders. Consequently, focusing only on identified sexual offenders means that even the most effective sexual-offender risk management efforts will only address a sliver of the overall sexual violence problem. Policies could make more efficient use of resources by recognizing that many sexual offenders pose no greater risk for sexually re-offending than non-sexual offenders, and that recidivism risk diminishes with time spent offence-free in the community. Further, even sexual offenders deemed at high risk for re-offence can be effectively managed in the community. Lastly, management strategies that are intuitively appealing may be ineffective and even counterproductive. Serious commitment to reducing sexual violence requires us to reconsider some of the current approaches to the case management of sexual offenders. There is sufficient research evidence to guide legislation that facilitates more effective risk management strategies.

References

Abel, G., Becker, J.V., Mittelman, M. et al. (1987). Self-reported sex crimes of nonincarcerated paraphiliacs. *Journal of Interpersonal Violence* 2: 3–25.

Adkins, G., Huff, D., Stageberg, P. et al. (2000). *The Iowa Sex Offender Registry and Recidivism*. Des Moines, IA: Iowa Department of Human Rights, Division of Criminal and Juvenile Justice Planning and Statistical Analysis Center.

Ambroziak, G., Kahn, R.E., Mundt, J.C. and Thornton, D. (2016). Recidivism outcomes of SVPs discharged following community supervised release. Unpublished raw data.

Anderson, A.L. and Sample, L.L. (2008). Public awareness and action resulting from sex offender community notification laws. *Criminal Justice Policy Review* 19: 371–396.

Anderson, A.L., Sample, L.L., and Cain, C.M. (2015). Residency restrictions for sex offenders: public opinion on appropriate distances. *Criminal Justice Policy Review* 26: 262–277.

Bailey, D.J.S. and Sample, L.L. (2017). Sex offender supervision in context: the need for qualitative examinations of social distance in sex offender-supervision officer relationships. *Criminal Justice Policy Review* 28: 176–204.

Bales, W., Mann, K., Blomberg, T. et al. (2010). *A Quantitative and Qualitative Assessment of Electronic Monitoring*. Tallahassee, FL: Florida State University.

Bandy, R. (2011). Measuring the impact of sex offender notification on community adoption of protective behaviours. *Criminology & Public Policy* 10: 237–263.

Barnes, J.C., Dukes, T., Tewksbury, R., and De Troye, T.M. (2009). Analyzing the impact of state-wide residence restriction law on South Carolina sex offenders. *Criminal Justice Policy Review* 20: 21–43.

Bates, A., Williams, D., Wilson, C., and Wilson, R.J. (2013). Circles South-East: the first ten years 2002–2012. *International Journal of Offender Therapy and Comparative Criminology* 58: 861–885.

Blood, P., Watson, L., and Stageberg, P. (2008). *State Legislation Monitoring Report*. Des Moines, IA: Criminal and Juvenile Justice Planning.

Bonta, J. and Andrews, D.A. (2017). *The Psychology of Criminal Conduct*, 6e. New York, NY: Routledge.

Boyle, D.J., Ragusa-Salerno, L.M., Marcus, A.F. et al. (2014). Public knowledge and use of sexual offender internet registries: results from a random digit dialing telephone Survey. *Journal of Interpersonal Violence* 29: 1914–1932.

Brouillette-Alarie, S., Proulx, J., and Hanson, R.K. (2017). Three central dimensions of sexual recidivism risk: understanding the latent constructs of Static-99Rand Static-2002R. *Sexual Abuse: A Journal of Research and Treatment* 30: 676–704.

Budd, K. and Mancini, C. (2015). Public perceptions of GPS monitoring for convicted sex offenders: opinions on effectiveness of electronic monitoring to reduce sexual recidivism. *International Journal of Offender Therapy and Comparative Criminology* 61: 1335–1353.

Burchfield, K.B. and Mingus, W. (2008). Not in my neighborhood: assessing registered sex offenders' experiences with local social capital and social control. *Criminal Justice and Behaviour* 35: 356–374.

Buttars, A., Huss, M.T., and Brack, C. (2016). An analysis of an intensive supervision program for sex offenders using propensity scores. *Journal of Offender Rehabilitation* 55: 51–68.

Calkins, C., Colombino, N., Matsuura, T., and Jeglic, E. (2015). Where do sex crimes occur? How an examination of sex offence location can inform policy and prevention. *International Journal of Comparative and Applied Criminal Justice* 39: 99–112.

Calleja, N.G. (2016). Deconstructing a puzzling relationship: sex offender legislation, the crimes that inspired it, and sustained moral panic. *Justice Policy Journal* 13: 1–17.

Chajewski, M. and Mercado, C.C. (2009). An evaluation of sex offender residence restrictions functioning in town, county, and city-wide jurisdictions. *Criminal Justice Policy Review* 20: 44–61.

Chen, L.P., Murad, M.H., Paras, M.L. et al. (2010). Sexual abuse and lifetime diagnosis of psychiatric disorders: systematic review and meta-analysis. *Mayo Clinical Proceedings* 85: 618–629.

Colombino, N., Mercado, C.C., and Jeglic, E.L. (2009). Situational aspects of sexual offending: implications for residence restriction laws. *Justice Research and Policy* 11: 27–43.

Colombino, N., Mercado, C.C., Levenson, J., and Jeglic, E. (2011). Preventing sexual violence: can examination of offence location inform sex crime policy? *International Journal of Law and Psychiatry* 34: 160–167.

Cram, J. and Ambroziak, G. (2016). Wisconsin SVPs – Residency restrictions, community notification, & outcomes. Paper presented at Wisconsin ATSA Conference in Madison, WI (2–3 June 2016).

Durose, M.R., Cooper, A.D. and Snyder, H.N. (2014). *Recidivism of Prisoners Released in 30 States in 2005: Patterns from 2005 to 2010* (NCJ 244205). Washington, DC: Bureau of Justice Statistics.

Duwe, G. (2013). Can Circles of Support and Accountability (COSA) work in the United States? Preliminary results from a randomized experiment in Minnesota. *Sexual Abuse: A Journal of Research and Treatment* 25: 143–165.

Duwe, G. (2014). To what extent does civil commitment reduce sexual recidivism? Estimating the selective incapacitation effects in Minnesota. *Journal of Criminal Justice* 42: 193–202.

Duwe, G. (2015). What has worked and what has not with Minnesota sex offenders: a review of the evidence. *Journal of Sexual Aggression* 21 (1): 71–85.

Duwe, G. and Donnay, W. (2010). The effects of failure to register on sex offender recidivism. *Criminal Justice and Behaviour* 37: 520–536.

Duwe, G., Donnay, W., and Tewksbury, R. (2008). Does residential proximity matter? A geographic analysis of sex offence recidivism. *Criminal Justice and Behaviour* 35: 484–504.

Edwards, W. and Hensley, C. (2001). Contextualizing sex offender management legislation and policy: evaluating the problem of latent consequences in community notification laws. *International Journal of Offender Therapy and Comparative Criminology* 45: 83–101.

English, K., Heil, P., and Veeder, G. (2016). The containment approach: a strategy for the community management of sex offenders. In: *Sexual Offending* (eds. A. Phenix and H.M. Hoberman), 713–743. New York, NY: Springer.

English, K., Pullen, S., and Jones, L. (1997). *Managing Adult Sex Offenders, Research in Brief.* Washington, DC: National Institute of Justice.

Erooga, M. (2008). A human rights-based approach to sex offender management: the key to effective public protection? *Journal of Sexual Aggression* 14: 171–183.

Finkelhor, D. and Jones, L. (2012). *Have Sexual Abuse and Physical Abuse Declined Since the 1990s?* Durham, NH: University of New Hampshire.

Fox, K.J. (2016). Civic commitment: promoting desistance through community integration. *Punishment & Society* 18: 68–94.

Freeman, N.J. (2012). The public safety impact of community notification. *Crime and Delinquency* 58: 539–564.

Gies, S.V., Gainey, R., Cohen, M.I. et al. (2012). *Monitoring High Risk Sex Offenders with GPS Technology: An Evaluation of the California Supervision Program.* Washington, DC: U.S. Department of Justice.

Hanson, R.K., Harris, A.J.R., Helmus, L., and Thornton, D. (2014). High-risk sex offenders may not be high risk forever. *Journal of Interpersonal Violence* 29: 2792–2813.

Hanson, R.K., Thornton, D., Helmus, L.M., and Babchishin, K.M. (2016). What sexual recidivism rates are associated with Static-99R and Static-2002R scores? *Sexual Abuse: A Journal of Research and Treatment* 28: 218–252.

Hare, R.D. (2003). *Manual for the Revised Psychopathy Checklist*, 2e. Toronto, ON: Multi-Health Systems.

Harris, A.J. and Lobanov-Rostovsky, C. (2010). Implementing the Adam Walsh Act's sex offender registration and notification provisions: a survey of the states. *Criminal Justice Policy Review* 21: 202–222.

Helmus, L., Thornton, D., Hanson, R.K., and Babchishin, K.M. (2012). Improving the predictive accuracy of Static-99 and Static-2002 with older sex offenders: revised age weights. *Sexual Abuse: A Journal of Research and Treatment* 24: 64–101.

Höing, M., Petrina, R., Duke, L.H. et al. (2016). Community support for sex offender rehabilitation in Europe. *European Journal of Criminology* 13: 491–516.

Janus, E.S. (2007). "Don't think of a predator" – changing frames for better sexual violence prevention. *Sex Offender Law Report* 8: 81–96.

Kahn, R.E., Ambroziak, G., Hanson, R.K., and Thornton, D. (2017). Release from the sex offender label. *Archives of Sexual Behaviour* 46: 861–864.

Kemshall, H. (2009). Working with sex offenders in a climate of public blame and anxiety: how to make defensible decisions for risk. *Journal of Sexual Aggression* 15: 331–343.

Kleban, K. and Jeglic, E. (2012). Dispelling the myths: can psychoeducation change publicattitudes towards sex offenders? *Journal of Sexual Aggression* 18: 179–193.

Lee, S.C., Restrepo, A., Satariano, A., and Hanson, R.K. (2016). *The Predictive Validity of Static-99R for Sexual Offenders in California: 2016 Update*. Sacramento, CA: SARATSO.

Letourneau, E.J., Levenson, J.S., Bandyopadhyay, D. et al. (2010). Effects of South Carolina's sex offender registration and notification policy on adult recidivism. *Criminal Justice Policy Review* 2: 435–458.

Levenson, J., Letourneau, E., Armstrong, K. and Zgoba, K. (2009). Failure to register: An empirical analysis of sex offence recidivism. Unpublished manuscript.

Levenson, J.S. (2008). Collateral consequences of sex offender residence restrictions. *Criminal Justice Studies* 21: 153–166.

Levenson, J.S. (2016). Hidden challenges: Sex offenders legislated into homelessness. *Journal of Social Work* 18 (3): 348–363.

Levenson, J.S., Brannon, Y., Fortney, T., and Baker, J. (2007). Public perceptions about sex offenders and community protection policies. *Analyses of Social Issues and Public Policy* 7: 1–25.

Levenson, J.S. and Cotter, L.P. (2005a). The effect of Megan's Law on sex offender reintegration. *Journal of Contemporary Criminal Justice* 21: 49–66.

Levenson, J.S. and Cotter, L.P. (2005b). The impact of sex offender residence restrictions: 1,000 feet from danger or one step from absurd? *International Journal of Offender Therapy and Comparative Criminology* 49: 168–178.

Levenson, J.S. and D'Amora, D.A. (2007). Social policies designed to prevent sexual violence: The emperor's new clothes? *Criminal Justice Policy Review* 18: 168–199.

Levenson, J.S. and Hern, A.L. (2007). Sex offender residence restrictions: unintended consequences and community reentry. *Justice and Research Policy* 9: 59–73.

Levenson, J.S. and Zgoba, K.M. (2016). Community protection policies and repeat sexual offences in Florida. *International Journal of Offender Therapy and Comparative Criminology* 60: 1140–1158.

Mancini, C. and Budd, K.M. (2016). Is the public convinced that "nothing works?" Predictors of treatment support for sex offenders among Americans. *Crime & Delinquency* 62: 777–799.

McCartan, K. (2016). Complexity and vulnerability in sexual harm more than a 'zero sum game'. http://sajrt.blogspot.com/2016/05/complexity-and-vulnerability-in-sexual.html (Accessed 20 August 2019).

National Offender Management Service (2014). *Merseyside MAPPA Annual Report 2013–2014*. London, UK: Author.

Omori, M.K. and Turner, S.F. (2015). Assessing the cost of electronically monitoring high-risk sex offenders. *Crime & Delinquency* 61: 873–894.

Payne, B.K. and DeMichele, M. (2011). Sex offender policies: considering unanticipated consequences of GPS sex offender monitoring. *Aggression and Violent Behaviour* 16: 177–187.

Prescott, J.J. and Rockoff, J.E. (2011). Do sex offender registration and notification laws affect criminal behaviour? *Journal of Law and Economics* 54: 161–206.

Sample, L.L., Evans, M.K., and Anderson, A.L. (2011). Sex offender community notification laws: are their effects symbolic or instrumental in nature? *Criminal Justice Policy Review* 22: 27–49.

Sample, L.L. and Kadleck, C. (2008). Sex offender laws: legislators' accounts of the need for policy. *Criminal Justice Policy Review* 19: 40–62.

Sandler, J.C., Freeman, N.J., and Socia, K.M. (2008). Does a watched pot boil? A time series analysis of New York State's sex offender registration and notification law. *Psychology, Public Policy and Law* 14: 284–302.

Schneider, J.E., Jackson, R.L., Ambroziak, G. et al. (2016). Annual survey of sex offender civil commitment programs. Paper presented at the Sex Offender Civil Commitment Programs Network Conference in Orlando, FL (3 November 2016).

Schram, D.D. and Milloy, C.D. (1995). *Community Notification: A Study of Offender Characteristics and Recidivism*. Olympia, WA: Washington State Institute for Public Policy.

Tennessee Board of Probation and Parole (2007). *Monitoring Tennessee's Sex Offenders Using Global Positioning Systems: A Project Evaluation*. Nashville, TN: Author.

Terry, K.J. (2015). Sex offender laws in the United States: smart policy or disproportionate sanctions? *International Journal of Comparative and Applied Criminal Justice* 39: 113–127.

Thornton, D. and Kelley, S.M. (2016). The value of protective factors for SVP programs. Webinar presentation conducted for the Sex Offender Civil Commitment Provider Network (SOCCPN) (3 November 2016).

Thornton, D., Mann, R., Webster, S. et al. (2003). Distinguishing and combining risks for sexual and violent recidivism. In: *Annals of the New York Academy of Sciences*, vol. 989. Sexually coercive behaviour: Understanding and management (eds. R.A. Prentky, E.S. Janus and M.C. Seto), 225–235. New York, NY: New York Academy of Sciences.

Turner, S., Chamberlain, A., Jannetta, J., and Hess, J. (2010). *Implementation and Outcomes for California's GPS Pilot for High Risk Sex Offender Parolees*. Irvine, CA: Center for Evidence-Based Corrections.

U.S. Department of Justice (2014). *Crime in the United States, 2013*. Clarksburg, West Virginia: Criminal Justice Information Services.

Vasquez, B.E., Maddan, S., and Walker, J.T. (2008). The influence of sex offender registration and notification laws in the United States. *Crime and Delinquency* 54: 175–192.

Vess, J., Day, A., Powell, M., and Graffam, J. (2013). International sex offender registration laws: research and evaluation issues based on a review of current scientific literature. *Police Practice and Research: An International Journal* 14: 205–218.

Wilson, R.J., Cortoni, F., and McWhinnie, A.J. (2009). Circles of support & accountability: a Canadian national replication of outcome findings. *Sexual Abuse: A Journal of Research and Treatment* 21: 412–430.

Wilson, R.J. and McWhinnie, A. (2013). Putting the "community" back in community risk management of persons who have sexually abused. *International Journal of Behavioural Consultation and Therapy* 8 (3–4): 72–79.

Wilson, R.J., McWhinnie, A., Picheca, J.E. et al. (2007). Circles of support and accountability: engaging community volunteers in the management of high-risk sexual offenders. *The Howard Journal* 46: 1–15.

Wilson, R.J., Picheca, J.E., and Prinzo, M. (2005). *Circles of Support & Accountability: An Evaluation of the Pilot Project in South-Central Ontario*. Ottawa, ON: Correctional Service of Canada.

Zandbergen, P.A. and Hart, T.C. (2006). Reducing housing options for convicted sex offenders: investigating the impact of residency restriction laws using GIS. *Justice Research and Policy* 8: 1–24.

Zandbergen, P.A., Levenson, J.S., and Hart, T.C. (2010). Residential proximity to schools and daycares: an empirical analysis of sex offence recidivism. *Criminal Justice and Behaviour* 37: 482–502.

Zevitz, R.G. (2006). Sex offender community notification: its role in recidivism and offender reintegration. *Criminal Justice Studies* 19: 193–208.

Zevitz, R.G. and Farkas, M.A. (2000). The impact of sex-offender community notification on probation/parole in Wisconsin. *International Journal of Offender Therapy and Comparative Criminology* 44: 8–21.

Zgoba, K. (2004). Spin doctors and moral crusaders: the moral panic behind child safety legislation. *Criminal Justice Studies* 17: 385–404.

Zgoba, K.M., Miner, M., Levenson, J. et al. (2016). The Adam Walsh Act: an examination of sex offender risk classification systems. *Sexual Abuse: A Journal of Research and Treatment* 28: 722–740.

25

Effective Systems and Processes for Managing Violent Offenders in the United Kingdom and the European Union

Hazel Kemshall[1] and Sarah Hilder[2]

[1] De Montfort University, Leicester, UK
[2] Nottingham Trent University, Nottingham, USA

Introduction

The community management of violent offenders is a challenging area of work, with blame and public scrutiny often following high-profile risk management failures. This chapter focuses on two key areas of work with this group of offenders: the multi-agency management of high-risk violent offenders in the United Kingdom (UK); and the increasing requirement to monitor and manage those violent offenders who travel across European Union (EU) borders to commit harmful offences.

The Origins of Multi-agency Working in England with Violent Offenders

Multi-agency public protection arrangements (MAPPA) began in the late 1990s in England, with a rapid extension across England and Wales from 2001 onwards (see Kemshall 2010a; Nash and Williams 2008, pp. 109–112 for a full history). MAPPA was formally established by the *Criminal Justice Act 2003* (sections 325-327B) and was 'designed to protect the public, including previous victims of crime, from serious harm by sexual and violent offenders' (para 1.1, Ministry of Justice 2016). Whilst initially driven by concerns about sexual offenders (see Kemshall 2003), violent offenders have increasingly come under the remit of MAPPA. Three categories of offenders fall under MAPPA: those who have committed violent and sexual offences; those offenders who are listed on the sex-offender register; and other offenders considered by the police and probation services to pose a serious risk to the public and others.

The Wiley Handbook of What Works in Violence Risk Management: Theory, Research and Practice,
First Edition. Edited by J. Stephen Wormith, Leam A. Craig, and Todd E. Hogue.

The Criminal Justice and Immigration Act 2008 added certain categories of terrorist and domestic extremist offences to MAPPA. The specific category of violent offender eligible for MAPPA is:

> An offender convicted (or found not guilty by reason of insanity, or to be unfit to stand trial and to have done the act charged) of murder, or an offence specified under Schedule 15 of the CJA 2003, who received a qualifying sentence or disposal for that offence (para. 6.6 parts A and B)' Ministry of Justice, *MAPPA Guidance* 2012 updated January 2016, para 6.1). For example, this includes serious sexual violence such as rape, and violent offences including grievous bodily harm.[1]

The offender must have received a term of imprisonment for 12 months or more, including indeterminate cases and sentences which are suspended. There are three levels of MAPPA management: level 1, which provides ordinary agency management, 'where the risks posed by the offender can be managed by the agency responsible for the supervision or case management of the offender'; level 2 with an active risk management of cases requiring 'active involvement and co-ordination of interventions from other agencies to manage the presenting risks of serious harm'; and level 3 for cases requiring more senior level input and the mobilization of 'significant resources at short notice'. These are cases where there is 'a high- or very high-risk of serious harm, a high likelihood of media scrutiny or public interest in the management of the case and a need to ensure that public confidence in the criminal justice system is maintained' (*MAPPA Guidance* 2012), paras 7.1–7.6).

The multi-agency assessment and management response to high-risk sexual and violent offenders has been the subject of three process evaluations in England and Wales (Kemshall et al. 2005; Maguire et al. 2001; Wood and Kemshall 2007), focussing on improvements to multi-agency meetings, the process of information exchange, the implementation of risk-assessment procedures and risk-management planning. Throughout the 2000s, these process evaluations were complemented by various other inspections organized along similar themes (Her Majesty's Inspectorate of Constabulary and Her Majesty's Inspectorate of Probation 2005; Her Majesty's Inspectorate of Probation 2006). This was paralleled by guidance, most notably the centrally-produced MAPPA Guidance (see *MAPPA Guidance* 2012). Despite an earlier process evaluation urging greater attention to engagement and motivation to change (Wood and Kemshall 2007), by 2010 Her Majesty's Inspectorate of Probation were concerned that risk-management plans were overly restrictive and the rehabilitative emphasis had waned. Whilst the inspectorate's comments were specific to sexual offenders, a number of the issues raised in the inspection report also applied to the management of high-risk violent offenders (see Kemshall 2010b). In particular, the inspection report marked a shift from restrictive measures towards an increased focus on the development of the individual offender's internal controls, the enhancement of their positive strengths and an increase in motivational work to encourage and sustain change (see desistance approaches: Healy 2010; Weaver 2013, 2014; *the Good Lives Model*, Ward and Fortune 2013; Purvis et al. 2011; *Therapeutic communities*, Day and Doyle 2010).

The Risk Management Authority (RMA) in Scotland has attempted to set standards for risk management that reflect a more balanced and holistic approach (Risk Management Authority 2007a). It defines risk management as 'a set of co-ordinated activities including: measures

---

[1] For the violent offences specified under Schedule 15 for MAPPA see: www.legislation.gov.uk/ukpga/2003/44/schedule/15.

taken to restrict the offender; to engage the offender and address their behaviours through treatment; to monitor behaviour and to protect potential victims' (Fyfe and Gailey 2011, p. 203). The RMA standards and guidance for risk management note the complex nature of risk and, in particular, those arising from violent and sexual offending:

> Violent and sexual offending are complex phenomena and so require individualised responses that are dynamic and derived from multi-faceted risk assessment. In turn this requires multi-layered and multi-modal risk management plans delivered through multi agency and multi-disciplinary collaboration. (Risk Management Authority 2007a, p. 4)

The potential tensions between risk management and human rights have been well documented (see Murphy and Whitty 2007; Royal College of Psychiatrists 2004). However, the RMA practice in Scotland endeavours to balance these tensions by stating key underpinning principles for risk-management decisions. These state that decisions should be:

- necessary;
- proportionate;
- prescribed by law;
- not arbitrary;
- balanced;
- evidence-based;
- transparent;
- recorded; and
- communicated.

(Risk Management Authority 2007a, p. 2).

In effect, risk management is based upon defensible decisions (Kemshall 2003) and proportionality (RMA 2007a). Within the Scottish model, risk management 'promotes the use of the least restrictive measures, rehabilitation and reintegration' (Fyfe and Gailey 2011, p. 203; Kemshall 2008). This has been described as 'blended protection' using 'protective integration' via a range of re-integrative measures running alongside community protection and restrictions (see Kemshall 2008, pp. 126–127). Risk-management planning in Scotland reflects these core principles and recognizes a 'spectrum of offending' and that the principle of rehabilitation should, wherever possible, be a core component of such plans (Scottish Executive 2000, p. 26). The RMA guidelines set out seven key areas to govern risk-management practice and they form the key standards:

- collaborative working across relevant partners with both a victim and offender focus;
- risk assessment, based on an evidential approach using proven, reliable risk assessment tools;
- risk formulation and risk scenario planning in order to articulate those 'strategies that will manage the risk posed in the current environment' (Risk Management Authority 2007b, p. 31). This stage focuses on preventive strategies and contingency measures;
- risk management strategies;
- accommodation;
- responding to change; and
- organizational support.

(Derived from Risk Management Authority 2007a).

The RMA actively reviews and publishes updates of the standards and guidance based upon research evidence (see RMA 2013); they promote best practice (see Farrington et al. 2008); evaluate the practical use of risk-assessment tools (see Darjee et al. 2016), providing an overview and 'rating' system (RMA 2007b); and a framework for collaborative practice on risk (RMA 2011). The RMA's work strongly underpins MAPPA practice and guidance in Scotland (see Scottish Government 2016) and has been instrumental in advising the Council of Europe on the sentencing and management of dangerous offenders (Council of Ministers 2014).

Evidence of Effectiveness for MAPPA

There are significant challenges in any attempt to demonstrate a direct correlation between MAPPA and reductions in re-offending. In the absence of a rigorous control group this remains particularly acute. However, the Home Office report on the English and Welsh arrangements: '*MAPPA- The First Five Years,*' painted a positive picture of effectiveness, based on reconviction rates for MAPPA cases. The report noted that the number of serious further offences committed by offenders managed at levels 2 and 3 in 2005/6 was only 0.44%. The biggest impact was noted at level 3, 'and such a low serious re-offending rate for this particular group of offenders is to be welcomed and supports the view that MAPPA is making a real contribution to the management of dangerousness in the community' (Home Office 2007, pp. 6–7). This was followed in 2011 by an internal evaluation by the Ministry of Justice. This was a limited reconviction study comparing two offender cohorts pre and post the introduction of MAPPA in England and Wales. Whilst the study did not fully meet the requirements of a long-term reconviction study and had some limitations in terms of constructing fully comparable cohorts, there was some evidence that MAPPA contributed to recidivism reductions (Peck 2011) and it is the first evaluative study of MAPPA impact on reconviction rates for sexual and violent offenders:

> Offenders released from custody between 2001 and 2004 (i.e. after the implementation of MAPPA) had a lower one-year reconviction rate than those released between 1998 and 2000. This remained true at the two-year follow-up for those cohorts where this had been calculated. The one-year reconviction rate had been declining before 2001, but fell more steeply after MAPPA was implemented.
> Immediately either side of MAPPA implementation, the one-year reconviction rate fell 2.7 percentage points for MAPPA-eligible offenders.
> Pre- to post-MAPPA implementation there was a comparatively large fall in the proportion of violent offenders reconvicted after one year and among those calculated to pose a high risk of reoffending. (pp. ii–iii).

Whilst recognizing the limitations of the study, these results are encouraging. The need for multi-agency, coordinated responses in the management of high-risk violent offenders are also replicated elsewhere, for example, in relation to issues of intimate partner violence (Fisher 2011). In a more recent analysis, Bryant et al.(2015) found that the one-year proven re-offending rate amongst Category 2 violent and other sexual offenders decreased from 26% in 2000 (pre-implementation of MAPPA) to 23% in 2004. It has remained relatively stable since, fluctuating between 22% and 24% from 2004 to 2010. In addition, the one-year proven re-offending rate amongst Category 1 registered sexual offenders decreased from 13% in 2000 to 10% in 2004. For each year between 2000 and 2010, Category 1 registered sexual offenders had a lower proven one-year re-offending rate than Category 2 offenders. Amongst new MAPPA, eligible offenders assessed as having a high risk of re-offending there was a 20% (17 percentage points) reduction in one-year proven re-offending between 2000 and 2010, with the re-offending rate falling from 83% to 66%. Between 2000 and 2010, the one-year serious re-offending rate of the highest risk of re-offending group decreased by 45% (13 percentage points), with the re-offending rate falling from 29% to 16%. In 2007, Wood and Kemshall found that offenders self-reported that they benefited from having their personal and social problems addressed, and that compliance with MAPPA with was generally positive. More recently, Weaver and Barry found that MAPPA supervision processes that engaged offenders positively with the process of change was more effective (Weaver and Barry 2014).

However, determining exactly how MAPPA is having this impact on re-offending rates is more difficult to establish. This makes replicating best practice challenging. However, interviews with offenders managed by MAPPA found that they valued and benefited from attention to their personal and social problems, and to their personal goals, needs and desires. Offenders were more likely to comply with external conditions that were explained to them, which they saw as legitimate and fair (Wood and Kemshall 2007). These findings were echoed by Weaver and Barry who found that engaging offenders more in the change process had increased benefits (2014).

Dealing with high-risk offenders has a number of hidden costs (Maguire et al. 2001). Currently, however, annual MAPPA reports do not routinely provide any comparative information of the unit costs of operation measured against the outcomes achieved. The current climate of 'value for money' requires the provision of MAPPA data which justifies the allocation of resources. However, to date, local MAPPA reports, have focused on: how many offenders have been subject to MAPPA; the number of panels and volume of offenders managed at different levels; and other more limited analysis of positive case storeys and reconviction data, where available.[2]

The Extension of Multi-agency Working with High-Risk Offenders: Integrated Response, Integrated Service (IRIS)

Multi-agency working with offenders is not the remit of MAPPA alone and during the 2000s the principle was extended to other areas of offender work, most notably to 'prolific offenders' under Integrated Offender Management and to high-risk offenders, particularly violent offenders, through Integrated Response, Integrated Service (IRIS) projects.[3]

IRIS projects are concerned with those offenders who are challenging to manage and who pose the highest risk of harm to others. Such projects are notable for their involvement of psychiatric services and those with expertise in personality disorder, an important addition for this cohort of offenders, where such a diagnosis often prevails. Teams are usually integrated and co-located to enable the exchange of information and joint working. The development of such systems for managing the most challenging violent offenders have been positively

[2] see: www.justice.gov.uk/publications/mappa.htm, accessed April 5th 2016). In 2010 the Ministry of Justice attempted to aggregate area statistics into an overarching annual statistical report (see www.justice.gov.uk/mappa-annual-reports.htm, accessed April 5th 2016).

[3] See (http://www.awp.nhs.uk/news-publications/trust-news/2012/june/introducing-iris; accessed 7 April 2016).

evaluated (see Her Majesty's Inspectorate of Probation and Her Majesty's Inspectorate of Constabulary 2014) although they also have some limitations, for example, healthcare agencies may have internal patient confidentiality protocols that hinder information exchange. The joint probation/police inspection in 2014 found that the police 'were usually the lead agency and in some cases, were attempting to fulfil both rehabilitative and control functions where Probation Trusts had not committed sufficient resources' (2014, p. 7). In some areas, the full integration of health services was also problematic.

The depth and intensity of supervision, 'disruption' tactics with high-risk offenders, end-to-end offender management, ensuring compliance and addressing personality disorders have all featured positively in evaluations of IRIS with each demonstrating positive outcomes (Williams 2014, p. 3). The co-location of agency partners was seen as providing added-value, expediting the exchange of knowledge and intelligence information, increasing trust across agencies, providing additional resources and ensuring prompt responses to enforcement issues and recalls to prison (Williams 2014, p. 61). However, the integration of psychology personnel has been more challenging, largely due to resourcing limits and patient confidentiality protocols preventing information exchange or joint management. Offenders subject to supervision by IRIS teams described positive experiences, with more time and focus provided to them by offender managers, a continuity of service delivery, with an emphasis on risks, needs and support to facilitate change (Williams 2014, p. 68). Overall, IRIS was seen as having a positive impact on high-risk offenders, although longer term evaluations based on reconviction outcomes are required.

These developments highlight the significant role that UK Police have come to play in the community management of violent offenders. They are central to the administration of VISOR (Violent and Sex Offenders Register) (Edwards 2003). This is the national IT system for the management of people who pose a serious risk of harm to the public and provides important information and intelligence on offenders to aid their effective management. Despite the centrality of ViSOR to the management of sex offenders, until recently, there had not been an in-depth evaluation on its utility, effectives and impact (O'Sullivan et al. 2016).

The management of violent offenders, however, extends beyond national borders and it is to the cross-border exchange of information across the EU community that this chapter now turns.

Effective Systems for Managing Violent Offenders Who Travel Across Countries

Increased global travel and the potential for national citizens to work and settle in other countries poses particular challenges to the effective management of violent offenders. This is markedly acute within the EU with an emphasis upon free movement of persons within the Schengen area.[4] The 'open space' of Schengen and the Freedom of Movement guaranteed by

---

[4] The Schengen Area enables EU citizens to move across national boundaries without the use of border controls and guarantees freedom of movement to some 400 million EU citizens. The Schengen Area encompasses most EU States, except for Bulgaria, Croatia, Cyprus, Ireland, Romania and the United Kingdom. However, Bulgaria and Romania are currently in the process of joining the Schengen Area. Of non-EU States, Iceland, Norway, Switzerland and Liechtenstein have joined the Schengen Area. See: http://ec.europa.eu/dgs/home-affairs/what-we-do/policies/borders-and-visas/schengen/index_en.htm; accessed April 21st 2016.

the EU has been characterized as a 'security risk' and a 'potential crime space' (Jacobs and Blitsa 2008; Parkin 2011) requiring strengthened police co-operation (Alain 2001; Finjaut 1993; International Centre for Migration Policy Development 2010). Such developments, however, have primarily focused upon large scale, organized crime such as terrorism, people trafficking, drug trafficking (Stelfox 2003; Council of EU 2010) and football hooliganism (Frosdick and Marsh 2005; ICFGHK 2013). However, high-profile cases such as the murder of Moira Jones by Marek Harcar in Glasgow in 2008 focused attention on the individual violent offender who moves around the EU. Harcar was originally from Slovakia, where he had 13 previous convictions, four for violence. Scottish Police were unaware of his previous convictions and he entered Scotland unmonitored.

There is an overarching permissive framework for law enforcement information exchange and co-operation across EU borders established by the EU Council Framework Decision 2006/960/JHA (Council of the European Union 2006) principle of availability (the 'Swedish Framework').[5] A number of mechanisms for the actual transfer of different types of criminality information currently exist, including the European Criminal Record Information System (ECRIS, Council Framework Decision 2009/316/JHA; Council of the European Union 2009), Interpol disseminations, communication via Central Bureau and Embassy staff and Europol National Units, with facilities for more general alerts possible via the Schengen SIS II system and INTERPOL Notices (International Criminal Police Organization see: https://www.interpol.int). INTERPOL covers 192 countries to work together to fight international crime including 'sexual tourism', child trafficking, and modern-day slavery. They can issue a Red Notice to globally search for serious violent offenders (e.g. murderers) and can issue a Yellow Notice to globally search for a missing or abducted child. A Green Notice can be issued to warn of offenders who are considered to be a threat to public safety, and a Blue Notice can be issued to gain information on a person's criminal history (see https://www.interpol.int for further details). Unlike EUROPOL (the European Union's Law Enforcement Agency), INTERPOL can operate globally.

Communication between prisons and probation across the EU primarily occurs in relation to the transfer of custodial (Council Framework Decision 2008/909/JHA; Council of the European Union 2008b) and community sentences (Council Framework Decision 2008/947/JHA [FD947]; Council of the European Union 2008c).[6] Some of the existing mechanisms have a specific function and serve to exchange certain types of criminality information, whereas others provide scope for a more versatile use. The ECRIS system for example exchanges conviction data, in order to retain a central record of a home national's offending in other EU Member States (MSs). In order to achieve this, MSs are obliged to electronically transfer all details of offences committed by a foreign EU national back to the offender's home Member State (MS) at the point of conviction. Requests can also be made via ECRIS to obtain information on an EU foreign national appearing in a court within another MS, although it is less well utilized in this respect. Other systems may be used to: disseminate information to find missing children (Interpol Yellow Notices); track down known offenders or other persons who may have absconded; exchange information for the purposes of detecting or preventing crime, or

[5] The principle of availability under the Swedish Framework Decision 2006/960/JHA, sets timescales for information exchanges across EU borders and advises that communication should not hampered by formal procedures, administrative structures and legal obstacle.
[6] For an over view of all existing Information exchange mechanisms see *European Union Information Exchange Mechanisms A Mapping Report of existing frameworks*, Hilder and Kemshall (2014) accessed via www.svdv.org.uk/somec-project.

in order to disrupt organized crime or other serious offences. In such circumstances, criminal intelligence data as well as convictions may be exchanged and circulated. Table 25.1 provides an overview of current information exchange systems and is derived from a review of information exchange mechanisms completed for the EU by Hilder and Kemshall (2014) under the project *Serious Offending by Mobile European Criminals (SOMEC)*.

However, managing criminality by co-operation and information exchange requires operational knowledge of such systems, access to them and a willingness to use them appropriately. Previous studies have shown a number of significant barriers to their operational use (ICMPD 2010), which has included a level of reluctance from some MS. Magee's (2008) review on the exchange of criminality information concluded that there was an apparent will for co-ordination to be achieved across the EU, but less willingness from MS to '*have themselves coordinated*' (2008, p. 62). There is evidence to suggest, therefore, that the provision of opportunities for these various types of exchange can be very different from an effective application of such measures (EC 2010; Walsh 2006). Research into information exchange, the monitoring and management of serious violent offenders within the EU found a series of barriers and challenges (see Kemshall et al. 2015a[7]). Most notably these were:

- There is a lack of consensus across the EU about those individuals who constitute serious violent or sexual offenders and about whom information should be exchanged if they travel to another MS.
- Formal risk-assessment tools are not commonly used across the EU in order to identify and assess serious violent or sexual offenders. A lack of communication between the judiciary, police, offender management/probation personnel can inhibit the accurate identification and assessment of such offenders. (See Kemshall et al. 2015a, section 7).
- A lack of knowledge about the range of existing mechanisms currently used for information exchange for police intelligence and investigation purposes. Levels of expertise and familiarity with these mechanisms varies across MS.
- EU law enforcement co-operation is well established during the investigation of a criminal matter. However, proactive information exchange in order to prevent further offending occurs less often and despite the Swedish Framework some MS remain reluctant to exchange intelligence and information on persons who *may* commit further offences.
- A number of MS are reluctant, and in some instances legally unable to, exchange information or monitor serious violent or sexual offenders once a custodial sentence has been completed. This position is exacerbated by a differential use of post-custody licence conditions across the EU.
- Once information has been exchanged, there can be a lack of national response to the information received. Internal dissemination systems within MS do not always support prompt and effective communication, inhibiting local responses to such offenders.

Addressing these issues requires action both at an EU strategic level and at the level of individual MS. The movement of serious violent or sexual offenders is now established, in some instances, for very genuine reasons such as a return to a home country, or travel for work or leisure. In other instances, travel is pursued in order to avoid regulation and oversight in a home MS, and/or to seek further offending opportunities (Thomas 2011, 2013). The Swedish

[7] Serious Offending by Mobile European Criminals (SOMEC) co-funded by the European Commission Directorate-General for Home Affairs - HOME/2011/AG/4000002521 30-CE-0519712/00–87 (January 2013–January 2015).

Table 25.1 Mechanisms for the Exchange of Criminal Information and their potential for a proactive/preventative approach (condensed version).

Mechanism	Primary purpose	Accessibility/Utilization across the EU	Challenges/Benefits	Potential for use in Proactive/ preventative exchanges
Interpol Dissemination processes	Interpol National Central Bureaux (ICB) Tracking wanted persons, international information exchanges for the detection and prevention of transnational crimes. Operates I-24/7 and other communication channels.	I 24/7 - A restricted access Internet portal for Global police communication. Predates Europol and accessible to countries outside of the EU. Other disseminations – Diffusions – a targeted email for single states, groups, regions or all Interpol members	A vast amount of information is contained on the I-24/7 which authorized personnel can access at a National level. With 190 Interpol Member States, information provided via the i-link has broad access outside of the EU. Targeted dissemination – allows for direct communications with other Member States relating to serious violent or sexual offenders. There is some reticence in the use of Interpol channels from some EU Member States, relating, in particular, to data protection outside the EU and advocating Europol as the primary source of exchange (EC 2010).	Whilst it is the case that I-24/7 is accessible to all States who are Members of Interpol, targeted disseminations can be made to single states/groups and regions. States can actively assess which form of Interpol communication is appropriate for the SOMEC exchange.
Interpol Green Notices	Provides warnings and criminal intelligence information on serious criminals who are likely to re-offend, posing a serious threat elsewhere.	Used for a variety of serious offences. Subjects who may be travelling extensively so requires systematic review by Interpol Central Bureaux.	Reportedly under-used for the tracking and monitoring of sexual offenders. However, the volume of notices issued overall is high (De Poubaix Lundin 2010); this can have operational challenges for individual Member States. There is no obligation for action upon receipt of a Green Notice and responses vary.	Potential to contribute to the management of serious sexual or violent offenders known to be travelling. However, operational challenges may currently hinder effectiveness.

(Continued)

Table 25.1 *(Cont'd)*

Mechanism	Primary purpose	Accessibility/Utilization across the EU	Challenges/Benefits	Potential for use in Proactive/ preventative exchanges
Europol (liaison officers, Information system)	Joint investigation of Organized Crime, terrorism and other serious crime affecting two or more Member States.	Primarily mandated to assist EU member states in combating serious organized crime. The Europol Information System (EIS)- a database of information supplied by Member States on crimes occurring/linked across EU borders. Member States engage through their Europol National Units (ENU) and (since 2011) other designated law enforcement authorities. SIENA- Europol's secure Information Exchange Network Application provides a mechanism for exchanges with Europol and between Member States, who each maintain a liaison bureau in the Europol Headquarters in the Hague. There are also specialist intelligence analysis units, called focal points, providing strategic and tactical intelligence reports on various areas of organized criminal activity. Analysis work files provide operational support to cross-border investigations.	There are European Commission proposals for a significant reform, to increase the role of Europol as a central co-ordination point of all types of information exchange between Member States. [EXIM] /*COM/2012/0735 final * / The Europol Council decision 2009/936/JHA sets out the criteria for information sharing across the EU via the Europol network. In addition to Terrorism and organized crime, a further annex list of serious offences which Europol may become involved with are also listed. Access to Europol data is defined and restricted by 4 Classifications, Restricted, Confidential, Secret and Top Secret. The data protection and management of information is clearly stipulated by Directive 95/46/EC (8).	It would need to be established that serious violent or sexual offenders would meet the criteria set out by the annexe list 2009/936/JHA for information exchange. Guidance may be required in terms of the level of detail provided and clarification of the imminent nature of a further serious offence being committed across EU borders. Europol's analytical function for these types of offenders may be limited due to current inconsistencies in utilizing this channel for this purpose.

SISII SIRENE	SIRENE Bureaux established in all Schengen States, following 'open border'. Alerts on persons and objects to maintain security.	A large-scale system, over 43 million alerts ((EXIM) /*COM/2012/0735 final */) accessible on a hit or no hit basis to front line officers. SIS II- alerts to support police cooperation between police and judicial authorities in criminal matters are accessible to all EU Member States.	Can be directly accessed on a hit/no hit basis by frontline operational law enforcement officers. Article 36 alerts. Discreet cheques and the seizure of evidence are possible where a serious threat to public security is identified 'a) where there is a clear indication that a person intends to commit or is committing a serious criminal offence. b) Where an overall assessment of a person gives reason to suppose that that person will also commit serious criminal offences in the future.' SIS II- currently more likely to be used for serious organized crime rather than the single transient offender.	Serious violent or sexual offenders are likely to require an assessment under criterion (b). There is potential to increase the relevance of SIS II for serious violent or sexual offenders but this may well require further guidance and agreement.
ECRIS	Conviction data exchange. Establishing a standardized electronic connection of criminal record databases across the EU.	A mandatory procedure across all EU Member States, to notify a Home Member State of convictions handed down to a national in another EU country. This is often a judicial function and the police do not have direct access to ECRIS. Deals with historical, factual information.	Managed by different types of personnel and departments in different states. Varying national laws as to whether convictions occurring in other member states can then be formally noted in the national state of origin.	Not directly relevant in relation to proactive/preventative exchanges.

(Continued)

Table 25.1 (Cont'd)

Mechanism	Primary purpose	Accessibility/Utilization across the EU	Challenges/Benefits	Potential for use in Proactive/preventative exchanges
PRÜM	Automated access to national databases for the exchange of DNA, finger prints and vehicle registrations.	Operates on a hit or no-hit basis in the first instance. A supplementary request for information is then made. A number of Member States have yet to engage with Prüm.	Assists with investigations, detection and confirming identities. Possible supplementary role in tracing a serious sexual or violent offender and/or quickly ascertaining their identity.	Reactionary rather than preventative, but can assist in identifying patterns of movement.
Embassy Liaison Officers	Law Enforcement Officers posted on behalf of their agency in another Member States.	Usually seconded to their country's embassy in the host member state.	The exact role of the liaison officer is subject to national differences and regulations in their host country. They can provide an intelligence and support role, facilitate joint investigations and requests for information sharing, arrests, extraditions.	Some Member States may prioritize this connection. Potentially useful for single high-risk cases. Potential challenges in terms of avoiding miscommunications and/ or a duplication of efforts. Would require clear guidance and protocols on how different issues of criminality are addressed.
Single Point of Contact (SPOC)	The central National co-ordination of all forms of EU information exchange on criminality.	Not an exchange mechanism but brings together all forms of cross border communication, i.e. SIRENE Bureau, ENU and Interpol National Central Bureau.	Places all key mechanisms for exchange together into a single organizational structure. It is thought that this makes it easier to ensure a prompt validation of a request and an appropriate response. Filters what is coming in and what goes out. Should improve efficiency rather than add an additional layer of bureaucracy.	A number of Member States already have SPOCs or integrated Bureaux and comment on their effectiveness (EC 2010). There may be resource implications and additional challenges for Member States with multiple jurisdictions. Connectivity between law enforcement and judicial departments may also need to be considered.

Formal Bilateral/ Multilateral	Formal exchange and mutual cooperation agreements between one or more Member States addressing particular criminal and judicial matters.	Various examples- Nordic, East European, and Memorandum of Understanding between UK and Republic of Ireland on mobile sex offenders.	Mainly addresses specific cross regional issues Benefits tend to be local or regional with limited pan European relevance In some instances, applied to serious organized crime only.	Further independent evaluations are required on the successes of such initiatives. The relevance to serious violent or sexual offenders is also likely to be determined at a political/policy level between Member States where recurring issues regarding travelling violent or sexual offenders are identified.
Informal regional arrangements	Where policing Units have close border geographical relations	Occurs informally, as part of other regional meetings, ad hoc communication	Informal arrangements are often seen to be more expedient by operational law enforcement officers. Relies on good local and regional relationships. Issues of accountability, rights and responsibilities and audit trails of decision making may occur.	The lack of formalization raises concerns regarding consistency and accountability. However, the benefits of joint training activities, shared understandings and consultations between key Law Enforcement personnel across EU Member States are useful considerations for serious violent or sexual offenders.

Framework Decision 2006/960/JHA, Council decision 2008/615/JHA and supplementary guidance for Interpol, Europol and Schengen Information exchange mechanisms and processes all highlight a facility for the exchange of information between MS for the prevention of a serious criminal offence. However, operational knowledge and confidence in using these mechanisms appropriately in relation to serious violent or sexual offenders is variable and, in some MS, remains in its infancy. This is largely due to the growth of the EU in recent times with some recently joined MS lacking internal systems for identifying and fully assessing serious violent and sexual offenders within their own state, and lacking the processes and systems to identify those who might travel and pose a risk (see Kemshall et al. 2015a for a review of key issues and difficulties; and Kemshall et al. 2015b for guidance on how to improve internal systems and information exchange processes).

The results of the research into European-wide information exchange systems and the barriers to effectiveness subsequently identified resulted in the following recommendations to the EU (see Kemshall et al. 2015a):

Improvements in the current situation may be achieved via the following courses of action:

- All EU MS to adopt a proactive approach to conviction data exchange via ECRIS, and Member States should recognize the importance of convictions acquired in other MS in accordance with Council Framework Decision 2008/675/JHA (Council of the European Union 2008a).
- The permissive EU framework and supporting governance guidelines for current methods of proactive/preventative exchange would be greatly improved if they were more widely understood. In addition, the Swedish Framework Decision 2006/960/JHA principle of availability for EU law enforcement exchanges should be more strongly embedded into all national legal frameworks.
- Higher levels of knowledge and expertise are achieved in the proactive use of all cross-border information exchange mechanisms to prevent future crime across the EU community, incorporating the SPOC model.[8]
- A standardized package of information is developed, which meets an agreed quality threshold to enable information exchanges across EU borders to occur and ensures a proactive response is both justified and defensible (see Kemshall et al. 2015b for guidance and templates).
- Further work is undertaken to ascertain the most appropriate channels for different types of proactive/preventative exchange, both where the destination of the offender is known and where a more general alert is required.

(Kemshall et al. 2015a, pp. 109–110).

Privacy rights and civil liberties' concerns were seen as a significant barrier to proactive information exchange in order to prevent crime in a number of MS and were most keenly felt in those MS with a history of State domination and/or an erosion of individual rights. The tension between risks, rights and freedom of movement presented by the increased regulation of serious sexual or violent offenders who are mobile across the EU is critical and should not be readily dismissed (see Padfield 2010). However, the issues raised are not necessarily

---

[8] SPOC stands for Single Point of Contact, a system used by police in international policing and information exchange. The system ensures that national exchanges go between Single Points of Contact who quality assure information sent and disseminate quickly information received.

insurmountable. The Council of Europe (2010) has recognized that the rights of victims and EU citizens to protection are fundamental, with crime prevention making a critical contribution to the reduction of physical and psychological harm. Current EU criminal justice and social policies and recent legal initiatives have established that the commission of serious violent or sexual offences is itself an infringement of the human rights of victims. This has been particularly apparent in EU responses to sexual tourism, sexual exploitation and violence against women and girls.[9] The key is to achieve a reasonable and defensible balance between the rights of (ex) offenders and victims, potential victims and citizens (see Kemshall et al. 2015b for guidance and practice standards). One person's right should not become another person's risk.

Brexit and Challenges to Effective Information Exchange Across the EU

The UK's decision to leave the EU on June 23rd 2016 has presented a number of challenges to continued information exchange between the UK and other EU Member States, including continued access to the Schengen Information System, and the continued, timely exchange of information about sexual and violent offenders. Whilst UK Law Enforcement agencies have argued that continued use of the information systems highlighted here is essential (House of Lords 2016), their immediate access to systems such as ECRIS, Prüm and the opt-in to SIS II is not guaranteed in the longer term. The direct access that the UK currently enjoys to systems such as European Information System (EIS) may no longer be available and individual requests may need to be made to Europol and Eurojust for the transfer of relevant data, no doubt resulting in delays. UK based law enforcement practitioners are concerned that without such direct access, vital information which currently takes a matter of hours to obtain, may take much longer to secure.

A bilateral treaty arrangement with the whole of the EU has been advocated as a way forward from this position, rather than a series of individual agreements with all other 27 EU Member States (House of Lords 2016) and comparisons have been made with the positions of Switzerland and Norway. However, such an approach leads to a country being bound by a treaty to certain EU arrangements without having any influence on the further development of policy frameworks (Deutscher Bundestag 2016). Whilst a more bespoke arrangement may be pursued, there is currently no precedent set for non-EU membership of SIS II and ECRIS and negotiating access with a presumption of an active involvement and continuing input in the shaping of EU frameworks appears incredibly ambitious and overly optimistic. The length of time required to establish and implement such agreements is also a cause for concern (Hilder 2017).

Conclusion

This chapter has reviewed systems for the management of violent offenders in the community, with a particular focus on the MAPPA arrangements in the UK and the current challenges to the effective management of mobile violent offenders across the EU. A number of issues appear to resonate across these systems, particularly in terms of effectiveness and successful

---

[9] See the Council of Europe (2011) *Council of Europe Convention on Preventing and Combating Violence Against Women and Domestic Violence* Strasbourg: Council of Europe.

implementation. In brief, these can be summarized as effective collaboration across relevant partners and indeed across countries; a balanced and holistic approach to risk management; a focus on proportionality, rehabilitation, wherever possible, and an informed balance of offender and victim rights. The RMA's approach in Scotland currently embeds many of these positive elements and could be used as a guide to future MAPPA developments, but also more broadly as a guide to good practice in Europe assisting with the establishment of standards and guidance on risk assessment and management practice (see Kemshall et al., 2015b for key examples). Risk-management strategies should seek to rehabilitate, change behaviour and meet the offender's needs as well as manage risks to others (Kemshall 2008). The tensions between risks and rights need not be incompatible if placed within a broader context of defensibility, proportionality and potential rehabilitation.

Acknowledgement

Thanks to the European Union for research grant *Serious Offending by Mobile European Criminals (SOMEC)*, EU Action Grant, 'Prevention of and Fight Against Crime', ISEC, 2011/AG/4000002521. The views expressed here are those of the authors.

References

Alain, M. (2001). Transnational police co-operation in Europe and in North America: Revisiting the traditional border between internal and external security matters, or how policing is being globalized. *European Journal of Crime, Criminal Law and Criminal Justice* 9 (2): 113–129.

Bryant, S., Peck, M., and Lovbakke, J. (2015). *Reoffending analysis of MAPPA eligible offenders. Ministry of Justice Analytical Series*. London, UK: The Stationary Office.

Bundestag, D. (2016). *Consequences of Brexit for the Realm of Justice and Home Affairs. Scope for future EU cooperation with the United Kingdom*. Berlin, GE: Author.

Committee of Ministers (2014). *Recommendation CM/Rec(2014)3 of the Committee of Ministers to member States concerning dangerous offenders*. Strasbourg, FR: Council of Europe.

Council of the European Union (2006). Council framework decision 2006/960/JHA of 18 December 2006 on simplifying the exchange of information and intelligence between law enforcement authorities of the Member States of the European Union. *Official Journal of the European Union* L386: 89–100.

Council of the European Union (2008a). Council framework decision 2008/675/JHA on taking account of convictions in the Member States of the European Union in the course of new criminal proceedings. *Official Journal of the European Union* L220: 32–34.

Council of the European Union (2008b). Council framework decision 2008/909/JHA on the application of the principle of mutual recognition to judgments in criminal matters imposing custodial sentences or measures involving deprivation of liberty for the purpose of their enforcement in the European Union. *Official Journal of the European Union* L327: 27–46.

Council of the European Union (2008c). Council framework decision 2008/947/JHA on the application of the principle of mutual recognition to judgments and probation decisions with a view to the supervision of probation measures and alternative sanctions. *Official Journal of the European Union* L337: 102–122.

Council of the European Union (2009). Council Framework Decision 2009/316/JHA on the establishment of the European Criminal Records Information System (ECRIS) in application of Article 11 of Framework Decision 2009/315/JHA. *Official Journal of the European Union* L093: 33–48.

Council of the European Union (2010). *Draft Internal Security Strategy for the European Union: "Towards a European security model.".* Brussels, BE: Author.

Darjee, R., Russell, K., Forrest, L. et al. (2016). *Risk for Sexual Violence Protocol (RSVP): A Real World Study of the Reliability, Validity and Utility of a Structured Professional Judgement Instrument of Sexual Offenders in South East Scotland.* Edinburgh, UK: NHS Lothian Sex Offender Liaison Service.

Day, A. and Doyle, P. (2010). Violent offender rehabilitation and the therapeutic community model of treatment: Towards integrated service provision? *Aggression and Violent Behavior* 15: 380–386.

Edwards, D. (2003). ViSOR – Violent and Sex Offender Register. *Criminal Justice Matters* 51: 28–28.

Farrington, D., Jolliffe, D., and Johnstone, L. (2008). *Assessing Violence Risk: A Framework for Practice. Final Report.* Edinburgh, UK: Risk Management Authority Scotland.

Fijnaut, C. (1993). The Schengen Treaties and European Police Co-operation. *European Journal of Crime, Criminal Law and Criminal Justice* 1: 37–56.

Fisher, E. (2011). Perpetrators of domestic violence: Co-ordinating responses to complex needs. *Irish Probation Journal* 8: 124–141.

Frosdick, S. and Marsh, P. (2005). *Football Hooliganism.* Cullompton, UK: Willan.

Fyfe, I. and Gailey, Y. (2011). The Scottish approach to high-risk offenders: Early answers or further questions. In: *Dangerous People: Policy, Prediction and Practice* (eds. B. McSherry and P. Keyzer), 201–216. London, UK: Routledge.

Healy, D. (2010). *The Dynamics of Desistance: Charting Pathways to Change.* Cullompton, UK: Willan.

Her Majesty's Inspectorate of Constabulary and Her Majesty's Inspectorate of Probation (2005). *Managing Sex Offenders in the Community: A Joint Inspection on Sex Offenders.* London, UK: Home Office.

Her Majesty's Inspectorate of Probation (2006). *An Independent Review of a Serious Further Offence Case: Anthony Rice.* London, UK: Author.

Her Majesty's Inspectorate of Probation (2010). Restriction and rehabilitation: getting the right mix. In: *An Inspection of the Management of Sexual Offenders in the Community.* London, UK: Author.

Her Majesty's Inspectorate of Probation and Her Majesty's Inspectorate of Constabulary (2014). *An Inspection of the Integrated Offender Management Approach.* London, UK: Author.

Hilder, S. (2017). Managing sexual and violent offenders across EU borders. In: *Contemporary Sex Offender Risk Management, Vol 2* (eds. H. Kemshall and K. McCartan), 93–112. Cham, CH: Palgrave MacMillan.

Hilder, S. and Kemshall, H. (2014). *European Union Information Exchange Mechanisms. A Mapping Report of Existing Frameworks: Report 2, part 1.* Leicester, UK: Serious Offending by Mobile European Criminals.

Home Office (2007). *MAPPA:* The First Five Years. A national overview of the Multi Agency Public Protection Arrangements 2001-2006 http://www.nomsintranet.org.uk/roh/official-documents/MAPPA%20-%20The%20First%20Five%20Years.pdf (Accessed 3 September 2019).

House of Lords (2016) *Brexit: Future UK-EU security and police cooperation.* House of Lords European Union Committee. 7th Report of Session 2016–17. London, UK: Author.

ICFGHK (2013) *Study on possible ways to improve the exchange of information on travelling violent offenders including those attending sporting events or large public gatherings.* Brussels, BE: European Commission.

International Centre for Migration Policy Development. (2010). *Study on the status of information exchange amongst law enforcement authorities in the context of existing EU instruments.* Brussels, BE: European Commission.

Jacobs, J.B. and Blitsa, D. (2008). Sharing criminal records: the United States, the European Union and Interpol compared. *International and Comparative Law Review* 30: 125–210.

Kemshall, H. (2003). *Understanding Risk in Criminal Justice.* Maidenhead, UK: Open University Press.

Kemshall, H. (2008). *Understanding the Community Management of High Risk Offenders.* Maidenhead, UK: McGraw-Hill and Open University Press.

Kemshall, H. (2010a). Community protection and multi agency public protection arrangements. In: *The Handbook of Public Protection* (eds. M. Nash and A. Williams), 199–216. Cullompton, UK: Willan.

Kemshall, H. (2010b). The role of risk, needs and strengths assessment in improving the supervision of offenders. In: *Offender Supervision: New Directions in Theory, Research and Practice* (eds. F. McNeill, P. Raynor and C. Trotter), 155–171. Cullompton, UK: Willan.

Kemshall, H., Hilder, S., Kelly, G., & Wilkinson, B. (2015a). *'Information exchanges, monitoring and management – A field work study of current responses by Member States. Report 2, part 2.* Leicester, UK: Serious Offending by Mobile European Criminals.

Kemshall, H, Kelly, G, Wilkinson, B., & Hilder, S. (2015b). *Offender management user guidance assessment and management of serious mobile European criminals.* Leicester, UK: Serious Offending by Mobile European Criminals.

Kemshall, H., Wood, J., Mackenzie, G. et al. (2005). *Strengthening Multi Agency Public Protection Arrangements (MAPPA).* London, UK: Home Office.

Magee, I.S. (2008). *The Review of Criminality Information.* London, UK: Review of Criminality Information.

Maguire, M., Kemshall, H., Noaks, L., and Wincup, E. (2001). *Risk Management of Sexual and Violent Offenders: The Work of Public Protection Panels.* London, UK: Home Office.

MAPPA Guidance (2012). MAPPA Guidance 2012, Version 4. https://www.justice.gov.uk/downloads/offenders/mappa/mappa-guidance-2012-part1.pdf (Accessed 3 September 2019).

Ministry of Justice (2016). *MAPPA Guidance 2012, Version 4.* London, UK: Ministry of Justice.

Murphy, T. and Whitty, N. (2007). Risk and human rights: ending slopping out in a Scottish prison. In: *Judges, Transition and Human Rights* (eds. J. Morrison, K. McEvoy and G. Anthony), 1014–1056. London, UK: Oxford University Press.

Nash, M. and Williams, A. (2008). *The Handbook of Public Protection.* Cullompton, UK: Willan.

O'Sullivan, J., Hoggett, J., Kemshall, H., and McCartan, K.F. (2016). Understandings, implications and alternative approaches to the use of the sex offenders register in the UK. *Irish Probation Journal* 13: 84–101.

Padfield, N. (2010). *The Sentencing, Management and Treatment of 'Dangerous' Offenders.* Strasbourg, FR: Council of Europe.

Parkin, J. (2011). *The Difficult Road to the Schengen Information System II. The Legacy of Laboratories and the Cost for Fundamental Rights and Rule of Law.* Brussels, BE: Centre for European Policy Studies.

Peck, M. (2011). *Patterns of Reconviction Among Offenders Eligible for Multi agency Public Protection Arrangements (MAPPA).* London, UK: Ministry of Justice.

Purvis, M., Ward, T., and Willis, G. (2011). The Good Lives Model in practice. *European Journal of Probation* 3: 4–28.

Risk Management Authority (2007a). *Standards and Guidelines for Risk Management. Version 1.* Paisley, UK: Author.

Risk Management Authority (2007b). *RATED: Risk Assessment Tools Evaluation Directory.* Paisley, UK: Author.

Risk Management Authority (2011). *Framework for Risk Assessment, Management and Evaluation: FRAME.* Paisley, UK: Author.

Risk Management Authority (2013). *Standards and Guidelines for Risk Management.* Paisley, UK: Author.

Royal College of Psychiatrists (2004). The psychiatrist, courts and sentencing: the impact of extended sentencing on the ethical framework of forensic psychiatry: council Report CR129. *Psychiatric Bulletin* 29: 73–77.

Scottish Executive (2000). *Report of the Committee on Serious Violent and Sexual Offenders. Chairman: Lord MacLean.* Edinburgh, UK: Author.

Scottish Government (2016). *Multi Agency Public Protection Arrangements (MAPPA) National Guidance 2016.* Edinburgh, UK: Author.

Stelfox, P. (2003). Transnational organised crime: a police perspective. In: *Transnational Organised Crime: Perspectives on Global Security* (eds. A. Edwards and P. Gill), 114–126. London, UK: Routledge.

Thomas, T. (2011). *The Registration and Monitoring of Sex Offenders.* London, UK: Routledge.

Thomas, T. (2013). The travelling sex offender. Monitoring movements across international borders. In: *The Wiley-Blackwell Handbook of Legal and Ethical Aspects of Sex Offender Treatment and Management* (eds. K. Harrison and B. Rainey), 445–461. Sussex, UK: John Wiley & Sons.

Walsh, J.I. (2006). Intelligence sharing in the EU: institutions are not enough. *Journal of Common Market Studies* 44: 625–643.

Ward, T. and Fortune, C. (2013). The Good Lives Model: aligning risk reduction with promoting offenders' personal goals. *European Journal of Probation* 5: 29–46.

Weaver, B. (2013). Co-producing desistance: who works to support desistance. In: *Understanding Penal Practices* (eds. I. Durnescu and F. McNeil), 193–205. Abingdon, UK: Routledge.

Weaver, B. (2014). Control or change? Developing dialogues between desistance research and public protection practices. *Probation Journal* 61: 8–26.

Weaver, B. and Barry, M. (2014). Risky business? Supporting desistance from sexual offending. In: *Responding to Sexual Offending: Perceptions, Risk Management and Public Protection* (ed. K. McCartan), 153–170. Cham, CH: Palgrave MacMillan.

Williams, M. (2014). *IRIS: An independent process and profile evaluation. Final report June 2014.* Portsmouth, UK: Institute of Criminal Justice Studies, University of Portsmouth.

Wood, J. and Kemshall, H. (2007). *The operation and experience of Multi agency Public Protection Arrangements (MAPPA).* London, UK: Home Office.

26

Beyond Core Correctional Practice
Facilitating Prosocial Change through the Strategic Training Initiative in Community Supervision

Guy Bourgon, Nick Chadwick, and Tanya Rugge

Public Safety Canada, Ottawa, Canada

Introduction

The use of community supervision (e.g. probation and parole) is a common practice in many industrialized countries. Community supervision is seen as a less expensive and possibly more efficient method of offender sanctioning. Recently, there has been an increased interest in the potential of community supervision to reduce re-offending and satisfy the ultimate goal of public safety. Most offenders are supervised in the community and the vast majority of incarcerated offenders will eventually be released and supervised in the community, including those convicted of violent offences. In the United States (US) there are nearly six million individuals supervised on probation and parole, representing approximately 70% of the country's entire correctional population (Glaze and Kaeble 2014), with approximately 20% of these supervised adults convicted of violent offences (Kaeble and Bonczar 2016). In England and Wales, 262 388 clients were supervised on probation with approximately 10% of the new admissions to community supervision sentenced for violent offences (Ministry of Justice 2017). The statistics for the type of offenders supervised in the community in Canada are scarcely available, but it is worth noting that in Canada, 69% of the federal offender population are serving a sentence for a violent offence (Public Safety Canada 2016). As highlighted earlier, most incarcerated individuals will eventually be supervised in the community, so it is likely that a large portion of community supervised individuals have a history of violent offending. Given that these percentages only include those with violent index *offences*, the number of violent *offenders* is likely higher as it does not include offenders who were sentenced for non-violent offences but also have a history/record of violence.

The Wiley Handbook of What Works in Violence Risk Management: Theory, Research and Practice,
First Edition. Edited by J. Stephen Wormith, Leam A. Craig, and Todd E. Hogue.
© 2020 John Wiley & Sons Ltd. Published 2020 by John Wiley & Sons Ltd.

Although it is believed that community supervision has positive benefits by minimizing the criminogenic effects of imprisonment and facilitating the community integration of offenders (Abadinsky 2009; Gibbons and Rosecrance 2005), evidence is equivocal about the effectiveness of community supervision to reduce offender recidivism. In a review of 15 studies that compared some form of community supervision with an alternative criminal sanction (e.g. prison sentence, fine), Bonta et al. (2008) found that recidivism was only two percentage points lower, on average, for offenders under community supervision. There was no decrease in violent recidivism associated with community supervision. Such findings, which contrast the more positive results found in reviews of the offender rehabilitation literature (see Andrews and Bonta 2010 for a comprehensive review), raise the question as to why this is so. To understand the inability of community supervision to have a measurable impact on re-offending, we must look behind the closed doors of community supervision and examine what it entails, and how it is conducted.

Looking Inside the Black Box of Community Supervision

One approach to assessing the likelihood that current supervision practices are related to reductions in recidivism is to examine adherence to the principles of risk, need, and responsivity (RNR). RNR principles have extensive empirical support (Bonta and Andrews 2017) and are the foundations of 'What Works' in offender rehabilitation. Briefly, the risk principle holds that the most effective correctional interventions are those provided to higher risk individuals, matching service dosage to risk. The need principle focuses on the targets of correctional services, specifically, services that target criminogenic needs (i.e. needs empirically associated with re-offending) are more effective. The responsivity principle stresses the importance of how the services are delivered, specifically whether services are provided in a style and manner that is responsive to the client to optimize learning and change. Of particular importance, the general responsivity principle states that effective services should utilize cognitive-behavioural intervention strategies. Services that employ techniques that target both thinking and behaviour have been shown to be most effective with criminal-justice-involved individuals (Bonta and Andrews 2017).

Relying on audio recordings of community supervision officers interacting with their clients, Bonta et al. (2008) explored inside 'the black box' of community supervision and found only modest adherence to the RNR principles. Results indicated that risk levels had only a minor association with service dosage as measured by contact frequency and were not related to the duration of face-to-face sessions. Regarding adherence to the need principle, discussions during these sessions often centred on the criminogenic needs of family and substance abuse, but rarely focused on the major criminogenic needs of attitudes, peers, and antisocial personality patterns. Limited adherence to the responsivity principle was also noted as officers made little use of skills and intervention techniques associated with creating optimal learning environments (e.g. establishing good relationships, using pro-social modelling and reinforcement). The almost non-existent use of specific cognitive-behavioural techniques (e.g. cognitive restructuring, role-playing, rehearsal, homework) was particularly worrisome. Notwithstanding typical efforts of community supervision to refer and place offenders into rehabilitation programmes, Bonta and colleagues concluded that this poor adherence to the RNR principles of effective correctional treatment during face-to-face supervision was the primary reason for the minimal reductions in re-offending associated with community supervision.

Although jurisdictions often attempt to adhere to the RNR model through various policies and practices, perhaps the greater challenge for officers is making the shift from the traditional case-management approach to a change-agent approach (Bourgon 2013). The traditional case-management approach emphasizes the administration of the sentence (e.g. ensuring compliance with the order), brokerage and referral to various services (e.g. connecting clients to employment services or treatment programmes addressing criminogenic needs), and the management of all this information (e.g. gathering, storing, and sharing of this information with other criminal justice partners). On the other hand, the change-agent approach emphasizes the officer actively facilitating change, with the officer providing 'treatment' during face-to-face supervision sessions (Bourgon 2013; Bourgon et al. 2011, Rugge and Bonta 2014). Such active efforts require officers to be knowledgeable about the RNR principles as well as understand how to apply them whilst interacting with offenders. Officers should be aware of how to be responsive to their clients and how to create an environment that is conducive to engagement, learning, and change. In order to accomplish this, it was reasoned that specialized officer training could enhance adherence to the RNR principles so that supervising officers could focus their efforts on higher risk clients, specific criminogenic needs, and applying skills and techniques that would enhance the interpersonal environment of supervision.

Training community supervision officers to facilitate change more effectively with their clients has gained considerable attention in recent years (Bonta et al. 2018). Drawing upon the empirical evidence of the 'What Works' literature as it pertains to the RNR principles and a few key studies that examined officer skills, a number of community supervision officer training programmes have been developed, piloted, and evaluated since 2010. A number of these programmes have been implemented on a wider scale in efforts to improve the effectiveness of community corrections to reduce reoffending (Bonta et al. 2018). The next section describes three such programmes.

Training Programmes for Community Supervision Officers

Strategic training initiative in community supervision (STICS)

Bonta et al. (2011) conducted a pivotal study that examined the training of probation and parole officers to be agents of change. Probation officers were randomly assigned to participate in the STICS or to a control group. Officers were asked to recruit and audio record three supervision sessions for six clients assessed as medium or higher risk on the validated risk assessment tool used in their jurisdiction. Officers assigned to STICS training participated in a formal three-day training on specific skills and intervention techniques to enhance their adherence to the RNR principles. In addition to the formal training, they were provided with ongoing support to enrich their learning. These supports included monthly meetings, in which different skills were reviewed and rehearsed, opportunities to receive individualized feedback of their skills (from trainers who would listen to and review their recorded supervision sessions), and annual refresher workshops. Officers assigned to the control group were provided with a short one-hour presentation of the RNR principles and their importance in the effectiveness of community supervision.

A total of 52 probation officers provided data on 143 clients. This included demographic and offence information, risk assessment results, and, importantly, almost 300 recordings of their face-to-face supervision sessions. Using a detailed coding manual, researchers listened to the recordings and coded the content area of the discussions between officers and clients (e.g. talking about clients' anger and aggressive behaviours), the skills or intervention techniques used by the officer (e.g. cognitive restructuring) and rated the quality of the skill or technique used on a scale of 1 (poor) to 7 (strong).

The analysis of the data focused on two primary questions. First, did the behaviour of officers change after receiving training? Or more specifically, did they demonstrate the skills and techniques taught in STICS training more often and with higher 'quality' than the control group? This was a critical empirical question because if the officers had not modified their interactions with probationers, then no change in the behaviour of the clients would be expected. In the end, the results were encouraging and demonstrated that trained officers used the skills and techniques more frequently and with better fidelity whilst interacting with their clients than the control group. Moreover, the trained officers showed greater adherence to the principles of RNR. The second primary question pertained to the effect of supervision on recidivism. A two-year follow-up showed a reconviction rate of 25.3% for the clients of the probation officers trained in STICS and a reconviction rate of 40.5% for the control clients.

Programmes derived from STICS

Similar approaches to training and research on the effectiveness of improving community supervision officers' skills are found in the US. This includes the Staff Training Aimed at Reducing Re-arrest (STARR) and Effective Practices in Community Supervision (EPICS) programmes, which are based on the STICS model. The developers of the STARR and EPICS training programmes had meetings with the STICS originators and access to the materials used in STICS (Bonta and Andrews 2017; Bonta et al. 2018). STARR (Robinson et al. 2011) and EPICS (Smith et al. 2012) consist of a similar length training (3–3½ days) and the training modules cover many of the same topics, skills and techniques found in STICS (e.g. prosocial modelling, role clarification, the use of effective approval and disapproval). All of the programmes include ongoing clinical support and development activities, such as coaching and booster sessions.

The results of STARR evaluations have been positive. Employing a research design identical to the STICS initial project (Robinson et al. 2011, 2012), results of audio recorded sessions between officer and clients demonstrated that the STARR trained officers significantly improved the frequency of use of the skills taught in training. Examining the 1-year recidivism rates for the two groups suggested that clients of STARR-trained officers re-offended at a lower rate (26%) compared to the clients of the control officers (34%). A follow-up study revealed lower 2-year recidivism rates for the clients of the STARR trained probation officers (28%) compared to the clients of the control officers (41%; Lowenkamp et al. 2014).

EPICS evaluations have been mixed and based on small samples. The first study consisted of 10 probation and parole officers supervising 52 adult and juvenile offenders (Smith et al. 2012) and the second study involved 44 officers who recorded 755 supervision sessions (Labrecque et al. 2013). These two studies focused primarily on change in officer behaviour as a result of training. Neither study used random assignment of probation officers or clients to training conditions nor did they report recidivism outcomes. Nevertheless, the results of both studies demonstrated that trained officers used the skills taught in EPICS more frequently than the comparison group officers. In a third study of EPICS, recidivism was reported (Latessa et al. 2013). Forty-one officers were randomly assigned to training or routine supervision. The results indicated that the behaviour of the trained officers changed in the expected direction but, the recidivism rate of the 141 clients supervised by the trained officers was actually *higher (24.7% vs. 22.9% for re-incarceration and 22.7% vs. 17.6% for arrests for new crime)* than the 131 clients of the officers using routine supervision practices. Further analysis of the recidivism rates found that the level of risk and actual application of the skills taught with the clients were important factors related to recidivism. High-risk offenders, who were supervised by officers who evidenced more frequent and higher quality use of skills (i.e. high fidelity use of Core Correctional Practise [CCP]), demonstrated lower recidivism rates (20.5% re-incarceration and 12.8% for re-arrest) than those who were supervised by officers who made less frequent or missed opportunities to utilize effective skills (i.e. low fidelity use of CCP; 32.4% re-incarceration and 14.9% for re-arrest).

Lessons Learned from Officer Training Programmes

Recognizing the flourishing research in this area, Chadwick et al. (2015) published a meta-analysis of 10 studies of structured training programmes and found that, on average, clients supervised by officers receiving this additional training demonstrated a 13% reduction in recidivism compared to those supervised by status quo officers (calculated from the reported odds ratio effect size of 1.48). Overall, these studies have provided a foundation for organizations and officers regarding how they can facilitate effective community supervision to reduce re-offending. Two critical factors appear to be important in enhancing adherence to the RNR principles.

The first factor concerns the attention placed on the value and importance of ensuring quality and fidelity to the training models. As mentioned, these new training initiatives include continuing educational and learning activities after the initial training. Significant investments are being made to provide ongoing feedback on the skills and intervention techniques taught during the formal initial training, in addition to providing coaching and regular refresher workshops to promote more frequent use and higher 'quality' use of those skills and techniques.

Empirically, results have shown that these investments do in fact enhance the quality and frequency of skill and technique use (Bourgon et al. 2010; Labrecque et al. 2015; Clodfelter et al. 2016). These particular studies focused on the impact of these ongoing activities on the officer's execution of skills and techniques taught in training. Bourgon et al. (2010) showed that officers with high levels of participation in these ongoing learning activities demonstrated higher 'quality' of the skills and intervention techniques. Quality of the skills and intervention techniques were assessed by trained raters who listened to recorded supervision sessions and rated the execution of the skills and techniques on a seven-point scale with higher scores indicating higher 'quality' (i.e. skills contained all of the steps and were executed appropriately). Table 26.1 presents client recidivism broken down by the level of participation in the ongoing supports (Bourgon et al. 2010). These results illustrate that client recidivism is lower when officer participation in these activities is high (see Table 26.1). This trend was evident for the clients as a whole as well as for violent offenders.

The second critical factor speaks directly to utilizing cognitive-behavioural techniques with clients, a key component of the responsivity principle. The importance of using cognitive-behavioural interventions in reducing recidivism is well-documented (see Cullen and Gendreau 1989; Gendreau and Andrews 1990; Lipsey et al. 2001; Schmucker and Lösel 2015; Wilson et al. 2005). All of the previously described training initiatives teach officers skills and

Table 26.1   Two-year recidivism rates of clients supervised by Strategic Training Initiative in Community Supervision (STICS) trained officers with low participation and high participation in ongoing professional development.

Clients supervised by	All Clients	Violent Clients[a]
Control Group Officers	40.5% (15/37)	31.8% (7/22)
STICS Trained Officers With Low Participation	27.7% (13/47)	37.5% (9/24)
STICS Trained Officers With High Participation	21.4% (6/28)	16.7% (3/18)

Source: Data source: Bourgon et al. (2010).
[a] Index offence includes violence.

Table 26.2   Two-year recidivism rates of clients exposed to Strategic Training Initiative in Community Supervision (STICS) cognitive intervention techniques vs. clients with no such exposure.

Cognitive Interventions	All Clients % (n/n)	Violent Clients[a] % (n/n)
Yes	19.0% (9/42)	21.4% (6/28)
No	37.1% (26/70)	36.1% (13/36)

Source: Data source: Bourgon and Gutierrez (2012).
[a] Index offence includes violence.

techniques to promote the use of cognitive restructuring with their clients. Cognitive restructuring is based on the theory that the interpretation of an event, rather than the event itself, determines the individual's behaviour. It aims to facilitate greater awareness of dysfunctional thoughts and to correct or replace those thoughts with more adaptive and rational cognitions (Beck 1970; Meichenbaum and Turk 1976). Published results demonstrate that officers make greater use of these techniques following training (Bourgon and Gutierrez 2012; Robinson et al. 2011).

The importance of the cognitive intervention techniques targeting procriminal cognitions (e.g. attitudes and cognitions supporting criminal activity and rule violations) to reduce re-offending was shown in the study by Bourgon and Gutierrez (2012). After statistically controlling for factors, such as risk and age, they found an approximately 24% difference in recidivism rates for clients exposed to specific cognitive intervention elements (e.g. identification of problem thinking, teaching cognitive restructuring skills) as measured by recorded supervision sessions compared to clients who had no such exposure. Table 26.2 presents the raw recidivism rates of clients exposed to cognitive intervention techniques and clients with no such exposure. Given that antisocial cognitions are seen as key contributors to aggressive behaviour (Polaschek et al. 2009), it is not surprising that the importance of addressing cognitions with cognitive intervention techniques was maintained when looking only at violent offenders (see Table 26.2).

With the increasing attention on the face-to-face work conducted during community supervision, the results have created an increased investment in what and how probation officers are trained and, arguably, an improvement in the effectiveness of community supervision to reduce re-offending. The investments into these initiatives are substantial; STICS has been implemented in Sweden and two large Canadian provinces with the training of 2000 officers. STARR has been rolled out across the US federal probation service with a plan to train over 4000 probation officers from 94 districts. EPICS has been embraced by many jurisdictions and has been delivered to 84 state/county correctional agencies and one international agency in Singapore (Labrecque et al. 2014). Nonetheless, we should remain cautious about concluding that these programmes will consistently produce a strong treatment effect, as there is much we still do not know regarding the critical components and best implementation practices. As a whole, these training programmes appear to work, but to further advance the practice of community supervision and continue to enhance its effectiveness, we need to understand more clearly why these change-agent training programmes work.

Understanding Why Change-Agent Supervision Can Work

To understand why change-agent supervision can reduce re-offending, one must examine exactly what officers are being trained in (i.e. knowledge, skills, and techniques) and why this training can be effective. Whilst the RNR principles are conveyed throughout these trainings, it is the specific skills and intervention techniques that are taught to officers and used with clients under supervision that translate RNR knowledge into practical application. In general, the set of skills and intervention techniques are based on what is known as CCPs (Dowden and Andrews 2004) as well as other evidence-based skills and techniques such as Motivational Interviewing (Miller and Rollnick 2012) and general cognitive-behavioural strategies.

The origins of CCP can be traced back to Andrews and Kiessling in the late 1970's (Andrews 1980; Andrews and Kiessling 1980; Kiessling and Andrews 1979). It is arguably the beginning of our empirical knowledge about the skills that are effective for community supervision. At that time, community supervision was conducted in Ontario, Canada, by probation officers and volunteers. In a study of Canadian Volunteers in Corrections (CaVIC; 1980), a variety of management, operational, and research issues were examined. This was perhaps the first study that explored the effectiveness of community supervision using audio recordings of the interactions of offenders and the individuals supervising them.

The CaVIC study is particularly noteworthy because its results were published one year *prior* to the seminal paper introducing 'What Works' and the RNR principles to the field (Andrews et al. 1990). Much of the theoretical underpinnings for the study stemmed from differential association theory (Sutherland and Cressey 1970), social learning theory and psychotherapy (see Andrews 1980). These theories drove the methodology and as a result, Andrews made a point of explicitly describing the in-session behaviours of the individuals who supervised the offenders and the hypothesized process that would promote change in intermediate targets of offending behaviour (i.e. attitudinal and related behavioural changes on what we now see as criminogenic needs). He also proposed the processes by which intermediate changes on attitudes and behaviours specific to other areas (i.e. criminogenic needs) were linked to changes in long-term criminal behaviour (i.e. recidivism). The methodology and findings of the CaVIC study provided some key elements worthy of review to fully understand where we are today and provided direction to moving forward. Five CCPs were broadly defined and included authority, anticriminal modelling and reinforcement, problem-solving, use of community resources, and quality of interpersonal relationships.

Authority refers to the explicit use of formal rules and sanctions (e.g. legal consequences). Authority is effective when rules and sanctions are vivid, understandable, and certain in their application. Anticriminal modelling and reinforcement refers to a combination of being a model of pro-social attitudes and behaviours (and linking such attitudes and behaviours to reinforcement) as well as a source of reinforcement for the client when they demonstrate pro-social attitudes, cognitions, and behaviours. Problem-solving refers to the practice of resolving personal, interpersonal, and/or community-based difficulties that reduced levels of satisfaction and rewards for noncriminal pursuits. All three of these practices can be viewed as direct and active officer-client interactions where the officer is embracing the change-agent role. In contrast, the use of community resources reflects the more traditional case-management role of community supervision officers. This practice captured activities where the officer is an advocate and plays a brokerage role for the client to various community programmes, services, and resources. The final practice is quality of interpersonal relationships and captures a variety of behaviours (e.g. expressions of warmth, concern, active listening, and empathy) that create conditions of trust and open communication (Andrews and Kiessling 1980). This practice recognizes the importance of the interpersonal relationship between client and helper (i.e. officer) in promoting change. The importance of the interpersonal relationship in treatment settings has also been highlighted in the psychotherapeutic literature (Baldwin et al. 2007; Elvins and Green 2008; Horvath and Bedi 2002; Martin et al. 2000; Ross et al. 2008). It is a precursor to the responsivity principle, as it contributes to creating an optimal learning environment for change that consists of relationship (i.e. a good working alliance) and structuring (i.e. cognitive-behavioural strategies) dimensions (Bonta and Andrews 2017; Bourgon and Bonta 2014).

The results of the CaVIC studies found that three of the five CCP practices (i.e. authority, anticriminal modelling and reinforcement, and problem solving) were found to be stand-alone predictors of recidivism (Andrews and Kiessling 1980). Subsequent research by Trotter (1990, 1994, and 1996) and Dowden and Andrews' (2004) meta-analysis eventually expanded and solidified CCP as evidence-based practice in corrections. However, these studies did not directly observe interactions, but rather inferred skills and practices from file reviews.

In an effort to replicate the CaVIC results, data from the original STICS project (Bonta et al. 2011; i.e. identified variables coded from the audio recordings that were approximations to Andrews and Kiessling's five CCPs) were examined. The results are presented in Table 26.3. Although caution is warranted as the variables were not coded identically to Andrews and Kiessling's original variables, there are some interesting similarities and differences in the results.

In terms of similarities, a number of distinct STICS variables were identified as capturing the anticriminal modelling and reinforcement practice. Although the modelling and reinforcement variables were not predictive, the two cognitive items were significantly related to recidivism, as expected. In addition, like the CaVIC results, no direct association was found between quality of relationship and re-offending. This aligns with Bourgon and Bonta's (2014) position that relationship quality is an indicator of adherence to the responsivity principle and would not have a direct relationship to re-offending. This is not to undermine the importance of a quality relationship, but rather highlight that it is likely associated with levels of client engagement and the effectiveness of client learning. If the officer and client have a quality relationship and they engage in effective change work (e.g. focus on criminogenic needs), then we would expect reductions in re-offending.

Table 26.3 Relationship of Core Correctional Practises (CCP) indicators with recidivism (N = 143).

Andrews and Kiessling's CCP Practices	Strategic training initiative in community supervision (stics) equivalent	Relationship to one-year Recidivism	
		Pearson r	Partial r (control risk)
Quality of Relationships	Item: Positive Relationship	0.02	0.03
	Score: Relationship Skills	0.05	0.05
Community Resources	Item: Community Partnerships	0.25**	0.25**
Problem Solving	Item: Problem Solving	0.08	0.12
	Item: Self-Management[a]	−0.17*	−0.20*
Authority	Item: Effective Disapproval	0.24**	0.22**
Anti-Criminal Modelling and Reinforcement	Item: General Modelling	0.00	0.02
	Item: Specific Modelling	0.07	0.05
	Item: Reinforcement	0.06	0.04
	Item: Behaviour Sequence[b]	−0.17*	−0.16

Source: Data source: Bonta et al. (2011).
*p < 0.05.
**p < 0.01.
[a] Self-Management refers to an officer-client interaction focused on identifying a problem situation and helping the client change their thoughts and behaviours to be achieve pro-social goals.
[b] Behaviour Sequence refers to an in-depth analysis of a situation to identify procriminal thinking, behaviour and their resulting consequences as well as to generate alternative pro-social thoughts and behaviours along with their potential consequences.

In terms of contradictory findings, we found Disapproval to be positively related to recidivism, which is in the opposite direction from what was found for authority in the CaVIC studies. There are at least two explanations for why this could be. One, the STICS sample was higher risk than the CaVIC sample (based on sample demographics and recidivism rates) and higher risk clients may respond very differently than lower risk clients to officer expressions of punitive consequences. Two, expressions of disapproval predict recidivism because they signal deteriorating client behaviour and eventual criminal activity (i.e. an officer disapproves more frequently because the client is noncomplying more often). Overall, the comparison between the CaVIC results and the STICS sample suggests that many of the initial relationships between the Core Correctional Practices and recidivism are replicated. This provides continued support for the importance of incorporating these skills into everyday supervision practice. As is discussed in the next section, doing so will assist in enhancing the overall adherence to the RNR principles.

How STICS Promotes RNR

Increasing adherence to the risk principle

Adherence to the risk principle involves matching the level of service to the level of risk, such that higher risk individuals receive more services (Bonta and Andrews 2017). All of the training initiatives described in this chapter taught officers about the risk principle. However, teaching does not guarantee adherence to the material being taught. For example, all officers in the control group of the original STICS pilot project received a short training about the importance of adhering to RNR, but this did not result in changes in their behaviour. In practice, enhancing adherence to the risk principle requires efforts from the officer *and* the organization. At the organizational level, adherence to the risk principle can be accomplished by developing policies that include contact standards (e.g. higher risk clients are required to report more often than lower risk clients, higher risk clients are required to utilize more treatment services than lower risk clients). Then quality assurance processes (e.g. management's monitoring of contact standards, case plans, and case progress) may ensure that more service is directed to higher risk individuals. It is common for organizations to have policies that direct more intense supervision to clients with specific index offences, regardless of the level of assessed risk (e.g. clients with sexual offences or domestic violence offences are to be supervised as if they were high risk). Although policies and directives will influence the degree of adherence to the risk principle, the officer's behaviour with each client also plays a role. As contact standards do not routinely dictate the minimum or maximum amount of time to be spent with a client during one supervision session, an officer can vary the actual amount of time contingent upon risk level (e.g. spending 40 minutes with higher risk individuals and 10 minutes with low-risk individuals).

One of our studies illustrates the potential disconnect between frequency of contact policy and practice (Bourgon et al. 2015). Despite policies that clearly define contact standards by risk level, the average amount of time spent in direct supervision over the course of a month demonstrated very little variation, with high-risk clients having only five minutes more face-to-face supervision time than low-risk clients (see Table 26.4). These results highlight the need to combine organization change (e.g. more closely aligning policy and practices with service provision) with staff training.

Increasing adherence to the need principle

Much of the research on the use of CCP has focused on its relationship with lower recidivism (Dowden and Andrews 2004; Trotter 2013). We hypothesize that it is not the simple application of the specific skills and interventions per se that directly results in reduced re-offending. Rather, it is the increased adherence to the need principle as these skills and techniques were operationally defined in a way that requires a criminogenic need target. For example, if we look at the operational definitions of the three CCP practices that were identified as empirically

Table 26.4 Supervision contacts standards and actual amount of time spent in direct supervision presented by risk level.

Risk Level	Policy Standards	Average amount of monthly time in face-to-face supervision (minutes: seconds)
Low Risk	Once per month	40:47 ($n = 21$)
Moderate Risk	Twice per month	43:48 ($n = 34$)
High Risk	Three times per month	45:30 ($n = 28$)

Source: Bourgon et al. (2015).

related to re-offending in the CaVIC studies, they showed that each was centred around a criminogenic need target and excluded non-criminogenic needs. Anticriminal modelling and reinforcement and authority required targeting criminal behaviour, procriminal attitudes, and/or encouraged alternative pro-social behaviours (i.e. antisocial orientation and/or procriminal peers). Problem-solving efforts focused on 'the areas of work, family, education, peers, finances, and housing' (Andrews and Kiessling 1980, p. 446), all of which are criminogenic needs.

Trotter's work (1990, 1994, and 1996) provides additional support for the hypothesis that adherence to the need principle is likely explaining the relationship between CCP and recidivism. Trotter developed a five-day training programme to increase community supervision officers' use of CCP identified by Andrews and Kiessling (1980). This training focused on pro-social modelling and reinforcement, challenging procriminal expressions and behaviours, problem-solving, and improving the client-officer relationship. To explore the impact of the training on officer behaviour and client outcome, Trotter gathered information on 366 clients and their corresponding officers through file review. Of the 366 clients, 104 clients were supervised by 12 trained officers who reported to use the model in their work and participated in ongoing training. The comparison group consisted of the remaining 262 clients, including 105 clients who were supervised by 12 trained officers who indicated that they did not use the model with their clients, and 157 clients who were supervised by a randomly selected sample of officers from the same community corrections centre but who did not receive the specialized training. The results indicated that clients supervised by officers who were trained and used the model had improved outcomes. Their clients' one-year breach rate was 28% compared to 44%, and the four-year recidivism rate was 46% compared to 64% for clients of officers who did not use the model.

The key 'skills' empirically related to reduced re-offending inferred from the file reviews by Trotter were those that directly targeted a criminogenic need and required enhanced adherence to the Need principle. For example, disapproval, reinforcement, and modelling practices promoted the expression of pro-social attitudes and behaviour were operationalized similarly to the anticriminal modelling and reinforcement CCP described by Andrews and Kiessling (1980) and required the targeting of a criminogenic need (e.g. procriminal attitudes, antisocial personality behaviours). Trotter found that when officers noted in their files that they provided reinforcement of pro-social attitudes and behaviours, disapproval of antisocial attitudes and behaviours, and/or modelled pro-social attitudes and behaviours, there was a positive relationship with reduced criminal behaviour (Trotter 1996). Such officer behaviour indicates greater adherence to the need principle by directing *what* the officer focuses on during supervision sessions. However, the specific behavioural details of *how* (i.e. the skill itself) is unclear as these practices were inferred from file notes and not from direct behavioural observation of the officers.

Trotter's (1996) 'Problem-Solving' was operationalized similar to Andrews and Kiessling (1980) but had one meaningful difference. Trotter assessed file information indicating generic collaborative problem-solving activities (i.e. evidence of any of eight identified steps/tasks of problem-solving). Unlike Andrew and Kiessling, Trotter did not require reference to any specific type of problem or goal, therefore the target was not necessarily criminogenic (Trotter 1994). This would imply that Trotter's measure of problem-solving was not as strong a proxy to adherence to the need principle as was the original CCP used in the CaVIC study. Not surprisingly, the results of the association between "Problem-Solving" and re-offending were mixed. After statistically controlling for risk relevant factors, there were no differences in recidivism in the first year of follow-up (32% compared to 31%) but significant differences emerged at the four-year mark (58% compared to 66%).

Like Trotter, Dowden and Andrews' (2004) meta-analysis of CCP did not directly observe or assess officer (or treatment provider) behaviour. Rather CCP were inferred based on information within research articles and other documentation available to them. This meta-analysis re-examined the original 154 treatment studies from the seminal 1990's 'What Works' meta-analysis of effective correctional treatment (Andrews et al. 1990) and added an additional 119 tests of human service. They also expanded the five CCP identified by Andrews and Kiessling (1980) and coded nine distinct CCPs: (i) Relationship Factors (e.g. staff characteristics associated with positive relationships such as warmth, empathetic, or humorous); (ii) Structuring Factors (e.g. directive, solution-focused or contingency-based communication); (iii) Effective Reinforcement (e.g. client immediately told why staff approved of behaviour); (iv) Effective Disapproval (e.g. staff immediately told why the staff disapproved of the behaviour); (v) Problem-Solving (e.g. engaged in problem-solving steps with client); (vi) Structured Learning (e.g. defined a skill, modelled the skill, or role-played); (vii) Effective Modelling (e.g. used a coping model to demonstrate the behaviour in a concrete or vivid way); (viii) Effective Use of Authority (e.g. message focussed on the behaviour not the client and was direct, specific, and specified choices and consequences); and (ix) Advocacy/Brokerage (e.g. job referral, speaking on behalf of client to external agency).

The results solidified these CCPs as empirically-supported skills of effective correctional workers. All but two factors (i.e. advocacy/brokerage and effective disapproval) were positively and significantly associated with reductions in recidivism *and* to a measure of 'appropriate treatment'. As no direct observations were made of the behaviour exhibited by those delivering the treatment, we should be cautiously optimistic about attributing this to staff skills as the causal factors in reducing re-offending. Again, close examination of the operational definitions provides insights that the 'skills' measured are likely elements of practice (i.e. change activities in human service) that target criminogenic needs, thereby enhancing adherence to the need principle. For example, effective reinforcement and effective disapproval captured differential reinforcement of pro-social/procriminal behaviour and attitudes. Effective modelling captured the use of a coping strategy to display similar challenges and pro-social self-corrective strategy. The clear target of these activities is procriminal thinking and behaviour. The presence of this CCP, compared to its absence, is greater adherence to the need principle.

Greater adherence to the need principle is one of the reasons why we see promising results from these new officer training programmes as officers are being trained to focus on the client's criminogenic needs. Many of the skills and techniques taught are those that will assist officers to directly target criminogenic needs (e.g. disapproval of procriminal behaviours, problem-solving focused on issues of peers, employment, or substance abuse). In the original STICS study (Bonta et al. 2011), the results demonstrated that training significantly improved adherence to the need principle with trained officers spending significantly more time during supervision discussing criminogenic needs. Nonetheless, these new training programmes are comprehensive and provide an integrated approach that requires drawing on skills and techniques that enhance adherence to responsivity as well. Many of these skills centre on building collaborative working relationships with their clients.

Increasing adherence to the responsivity principle

All of the aforementioned training programmes provide officers with certain skills to enhance adherence to the responsivity principle (e.g. relationship-building skills, cognitive-behavioural techniques). The goal of these skills is to teach officers *how* to intervene. We have already described recent results that demonstrated these training programmes increase officers' use of cognitive interventions and its relevance to recidivism. But the responsivity principle is also about creating an optimal learning environment, one that encourages the client to engage and learn through observation, dialogue, interaction, and experience (Bourgon and Bonta 2014). An important consideration when developing this learning environment is the relationship between the supervising officer and client (Bourgon and Gutierrez 2013).

The importance of an effective working relationship is not unique to community supervision. There is a long history of the importance of the therapist-client relationship in determining outcomes in psychotherapy (Horvath and Symonds 1991). The interpersonal relationship, often referred to as the therapeutic alliance (TA), can be described as a collaborative bond between therapist and client whereby positive change is achieved for the client via interpersonal processes that exist independent of specific treatment techniques (Green 2006; Martin et al. 2000). Evaluations of TA have shown that positive and stronger relationships lead to more positive therapeutic outcomes (Baldwin et al. 2007; Elvins and Green 2008; Horvath and Bedi 2002; Green 2006; Martin et al. 2000; Ross et al. 2008).

Although research on the relationship between community supervision officer and clients suggests that it may influence client outcome (Skeem et al. 2003, 2007), further study is warranted. Andrews and Kiessling (1980) recognized the importance of the relationship in their early work, concluding that officers who were warm, tolerant, flexible, and sensitive (i.e. adherence to the responsivity principle by means of building effective alliance with their clients) <u>and</u> targeted expressions of procriminal attitudes and behaviours (i.e. adherence to the need principle) were the most effective.

Contrary to Trotter's work which found no relationship between recidivism and empathy, Dowden and Andrews' (2004) review of CCP found the relationship factor to be associated with treatment effectiveness. The relationship factor described staff as having any of the following characteristics: warmth, genuineness, humour, enthusiasm, self-confidence, empathy, respect, flexibility, commitment to helping client change, engaging, maturity, and/or intelligence. Given these results with offender samples, combined with the abundant support found in the general therapeutic literature, it is understandable that relationship-building is a foundational component of today's new training programmes. Recognizing the possible conflicting roles of probation officers as administrators of a sentence (i.e. monitoring and enforcement of conditions and compliance) and as change-agents (Bourgon et al. 2011), many training programmes attempt to provide officers with strategies to navigate this dual role and build more collaborative alliances with their clients. This is accomplished through the use of techniques such as active listening, role clarification, and collaborative goal setting.

Our review of the evidence suggests that the practices/behaviours being encouraged by change-agent training programmes are contributing to reductions in re-offending because they result in officers' behaviours and activities that increase adherence to the RNR principles. This is largely accomplished through the increased adherence to the need principle with the skills and intervention techniques that target specific criminogenic needs, especially procriminal attitudes and cognitions. In combination, officers are provided with skills and techniques to optimize the learning environment which enhances adherence to the responsivity principle. These include formal efforts to create a more collaborative and respectful working relationship and by teaching techniques that are hallmarks of cognitive-behavioural interventions.

Whilst enhancing adherence to RNR principles is important, we have yet to critically evaluate the impact of these specific skills and, more importantly, the quality of their execution. For example, there are many similarities in the skills and techniques taught between the different training programmes but there are also many differences (Rugge et al. 2015). For example, both STICS and STARR train on a skill referred to as Feedback, but the skill is very different between the two programmes. Feedback in STARR involves seven steps including asking the client questions during its use. Feedback in STICS is a single step, an officer's verbal behaviour that follows three simple rules of how the feedback is phrased and delivered. Not only are the skills different, their goals are different as well. In STARR, one goal appears to be giving the client the opportunity to self-assess his/her behaviour or action. The goal of feedback in STICS is to provide the client with information about his/her behaviour from another person's point of view in a manner that increases the chances that it is heard and understood, with words that are respectful and non-judgemental. Given that each of these skills and techniques can vary in terms of their steps and goals, so too can the quality of execution during supervision (i.e. what determines differing degrees of quality of use of authority, problem-solving, and differential reinforcement).

If our goal is to continue to enhance the effectiveness of community supervision, we will need to better understand the differences between training models, the differences in the skills and intervention techniques taught, as well as the quality of their execution. Without such specifics, it will be difficult to be detailed and accurate when developing and/or refining training curriculum and the skills and intervention techniques taught. As the saying goes, 'the devil is in the detail'.

Lessons from Psychotherapy Research

Specific ingredients and common factors

As the field of corrections continues to move forward to expand our knowledge about 'what works', there are valuable lessons that can be drawn from the field of psychotherapy. Like RNR-based human services in corrections, the psychotherapeutic literature presents compelling empirical support related to client change (Wampold 2000). Moving beyond its effectiveness towards understanding the 'why' becomes critical, particularly in regard to improving training and assessing fidelity.

Whether the beneficial effects of psychotherapy are derived from the specific ingredients of treatment (e.g. identifiable skills and techniques of specific therapeutic models) or, more broadly, from factors common to all therapies (Ahn and Wampold 2001; Laska et al. 2014; Wampold 2000, 2015) has been heavily debated. The specific ingredient models are analogous to the medical model approach. That is, psychotherapy's efficacy is attributed to specific interventions of the therapist (e.g. effective reinforcement) with the client. The work on CCP and effective community supervision practices has embraced this 'specific ingredients' model, attempting to link specific behaviours engaged by the officers with their clients to re-offending outcomes. As Trotter's (2013) review of the CCP literature concluded, 'application of certain skills in probation supervision is likely to lead to lower recidivism when compared to their absence' (p. 48).

On the other hand, the common factors model of psychotherapy effectiveness holds that there are commonalities amongst all psychotherapies (and helping relationships) that are responsible for its effectiveness. This model hypothesizes five elements that are necessary and sufficient for change. The five common factors are (i) a confiding healing setting (i.e. a safe environment in which to interact), (ii) an emotionally charged bond between therapist and client (i.e. a collaborative and trusting relationship), (iii) an explanation for the problem that is psychologically derived and culturally embedded that is accepted by the client (i.e. a psychological model explaining the causes of behaviour), (iv) the explanation provides viable and believable options for overcoming the problem (i.e. the client can understand and acknowledge the specific course of action to deal with the problem), and (v) a set of procedures or activities engaged by the therapist and client that promotes uptake by the client (e.g. therapeutic activities such as cognitive restructuring that the client learns and practises). In this model, the specific ingredients (i.e. skills and techniques) are only one of the five factors involved. Importantly, although each factor contributes to success, the model holds that none of the factors is sufficient by itself (Laska et al. 2014). When therapy encompasses all of the factors, it should demonstrate effectiveness.

Research findings, including meta-analyses, substantially support the common factors model whereas empirical support for the specific ingredients has been lacking (see Ahn and Wampold 2001 and Wampold 2015 for critical reviews). The common factor model and its supporting evidence can provide direction and guidance to improve community supervision officer training programmes that focus on facilitating pro-social change and improving outcomes for offenders. The question is: How can this knowledge inform the work of community supervision officers?

Therapy is about facilitating change. The new training programmes for community supervision officers have reminded us of the importance of the change-agent's role and have brought attention to the skills and techniques that officers use to facilitate pro-social change. RNR has provided a framework to understand what is and what is not effective at reducing re-offending. The common factors approach can further refine the process of how probation officers can more effectively promote change by guiding training efforts to better align the skills and intervention techniques to deal directly with each of the common factors, particularly the third factor; providing the client with a psychological explanation for behaviour in general that is accepted and believed to be true by the client.

In corrections, the research to date has supported the efficacy of a cognitive-behavioural treatment approach. All of the new change-agent supervision training programmes teach officers skills and techniques to conduct cognitive-behavioural interventions and how to employ cognitive restructuring work. In STICS, one avenue to do cognitive restructuring with clients is through an interactive process called a 'behaviour sequence'. Through a detailed analysis of a specific behaviour in a given situation and its consequences, the officer and client identify 'tapes' (i.e. procriminal cognitions) that directed the behaviour and generate 'counters' (i.e. prosocial cognitions). In STARR and EPICS, restructured cognitions are called 'replacement thoughts' in their 'Cog Model' during a similar analysis of behaviour and corresponding thoughts. Although from the common factors perspective, the specific psychological model learned by the client is not a critical element of effectiveness, we know that the cognitive-behavioural model (i.e. a specific model), in comparison to other approaches, has been found to be effective with correctional clients (e.g. Lipsey et al. 2001). Why is this so? In addition to its alignment with the need principle (e.g. increased attention to procriminal cognitions and criminogenic needs such as substance abuse), we suggest that for correctional clients, the cognitive-behavioural model, in comparison to other theoretical models, is more likely an acceptable and believable explanation of behaviour for many offenders. A cognitive-behavioural explanation is congruent with correctional clients' experiences and understanding of the world because it is concrete rather than abstract, straightforward, easily understood, and recognizes the factors that are relevant to them (i.e. their thoughts, their behaviours, and the consequences they receive).

Although a cognitive-behavioural explanation may be easier to accept and believe compared to other explanatory models for correctional clients, this does not imply that once it is presented to them, clients will simply accept it to be true and valid. Even for officers who participate in training, simply learning about the model does not necessarily equate to personal acceptance. For example, training programmes educate officers about the importance of cognitions as determinants of behaviour and that cognitive-behavioural approaches are an evidence-based practice. Anyone who has provided training on RNR and/or cognitive-behavioural models and practices to correctional staff has no doubt observed their reluctance or outright resistance to accept the theory, principles, and empirical evidence of RNR because it contradicts their personal beliefs, experiences, and understanding of behaviour. The same reluctance and resistance can be seen in clients on community supervision.

The traditional approach of training officers about the cognitive-behavioural model is through education, presentation of theory, and the facts and evidence supporting the model. Once presented, training programmes teach a skill or technique followed by some form of rehearsal. Many training programmes do little in terms of ensuring officers' acceptance and belief of the explanatory model. This same educational approach is used with clients. Officers are trained how to 'teach' the cognitive-model to the client, and 'how to apply' the model with clients. The common factors approach highlights the importance of client belief and acceptance of the explanatory model. For that reason, training programmes may benefit from providing specific training on how to 'sell' the programme to ensure client 'buy-in'.

Spot, the dog: A STICS exercise

In STICS, we recognized the importance of the client's acceptance and belief in the fundamental assumptions of the cognitive-behavioural model. That is, cognitions are the primary determinants of behaviour and that individuals are responsible for their thoughts, feelings, and behaviour, which they personally have the power to change. In order to 'sell' and improve 'buy in', STICS trains officers in a technique called 'Spot, the Dog', an interactive exercise in which the officer guides a client on how to teach a dog to sit. Using this simple hands-on frame of reference to which most clients can relate (i.e. teaching a dog named Spot to sit), the client is encouraged to self-discover the main principles and assumptions of a cognitive-behavioural explanation of why people behave as they do. Through this exercise, clients learn simple, concrete language to identify and discuss the basic components of cognitive-behavioural learning.[1]

Although there are a number of lessons that the client learns in this exercise, the three primary learnings are as follows. One, the client is taught the basic components of learning (i.e. antecedent stimuli, internal events, behaviour, and consequences) and provided with a common language to identify, describe, and discuss these basic components. Following the responsivity principle, simple concrete language is preferred over technical or formal psychological terms. For example, antecedent or external stimuli are referred to as 'outside cues' and defined as everything outside of oneself. Internal stimuli such as cognitions, sensations, and feelings are referred to as 'inside cues' (i.e. everything inside of oneself). Whilst the term 'behaviour' and 'consequences' are the same traditional words that are easily understood, technical terms referring to types of consequences (i.e. reinforcer and punisher), are replaced with terms 'cookies' (i.e. things you like) and 'boots' (i.e. things you do not like). These STICS terms

---

[1] Further details of this exercise are available from the author upon request.

provide a visual image to assist in learning. In addition to types of consequences, Spot, the Dog also provides the client a learning opportunity to differentiate two sources of consequences (i.e. consequences from external sources called 'outside cookies' and 'outside boots' as well as internal consequences called 'inside cookies' and 'inside boots') and the importance of these different sources in learning.

The second primary learning in Spot, the Dog pertains to the assumptions of causality inherent in the cognitive-behavioural model. This exercise is designed to facilitate the client's self-discovery of these assumptions. For example, one critical assumption is the 'discovery' of the causal link of thoughts to behaviour and that thoughts cause behaviour. In addition, there is explicit recognition that outside cues, although important, are not causal factors of thoughts or behaviour. These are critical lessons for the client to accept. Often correctional clients hold onto the belief that external events (i.e. 'outside cues') are the cause of their behaviour, frequently denying responsibility for their actions and blaming others. Clients also discover that consequences, although an important component of learning, are an insufficient explanation of behaviour. It is not the result that causes the behaviour, but rather the thought, or anticipation, that a particular behaviour will lead to specific consequence that causes the behaviour.

The third primary learning in Spot, the Dog is that the client experiences and learns about empowerment, self-control, and self-efficacy. Throughout this exercise, the client discovers what they can and cannot control and, as a result, what they are and are not responsible for. Specifically, clients realize that they do not control 'outside cues' (e.g. a common belief of violent offenders is the thought that 'I can teach you to respect me') or 'outside consequences' (e.g. the belief that if I behave in a certain way, 'I can make her love me'). Conversely, they learn that they control their thinking, their behaviour, and the consequences that their thinking and behaviour generate for themselves.

This exercise aligns well with the common factors model in the sense that STICS provides officers with a strategy to 'sell' the cognitive-behavioural model to clients in the same way that they have bought into its explanatory scheme. In addition, it provides concrete and viable options for clients to change via explicit lessons about the ability to control one's own thoughts, feelings and behaviours (Factor 4 of the common factor model). To evaluate the importance of the Spot, the Dog technique, we re-examined the original data STICS data (Bonta et al. 2011). Reviewing all 295 recordings, we identified 14 of the 143 clients in the project who were exposed to the technique during a recorded session (i.e. an officer-client recording where the Spot, the Dog exercise took place). Interestingly, of the 14 clients, none of them re-offended after one year. Of these clients, none of the 13 of whom we had a two-year follow-up had re-offended. Although the sample size of this comparison is minimal, these preliminary findings may underscore the importance of teaching the model in a manner that clients can relate to, prior to applying it to their own thoughts and behaviours.

Conclusions

As our empirical knowledge continues to accumulate on what works in reducing re-offending, it is important that we ask why it works. The RNR principles have established a strong foundation for the development and administration of rehabilitative services to correctional clients. New community supervision officer training programmes have embedded these principles, providing skills and intervention techniques to officers so they can effectively implement RNR into their supervision sessions. The emerging evidence suggests that officers can be effective after receiving such training. However, we cannot and should not be satisfied with simply demonstrating that these training programmes work. Throughout, we have argued that we must continue to unravel the change processes that are inherent in officer-client interactions.

Our examination of the accumulated evidence on CCP suggests its effectiveness is a result of greater adherence to the RNR principles and not simply the execution of specific skills during supervision. As we have learned from the general psychotherapy research literature, we have suggested that there are other crucial factors in play. Of particular relevance is client belief and acceptance of the explanatory model as one of the common factors related to therapeutic effectiveness. It is our hope that by integrating the empirical evidence of RNR with that of psychotherapy, we may better understand why change-agent models of supervision are showing promise, in terms of improved client outcomes. By doing so, we can ensure that implementation efforts are centred on the most critical aspects to enhance the opportunity for success.

Acknowledgment

The views expressed are those of the authors and not necessarily those of Public Safety Canada.

We would like to thank James Bonta for his helpful comments on previous versions of this manuscript.

Correspondence concerning this article should be addressed to Guy Bourgon, 317 Catherine Street, Ottawa, Ontario K1R 5Y4.

References

Abadinsky, H. (2009). *Probation and Parole: Theory and Practice.* Upper Saddle River, NJ: Pearson Prentice Hall.

Ahn, H.N. and Wampold, B.E. (2001). Where oh where are the specific ingredients? A meta-analysis of component studies in counseling and psychotherapy. *Journal of Counseling Psychology* 48: 251–257.

Andrews, D.A. (1980). Some experimental investigations of the principles of differential association through deliberate manipulations of the structure of service systems. *American Sociological Review* 45 (3): 448–462.

Andrews, D.A. and Bonta, J. (2010). *The Psychology of Criminal Conduct,* 5e. New Providence, NJ: LexisNexis Matthew Bender.

Andrews, D.A. and Kiessling, J.J. (1980). Program structure and effective correctional practices: a summary of the CaVIC research. In: *Effective Correctional Treatment* (eds. R.R. Ross and P. Gendreau), 439–463. Toronto, ON: Butterworth.

Andrews, D.A., Zinger, I., Hoge, R.D. et al. (1990). Does correctional treatment work? A clinically relevant and psychologically informed meta-analysis. *Criminology* 28: 369–404.

Baldwin, S.A., Wampold, B.E., and Imel, Z.E. (2007). Untangling the alliance-outcome correlation: exploring the relative importance of therapist and patient variability in the alliance. *Journal of Consulting and Clinical Psychology* 75 (6): 842–852.

Beck, A.T. (1970). Cognitive therapy: Nature and relation to behaviour therapy. *Behavior therapy* 1 (2): 184–200.

Bonta, J. and Andrews, D.A. (2017). *The Psychology of Criminal Conduct,* 6e. New York, NY: Routledge.

Bonta, J., Bourgon, G., and Rugge, T. (2018). From evidence-informed to evidence-based: the Strategic Training Initiative in Community Supervision (STICS). In: *Evidence-Based Skills in Community Justice: International Perspectives on Effective Practice* (eds. P. Ugwudike, P. Raynor and J. Annison), 169–192. Bristol, UK: Policy Press.

Bonta, J., Bourgon, G., Rugge, T. et al. (2011). An experimental demonstration of training probation officers in evidence based community supervision. *Criminal Justice and Behavior* 38: 1127–1148.

Bonta, J., Rugge, T., Scott, T. et al. (2008). Exploring the black box of community supervision. *Journal of Offender Rehabilitation* 47: 248–270.

Bourgon, G. (2013). The demands on probation officers in the evolution of evidence-based practice: the forgotten foot soldier of community corrections. *Federal Probation* 77 (2): 30–35.

Bourgon, G. and Bonta, J. (2014). Reconsidering the responsivity principle: a way to move forward. *Federal Probation* 78 (2): 3–10.

Bourgon, G., Bonta, J., Rugge, T., and Gutierrez, L. (2010). Technology transfer: the importance of on-going clinical supervision in translating what works to everyday community supervision. In: *Offender Supervision: New Directions in Theory, Research, and Practice* (eds. F. McNeil, P. Raynor and C. Trotter), 88–106. New York, NY: Willan.

Bourgon, G., Chadwick, N., Rugge, T. et al. (2015). *The Living Laboratory Report Phase 1: Insights Into Community Supervision Practices at Edmonton Alberta Central Intake Probation Office*. Ottawa, ON: Public Safety Canada.

Bourgon, G. and Gutierrez, L. (2012). The general responsivity principle in community supervision: the importance of probation officers using cognitive intervention techniques and its influence on recidivism. *Journal of Crime and Justice* 35: 149–166.

Bourgon, G. and Gutierrez, L. (2013). The importance of building good relationships in community corrections: evidence, theory, and practice of the therapeutic alliance. In: *What Works in Offender Compliance: International Perspectives and Evidence-Based Practice* (eds. P. Ugwudike and P. Raynor), 256–278. Basingstoke, UK: Palgrave.

Bourgon, G., Gutierrez, L., and Ashton, J. (2011). From case management to change agent: the evolution of 'What Works' community supervision. *Irish Probation Journal* 8: 28–48.

Chadwick, N., DeWolf, A., and Serin, R. (2015). Effectively training community supervision officers: a meta-analytic review of the impact on offender outcome. *Criminal Justice and Behavior* 42: 977–989.

Clodfelter, T.A., Holcomb, J.E., Alexander, M.A. et al. (2016). A case study of the implementation of Staff Training Aimed at Reducing Rearrest (STARR). *Federal Probation* 80 (1): 30–38.

Cullen, F.T. and Gendreau, P. (1989). The effectiveness of correctional treatment: reconsidering the 'nothing works' debate. In: *The American Prison: Issues in Research and Policy* (eds. L. Goodstein and D.L. MacKenzie), 23–24. New York, NY: Plenum Press.

Dowden, C. and Andrews, D.A. (2004). The importance of staff practice in delivering effective correctional treatment: a meta-analytic review of core correctional practices. *International Journal of Offender Therapy and Comparative Criminology* 48: 203–214.

Elvins, R. and Green, J. (2008). The conceptualization and measurement of therapeutic alliance: an empirical review. *Clinical Psychology Review* 28: 1167–1187.

Gendreau, P. and Andrews, D.A. (1990). Tertiary prevention: what the meta-analyses of the offender treatment literature tells us about 'what works'. *Canadian Journal of Criminology* 32 (1): 173–184.

Gibbons, S.G. and Rosecrance, J.D. (2005). *Probation, Parole, and Community Corrections In the United States*. Boston, MA: Pearson Allyn and Bacon.

Glaze, L. and Kaeble, D. (2014). *Probation and Parole in the United States, 2013*. Washington, DC: Department of Justice.

Green, J. (2006). Annotation: the therapeutic alliance – a significant but neglected variable in child mental health treatment studies. *Journal of Child Psychology and Psychiatry* 47 (5): 425–435.

Horvath, A.O. and Bedi, R.P. (2002). The alliance. In: *Psychotherapy Relationships that Work: Therapist Contributions and Responsiveness To Patients* (ed. J. Norcross), 37–70. New York, NY: Oxford University Press.

Horvath, A.O. and Symonds, D.B. (1991). Relation between working alliance and outcome in psychotherapy: a meta-analysis. *Journal of Counselling Psychology* 38 (2): 139–149.

Kaeble, D. and Bonczar, T.P. (2016). *Probation and Parole in the United States, 2015.* Washington, DC: Department of Justice.

Kiessling, J.J. and Andrews, D.A. (1979). *Volunteers and the One-to-One Supervision of Adult Probationers: An Experimental Comparison with Professionals and a Field-Description of Process and Outcome.* Toronto, ON: Ontario Ministry of Correctional Services.

Labrecque, R.M., Luther, J.D., Smith, P., and Latessa, E.J. (2014). Responding to the needs of probation and parole: the development of the effective practices in a community supervision model with families. *Offender Programs Report* 18 (1–2): 11–13.

Labrecque, R.M., Schweitzer, M., and Smith, P. (2013). Probation and parole officer adherence to the core correctional practices: an evaluation of 755 offender-officer interactions. *Advancing Practices* 3: 20–23.

Labrecque, R.M., Smith, P., and Luther, J.D. (2015). A quasi-experimental evaluation of a model of community supervision. *Federal Probation* 79: 14.

Laska, K.M., Gurman, A.S., and Wampold, B.E. (2014). Expanding the lens of evidence-based practice in psychotherapy: a common factors perspective. *Psychotherapy* 51: 467–481.

Latessa, E.J., Smith, P., Schweitzer, M. and Labreque, R.M. (2013). Evaluation of the effective practices in community supervision model (EPICS) in Ohio. Unpublished manuscript.

Lipsey, M.W., Chapman, G.L., and Landenberger, N.A. (2001). Cognitive-behavioral programmes for offenders. *Annals of the American Academy of Political and Social Science* 578: 144–157.

Lowenkamp, C.T., Holsinger, A.M., Robinson, C.R., and Alexander, M. (2014). Diminishing or durable treatment of STARR? A research note on 24-month re-arrest rates. *Journal of Crime and Justice* 37 (2): 275–283.

Martin, D.J., Garske, J.P., and Davis, K.M. (2000). Relation of the therapeutic alliance with outcome and other variables: a meta-analytic review. *Journal of Consulting and Clinical Psychology* 68 (3): 438–450.

Meichenbaum, D. and Turk, D.C. (1976). The cognitive-behavioral management of anxiety, anger, and pain. In: *The Behavioral Management of Anxiety, Depression, and Pain* (ed. P.O. Davidson), 1–34. New York: Brunner/Mazel.

Miller, W.R. and Rollnick, S. (2012). *Motivational Interviewing: Helping People Change.* New York, NY: Guilford press.

Ministry of Justice. (2017). Offender management statistics quarterly: July to September, 2016. London, UK.

Polaschek, D.L., Calvert, S.W., and Gannon, T.A. (2009). Linking violent thinking implicit theory-based research with violent offenders. *Journal of Interpersonal Violence* 24 (1): 75–96.

Public Safety Canada (2016). *The Corrections and Conditional Release Statistical Overview 2016.* Ottawa, ON: Public Safety Canada.

Robinson, C.R., Lowenkamp, C.T., Holsinger, A.M. et al. (2012). A random study of Staff Training Aimed at Reducing Re-arrest (STARR): using core correctional practices in probation interactions. *Journal of Crime and Justice* 35: 167–188.

Robinson, C.R., VanBenschoten, S., Alexander, M., and Lowenkamp, C.T. (2011). A random (almost) study of staff training aimed at reducing re-arrest (STARR): Reducing recidivism through intentional design. *Federal Probation* 75 (2): 57–63.

Ross, E.C., Polaschek, D.L.L., and Ward, T. (2008). The therapeutic alliance: a theoretical revision for offender rehabilitation. *Aggression and Violent Behavior* 13: 462–480.

Rugge, T. and Bonta, J. (2014). Training community corrections officers in cognitive-behavioural intervention strategies. In: *Forensic CBT: A Handbook for Clinical Practice* (eds. R.C. Tafrate and D. Mitchell), 122–136. Chichester, UK: Wiley.

Rugge, T., Mitchell, D., Tafrate, R.C. et al. (2015). No sustain, no gain: Initiatives for community corrections officers. Symposium presented at the Annual International Community Corrections Association Research Conference in Boston, MA (8–10 November 2015).

Schmucker, M. and Lösel, F. (2015). The effects of sexual offender treatment on recidivism: an international meta-analysis of sound quality evaluations. *Journal of Experimental Criminology* 11: 597–630.

Skeem, J.L., Encandela, J., and Eno Louden, J. (2003). Perspectives on probation and mandated mental health treatment in specialized and traditional probation departments. *Behavioral Sciences & the Law* 21: 429–458.

Skeem, J.L., Eno Louden, J., Camp, J., and Polaschek, D. (2007). Assessing relationship quality in mandated community treatment: blending care with control. *Psychological Assessment* 19 (4): 397–410.

Smith, P., Schweitzer, M., Labreque, R.M., and Latessa, E.J. (2012). Improving probation officers' supervision skills: an evaluation of the EPICS model. *Journal of Crime and Justice* 35: 189–199.

Sutherland, E.H. and Cressey, D.R. (1970). *Principles of Criminology*, 3e. Philadelphia, PA: Lippincott.

Trotter, C. (1990). Probation can work. A research study using volunteers. *Australian Journal of Social Work* 43 (2): 13–18.

Trotter, C. (1994). The effective supervision of offenders. Unpublished PhD Thesis. LaTrobe University.

Trotter, C. (1996). The impact of different supervision practices in community corrections: cause for optimism. *Australian and New Zealand Journal of Criminology* 29 (1): 29–46.

Trotter, C. (2013). Reducing recidivism through probation supervision: what we know and don't know from four decades of research. *Federal Probation* 77 (2): 43–48.

Wampold, B.E. (2000). Outcomes of individual counseling and psychotherapy: empirical evidence addressing two fundamental questions. In: *Handbook of Counseling Psychology*, 4e (eds. S.D. Brown and R.W. Lent), 711–739. New York, NY: Wiley.

Wampold, B.E. (2015). How important are the common factors in psychotherapy? An update. *World Psychiatry* 14: 270–277.

Wilson, D.B., Allen Bouffard, L., and Mackenzie, D.L. (2005). A quantitative review of structured, group-oriented, cognitive-behavioral programs for offenders. *Criminal Justice and Behavior* 32: 172–204.

27

What Works in Risk Assessment in Stalking Cases

David V. James[1] and Lorraine P. Sheridan[2]

[1]Theseus LLP, Faversham, UK
[2]Curtin University, Bentley, Western Australia

Understanding the Nature of the Stalking Phenomenon

Stalking in the sense of obsessive harassment is a term that did not exist in the popular consciousness before 1990. It has been successful as a concept in encompassing a range of forms of incessant intimidation and pursuit, and rendering their overall effects understandable to the general public. But it is, in essence, a final common behavioural pathway reached by individuals setting out from different starting points, with very different motivations. It is associated with physical violence in a proportion of cases, yet it is not always associated with conscious malevolence or aggression. A person consumed with a grievance who stalks with the specific aim of causing harm differs from one whose motivation is amorous and whose actions are intended to further physical and emotional intimacy. This can make the phenomenon difficult for policing agencies to understand and evaluate in terms of risk: and it determines that special approaches to the assessment of violence risk (and that of other negative outcomes) need to be adopted in stalking cases, both in terms of initial screening and detailed evaluation.

Stalking is generally defined as a pattern of repeated, unwanted intrusion by one individual into the life of another, in a manner that causes distress, disruption or fear (Pathé and Mullen 1997; Pinals 2007). This can take the form of intrusive communications, physical intrusion or intrusion by a variety of other means. The fact that the behaviour is not only defined by the activities of the perpetrator, but also by the emotional reactions of the victim, makes stalking unusual in criminal justice terms. The individual behaviours that constitute stalking may seem innocuous in themselves as, for instance, with the making of telephone calls or sending letters

The Wiley Handbook of What Works in Violence Risk Management: Theory, Research and Practice,
First Edition. Edited by J. Stephen Wormith, Leam A. Craig, and Todd E. Hogue.

and gifts. It is only when they occur together in a particular context that they constitute something greater than the sum of their parts (James and MacKenzie 2017). In policing terms, many of the individual behaviours which together constitute stalking do not in themselves constitute criminal offences and this can make it difficult for law enforcement (and others) to realize their seriousness or recognize the risks involved.

In addition, stalking is in effect a social construct, in that it only has meaning in a specific social and cultural context. In western societies, the recognition of stalking as a social problem and its subsequent codification as a criminal offence were necessarily preceded by the recognition of the equal rights of women and by societal and prosecutorial intolerance of domestic violence. The concept of the stalking of women by men (as opposed to other combinations) is irrelevant and unrecognized in countries where women remain subservient to men. Indeed, before the changes in western societies in the second half of the twentieth century, the behaviour we now call stalking was often seen as socially acceptable, or indeed in the case of amorous intent, sometimes admirable.

There remain popular misconceptions about the nature of stalking victimization, which serve to confuse understanding. A consistent finding of prevalence surveys is that women are more commonly victims of stalking than men. Yet, this may be a circular, definitional issue. The problem of defining stalking in terms of distress or fear is that men may be less likely to experience these in response to intrusive events, or may be less willing to admit that they do so. Secondly, stalking cases may be viewed or categorized in terms of the previous relationship (if any) between stalker and victim: former sexual intimates, estranged family members and friends, acquaintances, and complete strangers. The popular image of the stalker suggests that former intimate partners are the largest group. However, the more stringent community surveys indicate otherwise. The 1998 British Crime Survey (BCS) found that only 29% of stalking cases involved ex-intimates (Budd and Mattinson 2000), and the combined BCS figures for 2013–2015 found that 43% of women victims had experienced stalking from an ex-partner, compared with 28.7% of male victims (Office for National Statistics 2016). The higher figures in some US surveys (e.g. Breiding et al. 2014: 60.8%) appear to reflect the inclusion of current intimates as well as ex-intimates in the scope of the survey, which arguably conflates two separate phenomena. For, stalking and domestic violence are separate entities, in that stalking occurs after a relationship has ended and domestic violence occurs before any end to a relationship. It cannot be assumed that the same risk factors are involved in stalking as in domestic violence (McEwan et al. 2017b). Nor is there reason to suppose that it is in any way helpful for the same specialist police units to deal with both phenomena.

There can also be some confusion as to the length of time that the behaviour should persist in order for cases to qualify as, and be risk-assessed as stalking, as opposed to short bursts of intrusive activity. The latter are generally characterized as harassment, with evidence being found by some researchers that this has a phenomenological cut-off at two weeks (Purcell et al. 2004a). However, legal definitions of stalking do not distinguish between stalking and harassment. Anti-stalking legislation has generally been codified in a similar manner in the increasing number of western countries in which it has been adopted (Purcell et al. 2004b). An offence is deemed to have been committed when an individual engages in certain types of intrusive activity which is repeated and which cause apprehension or fear, or would do so in the average person (Mullen et al. 2009, pp. 282–294). The element of repetition (or 'course of conduct') is generally defined as intrusive behaviour happening at least twice, although some jurisdictions allow a single protracted act (e.g. surveillance) to constitute stalking (Victoria, Australia; Belgium, van der Aa and Römkens 2013). However, it would be unusual in most jurisdictions for stalking legislation to be used with respect to short, completed bursts of activity which would require a different approach from stalking in terms of violence risk assessment.

The fear of violence is central to the experience of stalking victims. Yet, a particular difficulty for policing agencies and allied professions in evaluating risk in stalking cases is the volume (or potential volume) of complaints. Being stalked is a relatively common experience. Prevalence rates in different studies depend upon the definitions being used. In the US, surveys have found lifetime rates of 8% for women and 2% for men (Tjaden and Thoennes 1998); 4.5% for all adults – 7% of women and 2% of men (Basile et al. 2006); and 15.2% for women and 5.7% for men (Breiding et al. 2014). The BCS for the year ending March 2015 found a life-time prevalence of 15% for all adults, (20.2% of women and 9.8% of men) and a rate for the previous 12 months of 3.7% (4.9% of women and 2.4% of men; Office for National Statistics 2016). A German national prevalence study (Hellman and Kliem 2015) found a life-time prevalence of 15% (19.4% of women and 11.4% of men). An EU-wide prevalence survey of the stalking of women found a life-time rate of 18% and a rate for the previous 12 months of 5% (FRA 2014). If the above prevalence rates are translated into actual numbers of persons affected, these prove very high. This does not mean that most cases are currently reported to the police or that police take action if they are. In the US, only half of stalking cases were reported to the police, with less than 14% leading to prosecution and only 14% of these leading to conviction – in other words, 5.6% of stalking cases (Tjaden and Thoennes 2000). In the EU survey, only 25% of cases came to the attention of the police (FRA 2014, p. 53). In England and Wales, the BCS for 2015 (Office for National Statistics 2016) found that 1.1 million people aged 16–59 had been stalked in the past year: this contrasted with the fact that only 12 122 harassment and stalking convictions were initiated in the financial year 2014–2015 (CPS 2015). In the UK, poor police understanding of, and inadequate response to, stalking has been found to be a widespread problem (Her Majesty's Inspectorate of Constabulary 2017). The low proportion of cases coming to the attention of the police has been taken as evidence of a need for more police training, for better education of victims, and for a smoother mechanism of response by the criminal justice system (FRA 2014). Yet, any major increase in reporting would risk overwhelming current policing responses. This underlines the need for some simple and reliable means to assess risk and to triage cases when they are first reported to police.

Further problems have presented in relation to the use of the Internet and electronic media in stalking, such as e-mail, social media (e.g. Facebook, Twitter), blogs and chatrooms. These forms of communication are now ubiquitous. They can be used by stalkers, not only for direct communications with victims or their associates, but also for identity theft, the spreading of false information, and the recruiting of others to harass via the Internet. This phenomenon is known as cyberstalking, a concept which generally does not include mobile telephones or text messages which need not be Internet-based (Cavezza and McEwan 2014).

There are few reliable estimates of the prevalence of cyberstalking, but an EU survey of violence against women found that 5% had been cyberstalked at some point and 2% in the past year (FRA 2014). A 2016 British population survey (James and Persaud in submission) found that 5.3% of adults reported being stalked on-line, including 7% of women and 3.4% of men. However, three quarters of those who had been electronically stalked had also been subject to non-electronic stalking, confirming previous views that cyberstalking is not a discrete new phenomenon, but rather a technological update (Sheridan and Grant 2007; Cavezza and McEwan 2014). It should be noted that cyberstalking is a different phenomenon from what has come to be known as 'trolling', the sending of anonymous, malicious, abusive, derogatory or threatening messages through electronic means, such as Twitter, usually to someone not personally known to the sender (James and MacKenzie 2017). Trolling, whilst hurtful to the recipient, is generally limited to the expression of anger or the achievement of a sense of power through causing emotional pain and humiliation. Cloaked in an illusion of anonymity, there is little evidence thus far to associate it with any form of physical violence.

Understanding What Drives Stalkers

Motivation

Motivation is central to the assessment of risk in stalking. The most widely accepted classification is that of Mullen et al. (1999), which is generally accepted as the standard (Pinals 2007). It defines five categories of stalkers: the Rejected, Intimacy Seekers, the Incompetent Suitor, the Resentful and the Predatory. Subsequent studies have shown that associations of risk in stalking vary between the categories, with significant differences in rates of violence, persistence and recurrence, and in prevalence of psychosis and attachment problems (MacKenzie et al. 2008; McEwan et al. 2009a, b; James et al. 2010b; McEwan et al. 2016, 2017a). The motivational classification is incorporated into the structure of the Stalking Risk Profile (SRP; MacKenzie et al. 2009), a widely-used structured professional judgement (SPJ) tool for the assessment and management of risk in stalking. The motivational categories are defined as follows. *The Rejected* engage in stalking after the breakdown of an intimate relationship that was usually, but not always, sexually intimate in nature: the goal is one of reconciliation or retribution, or fluctuating mixtures of both. The *Intimacy Seeker* believes that he/she has, or is destined to have, a relationship or intense bond with the object of their affection, whatever evidence there may be to the contrary. The *Incompetent Suitor* also engages in stalking to establish a relationship, but unlike the Intimacy Seeker, the desire is simply for a date or a sexual encounter. The *Resentful Stalker* seeks to frighten or intimidate the victim to exact revenge for a perceived insult or injury. Unlike the Rejected, their grievance does not arise from rejection from an intimate relationship. Lastly, the *Predatory stalker* stalks in order to gain sexual gratification or in preparation for an attack, usually sexual. Consideration of the categories emphasizes that stalking is not a unitary construct.

Psychopathology

The common feature in stalking, whatever the underlying motivation or prior relationship, is that the stalker feels a strong sense of entitlement (MacKenzie and James 2011) – a belief that he or she has a right to fulfil their own desires and a right to their victim's attention and time. The 'right' to have their grievance heard, to pursue their love, to receive an 'explanation' or to be treated with 'respect' takes precedence over the interests and concerns of the victim (James and MacKenzie 2017). Stalkers show little concern for the feelings of their victims, except in cases where the causing of fear or distress is a goal of the stalking, from which the stalker derives pleasure. From the sense of entitlement, there arise justifications and rationalization of the stalker's behaviour. These are compounded by a variety of skills deficits which are common in stalkers, specifically anger and conflict resolution, a need for control, problem-solving and reasoning, social skills in general, and problems with emotional regulation. Stalkers are more likely to have insecure adult attachment styles (MacKenzie et al. 2008) and relatively poor verbal skills (MacKenzie et al. 2010), the latter being important in the design of management interventions. The identification and treatment of skills deficits is the basis of treatment in stalkers where no mental illness is present (MacKenzie and James 2011).

Mental illnesses are in fact relatively common in stalkers, with delusional disorders, schizophrenia, bipolar affective disorder and major depression frequently found in stalker samples (MacKenzie and James 2011). Disorders of personality are also often identified (Mullen et al. 1999; McEwan et al. 2017a). When delusions are present, they are commonly persecutory or erotomanic. The prevalence of psychotic illness has been found in a recent study to vary with relationship type, being present in one in three acquaintance stalkers, in one in 10 stranger stalkers and only in one in 50 ex-intimate stalkers (McEwan et al. 2017a). Mental state is an important consideration in stalking risk assessment and management, and these findings suggest that psychiatric assessment should be routine, at least in acquaintance stalkers. Treatment of any mental illness is understandably an important plank in the management of stalking cases.

The Expanding Evidence-Base on Stalking Risk

Before turning to specific tools for aiding in the assessment of risk in stalking, it is relevant briefly to review the expanding research base, upon which they depend (together with clinical expertise) for their construction. The focus of this volume is on risk of violence, but there are other forms of risk in stalking which also require assessment: the risk of persistence, in other words that stalking may continue for a lengthy period; the risk of recurrence of stalking activities, once they have stopped, either against the same or a different victim; the risk of psycho-social damage to the victim; and, finally, the risk of psycho-social damage to the stalker. The latter is of particular note, in that increasing such damage to the stalker is likely to increase other risks. However, it will not feature in the account below.

Risk of physical violence

The fear of violence is central to the experience of being stalked: but estimates of the prevalence of violence vary from 3 to 46% (Pinals 2007, p. 14), depending on definition and sample selection. Rates of violence are higher in forensic or police case series, and such results do not generalize. For instance, Mohandie et al. (2006) found in a sample of 1005 stalking cases that 28% had involved physical assault and 0.5% homicide or mass murder, which would translate into a ludicrously large homicide toll, if applied to the whole population of those experiencing stalking (James and MacKenzie 2017). It is probable both that cases involving assault are more likely to be reported, and also that stalking is less likely to be recorded or prosecuted in cases where homicide or serious violence occur. Overall, stalking-related violence appears rarely to result in physical injury, and most studies agree that homicide is rare, although it makes the headlines when it does occur. However, the converse does not hold true. Cases of serious violence or homicide are frequently preceded by stalking: a US study of 141 intimate partner femicides and 65 attempted femicides found the prevalence of prior stalking to be 76% in the femicide victims and 85% in the attempted femicide cases (McFarlane et al. 1999).

Early research on the associations of violence in stalking examined stalkers as a single group. The risk of violence was consistently found to be greater when the stalker was an ex-intimate

(Mullen et al. 1999; Farnham et al. 2000; Mohandie et al. 2006). A meta-analysis of 13 studies (Rosenfeld 2004) found violence in stalking to be associated with threats, substance abuse and the absence of a psychotic disorder. A later meta-analysis of a total of 5114 cases (Churcher and Nesca 2013) found eight significant associations with violence: the stalker being an ex-intimate, threats, absence of psychosis, presence of personality disorder, substance abuse, criminal history, violence history and stalker gender. There is no significant difference between male and female stalkers in rates of violence (Purcell et al. 2001). This was confirmed in a study by Strand and McEwan (2012), which also found that significant associations of violence were the same in both sexes: prior intimate relationship, threats, and approach behaviour. Associations may differ with the seriousness of the violence: a study by James and Farnham (2003) found that serious violence was associated with an absence of criminal convictions and with the stalker being in employment, however, there were no significant associations with substance abuse, previous convictions for violence, and personality disorder. The negative relation between violence and psychosis in stalking, contrasts with the general violence literature, in which psychosis is generally held to increase the risk of violence, particularly when paranoid ideation is present (Douglas et al. 2009; Coid et al. 2016). Overall, these studies indicate that the risk of violence varies substantially with type of former relationship with the stalker, and it appears that risk factors for violence in stalking may differ from those in the general population.

   Later studies have examined risk factors for violence in stalking separately based on different motivational types. McEwan et al. (2009b), using logistic regression in a sample of 211 stalkers referred to a specialist clinic, found that violence in ex-intimate cases was best predicted by a model comprising previous violence, threats and being employed (area under the curve 0.75). In non-ex-intimate cases, the model comprised age under 30 years, substance abuse at the time of the stalking, and prior violence (area under the curve 0.80). McEwan later expanded the case sample by 46 cases (unpublished data). On further analysis, she found that, in ex-intimates, violence was significantly associated with approach (odds ratio 13.8) and with threats (odds ratio 2.7). In non-ex-intimate cases, violence was associated with substance abuse (odds ratio 6.1) and with younger age. Such results indicate that structured violence risk assessment in stalking needs to take account of differences in previous relationship and motivation.

Psycho-social damage to the victim

The psychological effects of being stalked amount to emotional violence: distress or fear, is part of the very definition of stalking. Anxiety, apprehension, dread, the sense of loss of control, and feelings of violation constitute a toxic mix. Psychological and social damage in stalking is common. In a study of 100 stalking victims in Australia, Pathé and Mullen (1997) found that 83% reported increased levels of anxiety, 75% feelings of powerlessness, 74% sleep disturbance, 55% increased fatigue, 55% intrusive recollections and flashbacks, and 24% suicidal ruminations. Depressed mood, nightmares and appetite disturbances were also common. The criteria for post-traumatic stress disorder (PTSD) were fulfilled in 37% of cases and a further 18% demonstrated the clinical features, whilst the stressor criterion was absent. Similar results were later found in studies concerning the Netherlands, Germany and the European Union as a whole (Kamphuis and Emmelkamp 2001; Dressing et al. 2005; Kuehner et al. 2007; FRA 2014, p. 90). In a significant minority of cases, psychological effects continue long after the stalking has ceased (Purcell et al. 2005). The social and occupational effects of stalking can also be serious, with Pathé and Mullen (1997) finding that 94% of their sample had made major changes in their domestic and work lives, with 53% changing or stopping employment and 39% moving home. The degree to which victims of stalking suffer psychological sequelae has been found to be influenced by the presence of pre-existing vulnerability factors (Purcell et al. 2012) and by the length of the stalking (Purcell et al. 2005).

Risks of persistence and recurrence

In an analysis of stranger and acquaintance cases in a forensic sample, the strongest predictors of persistence were found to be psychosis and sending unsolicited gifts (McEwan et al. 2009a). Persistence beyond a year was associated with being acquaintances, being over 30 years of age and intimacy-seeking motivation. Ex-intimate partners tended to be moderately persistent, with the stalking lasting for months, rather than years. A study by James, McEwan, et al. (2010b) looked at two samples, inappropriate writers and approachers to the British Royal Family, and those with similar behaviours in a forensic sample. The associations with persistence proved similar in the two samples: psychosis, intimacy-seeking motivation, and multiple forms of communication. A later study found the associations of persistence to be previous acquaintance, delusional beliefs and the absence of any history of physical violence (McEwan et al. 2017a).

Stalking recurrence has proved more difficult to study, partly because of the difficulty in distinguishing between recurrence and persistence in cases under study. Studies of recidivism in stalking offer some evidence. Recidivism has been found to be associated with personality disorder (Rosenfeld 2004), and with increased diversity and severity of offending, and pre-existing mental disorder (Eke et al. 2011). A study specifically examining recurrence produced a predictive model comprising personality disorder, older age, criminal versatility and erotomanic delusions (McEwan et al. 2017a). In summary, the above studies demonstrate that the risk factors for persistence and recurrence differ from each other, and from the risk factors for violence.

What doesn't work in stalking violence risk assessment

Considering the research findings on violence in stalking, it is not surprising to find that standard tools for the assessment of risk of violence are considered unsuitable for use in stalking cases. This is because they ignore the relationship between victim and perpetrator, which is integral to stalking; they fail to take account of implicit threats; and they are not suited to assessing an activity which may go on for months or even years (Kropp et al. 2002). Looking at specific tools, the HCR-20 (Webster et al. 1997) included stalking as an act of violence, so making all stalkers at higher risk, which was clearly not the case; and the Level of Service Inventory – Revised (Andrews and Bonta 1995) was not specific enough, as high-risk stalkers did not necessarily have high levels of criminogenic need and so risked not being picked up by a general recidivism instrument (McEwan et al. 2011). Such instruments over-looked information which is central to risk in stalking (e.g. specific forms of delusional belief, threats, elevated anger) and included factors so common in stalkers as to have little discriminatory value (e.g. relationship instability). In addition, the stalking literature illustrates that some risk factors for general violence do not apply to stalking violence, for instance, the presence of psychotic illness (Kienlen et al. 1997; Harmon et al. 1998; Rosenfeld and Harmon 2002). But the fundamental weakness of general violence risk assessment instruments is that they fail to take account of the motivation of the stalker, which is central to evaluation of risk in stalking.

Finally, risk of violence is only one form of risk which needs to be addressed in evaluating risk in stalking, and other forms of risk are not addressed in existing instruments. For all the above reasons, risk assessment in stalking requires the use of specific tools designed for evaluation of risk in stalking cases.

Practical Risk Assessment in Stalking Cases

Given the complexities inherent in stalking situations, practical risk assessment involves heavy reliance on specialized instruments to aid in reaching risk formulations. Detailed case assessment is the bedrock of risk management, but there is also an evident need for methods to help policing agencies and other 'first responders' to sort out those cases which need urgent intervention from those that can be dealt with using standard procedures. For this reason, the account below will deal both with screening instruments and detailed risk assessment tools. The number available is small, but the stage has now been reached where the first reliability and efficacy studies on the main risk assessment instruments have been published. Two instruments of each type will be explored in detail below.

Screening instruments

Concern has been raised in different countries that police are failing to identify high-risk cases of stalking when they present. In consequence, there have been attempts to produce simple aids for the police to help identify and prioritize higher-risk cases. Whilst some of these efforts have been informal and remained unpublished, several groups of researchers have published studies of screening tools in peer-reviewed journals. Groenen and Vervaeke (2009) developed a preliminary, five-factor model for physical violence in stalking, based on examination of 204 judicial files. Sheridan and Roberts (2011) produced a set of 11 key questions to be asked when stalking cases present. These were derived from logistic regression modelling of factors associated with serious violence in an on-line questionnaire survey of 1565 stalking victims. The authors then examined 43 police files on stalking cases, completed the questions on the presenting information in each case, conducted a fuller assessment of each entire case file to allocate a risk level, then compared these risk levels with the number of positive responses to the key screening questions in each case. A highly significant level of correlation was found. The questions have been incorporated into the Domestic Abuse, Stalking and Harassment and Honour Based Violence (NPIA 2009) Risk Identification, Assessment and Management Model that has been used by a number of police forces in the UK. Subsequently, McEwan et al. (2015) produced a more refined screening tool, the *Screening Assessment for Stalking and Harassment* (SASH; McEwan et al. 2015), which incorporated Sheridan and Roberts' key questions and which will be described in more detail below. Such tools should be used routinely by policing and agencies, to which complaints of stalking present.

Screening assessment for stalking and harassment (SASH; McEwan et al. 2015)

The SASH is designed to help professionals who are not experts to prioritize resources in stalking or harassment cases. It is a screening or triage tool, rather than a risk assessment per se. It was initially developed in 2010 by a group of Australian, Swedish and British clinicians with expertise in stalking, and was tested and refined through a series of internal studies before a final version was published in 2015. A short user-manual was published in 2017 (McEwan et al. 2017c). The SASH is in use by police forces and other agencies in a number of countries: it is currently available in Dutch, Swedish, Danish and Italian, as well as English. The SASH incorporates 16 items which are intended to be completed by non-experts, based on information usually available at first presentation of a stalking complaint to front-line agencies. The items are sufficiently concise to fit on one side of a sheet of paper: the form used includes some guidance as to their interpretation on the reverse. The brief manual includes further clarification of the items, as well as guidance as to when the SASH should be used and how its results should be interpreted. Thirteen questions are completed on all cases: these concern: (i) Seeking proximity, (ii) Threats/intimidation/aggression, (iii) Unauthorized entry, (iv) Property damage/theft, (v) Breaching legal boundaries, (vi) Escalation, (vii) Last-resort thinking*, (viii) Unavoidable contact, (ix) Previous stalking/harassment, (x) Previous violence, (xi) Mental health problems, (xii) Problematic substance use, (xiii) Significant loss. A further three items are completed in cases involving an ex-intimate: (xiv) Victim fear*, (xv) Possessiveness/jealousy, (xvi) Disputes over children/property. Risk judgements are made as to whether the case is to be treated as being of low, moderate or high concern. The SASH includes two items (asterisked above) which, when either is present, automatically render the case of high concern, regardless of which other items are scored as present. A study of the reliability and predictive validity of the SASH was conducted by Hehemann et al. (2017) on 115 stalking cases from the Netherlands National Police. Untrained police officers, without access to the guidance manual, were able to score the SASH items in the same way 80% of the time. Concern levels with the SASH were then compared with judgements as to the severity of subsequent stalking behaviour, derived independently from the case-files. A SASH concern level of moderate or high correctly identified 83% of cases where the stalker went on to engage in behaviours of moderate or high severity. Overall, the results showed sufficient promise for the SASH to be adopted by the Netherlands National Police. The authors recommend that, where a SASH concern level of moderate or high is determined, detailed evaluation using an instrument such as the *SRP* (MacKenzie et al. 2009), which is described later, should be sought.

Communications threat assessment protocol (CTAP)

Some people receive letters and electronic messages from the general public, either because their job involves being in the public eye, or because of who they work for, or what they do. A significant minority of communications are strange or inappropriate in content and some are directly or indirectly threatening. The CTAP is a structured threat assessment tool designed to be employed by risk managers and supervisors who have received training in its use (James et al. 2014). It is designed to enable the user to: identify the presence in communications (written, spoken, online, published, broadcast) of specific risk factors associated with a higher risk of unwanted outcomes; use this information to allocate cases into one of three concern levels – low, moderate or high, which determine the necessary level and urgency of response; formulate initial management plans; and work towards a more detailed formulation of continuing cases. The CTAP covers not just violence, but a range of different types of risk.

The CTAP was developed by a group of forensic psychologists and psychiatrists, together with security personnel. It was based on three initial elements: a detailed survey of the international academic literature; an examination of the threat assessment procedures for communications adopted by various policing and security agencies around the world, and specific new research conducted by the authors and their associates. The current form of the CTAP was evolved over 10 years, through the assessment and management of 1000s of concerning correspondence cases at the Fixated Threat Assessment Centre (FTAC) (James et al. 2010a; James et al. 2014). The CTAP comprises two parts: a preliminary Quick Correspondence Screen (QCS), and the main CTAP itself. The QCS is designed to be completed by those to whom communications are addressed or their staff. It comprises 18 items concerning the content of the communication. If any item on the list is present, the letter should be referred to the security or threat assessment department for more detailed examination, using the CTAP. If none are present, the communication needs no further action. The CTAP itself is designed to be used by security managers or police who have undergone training in its use. It contains 25 items, each of which is associated with increased risk. The nature of each item is described in turn, with illustrations where necessary, and the reason for the importance of the item is explained. Guidance is given as to how to allocate cases into low-, medium- or high-concern categories. The CTAP is not totalled into a simple 'score'. Whilst a higher number of positives is likely to be associated with a higher level of concern, the items are not equal in value, nor in likelihood of occurrence. Some of the factors are rarely encountered: however, their significance when present is such that it is important that they are always considered. Five of the factors are associated with a high risk of violence, such that the presence of one item alone is sufficient to render the case of high concern until shown otherwise. The CTAP is a threat assessment, rather than a risk assessment tool, in that it deals with the real-time situation where little information is available, rather than a review setting, where there is little time pressure and a considerable amount of information about the case is available. A preliminary study on interrater reliability (as yet unpublished) has produced encouraging results. The CTAP and the CTAP manual are currently available in English and Dutch (through www.theseusllp.com). The CTAP is currently being used by police threat assessment centres in several countries and by the security departments of a range of international corporations.

Detailed risk assessment tools

Two SPJ tools for the assessment of risk in stalking cases have been published (Kropp et al. 2008; MacKenzie et al. 2009). Both are intended for detailed examination of cases in review settings, where considerable quantities of information are available, and to aid in the construction of management plans. The use of one or other of these tools is essential in any detailed assessment of stalking risk.

Stalking risk profile (MacKenzie et al. 2009: www.stalkingriskprofile.com)

The SRP, 'a relatively unique' tool (Churcher and Nesca 2013), is unusual in two ways: it requires separate risk judgements to be made for each separate risk domain – violence, persistence, recurrence, and psycho-social damage to the stalker; and, within each risk section, it incorporates differences in risk factors between different motivational types by treating them separately (McEwan et al. 2011). In addition, it has a section specific to assessing risk to public figures. In assessing violence, it incorporates 'red-flag' factors, these being items of such importance that the presence of one alone is sufficient to determine high risk. The SRP takes the form of a 100-page manual, complete with scoring-sheets. Between all domains of risk and types of stalker, there are a total of 81 risk factors in the SRP, with administration in a given case involving 32–40 items, depending on the stalker type and domains of risk being assessed. Apart from two dichotomous items, the presence of each SRP factor is rated on a three-point scale: absent, possibly or partially present, and definitely present. Using the risk categories set out by Webster et al. (1997), a 'low', 'moderate', or 'high' risk rating is then assigned for each relevant domain. These aid in the formulation of the case. The SRP is designed to identify dynamic risk factors which can then be used as treatment targets. It is intended for multiple administrations, so that any improvement during treatment can be tracked. The SRP was developed and refined over a number of years (Mullen et al. 2006). It was intended for use by mental health clinicians (e.g. psychologists, psychiatrists, psychiatric nurses and psychiatric social workers), but has also proved useful for specialist law enforcement officers (e.g. those in threat assessment teams), particularly where collaboration is possible with an appropriately qualified clinician. Attendance at a two-day training workshop is required before the SRP can be used. The SRP has been widely adopted in Europe and in the Antipodes. It is published in Dutch and German, as well as English.

A major study of the reliability and predictive validity of the SRP examined 241 stalking cases, using a mixed prospective and retrospective design, with police re-offending data available to the researchers (McEwan et al. 2016). The SRP was shown to have relatively good internal consistency, interrater reliability, correct classification of cases, and predictive validity in terms of discrimination between recidivists and non-recidivists over the total follow-up period (median = 39.2 months). Results at 6 months were less clear cut, possibly reflecting methodological difficulties, although high-risk stalkers still re-offended against their original victim(s) two to four times as often as low-risk stalkers. The study showed that the SRP has clinical utility, as well as indicating directions for further refinement.

Guidelines for stalking assessment and management (SAM)

The SAM is intended for use by criminal justice, security, and mental health professionals working in contexts where complaints of stalking present (Kropp et al. 2008). The SAM comprises 30 items which are rated as to their presence or absence, and divided into three equal sections: nature of the stalking, perpetrator risk factors and victim vulnerability factors. It does not present separate sets of risk factors for different domains of risk or incorporate into its structure categories of motivation. Users 'rate the relevance of each risk factor (i.e., the degree to which it is important for risk management plans), posit possible risk scenarios, and document recommended management strategies. Finally, users can document their conclusory opinions regarding case prioritization, risk for continued stalking, risk for serious physical harm, reasonableness of victims' fear, and whether immediate action is required' (Kropp et al. 2011, p. 306). Users of the SAM are required to attend training courses. The instrument is extensively used in Canada, the US, Norway and Scotland.

Preliminary reliability testing found that interrater reliabilities for the SAM risk factors and total scores ranged from fair to good, and that the structural reliability of the SAM was sound. However, a study of the predictive validity of the SAM was conducted in 69 cases, using stalking and violence outcomes acquired prospectively from several sources, for an average follow-up period of 2.5 years (Foellmi et al. 2016). The SAM clinical-risk ratings did not significantly predict stalking re-offending, and there were no significant associations between SAM scores and violent outcomes. The authors concluded that the study provided 'mixed support for the use of the SAM as a risk assessment tool for stalking offenders', (p. 600) and that further studies were warranted.

Practical Management in Stalking Cases

Risk assessment has little purpose without risk management. Equally, policing, criminal justice and mental-health agencies are unlikely to manage a stalking case effectively without adequate risk assessment. It is beyond the scope of this chapter to provide a detailed account of management possibilities. Rather, the basic principles will be set out concisely.

Early referral to the police is advisable in stalking cases. There are support agencies which can advise victims on the steps to take, including the gathering of evidence (Pathé 2002). Initial policing responses should ensure that stalking cases are recognized and not minimized by officers and that systems for identifying risk are incorporated into standard practice, in order that victims can be protected. Courts and prosecution agencies should seek detailed assessment of risk to inform decisions about prosecuting and sentencing. Specialized stalking risk-assessment arrangements (see below) are particularly effective in difficult cases.

Legal sanctions alone are often ineffective in preventing continued stalking because, in the absence of treatment, the fundamental problems driving the stalker remain unresolved.

Treatment of stalkers involves pharmacotherapy when mental illness is present, but the mainstay of treatment for non-psychotic stalkers is programmes of psychological intervention (MacKenzie and James 2011). These must generally be initiated on a compulsory basis, as a condition of parole, probation or a community treatment order. For the most part, group treatment is inadvisable: individual therapy is required, tailored to the person's needs in terms of identified skills deficits and responsivity factors (for which, see Ogloff and Davis 2005). A useful framework to assist in considering the stalker's motivation to change behaviour and in shaping the delivery of treatment is the transtheoretical model of intentional behaviour change (see MacKenzie and James 2011).

Given the importance of mental illness, psychological problems and personality factors in initiating and maintaining stalking behaviours, the involvement of mental-health professionals is necessary, if comprehensive and meaningful assessment and treatment is to be achieved in stalking and harassment cases. Several types of specialist units and models have arisen along these lines in recent years. One model is the establishment of a specialist regional psychiatric service to assist the police, the courts and the probation/correctional service in the assessment, management and treatment of problem behaviours. Such a service has long been established in the Australian state of Victoria, dealing with violence, sexual offences against adults or children, fire-setting, threatening, and stalking (see Warren et al. 2005). A second model is that of FTACs, which deal with threats, stalking behaviours and grievance-fuelled aggression towards public figures. This involves specialist police units jointly staffed with police and psychiatric personnel from the health service (James et al. 2010a, 2014, Pathé et al. 2015; James and Farnham 2016). This model was first developed in the UK in 2006 in relation to stalking and threats towards politicians and members of the Royal Family. It was then adopted in Australia, the Netherlands and New Zealand, where further FTACs were set up to deal with problems faced by politicians, and elements of the approach have influenced practice in many other countries. The model was then expanded to deal with stalking cases in the general population, the first unit being in the Netherlands, where the psychologists are directly employed in police units. It is also now being developed in a number of policing regions across the UK, with psychiatrists from the National Health Service involved in joint assessment and management of stalking cases alongside police officers in specialist police units. Initial results are encouraging. The assessment and management of risk in the area of problem behaviours, such as stalking, will never become a predictive 'science'. However, joint working between police and health services, aided by structured risk assessment models, appears to constitute a real advance in dealing with such phenomena and in promoting the mitigation and prevention of the serious forms of harm to which they can give rise.

References

Andrews, D.A. and Bonta, J. (1995). *Level of Service Inventory-Revised*. Toronto, ON: Multi-Health Systems.

Basile, K.C., Swahn, M.H., Chen, J., and Saltzman, L.E. (2006). Stalking in the United States: recent national prevalence estimates. *American Journal of Preventive Medicine* 31: 172–175.

Breiding, M.J., Smith, S.G., Basile, K.C. et al. (2014). Prevalence and characteristics of sexual violence, stalking, and intimate partner violence victimization – National Intimate Partner and Sexual Violence Survey, United States, 2011. *Centers for Disease Control and Prevention Morbidity and Mortality Weekly Report* 63: 1–18.

Budd, T. and Mattinson, J. (2000). *The Extent and Nature of Stalking: Findings from the 1998 British Crime Survey*. London: Home Office.

Cavezza, C. and McEwan, T.E. (2014). Cyberstalking versus off-line stalking in a forensic sample. *Psychology, Crime & Law* (10): 955–970.

Churcher, F.P. and Nesca, M. (2013). Risk factors for violence in stalking perpetration: a meta-analysis. *FWU Journal of Social Sciences* 7: 100–112.

Coid, J.W., Ulrich, S., Bebbington, P. et al. (2016). Paranoid ideation and violence: meta-analysis of individual subject data of seven population surveys. *Schizophrenia Bulletin* 42: 907–915.

Crown Prosecution Service (2015). *Violence Against Women and Girls 2014-2015*. London: Crown Prosecution Service.

Douglas, K.S., Guy, L.S., and Hart, S.D. (2009). Psychosis as a risk factor for violence to others: a meta-analysis. *Psychological Bulletin* 135: 679–706.

Dressing, H., Kuehner, C., and Gass, P. (2005). Lifetime impact and prevalence of stalking in a European population. *British Journal of Psychiatry* 187: 168–172.

Eke, A.W., Hilton, N.Z., Meloy, J.R. et al. (2011). Predictors of recidivism by stalkers: a nine-year follow-up of police contacts. *Behavioral Sciences & the Law* 29: 271–283.

Farnham, F.R., James, D.V., and Cantrell, P. (2000). Association between violence, psychosis, and relationship to victim in stalkers. *Lancet* 355: 199–199.

Foellmi, M.C., Rosenfeld, B., and Galietta, M. (2016). Assessing risk for recidivism in individuals convicted of stalking offenses: predictive validity of the guidelines for stalking, assessment and management. *Criminal Justice and Behavior* 43: 600–616.

FRA: European Union Agency for Fundamental Rights (2014). *Violence against Women: An EU-Wide Survey*. Luxembourg, LX: Publications Office of the European Union.

Groenen, A. and Vervaeke, G. (2009). Violent stalkers: detecting risk factors by the police. *European Journal on Criminal Policy and Research* 15: 279–291.

Harmon, R.B., Rosner, R., and Owens, H. (1998). Sex and violence in a forensic population of obsessional harassers. *Psychology, Public Policy, and Law* 4: 236–249.

Hehemann, K., van Nobelen, D., Brandt, C., and McEwan, T. (2017). The reliability and predictive validity of the Screening Assessment for Stalking and Harassment (SASH). *Journal of Threat Assessment and Management* 4: 164–177.

Hellman, D.F. and Kliem, S. (2015). The prevalence of stalking: current data from a German victim survey. *European Journal of Criminology* 12: 700–718.

Her Majesty's Inspectorate of Constabulary (2017). *Living in Fear – the Police and CPS Response to Harassment and Stalking*. London, UK: Author.

James, D.V. and Farnham, F.R. (2003). Stalking and serious violence. *Journal of the American Academy of Psychiatry and the Law* 31: 432–439.

James, D.V. and Farnham, F.R. (2016). Outcome and efficacy of interventions by a public figure threat assessment and management unit: a mirrored study of concerning behaviours and police contacts before and after intervention. *Behavioral Sciences and the Law* 34: 660–680.

James, D.V., Farnham, F.R., and Wilson, S.P. (2014). The fixated threat assessment centre: implementing a joint policing and psychiatric approach to risk assessment and management in public figure threat cases. In: *International Handbook of Threat Assessment* (eds. J.R. Meloy and J. Hoffman), 299–320. New York, NY: Oxford University Press.

James, D.V., Kerrigan, T., Forfar, R. et al. (2010a). The fixated threat assessment centre: preventing harm and facilitating care. *Journal of Forensic Psychiatry and Psychology* 21: 521–536.

James, D.V. and MacKenzie, R.D. (2017). Stalking and harassment. In: *The Routledge International Handbook of Human Aggression* (eds. J.L. Ireland, P. Birch and C.A. Ireland), 170–182. Abingdon, UK: Routledge.

James, D.V., MacKenzie, R.D., and Farnham, F.R. (2014). *Communications Threat Assessment Protocol*. London, UK: Theseus LLP.

James, D.V., McEwan, T.E., MacKenzie, R.D. et al. (2010b). Persistence in stalking: a comparison of associations in general forensic and public figure samples. *Journal of Forensic Psychiatry & Psychology* 21: 283–305.

James, D. V. & Persaud, R. (in submission). Cyberstalking in the UK: A prevalence survey.

Kamphuis, J.H. and Emmelkamp, P.M.G. (2001). Traumatic distress among support- seeking female victims of stalking. *American Journal of Psychiatry* 158: 795–798.

Kienlen, K.K., Birmingham, D.L., Solberg, K.B. et al. (1997). A comparative study of psychotic and nonpsychotic stalking. *Journal of the American Academy of Psychiatry and the Law* 25: 317–334.

Kropp, P.R., Hart, S.D., and Lyon, D.R. (2002). Risk assessment of stalkers: some problems and possible solutions. *Criminal Justice and Behavior* 29: 590–616.

Kropp, P.R., Hart, S.D., Lyon, D.R., and Storey, J.E. (2011). The development and validation of the guidelines for stalking assessment and management. *Behavioral Sciences and the Law* 29: 302–316.

Kropp, R.P., Hart, S.D., and Lyon, D.R. (2008). *Guidelines for Stalking Assessment and Management (SAM)*. Vancouver, BC: ProActive Resolutions Inc.

Kuehner, C., Gass, P., and Dressing, H. (2007). Increased risk of mental disorders among lifetime victims of stalking – findings from a community study. *European Psychiatry* 22: 142–145.

MacKenzie, R.D. and James, D.V. (2011). Management and treatment of stalkers: problems, options, and solutions. *Behavioral Sciences & the Law* 29: 220–239.

MacKenzie, R.D., McEwan, T.E., Pathé, M.T. et al. (2009). *Stalking Risk Profile: Guidelines for Assessing and Managing Stalkers*. Melbourne, AU: StalkInc. & Centre for Forensic Behavioural Science.

MacKenzie, R.D., Mullen, P.E., McEwan, T.E. et al. (2010). Stalkers and intelligence: implications for treatment. *Journal of Forensic Psychiatry and Psychology* 21: 852–872.

MacKenzie, R.D., Mullen, P.E., Ogloff, J.R.P. et al. (2008). Parental bonding and adult attachment styles in different types of stalker. *Journal of Forensic Sciences* 53: 1443–1449.

McEwan, T.E., Daffern, M., MacKenzie, R.D., and Ogloff, J.R.P. (2017a). Risk factors for stalking violence, persistence and recurrence. *Journal of Forensic Psychiatry and Psychology* 28: 38–56.

McEwan, T.E., Mullen, P.E., and MacKenzie, R. (2009a). A study of the predictors of persistence in stalking situations. *Law and Human Behavior* 33: 149–158.

McEwan, T.E., Mullen, P.E., MacKenzie, R.D., and Ogloff, J.R.P. (2009b). Violence in stalking situations. *Psychological Medicine* 39: 1469–1478.

McEwan, T.E., Pathé, M., and Ogloff, J.R.P. (2011). Advances in stalking risk assessment. *Behavioral Sciences & the Law* 29: 180–201.

McEwan, T.E., Shea, D., Daffern, M. et al. (2016). The reliability and predictive validity of the stalking risk profile. *Assessment* 25: 259–276.

McEwan, T.E., Shea, D.E., Nazarewicz, J., and Senkans, S. (2017b). Reassessing the link between stalking and intimate partner abuse. *Partner Abuse* 8: 223–250.

McEwan, T.E., Strand, S., MacKenzie, R.D., and James, D.V. (2015). *Screening Assessment for Stalking and Harassment (SASH)*. Melbourne, AU: StalkInc.

McEwan, T.E., Strand, S., MacKenzie, R.D., and James, D.V. (2017c). *Screening Assessment for Stalking and Harassment (SASH): Guidelines for Application and Interpretation*. Melbourne, AU: StalkInc.

McFarlane, J., Campbell, J.C., Wilt, S. et al. (1999). Stalking and intimate partner femicides. *Homicide Studies* 3: 300–316.

Mohandie, K., Meloy, J.R., McGowan, M.G., and Williams, J. (2006). The RECON typology of stalking: reliability and validity based upon a large sample of North American stalkers. *Journal of Forensic Sciences* 51: 147–155.

Mullen, P.E., MacKenzie, R., Ogloff, J.R.P. et al. (2006). Assessing and managing risks in the stalking situation. *Journal of the American Academy of Psychiatry and Law* 34: 439–450.

Mullen, P.E., Pathé, M., and Purcell, R. (2009). *Stalkers and Their Victims*, 2e. Cambridge, UK: Cambridge University Press.

Mullen, P.E., Pathé, M., Purcell, R., and Stuart, G.W. (1999). Study of stalkers. *American Journal of Psychiatry* 156: 1244–1249.

NPIA (2009). *DASH 2009 risk identification, assessment and management*. London: National Policing Improvement Agency.

Office for National Statistics (2016). *Compendium: Intimate Personal Violence and Partner Abuse*. London, UK: Office of National Statistics.

Ogloff, J.R.P. and Davis, M. (2005). Assessing risk for violence in the Australian context. In: *Issues in Australian Crime and Criminal Justice* (eds. D. Chappell and P. Wilson), 301–338. Chatswood, AU: Lexis Nexis Butterworth.

Pathé, M. (2002). *Surviving Stalking*. New York, NY: Cambridge University Press.

Pathé, M.T., Lowry, T., Haworth, D.J. et al. (2015). Assessing and managing the threat posed by fixated persons in Australia. *Journal of Forensic Psychiatry & Psychology* 26: 425–438.

Pathé, M.T. and Mullen, P.E. (1997). The impact of stalkers on their victims. *British Journal of Psychiatry* 170: 12–17.

Pinals, D.A. (2007). *Stalking: Psychiatric Perspectives and Practical Approaches*. Group for the advancement of psychiatry. New York, NY: Oxford University Press.

Purcell, R., Pathé, M., Baksheev, G.N. et al. (2012). What mediates psychopathology in stalking victims? The role of individual-vulnerability and stalking-related factors. *Journal of Forensic Psychiatry and Psychology* 23: 361–370.

Purcell, R., Pathé, M., and Mullen, P.E. (2001). A study of women who stalk. *American Journal of Psychiatry* 158 (12): 2056–2060.

Purcell, R., Pathé, M., and Mullen, P.E. (2004a). When do repeated intrusions become stalking? *Journal of Forensic Psychiatry and Psychology* 15: 571–583.

Purcell, R., Pathé, M., and Mullen, P.E. (2004b). Stalking: defining and prosecuting a new category of offending. *International Journal of Law and Psychiatry* 27: 157–169.

Purcell, R., Pathé, M., and Mullen, P.E. (2005). Association between stalking victimisation and psychiatric morbidity in a random community sample. *British Journal of Psychiatry* 187: 416–420.

Rosenfeld, B. (2004). Violence risk factors in stalking and obsessional harassment: a review and preliminary meta-analysis. *Criminal Justice and Behavior* 31: 9–36.

Rosenfeld, B. and Harmon, R. (2002). Factors associated with violence in stalking and obsessional harassment cases. *Criminal Justice and Behavior* 29: 671–691.

Sheridan, L. and Roberts, K. (2011). Key questions to consider in stalking cases. *Behavioral Sciences and the Law* 29: 255–270.

Sheridan, L.P. and Grant, T. (2007). Is cyberstalking different? *Psychology, Crime & Law* 13: 627–640.

Strand, S. and McEwan, T. (2012). Violence among female stalkers. *Psychological Medicine*. 42 (3): 545–556.

Tjaden, P. and Thoennes, N. (1998). *Stalking in America: Findings from the National Violence Against Women Survey*. Washington, DC: US Department of Justice.

Tjaden, P. and Thoennes, N. (2000). *Extent, Nature, and Consequences of Intimate Partner Violence: Findings from the National Violence against Women Survey*. Washington, DC: US Department of Justice.

van der Aa, S. and Römkens, R. (2013). The state of the art in stalking legislation: reflections on European developments. *European Criminal Law Review* 3: 232–256.

Warren, L., MacKenzie, R., Mullen, P.E., and Ogloff, J.R.P. (2005). The problem behaviour model: the development of the stalkers clinic and a threateners' clinic. *Behavioral Sciences and the Law* 23: 387–397.

Webster, C.D., Douglas, K.S., Eaves, D., and Hart, S.D. (1997). *HCR-20: Assessing Risk for Violence (Version 2)*. Vancouver, BC: Mental Health, Law, and Policy Institute, Simon Fraser University.

28

Managing Violent Offenders in the Community
Reentry and Beyond

Ralph C. Serin[1], Christopher T. Lowenkamp[2], and Caleb D. Lloyd[3,4]

[1] Carleton University, Ottawa, Canada
[2] Administrative Office of the US Courts, Washington DC, USA
[3] Centre for Forensic Behavioural Science, Alphington, Australia
[4] Swinburne University of Technology, Alphington, Australia

Introduction and Overview

Context

The community has substantial concerns regarding the risk posed by violent offenders,[1] especially those recently released from prison. It is reasonable to presume that the majority of violent offenders under some form of community supervision, whether parole or probation, had some period of prior imprisonment given the seriousness of their crimes. Thus, community corrections hold responsibility for managing a volatile and delicate transition to the community amongst offenders with prior known violence, which, in our view, also applies to violent clients who were assigned community supervision directly by the courts and/or clients who may have a prior conviction for a violent crime.

Kemshall (2008) nicely summarized three broad strategies considered by the Criminal Justice System to mitigate such concern (Connelly and Williamson 2000). She describes three contemporary models: community protection; clinical treatment; and, a justice model. Community protection, through the use of surveillance, monitoring, and mandatory treatment, emphasizes victim/community rights, which are prioritized over offender rights. This community protection model is most common in Canada and the United States (US).

The community protection model seems to assert these are bad people; in contrast, the treatment model emphasizes the offenders have done bad things. Hence, the provision of more intensive intervention and, especially in the UK, involvement of mental-health

---

[1] Throughout the chapter, violence will be used to denote offenders whose violence is non-sexual.

The Wiley Handbook of What Works in Violence Risk Management: Theory, Research and Practice, First Edition. Edited by J. Stephen Wormith, Leam A. Craig, and Todd E. Hogue.
© 2020 John Wiley & Sons Ltd. Published 2020 by John Wiley & Sons Ltd.

professionals, is intended to mitigate the risk violent offenders pose to the community. There is some slippage in this model as treatment is increasingly being mandated and not voluntary. Indeed, the Multi-Agency Public Protection panel (MAPP) in the UK is perhaps a hybrid of the community protection and treatment models. Wood and Kemshall (2008) refer to this as protective reintegration.

Third, the justice model perceives offenders as rational and their crimes volitional, emphasizing deterrence through longer sentences in order to mitigate risk to the public by limiting violent offender access to the community through imprisonment. These three approaches wax and wane in accordance with community tolerance and political ideology. Despite confusion regarding the terms risk and dangerousness (Brown 2000; Kemshall 2008) we support the criteria used by the Risk Management Authority in Scotland (2007) regarding the identification of risky clients. These include: likelihood; impact and scale of harm, sometimes referred to as seriousness; absence/presence of protective factors; the offender's motivation to change risky behaviours; and, the offender's ability to self-manage risk.

With this context in mind, the purpose of this chapter is to highlight recent work intended to refine risk assessment to include more acute dynamic risk factors to inform risk re-assessment and to review case and risk management strategies specific to non-sexually violent offenders, thereby mitigating offender risk.

Prisoner re-entry

In the US, *re-entry* is generally the term used to reflect the difficult transition offenders undergo following their time in prison and returning to the community. Similar terms are used in Canada, Australia, and New Zealand (*reintegration*) and the UK (*resettlement*). These terms are often a short-hand way to describe a set of complex and multi-faceted processes from multiple perspectives, which can encompass (i) interpersonal difficulties reuniting with pre-prison family and social groups, (ii) intra-individual challenges attempting to avoid temptation and stay clean, (iii) structural constraints such as securing housing and employment in the face of stigma due to a criminal record, and (iv) criminal justice agency concerns, such as providing through-care services to a complex parole population.

In addition to the ongoing reality of large numbers of ex-inmates re-entering the community following incarceration, in recent years, there has been increased discussion focusing on the systematic reduction of the prison population. Efforts to support this process of de-incarceration have been championed for both fiscal (prison is more expensive than community supervision) and policy (offender rehabilitation reduces rates of re-offending) reasons. In particular, in the US, federal initiatives such as the *Second Chance Act* and Justice Reinvestment Initiative have made significant progress, as reflected in decreased incarceration rates (Truman and Morgan 2016).

As such, community supervision encompasses a wide range of release contexts and client characteristics that may influence client outcome. However, typically, when the term *re-entry* is used, authors do not indicate the population of interest. For example, offenders on community supervision can be released by discretion such as in parole, or by statute/end of sentence. As well, probation is community supervision assigned by the courts in lieu of a custodial sentence. Some offenders who finish their sentence may also be required to complete a period of probation. Paroled cases imply an independent review such that those returned early to the community are only those who appear suitable for release in terms of acceptable public safety risk and rehabilitation effort. Conversely, end of sentence cases have met certain statutory requirements in terms of time served and are thereby returned to their community independent of estimated risk of reconviction. Potentially, these groups differ with respect to risk of recidivism, motivation, and programme completion, and it is not unreasonable to expect differential rates and time to failure.

In principle, probation, and parole are similar in terms of supervision practices, although they may vary in terms of risk profiles and consequent frequency of contacts between community supervision officers (CSOs) and clients. In some agencies, CSOs manage both parolees and probationers; as well, some CSOs manage specialized caseloads (e.g. sex offenders). Caseload ratios are often determined by some combination of risk profiles of clients and specialization requirements.

In addition to differences across types of release and caseloads, researchers make varied choices about whether to equate technical violations with new crimes when examining offender outcomes. Also, re-entry research has not thoroughly examined the potential trajectories of violent vs. non-violent offenders, thereby somewhat impeding assessment, intervention, and supervision strategies for violent offenders who return to the community.

In short, the re-entry transition is in many ways a catch-all concept, and not specifically defined. Compounding definitional issues of *re-entry*, serious violent offenders are themselves a poorly defined group, most typically designated by an arbitrary combination of scores on risk scales (not necessarily specific to violence), type of offence (serious violence, sexual crimes), and phase of release or re-entry (offenders are known to be higher risk during the months immediately following release).

The purpose of this chapter is to review community-based assessment and management of non-sexually violent offenders, with a view towards improved identification and management of violent offenders. Where possible, distinct subgroups of violent offenders are highlighted, if the empirical evidence suggests that attending to such heterogeneity will be informative. This chapter considers *which* offenders warrant more intensive community supervision, *what* appropriate strategies should be applied to mitigate risk of harm to the public, and *when* such strategies might be optimally applied.

Programming – does it work for violent offenders?

Consistent with the tenets of Risk-Need-Responsivity (RNR) intervention (Bonta and Andrews 2017), high-risk violent offenders merit intervention targeting risk factors prior to re-entry release. Intervention contributes in numerous important ways, from recidivism reduction to re-entry preparation. Examining reductions in recidivism, Jolliffe and Farrington (2007) conducted a meta-analysis of eight methodologically sound treatment studies for adult violent offenders (n = 1546). A small significant effect was found (six of eight studies reduced violent re-offending; two studies had a significant treatment effect). Overall, a small average effect size was found; mean d between 0.13 and 0.16 depending on whether the effects were calculated using a fixed or random effect model. Programmes that used the most effective strategies (i.e. using cognitive skills, role-play, and relapse prevention), increased the effect size (d = 0.33, or an 18% reduction in general recidivism). Overall, compared to untreated samples, the treated samples had lower rates for general offending (reductions by 8–11%) and violent offending (reductions by 7–8%). Second, such programming can help prepare offenders for re-entry; offenders with better release plans have better outcome (Polaschek et al. 2016). Third, RNR-type programming can be augmented by common re-entry efforts relating to accommodation and employment (Braga et al. 2009; Duwe 2014). Fourth, involvement in structured programming can inform case-specific or idiographic understanding of risk factors, which can be used to improve case planning and risk management (Polaschek 2019). Whilst not all violent offenders on community supervision will have received custodial programming, some rehabilitative effort could likely have numerous benefits, not the least of which is to augment amenability to further intervention, either in the form of boosters or additional programming.

Issues in the Assessment of Violent Offenders

Identifying high-risk violent offenders

In general, the field is somewhat split regarding the preferred approach to risk assessment (actuarial vs. structured professional judgement (SPJ)), and, hence there is no single preferred risk assessment measure. Certainly in corrections, risk, and need instruments seem most popular because they go beyond indicating likelihood of future offending to also identify criminogenic needs/treatment targets. A meta-analysis of the most popular violent risk instruments concluded predictive validity is essentially comparable across measures and that other factors such as training requirements, costs, and completion time are more important considerations for assessment adoption, compared to minor differences in predictive accuracy (Yang et al. 2010). Some efforts to provide agencies and individual practitioners with selection guidelines exist, but they appear to be the exception (Bonta 2002; Skeem and Eno Louden 2007; Serin and Lowenkamp 2015).

Using risk measures to identify individuals at risk for future violence involves two considerations. For an initial consideration of violence risk, the main model appears to be the development of a general risk measure (i.e. risk of any re-offending) and then examining its utility for predicting violent re-offending. This is the case for risk and need measures such as the Correctional Offender Management Profile for Alternative Sanctions (COMPAS, Brennan, Dieterich & Ehret, 2009), the Level of Service family of measures (Level of Service/Case Management Inventory [LS/CMI]; Andrews et al. 2004), the Ohio Risk Assessment Scale (ORAS, (Latessa et al. 2009), and the Post-Conviction Risk Assessment (PCRA, Lowenkamp et al. 2013). A second model suggests there may be unique predictors for violence that extend beyond the standard criminogenic needs to augment predictive accuracy (Mills et al. 2011).

The subsequent consideration has developed out of newer research on acute dynamic risks, which suggests there may be re-entry circumstances and client affective states that increase risk of violent re-offending in the short term (Lowenkamp et al. 2016). Hence, we have suggested changes in acute factors function much like a barometer that assesses change in barometric pressure, and hence predicts changes in weather (Serin et al. 2019). Of note, the implication of attending to proximal, short-term factors is that these must be re-assessed regularly in order to detect *changes* in risk.

Given that risk and need measures provide acceptable levels of predictive accuracy regarding violent re-offending, one might be tempted to simply limit assessment to a single measure of personal choice. This is problematic for several reasons. First, some measures, despite predictive validity, seem to capitalize on criminal history factors, whilst failing to include violence-specific factors. Moreover, violent offenders are not necessarily selectively specific in terms of their crimes; violent offenders often have prior non-violent crimes and some will commit non-violent crimes in the future. Additionally, specialized measures for intimate partner violence (IPV) yield greater predictive accuracy for IPV outcome (Gray 2012), necessitating a more case-specific consideration of risk assessment. Similar findings have been noted for sex offenders (Hanson 2009). This means staff must select measures based on various criteria, including the type of offender and outcome of interest.

Moreover, if staff wish to demonstrate diligence in their assessment, a consideration of credible violence predictors is warranted, especially if such factors are not reflected in the risk assessment measure. Recently, we demonstrated the utility of this viewpoint; certain violence-specific variables (e.g. victim access, anger/hostility considerations and negative affect) augmented prediction, reduced decision errors, and reflected unique predictors of violence beyond a credible risk and need measure (Serin, Lowenkamp, Johnson, and Polaschek, in preparation).

Despite being common practice in correctional policy, it is apparent that identification of violence propensity based solely on the index crime will be susceptible to over-predicting risk. Consider the following comparison of cases. Both cases involve a male offender of similar age and race, finishing a prison term for aggravated assault and returning to his old neighbourhood.

Mr. A has no prior criminal history, and had prior stable employment to which he will return. The crime involved Mr. A seriously assaulting the victim due to mistaken identity (Mr. A's car was vandalized many times over several months and he believed the victim was the vandal). The victim was briefly hospitalized.

In contrast, Mr. B has a long criminal history with numerous prior assaults where victims were injured but not admitted to hospital. These assaults occurred both when Mr. B was, and was not, under the influence of illicit substances. The current assault was a bar fight. Overall, Mr. B has been described as an angry person with a 'chip on his shoulder'. Whilst in prison, he talked repeatedly about settling scores upon release.

Despite a more serious index offence, Mr. A is clearly lower risk. If decisions were not made based on index offence, but made based solely on length of criminal history, Mr. B would be considered greater risk, but it is highly likely that a static risk assessment would not assist with the understanding that Mr. B's sense of entitlement is a key component within his offending. In this way, a consideration of violence-specific dynamic risk factors could enhance and better inform case management.

Refining violence risk assessment

As stated previously, assigning risk according to index crime category (i.e. more serious crime equates with higher risk) will likely over-predict risk and increase false positive errors (incorrectly predicting which individuals will fail). The application of structured risk assessment measures validated on the population of interest is the more common and empirically defensible approach. Such measures can be either actuarial instruments that weight items according to their association with recidivism (e.g. Violent Risk Appraisal Guide-Revised, VRAG-R; Rice et al. 2013) or SPJ measures (e.g. Historical Clinical Risk 20 Version 3, HCR-20 V[3]; Douglas et al. 2013). Risk and need risk instruments (e.g. COMPAS, Brennan and Oliver 2000; [LS/CMI]; Andrews et al. 2004 and ORAS, Latessa et al. 2009; and PCRA, Lowenkamp et al. 2013) have the additional advantage of systematically identifying criminogenic needs or risk factors for intervention. At its most simple level, offenders who score higher on these risk measures have increased estimated likelihood of failure. This estimate alerts a community supervision agency that differential case management is warranted according to offender risk level. For instance, an agency might determine that higher risk cases warrant more frequent contact with the CSO.

Phase of release is also a consideration in risk assessment. Of those who fail, a majority do so within the first six months (Brown et al. 2009). In addition, survival analyses illustrate that not only do higher risk offenders fail more often, they fail more quickly (i.e. steeper slope). Hence, community re-entry services should front-load services to mitigate risk. Such front-loading could include higher frequency of contact, longer contact time with CSOs, more programme referrals to treatment providers, increased number of supervision conditions that could be titrated over time, greater intolerance for failure to meet supervision requirements, and graduated sanctions relating to such failures (Carter and Sankovitz 2014). These strategies could be titrated such that with each successful 6 or 12 months of unproblematic supervision, conditions could be reduced.

Given the heightened concern regarding violent re-offending, there is an increasing risk aversive perspective regarding community supervision of violent offenders, as well as views that longer custodial sentences are required. Whilst incarceration has, at best, no impact on recidivism, it is certainly the case that offenders are greatly restricted from committing new violent crimes whilst incarcerated. Nonetheless, releasing high-risk violent offenders after a lengthy period of incarceration is not ideal either. This risk aversive climate, however, could mean that CSO's tolerance for lapses (i.e. breaches of conditions) is very low for serious violent offenders. That is, within the area of graduated sanctions, the nature of the breach and the risk level of the offender are often reviewed such that higher-risk violent offenders would be returned to custody for even minor transgressions (e.g. missed curfew, missed appointment, etc.).

By definition, re-entry describes the process by which an offender leaves prison and returns to the community. Depending on offenders' circumstances, there are likely pros and cons to returning to their previous community. Whilst they could have support of familiar pro-social peers, it is also likely that they would encounter criminal peers who might sabotage the offenders' efforts at becoming law abiding. Employment and accommodation could also be viable if the offender returns to his or her community. Ullrich and Coid (2011), examined re-entry efforts for a sample of 800 violent offenders with a three-year follow-up, reporting that strengths mitigated risk and these protective factors changed over time. Controlling for risk, protective factors in year one, reflected immediate concerns about accommodation and employment, whereas by year three, these had transformed to more intrinsic factors. This means the CSOs must be aware of an offender's phase of release and the differential impact of risk and protective factors over time.

Community supervision, whether parole or probation, is primarily concerned with false negatives (offenders who are presumed for success, but later fail). Increasingly, these situations are referred to as sentinel events (Doyle 2014), especially when a serious violent failure occurs. Whilst medicine and aviation have viewed sentinel events as an indication of the need to refine procedures to improve practice, in corrections, staff often view reviews of these failures as designed to assign blame. For serious violent offenders, such a perspective unnecessarily promotes a risk-aversion approach to supervision, providing few opportunities for staff or offenders to '*work through*' risk situations. Any apparent increase in risk would result in a more restrictive response, including, but not limited to, returns to custody even for technical violations. This approach has significant fiscal (jails cost more than community supervision) and personal (estrangement from potential positive community resources) costs. Nonetheless, for higher-risk, violent offenders, public safety should be the primary consideration in decision making.

Due diligence in the assessment of violent offenders

Due diligence refers to evidence that an agency and its representatives such as CSOs have met a standard of care to mitigate public safety concerns and to provide high-quality services intended to assist offenders' re-entry efforts. With respect to violent offenders, violence risk assessment instruments should include unique predictors of violent crime. Arguably, it is less than ideal to apply a general recidivism instrument that also has some validity (AUC > 0.70) in predicting violent recidivism.

We recently examined the utility of combining static violence-specific flags (e.g. gang affiliation, stranger victim, planning, weapon use, treatment noncompliance, IPV) in a sample of approximately 4000 federal probationers with a valid risk and need instrument (e.g. PCRA) to underscore the contribution of due diligence (Serin et al. 2019a). These initial findings indicated that even when the risk and need instrument has high validity for predicting serious violence in probationers (AUC = 0.77), the inclusion of the violent flags increases accuracy (AUC = 0.85). Moreover, the combined model (risk scale + violence flags) has a significant advantage over using only the risk scale in terms of correct decisions (62.18% vs. 41.23%). There is a slight decrease in sensitivity, but a noticeable increase in specificity (correctly identifying cases that succeed). Hence, the combined model improves prediction and reflects more violence-specific content within the assessment, which will assuage criticism in the event of a serious community failure. Obviously, this preliminary research requires replication but speaks to the potential utility of a multilevel risk assessment approach.

Two examples further highlight what is meant by due diligence. Consider the case of Mr. C; he is a 36-year-old male with four prior convictions for aggravated assault. These assaults occur at times of employment or family conflict, and when he has been drinking. He reports feeling his anger slowly build up, and then he explodes. He is often remorseful following the assault, realizing his aggressive response has been discrepant to his perceived level of provocation. An assessment approach that fails to consider current alcohol use, presence of purported triggers for drinking, and level of anger would be deficient, especially in the event of Mr. C subsequently assaulting someone.

In contrast, consider the case of Mr. D; he is a 36-year-old male with an exclusive history of IPV. He has four assault convictions across three different partners, one involved a weapon. Equally disconcertingly, he has two prior convictions for stalking and one conviction for breaching a no-contact order with one of his victims. He presents with misogynistic attitudes, commenting on poor prior working relationships with female probation officers, and still remarks about his ex-partner with expressions of jealousy. In light of his college degree, stable employment, noncriminal friends and appropriate leisure time activities, he could potentially be rated as moderate or even low risk on a traditional risk and need instrument. In contrast and for illustrative purposes only, a review of items on the Spousal Assault Risk Assessment (Kropp et al. 1999), indicates he would most likely be considered moderate to high risk for IPV. In addition, he reflects acute risk factors that should be addressed in both case planning and risk management considerations. Sole reliance on a non-IPV risk measure and failure to highlight these IPV-specific issues would fail to meet a standard of care. Thus, due diligence requires considerations beyond general recidivism risk.

Heterogeneity of violent offenders

Risk and *risk of violence* are often considered to be synonymous, but this is incorrect. High-frequency property offenders, such as those committing auto theft or break and enters, are high risk to continue criminal activity, but are not highly likely to commit new violent crimes. Disconcertingly, many, if not the majority of violent offender risk assessments incorporate empirical predictors without consideration of taxonomy or theory regarding violence propensity.

Specifically, existing assessments fail to consider the most common taxonomy of violence; that is, the distinction between expressive (i.e. hot emotion) vs. instrumental (i.e. cold emotion) goals (Cornell et al. 1996). For instance, several researchers have proposed that violent offenders characterized by either expressive or instrumental goals differ according to antecedent events, intent, affect, and function (Cima and Raine 2009; Meloy 2006; Merk et al. 2005). Specifically, expressive offenders' violence is described as arising from a provocation, such that the violence is impulsive, the offender experiences anger or loss of control, and the primary goal is to cause harm to the victim. In contrast, instrumental offenders' use of violence arises from the goal of reaching a specified positive outcome, such that the violence is premeditated, the offender does not experience anger, and the primary purpose is to achieve an external goal beyond the violence itself.

Although the utility of this theoretical dimension is less clear when attempting to determine the likelihood of future violence, it is reasonable to conclude that expressive – instrumental differences are relevant for informing strategies to manage the risk of released offenders. Different types of violent offenders imply the need for different intervention approaches to achieve comparable treatment effects across subgroups of offenders. Combining these disparate offenders within a common treatment curriculum would require some clinical finesse so that violent offenders' unique risk factors are sufficiently addressed.

Making the choice to manage offender subgroups in different ways requires theoretical and empirical support, but the distinction between reactive vs. instrumental offenders is not universally accepted because of concerns about temporal shift. Specifically, an offender can initiate one type of violence, but then exhibit another in a later context (Card and Little 2006). Over the past two decades, correctional intervention for violent offenders has moved from anger-based considerations to an appreciation that information-processing conceptualizations of violent offender deficits is more conceptually appropriate (Polaschek and Collie 2004). Expressive and instrumental violence are now considered to be a single dimension, such that each pure-defined goal sits on the opposite ends of a single continuum, and much violence can be placed in between the poles, since many violent acts have overlapping features (Woodworth and Porter 2002). Hence, generally violent offenders could potentially be characterized as using violence to achieve their goals, whereby the type of expression (expressive or instrumental) is more defined by the situation. Moreover, Anderson and Bushman (2002) proposed a definition that considers both proximate (intent to do harm) and ultimate (achievement of doing harm) goals. In this manner, harm is necessarily present when violence occurs, but harm may not be the primary goal (Tedeschi and Felson 1994).

McDermit et al. (2008), using a sample of inpatients, asserted that the predictors of short-term violence may be quite different from the predictors of longer-term recidivism and offending. Each of these findings has clear implications for community supervision, suggesting that (i) most of the current risk assessment approaches can generally identify violence potential, but (ii) attending to personality features characterized by different emotional expression may justify the use of different management approaches, and (iii) predicting short-term violence requires an enhanced assessment approach. There is a need for more complex approaches to theory, assessment, and management of violent offending.

Considering theory of general criminal offending (Bonta and Andrews 2017), these theories highlight the complex interaction amongst inter-individual factors (e.g. parental and social interactions, problem solving) and intra-individual (e.g. motivation, criminal attitudes, self-regulation, callousness) factors, with a strong emphasis on rewards or costs for continued criminal conduct or its cessation. Aggression theory (Anderson and Bushman 2002), albeit with a focus that is somewhat distinct from violence, highlights how the interaction amongst cognition, emotions, and behaviour leads to an aggressive act, either verbal or physical.

For violence in particular, there has been recent theoretical advancement (or construct refinement, at least) such that Polaschek et al. (2009)) reported specific thinking styles amongst violent offenders that might be instructive. Four violence-related implicit theories (or thinking styles) emerged from their analysis of offenders' views about violence: (i) *beat or be beaten*, (ii) *I am the law*, (iii) *violence is normal*, and (iv) *I get out of control*. Specifically, in this New Zealand sample, few offenders reported their violent behaviour as abnormal, or completely outside of their control, once initiated. These thinking styles or schema may activate violent behaviour but also justify its use after the fact.

Given the many commonalities across nations in the definitions, prevalence, and response to violence, this framework is broadly applicable, but this research has not been replicated. Nonetheless, it appears that several implicit theories held by violent offenders are inter-related through the widespread normalization of violence, leading to its continued expression. From a management perspective, it is unclear if these cognitions simply should be considered a more specific characterization of criminal thinking, which would only require simple tailoring of existing content, or if there are unique considerations that must be addressed. The sex offender field shares a similar challenge; there are unique predictors (e.g. sexual deviance, victim affiliation), and sex offenders report specific cognitive distortions to reduce dissonance and support criminal conduct. In sex-offender rehabilitation, specific cognitive distortions are considered key targets for treatment, but analogous approaches amongst non-sexually violent offenders are rare.

In summary, research regarding violent offender heterogeneity suggests there may be advantages to attending to specific violent offender subgroups (McDermit et al. 2008; Serin and Preston 2001) both in terms of correctional programming and community supervision.

Community Supervision of Violent Offenders

Assessment during community supervision

Whilst it would seem a straightforward process to assess criminogenic needs and risk and then apply them to a case-specific supervision strategy, there are sequential analytic steps that must be followed, like a logic model, in order to best determine an overall supervision strategy for an individual offender (Serin and Hanby 2017). Many CSOs engage the offender in a behavioural analysis through the use of an offence cycle exercise. This essentially assists offenders to review their criminal conduct and determine when they are most at risk. This activity identifies the individuals with whom they most commonly commit crimes, where these crimes most commonly occur, their intentions when committing crimes, and other exigent circumstances such as substance abuse. Part of supervision is to be alert to replication of these parameters, as these are indicators of increased risk. Ideally, the CSO is able to engage the offender to self-monitor such factors so they can take preventative steps as risk increases, as reflected in problem solving training. This is a core component of relapse prevention approaches that have been most often applied to subgroups where there are repetitive aspects to criminal conduct (i.e. sex offenders; Wheeler et al. 2005, and offenders with substance-abuse problems; Marlatt and Witkiewitz 2005).

Re-assessment of acute dynamic risk

Implicit within the paper thus far is the notion that dynamic factors are important for distinguishing amongst violent offenders. Traditionally, criminogenic needs have been discussed as synonymous with dynamic risk (Andrews and Bonta 2006; Serin et al. 2015), but dynamic risk is increasingly being described as either stable or acute (Hanson and Harris 2000). Criminogenic needs are often perceived as fairly stable dynamic factors (e.g. antisocial attitudes and peers); these factors can change, with effort, over months rather than days. Indeed, for peers, re-assessment is appropriate as circumstances change. Acute dynamic risks are more mercurial, potentially changing over hours or days (e.g. negative affect, substance use). This distinction is helpful in that stable dynamic risks (as well as static risk factors) indicate who is at risk, whereas acute dynamic risks are expected to indicate imminence of violence or when a person is at increased risk (Serin et al. 2019). Case planning and risk management are intended to identify which individuals warrant greater intervention and how such intervention might change over time to ameliorate or manage risk.

A recent archival study of approximately 1000 federal probationers in the US highlighted the incremental importance in assessing acute dynamic risks in the management of violent offenders on community supervision (Serin et al. 2019b). Reviewing archival monthly case file reports and coding for multiple violence-specific acute risks (e.g. anger, negative affect, victim access) for 18-months follow-up (12 months on average) was revealing. First, cases characterized by a higher total number of acute risks were significantly more likely to commit a serious violent crime (i.e. homicide, attempted homicide, sexual assault, robbery, and felonious assault), whilst on community supervision. High scorers had survival rates of about 2% compared to 52% for low scorers on acute risks. Second, after controlling for risk using a validated risk and need measure, high scores on the acute risk increased the odds of serious violent failure by up to 25 times in the short-term. Equally informative is which variables had *no* relationship with risk of violent re-arrest by themselves. Substance abuse, employment, interpersonal problems, and living situation failed to independently inform the likelihood of violent re-arrest, but do contribute as part of an overall dynamic risk score.

Case management during community supervision

It is apparent that unique acute dynamic risks could be assessed amongst violent offenders and then incorporated into case planning to make intervention and supervision more case-specific and effective. For instance, risk and need instruments fail to distinguish amongst types of violent offenders. Thus, case planning should consider traditional criminogenic needs, and violence-specific factors (stable and acute), and type of violent offender. Evidence from Jolliffe and Farrington's (2007) meta-analysis of interventions with violent offenders suggests that violent offender intervention can reduce post-programme violent recidivism, so each agency is tasked with considering and determining the extent to which its intervention matches violent offenders' distinct needs. One option is to implement two streams of intervention. The first would be a more traditional RNR approach to criminogenic needs, in which typical intervention targets such as criminal thinking, substance abuse, and poor self-regulation could be expanded to include additional sessions relating to violent offending (e.g. anger, hostile schema, victim selection, cost-benefits, and empathy development). A second option would be to have a subsequent, separate violent offender intervention that follows and augments the earlier generalized intervention. Both approaches potentially increase programme dosage, which would be appropriate for high-risk violent offenders.

Risk management during community supervision

Kemshall (2008) nicely underscores how case management evolves into risk management for high-risk cases, with a primary focus being on community protection concerns. In this manner, for serious violent offenders, case management involves more than rehabilitation. Specifically, risk management encompasses targeted surveillance, supervised accommodation, and proactive planning. Moreover, supervision sessions themselves can form an important part of a risk-management strategy. Table 28.1 reflects in-session and after-session considerations adapted from our earlier work (Lowenkamp et al. 2016), with elevations in anger and hostility as an exemplar. A CSO need not have incredibly sophisticated skills to recognize changes in acute dynamic risks. For instance, during a session with an offender, if the offender is agitated, and verbalizing hostility towards others (e.g. hostile ideation; feels people are 'screwing' with them; feels pre-emptive verbal or physical violence is warranted; feels increasing inability to regulate negative affect; feels like they may 'lose it'), then it is reasonable to conclude this is a problem area, even if similar behaviour has not previously been noticed. This elevation could be in response to recent interpersonal conflicts (fight with partner), recent disappointment

Table 28.1   Strategies for addressing anger concerns in offenders.

During Session	*Following Session*
Consider imminence for safety issues for self and others.	Telephone client to enquire about success in coping.
Identify emotional and situational triggers.	Contact possible targets of violence, if appropriate.
Review anger control and coping strategies.	Contact treatment provider, if applicable.
Problem solving to mitigate short-term consequences.	Advise supervisor of increased risk.
Role play self-talk.	Document analysis and action taken.
Consider instrumentality.	Investigate consequences.
Provide homework, handouts on anger control.	Review homework in next session
Behavioural contract regarding violence.	Reaffirm contract in next session

(fired from job), or recent stress (difficulty meeting conditions of supervision). Moreover, if these situations are similar antecedents to prior violence, sometimes referred to as offence parallelling behaviour (Daffern 2010), then it is of paramount importance that the CSO acts quickly.

CSOs are encouraged to develop similar strategies for other acute risk factors. Several aspects of this intervention warrant elaboration. First, as the offender's risk level increases, there is an increased requirement for more directive intervention during sessions and a necessity for documentation regarding the CSO's analysis and management of the case. Second, changes in acute dynamic risks necessitates the CSO to clearly indicate *how* they are going to manage the offender differently from earlier sessions, in light of recognizing a greater imminence of violence. This change or elevation in acute risk is akin to a flashing hazard signal, alerting someone to proceed with utmost caution. Prudence would suggest a CSO would rarely ignore such a warning; doing so, in the case of a subsequent violent failure by the offender, would be extremely challenging for all involved. Finally, taking action, even if it did not prevent subsequent violence in certain cases, is consistent with best practices.

Case planning is often considered at the start of supervision. Commonly, a risk and need assessment is completed and the identification of criminogenic needs drives referrals for intervention. In some cases, these need domains are incorporated into session activities by CSOs, although to our knowledge this is not routinely done (see Chapter 25, on Strategic Training Initiative in Community Supervision (STICS), for an exception). Essentially, the case plan is a roadmap designed to chart the expected path the offender will successfully navigate to exit the criminal justice system. This roadmap is not always smooth and occasionally accidents or roadblocks occur, necessitating a change in navigation.

Sometimes, these incidents warrant a change in strategies to mitigate or ameliorate risk. This is particularly critical in the case of serious violent offenders under community supervision. Failure to diligently monitor the case and respond in real time to observed changes in risk (e.g. presence of acute dynamic factors) can lead to increased victimization of the public. Offender level of risk is obviously and intricately linked to risk management approaches. Higher perception of risk, optimally informed by a valid risk scale, leads to greater oversight in the case. In this situation, greater oversight is equated with more supervision conditions such as more frequent CSO contacts, possibly unannounced work and home visits, tandem CSO contacts in the field, more frequent urinalysis testing, referral to rehabilitation programmes, residency in a hallway house, and so on. Also, there is lower tolerance for higher-risk violent offenders failing to abide by these conditions; return to jail for a breach would be more likely than for a lower-risk offender.

Given the evidence recidivism rates are higher during the early phase of re-entry, risk management of offenders may be titrated over time. As the offender maintains successful community supervision, conditions are commonly reduced or amended to reflect the lowered risk. Evidence from a large probation sample suggested that jail sanctions are not more effective than community sanctions in reducing the time to, the number of, or likelihood of future violations (Wodahl et al. 2015). Hence, it remains to be seen if these findings can be replicated amongst serious violent offenders who are sanctioned to community supervision.

For serious violent offenders, there is some evidence that re-entry planning is an important risk management approach (Polaschek and Kilgour 2013; Braga et al. 2009; Duwe 2014), potentially supporting generalization of treatment effects. Polaschek et al. (2015) followed a high-risk violent offender sample and noted longer (more than six months) supervision reduced reconviction rates, suggesting supervision can be an effective public safety strategy.

This has been more formally examined in probation more generally, where application of Core Correctional Practices (firm but fair approach by CSOs and targeting criminal thinking and peers during sessions; Dowden and Andrews 2004) reduced recidivism by 13% (Chadwick et al. 2015).

Summary and recommendations

Throughout this chapter, we posited that violent offenders are heterogeneous and that attending to these differences should inform assessment, intervention, and management. Evidence that intervention or programming in the community reduces violent re-offending is modest, but present (Jolliffe and Farrington 2007). Importantly, these programmes primarily reflect cognitive behavioural interventions that consider the intransigent personality features present in persistently violent offenders to be responsivity factors rather than the primary treatment targets (see Chapter 10, personality-based assessment, for more on personality as a responsivity factor). We also suggest that violent offenders in the community warrant an assessment and analysis of violence-specific factors, especially acute dynamic risks.

For those high-risk cases that are released from jail and prison, there are additional considerations beyond Core Correctional Practices (Dowden and Andrews 2004) to address re-entry challenges. Resources must be front-loaded, liaison with police and other agencies is critical (similar to Multi-agency public protection arrangements (MAPPA); Kemshall 2008), pre-release planning is desirable, development of a working relationship between client and CSO is essential, and the facilitation of social capital is also required. In combination, these strategies will improve success in high-risk cases by engaging such offenders in the pro-social change process and enhancing public safety.

References

Anderson, C.A. and Bushman, B.J. (2002). Human aggression. *Annual Review of Psychology* 53: 27–51.

Andrews, D.A. and Bonta, J. (2006). *The Psychology of Criminal Conduct*, 4e. Cincinnati, OH: Anderson.

Andrews, D.A., Bonta, J., and Wormith, J.S. (2004). *The Level of Service/Case Management Inventory*. Toronto, Canada: Multi-Health Systems.

Bonta, J. (2002). Offender risk assessment: guidelines for selection and use. *Criminal Justice and Behavior* 29: 355–379.

Bonta, J. and Andrews, D.A. (2017). *The Psychology of Criminal Conduct*, 5e. New York, NY: Routledge.

Braga, A.A., Piehl, A.M., and Hureau, D. (2009). Controlling violent offenders released to the community: an evaluation of the Boston reentry initiative. *Journal of Research in Crime and Delinquency* 46: 411–436.

Brennan, T., Dieterich, W., and Ehret, B. (2009). Evaluating the predictive validity of the COMPAS risk and needs assessment system. *Criminal Justice and Behavior* 36: 21–40.

Brown, S. (2000). Calculations of risk in contemporary penal practice. In: *Dangerous Offenders: Punishment and Social Order* (eds. M. Brown and J. Pratt), 93–108. London, UK: Routledge.

Brown, S.L., St. Amand, M.D., and Zamble, E. (2009). The dynamic prediction of criminal recidivism: a three-wave prospective study. *Law and Human Behavior* 33: 25–45.

Card, N.A. and Little, T.D. (2006). Proactive and reactive aggression in childhood and adolescence: a meta-analysis of differential relations with psychosocial adjustment. *International Journal of Behavioral Development* 30: 466–480.

Carter, M. and Sankovitz, R.J. (2014). *Dosage Probation: Rethinking the Structure of Probation Sentences.* Washington, DC: National Institute of Corrections.

Chadwick, N., DeWolf, A.H., and Serin, R.C. (2015). Effectively training community supervision officers: a meta-analytic review of the impact on offender outcome. *Criminal Justice and Behavior* 42: 977–989.

Cima, M. and Raine, A. (2009). Distinct characteristics of psychopathy relate to different subtypes of aggression. *Personality and Individual Differences* 47: 835–840.

Connelly, C. and Williamson, S. (2000). *A Review of the Research Literature of Serious Violent and Sexual Offenders.* Edinburgh, UK: Scottish Executive Central Research Unit.

Cornell, D.G., Warren, J., Hawk, G. et al. (1996). Psychopathy in instrumental and reactive violent offenders. *Journal of Consulting and Clinical Psychology* 64: 783–790.

Daffern, M. (2010). A structured cognitive-behavioural approach to the assessment and treatment of violent offenders using offence-paralleling behaviour. In: *Offence Paralleling Behaviour: A Case Formulation Approach to Offender Assessment and Intervention* (eds. M. Daffern, L. Jones and J. Shine), 105–120. Chichester, UK: Wiley-Blackwell.

Douglas, K.S., Hart, S.D., Webster, C.D., and Belfrage, H. (2013). *HCR-20V3: Assessing risk for violence—User guide.* Burnaby, BC, Canada: Mental Health, Law, and Policy Institute, Simon Fraser University.

Dowden, C. and Andrews, D.A. (2004). The importance of staff practice in delivering effective correctional treatment: a meta-analytic review of core correctional practices. *International Journal of Offender Therapy and Comparative Criminology* 48 (2): 203–214.

Doyle, J.M. (2014). Learning from error in the criminal justice system: sentinel event review. In: *Mending Justice: Sentinel Event Reviews* (eds. E.H. Holder Jr., K.V. Mason and W.J. Sabol), 3–19. Washington, DC: National Institute of Justice.

Duwe, G. (2014). A randomized experiment of a prisoner reentry programe: updated results from an evaluation of the Minnesota comprehensive reentry plan (MCORP). *Criminal Justice Studies* 27: 172–190.

Gray, A. (2012). Assessing risk for intimate partner violence: A cross-validation of the ODARA and DVRAG within a sample of incarcerated offenders. Masters thesis. Carleton University.

Hanson, K.R. and Harris, A.J. (2000). Where should we intervene? Dynamic predictors of sexual offense recidivism. *Criminal Justice and Behavior* 27 (1): 6–35.

Hanson, R.K. (2009). The psychological assessment of risk for crime and violence. *Canadian Psychology* 50: 172–182.

Jolliffe, D. and Farrington, D.P. (2007). *A Systematic Review of the National and International Evidence of Interventions with Violent Offenders.* London, UK: Ministry of Justice Research Series 16/07.

Kemshall, H. (2008). *Understanding the Community Management of High Risk Offenders.* Berkshire, UK: Open University Press.

Kropp, P.R., Hart, S.D., Webster, C.D., and Eaves, D. (1999). *Manual for the Spousal Assault Risk Assessment Guide*, 3e. Toronto, ON: Multi-Health Systems.

Latessa, E., Smith, P., Lemke, R. et al. (2009). Creation and validation of the Ohio Risk Assessment System. Final report. University of Cincinnati.

Lowenkamp, C.T., Johnson, J.L., Holsinger, A.M. et al. (2013). The federal post conviction risk assessment (PCRA): a construction and validation study. *Psychological Services* 10: 87–96.

Lowenkamp, C.T., Johnson, J.L., Trevino, P., and Serin, R.C. (2016). Enhancing community supervision through the application of dynamic risk assessment. *Federal Probation* 80: 16–20.

Marlatt, G.A. and Witkiewitz, K. (2005). Relapse prevention for alcohol and drug problems. In: *Relapse Prevention: Maintenance Strategies in the Treatment of Addictive Behaviors*, 2e (eds. G.A. Marlatt and D.M. Donavan), 1–44. New York, NY: Guilford Press.

McDermit, B.E., Quanbeck, C.D., Busse, D. et al. (2008). The accuracy of risk assessment instruments in the prediction of impulsive versus predatory aggression. *Behavioral Sciences and the Law* 26: 759–777.

Meloy, J.R. (2006). Empirical basis and forensic application of affective and predatory violence. *Australian and New Zealand Journal of Psychiatry* 40: 539–547.

Merk, W., de Castro, B.O., Koops, W., and Matthys, W. (2005). The distinction between reactive and proactive aggression: utility for theory, diagnosis and treatment? *European Journal of Developmental Psychology* 2: 197–220.

Mills, J.F., Kroner, D.G., and Morgan, R. (2011). *Clinician's Guide to Violence Risk Assessment.* New York, NY: Guilford Press.

Polaschek, D.L.L. (2019). Interventions to reduce recidivism adult violent offenders. In: *The Wiley International Handbook of Correctional Psychology* (eds. D.L.L. Polaschek, A. Day and C.R. Hollin), 503–514. Hoboken, NJ: John Wiley & Sons, Inc.

Polaschek, D.L.L., Calvert, S.W., and Gannon, T.A. (2009). Linking violent thinking: implicit theory-based research with violent offenders. *Journal of Interpersonal Violence* 24: 75–96.

Polaschek, D.L.L. and Collie, R.M. (2004). Rehabilitating serious violent adult offenders: an empirical and theoretical stocktake. *Psychology Crime and Law* 10: 321–334.

Polaschek, D.L.L. and Kilgour, T.G. (2013). New Zealand's special treatment units: the development and implementation of intensive treatment for high-risk male prisoners. *Psychology, Crime & Law* 11: 511–526.

Polaschek, D.L.L., Yesberg, J.A., Bell, R.K. et al. (2016). Intensive psychological treatment of high-risk violent offenders: outcomes and pre-release mechanisms. *Psychology, Crime & Law* 22: 344–365.

Polaschek, D.L.L., Yesberg, J.A. and Chauhan, P. (2015). Surviving the first year: An integrated examination of potential mechanisms for successful re-entry in high-risk treated and comparison prisoners on parole. Manuscript under revision.

Rice, M.E., Harris, G.T., and Lang, C. (2013). Validation of and revision to the VRAG and SORAG: the violence risk appraisal guide—revised (VRAG-R). *Psychological Assessment* 25: 951–965.

RMA (Risk Management Authority) (2007). *Standards and Guidelines for Risk Management (Version 1).* Edinburgh, UK: Author.

Serin, R.C., Chadwick, N., and Lloyd, C.D. (2015). Dynamic risk and protective factors. *Psychology, Crime & Law* 22: 151–170.

Serin, R.C. and Hanby, L.J. (2017). Client-based assessment of need and change. In: *The Wiley Handbook on the Theories, Assessment and Treatment of Sexual Offending* (ed. D.P. Boer), 1575–1592. Chichester, UK: Wiley.

Serin, R.C., Lloyd, C.D., and Chadwick, N. (2019). Integrating dynamic risk assessment into community supervision practice. In: *The Wiley International Handbook of Correctional Psychology* (eds. D.L.L. Polaschek, A. Day and C. Hollin), 725–743. New York, NY: Wiley Blackwell.

Serin, R.C. and Lowenkamp, C.T. (2015). *Selecting and Using Risk and Need Assessments.* Washington, DC: National Institute of Corrections.

Serin, R.C., Lowenkamp, C.T., Johnston, J. and Polaschek, D.L.L. (2019a). Introducing due diligence into violence risk appraisal: Validation of a multi-level risk assessment approach. Manuscript in preparation.

Serin, R.C., Lowenkamp, C.T., Johnston, J. and Polaschek, D.L.L. (2019b). Do changes in acute risk forecast sentinel events? Implications for violence assessment in a federal probation sample. Manuscript in preparation.

Serin, R.C. and Preston, D.L. (2001). Managing and treating violent offenders. In: *Treating Adult and Juvenile Offenders with Special Needs* (eds. J.B. Ashford, B.D. Sales and W. Reid), 249–272. Washington, DC: American Psychological Association.

Skeem, J. and Eno Louden, J. (2007). *Assessment of Evidence on the Quality of the Correctional Offender Management Profiling for Alternative Sanctions (COMPAS).* Davis, CA: Center for Public Policy Research.

Tedeschi, J.T. and Felson, R.B. (1994). *Violence, Aggression & Coercive Actions.* Washington, DC: American Psychological Association.

Truman, J.L. and Morgan, R.E. (2016). *Criminal Victimization, 2015.* Washington, DC: Bureau of Justice Statistics.

Ullrich, S. and Coid, J. (2011). Protective factors for violence among released prisoners-effects over time and interactions with static risk. *Journal of Consulting and Clinical Psychology* 79: 381–390.

Wheeler, J.G., George, W.H., and Stone, S.A. (2005). Enhancing the relapse prevention model for sexual offenders: adding recidivism risk reduction therapy to target offenders' dynamic risk needs. In: *Relapse Prevention: Maintenance Strategies in the Treatment of Addictive Behaviors*, 2e (eds. G.A. Marlatt and D.M. Donavan), 333–362. New York, NY: Guilford Press.

Wodahl, E.J., Boman, J.H. IV, and Garland, B.E. (2015). Responding to probation and parole violations: are jail sanctions more effective than community-based graduated sanctions? *Journal of Criminal Justice* 43: 242–250.

Wood, J. and Kemshall, H. (2008). Accountability and partnerships in criminal justice: the case of multi-agency public protection arrangements (MAPPA). In: *Applied Criminology* (eds. B. Stout, J. Yates and B. Williams), 135–153. London, UK: Sage.

Woodworth, M. and Porter, S. (2002). In cold blood: characteristics of criminal homicides as a function of psychopathy. *Journal of Abnormal Psychology* 111: 436–445.

Yang, M., Wong, S.C., and Coid, J. (2010). The efficacy of violence prediction: a meta-analytic comparison of nine risk assessment tools. *Psychological Bulletin* 136: 740–767.

Index

Page numbers in **bold** refer to Tables and *italics* refer to Figures

The Wiley Handbook of What Works in Violence Risk Management: Theory, Research and Practice,
First Edition. Edited by J. Stephen Wormith, Leam A. Craig, and Todd E. Hogue.
© 2020 John Wiley & Sons Ltd. Published 2020 by John Wiley & Sons Ltd.